CORPORATE LAW

EDITORIAL ADVISORY BOARD

CORPORATE LAW

ROBERT CHARLES CLARK
Professor of Law
Harvard University Law School

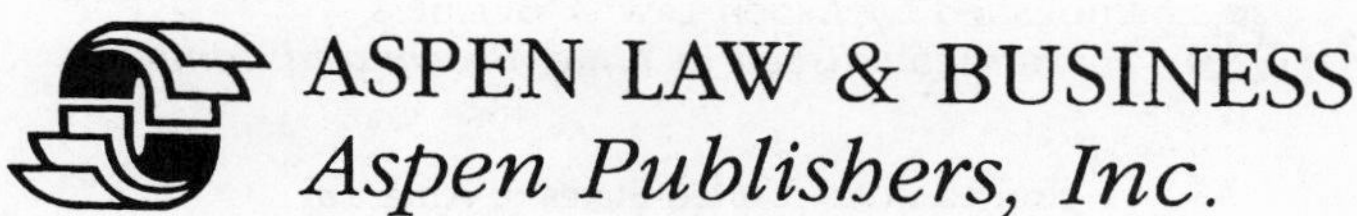
ASPEN LAW & BUSINESS
Aspen Publishers, Inc.

Library of Congress Catalog Card No. 85-81681
ISBN 0-316-144940

Thirteenth Printing

MV-NY

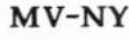

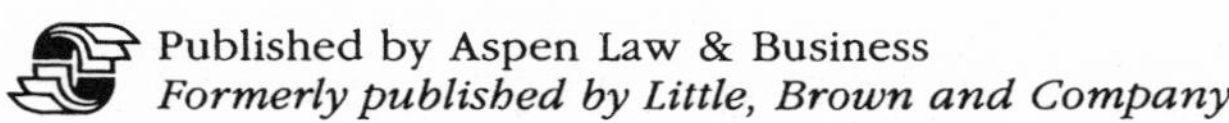

Published by Aspen Law & Business
Formerly published by Little, Brown and Company

Printed in the United States of America

To My Mother and Father

SUMMARY OF CONTENTS

CONTENTS

CHAPTER 5
BASIC SELF-DEALING 159

CHAPTER 6
EXECUTIVE COMPENSATION 191

CHAPTER 7
CORPORATE OPPORTUNITIES 223

CHAPTER 9
THE VOTING SYSTEM 357

CHAPTER 10
THE GROUND RULES OF CORPORATE COMBINATIONS 401

CHAPTER 13

CONTROL SHIFTS AND INSIDER RESISTANCE: TENDER OFFERS 531

CHAPTER 14

DISTRIBUTIONS TO SHAREHOLDERS 593

CHAPTER 18
CLOSE CORPORATIONS 761

PREFACE

Audience. This book is written primarily for law students taking the basic course in corporations. Its style and subject matter coverage are geared to students. Nevertheless, I hope that the book will reward many other kinds of readers. Parts of it should serve as a useful preparation to those who are about to embark on courses in securities regulation, corporate finance, or other specialized areas of study. Moreover, the book presents a distinctive vision of corporate law, and it aims to produce a fresh and unified understanding of basic principles and connecting themes. Consequently, it may prove helpful to lawyers and judges who are searching for new ideas and arguments about familiar topics, or who are trying to synthesize their hard-won stores of knowledge. Finally, the book may be an appropriate and friendly guide for businesspersons, economists, or non-lawyer academics who want to inform themselves about this important area of law. I have tried very hard to write a text that reads easily and forgives a lack of legal training.

Approach. Given its primary audience and focus, this book is not cast as a small encyclopedia. It does not purport to be a compilation of legal authorities that by itself could serve as a complete basis for concrete legal advice. The reasons for not attempting to write a treatise that both teaches and serves as a reference work are fairly obvious, even though they seem to have been forgotten by more than one author of a legal work: too much detail impedes learning, giving real legal advice requires exact knowledge of particular local law that is constantly changing in its details, and today loose-leaf services and computerized data banks often provide the best sources of detailed current information for the practitioner who already understands the basic legal doctrines.

Instead of questing for infinite completeness, this book tries to do what a one-volume introductory work can and should do. First, it explores major topics at length. Second, it gives the subject matter a coherent structure; it shows how all the major parts of corporate law fit together. Third, it examines the rationale of the major concepts and doctrines.

This emphasis on the organization of legal knowledge reflects my view of the nature of the expert knowledge possessed by truly competent lawyers. Becoming a good corporate lawyer, or a good lawyer in any field, is an ongoing process that never ends, but it is not a process of just piling up one legal nugget after another. Learning a technical subject is like building a house. If (but only if) the young professional has built a firm foundation and a properly laid out basic structure of understanding, later acquisitions of detailed knowledge or of new developments can easily be put into their proper place, thus letting the occupant move around efficiently. Those who throw up an awkward or incoherent structure in the beginning will later pay the price.

As compared to traditional hornbooks, this book may seem both more and less "theoretical." On the one hand, it often develops arguments for and against rules and pursues policy analyses, sometimes at great length, and it does so with the aid of economic theory and concepts. On the other hand, it relies greatly on examples, hypotheticals, and extended discussions of cases.

This latter feature of the book is deliberate and reflects its audience and purpose, as well as my beliefs about how students actually learn. The approach has certain risks. For example, some of my extended discussions of cases may be of cases that don't match those the student reads in her course or that will soon be dropped from casebooks or superseded by later developments. I regard this problem as far less important than the gains in understanding that are likely to come from abandoning the sterilized and deceptively permanent abstract statements of black-letter principles that dominate the pages of many traditional hornbooks. It is better to wrestle with a fleeting historical reality than to dally with an immortal but effete generalization. For the most part, I have chosen to discuss cases that are good vehicles for examining the operational meaning of legal rules and concepts, or of kinds of legal argument. Under this approach, some very old but interesting cases receive significant scrutiny.

The book tries to explain and illustrate a large quantity of rules, doctrines, and cases in a clear, concise, and fair way. Yet my own ideas and recommendations enter in several ways. First, there are explicit analyses of what the law should be, or how rules should be interpreted and related to one another. Examples are the concluding sections of the chapter on corporate opportunities, the concluding pages of the chapter on insider trading, and the first and last sections in the chapter on basic self-dealing. For the most part, these legal briefs are easy to spot and are kept separate from the expositional parts. The student anxiously concerned to learn "only what the law is" will find it easy to detect and skip over these parts if he so wishes. Second, I have made many value judgments in the course of selecting, weighing, and assessing opposing arguments about legal rules. Prime examples are my treatment of the pros and cons of insider trading and the pros and cons of management buyouts. The context should make it clear what conclusions belong to the courts, to the author, to other commentators, or to the general intellectual space of the subject. Third, my own view of corporate law as a whole is implicit in the selection and organization of topics. This viewpoint cannot be excised from the exposition itself. The reader who wants to examine it critically will have to do his own reflecting and cogitating.

Theme. Most of corporate law is concerned with the array of substantive rules and procedural devices that are aimed at controlling managerial slack and diversion while preserving adequate discretion to carry out business operations efficiently. Put in other words, the law displays a constant tension, and a constant striving for a good balance, between the fiduciary duties of care and loyalty on the one hand and the business judgment rule on the other. As is more fully explained in chapter 1, the book is organized around these topics.

Seen in this light, the study of corporate law is a study of the legal system's attempts to control managerial discretion in an important class of large, complex, formal organizations. It is a study that should offer important food for thought to anyone interested in the design of other large organizations in modern societies. The central problem of corporate law — the optimal control of managerial discretion — is a thoroughly pervasive one in all modern societies, whether they be capitalist or socialist in basic design. In all large formal organizations there are people (usually the top executives) who (1) possess a great deal of power to affect the operations of the organization and the fortunes of all of the affected participants, but who (2) are not given this power as something to be exercised principally for their own benefit. This is as true of labor unions, nonprofit hospitals, government agencies, and state-run enterprises as it is of stockholder-owned business corporations. Corporate law's major conceptual contribution to solution of the problem (the fiduciary principle), the major substantive rules it deploys to implement that concept, and its distinctive set of enforcement mechanisms (such as the derivative lawsuit, proxy voting, and the hostile tender offer) should be of great interest as a source of more general reflections about the allocation and control of power in highly organized societies.

Role of economics. Economic theory does not provide the organizing principle of the book. The book is for future lawyers, and the law has its own characteristic categories and ways of approaching problems that the lawyer *must* master on their own terms. Nor is the book immersed in economic jargon. On the other hand, it is suffused by a law-and-economics approach. More specifically, parts of the argument and analysis come from microeconomics, financial economics, and law review writing by law-and-economics scholars, or they at least have the flavor of a cost benefit analysis.

Numerous examples can be pointed out. Chapter 1 sketches a functional analysis that looks at the cost-reducing effects of legal principles. Chapters 1, 2, 4, 7, 11, and 12 all employ hypothetical contracts reasoning. Chapters 2 and 9 invoke the prisoners' dilemma of game theory. Chapters 8 and 12 present arguments cast as cost/benefit analyses. Chapter 10 uses valuation theory. Chapter 13 reviews economic theories about, and econometric studies of, the effects of tender offers and of defenses to tender offers. It and other parts of the book appeal to a modest version of efficient markets theory. Chapter 14, on dividends and repurchases, borrows arguments about optimal capital structure from the literature of financial economics. Chapter 16 takes a welfare-analytic approach to the functions of government and of corporations. Chapter 17 considers the extent to which information might be analyzed as a public good. Throughout the book, reliance is put on arguments about transaction costs, information costs, risk and uncertainty, and diversification. Finally, Appendix A is based on a theory about the minimization of types of information costs.

Omissions. Given the kind of book that I have tried to write, it is inevitable that I will have ignored or slighted the beloved topics of at least some professors of corporate law. Many of my silences about standard or semi-standard topics are quite calculated and deliberate; they rest mainly on the belief that it is not wise to try to cover everything, even everything that is arguably of practical importance, in the first pass through a subject. Some of the topics thus ignored or slighted have to do with the particular legal characteristics of different types of securities (bonds versus debentures versus preferred stock), the ALI's Corporate Governance Project, the proper drafting of articles and bylaws, and miscellaneous doctrinal areas such as conflict of law issues, the de facto incorporation cases, and state Blue Sky laws. These and similar omissions are obviously matters of judgment and taste, and as to their wisdom I am quite eager to receive feedback from my readers.

Robert C. Clark

April 1986

ACKNOWLEDGMENTS

I owe the greatest thanks to my colleague, Victor Brudney, for his inspiration and for the diligent and helpful way in which he responded to my request to read the draft manuscript of this book. Many other colleagues and law professors commented on parts of the manuscript at one time or another, and I am grateful to them all. The contributions of David Herwitz and Roberta Romano were especially helpful.

Several generations of Harvard law students have helped me by their research assistance or by writing unusually informative and perceptive papers under my supervision. The list of these noble co-workers includes Maria Galeno, Carol Westrich, Elliot Stein, Eric Richter, Michael Lyons, Peter Brody, Janet McKinnon, Marlene Stein, Richard Kahn, Krishnan Chittur, Lisa Sockett, Catherine Creech, and Christopher Grisanti.

I am deeply grateful to several sources of financial support that enabled me to complete this book: Harvard Law School, through its sabbatical and summer research programs; Stanford Law School, for making me a law and business fellow in the summer of 1984; and the John M. Olin Foundation, through its generous support of Harvard Law School's law and economics program.

I must also thank a number of organizations for graciously giving their permission to reprint portions of my previously published work:

The Duties of the Corporate Debtor to Its Creditors, 90 Harv. L. Rev. 505 (1977) (used in chapter 2). Copyright © 1977 by the Harvard Law Review Association.

Liability Insurance for Savings Association Directors, Officers, and Inside Counsel, 43 Legal Bulletin 57 (March 1977) (used in section 15.10). Reprinted from the LEGAL BULLETIN law review, March 1977, with permission of the United States League of Savings Institutions.

A New Look at Corporate Opportunities, 94 Harv. L. Rev. 997 (1981) (written with Victor Brudney) (used in sections 7.4-7.9). Copyright © 1981 by the Harvard Law Review Association.

Vote Buying and Corporate Law, 29 Case W. Res. L. Rev. 776 (1979) (used in section 9.5). Copyright © 1979 Case Western Reserve Law Review.

What Is the Proper Role of the Corporation?, from Brooks, Liebman, and Schelling's Public-Private Partnership: New Opportunities for Meeting Social Needs 195-220 (used in chapter 16). Copyright © 1984 by The American Academy of Arts and Sciences. Reprinted with permission from Ballinger Publishing Company.

In all but the last of these listed items, the previous work has been greatly revised and supplemented.

Finally, I must thank my family (Kathleen, Alexander, and Matthew) for bearing with me as I labored long on this project and for their cheerful assistance with the final stages of manuscript preparation.

SPECIAL NOTICE

SHORT CITATION FORMS

In order to reduce the bulk of the footnotes, the book departs from the formal citation practices of law reviews in a number of ways. The major differences are as follows:

1. Dates. References to statutory sources and securities law rules are usually undated. All such references are to compilations in force in 1985. Dates are used only when the statute has been superseded or the time of adoption is relevant.

2. State statutes. Frequently cited corporation laws are cited in abbreviated form as follows:

MBCA §8.01	Model Business Corporation Act, Section 8.01 (as approved June 1984).
Cal. §300	California Corporations Code, Section 300.
Del. §141	Delaware General Corporation Law, Section 141.
N.Y. §701	New York Business Corporation Law, Section 701.

Other statutes are cited in Blue Book form, except for the omission of dates.

3. State cases. I omit parallel citations and cite only the West regional reporters whenever possible. An unadorned abbreviation of a state's name means the decision was made by the state's highest court. For example, "493 A.2d 946 (Del. 1985)" cites a decision of the Delaware Supreme Court; "460 P.2d 464 (Cal. 1969)" cites a decision of the California Supreme Court. A lower court opinion is indicated by an added abbreviation in the parenthetical part of the cite, e.g., "(Del. Ch. 1985)" or "(N.Y. App. Div. 1969)".

4. Federal sources. References to the federal securities laws and rules under it are given in a short form familiar to practicing lawyers:

Securities Act §5	Section 5 of the Securities Act of 1933, which as a whole is codified at 15 U.S.C. §77a et seq.
Rule 144	Rule 144 under that act. The rules appear in 17 C.F.R. 230.xxx, where "xxx" means the number of the rule.
Securities Exchange Act §10(b)	Section 10(b) of the Securities Exchange Act of 1934, which as a whole is codified at 15 U.S.C. §78a et seq.
Rule 10b-5	Rule 10b-5 under that act. The rules appear in 17 C.F.R. 240.xxx, where "xxx" means the number of the rule.

CORPORATE LAW

CHAPTER 1

INTRODUCTION

§1.1 Dominance of the Corporate Form of Organization

Rise of corporations

Only a few centuries ago, the privately owned, for-profit business corporation did not exist.[1] At the beginning of the nineteenth century, most business and commerce was conducted by proprietorships and partnerships. Today, however, the corporation is the dominant form of business organization. As of a recent year, for example, although there were only about 3 million active corporations in the United States as compared to nearly 13 million proprietorships and 1 million partnerships, the corporations accounted for about 89 percent of business receipts.[2] Furthermore, the larger a particular business enterprise is, the more likely it is to be operated in corporate form. For example, among businesses with receipts of more than $1 million per year, a figure that is only modestly large by today's standards, corporations account for more than 96 percent of receipts.[3] True, the situation varies among industries.

Corporations are overwhelmingly predominant, in terms of the percentage of receipts they account for, in manufacturing, transportation, public utilities, and wholesale trade. They clearly predominate, by margins of two

§1.1 [1]See A. Chandler, The Visible Hand 14 (1977).
[2]U.S. Bureau of the Census, Statistical Abstract of the U.S. 532 (1984).
[3]Ibid.

to five, typically, in wholesale and resale trade and in services. However, they still account for only about a quarter of the receipts in agriculture, forestry, and fishing, where proprietorships are most important, and in certain large sectors of the economy, such as higher education and medical care, the nonprofit corporation is the dominant form of organization. But overall, the business corporation is the principal form for carrying out business activities in this country. A similar rise to dominance of the corporate form has either occurred or is occurring in other non-Communist industrialized or developing countries.

Puzzle of the corporation's dominance

What were the causes of this amazing historical transformation? What accounts for the continued preference for the corporate form of organization? Is this preference likely to be a fairly permanent feature of modern economies?

Explanations based on four main characteristics

I propose to sketch out one plausible answer to these questions. Briefly, what accounts for the corporation's success as a form of organization are its characteristics and a social environment that makes these characteristics useful. For convenience, I will identify four such characteristics:

(1) limited liability for investors;
(2) free transferability of investor interests;
(3) legal personality (entity-attributable powers, life span, and purpose); and
(4) centralized management.

Conditions favoring corporations

These four characteristics all serve the positive functions of greatly facilitating the efficient aggregation of very large amounts of capital from numerous investors and the efficient operation of a very large business with numerous owners and employees. Starting in the nineteenth century, I suggest, three conditions in society emerged so that an organizational form that could serve these functions was better fit to survive and grow than other forms of organization.

(1) Large firms

Technological advances led to great increases in economies of scale, that is, to an enormous increase in the number of workers and the amount of capital equipment that could be suitably combined in a single business organization. There was then a development toward very large business firms and, thus, a need for a form of organization that would be efficient for large firms. The railroads and the telegraph systems provide obvious examples of the new firms. In colonial times, there was a great amount of specialization among business firms, yet very few had more than a dozen employees.[4] In the late nineteenth and twentieth centuries, many firms employed thousands of people.

[4] See A. Chandler, note 1 supra, at 17.

Qualifications

The influence of technological developments on this shift to large size was strong but not simple or complete. In many industrial enterprises, for example, the technological innovations were such that a factory of fairly modest size could manufacture enough widgets to satisfy most of the demand in the reachable markets. Theoretically, entrepreneurs might simply have operated modestly large manufacturing firms and sold all their output through independent distributors. Yet many firms of this type "integrated forward"—they created or acquired their own distribution systems—and became even larger. According to a major historical analysis of the process,[5] they did this to better coordinate their manufacturing activities with the wholesaling and retailing process. Why in-the-firm coordination was then thought to be better than market or contractual coordination with outside distributors was itself linked to technological developments in communication and transportation. Managers came to perceive new ways to reduce the costs of coordinating complex business activities.[6]

Not all increases in business size were motivated by real economies of scale, of course; some were the product of an urge to suppress competition. What the mix of motives was is hard to determine with confidence, but the force of technologically based real economies was clearly great.[7]

(2) Dispersion of wealth

The second condition favoring the corporate form of organization was that the distribution of wealth, although by no means equal, was not extremely lopsided. This meant, and continues to mean, that the large amounts of money capital needed to launch and sustain large business enterprises must be collected and aggregated into usable pools. Business must solicit investors on a mass scale, not merely by private negotiations with a handful of very rich people.

(3) Private Property

The third condition was that private ownership of investment property was accepted as a social norm. This ruled out the alternative of solving the capital aggregation problem solely by having the government force savings and investment through taxation and government sponsorship of large business. Instead, promoters of large business somehow had to tap the savings of numerous private investors. Furthermore, the numerosity of the investor class made it inevitable that many of them would have little knowledge about and power over the actual running of large enterprises.

General result of the three conditions

The concatenation of these factors—large business units, numerous in-

[5] Id. at 285-286.

[6] See Williamson, The Modern Corporation: Origins, Evolutions, Attributes, 19 J. Econ. Lit. 1537 (1981).

[7] It has been suggested that, in the first wave of mergers in this country, the anticompetitive horizontal combinations rarely succeeded over the long run. See A. Chandler, note 1 supra, at 285.

vestors of relatively modest wealth, and the institution of private property—put a premium on forms of organization that facilitated the raising of large amounts of capital from numerous geographically scattered investors and that lent itself to the efficient management of a large firm with numerous employees and owners. In these respects the corporate form is clearly superior to its rivals: the proprietorship, the partnership, the limited partnership, and the business trust.

Because of its defining characteristics, the corporation had greater fitness for the environment in which it developed, and it in fact has survived and prospered. By the same token, if one or more of the three identified conditions of the social environment change radically in the future, the business corporation may well be eclipsed by something else.

The dark side

The growth of the corporation was not an unmixed good, however. Each of the four defining characteristics can be viewed as a thesis that has a deeply troublesome antithesis. The characteristics generate a predictable set of conflicts and problems that are a permanent structural feature of the corporate system. These conflicts and problems make up the bulk of the real problems dealt with under the headings of corporate law and securities regulation. In fact, corporate law is best understood as an attempt to synthesize these theses and antitheses—that is, to solve, mitigate, or sublimate these permanent and predictable sets of problems in the corporate system.

Why study the next section

In summary, if you

(1) want to understand what a corporation is, as distinct from other business forms;
(2) want to understand why the corporation has become so dominant a form of organization of collective activity;
(3) want to be able to give clients good advice about their choice between alternative forms of business organization; and
(4) want to unify and thus simplify your understanding of most of the particular problems and legal rules dealt with as the subject of corporate law;

you will be well advised to gain a careful understanding of those four characteristics.

§1.2 Comparison with Partnerships

Plan of study

To explore what each one of the four basic corporate characteristics means,

I will contrast it to the analogous attribute of the general partnership. I will ask what functions the corporate characteristics serve, and whether they are socially good ones. I will then introduce the problems that the characteristics create. The remainder of this book is a long exposition of these problems in their concrete forms.

Hypo of futuristic railroad

Consider an imaginary example. Colonists from the United States and Japan have settled on Titan, a satellite of Saturn, in a large number of scattered towns. Several entrepreneurs think that a transplanetary jet-propelled rail system would be a boon to heavy industry, and would be very profitable. They need an estimated $1.1 billion to build the rail system. The Bank of Titan is willing to lend $600 million, so they somehow have to raise another $500 million from individual investors. Conceivably, they could raise the money from the top 10 families on Titan, but unless the distribution of wealth is very skewed, not all large projects could be financed this way. Suppose instead that they must interest 50,000 middle class investors, each of whom will contribute $10,000 of discretionary funds in return for a chance to share in the profits of the rail system. They are now trying to decide whether to form a partnership organized under the Uniform Partnership Act (UPA)[1] or to form a corporation under Titan's version of the Model Business Corporation Act (MBCA).[2] (These stipulations are relevant ones today. Versions of the UPA exist in 48 states and the District of Columbia. The MBCA has influenced many states' laws, and it does not differ much from other states' corporate statutes in the matters relevant here.)

Partnership statutes vs. corporation statutes

The term *partnership* is defined as an association of two or more co-owners to carry on a business for profit.[3] In most vital respects, partners' rights and duties are determined by specific contracts. The statute is not technically necessary for the creation of a partnership, and it mainly fills in the blanks of the parties' agreements and understandings. By contrast, a corporation is a legal entity deemed to come into existence upon compliance with certain formal procedures, for example, filing articles of incorporation in the proper form with a secretary of state, who then issues a formal certificate of incorporation.[4] These procedures are taken pursuant to a corporate statute that is essential to the corporation's legal existence and that sets up some firm rules to govern the parties' rights and duties.

§1.2 [1]Unif. Partnership Act, 6 U.L.A §1 et seq. (1969) (hereinafter cited as UPA).

[2]The version cited was approved in June, 1984, but the previous version, which influenced many state statutes, is substantially similar in the matters covered in this chapter.

[3]UPA §6(1).

[4]MBCA §§2.01-2.03.

§1.2.1 Investor's Liability

Partners' liability in tort

As partners. If the promoters on Titan form a general partnership and each of the 50,000 investors becomes a partner, there will be unfavorable consequences with respect to tort liability, fiduciary misconduct, and contractual obligations. Traditionally, partners are said to be jointly liable for the partnership's contractual obligations and jointly and severally liable for its tort liabilities. To grasp the operational meaning of these catchwords requires some exposition. Suppose Edward, an investor-partner acting on behalf of the partnership, tries to speed the laying of jet-rail tracks by dynamiting the top of a mountain, which by his negligence falls the wrong way and smashes a town of 500 people. Their survivors want to bring wrongful death actions for damages of $1 million apiece. If willing to contend with the procedural problems of doing so, the survivors could bring a suit naming all 50,000 partners as defendants, or they could bring suits for the full amount of the liability due to Edward's negligence against any one of the partners.[5]

For breach of trust

Further, if partner David, who is in charge of collecting and disbursing the proceeds of the Bank of Titan loan, takes the money and absconds to Earth, the Bank of Titan could sue all of the partners upon whom it could get service and could collect the $6 million debt from the personal assets of each of the partners.[6]

For contract obligations

Suppose the jet-rail system, having been poorly managed by chief partner Rex, is a complete flop: The partnership spends the partners' contributions and the loan proceeds, gets zero revenues, sells the system as scrap for $100 million, and then has a bank loan liability $500 million greater than its assets. The bank can collect the shortfall from the partners.[7] According to the UPA, they are liable jointly, which seems to mean that they must all be joined in a suit by Bank of Titan (a difficult chore for the bank, since there are 50,000 partners), but statutes and courts vary on this point.[8] The

[5] UPA §§13, 15.

[6] UPA §§14, 15(a).

[7] UPA §15(b).

[8] Fifteen states and the District of Columbia have passed statutes specifically declaring partnership liability for all obligations to be joint and several. (Alabama, Arizona, Arkansas, Colorado, District of Columbia, Iowa, Kansas, Maryland, Minnesota, Mississippi, Missouri, New Mexico, North Carolina, Tennessee, Texas, West Virginia.) 6 U.L.A. 174-175. Courts in other jurisdictions may be strict in requiring that plaintiffs must join all the partners in a suit to recover a debt or obligation of the partnership. See Cunard Line Ltd. v. Abney, 540 F. Supp. 657 (S.D.N.Y 1982) (joint nature of contract gives joint obligor the right to insist that plaintiff join the other obligors if joinder is possible); Concra Corp. v. Andrus, 446 A.2d 363 (Vt. 1982) (trial court erred in holding defendant partners both jointly and severally liable, since under Vermont statute partners are only jointly liable for contract liability).

bank might sue the partnership as such, since each partner is supposed to contribute his share of the losses to the partnership so that creditors can collect on the partnership obligations due them.[9] As among the partners, the amount each of them has to contribute can be based on agreement. If there is no agreement, they split the losses in the same way they do the profits (which is not necessarily in proportion to their capital contributions). If there is no agreement about splitting profits, they are shared equally by all partners (which, again, is not the same as sharing pro rata in accordance with the size of each partner's capital contribution). In the hypothetical, each investor with sufficient assets would lose at least her original $10,000 investment plus another $10,000 from noninvested assets when the bank collected on its loan.

Unmet contributions

Furthermore, if the partnership were ended and some of the partners—say, half—cannot or will not make their contributions to the losses, the remaining partners have to make up this shortfall. Each of the responsible investors might then lose a third $10,000. That is, when all is said and done, each investor has potentially unlimited personal liability for the full amount of the partnership's contractual debts, not just for its tort liabilities. The investor does have a right to get contribution from fellow partners. Whether this right provides any actual comfort depends on the wealth of the other partners and the costs and trouble of bringing lawsuits to enforce contribution rights.

Mutual agency

A final ugly fillip is that all the above problems are made much worse by the fact that *all* of the 50,000 partners are agents of the partnership with respect to the partnership business and can therefore create partnership liabilities to third parties.[10]

In sum, any potential investor who appreciates the full extent of the possible liabilities as partner in the proposed jet-rail venture is apt to become very discouraged.

Shareholders' limited liability

As corporate shareholders. If the partnership idea is dropped and the 50,000 investors contract to buy shares of common stock in a corporation, each contributing $10,000 for 100 shares, they are liable only for the subscription price.[11] The corporation's agents and employees can run up sizable tort and contract liabilities, but the 50,000 passive investors will only lose their original $10,000 contributions. Their remaining personal assets will be safe.

[9] UPA §18(a).
[10] UPA §9(1).
[11] MBCA §6.22.

Does limited liability produce benefits?

Functions of corporate investors' limited liability. Smart students often doubt whether the shareholders' limited liability really produces a net gain, whether to the shareholders, the enterprise, or society. Consider this argument. If the bank loan is to go to the jet-rail enterprise organized as a corporation, the Bank of Titan will take account of the fact that it will not be able to collect the loan out of the individual assets of the 50,000 investors, whereas if the enterprise were organized as a partnership the bank could rely on these assets as providing some extra security for repayment. The bank may therefore charge a higher interest rate on the loan to the enterprise as corporation than to the enterprise as partnership. The investor-shareholders will endure less risk than if they were partners, but they will in effect pay more interest and get a smaller net return for themselves from the business. Have they gained? Could they ever gain from limited liability when there are perfectly competitive loan markets?

(1) Shifting risk to better bearers

The answer is yes, for three distinct reasons. First, limited liability often shifts risk to a better risk bearer, and this produces gains from trade. If the interest rate differential on the bank loan is 1 percent and each middle class investor therefore gives up about $100 a year by investing in a corporation as opposed to a partnership, the result is the equivalent of the investor's paying a $100 premium for a comprehensive personal liability insurance policy to protect her noninvested assets.

Buying insurance of this sort can be perfectly rational and can make both the investor and the insurer better off without making anyone else worse off. One reason has to do with the marginal utility of wealth. The average middle class investor of modest means will be much more upset about losing $10,000 worth of personal assets such as her personal automobile than about losing her $10,000 discretionary investment. Because of the declining marginal utility of wealth, the same dollar loss will not always create the same amount of disutility or suffering.

By contrast, the bank will find the slight risk of a $10,000 portion of its loan being unpaid because it cannot send a sheriff to get and sell an investor's automobile an unimpressive one, since it is a large entity with a diversified portfolio of loans and investments, and a $10,000 loss to it will not come out of its necessities of life. Another reason the bank may be a better risk bearer is that it is better at assessing and monitoring risks; risk assessment is one of its specialties.

(2) Reducing transaction costs

Second, limited liability eliminates the possibility of the incurrence of the huge transaction costs that would be created if the bank ever had to bring individual collection suits against 50,000 geographically scattered investors. Similarly, if the rule were unlimited liability and the bank were therefore going to rely on the investor's capacity to repay, it would want to assess the credit ratings of all of the 50,000 investors—a cumbersome and expensive task. Limited liability eliminates the need for doing this. The bank assesses only the corporation's capacity to repay and it sets the interest rate and other loan terms accordingly. Thus, limited liability greatly reduces two kinds of transaction costs of contracting about loans: the costs of credit evaluation and the costs of enforcement. In principle, eliminating these costs can make some or all those involved with the corporation better off without making anyone worse off.

Contract as good as statute?

At this point the observer who is innocent of the world but knowledgeable about some parts of economic theory may object that these two advantages of shareholder's limited liability are illusory because they are not restricted to shareholders. In principle, a partnership could simply agree to pay a higher interest rate on its loans and the bank could agree not to look to the partners' personal assets. The partners could thus achieve the two benefits of limited liability that were just mentioned. In fact, this strategy is legally possible, but it is not an impressive one. In a *large scale* business enterprise that has many lenders and suppliers and other potential creditors, achieving virtual limited liability by negotiation of specific contractual provisions with each creditor will be cumbersome, expensive, and risky to the investors. (What happens, for example, if the managing partners fail to reach agreement with a particular creditor?) It is more expeditious to have the legal system create a general presumption, or *form contract,* of the following sort: Everybody (meaning investors, lenders, and businessmen) dealing with businesses of a certain type (namely, corporations) must expect that limited investor liability is the rule and plan their affairs accordingly. This will save the expense of many time-consuming individual negotiations. If any lender or supplier dealing with a particular corporation does not like the general rule, it is free to try to negotiate personal guarantees by some or all investors. In effect, the corporate statute simply creates an efficient general presumption about the allocation of risks. Investors and creditors are free to bargain around the presumption, but how the presumption is set can make a big difference to the economic performance of the business sector.

(3) Avoiding tort liabilities

Moreover, the possibility of contracting against individual investor liability would not help to insulate partners' personal assets against tort liabilities generated by the business. This point in turn suggests a third function of limited liability. Shareholder limited liability sometimes keeps the investors from paying the full costs of the enterprise's external effects. If the enterprise damages consumers or bystanders and their tort claims cannot be satisfied out of corporate assets, the loss simply stays on the victims. Whether this possibility suggests that lawmakers concerned with the overall public interest ought to abolish the general rule of limited liability with respect to corporations' tort victims will be discussed in the second chapter.

At this point, it is worthwhile to add a note of realism about the significance of this theoretical problem. Despite some notable recent exceptions, it seems clear that, throughout most of the history of the modern corporation, very few *large* incorporated businesses have failed *because* of overwhelming tort liabilities, as opposed to contractual liabilities. It is much more plausible to criticize those rules that prevent tort victims from even getting a judgment against a corporation—for example, the old rules that, before the great judicial developments in strict products liability, prevented a consumer injured by a corporate product from getting recovery without proving negligence.[12] If, as some historians argue, [13] judges in the late nineteenth century fashioned rules to put many costs of businesses onto consumers and the public rather than on investors, the techniques by which they did so are to be found in tort law holdings rather than in the general institution of shareholders' limited liability.

§1.2.2 Investor's Ability to Transfer Interests

Partners' property rights

As partners. Suppose the jet-rail enterprise has been launched as a partnership, and one of the 50,000 investors, needing cash, wants to sell all her partnership rights to someone else. This is not a simple matter, because being a partner is not a simple thing. Under the UPA a partner's *property rights* are threefold.[14]

(1) She has rights in specific partnership property, that is, she has an undivided interest as *tenant in partnership* with the other partners in the enterprise's land, rails, jets, and the like.[15]
(2) She has an *interest in the partnership,* consisting of her right to share in the profits and surplus of the partnership.[16]

[12] For an interesting example of such a critique, see Justice Traynor's concurring opinion in Escola v. Coca Cola Bottling Co. of Fresno, 150 P.2d 436, 440-444 (Cal. 1944), which held in favor of a strict products liability standard. See also Restatement (Second) of Torts §402A (products liability rule).

[13] See M. Horwitz, The Transformation of American Law, 1780-1860, at 74-78 (1977). For a critique of this view of the history of tort law, see Schwartz, Tort Law and the Economy in Nineteenth-Century America: A Reinterpretation, 90 Yale L.J. 1717 (1981).

[14] UPA §24.

[15] UPA §25.

[16] UPA §26.

(3) And, absent contrary agreement, she has an equal right to participate in the management of the partnership.[17]

Not only are these three property rights severable; they cannot be transferred as a unit.

Problems selling interest in the partnership

Consider first the *interest in the partnership*, since that right, being a claim to a stream of future income, is what a new investor would be most interested in paying money to get. A partner can sell, or "assign," her interest in the partnership to a new investor. The other partners cannot object, and the assignment does not dissolve the partnership.[18] But there are serious flaws in this process. The assignee's rights to information about the partnership business are poor. She cannot invoke the sections of the UPA that give a full-fledged partner the right to inspect and copy partnership books,[19] to have other partners render on demand true and full information about all things affecting the partnership,[20] and to get a formal account as to partnership affairs under certain conditions.[21] The assignee's security about whether she is getting what she thinks she is paying for is quite imperfect, for an interest in the partnership is not embodied in a so-called negotiable instrument.[22] This means that even a good faith purchaser for value of such an interest may be subject to unknown claims against the interest that were created by the transferor or a prior owner.

Moreover, the assignee's right to receive income from the partnership is often doubly contingent, on the business success of the partnership and on the efforts and behavior of the particular partner who originally assigned the interest in question. Under many partnership agreements an individ-

[17] UPA §18(e).
[18] UPA §27(1).
[19] UPA §19.
[20] UPA §20.
[21] UPA §22.
[22] Common examples of negotiable instruments are checks drawn on banks, certificates of deposit, and promissory notes. A formal definition stipulating when such things are considered negotiable instruments is given in UCC §3-104(1). The concept of a negotiable instrument is best understood, however, by studying the legal consequences of calling a written document a negotiable instrument. Under UCC §3-301 the holder of such an instrument is able to transfer or negotiate it, whether or not he is the owner of it. As for transferees, UCC §3-305 declares that a holder in due course takes the instrument free from all claims to it on the part of any person and free from most defenses. Under §3-302(1) a holder in due course is defined as a holder who takes the instrument for value, in good faith, and without notice of claims to it or defenses against it. (In reading §§301 and 305 note that the term *instrument* means *negotiable instrument*. See §3-102(1)(e).)

Checks, promissory notes, and other things described by §3-104(1) do not exhaust the category of negotiable instruments, however. As the text will shortly point out, shares of stock in a corporation are also considered negotiable instruments. See UCC §§8-105(1), 8-102(1)(a). And there are other examples beyond our concern here.

ual partner's share in the profits (which is what the interest in the partnership is about) depends on how much business she brings in, how much work she does, and so forth.

If the interest in the partnership is viewed as a kind of investment security, it must therefore be viewed as having *two* issuers, a partnership and a particular partner, and an interest originating from one partner in a given partnership is *not* fungible with an interest originating from another partner in the same partnership. To put it mildly, this makes for a complicated market in partnership interests. Indeed, the fourth and most serious flaw in the transferability of interests in partnerships is that there are no efficient, highly organized trading markets in which such interests can be sold and bought.[23] This lack results from the other flaws—poor rights to information, non-negotiability, and the double issuer problem.

Rights in specific property

As for the original partners' rights in specific partnership property, they cannot be assigned by individual partners.[24] There is therefore no trading or "secondary" market in these rights, let alone an organized, efficient one. The rights have meaning only when items of partnership property, or proceeds from their sale, are distributed from the partnership to the partners—for example, when the partnership is terminated.

Management rights

Furthermore, a particular partner's management rights are also not transferable, and, absent contrary agreement, the only way a person can become a full-fledged new partner is by getting the consent of all the existing partners.[25] Even when the selection of new partners is delegated by agreement to a committee of partners, there is still no such thing as an individually salable right to vote or participate, and thus no easy way for an outsider to buy her way into control of a partnership by buying, for example, a majority of the interests in the partnership.

Relative illiquidity of partner's investment

Contemplating the cumbersome, fragmented, and incomplete methods of selling one's bundle of rights in a partnership, the potential investor is likely to place a substantial discount on the expected value of her investment because the investment will be so illiquid—that is, hard to sell quickly and at a price reflecting the rights' full intrinsic value—should the need to sell arise. This discount will make it hard for the promoters to raise the necessary funds. They will have to offer a higher expected return per unit of invested funds than if they could offer investors a more liquid investment.

[23] Trading of investor interests in *limited* partnerships is possible and does occur. See generally Revised Unif. Limited Partnership Act, 1984 Pocket Part, 6 U.L.A 189 et seq. (1976).

[24] UPA §§25(2)(b)-25(2)(d).

[25] UPA §18(g).

Shareholder's easily sold bundle of rights

As corporate shareholders. If the promoters offered the 50,000 investors shares of stock in a corporation, the situation would be radically different. The rights that characterize shares in corporations are multiple and varying. The corporate statutes allow corporations to issue classes of shares that have such relative rights, preferences, and limitations as are designated by the proper formal procedures.[26] But usually, what are referred to as shares of *common stock* possess the following three rights under state corporate law:

(1) the right to share pro rata (that is, the same amount for each share) in dividend payments, if and when the directors exercise their discretion to declare dividends,[27] and to share pro rata in distributions in liquidation of the enterprise;[28]
(2) the right to vote, on a one share–one vote basis,[29] upon the election of directors and certain major corporate changes such as mergers with other companies and liquidations;[30] and
(3) a restricted but not negligible right to information in the form of a shareholder's right to inspect corporate books and records.[31]

Absent contrary agreement or charter provision,[32] all of these rights are transferable (they can be sold by the individual shareholder) as a unit, and without the consent of other shareholders or the directors and officers of the corporation. The rights are usually embodied in a negotiable instrument.[33] There is only a single issuer: Because the corporate statute clearly separates the functions of investor and manager, the claim to a pro rata share of dividends depends simply upon ownership of stock. Whether or not the prior owner of a particular share of stock was and is a paid employee or officer of the corporation, and whether he now proceeds to add to or take away from the corporation's profitability, has no bearing on the

[26] MBCA §6.01(a).

[27] See MBCA §§6.40(a); 6.01(a), last sentence.

[28] See MBCA §6.01(b)(2).

[29] See MBCA §§6.01(b)(1), 7.21(a).

[30] MBCA §§8.03(d)(election of directors), 8.08 (removal of directors), 11.03 (merger), 12.02 (sale of substantially all assets other than in regular course of business), 14.02 (dissolution).

[31] MBCA §§16.02-16.04. See also §§7.20 (right to inspect shareholders' list), 16.20-16.21 (corporation's duty to furnish annual financial statements and certain other reports to shareholders).

[32] See MBCA §6.27. This authorization provides relatively clear guidelines for those (mostly participants in closely held corporations) who do want to impose restrictions on share transfers. The basic principle of free transferability is regarded as so obvious by modern draftsmen that they simply assume it or, as here, display it by negative implication.

[33] See MBCA §6.25; Uniform Commercial Code §§8-102, 8-105(1), 8-301(1), 8-301(2). Modern statutes, e.g., MBCA §6.26, also allow for the issuance of certificateless shares.

relative dividend rights of that share as opposed to other shares in its class. Shares of a certain class of stock in a certain corporation are basically fungible.

Why stock markets possible

Because of all these characteristics of corporate stock (free transferability of the whole bundle of rights, negotiability, and fungibility within classes) organized, efficient trading markets in corporate stock were able to arise and did arise. If the promoters of a new enterprise can offer shares that will be tradable on one of the organized stock markets, the potential investors will not place a substantial illiquidity discount on their investments, as they would on partnership rights.

Value of tradable shares

Functions of free transferability of shares. The chief function of the free transferability of corporate shares is to promote investor liquidity, and thus, indirectly to facilitate the capital formation process. This function appears especially important when one examines the chief alternative way of giving investors liquidity. This alternative is to give each investor a right to demand at any time that the enterprise buy back her interest for cash, perhaps at some value fixed by formula, such as book value, or by a set procedure, such as the fair value as determined by three independent appraisers. This right to force a buyout is routinely available to partners,[34] but giving investors in a *large, nonfinancial*[35] enterprise the right to be bought out at any time is a dangerous and potentially disruptive move. If a large number of investors exercise their right at once, the enterprise might only be able to meet its obligations by selling off property and disrupting operations and, thus, by destroying some of the firm's going concern value. (*Going concern* value is the firm's value as an integrated functioning business, and it is substantially greater in a successful business than the sum of the sale values of isolated items of property and other rights owned by the firm. A healthy business is worth more alive than dead.) Thus, the buyout right could provide liquidity to investors, but it could be extremely wasteful, both to investors as a class and to society, as compared to a world in which investors have liquidity because they can sell to other investors. Furthermore, the disruptiveness of the buyout right cannot be fully remedied by making the investors who trigger it pay for any disruption losses they cause to the other investors—this is the approach taken by the

[34] UPA §38.

[35] In a financial enterprise, such as an investment company or a commercial bank, assets are often broken up into many separate parts (particular stocks, bonds, and loans that the investment company or bank owns) that are fairly liquid. Selling financial assets to meet the claims of investors who are withdrawing from a financial enterprise is less likely to be fatally disruptive than selling assets in an industrial company.

UPA[36]—because the disruption losses that will still be caused despite this damage requirement are a dead weight loss to society, at least by comparison to the losses generated by an efficient secondary market in investor interests.

§1.2.3 Legal Personality

Economic value of legal fictions

One of the law's most economically significant contributions to business life, and one often ignored by lawyers because it generates less litigation than many other contributions, has been the creation of fictional but legally recognized entities or "persons" that are treated as having some of the attributes of natural persons. The process of creating fictions in our own image can be more or less thorough. Some legal persons are stunted beings with limited powers and no soul, like a handheld calculator. Others, like the ancient Golem or the futuristic robots of science fiction, not only have numerous powers but have a teleology or goal structure built into them. Partnerships and corporations fall into this latter category.

Partnership's powers

Of a partnership. The promoters of the Titan jet-rail system would find that putting their business in a partnership rather than a corporation would cause some problems because of the fact that partnerships are not treated as legal persons to quite the same extent as are corporations, although these problems would not be great by comparison to those already discussed. Under modern partnership law, powers important to operation of the business are often set in the entity. Thus, under the UPA any estate in real property may be acquired in the partnership name, and an estate so acquired may be conveyed by any partner executing a conveyance in the partnership name.[37] (Imagine having to list the names of 50,000 partners on every recorded deed of partnership property and having to change the deeds as new partners come in or old partners die, retire, or withdraw.) In addition, many states' procedural rules allow a partnership to sue or be sued as an entity.[38] Yet for some purposes a partnership is thought of as an aggregate of its members rather than a legal entity.[39]

[36] UPA §38(2).

[37] UPA §§8(3), 10(1).

[38] See, e.g., Cal. Civ. Proc. Code §388 (West 1973), Ill. Rev. Stat. Ch. 110 §2-411 (1983), Mich. Comp. Laws Ann. §600.2051 (West 1981), N.Y. Civ. Prac. Law §1025 (McKinney 1976), Utah R. Civ. Proc. Rule 17(d) (1977). The Illinois and Utah statutes say only that a partnership can be sued as an entity or by its common name, not that it can sue others in its firm name. In fact, Caliber Partners, Ltd. v. Affeld, 583 F. Supp. 1308 (D.D.C. 1984), held that a partnership could not sue in its firm name under the Illinois statute.

[39] The most important example is that, under the Internal Revenue Code, the federal

Partnership's purpose

The general purpose of any partnership is implied by the UPA's definition of *partnership:* an association of two or more persons to carry on as co-owners a business for profit.[40] The kinds of businesses that partnerships can legally carry on form a large and open-ended class. The restrictions come not from partnership law but from practical considerations and other legal restraints.

Partnership's life span: precarious

The life span of a partnership may be set by the partnership agreement, but each partner still has the power to kill or threaten the enterprise. For example, when the partnership agreement specifies no definite term or particular undertaking, any partner can cause the partnership's dissolution at any time without violating the partnership agreement and, absent contrary agreement, may have the partnership property applied to pay its liabilities and the surplus applied to pay in cash the net amount owed to

---

income tax is assessed against the profits of the individual partners. There is no separate partnership income tax, although there is a separate corporation income tax. Compare I.R.C. §701 with §11. (The partnership, however, does have to file an information return.)

In many other respects, aggregate treatment is a matter of history. Prior to the drafting of the UPA, the partnership was treated at common law as an aggregate of individuals. In 1907, the Commissioners on Uniform Laws appointed a committee to prepare a Uniform Act based on the entity theory of partnership, which was the basis of partnership law in civil law countries. Controversy ensued. Ultimately, in 1914, the UPA was adopted; it incorporated both the entity and aggregate theories of partnership. This compromise resulted in ambiguities in the law of partnership. See Jensen, Is a Partnership Under the Uniform Partnership Act an Aggregate or an Entity? 16 Vand. L. Rev. 377 (1963). As a result of the compromise, a partnership was defined in §6(1) as an aggregate of individuals but was treated as an entity in most of the substantive provisions. One notable exception in the UPA to the entity approach is the exclusion of the right of the partnership to sue or be sued in its own name.

The following sections of the UPA contain references to a partnership as an entity: §§8-10, 12-15, 18, 19, 21, 24-28, 30, 35(1)(b), 40(a)II, 40(h), and 40(i). These sections provide, inter alia, that the partnership may acquire property in its own name, that a partner is an agent of the partnership, and that a partnership has rights and liabilities under contract, tort, and property law. Notice to a partner constitutes notice to the partnership. The partnership is obligated to indemnify partners for personal liabilities incurred in ordinary business, but a partnership is insulated from separate creditors of the partners as individuals.

Under Rule 17(b) of the Federal Rules of Civil Procedure, the entity theory is applied, and actions arising under the Constitution or federal laws may be brought against the partnership. Serpa v. Jolly King Restaurants, Inc., 62 F.R.D. 626 (S.D. Cal. 1974). In diversity cases, the state procedural rule is followed. Roller Derby Assoc. v. Seltzer 54 F.R.D. 556 (N.D. Ill. 1972), Donald Manter Co. v. Davis, 543 F.2d 419 (1st Cir. 1976). Diversity is determined, however, in an aggregate sense by looking at the citizenship of each partner and not by looking at the citizenship of the partnership as an entity. Feldmann Insurance Agency v. Brodsky, 195 F. Supp. 483 (D. Md. 1961).

Under the Federal Bankruptcy Reform Act of 1978, 11 U.S.C.A. §101(30), the word *person* is defined to include a partnership. A partnership may be adjudged bankrupt separately from its partners.

[40] UPA §6(1).

the partners.[41] Even when it is in contravention of the partnership agreement, any partner may dissolve the partnership by "express will" at any time.[42] In this situation the dissolving partner is liable for damages caused by breach of the agreement, and the remaining partners may choose to continue the business as partners of each other. But they still have to pay the dissolving partner the value of her interest in the partnership (or secure payment by court-approved bond), minus the damages for which she is liable.[43] Thus, *dissolution* of a partnership means an ending of the partnership relationship among the partners; it does not imply that the underlying business has been terminated. But if enough partners choose to withdraw and dissolve the old partnership, the requirement of paying them off may lead to curtailment or termination of the business activities as well. The partnership's life is thus a precarious one, and this fact will give pause to those wanting to launch a large enterprise with large start-up costs.

Corporation's powers

Of a corporation. For legal purposes, a corporation is almost as much an entity as a natural person. Powers are set in the entity and are very extensive. Besides listing such chestnuts as the power to own real property in its own name and to sue and be sued, the MBCA gives a corporation "the same powers as an individual to do all things necessary or convenient to carry out its business and affairs. . . ."[44] The purposes of the corporation can be extremely varied, inclusive, and open ended, for the MBCA states that, unless a more limited purpose is set forth in the articles of incorporation, a corporation chartered under it has the purpose of engaging in "any lawful business."[45] In contrast to the situation under early incorporation statutes, most state statutes now allow a corporation's articles of organization to state its purpose as being to engage in any lawful business, without committing itself to any particular lines of activity.

Corporation's purposes

When the corporate statutes talk about corporate purposes, they really are referring to lines of business activity, not to the question of *whose* interests are to be served by the corporation. Although corporate statutes do not answer this question explicitly, lawyers, judges, and economists usually assume that the more ultimate purpose of a business corporation is to make profits for its shareholders. More precisely, corporate managers (directors and officers) are supposed to make corporate decisions so as to

[41] UPA §§31(1)(b), 38(1).
[42] UPA §31(2).
[43] UPA §38(2).
[44] MBCA §3.02.
[45] MBCA §3.01.

maximize the value of the company's shares,[46] subject to the constraint that the corporation must meet all its legal obligations to others who are related to or affected by it. These others include employees, creditors, customers, the general public (as affected by the company's pollution, for example), and governmental units. In other words, although the corporation has numerous and perhaps all-encompassing duties to these others, it is the shareholders who have the claim on the residual value of the enterprise, that is, what's left after all definite obligations are satisfied, and the managers have an affirmative open-ended obligation to increase this residual value, rather than the wealth of some other affected group (including

[46]This formulation (maximize share values) is less likely to give rise to an all-too-common misinterpretation of the vague maximize profits formulation, which some have understood to imply that companies are encouraged to focus only on short-run results and to ignore planning for the future. This view represents a serious conceptual mistake. The value of the corporation's shares depends on the discounted present value of its expected profits in the future. Stock market prices depend in significant part on the future prospects of companies, as perceived by investors. Thus, managers who attempt to maximize the market value of their company's common stock will take account of the probable long-range results of the company's activities as well as its bottom line in the current year.

Sometimes businessmen who fulminate about the way the profit-maximizing principle supposedly forces managers to eschew long-range planning and focus only on quick results (with devastating results in terms of the ability of U.S. companies to compete with more farsighted Japanese companies, etc.) are really just making a plea for a greater amount of power and discretion. Their real complaint is not with the legal concept but with the fact that *investors* as a class (i.e., the stock markets) *disagree* with them. That is, they must think that investors (1) place a higher discount rate on expected future earnings than they, the managers, think the investors should and/or (2) don't trust the managers' long term business strategies as much as the managers do.

It is not hard to see why these disagreements can come about. Managers of a company may be willing to take more business risks than the investors, because it is not primarily the managers' money that is at stake, and, of course, the proponents of a plan of future action (the managers) are more likely to give it credence than are dispassionate observers (i.e., market analysts). We can sympathize with managers who feel the frustration that stems from these disagreements, but this sympathy should not necessarily lead us to change legal rules in a way that would insulate them from the discipline of the stock markets. It is probably better for the corporate system to tell managers who think the market doesn't understand them or appreciate the wisdom of their plans to try harder to persuade the market of their viewpoint—for example, to communicate the bases for optimism about long-range plans. Investors have every reason to assess these managerial communications as accurately as possible.

It is also not hard to see why managers would want to disguise their disagreement with shareholders by complaining (nominally) about the short-sightedness of a profit-maximizing principle. Managers who make this kind of speech usually don't want to insult investors directly, so they try to obfuscate the real issues. And if there are managers who truly believe that the profit-maximizing norm in itself compels a neglect of long-term planning, they are simply confused.

Note also that some critics say *managers* are too short-sighted in their orientation. This alleged defect might be attributed to their incentive compensation plans or to flaws in their education at business school.

themselves). We shall have much more to say about this conception of corporate purpose in chapter 16.

Corporation's life span: durable

Modern statutes like the MBCA give corporations perpetual existence.[47] A better phrase might be "indefinite" existence"; the corporation's status as legal person does not terminate automatically upon the completion of a fixed number of years or a specified business venture, nor do charters have to be renewed periodically. Perpetual existence does not mean that corporations cannot terminate their existence but that they continue to exist as legal persons until some effective dissolution procedure is followed. Under the MBCA a corporation may be dissolved involuntarily by a court decree under certainly narrowly specified conditions,[48] or voluntarily by act of the corporation, that is, by a board of directors' resolution and a subsequent majority vote of the shareholders.[49] Unlike a partner, however, no individual shareholder (unless the shareholder controls the directors and owns the requisite majority of shares or has the benefit of certain close corporation provisions[50]) can unilaterally dissolve the entity and withdraw his investment. Shareholders get distributions of cash or property from the corporation when the directors decide to declare dividends, when a dissolution and consequent liquidating distribution occurs, or when the corporation decides to make a repurchase of certain shares or to exercise a right to redeem shares. Rarely do common shareholders in public corporations have a right to force the corporation to buy back their shares. Nor are they able, on their own initiative, to force the company to liquidate and thus pay all the shareholders. Consequently, there is no risk, as there is in a general partnership, that the joint exercise of such a right by a number of investors will kill the enterprise. Corporations have a more stable existence. They are more likely to preserve the going concern value of large projects.

Mechanical efficiencies

Functions of legal personality. The function of attributing powers to a fictional legal person is simple mechanical efficiency in the carrying out of legal acts. A good example is the ability of a corporation to own real estate in its own name. Without it, or some similar legal device, a forest products

[47]MBCA §3.02.

[48]MBCA §§14.30, 14.31. For example, the court might order dissolution when there is a deadlock among the directors or shareholders, something that hardly ever happens in the case of a publicly held corporation.

[49]MBCA §§14.02-14.07.

[50]See, e.g., MBCA §14.30(2) (allowing shareholder to petition court for dissolution on grounds of director or shareholder deadlock, oppressive conduct by controlling parties, or waste of corporate assets). Compare N.Y. §1002 (dissolution under provision in certificate of incorporation). See also section 18.4 infra.

company owning timberland in scores of counties and provinces throughout the United States and Canada might have to embark on the extraordinarily expensive procedure of listing all of its thousands of investors in dozens of real estate recording offices and frequently updating the lists. Legal personality effects a clear saving of transaction costs, and the cumulative effect of these mundane savings is very great.

Preservation of going concern value

As indicated, the function of the corporation's perpetual existence is to minimize disruption and to preserve the going concern value of business ventures. This effect is especially likely to yield a net social gain when, as is generally the case with public corporations, the shareholders can meet their liquidity needs by selling their interests to other investors on reasonably efficient stock markets.

Why profits are residual goal

The social value of making the single goal of a legal person to maximize the wealth of its owners is more debatable. One line of argument justifying the traditional view of the courts proceeds as follows. A single objective goal like profit maximization is more easily monitored than a multiple, vaguely defined goal like the fair and reasonable accommodation of all affected interests. It is easier, for example, to tell if a corporate manager is doing what she is supposed to do than to tell if a university president is doing what she is supposed to do. Assuming shareholders have some control mechanisms,[51] better monitoring means that corporate managers will be kept more accountable. They are more likely to do what they are supposed to do and do it efficiently. Better accountability thus encourages people to participate in large organizations, in which claims on the organization and the power to manage it are necessarily separated; it helps such organizations exist and function well. Large organizations are in turn often desirable for everyone. They increase social welfare, because without them certain large scale business ventures would be impossible or would be carried out in a wasteful way.

On the other hand, no one need be made worse off by the corporation's having a single goal of profit maximization. The interests of nonshareholder groups like employees can be protected by contract, common law developments, and special legislation. Negative externalities like pollution can be corrected by tort law or by pollution laws telling companies not to pollute or taxing them when they do. The production of public goods like defense and the redistribution of wealth from rich to poor can be better accomplished by actual governments, which have a more legitimate claim

[51] They do. The major control mechanisms are their ability to vote in new directors, to respond favorably to tender offers for control, and to bring derivative lawsuits. These three devices are discussed in chapters 9, 13, and 15.

to do these things. And corporate resources can still be diverted to these governmental activities, in small or great measure, as elected representatives see fit, because governments can tax both corporations and their shareholders. Considering both prongs of the argument—that a single, objective goal increases management's accountability but need not preempt direct governmental regulation of corporations to make them socially responsible—one might conclude that profit maximization is a legitimate and desirable goal for business corporations.

Doubts

Whether this chain of reasoning actually withstands analysis is a hard question that demands a great deal of background knowledge. I will therefore take it up after traditional corporate law has been explored.[52]

§1.2.4 Locus of Managerial Power

Assumptions of nonspecialization and equality

In a partnership. Basically, partnership law treats all partners as if they are normally expected to be both investors and managers. In a venture like that of our hypothetical jet-rail system on Titan, with its 50,000 investors, this starting assumption is absurd and dysfunctional. Specifically, the UPA declares that, absent contrary agreement, all partners have equal rights to manage the affairs of the partnership[53] and every partner is an agent of the partnership with respect to partnership business.[54] Under certain conditions, the partnership is bound by the admission of any partner,[55] by the knowledge of or the notice given to any partners,[56] by the wrongful act of any partner,[57] and by any partner's breach of trust.[58] One is reminded of the slogan, "All for one, and one for all." This may work fine for three or four musketeers, but it is too much to handle for a group of 50,000 capitalists.

Managerial power in directors and officers

Of a corporation. The single most important fact of corporate law is that managerial power is legally *centralized.* Traditionally, the board of directors has had the formal power to manage the business of the corporation.[59] In

[52] See chapter 16. Even there, we will not be able to come to closure on the issue.
[53] UPA §18(e).
[54] UPA §9(1).
[55] UPA §11.
[56] UPA §12.
[57] UPA §13.
[58] UPA §14.
[59] MBCA §8.01(b). Some modern statutes permit the articles to provide otherwise; they may even permit the articles to provide for management by stockholders. But this permission

recognition of the fact that in large corporations the directors play a passive role as compared to the top officers who actually manage the business, the more recent statutory formulations allow directors to play a supervisory role.[60] But the basic fact of legal centralization of authority remains. It is best understood by its negative aspects. Shareholders have little say in management except in the few situations where the statute gives them a vote, and employees have little formal say in management except where the directors or top officers have delegated authority to them or when they have authority with respect to third persons because of principles of agency law. The model behind corporate law's treatment of authority is one of a unilaterally controlled flow of authority from a single wellspring of power rather than a bubbling up and flowing together of many individual sources of personal power. The state has power; it chooses to delegate it to the board of directors of a corporation. They in turn may choose to delegate it to the officers and even to employees at a much lower level.

Shareholders' limited voting rights

Under the MBCA, shareholders have limited voting rights. They may elect directors,[61] approve mergers (but only when directors have chosen to submit merger proposals to them),[62] approve a sale of substantially all assets of the corporation (on similar conditions),[63] approve voluntary dissolutions,[64] and not much else. Accordingly, the relationship between shareholders and directors is not well described as being between principals and agents. (A principal is ordinarily understood to be one who has the power to direct the activities of his agent.)[65] Shareholders not only may not initiate

---

is often restricted to close corporations, e.g., Del. §351, and in any event all such permissions have been adopted for the purpose of responding to the unique needs of close corporations. See section 1.3 and chapter 18.

[60] E.g., MBCA §8.01(b): "All corporate powers shall be exercised by *or under the authority of*, and the business and affairs of the corporation managed *under the direction of*, its board of directors, subject to any limitation set forth in the articles of incorporation." (Emphasis added.)

[61] MBCA §8.03(d).

[62] MBCA §11.03.

[63] MBCA §12.02.

[64] MBCA §14.02.

[65] This point is embodied in a leading definition: "Agency is the fiduciary relation which results from the manifestation of consent by one person to another that the other shall act on his behalf and subject to his control, and consent by the other so to act." Restatement (Second) of Agency §1(1).

The point is explicated and driven home by cases and commentary. "The agent differs from most other fiduciaries such as executors, trustees, etc., in that he remains under the continuous control of the principal as to matters relating to the object of his agency, throughout the entire period of his agency. The agent has a duty, at all times, to obey the directions of his principal, even though the principal may have initially indicated he would not give such additional instructions." W. Sell, Agency 2 (1975). "Further, the agency relation differs from

or countermand specific business decisions of the managers, but they do not, may not, and, some would say, should not determine the corporation's ultimate goal, its specific lines of business, its business strategies, or even the identity of the top officers who actually manage it.

Employee power by delegation and agency law

As noted, employees basically have formal authority by delegation. A given corporation may be highly centralized or highly decentralized. It may be organized along functional lines or divided into independent profit centers. Employees at lower levels may have a great deal of actual authority. The important legal point is that the managers can control the nature, amounts, and recipients of delegated decision making authority. To protect third parties dealing with corporations, this control is limited. According to agency principles as applied in the corporate context,[66] the acts of employees may sometimes bind the corporation even when the managers have affirmatively denied those employees the authority to take those actions. If virtually all corporate purchasing agents in an industry can place orders for a certain number of widgets without getting prior approval from higher managers, for example, a supplier who in good faith ships that number of widgets on the order of a certain purchasing agent who actually was supposed to get the approval of his supervisors nevertheless has an enforceable contract against the corporation. The corporation's officers may then of course proceed to discipline the offending purchasing agent, perhaps by firing him. As between the agent and the corporation, his act was still a wrongful one, for within the corporation centralization of ultimate authority holds sway.

Benefits from specialization and reduction of redundancy

Functions of centralized management. The basic function of centralized management created by corporate law is to facilitate the specialization of roles. Although overlaps are possible, investors may be investors, pure and simple, and managers may be simply managers. Not only does this permit greater proficiency in launching and operating businesses, since those who are able to supply capital are not necessarily those who are best at managing businesses, but it also leads to a great reduction in expensive, redundant activity. A business run by two or three partners may be well-advised to arrange things so that each partner is fully informed of all the facts necessary to evaluate a particular business decision and to exchange

---

other fiduciary relations in that it is the duty of the agent to respond to the desires of the principal . . . even if the principal is guilty of a breach of contract by interfering, the agent will still commit a breach of duty by acting in a manner opposed to his principal's wishes." H. Reuschlein & W. Gregory, Agency and Partnership 11-12 (1979).

[66] See section 3.3 infra.

his views on resolution of the issue with the other partners. But making sure that each one of 50,000 or so public investors receives information fully adequate to evaluate and pass judgment upon every major, complex business decision would be extraordinarily wasteful. Any advantage that comes from the exchange of views could surely be achieved by a much smaller subset of decision makers.

Optimal networks

Another major function of centralized management is that it permits corporate managers to structure an optimal network of communication and control within the corporation. This point is a subtle and important one, although it proves elusive to many observers. It underlies the fact that many large organizations are perceived to be "hierarchical" rather than "democratic." It deserves much more elaboration than it usually gets. The pros and cons of hierarchical forms of organization are explored in Appendix A at the end of this book.

§1.3 The Special Nature of Close Corporations

Importance of size

As shown in Appendix A, the absolute size of an organization, whether measured by number of employees or number of capital suppliers, has many consequences for its structure and performance. Size differences also help explain why the law treats closely held corporations differently than public corporations. Corporate law cannot be intelligently understood unless the problems peculiar to close corporations are separately recognized. The lawyer who aims for such understanding must strive constantly to notice whether any particular judicial ruling concerns a close corporation and to decide whether the corporation's status was relevant to the outcome of the case.

Close corporations: what

Close corporations, as the closely held firms are called for brevity, may be defined as corporations that have only a small number (for example, fewer than thirty) of individual shareholders and whose shares are not traded on a recognized securities exchange or on the over-the-counter market.[1] In the

§1.3 [1]State statutes that have definitions of *close corporations* vary in their details, of course. Under Cal. §158(a), a close corporation is one whose articles stipulate its shares will be held of record by no more than a specified number of persons, not exceeding 35, and contain a statement, "This is a close corporation." A close corporation so defined will be affected by other sections of the California corporation law that specifically refer to close corporations. These other sections are scattered throughout the statute; a list of them is given in §158(g).

The definition in Del. §342 takes a similar approach, using a cutoff number of 30 rather than 35, but adds some conditions, e.g., that such a corporation shall make no "public offering" of securities within the meaning of the federal Securities Act.

United States, although not in many civil law countries, they have traditionally been chartered under the same business corporation statutes as publicly held, or public, corporations. Yet, in a sense they are not "real" corporations. The practices that their members either want to engage in, or find themselves forced to engage in, frequently contradict the four basic postulates of the corporate form of organization. For this reason, lawyers sometimes refer to them as *incorporated partnerships*.

Participants may not get limited liability

Thus, the stockholders of a small closely held corporation may be in favor of limited liability (why not take this comprehensive liability insurance policy that the state is willing to give away for the mere price of a filing fee?) but may find that major contract creditors, like the bank that lends the corporation money to buy buildings and equipment, insist on getting the stockholders' personal guarantees of the corporation's debts. As to these creditors, the shareholders will have the unlimited liability of partners.

May negate free transferability

The shareholders will often try to negate the presumptively free transferability of corporate shares: Each of them will want to have some power, similar to that possessed by partners, to pass upon the identity of new members of the club of shareholders. Consequently, the shareholders will be interested in being able to impose contractual restrictions on the transfer of shares—so-called buyout agreements. For example, under a right of first refusal agreement, a shareholder wanting to liquidate his investment by selling his stock may first have to offer it to the corporation or the other shareholders at a price fixed by formula or appraisal, and only if these offerees refuse to buy will he then be free to sell his stock to a third party. Some investors may desire to forbid absolutely any sale to outsiders. Others may want to contract so that the corporation or other shareholders have an obligation to buy their stock under certain conditions.

May not want perpetual corporation

The stockholders of a close corporation will want it to have many but not all components of legal personality. The chief stumbling block is the corporation's perpetual existence. In order to preserve the going-concern value of large enterprises, the business corporation statutes make it impossible except in special circumstances for individual shareholders or a minority coalition of them to dissolve the corporation or otherwise terminate it. But stockholders of a close corporation will more frequently want such power. Because his stock is not actively traded on a market, and perhaps also because it is subject to transfer restrictions, the stockholder who wants to

---

These and similar statutes define what a close corporation is and allow incorporators to elect close corporation status, for the purpose of determining whether certain special statutory rules will be applied.

liquidate his investment may desire to force the corporation to buy him out. If he is a substantial shareholder, a 25-percent shareholder perhaps, and the corporation has no large reserve of liquid assets (as it wouldn't if it were a thriving business), this may have the effect of causing the corporation to terminate or sharply curtail its business activities. In many of the situations where a shareholder wants to liquidate his investment, such as on retirement, death, or a falling out with the other investors, continuing to hold his stock and receive an indefinitely long stream of dividend income will not be an available or adequate substitute for a complete present conversion of his investment into cash. The shareholder will want something like a partner's right of withdrawal instead. For example, if the shareholder is also an officer of the corporation and receives most of his returns from the enterprise in the form of a salary (as is often the case for tax reasons), and now wants to retire, he may be afraid that the remaining members, other shareholders who will continue to be active officers and employees, will not begin voting for the payment of adequate dividends. They may decline to do this both because of the tax burden it will cause themselves, and because of a feeling that the retired person, since he no longer works in the business, does not "deserve" any of its returns.

May want to adjust centralized management

This latter point leads into some observations about the fourth postulate, centralization of management, and its corollary, the separation of ownership and control. The feeling that retired or inactive stockholders, or the widows, widowers, and other survivors of former active stockholders-employees, do not deserve to receive a large and indefinitely continuing share of the returns from the business, is strong in many close corporations. It results from the failure of the participants in these corporations to separate sharply the roles of investor and manager or employee (or the roles of capital and labor, to use the economist's terms). Many of the participants in a close corporation will have both of these roles, and each will have his own idea—or perhaps no idea—about the extent to which nominal salaries are in fact rewards for capital contributions and residual risk-taking, and the extent to which nominal dividends and repurchase payments are in fact rewards for behavioral contributions. Yet a major point of the corporation as an institution, a major factor in its additions to social efficiency, is precisely that it separates the capital supplying and managerial functions into distinct legal roles. By mixing up the roles, the participants in close corporations inevitably find themselves in situations where what they want to do violates the rules, or the spirit of the rules, that have evolved to govern the behavior of the directors, officers, and shareholders of public corporations.

Like many partners, participants in a close corporation will often want to share management rather than centralize it. Since there are smaller numbers, they might theoretically satisfy their desire by all becoming directors. But the rules evolved for public corporations will create problems. Each participant may want an effective contractual right to a directorship even if he does not own the requisite number of shares to insure his election under the governing corporation law rules. He may want a right as director or shareholder to veto some or all business decisions, rather than abide by simple majority rule. He may regard attendance at regular meetings of the board of directors, the requirement that corporate action be taken by the board at a meeting, and the need to keep minutes of meetings as bothersome formalities.

Why run closely held business as corporation?

Reasons for incorporation of closely held businesses. The history of the extent to which, and the ways in which, participants in close corporations have become legally able to solve the above-mentioned problems is a tortuous and fascinating one, which is treated elsewhere.[2] But we may legitimately ask why so many thousands—indeed, millions—of small businesses were incorporated in the first place. Why weren't most of them simply formed as partnerships or sole proprietorships? The basic answers appear to be two.

First, the corporation's limited liability is of some real use to investors who are concerned about unforseen, massive tort liabilities arising out of their business. Potential tort victims cannot negotiate specific contractual guarantees from close corporation shareholders.

Second, under certain circumstances, the corporate form may offer tax savings as compared to the partnership form.[3] Until fairly recently, qualified pension plans and some kinds of fringe benefits programs treated favorably under federal income tax law were better available if the business was a corporation.[4] And the interaction of the federal corporate income tax with the federal individual income tax has sometimes been such that high bracket taxpayers preferred to be shareholders rather than partners.[5] In

[2]See, e.g., F. O'Neal, Close Corporations: Law and Practice ch. 1 (2d ed. 1971 & ann. cum. supp.).

[3]See W. Painter, Corporate and Tax Aspects of Closely Held Corporations §§1.3, 10.1 (2d ed. 1981 & ann. supp.).

[4]Prior to changes made by the Tax Equity and Fiscal Responsibility Act of 1982 (hereinafter referred to as TEFRA), there were distinct tax advantages to the corporate form, so far as pension plans were concerned. But the advantages were largely eliminated, since TEFRA subjected both corporate pension plans and self-employed pension plans (such as those created by partners) to the same limitations on deductibility of contributions.

[5]Suppose, as was once the case, that the top marginal tax rates are: corporate income tax—48 percent; individual's ordinary tax—70 percent; the individual's tax on net long-term capital

any event, the theoretical extra burden of the corporate income tax has often been avoided by participants in close corporations, through tax planning devices, so there has at least been no fatal tax obstacle to using the corporate form.

Special rules

Legal consequences of close corporations. That so many close corporations have been formed has greatly affected the development of corporate law, in two major ways. The first way is obvious and has been recognized by all writers on corporate law. The close corporations gave rise to a special line of cases, to special charter provisions, and eventually to close corporation statutes or statutory provisions, dealing with problems peculiar to close corporations, or much more characteristic of them. Thus, case law delineated the kinds of stock transfer restrictions that were permissible and attempted to deal with the issue whether deadlock and other bitter conflict among close corporation shareholders would warrant dissolution. Statutes were passed to legitimize and regulate voting trusts and unusual allocations of decision making power.

Impact on general doctrines too

The second way in which close corporations affected the development of corporate law is more subtle, and seems generally to have gone unrecog-

gains—25 percent. Sally and Sam own a very profitable business and are in the top tax brackets.

(1) If they operate the business as a partnership, their tax on an additional $100 of income will be $70.
(2) If they operate the business as a corporation and distribute additional income as dividends, the total tax on the $100 will be $84.40, the corporate tax of $48 plus the individual income tax on the dividend of .7($100-$48), or $36.40.
(3) But if they operate as a corporation, have it retain the $52 of additional after-tax corporate income instead of paying it out as a dividend, and later sell some of their stock at a price reflecting the $52 increase in value, their total tax burden will be only $63, the corporate tax of $48 plus the extra capital gain tax on the stock sale of .25($52), or $13, and part of it (the capital gain tax) will be deferred.

Note, however, that strategy (3) doesn't help when, as at the present time, the top marginal rates are: corporate income tax—46 percent; individual's ordinary income tax—50 percent; individual's tax on net long-term capital gains—20 percent. With these rates, the corporate form looks disadvantageous, as compared to the partnership.

But, as suggested in the text, participants in close corporations have ways of negating the theoretical extra burden on the corporate tax. One whole set of ways consists of arranging things so that the corporation has no net taxable income. This might be done, for example, by paying the participants salaries equal to what would otherwise be corporate net income. (The IRS, however, might challenge truly unreasonable salaries.) Another alternative is to elect tax treatment under Subchapter S of the Internal Revenue Code, so that the corporation's income or loss is attributed and taxed to the shareholders. This treatment is *roughly* similar to that applied by Subchapter K to partnerships and partners.

nized. Because of the sheer number of close corporations, the tendency of their participants to become embroiled in conflict, and the tendency of many public corporation disputes to be cast in the legal form of disputes under the federal securities laws and litigated in federal courts, an overwhelming majority of the corporate law cases coming before most state courts have involved close corporations. When the state courts have created and elaborated judicial doctrines of general applicability to all corporations and their participants, they have often chosen rules that make good sense for close corporations but that are suboptimal for public corporations. That is, we can often identify an alternative rule or doctrine that would make more sense in the public corporation context, even though it would not be a suitable one for close corporation disputes. This is my own thesis, at any rate, and I will attempt to justify it at various points in this book—for example, by the analyses offered in the chapters on insider trading and corporate opportunities.[6]

Categorical vs. selective rules

An important aspect of my thesis is the belief that the proper rules for public corporations are frequently more categorical in nature, while the proper rules for close corporations are often more selective. By a categorical rule I mean one that is uniformly applicable—it doesn't permit many excuses or exceptions or unspecified "relevant facts and circumstances"—and yet is fairly precise and objective in its application. By a selective rule, I mean one that is not precise and that is uniformly applicable only when stated in a vague and general way. It usually leaves room for results to turn on an open-ended class of relevant facts and circumstances, including the reasonable understandings or expectations of the particular parties involved. The nature of this distinction, and the reasons for matching categorical rules with public corporations and selective rules with close corporations, are elaborated in section 7.4.

Implications for study and practice

The existence of close corporations means that the student reading a case in corporate law must be sensitive to whether it involves a close corporation and whether, if it did, that fact was important. Moreover, practitioners who deal with incorporated small businesses must learn not only the standard rules and doctrine of corporate law but also a whole host of *business planning* techniques (buyout agreements, employment contracts, voting trust agreements, key person insurance policies and the like) that are quite important to the efficient, trouble-free functioning of close corporations.[7] On the other hand, the person who mainly advises public

[6]See especially sections 8.12 (insider trading) and 7.4 (corporate opportunities) infra.

[7]See generally D. Herwitz, Business Planning: Materials on the Planning of Corporate Transactions (temp. 2d ed. 1984); W. Painter, note 3 supra.

corporations must become much better versed in the details of *securities regulation*.[8] The split is relevant even in fields like federal tax law. The rules that must preoccupy the close corporation practitioner concern incorporating transactions, excessive salaries, dividends, redemptions, partial and complete liquidations, and sales of the business. The public corporation practitioner is more likely to need to know the intricacies of the tax law governing corporate reorganizations (mergers, divisions, and the like), carryover of tax attributes, parent-subsidiary transactions, and the treatment of families of affiliated corporations.

In this book the main emphasis is on the public corporation and generally applicable corporate doctrines, but the special problems of close corporations are treated in chapter 18 and at various other points.

§1.4 Corporate Law Versus Other Laws Affecting Corporations

Limited focus of corporate law

Students studying corporate law for the first time are often puzzled or angered by the failure of the legal doctrines they encounter to do anything toward the effective solution of numerous social problems caused by corporations. As a result, they may object to the apparently unbridled power of corporate managers. Some, but by no means all, of the puzzlement may be dissolved when they realize that traditionally, the subjects of corporation law and securities regulation are simply defined to deal only with relationships between shareholders and managers (directors and officers), i.e., with the most capitalistic of relationships affecting capitalist enterprise. Business corporation statutes and the securities laws do not preclude laws regulating other corporate relationships. There are in fact a great many such laws, and it may be useful, in order to get a sense of what is not within conventional corporate law's jurisdiction, to mention some of them.

Other laws affecting corporations

We may organize this exercise by viewing the corporation as having relationships to a number of participants or affected persons other than shareholders and managers: employees, suppliers, creditors, customers, the general public, and governmental departments and agencies. General contract law and tort law principles affect all these relationships, of course, and they have sizable practical importance in all categories. The relationship between corporation and employee is heavily regulated by major

[8] See generally R. Jennings & H. Marsh, Securities Regulation: Cases and Materials (5th ed. 1982 & ann. supps.); L. Loss, Fundamentals of Securities Regulation (1983).

federal laws: the labor laws[1] and the extensive jurisprudence under them, the massive and detailed pension reform law known as the Employee Retirement Income Security Act,[2] and the Occupational Safety and Health Act.[3] Suppliers dealing with corporations are often protected by article 2 (on sales) of the Uniform Commercial Code. Creditors have the benefit of state laws concerning the individual collection of judgments,[4] article 9 (on secured transactions) of the Uniform Commerical Code, and the federal bankruptcy and reorganization statutes.[5] Customers are protected from physical injury by the Consumer Product Safety Act,[6] the Food, Drug and Cosmetic Act,[7] and similar preventive statutes; they may seek redress for injury under products liability law, now heavily developed in the courts of many states, and by resort to various consumer protection statutes. Their pocketbooks are supposed to be protected against monopolistic practices by the federal antitrust laws[8] and against unfair and deceptive sales practices by the Federal Trade Commission Act.[9] The general public is thought to be protected against some major negative externalities[10] of corporations, such as the pollution they create, by a set of extremely complex federal statutes and the rules and administrative activities thereunder: the Clean Air Act,[11] the Water Pollution Control Act,[12] the Noise Control Act,[13] and others. Corporations in many particular industries, from banking and insurance to utility companies and hospitals, are subject to other kinds of direct, substantive regulation. Finally, the relationship between corpora-

§1.4 [1]E.g., Anti-Injunction (Norris-La Guardia) Act, 29 U.S.C.A. §§101-115; National Labor Relations (Wagner) Act, 29 U.S.C.A. §§151 et seq.; Labor-Management Relations (Taft-Hartley) Act, 29 U.S.C.A. §§141 et seq.; Fair Labor Standards Act, 29 U.S.C.A. §§201-216, 217-219.

[2]Codified principally in 29 U.S.C.A. §§ 1001-1461.

[3]29 U.S.C.A. §§651-678.

[4]E.g., N.Y. Civ. Prac. Law §§5201-5252 (enforcement of money judgments).

[5]11 U.S.C.A. §§101-1330.

[6]15 U.S.C.A. §§2051-2083.

[7]21 U.S.C.A. §§301-392.

[8]Sherman Act, 15 U.S.C.A. §§1-7; Clayton Act, 15 U.S.C.A. §§12-27; Robinson-Patman Act, §§13-13b, 21a.

[9]15 U.S.C.A. §§41-58.

[10]Roughly speaking, the negative externalities of a business entity are the costs or burdens that it creates for others but for which it doesn't pay. In microeconomic theory, a system of free markets in goods and services will maximize social welfare only if certain conditions are met, one of which is that all costs are internalized. Hence, under such theory it may be a desirable function of government to intervene in markets to control negative externalities (by fining or taxing the generators of the externalities, by regulation, or otherwise).

[11]42 U.S.C.A. §§7401-7642.

[12]33 U.S.C.A. §§1251-1376.

[13]42 U.S.C.A. §§4901-4918.

tion and government is controlled by a variety of laws having enormous financial impact on the corporation: the laws establishing property taxes, sales taxes, income taxes, and others.

This brief listing will drive home the point that knowing corporate law is not enough to make you a good general corporate counsel nor to give you a full sense of how the legal system shapes corporate activities. And even if your aim is not to understand all of law's effects on corporate activities but only to grasp the basic legal "constitution" or make-up of the modern corporation, you must, at the very least, also gain a working knowledge of labor law.

§1.5 *Themes of This Book*

Theme (1): The problems flow from the postulates

Two major themes tie together many parts of this book. The first is the view that most of the major recurring problems of corporate law derive from, and in a sense were created by, the four basic postulates of the corporate form of organization. Accordingly, if presented and understood properly, the numerous topics dealt with in corporate law courses can be seen to form a surprisingly unified and coherent whole.

Abuse of limited liability

Thus, the institution of limited liability creates possibilities of abuse. It may be used as a shield to stop corporate creditors from doing anything effective about corporate transactions that were fraudulent or unfair as to them. It may seem to operate unfairly against certain classes of creditors, such as small trade creditors and tort victims. It may be used in ways that do not seem to further its basic purposes or functions, as when the parts of a single business enterprise are put into numerous separate corporate entities solely for the purpose of shielding enterprise assets, rather than the investors' personal assets, from liability. These problems are taken up in chapter 2.

Fraudulent transfers of shares

The free transferability of corporate shares results in much more voluminous trading in securities and therefore raises the frequency with which trades occur that are based on fraudulent or inadequate information. It seems to increase the importance of having a system of securities regulation aimed at insuring adequate disclosures and preventing fraud and manipulation. The basic rudiments of the federal securities laws' disclosure system, as applied to new issuances of stock, are taken up in chapter 17, but certain securities regulation topics, and in particular certain antifraud provisions, are considered at other points: most notably, insider trader provisions in chapter 8, the proxy rules in chapter 9, and the tender offer rules in chapter 13.

Troublesome (corporate) personalities

The postulate of legal personality creates the problem of deciding what, if any, limits should be placed on the powers and purposes that corporations may have. This is not only a problem of design of the business corporation statutes—for example, whether a corporation should be restricted to one line of business or to some size limit—but of judicial coping with the attempts of private and public parties to push corporations beyond pre-existing patterns of activity. What happens when corporate managers use the corporation to purport to take acts that are not permitted by the corporation's articles of organization? (This is a so-called ultra vires problem.) What happens when a state legislature declares by fiat that corporate expenditures to publish views about certain political referenda are illegal? (That is, does a corporation have a constitutional right of free speech, like a natural person?) What happens when a corporation's managers cause it, in lieu of maximizing profits, to make a large contribution to a charity? What happens when some shareholders want to request that a shareholder vote be taken on whether management should be directed or requested to take some course of action that is alleged to be socially responsible, even though it is not required by law and may reduce profits? Some of these issues are examined in chapter 16; related ones are examined at various other points.[1]

Abuse of managerial power

Finally, the postulate of centralized management creates a familiar dilemma, one that also affects policy makers concerned with other large, formal organizations, such as labor unions and regulatory agencies. For the purpose of increasing *organizational* efficiency, the top managers of large organizations are given enormous discretionary authority. Their business judgment (or union judgment, or regulatory judgment) is not to be second-guessed or countermanded on substantive grounds by outsiders like courts or even by their beneficiaries like stockholders. The discretion is never given for the *purpose* of enabling the top managers of large organizations to maximize their own well-being. All managerial jobs in large organizations only make sense—they can only be expected to maximize social welfare—on the premise that the role or function of the manager is to act on behalf of other persons' interests. Yet power corrupts. It can be turned to the personal use of the wielder of power in ways that hurt the other persons having claims on the organization. The problem, then, is how to keep managers accountable to their other-directed duties while nonetheless al-

§1.5 [1]See sections 3.1.3 (shareholders' right of inspection for non–profit-maximizing purpose); 3.5 (business judgment rule as possible shield for management's non–profit-maximizing purposes); 9.3 (shareholder proposals concerning non–profit-maximizing objectives); 13.6.3 (non–profit-maximizing goals as justifications for resisting takeover bids); 14.3 (bad faith test applied to non–profit-maximizing reason for withholding dividends) infra.

lowing them great discretionary power over appropriate matters. This is the major problem dealt with by corporate law.

The fiduciary principle

The most general formulation of corporate law's attempted solution to the problem of managerial accountability is *the fiduciary duty of loyalty:* the corporation's directors, officers, and, in some respects and situations, its controlling shareholders owe a duty of undivided loyalty to their corporations, and they may not so use corporate assets, or deal with the corporation, as to benefit themselves at the expense of the corporation and its shareholders. *The overwhelming majority of particular rules, doctrines, and cases in corporate law are simply an explication of this duty or of the procedural rules and institutional arrangements involved in implementing it.* The history of corporate law is largely the history of the development of operational content for the duty of loyalty. Even many cases that appear to be about dull formalities or rules of the road in fact involve disputes arising out of alleged managerial disloyalty. Most of chapters 4 through 14 are mainly concerned with problems of loyalty. Moreover, the chapter preceding these chapters lays out the allocation of powers that in a sense creates these problems. Chapter 15 deals with legal procedures for enforcing duties of loyalty.

Conflict-of-interest paradigms

My view, expressed as a subpart of the first theme, is that managerial loyalty problems can be usefully grouped into four different conflict-of-interest paradigms, each of which involves somewhat different problems and solutions. These paradigms are introduced in chapter 4, and they are important to understanding how particular conflict-of-interest problems are categorized and analyzed in chapters 5 through 14.

Theme (2): Importance of close/public distinction

The second major theme of the book, which will appear intermittently throughout, has already been mentioned. The existence of close corporations, and the generic differences between them and public corporations, has influenced the development of corporate law doctrine. In the United States, the distinction has also influenced, in a rough and imperfect way, the allocation of subject matters between federal and state law (both statutory and judicial) affecting corporations.

CHAPTER 2

DUTIES TO CREDITORS

§2.1 *Introduction*

Abuse of limited liability

As we saw in chapter 1, the institution of limited liability for shareholders has substantial economic advantages. It is not correct to see it as a mere device for subsidizing business. It doesn't just shift the costs of business around; it can actually reduce the total amount of those costs. By itself, however, limited liability seems to permit outrageous practices. Consider, for example, a case of blatant and deliberate misuse of the institution. Two stockholders form a corporation with a $1 million total equity investment, borrow another $1 million from a nearby savings and loan association, and run the business quite profitably for several years. Then they suddenly and deliberately pay out all of the corporation's assets (now $22 million) to themselves, labeling the payments dividends and salaries. As a result, the corporation cannot pay back any of its outstanding loan to the savings and loan association. Surely the law will provide a remedy for such conduct? Surely, that is, there is some limit to limited liability?

A common example

If there is, how does it apply to more common cases? Suppose, for example, your client controls a closely held corporation and wants to pay himself a salary that is at least twice as large as he could probably get for doing similar work with any other company, even though the large salary would mean that, should his company experience a moderately bad year, its ability to repay its bank loans would be severely jeopardized. If the corporation pays him the large salary, does he run a risk of personal liability for unpaid corporate debts?

Example involving tort victims

Consider also a somewhat different scenario, extreme in its facts but not in the underlying policy issues that it raises. A group of scientists and wealthy investors together form a for-profit corporation to do bioengineering research and development. They put in just enough invested capital each year so that the corporation can pay its expenses, such as the salaries of the researchers (who are all nonstockholding postdoctoral types) and rental payments for the laboratory and equipment. The researchers are engaged in work on bacteria. They negligently produce a mutant bacterium that escapes from the laboratory, multiplies geometrically, and causes the death of 200 children in a nearby school. The bereaved parents bring and win wrongful death actions but cannot collect on their judgments against the capital-poor corporation, which the investors have simply abandoned. Should the law allow the parents, despite the general rule of limited liability, to enforce their judgments against the stockholders? And if so, what would be the result in more common cases where modestly capitalized companies are hit with enormous tort judgments?

Creditors' contractual safeguards

Of course, ordinary contract law would provide a remedy to the savings and loan association in our first example if its officers had the forethought to impose restrictions on the company's payment of dividends and salaries in the loan agreement. Indeed, bank loan agreements and the lengthy debenture indentures under which debentures are issued to public investors typically contain elaborate and detailed recitals of all the things the borrowing corporation can't do while the loan is outstanding. The typical agreement contains many sorts of protection. For example, it might provide that, if the corporation's ratio of debts to net worth rises above a certain percentage, or if its ratio of current (short-term) assets to current liabilities falls below a certain figure, or if some other financial ratio test is not met, the lender will have the option of declaring the entire loan amount immediately due and payable (and thus will be able to go to court, get a judgment for the full amount of the loan, and start coercive collection proceedings).

Contracts the only source of norms?

Some economic analysts may be tempted by the availability and widespread existence of these voluntary agreements about permissible behavior of debtors to say that the equity investors in our first example should be able to get away with their scheme, as long as it didn't violate any express provision of their contract with the savings and loan association. If it is in the interest of creditors to contract against certain kinds of debtor behavior, so the argument goes, then surely they will do so.

Not entirely

The law does not accept this view entirely, however. In a variety of ways (which are discussed in sections 2.2 through 2.5 infra of this chapter), it provides automatically for a kind of "standard contract" consisting of a minimum set of creditor-protecting rules by which all parties are deemed to be bound, regardless of whether they bargain to be bound by them.

The instrumentality rule

Under what conditions, then, will the law call off limited liability? In a formal sense, the judicial opinions and commentaries on corporate law have a ready answer: The "corporate veil will be pierced," and the shareholders and/or the controlling parties will be subjected to personal liability for the debts of the corporation, when the corporation has served as the "instrumentality" or "alter ego" of shareholders or controlling parties. Courts give different general formulations as to when the instrumentality rule will be invoked. One typical formulation is as follows:

> The instrumentality rule requires, in any case but an express agency, proof of three elements: (1) Control, not merely majority or complete stock control, but complete domination, not only of finances but of policy and business practice in respect to the transaction attacked so that the corporate entity as to this transaction had at the time no separate mind, will or existence of its own; and (2) Such control must have been used by the defendant to commit fraud or wrong, to perpetrate the violation of a statutory or other positive legal duty, or a dishonest or unjust act in contravention of a plaintiff's legal rights; and (3) The aforesaid control and breach of duty must proximately cause the injury or unjust loss complained of. . . .[1]

The key part of this formula is the second element. In effect, it says that controlling stockholders and other controlling parties of a corporation may be liable for the corporation's debts when they have caused it to commit a "fraud or wrong." (Most litigated cases do not involve violation of "a statutory or positive legal duty," the other aspect of the second element of the formula.)

§2.1 [1]Zaist v. Olson, 227 A.2d 552, 558 (Conn. 1967).

The vagueness problem

Do you notice anything intellectually disturbing about this formulation? That's right; it's *vague*. It hardly gives you any concrete idea about which conduct does or does not trigger the doctrine—not enough of an idea, at least, to give you the ability to counsel clients in a meaningful way. Nor do any of the other general case law formulations do much better.

The immersion-in-cases solution

You could respond to this dilemma of the vague and unhelpful general formulation by reading a few dozen—or better yet, a few hundred—of the published judicial opinions in the alter ego area, in the hope that constant immersion in the facts of real cases, together with knowledge of their outcomes, will give you a feel for what the legal principles really mean. Your author has followed this traditional route. I report that it is sound and instructive but very unpleasant.

Thinking person's solution

There is another way. It is to recognize that the instrumentality doctrine, as well as certain other bodies of law designed to protect creditors of corporations (such as equitable subordination doctrine and dividend statutes), are ways of implementing the ideals set out in a very ancient, still applicable, body of law that applies to relationships between all kinds of debtors (not just corporations) and creditors. This body of law is the law of fraudulent conveyances. It *does* contain principles and rules that are easy to grasp and that have a fairly definite meaning when applied to real cases. Oftentimes, the best way to predict whether the instrumentality rule has been violated is to ask whether the behavior pattern in question violates any of the rules of fraudulent conveyance law. In doing so, you will often have to make guesses about some facts relevant to the fraudulent conveyance rules, but, since a court will often be faced with the same ambiguities and may make similar assumptions about them, the exercise is still worth doing.

Fraudulent conveyance law as the key

To be more specific, the thesis of this chapter is that the law of fraudulent conveyances[2] contains a few simple but potent moral principles governing the conduct of all debtors toward their creditors. These principles are expressed in rather specific rules, such as those found in the fraudulent conveyance statutes of individual states. When we understand these basic

[2] A succinct and general expression of fraudulent conveyance law appears in the Institutes of Justinian 4.6.6. A more recent expression was given by the statute of 13 Eliz., ch. 5 (1570). Modern statements include the Uniform Fraudulent Conveyance Act (hereinafter cited as UFCA), which has been adopted by about half of the states, and the Bankruptcy Code's own fraudulent conveyance statute, §548, 11 U.S.C. §548. Important commentary and discussion of case law is provided by G. Glenn, Fraudulent Conveyances and Preferences (rev. ed. 1940); 4 L. King, ed., Collier on Bankruptcy ¶¶548.01-548.11 (15th ed. 1985). See also Note, Good Faith and Fraudulent Conveyances, 97 Harv. L. Rev. 495 (1983).

principles well, we can see that a number of more modern doctrines concerning *corporate* debtors are substitutes for, or complements to, the law of fraudulent conveyances. In particular, we will see that the doctrines of equitable subordination and piercing the corporate veil are often applications of the same basic principles that underlie fraudulent conveyance law.

Compartmentalized thinking: why

There is very little sustained discussion in cases or in the writings of commentators of the relationships among these branches of the law. This near-silence is odd, in view of the importance that these doctrines have to attorneys.[3] My explanation is that the lack of comparative analysis has performed a practical function. The doctrines of equitable subordination and piercing the corporate veil are, in part, ways of overcoming the limitations of fraudulent conveyance law. Thus, the judges who initiated and developed these doctrines probably moved instinctively to portray them as applications of a respected tradition of equitable principles and rhetoric, rather than as a circumvention of the ancient and substantial body of law of fraudulent conveyances.[4]

Plan of chapter

The next section will introduce fraudulent conveyance law and will identify its distinct but related underlying principles—a task sorely neglected in literally hundreds of cases applying that body of law. In light of these principles, section 2.3 will show how equitable subordination is a functional substitute for fraudulent conveyance law under certain conditions and will then explain how that doctrine differs from fraudulent conveyance law and why it came about. Section 2.4 explores the doctrine of piercing the corporate veil and discusses whether it constitutes a significant expansion of the principles of fraudulent conveyance law. In section 2.5, common statutory restrictions on dividends are analyzed as a weakened means of implementing the principles of fraudulent conveyance law.

[3] Veil-piercing cases and equitable subordination are often treated together in courses on corporate law, and commentators have analyzed some of the interrelationships between these two doctrines. See generally the dialogue between Professors Landers and Posner: Landers, A Unified Approach to Parent, Subsidiary, and Affiliate Questions in Bankruptcy, 42 U. Chi. L. Rev. 589 (1975) (hereinafter cited as Landers I); Posner, The Rights of Creditors of Affiliated Corporations, 43 U. Chi. L. Rev. 499 (1976); Landers, Another Word on Parents, Subsidiaries and Affiliates in Bankruptcy, 43 U. Chi. L. Rev. 527 (1976) (hereinafter cited as Landers II). But sustained analysis of the relationship of these two doctrines to fraudulent conveyance law is rare indeed.

[4] This hypothesis does not require a belief that the judges who developed equitable subordination were consciously suppressing the doctrine's relationship to fraudulent conveyance law.

§2.2 *Fraudulent Conveyance Law*

Great breadth of fraudulent conveyance law (FCL)

The law of fraudulent conveyances, of which the Uniform Fraudulent Conveyance Act (UFCA)[1] is the principal but not exclusive embodiment, allows creditors to set aside certain transfers by debtors. Fraudulent conveyance

§2.2 [1]Because the UFCA is frequently cited in this chapter, it is here set forth in full:

Sec. I. *Definition of Terms.* In this act "Assets" of a debtor means property not exempt from liability for his debts. To the extent that any property is liable for any debts of the debtor, such property shall be included in his assets.

"Conveyance" includes every payment of money, assignment, release, transfer, lease, mortgage or pledge of tangible or intangible property, and also the creation of any lien or incumbrance.

"Creditor" is a person having any claim, whether matured or unmatured, liquidated or unliquidated, absolute, fixed or contingent.

"Debt" includes any legal liability, whether matured or unmatured, liquidated or unliquidated, absolute, fixed or contingent.

Sec. 2. *Insolvency.* (1) A person is insolvent when the present fair salable value of his assets is less than the amount that will be required to pay his probable liability on his existing debts as they become absolute and matured.

(2) In determining whether a partnership is insolvent there shall be added to the partnership property the present fair salable value of the separate assets of each general partner in excess of the amount probably sufficient to meet the claims of his separate creditors, and also the amount of any unpaid subscription to the partnership of each limited partner, provided the present fair salable value of the assets of such limited partner is probably sufficient to pay his debts, including such unpaid subscription.

Sec. 3. *Fair Consideration.* Fair consideration is given for property, or obligation,

(a) When in exchange for such property, or obligation, as a fair equivalent therefor, and in good faith, property is conveyed or an antecedent debt is satisfied, or

(b) When such property, or obligation is received in good faith to secure a present advance or antecedent debt in amount not disproportionately small as compared with the value of the property, or obligation obtained.

Sec. 4. *Conveyances by Insolvent.* Every conveyance made and every obligation incurred by a person who is or will be thereby rendered insolvent is fraudulent as to creditors without regard to his actual intent if the conveyance is made or the obligation is incurred without a fair consideration.

Sec. 5. *Conveyances by Persons in Business.* Every conveyance made without fair consideration when the person making it is engaged or is about to engage in a business or transaction for which the property remaining in his hands after the conveyance is an unreasonably small capital, is fraudulent as to creditors and as to other persons who become creditors during the continuance of such business or transaction without regard to his actual intent.

Sec. 6. *Conveyance by a Person About to Incur Debts.* Every conveyance made and every obligation incurred without fair consideration when the person making the conveyance or entering into the obligation intends or believes that he will incur debts beyond his ability to pay as they mature, is fraudulent as to both present and future creditors.

Sec. 7. *Conveyance Made With Intent to Defraud.* Every conveyance made and every

law, despite its name, has a very broad applicability. It is not restricted to conveyances, since virtually all transfers of property, and, under both the UFCA and the Bankruptcy Code, the incurrence of obligations, are covered.[2] Nor is it limited to fraudulent transactions, since unfair transfers made without deceptive intent[3] are included.

---

obligation incurred with actual intent, as distinguished from intent presumed in law, to hinder, delay, or defraud either present or future creditors, is fraudulent as to both present and future creditors.

Sec. 8. *Conveyance of Partnership Property*. Every conveyance of partnership property and every partnership obligation incurred when the partnership is or will be thereby rendered insolvent, is fraudulent as to partnership creditors, if the conveyance is made or obligation is incurred,

(a) To a partner, whether with or without a promise by him to pay partnership debts, or

(b) To a person not a partner without fair consideration to the partnership as distinguished from consideration to the individual partners.

Sec. 9. *Rights of Creditors Whose Claims Have Matured*. (1) Where a conveyance or obligation is fraudulent as to a creditor, such creditor, when his claim has matured, may, as against any person except a purchaser for fair consideration without knowledge of the fraud at the time of the purchase, or one who has derived title immediately or mediately from such a purchaser,

(a) Have the conveyance set aside or obligation annulled to the extent necessary to satisfy his claim, or

(b) Disregard the conveyance and attach or levy execution upon the property conveyed.

(2) A purchaser who without actual fraudulent intent has given less than a fair consideration for the conveyance or obligation, may retain the property or obligation as security for repayment.

Sec. 10. *Rights of Creditors Whose Claims Have Not Matured*. Where a conveyance made or obligation incurred is fraudulent as to a creditor whose claim has not matured he may proceed in a court of competent jurisdiction against any person against whom he could have proceeded had his claim matured, and the court may,

(a) Restrain the defendant from disposing of his property,

(b) Appoint a receiver to take charge of the property,

(c) Set aside the conveyance or annul the obligation, or

(d) Make any order which the circumstances of the case may require.

Sec. 11. *Cases Not Provided for in Act*. In any case not provided for in this Act the rules of law and equity including the law merchant, and in particular the rules relating the law of principal and agent, and the effect of fraud, misrepresentation, duress or coercion, mistake, bankruptcy or other invalidating cause shall govern.

Sec. 12. *Construction of Act*. This act shall be so interpreted and construed as to effectuate its general purpose to make uniform the law of those states which enact it.

Sec. 13. *Name of Act*. This act may be cited as the Uniform Fraudulent Conveyance Act.

Sec. 14. *Inconsistent Legislation Repealed*. Sections . . . are hereby repealed, and all acts or parts of acts inconsistent with this Act are hereby repealed.

[2]UFCA §§1, 4, 6, 7; Bankruptcy Code §§101(48), 548, 11 U.S.C. §§101(48), 548.

[3]See, e.g., UFCA §4; Bankruptcy Code §548(a)(2).

§2.2.1 Principles of Nonhindrance

Court opinions involving allegedly fraudulent transfers have often sounded muddled notes because of a failure to discriminate among the four distinct principles of conduct that this body of law seeks to implement. For convenience, I will label them the principles of truth, primacy, evenhandedness, and nonhindrance. Although more than one of these principles are usually involved in actual cases, what they are, and how they are related to the policy underlying the law of preferential transfers, can be seen through an examination of four simple situations.

Example of pure deception

1. Danny Debtor grants Freddy Friend a mortgage on Danny's small factory in return for a loan of $160,000, which Freddy actually makes to Danny. Danny wishes to discourage unpaid trade creditors who have $30,000 of claims against him from litigating them to judgment and seeking execution against the factory. He therefore persuades Freddy to have the recorded mortgage recite that it secures a debt for $200,000, which equals the well-known market value of the factory.[4] When the trade creditors' attorneys search the real estate records, they discover and give credence to the false mortgage. Knowing that Danny Debtor has few assets other than the factory, they become discouraged and cease pursuing him.

Principle of truth

Here, then, is a case of blatant fraud, involving a kind of behavior that has been recognized as wrong from time immemorial. Danny knew the transfer of the mortgage interest to Freddy was falsely described; he intended by his false representation to thwart legitimate creditors; and he actually did so. The keynote of the evil is the *actual deception* or falsehood practiced on the trade creditors to their detriment. By hypothesis, of course, Freddy did give full and fair consideration for the extent of the mortgage interest that he could enforce against Debtor. Further, the mortgage interest that he obtained did not actually render Debtor incapable of satisfying the remaining creditors. The ideal offended is simply that of *truth:* In connection with transfers of property rights to others, a debtor is forbidden to tell lies to his creditors that will lead to the nonsatisfaction of

UFCA §7

their claims.[5] This principle is expressed in a rule found in almost every

[4]In order to protect himself from possible double-crossing on the part of Freddy, Danny has Freddy sign a secret affidavit stating that as of the date after the recording he is owed only $160,000 by Danny, and the promissory note given by Danny is in only this amount. Given the affidavit and the note, Freddy's recovery would be limited to the $160,000 in any legal action.

[5]Finding fraudulent conveyance cases as to which we can be sure enough of the real facts to say that untruthful conduct *and nothing else* constituted the violation of duty to creditors is difficult. There are, however, many cases under UFCA §7 and similar rules in which the court decides against a defendant on the ground that he had an actual intent to defraud creditors in

fraudulent conveyance statute, that transfers made, or obligations incurred, with *actual intent* to hinder, delay, or *defraud* creditors is a fraudulent conveyance[6] and therefore may be set aside by the creditors or ignored when they attempt to levy execution on the property that was transferred or on which the obligation was imposed.[7]

Example of purely constructive fraud

2. Debbie Debtor has reached the point where $100,000 of her debts are due and payable, and her entire assets have a fair market value of the same dollar amount. Thinking that she would prefer that her husband and sister rather than her creditors get the benefit of her assets, she makes a deed of gift of all her possessions to those two fortunate relatives, and immediately delivers full and exclusive actual possession of the property to them, relinquishing any use or benefit from the transferred property. She makes no secret of the transaction or of her intentions. She reports the deed of gift in every conceivable recording office, and mails a copy by certified mail to each and every creditor, together with a detailed and accurate account of her motivations, purposes, and feelings towards her creditors. In this case, Debbie has made a transfer that, under the rules of any standard fraudulent conveyance statute or body of case law, would clearly be voidable, because (a) the transfer was made without fair and full consideration[8] and (b) she was insolvent immediately after the transfer.[9]

UFCA §4

More specifically, the relevant rules of statutes like the UFCA or the fraudulent conveyance Section of the Bankruptcy Code are threefold. First,

---

the sense of deceiving them and notes that *proof* of facts violating other principles of fraudulent conveyance law is therefore unnecessary. See, e.g., Linder v. Lewis, Roca, Scoville & Beauchamp, 333 P.2d 286 (Ariz. 1958) (transferee misrepresented himself as purchaser for value; transferor's insolvency need not be proved); Cooper v. Cooper, 335 P.2d 983 (Cal. App. 1959) (putting title in name of woman friend to conceal ownership from former wife-creditor was fraudulent; immaterial whether debtor rendered insolvent); Brown Packing Co. v. Lewis, 58 N.Y.S.2d 443 (Sup. Ct. 1943) (fair and adequate consideration irrelevant where there is actual intent to defraud); Sheffit v. Koff, 100 A.2d 393 (Pa. Super. 1953) (showing of insolvency and lack of fair consideration not necessary under §7).

[6] See, e.g., UFCA §7.

[7] See, e.g., UFCA §9.

[8] See UFCA §3 (definition of consideration).

[9] See UFCA §4. The same provision would be used to undo certain related types of transactions, such as a sale of her property while debtor is insolvent to relatives or to innocent nonrelated parties at less than the property's fair equivalent value. This would happen whether the sale was deliberately designed to satisfy moral obligations or perceived allegiances to or preferences for the transferees or was simply a bad bargain on the transferor's part, resulting from ignorance and incompetence. In the absence of preemptive statutes concerning the legality of dividends, this same provision, or the one concerning transfers without fair consideration that leave a business with "unreasonably small capital," see UFCA §5, would also vitiate dividends paid to shareholders on the eve of a corporation's insolvency, as well as a myriad host of bargain transactions with corporate insiders: excessive salaries, purchases and sales at prices that are bargains to the insider, phony loans, and so forth.

UFCA Section 4 makes a fraudulent conveyance out of a debtor's transfer of any property interest, or the debtor's incurrence of any obligation, when the debtor is or will thereby be rendered *insolvent* AND the transfer is made or the obligation is incurred *without* the debtor's receiving *fair consideration* in return. Fair consideration is defined in the statute. To simplify, it means that the debtor must receive something with a *fair equivalent value* for making the transfer or becoming obligated (that is, must get something of equal value that creditors can get at to satisfy their claims). Insolvency is also defined in the statute. While the terms are hardly free of ambiguity and do generate litigation, the rule as a whole is orders of magnitude more definite than the "don't use control to do wrong to creditors" formulation of the corporate veil-piercing cases.

UFCA §5

Second, UFCA Section 5 makes a fraudulent conveyance out of transfers of any property interest when the debtor-transferor will have *"unreasonably small capital"* afterwards AND does *not receive fair consideration* in return. This is like the first-mentioned rule, except that the small capital test is substituted for the insolvency test. The substitution means that it will be easier to find that a transaction is a fraudulent conveyance. But this section, unlike Section 4, only applies to debtors *in business*. It would apply to virtually all corporations, of course.

UFCA §6

Third, UFCA Section 6 makes a fraudulent conveyance out of a debtor's making a transfer or incurring an obligation when the debtor intends or believes that he will incur debts beyond his ability to pay as they mature.

Principle of primacy

The ideal offended by Debbie Debtor in the above example is not that of truthful conduct toward creditors. Debbie has been completely open with her creditors and has never tried to deceive them. (A diehard proponent of a "fraud" analysis might overstretch the notion of fraud and say that, when Debbie originally borrowed from her creditors, she "implicitly" promised to satisfy her legal obligations before her moral obligations and personal allegiances; that she has now failed to fulfill this promise; and that the failure is conclusive evidence that the promise was falsely and deceptively given. But this is a convoluted and fictionalized account of what she did. It is simpler and more honest to recognize that another ideal is served by fraudulent conveyance law.) The ideal can be captured by a cliche: Be just before you are generous.[10] The debtor has a moral

[10] This statement can be unpacked into a small family of commandments. Always act so that you can fulfill your legal obligations after any of the following: (1) transferring property to satisfy moral obligations and personal allegiances; (2) making inadvertent or coerced transfers for less than full value; and (3) retaining property for your personal benefit or, in the corporate context, transferring it to your shareholders. Considerations of human dignity, as evidenced

duty[11] in transferring her property to give *primacy* to so-called legal obligations, which are usually the legitimate, conventional claims of standard contract and tort creditors, as opposed to the interests of self, family, friends, shareholders, and shrewder or more powerful bargaining parties.[12] I will refer to this duty as the principle of primacy.[13]

Example of pure discrimination

3. Pierce is indebted to Twyne for $400 and to Calvin for $200. Pierce's nonexempt assets are worth only $300. Suppose that Pierce, simply because Twyne is the first to ask that he do so and because he dislikes Calvin, and for no other reason, transfers all of his property to Twyne. Suppose, contrary to the apparent facts in a similar, well-known case,[14] that Pierce makes the transfer openly and with much publicity and fanfare, so that no deception of any sort is practiced on Calvin, and that Pierce does not intend to and never does get a kickback of part of the transferred property or its use or any other kind of benefit from Twyne. Assume also that Twyne's claim is a completely valid, unobjectionable, due and payable, legal obligation of the most conventional sort.

Principle of evenhandedness

Pierce's transfer to Twyne does not run afoul of the principles of truth

---

by the exemptions available in bankruptcy proceedings, now obviously limit the third commandment.

[11] I describe the duties inherent in fraudulent conveyance law as "moral" for several reasons. First, they are standards of right and wrong in debtor-creditor relationships that have endured over many centuries and have governed extremely common transactions. The relation between debtors and creditors is as old as civilization, is only slightly less significant than relationships among family members, social classes, and races, has always occupied a substantial portion of the resources of legal systems, and has always been regulated in the commercial context by attitudes and emotions of a decidedly moral sort.

Second, these duties are, I think, not really perceived as *imposed* by the statutes and cases which reflect them—as are many modern legal obligations—but are perceived to be a part of normative custom.

Third, many actors in the commercial world have *internalized* the norms—they feel bound by them—and the norms are enforced to some extent by social as well as legal sanctions.

[12] Fraudulent conveyances of the sort under discussion may be buried amid obscuring factors. It often requires judicial imagination to see through the disguises and lawyerly caution to anticipate the possibilities. For instance, a bootstrap acquisition plan may give rise to voidable fraudulent conveyances when the acquired company later distributes assets, either directly to the seller or to the stock purchaser for use in meeting obligations to the seller, when the company is insolvent or possessed of small capital. E.g., Steph v. Branch, 255 F. Supp. 526 (E.D. Okla.), aff'd, 389 F.2d 233 (10th Cir. 1968) (*A* sold stock in corporation X to *B*, taking a note for most of purchase price; parties have X discharge *B*'s obligation by furnishing free materials to *A*).

[13] We could label this ideal the principle of loyalty to creditors. But the term *loyalty* has been preempted for use in the quite parallel context of a corporate director's duty to his corporation: The director must avoid abusive self-dealing and other conduct that puts his own interests, or that of a particular group or shareholders, above the interests of the shareholders as a whole.

[14] Twyne's Case, 3 Coke 80b, 76 Eng. Rep. 809 (Star Chamber 1601).

and primacy in dealing with creditors, because Pierce has fully and truthfully described the transaction and has given primacy to his legal obligations. Nevertheless, it seems objectionable for a debtor to satisfy fully the claims of just one creditor at a time when he lacks sufficient assets to meet his other legal obligations. A preferential payment of this sort hinders pro tanto the interest of all the other creditors. Many judges and other lawmakers have thought that, in such a situation, a debtor should deal equally with all his creditors. I will dub this ideal of debtor behavior the principle of *evenhandedness* toward creditors. But note that the term connotes equality of treatment of legal obligations in connection with liquidation proceedings.[15]

In law of voidable preferences

Evenhandedness, in its fullest expression, has two aspects. Whenever a debtor is or is about to become insolvent and thus unable to satisfy all his creditors in full, the debtor should refrain from preferring one creditor over another. Similarly, in such cases the creditors should refrain from seeking such a preference. In either instance, transfers resulting in better than equal treatment on the eve of liquidation proceedings should be undone. They may actually be undone in bankruptcy proceedings as voidable preferential transfers. Standard fraudulent conveyance rules, however, would not undo the transfers.

Unusual example of hindering creditors

4. Doris Debter, who owns 250 shares of stock, sold those shares to her husband for full value in illiquid assets. She was not insolvent at the time of the sale but the stock had been her only liquid asset. As a result of the transaction, she has no assets that creditors can easily reach. She made the transfer for the purpose of hindering her creditors but did not deceive them. This transaction would be avoided under the open-ended language of the UFCA,[16] which covers transactions made with actual intent to hinder or delay creditors.[17]

Residual principle of nonhindrance

Although Doris intends and accomplishes a transfer leading to a hindering of her creditors, her behavior does not, strictly speaking, offend the principles of truth, primacy, or evenhandedness, as developed above. The

[15] The principle of evenhandedness is not always adopted, especially in piecemeal liquidations, when individual creditors separately levy upon and exhaust the debtor's property. It is more commonly employed in collective liquidations such as dissolution and winding up of a corporation under state corporate law, straight bankruptcy proceedings under federal law, liquidating receiverships, and assignments for the benefit of creditors. The principle is sometimes enforced, as among creditors of the same class, in proceedings looking toward reorganization rather than liquidation of the distressed debtor—for instance, in reorganizations under Chapter 11 of the Bankruptcy Code, 11 U.S.C. §§1101-1174.

[16] See UFCA §7.

[17] This hypothetical is based on the facts in Klein v. Rossi, 251 F. Supp. 1 (E.D.N.Y. 1966).

scheme involves no actual deception, for she has truthfully informed all her creditors of the transaction. Moreover, the transfer of the shares is not for less than their fair value, nor does the transfer leave her insolvent, so the transfer does not violate the principle of primacy. Finally, the scheme results in no preference of any preexisting creditor over the others. Hence, we can say that there may be transactions that do not offend the three principles in their normal applications, but which are still fraudulent conveyances because they violate the more general expression of the ideal of which all three of the subsumed principles are specifications. The general ideal might be described as that of *nonhindrance* of the enforcement of valid legal obligations against oneself, in connection with transfers of one's property.

Summary

In summary, then, fraudulent conveyance law embodies a general ideal, in connection with a debtor's transfers of property rights and incurrences of new obligations, of nonhindrance of creditors. This vague ideal is made operational through the effectuation of the more specific principles of truth, primacy, and evenhandedness as well as a general, residual prohibition of conduct that hinders creditors in attempting to satisfy their claims. The principles are embodied in statutory rules and case law holdings.

§2.2.2 Evenhandedness

So far, I've presented evenhandedness as one of three particular duties derived from the general duty of nonhindrance, because a violation of the duty of evenhandedness operates to hinder the nonpreferred creditors. But we can also look at evenhandedness as a policy independent of, and on par with, a general ideal of nonhindrance. This way of looking at the policy has led to its development as a separate topic. Evenhandedness is the ideal behind what is referred to as the law of voidable preferences, and many cases assume or state explicitly that a preference is not a fraudulent conveyance.[18]

Idea of a voidable preference

The concept of a voidable preference is easy to grasp if you are careful to see it in relation to insolvency proceedings. Let's begin with some basic points. When a debtor's assets are less than his liabilities, each of his creditors may bring separate lawsuits to collect what they can from his assets. It's usually more efficient, though, if the creditors are able (or required) to place him in a single insolvency proceeding in which all of his

[18] E.g., Dean v. Davis, 242 U.S. 438 (1917); Coder v. Arts, 213 U.S. 223, 242 (1909); Pope v. National Aero Fin. Co., 46 Cal. Rptr. 233 (Cal. App. 1965); Johnson v. O'Brien, 144 N.W.2d 720 (Minn. 1966).

nonexempt assets are sold and the proceeds parcelled out among all the creditors in an orderly way. Some laws governing insolvency proceedings of this sort—such as the federal bankruptcy law—make it a basic principle (to which there are many exceptions) that all creditors should be paid an equal percentage of their claims. For example, each ordinary unsecured creditor in a bankruptcy proceeding might get 12¢ for each $1 of valid claims.

High cost of grabby behavior

Now, suppose that, shortly before the bankruptcy proceeding starts, one aggressive creditor prevails upon the debtor to pay *all* of his claim. This creditor has obviously grabbed himself a "preferred" status. His action might leave the other ordinary creditors with, say, only 3¢ for each $1 of valid claim. And, of course, the prospect of doing better than the other creditors will tempt each creditor of the troubled debtor to grab what he can, as quick as he can. But if every creditor scrambles to do this, they will probably run up legal costs, prevent an orderly sale of the debtor's assets that would yield their highest value, and thus reduce the total net payoff to the creditors as a group. The creditors will engage in individually rational but collectively self-defeating behavior. Their ability to get preferred treatment in the period immediately preceding bankruptcy threatens both to destroy the efficiency advantages of the bankruptcy process and to circumvent its goal of equal treatment.

Bankruptcy law's solution

Fortunately, bankruptcy law foresees the problem. It tries to deter such disruptive conduct by declaring that payoffs or other transfers in a defined prebankruptcy period that result in a creditor's getting preferred treatment may be "avoided" or undone in the bankruptcy itself. The details of this policy—exactly what does and doesn't count as a voidable preference, and so forth—are spelled out in the relevant statute and case law.[19]

Kinship between fraudulent conveyances and preferences

Despite the fact that there are separate and distinct rules about voidable preferences and about fraudulent conveyances, the fact situations in many fraudulent conveyance cases suggest that those cases might have been treated equally as well as instances of voidable preferences.[20] For example, one of the great ironies of legal history is that *Twyne's Case,*[21] which is widely regarded as the fountainhead of the modern Anglo-American law of fraudulent conveyances, does not, as presented in the reports, clearly involve anything more than a preference. The transaction offended the principle of evenhandedness, which was not then an ideal that the common law of individual collection efforts respected, but it is not clear that it

[19] See Bankruptcy Code §547 and annotations to 11 U.S.C.A. §547.

[20] See, e.g., Bullard v. Aluminum Co. of America, 468 F.2d 11 (7th Cir. 1972).

[21] 3 Coke 80b, 76 Eng. Rep. 809 (Star Chamber 1601).

offended the ideals of truth and primacy in any relevant way. The facts, which are roughly similar to those in the third example discussed above, do appear to include the circumstance that Pierce's transfer to Twyne was secret. But why a transaction that would be a mere nonvoidable preference if done openly should become a voidable fraudulent conveyance because done secretly is not at all clear, either from the report of the case or in logic.[22] Perhaps the secrecy led *C* (the injured creditor, like Calvin in our earlier example) to pursue his collection efforts longer than he would have had he known of the preference and thus to waste money. This possibility, it seems, could have been covered quite adequately by letting *C* recover the pointless expenses, rather than condemning the whole transfer to Twyne as a criminal act. It might well be that the key to the case was that Pierce violated the ideal of truth because he did not really transfer the entire amount of his property, but under a kickback arrangement with Twyne (who was apparently too slow of foot at that point to win his race against *C* via the use of judicial process) kept the use and benefit of certain property. Pierce was to keep some of his assets, although insolvent; Twyne was to obtain a larger percentage of his claim than if he resorted to legitimate collection procedures; and both were to defraud *C* in his collection efforts by pretending that Pierce no longer had any assets. The case may actually be understandable, then, as a case similar to the first example above, which involved actual, detrimental deception.[23]

Doctrinal differences

Despite their essential kinship, the fact that fraudulent conveyances and voidable preferences have emerged as distinct legal doctrines has significant consequences. While both fraudulent conveyances and prefer-

[22] For an interesting but unsuccessful attempt to argue that it may be a fraudulent conveyance to attempt to conceal a preference, see In re Cushman Bakery, 526 F.2d 23, 30-34 (1st Cir. 1975), cert. denied, 425 U.S. 937 (1976).

[23] This "kickback" interpretation is well supported by the text of the opinion. "[N]ot withstanding that [the deed of gift of all Pierce's goods and chattels to Twyne, in satisfaction of his debt] Pierce continued in possession of the said goods, and some of them he sold; and he shore the sheep, and marked them with his own mark. . . ." 76 Eng. Rep. at 811. "The donor continued in possession, and used them as his own; and by reason thereof he traded and trafficked with others, and defrauded and deceived them." 76 Eng. Rep. at 812-813. "[N]otwithstanding here was a true debt due to Twyne, and a good consideration of the gift, yet it was not within the proviso of the said Act of 13 Eliz. . . . it is not *bona fide,* for no gift shall be deemed to *bona fide* within the said proviso which is accompanied with any trust . . . [and] continuance of the possession in the donor, is a sign of trust." 76 Eng. Rep. at 814.

Twyne's case is the fountainhead of doctrines of fraudulent retention of possession, the ultimate development of which was to plague the development of the law governing security interests in personal property left in the debtor's possession. Indeed, a good number of the fraudulent conveyance cases decided under the "actual fraud" rubric involve transfers of property without a change of possession. See 2 G. Glenn, supra note 1 in §2.1, chs. XVIII(B)-XX (rev. ed. 1940).

ences are voidable in bankruptcy,[24] preferences can often be avoided only by a bankruptcy trustee while fraudulent conveyances are also voidable under state law at the behest of individual creditors.[25] Similarly, whereas many preferences must have occurred on or within 90 days before the filing of the bankruptcy petition in order to be voidable,[26] fraudulent conveyances that took place one year or possibly more before filing[27] may be set aside. And the list of technical requirements concerning the two branches of law could be differentiated at point after point.[28]

Evenhandedness less important?

Perhaps the key to the existence of the two great, "separate" branches of the law concerning the debtor's moral duties to his creditors is that the principle of evenhandedness has never been considered as important to the functioning of the commercial system as the principles of truth and primacy. Evenhandedness, therefore, has been relegated in part to a separate doctrinal category, where it can be diluted and adjusted by limited implementing rules, without affecting the other two principles. This strategy is reflected in such tired, and not entirely accurate or meaningful, saws as the one that there is nothing morally or legally "wrong" with giving or seeking a preference, although fraudulent conveyances should not be counselled by the debtor's or the creditors' attorneys.[29] It is also reflected,

[24] See Bankruptcy Code §§547, 548, 544(b).

[25] Indeed, in the area of piecemeal liquidation of insolvent estates, state law not only allows debtors to give creditors preferred treatment but permits creditors to seek to obtain it forcibly, by self-consciously rejecting the principle of equal treatment in favor of the "grab" principle. The notion is that diligence in the use of individual coercive collective procedures should be rewarded, so that the swiftest of wing—he who, or it which, first gets a judicial lien—should be first satisfied.

[26] See Bankruptcy Code §547(b)(4)(A). The period is extended to one year for insiders. Id. §547(b)(4)(B).

[27] The Bankruptcy Code's own fraudulent conveyance statute, §548, has a one year period. But transfers and obligations avoided by a trustee in bankruptcy under §544(b), which allows the trustee to invoke state fraudulent conveyance law, may have occurred much further in the past, depending on the applicable state statute of limitation.

[28] Extinguishment of an antecedent debt equal to the value of the transferred property can be fair consideration for fraudulent conveyance purposes; a transfer can be a preference only when it is given for or on account of an antecedent debt. Transfers may sometimes be voidable fraudulent conveyances even when the transferor is not afterwards insolvent; a preference can only be made by an insolvent debtor. Fraudulent conveyance rules apply to transfers made and obligations incurred; preference rules apply only to transfers.

[29] As the Supreme Court put it,

> The Statute recognizes the difference between the intent to defraud and the intent to prefer, and also the difference between a fraudulent and a preferential conveyance. One is inherently and always vicious; the other innocent and valid, except when made in violation of the express provisions of a statute. One is *malum per se* and the other *malum prohibitum*,—and then only to the extent that it is forbidden. [Van Iderstine v. National Discount Co., 227 U.S. 575, 582 (1913).]

of course, in the enormous number of exceptions made to the principle of equal treatment of creditors in bankruptcy—exceptions ranging from security interests through statutory priorities to contractual and other forms of subordination among creditors.[30]

§2.2.3 Balancing Fraudulent Conveyance Rules Against Other Legal Objectives

Relevance of transferee's good faith

The principles of nonhindrance, including the special evolution of evenhandedness in the voidable preference doctrine, have been presented above in a rather tidy and purified form. In actual implementation, the principles are often balanced against other objectives of the legal system, especially that of fairness toward the debtor's transferee. As is evident from a close reading of the UFCA, the good faith or absence of actual fraudulent intent of the transferee may have a bearing on the extent of the creditor's recovery.[31] It doesn't seem too harsh to ask an innocent transferee to disgorge the amount by which he "beat the market" when he paid less than fair value for transferred property, given that the transferor's innocent creditors would otherwise lose that amount. But to go further and ask him to disgorge everything the debtor transferred to him would be punitive and unfair. Moreover, in some old or odd cases the transferee's innocence may prevent recovery entirely, and under dividend statutes, the transferee's status as innocent public shareholder may protect him entirely.

FCL only one way of implementing principles

In addition, the legal system, in implementing the principles of nonhindrance, has had to go beyond the rules of fraudulent conveyance law, embedding the principles in other branches of the law. In theory, the principles could be effectuated in three radically different ways.

First, they could be expressed as a system of transactional rules. Decision of cases under the rules would necessitate examination of specific transactions and proof of a violation of a rule in each transaction. Fraudulent conveyance law fits this pattern.

The second mode of implementation is the gestalt approach. When transactions are complex or involve elements that are not normally covered under the transactional mode, this approach would permit a court to apply a remedy, albeit a crude one, to correct a pattern of fraudulent transfers or obligations that may reasonably be inferred. This mode of implementation

[30] See, e.g., Bankruptcy Code §§507 (priorities), 510(a) (subordination).
[31] See UFCA §§3, 9(2).

is, I will argue in section 2.3, exemplified by the doctrine of equitable subordination.

Finally, the principles could be embodied in a system of preventive rules. As mentioned briefly in subsection 2.3.5, the rule of automatic subordination proposed some years ago by the Bankruptcy Commission is an instance of this third mode of implementation.

§2.3 *The Doctrine of Equitable Subordination*

Three bases of subordination

In a bankruptcy proceeding, the court may order that the claims of a certain creditor not be paid off unless and until all or some of the other creditors are completely paid. Sometimes such a ruling is based on interpretation of governing contractual relationships among the debtor and its creditors, or on priority rules set out in a relevant statutory provision. But sometimes such a ruling that one creditor be subordinated to others is based simply on the general, open-ended equitable jurisdiction of the court—its power to do equity in the individual case.

Example of equitable subordination (ES)

For example, suppose the controlling shareholder of a corporation that is now in bankruptcy files a claim for unpaid compensation allegedly owed him for serving as chief executive officer of the corporation. The court finds that the executive's rate of pay was truly exorbitant and that it was raised to its extremely high level when there was serious question about the corporation's ability to meet its obligations to other creditors. The court, invoking the doctrine of equitable subordination, rules that the executive's salary claim be subordinated to the claims of other creditors. Since the bankrupt firm is quite insolvent, the result is that the executive receives nothing for his claim.

Basic points about ES

Compared to the law of fraudulent conveyances, the doctrine of equitable subordination is more modern, less widely adopted by legal systems, and basically applicable to a much narrower class of situations: federal bankruptcy proceedings involving debtors owned or controlled by persons who are also creditors of the bankrupt.[1] Typically, the court applies the doctrine of equitable subordination to the creditor claims of an insider or controlling party: A parent corporation, a sole shareholder, or a shareholder who in relation to other shareholders owns "debt" claims against

§2.3 [1] Equitable subordination now receives explicit statutory recognition in Bankruptcy Code §510(c). But the doctrine was developed in case law, and its meaning must still be found there. A leading article on equitable subordination is Herzog and Zweibel, The Equitable Subordination of Claims in Bankruptcy, 15 Vand. L. Rev. 83 (1961).

the insolvent corporation in the same proportion as his stock ownership. When the doctrine is applied, the claims of the controlling party are subordinated to those of bona fide outside creditors. The subordination is not automatic in our present law: An insider's claims as creditor against his corporation are not subordinated to those of other creditors merely because he is an insider. Rather, subordination is said to turn on the presence of one of the following: fraudulent conduct by the insider, mismanagement of the insolvent corporation, or inadequate capitalization of the corporation.[2]

Another vague formula

As in the veil-piercing cases, courts sometimes announce a three part general formula as to when a creditor will be subjected to equitable subordination. First, the claimant must have engaged in some type of "inequitable conduct." Second, the conduct must have resulted in injury to other creditors or conferred an unfair benefit on the claimant. Third, equitable subordination must not be inconsistent with provisions of the bankruptcy statute.[3] The phrase *inequitable conduct* is just as crucial, and just as vague and illuminating, as the word *wrong* in the veil-piercing cases.

In this section, I will first illustrate (in section 2.3.1) the functional equivalence between fraudulent conveyance law and equitable subordination doctrine in the largest group of equitable subordination cases: the fraud cases and most of the so-called mismanagement cases. I will then (in section 2.3.2) discuss why courts found it necessary to develop equitable subordination doctrine in these kinds of cases. Afterwards (in section 2.3.3 infra), a number of subordination cases that involve a modest expansion of the coverage of fraudulent conveyance principles will be analyzed. Cases involving inadequate capitalization will then receive special consideration (in section 2.3.4 infra).

§2.3.1 Parallels with Fraudulent Conveyance Law

We can see the similarity between equitable subordination doctrine and fraudulent conveyance law by comparing both the conditions under which

[2]Herzog and Zweibel classify the subordination cases into six categories. See Herzog & Zweibel, note 1 supra, at 90-112. With a few exceptions, the cases under three of their headings (fraud, fiduciary relationship, and instrumentality and alter ego cases) appear upon analysis of their facts to suggest actual or constructive fraud. One of their categories, the capital contribution cases, explicitly implicates the inadequate capitalization issue. Their other two categories are of tangential interest only. The consensual subordination cases simply involve courts in the process of finding or inferring an intent by a creditor to subordinate his claim to those of others—such cases are not within the ambit of equitable subordination as I construe the term. Finally, the remaining cases concern claims tainted by illegality.

[3]Matter of Mobile Steel Co., 563 F.2d 692 (5th Cir. 1977); Matter of Multiponics, Inc., 622 F.2d 709 (5th Cir. 1980).

they are applied and their results (as remedies). Let us first consider their conditions of application.

Similar behavior triggers ES and FCL

Conditions of application. Are equitable subordination doctrine and fraudulent conveyance law applied in response to very similar kinds of misconduct? Yes. The similarity is illustrated by almost all of the leading subordination cases. To take an example, the celebrated equitable subordination case, *Taylor v. Standard Gas and Electric Co. (Deep Rock),*[4] involved a complex series of inequitable or highly suspicious actions by Standard, the parent corporation in control of the debtor corporation (Deep Rock).

(1) Standard caused Deep Rock to enter into a lease with another subsidiary which was unfair to Deep Rock. The subsidiary was then required to turn the lease receipts over to Standard.[5]
(2) Standard caused Deep Rock to enter into a management contract with another subsidiary and pay it steep management fees.[6]
(3) Standard charged interest at a high rate on its open account with Deep Rock.[7]
(4) Standard caused Deep Rock to pay it dividends when Deep Rock could hardly afford them.[8]

Given the continuous inadequacy of Deep Rock's capitalization,[9] and assuming (as the Court undoubtedly did) unfairness in these transactions, all of them were fraudulent conveyances. They all involved Deep Rock in making transfers, or incurring obligations, without receiving fair consideration in return, at a time when Deep Rock was insolvent or would be left with unreasonably small capital.[10]

Another example

Pepper v. Litton[11] presents another example of the substitutability of the two doctrines. Scheming to defraud the corporation's creditors, a controlling stockholder accumulated large, unpaid salary claims owing to himself.

[4] 306 U.S. 307 (1939).
[5] Id. at 319-320.
[6] Id. at 311.
[7] Id. at 320.
[8] Id. at 317.
[9] See id. at 310 (from its organization "two jumps ahead of the wolf").
[10] See UFCA §5. The *Deep Rock* case also illustrates a use of equitable subordination doctrine that complements fraudulent conveyance law. The subordination of Standard's creditor claims *to the claims of Deep Rock's preferred shareholders* would not be possible under fraudulent conveyance law, simply because shareholders as such are not creditors. See generally section 2.3.3 infra.
[11] 308 U.S. 295 (1939).

Suing on them, he caused the corporation to confess judgment and used the judgment, as well as other delaying actions, to hinder a major creditor. The corporation's incurrence of the salary claim was, under the circumstances, a fraudulent conveyance.[12] Yet the case was treated as an occasion for announcing the equitable subordination doctrine.

[12]See UFCA §§1, 7. Other important cases also suggest that equitable subordination is a substitute for fraudulent conveyance law. In Comstock v. Group of Institutional Investors, 335 U.S. 211 (1948), the majority affirmed a plan of reorganization that accepted as valid the claim of a parent railroad company against its subsidiary on the basis of the lower court's finding of fair dealing. 335 U.S. at 230. The dissenters, however, pointed to 11 instances of loans by the parent to the subsidiary that were followed within a few days by dividends of similar or slightly smaller amounts from the subsidiary to the parent. Id. at 240. The dissent argued that compelling the subsidiary to pay dividends while it was debt heavy and cash poor was the type of "mismanagement" that should lead to equitable subordination. Id. at 247. The dissenters were rightly suspicious, although they would have been more persuasive if they had not focused on the dividend payments. If the loans are integrated with the dividends, it is seen that the parent was causing the subsidiary to *incur obligations* to itself without giving the subsidiary *fair consideration,* i.e., full equivalent value. To do this when it will leave the subsidiary with inadequate capital in relation to its debts is to cause it to effect a voidable fraudulent conveyance. See UFCA §§5, 7. The dissent's other bone of contention, that the parent for its sole benefit caused the subsidiary to assume obligations of another subsidiary without consideration and while the subsidiary was on the threshold of reorganization, also involved fraudulent conveyance, although again this analysis was overlooked.

A fascinating example of "bootstrapping" fraud, accompanied by an equally fascinating judicial response, is provided by In re Process-Manz Press, Inc., 236 F. Supp. 333 (N.D. Ill. 1964), rev'd on jurisdictional grounds, 369 F.2d 513 (7th Cir. 1966), cert. denied, 386 U.S. 957 (1967). Greatly simplified, the important facts were as follows. The shareholders of Manz sold their stock to Lithographers on an installment basis. Lithographers later found it financially difficult to make payments. An arrangement was worked out whereby Armstrong, a finance company, obtained a mortgage on the real estate of Manz and a security interest in some of its personal property. Of the loan proceeds given by Armstrong, however, about $1.5 million actually went to old, selling shareholders of Manz, discharging obligations of Lithographers. This transfer was accomplished by means of a redemption of Manz preferred stock held by Lithographers. 236 F. Supp. at 337-339. The $1,500,000 did not really benefit Manz, which therefore did not receive fair consideration for the note and security interests it gave. Armstrong wanted as security, not only the Manz stock, which its real borrower, Lithographers, could pledge to it, but also the assets of Manz, for it was only by an interest in the latter that it could hope to come ahead of Manz's creditors. Manz later went into Chapter XI proceedings. Because of Armstrong's knowledge and participation, the referee in bankruptcy, and the district court in affirming, explicitly held the mortgage *liens* void as violating various fraudulent conveyance rules. Id. at 346-347. The transfers were also found voidable as part of a conspiracy to cause an illegal stock redemption, illegal because of Manz's insolvency. Id. at 348.

In addition, the referee and district court invoked equitable subordination doctrine to subordinate the entire *claim* of Armstrong against Manz on an alter ego theory. Armstrong was not really a creditor of Manz but a holder, through its loans to Lithographers, of stock in Manz, and should therefore be paid only after the creditors of Manz were satisfied. Id. at 348. Strangely, although the discussions of fraudulent conveyance rules and equitable subordination were only a few paragraphs apart, the district court seems not to have noticed that the claims effectively might have been subordinated *under fraudulent conveyance rules* by voiding

Equivalent remedies, sometimes

Nature of the remedies. Analysis of a few examples will show that, given three restrictive conditions, equitable subordination is a functional substitute for fradulent conveyance law. These conditions are:

(1) a simple situation, which is here defined as one involving only one tainted transaction by the bankrupt corporation at the instance of a controlling party;
(2) a world in which corrective legal responses to tainted transactions take place without transaction costs;[13] and
(3) a policy decision that any rule attempting to undo the effects of a controlling creditor's influence should seek to accomplish the goal of corrective justice.

Full subordination vs. constructive distribution

The last condition may be satisfied by accepting a certain one of two facially plausible interpretations of equitable subordination doctrine. For convenience, let's call these interpretations the full subordination rule and the constructive distribution rule.

Under the full subordination rule, applying the doctrine of equal subordination automatically means that all creditor claims of the controlling party are fully subordinated to the claims of other creditors. As a result, the insider may in some cases be penalized in an amount greater than the unjust advantage he reaped from his controlling position.

The second interpretation is supposed to be corrective but not punitive, that is, the controlling party is to be subordinated only to the extent of the unfair advantage taken of the corporation.[14] Under this constructive distri-

---

them as obligations fraudulently incurred by Manz, with the result that Armstrong could share in the estate only as holder of Manz stock (which it was). If ever there were a case in which the functional substitutability of fraudulent conveyance law and equitable subordination doctrine could easily be observed, this was it; yet, the court does not observe the parallel.

See also Costello v. Fazio, 256 F.2d 903 (9th Cir. 1958); International Tel. & Tel. Corp. v. Holton, 247 F.2d 178 (4th Cir. 1957); In re Dean & Jean Fashions, Inc., 329 F. Supp. 663 (W.D. Okla. 1971). None of the above subordination cases expressly analyzed the relationships between fraudulent conveyance law and equitable subordination.

[13] As will become clear as the analysis unfolds, the assumption of a simple situation is important for legal doctrine because complex situations may entail very high transaction costs by making proof and analysis of particular facts quite expensive or impossible. In a sense, condition (1) is included in condition (2). However, I think it useful to treat the transaction costs generated by complex situations separately.

[14] The power of equitable subordination should

> not operate to take away anything punitively to which one creditor is justly entitled in view of the liquidation finality, and bestow it upon others, who in the relative situation have no fair right to it. It can therefore ordinarily go no farther than to level off actual inequitable disparities on the bankruptcy terrain for which a creditor is responsible, to

bution rule, the bankruptcy trustee would first compute the prorated shares of all creditors to the assets of the bankrupt corporation as if the tainted transaction had not occurred. He then deems the controlling party to have already received an anticipatory distribution of assets in the amount of his unjust benefit and adjusts the actual distribution accordingly. Although the case law and commentary on equitable subordination remedies have failed to properly distinguish between these two rules, a comparison of their effects in the examples which follow shows that the choice of rule has significant consequences for the remedy in the case.

1. *Situation A: Estate Insolvent Apart from Tainted Transaction.*

Hypo of insolvent estate

Milkable Corporation (M), which is controlled by a sole stockholder (*S*), owned assets with a fair salable value of $150. Previously, it had entered into a bona fide borrowing transaction at market interest rates with *S*, who thus became a creditor with a $100 claim. It had also bought goods on credit from a supplier who thus became an outside creditor (*OC*) with a claim of $100. There were and are no other creditors. In the absence of transaction costs, if, without more, M were to go into bankruptcy, *S* and *OC* would each receive $75. Let us refer to *S*'s $75 share in the bankrupt estate under such innocent conditions as *S*'s "just share" of the estate. This set of facts will be referred to as situation A.

Controlling party's unjust benefit

Suppose, however, that in fact *S* received a gratuitous or unfair benefit (an "unjust benefit") from M a few months before M goes into bankruptcy. The exact form in which *S* obtains a benefit without paying full consideration to M is not important. *S* may have caused M to pay $70 for services that *S* did not perform. M may have declared a $70 dividend to *S*. *S* may have sold goods to M at a price $70 in excess of the market price, or M could have sold goods to *S* at $70 less than the market price. *S* could have used the company's car or yacht for his personal use without compensation to the company. Further, the creation of the legitimate amount owed *S* and the illegitimate transfer of benefit to him may have occurred in the same transaction. For example, *S* may have made a credit sale of goods to M for $170, where the fair market value of the goods was only $100. Whether the creation of a legitimate and an illegitimate claim was linked together in this way is not crucial to our analysis (although it might be

---

the point where they will not create unjust disadvantages in claim positions and liquidation results.

In re Kansas City Journal-Post Co., 144 F.2d 791, 800-801 (8th Cir. 1944). See also Prudence Realization Corp. v. Geist, 316 U.S. 89, 97 (1942); Farmers Bank v. Julian, 383 F.2d 314 (8th Cir.), cert. denied, 389 U.S.1021 (1967). Note also that Bankruptcy Code §510(c) contemplates that "all or part of an allowed claim" may be equitably subordinated.

practically important, since it makes things harder to sort out). More generally, *how* the unjust benefit is taken is a secondary matter. All that is required at this point is an analytical ability to separate out *S*'s legitimate claim from the component of unjust benefit conferred. For concreteness, though, let's assume that *S* received $70 for services he didn't perform.

Result if injustice not remedied

If M's estate is distributed in bankruptcy without any attack on the $70 benefit paid to *S* for bogus services, *S* and *OC*, having equal creditor claims of $100, will each receive $40, or one half of the assets of the estate remaining after the payment for bogus services ($150 − $70 = $80), and *S* will keep his $70. As a result, *S* will have obtained $110 and *OC* will have obtained $40. If the transfer for bogus services had not occurred, however, each would have received one half of the company's $150 in assets, that is, his $75 just share.

Ideal result

Obviously, the legal system is called upon to make some sort of response to the bogus payment for services, since such payments by a debtor to a controlling person at the latter's direction violate the principle of primacy. Intuitively, if the proper legal response to *S*'s conduct is not a punitive one, it should lead to the result that would have occurred upon liquidation of M if *S* had not engaged in wrongful conduct. *S*, in other words, should wind up with neither more nor less than his just share of $75. How the parties will actually fare under the major remedial tools now available, fraudulent conveyance law and equitable subordination doctrine, turns out to depend on which of the two interpretations of equitable subordination is employed, and whether the amount of the unjust benefit is less than or greater than *S*'s just share of the estate. The following paragraphs illustrate these relationships.

Result if FCL applied

(a) Where amount of unjust benefit to the controlling party is less than his just share. Consider situation A when the amount of the payment to *S* for bogus services is, as supposed above, $70. Fraudulent conveyance law is precisely suited to correcting such bogus payments.[15] The trustee (*T*) in

[15] The text makes fraudulent conveyance law appear neater than it is. In a case where the transferee gave some but not fair consideration for the benefit conferred upon him, the analysis is more complicated. If the transferee acted "without actual fraudulent intent" he may retain the property transferred as security for return of the amount paid or consideration given. See Bankruptcy Code §548(c); UFCA §9(2). Usually, however, a controlling party who makes himself transferee for inadequate consideration will have displayed actual fraudulent intent within the meaning of these provisions, and with the result that the transfer will be voided in toto. This is *not* in theory a punitive result, however, since after surrendering the transferred property he can then prove an unsecured claim in bankruptcy for the amount of the consideration actually paid. On the other hand, this result is punitive in practice when compared to the happier fate of a controlling party who in one transaction with his corpora-

bankruptcy could sue (*S*) to recover $70 for the bankrupt estate.[16] In particular, he might invoke UFCA §4, since the transfer to *S* was without fair consideration while the estate was insolvent. The estate, now augmented to $150, would be divided equally between *OC*'s and *S*'s legitimate claims, and each would therefore receive $75.

Result under ES with full subordination

What would happen if *T* decided to invoke the doctrine of equitable subordination against *S*? This depends upon which interpretation of that doctrine one selects. If the full subordination rule were selected, *T* would bring no action for recovery of any amount from *S*, but would simply distribute the bankrupt estate, a nonaugmented $80, first toward satisfaction of *OC*'s $100 claim. There being no remainder, *S* winds up with $70, the amount of the bogus payment, which is $5 less than his just share. Thus, when the unjust benefit is less than the just share, *S* has been penalized relative to what he would have received were the law aimed solely at undoing his wrong.

Under ES with constructive distribution rule

But under the constructive distribution rule, *T* would *deem* the estate to contain $150, would compute each of the two creditors' shares as being $75, and would *deem* $70 of *S*'s share to have already been paid. Of the $80 actually left in the estate, *OC* would therefore obtain $75 and *S* would receive $5. The ultimate result is that *S* obtains exactly his just share, which is the result that a fraudulent conveyance action would have reached.

Results when unjust benefit relatively large

(b) Where amount of unjust benefit to the controlling party is greater than his just share. Now consider situation *A* when the amount of the payment for bogus services was $80. If *T* brings a fraudulent conveyance action this amount will be recovered for the bankrupt estate and *S* will wind up receiving his just share, as in the preceding case.

Under the full subordination rule, *T* simply attempts to satisfy OC's claim first. *OC* receives the amount of the nonaugmented estate, $70, while *S* keeps his $80 prior payment. Since *S*'s just share is only $75, he comes out ahead. *S*'s taking of the bogus payment has netted him an unfair advantage even after the application of the doctrine of equitable subordination. In contrast to the facts discussed in (a), the full subordination rule now leads to undercorrection rather than overcorrection.

---

tion paid equal value for a transfer and in a second transaction simply caused a transfer without giving any consideration: Upsetting only the second transaction, as seems feasible under a fraudulent conveyance approach, still leaves him with the benefit transferred in the first transaction, instead of with a provable claim on which he can hope to obtain only a few cents on the dollar. In other words, the rules work more harshly on those who integrate unfairness into their regular dealings than on those who keep their self-dealing clear and distinct.

[16] Bankruptcy Code §§548, 544(b).

Whether the constructive distribution rule will again, as in (a) above, avoid both undercorrection and penalties depends on the resolution of a new ambiguity. *T* deems the estate to contain $150, as it would had there been no payment for bogus services, computes *OC*'s and *S*'s shares to be $75 each, and deems *S* already to have received a bankruptcy distribution of $80 (the amount of the unjust benefit). The question remaining is whether *T* will regard this constructive bankruptcy distribution to *S* to be an irreversible fait accompli, even though excessive, so that *OC* will receive only the remaining $70 in the estate and suffer from a failure to achieve corrective justice, or whether T will invoke an asserted equitable power[17] to recover the amount of the $5 overpayment to *S*. Judicial opinions appear never to have focused sharply on these two alternatives, so that a definitive answer in terms of existing law cannot be given. If the overpayment recovery were explicitly considered and allowed—as I assume it would be—the process of doing so would certainly lead the court to an awareness of the essential similarity of equitable subordination doctrine and fraudulent conveyance law.

Another variation

2. *Situation B: The Tainted Transaction Creates Insolvency.*

Suppose that M had owned assets with a fair salable value of $200. As before, *S* and *OC* each have a legitimate creditor claim against M of $100. Each party's just share of M upon liquidation is $100. Let us refer to this set of facts as situation *B*.

If *S* were to take an unjust benefit from M of $90, which is less than the amount of his just share, M would be rendered insolvent and might go into bankruptcy. As in situation *A*, a fraudulent conveyance action by *T* against *S* would set matters exactly straight, as would application of the constructive distribution rule. But unlike the result in situation A where unjust benefit exceeded just share, the full subordination rule would now lead to a merely corrective result rather than a penalty. Thanks to the condition of solvency before the unfair transfer, full subordination and the resulting full satisfaction of *OC*'s claim does not give him more than his just share, with a resulting penalty upon *S*.

If, however, the unjust benefit taken by *S* had been $110, thus exceeding his just share, problems of undercorrection reemerge. Fraudulent conveyance law and the constructive distribution rule will again yield a simple

[17] Cf. In re Lilyknit Silk Underwear Co., 73 F.2d 52 (2d Cir. 1934) (without direct authority in Bankruptcy Act, court orders recovery of dividends paid out of the estate pursuant to an order later reversed).

corrective result.[18] The full subordination rule now leads to undercorrection—*OC* gets only the $90 left in the estate—as in situation *A*, part (b).

General result: full ES is rough, FCL is precise

The analysis just set forth suggests that the constructive distribution rule is the better of the two interpretations of equitable subordination. Since the full subordination rule can sometimes grant a boon to the wrongdoer rather than impose a punishment, we cannot justify that rule on the theory that fraud should be punished as well as corrected. Furthermore, the variations in outcome under this rule depend on mathematical relationships between unjust benefit and just share that have nothing to do with the legal policies involved. Indeed, from one point of view the relationships are positively counterintuitive, even shocking: Other figures being kept equal, the controlling party will maximize the legally retainable benefits from an unfair transaction by *increasing* the degree of unfairness![19] The constructive distribution rule, however, always results in exactly corrective justice. Therefore, if the constructive distribution rule is the chosen interpretation, the *results* of equitable subordination and of fraudulent conveyance law are equivalent.

[18] They will always yield a corrective response under the restrictive conditions governing this analysis.

[19] In some situations application of the full subordination rule will lead to the same result as a successful fraudulent conveyance action for reasons other than an accidental equivalence between unjust benefit and just share. One pattern is that presented when the prebankruptcy transfer of an unjust benefit to the controlling parties consisted of creating a nominal creditor claim on the part of those persons against the corporation, and the controlling parties have no other, legitimate creditor claims against it. The well-known case of Costello v. Fazio, 256 F.2d 903 (9th Cir. 1958), is a beautiful example of this pattern. Two of the partners in a failing business attempted to "withdraw" a substantial portion of their equity investment in the partnership by converting it into demand notes. The partnership was then incorporated, the notes were assumed, and the corporation marched straight into the valley of bankruptcy. If the business is regarded as having been one continuing business, and the switch from partnership to corporate form is therefore disregarded, the case presents a rather simple and straightforward example of a fraudulent conveyance: The business, while insolvent, transferred a benefit (the notes) to certain persons without receiving fair consideration. The response under fraudulent conveyance law would be that the trustee would seek to recover the benefit by bringing a suit to void the notes. In the actual case, equitable subordination, as operationalized by the full subordination rule, yielded the same result. The court, in fact, did not even mention that the transaction was a fraudulent conveyance, possibly because it overcautiously thought that the switch from partnership to corporate status created problems under that analysis.

§2.3.2 Why the Equitable Subordination Doctrine Was Developed

Why ES?

Since, in the vast majority of cases, equitable subordination operates as a functional substitute for fraudulent conveyance law, which a trustee in bankruptcy is well able to invoke, why did equitable subordination ever come into existence? Who needs it? When is it needed? The answer to these questions emerges when we begin lifting the three restrictive conditions that formed the context of situations *A* and *B* discussed above. Two of these conditions, which are obviously related, were no transaction costs and simple transactions.[20]

Different cost curves for ES and FCL

In actual cases, applying legal doctrines is always a costly process. When we move from simple to complex transactions, the costs of applying fraudulent conveyance law become extremely large, as compared to the costs of applying equitable subordination doctrine. This is because fraudulent conveyance law requires the person objecting to an insider's behavior and status with respect to a corporation to prove many specific, difficult points. He must identify each and every transaction he wishes to set aside or correct, and with respect to each transaction he must prove that the corporate debtor was insolvent or possessed of unreasonably small capital, that the terms of exchange were unfair, that the amount of the unfairness was thus-and-so, and so forth. Many of the equitable subordination cases—*Pepper v. Litton*[21] is a classic example—involved an incredibly complex series of controlling party transfers and other transactions. It would be extremely difficult and costly, if not impossible, to analyze separately each step in the series, to assess all the evidence relating thereto, to make the numerous separate findings as to insolvency and fairness of consideration, and to draw conclusions as to the proper amount of recovery at each step under the apparently exacting tests of the UFCA. Consider, for example, these remarks by the *Deep Rock* court:

> The basis of (the) claim (subordination of which was in question) was an open account which embraced transactions between Standard and Deep Rock from

[20] One set of transaction costs contributing to the early development of equitable subordination may have been no more than speculative, and it is now mainly of historical interest. Bankruptcy trustees appear to have believed that in order to recover fraudulently transferred property from claim filing creditors of the estate, they could not act within the so-called summary jurisdiction of the bankruptcy court, see Treister, Bankruptcy Jurisdiction: Is It Too Summary?, 39 S. Cal. L. Rev. 78 (1966), but rather had to initiate more expensive plenary proceedings. This fear should have subsided after the Supreme Court's opinion in Katchen v. Landy, 382 U.S. 323 (1966). The Bankruptcy Code of 1978 has made the problem even less serious.

[21] 308 U.S. 295 (1939).

the latter's organization in 1919 to the receivership in 1933. The account consists of *thousands of items* of debit and credit. . . .

. . . Many transactions entered in the account were attacked as fraudulent. . . .

Without going into the minutiae of the transactions between the two companies, enough may be stated to expose the reasons for our decision. . . .

. . . It is *impossible to recast Deep Rock's history* and experience so as to approximate what would be its financial condition at this day had it been adequately capitalized and independently managed and had its fiscal affairs been conducted with an eye single to its own interests.[22]

Though fraudulent conveyance law conceivably could be broadened to sanction a gestalt approach comparable to the step transaction doctrine in tax law,[23] rather than to require a transaction-by-transaction analysis and legal conclusion in all cases, it seemed less violent to tradition to invoke a more obviously amorphous doctrine to which the label equitable is attached.

The timing question

My theory of how equitable subordination came about may also help to explain when it came about. The timing question is, after all, a terribly puzzling one. Judges and lawmakers have made and applied fraudulent conveyance rules since Babylonian times. Why did they wait until the early twentieth century to invent the doctrine of equitable subordination?

Answer

The answer, in a nutshell, is that they had to wait for big business to come on the scene. The rise of large modern corporate enterprises created new opportunities for reducing the costs of enforcing creditor-protecting principles. These opportunities could be realized only by new specific rules implementing the old principles. For example, the managers of a large corporation with numerous subsidiaries could cause thousands of transactions to occur among the members of the corporate family. In an insolvency proceeding involving this corporate family, the facts about a fair

[22]Taylor v. Standard Gas & Elec. Co., 306 U.S. 307, 311-312, 315, 323 (1939) (emphasis supplied). Consider also the following, from another major subordination case:

> The vast extent of the railroad business carried on by the Missouri Pacific and the New Orleans during the long past period of alleged mismanagement and the intricate corporate structures of the railroads, inevitably presented most serious problems in the attempts of accountants to picture what their course of operations and financial transactions had been. . . . There was fundamental controversy as to what inferences should be drawn from the available accounts to establish the true financial condition of the New Orleans at different times. . . . [Comstock v. Group of Institutional Investors, 335 U.S. 211, 223-224 (1948) (quoting Comstock v. Group of Institutional Investors, 163 F.2d 350, 356 (8th Cir. 1947)).]

[23]The doctrine is discussed in section 10.4 infra.

sample of particular transactions, plus evidence that top management of the parent corporation had power to direct most of the transactions and an incentive to insist on terms that were biased in certain ways, may justify inferring the existence of a general pattern of transactions that were fraudulent or unfair to creditors of certain subsidiaries. In situations of this kind, the doctrine of equitable subordination offers a feasible remedy. Traditional fraudulent conveyance rules, because they require plaintiffs to prove each unfair transaction and to measure the amount of unfairness, do not. Before the rise of large corporate enterprises, the equitable subordination doctrine, which allows courts to look at an entire situation rather than at minutiae when defining a wrong and to substitute a shotgun for a rifle as the remedy, was less needed and less justified. The paradigmatic case was the failing business man who conveys title to his business and personal assets to his wife or to a friend just a short time before his creditors take him to court—or even, as in the deservedly famous *Twyne's Case*, while the sheriff is riding over to attach his goods. In these small-numbers situations, a sampling procedure is inapposite. But in a complex corporate insolvency, inferring a pattern of behavior from a sample of transactions may be not only economical but also justified.

Pressures to de-emphasize precision in remedies

The third restrictive condition used in our earlier analysis was that equitable subordination should seek to do corrective justice, eschewing both undercorrection of fraudulent and unfair transfers and punishment of the participants in them. Unlike the other two conditions, which are simplified assumptions about how the world is, this condition is a policy judgment about what the law's goal ought to be. Pressure to give up or de-emphasize the goal of precise corrective justice is, of course, generated by the very factual complexity which made the second condition unrealistic. Complexity not only drives courts to devise a doctrine that will avoid the necessity of applying all of the criteria of a fraudulent conveyance to each segment of a complicated series of transactions. It also pressures them to adopt the simple full subordination rule rather than the precisely corrective constructive distribution rule, since the latter obviously requires that a greater number of specific facts be determined.

Of course, a nonpunitive interpretation of equitable subordination—the view that the doctrine ought not to be applied in a way known to be punitive in the particular case—has much to be said for it. Many of the transactions characterized as fraudulent, both for purposes of fraudulent conveyance law and equitable subordination, involve conduct that is not clearly shown in litigation to be willfully wrong or criminal in nature or to betoken moral depravity in any ordinary sense. Although some cases involve intentional wrongs such as deliberate falsification of records,[24] most cases of fraud and mismanagement involve less obvious wrongs and may frequently be proven in court only in terms of mechanical financial tests. For example, the corporation may have paid, while insolvent, what is *now* found to be an excessive salary.[25] Because plaintiffs in civil cases are required to prove their cases by only a preponderance of evidence and because morally opprobrious fraud may be punished through other techniques, regarding fraudulent conveyance law and equitable subordination as basically corrective rather than punitive seems more reasonable and practical.

Costs of precision

Nonetheless, the fairness of requiring a careful and precise examination of evidence and computation of damages in an attempt to do corrective justice must be balanced against the cost of achieving precision and the mildly punitive attitude that the controlling parties should bear the risk of mistakes. At some point, it becomes obvious that a fraud or mismanagement case is so complex that one is justified in substituting a perception of an entire pattern of conduct for a sequence of focused looks at the elements and the shotgun for the rifle as remedy.[26] Furthermore, judges naturally feel that in uncertain and complex cases the fraudulent transferee should bear the risks of remedial imprecision. The lure of equitable subordination doctrine may be explained in part by the erroneous but understandable belief of judges that any imprecision in the corrective function of the doctrine typically bears down on and punishes a transferee who was in some sense at fault, as by causing the suspicious series of transactions.[27]

§2.3.3 Special Uses of Equitable Subordination

Special advantages of ES

I must now admit that equitable subordination can be used to achieve results that could not be reached under conventional fraudulent convey-

[24] Deliberate falsification of records is an intentional wrong that might be subject under ordinary tort principles to punitive damages, see W. Prosser, Handbook of the Law of Torts 683-686, 735-736 (4th ed. 1971), and criminal prosecution, see, e.g., 18 U.S.C. §152 (1970).

[25] Even a long history of spending as if there were no tomorrow will more readily trigger exasperation and a desire to oust the rascals than an impulse to jail them.

[26] A good example of how equitable subordination steps in when a course of conduct bothers the court, even though one prior, isolated transaction has been corrected by a trustee's action, is given by Bankers Life & Casualty Co. v. Kirtley, 338 F.2d 1006, 1011 (8th Cir. 1964).

[27] Moreover, the existence of equitable subordination may be partly explained by other judicial objectives, such as the desire to overcome technical restraints on fraudulent conveyance actions, for example, the statute of limitations. Such actions might not catch the earlier phases of a long history of abusive parent company dealings with its subsidiary.

ance rules. Specifically, it may be used to protect preferred or minority shareholders (who are not creditors within the meaning of the UFCA) or to remedy conduct that defeats the ideal of nonhindrance but does not involve a transfer of a property interest or the incurrence of an obligation.

Aid to shareholders

Conduct of a bankrupt corporation caused by controlling shareholders may violate ideals of truth, primacy, and evenhandedness with reference to other equity claimants against the enterprise (e.g., minority shareholders), even though those claimants cannot invoke the UFCA or similar law because they are not technically creditors.[28] In truth, there appears to be no good reason why the ideals of nonhindrance should not be imposed on corporate debtors as duties toward their equity claimants.[29] In this sense, equitable subordination doctrine may be viewed as a desirable finishing touch to fraudulent conveyance law.

Remedy for waste

One instance of the application of equitable subordination to a case not involving a transfer (or the incurrence of an obligation) is waste of corporate assets by controlling parties. If the waste does not cause some sort of transfer,[30] such as a salary payment to an idle officer, the situation would not trigger fraudulent conveyance law. Even if applicable, fraudulent conveyance law would often lead to only partial correction since the harm to

[28] That fraudulent conveyance law developed in such a limited way is understandable, given its ancient lineage and the relative modernity of the prevalent practice, via the corporate device, of having separate legal entities that can own property and conduct business but that are themselves owned by separate persons.

[29] The *Deep Rock* case involved subordination of parent company "creditor" claims to the claims of preferred shareholders, and those seeking subordination in Comstock, discussed in note 12 supra, merely had a security interest in the debtor corporation's stock. See also Bankers Life & Cas. Co. v. Kirtley, 338 F.2d 1006 (8th Cir. 1964) (subordination of dominant stockholders to minority public stockholders).

On the other hand, if fraudulent conveyance law and equitable subordination doctrine were expanded to cover all the myriad ways in which one (controlling) group of equity claimants achieved a non–pro-rata distribution from a corporation at the expense of other equity claimants of the same class, they would swallow up a very large part of corporation law. To note this is not to suggest that *Deep Rock* opened a floodgate that cannot be closed but to point out that there is an intimate structural and legal relationship between fraud or unfairness which harms creditors and that which harms shareholders. Cf. Superintendent of Ins. v. Bankers Life & Cas. Co., 404 U.S. 6 (1971) (Section 10(b) of the Securities Exchange Act of 1934 applies against deceptive practices even though creditors of the defrauded corporate buyer or seller of securities may be ultimate victims; controlling stockholders' fiduciary obligation extends to creditors as well as stockholders). A full comparison of fraudulent conveyance principles and insiders' fiduciary duties to minority shareholders remains to be made.

[30] Often it does. Suppose that the corporation's officers were simply lazy and did not work very hard to bring in corporate revenues. As a result, the corporation becomes insolvent. The conduct of the officers implies that their salaries were excessive, and thus, that they caused the corporation to make transfers of benefits to them that may be voidable under UFCA §4.

the corporation from sheer laziness in management, for example, may exceed the entire salaries actually paid to the officers.[31] It should be apparent, though, that the simplified remedy of equitable subordination may overshoot or fall short of the mark, depending on the relationship between the amount of the claims asserted in bankruptcy by the controlling parties and the actual amount of harm caused the corporation by their wasteful conduct.

§2.3.4 Inadequate Capitalization of Corporate Debtor

Inadequate capital a basis for ES?

Besides protecting minority shareholders and providing a shotgun approach to wasteful conduct of controlling parties, equitable subordination also *appears* to go beyond fraudulent conveyance law in the so-called inadequate capitalization cases. These are cases in which the court subordinates the creditor claims of controlling shareholders because they didn't put enough equity capital into the business. Often the reference is to initial capitalization, that is, the capital invested by the shareholders when they started the business. Small initial capitalization is a troublesome basis for subordinating the otherwise legitimate creditor claims of shareholders, because modern business corporation statutes *don't* usually require that any significant amount of equity capital be invested as a precondition of doing business in the corporate form. In the past, state statutes did have substantial capitalization requirements. The shift in statutes, it can be argued, suggests that shareholders should not be penalized merely because they took advantage of the statutory permission by putting up a minimal amount of capital.

Rarely sufficient

Although inadequate capitalization by itself has rarely been a sufficient condition to lead to subordination of the controlling creditor's claim (some courts have expressly held that it is not sufficient), thin capitalization quite often accompanies real deception.

Difficulty of determining harm

An interesting aspect of a case involving only inadequate initial capitalization is that it involves no transfer of benefits to the controlling parties.[32]

[31] If this is so, an action for waste would seem to be called for, and perhaps the officers would be responsible for the entire proximate damage to the corporation. Since the trustee in bankruptcy succeeds to all the causes of action of the bankrupt corporation, he could pursue this claim.

[32] One could draw an analogy to adequate capitalization followed later on by an unlawful dividend, which would violate the principle of primacy. The analogy is not accurate, because the actual presence of adequate capital during the interim between organization and the dividend later deemed unlawful would probably have helped the corporation to perform better and would thus have saved the creditors some loss.

Without a transfer of benefits that could in principle be measured and simply undone, choosing the scope of the creditors' remedy for the harm resulting from inadequate capitalization is difficult. Should there be automatic full subordination of the shareholders' creditor claims? Or should the court only compensate the outside creditors for that portion of the loss in value of their claim against the corporation proximately caused by the inadequate capitalization itself? In most cases, attempting the latter task would be too difficult. The court would therefore be driven to use a blanket subordination of all creditor claims of the relevant controlling parties. In any event, just as equitable subordination can substitute for a state court action based on wasteful conduct, it might also substitute for (though it is not equivalent to) a trustee action to pierce the corporate veil under state law. The substitution may not be adequate, since in some cases the outside creditors' harm from inadequate capitalization may not be corrected in full by a mere subordination of the controlling party's claims, and in other cases the response may be essentially punitive.

Should inadequate capital trigger ES?

As suggested, it is unclear that in actual cases equitable subordination ever results merely from inadequate initial capitalization of the corporate debtor.[33] Should it? In one view, the question resolves itself into one of full disclosure to outside creditors, with a meaningful opportunity given them to bargain for higher interest payments as compensation for the extreme risk of default (or for other forms of compensation and protection). This thought often leads lawyers to a distinction between contract and tort creditors. The former, it is said, shouldn't be able to object to mere inadequate capitalization. But inadequate capitalization without any deception might be a basis for subordinating insiders' claims to those of tort creditors,

[33] In neither *Deep Rock* nor Pepper v. Litton, nor in any of the cases cited in note 12 supra, did inadequate initial capitalization of a controlled subsidiary truly function as a sole and sufficient basis for subordination. There is language suggesting that inadequate initial capitalization was sufficient for subordination in the *Holton, Costello,* and *Dean & Jean Fashions* cases, but all of these cases involved an attempt to convert an equity interest into a debt interest in an ongoing business enterprise (thus producing inadequate capitalization): There was objectionable inadequacy of "initial" capital only if one focuses on the new corporate entities in those cases and not on the underlying businesses. Furthermore, some cases explicitly indicate that inadequate capitalization is not a sufficient basis for subordination. E.g., In re Brunner Air Compressor Corp., 287 F. Supp. 256, 262 (N.D.N.Y. 1968); accord, In re Branding Iron Steak House, 536 F.2d 299 (9th Cir. 1976); Rego Crescent Corp. v. Tymon, 7 C.B.C.2d 713 (B. Ct., E.D.N.Y 1982) (shareholder loans subordinated only when corporation was undercapitalized prior to loan, loans were really capital contributions, *and* conduct of lending shareholder was inequitable).

On the other hand, an occasional subordination case is difficult to explain as anything but a pure inadequate initial capitalization case. See, e.g., Arnold v. Phillips, 117 F.2d 497 (5th Cir.), cert. denied, 313 U.S. 583 (1941).

on the ground that organizers of corporations have a duty to provide a "reasonable" amount of net worth for the benefit of persons who might be injured by their tortious activities. But even here application of the law has lead to very mixed results.[34] (We shall return to the problem of inadequate capital and discuss it more fully in subsection 2.4.1.)

Summary

In summary, equitable subordination is not only a functional equivalent of conventional fraudulent conveyance law occasioned by the desire to reduce the transaction costs of enforcing the duties of corporate debtors. It also serves the purpose of expanding application of the principles of truth and primacy to situations that are not covered by technical fraudulent conveyance law because it is, perhaps arbitrarily, limited in its coverage to debt holder claimants against the debtor and to debtors who make or suffer transfers of benefits.

§2.3.5 Automatic Subordination?

Some years ago, the Commission on the Bankruptcy Laws of the United States made a recommendation that represents a third way of implementing the principles of truth, primacy, and evenhandedness: a system of preventive rules.[35] The Commission's proposal, which appeared in two sweeping bankruptcy bills that were not enacted by Congress,[36] would have automatically subordinated any claim of controlling shareholders to those of other creditors.

Arguments pro

What might justify replacing equitable subordination doctrine with a rule of automatic subordination of insiders' claims? One justification would be that the possibilities for insiders to violate the policy against hindrance of creditors by fraudulent and preferential transactions are so manifold, so difficult to discover and prove, and so tempting and likely to occur, that it is better not to burden the trustee in bankruptcy, and the outside creditors he represents, with the costs of a doctrine whose uncertainties invite litigation.

Arguments con

There are a number of arguments against automatic subordination, although some of them seem to dissolve when closely examined. Automatic

[34] See discussion of Walkovszky v. Carlton in section 2.4.3. infra

[35] Section 4406 of bill proposed in Report of the Commission on the Bankruptcy Laws of the United States, H.R. Doc. No. 93137, Part II, 93d Cong., 1st Sess. 115 (1973).

[36] H.R. 31, S. 236, 94th Cong., 1st Sess. (1975) (Bankruptcy Commission's bill); H.R. 32, S. 235, 94th Cong., 1st Sess. (1975) (bankruptcy judges' bill). Some older case law experimented with automatic subordination. See In re V. Loewer's Gambrinus Brewery Co., 167 F.2d 318 (2d Cir. 1948) (Frank, J.); but see Schwartz v. Mills, 192 F.2d 727 (2d Cir. 1951), and Gannett Co. v. Larry, 221 F.2d 269 (2d Cir. 1955).

subordination appears unjust as applied to those insiders who do in fact deal honestly, fairly, and nonpreferentially with their corporations. But would the rule really be unfair to them if they knew about it in advance? Automatic subordination prevents insiders from participating in their corporations as creditors on the same basis as outsiders and thus reduces their ability to have a portfolio of debt and equity securities so balanced as to meet their risk-return preferences. An investor should not be required to possess, in effect, only the status of a shareholder. The answer to this argument, of course, is that the capital markets of the United States are so richly diverse that a knowledgeable investor can surely create a portfolio consisting of stock in his controlled corporation and debt or equity securities of unrelated entities that will have the same risk-return characteristics as any given portfolio of stock and debt in his controlled corporation.

"Only lenders" argument

Another argument urged against an automatic subordination rule is that controlling shareholders are frequently—so it is said—the only persons willing to lend to a small, unknown corporation on "reasonable" terms. It is contended that if the insiders' creditor claim is not respected in bankruptcy, this source of funds may dry up and result in such small businesses' being deprived of the tax benefits of debt financing.[37]

Impacted information vs. efficient markets

The force of this argument is uncertain because it rests on unproven empirical assertions concerning the conduct of controlling insiders[38] and the magnitude of transaction costs involved in assessing and communicating risks of default on particular loans. If rational, disinterested outside lenders are unwilling to supply corporate "loans" on a given set of interest rates and other terms, an obvious conclusion is that a "loan" of that character would be made only by persons who, by virtue of concurrent stock ownership, could benefit from the inadequacy of the terms, and such "loans" to insiders should thus be treated like equity in distributing the bankrupt estate. True, situations may arise in which insiders (1) really do perceive more accurately that the "true" risk presented by a loan to a corporation on given terms is lower than outsiders recognize, and (2) are unable to articulate and convey the objective bases of their superior judgment to the prospective outside lenders at a reasonable cost. But, in view of the widespread belief in the general efficiency of our capital markets, we might well be agnostic about the notion that such situations are common. In short, objections to an automatic subordination rule based on the just

[37] Interest payments by a corporation are generally deductible for federal income purposes. I.R.C. §163. Dividend payments are normally not.

[38] Controlling insiders may continue to lend, because they are unaware of automatic subordination or because the corporation has no other creditors to whom they can be subordinated.

demands of small investors and small businessmen are of doubtful validity.

Doubt about proposal's benefits

Nevertheless, the advantages of a preventive rule must be viewed in a similarly agnostic fashion. We simply do not know the extent to which insiders who are also creditors abuse their controlling status by dealing dishonestly, unfairly, or preferentially with their corporations, to the detriment of outside creditors. Without such knowlege, the benefits to be expected from the automatic subordination rule are conjectural. This being so, a conservative adherence to equitable subordination is certainly defensible.

More remedial imprecision

Note also that an automatic subordination rule would imperfectly implement the basic principles behind fraudulent conveyance law. It would not always lead to an adequate correction of transactions that are unfair according to these principles, and it might lead to overcorrection by subordinating an insider's claims in the absence of a violation of the principles.

§2.4 *Piercing the Corporate Veil*

This section will examine a branch of law that mixes the narrow policy against hindering creditors when one is financially troubled with other policies. To a large extent, as we saw, fraudulent conveyance law and equitable subordination doctrine are different ways of implementing the same basic principles. The instrumentality doctrine sometimes appears to go farther toward an evolution of the underlying principles themselves.

Veil piercing (VP) often provoked by behavior raising FCL claim

Recall that, as a gloss on state corporation statutes, state and federal courts have developed a sizable body of case law dealing with the attempts of corporate creditors to satisfy their claims out of the personal assets of the corporation's shareholders, despite the general rule of limited liability.[1] Cases of this sort have been referred to by various metaphors, such as "alter ego" or "instrumentality" cases and attempts "to pierce the corpo-

§2.4 [1] Discussions of the case law are numerous. Among the more interesting treatments, drawn from different time periods, are I. Wormser, Disregard of the Corporate Fiction and Allied Corporation Problems (1927); Berle, The Theory of Enterprise Entity, 47 Colum. L. Rev. 343 (1947); Hamilton, The Corporate Entity, 49 Tex. L. Rev. 979 (1971); Krendl & Krendl, Piercing the Corporate Veil: Focusing the Inquiry, 55 Den. L.J. 1 (1978) (contains exhaustive review of cases); Landers II, §2.1 note 3 supra; Landers I, §2.1 note 3 supra; Latty, The Corporate Entity as a Solvent of Legal Problems, 34 Mich. L. Rev. 597 (1936); Posner, §2.1 note 3 supra; Comment, The Alter Ego Doctrine: Alternative Challenges to the Corporate Form, 30 U.C.L.A.L. Rev. 129 (1982); Note, Liability of a Corporation for Acts of a Subsidiary or Affiliate, 71 Harv. L. Rev. 1122 (1958); Note, Piercing the Corporate Law Veil: The Alter Ego Doctrine Under Federal Common Law, 95 Harv. L. Rev. 853 (1982).

rate veil."[2] Many of these cases are triggered by behavior that would invoke fraudulent conveyance law. Nevertheless, courts typically ignore the relationships between that body of law and the attempts to pierce.[3] There is some reference in the cases to the doctrine of equitable subordination, although careful analysis of the relationships between that doctrine and the instrumentality or alter ego rules is inevitably lacking. Moreover, the courts usually forgo any sustained attempt at a remedial theory or even a coherent exposition of the basis of liability, although descriptive summaries are occasionally attempted.[4]

[2] See, e.g., Walkovszky v. Carlton, 223 N.E.2d 6 (N.Y. 1966) ("instrumentality"); Goldberg v. Engleberg, 92 P.2d 935 (Cal. App. 1939) ("piercing corporate veil"). See also commentary cited in note 1 supra.

[3] See, e.g., Maryland ex rel. Goralski v. General Stevedoring Co., 213 F. 51, 72-79 (D. Md.), aff'd sub nom. Joseph R. Foard Co. v. Maryland ex rel. Goralski, 219 F. 827 (4th Cir. 1914) (subsidiary had small capital stock and parent took profits of business as a management charge that was apparently unfair); Goldberg v. Engllberg, 92 P.2d 935 (Cal. App. 1939) (piercing from behind: creditor of dominant stockholder reaches corporate assets where stockholder, after judgment was rendered against him, had deeded ranch to wife for "love and affection," and wife had later deeded it to corporation); Bartle v. Home Owners Coop., Inc., 127 N.E.2d 832, 834 (N.Y. 1955) (dissent) (parent cooperative organized building subsidiary with small capital and caused it to sell homes to parent's members at prices designed to yield no profit to subsidiary; prices presumably unfair to creditors).

An example of the technique of attempting to convert equity to debt in the context of a bootstrap acquisition is given by World Broadcasting System, Inc. v. Bass, 328 S.W.2d 863 (Tex. 1959), where shareholders sold their stock for cash and a $67,500 installment note. The note was secured by a mortgage on the corporation's assets and by a promise by the purchaser to dissolve the corporation. The court, not even mentioning fraudulent conveyance law, held that, since the selling stockholders had thus denuded the corporation of its assets, they were personally liable to its creditors to the extent of the funds received. Quite similar factual patterns were presented in Steph v. Branch, discussed in §2.2 note 12 supra, and in In re Process-Manz Press, Inc., discussed in §2.3 note 12 supra, but in the former the court explicitly invoked fraudulent conveyance rules and in the latter it partially invoked equitable subordination.

[4] It has been said that in order to make a parent corporation responsible for the acts of a subsidiary corporation under the instrumentality rule, there must be, in the absence of express agency, estoppel, or direct tort, three proven elements:

(1) control of the subsidiary by the parent;
(2) use of control by the parent to commit fraud or a dishonest and unjust act in contravention of legal rights, or to perpetrate a violation of statutory or other positive duty; and
(3) proximate causation of plaintiff's injury or loss by the controlling party's breach of duty.

See Fisser v. International Bank, 282 F.2d 231, 238 (2d Cir. 1960); Zaist v. Olson, 227 A.2d 552, 558 (Conn. 1967). The tripartite breakdown can be traced at least back to F. Powell, Parent and Subsidiary Corporations 4-6 (1931).

Despite the fact that different courts' lists of relevant factors bear a family resemblance to one another, a lawyer surveying a broad range of cases involving attempts to pierce the corporate veil might easily conclude that they are unified more by the remedy sought—subjecting to corporate liabilities the personal assets directly held by shareholders—than by repeated and consistent application of the same criteria for granting the remedy. In particular, some cases revolve, not around violations of the four principles of nonhindrance that we discussed in section 2.2 supra, but around violations of an alleged policy that corporations must be adequately or reasonably capitalized.[5] Because of the theoretical importance of this alleged policy, the next subsection examines it closely. Afterwards, I contrast the remedy in the veil-piercing cases (hereinafter, the piercing cases) with those afforded in fraudulent conveyance cases and in equitable subor-

But case law messy

Other courts have used similar formulations. E.g., Arrow, Edelstein & Gross v. Rosco Productions Inc., 581 F. Supp. 520, 525 (S.D.N.Y. 1984) (applying New York law; piercing is done where corporation formed for fraudulent, illegal, or unjust purposes or to mislead creditors); State Dept. of Environmental Protection v. Ventron, 468 A.2d 150, 164 (N.J. 1983) (disregard of corporate entity used to perpetrate a fraud or injustice); NCR Credit Corp. v. Underground Camera, Inc., 581 F. Supp. 609, 612 (D. Mass. 1984) (applying Mass. law; disregard of entity depends on control or intermingling of activities, plus need to prevent fraud, wrong, or gross inequity). Some courts express a more elaborate list of factors. E.g., Walter E. Heller and Co. v. Video Innovations, Inc., 730 F.2d 50, 53 (2d Cir. 1983) (under N.Y. law, criteria for piercing include

(1) absence of formalities of corporate existence,
(2) inadequate capitalization,
(3) personal use of corporate funds, and
(4) perpetration of fraud by means of the corporate vehicle).

[5]Richard Posner's article on veil piercing and equitable subordination seems to focus almost exclusively on the problem of adequacy of initial capitalization, and to constitute an elaboration and justification, in terms of microeconomic theory, of what I call the standard initial response to the problem. See Posner, §2.1 note 3 supra.

By contrast, the problem of coping with the possibility that the corporation will take steps to increase the riskiness of the loan after the terms have been set, which Posner calls the problem of supervision, are given relatively little attention. These problems of supervision are largely problems that lawyers have traditionally perceived to fall within the province of fraudulent conveyance law.

It should be noted, that the courts have generally been struggling, not with the relatively academic issue of adequate initial capitalization, but with the widespread phenomenon of self-dealing on the eve of insolvency. This is often so even when courts mention inadequate capitalization as a basis for decision. See notes 12 and 33 in §2.3 supra. As is often said, a fraudulent conveyance is but the reflex of an insolvent man. Anyone who reads and ponders a good sampling of the case law classified under the headings of equitable subordination and veil piercing should appreciate that fraudulent transfers and obligations have been the focus of litigation and legal doctrine.

dination cases. Section 2.4.3 then analyzes a leading case to show how the policies are mixed and treated in actual litigation.

§2.4.1 Broad Theory Versus Narrow Theory

Inadequate capital relevant but not sufficient for VP

Does inadequate capitalization by itself lead to a disregard of the corporate entity and subjection of shareholders to personal liability for corporate debts? A careful review of case law indicates this answer: "Very rarely, if at all. But many courts do consider it a relevant factor."[6] Yet commentators sometimes assume otherwise, and frequently analyze this factor at great length. Why? Because they see it as theoretically important. So let's restate the question. *Should* inadequate capitalization, by itself, result in piercing the corporate veil? If yes, what would this answer suggest about the theoretical basis for imposing rules on the debtor-creditor relationship? Does it depend, for example, on a radically different policy perspective than that which underlies fraudulent conveyance law?

Hypos for reflection

Discussions of these questions can easily become overly abstract, so I will begin by laying out two hypothetical cases, I'll call them the ordinary case and the hard case. Each involves a tort creditor and a contract creditor.

"Ordinary" case

The ordinary case involves the Plain Vanilla Corp., which is in the business of planting, harvesting, and marketing certain crops. It is owned and controlled by the Gentry family. It was founded 12 years ago with plenty of capital and has always earned quite substantial revenues. The Gentry family, however, has always taken pains to reduce nominal corporate net income to $0 each year by paying out, as "salaries" to family members, whatever amounts were needed to achieve $0 taxable income for Vanilla. Worn-out equipment has not been replaced; instead, family members have rented new equipment to Vanilla. Recently, Vanilla's pesticide-spraying machine exploded and seriously injured Maria and 11 other migrant laborers who happened to be walking along a nearby road. The Gentry family immediately called a board meeting and declared an extraordinary dividend in kind of the farmland and corporate cash owned by Vanilla. This action left Vanilla with very few leviable assets. The laborers sued Vanilla and won, but Vanilla could not pay the judgment. They then sued to pierce the corporate veil and get at the farmland and other assets of the Gentry family. In addition, Harriet, a local dairy farmer who supplied

[6]See, e.g., Carpentry Health & Welfare Fund of Philadelphia and Vicinity by Gray v. Kenneth R. Ambrose, Inc., 727 F.2d 279, 284 (3d cir. 1983) (undercapitalization "an additional factor which the court may consider"); West v. Costen, 558 F. Supp. 564, 585 (W.D. Va. 1983) (undercapitalization "a ground" for piercing, but no single factor sufficient).

natural fertilizer to Vanilla on credit, also sues the Gentry family to collect on several unpaid bills. Both veil-piercing suits are successful.

"Hard" case

The hard case involves Special Transport, Inc. A few months ago, Davida Defender set up this corporation to operate a mini-van service to take special needs children to and from their schools. The only client of the firm was the local public school system. Davida, the sole shareholder, contributed as her investment in the company only enough money to enable Transport to make a down payment on a van. Transport began operations. It has had minuscule net worth because it was so thinly capitalized and because it has yet to get off the ground. It pays only a modest salary to the driver it employs; Davida herself has never received any payment from the company. The driver negligently ran down Paula Plaintiff, who was seriously injured. She sued Transport and obtained a large tort judgment, only a fraction of which was paid. Transport ceased operations. Paula sued Davida under a veil-piercing theory. So did Penny Plaintiff, who owns a thriving and long-established chain of auto repair shops that has an outstanding unpaid bill for repair work done for Transport. Both Plaintiffs win.

Do the three principles of nonhindrance explain the hypos?

Can we explain the results in these hypothetical piercing cases in terms of our familiar principles of truth, primacy, and evenhandedness? Can we justify them by other policy considerations? Let's look at each of the three specific principles in turn.

None explained by actual deception

1. Truth. On the facts given, none of our plaintiffs' victories can be readily explained as applications of the principle of truth. Neither Vanilla nor Transport nor any of the controlling individuals practiced any deception—for example, a misrepresentation about the corporation's net worth or capitalization—on any of the plaintiffs.

Was there a more subtle form of deception? This too is hard to find. Tort victims, such as Maria in the ordinary case and Paula in the hard case, usually do not rely on the tortfeasor corporation's level of capitalization. When injured, they probably were not even aware of the existence of Vanilla and Transport. They could hardly claim to have "relied" in any real sense on an "implicit" representation that these corporations were "reasonably" capitalized. Any such finding of reliance would be a fiction, that is, a judicial policy decision based on some other policy consideration.

As for the contract creditors, Harriet in the ordinary case and Penny in the hard case, they might indeed have assumed that Vanilla and Transport had substantial capital. But in the absence of affirmatively deceitful representations of substantial net worth by the corporations or their controlling parties, we are tempted to remit these creditors to their own diligence. If they want to be sure that their client corporations can pay their bills, they should investigate. If their search efforts don't reassure them, they can refuse to deal, or assume the risk, or bargain for shareholder guarantees and other protections.

But VP sometimes based on fraud

Nevertheless, when the contract creditors are in a weak bargaining position, for example, small shippers claiming damages for breach of contract against a carrier, or where the complex of interrelated corporations is such that ordinary customers or creditors of one member of the complex might naturally be lulled into thinking that more assets were behind the contract or loan than the balance sheet of that member later shows, the courts have occasionally pierced the veil in favor of those customers or creditors.[7] This interference with the ostensibly consensual arrangements is based on a perception of unequal bargaining power or a kind of "soft-core" fraud. In our hypothetical ordinary case, this kind of treatment might be available to Harriet, who, let us suppose, is a relatively unsophisticated sole proprietor of a fertilizer-delivery business. (But there is a better reason for granting recovery to Harriet, as we shall soon see.)

Principle of primacy relevant?

2. *Primacy.* Does the principle that debtors should put the satisfaction of legal obligations ahead of donative impulses, personal concerns, "moral" obligations, and the like, help justify the outcomes in our hypothetical cases? Conceivably the principle could be interpreted quite expansively to embrace all the outcomes. But let's look more closely.

The hypothetical creditors' bargain

How should we go about trying to give specific content to the principle of primacy? As to contract creditors, one useful procedure is to ask this question: If all rational debtors and creditors were free to bargain with each other at no cost (and they don't overlook any important issues), what ground rules would they agree on to govern their conduct in almost all cases, even in the absence of explicit assent to these rules in particular cases? By establishing such ground rules, the parties could greatly cut down on bargaining costs in real situations and would also reduce uncertainty.

They'd agree on rules of FCL

Obviously, different people can imagine this hypothetical creditors' bargain coming out in different ways. But some outcomes seem more plausible than others. One that seems quite likely to me is an agreement on something like the specific rules of fraudulent conveyance law. The typical rational creditor who thought about the issue would insist that his would-be borrowers agree that, if a borrower should start to "go down the tubes" while the creditor's claim was unpaid, the borrower would refrain from wasting or giving away the assets, declaring lavish dividends, making above-market-price salary payments to key employees, and the like. He

[7] See, e.g., Luckenbach S.S. Co. v. W. R. Grace & Co., 267 F. 676 (4th Cir. 1920).

would probably define going down the tubes in terms of some conception of insolvency. He might well insist on a supplementary rule: no gratuitous or unfair transfers by the business debtor when the debtor would be left with unreasonably small capital (see UFCA Section 5). Why? Because the flexible concept of unreasonably small capital, which relates to insolvency in its pragmatic meaning, helps assure that mechanical balance-sheet tests of insolvency, which can be arbitrary and misleading, do not vitiate the primary rule.

Contract creditor in ordinary case should win

Given this hypothetical agreement about the ground rules of behavior, Harriet, the contract creditor in our ordinary case, could claim a breach by Vanilla and the Gentry family. When Vanilla was clearly in imminent danger of becoming insolvent, because of the tortious injury it had caused to the laborers, the controlling parties caused Vanilla to make a huge transfer of assets for which it received no leviable assets in return. Harriet had a right to expect that this kind of behavior would not be countenanced.

But not in hard case

On the other hand, Penny, the contract creditor in our hard case, could not claim any breach of the ground rule. Transport did not make any transfer resembling a fraudulent conveyance. This negative result leads us to return to the hypothetical bargaining table.

Why the hypothetical bargain wouldn't rule out thin initial capital

Would our rational creditors go even further in their hypothetical bargaining efforts? Could they get the assembled debtors to agree to a ground rule forbidding "thin *initial* capitalization" of business debtors that operate as corporations? Would the typical would-be incorporator at the table agree to so capitalize and run her corporate businesses as not to raise the risk of failure presented to outside creditors beyond a certain maximum point, *X*? Perhaps not. She would observe that the concept of *X*, the maximum risk level to outside creditors, as well as the concept of adequate capital, are quite vague. More importantly, the amount of capital that actual creditors and incorporators would agree should be put into a corporation at its inception would surely differ greatly from case to case, depending on the circumstances.

Problems with minimum initial capital requirement

If the corporation were formed to carry on business in a relatively stable industry, which the principals had carried on successfully as individuals, the lender might not care that the corporation was being set up with minimum equity capital. If the individuals were to enter a business in which they lacked experience, and in which devastating product liability claims were not uncommon, the lender's attitude would be very different. Even then, the lender might choose to take care of the risk by insisting on a higher interest rate, a security interest in specific collateral, frequent business reports by the debtor, a personal guarantee by one of the stockholders, and other measures. The lender would not necessarily insist that the debtor's shareholders put in any particular amount of capital beyond what they wished to contribute. He might well regard that as a rather trivial issue.

Therefore, the typical would-be incorporator at our bargaining table would argue, there should *not* be any universal ground rule imposing a specific minimum capital requirement or even a vague "adequate capital" requirement on all corporations. This sort of requirement should be bargained about in individual cases. And if certain particular forms of this requirement often seem to make mutual sense to creditors and debtors in a particular industry or recurrent situation, the parties can economize on bargaining costs by developing form contracts for those contexts.

Let's assume that this argument would carry the day. The principle of primacy, the adopted ground rule, would be interpreted along the lines of standard fraudulent conveyance rules. Inadequate *initial* capitalization would *not* violate the principle. Under this analysis, letting Penny pierce the corporate veil in our hard case was a mistake. Penny, unlike Harriet, cannot point to any gratuitous or unfair transfer by the corporate debtor on the eve of insolvency.

Minimizing costs of accidents

Now we turn to the tort victims. Here we cannot resolve the issue by continuing to imagine the progress of our hypothetical debtor-creditor bargain: The tort victims are not at the table. We could imagine them there, of course, but opening the process this way gets us into a more open-ended "social contract" analysis that is much harder to manage. Let us simply assume that our goal as policy makers is to minimize the total costs of accidents. Assume further that this consideration leads us, among other things, to favor loss spreading by compensation of tort victims. Does this policy preference imply that judges should give tort victims a right to pierce the corporate veil simply on the basis of inadequate initial capitalization?

Many approaches; VP probably not best

Not necessarily, because there may well be better solutions to the problem of compensation. Consider some of these alternatives. First, if a state legislature felt that tort victims needed greater protection against the vagaries of limited liability, it might require higher initial legal capital requirements for corporations and might impose capital maintenance rules as well.

Second, it might mandate the carrying of greater amounts of liability insurance than are presently required. Either alternative, if imposed in the form of a universal requirement, might entail provision of excessive tort victim security in some lines of corporate business and inadequate provision in others. Consequently, the requirements might have to be varied for types of business.

To avoid the regulatory burden and clumsiness of such a scheme, a third alternative that the federal government might mandate would be a requirement that contract creditors, including secured creditors, be automatically subordinated in insolvency proceedings to all tort creditors. Given such an absolute rule of subordination, the burden of prodding debtors into securing "adequate" capital or insurance to take care of tort victims would be partially shifted to those contract creditors, for example, outside lending institutions, who are in a strong bargaining position vis-à-vis the debtor. The debtor and his creditors would arrange whatever amount of protection against tort victims was judged adequate for them. Such a rule would give an incentive to control or insure risks not only to controlling shareholders (who are typically small businessmen willing to take high risks) but also to powerful and conservative outside parties (such as lending banks). It might well have more impact on corporate practices than even an activist expansion of the doctrine of piercing the corporate veil.

Finally, a fourth alternative might be to provide for tort victims in some way other than by increasing the likelihood of there being a person sufficiently solvent to make a defendant in a tort action. First-party compensation schemes such as no-fault insurance are an obvious example. If one focuses not on "tort creditors" generally, but on types of accidental injury problems—for example, the problem of automobile accidents—a scheme to lower the high transaction costs and spotty results associated with the fault system may well seem the preferable alternative.

But sometimes a handy second best

None of this is to deny that, where the need for redress is great, a court may well consider the possibility of better, alternative compensation schemes to be academic and, on something like a theory of the second best, to permit recovery. In one old case, for example, the veil of a shell corporation was pierced for the benefit of a widow and six dependent children of an employee killed in the course of the company's coal mining operations.[8]

Judicial deference re initial capital

But the basic point is that, in view of the wide array of alternative solutions, a court with anything less than a wildly activist vision of its role might decide to refrain from qualifying the statutory rule of limited liability by a judge-made rule that tort victims can sue the controlling parties of thinly capitalized corporations. To be sure, a legislature might properly decide, despite the competing interests and uncertain facts, that limited liability should not shield controlling investors from their corporations' tort liabilities. But so far no legislature has been willing to make this judgment.

So tort creditor in hard case loses

In terms of our hypothetical hard case, this analysis means that tort victim Paula probably should not have won her veil-piercing suit.

[8] Dixie Coal Mining & Mfg. Co. v. Williams, 128 So. 799 (Ala. 1930).

But wins in ordinary case

But what about Maria, the tort victim in our hypothetical ordinary case? Was her victory justified? Her veil-piercing action, like that of Harriet, was actually just a substitute for a fraudulent conveyance action. Fraudulent conveyance law, with its relatively narrow and specific conception of the primacy of legal obligations, *is* reflected in a legislative judgment in most jurisdictions, and in any event, its principles have been accepted by legal systems from time immemorial. A judge could not be accused of arrogating legislative power by simply applying those principles, in a more flexible way and in slightly different linguistic garb, in the related context of a veil piercing suit. A deeper question is whether applying the principles to tort victims contributes to minimization of the total costs of accidents. That question I leave you to ponder.

Why evenhandedness might imply adequate initial capital

3. *Evenhandedness.* The principle of evenhandedness could be said to be involved in many inadequate initial capitalization cases in an indirect way. We could characterize a corporation like Transport in our hard case as having been organized so as to create a higher probability of satisfying the claims of some creditors—those who investigate the corporation's financial situation before lending and take precautionary measures—than of satisfying the claims of other creditors: tort creditors and contract creditors, such as small trade creditors, who made weaker credit checks. Arguably, we could describe this state of affairs as operating in a manner "unfairly preferential" to some creditors.

Why the argument fails

But the argument seems both troublesome and odd. For one thing, it is misguided to suggest that creditors who engage in diligent investigation and self-protection get an "unfair" advantage; such activity deserves to be rewarded. Moreover, conventional preferences often involve an intent of the debtor to favor one creditor over others or a conscious effort by one creditor on the eve of insolvency or bankruptcy to grab payment or security before the other creditors do. Transport's inadequate capitalization resulted from neither of these motivations. Furthermore, there seems to be no good way to decide when a way of doing business raises the probability of satisfying one unsecured creditor so high relative to the probability of satisfying another unsecured creditor that some drastic legal remedy such as piercing the corporate veil ought to be invoked.[9] And differences in

[9]Not just the decision to capitalize thinly, but other business decisions could cause this divergence of probabilities of satisfaction. For instance, the decision to settle all customer claims quickly and without dispute, rather than to fight and delay them, could result in a relatively small number of such claimants being subjected to the meager payout of straight bankruptcy. Are all such decisions to be a basis for piercing the corporate veil in favor of the relatively disadvantaged creditors? Why restrict relief to the decision to put in less capital than that needed to reduce such divergences?

probabilities of satisfaction of sophisticated, bargaining creditors and satisfaction of tort or trade creditors could vary greatly, depending on the extent of capital inadequacy and many other factors. Thus, even if it were wise in principle to require corporations to operate so as to maintain an equal chance of satisfying all creditors, it would be difficult or impossible to implement the idea.

Summary

Let us summarize to this point. Some piercing cases (like our easy case) are simply substitutes for fraudulent conveyance actions. In those that are not, *and* that genuinely turn upon inadequate initial capitalization (like our hard case), the principles of truth, primacy, and evenhandedness are often implicated weakly or not at all. Such cases can be interpreted as expanding the ideal of nonhindrance to a new ideal of *affirmative* support of creditors' interests through the requirement of an adequate capital structure. Put another way, the thin capitalization cases have experimented with the notion of placing upon business creditors an *affirmative duty of cooperation* with creditors. But as the near absence of cases basing veil piercing solely on inadequate initial capitalization suggests, courts have not gone very far toward accepting this notion.[10]

§2.4.2 Comparison of Remedies

VP imprecise and somewhat punitive

The piercing cases appear to employ a shotgun remedy, that is, a remedy less precisely responsive than those invoked in fraudulent conveyance cases. But it is a remedy more biased toward a punitive result than that invoked by the doctrine of equitable subordination.

Courts in piercing cases often assume either that the proper remedy is simply the complete revocation of limited liability. An obvious alternative,

[10]Unlike the New York courts, see section 2.4.3 infra, the California courts have given significant weight to inadequate capitalization—at least in the past. See, e.g., Automotriz del Golfo de California S.A. de C.V. v. Resnick, 306 P.2d 1 (Cal. 1957); Minton v. Cavaney, 364 P.2d 473 (Cal. 1961). These cases relied heavily on Ballantine's wishful reading of prior cases:

> It is coming to be recognized as the policy of the law that shareholders should in good faith put at the risk of the business unincumbered capital reasonably adequate for its prospective liabilities. If the capital is illusory or trifling compared with the business to be done and the risks of loss, this is a ground for denying the separate entity privilege. [H. Ballantine, Corporations 303 (rev. ed. 1946).]

It should be noted that, at least in recent years, inadequate capitalization per se does not trigger veil piercing in California, and the courts apply the principles of *Resnick* in a fairly strict fashion. Characteristic and instructive cases are Walker v. Signal Companies, Inc., 149 Cal. Rptr. 119 (Cal. App. 1978); United States v. Healthwin-Midtown Convalescent Hospital & Rehabilitation Center, Inc., 511 F. Supp. 416 (C.D. Cal. 1981), aff'd without op., 685 F.2d 448 (9th Cir. 1982).

where state decisional law recognizes the inadequate capitalization factor, is to limit recovery to the amount of the inadequacy of the capitalization. Either approach may fail to compensate completely outside creditors for harm wrongfully caused them if the personal assets of the defendants are insufficient to fill the need. Of course, this possibility is also present in a fraudulent conveyance action. On the other hand, if the personal assets of the defendants exceed either the amount of funds improperly transferred to them from the corporation or the size of the inadequacy of the corporation's capitalization, piercing the veil and imposing liability to the full extent of their personal assets will overcompensate the creditors for the harm traceable to the defendants' provable or wrongful acts. This result has the effect of penalizing the defendants.[11] A little thought shows that this punitive bias differs significantly from the remedial imprecision of equitable subordination doctrine.[12]

[11] A better remedy would be recovery of the amount of harm proximately caused to outside creditors by the relevant misbehavior of the controlling shareholder, whether it was failure to capitalize adequately, wasteful management, or self-dealing and confusion of roles. To be sure, the notion of proximate causation is itself perplexing and largely functional in its orientation, see Calabresi, Concerning Cause and the Law of Torts: An Essay for Harry Kalven, Jr., 43 U. Chi. L. Rev. 69 (1975), but it suggests the remedial path to be taken in piercing cases.

[12] Assume that M corporation has assets of $100 and an outside creditor claim of $150, held by Connie. Sam, the controlling shareholder, has committed acts that will trigger the doctrine of equitable subordination as well as that of piercing the corporate veil. Assume first that Sam has no legitimate creditor claim against M but owns nonexempt personal assets worth $50. If M is placed into straight bankruptcy and the trustee in bankruptcy raises no objections, Connie receives $100, which is all of M's assets. Even if the trustee could successfully invoke equitable subordination and the interpretation of that doctrine as calling regularly for full subordination of the total creditor claims of the controlling party, he would not improve the proceeds available to Connie.

Now suppose that M has not gone into bankruptcy and Connie simply sues M. She again collects $100 from M. But if she also pierces the corporate veil successfully, she will reap an additional $50 in satisfaction of her claim. The extra $50 recovery may conceivably put her in a position that matches the result that would have occurred had Sam not engaged in the wrongful conduct, although her position may just as easily be better or worse than that result. In any event, she fares better than she would if only equitable subordination were invoked on her behalf.

If the controlling shareholder's posture is reversed—if he is assumed to be asset-poor but possessed of a large legitimate creditor claim against his corporation—the result for the outside creditor under the two doctrines is *not* the opposite of that described in the preceding two paragraphs. Assume, for instance, that Sam has a legitimate creditor claim against the corporation of $50 but no (other) nonexempt personal assets. If M goes into bankruptcy and the trustee does not object to Sam's creditor claim, Connie will receive 150/200 of the assets, or $75. If equitable subordination is successfully invoked, she will receive $100.

In contrast to the role of equitable subordination in the previous example (where Sam had no creditor claim to be subordinated), that doctrine now does better Connie's recovery. Yet it does not follow that the doctrine of piercing the corporate veil will now yield her a worse recovery. Absent a bankruptcy, Connie's recovery in a suit against M will depend on a

§2.4.3 An Illustrative Case: *Walkovszky*

Walkovszky case

A brief discussion of one of the better known piercing cases may illustrate the difficulties perceived by courts that think they are being asked to go beyond nonhindrance to imposing on debtors an affirmative duty of cooperation with their creditors. In *Walkovszky v. Carlton,*[13] the plaintiff was a seriously injured tort victim of the employee of a corporation that owned two taxicabs and carried only the minimum amount of automobile liability insurance. The corporation was owned by Carlton, who also owned nine similar corporations, each with two taxicabs and minimal liability insurance. The cabs were all operated out of a single garage, so it seemed clear that Carlton had set up a number of separate corporations precisely in order to insulate at least nine-tenths of the assets of his business from any given tort claim. The plaintiff attempted to have liability imposed on the nine affiliated corporations and on Carlton. Plaintiff alleged that Carlton had systematically "milked" and siphoned off the profits of the corporation for the purpose of further minimizing the assets of the business that would be exposed to tort claims. The New York Court of Appeals appeared to rule that Walkovszky could succeed only on a fraud or an agency theory, neither of which he had alleged with sufficient particularity. The apparent negative implication was that a tort creditor in New York cannot pierce the corporate veil solely on grounds of inadequate capitalization.

---

number of factors. If she wins the "race of diligence" under state law concerning collection remedies, as by being the first to get a judgment or execution lien on M's property, then she will recover $100. If Sam qua creditor wins the race, however, Connie will recover only $50. If there is no race and an assignment for the benefit of creditors is made, both may share pro rata, so that Connie receives $75. If, however, Connie sues M and also successfully pierces the corporate veil, she will have access to Sam's personal assets. By the terms of our second example, his only asset is his claim against M. If, as may often be the case, that claim is not exempt from creditors' process (at least in a piercing case), then Connie will get the benefit of Sam's claim, and thus recover $100, the full amount of the assets of the corporation.

Assuming, then, that the outside creditor who pierces the corporate veil can obtain not only the shareholder's ordinary personal assets but also any creditor claim of the shareholder against the corporation, the doctrine of piercing the corporate veil will never yield a result less favorable to the creditor than equitable subordination and may often yield a more favorable one. From the debtor's standpoint, of the two shotgun approaches to remedying the debtor's violation of his moral duties to creditors, piercing the corporate veil is more likely to yield a punitive result.

[13] 223 N.E.2d 6 (N.Y. 1966). Cases applying New York law have continued the strict approach of this case to veil piercing. See, e.g., Brunswick Corp. v. Waxman, 459 F. Supp. 1222 (E.D.N.Y. 1978), aff'd, 599 F.2d 34 (2d Cir. 1979) (severe undercapitalization deemed irrelevant); Bank Saderat Iran v. Amin Beydoun, Inc., 555 F. Supp. 770, 774 (S.D.N.Y. 1983) (piercing requires fraud or disregard of corporate form, as by intermingling corporate and personal funds); Billy v. Consolidated Machine Tool Corp., 412 N.E.2d 934, 941 (N.Y. 1980) (avoidance of personal liability is a "fundamental purpose" of incorporation).

Application of "fraud" theory

Since the court disposed of the alleged milking in a footnote—without evident awareness of the relevance of fraudulent conveyance rules to the allegation—on the questionable grounds that it was premature and unspecific,[14] it is not clear just what Walkovszky could have alleged in particular to invoke the so-called fraud theory of piercing.[15] Inadequate capitalization alone generally does not fall under the rubric of actual or constructive fraud. Moreover, violations of the principles of truth or primacy are difficult to maintain in connection with inadequate initial capitalization. Though later withdrawals of profit might be argued to violate the principle of primacy, the court's footnote on the milking claim seems to reject this argument, at least as applied to tort victims who were not such on the dates of withdrawal.

We might be tempted to conclude, then, that the court's opinion amounts to a rejection of the piercing lawsuit in New York, leaving unfair transfers for fraudulent conveyance actions and inadequate capitalization for redress by the legislature, if at all.[16] Such a conclusion would be unjustified, however, because the court did contemplate that plaintiffs could invoke the agency theory. That is, the plaintiff can attempt to prove that the corporation was merely an agent or "instrumentality" of the individual shareholder in the latter's carrying out of what was in reality his own business.[17] The function of this theory in practice is to loosen up the

[14] Id. at 10 n.3. The charge was thought premature because plaintiff was not yet a judgment creditor of the corporation. If he should become such, asserted the court, he might then sue under the dividend restriction and similar rules of the business corporation statute. The court overlooked the possibility of suit under New York's version of the UFCA, it having been held long before that a prior judgment is *not* a procedural prerequisite to suit under that statute. American Surety Co. v. Connor, 166 N.E. 783 (N.Y. 1929). (This has also been the consistent interpretation in other states of the UFCA. Note, Fraudulent Conveyances—Necessity of Judgment to Set Aside, 11 Mont. L. Rev. 60 (1950); see Note, Joinder of Parties and Causes under Uniform Fraudulent Conveyance Act, 32 Mich. L. Rev. 705 (1934).) Furthermore, New York fraudulent conveyance law has been applied to remedy milking and diversion of corporate assets, even where one of the devices was payment of dividends. United States v. 58th Street Plaza Theatre, Inc., 287 F. Supp. 475, 498 (S.D.N.Y 1968).

[15] In fact, newly added allegations in Walkovszky's amended complaint were later held to state a cause of action, but on the theory that the individual defendants were really conducting business in their individual capacities—a theory which corresponds to the agency or instrumentality theory discussed in the text. Walkovszky v. Carlton, 287 N.Y.S.2d 546 (App. Div. 1968), aff'd, 244 N.E.2d 55 (N.Y. 1968).

[16] See the discussion of legislative alternatives in section 2.4.1. That discussion suggests that New York's enactment of a no-fault insurance law, N.Y. Ins. Law §§5101-5108 (Consol. 1985), constitutes, among many other things, a response to the problem of the two-cab corporation, a response that may turn out to be better than reversal of the decision in *Walkovszky*.

[17] This approach derives perhaps from Justice Cardozo's opinion in Berkey v. Third Avenue Ry., 155 N.E. 58 (N.Y. 1926). Ironically, Cardozo thought that this mechanistic and opaque "agency" theory of liability would be better than what he referred to as the "mists of metaphor." See id. at 61.

level of proof and the atomistic nature of the analysis that would be required in a fraudulent conveyance action. Using the theory, the court does not focus sharply on each dealing of the defendant corporation with its controlling shareholders, nor does it confront directly the doctrinal argument for and against making inadequate capitalization a basis for calling off limited liability. Instead, the court looks for random instances of self-dealing and mismanagement in a context where the shareholder has failed to keep corporate books and observe corporate formalities, or has mingled corporate and personal assets, or has engaged in other acts that suggest too weak a faith in the reality of the corporate fiction.[18] All the latter kinds of signs of agency (the inattention to formalities and the mingling of affairs and assets) are, on analysis, singularly lacking in *direct* relevance to the question of the existence, and the amount, of harm caused the outside creditor by the misbehavior of the controlling shareholder. Yet these signs at least *suggest* that fraudulent transfers may have taken place, or that creditors justifiably relied on the creditworthiness of the dominant stockholder or an affiliated corporation. When sufficiently suffused with intimations of some actual self-dealing, the presence of these signs of agency may create the appearance of a justification for going beyond the limits imposed by rules that require a more careful analysis and a precise remedy.

VP as loose version of FCL

In summary, the agency theory enunciated in the piercing cases serves a practical function similar to that of equitable subordination doctrine. Both avoid the perceived restraints of fraudulent conveyance law. They make it easier for plaintiffs to prove their cases, and they give judges more flexibility and discretion. Understandably, then, the piercing cases suppress mention of fraudulent conveyance law.[19]

[18] See Douglas & Shanks, Insulation from Liability through Subsidiary Corporations, 39 Yale L.J. 193 (1929); H. Ballantine, supra note 10, §§123, 137, at 294-295, 314-318.

[19] It should also be mentioned that the technique of doctrinal suppression can be invoked not only to hurt but to help controlling shareholders, when the court feels for whatever reasons that the shareholders should be helped but might be unduly disadvantaged by an analysis in conventional fraudulent conveyance terms. A nice example is given by one of the major New York cases dealing with the attempt of contract creditors of a subsidiary corporation to pierce the corporate veil and obtain access to the assets of the parent corporation. In Bartle v. Home Owners Coop., Inc., 127 N.E.2d 832 (N.Y. 1955), the creditors of the subsidiary corporation, a company in the business of building homes that were to be sold to the parent company's shareholders (who were mostly veterans), claimed that the parent corporation had dominated the subsidiary and had run it not in the best interest of the subsidiary itself but for the interest of the parent and its shareholders. In an opinion that is far from satisfactory in its explanation or motivations, the court rejected this claim, which was a standard way of expressing the agency theory. Most interestingly, it completely brushed over the fact that plaintiffs had alleged that the subsidiary had sold its homes at cost to the veterans, see 127 N.E.2d at 834 (Van Voorhis, J., dissenting) and thus ignored the very real

§2.5 *Dividend Statutes*

Dividend statutes as specific kind of FCL

The moral duties of the business debtor are also expressed in provisions of business corporation laws that restrict a corporation's ability to pay dividends or make other kinds of distributions to its shareholders. While perhaps most corporate lawyers perceive a relationship between these restrictions and general fraudulent conveyance law principles, there has been no close analysis of how this relationship may weaken the protection afforded by fraudulent conveyance law. The topic bears some discussion, not only because corporate distributions are of great economic significance, but also because these particular restraints raise the interesting general problem of the role of bright lines in corporate management.

Legal restraints on corporate distributions are treated more fully in a later chapter, where the concepts are illustrated by numerical examples; but a few anticipatory remarks are desirable here. (If you are a true neophyte to this subject and find this section hard to understand, you can simply return to it after reading chapter 14.)

No dividends when corporation insolvent

Under the MBCA, as well as the actual laws of may states, a corporation may not pay a dividend to its shareholders if, just after the distribution, the corporation would be insolvent.[1] (The same restraint applies to other kinds of corporate distributions to shareholders, e.g., payments to shareholders who are selling their stock back to the corporation.) And, of course, a corporation in an actual dissolution proceeding must pay its creditors before distributing anything to shareholders.[2] The existence of these restraints on corporate distributions is not surprising, for they are a straightforward expression of fraudulent conveyance principles. Under the fraudulent conveyance principle of primacy for creditors, a debtor may not make a gratuitous or unfair transfer if, just after the transfer, he would be insolvent[3] in a modified balance sheet sense.[4] The specific restraints on corporate distributions simply remove all doubts as to whether a dividend

possibilities that a fraudulent conveyance action could be brought to set aside these sales, or to recover the excess of market value over cost from the veterans, or to recover the excess amount from the parent corporation on the theory that it, as controlling party, was the fraudulent transferor or at least an aider and abettor. Had the court recognized these possibilities, it might have been forced to acknowledge that the case before it was in substance one seeking to recover from the parent as a fraudulent transferor and, therefore, the fact that the homes were to be sold at cost to the veterans was crucial.

§2.5 [1]See, e.g., MBCA §6.40; Cal. §501; N.Y. §510(a).

[2]See, e.g., MBCA §§14.05(a)(3), 14.04(a)(4); Cal. §§2004, 2005; N.Y. §1005(a)(3).

[3]See UFCA §4.

[4]See UFCA §2.

to shareholders is a "transfer without fair consideration" within the meaning of general fraudulent conveyance law.

FCL's "unreasonably small capital" rule

The UFCA, however, as well as the Bankruptcy Act, go a significant step further in the protection they would give the creditors of *business* debtors. UFCA Section 5 declares fraudulent any gratuitous or unfair transfer by a debtor in business if, after the transfer, the property remaining in the debtor's hands is "an unreasonably small capital." The debtor's post-transfer situation must be such that not only do its assets exceed its liabilities, but the amount of the excess—the debtor's net worth, or, in the loose usage of the statute,[5] *capital*—must not fall below some reasonable, minimum amount. What constitutes a reasonable amount of capital is not specified in the statute. Although we can hardly extract rules of thumb from the case law, we can conclude that the concept of capital is a flexible notion derived from all relevant facts and circumstances in a particular case. The thrust of the notion is a realistic and purposive one: The court must do its best to determine a level of capital that would provide a reasonable minimum level of protection against future decreases in the value of the debtor's assets and its subsequent inability to meet obligations to creditors. Obviously, creditor protection against adverse developments is a matter of degree. In practice, courts must make very rough estimates indeed of the amount of protection afforded to creditors in a particular case. Moreover, how much protection is legally required is a normative stipulation rather than an economic matter.

Compare "earned surplus" tests for dividends

General business corporation statutes often contain restraints on dividends that are apparently based on the notion that a business debtor ought to keep a minimal capital cushion in the business to protect its creditors. Under an older version of the MBCA—in a provision repealed in 1979, but still reflected in the law of many states[6]—dividends could only be paid out of "earned surplus," or put negatively, not out of legal capital and capital surplus. Nevertheless, the restraints were virtually meaningless for two major reasons: first, because they could be avoided if proper statutory procedures were followed; second, because they were founded on formalistic accounting conventions rather than the UFCA's equity-oriented, purposive concept of capital, which is much more relevant to the question of risk actually posed to creditors. (The discussion in chapter 14, section 14.3 shows how the earned surplus test works and how it can be evaded.)

[5]The UFCA does not define what it means by *capital* as it appears in the phrase "unreasonably small capital," but common sense suggests that it must mean something like *capital* as the word is used in discussion of commercial bank capital adequacy or of reasonable capital in veil-piercing cases. In other words, it has to do with net worth, not just legal capital.

[6]See section 14.3 infra.

Not much litigation

The porosity of ordinary corporation law's barriers against outflows of a corporation's minimum cushion of capital for creditors and the use of irrelevant legal-accounting methods of computing the cushion have had a number of consequences. First, the statutory restrictions probably lead to less litigation than would a less mechanical test. (Consider, for example, a rule requiring corporations to "maintain a net worth reasonable in light of the nature of the particular business and its liabilities." Dividend-restricting statutes are easier than fraudulent conveyance law for courts and shareholders to apply.

And not much protection for lenders

Second, most lenders to corporations, if at all sophisticated, do not rely on the statutory capital cushions. If it is worth their while to obtain protection beyond that afforded by the overarching insolvency test, they will bargain to obtain security interests or protective provisions in their loan agreements containing more effective restrictions on dividends and other distributions.

Or tort victims

A third consequence is that it is possible for tort creditors of a corporation to be adversely affected by the weak dividend restraints of ordinary business corporation law. At the time a tort claim arises, the corporation's net worth, and even the assets available for creditors who are not secured, may have fallen so low because of past dividend payments that the tort creditor's claim will not be satisfied to any significant degree.[7]

Do dividend statutes preempt UFCA §5?

Ordinary business corporation law's weak and arbitrary restraints upon shareholder distributions force us to examine the relationship between these restraints and UFCA Section 5. Does compliance with these statutory restraints preclude an attack on a distribution to shareholders under the more general rule embodied in UFCA Section 5? Furthermore, why should distributions to shareholders be singled out for treatment that is different from that accorded all other kinds of transfers without fair consideration made by a corporate debtor?

Author argues no

I would argue that, when a trustee invokes the fraudulent conveyance rules of the federal Bankruptcy Code, a court can and should hold that the Code's fraudulent conveyance rules preempt the dividend rules of state corporation laws. I would also argue that, when a state has enacted a fraudulent conveyance statute, it ought to be interpreted as providing an *additional* set of restrictions that dividends and similar distributions must

[7] Of course, the veil-piercing cases do not provide a complete solution to the tort victim's problem. Most courts don't accept unadorned inadequate capitalization as a basis for piercing. Moreover, those that do have focused mainly on the adequacy of the corporation's initial capitalization, rather than on the maintenance of a capital cushion over time. In any event, the shareholders' personal assets may be exempt, inadequate, or pledged to contract creditors.

satisfy. There is nothing inherently problematic about barring dividends when a corporation is insolvent either in the dividend statute's sense or the UFCA's sense, or when either an "impairment of legal capital" or an "unreasonable capital" for the particular business would afterwards obtain. Mechanical rules and flexible rules can co-exist, just as law and equity can. As for the statutory protections afforded "innocent" shareholders who receive illegal dividends, they might be conceded to be preemptive, but they would usually be of no avail to controlling parties.

Opposite view

This argument now has case law support.[8] Unfortunately, some courts might yet decide that the corporation statute's rules concerning dividends preempt the rules of general fraudulent conveyance law.[9] This would probably happen because the dividend statutes continue in existence for reasons other than the protection of creditors. One possible other reason is precisely that statutory restrictions on dividends supplant more stringent general restrictions on transfers without fair consideration with a set of lax rules that give management and shareholders greater freedom of action. Less cynically, the statutory restrictions are easily administered mechanical tests that facilitate corporate planning and decision making, whereas UFCA Section 5 provides a vague and uncertain standard. The relevance of the restrictions to their goal and their efficacy as means have been sacrificed to management's desire for clarity and bright lines. This latter

[8] See Wells Fargo Bank v. Desert View Building Supplies, Inc., 475 F. Supp. 693 (D. Nev. 1978), aff'd without op., 633 F.2d 221 (9th Cir. 1980).

[9] The great commentator Glenn, succumbing to the temptation to rationalize this realistic intuition, once nodded and made the rather formalistic argument that the theory of fraudulent conveyances will not fit the case of an improper dividend because the stockholder is not within either of the simple categories (donee and purchaser) that are part of the law of fraudulent transfers, but is an investor. Otherwise, he simply asserted that "the law of the corporation's being" should govern. 2 G. Glenn, §2.1 note 2, §604, at 1043-1047. Glenn's argument is unconvincing for at least two reasons.

First, at least under the UFCA and the Bankruptcy Act, nothing in the language or theory of the statutes requires the fraudulent transferee or obligee to have the status of donee or purchaser: These are commentators' classifications for purposes of convenience.

Second, Glenn did not explain why one set of rules should govern unfair dealings by controlling stockholders to the detriment of corporate creditors when the technique of unfairness is a dividend payment, and another set when the technique of unfairness is any other form of transaction, such as a sale of property to the corporation at an excessive price.

Nevertheless, the argument that might persuade some courts as to the exclusivity of corporate law is that a specific statute should be construed to preempt a more general one. See D. Kehl, Corporate Dividends 36 (1941). Supporting this argument are provisions in corporate laws specifically stating the conditions under which stockholders may be liable to corporate creditors for improper dividends received. Some of these provisions are clearly more lenient than those applicable to the ordinary fraudulent transferee, e.g., provisions immunizing from any duty to disgorge dividends those stockholders who were ignorant of the impropriety of the dividends, even when the dividends were paid while the corporation was insolvent.

observation also provides whatever answer might be given to the question as to why distributions to shareholders are treated differently from other transfers for which the corporation does not receive equal value in return. Management especially wants bright lines concerning the chief recurrent transfers without fair consideration that a corporation makes—dividends and other distributions to shareholders.

No capital maintenance rule

Perhaps the most significant observation to be made about restrictions on distributions to shareholders is that even if they were modeled after UFCA Section 5, and the concept of reasonable capital was given a strong content, the protection afforded creditors would still be incomplete. When a business corporation's capital sinks below some level that would provide creditors with a legally minimal protection against future adversities, a complete legal response would be to tell the corporate debtor that it must not

(1) pay dividends or make other distributions to shareholders;
(2) incur additional debts unless they would improve ability to meet existing obligations; or
(3) fail to obtain additional equity capital within a reasonable period of time.

The absence of any requirement in the nature of (3), in the case of ordinary business corporations,[10] indicates that the statutory restrictions, as well as fraudulent conveyance law, are based on a distinction between misfeasance and nonfeasance. Although shareholders cannot pay themselves before paying the company's creditors, there is no affirmative duty on their part to supply an additional investment to a dying corporation. Such a duty would be in fundamental contradiction to the policy of permitting limited liability. Not even the rare veil-piercing cases decided for plaintiffs on grounds of inadequate initial capital are inclined to carry the affirmative duty of cooperation to the full flowering of a capital maintenance rule.

[10] It is only in the case of certain financial intermediaries, such as banks, savings and loan associations, and insurance companies, that the law strives toward something like an affirmative action program with respect to capital adequacy. Legal protection of the creditors of financial intermediaries is taken more seriously than that given to ordinary commercial lenders to industrial corporations because the public creditors of the intermediaries—basically, depositors and policyholders—are treated as in need of a special level of protection. See Clark, The Soundness of Financial Intermediaries, 86 Yale L.J. 1 (1976).

§2.6 *Conclusion*

Aim: show relationships among four bodies of law

This chapter has dealt with two problems in the prior writing about duties to creditors: the lack of clarity in the case law about the purposes of fraudulent conveyance law and the dearth of explicit analysis in the case law and commentary of the relationships among fraudulent conveyance law, equitable subordination doctrine, the doctrine of piercing the corporate veil, and statutory restraints on dividends. My view is that the law of fraudulent conveyances, together with the law of voidable preferences, embodies a coherent set of conceptually distinct moral principles that should govern the conduct of debtors toward their creditors. I called these the principles of truth, primacy, and evenhandedness, and they may be grouped under a more general duty of nonhindrance.

Summary of the analysis

The intellectual progression from fraudulent conveyance law to equitable subordination and to the sometimes proposed rule of automatic subordination can be seen as an evolution of ways of implementing the same principles. The principles of truth and primacy are specified by fraudulent conveyance law in rather precisely conceived tests, and their violation calls for equally precisely conceived, nonpunitive remedial action. But fraudulent conveyance law is limited in the scope of the protection it gives by the concept of a transfer and by its restriction to formal creditors (a restriction that excludes minority or preferred shareholders). These same principles were given expression in a distinct, bankruptcy-related doctrine, that of equitable subordination, precisely in order to overcome the limits of fraudulent conveyance law. Where atomistic, transactionally oriented proof of violations of the principles would be too costly; where precisely conceived, nonpunitive remedies were felt to be infeasible; where violations of the principles occurred without a transfer; and where the duties were owed to obligees who were not legal creditors, new doctrine had to be developed. The courts have avoided characterizing these developments in the doctrines of equitable subordination and of piercing the corporate veil as an expansion or "weakening" of fraudulent conveyance rules. Indeed, courts deciding cases invoking these doctrines have almost always failed to draw the rather obvious parallels between what they were doing and the extensive case law concerning fraudulent conveyances.

Furthermore, in some veil-piercing cases, courts have experimented with an evolution of the principles themselves, from ideals of nonhindrance toward ideals of affirmative cooperation with creditors. Statutory restrictions on distributions to shareholders, by contrast, reflect a mechanization and weakening of the principles.

Go forward but respect the old and great

Courts will continue to develop the doctrines of equitable subordination and veil-piercing. Ideally, they should do so with explicit awareness of the extent to which plaintiffs resort to these doctrines as a way of avoiding the requirements of fraudulent conveyance law. As indicated throughout this chapter, modifications of these requirements may be quite justified. But the usual justifications will not extend to relatively simple cases of fraudulent transfers. With respect to those courses of conduct of insiders that can be readily unpacked into untruthful or unfair transactions, the ancient leviathan of commercial law doctrines gives a clearer analysis and a better remedy.

CHAPTER 3

THE BASIC ALLOCATION OF POWERS AND DUTIES

This chapter provides an introduction to the basic distribution of power among shareholders, directors, and officers. It also explores two fundamental doctrines, the duty of care and the business judgment rule.

§3.1 Shareholders

The important powers of shareholders can be put under three headings: voting rights, rights to sue, and rights to information. The first two are treated quite briefly in this chapter.

§3.1.1 Voting Rights

What shareholders vote on

Shareholders vote to elect the directors[1] and to approve extraordinary matters like mergers,[2] sales of all assets,[3] dissolutions,[4] and amendments of the articles of incorporation.[5] They may also vote to adopt, amend, and repeal bylaws;[6] to remove directors when cause for doing so exists or the right to remove has been preserved;[7] and to adopt shareholder resolutions, which may ratify board actions or request the board to take certain actions. Particular rules governing the voting process are explored in the chapters on proxies (chapter 9) and on mergers (chapter 10). As indicated previously, a perception of the advantages of separation of ownership and management, plus the practice of making corporate law rules into a standardized form contract, have led courts to hold that shareholders cannot order the directors to follow particular business policies and practices.[8]

Shareholder passivity

One advantage of centralized management is the elimination of the greatly multiplied costs that are incurred when thousands of shareholders all make themselves sufficiently well informed to vote intelligently on a key corporate decision. Coupled with this advantage is something that economists call the *free rider problem* — the temptation faced by each individual member of a large group, like the shareholders of a public corporation, to fail to make the effort needed to contribute to a group action, because he hopes that the others will do the work and he will benefit anyway. These factors, the rationality of shareholders' delegating authority rather than voting intelligently and the free rider problem, suggest that many shareholders in public corporations will often be apathetic and sheeplike in their voting, even with respect to matters like the election of directors and mergers. Observers of the corporate scene have confirmed that this theoretical prediction has been borne out in practice. In most matters, small individual shareholders in public corporations simply vote for whomever and whatever management recommends.[9]

§3.1 [1]MBCA §8.03(d); Cal. §301; Del. §211(b); N.Y. §703(a).

[2]MBCA §11.03; Cal. §1201; Del. §251(c), (f); N.Y. §903(a).

[3]MBCA §12.02; Cal. §1001; Del. §271(a); N.Y. §909(a).

[4]MBCA §14.02; Cal. §1900; Del. §275(b); N.Y. §§1001, 1103.

[5]MBCA §10.03; Cal. §903; Del. §242(b); N.Y. §803.

[6]MBCA §10.20(b); Cal. §211; Del. §109(a); N.Y. §601(a).

[7]MBCA §8.08; Cal. §303; Del. §141(k); N.Y. §706.

[8]Automatic Self-Cleansing Filter Syndicate Co., Ltd. v. Cunninghame, 2 Ch. 34 (C.A. 1906); Continental Sec. Co. v. Belmont, 99 N.E. 138 (N.Y. 1912); Associated Grocers of Alabama, Inc. v. Willingham, 77 F. Supp. 990 (N.D. Ala. 1948); Amdur v. Meyer, 224 N.Y.S.2d 440 (App. Div. 1962).

[9]Manning, Book Review, 67 Yale L.J. 1477, 1485-1496 (1958); Latham, The Commonwealth

Reformist and cynical reactions

The responses of practitioners and commentators to this fact have tended to be of two kinds. One is to lament the apparent lack of meaningful use of the shareholder voting process and to propose a battery of changes, usually modest ones, that might shore up "shareholder democracy."[10] The other response is to suggest cynically that the whole institution of shareholder voting is a fraud, or a mere ceremony designed to give a veneer of legitimacy to managerial power, and that in a more forthright world the institution would simply be dropped.[11]

Key role of voting rights

Both of these responses miss the true value of voting rights. That value is related to the ease with which the control and authority of individual directors and officers can be forcibly wrested away from them. Since voting rights can be sold along with the shares they accompany, they facilitate the displacement of incumbent managements. Although the public shareholders of a corporation may devote little effort to the exercise of informed judgment in voting on routine matters, they may be persuaded to sell their shares to an outside corporation or group of individuals who, then possessing a majority of the votes, will proceed to vote in new directors, who will in turn appoint new officers.[12] This process occurs fairly frequently in the transactions publicized as corporate takeovers and tender offers. The key legal facts in understanding their existence are that outsiders can appeal directly to shareholders to sell their shares and votes, and the shareholders can sell without director approval. The possibility of displacement acts both as a disciplinary force on existing managements and as a mechanism by which suboptimal managements can be corrected. To be sure, takeovers and shifts in control are often fraught with questionable attributes. Both their good side and their bad side will receive much more attention in later parts of this book (chapters 9 through 13). For the moment it is enough to realize the crucial link between voting rights and the possibility of managerial displacement.

of the Corporation, 55 Nw. U.L. Rev. 25 (1960). But see M. Eisenberg, The Structure of the Corporation: A Legal Analysis 64-65 (1976), stressing that in most public corporations large blocks of stock are held by sophisticated institutional investors, wealthy individuals with substantial holdings, and/or a control group. Indeed, Eisenberg stresses that although shareholders return proxies and usually rely on management proposals, in the presence of a contest they will not support management by reflex. He cites proposals that have failed, been withdrawn, or passed by narrow margins because of shareholder opposition. Id. at 65 n.1.

[10] Small, The Evolving Role of the Director in Corporate Governance, 30 Hastings L.J. 1353 (1979).

[11] Chayes, The Modern Corporation and the Rule of Law, *in* The Corporation in Modern Society 25 (E. Mason ed. 1959).

[12] See M. Eisenberg, note 9 supra, at 66-68.

§3.1.2 Rights of Action

Shareholders' suits

Besides being able to sue corporations, directors, and officers for wrongs committed directly against them, individual shareholders may bring derivative suits, or suits on behalf of the corporation, under the proper conditions.[13] Usually these suits are brought against directors and officers for violation of their fiduciary duty of loyalty, that is, because they are alleged to have taken advantage of their power to their own benefit and to the detriment of the corporation. (Contrast the corporate takeover, where perfectly honest and hardworking managers may be thrown out because the new owners think that they or their appointees can run the business better.) The function of the shareholder's power to sue is to provide a check on disloyal managerial behavior. It does this by allowing any individual shareholder to appoint himself a policeman for all the others. The law provides incentives by allowing the plaintiff shareholder's expenses and attorney's fees to be paid out of any corporate recovery.[14] In the paradigm cases for which it was designed, and in view of the restrictions placed upon it in practice, the shareholder's right to sue derivatively is not at odds with the principle of centralized management. The assumption behind such suits is that the managerial process has been corrupted: management exercised, not "business" judgment, but "personal, self-interested" judgment.[15]

§3.1.3 Rights to Information: Right of Inspection and "Proper Purpose"

Need for information

Shareholders can hardly exercise their rights to sell their stock, to vote or to solicit others to vote, and to bring derivative suits in an intelligent way unless they have adequate information about their corporation. The federal securities laws give public shareholders rights to a wide range of information and various protections against frauds. These protections will occupy us in other parts of the book.[16] One kind of information right, the share-

[13] MBCA §7.40; Cal. §800; Del. §327; N.Y. §626.

[14] Trustees v. Greenough, 105 U.S. 527 (1882); Sprague v. Ticonic Natl. Bank, 307 U.S. 161 (1939); Hornstein, The Counsel Fee in Stockholder's Derivative Suits, 39 Colum. L. Rev. 784 (1939); Hornstein, Legal Therapeutics: The "Salvage" Factor in Counsel Fee Awards, 69 Harv. L. Rev. 658 (1956); Jones, An Empirical Examination of the Resolution of Shareholder Derivative and Class Action Lawsuits, 60 B.U.L. Rev. 542 (1980). See section 15.8 infra.

[15] Derivative suits are explored at length in chapter 15.

[16] Chapter 8, on insider trading; section 9.2, on the proxy rules; chapter 17, on issuances of securities.

holders' right of inspection that is provided by the state statutes and cases,[17] will be taken up here.

Common law right of inspection

As a common law matter, a shareholder, on proof of a proper purpose for wanting to inspect corporate books and records, can obtain a court order compelling the corporation and its officers to make the records available for inspection.[18]

Statutory modifications

Statutory provisions often modify or affect the right to inspect, while leaving room for continued case law development.

MBCA's provisions: record keeping

The Model Act's provisions seem to add three things to the common law right. First, MBCA Section 16.01 affirmatively requires the corporation to make and keep certain sorts of records: minutes of meetings of shareholders and directors; "appropriate accounting records;" a record of shareholders' names, addresses, and holdings; and, at its principal office, its articles, bylaws, board resolutions creating classes of stock or fixing their relative rights, minutes of shareholders' meetings for the last three years, written communications to shareholders in the past three years, a list of names and addresses of current directors and officers, and its most recent annual report furnished to the secretary of state.

Peremptory right to inspect

Second, MBCA Section 16.02(a) gives shareholders a rather peremptory right to inspect certain kinds of records, namely, those listed in the previous paragraph as being required to be kept at the corporation's principal office. The statute requires the shareholder to give five days' written notice and to pay a reasonable charge for copies of these documents, but it doesn't provide for inquiry into his motives or purposes. In this latter respect it makes his task easier than at common law.

Need "proper purpose" to see X-rated documents

Notice, however, that the list of things subject to the "easy" inspection right leaves out some important items, including those that management might be most reluctant to show. The accounting records and the minutes of the directors' meetings, for example, are records in which a shareholder contemplating a lawsuit against management would be most interested. The record of shareholders might be of special interest to a shareholder

[17] MBCA §§16.02-16.04; Cal. §§1600, 1601; Del. §220; N.Y. §624; Soreno Hotel Co. v. State ex rel. Otis Elevator Co., 144 So. 339 (Fla. 1932); State ex rel. Pillsbury v. Honeywell, Inc., 191 N.W.2d 406 (Minn. 1971); Note, Inspection of Corporate Books and Records in Delaware, 41 Va. L. Rev. 237 (1955); Note, Shareholders' Right to Inspection of Corporate Stock Ledger, 4 Conn. L. Rev. 707 (1972); Starr & Schmidt, Inspection Rights of Corporate Stockholders: Toward a More Effective Statutory Model, 26 U. Fla. L. Rev. 173 (1974); Symposium: Corporation Notes, Shareholders' Inspection Rights, 30 Okla. L. Rev. 616 (1977); R. Stevenson, Corporations and Information: Secrecy, Access, and Disclosure (1980).

[18] See, e.g., Albee v. Lawson & Hubbard Corp., 69 N.E.2d 811 (Mass. 1946); Durnin v. Allentown Fed. Sav. and Loan Assn., 218 F. Supp. 716 (E.D. Pa. 1963).

contemplating a proxy contest against management or a hostile takeover bid. When may a shareholder inspect and copy any of these items? According to Section 16.02(c), he may do so only if his demand is "made in good faith and for a proper purpose," he describes with "reasonable particularity" his purpose and the records he wants to inspect, and the records are "directly connected" with his purpose. In tone, at least, these preconditions seem slightly more strict than those imposed at common law.

Costs

Third, MBCA Section 16.04(c) puts some teeth into the right to inspect by providing that, if a court has to order the corporation to allow the inspection, it shall also order the corporation to pay the shareholder's costs, including reasonable counsel fees. The corporation can avoid this imposition of costs, however, if it can prove that it refused inspection in good faith because it had a "reasonable basis" for doubt about the right of the shareholder to inspect the records demanded.

Statute not exclusive

The statute is quite explicit that Section 16.02 does not affect rights of inspection of parties in litigation (for example, discovery rights created by the applicable rules of civil procedure). Nor does it affect the power of a court, independently of the Model Act, to compel the production of corporate records for examination.[19] Presumably, then, the common law right to inspect on proof of proper purpose survives the statute.

It should be noted in passing that, under MBCA Section 7.20, shareholders sometimes have a right to get a rather specific version of the shareholders' list. After fixing the record date for a shareholders' meeting, a corporation has to prepare a list of shareholders entitled to vote at it. Starting two days after notice of the meeting is given and continuing through the meeting, a shareholder or his attorney is entitled to inspect and copy the list. (This right is subject to the proper purpose and other requirements of Section 16.02(c).) Consequently, a shareholder wishing to solicit proxies from all and only those shareholders entitled to vote will be able to do so.

New York approach

Section 624 of the New York Business Corporation Law, as well as the inspection rights provision of the preceding version of the Model Act (Section 52), display an interestingly different pattern. Different rules apply to smaller and newer shareholders than to those who have been shareholders of record for at least six months or who hold at least 5 percent of any class

[19] Varney v. Baker, 80 N.E. 524 (Mass. 1907); Commonwealth ex rel. Wilde v. Pennsylvania Silk Co., 110 A. 157 (Pa. 1920); State ex rel. Watkins v. Cassell, 294 S.W.2d 647 (Mo. Ct. App. 1956); Sanders v. Pacific Gamble Robinson Co., 84 N.W.2d 919 (Minn. 1957); Wyman v. Sombrerete Mining Co., 222 N.Y.S.2d 996 (Sup. Ct. 1959); Brandt Glass Co. v. New Orleans Housing Mart, Inc., 193 So. 2d 321 (La. Ct. App. 1966).

of stock. The New York statute gives these older and bigger shareholders the right to examine a record of shareholders and the minutes of shareholders' meetings, without proof of proper purpose. (If requested, however, the shareholder has to furnish an affidavit that the inspection is not for a purpose that is in the interest of a business other than the business of the corporation and that he has not within five years sold a shareholders' list.) This is a rather special and incomplete rule, of course. The statute goes on to declare that it doesn't impair the power of courts to compel the production of books and records of a corporation. Thus, the common law right still covers many situations, such as requests by small shareholders or requests by any shareholders to inspect accounting records or minutes of directors' meetings.

Treat older and bigger shareholders differently?

The reasoning behind statutes giving advantages to the bigger and more longstanding shareholders is not completely persuasive. The thought seems to be that frivolous and harassing inspection requests are more likely to be made by smaller and more recent shareholders, since this class contains those who became shareholders simply because some attorney suggested that they buy a few shares in order to permit the exercise of inspection rights and the subsequent initiation of a shareholder resolution or a derivative suit. But even if attorney-instigated stock purchases are usually small and occur soon before a request for inspection, the statutory rule discriminates against all of the small, recent shareholders who bought on their own motion and who now have bona fide suspicions or causes of complaint against corporate managers. Furthermore, it seems unlikely that plaintiffs' attorneys systematically suggest "qualifying" purchases of small amounts of stock on the basis of frivolous suspicions of managerial wrongdoing. It is in the attorney's own interest to make such suggestions only when his preliminary research indicates that a valid reason exists for doubting management's wisdom or integrity.

Delaware approach

To its credit, the corresponding Delaware statute, Section 220 of the Delaware General Corporate Law, makes no discriminations among shareholders on the basis of size or length of holdings. Rather, its approach is based on another dichotomy: corporate "books and records" versus the list of shareholders. When seeking to inspect the former, the shareholder must prove a proper purpose; when seeking to inspect the shareholder list, the corporation has the burden of proving an improper purpose. This differentiation may reflect the Delaware legislature's perception of the nature of the situations in which there is bitter conflict over inspection requests about the two kinds of records. Shareholders often want a shareholder list in order to mount a proxy contest or to make a tender offer, both of which are viewed with horror by incumbent management but may very well be in the economic interest of all the shareholders. In these situations management almost instinctively resists inspection, even though there is little or no legitimate basis for delay. Moreover, a shareholder's viewing and copying a shareholder list is unlikely to disrupt company operations or lead to dissemination of trade secrets and other sensitive information. By contrast, in recent times some prominent requests for inspection of books and records have come from persons who were concerned not so much with the corporation's economic well-being as with the social consequences of the corporation's actions.[20] Inspection might be the first step in a chain of actions that would injure the corporation's business, and the inspection itself might jeopardize the secrecy of sensitive business information or otherwise disrupt operations.

Proper purpose the usual substantive test

Whatever the variations in statutory procedure, proper purpose has become the substantive touchstone in most jurisdictions. Its meaning and purpose become clear in the case law.[21] The MBCA provision does not define the term, although the Delaware one describes it as "a purpose reasonably related to such person's interest as a stockholder." Since this language does not say "financial interest às a stockholder," linguistic room has been left for debating what a stockholder as such may be properly interested in.

Four kinds of purposes

The case law on the meaning of the proper purpose test may be grouped into four categories, based on what motivates the shareholder:

(1) the desire to evaluate his investment;
(2) the desire to deal with other shareholders, qua investors;
(3) the desire to obtain noninvestment-related personal benefits; and
(4) the desire to promote social responsibility goals.

In most cases, the first two purposes would be proper purposes for inspection, while the second two would not.

Examples of first kind

In the first category are cases in which the shareholder wants to determine the reasons for nonpayment of dividends,[22] to investigate possible mismanagement where some evidence is offered to justify the concern,[23] to

[20] State ex rel. Pillsbury v. Honeywell, Inc., 191 N.W.2d 406 (Minn. 1971); National Consumer's Union v. National Tea Co., 302 N.E.2d 118 (Ill. App. 1973).

[21] See, e.g., Insuranshares Corp. of Delaware v. Kirchner, 5 A.2d 519 (Del. 1939); State ex rel. Thiele v. Cities Serv. Co., 115 A. 773 (Del. 1922); Winter v. Southern Sec. Co., 118 S.E. 214 (Ga. 1923); Goldman v. Trans-United Indus., 171 A.2d 788 (Pa. 1961).

[22] Laher Spring & Tire Corp. v. Superior Court of Alameda County, 126 P.2d 391 (Cal. Ct. App. 1942); Briskin v. Briskin Mfg. Co., 286 N.E.2d 571 (Ill. App. 1972).

[23] Guthrie v. Harkness, 199 U.S. 148 (1905); Varney v. Baker, 80 N.E. 524 (Mass. 1907);

determine reasons for an apparent disparity between the value implicit in the company's published annual report and the market price of its stock,[24] and otherwise to investigate the corporation's true financial condition.[25]

Examples of second kind

In the second category are the important cases, often involving potential shifts in control, in which the shareholder's immediate objective is to inspect a stockholder list so that he knows who the other shareholders are, and his purpose is then to make a tender offer to the other shareholders or to urge that they accept one,[26] to solicit proxies from them,[27] or to communicate with them regarding the affairs of the corporation, provided that the substance of the communication — such as the possible need to change management in order to effect a merger[28] — is stated. These cases differ from those in the first category in that the shareholder is not primarily concerned with getting more information about the corporation's activities and operations. Managers have tried, to no avail, to make this difference into a successful defense.[29] The courts have been more impressed by the fact that, as in the first category, the shareholder's inspection related ultimately to actions affecting the economic value of stockholder investments. Courts seem sensitive to managers' tendencies to resist shareholder requests with all their energy, for it has been held that if a shareholder shows a proper purpose, the fact that he may also be motivated by an improper purpose is irrelevant.[30] This holding is supported by the argument that any improper use of the corporate information by the shareholder can be remedied if and when it later occurs.

Martin v. Columbia Pictures, 133 N.Y.S.2d 469 (Sup. Ct. 1953), aff'd, 130 N.Y.S.2d 300 (App. Div. 1954), aff'd, 123 N.E.2d 572 (N.Y. 1954), reh. denied, 125 N.E.2d 103 (N.Y. 1955), modified, 145 N.Y.S.2d 484 (App. Div. 1955); Skouras v. Admiralty Enterprises, Inc., 386 A.2d 674 (Del. Ch. 1978); Skoglund v. Ormand Indus., Inc., 372 A.2d 204 (Del. Ch. 1976).

[24] Homestake Mining Co. v. Superior Court of San Francisco, 54 P.2d 535 (Cal. Ct. App. 1936); cf. State ex rel. Rogers v. Sherman Oil Co., 117 A. 122 (Del. 1922) (where shareholder's purpose was to ascertain the value of stock having no ready market).

[25] Guthrie v. Harkness, 199 U.S. 148 (1905); Cooke v. Outland, 144 S.E.2d 835 (N.C. 1965); Weigel v. O'Connor, 373 N.E.2d 421 (Ill. App. 1978). But see State ex rel. Jones v. Ralston Purina Co., 358 S.W.2d 772 (Mo. 1962) (right of inspection may not extend to analyses or tentative studies prepared purely for the information of management, such as preliminary profit and loss statements or tentative balance sheets).

[26] Crane Co. v. Anaconda Co., 346 N.E.2d 507 (N.Y. 1976); Mite Corp. v. Heli-Coil Corp. 256 A.2d 855 (Del. Ch. 1969).

[27] General Time Corp. v. Talley Indus. Inc., 240 A.2d 755 (Del. Ch. 1968); Fears v. Cattlemen's Inv. Co., 483 P.2d 724 (Okla. 1971).

[28] Hanrahan v. Puget Sound Power & Light Co., 126 N.E.2d 499 (Mass. 1955).

[29] Crane Co. v. Anaconda Co., 346 N.E.2d 507 (N.Y. 1976).

[30] CM&M Group, Inc. v. Carroll, 453 A.2d 788 (Del. 1982); General Time Corp. v. Talley Indus., Inc., 240 A.2d 755 (Del. Ch. 1968); Skoglund v. Ormand Indus., Inc., 372 A.2d 204 (Del. Ch. 1976).

Examples of third kind

In the third category of cases are those in which the shareholder wanted to get access to trade secrets,[31] to obtain knowledge of the corporation's inner workings and to supply it to a competitor or embarrass the corporation,[32] or to sell any stockholder list to persons who would use it as a list of possible customers or donors (and possibly flood the shareholders with junk mail).[33] Since many of these purposes are adverse to the corporation's interest the courts have had little trouble conceiving them as improper. But they have been wary of management claims that these purposes are actually present and controlling.

Example of fourth kind: *Pillsbury* case

It is the fourth or social responsibility category that is most troubling and interesting. In *State ex rel. Pillsbury v. Honeywell, Inc.*,[34] the shareholder sought to inspect the corporation's shareholder ledger and all of the corporate records dealing with weapons and munitions manufacture. He had purchased one share of stock for the sole purpose of trying to stop the corporation from producing munitions. He was unconcerned with whether the stock was a good investment but was interested in impressing his political viewpoint on the corporation and its shareholders. He argued that any shareholder who disagreed with management had an absolute right to inspect the records in order to solicit proxies, that is, that solicitation in opposition to management is a per se proper purpose. The court rejected this contention and adopted the narrower view that in order to be proper the purpose must concern economic or investment return. The shareholder was not entitled to inspect the records because "[h]is sole purpose was to persuade the company to adopt his social and political concerns, irrespective of any economic benefits to himself or Honeywell."[35] However, a shareholder with an investment interest could bring the suit "if motivated by concern with the long or short-term economic effects on Honeywell resulting from the production of war and munitions. Similarly, this suit might be appropriate when a shareholder has a bona fide concern about the adverse effects of abstention from profitable war contracts on his investment in Honeywell."[36] In other words, the social concern must ulti-

[31] In re H. Verby Co., 330 N.Y.S.2d 92 (App. Div. 1972); see also Fownes v. Hubbard Broadcasting, Inc., 225 N.W.2d 534 (Minn. 1975) (suggesting protective order to shield company's trade secrets).

[32] Schulman v. Louis Dejonge & Co., 59 N.Y.S.2d 119 (App. Div. 1945); RDR Assoc., Inc. v. Media Corp. of America, 405 N.Y.S.2d 702 (1st Dept. 1982); Hutson v. Brown, 26 So. 2d 907 (Ala. 1946).

[33] State ex rel. Thiele v. Cities Serv. Co., 115 A. 773 (Del. 1922).

[34] 191 N.W.2d 406 (Minn. 1971).

[35] Id. at 412.

[36] Id.

mately be tied to a long-range impact on corporate profits. (And if a socially concerned shareholder is willing to perjure himself, he can almost always allege such a connection.) Similarly, a shareholder's desire to inspect the corporation's records in order to sensitize the corporation to consumer demands was also declared not to be a proper purpose.[37]

Fears of disruption and corporate harm

In these cases the courts are ostensibly concerned with the possible *extent of the disruption of internal corporate affairs* that might result from holdings in favor of plaintiffs. The basic reason for a shareholder inspection right is to insure managerial accountability to shareholders. The right assists shareholder efforts to protect themselves when managerial discretion has led to their having inadequate information about when and on what terms to sell, how to vote, and whether to sue. The basic reason for limitations on shareholder inspection rights is to prevent intrusions into the corporation's internal communication and control network that (1) will have ultimately adverse consequences to the corporation's operations or (2) will be too costly and disruptive in themselves. It can be argued that, in view of the extensive disclosures of corporate information required of public corporations by the federal securities laws, inspections made with the ultimate aim of evaluating one's investment, that is, second guessing the stock market's valuation, will be relatively rare in the case of public corporations. Furthermore, requests by potential tender offerors for shareholder lists are only mildly disruptive of the corporation's internal operations. As for close corporations, the intrusions caused by shareholder inspections may be relatively frequent and severe, but they are essential to prevent unjust oppression of minority shareholders. By contrast, inspections aimed at challenging the propriety of the corporation's impact on numerous nonshareholder interests, or on the public interest generally, are an open-ended class whose cumulative impact on a corporation could be extremely disruptive. Labor unions, consumer activists, antiwar groups, conservationists, antivivisectionists, and so forth might all buy a single share of a public corporation in order to then proceed to take it to task for actions allegedly infringing their interests and to harangue its shareholders.

Allow "socially" motivated inspections when disruption modest?

This view gives rise to an instructive counterargument. If the goal of limitations on inspection rights is to prevent undue disruption of a corporations' internal communication and decision making networks — the army of irate plaintiffs dragging fishing lines through the corporation's papers and computers — then the proper purpose test is both underinclusive and overinclusive. It is underinclusive because it could happen, at

[37]National Consumer's Union v. National Tea Co., 302 N.E.2d 118 (Ill. App. 1973).

least in theory, that profit maximizing shareholders would overburden the corporation with simultaneous requests to inspect, without running afoul of the test. It is overinclusive because socially concerned shareholders could make requests for inspections that would not greatly disrupt intracorporate functioning, and yet would be barred by the proper purpose test, even though its alleged rationale of preventing disruption was not being furthered in the particular instance. Why not adopt a test geared more directly to the disruption danger? For example, the courts could be given discretion to deny requests to compel inspection whenever they find that, in view of the nature of the request and the kind and character of any other inspections already under way, the corporation would be unduly burdened.

Systemic costs of doing so

The best rebuttal to this counterargument focuses on the entire *system* of governmental and citizen efforts to control the bad consequences (or negative externalities) of corporate business. The inspection activities of a few socially concerned shareholders with respect to a given corporation may not be a crushing burden, but if similar inspections are being made of many public corporations, the overall costs to society may be very large. It must be remembered that, once it becomes the practice that those requesting inspection need not be moved by the goal of protecting the economic value of their investment, the number of public inspectors and the reasons for their wanting to inspect can increase astronomically. Any person or group concerned with any apparent social problem in which any number of corporations has been involved could buy one share in all of those corporations and then have a free right to inspect the company's internal documents. Indeed, if such motivations were held proper, the requirement of holding a share of stock becomes a mere formality and should be discarded. The law would then have made a clear substantive decision that any citizen could inspect any corporation's internal records if he or she could allege some nonfrivolous basis of public concern with that corporation's activities.

Political question: where should investigatory power reside?

So let us face the real issue directly: Why should lawmakers not make such a substantive decision? The basic reason, which may be hard for people living in a democracy to admit and accept, is that sharp limits on the forms and forums of participation in governmental decision making is socially efficient. By governmental decision making I mean decisions as to what are public goods and how they should be subsidized or encouraged, what are really negative externalities and how they should be corrected, and what kinds and amounts of redistribution of resources should occur. One part of our traditional model of a proper political process is that governmental decision making in this sense is a specialized task that requires enormous amounts of system-wide information and a continuing effort to coordinate the parts into a whole. It ought to be concentrated in the hands of legitimated, democratically elected governmental bodies and in the regulatory agencies to which they delegate specific tasks. Moreover, one should presume that the proper persons to make costly accusatory investigations into the alleged bad consequences of corporate actions are legislative committees, regulatory agencies, and private plaintiffs who have found themselves specifically injured by corporate violations of existing law and are making use of discovery rules. Furthermore, when legislators want to enlist private citizens in the task of finding out about possible bad external consequences of corporate actions, they can, and in various contexts have, added new reporting requirements and disclosure requirements,[38] as well as new causes of action. Increasing the public interest burden on corporate information networks in this way — by the considered, explicit judgments of actual governmental bodies who have some view of all alleged social problems and their relative importance — seems preferable to the alternative of granting all citizens the right to rummage through the documents of any public corporations on behalf of their visions of the public interest.

§3.2 Directors

§3.2.1 Powers

Election and powers of directors

Shareholders usually elect directors who have the formal legal power to manage the corporation.[1] The directors usually serve one-year terms (and may be re-elected), although many statutes permit a classified board of directors, — for example, nine directors, three of whose terms expire in year one, another three in year two, the other three in year three, and so forth.[2] Directors may be removed by shareholders "for cause" and, if the statute allows, without cause.[3] As a formal legal matter, the directors, acting as a board at properly called meetings, have extremely broad powers and responsibilities. These include the appointment, supervision, and re-

[38] See, e.g., Clean Air Act Amendments of 1977, 42 U.S.C. §§7414, 7542; Clean Water Act of 1977, 33 U.S.C. §1318.

§3.2 [1] MBCA §8.01(b); Del. §141; Cal. §300; Ill. Rev. Stat. c. 32, §157.33; Mass. Ann. Laws c. 156, §156, §25; N.Y. §701.

[2] MBCA §8.06; Del. §141(d); N.Y. §704; Wash. Rev. Code Ann. §23A.08.360.

[3] MBCA §8.08 and Del. §141(k) allow removal with or without cause. Cal. §303 allows removal without cause subject to certain restrictions; see also Cal. §304 (for cause). N.Y. §706 allows removal for cause and, if the articles so provide, without cause.

moval of the officers who actually run the corporation; the fixing of the officers' compensation; the delegation of decision making authority to subcommittees of the board of directors, to the officers, and to others; the decision whether, in their discretion, to declare and pay dividends on the corporation's stock; the adoption, amendment, and repeal of bylaws (a power that may also reside in shareholders[4]); the initiation and approval of certain extraordinary corporate actions, such as amendments to the articles of incorporation, mergers, sales of all assets, and dissolutions, before such matters can be submitted to the shareholders for their approval; and, more generally, the making of major business decisions, such as policies concerning what products and services the company will offer, what prices it will charge and wages it will pay, what major financing agreements it will enter, and the like.[5] In a word, the board is supposed to supervise the entire operation of the business. Directors also have some rights that may be individually exercised: a right to inspect corporate books and records, (called absolute in some states and qualified in others),[6] and, sometimes, a right to bring derivative actions on behalf of the corporation.

Actual role in public corporations

In the case of public corporations, however, the actual functions carried out by boards of directors are much more modest than is suggested by these formal legal powers. This observation, which has been made by numerous attorneys and businessmen,[7] is supported both by experience and by analysis. On the empirical side, a leading source of evidence is a three-year field study of the activities of directors of manufacturing, retailing, and mining corporations that was conducted over a decade ago by Professor Myles L. Mace of the Harvard Business School.[8] He found that in

[4]See note 6 to section 3.1 supra.

[5]See generally Eisenberg, The Legal Roles of Shareholders and Management in Modern Corporate Decisionmaking, 57 Calif. L. Rev. 1 (1969); 1 & 2 G. Hornstein, Corporation Law and Practice 199-205, 366-367, 577-578, 630-631 (1959 & Supp. 1968).

[6]Cal. §1602 (absolute); Machen v. Machen & Mayer Elec. Mfg. Co., 85 A. 100 (Pa. 1912) (absolute); Murphy v. Fiduciary Counsel, Inc., 336 N.Y.S.2d 913, (App. Div. 1972), aff'd, 300 N.E.2d 154 (N.Y. 1973) (former director has qualified right covering period of directorship where he makes proper showing that inspection is necessary to protect personal responsibility interest); Matter of Cohen v. Cocoline Products, Inc., 127 N.E.2d 906 (N.Y. 1955), noted in 9 Vand. L. Rev. 95 (1955) (absolute right of directors in office, qualified right of former directors).

[7]Conard, Mace, Blough & Gibson, Functions of Directors Under the Existing System, 27 Bus. Law. 23 (1972); Eisenberg, Legal Models of Management Structure in the Modern Corporation: Officers, Directors, and Accountants, 63 Calif. L. Rev. 375 (1975).

[8]M. Mace, Directors: Myth and Reality (1971); Mace, The Changing Role of Directors in the 1970s, 31 Bus. Law. 1207 (1976); Mace, Directors: Myth and Reality — Ten Years Later, 32 Rut. L. Rev. 293 (1979); Interview with M. Mace on Directors: "Good Ones Don't Have to Worry," Forbes, May 12, 1980, at 129.

medium and large widely held corporations where little stock was owned by management and directors, the directors acted as advisers and counsellors to the president, as a source of discipline or a corporate conscience (the very fact that the officers had to prepare and articulate presentations for outside directors helped keep them more rational and honest), and as decision makers in times of crisis. (For example, they might fire the president when the company was on the brink of disaster.) A few boards established, or at least studied and appraised, corporate objectives, strategies, and policies such as product line changes, diversification moves, and labor agreements; but most did not. A few directors asked discerning questions of management; but most did not. Moreover, in most cases the board did not really select and de-select the president, nor did the directors monitor and evaluate his performance.

Changing practices

Since Mace's original study, the situation appears to have changed somewhat, partially as a result of lawsuits against directors and scandals such as that involving the widespread foreign bribes and questionable payments discovered to have been made by American corporations in the early 1970s.[9] Most publicly held corporations now appear to have boards a majority of whose members are outside directors (those who are not also officers),[10] audit committees composed mostly of outside directors who make a more serious effort to review audits of the corporation's and the officers' performance,[11] and compensating and nominating committees containing a majority of outside directors. They also pay their directors

[9] Kane & Butler, Improper Corporate Payments: The Second Half of Watergate, 8 Loy. U. Chi. L.J. 1 (1976); Stevenson, the SEC and Foreign Bribery, 32 Bus. Law. 53 (1976); Duncan, Corporate Payoffs Abroad: Issues and Answers, 1 Directors & Boards (no. 3) 12 (1976); Holt & Aldridge, Improving the Audit Function: A Director's Guide to Compliance with the Accounting Provisions of the Foreign Corrupt Practices Act of 1977, 4 Directors & Boards (no. 3) 42 (1979); Baruch, The Foreign Corrupt Practices Act, 57 Harv. Bus. Rev. 32 (Jan.-Feb. 1979); Sumutka, Questionable Payments and Practices: Why? How? Detection? Prevention?, J. Accountancy, March, 1980, at 50; SEC Commentary — The Foreign Corrupt Practices Act of 1977: An Auditor's Prespective, CPA J., May, 1978, at 71.

[10] See Haft, Business Decisions by the New Board: Behavioral Science and Corporate Law, 80 Mich. L. Rev. 1, 3 (1981); but compare Coffee, Beyond the Shut-Eyed Sentry: Toward a Theoretical View of Corporate Misconduct and an Effective Legal Response, 63 Va. L. Rev. 1099, 1233 (1977) (role of chief executive in selecting outside directors). See generally Brudney, The Independent Director — Heavenly City or Potemkin Village?, 95 Harv. L. Rev. 597 (1982); Solomon, Restructuring the Corporate Board of Directors: Fond Hope — Faint Promise?, 76 Mich. L. Rev. 581 (1978).

[11] See Leech and Mundheim, The Outside Director of the Publicly Held Corporation, 31 Bus. Law. 1799 (1976); SEC Rel. No. 34-13346 (Mar. 22, 1977) (urging audit committees of independent directors); ABA Committee on Corporate Laws, Corporate Directors' Guidebook, 33 Bus. Law. 1595, 1624-1627 (1978) (urging significant number of nonmanagement directors on audit, compensation, and nominating committees).

better to encourage them to engage more seriously in monitoring corporate and executive activities. But it is still unrealistic to view directors as making any significant number of basic business policy decisions. Even with respect to the broadest business policies, it is the officers who generally initiate and shape the decisions. The directors simply approve them, and occasionally offer advice or raise questions.

Supervisory role permitted

In view of the increasing publicity given to these realities, the custodians of the MBCA, in a display of the super-caution that is the hallmark of practicing corporate lawyers, amended former Section 35 in 1974. The clause stating that "the business and affairs of a corporation shall be managed by a board of directors" was amended to read "the business and affairs of a corporation shall be managed *under the direction of* a board of directors." The idea was to preclude any possibility — no realistic possibility existed — that the section might be interpreted to require active involvement by boards in day-to-day affairs of corporations.[12]

Reasons for board's modest role

As a matter of analysis, the findings about the actual roles of directors in large diversified corporations should come as no surprise. As traditionally structured, the board of directors suffers from serious constraints on its time, information, and budget; from a lack of strong personal incentives to act diligently on behalf of shareholders; and from a selection process that is effectively controlled by the officers.

Time, information, and budget constraints

The directors of a large corporation characteristically meet for only a few hours every month. It is thus impossible for them to deal in a thorough way with the merits of any significant number of complex corporate business decisions. Nor can they second guess, in an effective, detailed way, the judgments and arguments of the corporation's full-time officers, who are intimately versed in the company's business affairs. The directors often receive their information about the corporation from documents and presentations put together by the full-time officers. Sometimes the information supplied is too sketchy for them to evaluate the wisdom of the corporation's business policies. Sometimes it is so voluminous that it simply cannot be digested. In all cases the fact that the officers selected the information creates some risk that the picture seen by the directors may be distorted, but not recognized as distorted. Finally, the directors typically have no staff that is responsible only and directly to them.

Weak incentives

As for incentives, the directors typically receive a flat yearly fee that is

[12]Report of Committee on Corporate Laws, Changes in the Model Business Corporation Act, 29 Bus. Law. 947, 949-950, 952-953 (April 1974); Report of Committee on Corporate Laws: Changes in the Model Business Corporation Act, 30 Bus. Law. 501, 502-505 (1975). The current MBCA provision, §8.01(b), continues to reflect this linguistic change.

unrelated to their performance on behalf of the shareholders. Though significant, the fee will appear modest to many of the kinds of people who actually become directors of large corporations.

Biased selection

As for the selection procedure: It is a notorious fact that in the overwhelming majority of elections for directorships in public corporations the public shareholders simply vote for whomever is proposed by the corporation's official nominating committee. At least in the past, this committee of the board was often made up of directors who were officers, or friends of the officers, and it was careful to nominate only candidates who were likely to be well disposed to incumbent management. Nominees tended to be agreeable, chummy persons, usually of the same social class as the incumbents. They might bring some special experience to their role or represent some special relationship, but they could be counted on to take a cooperative rather than an adversarial or supervisory stance toward the officers. In effect, boards were self-perpetuating and usually congenial to the officers. This characterization frequently had to be qualified, however, when the corporation had a large shareholder whose director-representatives were really looking out for that shareholder's interest. Today, it may be the case that the characterization is becoming less valid more generally, because more nominating committees contain a majority of outside directors. But since most outside directors on these committees were originally identified by officers, and since there is a kind of social compact among most businessmen at the top-officer and director level, substantial change in the intensity and seriousness with which boards act as monitors may be slow in coming.

§3.2.2 Procedures

Basic points

Directors usually must act as a board (i.e., as a group), by majority vote at formally held meetings, and their decisions are formally recorded in the minutes of those meetings.[13] Proper notice of these meetings must be given and a quorum must be present; the bylaws of the corporation usually specify what constitutes proper notice and a quorum.[14] Each director has

[13]See MBCA §§8.20-8.25, 16.01(a); Cal. §307; Del. §141; N.Y. §708(a). The statutes usually assume the requirement that action will be taken at a meeting — as is evident by their making an exception for action by unanimous written consent — rather than state it explicitly.

[14]See MBCA §§8.22 (default rules for notice if articles or bylaws don't provide otherwise: none for regular meetings, two days for special meetings), 8.24 (default rule for quorum: majority of directors; articles or bylaws can't authorize quorum of less than one-third of directors); Cal. §307(a); Del. §141(b); N.Y. §§707, 708, 711.

one vote and, unlike shareholders, may not vote by proxy.[15] Almost all states now provide that, in lieu of traditional board action, the directors may act without a meeting by giving their *unanimous written* consent to the corporate action in question.[16] These provisions were enacted principally to accommodate the realities of practice in close corporations, where it is frequently hard to get the participants to live by the formalities adopted for public corporations. Some statutes also permit directors to hold a meeting by conference telephone,[17] but this is an acknowledgment of possibilities created by new technology rather than a repudiation of the notion that directors should act at a meeting.

Why have meetings?

Why has corporate law insisted for so long that directors must act at meetings at which a quorum of them is present? Why shouldn't it be enough for the director or officer initiating an action to have it individually approved by a majority of the directors, whose approval is obtained at different times and places? The traditional answer is that the decision making process is likely to function better when the directors consult with and react to one another. A group discussion of problems is thought to be needed, not just a series of yea or nay responses.

Sociological support

In fact, the traditional answer is supported by the empirical work of sociologists who have studied groups and organizations. As one early but still valuable review of the literature[18] put it, individuals are often superior at tasks requiring the creation and construction of a coherent, highly integrated plan or project (How many great novels or symphonies were written by committees?), but small groups are distinctly superior to individuals at revealing the errors and problems associated with proposals put forward by individuals. It often takes someone else, operating from a different frame of reference, to spot the obvious flaws in one's bright ideas. Thus, the rule that directors must act at meetings should not be viewed as a mere formality; it is an important formality.

Example of *Baldwin v. Canfield*

It is also a rule whose actual role in litigated cases can be quite surprising. The venerable case of *Baldwin v. Canfield*,[19] an inadequately appreciated jewel that long graced the pages of the major corporate law case book,[20] provides a good example. One King acquired all of the stock of the

[15] An unusual exception is found in La. Rev. Stat. Ann. §12:81(E) (proxy voting by directors permissible if articles provide for it).

[16] MBCA §8.21; Cal. §307(b); Del. §141(f); N.Y. §708(b).

[17] MBCA §3.20(b); Cal. §307(a)(6); Del. §141(i); N.Y. §708(c).

[18] P. Blau & R. Scott, Formal Organizations 116-121 (1962).

[19] 1 N.W. 261 (Minn. 1879).

[20] W. Cary, Cases and Materials on Corporations 176 (4th ed. unabr. 1969), opinion inexplicably omitted in W. Cary & M. Eisenberg, Cases and Materials on Corporations (5th ed. unabr. 1980).

Minneapolis Agricultural and Mechanical Association (MAMA), an inactive corporation whose sole valuable asset was some fair grounds property. Through an involved and indirect series of transactions, King borrowed about $30,000 on the security of this stock, which was then held by a Minneapolis Bank and its cashier, Baldwin, as pledgees. King next negotiated a deal with Canfield, who was willing to pay $65,000 (in the form of readily marketable securities — railroad bonds) to get the fair grounds property. The written agreement provided that *King* would sell the property and execute a warranty deed conveying it. Because Canfield knew that King did not then personally own the property, and was told that King owned all of the MAMA stock (but was not told of the pledges), it was orally agreed at the time of signing the written agreement that, at the closing, King would transfer the stock to Canfield *and* get a deed of the property from MAMA to Canfield. The closing was to occur not in Minneapolis but in New York. King then contacted Baldwin and convinced him to send all the pledged MAMA stock to an escrow agent in New York City, the Park Bank, which was instructed to release the stock to Canfield upon his handing over enough of the railroad bonds to pay off King's loans. Unfortunately, this plan was never effectively communicated to Canfield. (Baldwin apparently relied upon King to tell Canfield about it.) King proceeded to get the ten directors of inactive MAMA to sign a deed purporting to transfer the fair grounds property to Canfield. The signatures were gotten separately and at different times, whenever King or his attorney happened to catch up with the directors; no meeting authorizing the sale was held.

A disastrous closing

Ultimately, the closing occurred in New York. King handed over the deed from MAMA, threw in a guaranty deed from himself for good measure, and received the railroad bonds. Canfield, through inadvertency, did not also demand the MAMA stock pursuant to the oral agreement. (Perhaps that would have seemed like gilding the lily.) Indeed, the escrow agreement and the Park Bank were ignored; the MAMA stock just sat there. The Park Bank did not receive any of the railroad bonds; King's loans were not repaid in this or any other manner; King did not turn the railroad bonds over to MAMA but kept them for himself; and King subsequently became unavailable for lawsuits. (One can imagine him, after the real estate closing, walking over to Wall Street and selling the railroad bonds, buying a satchel to put all his money in, and then catching a boat to Brazil.) King had succeeded in extracting some $85,000 from various parties, but all that was left behind was property worth about $65,000. In other words, the facts of the case suggest a rather remarkable fraud by a clever con man. The court's task was to decide how to allocate the loss between the two unfortunate people, Baldwin and Canfield, whom he left holding the bag. The court accomplished the allocation by invoking the rule that directors must act at a meeting. The deed was therefore invalid, and Canfield lost to Baldwin.

Assessing this use of the rule

Although one can argue that a meeting would not have made any difference, perhaps this ruling does express the purpose of the formal meeting rule. If there had been a serious directors' meeting, the directors might have learned of King's pledges of stock and examined the deal with Canfield. They might then have required that the written contract for sale be recast with MAMA as a party and provided for safeguards to insure that consideration would be payable to and received only by the corporation, out of which it might later be paid as dividends to the holders of the stock. (Assuming that Baldwin and his bank had a good pledge agreement and had gotten themselves listed as owners of record, they would be the holders of the stock and would have received the dividends, which they could apply against King's debts.) And in view of the general virtues of the formal meeting rule, even outsiders like Canfield may be regarded fairly as acting at their own peril when they do not take the normal documentary precautions that any well advised third party about to buy substantially all of a corporation's assets would take.

A business planning moral

Let us dwell briefly on the latter point, since it contains an important practical lesson. Today, most lawyers for the buyer would negotiate a rather specific contract for sale and would require the selling corporation's officials to produce at least all of the following:

(1) a copy, certified by an appropriate state official, of the corporation's articles of organization, and a certificate of existence and good standing with respect to taxes, also from a state official;
(2) an up-to-date copy of the bylaws, certified by the corporation's secretary;
(3) a copy of the resolution of the board of directors authorizing the sale, accompanied by a certificate from the corporate secretary reciting that the action was taken by a proper majority of the directors at a meeting for which due notice was given and at which a quorum was present, and that there has been no substantive action affecting the resolution since then; and
(4) miscellaneous certificates attesting to the validity of certain signatures, to the identity of certain officers, and to the up-to-date character of the other documents.

Young corporate lawyers often view all of this as a lot of formalistic hocus pocus. But this is only because they are too inexperienced to appreciate how strongly the dark force of fraud can pull on the heart of man.

A moral for future Baldwins too

In favor of the outcome in *Baldwin,* one can point out not only that Canfield acted in somewhat sloppy and imprudent way (perhaps he could have sued his attorney for malpractice) but also that Baldwin's interest was first in time and that the formal meeting rule allocated the loss in an impartial and principled (though arbitrary) way. "First in time, first in right" seems an acceptable priority rule when no other convincing ones are available. On the other hand, Baldwin and his bank may not have been completely prudent either. Perhaps they could have compelled King, as full beneficial owner of MAMA, to take the property out of the corporation and mortgage it to them. The facts are insufficient to allow one to decide if this was feasible. But if it were, no good lawyer would have advised them to get a pledge of all of a corporation's stock instead of a mortgage or security interest directly in the corporation's assets. To do otherwise is to run a needless risk of subordination to the interest of later creditors of the corporation.

The violence behind the black letter façade

In any event, *Baldwin v. Canfield* illustrates a recurring characteristic of corporate law cases. Although the legal dispute may appear to revolve around the dullest imaginable rule of procedure, the controversy is often based upon a fraudulent or unfair assault by some human beings (usually controlling insiders) upon the financial interest of others.

§3.3 *Officers*

Appointment and removal

The board of directors usually has the power to appoint the corporation's officers.[1] It may also remove them with or without cause, even when the officers have an employment contract for a longer term.[2] Removal without cause in breach of such a contract might subject the corporation to liability for damages, of course. But in some cases the board might well prefer to pay damages than to retain the objectionable officer.

Who are officers

By and large, the directors have the power to carve up and delegate authority to such officers as they see fit. The traditional officers are the president, vice presidents, treasurer, and secretary. But a number of others are now common: chairman of the board, general counsel, division man-

§3.3 [1]MBCA §8.40; Cal. §312(a); Del. §142(b); N.Y. §715(a).
[2]MBCA §§8.43, 8.44; Cal. §312(b); Del. §§142(b), 142(e); N.Y. §716(a), (b).

agers, executive vice presidents, and so forth. Generally, only the more important executives in the corporation are called officers. Where the line is drawn is not always clear, and it may be different for different purposes. The term *officer* might be interpreted one way in connection with a statutory rule subjecting directors and officers to liability for profits made on purchases and sales of their company's stock within a six month period[3] and in a slightly different way in connection with a liability insurance policy covering directors and officers.[4] Frequently, a corporation's officer positions are set out in its bylaws, and one can usually identify officers as those executives who receive their formal appointments directly from the board of directors. In any event, for purposes of deciding whether many corporate law fiduciary doctrines are relevant, the distinction is not crucial. Unlike directors, who have a special status, officers may unquestionably be labeled agents of their corporations, as are lesser executives and ordinary employees, and they are subject to the fiduciary duty of agents.[5]

§3.3.1 Agency Principles

Agents and authority

Generally speaking, an agent is a person who acts on behalf of another, his principal, within the scope of his authority to so act and, even when granted discretion in carrying out his agency, is subject to the principal's control.[6] (In the present context the principal is the corporation considered as a legal person; but obviously, the specific controls over corporate officers are exercised by the board of directors.) Calling officers agents naturally leads lawyers to focus on their authority or legitimate power to bind the corporation to others or to take other action affecting the corporation's legal position. The conventional description, which follows agency law

[3] Securities Exchange Act §16(b). See Merrill Lynch, Pierce, Fenner & Smith, Inc. v. Livingston, 566 F.2d 1119 (9th Cir. 1978) (liability under §16(b) of the Securities Exchange Act is not based upon a person's title within a corporation, but on the existence of a relationship with the corporation that makes it more probable than not that the individual has access to insider information); Hurley, Who Is An "Officer" for Purposes of the Securities Exchange Act of 1934 — Colby v. Klune Revisited, 44 Fordham L. Rev. 489 (1975).

[4] For example, the term may be defined to mean company employees who are appointed to their jobs by the board of directors itself (or, in an odd case, by the stockholders). See New Lloyd's Policy Form for Directors' and Officers' Liability Insurance ("Lydando No. 1"), clause 2(A), reproduced in J. Bishop, The Law of Corporate Officers and Directors: Indemnification and Insurance, App. 77 (1981).

[5] See, e.g., N.C. Bus. Corp. Act §55-35: "Officers and directors shall be deemed to stand in a fiduciary relation to the corporation and to its shareholders and shall discharge the duties of their respective positions in good faith, and with that diligence and care which ordinarily prudent men would exercise under similar circumstances in like positions."

[6] Restatement (Second) of Agency §1 (1958).

terminology, is that officers' authority is of two types: *actual* authority and *apparent* authority. Actual authority is itself divided into two types — *express* and *implied*. The acts of an agent who lacks both actual and apparent authority may nevertheless be legally effective if they are properly *ratified* by appropriate representatives of the principal — for example, the directors or the shareholders.

Express actual authority

Express actual authority is usually given in the corporation's bylaws or in resolutions of the board of directors. Most corporations' bylaws list the officer positions and describe, in a general way, what each officer's powers are to be. For example, the president is often described as being the general manager or chief executive of the corporation. From time to time the board of directors will vote resolutions authorizing named officers to undertake certain unusual or especially important tasks. For example, they may authorize the president and executive vice president to try to negotiate an agreement to merge the corporation with another company. Express authority may also stem from provisions in the corporate statute or in the articles of incorporation, but this is rare. Most statutes, for example, MBCA Section 8.41, simply say that officers shall have such authority as may be provided in the bylaws or by resolution of the board of directors not inconsistent with the bylaws.

Implied actual authority

Implied actual authority, a more interesting concept, is often described as authority which is inherent in the office. It is based on what courts have recognized as customary in the corporate world or on the regular practice of a specific corporation when the directors or shareholders have known of it and have not objected.[7] Thus, the office of corporate secretary, by itself, is not generally considered to give the holder of it authority to bind the corporation.[8] The secretary's role is rather to keep the minutes of the director and shareholder meetings, to give notices, and to certify corporate records.[9] The treasurer also has no implied authority to bind the corporation, in most jurisdictions.[10] His role is to receive and keep the monies of the corporation and to disburse them as authorized.[11] For example, the treasurer may be empowered or directed to sign all checks drawn on the corporation's chief bank account, but that does not mean that he has authority to decide that the corporation should order certain goods and ser-

[7] See Note, Inherent Power as a Basis of a Corporate Officer's Authority to Contract, 57 Colum. L. Rev. 868 (1957); Note, Inherent Powers of Corporate Officers: Need for Statutory Definition, 61 Harv. L. Rev. 867 (1948); Restatement (Second) of Agency §8A (1958).

[8] Hollywyle Assn. Inc. v. Hollister, 324 A.2d 247 (Conn. 1973).

[9] 2A W. Fletcher, Cyclopedia Corporations §636 (perm. ed. 1975 & supp).

[10] United States v. Marin, 651 F.2d 24 (1st Cir. 1981).

[11] 2A W. Fletcher, Cyclopedia Corporations §654 (perm ed. 1975 & supp.).

vices and thus become liable to pay for them. Vice presidents are an even less favored lot; some cases say that they have no authority simply by the virtue of their office.[12] As for corporate presidents, the older cases took the niggardly view that a corporate president's implied authority consisted only of the power to preside at director and shareholder meetings.[13] But later cases, reacting to the obvious force of custom, began to recognize that corporate presidents usually should be viewed as having the powers of a general manager and, therefore, authority to bind the corporation in all ordinary business transactions.[14]

Ordinary vs. extraordinary acts

The distinction between ordinary and extraordinary business transactions and corporate actions can be elaborated by a variety of verbal formulae, and there are some relatively clear examples suggesting what the concepts mean. Few well-informed businessmen would suppose that a corporate president, merely by virtue of his office, has authority to commit his company to the sale of all its assets, or to a public sale and distribution of a new series of stock. But most would suppose that he could commit the corporation to the purchase of raw materials used in the corporation's regular operations so long as the purchase was not of extraordinary magnitude. But the scope of presidential authority is inevitably unclear. One cannot, by consulting either reason or practice or case law, draw up a definitive list, valid for all corporate presidents in all industries, of the particular kinds of actions that corporate presidents may properly take, simply by virtue of their office. The authority that is fairly implied does and should vary with the size and nature of the business, industry practice, and the like, and it can be expected to vary over time.

Apparent authority

The role of custom and ordinary practice is also important to the concept of apparent or ostensible authority. Under this concept, a corporation may be bound by the actions of an officer when the corporation somehow manifests to a third party that the officer may act in its behalf and the third party in good faith relies on the existence of such apparent authority.[15] Often the manifestation consists of a course of past conduct by the corporation and its officer. But industry custom may have a bearing on whether a particular corporate act should be interpreted as being such a mani-

[12] Russell v. Washington Sav. Bank, 23 App. D.C. 398 (1904); 2A W. Fletcher, Cyclopedia Corporations §627 (perm. ed. 1975 & supp.).

[13] See Note, Authority of a Corporation President to Bind the Corporation by Virtue of His Office, 50 Yale L.J. 348 (1940).

[14] Perlmuter Printing Co. v. Strome, Inc. 436 F. Supp. 409 (N.D. Ohio 1976); Ruscito v. F-Dyne Electronics Co., Inc., 411 A.2d 1371 (Conn. 1979); 2A W. Fletcher, Cyclopedia Corporations §553 (perm. ed. 1975 & supp.).

[15] Restatement (Second) of Agency §§8, 27 (1958).

festation. For example, by appointing an officer called "the president" of itself, X Corporation, a company manufacturing widgets, may be construed as signaling to the world that the officer has authority to negotiate contracts for the sale of widgets in customary amounts, say, in orders ranging from one hundred to one million widgets. The belief exists, let us suppose, because all other widget companies have been willing to sell up to one million widgets without pausing to seek board approval or to bring in lawyers to design the transaction, and purchasers have always dealt solely with widget company vice presidents for sales or, at most, with the company president. Suppose that X Corporation's directors have in fact adopted a resolution directing its president to seek board approval for all contracts for the sale of 100,000 widgets. The corporation has expressly negated *actual* presidential authority — *including implied actual authority* — to make larger sales. But if a purchaser does not know of this limitation and in good faith negotiates a sale with X Corporation's president for 500,000 widgets, it is unlikely, given the doctrine of apparent authority, that the corporation could disclaim the contract and avoid having to perform or pay damages. In effect, if the directors want to create a unique distribution of powers between themselves and their president, it is up to them to communicate this arrangement effectively to the outside world.

§3.3.2 Kinds of Litigation About Authority

Forces limiting litigation

It should be clear that, despite the vagueness of the concepts of implied and apparent authority, many factors operate to keep issues about officers' scope of authority from becoming litigated. Corporate bylaws do offer some guidance. Many corporations are cautious: They make it a practice to issue board resolutions authorizing officers to do specifically identified important tasks, even when the resolutions may not be necessary. Industry practice does often provide clear guidance about whether recurring transactions fall within the inherent authority of certain officers. Corporate officers may do something unusual and not clearly authorized, but the board may then agree that it was a good step to take and may authorize or ratify the action.[16] Alternatively, corporate officers may do something unusual and not clearly authorized, but then be prevented by their board or superior officers from doing it again; and the misstep may not have created a litigable problem with the third party.

Kinds of litigation about authority

In fact, there are only a few conditions under which uncertainty over the scope of authority is likely to create litigation. Two patterns stand out. First, one of the parties to a relationship may regret having entered (or not

[16] See 2A W. Fletcher, Cyclopedia Corporations §§750-785 (perm. ed. 1975 & supp.).

entered) a contract with the other. Thus, the corporation may want to weasel out of a bad deal made on its behalf by some officer and may try to use the alleged lack of authority of its officer as an excuse for doing so. Correlatively, the third party may want to take advantage of an alleged good deal and may insist that its expectations about the authority of the person acting for the corporation were not disingenuous or unreasonable.

Second, the dispute over scope of authority may reflect a conflict among major participants in the enterprise: It may be a form in which internecine warfare expresses itself. For example, such conflicts are often at the bottom of the cases dealing with the question whether a corporate president or other officer may initiate litigation or arbitration in the corporation's name. In the terminology developed in the next chapter, these cases involve a conflict of interest falling within the mixed motive category.

Example

As an example of the first kind of dispute, with a third party invoking apparent authority to claim the benefits of an alleged (unusually sweet) deal, consider *General Overseas Films, Ltd. v. Robin International, Inc.*[17] Reisini, chief executive officer of Robin, prevailed upon a company (GOF) that had lent money to Robin to extend the loan, partly by having one Kraft, a vice president and the treasurer of Anaconda, a large public corporation, represent to GOF that Anaconda would guarantee repayment of the extended loan. When GOF tried to enforce the alleged guarantee, Anaconda defended on the ground of Kraft's lack of authority, and won. GOF claimed Kraft had apparent authority, since Anaconda had placed him in a "high and visible corporate position" and its bylaws gave the treasurer authority to sign checks, notes, and other evidences of indebtedness. The court rightly rejected these arguments. It pointed out that they might have force if the transaction in question was a normal one but that it was extraordinary. For-profit, nonfinancial business corporations like Anaconda do not habitually give uncompensated guarantees of the debts of unrelated corporations! Any businessman hearing Kraft's promises should have been suspicious and should therefore have made inquiry into his authority before relying on them. (Good practice would call for him to demand a certified copy of an Anaconda board resolution explicitly granting Kraft the authority to sign a particular guarantee agreement expressly covering the extended loan.) In short, reliance on Kraft's representations was, under the circumstances, unreasonable.

Another example

Now consider an example of the first kind of dispute, which involved the corporation claiming *lack* of authority in order to weasel out of a deal

[17] 542 F. Supp. 684 (S.D.N.Y. 1982), aff'd without op., 718 F.2d 1085 (2d Cir. 1983).

that turned sour: *Yucca Mining & Petroleum Co. v. Howard C. Phillips Oil Co.*[18] Yucca and Phillips had a contract whereby Yucca was to pay Phillips $12,000 to drill two wells on certain leased land. According to that version of the conflicting testimony accepted by the trial court, after one dry well was dug, Yucca's president agreed that further drilling on the originally identified land would be inadvisable, and drilling was then done at a different location. The second hole was also dry. Yucca's disappointed board of directors caused it to bring suit for damages for breach of contract, or for rescission, arguing that the corporation should not be bound by the action of its president, that is, his alleged oral modification of the contract. Not surprisingly, the court denied relief.

Corporate benefit as key?

The interesting point about the case is that the court seemed to feel it was not worth the effort to decide which of the traditional concepts — apparent authority, implied authority, waiver, estoppel, or the like — ought to be invoked. Instead, it seemed to enunciate the unusual view that so long as the officer acts for the benefit of the corporation the latter is bound.

> In the instant case, all of the actions of [Yucca's president, a liaison director, and its geologist] were for the benefit of the corporation, which would have profited if the drilling had been successful. Under such circumstances, the corporation was bound by the actions taken on its behalf, and cannot be relieved by claiming lack of authority. . . . Yucca was to have the benefits of the contract as modified, so it must also be charged with the burdens, and it is unnecessary for us to determine under which one or more of the aforementioned theories such result is reached. . . . [19]

A weak theory

This corporate benefit reasoning simply cannot serve as an adequate guide to what the case law is or should be, however. Consider Jack, the young president of New England Dairy Corporation, who agrees with Oldman to sell the corporation's entire assets — 1 million dairy cows — to Oldman in return for six small magic beans. Though terribly naive, Jack does think he is acting for the benefit of the corporation. Under the *Yucca* reasoning, if taken at face value, that would end the matter: the corporation would be bound to comply with the absurd and unfair contract. But, let us suppose, Oldman knew that Jack was naive, that he was making a serious mistake, and that corporate presidents generally have to seek board approval before they contract to sell their company's entire assets. Surely Oldman would not be allowed, even by the *Yucca* court, to keep his

[18] 365 P.2d 925 (N.M. 1961).
[19] Id. at 929.

bargain. Indeed, even if Oldman also believed the beans were magic and very valuable (because he was daft), and he honestly believed that Jack had authority to conclude the contract for sale (because he was ignorant of the customary corporate practice), it is probable that most courts would still not uphold the bargain.

Expectations should be reasonable

This last point is supported by a Delaware case famous for its jury instructions on an officer's authority.[20] The court declared that authority may stem from a statute, corporate charter, bylaw, board resolution, a course of conduct on the part of the officer and the corporation, or, in the case of "acts of an ordinary nature," from "usage or necessity." (The last-mentioned kind of authority might be classified as implied rather than apparent authority.) It gave no intimation that any honest expectation of a third party will suffice to bind the corporation to the acts of its agents. In effect, the traditional case law requires third party expectations to be not only genuine but also *reasonable*, that is, in accord with customary conceptions as to the distribution of authority within corporations.

Why a requirement of reasonableness

Why, one may ask, does traditional agency law require third parties to be reasonable in this sense? Why don't courts follow the minority view expressed in the North Carolina statute,[21] which is very liberal in protecting third parties, or the expansionary conception of authority put forward by some commentators?[22] The general answer is that they are trying to effect an *efficient* accommodation of competing interests. On the one hand is the interest of corporate investors in legal rules that help preserve the integrity of the presumably efficient system of centralized management. The shareholders expect — or rationally ought to want it to be the case — that their elected representatives, the directors, will have ultimate control over the allocation of power within the corporation. For efficiency's sake, corporate presidents should not be able to unilaterally expand the scope of their jobs. On the other hand are the interests of parties who deal with

[20]Joseph Greenspon's Sons Iron & Steel Co. v. Pecos Valley Gas Co., 156 A. 350 (Del. Superior Ct. 1931) (jury charge of Rodney, J.).

[21]N.C. Bus. Corp. Act §55-36, which validates, for "innocent third parties," all deeds, mortgages, contracts, notes, and so forth so long as signed "in the ordinary course of business" by a president or a vice president and attested or countersigned by a secretary or assistant secretary. The statute doesn't state that the innocent third parties must have reasonable beliefs about usage and custom, or that they should have relied on a certain course of conduct.

[22]See Note, Inherent Power as a Basis of a Corporate Officer's Authority to Contract, 57 Colum. L. Rev. 868, 886 (1957) (urging inherent authority be found where third party knows of no irregularity, or has no reason to know of an irregularity in the officer's authority, even though basic elements of apparent authority are absent and corporation is completely faultless).

corporations. These parties do not want to be put to the choice of either continually finding out about the formal authority structures of each corporation with which they deal — a costly and cumbersome process — or acting with these corporations' apparent agents at their peril. For the most part, net social efficiency calls for respecting third parties' interest. It is obviously more expeditious to have a legal rule that allows third parties to rely on what is the customary division of authority, without making formal checks, unless they receive specific notice to the contrary. This is especially true when the corporation that wants to institute an unusual division of powers can set up its own inhouse methods of disciplining errant officers.

Third party sometimes cheapest cost avoider

The exceptions to the principle of letting corporations be responsible for enforcing their own systems of delegated authority only come about when the third party is in a better position to enforce them, that is, when the cheapest action to avert a threat to the socially valuable system of centralized management seems to be an action on the part of third parties. The board of directors cannot be constantly monitoring the corporate president's actions, to see whether he exceeds his authority. Yet a third party negotiating a particular deal cannot help but notice what the corporation's officer is purporting to be able to do. He will usually notice when the president is attempting to do something quite unusual in terms of the customary practice of the corporation or the industry. His marginal cost, at that point, of making further inquiries or seeking proof of authority to do unusual acts is rather small. Thus, it does not seem too much to hold third parties to the consequences of a rule that puts the risks on them when they enter an arrangement knowing (or having reason to know) that the actions of the officer on the other side probably exceed the authority granted by his corporation or the authority typically assumed to be possessed by similar officers. Nor is it harsh to charge third parties who are businessmen with knowledge of what is customary or inherent authority within the industries in which they operate. For virtually all businessmen will in fact have such knowledge; it is desirable to encourage them to have it; and a rule based on what each third party in fact believed would simply invite litigation and perjury.

Example of intracompany dispute

The second kind of dispute about officers' authority reflects conflicts among the participants in a company.[23] The setting is usually a close corporation. Suppose Andy and his spouse own half the stock of Excellent Cor-

[23]See, e.g., the following interesting sequence of four cases: Sterling Indus., Inc. v. Ball Bearing Pen Corp., 84 N.E.2d 790 (N.Y. 1949); Rothman & Schneider, Inc. v. Beckerman, 141 N.E.2d 610 (N.Y. 1957); Paloma Frocks, Inc. v. Shamokin Sportswear Corp., 147 N.E.2d 779 (N.Y. 1958); West View Hills, Inc. v. Lizau Realty Corp., 160 N.E.2d 622 (N.Y. 1959).

poration and are two of its directors; Barbara and her spouse own the other half of the stock and are the other two directors. Andy is the president of the company; Barbara is the vice president, secretary, and treasurer. Barbara wants to bring a suit in the name of Excellent Corporation against Chumly, Andy's son-in-law who was made a sales employee of the corporation at Andy's insistence. The claim is that Chumly wrongfully converted corporate assets to his own use. Andy and his spouse object to the bringing of the litigation. Chumly defends on the ground that Barbara does not have authority to initiate the suit.

In cases like this, courts have seemed to accept the issue as being one of authority. They have purported to find it relevant whether the suit was against an insider or not (a suit against Andy himself would presumably be easier to permit than one against Chumly), and whether the board of directors actually voted that the suit not be brought (in which case, apparently, their decision would be respected) or whether the board was deadlocked or did not formally vote on the matter at all (in which case the suit might proceed despite the fact that a majority of directors does not affirmatively support the bringing of a suit).

Real issue is conflict of interest

What is really at issue in these cases, of course, is not primarily a question of authority, but a conflict of interest. It is clear that *ordinarily* the board of directors may vote to preclude the bringing by the corporation of a suit and may thus override the corporate president. It is also clear that corporate presidents ought to be able, without explicit board approval, to cause their corporations to bring a variety of lawsuits in the *ordinary* course. The trouble arises — and the case therefore becomes *non*ordinary and thus legitimately subjected to *different* rules — where the directors have mixed motives. Andy and his spouse may have opposed the lawsuit in our example, not because they believe it would not be in Excellent's best interest, but because they want to protect their son-in-law. Indeed, the conversion by Chumly of Excellent's assets may actually have been in their own interest if they were intending to make a substantial gift to Chumly and his wife. For a dollar taken by Chumly from the company only costs them 50 cents (the other half coming from the stockholder claims of Barbara and spouse), whereas a dollar from their own assets would cost a dollar. In this kind of situation, it is not surprising that courts find a way to let the lawsuit proceed — even despite apparently contrary precedent.[24] What is surprising is that their reasoning seems confined to the language of presumptive

[24] See, for example, how the court in *Rothman & Schneider,* which resembles the hypothetical in the text, dealt with the prior opinion in *Sterling Industries.* (Both cases are cited in footnote 23 supra.)

or inherent authority. It might be better for courts to simply say that, when director opposition to the bringing of a corporate suit is infected with a conflict of interest, any officer acting in good faith may initiate the suit.

§3.4 *The Duty of Care Versus the Business Judgment Rule*

Duty of care

Nowhere is the tension between the policies of giving managers ample discretion and trying to keep them accountable as obvious as in the cases invoking the duty of care, the business judgment rule, or both. Statutes and case law say that directors and officers owe their corporations a duty of care: They must exercise that degree of skill, diligence, and care that a reasonably prudent person would exercise in similar circumstances.[1] At times, some authorities have applied the stricter formulation that the director or officer must act as a reasonably prudent person would act in the conduct of his own affairs.[2] It is doubtful whether this difference in standard has affected the outcome of cases. In any event, by analogy to the duty of care concept used in tort law, violation of the director's or officer's duty of care is frequently described as negligence.

Business judgment rule (BJR)

In contrast to this worrisome doctrine, the mere mention of the business judgment rule brings smiles of relief to corporate directors. In a sense, the business judgment rule is just a corollary of the usual statutory provision that it is the directors who shall manage the corporation.[3] The rule is simply that the business judgment of the directors will not be challenged or overturned by courts or shareholders, and the directors will not be held liable for the consequences of their exercise of business judgment — even for judgments that appear to have been clear mistakes — unless certain exceptions apply. Put another way, the rule is "a presumption that in making a business decision, the directors of a corporation acted on an

§3.4 [1]MBCA §8.30(a) (director's duty to act in good faith, with due care, and in manner he reasonably believes to be in the best interests of the corporation); Cal. §309; N.Y. §715(h); Guth v. Loft, Inc., 5 A.2d 503 (Del. Ch. 1939), aff'd, 19 A.2d 721 (Del. 1941). See generally American Law Institute, Principles of Corporate Governance: Analysis and Recommendations, tent. draft no. 3 (April 13, 1984), at 1-84 (part on duty of care and business judgment rule) (hereinafter cited as ALI Corp. Gov., t.d. no. 3).

[2]See Comment to N.Y. § 717, "Duty of Directors and Officers" (McKinney 1963); former Pa. Bus. Corp. Law §408, discussed in Selheimer v. Manganese Corp. of America, 224 A.2d 634 (Pa. 1966).

[3]Smith v. Van Gorkom, 488 A.2d 858, 872 (Del. 1985).

informed basis in good faith and in the honest belief that the action was taken in the best interests of the company."[4]

Challenges not precluded by BJR

By any reckoning, the kinds of actions and judgments not protected by the business judgment rule are extremely important, although courts do differ in their formulation of the exceptions. Some say that no challenge to the directors' judgments will be considered on the merits unless the judgment in question was tainted by fraud, conflict of interest, or illegality;[5] others say, unless the alleged defect in the directors' judgment rises to the level of fraud;[6] still others, unless it rises to the level of gross negligence.[7] The basic idea of the fraud and conflict of interest exceptions is that, when directors are shown to have been trying to further their own personal ends, or to have been strongly tempted to bias the terms of a transaction in their own interest, their judgments are not really within the class of discretionary exercises of power on behalf of the corporation that we want to protect. The idea behind the illegality exception is that shareholders' derivative suits can be a useful supplement to the enforcement activities of public prosecutors and regulatory agencies.

Tension between duty of care and BJR

At first blush, the business judgment rule seems to take away much of the force of the duty of care. Virtually all courts agree that directors will not be held liable for "honest mistakes" of judgment. But most of them also say, in effect, that directors cannot act negligently (or in a grossly negligent way). Is the duty of care simply gobbledygook, then, or a mere exhortation rather than an enforceable legal duty? Linguistically, one can construct an accommodation of the two ideas that makes them *logically* consistent with each other. Here is one such formulation: the directors' business judgment cannot be attacked unless their judgment was arrived at in a negligent manner, or was tainted by fraud, conflict of interest, or illegality. Put another way (as courts have sometimes put it), the business judgment rule presupposes that reasonable diligence lies behind the judgment in ques-

[4] Aronson v. Lewis, 473 A.2d 805, 812 (Del. 1984). See also Pogostin v. Rice, 480 A.2d 619 (Del. 1984); Zapata Corp. v. Maldonado, 430 A.2d 779 (Del. 1981); Gimbel v. The Signal Companies, Inc., 316 A.2d 599 (Del. Ch. 1974), aff'd, 316 A.2d 619 (Del. 1974).

[5] E.g., Shlensky v. Wrigley, 237 N.E.2d 776, 780 (Ill. App. 1968). See also Maldonado v. Flynn, 413 A.2d 1251, 1255-1256 (Del. Ch. 1980), rev'd, 430 A.2d 779 (Del. 1981).

[6] Auerbach v. Bennett, 393 N.E.2d 994, 1000 (N.Y. 1979).

[7] Bucyrus-Erie Co. v. General Prod. Corp., 643 F.2d 413 (6th Cir. 1981); see also Smith v. Van Gorkom, 488 A.2d 858, 873 (Del. 1985). Note that decisions such as this do *not* mean to imply that the business judgment rule precludes a suit based on fraud or self-dealing by the directors. The "gross negligence" formulation is concerned only with adjusting the business judgment rule to the fiduciary duty of care; the duty of loyalty (see chapter 4) is another matter.

tion.[8] But making the concepts *practically* consistent is another matter: drawing the line between an honest mistake and a negligent one can be difficult.

§3.4.1 Case Law Development of Duty of Care

Liability for inactive directors

Violation of the duty of care might arise from inactivity, from grossly negligent behavior, or from simple negligence. The distinction might be compared to three levels of bad acting: going on stage but failing to say one's lines, because one didn't even try to memorize them; going on stage and murdering one's lines, because one learned the lines poorly; and going on stage and saying the lines correctly but doing a bad job of acting, because one lacks talent or did not rehearse enough. As a general matter, most successful attacks on directors resemble the first level, that is, a simple failure, after having become a director, to engage in the basic activities of that role. Directors have been found to violate their duty of care when they failed to attend meetings, to learn the basic facts about the business of the corporation, to read a reasonable quantity of reports, to seek needed help when a danger signal appeared, or when they have otherwise neglected to go through the standard motions of diligent behavior.[9] The

[8] The classic statement of this point is in Casey v. Woodruff, 49 N.Y.S.2d 625, 643 (S. Ct. 1944). A representative recent case is Lussier v. Mau-Van Development, Inc., 667 P.2d 804, 817 (Hawaii Ct. App. 1983). See also ALI Corp. Gov., t.d. no. 3, at 56-69 (discussing prerequisites to the protection afforded by business judgment rule:

(1) a conscious exercise of judgment;
(2) an informed decision;
(3) good faith and no self-interest; and
(4) a rational basis).

[9] A good example is given by Francis v. United Jersey Bank, 432 A.2d 814 (N.J. 1981), where a director and the largest shareholder of a corporation, after the death of her husband, took no interest in the company, thus giving her sons the opportunity to embezzle corporate funds. (Plaintiffs were trustees in bankruptcy of the corporation and therefore represented its creditors. Note that in an insolvent corporation creditors acquire the status of residual claimants and can enforce duties principally designed for the benefit of shareholders.) The court was unimpressed by the claims that she was old, depressed, alcoholic, and ignorant of business affairs; such a person should not become a director. (In fact, since the trustees were simply trying to get at the assets in the estate of the deceased husband, who was the prime mover in the corporation, the holding was not as hardnosed as it seems.)

From a planning perspective, the opinion in *Francis* offers useful guidelines as to what every director should do:

(1) get a rudimentary understanding of the business;
(2) keep informed about the corporation's activities;

courts often talk tough in these cases and warn so-called figurehead directors — those who become directors at the request of spouses or friends and as an "accommodation" — that the law will not excuse them for failing to behave like real directors. Even here, however, the inactive or naive director sometimes gets off the hook.[10] And in other cases, the undoubted negligence of directors may not result in liability if the plaintiff cannot show that the negligence proximately caused damages to the corporation.[11]

Liability for simple negligence rare

Cases in which active directors are nevertheless held liable are rarer. In fact, the total number of reported cases in which derivative actions against directors of nonfinancial corporations were actually won on the merits on the basis of simple negligence uncomplicated by any fraud or self-dealing is small. Professor Bishop, in a search of cases over several decades, found only four.[12] To be sure, the number of decided cases does not tell the whole story, since most suits against directors, whether based on negligence or something else, are settled, and since all the cases brought, if publicized within the corporate world, may terrify other directors into being more careful. But the case law experience must still lead us to wonder whether the courts are serious when they say directors may be held liable for negligence.

Cases sometimes suggest self-dealing

This feeling is reinforced when we examine some of the better known cases in a critical way. Not infrequently, the facts suggest that the directors were actually being sued and held liable because of wrongful self-interested conduct — for a violation of their fiduciary duty of *loyalty* — and the courts' talk about duty of care is simply a way of letting the plaintiffs win without having to prove all the elements of a wrongful conflict of interest transaction.[13] (Such proof may be difficult and the evidence may be within the defendants' control.)

---

(3) engage in "a general monitoring of corporate affairs and activities";
(4) attend board meetings regularly;
(5) review financial statements regularly; and
(6) make inquiries into doubtful matters, raise objections to apparently illegal actions, and consult counsel and/or resign if corrections aren't made.

[10] See, e.g., Allied Freightways, Inc. v. Cholfin, 91 N.E.2d 765 (Mass. 1950) (passive accommodation director — the wife of another director — escapes liability under gross negligence standard).

[11] See Barnes v. Andrews, 298 F. 614, 616-617 (S.D.N.Y. 1924) (Learned Hand, J.).

[12] Bishop, Sitting Ducks and Decoy Ducks: New Trends in the Indemnification of Corporate Directors and Officers, 77 Yale L.J. 1078, 1099-1100 (1968). See also Cohn, Demise of the Director's Duty of Care: Judicial Avoidance of Standards and Sanctions Through the Business Judgment Rule, 62 Tex. L. Rev. 591 (1983). An important later case, Smith v. Van Gorkom, will be discussed shortly.

[13] See Bishop, note 12 supra, at 1100, for a similar analysis of the Selheimer case cited in

In *Litwin v. Allen*,[14] for example, the directors of the Guaranty Trust Company had approved the purchase of certain convertible debentures with an option in Allegheny Corporation, the seller, to repurchase. The directors were among the most experienced risk assessors in the investment or commercial banking communities. Yet a New York court found that their approval of the bond purchase was negligent. Specifically, it found that the entire arrangement was so improvident, so risky, so unusual and unnecessary as to be the contrary to fundamental conceptions of prudent banking practice.[15] But the court's reasoning is not persuasive, even on its own terms.

Example of *Litwin v. Allen*

First, the fact that a transaction is unique can hardly be a basis for finding that it is negligent to undertake it.

Second, the transaction was not really very unique. A repurchase agreement of the sort involved simply means that in effect the Guaranty Trust Company was making a *secured loan* to the Allegheny Corporation. In fact, the transaction clearly was a substitute for a loan, which Allegheny Corporation was prohibited from accepting directly because of a borrowing limitation in its charter.

Third, it is of course possible that directors could be negligent because they approve a loan that is excessively risky, or more precisely, that has a risk that is excessive in relation to the risk that would be incurred in other investments with comparable expected return. But the court in fact made no serious inquiry into this question, which in any event would seem to fall clearly within the ambit of the business judgment rule.

Clue to the result

The clue as to why the court resorted to such a formalistic and erroneous application of the duty of care is that the Guaranty Trust Company was an affiliate of, and controlled by, the J. P. Morgan Company, and the Allegheny Corporation was part of the so-called Van Sweringen business empire. J. P. Morgan and Company and all its affiliates together had quite an investment in the Van Sweringen empire, and a decline in the value of Allegheny stock was threatening the stability of all these investments. Thus, although the risk inherent in the debenture purchase transaction was the potential decrease in the value of the debentures, a risk that would be borne solely by Guaranty Trust Company, the potential benefit was the avoidance of the even greater loss of the total investment of the J. P. Morgan affiliates in the Van Sweringen empire, a benefit that would

note 2 supra. On its face it is a duty of care case, he says, but "the facts are heavy with the odor of self-dealing. . . ."

[14] 25 N.Y.S.2d 667 (S. Ct. 1940).

[15] Id. at 699.

accrue to various parts of the Morgan complex. In other words, the transaction could be seen as one that was not being effected *for the best interest* of the Guaranty Trust Company. It was a transaction in which there was an apparent conflict of interest between the injured corporation and other companies that controlled it.

Why talk negligence instead of self-dealing

Why didn't the court deal with the conflict of interest problem directly? The court's own words suggest the answer: "There is *no evidence* in this case of any improper influence or domination of the directors or officers of the Trust Company or of the Guaranty Company by J. P. Morgan & Co. . . . "[16] Evidence of how Morgan's top management might have influenced the directors of the Trust company would be very difficult for the plaintiffs, who were shareholders of the Trust Company, to get. In addition, evidence needed to show *wrongful* self-dealing, that is, evidence about the actual riskiness, expected return, and hence true value of the convertible debentures, would have been equally difficult to present in a conclusive way. One may suspect, then, that the court's twisted reasoning toward the conclusion that there was a violation of the duty of care was simply a way of giving the plaintiffs a break in a situation where equity seemed to require it.

Example of *Smith v. Van Gorkom*

In view of this case law background, the Delaware Supreme Court's controversial 1985 decision in *Smith v. Van Gorkom*[17] is quite striking. Shareholders brought a class action seeking rescission of a cash-out merger of their company into another or, in the alternative, damages from defendant members of the board of directors whom they charged with breach of their duty of care in approving the merger. The court of chancery held for defendants on the grounds that the directors were protected by the business judgment rule and the shareholder vote on the merger was fully informed. But the Delaware Supreme Court reversed and directed judgment for the plaintiffs. It held that the board's approval of the merger agreement wasn't the product of an informed business judgment, that the board's subsequent curative efforts were ineffectual, and that the board didn't deal with "complete candor" with the shareholders.

Duty to become informed

Perhaps the key legal proposition of the case is that, though the business judgment rule does create a presumption that the board's decision was an informed one, plaintiffs can rebut the presumption (and they did, in the *Van Gorkom* case) by showing that the directors failed to meet their duty to inform themselves "prior to making a business decision, of all material

[16] Id. at 694 (emphasis added).
[17] 488 A.2d 858 (Del. 1985).

information reasonably available to them."[18] The business judgment rule doesn't shield unadvised judgments. This duty to become informed is, of course, an aspect of the duty of care. The court stated that the concept of gross negligence was the proper standard for determining whether the board's business judgment was an informed one.

Factors in the result

The opinion in *Van Gorkom* is heavily oriented to the facts. Of obvious importance to the result was the fact that the directors approved the merger at a relatively brief, quickly called meeting upon the basis of a 20 minute oral presentation by Van Gorkom, the chairman and chief executive officer, without having or reviewing the merger documents and without having or calling for a serious valuation study, either by directors and officers or by an outside investment banking firm. Of apparent importance to the result (on my reading) is the circumstance that Van Gorkom seems to have been a rather autocratic leader who acted and made decisions in a solitary rather than a consultative fashion, without soliciting substantial discussion with and feedback from the company's top officers and board members. The court apparently thought it was an abdication of duty for the other directors to submit to this kind of domineering leadership.[19] The court also discounted the significance of the fact that the cash-out merger price was at a premium over the previous market price of the company's stock, since the merger price was not based on any serious effort to value the company. It also discounted the fact that the merger proposal was subjected to a market test (the directors reserved time in which to consider other, better offers), since the test was "virtually meaningless" in light of the terms and time limitations governing it. And it rejected the defense that the directors were highly sophisticated and experienced persons (they were) on the ground that their general expertise did not give them a license to shoot from the hip in such an important transaction.

§3.4.2 Duty of Care as Responsibility for Systems

The monitoring model

In large corporations, the directors' role seems confined in practice to giving advice and counsel to the president, acting in crisis situations, and reviewing broad policy decisions. Commentators have used this fact as

[18] Id. at 872, quoting Aronson v. Lewis, 473 A.2d 805, 812 (Del. 1984).

[19] Recall our discussion earlier in this chapter of Baldwin v. Canfield. Of course, one could take the view, implicit in the *Van Gorkom* dissent, that strong leadership, quick action, and avoidance of committees and red tape make the business world work better or, at the least, that it should be permissible for directors of particular companies to allow them to be run under such a philosophy.

part of an argument for explicit legal recognition of a "monitoring" model of the board, plus reforms to encourage real monitoring by directors of officers' performance.[20] There has been resistance to the policemen image conjured up by the monitoring model, and even counterargument to the effect that there is a substantial role for the board of the large modern corporation to play in substantive business decision making.[21] But even under the latter approach, directors would principally make strategic decisions rather than direct day-to-day operations.

Nature of monitoring duties: the *Allis-Chalmers* case

A question raised by the inevitably general, even detached, role of the board in very large corporations is, What is the nature of the directors' responsibility for the misconduct of operating level managers and employees? This question was presented to the Delaware Supreme Court in *Graham v. Allis-Chalmers Manufacturing Co.*,[22] a case arising out of the notorious electrical equipment price-fixing conspiracy.[23] The Department of Justice obtained indictments charging criminal violation of the federal antitrust laws by the price fixing activities of various middle level executives of Allis-Chalmers and other companies in the heavy electrical equipment industries. Pleas of guilty were entered by the corporation and certain of its employees, who went to jail. Certain shareholders brought a derivative suit in the Delaware courts to recover, from the directors and from nondirector employees, damages Allis-Chalmers was claimed to have suffered by reason of the antitrust violations and the ensuing imposition of penalties. The Delaware Supreme Court confirmed a Vice Chancellor's ruling that the defendant directors were not liable. It characterized the plaintiffs' proposed interpretation of the duty of care as calling for an affirmative duty to install a system of internal monitoring of the legality of employees' conduct, and it rejected the idea.

> The precise charge made against these director defendants is that, even though they had no knowledge or any suspicion of wrongdoing on the part of the company's employees, they still should have put into effect a *system of watchfulness* which would have brought such misconduct to their attention in

[20] The major pioneer in developing this model is Professor Melvin Eisenberg. See his The Structure of the Corporation: A Legal Analysis (1976). See also Dent, The Revolution in Corporate Governance, the Monitoring Board, and the Director's Duty of Care, 61 B.U.L. Rev. 623 (1981).

[21] Haft, Business Decisions by the New Board: Behavioral Science and Corporate Law, 80 Mich. L. Rev. 1 (1981).

[22] 188 A.2d 125 (Del. 1963).

[23] See Geis, On White-Collar Crime: The Heavy Electrical Equipment Antitrust Cases of 1961, in Corporate and Governmental Deviance: Problems of Organizational Behavior in Contemporary Society 123 (M. Erman & R. Lundman eds., 2d ed. 1982).

> ample time to have brought it to an end. However, . . . directors are entitled to rely on the honesty and integrity of their subordinates until something occurs to put them on suspicion that something is wrong. If such occurs and goes unheeded, then liability of the directors might well follow, but absent cause for suspicion there is no duty upon the directors to install and operate a corporate system of espionage to ferret out wrongdoing which they have no reason to suspect exists.[24]

The court's arguments

In reaching this result, the court was influenced by several factors. Allis-Chalmers' large size — its 31,000-plus employees, 24 plants, and 145 sales offices, for example — confined the directors' role, according to the court, to "the broad policy decisions." Its policy of decentralizing decision making authority was also noted by the court, which apparently thought it to be a good idea and somehow inconsistent with top-down monitoring systems. An internal monitoring system also connotes, to some persons, unwholesome snooping, a gratuitous insult to the dignity and integrity of corporate employees, and a business policy that may create more costs in terms of bad employee morale than it is worth. All of this may be implicit in the court's exaggerated rhetorical description of the plaintiff's proposal as being to establish a system of "espionage." And finally, the directors were entitled to rely in good faith upon books of account or reports made by officers, as well as upon other corporate records, under a statutory provision now appearing as Section 141(e) of the Delaware General Corporation Law, which has analogues in MBCA Section 8.30(b) and the statutes of other states.[25]

Rebuttals

Of course, none of these considerations really clinched the court's conclusion. The fact that giant size confines directors to broad policy decisions is beside the point. A decision by the directors ordering the corporation's legal counsel to design and implement a systematic legal compliance or legal audit program, as it is sometimes called, *would* be a broad policy decision. No one expects the directors to design or implement the program themselves. Furthermore, a policy of decentralizing decision making authority is not in fact inconsistent with a policy of monitoring whether employees obey the law, any more than it is inconsistent with internal accounting controls designed to make sure that employees do not steal the company's inventory or cash. A monitoring system might cause discomfort to employees who do not like to be watched. But it is a discomfort that may necessarily attend all efforts at supervision and control, and the cost seems warranted in light of widespread reports of corporate illegality. Moreover,

[24] 188 A.2d at 130 (emphasis added).
[25] E.g., Cal. §309; N.Y. §717.

no rational employee should feel personally insulted by an impartial system of controls applicable to virtually all of the corporation's employees. And finally, the statutory provisions about reliance upon corporate records are qualified by the condition that reliance must be in good faith. The good faith proviso can be interpreted to mean that directors may not rely when they spot something they should regard as suspicious or inadequate about the particular records or reports in question *or* about the corporation's system of procedures for generating records and reports. (In any event, policy makers might well consider clarifying the statutes to spell out this latter interpretation.)

A *judicially* required legal compliance program?

Despite the weakness of its reasoning, the Delaware court did seem to reject a general affirmative duty on the part of directors of large corporations to order implementation of a proactive legal compliance *system* of some sort and restricted their investigative duties to those arising when some suspicious *triggering event* occurs. Why?

Arguments against the idea

Perhaps a deeper motivation for the court's holding is to be found in the belief that the net result of the middle managers' price fixing activities actually was beneficial to the company and its shareholders. At least this may have been true prospectively, at the times when these managers made the relevant decisions. It may even have remained true after the discovery and the ensuing law suits! After all, undiscovered antitrust violations hurt consumers but help the offending corporation and its shareholders. Whether a violation is likely to be discovered and sanctioned, and if so, whether the risk is worth running, are questions of business judgment. Given these assumptions, the directors' institution of an effective legal compliance program would amount to an act that was wasteful, rather than careful, skillful, and diligent, as regards the interests of the corporation and its shareholders. No court would countenance a directorial decision ordering middle managers to violate important criminal statutes, of course, or a deliberate refusal of the directors to do anything about known continuing violations. But a court might think that a decision to have corporations incur the cost of creating a non–profit-maximizing legal compliance program should be expressly compelled by the legislature that enacted the laws whose compliance is in question, or at least left to management's discretion, rather than judicially made by reading an affirmative, specific duty to advance the public interest into *corporate* law duties whose historical purpose has been to ensure managerial regard for the interest of shareholders. If antitrust policies are so important, and if Congress thinks that the antitrust monitoring and enforcement devices that it explicitly legislated are inadequate, it has the option of deciding that a new law requiring corporate directors to monitor antitrust compliance would be a good way to help solve the problem. According to this argument, *judicial* creation of enforcement systems for regulatory statutes is a task that should be approached with caution, especially when the statute is federal and the court is a state court.

Internal accounting controls are a different matter

If this reading of the motivations behind the *Allis-Chalmers* result is correct, it would mean that the Delaware Supreme Court might yet find that directors of large corporations can violate their duty of care by failing to insure the existence of a system of *internal accounting controls.* Not having such a system might very well be thought to result in a risk of injury to shareholders that no reasonable director would normally incur. In so finding, the court would not be mandating an enforcement system for a regulatory statute aimed at protecting nonshareholder interests. Therefore, it would not contradict the spirit of *Allis-Chalmers.*

Federal requirement of such controls

Ironically, public corporations are now subject to federal statutory requirement that they devise and maintain a system of internal accounting controls. The requirement grew out of the foreign bribery scandals of the mid-1970s. It came to light that hundreds of U.S. corporations, through employees and agents, had made bribes of many millions of dollars to foreign government officials and politicians, in hopes of obtaining governmental purchase orders and regulatory favors that would enhance their business volume and profit.[26] The main concern of most investigators and reformers was not with corporate shareholders, despite some lip service in their direction, but with the impropriety of letting U.S. corporations contribute to the corruption of foreign governments. In many cases, the bribery may have helped corporate profits.

Foreign Corrupt Practices Act

Congress's response was the Foreign Corrupt Practices Act of 1977.[27] The key provision was one making it unlawful for U.S. corporations or their directors, officers, or agents (1) to make a bribe to a foreign official or foreign political party or party official or (2) to make payments to agents who they have reason to know will make such bribes, in order to assist the corporation in getting or retaining business for or with any person.[28] The definition of foreign official does *not* include any foreign government employee whose duties are essentially ministerial or clerical. Thus, so-called grease money payments such as those made to customs officials in many countries are not made illegal by this act.

[26] See SEC, Report on Questionable and Illegal Corporate Payments and Practices (Comm. Print 1976) (submitted to the Senate Committee on Banking, Housing and Urban Affairs, 94th Cong., 2d Sess.); Business Without Bribes, Newsweek, Feb. 19, 1979, at 63; Note, Effective Enforcement of the Foreign Corrupt Practices Act, 32 Stan. L. Rev. 561 (1980).

[27] 15 U.S.C. §§78a, 78m(b)(2)-78m(b)(3), 78dd-1, 78dd-2, 78ff.

[28] 15 U.S.C.A. §§78dd-1, 78dd-2.

Exchange Act §13(b)(2)

Because in many of the reported bribery cases various directors and top officers claimed not to have known what was going on, Congress also added an accounting controls provision. This provision, which became Section 13(b)(2) of the Securities Exchange Act, applies to all corporations having securities registered under the Act, or having to file reports under it, that is, to most public corporations in the United States. Such corporations have to make and keep books, records, and accounts that, in reasonable detail, fairly and accurately reflect their transactions and the dispositions of their assets. They must also "devise and maintain a system of internal accounting controls sufficient to provide reasonable assurances" that four conditions are met:

(1) Transactions are executed in accordance with management's general or specific authorization.
(2) Transactions are recorded as necessary (a) to permit preparation of financial statements in conformity with generally accepted accounting principles or any other criteria applicable to such statements and (b) to maintain accountability for assets.
(3) Access to assets is permitted only in accordance with management's general or specific authorization.
(4) The recorded accountability for assets is compared with the existing assets at reasonable intervals and appropriate action is taken with respect to any differences.

Potential impact

Two comments must be made about Section 13(b)(2). First, as a formal matter, its potential impact on corporations is great. Despite its genesis, the provision applies to virtually all public corporations, not just those engaging in foreign trade. It applies to accounting controls with respect to all kinds of corporate transactions and uses of assets; it is not at all restricted to controls that might uncover foreign bribes. Because of its generality and its apparently formless wording, corporate managers and attorneys later began to fear that the SEC, by virtue of its ability to make rules spelling out and implementing the provision, would use it to embark on a sweeping program of mandated reforms of corporations' internal communication and control systems. Thus far, however, the SEC has done little to substantiate these fears.

Aids to interpretation

Second, the list of four conditions that a system of internal accounting controls is supposed to assure was taken almost verbatim from Statement of Auditing Standards Number One of the American Institute of Certified Public Accountants, the chief trade association of the nation's independent certified public accountants, who do the work of auditing corporations' financial statements. There is a considerable lore on what auditors do or should do that may therefore be availed of by the SEC or the courts in their efforts to give meaning to Section 13(b)(2). Textbooks on auditing procedures,[29] for example, identify numerous specific tasks that an auditing firm must carry out in fulfillment of its duty to evaluate the audited company's system of accounting controls. What good accounting firms actually do, and which specific tasks are considered most important in the profession, can be explored via expert testimony of qualified accountants.[30]

Significance of state/federal contrast

The contrast between state law and the federal statute is instructive. It illustrates the tendency of state courts to fail to adopt rules that are suitable for the governance of large public corporations. Leaving corporate managers the discretion to decide whether to adopt a triggering event approach or a systemic approach to internal monitoring is a policy choice that makes eminent sense if the rule one adopts is going to govern the affairs of many close corporations. This is so because in a close corporation, where the small number of key participants and their greater incentive makes informal monitoring and cross-checking more feasible, the cost of adopting a formal system of internal accounting controls could be far out of proportion to any expected benefits. There are economies of scale that apply to the benefits that may be expected to flow from a formal, rule-governed system

[29] E.g., Burton, Palmer, & Kay, eds., Handbook of Accounting and Auditing chs. 9-16 (1981 & supp.). For an overview of auditing, see S. Siegel & D. Siegel, Accounting and Financial Disclosure 129-143 (1983).

[30] Of course, it is the courts that must finally declare the meaning of the law. They may decide for themselves that any particular auditing procedure was or was not called for by the statute in the circumstances of a given case, and they might decide that certain generally followed auditing procedures (as opposed to the more abstractly formulated generally accepted auditing *standards*) are simply too lax to constitute compliance with the statute. Moreover, even if a court or the SEC wants to give great deference to received standards within the auditing community, it may find itself with important unanswered questions. It is said by some experts, for example, that various factors "contribute" to effective internal control, such as competent personnel, a clear-cut organizational structure, a well-designed accounting system, limited access to assets by unauthorized persons, and the existence of an effective internal auditing staff. Suppose a large corporation has no separate internal auditing staff: Should that by itself mean that it has violated §13(b)(2)?

Or consider that Statement of Auditing Standards Number One distinguishes between accounting controls and administrative controls. It defines administrative controls to include "the plan of organization and the procedures and records that are concerned with the *decision processes* leading to management's authorization of transactions." As a matter of statutory interpretation, should the SEC and the courts follow this or a similar distinction in implementing §13(b)(2) and therefore limit the potential range of the provision by not embracing within it anything that should properly be classified as an administrative control? Certainly a strong case could be made that the statute does not authorize the SEC to require corporations to set up *general legal* compliance programs or legal audit programs.

of controls. On the other hand, that a large public corporation with thousands of employees could decide to do without internal auditors is a possibility that ought to be discouraged or ruled out of existence.

§3.5 *The Limits of the Business Judgment Rule*

In subsection 3.4.1, we saw how directors may be held liable for negligence, or gross negligence, despite the business judgment rule. The application of the business judgment rule to two special phenomena that have generated great controversy, derivative lawsuits and defensive maneuvers to takeover bids, will be dealt with later (in sections 15.2 and 13.6.2, respectively). In this section I focus on some rather different, general aspects of the rule's limits.

Four kinds of challenge to decision of directors

Judicial deference to directors' business judgment might mean not only that courts will not closely scrutinize directors' carefulness, but also that they will not weigh the directors' decisions against competing goals and policies. Is this what in fact happens? It is to this question that we now turn. We have already given a statement of the business judgment rule. Let us consider, in order, cases in which a business judgment conflicts or competes with

(1) another business judgment,
(2) a social or personal goal of the managers,
(3) the managers' self interest, and
(4) specific legal rules and policies.

(1) Decision was wrong

As an example of the first conflict, the directors and officers of a corporation owning a baseball team may honestly think that restricting games to those held in the daytime is in the shareholders' best interest, whereas some shareholders, armed with statistics about what other teams do, may earnestly believe that night games are the key to adequate profits. In this situation a court would simply not permit a shareholder challenge to the managers' judgment to go forward, even if it suspected or believed that the shareholders' business arguments would be much more persuasive than those of the managers. This is a primary or paradigmatic application of the business judgment rule.

(2) Decision aimed at social goal, not profits

But let us change the facts to create the second kind of conflict. Suppose, as happened in *Shlensky v. Wrigley,*[1] the shareholders' complaint included

§3.5 [1] 237 N.E.2d 776 (Ill. App. 1968).

the charge that Wrigley, the president and 80 percent shareholder of the corporation owning the Chicago Cubs, refused to install lights at Wrigley Field and thus make night games there possible, not because of his interest in the corporation's welfare but because of his personal convictions that daytime games were better for the neighborhood around Wrigley Field and that they fit the concept of baseball better. The court, while appearing to concede that directors ought not to act for reasons unrelated to the corporation's financial interest, nevertheless affirmed dismissal of the plaintiffs' complaint. It said it was "not satisfied that the motives assigned to [Wrigley and the other directors] are contrary to the best interests of the corporation and the stockholders."[2] It sketched a scenario in which concern for the neighborhood would be in the corporation's long-run interest but then quickly denied it was deciding that the directors' decision had been a correct one in fact. "We are merely saying that the decision is one properly before directors and the motives alleged in the amended complaint showed no fraud, illegality or conflict of interest in their making of that decision."[3]

Ambiguity of *Wrigley* case

The *Wrigley* case seems to stand for the proposition that the business judgment rule precludes a shareholder attack on the directors' business decisions on the grounds that the decisions were actually motivated by the directors' perception of social values. But the court seemed reluctant to hold outright that corporate managers are perfectly free to use corporate assets to implement their vision of the social good, at the expense of the shareholders. After all, the shareholders contributed the capital, own the residual claim on the assets, and may have a very different vision of the social good. The *Wrigley* holding is therefore puzzling.

Possible reasons for limiting challenges

The case may be construed as a decision based on considerations of appropriate judicial process. The point would be that courts should usually prohibit shareholders from attempting to prove management's real motivations in this kind of case. The reasons for this prohibition might be several.

First, real motivations are very difficult to prove.

Second, allowing shareholder to challenge directors' decisions on the basis of real motivations will simply tempt management to perjury at the time of trial. They will say, always with some plausibility, that they actually thought that a given decision was in the corporation's long-run interest.

Third, well-advised managers will easily forestall all such challenges by couching all documentation about corporate decisions in vague rhetoric

[2] Id. at 780.
[3] Ibid.

about the corporation's long-run interest. (So why discriminate against managers with less sophisticated legal advice?)

Fourth, managers' decisions to further their social values at the shareholders' expense are in fact rare and systemically unimportant. When such decisions do occur, their purpose may be publicly and clearly announced,[4] in which event a court heartened by the clear absence of difficult problems of proof might indeed allow a shareholder challenge.

(3) Decision was tainted by self-interest

A third conflict involves competition between business policies and managerial self interest. Suppose that the directors and officers of Toy Corporation cause it to buy a ton of expandrium, a new multipurpose raw material, from the Nightflyer Company for $1 million. Shareholder Small brings a derivative suit against all the directors and officers, claiming that they had a substantial personal financial interest in Nightflyer and that the purchase was unfair to Toy Corporation. This suit would *not* be dismissed because of the business judgment rule, because the rule does not apply to such a cause of action. This is an important point to grasp, for the vast body of case law on conflicts of interest and self-dealing that is discussed in subsequent chapters depends on it. The charge is not simply that the managers' business judgment was wrong, but that it was corrupt. In a sense, the plaintiff is arguing that the managers' decision was not a *business* judgment at all but a self-interested *personal* judgment. In contrast to the *Wrigley* court's attitude toward the social values allegedly motivating managers, the courts have shown little reluctance about letting shareholders try to prove that managers were really motivated by selfish personal goals. Perhaps the difference lies in the courts' perceptions that the selfish brand of ulterior motivation is much more frequent and serious.

Caveat

An important caveat to the preceding paragraph is that, if not all of the Nightflyer directors were personally interested in the expandrium sale, the defendant directors and officers might be able to get back under the business judgment rule by invoking the informed approval of the deal by the disinterested directors. (This important possibility is considered at various points in subsequent chapters.) They might even benefit by the recommendation to a court by the disinterested directors that a derivative suit against them be dismissed (see subsection 15.2.3).

(4) Decision was illegal: example of *AT & T* case

Finally, consider conflict between business goals and legal policies. In *Miller v. American Telephone & Telegraph Co.*,[5] the stockholders brought a

[4] See, e.g., Dodge v. Ford Motor Co., 170 N.W. 668 (Mich. 1919).

[5] 507 F.2d 759 (3d Cir. 1974), on remand, 394 F. Supp. 58 (E.D. Pa. 1975), aff'd without op., 530 F.2d 964 (3d Cir. 1976).

suit against AT & T's directors on account of the company's failure to collect an outstanding debt of $1.5 million owed it by the Democratic National Committee for communication services provided during the 1968 Democratic National Convention. The plaintiffs claimed not only that the directors negligently failed to pursue a valid corporate claim, but also that the failure amounted to AT & T's making a contribution to the committee in violation of a federal law about corporate campaign spending. The Third Circuit reversed a dismissal of the complaint, holding that the business judgment rule could not insulate the directors from liability if they did in fact violate the federal statute. It based its result both on the underlying purposes of the federal statute, which included destruction of corporate influence over elections *and* checking the practice of using corporate funds to benefit political parties without the stockholders' consent, and on the New York law regarding illegal acts. (AT & T was a New York corporation.) Under that state's decisions, illegal acts may amount to a breach of fiduciary duty by the directors and officers even when committed to benefit the corporation, because directors should be restrained from engaging in activities that are against public policy.[6] These holdings go beyond the platitude that courts will not hold that directors' violations of criminal statutes are proper if done for a corporate purpose, because they add the private enforcement activities of interested shareholders to the efforts of public prosecutors and regulators.

"Hands off" the key concept?

Perhaps the main impression arising out of the duty of care and business judgment cases is that under these notions courts place fairly limited restraints on private decision making. *Allis-Chalmers* suggests that courts are loath to *require* directors to design a monitoring system to enforce non–profit-maximizing legal policies, in the absence of a legislative judgment to that effect; but *Wrigley* suggests that in practice courts will *allow* directors to temper business decision making with their perceptions of social values; and the *AT & T* case suggests that they will *allow* shareholders to use the derivative suit mechanism to enforce general legal policies, not just to protect the financial welfare of the corporation. Therefore, although the official purpose of the business corporation may be to maximize profits, legal doctrine may leave managers and shareholders leeway to grind other axes. It is important not to overstate this point, of course. We have discussed only a few cases, and they may not predict well what most state courts would do in similar situations. (In particular, note that *Wrigley* is a

[6]See Abrams v. Allen, 74 N.E.2d 305 (N.Y. 1947), reh. denied, 75 N.E.2d 274 (N.Y. 1947); Roth v. Robertson, 118 N.Y.S. 351 (Sup. Ct. 1909).

decision of one lower court in one state; and similar holdings elsewhere appear nonexistent.)

In any event, there is one major, indeed all-important, class of cases that falls outside the protection of the business judgment rule: those involving managerial fraud and self-dealing. It is to this vast body of legal material that we now must turn.

CHAPTER 4

INTRODUCTION TO CONFLICTS OF INTEREST

§4.1 *The Conflict-of-Interest Paradigms*

Fiduciary duty of loyalty

Directors, officers, and, in some situations, controlling shareholders owe their corporations, and sometimes other shareholders and investors, a fiduciary duty of loyalty. This duty prohibits the fiduciaries from taking advantage of their beneficiaries by means of fraudulent or unfair transactions. They may not abuse the beneficiaries in situations in which they have a conflict of interest. In some contexts, they may act improperly simply by maintaining a state of affairs in which they have a conflict of interest. Most importantly, this general fiduciary duty of loyalty is a residual concept that can include factual situations that no one has foreseen and categorized. The general duty permits, and in fact has led to, a continuous evolution in corporate law.[1] At the same time, the courts and legislatures have developed more specific rules, or particular fiduciary duties, to deal with many recurring situations involving a conflict of interest.

Four paradigms

I find it useful to group the recurring situations into four clusters. Each cluster implicates somewhat different dangers and calls for a somewhat different legal response. In this section I will introduce each cluster by a

§4.1 [1] For efforts to identify and analyze the elements of the fiduciary duty of loyalty in a general way, see Clark, Agency Costs Versus Fiduciary Duties, in Principals and Agents: The Structure of Business 55, 71-79 (J. Pratt & R. Zeckhauser eds. 1985); Frankel, Fiduciary Law, 71 Calif. L. Rev. 795 (1983).

pure and simple example, or paradigm, that contains the essential features of that cluster. I will then present a more abstract analysis of conflicts of interest, and will explain how the four different conflict-of-interest patterns differ in the problems they present for lawmakers interested in the design of proper legal rules.

The four paradigms are labeled:

(1) basic self-dealing;
(2) executive compensation;
(3) the taking of corporate or shareholder property; and
(4) corporate action with mixed motives.

(1) Basic self-dealing

The first paradigm is represented in Figure 4.1-A. Twenty-five percent of the stock of Public Corporation is owned by Insider, who is also a director and president of the company, but the rest is owned by thousands of unrelated public shareholders. Insider also owns all of the stock of Private Corporation. Private Corporation sells Public Corporation 50 acres of land for $1 million. There is a risk that Public Corporation will be cheated in this transaction — that it will pay an excessive price — because Insider can control the actions of both corporations but is personally more interested in the welfare of Private Corporation. If any given dollar is left in Public Corporation and later paid out to shareholders as a dividend, Insider will get only 25 cents, and the public shareholders will get the rest. If the dollar is transferred to Private Corporation and then paid out as a dividend, Insider will get all of it and the public shareholders of Public Corporation will suffer.

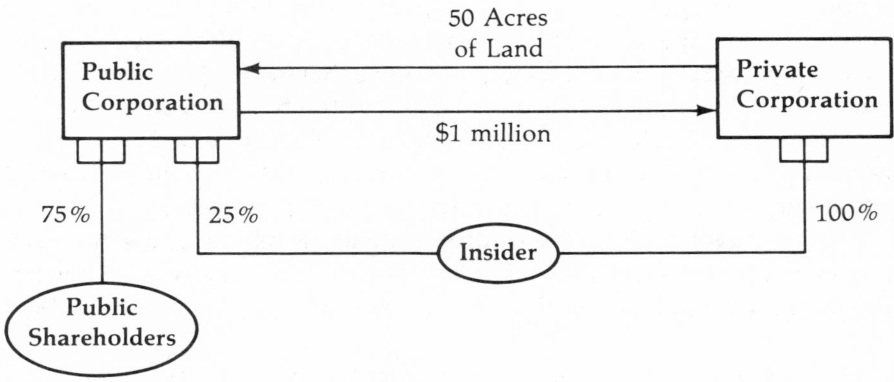

Figure 4.1-A
Basic Self-Dealing

Unfairness often not obvious

Of course, if Insider simply compels Public Corporation to make a transfer of money or property to Private Corporation, and Public Corporation receives nothing in return, it will be fairly obvious that Insider is stealing from Public Corporation. But if an uncompensated transfer by Public Corporation is folded into an apparently legitimate transaction (for example, if the price paid by the corporation for the land is simply inflated to an unfairly high level) the existence of a wrongful taking will not be so obvious to the public shareholders and other outside parties. It may even be less obvious to Insider himself, for he may more easily rationalize an inflated purchase price than outright stealing. It is frequently possible to identify and exaggerate some reasons why Public Corporation should pay dearly for some particular piece of land or property. That having been done, Insider may continue to think of himself as a just and honorable man. That this possibility is of enormous practical importance is suggested by the empirical work on the importance of rationalization and maintenance of self-respect to white collar criminals. (For example, a famous sociological study showed that even convicted embezzlers seem always to have a set of excuses by which they justify to themselves the proposition that what they did was not "really" wrong or criminal.[2])

Basic self-dealing is explored more fully in chapter 5.

(2) Executive compensation

The second paradigm is the fixing of executive compensation, and is represented by Figure 4.1-B. In a given year, Public Corporation gives compensation valued at $1 million to Insider, who is its president and chief executive officer. This amount includes fringe benefits and the estimated value of items of "incentive" compensation such as stock options and stock appreciation rights."[3] There is some risk that the compensation is excessive because the executive has at least a de facto influence on the corporation's decision making with respect to his own salary and an obvious interest in getting the better of the deal. His power over or influence on the *corporation*'s actions in "bargaining" with himself arises because of the weaknesses in the institution of the board of directors, which formally acts on behalf of the corporation in the setting of executive compensation. These weaknesses, which concern the process by which directors are selected as well as the severe constraints on the directors' incentive and ability to maximize the corporation's interest, were introduced in section 3.2 and are taken up at later parts of the book.[4] One of the implications of these flaws is that, to the extent that they affect the compensation-setting process, the

[2]See D. Cressey, Other People's Money ch. 4 (1953).
[3]See chapter 6.
[4]See, e.g., subsections 5.4.1, 6.3, 7.6.4, 13.6.2, 13.6.3, 15.2 infra.

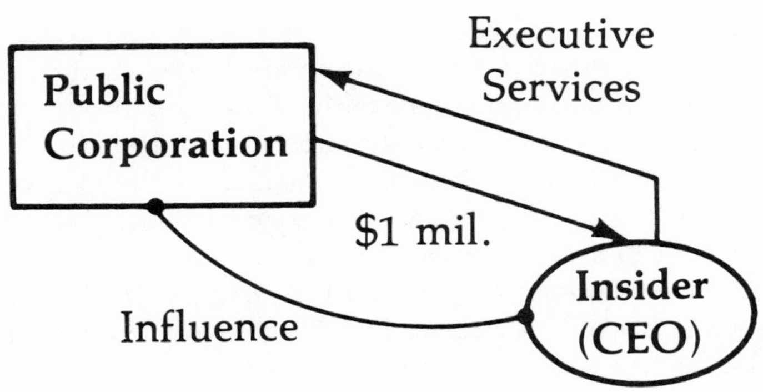

Figure 4.1-B
Executive Compensation

executive's compensation is not really being set in a market. The term *market* implies a context in which bargaining occurs and contracts are made. But there is no real contract or bargain in a case where there are not two or more independent bargaining parties. Indeed, this is the root meaning of the term *self-dealing*: a transaction appears to be between two or more parties but actually involves only one decision maker.

The problem of executive compensation is explored more fully in chapter 6.

(3) Taking of corporate or shareholder property

The third paradigm is the taking of corporate or investor property. It is represented in Figure 4.1-C. Insider, the president of Public Corporation, uses the company's yacht for his personal pleasure during an entire month. The use was not part of his official compensation package that was approved by the directors. The yacht has a monthly rental value of $5,000, and the company might have rented it out or put it to use on company business. Obviously, Insider's action is a short step away from an outright theft of $5,000 from Public Corporation's treasury. The difference is that he may argue that his personal use of the yacht is one of the customary perquisites of being chief executive officer of a corporation like Public Corporation, that it was in effect, if not technically or officially, part of his compensation package, and that the directors' failure to approve it specifically should be irrelevant. In other words, there may be an argument about whether he actually took *corporate* property or merely something that was rightfully available to him.

Kinds of uncertainty as to existence of wrong

As in the previous two paradigms, there is a crucial element of murkiness or ambiguity that permits rationalization and apparent justification of what was done. In each paradigm, the nature of the ambiguity is differ-

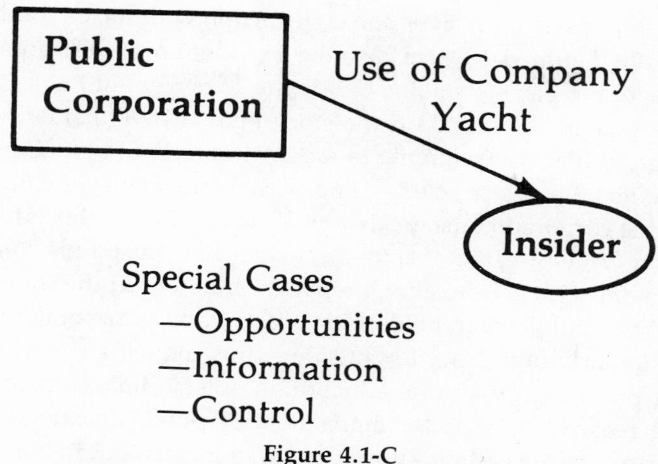
Public
Corporation
Use of Company
Yacht
Insider
Special Cases
—Opportunities
—Information
—Control

Figure 4.1-C
Taking of Corporate (or Shareholders') Property

ent. In the basic self-dealing paradigm, the chief difficult question is, "Was the price *unfair*?" In the executive compensation paradigm it is, "Was approval of the compensation *informed and independent*?" In the taking-of-propety paradigm it is, "Was the thing of value that was taken really *corporate or shareholder property*?"

Broad reach of the taking paradigm

The difficulty of determining what things of value ought to be deemed not to belong to the fiduciaries but to the corporation or its investors is what allows the taking-of-corporate-property cluster of cases to become an interesting, major component of corporate law. As we shall see (chapter 7), a substantial body of case law has dealt with the question whether a given business opportunity should be treated as a *corporate opportunity* that corporate fiduciaries are forbidden to take for themselves. Moreover, when corporate fiduciaries buy and sell stock in their corporation on the basis of undisclosed *inside information* (discussed in chapter 8), one important way of viewing their behavior is as a taking of something that rightfully belonged to a specifiable class of public investors in corporations. That is, it may be viewed as a taking of investor property, if not of corporate property. This view extends the concept of the third paradigm, but good reasons can be given for doing so. Another extension is conceptually more difficult: the notion that *corporate control* should itself be viewed as a corporate asset or, more accurately, as an asset whose fruits belong to all the corporation's shareholders. Chapter 11, on insider overreaching during control shifts, and chapter 12, on insider unfairness in the extension and consolidation of control, consider whether control can be examined from this perspective.

(4) Mixed motives

The fourth paradigm involves corporate action with mixed motives. It is represented by Figure 4.1-D. Insider, the president of Public Corporation, causes the latter to pay $50 million to buy the 20 percent of Public Corporation's stock recently acquired on the stock market by Outsider. Outsider had announced that he was trying to acquire control of Public Corporation and change its business policies — and perhaps its management. His sale of stock to the corporation means that he is now giving up this intention. In street jargon (Wall Street's, of course), Insider has caused his company to buy off a raider with greenmail. One danger inherent in the transaction is dilution of the public shareholders' interest: Public Corporation may be paying an unfairly high price to Outsider, thus reducing corporate assets by a larger proportion than the reduction in outstanding stock and consequently decreasing the value of shares held by public investors.

To take an extreme case, if Public Corporation pays out half of its assets to repurchase Outsider's shares, and the continuing public investors' holdings now constitute 100 percent rather than 80 percent of the outstanding stock, the value of their stock will be only 62.5 percent of what it was before the purchase (that is, original value times 1/2 times 10/8).

A second danger is what economists call an opportunity cost: Public Corporation may be foregoing an increase in value that Outsider would have brought about had he succeeded in taking control and putting in better management and better business policies.

More uncertainty

These two dangers are real because Insider may actually have been motivated, in causing Public Corporation to buy Outsider's shares, by the fear of losing his job. He will say, of course, that he acted in the corporation's best interest and that the true purpose of the repurchase was simply to eliminate a threat to the good business practices of Public Corporation. That is, he will say he wanted to prevent a takeover that in his business

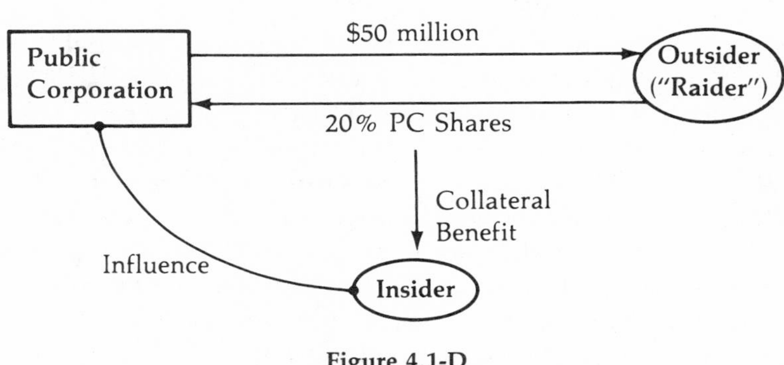

Figure 4.1-D
Mixed Motives Situation

judgment would have been disastrous for the corporation and its shareholders. Once again, the questions raised by a paradigm are often extremely difficult to answer with certainty. The main question in this paradigm may be phrased in a number of ways. What was Insider's real motive or purpose? Or: Were the corporation or its public investors harmed, compared to what would have happened if Insider had acted in some other feasible way with respect to Outsider's takeover attempt?

Cases related to the fourth paradigm will be explored primarily in chapter 13, on insider resistance to control shifts, and in chapter 14, on distributions to shareholders.

Self-dealing defined

We now ought to analyze transactions involving a conflict of interest in a more precise and more abstract way. Because the common phrase *conflict of interest* is used in many different ways — sometimes to refer to a situation, sometimes to a transaction, sometimes to a wrongful transaction — I prefer to use somewhat different terminology in formal analysis. In my view, *self-dealing* occurs when three conditions are satisfied.

First, there is a *transaction* between the referent corporation (or group of public investors) and some other person. By *referent* corporation or investors I simply mean the corporation or shareholders whose interest may be in jeopardy. By *person* I mean both natural and artificial persons: individuals as well as corporations or partnerships.

Second, a certain individual (or group of them) has *decision making influence* with respect to the actions taken by the referent corporation or group of investors. The influential person will often be a corporate director, officer, or controlling shareholder and may be colloquially referred to as a manager or insider. He may or may not be the other person referred to in the first condition.

Third, this influential individual or group has a greater *personal interest* in the welfare of the other person involved in the transaction, or in certain collateral consequences of the transaction, than in the welfare of the referent corporation or group of investors.

Concept of unfairness

Any particular self-dealing transaction may or may not be disadvantageous or suboptimal to the referent corporation or group of investors. Accordingly, a self-dealing transaction will be described as *unfair* or *abusive* if and only if a fourth condition is also satisfied: The transaction is in fact unfair to the referent corporation or group of investors. Unfairness in a self-dealing transaction may be identified in one or both of two related ways: by comparison of the transaction to a hypothetical other-dealing transaction or by comparison to actual transactions in a well-functioning competitive market. Thus, a self-dealing transaction is unfair to the referent corporation or group of investors if the outcome to them is less advantageous than the outcome would have been if the transaction had been agreed to, on their behalf, by a rational, well-informed decision maker who was independent and loyal, that is, not affected by a conflict of interest. This is the arms'-length bargain comparsion. It is a hypothetical exercise, but it is very useful when unquestionably comparable market data are not available. Alternatively, or in addition, a self-dealing transaction is often adjudged unfair to the referent corporation or group of investors if the outcome to them is less advantageous than the outcome of clearly comparable transactions between independent parties in a reasonably competitive market. This is the competitive market comparison. It resorts to objective data, but it may founder if the self-dealing transaction, or the situation and needs of the parties to it, is not truly comparable to those of parties in the market. It may also be an impossible comparison if there is no relevant competitive market to turn to for reference.

Differences among the paradigms

These defining characteristics of unfair self-dealing may now be applied to my four conflict-of-interest paradigms. The two most important notions for distinguishing the paradigms are transactions and unfairness. The paradigms differ in the nature of the transactions they involve and in the kind of remedial approaches that the law might feasibly take toward the risk of unfairness in the transactions.

Two-way exchange and two remedial options

In the basic self-dealing cluster of cases, the transaction is a *two-way exchange* between the referent corporation and some other person, who might or might not be identical with the influential Insider. Thus, for example, this class of cases includes sales of widgets between the corporaton and a director or officer, as well as sales between the corporation and a private company in which the corporation's president has a great personal interest. As for possible remedies, the legal system may try to control unfairness in such transactions by one of two ways: by forbidding them entirely or by subjecting them to approval or disapproval under some substantive test — for example, fairness — that is applied by special decision makers such as disinterested directors or courts.

Two-way exchange and one remedial approach

In the executive compensation paradigm, the transaction is also a two-way exchange (executive services for pay), but it is always directly between the corporation and the influential, self-interested insider. Moreover, it differs from the transaction in the first paradigm in that the law *could not prevent it.* No rational person who is not a major stockholder would consent to become a full-time officer of a public corporation if he could not expect to receive executive compensation. The range of legal responses available for dealing with this kind of self-dealing is therefore limited: The law may only regulate the terms of executive compensation or the procedures for determining and questioning it. By contrast, it is perfectly possible simply to forbid an officer of a corporation from also becoming a supplier of goods to it — that is, to flatly prohibit basic self-dealing, whether or not it is unfair — and some important legal rules did or do forbid such dual relationships.[5]

One-way transaction and one remedial approach

In the third or taking-of-corporate-or-investor-property paradigm, the transaction is a *one-way transaction*. The president uses the company yacht, giving nothing in return, or unilaterally expropriates a business opportunity, like the chance to buy a new factory, that should have been taken by the corporation. The transaction is always unfair *if* corporate or investor property is actually being diverted. In contrast to the feasible legal treatments of the second paradigm, the law can forbid such transactions. In contrast to the actual range of treatments for the first paradigm, it always forbids them.

Two-way with side effects and multiple options

Finally, the transaction in the fourth or mixed-motive paradigm is usually a two-way transaction between the referent corporation and some outsider in whose welfare the influential insider has no particular interest. Rather, the insider has some interest in a *side effect* of the transaction: The corporation's repurchase of an insurgent's shares, for example, may result in the insider's retaining control and continuing to reap the rewards of control. As far as feasible legal responses are concerned, the situation is similar to that with respect to the first paradigm. That is, the law may either forbid *or* regulate mixed-motive transactions. But there is more pressure here for subcategorization and for regulatory tests other than fairness. As we shall see,[6] some types of corporate defenses against takeover attempts, such as the issuance of new voting shares to the incumbent management's friends, seem to be much more suitable candidates for outright prohibition than others, such as corporate press releases explaining why incumbent management believes that it would be unwise for the shareholders to accept a takeover bid. Moreover, because of the great complexities typically involved in figuring out the effects of a mixed-motive transaction — whether it was worse for a corporation than some feasible alternative course of action — courts have tended to invent regulatory tests that look more to evidence of unwholesome insider *purposes* than the substantive fairness or business wisdom of the transaction in question.

The influence and self-interest elements

Thus far I have talked about how the four paradigms differ with respect to the kinds of transactions involved and the susceptibility to legal control

[5] An important example is the set of rules prohibiting certain conflict-of-interest transactions between pension plans and their sponsoring corporations, 29 U.S.C.A. §1106. See also section 5.4 infra.

[6] Section 13.6 infra.

of the dangers they present. In most respects, it is fairly easy to see how the other two notions that are key to the concept of self-dealing — an insider with decision making influence but with some personal interest in a transactional outcome that is suboptimal to the referent corporation or group of investors — apply to the conflict-of-interest patterns. In each of my four paradigms I referred to a corporate president since that officer is usually one of the most influential decision makers with respect to a corporation's actions. In each instance it was obvious that he might have been strongly tempted to do something that would hurt his corporation but help himself. In some of the cases that cluster around these paradigms, however, the applicability of these notions may be less clear.

Fraud as influence

To use an example that arguably falls into the wrongful taking-of-property category: In what respect does a corporation's president have decision making influence over the actions of a group of the company's shareholders (the referent group of investors) when he buys their stock cheaply on the basis of undisclosed but valuable inside information about the corporation's financial condition? Obviously, the president does not coerce the shareholders into selling, to their detriment, in the way that he might compel a corporate action — by authorizing a transaction, for example, or by threatening the nominal decision makers (subordinate officers, for example) with subtle penalties if they do not comply with his wishes. But by withholding information from the shareholders, information that we are now assuming belonged to them, he causes them the same kind of loss. Similarly, whether the company president approves a self-dealing transaction himself, brow-beats the directors into approving it, or simply lies to them so that they approve it, the result may be the same. An insider can influence corporate or investor decisions not only by force of formal authority but also by fraud. And unfair failures to reveal information can be classified as a form of fraud.

§4.2 *Why Fraud and Unfair Self-Dealing Are Considered Wrong*

Why this section

It may seem odd to pause for a reflection on the wrongfulness of fraud and unfair self-dealing. Surely everyone agrees that fraud is wrong? Perhaps. But the aim of my inquiry is not to convince doubters but to get a more precise notion of the *reasons* for our common belief. Having a certain conception of the reasons, or having none at all, is practically important. Different notions of why fraud is wrong, for example, will lead us to very different notions about the proper legal reach of the concept and about the proper legal remedies for violations.

§4.2.1 Objections to Fraud

Fraud makes markets imperfect

The objections to fraud can be put under two headings, one going to its impact on basic resource allocation and the other going to its impact on transaction costs. The first point simply applies the familiar notion of economists that perfect or competitive markets, which are assumed to be socially desirable, generally depend on participants who possess full and correct information relevant to their decision making. Fraud, in the sense of deceit, causes participants to make decisions on the basis of incorrect information, and thus tends to make markets imperfect, and resources to be allocated inefficiently.

Affirmative disclosure duties too?

The notion that information helps make markets perfect opens the way for arguments in favor of legal rules that impose affirmative duties on certain persons to disclose information to others. That is, it leads the way to the view that some types of nondisclosure should be treated as wrongful fraud. Among the roles to which such duties should be attached are those in which the inhabitants are often the cheapest and likeliest sources of relevant information and have assumed the task of generally acting on behalf of a class of other persons who can make use of the information. Accordingly, one finds that many kinds of fiduciaries are viewed by the law as having certain affirmative disclosure duties to their beneficiaries. In the corporate context, the law has long struggled, sometimes fitfully, to give content to the general notion that corporate managers owe specific disclosure duties to shareholders and potential investors.

Questions of scope

To be sure, how far these duties should reach and how elaborate the disclosures should be are difficult questions that demand a finer analysis of potential costs and benefits than we can undertake here. Consider, for example, whether managers should only have to make affirmative disclosures when they are about to engage in conflict of interest transactions or also in other contexts. (Whether the law should require corporations, acting through their managers, to make elaborate financial and business-related disclosures to investors when they sell new securities, and at periodic intervals throughout its existence, is a question taken up in subsection 17.5.3.) In any event, it is clear that, in some contexts, corporate managers do have an affirmative duty to make detailed disclosures. In the case of public corporations, the duty has not been based on any notion that actual shareholders as principals have specifically contracted with particular managers as agents for the right to receive relevant information.[1] Rather, it has been based on a kind of hypothetical social contract, a notion that shareholders as a group, if rational and well-informed and able to contract about the question free of transaction costs, would have insisted on obtaining a promise from managers, as a group, to supply certain corporate-generated and other information relevant to shareholder decision making. That is, such bargaining as can be postulated to justify legal rules is hypothetical and relates to roles, not individuals. The hope is that the legal system's use of hypothetical bargains of this sort is more efficient than a more literally contractualistic approach.

Other theories

This first objection to fraud should be contrasted with some other conceptions about what is wrong with fraud. Other conceptions, by themselves, may not support the idea that affirmative disclosure duties should be created. This is true of the objection to fraud developed in the next paragraph, for example. It is also true of the notion that fraud is wrong because it is immoral or against God's will. Furthermore, it is rather difficult to derive support for affirmative duties of disclosure from the notion that fraud is wrong because it constitutes an affront to the autonomy of the person whom one is defrauding.[2]

Fraud increases transaction costs

The second objection to fraud is that it increases transaction costs. By undermining credulity and trustworthiness, a fraudulent act — or better, "some critical mass" of fraudulent acts — will lead market participants to invest in costly procedures for checking and verifying the information supplied by other persons and/or will cause them to obtain and pay for guarantees of truthfulness or insurance against losses stemming from untruthful information received from others.

Social utility of truthfulness

That these costs will become costs of enormous magnitude, if the per-

§4.2 [1]Since shareholders generally lack control over the actions of directors, a basic feature of the agency relationship is absent. Restatement (Second) of Agency §14C, Comments a, b (1958).

[2]Consider the interesting argument that Charles Fried makes against lying, as distinguished from nondisclosure:

> Lying is wrong because when I lie I set up a relation which is essentially exploitative. It violates the principle of respect [for persons], for I must affirm that the mind of another person is available to me in a way in which I cannot agree my mind would be available to him — for if I do so agree, then I would not expect my lie to be believed. When I lie, I am like a counterfeiter; I do not want the market flooded with counterfeit currency; I do not want to get back my own counterfeit bill. Moreover, in lying to you, I affirm such an unfairly unilateral principle in respect to an interest and capacity which is crucial, as crucial as physical integrity; your freedom and your rationality. When I do intentional physical harm, I say that your body, your person, is available for my purposes. When I lie, I lay claim to your mind. [C. Fried, Right and Wrong 67 (1978).]

ceived likelihood of fraud becomes very significant, can be appreciated by considering the vast social utility of the opposite practice — an established pattern of truthfulness. Clearly, the benefits of human society depend entirely on cooperative behavior, and cooperative behavior depends greatly on communication. The overwhelming majority of the facts we know, and by which we orient our own self-seeking action, are learned not from our observations and direct experience but derivatively through the spoken, written, and televised reports of others. The same is true of our generalizations, hypotheses, theories, opinions, and values — all of which are captured, perhaps, in the term *information*. Very few of these things are traceable to our original cogitations or personal experience. At any given moment, almost all of our valuable technology and culture is old stuff being transferred to new custodians. This massive cultural process, the transmission of information, could not serve its function unless most people told the truth about most things most of the time. It is a significant social danger that the quantity of lies may become so great that people in general will lose a significant amount of their credulity, with an ensuing collapse of effective, or at least inexpensive, communication. Yet, despite the enormous social value of truthfulness, it is clear that many persons will often find it to be to their individual advantage to lie and to get away with it. There is a serious free-rider problem: Each self-seeking individual, if amoral, prefers a situation in which virtually everyone else tells the truth, thus enabling the vast benefits of social cooperation to be created, while he himself frequently tells lies in order to secure a greater part of those benefits. If everyone acts on this impulse, of course, the whole system will be jeopardized. Thus, a cultural pattern of truthfulness is in the nature of a public good; individuals left to themselves may not produce it.[3]

Fraud and punishment

Hence, fraud may cause damage extending beyond the harm done to particular defrauded persons. It may have extensive negative externalties;

[3]Public goods are characterized by three related features.

(1) If available at all, they are available to all individuals (nonappropriability).
(2) One individual can increase his "consumption" of the good without reducing the benefits available to others (nonrivalry in consumption).
(3) No individual can be prevented from benefiting from a public good (nonexcludability).

These features imply that public goods cannot be sold at a price, so they will not be produced by private enterprise. Like the paradigm public good, national defense, they may be provided by government. J. Due and A. Friedlander, Government Finance: Economics of the Public Sector 22-23 (6th ed. 1977). Of course, many goods may not possess the three features perfectly — they may not be pure public goods — but may come close enough that analysis of them in terms of these features is quite useful.

it is a kind of public bad. Consequently, the damage actually suffered by a particular defrauded plaintiff will not be an adequate measure of the full social cost of fraud. To the extent that lawmakers perceive this, there will be, as there occasionally has been, pressure to subject fraudulent defendants to deterrence oriented or punitive measures of damages, and to special sanctions. And because of the inadequacy of conventional legal devices in measuring and imposing the full social cost of fraud upon the defrauders, there is pressure to supplement legal sanctions with social santions. Thus, fraud is considered morally wrong, not just legally wrong, and is subject to disapproval. Social disapproval, in turn, can lead persons to develop an internal, emotional, or moral sense of the badness of fraud. This mix of legal and moral sanctions may reflect a pervasive drive for social efficiency. For up to some point, it is cheaper for society to control fraud by getting its members to "internalize" a sense of its badness through social conditioning than to invest in external monitoring and enforcement arrangements.

Two nonobvious conclusions

Our reflections on what makes fraud wrong thus leads to two general conclusions that very certainly have not been clear to everyone or free from controversy.

First, it can be socially efficient, at least in some contexts, to impose affirmative disclosure duties on corporate managers. This follows from the resource-allocation argument.

Second, it can be socially efficient to subject defrauding persons to sanctions more severe than the imposition of conventionally conceived compensatory damages. This follows from the transaction costs argument.

§4.2.2 Objections to Unfair Self-Dealing

Taking vs. bargaining

The basic objection to all forms of self-dealing that are unfair (that is, not as advantageous to corporations or investors as other-dealing or market transactions) derives from the fact that the unfair element constitutes a *unilateral* taking of property rather than a bargained-for distribution of it. The practical differences between an insider's special benefits from self-dealing and an equal amount of overt, additional compensation also derive from this fact. (Of course, a benefit can be unilaterally taken even though there are two *ostensible* bargaining parties — the insider and the board of directors, say — if there are defects in the information, incentives, or practical power of one party.) Furthermore, the disapproval of unilateral takings is what really lies behind the ancient prohibition against a trustee's taking secret profits. Consequently, the wrongness of unfair self-dealing can be understood if we can understand what is wrong about the pure case of outright theft.

Example of Cain's taking

Consider this problem. Suppose Cain, president of The Garden Corporation, takes $100,000 from the corporate treasury for his own purposes without telling anyone or asking anyone's permission. Cain does have an employment contract with the corporation and has collected the salary due thereunder. But he has been an extremely good businessman and under his presidency the corporation has done much better than anyone expected. Why shouldn't the $100,000 taken by Cain be construed as additional compensation, which in this case was well deserved? Why shouldn't the law deem his action to be one as to which no individual director or shareholder may raise an actionable objection?

The answer is that Cain had an alternative way of seeking additional compensation for alleged superior performance (that of *bargaining* for additional above-board compensation directly with the board of directors) and this alternative is socially more efficient.

Taken amounts may be monopoly rents

To see this, let us examine Cain's alternative course of action from a prospective viewpoint, that is, at the moment when he was just about to decide to take the $100,000. For simplicity, assume that if he were then to seek explicit, formal approval of a $100,000 bonus for superior peformance (past or future), his request would be either denied or granted. Denial would be a sign that Cain's services were not valued as highly as he thought or that the bonus was excessive in relation to the estimated value it would induce him to create for the company. Now, paying people just enough to supply their labor or products to the payor, and no more, is not a bad thing, but the avoidance of monopoly profits; it is what we would expect everyone to be doing to each other in a productive, well-functioning, competitive economy. And there is no reason to suppose that, for institutional reasons, boards of directors will be systematically too harsh in their dealings with officers about explicit compensation; quite the opposite is true. Thus, under this scenario, Cain would make more money by resorting to theft than by negotiating additional above-board-pay (after all, that is why managers sometimes steal) but his private gain would reflect a social inefficiency.

But suppose a neutral observer would honestly say, at the time of Cain's theft, that a request for additional overt compensation in the amount of $100,000 *would* have been granted. Does the problem then disappear? No, for several reasons.

First, there is always some risk that such a prediction about the outcome of a hypothetical course of action is wrong and that Cain by his taking was getting something a well-informed and well-motivated group of directors or shareholders would not approve. There is little reason for the investors to take that risk unless they are being paid for taking it, which they are not. Remember, the risk in question is absent when all compensation is aboveboard. Consequently, one may postulate that rational shareholders, when designing the hypothetical social contract that constitutes basic corporate law, would have insisted on a rule that managers may not unilaterally determine their own compensation. The taking of secret profits is a violation of that rule.

Second, even if shareholders as a class have a fairly good idea of the amount of secret profits taken by managers in the aggregate, and have come to expect this level of unilateral takings to continue, their expectations hardly justify the takings. After all, shareholders also have *expectations about what their legal rights are.* As long as this is true, expectations about what will actually happen to them cannot be used as the basis for defining their rights. One of the things shareholders expect is, of course, that if any particular manager is caught at unfair self-dealing he will have to respond in damages. The defendant could hardly expect to win his case by arguing, although some have tried,[4] that what he did was common practice among managers in his industry, or that investors had come to expect a certain amount of pilfering.

Takings create unproductive uncertainty

Moreover, investor expectations about what the frequency and the amount of unfair self-dealing will be are always *estimates,* and their estimates are accompanied by a substantial amount of *uncertainty.*[5] The measure of uncertainty is likely to be quite substantial, given the nature of unilateral takings and unfair self-dealing. Thus, each investor faces substantial uncertainty about the amount of secret profits that will be taken and, therefore, about his own expected rate of return on his stock investment. This uncertainty is over and above all other risks and uncertainties he must confront as stockholder. Now, it is generally thought in modern valuation theory that investors demand compensation for risk and uncertainty. The greater the risk, the greater the average or mean expected return that they demand. Additional uncertainty will therefore raise the

[4]E.g., United States v. Brookshire, 514 F.2d 786 (10th Cir. 1975).

[5]In technical terms, the expectations can be seen as probability distributions. Investors, to the extent they think about it, will assign different subjective probabilities to each of a large number of possible levels of future unfair self-dealing. The best estimate of the level of future unfair self-dealing will simply be a weighted average of these probabilities times their associated levels. In principle, the amount of risk or uncertainty associated with the best estimate could be determined by applying certain statistical measures to the investors' probability distributions.

cost of capital and perhaps depress the level of investment in productive enterprise. This is a bad effect when the uncertainty is basically unnecessary and unproductive — as is the uncertainty created by the prospect of variable secret profits.[6]

Not eliminated by diversification

Note that the uncertainty we are talking about is not one that can be eliminated by investors' putting together fully diversified portfolios. There is uncertainty associated with the investors' best estimate of the *total* amount of future unfair self-dealing by managers of all corporations, not just uncertainty about the amount of unilateral takings by managers in particular corporations. Of course, individual investors may better their position by diversifying against the risk of holding stock in companies that become subject to unusually great amounts of self-dealing. And to the extent that all investors are not in fact fully diversified, they may suffer losses they could avoid. But the main point of interest from a policy making perspective is the unproductive uncertainty associated with unfair self-dealing in the whole system. Corporate law attempts to reduce this uncertainty by rules against unfair self-dealing.

Summary

In summary, unfair self-dealing is wrong because it leads either to (1) managers collecting unwarranted monopoly rents or (2) the creation of unproductive uncertainty, which in turn may raise the cost of capital. To mitigate these problems, corporate law has in effect stipulated that corporate managers (of public corporations, at least), by voluntarily entering their roles, promise not to engage in unfair self-dealing. Like our analysis of what is wrong with fraud, this analysis has important practical implications.

Two may be mentioned here. First, actual shareholder expectations of the prevalence of managerial takings of secret profits should not be construed to justify the practice.

Second, because beliefs about the current level of such takings do not justify them, the introduction of new legal rules or procedures that will more cheaply or effectively control the takings is not unfair to managers.

[6] Of course, correct pricing of uncertainty is, in itself, a good thing. And much uncertainty is the inevitable byproduct of productive activities. It is *unproductive* or *avoidable uncertainty* that is objectionable.

CHAPTER 5

BASIC SELF-DEALING

Types of basic self-dealing

Basic self-dealing, as I use the term, includes four things:

(1) transactions between a corporation and its directors or officers;
(2) transactions between a corporation and a business entity in which the directors or officers have a significant direct or indirect financial interest;
(3) transactions between a partially owned subsidiary corporation and its parent corporation; and
(4) transactions between a corporation and another one with common or "interlocking" directors or officers.

For the sake of simplicity, in this chapter I will often focus on the first type of transaction.

Basic self-dealing is currently governed both by statute and by case law. In this chapter (sections 5.2 and 5.3 infra,) we examine closely some typical specimens of each. In order to understand them correctly, however, it is quite important to have some idea of the history of the law on this subject.

The history is therefore considered in the first section. The final section (5.4 infra) offers some suggestions for law reform.

§5.1 *The Historical Puzzle*

Three stages

According to Harold Marsh, author of a well-known law review article,[1] the law in the United States since the mid-nineteenth century concerning contracts between a director and his corporation has evolved in three distinct stages. In 1880, the first stage, the rule was that any such contract was voidable at the instance of the corporation or its shareholders, without regard to the fairness or unfairness of the transaction. A similar rule governed contracts between parents and subsidiaries and between corporations with interlocking directorates. In effect, most basic self-dealing was simply prohibited. By 1910, the second stage, however, "the general rule was that a contract between a director and his corporation was valid if it was approved by a disinterested majority of his fellow directors and was not found to be unfair or fraudulent by the court if challenged; but that a contract in which the majority of the Board was interested was voidable at the instance of the corporation or its shareholders without regard to any question of fairness."[2] Finally, by 1960, the third stage, the rule had become more lenient: Contracts with interested directors are generally valid unless found to be unfair by a court if challenged.

A possible fourth

Perhaps a fourth, even more lenient stage has begun since Marsh wrote, for in 1975 California adopted a comprehensive new corporate code containing a provision that can be read to exclude the need for an interested transaction to pass a judicial test of fairness. Section 310 of that code requires a transaction to be "just and reasonable" for it to stand alone or be approved by the Board of Directors but omits that requirement with respect to *shareholder ratification*. In context, the omission suggests that a transaction properly ratified by shareholders is immune to a judicial inquiry into the fairness of its terms.[3]

In sum, the law seems to have evolved through three or four rules:

(1) a flat prohibition against basic self-dealing;

§5.1 [1] Marsh, Are Directors Trustees? Conflict of Interest and Corporate Morality, 22 Bus. Law. 35 (1966).

[2] Id. at 39-40.

[3] See Bulbulia and Pinto, Statutory Responses to Interested Directors' Transactions: A Watering Down of Fiduciary Standards?, 53 Notre Dame Law. 201, 218-223 (1977).

(2) a rule allowing basic self-dealing that is approved by a majority of disinterested directors and is fair;
(3) a rule allowing basic self-dealing that is fair, as found by a court; and
(4) in some states, perhaps, a rule allowing basic self-dealing that is fair *or* that is approved by a majority of properly informed shareholders.

One naturally wonders about the meaning of these changes. What, if anything, explains these historical shifts? Are the rules that have survived this evolutionary process justified? Are they optimal? These questions deserve the greatest attention by those trying to understand the forces that shape corporate law.

Explanation not obvious

Professor Marsh himself seemed at a loss to provide an explanation. He pointed out that the courts that first enunciated second stage-type holdings gave no convincing reasons for changing the rules, whereas courts applying the voidability rule of the first stage gave numerous strong arguments. The early courts, which saw themselves as adopting a sound principle of trust law, and which may have been influenced by the proliferation of notable railroad frauds in the 1860s and 1870s, saw the risk of abusive conflicts of interest as very real. They also saw the alternative to a voidability rule — approval of interested transactions by disinterested directors — as inadequate. Some, like Justice Field, thought that humanity was so constituted that in the majority of cases involving a conflict of interest, duty would be overborne by self-interest.[4] Furthermore, the courts thought that detecting unfairness in real-world transactions was extremely difficult. They said it was impossible to measure the influence that a director might have over his fellow directors, even though he ostensibly abstained from discussing the proposed transaction or voting on it. They also disliked a rule that would put the remaining directors in the embarrassing and invidious position of having to scrutinize and pass upon the transactions of one of themselves.

Courts' weak arguments

The courts that later altered the voidability rule never really answered these arguments. At most, they made technical, analogical arguments. For example, they pointed out that a trustee, while forbidden to deal for himself with trust property, could deal with the cestui que trust if he made full disclosure and took no unfair advantage. According to these courts, a director who abstained from representing his corporation in a particular transaction and dealt in his personal capacity with a majority of disinter-

[4] Wardell v. Union Pac. R.R., 103 U.S. 651, 658 (1880).

ested directors was analogous to such a trustee, and the same rule ought to apply.

Three possible explanations of the long-run shift in rules about basic self-dealing may be considered. The first two focus on changing power relationships among people influencing the growth of law; the third focuses more on the merits of the substantive arguments for and against the alternative legal rules — that is, on the internal logic of the law.[5]

Managerial influence theory

The first explanation is that the courts and legislators were in some sense captured by corporate managers. Let us call this the managerial influence theory. According to this theory, the common element marking each shift from one stage to the next is increasing leniency to corporate fiduciaries. The later rules made it easier for corporate managers to get what they wanted: an increase in their personal welfare at the expense of public investors or minority shareholders. For although the third-stage rule requires basic self-dealing transactions to be fair, in practice the rule will allow much unfairness to occur and go undetected or uncorrected. The later rules came about, according to this explanation, because courts were somehow induced to adopt rules favoring the interests of corporate managers. Perhaps they felt a sense of class loyalty to corporate managers, as opposed to noncontrolling investors.

Problems

This managerial influence theory is fraught with difficulties. It is virtually impossible to show the extent to which the new rules actually benefited influential corporate managers. One suspects that other legal and economic changes had much greater significance for the financial welfare of the average corporate manager. Moreover, it is difficult to identify a convincing mechanism by which to show exactly how lawmakers came to adopt and further the personal interests of corporate managers. Direct, tangible influences by corporate managers on the courts and legislatures need to be documented. And one certainly wonders about what the real class identifications and loyalties were. Both controlling corporate managers and noncontrolling shareholders tend to be wealthy, upper class people. It is therefore not obvious that judges, if they did want to curry favor with the upper classes, would systematically favor corporate managers over corporate investors. In this respect, the situation is unlike that with respect to tort rules, which could have an important bearing upon the distribution of accident losses as between the ordinary consuming public and the large corporations (alias *both* managers *and* investors).[6]

[5] See Fried, The Laws of Change: The Cunning of Reason in Moral and Legal History, 9 J. Leg. Stud. 335 (1980).

[6] See generally, M. Horwitz, The Transformation of American Law 1780-1860 ch. 3 (1977).

General shift to flexible rules?

A second explanation emphasizes the proposition that the shift in self-dealing rules is really just an instance of a much larger pattern of change in the law and perhaps in social attitudes generally. In this view, legal rules in many fields were becoming less absolute and rigid and more qualified and flexible. Instead of mechanical, unqualified rules that brooked of no exceptions and were relatively cheap for lawyers and courts to apply, one began to see courts adopting open-ended principles that depended more on the facts and circumstances of the particular case and were likely to cause the consumption of greater legal and judicial resources. The shift in self-dealing rules fits this view well, for a fairness rule does leave more scope for argument and adjudication than does a voidability rule.

Lawyers' influence theory

But what were the forces underlying this supposed general shift to less absolute legal rules? One hypothesis is that lawyers (like other professionals) were becoming increasingly powerful in society and that they, with the increasing affluence of the U.S. public, were able to convince clients to tolerate less certain, and thus more expensive, legal rules.[7] It was obviously in the interest of the lawyers as a class to opt for less certain rules, since these would generate more business. Somehow, they were able to get the courts to adopt their preferences for kinds of rules. Let us call this view the lawyers' influence theory.

Problems

This theory, like the managerial influence theory, has some plausibility but leaves one with difficult and troubling questions. Foremost is the question: Why did the judges go along with the shift? After all, it was the judges, not the practicing lawyers, who had the power to declare new rules in their judicial holdings. But once any particular judge is appointed to the bench, why would it be in his self-interest to adopt rules that would tend to increase his own workload?[8] Judges, unlike private practitioners, are paid on a salaried basis rather than on a fee-for-service basis, so one would expect them, if anything, to adopt new rules that cut down on litigation. One might respond that the new rules, like the fairness rule for basic self-dealing, were so open-ended and spongy that they discouraged plaintiffs from bringing cases. This is an intriguing, if somewhat implausible, conjecture. But even if it is valid, it simply seems to discredit the lawyer-capture

[7] Indeed, over the period in question, other professionals also seemed to be growing in their economic power relative to ordinary workers. Physicians, for example, acquired greater relative prestige, greater relative income, and an apparent ability to create demand for their services. See generally P. Starr, The Social Transformation of American Medicine (1982). The whole era might be said to have been characterized by "the rise of the professions."

[8] One possible explanation: The bureaucrat who makes extra work may then appeal for approval to hire new subordinates, whose existence will give him greater status. C. Parkinson, The Law ch. 1 (1979).

thesis from another angle: Lawyers, whatever their intentions, did not succeed in having rules adopted that increased their litigation business.[9]

Another troubling question for the lawyers' influence theory of the shift to fairness rules concerns the alternatives available to the lawyers. Couldn't they have achieved a faster and greater increase in legal business by lobbying for the multiplication of legal rules, as opposed to the loosening up of old ones? Why, then, did the push for complicated regulatory statutes like the federal securities laws come much later in history?

The point of asking these questions is not to clearly disprove the managerial influence and lawyers' influence theories but to suggest how much work would be involved in trying to confirm them in anything like a scientific way.

Judicial enlightenment theory

The third explanation for the shift in self-dealing rules is that courts increasingly came to appreciate the positive values of some self-dealing transactions. Let us call this the judicial enlightenment theory. In this view, the original voidability rule was a result of the court's straightforward borrowing of an existing rule from trust law, plus the arguments about human nature and the difficulty of judicial second-guessing of directors' relationships and actions that they articulated in their opinions. But the increasing use of the corporate form inevitably caused the courts to be exposed to a greater number and variety of self-dealing transactions. They then began to realize the certain self-dealing transactions might be not only normal and virtually unpreventable but also positively better than comparable other-dealing, or market, transactions. Accordingly, they adopted more selective rules in order to allow the nonabusive self-dealing transactions to occur. Note that a shift in judicial attitudes of this sort is consistent with a larger pattern of shifts to more open-ended legal rules, although it does not require such a larger pattern. What the third theory suggests is that some or all such shifts resulted from courts' perceptions of the social or economic advantages of open-ended rules.

Related to close/public distinction

No one has conclusively demonstrated the validity of the judicial enlightenment theory. Nevertheless, it is possible to reason about the kinds of past patterns of litigation that would tend to confirm it and then to see if those patterns actually occurred. One inference of this sort has to do with close corporations. My view is that a voidability rule makes more sense for

[9]On the other hand, a fairness rule, even though it might generate the same or less *litigation* than a voidability rule, might require corporate lawyers to spend more time in *corporate counseling* with respect to proposed particular transactions. Perhaps, then, the lawyer-capture theory could be rehabilitated by focusing on the increasing power of some *subpart* of the bar: here, the corporate departments of large firms, as opposed to their litigation departments and the smaller firms of plaintiffs' attorneys.

public corporations than for close corporations. Let us call this the first proposition. The reasoning behind this proposition is explored in section 5.4 infra. For now, the idea can be grasped intuitively by a simple contrast. Consider a director who wants permission to make a loan of $1 million, at the going interest rate, to the corporation on whose board he sits. If the corporation is General Electric, is it plausible to argue that the corporation needs to enter this self-dealing transaction, or that the transaction will produce advantages it can't get in the financial markets? Of course not. General Electric has access to many sources of financing, and it can shop around for a low, competitive rate. If the corporation is the small, young, closely held Jones Mattress Company of Podunk, Alaska, might the self-dealing loan represent an advantage to the corporation not easily obtained elsewhere? It might very well represent such an advantage. This suggests that self-dealing transactions may occasionally be good things for close corporations and that, with appropriate safeguards, they ought to be allowed.

And judges' goals and psychology

Now assume two additional propositions. The second proposition is that, since at least the time of the Civil War, state judges have generally tried to adopt rules that are socially efficient. (This proposition is implicit in the judicial enlightenment theory.) The third proposition is that judges usually construct rules that (in their view) make sense when applied to the particular kinds of factual context they see most often in their courts. (This is a psychological assumption. It is supported by current psychological research, which shows that people are much more influenced by the concrete examples they observe than by the general verbal formulations they hear and use.[10]) Furthermore, judges may decide cases without classifying the factual contexts explicitly and may therefore make rules that on their face apply to contexts they rarely see, even though the rules are not so sensible for those rare contexts. Given our three propositions, we can then hypothesize why judges, around the turn of the century, began to change the self-dealing rules: *because the proportion of self-dealing cases involving close corporations became much greater than the proportion of self-dealing cases involving public corporations.* Here, then, is a testable proposition that might confirm or disconfirm the judicial enlightenment theory.

Supported by changing case mix

Is the proposition true? One research study provides strong evidence that it is.[11] Examining all the reported opinions in basic self-dealing cases

[10] See Richard Nisbett & Lee Ross, Human Inference: Strategies and Shortcomings of Social Judgment ch. 3 (1980).

[11] John C. Dugan, The Decline and Fall of the Corporate Prophylactic Rule: An Empirical Inquiry (1981) (unpublished manuscript on file at Harvard Law School library).

decided by six major state supreme courts and all the federal courts between the Civil War and about 1950, it found a sharp change in the kind of cases coming before the courts. Indeed, around 1880 virtually all of the opinions involved public corporations; around 1910, virtually all of them involved close corporations; in between the proportions changed, faster in some jurisdictions than others. All this is consistent with the judicial enlightenment theory.

Room for debate

This kind of evidence hardly proves the theory, of course. Moreover, it doesn't prove that there is no validity to the other two theories. And this uncertainty over the empirical support for the three competing theories is important. Those attracted to the first two theories are likely to be cynical about existing corporate law rules and will see these theories as validiating their attitudes. Those who take the view of the world implicit in the third explanation, which sees positive values in apparently inevitable and common business practices, would tend to use that explanation to legitimize the present approach of corporate law rules.

Fortunately, historical explanations are not the only intellectual tools one can use in criticizing or justifying existing legal rules or in pondering how to design better ones. The pros and cons of existing legal rules can be debated and used as a basis for legal reform, regardless of whether perceptions of these factors actually caused past lawmakers to adopt the rules that they did. I will undertake the more abstract, atemporal analysis of self-dealing rules in section 5.4 infra. Meanwhile, we must learn more about specific rules and cases.

§5.2 *Present Law: The Fairness Test*

§5.2.1 Delaware Law and MBCA Section 8.31

Section 144 of the Delaware General Corporation Law, which is similar to MBCA Section 8.31 and to the statutory rules in many states, governs corporate transactions involving interested directors and officers.[1] In es-

§5.2 [1]Del. §144 reads as follows.

(a) No contract or transaction between a corporation and one or more of its directors or officers, or between a corporation and any other corporation, partnership, association, or other organization in which one or more of its directors or officers, are directors or officers, or have a financial interest, shall be void or voidable solely for this reason, or solely because the director or officer is present at or participates in the meeting of the board or committee which authorizes the contract or transaction, or solely because his or their votes are counted for such purpose, if:

sence, it provides that no contract or transaction is voidable *solely* because it is a basic self-dealing transaction (as I have defined that concept), as long as one of three conditions is satisfied.

Coverage

Thus, the section explicitly covers transactions directly between a corporation and its directors or officers and transactions between a corporation and another business entity in which some of its directors or officers have a financial interest or of which they are directors or officers. This would include many transactions between subsidiaries and their parent companies, because these companies often have common or interlocking directors and officers. The section also provides, subject to the same qualification, that basic self-dealing transactions are not voidable solely because an interested director or officer is present at or participates in the meeting of the board or committee that authorizes the transaction or because his vote is counted.

Conditions

The three conditions, one of which must be met if the fundamental effect of Section 144 is to be obtained — namely, that a particular instance of basic self-dealing is not automatically voidable — make for tricky reading and interpretation. They may be described briefly as follows:

(1) disclosure plus approval by disinterested directors;
(2) disclosure plus shareholder approval; and
(3) fairness.

Under the first alternative, the material or important facts as to the conflict of interest *and* as to the contract or transaction itself must be disclosed to the board of directors (or appropriate committee)[2] or known to them. For

---

(1) The material facts as to his relationship or interest and as to the contract or transaction are disclosed or are known to the board of directors or the committee, and the board or committee in good faith authorizes the contract or transaction by the affirmative votes of a majority of the disinterested directors, even though the disinterested directors be less than a quorum; or

(2) The material facts as to his relationship or interest and as to the contract or transaction are disclosed or are known to the shareholders entitled to vote thereon, and the contract or transaction is specifically approved in good faith by vote of the shareholders; or

(3) The contract or transaction is fair as to the corporation as of the time it is authorized, approved or ratified, by the board of directors, a committee, or the shareholders.

(b) Common or interested directors may be counted in determining the presence of a quorum at a meeting of the board of directors or of a committee which authorizes the contract or transaction.

[2]Modern statutes allow some or all of the board's powers to be delegated to designated committees of board members. E.g., MBCA §8.25; Cal. §311; Del. §141(c); N.Y. §712.

example, if Chip Company were about to buy 100 tons of potatoes from a farm in which the president of the company had a one-third interest as limited partner, the board of directors, when approving the transaction, would have to know all the important facts about the president's interest in the farm and about the potato contract. Presumably, material facts as to the latter include not just the bare terms of the contract itself but the information relevant to assessing its business wisdom. Moreover, the board or committee must then authorize the transaction in good faith and by a *majority* of the *disinterested* directors.

Director approval

It is not necessary that the disinterested directors make up a quorum. For example, if in Chip Company four of the seven directors had personal financial interests in a potato farm from which Chip was about to make purchases, at least two of the three other directors would have to vote for the transaction. (Since the three disinterested directors would not usually make a quorum, it appears that one or more of the interested directors would have to be present and vote at the meeting dealing with the purchase transactions in order to satisfy the formalities for achieving corporate action.)

Shareholder approval

Under the second alternative, the material facts about the conflict of interest and the transaction itself must be known to the shareholders entitled to vote upon it, and the transaction must be "specifically" approved "in good faith" by vote of the shareholders. There is no statutory requirement of approval by a majority of disinterested shareholders; interested and disinterested shareholders are left undistinguished under this alternative. The second alternative, which may be more expensive and risky (to the interested director) than the first, seems designed for use when (1) there are no disinterested directors, (2) they are unwilling for whatever reasons to approve the transaction, or (3) the directors as a whole want to pass the buck and seek extra, or hopefully greater, legitimacy for a self-dealing transaction.

Fairness

The third alternative in the statute seems to offer the interested director or officer much more intriguing possibilities. Under it, the transaction must simply be "fair" as to the corporation "as of the time authorized, approved or ratified, by the board of directors, a committee thereof, or the shareholders." The latter phrase suggests, although it does not say, that every basic self-dealing transaction that is to avoid automatic voidability must receive director or shareholder approval at some point in time, but it clearly recognizes that after-the-fact approval (ratification) may be given. Moreover, the third alternative does not, by its terms,[3] require the disinterested director

[3]But see the *Hayes Oyster* case, discussed in the text accompanying notes 6 and 7 infra.

or officer to disclose anything, or the approving persons to know anything about the conflict of interest. Of course, the third alternative was not offered for the purpose of giving interested managers an incentive to deliberately conceal conflicts of interest. Rather, it seems designed to cover two special situations: (1) cases where all of the directors are interested in the transaction (so that the first alternative is unavailable), but where seeking shareholder approval (the second alternative) would be cumbersome, expensive, and not really meaningful; and (2) cases where a conflict existed at the time the transaction was entered into but where, through inadvertence, proper disclosure and approval were not obtained. In any event, the effect of the third alternative is that the interested party can always defend a basic self-dealing transaction against a charge of automatic voidability by arguing that it was fair, whether or not there was adequate disclosure of this conflict of interest or any prior approval of the transaction. This is one reason why the usual modern rule about basic self-dealing is often called, for simplicity, the fairness rule.

Statute's limited role

There is another reason, and it is more important. The basic test for evaluating basic self-dealing really comes from case law, not statute, and it is a fairness test. To see this, reconsider what the statutes do and don't do. Throughout the preceding discussion, I have referred to Section 144 as shielding self-dealing against charges of automatic voidability. That is, if the section operates, a corporation (acting by a board decision or at the instance of a court order in a derivative suit brought by shareholders) may not undo the transaction *simply* because there was a conflict of interest. And that is indeed the obvious function of the statute — to make it clear that the late nineteenth century rule of voidability is no longer the law.

No preclusion of judicial scrutiny

A key question then arises. Does the statute have any function beyond this negative one? Specifically, if the first or second conditions — disclosure plus disinterested director approval or disclosure plus shareholder approval — are met in a given instance, does that mean that the transaction is completely shielded from shareholder attack and that a court is *precluded* by the statute from examining the fairness of the transaction and possibly invalidating it? The Delaware Supreme Court has given a clear answer: No. In *Fliegler v. Lawrence,*[4] the court rejected the defendants' argument that they were relieved of the burden of proving fairness in a self-dealing transaction by reason of shareholder ratification of the board's decision to enter the transaction in question. The court said, "[Section 144] merely removes an 'interested director' cloud when its terms are met and provides against invalidation of an agreement 'solely' because such a direc-

[4] 361 A.2d 218 (Del. 1976).

tor or officer is involved. Nothing in the statute sanctions unfairness to Agau [the corporation] or removes the transaction from judicial scrutiny."[5]

Confusing statute

The *Fliegler* case highlights a confusion inherent in the way the Delaware interested director provision is drafted. The statute starts out as if its only purpose were to negate a rule of automatic voidability, and not also to lay out the rules that courts should apply in evaluating basic self-dealing: "no transaction is voidable *solely* because it constitutes basic self-dealing *if* . . . ." The form of the provision suggests that when the *if* clause is satisfied, a self-dealing transaction is not voidable as such but seems to leave it open for courts to develop tests for the propriety of such transactions. (For example, a court might decide that a self-dealing transaction is voidable unless the directors first tried to get outsiders to enter the transaction on terms comparable to or better than those offered by the insider.) But the actual content of the *if* clause — specifically, the third or fairness condition — suggests that the draftsmen were also trying, somewhat halfheartedly, to lay down tests for self-dealing transactions. The net result is odd. Because of the third condition, *failure* of an interested officer to make disclosure and get director or shareholder approval of a basic self-dealing transaction will not make the transaction automatically voidable. Yet, under the *Fliegler* case, *compliance* with the disclosure and approval procedure will not make the transaction automatically valid. In both cases the transaction stands or falls depending on whether it is fair.

A clearer approach

The Delaware and MBCA provisions, and those in many other states, would be clearer if they were recast to separate the two legislative tasks — negating the old rule and specifying a new one — and to specify the role of disclosure and approval more accurately. A better drafted interested director provision might sensibly start with three distinct subsections.

The first would say that basic self-dealing transactions are not voidable as such, period.

The second would say that a basic self-dealing transaction is voidable, or may give rise to a suit for damages, under certain specified conditions, such as when the interested directors or officers fail to sustain the burden of proving that it is fair to the corporaton. (This is not the substantive test that I favor, however. See section 5.4 below.)

The third would identify factors that courts should or might consider in applying this substantive test. For example, it could say that, in determining whether a transaction was fair, the court should give such weight to whether material facts concerning the conflict of interest and the business merits of the transaction were fully and adequately disclosed, and whether

[5] Id. at 222.

disinterested director or shareholder approval was given, as seems reasonable under the circumstances.

§5.2.2 Disclosure

In the above discussion, the impression may have been created that two fairly distinct routes to legitimating a self-dealing transaction are available. One is to make the transaction into something like a true other-dealing transaction by the device of full disclosure of the facts and approval by some relatively independent bargaining party (disinterested directors or shareholders). The other way is to set the transaction's terms so as to be fair, that is, comparable to those of an other-dealing transaction. The case law readily shows how these concepts are in fact intertwined. Indeed, in the *Hayes Oyster* case,[6] the court faulted the transaction because the conflict of interest had not been adequately disclosed: "non-disclosure by an interested director or officer is, in itself, unfair."[7] This is a rather startling holding for a modern court to have made, for in effect it transforms a stage three fairness rule into something very much like the stage two rule of fairness plus disclosure and approval. Whether this approach will be followed in many jurisdictions is doubtful.

Example of *Globe Woolen*

Other cases depend on nondisclosure, not of the conflict of interest but of information relevant to the business merits of the transaction. They show how readily the courts will object to the insider's acting passively with respect to his corporation while bargaining diligently for himself. In the old but still instructive case of *Globe Woolen Co. v. Utica Gas & Electric Co.*,[8] the New York Court of Appeals affirmed a judgment that an electric company could not be forced to fulfill a losing self-dealing contract that it had made. One Maynard, who was a director and a chairman of the executive committee of the electric company, was also the chief stockholder, the president, and a director of the other party to the contract, a textile manufacturing company. Maynard caused the electric company to enter a contract to supply all needed electric power to operate the mills of the textile company, which had been operating on steam power. Under the contract, the electric company *guaranteed* the textile company a substantial, continuing cost saving of a flat dollar amount per month from the switch to electric power, but there was no limitation in terms of the scope and nature of the operations in the textile mills. As it turned out, the mills changed the mix of

[6] State ex rel. Hayes Oyster Co. v. Keypoint Oyster Co., 391 P.2d 979 (Wash. 1964).
[7] Id. at 984.
[8] 121 N.E. 378 (N.Y. 1918).

their operations after the contract was entered. There was more yarn dyeing, which was energy intensive, and less slubbing, which required less energy. For these and other reasons, the electric company lost money on its contract and actually owed the textile company substantial sums under the guarantee. Maynard may have known that these changes were forthcoming. In any event, according to the court, he must have known that the contract was terribly one-sided.

Fiduciary's affirmative duty to disclose

Judge Cardozo took the position that it was not enough for Maynard to disclose his own interest in the contract to the approving directors of the electric company and to abstain from voting. It was not enough to refrain from lying and to give the ostensibly disinterested directors a fair chance to bargain with himself. (Incidentally, the facts of the case illustrate how cursory and superficial the approval of such directors often is.) He also had an *affirmative* duty to disclose the risks and one-sidedness of the proposed transaction itself. He could not be silent about the business improvidence of the contract simply because he was not voting on it; a fiduciary cannot thus get rid of his duty to warn of danger and error. The concluding paragraph suggests an even stronger principle: "We hold that a constant duty rests on the trustee to seek no harsh advantage to the detriment of his trust, but rather to protest and renounce if through the blindness of those who treat with him he gains what is unfair."[9]

This case does not mean that the disinterested director cannot make a profit on a self-dealing transaction, however, or that any self-dealing contract that turns out badly for the corporation can be avoided. If the insider makes full disclosure, if he presses for no harsh advantage, if the contract is fair as of the time it was entered, and if it turns out be an unusually good deal for him solely because of unforeseen developments, then, apparently, he can keep his bargain. Moreover, not all courts have been as strict in their rhetorical tone or their actual holdings as Judge Cardozo's.[10]

§5.2.3 Division of Gains

One additional aspect of the fairness test that bears mention is the question: How should the positive benefits (if any) of a self-dealing transaction be divided or shared among the parties? An important argument for allowing any self-dealing at all is that it sometimes yields the parties benefits not otherwise obtainable. In some situations, the special benefit can actually be

[9]Id. at 381.

[10]See, e.g., Puma v. Marriott, 283 A.2d 693 (Del. Ch. 1971) (business judgment rule protects contract between corporation and inside director when approved by disinterested outside directors); Brigham v. McCabe, 232 N.E.2d 327, (N.Y. 1967).

measured in dollar terms, and the question as to who gets it becomes acute.

Parent-subsidiary hypo

Suppose, for example, X Company, which has been losing money, owns 80 percent of the stock of Y Company, which has been earning income. By the filing of consolidated tax returns, under which the two companies are treated as one for certain federal income tax purposes, the companies will be able to offset X's losses against Y's income, and thus produce a tax saving. If X has been losing $10 million a year, and Y has been earning the same amount, for example, consolidation may free Y from the payment of $4.6 million in taxes. As a matter of corporate law, which company should get the saving, or how should it be divided? (Federal tax law does not constrain the allocation although it does direct refunds to the parent corporation.[11]) Bear in mind that the decision to consolidate tax returns and to divide the tax savings in a certain way is likely to involve a serious conflict of interest. The parent corporation's management will often have strong decision making influence on the actions of the subsidiary, either because there are common directors or officers or because the parent company managers have the power to vote in directors for the subsidiary that are to their liking. Yet the parent's management will often have a greater personal interest in the financial well being of the parent corporation. Parent company officers, for example, will often have stock options or stock appreciation rights that make them personally concerned with the value of the parent company stock. If a given dollar of tax savings is owned by the parent company, its shareholders, including the officers, have the residual claim to all of it, but if it is owned by the subsidiary, the minority shareholders of the subsidiary have a claim to 20 percent. There will therefore be a temptation for the officers to direct most of the tax saving to the parent.

Usual tests unavailable

The problem cannot be readily solved by resort to the usual arm's-length bargain or competitive market tests of fairness. The outcome of an arm's length bargain about the division of a jointly produced savings of this sort would depend very much on the individual bargaining skills of the two parties, and is difficult to predict. (Game theorists have been working on similar problems with some success.[12]) Moreover, there seems to be no good market comparison available. The results of other parent-subsidiary agreements about tax savings are irrelevant, since it is likely that they also involved self-dealing rather than independent bargains. And data on the purchase prices paid by healthy independent companies for tax loss corpo-

[11] Treas. Reg. §1.1502-77(a).

[12] See, e.g., Roth & Malouf, Game-Theoretic Models and the Role of Information in Bargaining, 86 Psychological Rev. 574 (1979).

rations is skimpy because the corporate tax law discourages trafficking in loss corporations.[13]

Alternative approaches

Courts could take several alternative approaches to the problem of allocating the tax saving. One would be that the company that has the income to be offset should get all of the saving, since it is the one that would otherwise have paid the tax. This rule is a narrow one, geared only to the tax saving situation, not to cases of self-dealing surplus generally. It also seems unfair, since the other company contributed something equally important — an operating loss — to the creation of the tax saving. Both companies were necessary but individually insufficient to the creation of a tax saving: It cannot be said to have been caused more by one than the other.

Another approach is to "lean against" the conflict of interest by adopting a rule strictly protective of the subsidiary. The subsidiary would always have to get the full advantage of the tax saving, and the parent company would only share in this increasing value by means of its stock ownership in the subsidiary. But this rule seems needlessly harsh to the parent's public shareholders. A less drastic alternative that would also protect partially owned subsidiaries would be a neutral sharing rule applied generally to self-dealing surpluses generated by parent-subsidiary interactions. A specific sharing rule might say, for example, that the surplus should always be shared in proportion to the relative asset sizes of the two companies.[14] Arguably, this rule is arbitrary, since there is no logically defensible way of measuring the relative value of each company's contribution to the surplus. But this difficulty is inherent in all gains produced by jointly necessary causes and does not reflect any flaw in legal analysis. A neutral sharing rule still seems better than none.

Finally, a court wanting to avoid even the relatively modest work entailed in enforcing a sharing rule, or worried about the institutional propriety of a court adopting a formula as a response to a problem, might adopt the rule that any allocation of the tax saving or other self-dealing surplus will be considered fair so long as the subsidiary gets some not insignificant part of it (or even as long as the subsidiary is not worse off then before the self-dealing transaction).

The *Case* case

This last alternative is, perhaps unfortunately, the approach taken in the noted case of *Case v. New York Central Railroad*.[15] But the facts there suggest that the court was heavily influenced by the long-standing existence of a

[13] See I.R.C. §382.

[14] This idea of sharing is discussed in the context of mergers in chapter 11.

[15] 204 N.E.2d 643 (N.Y. 1965).

rental agreement between the parent and subsidiary that was unfavorable to the former. The court may have felt that the parent needed relief from a serious past mistake. And there is authority contrary to the view in *Case*.[16]

Burden of proof and remedy

Two final points need mention. First, the usual rule is that the party seeking to uphold the validity of a basic self-dealing transaction has the burden of proving its fairness.[17]

Second, the remedy now usually granted with respect to a faulty self-dealing transaction is that it is avoided, or the interested party has to pay damages in the amount of the unfairness of the transaction.[18] For example, when an officer sells property at an unfair, inflated price to his corporation, he becomes liable for the difference between the actual price and the fair value of the property.[19]

§5.3 *Present Law: Authorization and Ratification*

Desire for immunity from suit

Managers may try to protect their self-dealing transactions from effective attacks by appeal to the acquiescence of the shareholders at large. They may arrange to have provisions in the certificate of incorporation that authorize and insulate self-dealing transactions to a greater extent than general corporate law rules do. They may also seek shareholder approval or ratification of particular self-dealing transactions. The next section explores the possibility that, as a matter of policy, shareholders may not be a good group to possess final decision making authority in such matters and

[16]Alliegro v. Pan American Bank of Miami, 136 So. 2d 656 (Fla. Dist. Ct. App.), cert. denied, 149 So. 2d 45 (Fla. 1963) (parent corporation ordered to return payment made by partially owned subsidiary; payment represented taxes saved by subsidiary as a result of consolidated return).

[17]Sisk v. Jordan Co., 109 A. 181 (Conn. 1920); Patron's Mutual Fire Ins. Co. v. Holden, 222 N.W. 754 (Mich. 1929); Mountain Top Youth Camp, Inc. v. Lyon, 202 S.E.2d 498 (N.C. App. 1974). Contra, Murphy v. Hanlon, 79 N.E.2d 292 (Mass. 1948).

[18]Shlensky v. South Parkway Bldg. Corp., 166 N.E.2d 793, 802 (Ill. 1960). See also Bliss Petroleum Co. v. McNally, 237 N.W. 53 (Mich. 1931) (corporation did not rescind but recovered difference between price paid and fair value); Ripley v. International Rys. of Central America, 171 N.E.2d 443 (N.Y. 1960) (recovery for fair value of services provided and reformation of contract for future services). Although the decisions are rarely explicit on this point, it appears that the plaintiff may elect either rescission or damages. But see Mariani v. Mariani, 93 N.Y.S.2d 370 (App. Div. 1949) (rescission appropriate only in case of fraud; inadequacy of consideration remedied by damages).

[19]Some early decisions held that if full rescission was possible, it was the only relief available. Thus, if the corporation wished to retain property it bought from a director, it had to pay the agreed price, even if this resulted in exorbitant profits for the director. New York Trust Co. v. American Realty Co., 155 N.E. 102, 105 (N.Y. 1926); Barr v. New York L.E. & W.R.R., 26 N.E. 145 (N.Y. 1891).

that their votes for or acquiescence in ratification proposals and charter provisions should not foreclose courts from scrutinizing and evaluating self-dealing transactions. In this section, however, I shall simply comment on the muddled state of existing law.

§5.3.1 Charter Provisions

Example of *Everett v. Phillips*

One can cite cases as having sustained charter provisions immunizing management from what would otherwise be an actionable breach of fiduciary duty, just as one can cite decisions that say such provisions offer no protection against liability when bad faith is present or that they do not always foreclose a judicial inquiry into the fairness of the transaction.[1] But the cases, when closely read, do not give management much comfort. For example, one of the leading cases in this area, *Everett v. Phillips,*[2] involved a charter provision of the Empire Power Corporation which said that no transaction with another corporation would be "affected or invalidated by the fact that" the directors or officers were connected with or interested in the other corporation. This was at a time when New York did not yet have a statutory provision that clearly negated the old automatic voidability rule for basic self-dealing.[3] A minority shareholder of Empire sued its directors for failing to demand repayment of loans made by Empire to the Long Island Lighting Company, in which the directors held a majority of the stock. The claim was that the directors had a conflict of interest and had breached their fiduciary duty. The court rejected the claim, and seemed to base its result partly on the charter provision.

Interestingly, the business rationale for the loans was avoidance of regulation. Long Island Lighting needed money, but to issue bonds it would have had to seek approval from the Public Service Commission and would have become subject to various restrictions. Short-term loans would avoid these problems but would of course create a problem of frequent need for refinancing. By virtue of the interlocking director connection, Long Island Lighting was able to arrange loans that were technically and legally short-term, but that it could comfortably expect to be renewed — thus avoiding

§5.3 [1]Compare Breswick & Co. v. Harrison-Rye Realty Co., 154 N.Y.S.2d 625 (App. Div. 1956), aff'd, 148 N.E.2d 299 (N.Y. 1958) (charter provision bars derivative suit to avoid unfavorable contact) with Abeles v. Adams Engineering Co., 173 A.2d 246 (N.J. 1961) (transaction subject to judicial scrutiny for fairness despite charter authorization).

[2]43 N.E.2d 18 (N.Y. 1942).

[3]New York enacted such a statute in 1961 as §713 of its Business Corporation Law, 1961 N.Y. Laws ch. 855.

both problems. Perhaps, then, the transaction could be viewed as creating a form of self-dealing surplus and should have been looked upon favorably for just that reason. Moreover, the court's statement about the significance of the charter provision must be read in context:

> The dual position of the directors . . . should lead the courts to scrutinize these transactions with care. . . . It does not, however, *alone* suffice to render the transactions void, and the provision of the certificate of incorporation of Empire Power Corporation expressly authorizing the directors to act even in matters where they have dual interest, has the effect of exonerating the directors, *at least in part*, "from adverse inferences which might otherwise be drawn against them."[4]

Limited nature of result

Thus, although the court did not dismiss the charter provision and seems to have given it some weight, several qualifications must be noted.

First, the court was dealing with a provision that simply anticipated later statutory confirmation of an ongoing shift from the automatic voidability rule to the present fairness rule about self-dealing transactions. There is no indication that charter provisions may generally substitute for clearly established rules governing conflicts of interest.

Second, the provision wasn't seen as foreclosing judicial scrutiny — indeed, *careful* scrutiny — of the transaction.

Third, it was not clear what legal effect the provision did have. What were the "adverse inferences" from which the defendants were freed? Did the court simply mean that the burden of proof was shifted to the plaintiffs?

Fourth, it seems likely that without the provision the case might nevertheless have been decided the same way. Of interest in this connection is the fact that there was a business purpose or self-dealing surplus for the loans (admittedly, not one that the Public Service Commission would have cherished). Perhaps even more importantly, the individual defendants' personal interests in Empire, the referent corporation, seemed as great or greater than their interests in the lighting company. In other words, the case might be characterized as not actually involving self-dealing. This is because one of our three defining characteristics of self-dealing (see section 4.1 supra), a greater interest on the part of the insiders in the other corporation than in the referent corporation, seems not to have been satisfied. Although not casting the point in these terms, the court was clearly in-

[4] 43 N.E.2d at 22.

fluenced by the underlying fact of the defendants' sizable self-interest in the welfare of Empire.[5]

Other cases are similarly unclear about the precise legal effect of a charter provision authorizing self-dealing.[6]

§5.3.2 Ratification

Effect of ratification

Shareholder ratification of basic self-dealing transactions raises at least four important questions. First, what legal effect does proper shareholder ratification have? The main alternatives are that ratification will simply immunize the transaction from attack on the ground that it was not properly authorized; that it will shift the burden of proof on the issue of the fairness of the transaction to a plaintiff who attacks it; or that it will immunize the transaction against attack on the grounds that it was unfair. Judicial opinions, to the extent that they are clear, seem to distribute themselves between the latter two alternatives.[7] But even courts that clearly give substantial weight to ratification often leave an out for the plaintiff who can prove something worse than unfairness. For example, they might say that ratification does not prevent the setting aside of a transaction that amounted to "fraud,"[8] "overreaching,"[9] or a "waste or gift of corporate assets."[10] To a large extent, the difference between these forms of misconduct and ordinary unfairness is just a matter of degree. In practice, the courts seem to have a great deal of latitude in deciding how much weight

[5]Right after its adverse inferences passage, the court says, "We may point out here also that if by reason of these loans Empire Power Corporation should sustain a loss, the loss would fall primarily upon these defendants as owners of the entire capital stock. The proportion of stock of all classes owned by these defendants in Empire . . . is . . . much greater than the proportion of stock owned by them in Long Island Lighting. . . ." Id. at 22.

[6]E.g., Spiegel v. Beacon Participations, Inc., 8 N.E.2d 895 (Mass. 1937).

[7]Compare Cohen v. Ayers, 596 F.2d 733 (7th Cir. 1979) (applying New York law) and Michelson v. Duncan, 407 A.2d 211 (Del. 1979) (ratification shifts burden of proof to plaintiff) with Kirwan v. Parkway Distillery, Inc., 148 S.W.2d 720 (Ky. 1941) and Russell v. Henry C. Patterson Co., 81 A. 136 (Pa. 1911) (ratification precludes review for fairness). But see Pappas v. Moss, 393 F.2d 865 (3d Cir. 1968) (under New Jersey law, defendant must prove fairness despite shareholder ratification).

[8]Continental Sec. Co. v. Belmont, 99 N.E. 138 (N.Y. 1912); American Timber and Trading Co. v. Niedermeyer, P.2d 1211 (Or. 1976). Contra, Claman v. Robertson, 128 N.E.2d 429 (Ohio 1956).

[9]Chambers v. Beaver-Advance Corp., 140 A.2d 808 (Pa. 1958).

[10]Schreiber v. Bryan, 396 A.2d 512 (Del. Ch. 1978); Eliasberg v. Standard Oil Co., 92 A.2d 862 (N.J. Super. 1952), aff'd mem., 97 A.2d 437 (N.J. 1953).

to give to shareholder ratification and what effect it will have on the outcome of a particular case.

Varies by kind of case?

The second question is whether the effect of ratification varies with the kind of self-dealing transaction under attack. It may well be, for example, that ratification is more likely to be treated as dispositive of a case involving alleged directorial negligence[11] or a transaction between corporations having common outside directors but not involving serious conflicts of interest (because, for example, the common directors have little financial interest in either company). This would be in contrast to cases involving a corporate transaction with an interested director or officer or with a corporation in which an officer had a significant personal interest.[12]

Interested shareholders

The third question is whether ratification's effect, whatever it is, is contingent upon nonvoting by the interested shareholders or upon the interested shareholders' not being needed for a majority vote. Some case authority says no, if the terms of the transaction are fair.[13] This statement of the matter is obviously very confusing, if not self-contradictory. The proviso about fairness seems to suggest that, where the interested shareholders hold majority voting power the ratification is nevertheless valid but the plaintiff can attack the transaction as unfair. But the main, hoped-for-effect of ratification is to immunize against a fairness attack. Perhaps the courts mean only that the plaintiff has the burden of proof.

Need for full disclosure

The fourth and most important question concerns disclosure. Whatever the legal effect of a proper shareholder ratification may be, ratification is clearly considered improper if the shareholders do not receive full and adequate disclosure of matters material to what they are voting on. All courts agree on this and, as a practical matter, much litigation about ratified self-dealing transactions, at least in the case of public companies, focuses on whether there was adequate disclosure of a conflicting interest — as required under the federal proxy rules, for example[14] — rather than on the effect that ratification should have.[15] Of course, there can be much debate about what does and what does not constitute adequate disclosure in a particular case.

[11] Smith v. Brown-Borhek Co., 200 A.2d 398 (Pa. 1964).

[12] Rankin v. Frebank, 121 Cal. Rptr. 348 (Cal. App. 1975).

[13] Bjorngaard v. Goodhue Country Bank, 52 N.W. 48 (Minn. 1892); Russell v. Henry C. Patterson Co., 81 A. 136 (Pa. 1911).

[14] See chapter 9.

[15] E.g., Galfand v. Chestnutt, 402 F. Supp. 1318 (S.D.N.Y. 1975), aff'd in part, remanded in part on other grounds, 545 F.2d 807 (2d Cir. 1976), aff'd mem., 573 F.2d 1290 (2d Cir. 1977).

§5.4 *The Search for a Better Rule*

Argument for a flat prohibition

In the context of the modern publicly held corporation, one can make a good case for the view that there is no excuse for permitting any basic self-dealing. There are two prongs to this argument, discussed in subsections 5.4.1 and 5.4.2. On the one hand, all basic self-dealing presents a significant danger of abuse or unfairness, and the danger is not made insignificant by the safeguards in the prevailing legal rules or by other controls over managerial misconduct. On the other hand, there often appears to be no positive corporate or social purpose served by fair self-dealing transactions that could not be served by fair transactions with true outsiders. Now, if self-dealing transactions do not make the corporations involved positively and significantly *better* than they would be without self-dealing, there is no reason to permit any nontrivial danger of unfair self-dealing. For to do so is only to expose corporations and their investors to an unproductive and unnecessary risk. Given this argument, it is irrelevant to contend that most directors and officers are honest and most self-dealing transactions do not hurt the corporations involved. These facts may well be true, but they do not explain why corporate managers should be allowed to expose their investors to unnecessary and unproductive risks.

This section attempts to evaluate the argument just sketched.

§5.4.1 Imperfect Controls

Imperfect nonlegal controls

The two parts of the argument need considerable expansion. The first part states that the current system leaves some nontrivial risk that unfair transactions will occur and go uncorrected. One subpart of it is that nonlegal controls, such as market and moral forces, are imperfect. They leave managers with a not insignificant amount of slack or leeway to engage in unfair self-dealing. Product markets, capital markets, and the market for managerial talent do exert a restraining force on managers, but they do not eliminate managerial discretion. How much is left? Perhaps a clue to this question is to focus on the form of market control most economists think is best: the hostile takeover bid. It is fairly clear from empirical studies[1] that company values can decline quite substantially before a takeover bid is provoked. The average amount of safe decline is a rough measure of the amount of slack left by market controls.

§5.4 [1]For a good literature review, see Jensen & Ruback, The Market for Corporate Control: The Scientific Evidence, 11 J. of Fin. Econ. 5 (1983).

Imperfect legal rules

Another subpart of the argument about the danger of self-dealing is that the prevailing *legal* rules about basic self-dealing do not reduce the risk that undetected or uncorrected unfairness will occur to insignificance. Since the rules give some weight to shareholder approval and director approval of basic self-dealing, and they rely on the possibility of judicial scrutiny, it is useful to see how well each of these three mechanisms can be expected to work.

Hypothetical of Jones

Consider shareholder approval. Suppose that Jones, president of a large publicly held electric company, uses his influence to have the corporation negotiate a contract with a coal mining company, in which Jones and members of his family have a substantial financial interest. Under the contract, the coal company will supply the electric company with all its requirements for coal for five years at a specified price. Jones, anticipating challenge by some dissident shareholder and his hungry "plaintiff's attorney," takes pains to get shareholder approval of the contract. He causes the annual proxy statement[2] of the electric company to describe the proposed contract and his own relationship to the coal company. The shareholders can approve the contract by checking a yes box rather than a no box on the appropriate line of the proxy card that comes with the statement. The card also calls for votes on other matters, such as the annual election of directors.

Problems with shareholder approval

Is this shareholder approval process a good one for passing judgment on the contract? No. To make a sound judgment that the contract is fair to their corporation, the shareholders would have to possess a great deal of background information and would have to engage in time consuming analysis. Obviously, besides knowing about the contract's terms, they should know whether the price of coal in the contract is the same as or better than the current market price of the same general kind of coal. But this information is clearly not enough; *simple comparison with market prices is almost never an adequate inquiry into the fairness issue.* The intelligent shareholder will think of many additional relevant questions. Is the market price of coal expected to go up or down in the next five years? If the latter, the electric company may be locked into an unfortunate arrangement. How important is it in the electric company's planning to have a requirements contract? Are there better arrangements, such as a requirements contract priced on a variable price formula? Is the coal company more or less reliable about making deliveries than other coal companies? Can it handle an unex-

[2] A proxy statement is a document in which the corporation is required to provide the shareholder with information related to a proposed corporate action for which the shareholders must vote their approval. See section 9.2 infra.

pected surge in demand as well as other companies? Is its coal actually of adequate and uniform quality? Is it more subject than other companies to labor, financial, or regulatory troubles? Are there sizable transportation costs in addition to the basic market price? If so, are the coal company's facilities as well located in relation to the electric company's utility plants as are those of other coal companies? Will the arrangement somehow induce the electric company to be slow in switching to other kinds of fuel, should that become necessary or desirable? How likely are such possibilities? And so forth.

Superficiality vs. waste dilemma

For every shareholder to assemble the background information and to exert the thought necessary to answer these questions in an informed, sound way would require an effort that, in the aggregate, would be monumental in terms of the time and money expended. Without these massive expenditures, the shareholders, if they all act independently and sum their opinions in a collective vote, cannot pass a sound business judgment on the fairness of the contract. And if they do make the expenditures, the aggregate costs may well exceed any conceivable value attributable to the prospect of detecting and preventing unfairness in the contract. In effect, shareholder approval is doomed to be either superficial or wasteful. (To make matters even worse, shareholders are beset with so-called free rider problems: Many of them will be tempted to gamble on the prospect that the other shareholders will do the reading and thinking for them.)

Not surprisingly, shareholders characteristically choose superficiality over waste. As many observers of the corporate scene have noted, shareholders in public corporations rarely make the kind of intensive effort a true judgment on matters such as the fairness of a specific contract would require, and usually either go along with management or do nothing. Their doing so actually fits well with a basic design principle for the large public corporation: The roles of business decisionmakers and investors are to be purified and separated. As we have seen (in chapter 1 supra), this division of labor has great efficiency advantages. Since the shareholders of the electric company have already hired a much smaller number of persons (the managers) to make informed business decisions for them, to expect them to monitor their managers by becoming additional managers — which is what they are when they go into details about the business wisdom of a contract — is to expect a very bad social arrangement to arise.

To summarize about the shareholder approval procedure as a way of policing basic self-dealing transactions: It would be perverse for the legal system to have many such matters taken to the shareholders; folly to expect the shareholders to pass upon them in a careful, well informed way; and wrong to hold them to the consequences of their failing to do so.

Problems with director approval

Now consider director approval. This process fails because, under conventional (although perhaps alterable) arrangements, the independent directors may not really be independent, or may not have adequate resources and incentives for doing a good job of review. On many boards, the chief executive officer, such as Jones in our example, is the dominant personality. Many board members are corporate employees and depend for their jobs, promotions, and so forth on the dominant personality. The nominations for outside directors are controlled by a nomination committee of existing directors, which may be in turn controlled by inside directors or by outside directors who were selected by and acceptable to the insiders. Nomination of a person by the official committee virtually insures his election by the shareholders. The persons nominated are in fact often friends of the chief executive officer or other insiders, or at least they are in the same social class and share the same basic attitudes. Among special-status directors, such as academics, women, and members of minorities, attitudinal selection is very careful. Some of the less wealthy of these directors may be influenced by the fear of not being renominated and thus losing the fee accompanying the directorships. Many apparently independent directors, such as a lawyer with the corporation's outside law firm or an investment banker with the corporation's securities underwriter, in fact have a key financial interest in their firm's relationship with the corporation. This relationship is often controlled by the chief executive and other insiders. Furthermore, the social atmosphere of directors' meetings favors clubbiness and mutual support. It is not "nice" to withhold affirmation of the inside executives, to take an adversarial stance, or to ask and pursue "discerning questions." Finally, the amount of time spent on the corporation's business affairs by independent directors is small — a few hours or a day or two a month — and the range of complex matters that must be considered can be very large.[3]

To be sure, by expending effort, a relatively small number of truly independent directors might be able to put themselves into a position where they could make an informed judgment about the fairness of a basic self-dealing transaction. The cost of their doing so, though not so extravagant as the cosι of independent decision making by all of the shareholders, would be considerable. One would then wonder why the corporation should incur this considerable cost: If the proposed contract is merely fair — no worse than an alternative other-dealing transaction — the corporation gains absolutely nothing by incurring the cost.

[3]See generally Note, The Propriety of Judicial Deference to Corporate Boards of Directors, 96 Harv. L. Rev. 1894 (1983).

In summary, the director approval procedure for basic self-dealing transactions suffers from the risks that the directors are not truly independent and that they lack adequate personal incentives to act vigorously in the best interest of the shareholders; from the time, information, and budget constraints on directors; and from the fact that the cost of getting them into the position of being truly competent to pass judgment on the business wisdom of a self-dealing transaction presented by insiders is considerable but often unproductive for the corporation.

Problems with judicial scrutiny

Finally, consider the flaws in the procedure of judicial scrutiny of the fairness of basic self-dealing transactions. First, judicial scrutiny of self-dealing will often not occur. Some strongly motivated shareholder or director must first find prima facie evidence of unfairness in the transaction. In many or most self-dealing situations, the probability of this happening is not high.

Second, judicial scrutiny of fairness is terribly expensive. As the discussion of shareholder approval showed, many pieces of information are logically relevant to the passing of a sound judgment on the fairness of a contract. This information must somehow be gotten before the court, and argued about. Even if the burden is on the defendant to show fairness, he may do quite well by documenting the facts about a few of the obvious features — in our example, price under the contract as compared to some apparently comparable market price, an industry practice of having requirements contracts, and a few other matters. The plaintiff will still have to deal with the open-ended number of nonobvious but potentially relevant questions. Answers to these questions can, of course, be sought through the pretrial discovery process. The plaintiff can take depositions from Mr. Jones and others, require various persons to answer lengthy interrogatories, and seek to get copies of volumes of documents. In retaliation, the defendant can do likewise. Indeed, the pretrial discovery process is well suited for deliberate strategic use, and it not infrequently results in enormous delay and expense.

Third, judicial scrutiny of fairness is a process that may be corrupted or diverted in various ways. For example, it may often be more profitable for the lawyers involved to settle the case instead of litigating it to the end, even though full litigation would better serve the interests of the shareholders.

§5.4.2 Self-Dealing Surplus

Review of argument so far

The preceding discussion indicates that the very real danger of unfair self-dealing that survives market and moral controls is not reduced to a negligibly small danger by the safeguards of the prevailing legal rules. We need not be too precise about this conclusion. Given any significant danger of unfair self-dealing, the argument for a flat prohibition against all basic self-dealing is strong, *unless* we can show clearly that self-dealing often has significant positive value. It is this possibility that we must now examine.

Self-dealing surplus

Some self-dealing transactions are less costly than any reasonably substitutable other-dealing transactions. I will call the difference in cost the self-dealing surplus. It is rational for a corporation to prefer a self-dealing transaction over any available other-dealing transaction if there is a self-dealing surplus and if, under the terms of the deal, the corporation will share in it.

Two types

It is useful to divide the sources of self-dealing surplus into savings in transaction costs and savings in production costs. The term *transaction costs* includes all the resources expended by the corporation and the other bargaining party in searching out each other, getting information about each other as to such matters as productive capacity, reliability, creditworthiness, style of operation, and so forth and establishing a groundwork of communication channels and social acceptance among individuals in the two organizations, upon which groundwork particular deals can be expeditiously made. Thus, in our previous example, Mr. Jones might make additional arguments for the contract between the electric company and the coal company if there were already an established pattern of relationships between the companies. Perhaps the people in the electric company's purchasing department have already learned which specific individuals at the coal company it would be best to call when placing an order or trying to resolve a confusion or dispute. Perhaps they have already learned how much lead time should in fact be given the coal company for various sizes of orders at different times of the year. Although difficult to articulate, these advantages may be real. In this particular case, they may seem rather unimpressive.

Example

A more dramatic case would be presented if it were proposed that the corporation sell a piece of land for $100,000 — the alleged fair market value as determined by an appraiser — to the president, Mr. Jones, rather than to anyone else, in order to save a 6 percent real estate brokerage commission. The source of the saving can be readily identified. In the course of normal corporate activities, Jones and the corporate directors have *already* consumed valuable resources in establishing a relationship and learning about each other's needs and capacities. These past expenditures, or sunk costs, have had the effect that now the additional or marginal cost of dealing with the interested person is lower than that of dealing with an sider. Since, in making a rational decision at any given moment, sunk costs should be regarded as bygones and only marginal costs considered, the sale to Jones appears to be positively desirable.

Points about transaction cost savings

Several observations may be ventured about transaction cost savings that result from self-dealing. First, such savings are likely to be frequent but often small and hard to identify and measure. The example of the established relationships between the electric company and the coal company suggests this.

Second, such savings will often be one time in nature and fortuitous, because the same kinds of savings can usually be achieved in transactions with true outsiders. The electric company, for example, might just as well have consumed resources in established smooth working relationships with an *independent* coal company. Once this was done, there would be transaction cost savings in continuing to deal with that independent company rather than switching.

Third, and most importantly, to the extent that self-dealing permits sizable savings in transaction costs, it tends to lessen the chances of an inexpensive, objective evaluation of the fairness of the transaction. This relationship arises because the transaction costs of dealing with independent persons are relatively high precisely in those cases that do not involve homogenous products sold in an active, competitive market. It is no accident that the appealing cases, like the example in which the corporation and Jones would save a 6 percent brokerage fee, involve matters such as the sale of *land,* the archetypical unique product. Little worldly experience is needed to appreciate how "soft" real estate appraisals can be, how gossamer is the independence of an appraiser selected by self-interested individuals, and how difficult it therefore is to judge the fairness of a land sale that was not in fact at arms' length. Conversely, when, as in the case of the sale of fungible commodities that are traded in a competitive market, it is fairly easy to determine the relevant market prices of the goods involved (and market price is a key element of the fairness inquiry) the transaction costs savings of self-dealing are likely to be small or nonexistent, because the transaction costs of a true market transaction would be relatively small.

Production cost savings

The other conceivable type of self-dealing surplus is a saving in production costs. On some occasions an insider may be able to offer a better deal than anyone else, or even the only deal of a certain kind, because he possesses some degree of monopoly power as producer of the good or service that the corporation wants. Real estate again furnishes a convenient example. Suppose the electric company wants to expand its physical facilities and obtain land for a nearby parking lot. It may happen that Mr. Jones is the owner of the only available and suitable plot of land. Letting him sell the company that land seems quite sensible.

Limited role of concept

The unique producer argument will not often be a convincing one for most goods and services. It will be especially suspicious when the insider is asserting that he is the only one willing and able to finance the exploits of the corporation, that is, lend money to it. At least with respect to public corporations, this claim flies in the face of the widely accepted proposition that financial markets in the United States are fairly efficient.

Indeed, the most important observation to be made about production cost savings from self-dealing is almost the opposite of the one made about transaction cost savings: Although in specific instances production cost savings may be quite large, they are probably infrequent. In most situations, it is fairly easy to concoct some prima facie reason why an insider or an affiliated entity is the "only" feasible party with which the corporation should deal. But careful analysis of the evidence and arguments will often cast serious doubt on such claims.[4]

[4]Consider the following application by a profit-sharing plan to the Department of Labor for a variance from the regulations imposed by the Employee Retirement Income Security Act of 1974, cited in note 7 infra. The plan requested permission to purchase, from the sponsoring employer corporation, loans made by the employer to customers. That is, it sought to refinance the employer's credit-sale business operations. The claim was that this "unique investment opportunity" had been utilized by the plan for 15 years and had shown an average return of 8.75 percent. Furthermore, the plan was not in the business of making loans and the start-up costs for the operation would have been very high, so the plan could not compete with the employer. Application No. D-198, June 23, 1975.

The application for a variance was denied. Those who requested it probably thought the denial was terribly unreasonable. Nevertheless, the argument for the exemption was incomplete. Rationally, to assess the fairness of the refinancing operations to the profit-sharing plan one has to compare those operations to other relevant opportunities. Most modern managers of institutional investors such as pension and profit-sharing plans would argue that they should consider only a few abstract financial characteristics of possible investments: their risk, their return, and their impact on the investor's liquidity needs. In this view, the supposedly unique refinancing opportunity has to be compared with virtually all opportunities to invest in financial assets — stocks, bonds, and government securities of every description. The refinancing investment would be uniquely better only if it offered a higher return *per unit of risk* than other financial assets. In general, given reasonably efficient financial markets, uniqueness of this sort is simply implausible. In any event, it cannot rationally be found to exist until the party requesting the variance (1) gives reliable information about the riskiness of the refinancing operations and (2) gives information about the risk-return characteristics of other available financial assets in which the plan could invest.

Furthermore, even risk-return comparisons may be inadequate. For example, pension plans, like life insurance companies, usually have relatively small and highly predictable liquidity needs; they therefore can and usually should invest heavily in long-term investments, to an extent that would be very dangerous for institutions like banks. Accordingly, if a pension plan already has enough liquidity, the fact that a short term note issued by an affiliated corporation has a better-than-market interest rate for its riskiness and term to maturity may not be enough to overcome the cost of forgoing longer term investments.

§5.4.3 A Proposal

Review

The previous two subsections suggest that the possibility of self-dealing surplus does not justify a legal rule giving blanket permission to engage in basic self-dealing, subject only to rare or superficial reviews of the fairness of the transaction by a court, a board of directors, or the shareholders. It is doubtful whether the value of self-dealing surpluses *generally* exceeds the disvalue stemming from the fact that unfairness may occur and go undetected or uncorrected. On the other hand, the discussion casts doubt on the wisdom of a rule flatly prohibiting basic self-dealing, without any exceptions. What kind of rule does seem warranted?

Proposed approach

Many of the major opportunities for realizing self-dealing surpluses could be exploited in a legal system that (1) basically adopted a flatly prohibitory rule against basic self-dealing but (2) provided for administrative approval, through class exemptions and specific variances, of transactions that meet appropriate standards of justification. For a variety of reasons,[5] the Securities and Exchange Commission may be the best regulatory agency to administer this proposed exemption-making process.

Examples of similar approaches

The combination of flat prohibitions with a variance system is not a new idea. In the case of large, special segments of the corporate world, it already exists. The Employment Retirement Income Security Act of 1974 adopts such a system for most private pension plans in the United States,[6] and a similar, but less elaborate, scheme exists with respect to investment companies (mutual funds and the like) under the Investment Company Act of 1940.[7] The proposal that I am making would insist, however, on a more exacting standard of approval than is typically contained in such statutes. A variance should be granted for a self-dealing transaction, not when it is shown to be fair but only when (1) it is shown to be better than fair, that is, substantially certain to give rise to a self-dealing surplus, *and* (2) the referent corporation or entity will share in the surplus. Furthermore, the administrative mechanics of any such variance system should be — and they can be — designed with great care to achieve substantial efficiency in operation. The procedures under the Investment Company Act and ERISA are quite defective in terms of this ideal.[8] But the major defects are not

[5]State securities commissions, as presently constituted, are not sufficiently well funded or staffed to handle such a program. Some courts have allowed disinterested outside directors to perform this role, e.g., Puma v. Marriott, 283 A.2d 693 (Del. Ch. 1971), but our discussion in subsection 5.4.1 supra raises questions about the wisdom of this.

[6]29 U.S.C. §§1106-1109.

[7]15 U.S.C. §80a-17(a), 80a-17(b).

[8]The ERISA variance procedure involves both the Department of Labor and the IRS. The standard of review of the transaction is complex and requires extensive evidentiary examina-

inherent in the concept of a variance system and may be avoided in future legislation.[9]

tion, but it is not precise enough to produce predictable results. Long delays in processing of applications often result in the proposed transaction becoming unavailable. See Note, At Variance with the Administrative Exemption Procedures of ERISA: A Proposed Reform, 87 Yale L.J. 760 (1978). Similar objections have been raised regarding the Investment Company Act. Rosenblat and Lybecker, Some Thoughts on Federal Securities Laws Regulating External Investment Management Arrangements and the ALI Federal Securities Code Project, 124 U. Pa. L. Rev. 587, 634-643 (1976).

[9] A variance system should be administered by a single agency. The standard by which proposed transactions will be judged should be clear and objective. It might be appropriate to require that the administering agency reply to an application within some specified time.

CHAPTER 6

EXECUTIVE COMPENSATION

§6.1 The Test of Reasonableness

"It ain't peanuts"

In former times, directors of corporations served without pay, perhaps because they were often large shareholders in their own right and thus had strong personal incentives to become directors. Many corporate statutes now allow them to fix their own compensation,[1] as well as that of the officers. In many small- and medium-sized corporations, directors' fees are still nonexistent or nominal, but fees paid to directors of very large public corporations have become fairly significant.[2] Corporate executives are paid much more handsomely, of course, especially in the large corporations.[3] Considering the average compensation of chief executive officers of large

§6.1 [1]MBCA §8.11; Del. §141(h).

[2]Directors of corporations with annual revenues of at least five billion dollars earned an average yearly fee of $34,300 in 1984. Wall St. J., June 14, 1985, at 7, col. 1. Directors also receive a fee for each monthly board meeting attended. For example, Citicorp pays its directors $850 per meeting; Dupont pays $700. Wall St. J., May 8, 1984, at 1, Col. 5.

[3]The 1985 survey of executive pay by Forbes magazine covered chief executive officers (CEOs) in 785 large companies in 42 industry groupings. The median annual remuneration ranged from $414,000 for CEOs in the age group under 40 to $672,000 for CEOs in the 65-and-over category. Of the 785 CEOs, 133 made $1 million or more. Forbes, June 3, 1985, at 114-115.

corporations as a multiple of the average compensation received by U.S. workers,[4] a detached observer may wonder whether and how the disparity can be justified. Is executive compensation "excessive" in terms of some accepted social or economic norm? If so, how has this come about, and why doesn't the legal system respond?

Reasonable relationship test

A conventional statement of the chief judge-made limitation on executive compensation is that it must be based on services performed for the corporation and must be "reasonable" in amount. Put another way, the amount of compensation must bear a "reasonable relationship" to the value of the services performed for the corporation.[5] Since the fixing of executive compensation often involves some element of at least de facto self-dealing (see section 4.1), one may wonder why the courts do not simply deploy the fairness test used in the scrutiny of basic self-dealing (see section 5.2). Does the difference in terminology have any significance? Yes; it marks a real difference in judicial practices. Executive compensation is scrutinized in a less exacting way than are other contracts with interested officers. It is harder for plaintiffs to successfully mount an attack on the amount of executive compensation on the simple ground that it is unreasonable, than it is to attack a basic self-dealing transaction on the ground that the terms are unfair.

The relatively loose scrutiny of executive compensation under corporate law principles reflects the difficulty of constructing a set of legal controls that are both justified and meaningful. Many courts are undoubtedly influenced by the belief that any self-dealing involved in the setting of most executive compensation is of a mild kind. Formally, for example, the top officer's pay may be approved by a board of directors containing a majority of apparently disinterested directors, at a meeting at which the top officer is absent. Moreover, the existence of executive headhunter firms and the switching of executives from one corporation to another means that there is something like a market for executives and, therefore, a mechanism for helping to make sure that executives are paid competitive rather than monopolistic salaries. How close this "market" comes to the economists' ideal of a competitive market is an open question.[6] But even if we believe

[4]The annual salary of a typical worker in a manufacturing industry is given as about $18,650 [based on an average weekly salary of $373 in U.S. Bureau of the Census, Statistical Abstract of the United States (105th ed. 1985), at 417]. Using the data in the previous note, this suggests that CEOs typically make between 22 and 36 times the pay of such a worker.

[5]Glenmore Distilleries Co. v. Seideman, 267 F. Supp. 915 (E.D.N.Y. 1967) (applying New York law); Beard v. Elster, 16 A.2d 731 (Del. 1960); Black v. Parker Mfg. Co., 106 N.E.2d 544 (Mass. 1952); Berman v. Meth, 258 A.2d 521 (Pa. 1969).

[6]Compare the extraordinarily optimistic view of Fama, Agency Problems and the Theory

that top executives' pay is influenced by factors making the pay setting process something less than a true bargain in a perfectly competitive market, this merely aggravates the operational aspects of judicial scrutiny. If the average pay to top executives of apparently comparable companies is itself a tainted and suspect figure, with what is a given top executive's pay to be compared, for the purpose of assessing its fairness? One might toy with the idea that executive compensation should be set by a regulatory agency, in the manner that utility rates are set. But several factors lead most observers to reject the regulatory alternative: the extreme conceptual and practical difficulties of determining the value of labor other than in a market; the serious implementation problems and side effects of most existing public utility-type rate regulation;[7] and the perception that the problem of excessive executive compensation is not nearly as serious a social problem as those leading lawmakers to impose price regulation in many other areas.

Law's middle way

Instead, the legal system chooses a middle way between intrusive regulation and complete laissez faire. The approach has two aspects: market-enhancement measures and a fail-safe device. The enhancements focus on disclosures and decision making. If the market for executives is to be a good one, accurate information about executive compensation must be readily available. The SEC's rules require disclosure of compensation arrangements in the annual proxy statements sent to shareholders.[8] Since the information about a corporation's officers is public, it is also available to securities analysts, headhunter firms, the directors of other corporations, and other decision makers. A market for executives also requires true bargains between independent parties. Accordingly, commentators[9] and the

of the Firm, 88 J. Pol. Econ. 288 (1980), with the more sober assessment of Vagts, Challenges to Executive Compensation: For the Markets or the Courts?, 8 J. Corp. L. 231 (Winter 1983). Contrary to impressions created by some popular writers, there now is some carefully analyzed empirical evidence for the proposition that managerial compensation is significantly and substantially correlated with company performance. See Jensen & Zimmerman, Managerial Compensation and the Managerial Labor Market, 7 J. Accounting & Econ. 3 (1985), which reviews a set of empirical studies reported in the same volume; see especially Murphy, Corporate Performance and Managerial Remuneration: An Empirical Analysis, 7 J. Accounting & Econ. 11 (1985). The correlation is far from perfect or complete.

[7] See F. Scherer, Industrial Market Structure and Economic Performance 481-486 (2d ed. 1980).

[8] Securities Exchange Act Rules, Schedule 14A, item 7. See also Ferrara, Starr, & Steinberg, Disclosure of Information Bearing on Management Integrity and Competency, 76 Nw. U.L. Rev. 555 (1981).

[9] See, e.g., Cohen, The Outside Director—Selection, Responsibilities, and Contribution to the Public Corporation, 34 Wash. & Lee L. Rev. 837 (1977).

SEC[10] have long been pressing for reform of boards of directors. It now appears that in most large public corporations, outside directors make up a majority of the board.[11] If and when they obtain exclusive control of the corporation's audit committee, proxy machinery, and compensation setting process, their presence may have a significant impact on compensation practices. For their part, the courts seem disposed to judge executive compensation more or less strictly depending upon the degree of apparent involvement of insiders and outsiders. An officer is ill advised to be present and vote at the directors' meeting at which his compensation is set, especially if his vote is needed to carry the measure.[12] And shareholder ratification will often have some practical or procedural effect, if not an impact on the substantive test of the validity of compensation. The Delaware rule, as evidenced in *Saxe v. Brady*,[13] appears to be that, although defendant officers or other fiduciaries usually have the burden of showing that their compensation is reasonable, shareholder ratification shifts the burden to the plaintiff of showing that the compensation was so excessive as to constitute waste.

Besides all these measures, the legal system provides, as a kind of failsafe device similar to the relief valve on a boiler, the possibility of judicial redress for compensation that is so excessive as to be unreasonable or wasteful, that is, for compensation that has somehow slipped through the normal array of market forces and process-oriented legal controls.

[10] The efforts of the SEC have focused on disclosure of information related to individual directors and their relationships with the company, and to the structure and organization of the board. See SEC Release No. 34-15384, 43 Fed. Reg. 58,522 (1978); SEC Release No. 34-16356, 44 Fed. Reg. 68,764 (1979); SEC Release No. 34-17518, 46 Fed. Reg. 11,954 (1981); SEC Release Nos. 33-6592, 34-22195, 35-23752, 50 Fed. Reg. 29, 409 (1985).

[11] A Survey of 487 large corporations indicated that 87.6 percent had a majority on the board consisting of directors who were not officers or employees of the company. Independent outsiders, those with no family or business ties with the company, were a majority on 55 percent of the boards. Wall St. J., Nov. 3, 1980, at 33, col. 3.

[12] See Wilderman v. Wilderman, 315 A.2d 610 (Del. Ch. 1974) (burden of showing reasonableness is on executive when his vote was necessary to approve his compensation); Bennett v. Klipto Loose Leaf Co., 207 N.W. 228 (Iowa 1926) (executive employment contract held void where the executive's vote was needed for approval); Dowdle v. Texas American Oil Co., 503 S.W.2d 647 (Tex. Civ. App. 1973) (compensation agreement voidable at option of corporation where executive's vote was needed for approval).

[13] 184 A.2d 602 (Del. Ch. 1962). See also Gartenberg v. Merrill Lynch Asset Management, Inc., 528 F. Supp. 1038 (S.D.N.Y. 1981), aff'd, 694 F.2d 923 (2d Cir. 1982) (on the meaning of a "fiduciary duty with respect to the receipt of compensation" in the Investment Company Act).

§6.1.1 Past Services

Emphasis on process

Although cases on the unreasonableness of executive compensation for income tax purposes are numerous, cases invalidating executive compensation on corporate law principles are fairly infrequent. Because of the difficulty of assessing the reasonableness of the outcome of a compensation setting process, the courts often give substantial weight to apparent defects in the *process* itself. One illustrative category of cases involves unbargained-for compensation for past services. In *Adams v. Smith*,[14] for example, a minority shareholder successfully challenged payments that the corporation's board of directors ordered to be made to the widows of the deceased president and the deceased comptroller. The objection was that the payments were without consideration—the corporation did not receive anything from the widows—and so constituted an illegal waste or gift of corporate assets. Defendants, building on the obvious point that the payments could be construed as an end-of-career bonus or ersatz pension plan with survivor benefits, and thus as actually being given for past services of the deceased executives, noted that directors generally have the power to make bonus or retirement payments to corporate officers or employees. The court rejected this response because the corporation in this case had no contract to make the payments in question. Thus, the court seems to have been laying down a process control: Compensation may be paid for past services, but only when the recipients' identity and at least some of the specific arrangements for making such payments have been agreed to beforehand.

Example of past services

Relation to four paradigms

In terms of my four conflict of interest paradigms, the case resembles the second because it involved something that could be construed as executive compensation; the third because it involved an alleged transfer without consideration of corporate assets; and the fourth because the directors' motive for ordering the payments may have been to satisfy their personal desires to help the widows rather than to boost the corporation's reputation as a generous employer so as to better recruit good executives in the future.

Reasons for result

The court's decision in *Adams v. Smith* seems to be founded upon several insights. First, executives can hardly be deemed to have worked harder and better because of the vague prospect that they or their survivors might be given bonuses that they had no good reason to expect. A "good reason" might be a contract, a formally adopted bonus plan, or an established company practice. Consequently, payments exceeding the executives' con-

[14] 153 So. 2d 221 (Ala. 1963).

tract rights and reasonable expectations are in fact economically wasteful to the corporation; they are not needed to get the executives' services.

Second, the apparent harshness to the widows should not deter prospective employees of the company, for they can simply demand explicit fringe benefit packages before working for the company. Or they can bargain for higher straight compensation and then buy as much life insurance or annuity insurance as they wish.

Third, the results of the no gift rule will usually not offend instinctive notions about justice to deceased or superannuated employees when, as happens in these cases, they were paid handsome salaries for many years and could have made their own provisions for death or retirement.

***American Woolen* case**

A similar judicial attitude is discernible in *Fogelson v. American Woolen Co.*[15] The court was faced with a retirement plan that provided a very large pension to an officer (more than seven and a half times the amount receivable by the employee with the next largest pension) who served to within one year of retirement age without any expectation of receiving a pension. The court thought the plan was analogous to a gift or bonus and that the directors' decision to approve it was therefore not shielded by the business judgment rule. It stressed the points that the pension had not induced the officer's past efforts for the company and that considerations of justice to an aged employee were irrelevant, since the officer had been receiving a generous salary.

Doubts about courts' attitude

Lingering doubt about the correctness of *Adams v. Smith* comes from the observation that the decision's process-oriented restraint will not necessarily restrain large corporate payments to survivors of deceased executives. A well-advised corporation may establish generous life insurance and pension plans for its executives. A rule against unbargained-for payments for past services will tend, however, to penalize those companies and executives who do not plan ahead to avoid the rule. These nonplanners may well be small businessmen who fail to purchase expert legal advice because of the expense or because of their inability to identify good legal talent. One therefore wonders whether the rule's only function is to increase business for lawyers. This doubt is reinforced when one considers how a corporation that has a clever lawyer *can* make up for its past failure to plan ahead.

Avoidance strategy

Suppose Host Corporation has long employed Opec, its chief executive, at a generous rate of compensation but has failed to adopt a formal pension plan or similar arrangement affecting Opec. Opec now wants to retire but would like an income greater than that available solely from his personal

[15] 170 F.2d 660 (2d Cir. 1948).

savings. The directors of Host think that "in fairness" they should give Opec a pension in recognition of his many years of service. How can they do this without violating the rule against giving away corporate assets? Answer: they can cause the corporation to enter a so-called consulting and noncompetition agreement with Opec. He will agree, say, to "hold himself available for consultation and advice" to the company and its officers for the rest of his life and not to engage in or work for any business that competes with his former employer. The corporation will agree, let us say, to pay him $50,000 a year for life. Case law indicates that it is difficult to attack such an arrangement successfully.[16] Even though a dispassionate observer might be extremely skeptical of the high value placed on a 70-year-old chief executive's promise to refrain from competition and to be available for advice, and even though it turned out, after the contract terms were set, that the retiring executive soon became physically and mentally incapable of producing serious advice or competition, or for whatever reason did not in fact give much advice, it cannot be denied that in most cases the promise has some prospective value for which a rational corporation would willingly pay. There is thus no realistic basis for rejecting the consulting and noncompetition agreement on the ground that consideration was lacking and the payments constituted an illegal gift. And given the difficulty of a judicial inquiry into the fairness of the amount of payments under the contract—whether they were reasonably equivalent in value to the executive's promises—the courts are apt to hold that the contract was fair or reasonable as long as it was approved by the board of directors and there was no evidence of collusion among the directors, bad faith, or dishonesty.[17]

§6.1.2 Outmoded Formulas

Case of *Rogers v. Hill*

A second kind of situation illustrating the weight given by the courts to process controls involves compensation paid in accordance with a long standing formula, that is, a formula that has not been adjusted to reflect later and unforeseen developments. The famous case of *Rogers v. Hill,*[18] which is usually cited as one of the few cases striking down executive compensation simply on the ground that it was excessive, in fact involved this situation. In 1930, the president of the American Tobacco Co. received

[16] Osborne v. Locke Steel Chain Co., 218 A.2d 526 (Conn. 1966); Good v. Modern Globe Inc., 78 N.W.2d 199 (Mich. 1956).
[17] See cases cited in preceding note.
[18] 289 U.S. 582 (1933).

a salary of $168,000, a bonus of $842,507, "special cash credits" of $273,470, plus options to purchase stock at $87 per share below market value. All this occurred at a time when the purchasing power of a dollar was much greater than it is today.[19] The Supreme Court adopted as its own the rule proposed to the appellate court by Judge Swan in his dissent: "If a bonus payment has no relation to the value of services for which it is given, it is in reality a gift in part and the majority stockholders have no power to give away corporate property against the protest of the minority."[20] The Court also argued that the bylaw authorizing the bonus plan could not justify a sum so large "as in substance and effect to amount to spoliation or waste of corporate property."[21] Yet the Court obviously felt strengthened in making its decision by the fact that the bonus payments were not the product of a current, conscious decision by the directors or majority stockholders, but rather it resulted from the mechanical application of an outmoded rule. In 1912, the shareholders had adopted a bylaw providing for an annual bonus to the president of 2½ percent of net profits (and 1½ percent to each of five vice presidents). The Court recognized that the bonuses under this formula were reasonable at that time; indeed, the plaintiff did not complain of any bonuses made prior to 1921. The problem was created by an enormous increase in the company's profits over the years.

Pro and con the result

Abstractly, one could argue that shareholders should be free to contract for as long as they want into the future and ought to be bound by such contracts. After all, the percentage-of-profits-bonus formula in the *Rogers v. Hill* case was obviously designed to induce the officers to do their best to make the company profitable, and it did become profitable. Why, then, should we now undo the deal? Why should we now consider, in effect, whether the officers' efforts have caused the increase in profits or were otherwise "worth" what the formula would yield them by way of bonuses? The Court's rule reflects, however, a more realistic view of the meaningfulness of director or shareholder consent. Its implicit ruling—that compensation will be examined more strictly when not subjected to reasonably frequent review—seems to be a sensible, process-oriented safeguard against the consequences of giving legal effect to such consent. The courts' notion may be that, in the case of consent by outside directors or public shareholders, greater frequency may offset poor quality.

[19] Income taxes would reduce the president's compensation from about $1,300,000 to $1,050,000. After adjustment for cumulative inflation from 1930 to 1981, this would be equivalent to $5,250,000 in 1981 after-tax dollars. To provide this amount after tax, an executive in 1981 would have had to receive almost $10,500,000. See Vagts, note 6 supra, at 255 n.111.

[20] 289 U.S. at 591-592 (quoting 60 F.2d 109, 113 (2d Cir. 1932) (Swan, J., dissenting)).

[21] Id. at 591.

It should also be noted that *Rogers v. Hill* was decided during the Great Depression, when many people would be outraged at the spectacle of some persons receiving astronomical salaries while others languished in the bread lines.

§6.1.3 Tax Cases on Compensation

The problem under tax law

Under Section 162 of the Internal Revenue Code, corporations are allowed to take a deduction against their gross income for ordinary and necessary expenses paid or incurred in carrying on their business, including a "reasonable allowance for salaries or other compensation for personal services actually rendered." As we have seen, the roles of managers and investors are sharply distinguished in the modern public corporation, and one encounters little trouble in telling a payment for executive labor from a payment for investment capital. But in many close corporations, the shareholders are also officers or employees of the company. It is intrinsically difficult to specify how corporate net income before any payments to key participants should be divided as between returns to labor and returns to capital. The participants usually prefer, however, not to take out the business's earnings in the *form* of dividends on their stock. For this would subject the earnings to taxation at two levels: a corporate income tax on the corporate net income out of which the dividends are to be paid and an individual income tax on the dividends received by the shareholders. Instead, they may try to reduce apparent or nominal corporate income, and therefore the corporate income tax, to virtually nothing by the simple expedient of inflating their salaries. In such a situation only one level of taxation—the individual income tax on the salaries—is paid. Because of this and other techniques, many thriving close corporations pay little or no corporate income tax. The Internal Revenue Service tries to restrain the practice by attacking deductions for executive salaries as unreasonable. In many cases, the excessive portion of an unreasonable salary should be treated as a disguised dividend, or payment to an officer in his role as investor. It should therefore be nondeductible by the corporation, although taxable to the individual officer.

Beyond process, in this area

In the many cases dealing with allegedly excessive compensation under Section 162, the federal courts *have* focused not only on the quality of the process by which executive compensation is set but also on the reasonableness of the outcome. As a rough generalization, they have relied most heavily on *comparative* analyses.[22] For example, they have given weight to

[22] See generally Vagts, note 6 supra, at 257-261.

whether the executive's compensation was unusually great in relation to the average compensation paid to executives doing comparable work in a comparably sized firm in the same industry and region.[23] Clearly this approach may simply catch those extraordinary close corporation participants who are far greedier than the rest, without doing much about the overall problem of avoidance by close corporations of the corporate income tax. In an industry composed mostly of close corporations, the average executive pay may itself be tainted by the universal practice of verbally transmuting return on investment into return on labor. In an industry containing closely held and publicly held firms, the latter, especially if bigger on average, may have more elaborate divisions of executive labor that make comparisons between the pay of a close corporation chief executive and any particular officer in the public corporation's hierarchy of personnel a difficult and questionable task. These difficulties are endemic, so the efforts of the Internal Revenue Service to attack unreasonable salaries have the quality of skirmishes that can never be expected to finally resolve the war. It is worth noting, however, that the agency has won many of the skirmishes.

§6.2 *Incentive Compensation Plans*

Personal contingency plans

Besides receiving straight salaries, executives in public corporations enjoy a wide variety of less simple benefits as part of their compensation. Some of these reflect planning for personal contingencies. They include participation in the corporation's group health plan, its group life and disability insurance policies, and its qualified pension plan. These benefits are typically shared by many other employees, but exceptions may occur, as in the case of certain deferred compensation arrangements available only to the top officers. These benefit packages, whose dollar size and increasing importance at the present time make the label "fringe benefits" a very misleading one,[1] are often constructed with a view to tax rules. They may also

[23] Elliots, Inc. v. Commissioner, 40 T.C.M. (CCH) 802 (1980); Drexel Park Pharmacy, Inc. v. Commissioner, 39 T.C.M. (CCH) 788 (1979); Good Chevrolet v. Commissioner, 36 T.C.M. (CCH) 1157 (1977).

§6.2 [1] For salaried employees, noncash compensation in 1979-1980 ranged between 30 and 42 percent of cash compensation, depending on salary level and type of organization. Compensation Rev., 1st quarter, 1981, at 5-6. For example, top management in large corporations earn retirement benefits equal to 65 percent of final five-year average gross pay as well as life insurance policies three times their base salary. J. Wright, The American Almanac of Jobs and Salaries 441 (1984).

be based on the efficiency advantages of a group solution to the common need to plan for the financial strains of accidents and distant personal contingencies like death and retirement. For example, it is cheaper for one representative of a group to shop around for life insurance protection than for each member of the group to undertake his own search and selection of a policy. Also, the selection of a policy by an expert representative is likely to be much better than the selections made by average group members, given the enormous variety and complexity of life insurance policies and the consequent difficulty of making valid price comparisons.

Incentive plans

Another major category of benefits consists of incentive compensation schemes. They are often, though not always, limited to upper and middle-level executive personnel. They include cash and stock bonuses, profit-sharing plans, stock option plans, stock appreciation rights, employee stock purchase plans (in which many nonofficer employees participate), and certain deferred compensation arrangements. These will be examined presently. As in the case of personal contingency benefits, these plans are often the product of the tax laws, and they may be shaped in view of other technical and practical considerations, such as SEC rules. But they are also aimed at the business goal of increasing executive morale and productivity.

Complexity and its problems

Both types of benefit plans, the personal contingency packages and the incentive compensation schemes, have the effect of making executive compensation a complex matter. This complexity creates problems—for markets, for firms, and for courts trying to define the legal rights of shareholders. Thus, like product variation in many markets, the variety of compensation arrangements for executives makes it difficult to compare "prices," that is, the total value of the compensation paid to different executives, and so may hinder the achievement of a fully competitive market for executive talent. Even if an executive's salary is not ultimately incommensurable with his rights in a stock option plan, the valuation of the latter is often a difficult process. Reducing the elements of a compensation package to a common denominator will at least generate transaction costs and uncertainty. Moreover, economic efficiency in the operation of particular firms requires the designers of complex compensation plans to engage in correct analyses of the tax and other consequences of alternative possible plans. The optimal analysis is by no means sure to be made. Finally, the shareholders may find the complexity of the schemes a barrier to assessment and challenge. A shareholder can make the usual attack on the ground that compensation under a certain plan is excessive or unreasonable or was presented to directors or shareholders in a fraudulent way. But argument and proof may be harder in the case of incentive plans.

New legal questions

In addition, the greater complexity prompts new questions. May the shareholder, despite the business judgment rule, attack an incentive compensation scheme on the ground that the underlying analysis of tax and other technical factors was clearly wrong? May the shareholder make out a claim that the plan was inadequately presented to approving directors or shareholders by showing that there was no disclosure of a full, correct *analysis* of the tax and other factors bearing on the business wisdom of the plan? Subsection 6.2.2 will take up these questions, but I will first describe (in subsection 6.2.1) a variety of common incentive compensation schemes and their principal merits and demerits. In the final subsection (6.2.3), I will consider a simpler but deeper and less tractable set of problems raised pointedly by incentive compensation—the problems of measuring and valuing individual contributions to corporate prosperity.

§6.2.1 Types of Plans

Incentive compensation plans usually seek to give the executive a long-term reward that is linked to some measure of company performance. The performance measure might be the market price of the company's stock or the operating results (as indicated by financial statements) of the company or of the particular subsidiary or unit for which the executive works. Most plans may be put into one of two categories, depending on whether or not they envision that the executive will receive actual shares of stock in the company. As we shall see, this difference goes along with differences in certain legal and practical considerations. But within each category, importantly different tax rules may apply to the different plans.

Plans involving actual shares

In the actual shares category, I will mention six related types of plans. The first four involve stock options, that is, rights to purchase the company's shares in the future at a set price.

For example, Purse Corporation might grant Sowsear, an executive, an option to buy 1,000 shares of Purse stock at any time within five years of the date of the grant of the option to him, as long as he is still employed by Purse (or was employed by it less than three months before the purchase), at the price of $10 per share, which is the market value of Purse stock at the time of the option grant. Sowsear is now interested in making the company perform so as to be well received by securities analysts and investors, for he may make a profit if the market price of Purse stock increases. If the price goes to $25, for instance, then with an outlay of $10,000 he may purchase from the company stock that has a market value of $25,000. If the higher market price is sustained, he will cash in on this gain when he later sells the stock. But let us turn to the variations.

Restricted stock options

(1) *Restricted stock options* were tax favored options that were made possible by the 1950 amendments to the Internal Revenue Code and were allowed until the 1964 amendments. Since leading case law on corporate aspects of stock options involves these options, it is still useful to know something about them. The 1950 amendment provided that if a company's stock option plan met certain requirements, the executives receiving options did not have to recognize any income until they *sold* or otherwise disposed of the shares obtained through exercising their options and could treat their entire profit as capital gain.[2] The restrictions seemed designed to insure that executives would be given an investment-oriented interest rather than an occasion for speculative trading, since the incentive goal of the plans seems more consistent with the former.[3]

Example of their treatment

Thus, suppose that the option received and exercised by Sowsear in our earlier example did qualify as a restricted one. During the 1950s, he sold all the stock he had purchased pursuant to the option for $45,000, there having been an advance in the market price of Purse stock since the time he exercised the option. Sowsear would not recognize taxable income when he received the option, even though it had a readily ascertainable market value (say $800) and he was free to exercise it right away. He would not recognize taxable income when he exercised the option by buying Purse shares, even though he realized a gain of $15,000 at that point ($25,000, the value of the securities received, less his $10,000 purchase price). He *would* recognize taxable income at the time he sold the stock, in the amount of $35,000 (the $45,000 sales proceeds less his original outlay, or basis, of $10,000). But that amount would be treated as capital gain and, if he had held the stock long enough, would be taxed to him at a rate much lower than the ordinary income tax rate applied to his salary and straight cash bonuses.

Given very high marginal tax rates on individual income, a substantial majority of large public corporations adopted restricted stock option plans during the 1950s and 1960s.

Qualified stock options

(2) *Qualified stock options* were what the tax-favored stock options were called after the 1964 Amendments to the Internal Revenue Code.[4] These amendments tightened the requirements that a stock option plan had to meet in order to qualify for special tax treatment. The special tax treatment

[2]Revenue Act of 1950, §218(a), 64 Stat. 942 (1950) (replaced by current provisions in I.R.C. §§421-425).

[3]S. Rep. No. 2375. 81st Cong., 2d Sess., reprinted in [1950] U.S. Code Cong. Serv. 3053, 3114.

[4]I.R.C. §§421-425.

remained essentially as outlined above. To be qualified, a plan had to provide that the shareholders would approve it; that options would be granted within 10 years of the plan's adoption or approval by shareholders (whichever was earlier); that the option could not be exercised more than five years after being granted; that the option price was not less than the stock's fair market value at the time of grant; that the receiving executive could not transfer the option other than by his death; that he could not own more than 5 percent of the company's stock after the grant; and that he must hold the shares purchased pursuant to the option for at least three years.[5] If these rules made any sense, it was as a set of safeguards against possible abuse of shareholders rather than as an expression of some notion of the ideal income tax treatment of stock options. In any event, these conditions, plus a sharp decrease in the difference between ordinary income tax rates and the long-term capital gain rates,[6] reduced the attractiveness of tax favored stock option plans during the late 1960s and early 1970s. Many large companies did continue to have them. But the tax law was amended yet again, this time to abolish the provisions for qualified stock option plans, effective May 20, 1976.[7] Henceforth, newly adopted stock option plans were to be neither bound by elaborate tax law preconditions nor favored by special tax treatment.

Nonqualified stock options: how treated

(3) *Nonqualified stock options*, as those remitted to ordinary principles of taxation are sometimes called, are occasionally issued by corporations. Generally, the executive recognizes no taxable income at the time a nonqualified stock option is granted to him.[8] At the time the executive exercises the option, he recognizes taxable income in the amount of the difference between the fair market value of the stock purchased and the exercise price that he pays for the stock, and this income is taxed at his *ordinary* individual income tax rate. In our example, Sowsear, if his option was nonqualified, would recognize $15,000 of ordinary income when he exercised the option and thus bought Purse stock at a bargain rate. This is

[5] I.R.C. §422. Qualifications and refinements have been omitted.

[6] In 1954, the maximum tax rate on ordinary income was 91 percent (on income in excess of $200,000) and the maximum rate on long-term capital gains was 45.5 percent. In 1970, the maximum rate on earned income (e.g., salary) was 50 percent and the maximum capital gains rate was 35 percent. The gap had, therefore, narrowed from 45.5 percent to 15 percent. More recently, the trend has reversed. Under the Economic Recovery Tax Act of 1981, Pub. L. No. 97-34, 95 Stat. 172 (1981), the two maximum rates are 50 percent and 20 percent, respectively.

[7] Tax Reform Act of 1976, §603, 90 Stat. 1520, 1574 (1976).

[8] More exactly, this is true if the option has no readily ascertainable fair market value, or if there is no election to be taxed currently. When there is ascertainability of value and an election, the executive recognizes ordinary income in the amount of the difference between the fair market value of the option and the amount paid (if any) for it.

the treatment that one knowing general principles of individual income taxation would expect: By transferring marketable stock to Sowsear at a price that is designed to be a bargain to him, Purse Corporation is actually paying him compensation for his services in the amount of the "bargain" element. Finally, after the exercise, the executive is treated as any other shareholder. If he later sells his stock, his gain is capital gain, which will be short-term or long-term depending on how long he held the stock, and it may therefore qualify for the favorable tax rates applied to long term capital gains. In our example, Sowsear, when he later sold his nonqualified stock, would have capital gain of $20,000 (the $45,000 sales proceeds less his $25,000 basis, which is made up of his $10,000 outlay at the time of exercise and the $15,000 of compensation income on which he has already been taxed).

Incentive stock options

(4) *Incentive stock options* are authorized by Section 422A of the Internal Revenue Code, added by the Economic Recovery Tax Act of 1981.[9] The statute restores essentially the same preferential tax treatment that was available until 1976 for qualified options. Requirements that an option plan must meet are similar to those for the old qualified plans, but in several respects are more generous to taxpayers. For example, bigger shareholders (those with 10 percent or less of the company's stock rather than 5 percent or less) may now get tax-favored options—provided, of course, they are also employees. The option may be written to last up to 10 years, not just 5. And the employee only has to wait 1 year, not 3, before selling stock he gets by exercising the options. There is a limit of $100,000, however, on the value of shares on which an individual can be given incentive options in any year; no such limit applies to qualified plans.

Conditions for favorable treatment

It may be helpful to present the major requirements for treatment of options as incentive options in the form of a list:

1. Stock bought pursuant to the option can't be sold in the two years after the option was granted.
2. Such stock can't be sold in the one year after the option was exercised.
3. If all requirements in this list except the previous two are met, then the employee is taxed when the stock is sold rather than when the option is exercised (in this respect, it's like a tax-favored option), *but* the gain is treated as ordinary income and the corporation gets a deduction for it (in these respects, it's like a nonqualified option).
4. The recipient of the option must be employed by the company

[9] Pub. L. No. 97-34, §251, 95 Stat. 256 (1981).

continuously from the date of grant until three months before the date of exercise.

5. The option plan must specify the number of shares that may be issued pursuant to the options and the employees eligible to receive the options.
6. Shareholders must approve the option plan within 12 months before or after it is adopted.
7. The options must be granted within 10 years of the plan's adoption date or shareholder-approval date, whichever is earlier.
8. By their terms, the options must not be exercisable after 10 years from the date of grant.
9. The option price can't be less than the stock's fair market value at the time an option is granted.
10. The options may not be transferable, except by death of the employee.
11. At the time of grant, the employee may not own more than 10 percent of the combined voting power of all the company's classes of voting stock. (There are certain refinements and exceptions to this.)
12. The employee must exercise the options in the order they are granted to him.
13. There is a $100,000 limit on optioned shares per year per employee, as mentioned above.

Employee stock purchase plans

(5) *Employee stock purchase plans* allow employees to purchase shares in the company, usually at bargain prices payable in installments. They still may be "qualified" for tax purposes, in which case favorable tax consequences will ensue.[10] The qualification requirements are designed to insure that there is no discrimination in favor of higher paid employees and that there is a broad coverage, that is, most employees may participate.[11] There are limits on the amount that may be invested by an employee in a given year.[12] These plans do not satisfy the demand for incentive compensation of executives.

[10] For example, the employee recognizes no income when he makes a purchase, even though the plan may provide for the option to purchase at a discount of up to 15 percent from the fair market value at the time the option is granted. Income recognition occurs when the shares are sold. I.R.C. §423.

[11] Highly compensated employees, managers, part-time employees, and those who have worked for the company less than two years may be excluded without disqualifying the plan; all other employees must be included. I.R.C. §423(6)(4).

[12] In a given year, the employee may be granted rights to purchase shares worth up to $25,000, with the value measured by fair market value at the time of the grant. I.R.C. §423(b)(8).

Performance share plans

(6) *Performance share plans* provide for receipt by the executive of a stock bonus with the right to the shares contingent upon achievement of specified operating goals. The bonus may be based on a combination of operating results and stock price, and the number of shares awarded may vary with the quality of the results. There is no special tax treatment: The market value of the bonus shares is taxed to the executive as ordinary earned income when the shares are issued to him, although later increases in the value of the shares will be treated as capital gain. The chief advantage as compared to stock option plans is that the executives do not have to find money to purchase the shares because they receive them outright.

Problems with all "actual shares" plans

All of the incentive plans involving actual shares pose certain nontax problems which, unless there are offsetting tax advantages, tend to chill corporate enthusiasm for them. First, stock option plans generally require shareholder approval, a process that creates delay, expense, and risk for the corporation. The requirement may stem from corporate statutes,[13] stock exchange rules,[14] or the Internal Revenue Code in the case of incentive plans;[15] and in any event the relevant information must be included in annual proxy statements[16] and reports to the SEC.[17]

Second, the stock to be sold under the option plan must be registered under the securities laws, and this process is expensive.[18]

Third, insider trading rules will apply to the executives,[19] including the mechanical, no-fault rule against sale-purchase combinations within six months,[20] and this prospect annoys executives and creates legal complexities.[21]

Fourth, with the option or purchase plans as opposed to the stock bonus plans, the executive must arrange for financing his purchase of shares. This factor may be especially discouraging to young, middle level executives with large current expenses. For all these reasons, the abolition of the tax qualified stock option led many large corporations in the later 1970s to

[13] E.g., N.J. Stat. Ann. §§14A:7-7, 14A:8-2; N.Y. §505(d). But see Del. §157 (no shareholder approval required).

[14] N.Y. Stock Exchange Company Manual §A7; 2 Am. Stock Exchange Guide (CCH) 3561.

[15] I.R.C. §422A(b)(1).

[16] 17 C.F.R. §240.14a-101, item 7 (Schedule 14A).

[17] See Securities Exchange Act, Form 10-K, item 10; Securities Exchange Act §13(b).

[18] Stock to be issued under an employee stock option plan may be registered using Form S-8 rather than the more complex and expensive S-1. See Johnson, SEC Registration Form S-8: An Interpretive Guide, 33 Bus. Law. 2199 (1978).

[19] See sections 8.6-8.10 infra.

[20] Securities Exchange Act §16(b).

[21] For example, the problem of interpreting the words *sale* and *purchase* in connection with option grants and exercises. See Silverman v. Landa, 306 F.2d 422 (2d Cir. 1962); Blau v. Ogsbury, 210 F.2d 426 (2d Cir. 1954); Prager v. Sylvestri, 449 F. Supp. 425 (S.D.N.Y. 1978).

adopt incentive plans that do not involve the actual issuance of shares. We will consider three of these plans.

Phantom stock plans

(7) *A phantom stock plan* treats the executive almost as if he were currently receiving a bonus in the form of a certain number of shares of the company's stock that could not be sold until some specified time in the future. It thus gives him an incentive to work so as to help cause the company's stock price to rise. In the conceptualization of an actual plan, he may be said to receive nontransferable "units of participation" (more imaginatively, "phantom" stock) whose value is linked or equated to the market price of the company's actual stock. When the units become payable in the future, he will be entitled to have the corporation pay him in cash the then current market value of the corresponding number of real shares. (In practice, of course, the value of the units will have to be adjusted to reflect events like stock splits and dividends. For example, the executive with a unit of phantom stock may be treated as if he had received phantom dividends on it that correspond to real dividends, and had reinvested them in new phantom stock.) The executive does not buy and sell real shares, though, and consequently, the units do not give him the noneconomic rights of a shareholder, such as voting rights, inspection rights, or the right to sue derivatively. His right under a phantom stock plan is thus a right to a deferred cash bonus, with the amount of the bonus linked to future stock price.

Stock appreciation rights

(8) *Stock appreciation rights* (often labelled SARs) are very similar, but here the amount of the deferred cash bonus is based on any *increase* in the market price in the company's stock, between the time the company grants the unit or right to the executive and the time that it becomes payable. Thus, the executive who receives SARs may get no future cash bonus if the stock price simply remains the same. The plan need not link the amount of the bonus to stock price increases in a perfectly linear way; the bonus may be augmented or diminished depending on the size of the stock price increase. For example, an executive with one unit of SAR may get cash exactly equal in amount to the increase in the price of one share of stock, if the increase is less than 15 percent, but twice the amount of the increase if the latter was more than 15 percent.

Participating units

(9) *Participating units* are also deferred cash bonuses, but here the amounts paid in the future are based not on stock prices but on future operating results of the relevant company, subsidiary, or unit. Plans giving such units are especially useful in large, diversified corporations that want to give incentive compensation to hundreds of their executives. For all but the few top officers of the entire corporate enterprise, it makes more sense to link incentives to measures of performance of subunits, since individual

executives will feel that they have more chance of affecting such measures. In a plan with stock appreciation rights, by contrast, the vice president of one division of one subsidiary of the giant public corporation may work furiously to improve the performance of his division and may do so, only to find his potential cash bonus negated by the poor performance of other divisions or the vagaries of the stock market, which may set prices partly on the basis of general factors (like interest rate changes) that have little to do with changes in the company's operating efficiency. On the other hand, it should be acknowledged that linking compensation to a subunit's performance may cause executives to work for the good of the subunit even when doing so is bad for the corporation as a whole.[22]

Advantages of such plans

All of these popular plans—for phantom stock, stock appreciation rights, and participating units—avoid the problems of shareholder approval, stock registration, applicability of insider trading rules, and the need for financing by individual executives. In each of them, the executive is taxed on the cash bonus only when it is paid. The executive thus does get, as compared to his treatment under a current cash or stock bonus, the benefit of deferred taxes, which may have considerable value. But the amount he is paid is taxed as ordinary earned income. As for the corporation income tax, the corporation only gets a deduction from its income when it pays the cash bonus.[23]

§6.2.2 Tax Analysis of Plans

"Tax favored" plans not always best

In the discussion of stock option plans, I consciously refrained from discussing the tax consequences of the various plans to the sponsoring corporations. Such silence may give rise to the impression, which undoubtedly was held by numerous public investors in the last three decades, that it is clearly better for all public corporations to adopt the tax-favored stock option plans rather than nonqualified stock option plans. If questioned, those making this assumption would probably agree with this explanation of what should be meant by a "clearly better" stock option plan: Plan A is better than Plan B if it allows the corporation, at no greater cost to itself, to deliver more after-tax compensation to its executives or, conversely, if it allows the corporation to deliver the same after-tax compensation to the executives at a lesser cost to itself. But in fact the common assumption is not correct. The business wisdom of restricted, qualified, or incentive stock options depends crucially upon the relationships among

[22] See, e.g., O. Williamson, Corporate Control and Business Behavior 125-127 (1970).
[23] I.R.C. §404(a)(5).

three different tax rates: the corporation's marginal income tax rate, the individual executives' marginal tax rate on earned or ordinary income, and the executives' rate on long term capital gains. These rates vary among companies and executives and their typical interrelationships have changed over time. The reason why these relationships matter is that the tax treatment of the corporation differs between the tax-favored and the nonqualified option plans. In the latter, but not in the former, the corporation may take a deduction for the element of compensation that is given to the executives.

Fiscfry hypo

Consider this example. Fiscfry Corporation has a flat marginal tax rate of 46 percent.[24] The executives who are to be included in a new stock option plan are in personal circumstances such that they will be taxed on additional ordinary income at 50 percent and on additional long-term capital gains at 20 percent. The board of directors of Fiscfry has before it two proposed plans. Each of them would give the covered executives options to buy stock at $10 a share, the current market price of the company's stock. Under Plan A the options would be tax qualified "incentive" options. Each Plan A option would entitle its holder to buy 100 shares. Under Plan B, the options would not be qualified, but each option would entitle its holder to purchase 185 shares. Under each plan, each executive would receive the same number of options. The board wants to minimize the total tax cost of its incentive compensation plan, that is, the total tax cost to the company and the executive. Thus, if two plans entail the same after-tax burden to the company, it will choose the one that promises to give the greater amount of after-tax dollars to the executives, since that plan will presumably have a more powerful incentive effect on the executives. Should the Fiscfry board of directors choose Plan A or B?

Consider impact on *both* corporation and executives

The better answer may well be Plan B, the nonqualified plan. Suppose each executive exercises his options when the market price of Fiscfry stock has risen to $30 and then sells his stock at that price.[25] Under Plan A an executive receives a profit of $20 with respect to each share bought and sold pursuant to the options, but pays only a $4 tax on the profit. With respect to a single option covering 100 shares, this means that the executive has a $2,000 gross profit, a $400 tax liability, and, therefore, a net gain of $1,600. The corporation, however, receives no tax benefit for creating the option since it takes no deduction either on account of the grant or the

[24] See I.R.C. §11.

[25] The value and tax treatment of further stock price increases after the day of exercise of an option are the same under the two plans, so it is a legitimate simplification of the problem to assume that exercise price and subsequent sales price are the same.

exercise of the option. Yet the company, or the public shareholders as a group, has incurred a cost of $2,000 by creating the option.

Costs of option plans to shareholders

The last point may not be obvious, since when the company issues an option or sells stock it does not deplete its checking account balance or its store of real assets. But the truth of the proposition can be readily understood in either of two ways. When Fiscfry, pursuant to an option, sells an executive 100 shares in itself for $1,000, it incurs an opportunity cost of $2,000; for, at least theoretically, it could have sold those shares in the market place for $3,000. Looked at another way, the sale to an executive of stock at a bargain price dilutes the aggregate value of the existing shareholders' stock by the amount of the bargain element. If a group of executives buys 20,000 shares from the company for $200,000 when the prepurchase market value of that many shares was $500,000, it seems clear that the value of each preexisting shareholder's claim to dividends has been reduced by more than his share of the company's $200,000 gain in real assets and that, in a well functioning stock market, the market price of the company's stock would drop accordingly. The bargain sale of stock thus amounts to an almost direct transfer of wealth from the shareholders to the executive; that is why the nonreduction of real corporate assets is irrelevant. To be sure, the loss to the shareholders will be *precisely* equal to the gain to the executives only if certain conditions are completely met—for example, the stock market must perceive and react efficiently to all dilutions. Moreover, the analysis is based on the premise that the way claims against a corporation are carved up does not fundamentally affect the total market value of the corporation. But even if these premises and conditions do not hold perfectly true, it is abundantly clear that the executive compensation given under stock option plans is not being created out of thin air. And this point applies equally well to both tax-favored and nonqualified plans.

Under Plan B, the nonqualified plan covering 185 shares per option, an executive also receives a gross profit of $20 with respect to each share of Fiscfry purchased pursuant to an option, but he pays a $10 ordinary income tax on that profit. With respect to each option he exercises, this means a $3,700 gross profit, an $1,850 tax liability, and, therefore, an $1,850 net gain. Contrast this with his net gain of only $1,600 per option under Plan A. Option for option, he does $250 better under Plan B. Since he gets the same number of options under each plan, he should clearly prefer Plan B. Yet the company's net cost per option is almost the same as under Plan A. Indeed, it is slightly less: the corporation (or the shareholders as a group, if you prefer) incurs a gross cost of $3,700 when it sells 185 shares at a bargain price, but since it gets a tax deduction for that amount, it reaps a

Table 6.2-A
Competing Stock Option Plans*

	Plan A *Incentive Option* *For 100 shares*	*Plan B* *Nonqualified Option* *For 185 shares*
Corporation		
Option's cost	$(2000)	(3700)
Tax benefit	—	1702
Net cost	(2000)	(1998)
Executive		
Option profit	2000	3700
Tax cost	(400)	(1850)
Net gain	1600	1850

*The option's exercise price is $10 per share. The option is exercised, and the shares later sold, when the market price of a share is $30. Corporation's tax rate is 46 percent; executive's, 50 percent for ordinary income and 20 percent for long-term capital gains.

partially offsetting tax benefit of $1702 (that is, $3,700 × .46, its tax rate). So its after-tax cost is only $1998. The analysis is summarized in Table 6.2-A.

Refinements

The analysis just made ignores some refinements. For example, since under Plan B the executive recognizes taxable income when he exercises an option but under Plan A he recognizes taxable gain only when he later sells the stock, the analysis ignores the present value of the qualified plan's capacity to permit tax deferral. Yet unless this effect is so great as to cause the present value of the executive's prospective capital gains tax of $400 per option to fall below $150,[26] it would not destroy the point made by the example. Whether the effect is that great depends on how long, on average, the executive expects to hold his stock after exercising his option, and on the rate of discount used to figure present values. Thus, after a really complete analysis, Plan A might yet seem superior to Plan B. Then again, it might not. (One should also note that, under some past patterns of tax rates—when corporate rates and long-term capital gain rates were higher relative to the marginal ordinary income rate for most executives—the scales were tipped more in favor of nonqualified plans.)

Point of the hypo

The purpose of the preceding example is *not* to suggest that adopting incentive stock option plans is irrational. In most cases the adoption of such plans is probably quite sensible. The point of the example is a much

[26] That is, $400, the capital gain tax burden, less $250, the amount of additional after-tax compensation per option received under Plan B.

weaker, but important, one: Under some sets of circumstances, most rational plan analysts would agree that a nonqualified stock option plan is better than a tax-favored plan when the tax effects on the corporation and the executives are both taken into account.

Relation to corporate law issues

If this is so, why should stock option plans give rise to any corporate law problems? How could it ever come about, for example, that Fiscfry Corporation would adopt Plan A instead of Plan B? The answer is twofold.

First, the promoters of Plan A may have simply made a mistake. For instance, they may have jumped on the incentive-stock-option bandwagon and blindly copied other companies' plans without making a careful, complete analysis in relation to their own company's situation.

Second, the promoters may be tainted by a conflict of interest, albeit a low grade one. Plan B requires them to seek shareholder approval for the issuance of almost twice as many shares. They may fear that the greater number will prompt more shareholders to vote against the plan. They may therefore wish to propose some kind of tax-favored plan and try to conceal its real inferiority from a tax standpoint, rather than risk the possibility that they could not successfully persuade shareholders of the true merits of a much larger nonqualified plan. Similarly, if the given element of the situation is that any plan adopted will convey a fixed amount of expected after-tax compensation to the executives, and the choice to be made primarily affects only the cost to the corporation, executives will note that the nonqualified plan requires them to arrange for more financing to exercise their options, and they may regard this as an unacceptable nuisance. They might therefore press the board of directors for adoption of a qualified plan despite its tax inferiority from the company's standpoint.

Example of *Eliasberg v. Standard Oil*

With this background we are finally in a position to appreciate the issues involved in the early New Jersey case of *Eliasberg v. Standard Oil Co.*[27] A small shareholder attacked the legal validity of restricted stock options granted to 80 executives of Standard Oil Company of New Jersey—options that covered nearly 164,000 of the company's 60 million shares. The plan under which the options were granted was recommended by unanimous vote of the directors and adopted by vote of shareholders holding over 78 percent of the outstanding shares. In response to plaintiff's argument that, since the plan provided for no increase in executives' responsibilities or duties, the options were without consideration and an ultra vires gift of corporate property, the court pointed out that the plan required optionees to perform at least one year of service before being able to exercise their

[27] 92 A.2d 862 (N.J. Super. Ct. Ch. Div. 1952), aff'd, 97 A.2d 437 (N.J. 1953).

options. The options were ostensibly designed, that is, to induce executives to remain with the corporation.

On the question of reasonableness the court clearly expressed a deferential attitude:

> Because of the stockholders' ratification the court will look into the transaction only far enough to see whether . . . the value of the service bears a reasonable relationship to the amounts to be paid under the plan; whether the value to the company of the benefits which it would receive from any optionee was so much less than the value of the options granted to him that no person of ordinary business judgment could be expected to entertain the view that the consideration furnished was a fair exchange for the options conferred.[28]

Duty to disclose *analysis* of plan?

But the plaintiff's most interesting argument was that there had been a failure of full and fair disclosure to the shareholders, since neither the plan nor the proxy statement revealed to them the tax effects of the plan, including the special capital gain treatment of the executives and the corporation's inability to take any deduction for the cost of performing under the option agreement. In effect, said the court, the plaintiff was arguing that "it is the duty of a director who submits to the shareholders a full text of a proposal to accompany it with an analysis of the beneficial and detrimental aspects of the proposal."[29] The court rejected this view and declared that the stockholder receiving an involved or technical proposal had the obligation to make his own inquiries, perhaps by seeking the advice of his lawyer or accountant.

Query court's flat answer

The court gave no reason for its apparently sweeping rule that directors need not disclose the analysis of pros and cons that underlies their recommendation to the shareholders of a proposal requiring a vote. One wonders whether this was a sensible position. Granted, in many contexts it might be wasteful and unnecessary to require directors to spell out or guess the implications of information generated within the corporation. It would also be chancy, since doing a good analysis would often require them to show how certain information or circumstances not generated by the corporation—such as general interest rate changes, political events or various laws and regulations—would affect future corporate welfare. But, as we have seen, shareholders vote on relatively few matters, and the most common occasion for voting, the annual election of directors, does not concern involved technical questions. A rule requiring full disclosure of the

[28] Id. at 871-872.
[29] Id. at 868.

analysis of pros and cons that supposedly underlies the directors' recommendation that the shareholders vote for a complex proposal (one involving stock option plans, mergers, liquidations, or the like) would not be very costly. This is so because the occasions on which the rule would operate are relatively rare, and because the *marginal* cost of printing and sending to the shareholders an account of the analysis, which the directors presumably have already done, would be small. Given the importance of the proposals, the wastefully duplicated effort that would occur if thousands of shareholders actually did ask their attorneys or accountants to analyze each proposal, and the unlikelihood that shareholders receiving a mere description of a complex proposal would have any reasonable basis for suspecting that something was wrong, the court's decision to restrict required disclosure to facts but not analysis seems questionable indeed.

Understanding the court

Why did the court not perceive the weakness of its argument? Perhaps the court, like most investors, simply did not see (a) the analytical point, that under certain combinations of corporate and executive tax rates, a restricted stock option plan could be clearly less desirable than a nonqualified stock option plan, and (b) that the directors recommending the plan might have a conflict of interest that influenced their recommendation of a restricted option plan. There is nothing in the opinion to suggest that the court appreciated these possibilities, or that the plaintiff's attorney called them to the court's attention in a clear, forceful, and effective way. This situation seems unfortunate: a fairly modest amount of information—the corporation's marginal tax rate, and representative marginal tax rates on ordinary income and capital gain for the executives involved—might have enabled the court to deal with the first possibility rather quickly.

§6.2.3 The Problem of Causal Knowledge

***Beard v. Elster's* two-pronged rule**

A major function of the leading cases dealing with stock option plans was simply to bless the trend among public corporations to adopt large scale restricted or qualified stock option plans, that is, to assure everyone that these creatures of the tax law were not impermissible per se as a matter of corporate law. The Delaware Supreme Court, in its 1960 decision in *Beard v. Elster,*[30] performed this function decisively. The case involved American Airlines' restricted stock option plan, which covered 250,000 shares and under which options were issued to 289 employees. The court purported (not very convincingly) to reconcile its holdings in favor of the

[30] 160 A.2d 731 (Del. 1960).

company with two prior decisions, and it characterized itself as "restating" a fundamental, two-pronged rule for stock option plans.

> All stock option plans must be tested against the requirement that they contain conditions, or that surrounding circumstances are such, that the corporation may reasonably expect to receive the contemplated benefit from the grant of the options. Furthermore, there must be a reasonable relationship between the value of the benefits passing to the corporation and the value of the options granted.[31]

Application

With respect to the first prong, the court was impressed by the fact that optionees could generally exercise their options only while still in the employ of the company. As usual, the court was influenced by the fact of disinterested director approval and shareholder ratification of the plan. On the reasonable relationship test, the court noted the fact that comparable salaries of employees of other corporations were higher and gave "utmost consideration" to the fact that a disinterested board of directors made a "business judgment" that the plan was adequately designed to further the "corporate purpose" of securing the retention of key employees' services.

Attacking the link between plan and company benefit

This appeal to business judgment rather than the substantive merits of the issue of reasonableness was bound to strike some observers as bland and perhaps unconvincing. Some plaintiffs tried an argument that seemed as if it would surely push through the thin crust of rationality into the sticky miasma below. In *Lieberman v. Becker*,[32] for example, the Delaware Supreme Court was confronted by a plaintiff who, in attacking a phantom stock plan, insisted on developing the argument that there was no reasonable relation between the value of the benefits conferred on the employee by the plan and the value of his services to the corporation. Under the plan, an employee's deferred compensation would depend on appreciation in the market value of the company's stock between the time the employee entered the plan and the time he terminated employment with the company. The plaintiff argued that market value of common stock is "too speculative" a thing to form a reasonable basis for fixing executive compensation. He correctly pointed out that a whole host of factors other than the employees' best efforts might influence the market value of the company's stock: interest rates, corporate earnings, the business cycle, commodity prices, the psychology of the buying public, labor relations, and so forth. The plaintiff even submitted evidence and arguments for the

[31] Id. at 737.
[32] 155 A.2d 596 (Del. 1959).

view that the market value of the company's stock was not determined to any large extent by the services of its employees (as a group), even though the difficulty of distinguishing one employee from others would alone have raised the basic problem. That problem was the impossibility of stating a truly rational justification of the amount of the compensation to be awarded to an employee by the plan, given the difficulty of identifying the true causes of market price appreciation, and the even greater difficulty of measuring the amount of the appreciation that ought to be attributed to each cause.

Evasive judicial response

The Delaware court responded to the argument by boldly and unashamedly side-stepping it. Essentially, the court argued that the phantom stock plan was no more liable to attack on the ground of a lack of reasonable relation between compensation and the value of services than is an ordinary stock option plan (a correct premise); that ordinary stock option plans had survived shareholder attacks on the ground of unreasonableness (also a correct proposition); and that the phantom stock plan ought then to survive such an attack (a non sequitur). The court refused to consider the obvious alternative of finding both types of plans fatally flawed. Its only remarks relevant to this implicit decision were in its customary invocation of the importance of giving weighty consideration to a decision by responsible businessmen after they have given careful consideration to numerous factors. If the court meant to suggest by these remarks that businessmen have somehow solved the problem of rationally linking portions of stock price increases to the efforts of particular employees, or if it meant that in their subconscious and therefore inaccessible wisdom they can make such linkages, it was simply being silly. It is doubtful, however, whether this is what the court meant to suggest.

Contrary authority

The Delaware view seems to have carried the day, but there is contrary authority. *Berkwitz v. Humphrey*[33] held invalid a similar phantom stock plan, and the court was heavily influenced by the causation problem. It viewed the amount of benefits a retiring employee would receive under the plan as governed by "aleatory considerations," that is, chance, and said that the plan rested on the "demonstrably false" postulate that an increase in the stock's market value was attributable solely to the extraordinary services rendered by plan participants in response to the incentive of additional compensation.

But Delaware view better

Which view is better? In my opinion, that of the Delaware court. Its conclusion should be supported by additional considerations, however. For one thing, the argument by analogy between phantom stock plans and

[33] 163 F. Supp. 78 (N.D. Ohio 1958).

ordinary stock option plans should be greatly extended. In point of fact, finding a rational relationship between an employee's *straight salary* and the value of his services, in the sense of accurately measuring that part of the corporation's value that his efforts can be defensibly said to have caused, is also impossible. The salaries of particular employees within a large corporation are clearly based on many objective factors that do not directly or necessarily relate to any such "intrinsic value" of their services. These factors include seniority and the relative position of employees in the corporate hierarchy.[34] It is sometimes said, for example, that the compensation of a corporation's chief legal officer tends to be a fixed proportion—say, 40 percent—of the compensation of the chief executive officer. And the overall level of compensation in a corporation—as determined downward from the compensation of its top executive—varies with the size of the corporation and the industry in which it operates.[35] One wonders whether a dozen corporate vice presidents getting the same salary can ever be shown to have contributed equal portions of the corporation's market value.

Problem of causal knowledge

More fundamentally, measuring the relative causal importance of the efforts of different participants in a cooperative effort is often *logically* impossible. For example, if five executives' efforts were jointly necessary but individually insufficient to the production of a good corporate result—say, a $1 million profit on a given project—there is simply no scientific way to say that any individual executive caused a given percentage of the gain. Thus, to stipulate the relative value of each executive's efforts in connection with the project would inevitably involve a host of considerations, many of them subjective, other than the determination of who "produced" or was "responsible for" what amount of gain. And since large corporations are, above all else, systems of cooperative action, this difficulty is a thoroughly pervasive one.

Relation to broader economic theories

Indeed, the entire effort to link monetary remuneration to the value created by particular employees suffers from the same difficulties that have plagued the labor theory of value espoused by Karl Marx and some of his disciples.[36] That theory has not been found useful by the neoclassical economists, who have preferred to embark on the more operational task of

[34] E. Mruk & J. Giardina, Executive Compensation 5 (1979).

[35] Id. at 34.

[36] A pure labor theory of value, which would equate the value of goods (for purposes of exchange and distribution) with the labor needed for their production, is usually rejected for its failure to recognize the effect of scarcity of other resources (e.g., land) used in varying proportions to labor in producing different goods. See P. Samuelson, Economics 728-734 (10th ed. 1976).

analyzing how prices (alias values) are set by the intersection of supply and demand curves.[37] Their view suggests the application that, in the case of an executive, the most workable index of his value is the price that he would fetch in a reasonably competitive market for executive talent. Because the nonoperational character of alternative standards of value draws them to this view, judges understandably find themselves engaged in the comparative approach—comparing suspect salaries with those of comparable executives elsewhere—and lawmakers in general are drawn to the strategy, not of regulating compensation directly, but of trying to make the market for executives perfect.

Judicial strategy

The Delaware court's interpretation of the reasonable relationship test fits with these strong tendencies. In effect, the court rejected something like the labor theory of value, but it did not fail to adopt a strategy. It left the wisdom of particular attempts to get useful employee services by adopting complex compensation schemes to corporate managers, but maintained the safeguard that courts could be persuaded to make market comparisons of compensation and to encourage the adoption of practices (like disclosure to and approval by disinterested directors) that might help insure that true bargains were being made. This basic strategy is defensible, though commentators and future courts may—and hopefully will—devise better ways of implementing it.

§6.3 *Close Versus Public Corporations*

A possible rule for public corporations

In view of the importance of trying to make the market for executives perfect, it seems desirable to govern public corporations by a rather categorical, process-oriented rule. Here is an example of such a rule: The compensation arrangements of corporate officers will be invalid unless (a) the arrangements have been entered into for the corporation by a committee of the directors composed entirely of outside directors (defined in a stringent way)[1] and (b) the board's committee for nominating new directors and directors for reelection is composed entirely of outside directors; moreover, shareholders may sue derivatively to collect a penalty (say, 10 percent of the invalid compensation) from offending executives and directors, and to obtain an injunction against future violations. Although courts

[37] P. Samuelson, Economics 355-383 (11th ed. 1980); G. Stigler, The Theory of Price (2d ed. 1966).

§6.3 [1] The term *outside director* is usually used to mean only that the director is not also an officer or employee of the corporation. A more appropriate definition would require additionally that the director have no family or business ties with the company.

do give "weight" to disinterested director approval, they have adopted no such categorical rule. Why is this so?

Explanation of its nonadoption

One answer might be that the cost of the rule would exceed any possible benefits because it would force corporations to seek out and pay for more outside directors. Outside directors, it might be argued, are scarce, hard to get, and not as well informed about the companies' businesses as are insiders. But this objection is not persuasive. Qualified potential outside directors of public corporations are numerous. Consider that most executives in public corporations who serve as outside directors serve as outside directors of other, noncompetitor corporations in which they or their primary corporation have no financial interest. In addition, directors can be sought among the ranks of unaffiliated professionals and academics, and the pool of retired chief executives may provide a rich source of able outside directors. Nor is the lack of intimate familiarity with the details of a corporation's business a serious flaw in outside directors. The corporation's officers will still be versed in these operational matters, they can still base business decisions on their special knowledge and expertise, and they can still justify their actions to outside directors by calling upon their vast reservoirs of particularistic knowledge. The main function of the directors is not to make specific business judgments but to monitor the performance of the insiders and to make those important but relatively infrequent decisions as to which the insiders have a conflict of interest. Excellent performance of these functions requires intelligence, diligence, probity, and a good general understanding, based upon experience, of human nature and the ways of business, but it does not require that the director have an insider's familiarity with the company. Indeed, the outside perspective may be crucial for the generation of fresh, innovative reactions to the ingrown routines of thought and action into which insiders are tempted to fall.

Better explanation

There is a second, more plausible answer to the question about the courts' failure to adopt some apparently better categorical rule about executive compensation. It is that a categorical rule would not be suitable for close corporations. Since state courts deal with a relatively greater number of close corporation cases, yet have systematically failed to realize the viability of adopting different specifications of the fiduciary principle for close corporations, the courts have declined to adopt such a rule.

The close/public distinction

In the public corporation, the executives and the shareholders are distinct, and the clear function of the directors is to serve as bargaining representatives of the shareholders. It therefore makes sense to insure their independence from the executives and even to put them into an adversary position with respect to matters like executive compensation. In many close corporations, however, the investors and the chief employees are the same persons, or their members significantly overlap, and the question of executive compensation is but a part of the larger problem of dividing the fruits of the business among the various participants. Basically this division is accomplished by bargaining among all the participants. Since the board of directors is formally the ultimate decision making body in a corporation, it makes sense to allow all the participants a position on the board. When outsiders are needed in the close corporation, it is rarely to represent shareholders as a class against executives as a class but to serve as a referee among squabbling participants, many of whom have multiple formal roles. In many well planned or otherwise happily functioning close corporations, mandating the presence of an outsider referee would be totally unnecessary and even obstructive of the parties' best interest. And when referees are needed, they need not take the form of outside directors. (A court might appoint a receiver in case of deadlock among the participants, for example.)

Costs of strict process to close corporations

Another factor becomes important if we insist (as we ideally would, in the case of public corporations) on defining outside directors to exclude not only corporate executives and employees but also persons, like the corporation's lawyers and suppliers, who have a financial interest in its decisions. Some close corporations may be small businesses operating in relatively small markets. It could be difficult and expensive for them to interest qualified persons in becoming their outside directors (in this strict sense). In a small town, for example, there may be only one significant corporation engaged in manufacturing or commerce. The only readily available "outsiders" with general business experience may be the principals in the town's bank and real estate firms, which will probably have relationships with the corporation. In such a situation, the desire to get directors who will bring a different perspective, plus the expense of searching in other communities for "purer" candidates, may well be thought to override conflict of interest dangers.

In sum, the failure of state courts to be more categorical in their imposition of process restraints on the fixing of executive compensation may simply reflect courts' desire to make rules that are suitable for close corporations, even though they are generally applicable to all corporations. In this perspective, it should not be surprising that the increasingly successful drive to have public corporations recruit boards consisting mainly of outside directors has come from academic commentators and the SEC, both of whom are more accustomed to thinking about the problems of public corporations and the solutions most appropriate to them.

CHAPTER 7

CORPORATE OPPORTUNITIES

§7.1 Introduction

Basic concept

If a business opportunity is deemed to be a corporate opportunity of a given corporation, then the fiduciaries of that corporation — its directors, officers, and controlling shareholders — may not take or usurp the opportunity for themselves. Thus, if the chance to buy a particular glassworks factory would be found by a court to be a corporate opportunity of Wine, Persons, and Song Company (WPS), then Luce, the president of the corporation, could not lawfully buy it himself. What makes something a corporate opportunity will be discussed later. But note here that the opportunity need not be corporate property in the strong sense that the corporation could legally object to its being taken and developed by independent third parties. The point is only that, as between the corporation and its fiduciary, the opportunity belongs to the corporation. Thus, Omar Khayyam, a wealthy Arab with no connections to WPS, might rightfully buy the glassworks factory before WPS can act, even though Luce could not do this.

Defenses

In many but not all jurisdictions the fiduciary may raise the defense that the corporation was financially or legally unable to take the opportunity. If he proves such corporate incapacity, then his taking was not wrongful. He may also defend himself by showing that the corporation rejected or abandoned the opportunity or that it explicitly approved his taking it.

Remedy

If a fiduciary does take a corporate opportunity, and has no good defense, the corporation may recover the appropriated asset or business project from the usurper or the profits that he made on it.[1] The remedy, which is derived from the law of trusts, is a strict one. The usurping fiduciary gets no offset because of the fact that the later value of the project (or the size of the profits made) increased as much as it did because of his personal efforts.

Relation to paradigms

Usurpation of a corporate opportunity fits with our third conflict of interest paradigm, the taking of corporate property.[2] Accordingly, if a manager engages in such usurpation, he has done wrong, ipso facto. There is no question of looking into the fairness or the reasonableness of some exchange between the corporation and the manager, for his behavior is viewed as not involving an exchange. At a general level, therefore, the reasons for considering a manager's taking a corporate opportunity to be wrong are the same as the reasons for considering outright theft from the corporate treasury to be wrong: Secret, unilateral takings by managers create unproductive uncertainty and may amount to monopoly rents.[3]

The foregoing general statements are not very illuminating. As with other variants of the third paradigm, the difficult issue is to determine

§7.1 [1]On imposition of a constructive trust, see Guth v. Loft, Inc., 5 A.2d 503 (Del. 1939); Weissman v. A. Weissman, Inc., 97 A.2d 870 (Pa. 1953); Beatty v. Guggenheim Exploration Co., 122 N.E. 378 (N.Y. 1919). On accounting for profits realized by the fiduciary, see Hill v. Hill, 420 A.2d 1078 (Pa. Super. 1980); Irving Trust Co. v. Deutsch, 73 F.2d 121 (2d Cir. 1934), cert. denied, 294 U.S. 708 (1935), petition for relief denied, 294 U.S. 733 (1935); Regal (Hastings), Limited v. Gulliver, [1942] 1 All E.R. 378 (H.L.); Sialkot Importing Corp. v. Berlin, 68 N.E.2d 501 (N.Y. 1946).

[2]See section 4.1 supra. Again, "property" is used here in a nontechnical sense.

[3]See section 4.2 supra.

what should be deemed, as between corporation and fiduciary, to belong to the corporation, and why. In short, what *is* a corporate opportunity? The answers worked out in the case law will be discussed in the next section. These answers turn out to create certain riddles (which are discussed in section 7.3 infra), and the attempt to resolve them will lead to a discussion of the differences between kinds of corporations (section 7.4 infra) and of the kinds of corporate opportunity rules that are most appropriate to different categories of situations (sections 7.5-7.8 infra).

§7.2 *The Traditional Tests*

§7.2.1 Interest or Expectancy

General statement

Perhaps the oldest judicial test of a corporate opportunity, and one that is still widely used, is that a corporate opportunity is a business opportunity in which the corporation has an *interest* or *expectancy* or which is *essential* to the corporation. Since the three key terms used in this statement are terms of art, it will be useful to give examples of each of them and of their judicial explanations.

Meaning of "interest"

In a classic Alabama decision rendered in 1900,[1] the court faced a situation which resembled an exam question written by a tidy law professor. The corporation owned a one-third interest in a limestone quarry, had a contract to buy a second one-third interest in it, and had no formal arrangements with respect to the final one-third interest. Certain corporate fiduciaries (directors and majority shareholders) bought the two one-third interests that the corporation did not already own. The court found that they violated their fiduciary duty to the corporation by personally purchasing the one-third interest under contract with the corporation but not by purchasing the final one-third interest. The court said that directors and officers need only turn over to their corporation property they have purchased from third parties when it is "property wherein the corporation has an interest already existing or in which it has an expectancy growing out of an existing right . . . where the officers' interference will in some degree balk the corporation in effecting the purposes of its creation."[2] Apparently the second one-third interest could not be taken by the insiders because the corporation had an interest in it.

Expectancy

A slightly later case shows what is meant by a tangible expectancy

§7.2 [1]Lagarde v. Anniston Lime & Stone Co., 28 So. 199 (Ala. 1900).
[2]Id. at 201.

arising out of an existing interest. The corporation had leased property important to itself, but insiders bought the lease renewal rights themselves. Their doing so was found to be a wrongful usurpation of a corporate opportunity.[3]

Necessity

A good example of an opportunity deemed essential, or extremely important to the corporation in effecting its purposes, was provided by an early case[4] in which the executives acquired rights to divert a river at a point just upstream from one of the corporation's hydroelectric power plants.

Negative conception of duty

These three holdings reflect a modest, negative conception of a fiduciary's duty. The fiduciary should not deliberately harm his corporation. He is not supposed to take steps to further his own interest that will rather clearly and directly thwart the corporation's interest. Thus, he should not interfere with efforts already begun by the corporation to acquire new property (the quarry case), even though a nonfiduciary third party might legally compete with the corporation and interfere with its plans. He should not exploit the market power that third parties have over his corporation but which, for whatever reasons, they have so far failed to exploit. It will therefore do the insiders no good, in cases like those involving the lease renewal or the upstream rights, to argue that some third party already possessed the power either to make the corporation pay a premium to secure achievement of its ends or to sell important rights to a higher bidder than the corporation and that such third party would probably have exercised his market power eventually. There may be a real risk that a corporation's lessor will threaten to lease the corporation's property to someone else, or that an upstream owner will threaten to divert the stream to another plant owner, unless paid a requested sum. But the fiduciary may not trigger or accelerate the process; he may not be the one who translates the risk into a reality. Prohibiting him from doing so may mean that the corporation will do better, and it will not lead the corporation to fare worse. Fiduciaries will often have better information than independent third parties do about the corporation's needs and vulnerabilities — its true demand curve — and may therefore be superior exploiters of market power against their corporation. They may know better than the existing upstream owner, for example, how desperately the corporation needs water flow from the river. But fiduciaries can no more reap the advantage of informed market power against their corporations than they

[3]Pike's Peak Co. v. Pfunter, 123 N.W. 19 (Mich. 1909).
[4]Nebraska Power Co. v. Koenig, 139 N.W. 839 (Neb. 1913).

can exploit their control power in a basic self-dealing situation to get an exceptional deal for themselves.

In sum, the gist of the interest or expectancy test is that it defines the concept of corporate property in light of the general principle that a fiduciary may not harm, compete with, or take advantage of his beneficiaries. It is an easier test for executives to meet than is the next one to be discussed.

§7.2.2 Line of Business

Example of *Guth v. Loft*

In *Guth v. Loft, Inc.*,[5] a leading Delaware case decided in 1939, the court defined corporate opportunities more broadly to include virtually any business opportunities that are within the subject corporation's "line of business." Guth, the president and executive head of Loft, Inc., a manufacturer and seller of beverages, acquired for himself, through ownership of a majority of the shares of another corporation, an interest in the secret formula and trademark of the bankrupt National Pepsi-Cola Company. He developed the Pepsi-Cola business and even had it sell large quantities of the product to Loft. The court held that his Pepsi-Cola shares were a corporate opportunity of Loft and had to be turned over to it.

There were a number of factors besides the affinity in lines of business that probably would have led independently to the result. The opportunity to acquire Pepsi-Cola shares came to Guth because of his connection with Loft, Inc. Moreover, he used the latter's funds and plant facilities to purchase and develop the Pepsi-Cola business. Use of corporate resources to develop and acquire an opportunity for oneself is a frequent ground for finding a wrongful taking. But the court's opinion implied that the Pepsi-Cola opportunity was a corporate one of Loft even apart from Guth's use of corporate resources.

Meaning of "line of business"

Note that when courts examine whether an opportunity is within a company's existing "line of business" they are not engaged in a mere exercise in conceptual classification or analogical reasoning but in a rough and ready inquiry into economic efficiency. They are looking to see whether the opportunity presents some especially favorable business prospects because of the way it would "fit in" with the company's existing assets and talents. Thus, the Delaware Supreme Court stated that

> [w]here a corporation is engaged in a certain business, and an opportunity is presented to it embracing an activity as to which it has fundamental knowledge, practical experience and ability to pursue, which, logically and natu-

[5] 5 A.2d 503 (Del. 1939).

> rally, is adaptable to its business having regard for its financial position, and is one that is consonant with its reasonable needs and aspirations for expansion, it may be properly said that the opportunity is in the line of the corporation's business.[6]

Under this concept of line of business, a plaintiff might argue, for example, that a business engaged in manufacturing and selling contact lens wetting solution would fall sufficiently within the same line as a corporation engaged in making and selling cold medicines to invoke the corporate opportunity doctrine. The argument would be that the methods of marketing and distributing the products — through drug stores, for example — overlapped enough to permit significant economies of scale if the businesses were to be combined. He might or might not win such an argument, for the line of business formula could be interpreted very narrowly or very broadly by an individual court. But his claim could hardly be treated as a frivolous one. It could not be effectively rebutted by the simple observation that wetting solution and cold medicines are different products.

Other jurisdictions have adopted the line of business test.[7] Later Delaware decisions affirm the view that the Delaware test is cumulative; an opportunity is a corporate one if it meets either the interest or the expectancy or the line of business tests.[8]

§7.2.3 Fairness

Open-ended test

In 1948 a Massachusetts Supreme Judicial Court decision adopted the view of a then-contemporary commentator, Ballantine,[9] that the "true basis" of the corporate opportunity doctrine was the "unfairness on the particular facts" of a fiduciary taking an opportunity when the corporation's interests call for protection and that the courts ought to apply "ethical standards of what is fair and equitable to particular sets of facts."[10] Since the postulated "ethical standards" are never set forth in the words of either court or commentator, this position seems mostly to reflect despair at the prospect of trying to sum up in some more definite verbal formula all the factors that have in fact been cited by courts in their justifications for

[6] Id. at 514.

[7] Rosenblum v. Judson Engineering Corp., 109 A.2d 558 (N.H. 1954). See generally 77 A.L.R.3d 961 (1977).

[8] Equity Corp. v. Milton, 221 A.2d 494 (Del. 1966); cf. Fliegler v. Lawrence, 361 A.2d 218 (Del. 1976).

[9] H. Ballantine, Ballantine on Corporations 204-209 (rev. ed. 1946).

[10] Id. at 205; Durfee v. Durfee & Canning, Inc., 80 N.E.2d 522, 529 (Mass. 1948).

holdings in corporate opportunity cases. Although regrettable, this position is also understandable.[11]

§7.2.4 Two-Step Analysis

Minnesota's two-step approach

In 1974 the Minnesota Supreme Court devised a test that combines the line of business test with the fairness test.[12]

The first step is to determine whether the opportunity is a corporate one. This is done by asking whether it was so closely or intimately associated with the corporation's existing or prospective activities as to fall within its line of business. If the answer is yes, the second step is taken: determining whether the officer who took the corporate opportunity violated his fiduciary duties of loyalty, good faith, and fair dealing towards the corporation. Plaintiff has the burden of proof with respect to the first step; defendant has it with repect to the second.

Problems with it

The Minnesota court's opinion was a scholarly and carefully considered one. In my view, however, it muddied the waters in several ways: semantically, by changing accepted usage so that an opportunity found to be a corporate one might nevertheless be taken by a fiduciary if his doing so is "fair"; and substantively, by relying on an "all relevant factors" fairness approach without explicitly recognizing the key importance of determining what expectations and understandings the parties had, or ought to be deemed to have had, in the particular case. (See section 7.4 below.)

But result proper

Nevertheless, the result reached in the case is the intuitively correct one.

[11] Ballantine noted seven factors considered by courts in applying corporate opportunity doctrine:

(1) Is the opportunity of special or unique value (e.g., patents or real estate) or is it necessary for the corporate business or expansion?
(2) Was the opportunity presented to the officer due to his official position?
(3) Was the company actively pursuing the opportunity, and if so, had it abandoned its effort?
(4) Was the officer explicitly made responsible for acquiring such opportunities for the company?
(5) Did he utilize corporate funds or facilities to obtain or develop the opportunity?
(6) Did taking the opportunity place the officer in a position adverse to the corporation? Did he intend to resell to the corporation?
(7) Did the corporation have the ability, financial and otherwise, to take advantage of the opportunity?

Ballantine, note 9 supra, at 206.

[12] Miller v. Miller, 222 N.W.2d 71 (Minn. 1974).

The dispute involved a son who left the family business to become a securities analyst and then, many years later, after the parents had died, sued to get some of the benefits of some separately incorporated side ventures that his two brothers had started. The two brothers, unlike the plaintiff, had slogged along as active workers in the family business; plaintiff's claim rested solely on his status as shareholder. (Why this is relevant is explored below.) The case thus illustrates some common themes in close corporation cases: the confusion of roles between investors and executives and the strength of sibling rivalry, which appears to persist throughout life and to flourish when the parents are not around.

§7.2.5 Other Relevant Factors

Use of resources and status

As noted, courts have treated the insider's use of corporate resources to acquire and develop an opportunity for himself to be equivalent to a wrongful taking of a corporate opportunity. This factor might be treated as a separate, additional test. Some courts, like those in Delaware, appear to give considerable weight as to *how* information about an opportunity comes to the attention of the corporate fiduciary: in his official capacity, that is, by virtue of his connection with the corporation, or in his individual capacity. If the former, he may be bound by the stricter line of business test;[13] if the latter, only by the interest or expectancy test.[14] This distinction in effect treats some information as corporate property (as between corporation and fiduciary), namely, information received by an insider by virtue of his playing the role of fiduciary for the corporation. The cases based on the distinction are therefore a subcategory of the use-of-corporate-resources cases.

The distinction between official and individual capacities can create endless argument about the proper characterization of facts. For example, suppose Able is invited to a cocktail party at a private individual's home. While there, he hears of a business opportunity that would be profitable if purchased by someone like himself or by a corporation like the one he serves. If it is clear that the hostess invited him only because he is the chief executive of a large local corporation, should we say that he received the information in his official capacity? The problem is a general one, because it is often difficult to decide when an executive has stepped completely outside his role.

[13] Guth v. Loft, Inc., 5 A.2d 503 (Del. 1939).
[14] Kaplan v. Fenton, 278 A.2d 834 (Del. 1971).

§7.3 *Two Riddles: Of History and Outcomes*

Historical riddle

Consider this contrast in the history of conflict of interest rules. Between the 1880s and the mid-twentieth century, most U.S. courts essentially changed the rule governing basic self-dealing transactions from an automatic voidability rule to a fairness rule (via an intermediate, proceduralistic disclosure-plus-fairness rule). Within that same period, many courts in commercially important states expanded the rule for defining corporate opportunities from an interest or expectancy test to the line of business test. In the one case, the rule became more permissive from the corporate manager's point of view; in the other, it became more strict. How are we to best understand this apparent inconsistency in changing judicial attitudes? Is there any clue in the fact that *Delaware* led the way in adoption of the new test for corporate opportunities?

Riddle of inconsistent but correct cases

A second puzzle is that *both* of the major tests of a corporate opportunity sometimes yield case law results that seem intuitively to be correct but that would *not* have followed from normal application of the other test.

Example dependent on line of business test

For example, consider the following pair of cases. In *Kerrigan v. Unity Savings Association,*[1] five controlling directors of a savings and loan association had organized an insurance agency and caused it to lease office space in the building owned and occupied by the savings association. The association would then refer its home loan borrowers to the agency, which would sell the borrowers their homeowners' insurance and other forms of insurance related to mortgage loans. A shareholder of the association brought a derivative suit alleging that the directors and the insurance agency had thereby appropriated a business opportunity that belonged to the association. The defendants argued, and the trial court agreed, that the savings association was forbidden by statute to write insurance, but this holding was reversed by the intermediate appellate court and the Illinois Supreme Court.

More important, the Supreme Court insisted that the directors should have presented the association (meaning its disinterested directors or shareholders) with the pertinent facts about the opportunity and thus should have given it the chance to make its own judgment on the question of legal capacity to either seize or reject the opportunity. "(T)he corporation or association must be given the opportunity to decide, upon full disclosure of pertinent facts, whether it wishes to enter a business that is *reasonably incident to its present or prospective operations.*"[2] In my view, the

§7.3 [1] 317 N.E.2d 39 (Ill. 1974).
[2] Id. at 43 (emphasis added).

court here was applying a line of business test. Making home mortgage loans and selling homeowners' insurance are separate and distinguishable activities, of course. But they can be construed as falling within the same line of business because they are functionally related: A business may find it advantageous to be able to offer its customers both services at the same location.

By contrast, the interest or expectancy test, at least as construed and applied in the older cases, would most likely have saved the defendants from liability. Before the insurance agency was organized, the association had no interest in it. Nor did it later acquire one by entering a contract or beginning exploratory investigation and negotiations concerning the possible establishment of an insurance agency. Nor could it be said that the association acquired a "tangible expectancy growing out of an existing interest" (as in the lease renewal cases), unless we want to expand the expectancy concept so far as to engulf the line of business test. "The corporation has an expectancy concerning every opportunity in its line of business" is simply not a way in which the courts have used the word *expectancy* when applying the simple interest or expectancy test. Furthermore, the insurance agency was not essential to the association's existing business. At most, the agency would have been a profitable but minor portion of the association's overall business.

Example dependent on interest or expectancy test

An apparently contrasting case is *Burg v. Horn*,[3] a tale of two once friendly families. The Horns, who already owned three low rent buildings in Brooklyn through wholly owned corporations, urged their friends, the Burgs, to "get their feet wet" in real estate. Accordingly, in 1953 they formed a corporation that immediately purchased a low rent building in Brooklyn. The stock was issued equally to George Horn, Max Horn, and Mrs. Burg. Mr. Burg served as the corporation's accountant and tax planner, and the Horns served as the active real estate managers. A few years later, this corporation sold its original building and bought another; it subsequently bought two more. Meanwhile, the Horns were acquiring nine other, similar properties individually or through wholly owned corporations. Eventually the Horns moved to California; there was a falling out, and Mrs. Burg brought a derivative suit against the Horns, claiming that their post-1953 purchases of low rent properties in Brooklyn were a usurpation of corporate opportunities of the jointly owned corporation. The Burgs testified that they expected the Horns to offer any low rent properties that they found in Brooklyn to the corporation. But the district court said that there was no agreement to that effect; that the Burgs had been

[3] 380 F.2d 897 (2d Cir. 1967).

aware of the Horns' pre-1953 acquisitions; that they became aware of some of the Horns' post-1953 acquisitions as they were made; and that Mr. Burg had even participated in some of the latter by making loans to one of the Horns. In other words, the Burgs' objections seem pretty clearly to have arisen well after the essential facts.

Applying New York law, the Second Circuit affirmed the holding that there had been no wrongful taking of corporate opportunities. In doing so, it applied the interest or expectancy test and explicitly rejected the line of business test, attributing it to "commentators" and decrying it "as too broad a generalization." It said that the interest or expectancy test was more consistent with "our holding that the scope of the director's duty to offer opportunities he has found to his corporation must be measured by *the facts of each case*. . . ."[4] As usual when courts make such statements, the reader is given no listing of all the possibly relevant kinds of facts, no specification as to their real weight and priorities, and no clear reason for thinking they are relevant.

Obviously, if the court had interpreted New York law so as to embrace the line of business test, it would probably have come out with the opposite result. All of the crucial transactions involved purchases of similar properties within a reasonably small geographical area; the Horns had taken opportunities in the jointly owned company's line of business. Yet this opposite result would have been unfair.[5] The court's opinion seems to rest upon the appealing view that the Burgs had no *reasonable expectation* that the Horns would offer all chances to buy low rent buildings to the corporation (and perhaps no such expectation at all), because they had no explicit agreement to that effect and, given all they knew, could not have had an implicit agreement or mutual understanding. But this assessment of the case's outcome poses our second riddle: How can *Kerrigan* and *Burg* both be correct?

Solution in close/public distinction

The answer to both riddles, I suggest, lies in the differences between close and public corporations. The Delaware courts developed the line of business test, even though it may have seemed harder for managers, because they realized, at some level, that it is a more suitable rule for public corporations. (But it is not a perfect one.) Since Delaware is the preeminent

[4] Id. at 900 (emphasis added).

[5] But see id. at 902-903 (Hays, J., dissenting, arguing that, even in the absence of explicit agreement, the Horns were under a fiduciary duty to offer the properties to the corporation, and disputing the factual conclusion that the Burgs were aware of the Horns' purchases); Note, Corporate Opportunity in the Close Corporation — A Different Result? 56 Geo. L.J. 381 (1967); 43 N.Y.U.L. Rev. 187 (1968) (noting that most jurisdictions, but not New York, hold directors of close corporations to a higher standard of duty than those of public corporations).

place of incorporation for large companies, its courts are naturally more conscious of the problems characteristic of large public corporations. Their consciousness was undoubtedly raised after the modern publicly held business corporation was firmly established, and a trickle of cases involving its peculiar problems began to come before the courts. As for the second riddle, note that *Burg v. Horn* involved a close corporation. The court's approach — looking at what expectations or mutual understandings existed or would have been rational on the facts of the individual situation — was suitable, I will argue, for a close corporation. *Kerrigan,* however, involved a corporation with outside shareholders who needed to be protected by a more sweeping rule based on categorically imputed understandings.

The rest of this chapter elaborates this proposed solution of the two riddles.

§7.4 *Different Rules for Different Corporations*

Categorical rule

Rules specifying the corporate manager's general fiduciary duty of loyalty tend toward one of two polar types, categorical rules and selective rules. A *categorical* rule is one that applies uniformly to a rather broad category of situations — for example, all takings by corporate officers of business opportunities for themselves — even though it is fairly precise and specific. The uniformity component of this definition means that the rule adopts a strict stance towards pleas for variations, exceptions, and defenses. The precision component means that the rule does not rely very much on unspecified, unweighted, or vague factors like "the particular facts and circumstances of the case." Examples of relatively categorical rules are the strict rule forbidding trustees to deal personally with trust property;[1] the automatic voidability rule that once governed basic self-dealing transactions; and a proposed corporate opportunity rule that would deny all full time officers of corporations the right to take for themselves any active business opportunities, that is, opportunities in which they would have significant decision making influence over the operation of the business.

Selective rule

A *selective* rule is one that allows for more differentiation in the treatment of cases falling within a general category of situations and that is not

§7.4 [1] "No trustee shall directly or indirectly buy or sell any property for the trust from or to itself or an affiliate; or from or to a director, officer, or employee of such trustee or of an affiliate; or from or to a relative, employer, partner, or other business associate." Uniform Trusts Act §5 (1937). See 2 A. Scott, Scott on Trusts §§170-170.25 (3d ed. 1967 & Supp. 1981).

precise or specific in its identification or weighting of operative facts. Exceptions and defenses abound, and the facts and circumstances that are relevant to determining what is right conduct form a large, open-ended, and inexactly specified class. Examples of selective rules are the fairness test governing basic self-dealing and the traditional tests of a corporate opportunity. For example, the interest or expectancy test "selects" some but by no means all takings of active business opportunities by corporate fiduciaries for condemnation. Although its principles of selection can be summed up in a short verbal formulation, the formula leads courts into some rather involved but ill-defined factual investigations.

A difference of degree

The difference between categorical and selective rules is one of degree, of course. Often one can make the contrast only after stipulating a relevant category of situations, for example, "personal takings of business opportunities by corporate officers." Then one can make the point that, within that domain, the line of business test is a "more" categorical rule than the interest or expectancy test or the fairness test.

Related distinctions

The categorical-selective distinction is similar to that between rigid and flexible rules. But, as a logical matter, it should not be equated with the distinction between strict and lax rules. Strictness may mean that it is difficult or burdensome for a fiduciary to comply with the rule or that the rule offers unusually good protection to beneficiaries against a real risk of abuse of discretionary power. Categorical rules may often be strict in these senses, but they need not be. For example, the business judgment rule is a relatively categorical one — in essence, all business decisions are insulated from judicial scrutiny unless tainted by fraud or conflict of interest — but it is not a strict one. Conversely, a basically selective legal approach to a category of situations may be strict — because, for example, a heavy burden of proof is placed on the managers or other fiduciaries.

Differences between close and public corporations

The point to recognize is that the choice between categorical and selective rules depends in part on characteristic differences between close and public corporations. Let us review these differences. (1) Stockholders of close corporations have a greater real ability than do stockholders of a public corporation to select fiduciaries to whom they entrust their capital. (2) They also have a greater ability to monitor their managers' contributions to (and diversions from) the enterprise. Investors in public corporations are usually passive and widely scattered contributors of money to be managed by preselected officers to whom they effectively delegate full decision making power over operating matters. In contrast, investors in close corporations are fairly small in number and tend to know one another.[2] They make

[2]See generally Soderquist & Vecchio, Reconciling Shareholders' Rights and Corporate

more conscious choices when selecting managers from among themselves. They are likely to be active participants rather than merely passive contributors of funds. And they can also consent in a more meaningful way to diversions of corporate assets by fellow participants, either when they form or join the enterprise or on the occasion of the diversion. They may therefore have less need of categorical rules against diversions by fellow participants.[3]

More differences

Moreover, both (3) the scope of the duties and (4) the nature of the compensation of the managers differ as between the two types of corporations. The duties of the executives of a public corporation normally require full-time application of their managerial talents and energies and leave no room for active participation in the development or operation of other businesses. Their compensation arrangements are usually such that neither equity nor efficiency requires them to be allowed to take covert indirect compensation as they see fit. But with respect to many close corporations, other expectations may be more reasonable. The participants may sometimes agree, or assume in the initial arrangements, that their managing colleagues are not to work only for the particular corporation but are free to engage in other activities.[4] In any event, it is feasible in close corporations (as it is *not* in public corporations) to obtain the consent of all the participants to such part-time employment by the managing participants. Such consent may even be inferred in close corporations when some participants are undercompensated in relation to others. As often noted, the formal compensation arrangements in a close corporation may not clearly separate the role of a participant's talents and efforts from the role of his capital contributions in determining his returns from the business. In such a situation, it may well be found that the participants agreed or understood — or probably would have agreed had they thought of the matter — that their financial reward should reflect variations in their continuing active efforts in the business, as well as in their initial capital contributions, and that this understanding implies some consent to outside activities on the part of some participants.[5]

Responsibility: New Guidelines for Management, 1978 Duke L.J. 819; Soderquist, Reconciling Shareholders' Rights and Corporate Responsibility: Close and Small Public Corporations, 33 Vand. L. Rev. 1387 (1980).

[3]See, e.g., LaSalle Street Capital Corp., 44 S.E.C. 655, 661-662 (1971).

[4]Compare Wilshire Oil Co. v. Riffe, 381 F.2d 646 (10th Cir.), cert. denied, 389 U.S. 822 (1967), and Michigan Crown Fender Co. v. Welch, 178 N.W. 684 (Mich. 1920), with Robinson v. Brier, 194 A.2d 204 (Pa. 1963).

[5]For example, if events after formation of the enterprise result in withdrawal from active participation by some participants, the efforts of those continuing to manage the firm may not

Finally, (5) differences between the opportunity sets of the two types of enterprise imply different constraints on their managers. A publicly held enterprise may be treated as large and flexible enough to accept any new investment opportunities that offer an appropriate return per unit of risk. Hence, its opportunity set embraces virtually any business in which its executives might want to invest and take an active role. The opportunity set of a close corporation is not nearly so broad. Market imperfections and transaction costs may impede such corporations' efforts to accept projects unrelated to their existing experience or talent[6] or far beyond their existing financial capacity.[7] There may be many businesses that the officers of a closely held company may develop on their own time which would not deprive the enterprise of any opportunity it could reasonably hope to exploit.

Implication of differences

All these differences between close and public corporations — in size of opportunity sets; in investors' ability to select and monitor their managers and contract with one another; and in the nature of managers' duties and compensation arrangements — are mainly a consequence of differences in size. They suggest that lawmakers generally ought to construct corporate law doctrines with a different jurisprudential orientation in the two contexts. As a rough but fair generalization, the basic characteristics of the corporate form of organization and the related statutory rules are best suited for large scale enterprises owned by numerous public investors. (See chapter 1 supra.) In this context, legal rules often can and should be categorical: uniformly applicable to general categories of situations even when they are fairly precise and specific. The rules of corporate law, which define the relationships of stockholders to each other and to management, constitute something like a standard contract to which all the actors who play the standard roles of shareholder, director, and officer automatically agree by assuming those roles. The outcome of legal disputes governed by public corporation law should leave little play for the vagaries of particular understandings and arrangements.

Categorical rules for public corporations

be adequately rewarded, unless their returns are increased. In light of the continued level of returns to the withdrawn former participants, participation in other enterprises may offer a proper supplement to the returns payable to the managers. See Miller v. Miller, 222 N.W.2d 71 (Minn. 1974). Put another way, in the context of public corporations, the market for managers, whatever its limitations in absolute terms, may be a more real—and more efficient—mechanism by which to determine their compensation than in the context of private ventures, where the managers are also likely to be entrepreneurs and therefore expect returns that are not easily separable between capital and managerial talent.

[6]See Robinson v. Brier, 194 A.2d 204 (Pa. 1963).

[7]Cox & Perry, Inc. v. Perry, 334 So. 2d 867 (Ala. 1976); Gauger v. Hintz, 55 N.W.2d 426 (Wis. 1952).

But the notion that corporate participants should be viewed as entering voluntarily into a standard contract, or pre-fixed set of roles and relationships, has much less relevance to close corporations. The close corporation "deal" simply does not have to be the same for all close corporations. The roles of the investor and the manager are more likely to be mixed and shared by the participants. The range of variations in the terms of participation is likely to be greater. These points are a straightforward consequence of size differences. The small number of players (directors, officers, and shareholders) in the typical close corporation makes possible a far greater amount of real communication and agreement among all players about their particular situations and objectives. As the number of players increases, however, the number of communication channels needed to connect all of them with each other increases astronomically.[8] Public corporations simply cannot have a meaningful system of open communications and particularized agreements among all their players.

Selective rules for close corporations

What this analysis suggests is that rules like those governing corporate opportunities should leave more room in the close corporation context for results to turn on the special facts, arrangements, and understandings of each situation. Lawmakers should assume that the parties are better able than in the case of public corporations to make individualized bargains. By contrast, courts dealing with alleged violations of the fiduciary duties of public corporation managers ought not to focus crucially upon the nuances of the factual situations before them or on what the actual expectations of shareholders were. Rather, they should concentrate on determining the rights and duties that rationally ought to govern all players of the roles in question.

We turn now to some suggested rules that are based on these principles.

§7.5 *Close Corporations: Restatement of the Law*

Guidelines for gaps

Unfortunately, to determine the duties of a close corporation fiduciary with respect to the taking of business opportunities, it is not enough to say that

[8]More precisely, the number of channels needed to connect all persons in a group directly with each other is given by the formula

$$C = \frac{P^2 - P}{2}$$

where C means number of communication channels and P means the number of persons. Obviously, C increases much faster than P.

the duties are fixed by the actual contract, mutual understandings, or reasonable expectations of the parties involved. This is inadequate because, when a close corporation is formed or its cast of characters reset, the participants usually do not envision all the contingencies against which they would contract if they could foresee the future. Courts need to fill in the gaps in actual agreements. In the present context, this means constructing judicial tests of a corporate opportunity that amount to presumptive guidelines. A useful procedure to follow in developing these guidelines is to focus on what rational participants could be deemed to have expected and agreed to at the beginning of the venture. If the participants had contemplated a certain possibility which later materializes, would they have contracted to prevent it and, if so, how?

§7.5.1 Guidelines

Defending traditional tests

In the close corporation context, the traditional corporate opportunity tests can be defended by the procedure of reconstructing a rational original understanding. Consider, for example, the test of essentiality. New participants probably would have contracted against the appropriation by some participants of projects that are essential to the continued viability of the enterprise. They might not, however, have contracted against the taking by participants of *all* essential opportunities; they might have excluded those wholly unrelated to the business of the enterprise, even if letting the corporation take the opportunities might avoid insolvency.

A more inclusive but still reasonable expectation to impute to the original participants is that their company would be entitled to, as against the individual participants, new projects that are within the corporation's line of business or its set of functionally related operations. And finally, we can suppose that they would have sought to protect their collective right to opportunities which the corporation should reasonably expect to acquire, such as the renewal of a lease, or which it has taken overt steps to obtain, as by negotiating or by making studies or inquiries — that is, opportunities in which it has an interest or expectancy.

A restatement

On the premise that the law should vindicate these imputed expectations, we[1] propose that the following guidelines, which the case law often acknowledges, should govern the taking of business opportunities by participants in close corporations:

§7.5 [1]The recommendations throughout sections 7.5-7.8 were proposed by Professors Brudney and myself in a law review article. Brudney & Clark, A New Look at Corporate Opportunities, 94 Harv. L. Rev. 997 (1981). Hence the use of the term *we*.

(1) If the disputed opportunity is functionally related to the corporation's business, then, whether or not it is necessary or of special value, the individual participants may not take it.
(2) If the corporation has an interest or expectancy in the opportunity, the individual participants may not take it.
(3) If the participants consent in advance or contemporaneously to diversion of the new project,[2] an individual participant can take it, even though it would otherwise run afoul of (1) or (2), provided, however, that nothing less than express contemporaneous consent will permit the taking of a functionally related opportunity whose acceptance is necessary to prevent loss or injury to the corporation.
(4) If the new project is not covered by the preceding rules, it may be taken by some individual participants, without sharing with the others and without the consent of the others.

Functional relationship

Some comments are necessary to indicate how this restatement would clarify or modify current law. First, "functional relationship" would replace "line of business" in order better to connote what should be the focus of lawyers' and courts' attention. The courts should be concerned with whether the new project, because of the nature of its manufacturing or sales processes or of its resources, will overlap with the corporation's existing business so as to produce nontrivial synergistic gains.[3] This is a difficult factual question, of course, and may unfortunately cause protracted litigation.[4]

Harm vs. lost profits

Second, the guidelines cut back on the significance given by decided cases to the distinction between an opportunity whose taking by a

[2] A requirement of contemporaneous consent could be cast in terms either of board consent or of stockholder consent by vote, either unanimously or by a simple majority.

[3] The gain may come from complementary values (such as may flow from a manufacturer's ownership of a sales outlet), Gottlieb v. Mead Corp., 137 N.E.2d 178 (Ohio Ct. C.P. 1954), aff'd per curiam, 137 N.E.2d 211 (Ohio Ct. App. 1955); Tennessee Dressed Beef Co. v. Hall, 519 S.W.2d 805 (Tenn. Ct. App. 1974); Guth v. Loft, Inc., 5 A.2d 503 (Del. 1939); or from parallel opportunities (as in producing or selling comparable products), Rosenblum v. Judson Engineering Corp., 109 A.2d 558 (N.H. 1954); Hubbard v. Pape, 203 N.E.2d 365 (Ohio App. 1964); or from the exploitation of additional sources of natural resources or quantities of the same product.

[4] The case law conception of line of business, which is analogous to functional relationship, is ephemeral, sometimes as broad as the corporate charter and other times limited by the firm's actual operations. Compare Weismann v. Snyder, 156 N.E.2d 21 (Mass. 1959) (to breadth of corporate charter), and Production Mach. Co. v. Howe, 99 N.E.2d 32 (Mass. 1951), with Lancaster Loose Leaf Tobacco Co. v. Robinson, 250 S.W. 997 (Ky. 1923) (demanding past experience in line).

fiduciary would cause a loss or contraction of the corporation's business and one whose taking would merely deprive the firm of increased profits.[5] That an opportunity is necessary to the corporation's functioning would only bear on whether the insider, before taking it, must obtain the explicit, contemporaneous consent of the other participants in the corporation.

Role of consent

Third, consent could be used rather broadly to justify the taking of a business opportunity. With the just-mentioned exception, the taker of an opportunity could try to show that the participants originally understood, or should have expected, that he would be free to seek out other projects of the sort in question. Thus, the court faced with a situation like *Burg v. Horn* would not have to see the issue as involving a choice between the interest or expectancy test and the line of business test. Instead, it would inquire into the parties' reasonable expectations.

Burden of proof

Fourth, in order to provide a strong degree of protection for the often vulnerable minority shareholders of close corporations, the defendant fiduciary in corporate opportunity cases would have a heavy burden of proof. After a plaintiff had established that the defendant was a fiduciary and had taken the opportunity in question, the defendant would have to show that (1) the opportunity taken by him was not one in which the corporation had an interest or expectancy and not one that was functionally related to the corporation's business or (2) there was consent — original or contemporaneous, express or implied — to the taking. The fact that the fiduciary can always seek explicit consent to his taking an opportunity should remove the seeming harshness of this burden of proof rule.

"Fairness"?

Fifth, and most important, the suggested guidelines omit use of the generalized notion of fairness. In this context, the notion simply gives courts boundless discretion without instructing corporate counsel and their clients. The guidelines also omit the defense of corporate incapacity. This last point requires special mention.

§7.5.2 Corporate Incapacity

Conflicting case law

A substantial body of case law permits diversion by officers of corporate opportunities when some showing is made that the corporation is unable to take the opportunity because of limitations in its charter or contracts,[6]

[5] Compare Golden Rod Mining Co. v. Bukvich, 92 P.2d 316 (Mont. 1939), with Colorado & Utah Coal Co. v. Harris, 49 P.2d 429 (Colo. 1935), and Carper v. Frost Oil Co., 211 P. 370 (Colo. 1922). See also Austrian v. Williams, 103 F. Supp. 64, 79-80 (S.D.N.Y.), rev'd on other grounds, 198 F.2d 697 (2d Cir.), cert. denied, 344 U.S. 909 (1952).

[6] Alger v. Brighter Days Mining Corp., 160 P.2d 346 (Ariz. 1945); Urban J. Alexander Co. v.

external legal constraints,[7] inability to finance the acquisition,[8] or the unwillingness of the person offering the opportunity to deal with the corporation.[9] Other courts, such as the Second Circuit in its notable opinion in *Irving Trust Co. v. Deutsch,*[10] have rejected this kind of defense. They recognize that allowing the defense creates problems of proof, reduces the incentives on fiduciaries to improve corporate capacities, and often allows inherently implausible claims to carry the day.

Incapacity defense permits diversions

As some courts have pointed out, if financial disabilities or third party refusals to deal with the corporation are accepted as tests, the inevitable result will be to permit the diversion.[11] This happens because courts must decide on the basis of a set of facts largely in the control of the diverter. For example, when management argues that the corporation could not have financed the purchase of a particular opportunity, the ability of outsiders to show that the corporation could have raised the money is usually limited. Or suppose a legal inability is alleged to justify the corporation's not taking a bargain. The relevant question may be taken to be, not who is legally

---

Trinkle, 224 S.W.2d 923 (Ky. 1949); Lancaster Loose Leaf Tobacco Co. v. Robinson, 250 S.W. 997 (Ky. 1923); Diedrick v. Helm, 14 N.W.2d 913 (Minn. 1944).

[7] Thilco Timber Co. v. Sawyer, 210 N.W. 204 (Mich. 1926); Gross v. Neuman, 337 N.Y.S.2d 623 (App. Div. 1972). Compare Diedrick v. Helm, 14 N.W.2d 913 (Minn. 1944), with Goodman v. Perpetual Bldg. Assn., 320 F. Supp. 20 (D.D.C. 1970), and Kerrigan v. Unity Sav. Assn., 317 N.E.2d 39 (Ill. 1974); Fliegler v. Lawrence, 1 Del. J. Corp. L. 145, 147-149, 154 (Del. Ch. 1974), aff'd, 361 A.2d 218 (Del. 1976), with Grossman, Faber & Miller, P.A. v. Cable Funding Corp. (1974-1975 Transfer Binder), Fed. Sec. L. Rep. (CCH) ¶94,913, at 97, 112-125. See also the following cases, in which the corporation was not made—and could not be made—lawfully able to acquire the opportunity. Case v. Kelly, 133 U.S. 21 (1890); Diamond v. Oreamuno, 248 N.E.2d 910 (N.Y. 1969).

[8] City of Miami Beach v. Smith, 551 F.2d 1370 (5th Cir. 1977); Presidio Mining Co. v. Overton, 261 F. 933 (9th Cir. 1919), aff'd, 270 F. 388 (9th Cir.), cert. denied, 256 U.S. 694 (1921); Rankin v. Frebank Co., 121 Cal Rptr. 348 (Cal. App. 1975); Katz Corp. v. T.H. Canty & Co., 362 A.2d 975 (Conn. 1975); A.C. Petters Co. v. St. Cloud Enterprises, Inc., 222 N.W.2d 83 (Minn. 1974) (per curiam); Gauger v. Hintz, 55 N.W.2d 426 (Wis. 1952).

[9] Davis v. Pearce, 30 F.2d 85 (8th Cir. 1928); Bisbee v. Midland Linseed Prods. Co., 19 F.2d 24 (8th Cir.), cert. denied, 275 U.S. 564 (1927); Washer v. Seager, 71 N.Y.S.2d 46 (App. Div. 1947); Hauben v. Morris, 5 N.Y.S.2d 721 (App. Div. 1938). Contra, Twin Falls Farm & City Distrib., Inc. v. D & B Supply Co., 528 P.2d 1286 (Idaho 1974).

[10] 73 F.2d 121 (2d Cir. 1934), cert. denied, 294 U.S. 708 (1935).

[11] See, e.g., Borden v. Sinskey, 530 F.2d 478 (3d Cir. 1976); W.H. Elliott & Sons v. Gotthardt, 305 F.2d 544 (1st Cir. 1962); Irving Trust Co. v. Deutsch, 73 F.2d 121 (2d Cir.), cert. denied, 294 U.S. 708 (1935); Toledo Trust Co. v. Nye, 392 F. Supp. 484 (N.D. Ohio 1975); Knutsen v. Frushour, 436 P.2d 521 (Idaho 1968); Durfee v. Durfee & Canning, Inc., 80 N.E.2d 522 (Mass. 1948); Electronic Dev. Co. v. Robson, 28 N.W.2d 130 (Neb. 1947); cf. Young v. Columbia Oil Co., 158 S.E. 678 (W. Va. 1931) (opportunity to be offered to all shareholders if corporation does not take it).

"correct" but, whether the managers were unreasonable in believing their (self-serving) legal conclusion.[12] Managers can almost always offer reasons to support such judgments. Or perhaps the issue is whether they could have overcome the legal disability by amending the charter or security registration statement, forming a subsidiary, or procuring revocation of the offending legislation.[13] Once again, the question of the avoidability of the obstacle turns on variables substantially within the control of the diverter.

Creates bad incentives

To permit claims of disability to become the subject of judicial controversy when they can only be disproven by outsiders with great difficulty and at considerable expense is to tempt participants to actions whose impropriety is visible but rarely subject to effective challenge. In addition, availability of the defense reduces their incentive to solve corporate financing and other problems.

Is often implausible

Moreover, some types of claimed incapacity are simply implausible as a general matter. If a new business opportunity is prospectively so good that the fiduciary wants to take it himself, why can't he convince a bank or other investor of this fact in order to obtain financing for the corporation to take it?

Is not necessary

Again, our guidelines may seem harsh at first glance; in this case, because they don't allow the defense of corporate incapacity. But this apparent harshness disappears when you consider that a fiduciary who wants to take an opportunity that the corporation feels unable to exploit can simply seek the consent of the other participants. Indeed, if he offers to assist in curing an apparent corporate incapacity and the others reject his offer, this fact might support an inference that they consented to his taking the opportunity.

§7.6 *Public Corporations: Full-time Executives*

"No active opportunities" rule

It is recommended that full-time executives — that is, officers and upper level executives — be governed by the following categorical rule: Such an executive may not take for himself any active business opportunity.

At least three lines of argument support this proposal.

[12] See Tennessee Dressed Beef Co. v. Hall, 519 S.W.2d 805, 808 (Tenn. Ct. App. 1974). But see Blaustein v. Pan Am. Petroleum & Transport Co., 56 N.E.2d 705 (N.Y. 1944).

[13] See New v. New, 306 P.2d 987 (Cal. App. 1957); Kerrigan v. Unity Savings Assn., 317 N.E.2d 39 (Ill. 1974). See also Lancaster Loose Leaf Tobacco Co. v. Robinson, 250 S.W. 997 (Ky. 1923).

§7.6.1 Comparison of Rule to Rules Governing Trustees

Trustees and categorical rules

One argument starts with a consideration of the traditional trustee, such as a lawyer appointed to administer a trust set up for the settlor's children. Such a trustee is usually governed by a categorical rule against self-dealing. Most of the reasons that can be given to support such a rule apply with equal or greater force in the case of full-time corporate executive. Therefore, if we assume that the categorical approach to traditional trustees is valid, then we should also apply that approach to the full-time executive, unless there is some compelling counterargument.

Pro-categorical factors present

Let's expand this *a fortiori* argument. Some factors are usually taken to point toward a categorical approach. For example, beneficiaries depend or rely heavily upon trustees; but so also do shareholders depend and rely upon full-time executives. Beneficiaries often have little ability to monitor their trustees; but in practice, the ability of shareholders to police managerial derelictions (especially those of the one-shot variety) is also weak. A trustee is expected to devote such a portion of his working time and energy as is needed to the conduct of the trust; but the standard expectation about the top level corporate executive is even more stringent, namely, that she will devote her full working time, and her full managerial prowess, to the affairs of the corporation. Both trustees and executives are usually free to negotiate their initial compensation and may refuse to take on their roles if their explicit compensation will be unacceptable to them. Thus, there is no obvious need (in order to induce their best performance) to allow them the opportunities for additional, covert "compensation" that a selective rule would permit.

Contra-categorical factors absent

Other factors seem to cut against a categorical rule, but they affect public shareholders less than they do settlors of trusts. For example, a settlor often has some ability to identify diligent and loyal trustees before appointing one; but the shareholders' collective ability to select diligent and loyal directors, and thus to increase the probability that diligent and loyal officers will be appointed, probably is not as great. Settlors often choose trustees for their caution and scruples; but full-time executives are often chosen because of their ambition and their willingness to take risks, and this may mean that a greater proportion of managers will succumb to the temptation to take unfair advantage of their positions.

§7.6.2 Comparison with Case Law Principles

Ambiguity of traditional rules

A second argument for our proposed rule is that it has advantages over existing corporate opportunity doctrine. The traditional tests are extremely ambiguous and uncertain in their application. This tolerance for ambiguity seems justified in the case of close corporations, where courts must leave themselves room to discern and enforce varying individual contracts and understandings. But it is not appropriate for public corporations. Realistically, in this context the ambiguities in doctrine cannot be resolved by looking to particular understandings. They therefore permit executives to divert economic benefits that they do not need as incentives and that the public shareholders should receive.

Ineffectuality

Moreover, the incapacity defense makes the traditional rules toothless. This defense is even less tenable here than in the close corporation context. It inevitably depends on self-serving managerial claims that there exists no viable way to overcome the stated corporate disability, and it is virtually impossible for public stockholders to negate such claims. Moreover, claims of inability to finance a business opportunity that is a good one on the merits are simply implausible in the case of public corporations, which can seek money in efficient, large financial markets. Similarly, public corporations are often able to overcome legal obstacles when they really try. The main effect of allowing the incapacity defense is to tempt the officers to fail to exercise their best efforts to make the corporation able to overcome its disabilities.

Conceptual failure

The traditional tests also fail to follow through on the basic notion that fiduciaries should do no harm to their corporations by interfering with their operations or competing with them. Any kind of business opportunity is a potential project for most publicly held corporations. In economic theory, and in practice as evidenced by the growth of conglomerates, the modern publicly held corporation should accept *any* opportunity that it expects to produce a risk-adjusted rate of return that is not worse than that of its current operations. To be sure, there is always the question whether it wishes to take advantage at a given time of any particular opportunity. But the corporation's opportunity set includes all possibilities of acquiring a business with an attractive rate of return and risk level. Unfortunately, the courts have not yet caught up with this perception. Neither the interest or expectancy test, nor the line of business test, nor the fairness test, embodies it. Even the line of business test seems to presume that a publicly held corporation should be confined to a single line of business—or at least a fixed set of lines. But why, in the modern business world, should one assume that an enterprise that starts out in the electronics business is precluded from moving profitably into the beer-bottling business?

In summary, the traditional rules impose heavy policing costs because they are uncertain in scope and application; and to some indeterminate extent, they fail to interdict the taking by officers of opportunities that are legitimate aspirations of publicly held corporations. The proposed categorical rule is better in both respects.

§7.6.3 Costs and Benefits of Proposed Rule

Proposed rule's costs and benefits

A third argument, which is really just a continuation and completion of the second, is that the costs of the proposed rule are not so great as to outweigh its advantages.[1] The two principal costs that could result from it are that some socially desirable opportunities may go unexploited and that duplicate costs may be incurred when other people develop opportunities rejected by firms and denied to their officers.

Unexploited opportunities?

The first kind of cost is not apt to be significant.[2] The seller of an opportunity will rarely give up his efforts just because one particular corporation and its officers decline to buy it. There are usually many potential exploiters of an opportunity.

Duplicated search costs?

The second kind of cost seems somewhat more likely. A corporation expends resources investigating a business opportunity; in the course of this, some of its officers learn all about the opportunity; but the corporation, for various business reasons, decides to reject the opportunity. The

§7.6 [1]It may be noted that the cost of the sweeping definition of corporate opportunity we propose is likely to be less than the cost of imposing a categorical rule against basic self-dealing. There may be a net social gain from self-dealing transactions if the insider is a sole source of goods or services (for example, if the director on the board of the local industrial enterprise is the president of the only bank in town or the only available supplier of particular goods or services to the enterprise), or a more reliable customer or supplier than available outsiders, or because of the savings in information flows and risk perceptions that come when a buyer or supplier is on the board. See subsection 5.4.2 supra.

Moreover, if a selective rule against self-dealing is defined in terms of some conception of fairness, it is easier to police than a selective rule on appropriation of corporate opportunities. In the former case, there is available (always in theory and often in fact) a market or other basis for comparing the self-dealing transaction with an arm's-length transaction. No such benchmark is available for measuring the divertibility of the corporate opportunity.

This contrast between the self-dealing and the corporate opportunity contexts doesn't mean, of course, that we can't favor self-dealing rules that are less rigid for close corporations than for public corporations. Close corporation participants may have a better ability to police self-dealing and to cause any surplus created by it to be shared.

[2]If the opportunity is of the sort that the corporation does not find it profitable to accept but that a more venturesome entrepreneur would accept if he knew of it, there might be a net social loss from total failure to exploit the opportunity. And the loss would be greater if the opportunity could have created competition with the corporation. Most corporate opportunities, however, are not internally generated trade secrets but business opportunities offered by third persons to the world at large. Hence, they are not as likely to go unexploited as are trade secrets. By the same token, the number of especially risky opportunities that a risk-loving executive would take, but that our rule would leave for other risk lovers to discover and take if he and his corporation do not take it, is unlikely to be large.

executives are willing to develop the opportunity on their own but are deterred from doing so by the "no active business opportunity" rule. Some outside third party then takes advantage of the opportunity but in doing so incurs exploration and information costs that may duplicate the expenditures previously made by the corporation. (There need not be duplication in all such cases, of course. The third party may have investigated the opportunity concurrently with the corporation. Since his investigation costs would have been incurred even if the executive got the opportunity, they cannot be attributed to the proposed rule.)

Suboptimal development?

A third kind of cost could occur when the executive affected by the rule would be better able than both the corporation and all available third parties to develop the opportunity. In such a case, if he is prevented from developing the opportunity, some value that could have been created will be lost. It seems extremely doubtful, however, that there are many situations of this kind. And when one does arise, the cost could be avoided if the law allows the corporation to give its express contemporaneous consent to the executive's taking the opportunity.

The benefits

Offsetting these costs are three related benefits from the proposed rule: helping to keep executives single-mindedly devoted to the corporation, eliminating the high policing costs of current rules, and lowering the cost of capital by avoiding investor fears of the improper diversions of assets that the current rules permit.

The balancing problem

In a sense, the problem of choosing between the proposed categorical rule and the traditional ones comes down to an effort to weigh two kinds of costs against each other: On the one hand, the waste represented by unexploited opportunities or by duplicated expenditures on exploratory efforts that might occur in some situations under the categorical rule; and on the other, the monitoring and enforcement costs (including litigation expenses) of the ambiguous, selective rules and the increased cost of capital that stems from the rational fears of diversion that they permit. Although it is impossible to demonstrate quantitatively that the latter costs are greater, it is not hard to recognize that we are dealing with indeterminancies in which, institutionally, the scales are weighted in favor of misappropriating insiders. For that reason alone, the law might properly put its finger on the other side of the scales.[3] And when the positive benefit of the categorical

[3]There is a prevalent notion that apparently conflicts with our analysis: the view that the fiduciary principle should—and does—operate more "rigorously" to restrict overreaching by partners or participants in close corporations than similar conduct by executives and directors of public corporations. See, e.g., Donahue v. Rodd Electrotype Co., 328 N.E.2d 505, 515-516 (Mass. 1975); Wilkes v. Springside Nursing Home, Inc., 353 N.E.2d 657, 661-663 (Mass. 1976);

rule—encouraging single-minded devotion by executives to their corporations by removing the temptation to divert their energies—is added to the scales, the appropriate choice seems even clearer.

§7.6.4 Corporate Consent

Problems with "corporate consent"

If the corporation knowingly and freely rejects an opportunity, and also consents to the executive's taking it, there is little basis in theory for precluding the executive from enjoying it. At least for publicly held corporation, however, this abstract statement conceals three difficult questions.

Note, Corporate Opportunity in the Close Corporation—A Different Result?, 56 Geo. L.J. 381 (1967); 43 N.Y.U.L. Rev. 187, 190-192 (1968). It is true that our proposals permit executives and directors of close corporations to take opportunities that could not be taken by executives and directors of public corporations. *A selective approach does not, however, amount to a denial of fiduciary protection to the stockholders of close corporations—or to partners.* It merely alters the emphasis of the protective rules in deference to the differences between the needs of (and costs to) participants in partnerships or close corporations and those of stockholders in public corporations.

To be sure, the minority shareholder in a close corporation is apt to have a greater personal stake in his investment than does a minority public shareholder and far less ability to shift out of his investment. Therefore, he may be injured more seriously by a violation of any rule or doctrine designed to protect him. On the other hand, he is in a better position than a public investor to achieve individualized contracts and understandings and to protect himself by such provisions. Therefore, relaxation of categorical prohibitions—rules that are uniform, precise, and intolerant of exceptions—is more desirable, since it may permit the realization of social gains without imposing great risks on people unable to protect themselves by contract. *Rules and doctrines can be strict in the sense of offering great protection to minority participants without being categorical in the sense just described.* This is evident from the array of rules protecting minorities in close corporations. Compare the solutions for the freezeout problems discussed in Gabhart v. Gabhart, 370 N.E.2d (Ind. 1977), and Hetherington & Dooley, Illiquidity and Exploitation: A Proposed Statutory Solution to the Remaining Close Corporation Problem, 63 Va. L. Rev. 1 (1977), suggesting special rules giving minority shareholders in close corporations a "put" to the majority, with those discussed in Brudney & Chirelstein, A Restatement of Corporate Freezeouts, 87 Yale L.J. 1354 (1978).

Similarly, the fiduciary principle has been the source of a number of more particular rules governing close corporations that recognize the limitations of the capacity of participants in close corporations to protect themselves against one another in various contexts. See F. O'Neal & J. Derwin, Expulsion or Oppression of Business Associates (1961); Brudney, Fiduciary Ideology in Transactions Affecting Corporate Control, 65 Mich. L. Rev. 259, 290-291 (1966). Moreover, fiduciary considerations demand no less disclosure by insiders of close corporations than by those of public corporations for dealings relating to the corporation. Indeed, considering the wider range of matters on which consent may be realistically given in the former case, even more extensive disclosure may be required. Cf. Goodwin v. Agassiz, 186 N.E. 659 (Mass. 1933) (dictum) (when director personally seeks stockholder to purchase his shares without disclosing material facts solely within director's knowledge, the transaction will be closely scrutinized and relief may be granted).

(1) Can we simply *presume* that public corporations usually consent, if only implicitly, to executives' taking of opportunities, in return for concessions from the executives?
(2) May consent be lawfully given by less than unanimous stockholder action?
(3) Does the process by which consent is ostensibly given generate a free and informed choice?

Implicit "settling up"?

As to the first question, some commentators do imagine that when a corporate manager takes a corporate opportunity for himself, there is a "settling up" between the manager and the corporation: Either before or after the taking, the manager's compensation is adjusted downward in implicit recognition of his active outside interests.[4] But imagining such implicit contracts seems like a purely gratuitous speculation. If the corporation wants to settle up with its moonlighting managers, and is practically able to do so, why doesn't the settling up take the form of an *explicit* compensation contract approved by disinterested decision makers? Certainly the law expects such explicitness. The very concept of the fiduciary duty of loyalty is essentially based on a profound hostility to secret profits—that is, to all claims that positional advantages are "implicitly" part of the fiduciary's compensation package.

Unanimous approval?

The second question requires some explanation. If by giving up an opportunity the corporation surrenders a thing of value, and in effect enhances the officer's compensation, it may be making a gift without consideration. Under traditional corporate law principles, such an act usually requires unanimous stockholder approval. But is the corporation's conferral of a benefit in this context a gift? Arguably it is. In any event, the compensation offered when an executive takes an opportunity—unlike many other modes of compensation such as stock options or bonuses, which are tied by some string to the employee's contributions to the profitability of the enterprise—bears no relationship at all to the officers' efforts on behalf of the enterprise. Indeed, quite the opposite is true. Since we are concerned with active business opportunities that entail a more continuous effort than does a merely passive investment, allowing the executive to take the opportunity may well divert his energies from the affairs of the corporation.

It is possible, of course, to increase an officer's compensation by mone-

[4] Easterbrook & Fischel, Corporate Control Transactions, 91 Yale L.J. 698, 734 (1982).

tary rewards that are not related directly to his increased contribution to the enterprise. He may simply be given money as a reward for great diligence and ingenuity or in the hope that he will be grateful and put forth greater effort in the future. But in such a case, there must be some quantitative similarity—however imprecisely measured—between the value of the reward and the value of his services, if the compensation is to be upheld. In the case of rejected corporate opportunities, the value given to the officer is often so uncertain as to be virtually unmeasurable. Since the uncertain benefit is functionally unrelated to his efforts on behalf of the corporation, and the corporation will not share in the benefits of a favorable resolution of the uncertainty, there is no good basis for ignoring those difficulties in quantitative measurement.

In short, the officer's taking a corporate opportunity approaches the kind of waste for which unanimous stockholder approval is traditionally required.[5]

Adequate procedures?

As for our third question, there is also reason to doubt the adequacy of any feasible procedure to effect consent. There is serious question whether, in practice, a publicly held corporation can often be expected to reject an opportunity in a knowing and free way and to give its voluntary consent to an officer's appropriation of it. Presumably, the corporation can only act through its officers, directors, or stockholders. If any of these organs is dominated by persons who benefit from the corporate rejection and the officer's acceptance of the opportunity, their consent cannot constitute free and knowing corporate consent. But even if the decision making body is formally disinterested, it is not very likely to give consent that is adequately informed and impartial. The consent of fellow officers may well suffer from lack of objectivity; the consent of stockholders, from lack of knowledge; and the consent of outside directors, from lack of proper incentives.

In sum, both its substantive and its procedural defects make corporate consent a poor filter to use for restraining improper diversion of corporate opportunities to executives of public corporations. Its use will inevitably permit some "improper" diversions.

Nevertheless, because a categorical rule would occasionally have adverse results, lawmakers might decide that the safety valve of corporate

[5]See, e.g., Schreiber v. Bryan, 396 A.2d 512, 518 (Del. Ch. 1978); Gottlieb v. McKee, 107 A.2d 240 (Del. Ch. 1954); cf. Michelson v. Duncan, 407 A.2d 211, 223 (Del. 1979) (summary judgment for defendant reversed on charge of waste in connection with granting of stock options, when there had been less than unanimous shareholder ratification); Cohen v. Ayers, 596 F.2d 733, 740 (7th Cir. 1979) (dictum) (shareholders cannot, by less than unanimous vote, ratify waste).

consent is needed for those exceptional cases. But the law should at least require that consent be explicit, contemporaneous with the executive's taking, and given on behalf of the corporation by disinterested decision makers.

§7.6.5 Passive Investments

Passive investments proper

Our reasoning about the corporate opportunity doctrine does not suggest that corporate officers should be precluded from making passive investments. The fact that officers are adequately compensated does not justify curtailing their ability to save and to put their savings into passive investments. Nor does the corporation's need for their faithful, full-time service imply such curtailment. Since the corporation normally has no special interest in making passive investments, to give the executive wide freedom in making such investments will not interfere with corporate interests.

Meaning of passive investment

A permissible, passive investment of savings may be defined as one the making of which does not require or entitle the investor to participate in decision making with respect to operations of the entity in which investment is made. Thus, if the investing officer does not actually participate in the affairs of the venture involved, and he is not vested with the power to make or affect substantially any of its business decisions, it is a permissible, passive investment. The officer may purchase government bonds, for example, or noncontrolling blocks of stock in publicly traded companies. This contrasts with the active interest he has when he buys control of an operating business, in which case he will be drawn toward the kind of decision making that is typical of an entrepreneurial venture.

Distinction not fatally ambiguous

The active-passive distinction, like many other dichotomies in legal doctrine, will entail some difficulties when applied to borderline cases. But this fact does not impugn the validity or value of the rule for most cases. Its ambiguities are modest when compared with the difficulties of understanding and applying the traditional corporate opportunity rules.

§7.6.6 The Special Case of Financial Intermediaries

Special approach needed

The rule against taking active business opportunities would pose few real problems when applied to executives of industrial or commercial companies. It would present problems, however, if applied to executives of financial intermediaries. The entire business of these companies is to acquire passive investment interests in other enterprises, rather than to control them. Since we define financial intermediaries to include investment companies, insurance companies, pension funds, thrift institutions, banks, and similar institutions, the special case is a large and important one. Fortunately, the policy decisions behind our rule suggest a similar categorical rule for these institutions. The proposed rule is as follows: The full time officers of a financial intermediary may not make investments that are within the intermediary's scope of operations. In effect, the officer would be relegated to real investments, investments in his own and similar financial intermediaries, and direct financial investments of a type not dealt in by his intermediary. The rationale for this proposal is elaborated elsewhere.[6]

§7.7 *Public Corporations: Outside Directors*

Outside directors in separate category

Directors of a public corporation who are not also executives of it should be governed by a different rule than that applicable to the corporation's full-time executives. The outside directors typically are not paid a salary. Nor are they expected to devote much time, let alone full time, to the affairs of the corporation on whose board they serve. Therefore, a major premise of the prohibition against active business ventures by full-time officers does not apply to them. They are not disentitled, by reason of their directors' fees or commitments to the corporation, to participate actively in other ventures. Indeed, they are often made outside directors precisely because they are executives of other corporations.

No use of resources rule

What, then, should be the limits on the outside director's right to take opportunities for himself? We suggest this limited restraint: He may not *use the corporation's resources, including its information,* to develop or acquire personal business opportunities. The relevant conception of corporate property or assets, which he may not divert, will usually be defined by reference to information that the corporation has about opportunities, unencumbered by additional factors like the corporation's interests or expectancies, its line of business, special values, or corporate incapacity.

While it may be hard to determine the capacity in which a person acquires information, the problem is more tractable when it involves outside directors. The problem could be reduced even further if we were to add the stipulation that when both the corporation and the outside director independently learn of an opportunity, only the corporation may try to acquire it.

[6]Brudney & Clark, A New Look at Corporate Opportunities, 94 Harv. L. Rev. 998, 1037-1042 (1981).

The question just discussed here should not be confused with the question of the rights and duties of the outside director in allocating opportunities between the various corporations with which he is involved—for example, that of which he is merely a director and that which employs him. We can devise other rules to accommodate these different roles.[1] Another situation that requires separate analysis is that of the person who is a part-time executive of more than one public corporation.[2]

Related issues distinguished

§7.8 *Parents and Subsidiaries*

This section considers the proper policy to take toward business opportunities that could be allocated to one of two or more affiliates of a publicly owned corporation or to the public corporation itself. To simplify the anal-

§7.7 [1]From the viewpoint of his relation with his employer, the hard question for the executive is not whether he may reveal opportunities that he discovers as an employee to the other corporation he serves as outside director. Plainly, the considerations underlying our analysis forbid it. But, if he has a presumptive obligation to report to his employer all business opportunities he learns about, even apart from his work efforts for his employer, as long as the latter might reasonably desire to examine them, is he permitted or obliged to reveal to his employer opportunities of which he learns as an outside director? Presumably, loyalty to the outside corporation precludes his reporting to his employer; and his employer's consent to that arrangement is appropriately inferred from its knowing acquiescence in his serving as outside director. Finally, we may ask another question. To which enterprise must he deliver opportunities of which he learns other than in his role as employee or as outside director? Under our proposal, if they belong to anyone (that is, if he must report them), they belong to his employing corporation, and he cannot reveal them to the other corporation, whose consent to this arrangement is also implied. In all of this, there is no need to narrow the definition of corporate opportunity by reference to the received learning on interest or expectancy, line of business, or corporate inability to exploit.

Suppose instead that the problem is to define the outside director's obligations as between two corporations, each of which he serves only as outside director. Again, there is no need to import the received learning. We would prohibit him from informing either firm about the affairs and expectations, however remote, of the other. Any such conveyance of information could be a basis for the recipient of the information's usurping an expectation of the other. A somewhat different question is presented by opportunities he discovers other than in his role as director of either. To which of the two corporations is he permitted or obliged to turn over such opportunities? We believe he should not be obliged to turn over such opportunities to either corporation, because he is not working for them; such commitments as he has to them do not include an undertaking to supply them with discoveries made on his own time and in some nondirector role. We feel less certain about permitting him to reveal such opportunities to either corporation, because of the possibility that he will systematically and unfairly favor one over the other, but we see no clear-cut case for denying him the permission. Accordingly, unless unfairness is apparent in the facts of the particular situation, the director could exploit the opportunity himself or reveal it to either or both of the corporations.

[2]See Brudney & Clark, A New Look at Corporate Opportunities, 94 Harv. L. Rev. 998, 1044-1045 (1981).

ysis, we will focus only on the problem of allocating a business opportunity between a publicly owned parent company and one partially owned subsidiary of it.

Why a separate category

Although parent corporations ought to be treated as fiduciaries with respect to their subsidiaries, the problem of corporate opportunity is different in this context than in the others we have analyzed. The basic reason is that the interests of the parent corporation's public investors must also be taken into account. Unlike the subsidiary's full-time executives, the parent's public investors are not agents of the subsidiary whose compensation suggests a basis for categorically denying them access to all opportunities the subsidiary might take. As investors, they have legitimate expectations that their company will have opportunities of its own. This suggests that legal rules should leave room for both the parent's public stockholders and the subsidiary's minority stockholders to get the benefits of at least some opportunities.[1]

The guidelines derived from close corporation cases are also not appropriate to the public parent-and-subsidiary situation. The genuine ability of participants in close corporations to tailor arrangements to their individual needs by contract is lacking here. Getting a meaningful consent from the public investors in a subsidiary to a particular taking of an opportunity by a parent is as chancy as getting such consent to an officer's takings. In short, the contractual solution is not realistically available to govern the allocation of corporate opportunities between public parent and subsidiary.

§7.8.1 Analysis of the Problem

The situation for analysis

For analysis, assume a case where an identifiable group of managers is de facto in control over the decisions of both corporations. Assume that these managers have a greater personal interest in the financial well-being of the parent company, because their own compensation plans feature parent company stock options or because they and their relatives own personally significant amounts of stock in the parent company. Assume

§7.8 [1]The entitlements of the public investors in a publicly held parent are not quite the same as those of an individual controlling stockholder of a publicly held corporation. Denial to the latter of the rewards of other business opportunities could be meliorated by adjusting contractual compensation for services or even for forbearance. Or the controlling shareholder might be required to share the rewards of taking a new opportunity. For examples of mandated sharing between controlling stockholders and minority stockholders, see Perlman v. Feldmann, 219 F.2d 173 (2d Cir.), cert. denied, 349 U.S. 952 (1955); Lebold v. Inland Steel Co., 125 F.2d 369 (7th Cir. 1941), cert. denied, 316 U.S. 675 (1942); Jones v. H.F. Ahmanson & Co., 460 P.2d 464 (Cal. 1969); cf. Young v. Columbia Oil Co., 158 S.E. 678 (W. Va. 1931) (required sharing between directors and stockholder plaintiffs).

there is some legal norm that governs allocation of new opportunities between parent and subsidiary. For the purpose of simply defining the problem, we really do not need to assume any particular norm. But to focus discussion, let's start with the rule that the opportunity should go to that corporation with whose line of business it fits best.

Problems it creates

In this paradigmatic situation, the managers experience a conflict of interest. It is in their interest to allocate opportunities to the parent company even when the legal rule dictates otherwise. Moreover, they will often be able to get away with such actions, because situations will arise whose disposition under the rule is unclear and depends on individual judgment. Of course, if the parent company makes aluminum cans and nothing else, and the subsidiary makes men's shoes and nothing else, an opportunity to acquire a manufacturer of men's shoes would clearly belong to the subsidiary, under an unadorned line of business test. But the test as actually developed by the courts is tempered by other considerations, such as the subsidiary's ability to purchase the opportunity, the circumstance that the offer to sell the business was directed specifically at one or the other corporation, and so forth. Reasonable persons may differ about the applicability of these factors and the balance to be struck among them. Moreover, even an unadorned line of business test would often be indeterminate. What if the new business opportunity is a jewelry store? Does it belong to the can company or the shoe company? What if, as is common among larger companies, both parent and subsidiary have numerous lines of business and the new opportunity is arguably similar to, or "fits in with," a division of each corporation? What if the parent and the subsidiary are in the same line of business?

Danger to subsidiary's minority shareholders

Whenever the situation calls for a response that cannot be obtained by a robotic application of mechanical rules, management will be tempted to overreach the subsidiary's minority shareholders. Moreover, since the parent company shareholders will benefit from the overreaching, they are unlikely to object to it. Nor do market forces greatly alleviate the problem. The existence of competitive product markets provides no control over this sort of managerial misbehavior. And the subsidiary's minority shareholders may have become such unexpectedly or involuntarily[2] or without having had a feasible opportunity to bargain beforehand with the parent company for its obedience to a more mechanical and more favorable allocation rule.

[2]For example, their status may have arisen when a majority of the other individual shareholders sold out to a tender offeror.

Inadequacy of traditional rules

The traditional legal approach, both in Delaware and elsewhere,[3] invites all these problems because it simply applies to the parent-subsidiary context the same rules that were developed for close corporations. The problems are compounded when, as a key Delaware decision suggests, the matter is to be viewed by the courts as one of business judgment.[4] Of course, this view has some advantages, such as reduction in strain on judicial resources. But if one could construct an alternative approach that is responsive to all of the major policy goals—reducing the risks of unwarranted judicial second-guessing of business decisions, cutting back on excessive litigation, and yet reducing the risk of unfairness to the subsidiary's public shareholders—it would commend itself to the courts.

Distinguish kinds of opportunities

To start thinking about what a better approach might be, let us first distinguish three kinds of business opportunities. One kind could be called the differentially valuable opportunity, that is, an opportunity that would cause a greater increase in risk-adjusted return if placed with one of the two corporations rather than the other. This could result if combination of the opportunity with the existing business of the one corporation permits elimination of duplicate activities, fuller realization of the economies of scale, or other operating synergies. This kind of opportunity naturally suggests a highest value rule of corporate opportunities: The opportunity should be placed with that one of the parent or subsidiary with which it will lead to the greater increase in value. The rule makes sense here because it promotes economic efficiency. It also seems like a neutral, fair way of allocating opportunities. (In the long run, though, one or the other of the two companies might happen to get more opportunities than the other under this rule.)

[3]See Schreiber v. Bryan, 396 A.2d 512 (Del. Ch. 1978); Blaustein v. Pan Am. Petroleum & Transport Co., 56 N.E.2d 705 (N.Y. 1944); Knauff v. Utah Constr. & Mining Co., 277 F. Supp. 564, 575 (D. Wyo. 1967), aff'd, 408 F.2d 958 (10th Cir.), cert. denied, 396 U.S. 831 (1969). Compare Case v. New York Cent. R.R., 204 N.E.2d 643 (N.Y. 1965), and Horsman Dolls, Inc. v. Premier Corp. of Am., 312 N.Y.S.2d 150 (App. Div. 1970), and Greenbaum v. American Metal Climax, Inc., 278 N.Y.S.2d 123, 129-130 (App. Div. 1967), with Alliegro v. Pan Am. Bank, 136 So. 2d 656, 658-662 (Fla. Dist. Ct. App. 1962). See also Shreiber & Yoran, Allocating the Tax Saving Derived from Filing Consolidated Corporate Tax Returns, 29 Baylor L. Rev. 243 (1977); Note, Corporate Fiduciary Doctrine in the Context of Parent-Subsidiary Relations, 74 Yale L.J. 338 (1964).

[4]Sinclair Oil Corp. v. Levien, 280 A.2d 717 (Del. 1971). The *Sinclair* approach relieves the courts of the necessity of weighing considerations of business judgment, which they are forced to do when a transaction is treated as one involving a significant conflict of interest, that is, as self-dealing, and therefore triggering the intrinsic fairness test. The *Sinclair* approach also reduces incentives to make litigious and costly challenges to managerial judgments. It may also reduce incentives to settle dubious claims on behalf of the subsidiary's shareholders at the expense of the parent company shareholders.

A second kind of opportunity might be called the equally valuable but normal opportunity. Such an opportunity's value would not depend on whether it was taken by the parent or the subsidiary, and it would offer only a normal expected return. Since normal opportunities are presumably common, the parent's taking any particular one could not be seen as an injury to the subsidiary. The law might therefore respond to this type of opportunity with the business judgment rule: Management, in its business judgment, may allocate such an opportunity to either company.

Different rules for different kinds

A third kind of opportunity is the equally valuable but superior opportunity: one whose value doesn't depend on whether the parent or the subsidiary owns it, but which is available at a bargain price, so that it will yield an unusually high risk-adjusted return. Here one may be tempted to propose a sharing formula: Every such exceptional opportunity should be developed as a joint venture between the parent and subsidiary. Each corporation would have a claim to a proportion of the returns from the opportunity that corresponds to the proportion that its fair market value at the time of forming the venture bears to the total fair market value of the two corporations at that time. We need not require that legally separate joint venture entities be created. All that is really necessary is that a correct bookkeeping account be kept of costs and revenues attributable to each such opportunity taken and that the corresponding profits be allocated according to the rule. The opportunity might technically be owned by either parent or subsidiary rather than both, and it might be under the exclusive direction and management of the owner corporation's officers and employees.

Impracticality of such an approach

Should the law adopt this three-part distinction and the three corresponding rules? No. Doing so would be quite impractical because it would be extremely difficult to decide how to classify many particular opportunities in particular situations. And although managers might often have adequate information and expertise to make a reasonable judgment about the classification question, in most cases it would be very difficult for outside shareholders and courts to show that the self interest of managers led them to make the classification in an unreasonable way.

A sharing rule?

We might try to salvage the essence of the tripartite system by simplifying it. Only one rule, rather than three, would remain. For example, all opportunities could be governed by the sharing rule. When this rule leads to sharing of an equally valuable but superior opportunity, the result simply reflects the original policy intuition. When it leads to sharing of equally valuable but normal opportunities, neither company's shareholders can complain. When it leads to sharing of the returns from a differentially valuable opportunity, no one can complain that the rule requires an efficiency loss from suboptimal placement of the opportunity; under the sharing rule as explained above, managers are still free to cause either operation to own and manage the opportunity.

Costs of sharing rule

Unfortunately, however, the sharing rule imposes a set of restraints on managerial behavior that will continue indefinitely, yet it does not eliminate the underlying conflict of interest. The two corporations will incur accounting costs in carrying out the sharing rule on a continuing basis. The minority shareholders of the subsidiary will incur costs in the course of monitoring and enforcing compliance with the rule. Given the many cost accounting problems that could arise in such an arrangement and the difficulties of detecting unfairness in the inevitable transactions among the joint venture and the two corporations, both sets of costs may be far from trivial.

Frustration with these difficulties leads to yet another proposal.

§7.8.2 A Proposed Rule

A presumed entitlement rule

Our proposed rule, which is easier than a sharing rule to administer and creates desirable incentives, provides as follows: all business opportunities that may be taken by either a parent company or its partially owned subsidiary are deemed to belong to the subsidiary and their taking by the parent is therefore a wrongful usurpation, unless the parent company shows by clear and convincing evidence that the opportunity would have a substantially higher value if taken and developed by the parent company than if taken and developed by the subsidiary. The special burden of proof and the reference to "substantially" higher value are intended to prevent the exception from swallowing the basic rule.

Higher value defense

To take advantage of the higher value defense, the parent company would have to adduce specific evidence and arguments about how the project would fare as part of the parent's operations and equally detailed, comparable evidence and arguments about how it would fare as part of the subsidiary's operations. Ideally, the parent's directors would collect this evidence in documented form and make a formal, recorded decision that the higher value defense applies before the parent could commit itself to taking the opportunity. The presumptive entitlement rule could be generalized to a family of corporations in which one or more partially owned subsidiaries exist.[5] The alleged financial inability of the subsidiary to take

[5] Under the generalized rule, all opportunities would go to the subsidiary in which the parent's percentage interest was the lowest, unless it could be shown by clear and convincing evidence that the opportunity would have a substantially higher value if it went to the parent

the opportunity would not be a permissible defense, although a clear, irremediable legal inability might be.

Advantages of rule

Since the suggested rule places a heavy burden of proof on parent companies and should discourage them from attempting questionable taking of new opportunities, judges will be less frequently called upon to evaluate private business judgments than under the present rules. And when judges are called upon to do so—because a parent company that followed the proper procedures for the higher value defense is nevertheless being sued—their task will be more rational and manageable than under the present rules and less costly than under a sharing rule with its continuous policing problems. The rule will also limit occasions for litigation by narrowing the range of litigable issues. For example, the courts will *not* consider any of the following issues: the subsidiary's alleged financial inability to take the opportunity (which is, as the cases show, a favorite last ditch argument of defendants, especially those under whose control the corporation in question has suffered serious setbacks); the validity and effect of a rejection of the opportunity by the subsidiary's supposedly independent directors; the usually specious question as to which entity the opportunity was presented; and the intractable debates about whether the opportunity was analogically closer to a line of business of the parent or more clearly within its geographical or other jurisdiction. The rule might further limit occasions for litigation by reducing the number of partially owned subsidiaries—an effect to be discussed shortly. And the rule, once established and known, could not really be argued to be unfair to parent company shareholders.

Incentive to change situation

An interesting virtue of the rule is that it would create an additional incentive for managers not to establish or maintain a *generally* undesirable relationship—that between a parent and a partially owned subsidiary. Given the presumed entitlement rule, managers contemplating creation or maintenance of a partially owned subsidiary will be more likely to examine alternative courses of action (since these would avoid the rule).

(1) The parent company could refrain from buying any stock in a putative target company.
(2) It could buy a less than controlling block of stock (if it were content to be a passive investor).

---

or one of the other subsidiaries. The possibility of giving the opportunity to another subsidiary if this showing could be made would prevent the rule from operating unfairly against the minority stockholders in subsidiaries other than the one with a presumptive entitlement to all opportunities.

(3) It could buy all of the company's stock, or most of it.[6]
(4) Most importantly, if the parent acquired a controlling block of the subsidiary's stock, whether recently or long ago, it could obtain complete control by effecting a parent-subsidiary merger in which the subsidiary's minority shareholders are squeezed out of the subsidiary.[7]

Desirability of such change

At first glance, it may seem odd to justify a proposed rule partly on the ground that it will encourage apparent squeeze-out mergers. Consideration of two points may help assuage the fears raised by this prospect.

First, the continued existence of a minority shareholder interest in a subsidiary creates many problems of fairness other than the problem of allocating corporate opportunities. Parents and subsidiaries often have many relationships and dealings with each other. When, as with a partially owned subsidiary, there is an ever present conflict of interest, all such relationships and dealings may be the cover for abuse of the subsidiary. Given a large number of connections between the entities, effective policing of unfair transactions becomes extremely difficult. Thus, this rule about corporate opportunities might help to mitigate a whole host of other problems.

Second, valid fears about squeeze-out mergers can be taken account of by proper design of rules concerning parent-subsidiary mergers. This topic is explored later in chapter 12.

No impediment to diversification

On first examination, the presumed entitlement rule may seem to create a serious impediment to desirable efforts of corporations to diversify. For example, since the rule creates an incentive to eliminate minority shareholders, it seems to mean that a company that would have preferred to use a fixed amount of its wealth to acquire 60 percent ownership of five equally sized subsidiaries will now be pressured to acquire 100 percent ownership of three of these subsidiaries, that is, to become less diversified than it

[6] Allocation of all opportunities to the subsidiary does not mean that the parent company shareholders do not benefit from them. If the parent owns 97 percent of the subsidiary's stock, the parent's shareholders will receive 97 percent of the return generated by each opportunity. Thus, mitigating the burden created by the recommended rule is the fact that it is not an all-or-nothing proposition.

[7] Often, under short-form merger statutes, the parent company's board of directors could do this unilaterally, without a vote of either company's shareholders. The subsidiary could be merged directly into the parent, or, if it were desired to keep the business assets separately incorporated, it could be merged with a newly formed, wholly owned subsidiary of the parent in exchange for parent company stock or other consideration supplied by the parent company.

would have preferred. The rule, however, is not really a serious impediment to firms' efforts to diversify. It does not interfere with diversification by internal growth or by acquisition of many noncontrolling interests in other companies. Moreover, it will often cost only slightly more in terms of the corporation's real assets to acquire 100 percent ownership of a company than 60 percent ownership, since the extra 40 percent may be acquired for stock in a controlled merger. Apart from the transaction costs of the merger itself, then, the company need not expend retained earnings or use up borrowing power.

In summary, the proposed rule both sets up a countervailing force against the conflict of interest inherent in the parent-subsidiary situation (by assigning opportunities to the vulnerable entity, with few questions asked or allowed) and creates an incentive, but not a compulsion, to rearrange matters so as to eliminate the conflict.

§7.9 Conclusion

Review of close/public distinction

Because of the small number of participants in close corporations, these companies typically differ from public corporations in the ability of the participants to select and monitor managers and to negotiate special arrangements with each other; in the nature and variety of their understandings with respect to managers' duties and compensation; and in the size of their opportunity sets. These differences indicate that it is often appropriate to govern the behavior of fiduciaries of close corporations with selective rules, but it is better to control the fiduciaries of public corporations with categorical rules. In the context of the doctrine of corporate opportunities, the current law's basic approach is suitable for close corporations, if modified by limited versions of the "interest or expectancy" and "line of business" tests for determining what is a corporate opportunity, a large role for consent to the taking of corporate opportunity, and certain burden-of-proof adjustments.

New rules for public context

In the public corporation context, we were led to distinguish three categories of cases. Because of the sharp, characteristic differences in the nature of their duties and compensation arrangements, full-time executives were separated from outside directors. For the former, a rule forbidding the taking of any active business opportunity is recommended; for the latter, a rule forbidding only use of the corporation's resources (including its information) in the acquisition of an opportunity. Both of these fiduciaries must be further distinguished from parent corporations. The managers of a parent corporation must accommodate the claims and expectations of the parent's public shareholders as well as those of the vulnerable minority shareholders of the subsidiary. After considering a number of possible alternatives, I recommend a rule that all business opportunities are presumed to belong to the subsidiary except when the parent company clearly proves that the opportunity will have a substantially higher value in the hands of the parent.

Larger significance of analysis

This exercise with respect to one general doctrine of corporate law points to issues of much larger significance. The formulation of corporate law doctrines by state courts has been *pervasively* influenced by the fact that the overwhelming majority of corporate cases coming before state courts have involved close corporations. It is widely noted, of course, that the earlier state statutory rules, which upon analysis seem geared to the paradigm of the public corporation, imposed rigidities that had to be struggled with and modified by courts and legislators to accommodate the needs of close corporations. But the press of close corporation cases has had an equally great, albeit inappropriate, effect on rules governing public corporations: With respect to a number of important doctrines, the judicially developed rules of *general* applicability—to all corporations—are more suited to close corporations. In these situations, clearly better rules can be formulated to govern the public corporations. Future scholarship and analysis should help to demonstrate this thesis. It has broad implications for future efforts to rethink how regulatory and judicial authority over corporations should be divided between the state and federal governments.

CHAPTER 8

INSIDER TRADING

§8.1 Introduction

Basic concept

In ordinary usage, "insider trading" is said to occur when a person buys or sells securities of a corporation on the basis of material inside information. Usually the information is "inside" in the sense that it concerns a new development in the corporation's business but is not yet widely known by the general investing public — in particular, the corporation's public security holders and those investors who are interested in buying its securities. The information is "material" or important in that, if it were publicly available, it would influence the market value of the corporation's securities or, at the least, would probably be considered an important factor by investors considering whether to buy or sell the corporation's securities. The person who buys or sells on the basis of material nonpublic information is usually someone who would be colloquially termed an "insider": a director, officer, or controlling shareholder of the company or a person who has received the inside information from them (a tippee). Insider trading may be based on undisclosed bad news as well as undisclosed good news.

Example: good news

Insider trading may be illustrated by a simple example. On April 1 the research scientists of X Drug Company inform the president of the company that they have discovered a cheap way of manufacturing intervenon, a substance thought to be effective in fighting cancer. The information is valid, the president has no doubts as to its validity, and the company will not suffer any competitive harm by prompt disclosure to the public of its discovery, since the manufacturing process itself can still be kept secret. Furthermore, the president realizes that if the news of the discovery is released, the price of X stock will skyrocket from its current price of $30 per share. Instead of issuing a press release, the president keeps the good news under wraps while he buys as much X stock as he can, at the current price. On April 15 he finally causes a press release to be issued. The market price of X stock immediately jumps to $100. Several days later, the president sells his shares at that price. Obviously, as compared to what would have happened had the president disclosed the corporate good news on April 1 before he bought large amounts of X stock, (1) the president has done much better for himself and (2) those X shareholders who happened to *sell* their stock during the April 1 to 15 period of nondisclosure did worse.

Example: bad news

Suppose, however, that on May 1 X's research scientists announce to the president that, unfortunately, manufactured intervenon now seems to be of modest promise in fighting cancer in humans, because large injections of it stimulate the body's immune system to destroy normal cells too. Again the president delays release of the information to the public without having any good corporate business purpose for delay. But he passes the information along to all his senior vice presidents, who immediately sell their X stock on the market for $100 a share. On May 15 the bad news is released and the price of X stock falls back to $30. In this situation, as compared to what would have happened had there been prompt disclosure of the corporate bad news, (1) the vice presidents fare much better and (2) public investors who happened to *buy* X stock during the May 1 to May 15 period of nondisclosure suffer a loss.

Three legal approaches

The legal system of the United States has evolved three noteworthy remedial approaches to deal with insider trading of the sort represented by our two paradigm cases: the federal approaches under Sections 16(b) and 10(b) of the Securities Exchange Act of 1934 and the state law approach introduced by the New York Court of Appeals. Both federal approaches have spawned a sizable jurisprudence. But in order to properly understand or assess these legal rules, it is necessary to grasp the policy arguments behind the legal condemnation of insider trading. Perhaps surprisingly, this task is both difficult and controversial. To a number of commentators, it has not been at all obvious that insider trading is bad or that the legal system should attempt to do anything about it. Accordingly, in the next four sections of this chapter, four important general questions are considered:

(1) Who or what is harmed by insider trading?
(2) Does insider trading yield positive benefits?
(3) Is insider trading extremely widespread and virtually impossible to stop, and are legal rules against it therefore bad, since attempts to enforce them will surely generate costs even though they achieve no results?
(4) Do all or any of the three major legal approaches to insider trading respond appropriately to the harms caused by insider trading?

§8.2 Harms of Insider Trading

Because the reasons for rules about insider trading that one finds in judicial opinions are often cast in conclusory language and are likely to create a false sense of understanding, it is desirable to look at the issue as if it had just been raised for the first time and to scrutinize the potential reasons carefully.

§8.2.1 Corporate Harm

Corporate harm not obvious

A first possibility is that insider trading harms the corporation involved. In most cases, however, as illustrated by our example of the X Drug Company, the insider trading and the associated period of nondisclosure of good or bad corporate news does not directly harm the corporation's business.

Benefit sometimes argued

Indeed, it is sometimes argued that the extra period of secrecy caused by insiders who wish to trade for their own profit may actually help the corporation, by preserving its informational advantage over competitors or parties with whom it will bargain. A minerals company that has just discovered copper on a plot of land may legitimately want to delay announcement of the news until it buys the surrounding plots of land lest it pay a higher price for the land and lose much of the value created by its own exploratory work.[1] But this argument is a red herring. No one has proposed or enacted an insider trading rule that requires a corporation or its insiders to publicize information that is not "ripe" for publication. In this context, ripeness means that management is reasonably certain of the information's validity and that release of the information would not deprive the corporation of a profitable opportunity. Actual insider trading rules usually give insiders the option of disclosing material information *or* abstaining from trading. If the ripeness of certain information is uncertain, they can obey the rules without making premature disclosures.

Reputational harm

Some courts have argued that insider trading may indirectly harm the corporation involved.[2] Public shareholders who become aware of the practice may feel they are being treated unfairly and that management lacks integrity. Their loss of confidence may lead to devaluation of the company's stock and impede its effort to finance desired new ventures. Although this view has some plausibility, it is not clear that in practice the postulated impact of insider trading is either common or important. Consequently, many courts and commentators seem disinclined to believe that rules against insider trading are justified on the theory that the trading harms the corporation.[3]

§8.2 [1]SEC v. Texas Gulf Sulphur Co., 401 F.2d 833, 850 n.12, (2d Cir. 1968), cert. denied, 394 U.S. 976 (1969).

[2]Diamond v. Oreamuno, 248 N.E.2d 910, 912 (N.Y. 1969). For a related argument, see Haft, The Effect of Insider Trading Rules on the Internal Efficiency of the Large Corporation, 80 Mich. L. Rev. 1051 (1982).

[3]Schein v. Chasen, 313 So. 2d 739 (Fla. 1975).

Excessive risk taking?

Another conception of possible corporate harm is that, in their eagerness to make large personal profits on stock trades, managers may run their companies at an excessively high risk level. But if there is such a perverse incentive — the point can be vigorously debated — it would seem to stem, not from trading on inside information but from the mere fact that managers of public companies are allowed to be shareholders in them as well.

Yet another possibility is that, in order to buy stock in their companies cheaply, the managers may run it badly so as to depress its stock price. But managers who do this would be shooting themselves in their feet; they will get stock worth only the low price they pay. To buy at a real bargain price, they must make the investing public *think* the stock is worth less than it really is by manipulating information disclosed to the public or signals (e.g., dividend payouts) that are given to it, not by hurting their companies.

§8.2.2 Investor Harm from the Trading Activity

Induced trading theory

A second possibility is that insider trading misleads and cheats *some* people trading in the corporation's securities during the period of nondisclosure. In the good news hypothetical, for example, it could be argued that the flurry of trading activity created by the president of X Drug Company might itself raise the market price of the X stock somewhat and thus induce selling by some shareholders who otherwise would have stood pat, and eventually reaped the benefit of the good news, when the latter was announced and caused the stock price to jump up quickly.[4]

How the insider's trading activity might lead to a price change is a separate question that is worth reflecting on. Presumably, a mere temporary increase in the supply of buy orders for a stock need not cause holders of the stock to revise their estimates of the stock's value. But if the orders are known by some holders to emanate from an insider, those in the know may guess that the insider is buying on inside information. They will take the fact that an insider is buying as a valuable signal. They may then start buying more stock for themselves. In their haste to get more stock before the news comes out, they will be willing to buy at prices above the prevailing market price, and the market price will creep up.

Difficulties

In any event, the view that harm is caused by the insider's addition to the level of trading activity suffers from difficulties of practice and princi-

[4]See Schotland, Unsafe at Any Price: A Reply to Manne, 53 Va. L. Rev. 1425, 1447-1448 (1967).

ple. One would be hard pressed to identify the misled shareholders, as distinguished from the selling shareholders who would have sold during the nondisclosure period regardless of the price rise caused by the extra trading. It is therefore difficult to assess the extent of the alleged harm, either in general or in particular cases. Furthermore, it is not clear that the shareholders induced to sell because of the extra trading activity should be characterized as having been wrongfully misled. Arguably, the legal system could tell investors that they must interpret the significance of fluctuations in trading activity at their own peril, for otherwise too many mere expectations might be transmuted into legal rights.

§8.2.3 Market Harm from Delayed Disclosure

Bias against prompt disclosure

The third possibility is more important. In essence the argument is that the prospect of insider trading gains creates a bias against prompt disclosure of ripe corporate information and that this bias leads to inefficiency and unfairness. On this view, the harm is a quite general one, because the pricing mechanism of the securities market is knocked off its efficient course; it then runs like an automobile engine that is out of tune, and this has numerous undesirable consequences.

Related view

A related view, which seems to underlie or at least rationalize the reasoning of many judicial opinions, tries to visualize the harm in a more concrete way. There is an implicit assumption that public investors have a *right* to prompt disclosure of ripe information, that is, a right to what they would get in a well functioning, fully efficient securities market. Therefore, those who should be viewed as "harmed" by insider trading are all those public shareholders who traded in the opposite direction from the insider during the period of nondisclosure. In our good news hypothetical, this means all those who sold stock during the 15-day period when the president of X was trying to round up shares for himself. In our bad news hypothetical, it means all those who bought X stock during the 15-day period of nondisclosure of the ripe bad news. In either case, the sellers (or buyers) were harmed relative to what would have happened to them had there been prompt disclosure of the corporate developments.

The injured class

Note that, unlike the second view, this view considers *all* rather than some of the selling (or buying) shareholders during the period of nondisclosure of good (or bad) news to have been harmed. It thus poses no unmanageable identification problem. Note also that it considers only the selling (or buying) shareholders to have been harmed. In either variant of the hypothetical, the nontraders — those who sat there like bumps on a log, holding their X stock since before the period of nondisclosure started until after it ended — are in no way injured. Thus, it is inaccurate to construe the insider trading as harming all shareholders as a class or, a fortiori, as harming the corporation. Instead, it harms a significant, objectively defined subclass of shareholders. This third view thus has profoundly different remedial implications than the first. It seems to call for a remedy on behalf of a subclass of shareholders, while the corporate harm theory calls for a recovery on behalf of the corporation, as in a derivative suit. The third view also calls for a different conception of insiders' fiduciary duties, as being owed not only to the corporation and to the public shareholders as a class but also as being owed to major subclasses of investors.

The causal connection

In the third view, the *immediate* cause of harm to selling (or buying) shareholders is a violation of some supposed ideal of *timely disclosure* of ripe corporate information, rather than the insider's trading for his own account on the basis of inside information. Nevertheless, it is the prospect of gaining personal profits from insider trading that creates constant pressure on insiders who have influence over corporate decision making to delay official disclosure of corporate information. Thus, by systematically generating tardy disclosures, insider trading indirectly causes the harm to the trading shareholders.

In order to assess this view of the nature of the harm caused by insider trading, three important questions must be pursued:

(1) Why is prompt disclosure an ideal?
(2) Why isn't it enough to mandate prompt disclosure directly rather than by outlawing insider trading?
(3) Doesn't insider trading itself lead to a reflection of the inside information in market prices, thus promoting efficient pricing?

Efficiency of prompt disclosure

Why prompt disclosure? The answer to the first question can be cast in terms of efficiency or equity. As for efficiency, prompter disclosure of information relevant to the valuation of corporate securities will lead to stock prices being more often correct. As with goods and services generally, better information leads to better pricing and more accurate signals as to where and in what amounts resources should be allocated. This is rather easy to grasp in the context of primary[5] financing markets. If Y Corporation and Z Corporation are both drilling companies attempting to raise money

[5] "Primary market" refers to the market in which corporations raise new capital through the issuing of securities. Investor trading in already existing securities takes place in the "secondary market."

by selling new stock to the public, and Y but not Z has already discovered proven oil reserves, public disclosure of this information will enable Y to raise the new money more cheaply and easily. This seems perfectly proper, since resources ought to flow more freely into the better prospect.

In secondary markets too

The point is somewhat harder to grasp in the context of secondary markets, where stock has already been issued by corporations and the function of information is to affect the price at which it changes hands among investors rather than the ease with which the corporation can raise new equity. But presumably the efficiency effect of accurate, publicly available information, although indirect, is still there. Thus, if the outstanding stock of Y and Z is priced on the stock market in light of accurate information, Y will more readily obtain bank loans and its managers who are linked into stock-based incentive compensation plans will have been better compensated, which is as it should be. Furthermore, misinformation-caused inflation of secondary market stock prices may mean that investors' money is being diverted from more deserving primary market investments. The opposite bad effect may occur when stock prices are wrongly deflated.

(I am focusing here on reasons for *prompt* disclosure of information. For completeness, I should also mention the more basic underlying point that, from an efficiency point of view, it may sometimes be desirable for the law to mandate disclosures of information, rather than simply to rely on market forces. We touched upon the information-is-a-public-good theory for such a viewpoint in section 4.2.1, and the arguments for and against affirmative disclosure requirements will be treated more fully in subsection 17.5.3.)

Equity argument

We turn to an answer to the question of timely disclosure that is couched in terms of equity. The argument has two steps. Prompt disclosure of material corporate information should be a norm because (1) all corporate investors should have *equal access* to relevant information (or at least to information generated by the corporations in which they are asked to invest)[6] and (2) it is practically necessary and psychologically natural to implement this equal access principle by a prompt disclosure rule.

Link to timely disclosure ideal

Theoretically, if one were concerned only that all investors be treated equally, one might be satisfied with any one of an infinite number of

[6] A distinction has been drawn between information regarding a company's assets or earnings and "market information" (e.g., that the company's shares will be the object of a tender offer). See Chiarella v. United States, 445 U.S. 222, 231-235 (1980); Fleischer, Mundheim, and Murphy, An Initial Inquiry into the Responsibility to Disclose Market Information, 121 U. Pa. L. Rev. 798 (1973).

disclosure timing rules. Why not say, for example, that "Every corporation must disclose new material information simultaneously to all shareholders and potential investors on the thirteenth day after the information is ripe for disclosure?" Or, "Every corporation may decide when to release new material information, so long as it makes the information available to all investors simultaneously"? It should be obvious that most such systems would break down in practice. Between the ripeness date and the thirteenth day there would inevitably be leaks and, therefore, violations of the equal access principle. Since the longer the lag, the more likely the leaks, one turns naturally to a rule of prompt disclosure: There should be no lags between the ripeness and the public announcement of the news. In addition, as a psychological matter, prompt disclosure undoubtedly seems more natural and less arbitrary than a rule like the 13th-day rule.

Basis of equality ideal

On the ideal of equality itself, as distinct from the timing aspect of a disclosure rule, many people, including judges and legislators, feel no need to say anything further. It is simply obvious to them that it is unfair for some investors (insiders and their tipees) to have preferential access to information, and no more need be said. But others (including myself) find unfairness to be an opaque notion that should itself be tied back to more basic considerations.[7] One such link that is frequently made is that when public investors perceive themselves being treated unequally and disadvantageously as compared to insiders, they lose confidence in the stock market and do not invest as readily, which in turn harms the functioning of the stock markets and the vital economic process of capital formation. I shall return to this argument in connection with the fourth view of the harm caused by insider trading.

Enough to require prompt disclosure?

Why not direct regulation? The second major question to be asked about the view that insider trading creates an inefficient and unfair bias against prompt disclosure of corporate information is why the law does not simply rely on direct regulation of prompt disclosure. Since violation of the timely disclosure ideal is the immediate cause of harm to selling or buying shareholders, why not focus legal remedies directly on violations of that ideal? Why not simply tell corporations and certain specified officers within them, "You have a legal duty to announce all ripe material information promptly to the investing public"? Why *also* tell them, "You have a legal duty not to buy or sell company stock while you are in possession of this undisclosed material information"?

[7] For a critique of fairness as the source of the obligation to disclose, see Easterbrook, Insider Trading, Secret Agents, Evidentiary Privileges, and the Production of Information, 1981 Sup. Ct. Rev. 309, 323-330.

Need to shape incentives

The basic answer is that the law simply cannot devise a meaningful and enforceable duty of prompt disclosure — certainly not one that can be applied in a reliable way in litigation — and therefore must focus on attacking *incentives* to distort or delay the release of information. No court or legislator wants to impose a rule forcing corporations and their insiders to announce information that is not ripe. "Ripe" information is that (1) about which the managers are reasonably certain and (2) as to which there is no longer a business reason for secrecy. But ripeness is preeminently a matter of business judgment. There are inherent limits on the ability and willingness of courts to scrutinize such judgments carefully.

Timely disclosure policies

To be sure, the timely disclosure ideal is not a figment. There are policy statements and legal principles calling for prompt disclosure of new material corporate information. Such disclosure is called for in SEC releases[8] and by the rules of major stock exchanges such as the New York Stock Exchange and the American Stock Exchange.[9] And in an important 10b-5 case,[10] it was indicated that, at least in principle, a shareholder trading during a nondisclosure period can sue the nontrading *corporation* for silence or wrongful delay in releasing material information. But the plaintiff in that case lost, and the court's opinion illustrates how very hard the business judgment principle makes it for the shareholders to win on the wrongful nondisclosure theory. It is not enough for the plaintiff to show that the managers made a clear error in deciding when to disclose the information or that they had a personal motive to delay this disclosure. He must show that they actually delayed for the improper reasons.[11]

The upshot is that the law, if it is to have any chance of being effective, must not only embody general principles mandating prompt disclosure but must also try to remove the sources of bias in management's business judgments about when information is or is not ripe for disclosure. Since the hope of insider trading profits does tend to distort those judgments, the law outlaws those profits and remits managers to their above-board, openly negotiated compensation arrangements.

Counterargument

One attack on the view of insider trading as creating a bias toward untimely disclosure of information relevant to investment decisions was launched fully two decades ago by Professor Henry Manne.[12] He argued

[8] Sec. Exch. Act Release No. 34-8995 (1970), 2 Fed. Sec. L. Rep. (CCH) ¶23,120A.

[9] N.Y.S.E. Company Manual A-18, 2 Fed. Sec. L. Rep. (CCH) ¶¶23,121-23,123. American Stock Exchange Co. Guide §401-05, id. at ¶¶23,124A-D.

[10] Financial Indus. Fund. v. McDonnell Douglas Corp., 474 F.2d 514 (10th Cir.), cert. denied, 414 U.S. 874 (1973).

[11] 474 F.2d at 521-522.

[12] See generally H. Manne, Insider Trading and the Stock Market (1966).

that the distortion of correct stock pricing is not very great since the insiders need only a day or two of delay in order to make their killing, and it is not worth worrying about. Others would disagree,[13] and in any event Manne's response does not assuage those who are most concerned about equality of access to investment information.

Ways of adjusting prices

Whether insider trading promotes better pricing. Can't it be argued that insider trading actually helps the market to run efficiently since it will tend to result in stock prices moving toward where they should be, in light of the inside information? Yes, of course; the argument can be made because insider trading does have the effect stipulated. Even if the trading activity has no effect by altering the supply of buy or sell orders, the fact that insiders are trading may signal the market that prices should be different. But as Professors Gilson and Kraakman have argued, insider trading is a relatively inefficient way of getting information reflected in prices.[14] It seems better if the appropriate corporate officers simply disclose the information to the public and have no incentive to delay. And if the indirect signal is desired for some reason, it would at least be better to change current reporting rules applicable to insiders so that they would be required to disclose *beforehand* that they intend to trade and in what amounts. A counterargument to these claims would be the claim that new information will be impounded in prices more quickly when insiders are spurred on by the hope of making extraordinary insider trading profits than under a system that prohibits such profits and simply threatens to punish them for tardy disclosures. The truth of this empirical claim is hard to assess.

§8.2.4 Harm to Efficiency Caused by the Taking of Secret Profits

A unilateral taking analysis

The fourth view is that insider trading harms economic efficiency because it amounts to the taking by corporate fiduciaries of what trust law refers to as "secret profits." Under this view, insider trading is objectionable basically for the same reasons that apply to managerial self-dealing in general. It is founded on the observation that if insider trading were per-

[13] E.g., Schotland, supra note 4. See also Hetherington, Insider Trading and the Logic of the Law, 1967 Wis. L. Rev. 720; W. Painter, Federal Regulation of Insider Trading (1968).

[14] Gilson & Kraakman, The Mechanisms of Market Efficiency, 70 Va. L. Rev. 549, 629-634 (1984). A different but related view is that a rule against insider trading will diminish the efficiency of the price system in reflecting the value of firms, but the diminution is small if the market draws appropriate inferences from insiders' inaction as well as their actions. Easterbrook, supra note 7, at 335-337.

fectly proper, insiders would be in a heads-I-win-tails-you-lose position. In our good news hypothetical, the president of the X Drug Company could appropriate from the other shareholders an *indefinitely* large part of the value of the new corporate development. His only constraints are the pragmatic ones: how much financing he can get and how many shares can he purchase at prices that still make it worth his while. In a particular case, the amount of the value of new developments unilaterally appropriated by the insiders from the outsiders could be an enormous portion of the total. Giving legal permission to take insider trading profits amounts to giving the insiders permission to take whatever extra compensation they feel is appropriate out of the corporate treasury in secret. It is as if they were given a blank check to be exercised unilaterally and secretly.

Why rational shareholders won't consent

As stated in other contexts in this book, rational public shareholders ought to be alarmed by this sort of arrangement.[15] The compensation taken by managers of corporations in such a regime might be larger in the aggregate than if the compensation were paid pursuant to openly negotiated bilateral contracts. But there is a more important point. Even if the long run average total amount of managerial compensation is the same when insider trading is allowed, the amount that companies and their shareholders will pay by means of insider trading gains is more *uncertain* than open compensation. Yet this uncertainty is avoidable, unnecessary, and unproductive.

Possible impact on capital formation

Since blanket permission of insider trading means that the public shareholders' net expected returns from their stock investments are more uncertain, they will demand a higher rate of return to compensate them for bearing the uncertainty. Put another way, the price of capital will be higher. And if the demand for capital is price elastic, the higher price in turn means that there will be less investment and less capital formation. Less technically, the uncertainty will chill and reduce participation in the stock market, and that may ultimately impair the investment process.

An empirical question

But by how much?, one may ask. The honest answer seems to be that no one really knows. There is much room for each analyst to make his own empirical guesstimate. Professor Manne made the argument, since seconded by others, that the investor discouragement argument is obviously trivial because millions of people have participated in the U.S. stock markets even though everyone knows there is widespread insider trad-

[15] An argument similar to the one I make in this and the next paragraph is made in Scott, Insider Trading: Rule 10b-5, Disclosure and Corporate Privacy, 9 J. Leg. Stud. 801, 808 (1980). Conversely, in our bad news hypothetical, insiders who already own stock can avoid sharing in the loss created by the new corporate development, while the other shareholders suffer the loss. They may even benefit from the bad development by selling stocks short.

ing.[16] This observation is suggestive, but it doesn't prove anything, of course: The more relevant inquiry would be as to how much more participation there would be, if any, and on what terms, if there were no insider trading. Furthermore, although legal remedies against insider trading seem remarkably ineffective on both a priori and empirical grounds, there seems to have been, both before and after the enactment of the federal securities laws and before and after specific landmark decisions on insider trading, a general ethical consensus in the business community that insider trading is improper. This general ethical sense may very well inhibit the overall level of insider trading. In other words, we really do not know what would happen to investor confidence and capital formation if everyone were suddenly persuaded to believe that insider trading in unlimited amounts is absolutely proper. The results could be quite bad.

Perverse incentives argument

An argument related to my secret profits analysis is that of Judge Easterbrook, who claims that insider trading may generate "perverse incentives." One such incentive derives directly from the heads-I-win-tails-you-lose nature of insider trading. Insiders may cause the firm to engage in riskier ventures than the shareholders would prefer or find warranted by a present-value analysis, since if a venture pays off they can capture much of the gain by insider trading, but if it flops they can let the shareholders bear the loss. The insiders might also cause the corporation to incur costs to keep inside information leakproof while they complete their trading, although this point seems a minor one.[17]

§8.2.5 Relevance of Private Regulation

Absence of contracts proves what?

Sometimes commentators ask the following question: If insider trading is so bad, why is it that corporations seem only rarely to adopt *explicit* charter, bylaw, or contractual provisions making it improper for their managers to do it?[18] This question serves a useful heuristic purpose. But to take the fact that explicit private contracts against insider trading are rare as strong evidence that insider trading is not harmful would be a mistake, evincing either a distorted view of the importance of actual contracts in modern society[19] or confusion about the nature of law. One could, after all, ask why firms don't usually contract expressly against fraud and theft.

[16] Manne, Insider Trading and the Law Professors, 23 Vand. L. Rev. 547, 577 (1970).

[17] See Easterbrook, supra note 7, at 332-333.

[18] E.g., Dooley, Enforcement of Insider Trading Restrictions, 66 Va. L. Rev. 1, 45-47 (1980); Carlton & Fischel, The Regulation of Insider Trading, 35 Stan. L. Rev. 857, 861-866 (1983).

[19] For a critique of extreme contractualistic viewpoints in the corporate context, see Clark, Agency Costs versus Fiduciary Duties, in Principals and Agents: The Structure of Business 55 (J. Pratt & R. Zeckhauser eds. 1985).

A reason for collective action

One reason why insider trading may need to be dealt with by collective action (such as legal rules) rather than by private contracts is that individual firms may lack sufficient incentive or ability to curb the practice. Suppose that our preceding analysis is correct: Insider trading usually causes little obvious or significant direct harm to the corporation whose securities are being traded, but in the aggregate insider trading creates unproductive uncertainty that reduces the efficiency of the securities markets. If so, it could be in the interest of corporations and investors as a group to curtail the practice. Legal restrictions, assisted by a widespread sense that insider trading is unethical and subject to social disapproval, might help do this. Yet an individual corporation's board of directors might see little direct point in devoting serious effort and resources to preventing the company's own managers from engaging in insider trading. Indeed, the board may be dominated by persons who personally stand to gain from insider trading and whose interests and incentives are far from identical to those of public investors. And as long as there are a fair number of such boards, individualistic restrictions may be futile. If a corporation's board really cracks down on insider trading, its officers may simply seek employment at other firms that are not so strict. Yet the whole system might benefit from prohibiting insider trading.

Analogy to fraud and theft

Consider why fraud and theft aren't usually prohibited by explicit private contracts. One reason is, of course, that the law already prohibits these things. This fact in turn reflects a belief that collective action is a superior way of dealing with these behaviors. Another reason is that people simply assume that they are wrong, as a matter of morals or custom, and are subject to social disapproval. It does not occur to them to think that anyone could honestly believe the opposite or that the mores either can be or must be validated by actual contracts. I believe that, despite the prevalence of insider trading, the community of investors generally considers it unethical and improper.[20] Incidentally, and contrary to the suggestions of some commentators, this attitude toward insider trading has gradually spread to other countries with developed or developing securities markets, such as Japan, South Korea, Brazil, and Mexico — in all of which there are rules or norms against insider trading.[21]

[20] A related point, made in different jargon, would be that there is an implicit contract between investors and managers, and the terms of that contract specify that managers will not take secret profits, including insider trading profits.

[21] See generally Hopt, Insider Trading on the Continent, 4 J. Comp. Corp. L. & Sec. Reg. 379 (1982); Lee, Law and Practice with Respect to Insider Trading on Market Information in the United Kingdom, 4 J. Comp. Corp. L. & Sec. Reg. 389 (1982); Eizirik, The Role of the State in the Regulation of the Securities Markets: The Brazilian Experience, 1 J. Comp. Corp. L. &

In any event, the perception of investors and lawmakers is such that the agreement made between public investors and corporate managers, through the standard form contract of the corporate and securities laws, provides that corporate agents and fiduciaries undertake not to capture the value of corporate developments by means of insider trading.

Best theories

Summary. The best arguments against insider trading are that (1) it creates a systematic bias against prompt disclosure of information relevant to investment decision making, with resulting inefficiency and unfairness to public investors and (2) it constitutes an inefficient taking of secret profits by corporate fiduciaries, inefficient because such takings create avoidable and unproductive uncertainty.

§8.3 *The Positive Virtues of Insider Trading?*

§8.3.1 Rewarding Entrepreneurs

Entrepreneurship depends on insider trading?

Perhaps the most provocative of all apologias for managerial practices is that of Henry Manne, who argues that insider trading is a positively good thing.[1] Somewhat reconstructed, his most interesting line of argument proceeds as follows. There exists a class of men who are entrepreneurs. They are capable of innovating and of managing and galvanizing modern business enterprises; they are socially important creators of real value. Unfortunately, these men are rare. Even more unfortunately, corporations do not pay them adequately for their efforts. Existing incentive compensation schemes do not reward them enough to induce them to give their socially productive best to the economy. Happily, though, insider trading profits are able to take up some of the slack and keep these Nietzschean *Übermenschen* from picking up their marbles and dropping out of the business game. (Otherwise they might become doctors instead of businessmen or, even worse, they might work for the government.) Without insider trading, says Manne, the corporate system might not survive.[2]

Implausibility objection

At least six substantial objections can be directed against Manne's thesis.[3] First, it is simply implausible to believe that explicit executive com-

Sec. Reg. 211, 217 (1978); Tatsuta, Enforcement of Japanese Securities Legislation, 1 J. Comp. Corp. L. & Sec. Reg. 95, 107 (1978).

§8.3 [1]H. Manne, Insider Trading and the Stock Market (1966).

[2]Id. at 110.

[3]See O. Williamson, Corporate Control and Business Behavior 93-96 (1970); Schotland, Unsafe at Any Price: A Reply to Manne, 53 Va. L. Rev. 1425 (1967).

pensation schemes are inadequate to induce managers to work vigorously for corporations. Beside the fact that the reported compensation of top corporate officers seems rather high, and much of it seems linked to company performance, there is the institutional reality that executives actually have a large influence in the process of determining their own compensation. They bargain not with a single, rational "capitalist" with a powerful self-interest in the outcome of the bargain, but with a multiple, perhaps chummy board of directors who suffer from information, budget, and time constraints and often experience no deep link between their personal fortunes and those of the stockholders whose interests are affected by the bargaining process.[4] Nor is it obvious why one cannot select devices from the existing array of stock option and stock bonus plans, stock appreciation rights, and the like that will provide incentives to managers as good as those provided by the lure of insider trading profits.

Objection to profiteering on bad news

Second, insider trading allows managers to profit from their bad management, and from the misfortunes of their companies, a result whose social utility is not obvious. By using advance knowledge that the company's fortunes have taken a turn for the worse, they can sell their shares and avoid participating with the other shareholders in the disaster. Reported cases illustrate this possibility.[5] It is hard to see why our capitalist system requires that any of the individuals sued in these cases should have received a covert entrepreneurial-type reward for their behavior. By employing the technique of the short sale,[6] the trading insider may actually make a profit of the bad news, at the expense of buyers, those incoming shareholders during the period of nondisclosure.

It can be argued in response to this second point that managers are usually *too* risk averse — they are afraid of being blamed if projects they cause their firms to undertake turn out badly — and their personal ability to profit by insider trading from their firms' bad outcomes will redress this tendency.[7] Whether this argument has any real-world force depends on unanswered empirical questions. The argument does seem quite strained.[8]

[4]See section 5.4.1 supra.

[5]Diamond v. Oreamuno, 248 N.E.2d 910 (N.Y. 1969). Cf. SEC v. Shattuck Denn Mining Corp., 297 F. Supp. 470 (S.D.N.Y. 1968) (company president sold his stock before correcting false and misleading press release).

[6]An investor sells short by selling securities that he has borrowed (usually through a broker); the borrowed securities will be replaced with securities bought later. Since the sale precedes the purchase, the shortseller profits if prices fall.

[7]See Carlton & Fischel, The Regulation of Insider Trading, 35 Stan. L. Rev. 857, 872 (1983).

[8]Both the allegedly excessive fear of risk taking and the assumed inability to deal with it in some other way (e.g., by giving managers *very great* rewards for positive outcomes to risky ventures) seem doubtful to me.

Does "insider" equal "entrepreneur"?

Third, for Manne's argument to work well, we would have to believe that, by and large, the executive promotion system in large corporations is such that only true entrepreneurs, those who create substantial value by innovating, managing, and taking risks, get to the top or, more precisely, to those spots where they can receive inside information. But even slight experience with bureaucracies, as well as analysis of the facts of actual insider trading cases, should make us doubt whether the great majority of those who actually get and use inside information fall into the entrepreneurial category.

A comeback to this third point might be that identifying true entrepreneurs is expensive, so we have to use rules of thumb. But why not let the compensation committees of boards of directors apply the rules of thumb, rather than let each bureaucrat decide for himself whether he deserves some extra (and secret) compensation for being so entrepreneurial?

The behavior/stock price link

Fourth, the large *size* of modern corporations attenuates the relationship between any individual insider's entrepreneurial behavior and stock market performance. In a very large corporation with several major divisions, a divisional head may in fact have done a poor or mediocre job, even though success in the rest of the enterprise allows all the top officers to anticipate, and by insider trading to profit personally from, a rise in stock prices. Conversely, a divisional head who has performed superbly may be unable to reap an entrepreneurial reward by buying the company's stock on inside information, if all the other divisions have been performing in a mediocre way. The point is even stronger, of course, with respect to lower level line officers and staff personnel who may come across inside information.

This problem of trying to *attribute* created value to individual participants in an organization which has hundreds or even thousands of "managers" is a problem affecting corporations with explicit compensation schemes, of course. It is always hard, if not impossible, to say who was responsible for what amount of profit or loss of an essentially cooperative venture.[9] But at least some explicit compensation schemes seem to offer a much better shot at fair attribution of results than does insider trading. For example, many current compensation schemes go beyond simple stock appreciation rights to link the amount of incentive compensation received by executives to the performance, not of the price of the company's stock, but to the financial results of the particular division of the company in which the executives work.[10]

[9] C. Barnard, The Function of the Executive (1968); O. Wiliamson, note 3 supra, at 151-152.

[10] See, e.g., Pursell, Administering Divisional Incentive Compensation, Compensation Rev., 1st Quarter, 1980, at 15. Such compensation schemes create a risk of counterproductive

Delay

Fifth, the hope of insider trading profits may lead insiders to delay release of information even when doing so would be harmful to the corporation. This is not a problem with explicit incentive compensation schemes.

Distraction

Sixth, the energy diverted into pursuit of individual profit-making through insider trading activities may deprive the company of the benefits of more constructive behaviors.

Despite all of these objections, the managerial compensation argument has been resurrected in recent years by Professors Carlton and Fischel.[11] In addition to trying to rebut the objections, they stress the point (discussed in subsection 8.2.5) that private contracts usually don't expressly prohibit insider trading.

Absence of contracts

One is tempted to ask why private contracts don't expressly provide *for* compensation by means of insider trading profits. Surely one may argue that the absence of such provisions in executive compensation agreements means that such compensation was not agreed upon by the bargaining parties. Indeed, the entire law of fiduciary duties — not just the part that has blossomed into the federal law on insider trading — is premised on just such an assumption. Fiduciary law displays an unyielding hostility to the notion of "implicit compensation arrangements" for fiduciaries. Not to see this is to fail to perceive the very essence of corporate law.

§8.3.2 Getting Information Reflected in Market Prices

Another positive argument for insider trading is that it helps get the inside information reflected in the market price of the traded security, a result that is economically desirable. As explained above (in section 8.2.3), however, there are more direct, and apparently more efficient, ways of achieving this result. One could argue in reply that in some circumstances insider trading is the preferred method. For example, the corporation in question might be harmed, as against its competitors, if the inside information is directly disclosed. How important this point is empirically is an open question. In any event, it seems that there will often be ways of signalling that material events have occurred within a firm without revealing valuable proprietary information. Remember the example of the X Drug Company: It could disclose that its scientists had discovered a breakthrough product without giving out the formula or the method of production.[12]

Sometimes best method?

---

competition among divisions within the corporation; see O. Williamson, supra note 3, at 126-127; R. Cyert and J. March, A Behavioral Theory of the Firm (1963).

[11] See Carlton & Fischel, supra note 7.

[12] In response to this point, it could be argued that many people won't believe the claim of

§8.4 *Prevalence and Preventability of Insider Trading*

Rampant and unstoppable?

Perhaps the most sensible arguments against regulation of insider trading revolve around the alleged facts that "everybody does it" and the legal system cannot stop it. More precisely, the costs of doing something *effective* about insider trading, according to this argument, are so enormous that they would far overshadow any benefits that might be created. Consequently, even if insider trading is bad, it is better to do nothing about it than to waste resources by maintaining a litigation-promoting but basically toothless set of legal controls against it. (Professor Manne also made this argument.)

Evidence of prevalence

Beyond anecdotes, there is some good systematic evidence that indirectly suggests that many insiders do engage in trading on insider information. Economists who have studied the trading reports filed by statutory insiders (directors, officers, and 10 percent controlling shareholders) under Section 16(a) of the Securities Exchange Act of 1934 have concluded that those insiders consistently obtain a higher risk-adjusted rate of return on their trades in their companies' stocks than do public investors generally.[1] In view of the substantial evidence in support of a limited version of the efficient markets thesis,[2] according to which no public investors *systematically* outperform the market, the results concerning the trading profits of insiders suggest that many of them illegally base their activities on material nonpublic information. On the other hand, an indeterminate amount of their superior gains may be due not to illegal trading on the basis of specific inside information but to a better developed sense of their company's future prospects. This intuitive sense may arise out of actually living within

---

a "breakthrough" unless these sensitive details are also disclosed. How often such a problem arises, and how serious it is, are other unanswered questions.

§8.4 [1]See Baesel & Stein, The Value of Information: Inferences From the Profitability of Insider Trading, 14 J. Fin. & Quan. Anal. 553 (1979); Finnerty, Insiders and Market Efficiency, 31 J. Fin. 1141 (1976); Keown & Pinkerton, Merger Announcements and Insider Trading Activity: An Empirical Investigation, 36 J. Fin. 855 (1981); Lorie & Niederhoffer, Predictive and Statistical Properties of Insider Trading, 11 J. Law & Econ. 35 (1968); Penman, Insider Trading and the Dissemination of Firms' Forecast Information, 55 J. Bus. 479 (1982).

[2]An efficient market is one in which prices always fully reflect all available information and which adjusts instantaneously to news. There are three forms of the efficient market thesis. The weak form asserts that changes in stock prices are substantially independent, implying that future price movements cannot be usefully predicted from price history. The semistrong form (referred to in the text) asserts that stock prices reflect all *public* information. The strong form asserts that prices reflect public and private information; the articles cited in note 1 supra provide evidence against this form. For surveys of empirical studies, see J. Lorie, P. Dodd, & M. Kimpton, The Stock Market: Theories and Evidence 55-79 (2d ed. 1985); K. Garbade, Securities Markets 241-266 (1982).

a company and absorbing, both consciously and unconsciously, untold numbers of bits of information, some of which are known and appreciated by outsiders and others that are not.

Apparent noneffect of regulatory changes

On the question of regulation's effects, there is a study which indicates that certain landmark legal decisions about insider trading had no detectable impact on the level of insider trading as inferred from the Section 16(a) reports filed by statutory insiders.[3] The study by itself hardly proves that legal rules and remedies cannot cut down the amount of insider trading significantly. For one thing, the measure of insider trading it used tells us nothing about unreported insider trading activities or about trades carried on by nonstatutory insiders, those who are tipped by a statutory insider or other inside source and those, such as the spouse of a corporate officer, who carry out trades at the suggestion and indirectly for the benefit of a statutory insider.

No proof of unstoppability

More importantly, there really was no strong reason to expect that the particular legal decisions tested in the study would have a deterrent effect on insider trading. Those decisions under Section 10(b) and Rule 10b-5 established the disclose or abstain rule: An insider in possession of material nonpublic information must either disclose the information to the public before trading in the company's securities or refrain from trading. But they did not establish that an insider found to have violated the rule would have to do any more than disgorge his illicit profits. As we shall see, even the current case law threatens little more than disgorgement. As long as the probability of getting caught and made to pay up for one's insider trading is significantly less than one, even a modestly daring insider may feel that he has nothing to lose, and much to gain, by trying to get and keep insider trading profits. Furthermore, the legal decisions in question did nothing to increase the probability that illegal insider trading would be *detected* and subjected to successful legal proceedings. Put another way, the legal developments tested in the study involved a change in substantive legal rules, but not in the monitoring, enforcement, and sanctioning phases of the legal process. Consequently, they could have been expected to lead to further litigation (they did) but not necessarily to a decrease in the quantity of insider trading.

These remarks have practical implications. For example, if the damages rule were that insiders found to have reaped illegal insider trading profits must pay not only their gains but some *multiple* thereof, and if the multiple

[3] Jaffe, The Effect of Regulation Changes on Insider Trading, 5 Bell J. Econ. & Man. Sci. 93 (1974). The decisions in question were the *Cady, Roberts* and *Texas Gulf Sulphur* decisions, which are discussed in section 8.10 infra.

damages rule became widely known, then the amount of insider trading that occurs might indeed be significantly curtailed. There is no analytical or empirical reason for concluding that a damages formula with a high enough multiplier could not work.

Problems of optimal deterrence strategy

To be sure, even with a multiple damages formula, real and difficult policy questions would persist. Would a multiplier adequate to achieve some deterrence have to be so high that it would raise severe problems of fairness to defendants? Would it be self-defeating with respect to the many defendants who simply could not pay the judgments assessed against them? What is the proper balance between the two major deterrence increasing strategies, devoting resources to detection and prosecution of insider trading violations or simply increasing the damages multiplier? The former strategy could increase the *probability* that insider trading would be caught and sanctioned. The latter strategy would increase the *penalty* imposed on miscreant insiders who are caught.[4]

In any event, since legal developments to date have focused on identifying the proper elements of the substantive legal rules about insider trading, with less attention paid to developing legal incentives for more potent detection methods, enforcement proceedings, and remedies, it seems premature to declare that insider trading cannot be stopped or that the cost of curtailing it will "obviously" exceed the benefits.

§8.5 The Fit Between Remedies and Harms

§8.5.1 Introduction

Dimensions of remedies

The three major remedies for insider trading differ along key variables. Under the case law developing Rule 10b-5 and the state law approach of *Diamond v. Oreamuno*,[1] a defendant insider may be sued for a single transaction — say, a stock purchase before good news is publicly announced — even though the insider then holds the stock indefinitely rather than monetizing his gain. But the plaintiff must prove that the defendant actually used that information. Under Section 16(b), the plaintiff must show that the defendant insider engaged in a double transaction, — a purchase followed by a sale or a sale followed by a purchase, with both events occurring within a six month period. But the plaintiff need not show that the

[4]See generally Polinsky & Shavell, The Optimal Tradeoff between the Probability and Magnitude of Fines, 69 Am. Econ. Rev. 880 (1979); Landes & Posner, The Private Enforcement of Law, 4 J. Leg. Stud. 1 (1975).

§8.5 [1]248 N.E.2d 910 (N.Y. 1969).

insider actually had access to inside information or made use of it. On the other hand, the *Diamond* and the Section 16(b) approaches contemplate that damages will be paid by the insider to the corporation in whose securities he traded. But the 10b-5 cases provide, among other things, for the insider to pay damages to certain classes of shareholders.

Corporate vs. shareholder recovery

The primary purpose of this section is to analyze whether corporate recovery or shareholder recovery makes more sense in light of the earlier discussion of the harms caused by insider trading. I will ask first whether corporate recovery is more sensible than shareholder recovery when insider trading is viewed as creating a bias against carrying out the ideal of timely disclosure. From this perspective, one should consider who bears the gain or loss represented by new corporate developments (those that are the subject of the inside information) under three conditions:

(1) when events have occurred ideally, that is, when the information about the new development is publicly disclosed just as soon as it is ripe, and there is therefore no insider trading;
(2) when insider trading occurs but is not corrected by any legal remedies; and
(3) when insider trading occurs but is remedied by the particular legal approach under analysis.

I will also ask whether the fiduciary misconduct or self-dealing theory of insider trading adds anything to the various arguments.

Hypo for analysis

Since even a pure and abstract analysis requires us to make numerous distinctions, first consider the simplified example outlined by Figure 8.5-A. X Corporation, whose shares are publicly traded, discovers oil at a time when the company's stock is trading at $50 per share. Suppose we are sure that if the good news were accurately and promptly disclosed to the public, the price at which X shares would change hands would quickly jump to $80. In fact, however, announcement of the good news is delayed and insider *I*, the president of the company, buys a large quantity of the stock at $50. The discovery is eventually announced and the market price of X stock immediately jumps to $80, at which point *I* sells his stock at the new price.

For the sake of simplicity, we are assuming that nothing else but the oil discovery announcement is operating to change the stock's market price. In real situations, of course, various other things within the company and the market are occurring, and one cannot be certain that the stock's intrinsic or true value during this period of nondisclosure of the ripe good news is accurately measured by looking at the market price to which the

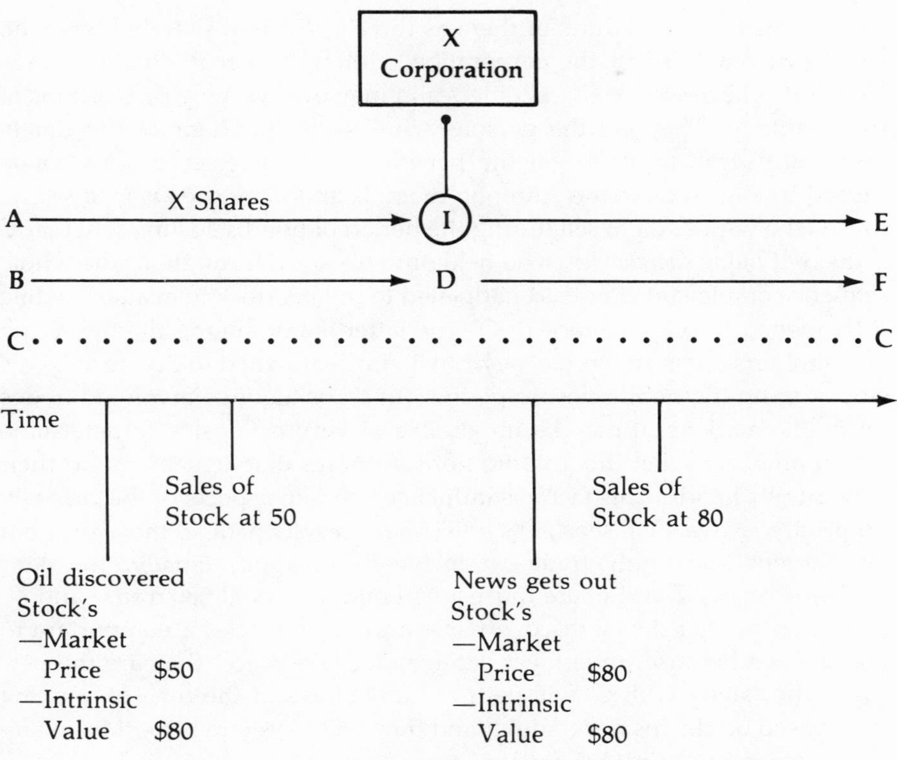

Figure 8.5-A
Insider Trading: Responsiveness of Remedies to Harms

stock moves shortly after disclosure is finally made. In other words, the $80 price at which X stock is *observed* to sell after announcement of the oil discovery only indicates, but does not demonstrate, that the stock would have been sold at $80 if, contrary to fact, the news had been released as soon as it was ripe. As we shall see,[2] this evidentiary problem of real life causes courts great difficulties in choosing a sound but practical formula for computing damages. But it does not affect our analysis here.

Cast of characters

The cast of relevant characters includes others besides the corporation and the insider. The owners of X's stock at the moment when the oil discovery should have been disclosed but was not are *A*, *B*, and *C*, who will be referred to collectively as the *deserving shareholders.* (Admittedly, this label may connote an exaggerated notion of the significance of their claim.)

[2]See section 8.11.3 infra.

For simplicity we can think of them as three individual shareholders who each own one-third of the corporation, although in real situations they constitute subclasses of shareholders and may own varying proportions of the company. They are the persons who, under the logic of the timely disclosure ideal, *ought* to get the benefit of the increase in stock value caused by the oil discovery. Among them, *A* and *B* are the *innocent sellers,* those who happened to sell during the period of nondisclosure, whereas *C* is the *continuing shareholder,* who held onto his stock throughout the whole sequence of relevant events. *A* happened to sell his stock to insider *I,* while *B* happened to sell his stock to *D.* The latter is not among the deserving shareholders but is an *innocent buyer,* who just happened to decide to buy X stock during the nondisclosure period. (In real situations involving trades on public markets, it may be impossible or very expensive to determine which innocent seller did and did not sell shares that actually found their way into I's hands. This fact has influenced certain aspects of the case law on privity, as we shall see.[3]) *D*'s investment results parallel those of *I,* but he did not knowingly trade on inside information. Finally, the *post-disclosure buyers, E* and *F,* are those who bought stock at $80 from *I* and *D,* respectively, after the oil discovery was announced. They are important to the analysis because, unless yet other trades take place, they are the persons who, along with *C,* will be the shareholders at the time of any law suits based on the insider trading, and they will therefore benefit from any recoveries paid to the corporation.

Outcomes in ideal situation

Table 8.5-A displays how, under various conditions, the gain in the company's value that was caused by the oil discovery is distributed among the characters in the game. The first column (ideal situation) reports that, if the oil discovery had been announced when it should have been, the deserving shareholders *A, B,* and *C* would each have benefited by $30, the immediate increase in the market value of their stock, whereas the insider *I* and the later purchasing shareholders *D, E,* and *F* would have received no gain or loss on account of the oil discovery.

Outcomes with insider trading

By contrast, if insider trading occurs and nothing is done about it, then, as indicated in the second column of Table 8.5-A, two of the deserving shareholders, the innocent sellers *A* and *B,* are deprived of their gains, which are instead reaped by *I,* the insider who deliberately appropriates part of the gain, and by *D,* the innocent buyer who gets a windfall of sorts because he traded in parallel to *I.* But the continuing shareholder *C* is not deprived of his gain because of the insider trading. All that happened to him is that the market value of his stock increased later than it should have.

[3]See section 8.10.6 infra.

Table 8.5-A
Allocation of Stock Price Gain Based on Information About a Good Corporate Development

		Insider Trading Plus —			
				Shareholder Recovery with Damages Based on —	
	"Ideal" Situation (Prompt Disclosure)	*No Remedy*	*Corporate Recovery*	*Defendant's Gain*	*Plaintiff's Harm*
A	$30	0	0	15	30
B	30	0	0	15	30
C	30	30	40	30	30
I	0	30	0	0	−30
D	0	30	30	30	30
E	0	0	10	0	0
F	0	0	10	0	0

But since he was simply holding on to his investment, this effect did not constitute an injury to him.[4] Moreover, the post-disclosure shareholders *E* and *F* are neither injured nor benefited, relative to the ideal situation, because they bought in after the stock's market price fully reflected the information in question. Thus, *none* of the shareholders who are shareholders after the insider trading has occurred and the oil discovery has been announced have been injured by violation of the timely disclosure ideal.

§8.5.2 Corporate Recovery

Outcomes after corporate recovery

The last remark helps us appraise the third column, which gives the distribution of gains when insider trading occurs but is then "remedied" by application of a corporate recovery approach, whether that of the *Diamond* case or of Section 16(b).[5] In this case, *I* is forced to pay his insider trading gain of $30 to X Corporation; the payment is presumed to cause a $30 aggregate increase in the market price of all of X's shares; and the

[4] To be sure, situations can be imagined where *C* would have been hurt by delay in the release of the information. For example, he might have pledged his stock as collateral for a loan during the period of nondisclosure and would have gotten a bigger loan or better terms if the stock's market price had been higher. But in this context the pledge functions much like a sale, so the example can be assimilated to the situations of *A* and *B*.

[5] Section 16(b) is discussed more fully in sections 8.6 and 8.7 infra. If *I* sells his shares less than six months after purchasing them, he will be liable under §16(b) to the corporation for his profits. If *I* simply holds his shares after the discovery is disclosed, §16(b) does not apply.

beneficiaries of this increase are those who own X stock at the time the judgment is paid. The results of this procedure are far from those in the ideal situation. The injured innocent sellers *A* and *B* are not compensated for the loss of their share in the gains. The innocent buyer *D* gets to keep his windfall. Furthermore, each of the shareholders at the time of the lawsuit, (*C, E,* and *F*) gets an undeserved $10 windfall that is created by the remedy of corporate recovery. The only result that conforms to the ideal is that insider *I* is forced to disgorge his ill-gotten gains. But note that even here there is no penalty imposed on *I;* he only coughs up his profits if he gets caught. It is therefore doubtful whether the remedy acts as an effective deterrent for most insiders. Deterrence is, of course, a goal that would arise whether the harm of insider trading is viewed as consisting of a violation of timely disclosure principles or a violation of principles of fiduciary loyalty.

Little apparent sense

Thus, the corporate recovery approach seems to make little sense, whether viewed as an instrument of compensation or deterrence. It pays the wrong persons (X and, indirectly, *C, E,* and *F*), does not help the injured persons (*A* and *B*), and gives the losing *I* a conciliatory handshake rather than a slap on the wrist.

But fits one theory

After these rationalistic remarks, you may wonder how lawmakers could ever have been so stupid as to provide for corporate recovery of insider trader profits. Can anything good be said about the idea? In fact, there is a great deal to be said in favor of the Section 16(b) and *Diamond* approaches. First, and most obviously, corporate recovery makes sense to those who, like the judges of the New York Court of Appeals, can persuade themselves that a valid objection to insider trading is that it harms the corporation involved, as by making it difficult for the corporation to gain the trust and confidence of its investors, suppliers, and customers.

Offers some deterrence

Second, in a real life context the corporate recovery approach actually may deter some insider trading. A 16(b) or *Diamond* lawsuit may not only force disgorgement of gains but impose various collateral costs on the defendant. He may be shamed before his peers and perhaps made to incur legal and other expenses that are not fully recoverable by indemnity, insurance, and tax deductions.[6] The probability of getting caught and made to suffer these collateral costs may be great enough to deter those insiders who are already fairly law abiding and risk-averse, those basically honest

[6]See Johnston, Corporate Indemnification and Liability Insurance for Directors and Officers, 33 Bus. Law. 1993, 2007-2009, 2018-2019 (1978) (indemnification unlikely in view of public policy; standard insurance coverage exludes claims arising from §16(b) violation); cf. Locke v. Commissioner, 568 F.2d 663 (9th Cir. 1978) (no tax deduction for legal fees in successful defense of 10b-5 action for fraud).

men and women who need just an additional threat or two to keep themselves in line. Thus, the threat of having to disgorge trading profits and suffer collateral costs does add something to a situation where the law provides no other remedy that is likely to be applied.

Is procedurally efficient

Third, the corporate recovery approach is enforced by means of a shareholder's derivative suit. At least in the current state of the law, this device has efficiency advantages over a class action, which is the device that is used to get a recovery on behalf of the *A*'s and *B*'s of this world. For example, class actions can readily cause an enormous amount of the legal system's resources to be devoted to the task of class definition and certification, the giving of notices, and the processing and administration of individual claims. The derivative suit elegantly sidesteps these problems. The attributes of derivative suits will be explored at a later point in this book.[7] The point to be made here is that the differing costs of class actions and derivative suits lend plausibility to the notion that corporate recovery of insider trading gains is a sensible remedial approach. It may be the best practical approach to the problem, once all factors are considered. At the least, corporate recovery can be defended as a supplement to other remedies against insider trading.

Query importance of windfall problems

Fourth, the various windfall problems that are unaddressed or caused by corporate recovery may be seen as something that should cause us little concern. Corporate recovery does not take the windfall away from innocent lucky trader *D*, but there seems to be no other feasible remedial approach that does anything about this windfall. One is hard pressed to imagine a legal proceeding in which the parties try to identify and track down all the innocent public traders who happened to trade during a period of tardy corporate disclosure and make them give up some of the trading gains that they assumed were theirs. Since this kind of windfall is one that we simply have to endure, it cannot be used as a basis for comparisons among remedies. Furthermore, the windfalls obtained by shareholders like *C*, *E*, and *F* after a corporate recovery may be individually small if the insider's trading was modest in relation to the company's total outstanding stock. And finally, how sorry can we feel about selling shareholders *A* and *B*? Their claim to compensation is based on the notion that they would have been better off if a certain rule of the road (timely disclosure) had been followed. Somehow, this seems less compelling than a claim based on some specific, bargained-for promise of benefits to them. If the timing of the oil discovery had been a little later, then, with or without insider trading, they would have been out of luck anyway. (On the other

[7] Chapter 15.

hand, it is quite clear that a large part of the gain that they would have gotten if the rule had been followed has been deliberately taken by an insider who is understood by all concerned to have no right to do such a thing and to be a fiduciary toward them and the other public shareholders).

§8.5.3 Shareholder Recovery

Outcomes with shareholder recovery

The fourth column of Table 8.5-A shows the distribution of gain if insider trading occurs but the *A* and *B* shareholders bring a successful class action under Rule 10b-5 against the insider and obtain a recovery based upon the insider's illegal profits. The fifth column shows results of the same case except that now the court awards damages based not on disgorgement but on the harm suffered by all the plaintiffs in the class, and harm is measured in relation to outcomes in the ideal situation. The distinction shown by these two columns needs to be made because it represents a fundamental difference in approach to the proper measure of damages in 10b-5 cases — a subject to which we shall return.[8]

Like corporate recovery, both of these shareholder-oriented remedial approaches let *D* keep his windfall. Unlike corporate recovery, they do not give a windfall to continuing shareholder *C* or to post-disclosure buyers *E* and *F*, and they both provide at least some compensation to the selling shareholders *A* and *B*. The difference between them is with respect to the question: Who (the wrongdoing insider or the innocent sellers) is to bear the unhappy burden of the fact that lucky *D* has captured part of the value of the corporate development but realistically cannot be made to give it up? The disgorgement approach throws this burden on the innocent sellers. The full compensation approach throws it on the insider, who in some sense caused the problem.

Full compensation vs. disgorgement

The full compensation approach may seem the obviously correct one at first glance. But this becomes uncertain when we consider the effects of relative trading volumes. If, as happens in some real cases,[9] the insider's trading during the period of nondisclosure constitutes only a small portion of the trading during the period, forcing him to pay the innocent sellers enough to put them all in the position they would have been in had the ideal situation of prompt disclosure occurred would impose an *enormous* penalty upon him, one that would be a very high multiple of his ill-gotten gains. In a particular case, the trading gains illegally taken by the insider could amount to a few thousand dollars, while the amount shifted because

[8] See sections 8.10.5-8.10.7 infra.

[9] E.g., Fridrich v. Bradford, 542 F.2d 307 (6th Cir. 1976), cert. denied, 429 U.S. 1053 (1977).

of tardy disclosure of good corporate news from innocent sellers to innocent but lucky buyers like *D* could run into millions of dollars. In such cases, the full compensation rule, which might be called the standard tort law approach, might occasionally provide actual full compensation to the innocent sellers (in those cases where the defendant had enough wealth to satisfy the enormous judgment), and it might indeed provide extra deterrence against future insider trading, but with a vengeance that should disturb even the most hard-hearted of legal reformers.

§8.5.4 Workable Deterrence

A balanced approach

Perhaps the best insider trading remedy would be one that tried to achieve deterrence without imposing unnecessary penalties. Instead of opting for full compensation of all those who are victims under the timely disclosure analysis or for simple disgorgement of the insider's profits, it would impose liability on the insider in an amount that is some fixed *multiple* of his trading profits. Ideally, the exact multiple — whether three or five, for example — would depend on what insiders perceive to be the probability of getting caught and sanctioned for insider trading. But in default of good evidence on this point, the law could simply imitate the treble damages formula of the antitrust laws.

Priorities among plaintiffs

At the same time, the ideal insider trading remedy would give priority to recovery by the relevant class of suing shareholders but would preserve the possibility of corporate recovery for situations in which a shareholder class action was not forthcoming. How the two kinds of suits might be accommodated is a subject that is illuminated by the analogous discussion in the law review literature of the insider's possible multiple liability under existing law, for example, when 10b-5, 16(b), and state law suits are all brought with respect to the same insider and the same set of events.[10] In general, the basic guidelines in an ideal world would be that a shareholder class action precludes a derivative action against the insider for insider trading and that when a derivative action results in a recovery, the amount recovered should be held in a separate fund by the corporation for a modest period of time so that the individuals really injured by the insider trading can make a claim against it.

Insider Trading Sanctions Act

In fact, the Insider Trading Sanctions Act of 1984 has provided for treble damages in certain situations. The Act added Section 21(d)(2) to the Securi-

[10] Note, A Comparison of Insider Liability under Diamond v. Oreamuno and Federal Securities Law, 11 B.C. Ind. & Com. L. Rev. 499 (1970); Note, Common Law Corporate Recovery for Trading on Non-Public Information, 74 Colum. L. Rev. 269, 289-294 (1974); Note, 55 Va. L. Rev. 1520, 1531-1533 (1969).

ties Exchange Act. That provision allows the SEC to seek, and a federal court to impose, a civil penalty for insider trading. The court has discretion in imposing the penalty, which may not exceed three times the profit gained or loss avoided by the insider trading. But the provision was not made available to private plaintiffs.

§8.5.5 A Postscript on Bad News

Different analysis with bad news?

The hypothetical that formed the basis of the analysis in this section dealt with an insider who traded on undisclosed information about a good corporate development that would eventually increase the price of the company's stock. The question arises as to whether the analysis would be different if the insider had traded on the basis of undisclosed bad news. Suppose, for example, the company's president suppressed release of disastrous financial results long enough to sell his own stock at a good price before the bad news could have a chance to depress the price of the company's stock. In this context, the points made about corporate versus shareholder recovery with respect to the good news hypothetical remain essentially valid, although they must be modified somewhat.

Similarities

In both cases, both corporate and shareholder recovery involve taking away the insider's trading profit (and perhaps more). In the bad news case, of course, the profit consists in the amount of loss that the insider averts by selling early. In both cases, both shareholder and corporate recovery do not result in taking away windfall gains from those innocent lucky traders who happen to trade in the same direction as the insider during the period of nondisclosure. As was mentioned earlier, it is unfeasible to do anything about the gains to such traders.

Differences

In the good news case, as we saw, when there is *corporate* recovery of the insider trading profits, the continuing shareholders and the post-disclosure shareholders get a windfall, whereas the innocent selling shareholders who are harmed by the nondisclosure are not compensated. In the bad news case, however, corporate recovery will reduce the harm to those who bought during the nondisclosure period, but it will only do so partially and only if they are still shareholders at the time of recovery. Corporate recovery will still give a windfall — in this context, an undeserved reduction of loss — to continuing shareholders. In general, the larger the amount of stock held by continuing shareholders in relation to the amount bought by innocent buyers during the nondisclosure period, the more inadequate will be the compensation of the buyers' harm afforded by corporate recovery. Thus, corporate recovery makes more sense, although not much more, than in the good news case.

Finally, in both the good and bad news cases a shareholder class action can theoretically lead to greater compensation of the defrauded traders (sellers or buyers, depending on the case) and to full compensation if the courts do not hesitate to impose damages exceeding the insider's profit. In both cases, shareholder recovery will also avoid giving a windfall to the continuing shareholders.

§8.6 *Section 16(b): Basics*

§8.6.1 Introduction

Basic concept

Section 16(b) of the Securities Exchange Act[1] is designed to make certain categorically defined insiders liable to pay to their corporations any so-

§8.6 [1] The full text of subsections (a) and (b) of Section 16 is as follows:

Sec. 16. (a) Every person who is directly or indirectly the beneficial owner of more than 10 per centum of any class of any equity security (other than an exempted security) which is registered pursuant to section 12 of this title, or who is a director or an officer of the issuer of such security, shall file, at the time of the registration of such security on a national securities exchange or by the effective date of a resignation statement filed pursuant to section 12(g) of this title, or within ten days after he becomes such beneficial owner, director, or officer, a statement with the Commission (and, if such security is registered on a national securities exchange, also with the exchange) of the amount of all equity securities of such issuer of which he is the beneficial owner, and within ten days after the close of each calendar month thereafter, if there has been a change in such ownership during such month, shall file with the Commission (and if such security is registered on a national securities exchange, shall also file with the exchange), a statement indicating his ownership at the close of the calendar month and such changes in his ownership as have occurred during such calendar month.

(b) For the purpose of preventing the unfair use of information which may have been obtained by such beneficial owner, director, or officer by reason of his relationship to the issuer, any profit realized by him from any purchase and sale, or any sale and purchase, of any equity security of such issuer (other than an exempted security) within any period of less than six months, unless such security was acquired in good faith in connection with a debt previously contracted, shall inure to and be recoverable by the issuer, irrespective of any intention on the part of such beneficial owner, director, or officer in entering into such transaction of holding the security purchased or of not repurchasing the security sold for a period exceeding six months. Suit to recover such profit may be instituted at law or in equity in any court of competent jurisdiction by the issuer or by the owner of any security of the issuer in the name and in behalf of the issuer if the issuer shall fail or refuse to bring such suit within sixty days after request or shall fail diligently to prosecute the same thereafter; but no such suit shall be brought more than two years after the date such profit was realized. This subsection shall not be construed to cover any transaction where such beneficial owner was not such both at the time of the purchase and sale, or the sale and purchase, of the security involved, or any transaction or transactions which the Commission by rules and regulations may exempt as not comprehended within the purpose of this subsection.

called short-swing profits, that is, profits from in-and-out trading in the company's stock. Specifically, it provides that certain issuers (including most publicly held corporations) can recover any profit realized by specified insiders from any purchase and sale, or sale and purchase, of any nonexempt equity security of the issuer within any period of six months. The insiders covered by the rule are the *directors* and *officers* of companies that have any class of equity securities registered pursuant to Section 12 of the 1934 Act, as well as all direct or indirect *beneficial owners* of more than 10 percent of any such class of equity security other than an exempted security. Since Section 12 covers all securities on national securities exchanges like the New York Stock Exchange, American Stock Exchange, Pacific Coast Stock Exchange, and other regional exchanges and also requires all corporations with assets in excess of $3 million and a class of equity security held of record by 500 or more persons to register with the SEC,[2] Section 16(b) applies to virtually all directors and officers of publicly held United States corporations and to virtually all ten percent beneficial owners of their publicly held equity securities.

Enforcement

Section 16(b) recovery can only be sought in the federal courts.[3] The SEC has no jurisdiction to enforce it,[4] but it may adopt rules exempting certain transactions as not being within the purpose of the subsection.[5] Suit to recover the short-swing profits may be brought by the corporation or, more importantly, by any security holder of the corporation on its behalf, if the corporation fails or refuses to bring the suit within 60 days after request or fails diligently to prosecute it. This permission to bring a derivative suit is not hampered, as derivative suits often are, by the ability of the corporation's independent directors to foreclose the suit by deciding that pursuing it would not be "in the best interest of the corporation." Cases have also held that certain derivative suit preconditions such as contemporaneous ownership requirements[6] and security-for-expenses statutes[7] do not apply to 16(b) suits. Since recovery under 16(b) goes into the corporate treasury and rarely increases the market value of any particular shareholder's stock dramatically, the motivation for bringing 16(b) suits resides in the attor-

[2]Securities Exchange Act §12(g); Rule 12g-1 (raising amount to $3 million).

[3]Securities Exchange Act §27. Lincoln Natl. Bank v. Lampe, 414 F. Supp. 1270, 1279 (N.D. Ill. 1976).

[4]But see 2 L.Loss, Securities Regulation 1053-1054 (2d ed. 1961) (suggesting that the SEC should be given enforcement powers).

[5]See 17 C.F.R. §240.16b-1 to 240.16b-11.

[6]Dottenheim v. Murchison, 227 F.2d 737 (5th Cir. 1955), cert. denied, 351 U.S. 919 (1956).

[7]Truncale v. Blumberg, [1948-1952 Transfer Binder] Fed. Sec. L. Rep. (CCH) ¶90,470 (S.D.N.Y. Oct. 24, 1949); cf. McClure v. Borne Chem. Co., 292 F.2d 824 (3d Cir.) (no security required for action under §10(b)), cert. denied, 368 U.S. 939 (1961).

neys who bring them in the hope of getting fees out of the corporate recovery. There is nothing unseemly about this; the courts recognize it as the mechanism for enforcement of the statute.[8]

Purpose

The purpose of 16(b), as stated in the statute itself, is to prevent "the unfair use of information which may be obtained by [the statutory insider] by reason of his relationship to the issuer." Thus, it aims to help stamp out paradigmatic insider trading of the type discussed in previous sections of this chapter. Nevertheless, the insider is liable under 16(b) for his short-swing profits whether or not he had inside information or acted upon it, and whether or not he had any intention, when he made any particular purchase or sale, of making a later sale or purchase within six months. If a director of X Corporation buys some X stock on January 1 and sells some X stock at a higher price within the next six months, he is liable. If he sells some X stock on January 2 and buys some X stock at a lower price within the six months after that date, he is also liable. It does not matter what information he possessed or what his intentions were or even whether the net result of all his transactions in a given six month period is profitable or not. Thus, the Section 16(b) rule is routinely described by courts and commentators as "flat," "arbitrary," "sweeping," "strict," "objective," and "prophylactic."

Objective approach

Did Congress decline to make the rule turn on the insider's knowledge and intent because it thought these things to be theoretically irrelevant? Because it was interested in some evil other than insider trading? The answer to both questions is no, of course. Congress simply wanted to enact a rule that was capable of easy administration.[9] The ease of administration was to be achieved by eliminating the need for proof of elements of misbehavior that are costly and difficult to prove. The flatness, objectivity, and so forth are deliberate. They reflect Congress's belief that the possibility of abuse of inside information was intolerably great in short-swing trading situations and that a hard-headed, "no excuses" rule against it was necessary if anything effective was to be done about the problem.

Overinclusive and underinclusive

Like many other legal rules that are designed to be mechanical or objective, Section 16(b) catches defendants who did not violate the policy decision underlying the rule (here, the decision that trading on inside information is unfair), and it fails to catch other defendants who did violate it. For example, if the president of X Corporation buys half of the company's stock on the basis of undisclosed good news about the company's

[8]Smolowe v. Delendo Corp., 136 F.2d 231, 241 (2d Cir.), cert. denied, 320 U.S. 751 (1943).

[9]It may also have thought that an insider's making a quick in-and-out set of trades was especially likely to be based on inside information.

prospects and simply holds onto it for more than six months, then he is untouched by 16(b), no matter how great his unfair gains, how important the undisclosed information, or how deliberate and outrageous the nondisclosure of the good news and the decision to purchase. For 16(b) requires at least *two* transactions within six months: a purchase followed by a sale or a sale followed by a purchase. Such is the price of easy administration.

Ambiguities

Like other statutory rules, whether mechanical or not, 16(b) has generated its share of case law dealing with the inevitable ambiguities in the meaning of the statute's terms. It may be instructive to consider developments with respect to three of the more important terms: "beneficial owner," "equity security," and "any profit."

§8.6.2 "Beneficial Owner"

Timing question

The last sentence of Section 16(b) states that the

> subsection shall not be construed to cover any transaction where such beneficial owner [that is, one who owns 10 percent of any class of registered, nonexempt equity security of the issuer] was not such *both at* the time of the purchase and sale, or the sale and purchase of the security involved. . . . [Emphasis added.]

It might seem that there would be little doubt about the meaning of the words "at" and "the time of" a purchase or sale, but the case law shows otherwise.

***Reliance Electric* case**

In *Reliance Electric Co. v. Emerson Electric Co.*,[10] the following sequence of events occurred within a six months period.

(1) Emerson bought 13.2 percent of the stock of Dodge Manufacturing Co. pursuant to a tender offer.
(2) Dodge shareholders approved a merger of Dodge into Reliance, a move that would frustrate Emerson's hopes of taking control of Dodge.
(3) Emerson, now a defeated tender offeror hoping to withdraw from the takeover battle, sold 3.24 percent of Dodge's stock.
(4) Emerson then sold the remaining 9.96 percent of Dodge stock.

After the merger, Reliance was not content to simply bask in its victory in the battle for Dodge but, having knocked its rival to the ground, as it were,

[10] 404 U.S. 418, reh. denied, 405 U.S. 969 (1972).

proceeded to kick it vigorously. As successor to the rights of Dodge, it brought suit against Emerson to recover the latter's profits from trading in Dodge stock, on the theory that Emerson had been a 10 percent beneficial owner and the step (1) purchase could be paired with the sales at steps (3) and (4). It was not being disputed that step (1) was a covered purchase (although later cases effectively challenged this assumption) or that step (3) was a covered sale, therefore profits from the latter were found recoverable in the courts below. In effect, those courts decided that being a beneficial owner "at" the time of the sale meant having more than 10 percent of the stock "just before" the sale, rather than "just after" it. The only issue before the Supreme Court was whether the court of appeals was right in holding that Emerson was not liable for the profit it made when it sold stock at step (4) on the ground that Emerson was not a 10 percent shareholder at that point in time. Reliance's argument was that steps (3) and (4) should be viewed as constituting only one sale: The apparent immunity of the second sale profits should be lost where the two sales are interrelated parts of a single plan. While this common form of argument — that a sequence of transactions ought to be "integrated" into a whole for purposes of applying some statute or doctrine — carries the day in many contexts involving issues of tax law and corporate law, the Supreme Court refused to accept it here. It held for Emerson and argued that the integration analysis, based as it was on proof of the seller's subjective intent (the plan aspect), was not in harmony with the congressional design of basing liability upon an objective measure of proof.

Timing question at front end

A later case suggests that a defeated tender offeror like Emerson is able to do even better than *Reliance* suggests. Consider a *purchase* of X Corporation stock, which is later sought to be characterized as the first part of a purchase-sale sequence covered by Section 16(b). For the purchaser to be liable, he must be a more than 10 percent shareholder of X at the time of the purchase. But does that mean that it is enough if the purchase in question put the purchaser over the 10 percent mark, even though he previously held little or no stock? That is, does "at the time of" mean "just after" the purchase? Or must the purchaser have already been a more-than-10 percent shareholder? That is, does "at the time of" mean "just before" the purchase?

***Foremost-McKesson* case**

In *Foremost-McKesson, Inc. v. Provident Securities Co.,*[11] the Supreme Court held that the 10 percent test must be satisfied just before the purchase. Among other things, the Court said that Congress viewed trading by mere stockholders (as opposed to directors and officers) as subject to

[11] 423 U.S. 232 (1976).

abuse "only when the size of their holdings afforded the potential for access to corporate information" and that it would be inconsistent with this view to impose liability on the basis of a purchase made when the percentage of ownership requisite to insider status (and thus presumptive access to information) had not already been acquired.[12]

Reliance on statutory purpose

Although *Reliance* and *Foremost McKesson* are often spoken of as cases embodying an objective or mechanical approach to the interpretation of Section 16(b), the preceding remarks should indicate that the choices made by the Court in settling the statute's ambiguities are heavily based on its notions as to what will further the *purpose* of the statute. Taking the cases together, the pattern that emerges is that, when an investor buys and then sells a corporation's stock within six months, his status as beneficial owner for purposes of 16(b) is to be determined by looking at how much stock he owned just before the purchase and just before the sale. If he had more than 10 percent at both points, he is caught, and what he owned just after each step of the sequence is irrelevant. This pattern makes fairly good sense. The 10 percent test is a rule of thumb to determine when someone probably has access to inside information. But probable access to information is only relevant to an insider trading rule if the access exists *at the time of the investment decision* (the buy-sell decision) by the investor in question. The decision to buy or sell stock always occurs sometime before the action of executing a purchase or sale. Hence the 10 percent test should apply to the trader just before the purchase and the sale.

§8.6.3 "Equity Security"

Counting convertibles problem

Section 16(b) only applies to trading in equity securities. The definition of *equity security* in the 1934 Act, however, includes any security, such as a bond or debenture, that is convertible into stock. Suppose an investor owns more than 10 percent of a class of X Corporation's outstanding convertible debentures, although if the debentures were converted the investor would possess less than 1 percent of X's outstanding common stock. For 16(b) purposes, are the convertible debentures to be considered by themselves as a class of any equity security? If so, the investor has 10 percent beneficial owner status, and any purchases and sales of X stock or X convertible debentures during a six month period could give rise to Section 16(b) liability. This view was rejected in *Chemical Fund Inc. v. Xerox Corp.*,[13] which decided that the investor would only have Section 16(b)

[12] 423 U.S. at 253-254.
[13] 377 F.2d 107 (2d Cir. 1967).

insider status if its total position in a class of stock in the company (including stock owned separately from debentures) following full conversion of the debentures would be more than 10 percent of that class of stock then outstanding. In other words, the court viewed the proper class as consisting of the common stock augmented, as to the investor in question, by any common stock into which its debentures were convertible.

Resort to statutory purpose

Once again, the basis of judicial decision of an apparently mechanical point was a conception of the purpose of the statute. The court said that "the reason" why the Section 16(b) statutory insiders were made liable for short-swing profits is that "they are the people who run the corporation, and who are familiar with its day to day workings," whereas "there is no reason whatever to believe that any holder of any Convertible Debentures would, by reason of such holding, normally have any standing or position [so as to be] the recipient of inside information."[14] The SEC refused to accept the court's result for purposes of Section 16(a) reporting purposes, and it has been argued that the court ignored the fact that the 10 percent holder of a registered nonvoting, nonconvertible equity security is clearly subject to Section 16(b), a fact that supposedly suggests that "Congress was not exclusively concerned with actual or potential control."[15] Like many other arguments that try to prove or disprove a legislative purpose by insisting that the legislature must have tried to execute whatever its purpose was with logical consistency, this counterargument is rather unconvincing. For a variety of reasons, nonvoting, nonconvertible stock is comparatively uncommon among publicly held corporations, and Congress, or the draftsmen of Section 16(b), may have given it little or no thought. Yet it is abundantly clear that much thought was given to determining which persons probably have access to inside information.

§8.6.4 "Any Profit"

Highest profits computational approach

Since an insider may engage in numerous purchases and numerous sales of a company's stock within any six month period, and since hundreds of six month time periods can be identified by varying the starting date, the computation of short-swing profits can be conceptually difficult. Relying on a presumed legislative intent "to squeeze all possible profits out of stock transactions" covered by Section 16(b), the court in *Smolowe v. Delendo Corp.*[16] adopted a "lowest in" — "highest out" approach to com-

[14] 377 F.2d at 110-111.

[15] 3B H. Bloomenthal, Securities and Federal Corporate Law §10.04 (1985).

[16] 136 F.2d 231 (2d Cir.), cert. denied, 320 U.S.751 (1943). See also Gratz v. Claughton, 187 F.2d 46 (2d Cir.), cert. denied, 341 U.S. 920 (1951).

puting profits for Section 16(b) purposes: The court matches the highest price sales against the lowest price purchases so that the insider may be held liable for profit even when he suffered an overall trading loss during the six month period in question.[17] In doing so, the court rejected various other alternatives, such as matching the purchase and sale price of particular stock certificates, treating stock first acquired as first to be sold, and using an average sale price and average purchase price during the six month period. Although consistently followed by the courts, the *Smolowe* rule has been subject to criticism by commentators.[18]

§8.7 *Section 16(b): Unorthodox Transactions*

Curbing litigation: How much?

One of the intriguing questions raised by a study of lines of case law development is whether, in a common law system, a legislative attempt to promote ease of administration and thereby to curb litigation is doomed to be compromised, if not totally frustrated, by the combined efforts of courts and disputing parties acting upon the complex variety of transactions that actually occur. In the insider trading context, one wonders whether a supposedly flat prophylactic rule like Section 16(b) can long retain its objective character in such a system of adjudication. For example, the statute clearly covers classic cash purchases and sales of stock. But what about less orthodox transactions? Suppose a statutory insider buys stock of X Corporation and within six months the stock is exchanged for cash or stock of Y Corporation in a merger.[1] Is the exchange of X for Y stock in the merger a

[17] Suppose a director trades in the corporation's shares as follows:

March 5	Purchases 100 at $14
March 20	Sells 100 at $11
June 1	Purchases 200 at $8
June 15	Sells 200 at $9

The net result of these transactions is a $100 loss. Under the lowest-in-highest-out rule, however, the March 20 sale may be matched with 100 shares of the June 1 purchase ($300 gain), and the other 100 shares from June 1 may be matched with 100 shares of the June 15 sale ($100 gain). No offset is allowed for the loss ($500) from the remaining transactions. The director is liable under §16(b) for $400.

[18] See, e.g., W. Painter, Federal Regulation of Insider Trading 29-39 (1968).

§8.7 [1] Merger is a statutory procedure for combining two (or more) corporations. The merging corporation (X, in the example in the text) ceases to exist as a separate legal entity. All of its assets and liabilities, including legal rights and duties, are absorbed by the surviving corporation. In exchange for their shares, X shareholders usually receive securities of the surviving corporation or another, related corporation, cash or cash-equivalent assets, or some combination of these. What they receive is determined by the terms of a merger agreement between the two companies. See chapter 10.

sale for Section 16(b) purposes so that the insider's profit on the exchange is recoverable by the surviving company Y in its role as successor to the rights of X?

Kern County **facts**

The problem can be better appreciated by examining the facts and results in *Kern County Land Co. v. Occidental Petroleum Corp.*,[2] a case that, like *Reliance Electric,* involved a hostile takeover attempt that was defeated by a defensive merger of the target company into a "white knight" company (so called, presumably, because it snatches the target from the fire-breathing jaws of the hostile tender offeror). Within a six month period, the following events happened.

(1) Occidental, the raider, made and extended a tender offer for the shares of Kern County Land Co. (Old Kern), the target, and acquired about 20 percent of the latter's stock.

(2) Old Kern's management negotiated a defensive merger deal with Tenneco, whereby Old Kern would merge into a newly formed shell subsidiary of Tenneco and all the shareholders of Old Kern would receive Tenneco preference stock in exchange for their Old Kern shares.[3]

(3) Sensing that it might lose the takeover battle, and not wanting to be a substantial minority shareholder in an enterprise controlled by its rival Tenneco, or to endure the antitrust problems thereby created,[4] Occidental decided to come to terms with Tenneco. It entered into a call option agreement whereby, for a payment of nearly $9 million, it gave a Tenneco subsidiary the right to buy, at a fixed price, the Tenneco preference stock that Occidental would receive if the defensive merger went through. The option was not exercisable, however, before six months and one day after expiration of Occidental's tender offer.

(4) Old Kern merged into the new Tenneco subsidiary (New Kern), and all Old Kern shareholders, including Occidental, received Tenneco preference stock in exchange for their old Kern stock.

Then, outside the six month period starting with expiration of the tender offer of step (1), the option was exercised, and Occidental sold its Tenneco preference stock to a Tenneco subsidiary at a profit of about $19.5 million. (Being a defeated tender offeror isn't entirely bad!) Finally, New Kern, displaying the same vengeful tendencies as the victor in the *Reliance* case,

[2] 411 U.S. 582 (1973). See also Note, Exceptions to Liability Under Section 16(b): A Systematic Approach, 87 Yale L.J. 1430 (1978).

[3] Actually, it was a "practical" rather than a statutory merger. See chapter 10.

[4] Section 7 of the Clayton Act, 15 U.S.C. §18, forbids one company to acquire stock in another "where in any line of commerce or in any activity affecting commerce in any section of the country, the effect of such acquisition may be substantially to lessen competition, or to tend to create a monopoly."

sued Occidental under Section 16(b), presumably with the blessing and encouragement of Tenneco management. (Knighthood, maybe; chivalry, no.) The theory was that Occidental's step (1) purchase of Old Kern stock could be matched with either the merger or the giving of the option, both of which could be construed as sales of Occidental's Old Kern stock.

Merger not a sale here

No legal precedent or general understanding of terms prevented the Supreme Court from deciding that a merger exchange is within the concept of a sale of stock. The 1934 Act states sweepingly that the term *sale* includes "any contract to sell or otherwise dispose of."[5] The Court had already held that a merger is a sale for purposes of Section 10(b), the chief antifraud provision of the 1934 Act.[6] For a long time the SEC treated mergers as not being sales for purposes of the registration provisions of the 1933 Act, although that interpretive position was subject to change, and it did change.[7] But the Supreme Court, while not laying down a categorical rule for all mergers, refused to treat the Old Kern — New Kern merger as a sale.

> We do not suggest that an exchange of stock pursuant to a merger may never result in §16(b) liability. But the *involuntary nature* of Occidental's exchange, when coupled with the *absence of the possibility of speculative abuse of inside information,* convinces us that §16(b) should not apply to transactions such as this one.[8] (Emphasis added.)

Involuntary as to defendant

Voluntariness is relevant not only because the term *selling* ordinarily connotes a voluntary act (something one does, not something one endures) but also because a person can hardly have been influenced by inside information in his decision to sell stock if in fact he makes no such decision. The merger exchange was involuntary as to Occidental because the merger was arranged by Old Kern's and Tenneco's managements, and Occidental's votes were *not* needed to approve the merger. In fact, Occidental abstained from voting on the merger agreement, a posture that was tantamount under state law to voting against it.

No possibility of abuse

The other factor cited by the Court, absence of possibility for abuse of inside information, is more troublesome. On the one hand, it seems clear that the drafters of 16(b) were concerned about reaching the short-swing profits of investors with access to inside information. It also seems clear that the Court was right in arguing that under the particular factual circum-

[5] Securities Exchange Act §3(a)(14).

[6] SEC v. National Securities, Inc., 393 U.S. 453, 465-468 (1969).

[7] Compare the old Rule 133, 17 C.F.R. §230.133 (rescinded Jan. 1, 1973) with the present Rule 145, 17 C.F.R. §230.145.

[8] 411 U.S. at 600.

stances before it, Occidental was unlikely to have had access to any confidential information about Old Kern, because Occidental was a hostile tender offerer seeking to get control of Old Kern and displace its management and old Kern's management immediately and vigorously opposed those efforts. But Section 16(b) principally measures access to inside information by the admittedly blunt rule-of-thumb method of designating certain classes of investors as statutory insiders: directors, officers, and 10 percent beneficial owners. It seems doubtful that a person who is a director for state corporate law purposes could argue that he should not be considered a director for Section 16(b) purposes because, under the particular circumstances in which he operated, he actually had no access to inside information. If he cannot so argue, does it make sense to allow him to argue his de facto lack of access as a factor relevant to how the word *sale* should be interpreted? Access or the lack thereof seems a quite logically relevant consideration to use in filling in the ambiguities of the concept of a 10 percent beneficial owner but seems beside the point in connection with the concept of sale. The counterargument, of course, is that one should not focus so narrowly on particular words in the statute but should consider it as a whole and determine whether it makes sense to apply the statute to certain classes of transactions.

Doubts about approach

Reach of *Kern*?

But *what* classes of transactions? When the Supreme Court said that Section 16(b) should not apply to "transactions such as this one," what did it mean? Is *Kern* only a case about defensive mergers following hostile takeover attempts? Or does it govern all mergers in which the two factors of nonvoluntariness and nonaccess to information are present? Does it extend even further and apply to all "unorthodox" transactions in which the two factors are present? If so, what are unorthodox transactions?

Later developments

The case law after *Kern* attempts to grapple with these questions. Some of the results are startling. In *Gold v. Sloan,*[9] the court characterized a merger transaction as unorthodox even though the merger was not extraordinary; it proceeded to base its conclusion as to whether a merger exchange of stock was a purchase for Section 16(b) purposes on the particular situation of each director and officer involved. Consequently, it held that a principal negotiator of the merger was liable under Section 16(b) but not the other individual defendants. Clearly, some courts have come a long way from the tough talk of objectivity in *Reliance Electric.*

Sale when option granted?

Two points remain to be explored about the *Kern* case: (1) the option agreement in that case and (2) whether the overall pattern of Section 16(b)

[9] 486 F.2d 340 (4th Cir. 1973), on petition for rehearing, 491 F.2d 729, cert. denied, 419 U.S. 873 (1974).

case law results with respect to takeover battles makes good sense. In response to the argument that the option arrangement in *Kern* should be considered a sale, either because options to sell should always be considered sales or because options that are virtually certain to be exercised in fact should be so considered, the Court argued that the mere execution of an option to sell is not generally regarded as a sale; it stressed the absence of "measurable possibilities for speculative abuse" with respect to the option agreement before it. It pointed out that Occidental's motivation, to avoid becoming a minority shareholder in a rival's enterprise, did not smack of insider trading. It noted that, because Tenneco had a right but not an obligation to buy at a fixed price, Occidental was not going to share in a rising market. It also pointed out that the stock to be sold under the agreement was Tenneco preference stock, yet if Occidental had any inside information it was about Old Kern, not about Tenneco. And it refused to disturb the lower court's rejection, on the basis of its factual findings, of the argument that the option was a de facto sale because the premium paid was so large as to make exercise a virtual certainty.

Altered facts

Was it necessary for Occidental to make the option nonexercisable for six months and a day? Consider the case where the following events occur *within* a six month period.

(1) Raider buys 20 percent of Target Company stock at $50 per share pursuant to a hostile tender offer vigorously resisted by Target management.
(2) Target company arranges and effects a defensive merger into Ally Company. Pursuant to the merger, Raider's stock in Target is converted into shares of Ally stock on a one-for-one basis. Raider winds up with eleven percent of Ally stock.
(3) Raider sells its Ally stock for $80 per share.

Merger not a purchase

Suppose Ally now wants to sue Raider under Section 16(b). Can it match steps (1) and step (2)? No, according to the reasoning of the *Kern* case. Can it match steps (2) and (3), the merger being a purchase by Raider of Ally stock and the sale being the second part of a forbidden sequence? Again the answer appears to be no. If the merger is not a sale for Section 16(b) purposes, because Raider's participation is involuntary and it lacks access to inside information, then it is hard to see how it could be a purchase for Section 16(b) purposes.

Different issuers' securities not matched

Finally, can steps (1) and (3) be matched? There is no doubt that step (1) is a classic rather than an unorthodox purchase and that step (3) is a classic rather than an unorthodox sale, so questions of volition and access to inside information are presumably irrelevant. But the problem now is that the purchase and sale are of different stock (Target's in the one case, Ally's in the other). One might argue that this point should be ignored because Target's assets passed over into Ally's hands by virtue of the merger, so that, at step (3), Ally's stock represents an interest in the old underlying business of Target Company. But Ally's stock also represents an interest in Ally's previously existing lines of business, so it simply is not true that Ally's stock is basically the same as Target stock. Moreover, Section 16(b) refers to trades in the equity security "of such issuer." This use of the singular suggests that matching a purchase of merging company stock with a sale of surviving company stock is improper. And so the court held in *American Standard, Inc. v. Crane Co.*[10]

Moreover, the holding of *Foremost-McKesson* — which, perhaps unfortunately, was decided after the *Kern* and *Crane* cases — would also help Raider greatly. Neither step (1) nor step (2) could be considered a purchase for Section 16(b) purposes if it put Raider over the 10 percent mark and Raider was not already a statutory insider by virtue of some other theory.[11]

Remaining problem for offerors

Indeed, perhaps the only situation that hostile tender offerors have to worry about after these three cases occurs when the tender offeror buys some target stock in a discrete purchase occuring after it first acquires 10 percent beneficial ownership — for example, it acquired 11 percent of the target in one tender offer and another 20 percent by a later offer — and within six months sells the target stock for cash — for example, because it does not want to wait for the actual execution of a defensive merger. Arguably, if the law's objective is to achieve consistent, sensible treatment of takeover situations, even this pattern ought to escape Section 16(b). But in *Allis Chalmers Mfg. Co. v. Gulf & Western Industries, Inc.*,[12] the court decided that *Kern*'s rationale did not extend to a simple sale for cash by a tender offeror after the defensive merger was announced but before it was completed. Since a sale for cash is not an unorthodox transaction, according to the court, an objective rather than a pragmatic approach was required.

Case law costly but sensible

The entire line of cases involving the applicability of Section 16(b) to stock transactions and takeovers illustrates two propositions that have general significance in corporate law, and perhaps in law generally. First, the overall position worked out so laboriously and in such a piecemeal, expensive way by the case law developments is basically correct, and it probably

[10] 510 F.2d 1043 (2d Cir. 1974), cert. denied, 421 U.S. 1000 (1975).

[11] E.g., Feder v. Martin Marietta Corp., 406 F.2d 260 (2d Cir. 1969) (the "deputization" theory), cert. denied, 396 U.S. 1036 (1970).

[12] 527 F.2d 335 (7th Cir. 1975), cert. denied, 424 U.S. 928 (1976).

would have been accepted with little fuss if it had been proposed to draftsmen and legislators from the beginning. The position is essentially as follows. Section 16(b) is supposed to be a flat rule against short-swing profits in situations where trading on inside information is likely to have occurred. When a hostile tender offeror buys stock of a target and later finds it converted in a merger exchange, because of defensive maneuvers of the target, it is unlikely that it will have been trading on inside information. Furthermore, such sales by defeated tender offerors are fairly easy to identify. Therefore, we will exclude such sales from the ambit of Section 16(b).

Drafters not seers

The second proposition is that the statute's ambiguity with respect to the hostile takeover situation is probably due to the draftsmen's inability to anticipate the problem. This inability may simply reflect the fact that takeovers, as a species of recurring corporate behavior, only became common and salient after the statute was passed. Statutes are like that: Their most serious ambiguities are often *not* the result of "poor draftsmanship" — we probably could not have avoided the *Kern* case by exhorting the sponsors of the 1934 Act to draft more carefully and completely — but of *uncertainty* about the nature and prevalence of future patterns of behavior on the part of those sought to be regulated by the law. Case law adjudication, whatever its costs, at least responds to the unpredicted.

§8.8 State Law Approaches: The Agency Theory

***Diamond* approach**

As in many other areas of corporate law, the state courts' common law approach to insider trading vividly reflects the state courts' basic orientation to small-numbers situations and rights among individuals, rather than a focus on the mass production aspects of public stock markets that are essentially national in scope.

In *Diamond v. Oreamuno,*[1] the New York Court of Appeals decided that a stockholders' derivative suit could be maintained to seek corporate recovery of the profits (including averted losses) made by corporate agents (a director and an officer, in the case) by trading on the basis of undisclosed inside information. The corporate recovery aspect is of course reminiscent of 16(b). But the Court did not require a two-part sequence of transactions: On the basis of undisclosed bad news, the insiders in question sold stock that they had held for more than six months. Furthermore, the Court did contemplate proof of actual use of inside information.

§8.8 [1] 248 N.E.2d 910 (N.Y. 1969).

Until fairly recently, it was not uncommon for SEC releases and opinions and federal court opinions discussing insider trading to stress the fairness and perhaps the efficiency that flows from giving all investors participating in the public stock markets equal access to important information or the need to bolster incentives to prompt disclosure. (As will become apparent later, especially in sections 8.10.2 and 8.12, this theme has been downplayed since the Supreme Court decision in the *Chiarella* case.) But in *Diamond,* the state court grounded its decision squarely upon the fiduciary misconduct view of what is wrong with insider trading. It asserted,

Fiduciary misconduct

> It is well established, as a general proposition, that a person who acquires special knowledge or information by virtue of a confidential or fiduciary relationship with another is not free to exploit that knowledge or information for his own personal benefit but must account to his principal for any profits derived therefrom. This, in turn is merely a corollary of the broader principles, inherent in the nature of the fiduciary relationship, that prohibits a trustee or agent from extracting secret profits from his position of trust.[2]

It supported its argument by quoting from Restatement (Second) of Agency §388, comment c, which makes the same point about use of confidential information by an agent and explicitly applies it to a corporate officer possessing inside information.

Arguments for corporate recovery

Recognizing that corporate recovery did not seem to help all and only those who most obviously seemed to be harmed by insider trading, the court tried to justify corporate recovery in several ways. First, it asserted that a function of an action founded on breach of a fiduciary duty is not merely to compensate injured plaintiffs but to deter such breaches by taking away the defendants' hope of gains. It argued that insider trading might cause some harm to the corporation as such, since the latter might well have an interest in maintaining a reputation for managerial integrity. Oddly, it did not then analyze the factors that may make a derivative suit a more realistic remedy than a common law–based class action by injured stock purchasers. Instead, it then argued that it was especially appropriate to affirm the existence of some common law remedy in light of the gaps existing in federal law under Section 16(b) and Section 10(b). It proceeded to defend this view against the specter of possible double liability by noting that the defendants can interplead injured stock purchasers if they fear the latter may have a superior claim (as against the corporation) to the agents' illicit profits.

Problems

These arguments probably did, and should have, left many observers

[2] 248 N.E.2d at 912. See also Brophy v. Cities Service Co., 70 A.2d 5 (Del. Ch. 1949).

feeling uneasy. In effect, the *Diamond* court failed to face up to the conceptual problems of fitting insider trading under a traditional, narrowly defined conception of fiduciary misconduct. Many people, including the New York Court of Appeals, probably would view the parties primarily injured by the insiders' conduct in that case to be the investors who bought into the company's stock while the corporate bad news should have been, but was not, disclosed. Why didn't the court consider the advisability of putting the common law remedy in the hands of that class of persons? One reason is that many of those purchasers may have bought after the insiders sold their own stock on the basis of inside information. The court would have to have been willing to say that insiders owe fiduciary duties to persons who are not yet shareholders. Another is that continuing shareholders would not have been in the class. The court would have to have been willing to say that the fiduciary duty runs not to the corporation but to shareholders and, indeed, to a subclass of them.

Need different concept of fiduciary

Now, there is nothing logically insuperable or practically untenable about saying that fiduciaries and agents of a publicly held corporation have a fiduciary duty *running to all investors who trade in the corporation's securities* and should refrain from trading against them on the basis of confidential inside information. Indeed, in the context of giant corporations and national securities markets, it seems fitting to view managers as a class as owing duties to public investors in general. The state courts' difficulty in viewing matters in this light seems a consequence of their relative immersion in close corporation cases and in other disputes involving small numbers of definite, identifiable participants.

***Diamond* not followed**

In any event, *Diamond*'s failure to fully explore and analyze the nature of the possible fiduciary duties that could be placed on insiders of public corporations came home to roost in *Schein v. Chasen.*[3] In that case, the Florida Supreme Court not only declined to extend the *Diamond* theory to tippees of corporate agents, on the ground that mere tippees could not be fairly characterized as fiduciaries with respect to a corporation of which they were not directly officers, employees, or the like, but also refused even to adopt the basic *Diamond* approach on the ground that a derivative suit is only appropriate where the plaintiff alleges actual damages to the corporation. To the Florida court, the possible indirect damage that insider trading might cause to a corporation's well-being, via the reduction of potential investors' confidence in management's integrity, seemed too

[3]313 So. 2d 739 (Fla. 1975). Similarly, a federal court applying Indiana law opined that Indiana courts would not follow the *Diamond* approach. Freeman v. Decio, 584 F.2d 186 (7th Cir. 1978).

speculative and uncertain to count. Once again, the problem seems to be a lack of vision in a court used to close corporation cases: The failure to recognize that fiduciary duties can be owed to the general investing public and not just to specific corporations and to known co-adventurers.

§8.9 *Rule 10b-5: Introduction*

A catchall antifraud provision

The federal securities laws contain a number of provisions directed against fraud and manipulation in securities transactions. Section 10(b) of the 1934 Act, which was designedly a catchall provision, is the most open-ended and the most important. It declares it unlawful for any person to employ, in connection with the purchase or sale of any security, "any manipulative or deceptive device or contrivance" in contravention of SEC rules.[1] The subsection does not prohibit anything unless there is an SEC rule implementing it. In 1942, in order to deal with the *purchase* by a corporate president of a company's securities on the basis of misrepresentations about its financial condition, the SEC adopted Rule 10b-5. The language of the rule is based upon Section 17(a) of the 1933 Act, which, because that act was aimed mainly at regulation of the initial offering and distribution of securities to the public, prohibited fraud only in connection with *sales* of securities. The text of Rule 10b-5 is as follows:

> It shall be unlawful for any person, directly or indirectly, by the use of any means or instrumentality of interstate commerce, or of the mails, or of any facility of any national securities exchange,
>
> (1) to employ any device, scheme, or artifice to defraud,
> (2) to make any untrue statement of a material fact or to omit to state a

§8.9 [1]Sec. 10:

> It shall be unlawful for any person, directly or indirectly, by the use of any means or instrumentality of interstate commerce or of the mails, or of any facility of any national securities exchange . . .
>
> (b) To use or employ, in connection with the purchase or sale of any security registered on a national securities exchange or any security not so registered, any manipulative or deceptive device or contrivance in contravention of such rules and regulations as the Commission may prescribe as necessary or appropriate in the public interest or for the protection of investors.

Unlike §16(b), §10(b) applies to *all* securities, not just to equity securities of registered companies, and to *all* persons not just to directors, officers, and ten percent shareholders. The jurisdictional requirement of the use of the mails or an instrumentality of interstate commerce has been broadly interpreted to give the statute maximum scope. See, e.g., Dupuy v. Dupuy, 511 F.2d 641 (5th Cir. 1975) (jurisdictional requirement satisfied by intrastate telephone call), cert. denied, 434 U.S. 911 (1977).

material fact necessary in order to make the statements made, in the light of the circumstances under which they were made, not misleading, or

(3) to engage in any act, practice or course of business which operates or would operate as a fraud or deceit upon any person in connection with the purchase or sale of any security.

Such a vast jurisprudence has arisen under this rule that it has been referred to as an acorn that grew into a mighty oak.

Coverage and origin

Rule 10b-5 covers insider trading of the paradigmatic kind discussed in section 8.1, but it goes well beyond it to include frauds and misrepresentations of many kinds, such as stock manipulation schemes and false or misleading press releases issued by corporations. These other kinds of fraudulent activity will be discussed in section 8.11. At present, it is sufficient to note that 10b-5 originated in the need, which became more pressing with the rise of the modern corporation and the national securities markets, to transcend the gaps and limits of the common law actions available to securities traders injured by false representations or failures to disclose.

Action for deceit

The most important of the common law remedies was the cause of action based on deceit. Although summarization ignores intertemporal and jurisdictional variations, the plaintiff in such an action basically has to prove that the defendant

(1) made a false representation
(2) of a material fact
(3) with knowledge of its falsity or with reckless disregard for its truth; and
(4) with the intention that the plaintiff act in reliance upon the representation; and that
(5) the plaintiff did justifiably rely on the representation; and
(6) thereby suffered damages.[2]

Unsatisfying regarding insider trading

In most situations, therefore, the action of deceit was not available to deal with insider trading. The general rule in commercial matters seems to have been that mere silence or failure to disclose facts did not amount to deceit — silence was not a representation — unless the parties stood in some confidential or fiduciary relationship to one another or other special

[2] W. Prosser, Handbook of the Law of Torts 728 (5th ed. 1984).

factors were present.[3] But the majority rule appears to have been that corporate directors and officers owe their fiduciary duties to the corporation, not to the shareholders personally, so that shareholders selling to an officer who purchased on the basis of inside information would ordinarily have no remedy.[4] There was a contrary minority rule,[5] to be sure, and some courts adopted an intermediate stance known as the special facts doctrine under which corporate directors and officers have a duty to disclose information to selling shareholders where "special circumstances or facts" exist that would make nondisclosure "inequitable."[6] But these occasional and vague developments were hardly satisfying.

Furthermore, virtually no cases were ever brought by those buying stock from corporate managers who *sold* on the basis of inside information, apparently because everyone assumed that, whether or not managers owe existing shareholders a direct fiduciary duty, they do not owe such a duty to those who are not yet shareholders.

Especially on stock markets

And finally, common law cases rejected the proposition that managers owe a duty of disclosure to selling shareholders when they buy shares in faceless transactions in the stock markets, that is, in transactions where the buyer is not aware of the identity of the prior owner of the stock he

[3]But see Keeton, Fraud — Concealment and Nondisclosure, 15 Tex. L. Rev. 1 (1936) (developing "ordinary ethical person" standard), arguing that a broader basis for imposition of a duty to disclose existed in the case law. In any event, in more recent years courts deciding tort cases have often found a duty to disclose after an inquiry into several factors, the relationship between the parties being only one of them. See, e.g., Jim Short Ford Sales, Inc. v. Washington, 384 So. 2d 83, 86-87 (Ala. 1980): "A duty to speak depends on the relation of the parties, the value of the particular fact, the relative knowledge of the parties, and other circumstances. Thus, each case must be individually examined to determine whether a duty of disclosure exists; a rigid approach is impossible." Courts have recognized in sellers a duty to disclose certain material facts to buyers with whom they have had no prior dealings, relying heavily upon the findings that the facts are available only to the seller and that the buyer would clearly want to know the information but cannot himself discover it. Anderson, Fraud, Fiduciaries and Insider Trading, 10 Hofstra L. Rev. 341, 351-353 (1982); Levmore, Securities and Secrets: Insider Trading and the Law of Contracts, 68 Va. L. Rev. 117, 133-134 (1982). See, e.g., Obde v. Schlemeyer, 353 P.2d 672 (Wash. 1960).

Oddly, in view of these modern developments, the United States Supreme Court, in Chiarella v. U.S., 445 U.S. 222, 232 (1980), adopted the view that a duty to disclose (under Section 10b-5) could only arise from a fiduciary or similar relationship. See section 8.10.2 infra.

[4]E.g., Board of Comm. v. Reynolds, 44 Ind. 509 (1873); Goodman v. Poland, 395 F. Supp. 660 (D. Md. 1975) (Maryland law); and cases cited in 3A W. Fletcher, Cyclopedia Corporations §1168.1 (perm. ed. 1975 & supp.).

[5]E.g., Hotchkiss v. Fischer, 16 P.2d 531 (Kan. 1932); and cases cited in 3A W. Fletcher, note 4 supra, at §1168.2.

[6]Strong v. Repide, 213 U.S. 419 (1909). See also cases cited in 3A W. Fletcher, note 4 supra, at §1171.

acquires and vice-versa.[7] This rejection may have resulted from the courts' familiarity with and psychological attachment to the basic factual paradigm of the deceit action, where a particular defendant was alleged to have tried to deceive a particular plaintiff. But, as we shall see later (section 8.10), traditional notions of reliance and privity were simply ways of conceptualizing the causation requirement of tort actions; they do not constitute necessary elements of a sensible antifraud cause of action.

In any event, the reasoning of the court in the major case of this sort, *Goodwin v. Agassiz,*[8] is supremely unconvincing. It assumed that a duty to disclose would mean that the director would have to seek out the other actual party to the stock trade and disclose "everything which a court or jury might later find that he then knew affecting the real or speculative value of such shares,"[9] and that this "onerous" requirement would deter honest, experienced, and able men from becoming directors. The court blithely ignored the possibility that the director could simply abstain from trading until a public announcement — by means of a press release, for example — of all important corporate information had been made.[10]

Enter Rule 10b-5

Against this bleak common law background, the SEC adopted Rule 10b-5. This made it possible for the SEC to enforce an open-ended antifraud provision by seeking an injunction in the federal courts or by referring the matter to the Department of Justice for possible criminal prosecution.[11] It opened the way for later decisions that applied the rule to insider trading.[12]

Private civil actions allowed

But perhaps the main impetus for the growth of a liberal antifraud jurisprudence was a 1946 decision permitting a private party to bring a civil action based on Rule 10b-5. That decision, *Kardon v. National Gypsum Co.,*[13] purported to be merely applying an accepted canon of statutory interpretation. As every first year law student should know, there is a standard collection of tort cases[14] dealing with the implications for civil tort actions of

[7]Goodwin v. Agassiz, 186 N.E. 659 (Mass. 1933).

[8]See id.

[9]186 N.E. at 661.

[10]The court's extreme statement of a possible disclosure duty and its bad effects is a classic illustration of the hyperbole that characterizes much of the rhetoric supporting management's discretion to determine its own share of enterprise profits.

[11]See 1 A. Bromberg & L. Lowenfels, Securities Fraud and Commodities Fraud, §2.2 (410-420) (1984).

[12]The seminal decision was In the Matter of Cady, Roberts & Co., 40 S.E.C. 907 (1961).

[13]69 F. Supp. 512 (E.D. Pa. 1946). See also Wachovia Bank & Trust Co. v. National Student Mkt. Corp., 650 F.2d 342 (D.C. Cir. 1980), cert. denied, 452 U.S. 954 (1981).

[14]E.g., Ross v. Hartman, 139 F.2d 14 (D.C. Cir. 1943), cert. denied, 321 U.S. 790 (1944); Osborne v. McMasters, 41 N.W. 543 (Minn. 1899); Martin v. Herzog, 126 N.E. 814 (N.Y. 1920). See generally W. Prosser, Handbook of the Law of Torts §36 (5th ed. 1984).

the fact that a defendant violated a criminal statute: whether the violation constitutes conclusive proof of negligence, creates a presumption, or is merely admissible evidence of negligence; whether and under what condition a person injured as a result of the defendant's violation may base a civil suit thereon; and so forth. The *Kardon* court relied upon the summary of the law in Section 286 in the Restatement of Torts, which made the violator liable in a tort action if the intent of the statute was exclusively or in part to protect an interest of the other individual and the interest invaded is one that the statute was intended to protect. Put differently, if the plaintiff fell within the class of persons intended to be protected by the statute, and his alleged harm was within the class of harms the statute was directed against, he could sue, despite the fact that the legislature did not provide for a civil remedy. Although this species of reasoning is not unusual in the common law legal system, its application to create a private civil action under Rule 10b-5 has been strongly criticized.[15]

Squaring express and implied remedies

One of the major conundrums facing the courts in cases in which plaintiffs sought to pursue civil remedies was that of trying to enunciate a holding consistent with other provisions of the federal securities laws. The key fact is that the 1933 Act provides *express* causes of action by defrauded or misled buyers of securities, but these remedies are carefully circumscribed and limited by the statute.[16] According to the notable opinion

[15] E.g., Ruder, Civil Liability under Rule 10b-5: Judicial Revision of Legislative Intent? 57 Nw. U.L. Rev. 627 (1963).

[16] Section 11 of the Securities Act prohibits material misstatements and omissions in registration statements. Any purchaser of a security registered under a defective registration statement can sue for the difference between the purchase price (not exceeding the public offering price) and the value at the time of suit or, if the plaintiff has sold, the sale price. The statute specifies the persons liable, including the issuer, its directors, the underwriters, and certain experts (e.g., accountants) who participated in the preparation of the registration statement. The plaintiff is not required to prove reliance on the misstatements or omissions, unless he purchased after the issuer made available an earnings report covering a one year period commencing after the date of the registration (§11(a)).

Liability may be avoided by proving that the plaintiff knew of the misstatement or omission at the time of purchase (§11(a)), or may be reduced by proof that all or part of the decline in the security's price was due to causes other than the defective registration statement (§11(e)). Defendants (other than the issuer) may escape liability by establishing that they acted with "due diligence" (§11(b)); this standard of care varies according to the defendant's relationship with the issuer and connection with the registration statement.

Section 12(2) of the Securities Act imposes liability on a *seller* of registered or unregistered securities for material misstatements or omissions (not known to the buyer) in any communication, written or oral, through which the securities are offered or sold. The specified remedy is rescission, or damages if the plaintiff no longer owns the securities. A defense of "reasonable care" is allowed.

See generally section 17.4 infra.

in *Ellis v. Carter,*[17] this left the courts with essentially four options, none of which was entirely satisfactory.

First, they could refuse to imply any private right of action under Rule 10b-5. But this would leave defrauded sellers without a remedy under the securities laws.

Second, they could imply a private right of action only for sellers. But this seems logically indefensible, since Section 10(b) refers indiscriminately to frauds "in connection with the purchase or sale" of any security.

Third, they could imply private rights of action for both sellers and buyers, but import procedural and other limitations on express rights of action under the 1933 Act to the implied actions brought by buyers, in order not to permit circumvention of those limitations. Again, the problem of consistency with the language of Section 10(b) arises.

Fourth, they could imply private rights of action for both buyers and sellers, without any distinctions, and free of the restrictions imposed under the 1933 Act. This creates at least the appearance of fashioning a judicial remedy that partially nullifies provisions in a related statute, but it is the alternative chosen by the court in *Ellis.* So much for the perfect internal consistency of the federal securities laws.

Of course, the decision in *Ellis* can hardly be evaluated fairly in terms of whether or not it left us with a consistent matrix of remedies. No matter what it did, the court was bound to offend some interest. Although it sacrificed some intrastatutory consistency, it did not sacrifice the general common law tradition of creating specific tort actions at the suggestion of legislative enactments, nor did it sacrifice the interests of defrauded public investors.

Thereafter, the propriety of a private right of action under Rule 10b-5 was generally accepted without serious question during the later 1960s and the 1970s.[18] But with the perceived shift of the Supreme Court toward stricter construction of the securities laws, unhappy defendants pressed the issue again. Since an argument that private actions should *never* be allowed under Rule 10b-5 seemed unlikely to prevail, the attack focused on

[17] 291 F.2d 270 (9th Cir. 1961).

[18] By 1961, the time of the *Ellis* decision, four courts of appeal and several district courts in other circuits had recognized a private remedy under Rule 10b-5, and only one district court decision had reached a contrary conclusion. See 3 L. Loss, Securities Regulations 1763 -1764 and nn. 260-263 (2d ed. 1961). By 1969, 10 of the 11 courts of appeal had recognized the private cause of action. See 6 L. Loss, Securities Regulation 3871-3873 (2d ed. supp. 1969). The Supreme Court itself acknowledged, albeit without discussion, the existence of the private action on several occasions. Ernst & Ernst v. Hochfelder, 425 U.S. 185, 196, reh. denied, 425 U.S. 986 (1976); Superintendent of Ins. v. Bankers Life & Cas. Co., 404 U.S. 6, 13, n.9 (1971).

those factual situations where plaintiffs had an alternative, express remedy. The basic argument was that a private action under Rule 10b-5 would simply weaken the constraints and procedures embodied in the express cause of action. Nevertheless, in 1983, in *Herman & MacLean v. Huddleston,*[19] the Supreme Court held that purchasers of registered securities who alleged that they were defrauded by misrepresentations in a registration statement may maintain an action under Section 10(b), notwithstanding the apparent availability of the express remedy for misstatements and omissions in registration statements granted by Section 11 of the Securities Act of 1933.

***Herman & MacLean* case**

Court's rationale

But doesn't this holding wreak havoc with the scheme of express remedies in these securities laws? The Court thought not. Its principal argument on this issue is that Section 10(b) and Section 11 actions are complementary rather than conflicting, because they involve different but related policy tradeoffs. Section 11 is limited in scope but places a relatively light burden on plaintiffs. Section 10(b) is a sweeping, "catchall" antifraud provision but requires plaintiffs to carry a heavier burden. Specifically, in a Section 10(b) action the plaintiff has to prove that defendant acted with scienter, that is, with intent to deceive, manipulate, or defraud, whereas the Section 11 plaintiff does not. It is as if the scienter requirement compensates for the possibilities of abuse inherent in a catchall cause of action. (See also section 8.10.3 infra.)

Other possible conflicts

The reasoning in *Herman & MacLean* leaves room for case-by-case adjudication of other possible conflicts between the implied private right of action under Section 10(b) and various other express causes of action under the securities laws, because the Court's method of analysis — asking whether the two causes of action are complementary rather than conflicting —may not yield the same answer for each possible conflict. Thus, for example, a district court later held that (1) there is no private Section 10(b) action against a broker-dealer when a 1934 Act Section 15(c) action lies against it for the same conduct; but (2) a Section 10(b) action is proper even though a 1933 Act Section 12(2) action might also lie; and (3) an implied right of action under 1933 Act Section 17(a) is in addition to any express remedies purchasers may have.[20]

An endless game

After noting the third of these just enumerated holdings, the perceptive reader will ask whether this game might be played on a grander scale. Section 10(b) is only one provision. Might not the courts have to decide

[19] 459 U.S. 375 (1983).

[20] Amunrud v. Taurus Drilling Ltd., Fed. Sec. L. Rep. (CCH) §99,649 (D. Mont. Dec. 23, 1983).

whether there should be implied private rights of action under numerous other provisions of the securities laws? Might not the decisions be complicated by considerations of possible overlap and conflict with other, express rights of action granted by those laws? Might not the existence of overlaps depend on certain kinds of factual patterns, so that general answers to the preceding two questions will be difficult? In short, do we not have here a rich mine of possible legal issues that can serve as the basis for protracted litigation which will generate substantial income for lawyers? The answer to all these questions is yes. There is a vast and dreary jurisprudence on these issues.[21]

§8.10 Rule 10b-5: Elements of the Cause of Action

Issues for resolution

Once a private right of action under Rule 10b-5 was implied and recognized, there was bound to be a period of painful growth, as the courts struggled to give shape and meaning to the standard list of elements of a tort action as applied to the new context. Who was to have standing to bring private actions? Who could be sued? What exactly would constitute the duty imposed? What would be needed to show a violation of the duty and causation of injury? What would the measure of damages be? Interestingly, the case law developments show clearly the importance of a conservative versus a liberal orientation in the Supreme Court. They also illustrate the importance of having one conception or another of the harm caused by insider trading (see section 8.2 above).

§8.10.1 Who Can Sue: The Purchaser-Seller Doctrine

***Blue Chip Stamps* case**

For roughly 15 years prior to 1975, the federal courts had been expanding the reach of Rule 10b-5 and generally upgrading standards of conduct affected by the rule. In that year, however, the Supreme Court, recently constituted to have a conservative majority, inaugurated a series of securities law holdings whose common theme seemed to be that plaintiffs always lost.[1] The watershed case, *Blue Chip Stamps v. Manor Drug*

[21] See generally Aldave, "Neither Unusual Nor Unfortunate": The Overlap of Rule 10b-5 with the Express Liability Sections of the Securities Acts, 60 Tex. L. Rev. 719 (1982); Steinberg, The Propriety and Scope of Cumulative Remedies under the Federal Securities Laws, 67 Cornell L. Rev. 557 (1982).

§8.10 [1] E.g., Blue Chip Stamps v. Manor Drug Stores, 421 U.S. 723, reh. denied, 423 U.S. 884 (1975); Ernst & Ernst v. Hochfelder, 425 U.S. 185, reh. denied, 425 U.S. 986 (1976); Santa Fe Industries v. Green, 430 U.S. 462 (1977); Chiarella v. United States, 445 U.S. 222 (1980);

Stores,[2] concerned a question of standing to bring suit. The facts were unusual. Pursuant to an antitrust consent decree, a trading stamp company agreed with the Department of Justice to offer to sell stock in itself on favorable terms to a certain class of retailers, who were the alleged victims of the company's anticompetitive practices. The offering was made, and more than 50 percent of the offered units were purchased. Two years later, one of the offerees who had not bought the stock brought suit on behalf of itself and other such offerees under Rule 10b-5, alleging that the prospectus given to the offerees had been made unduly pessimistic precisely in order to discourage them from buying, so that the rejected shares could later be offered and sold to the general investing public at a higher price. The Supreme Court held that the plaintiff was not entitled to sue for violation of Rule 10b-5 because persons who are not actual purchasers or sellers of securities involved in the allegedly fraudulent transaction or scheme cannot base a private action on the rule.

Purchaser-seller doctrine

From an historical perspective, the Court viewed itself as reaffirming the purchaser-seller doctrine, which had been enunciated in 1952 by an outstanding panel of Second Circuit judges in the case of *Birnbaum v. Newport Steel Corp.*[3] but which had been attacked by the SEC and certain commentators.[4] From the point of view of an original legal analysis, the matter was not free from doubt. Section 10(b) outlaws frauds "in connection with the purchase or sale" of securities, but it does not specify what kind of connection there must be, nor does it say that particular plaintiffs or defendants must actually have bought or sold securities. Indeed, even after *Blue Chip* no one suggests that *defendants* in Section 10(b) actions must have bought or sold a security.

Rationale

Justice Rehnquist, who wrote the majority opinion in *Blue Chip*, tried to support the purchaser-seller doctrine in two major ways. First, he deployed the usual army of reasonable but inconclusive arguments concerning the language of the statute, the past practice of the courts, the implications suggested by other provisions of the securities laws, and the apparent intent of Congress. As Rehnquist recognized, this tactic could have only limited success. One argument as to the intent of Congress, for example, was that Congress had twice failed to enact SEC-sponsored securities law amendments that included a proposed addition to Section 10(b)

Aaron v. SEC, 446 U.S. 680 (1980). See also 1 A. Bromberg & L. Lowenfels, Securities Fraud and Commodities Fraud § 2.2 (463) (1984).

[2] 421 U.S. 723 (1975).

[3] 193 F.2d 461 (2d Cir.), cert. denied, 343 U.S. 956 (1952).

[4] E.g., Lowenfels, The Demise of the *Birnbaum* Doctrine: A New Era for Rule 10b-5, 54 Va. L. Rev. 268 (1968).

of the words "or any attempt to purchase or sell" (any security) after the words "in connection with any purchase or sale." Anyone familiar with the workings of Congress would of course be skeptical as to whether anything was proved by these episodes.

Vexatious litigation theme

Second, however, Rehnquist composed a long fugue on the theme of vexatious litigation. He argued that there was "widespread recognition" that litigation under Rule 10b-5 presents a danger of vexatiousness different in degree and in kind from that which accompanies litigation in general. In his view, the likelihood of strike suits — those brought without merit but which nevertheless have a settlement value because the plaintiff can force the defendant to submit to costly discovery proceedings — and the need to rely on hazy oral testimony were especially great if the purchaser-seller limitation were abandoned. Thus, Rehnquist viewed the purchaser-seller rule as a kind of filter to strain out suits that were most likely to be unmeritorious.

A parade of horribles

In his concurring opinion, Justice Powell, with whom Justices Stewart and Marshall joined, articulated a version of the argument that is more moderate in tone. Powell paraded a horrible picture of what would happen if the court were to abandon the *Birnbaum* rule in favor of that argued for by the dissent. Every time that a company offered the public new securities that later enjoyed a large price increase, the alternative rule would "invite" all nonbuyers of the securities to sue and claim that the prospectus wrongly understated the securities' value. The number of possible plaintiffs with respect to each security offering would be virtually unlimited. It would be hard to refute plaintiffs' assertions that they read and relied on the prospectuses. And the claims of understatement would often appear nonfrivolous because the SEC's policy with regard to prospectuses has long been the negative one of encouraging great caution in the statements made by offerors in their prospectuses. Thus, without the *Birnbaum* rule, many fraudulent and baseless suits might be filed.

Skeptical reaction

Powell's worst case scenario may seem to prove that the *Blue Chip* result is quite reasonable or even necessary. But this impression changes when one considers two other factors: (1) the normal structure of incentives to engage in fraudulent misrepresentations in connection with securities transactions and (2) the existence of alternative mechanisms for filtering out vexatious suits. The plaintiffs in *Blue Chip,* we must remember, were in a rather unusual position. In the ordinary case, what the fraudulent seller of securities wants to do is conceal bad information about the issuing corporation and make it appear better than it is, so that the buyers will pay a higher price. Consequently, the persons injured by his fraud are *actual* buyers of the securities, and so they are fixed in number and easily identified. Those who considered buying but who, for whatever reason, did not buy, were simply lucky; they escaped the consequences of the fraud and clearly have no basis for a lawsuit. Similarly, what a fraudulent buyer of securities usually wants to do is conceal good information about the issuer or paint an erroneous bad picture of its fortunes in order to buy the securities cheaply. Again, all the injured persons are actual sellers.

Oddity of *Blue Chip* facts

The *Blue Chip* plaintiffs had a plausible claim only because of a fairly peculiar fact situation. (In general, the situations in which liberalizing or abandoning the purchaser-seller rule would make a difference are rare.) The offeror in *Blue Chip* was in the unusual position of having to offer to sell stock at a *fixed price* that was designed to be a bargain to the offerees, while knowing that the unsold stock could later be marketed to the public at a higher price. It therefore had an incentive, quite opposite the normal one for sellers, to disparage its own stock. Furthermore, the class of people to whom it directed a message and as to whom it had this perverse incentive was quite definite and limited — the offerees who were made such by virtue of the antitrust consent decree. Thus the Court, even though it was gravely concerned about floods of strike suits under Rule 10b-5, might reasonably have reached one of two conclusions other than its actual one.

First, and most cautiously, it might have reaffirmed the purchaser-seller limitation in general while interpreting the term *purchaser* to include, for the purpose of applying this judge-made limitation, any class of offerees possessing the essential characteristics of the offerees in *Blue Chip,* — that is, offerees who were objectively *limited* in number and faced with an offeror who had a specifically identifiable, nontrivial incentive to downplay the value of the offered securities. Such an interpretation would not exceed the bounds of permissible linguistic propriety. The securities laws define *sale* as including a contract for sale,[5] and in practical terms the offerees in *Blue Chip* were very much like persons holding a contractual option to buy. Thus, the Court could have kept the dike safe against the fearsome floods of specious litigation while nevertheless doing justice in the particular case.

Fear of erosion

Why did it not do at least this much? The answer, I think, is that the conservative members of the Court were afraid of embracing a case-by-case, common law method of adjudication in this area. They feared that the relief valve of policy-oriented but fact-dependent exceptions might easily be eroded into a fatal leak through which the invading plaintiffs' attorneys would pour. Indeed, precisely in the context of rejecting the Court of Appeals' expanded reading of *Birnbaum,* Justice Rehnquist speaks with

[5]Securities Act §2(3); Securities Exchange Act §3(a)(14).

obvious horror of "endless case-by-case erosion."[6] Thus, we can see the importance of the Supreme Court's using a case in which the actual plaintiffs' position was a fairly appealing one as the occasion for reaffirming *Birnbaum*. *Blue Chip* is as significant for its effort to adopt a flat, objective, tough rule as it is for a holding about the purchaser-seller limitation.

Other filters of frivolous suits

The point becomes clearer if we consider the second approach the Supreme Court could have taken given the *normal* structure of incentives faced by potentially fraudulent securities traders. Why didn't the Court simply abandon the purchaser-seller rule entirely and rely on other elements of the cause of action, or various procedural resources, to filter out unmeritorious suits? After all, it is hard to believe that plaintiffs who alleged that they bought or sold stock because of the defendant's false statements or omissions are almost always the serious plaintiffs, while plaintffs who allege that they were tricked into not buying or not selling because of the defendant's false statements or omissions are almost always the frivolous plaintiffs. If there is this fit between the categories it is undoubtedly a loose one. The question then becomes: Isn't there a better filter than actual purchaser-seller status that can be used to strain out unmeritorious plaintiffs? The answer is that there are better filters and that, remarkably, one of the best of them was adopted by the Supreme Court in the year after the *Blue Chip* decision. If that filter, the scienter test discussed in subsection 8.10.3, had been firmly in place when the Court decided *Blue Chip*, one wonders whether the Court's vexatious litigation argument would have carried much persuasive force.

§8.10.2 Who Can Be Sued: Fiduciaries, Tippees, and Others

Disclose or abstain duty

In a sense, the persons who can be sued under Rule 10b-5 are obvious: those who violate the duties it imposes. It is apparent from the language of the rule that this includes all persons who make misrepresentations and misleading omissions in connection with the purchase or sale of securities. Some aspects of these duties are explored below in section 8.11. But what about persons engaged in classic insider trading? Are they covered by Rule 10b-5? Yes. They are governed by the duty to "disclose or abstain": Insiders in possession of material inside information must either disclose the information before trading in the securities whose value may be affected by the information, or, if unable or unwilling to do so, must refrain from

[6] 421 U.S. at 755.

trading in those securities until the information is made public in some other way. This disclose or abstain duty was declared to be an implication of Rule 10b-5 by the SEC in its *Cady, Roberts* opinion,[7] was adopted by the Second Circuit in the important case of *SEC v. Texas Gulf Sulphur Co.*[8] and then by other courts, and has been recognized with greater or lesser degrees of directness by the United States Supreme Court.[9]

Questions of scope

As formulated above, the disclose or abstain duty leaves open a number of questions. Some are questions of detail. If one bound by the duty chooses to disclose, how does he go about it? (A press release should usually do the trick.) Does he have to wait until the market has had time to "digest" the information before he trades? (Yes.) Two other questions go more to the basic scope of the duty.

First, should the duty be phrased in terms of all material nonpublic information, whatever its source, or only in terms of inside information in the narrower sense of information generated by or arising within the particular corporate hierarchy? Consider, for example, the information that the Federal Reserve Board will change monetary policy in a way that will depress the price of Ajax Company's stock, which Ulysses, a vice president of Ajax, has learned from a faithless governor of the Board. Contrast this with the information that Ajax will soon release a dreary quarterly report that will also depress its price, which Menelaus, another vice president, learns because he helped prepare the report as part of his job. The question whether these situations should be treated differently will be explored in section 8.12.

Only conventional insiders?

Second, does the disclose or abstain duty apply to *anyone* in possession of material inside (or nonpublic) information, or only to those who are insiders in some more conventional sense, such as officers and employees of the corporation in question? This is the question that is explored in this subsection.

Supreme Court cases

Two Supreme Court cases bear directly on the issue. *Chiarella*[10] established that persons who merely trade on material nonpublic information, without violating some specific fiduciary duty or similar duty, do not thereby violate Rule 10b-5. *Dirks*[11] established that a tippee's liability is derivative from that of his ultimate tipper.

Facts of *Dirks*

Dirks is instructive on both points. Mr. Dirks was an officer of a broker-

[7] In the Matter of Cady, Roberts & Co., 40 S.E.C. 907 (1961).

[8] 401 F.2d 833 (2d Cir. 1968), cert. denied, 394 U.S. 976 (1969).

[9] See, e.g., Chiarella v. United States, 445 U.S. 222, 227 (1980).

[10] See note 9 supra. See Langevoort, Insider Trading and the Fiduciary Principle: A Post-*Chiarella* Restatement, 70 Calif. L. Rev. 1 (1982).

[11] Dirks v. SEC, 463 U.S. 646 (1983).

dealer firm and specialized in doing investment analyses of insurance company securities for institutional investors. Secrist, a former officer of Equity Funding, an insurance company that sold a once hot product that combined life insurance with an investment in a mutual fund, told him that Equity Funding's assets were vastly overstated as a result of widespread fraudulent practices. (Among other things, Equity Funding employees would hold forgery parties at which they would make up imaginary insurance contracts, which the company would then resell to other institutions.) Dirks was also informed that various regulatory agencies had failed to act on similar charges by company employees. He proceeded to investigate. Some company employees corroborated the fraud charges; senior management denied them. Dirks tried to get the Wall Street Journal to publish a story about the fraud allegations, but it declined to do so.

Throughout his investigation, Dirks discussed the information he had obtained with a number of clients and investors. Some of them sold their holdings in Equity Funding. Thus, the case involved trading on material nonpublic information by secondary tippees. Secrist and the other Equity Funding employees who talked to Dirks were insiders and tippers; Dirks was a tippee and tipper; his clients were secondary tippees.

Eventually the fraud came to light. Equity Funding's stock fell in price; the New York Stock Exchange halted trading in it; state insurance regulators impounded the company's records and uncovered evidence of massive fraud; the SEC filed a complaint against the company; the Wall Street Journal finally published a story on the fraud, based largely on information assembled by Dirks; and sociologists of white collar crime rushed to do case studies.

Legal proceedings

After a hearing, the SEC found that Dirks had aided and abetted violations of Rule 10b-5 and other provisions by tipping the investors who then traded on the nonpublic information. In light of his role in exposing the fraud, however, it only censured him. On appeal, the Court of Appeals entered judgment against Dirks. But the Supreme Court reversed. It reaffirmed the point in *Chiarella* that the disclose or abstain duty does not arise from the mere possession of material nonpublic information but from the existence of a fiduciary relationship. The Court observed that Dirks had no pre-existing fiduciary relationship to Equity Funding's shareholders.

When tippee has duty

The Court went on to examine Dirks' possible duties as a tippee. It held that the duty of the typical tippee, who has no independent fiduciary duty to the corporation and its shareholders, is derivative: There must be a breach of the insider/tipper's fiduciary duty before the tippee inherits the duty to disclose or abstain. Here, the insider-tippers, Secrist and the other Equity Funding employees, did not violate their fiduciary duties to the company and its shareholders by giving the nonpublic information to Dirks, because they were simply trying to help expose the fraud. The Court opined that whether the insider's tip amounted to a breach of his fiduciary duty depends in large part on whether he receives a *personal benefit* as a result of the disclosure. Absent an improper purpose, there is no breach by the insider and therefore no derivative breach by the tippee.

Hypo for analysis

To see the ramifications of this case, let's explore a hypothetical case. Employees at Hopeful Mining Co. have discovered a rich and valuable vein of copper ore. News of the discovery has not yet been made available to the general investing public, but when it is the impact on the market price is sure to be great. Various people who do know about the good news are considering buying substantial amounts of Hopeful stock. They can be classified into four groups: insiders, outsiders, tippees, and second-order tippees.

Company president

Consider first Alan, the corporation's president. His is an easy case. Prototypical insiders, like Hopeful's directors and officers, who get the information by virtue of their corporate positions, are clearly bound by the disclose or abstain rule. Alan may be sued not only by the SEC but by shareholders who were selling Hopeful stock while he was buying. Alan has a fiduciary relationship to the corporation and its shareholders, by virtue of which he may not misappropriate corporate-generated information for himself.

Lower level employee

But what about others who work for the corporation? Are they also bound by the duty? Consider Bruce, Alan's secretary, who finds out about the undisclosed good news by nosing around his desk. Is he enough of an insider to be covered? Probably yes. Although not a director or officer of Hopeful, Bruce is an employee and probably has a duty under state law to keep such information confidential and not to exploit it for his own benefit.[12] Thus, he appears to be an insider within the meaning of the *Chiarella* and *Dirks* decisions.

Outside attorney

Consider also Clare, an outside attorney who does legal work for Hopeful and in that connection learned of the discovery of ore. She too would be subject to the duty. She is more like an independent contractor than an employee with respect to Hopeful, and she isn't a full fledged fiduciary to it in the way that Alan is. But by becoming counsel to the corporation she entered a special confidential relationship with it and was given access to inside information for corporate, not personal, purposes. Indeed, footnote 14 of the *Dirks* opinion is rather clear that she would be bound by the

[12]See Restatement (Second) of Agency §388, comment c (1957); Brophy v. Cities Service Co., 70 A.2d 5 (Del. Ch. 1949); Diamond v. Oreamuno, 248 N.E. 2d 910 (N.Y. 1969).

disclose or abstain duty, and would view her as an "insider" rather than as a "tippee." The same analysis would apply to a company's accountants, underwriters, and consultants.

Independent analyst

At the other end of the spectrum are the relatively pure outsiders. Assume that Janice, a brilliant and diligent stock market analyst, has researched technical but publicly available geological data and has predicted that Hopeful will soon make a major ore discovery in one of the fields it is investigating. She could certainly trade on the basis of this prediction, even if it is embodied in a nonpublic report and might itself be construed as material nonpublic "information." So could her clients. This result follows because she is not an insider with respect to Hopeful and is not trading on nonpublic information obtained from any insiders. She is not trading on the basis of inside information in the sense of information generated by or arising within the corporation but not yet made public. Moreover, she has no duty to Hopeful or to the investing public to share her inferences, opinions, and predictions made on the basis of publicly available data. Indeed, it seems economically efficient to insist that she be able to reap the rewards of her own diligent searching and cogitating.

Accidental recipient

A somewhat less appealing case is the windfall recipient of genuine inside information. Consider Isidore, a rock musician with no connection to Hopeful or its shareholders, who, while sitting alone in an elegant bar, happens to overhear Hopeful's president telling a friend about the discovery of copper ore. Does he remain an outsider not bound by the disclose or abstain rule? The post-*Chiarella* answer is fairly easy: yes. Under current legal conceptions (but see section 8.12 below), he has no fiduciary or confidential relationship to Hopeful, to its shareholders, or to the investing public. It is true that, if he buys Hopeful stock on the basis of the conversation he overheard, he will be trading on the basis of material nonpublic information. But that alone is not enough to make him liable under Rule 10b-5.

Now that we've seen the polar cases, what about tippees? Tippees can be described as people who are themselves not insiders but to whom insiders consciously give inside information. Are they bound by the disclose or abstain duty? Some types of tippees, whom I would call reciprocating tippees and donee tippees, clearly are bound. Consider Douglas, a food company executive with no formal connection to Hopeful but who lives next door to Alan, its president. Douglas and Alan have a mutual understanding that each will give the other valuable tips about his business. Alan tells Douglas about the ore discovery and Douglas buys Hopeful stock on the basis of this information. A few months later, Douglas reciprocates for the tip by telling Alan about a fantastic new candy bar that his

Reciprocating tippee

company is about to market. *Dirks* suggests strongly that Douglas is liable for trading in Hopeful stock because he knew that Alan gave him the inside information for Alan's own personal benefit (Alan expected reciprocal tips, and they both knew this) and therefore breached his fiduciary duty to Hopeful.

Note, then, that although *Chiarella* and *Dirks* represent a move to restrict Rule 10b-5 disclose or abstain duties to persons with a fiduciary-like relationship to the relevant corporate issuer of securities, they do not eliminate all tippee liability. Even tippees who do not pay for tips or reciprocate for them in a fairly specific way may be liable. Suppose Alan, caught in a surge of benevolent feelings, tells Ernie, his best friend, about the ore discovery. Is Ernie bound by the disclose or abstain rule? Quite possibly, yes. Justice Powell, writing for the Court in *Dirks,* indicated clearly that the requisite elements of fiduciary duty and exploitation of material nonpublic information "also exist when an insider makes a gift of confidential information to a trading relative or friend."[13]

Donee-tippee

On the other hand, a tippee will escape liability if the insider-tipper was not violating a duty by giving the tip. The *Dirks* case itself illustrates this point. Secrist, the chief insider-tipper, gave Dirks the bad news about Equity Funding not to get a payoff of some kind or to make a gift to a friend but to cause exposure of the giant fraud occurring within the company. A less dramatic variant of this story might involve simple loss of self-control by the tipper. Suppose Alan is having drinks with Francine, a reporter; he drinks several too many and starts blabbing about numerous corporate matters, including the ore discovery. It might be that Francine could legally trade on this information. Under *Dirks,* her breach of duty and resulting liability would have to "derive" from those of Alan. Her argument would be that Alan didn't breach his duty to Hopeful in the sense required by *Dirks,* because he wasn't leaking the information for his own personal gain, or as a gift, but because he was drunk.

Derivative nature of duty

Secondary tippees are those who get their tips indirectly from an insider-tipper — for example, through an intermediate tippee. Suppose Alan, in breach of his duty, tips Douglas, who in turn tips Gail, who tips Harry. All buy Hopeful stock and make lots of money. Presumably, the analysis with respect to Gail and Harry is similar to that with respect to Douglas: Did they know that they were getting material nonpublic information and that the ultimate source of it was a person (Alan) who was violating his fiduciary duty to the corporate issuer by releasing that information?

Secondary tippee

[13] 463 U.S. at 664.

Of course, many additional cases can be imagined that are hard to classify or that raise new issues, and some of these are sure to arise in practice. That is why case law never stops growing.

§8.10.3 Scienter

Scienter needed

In *Ernst & Ernst v. Hochfelder,*[14] the Supreme Court held that a private cause of action for damages will not lie under Section 10(b) and Rule 10b-5 in the absence of any allegation of scienter, that is, intent to deceive, manipulate, or defraud. In so doing, it disposed of the views of some courts and commentators in prior years that negligent conduct alone was sufficient for such a cause of action. More specifically, it removed a large class of threats to professional firms like those of accountants and lawyers, who minister to corporations and their insiders and who possess deep pockets of wealth to which injured plaintiffs would like to have access.

Facts of *Ernst & Ernst*

The facts of *Ernst & Ernst* illustrate this latter point. The plaintiffs were customers of a small brokerage firm who had invested in a fraudulent security scheme perpetrated by its president (who later committed suicide, when the scheme became unviable). The brokerage firm being unable to respond in damages,[15] the plaintiff sued the large accounting firm — *Ernst & Ernst* is one of the Big Eight — that had audited its books and records, alleging that the accountants had negligently failed to utilize appropriate auditing procedures, which if used would have led to discovery of suspicious practices within the brokerage firm[16] and perhaps of the fraudulent scheme, and that the accountants therefore aided and abetted a fraud in violation of Rule 10b-5. The Supreme Court's rejection of this claim as a matter of law must certainly have sent cheers up and down Wall Street, and one can only imagine how many bottles of scotch were consumed by the thousands of celebrating accountants in the Big Eight firms. For the *Ernst & Ernst* holding was a setback to the SEC's policy (at that time) of trying to focus more legal responsibility for monitoring the conduct of corporate insiders on outside lawyers and accountants.[17]

[14] 425 U.S. 185, reh. denied, 425 U.S. 986 (1976).

[15] The equitable receivership commenced by the SEC in 1968, one week after the suicide, was still in progress in 1976. See SEC v. First Securities Co. of Chicago, 507 F.2d 417 (7th Cir. 1974).

[16] For example, the president of the firm insisted that only he could open certain kinds of mail, even when he was away from the office. Hochfelder v. Ernst & Ernst, 503 F.2d 1100, 1109 (7th Cir. 1974). To an auditor who had read or heard about Ponzi schemes, this might have sounded a warning bell. See generally A. Leff, Swindling and Selling (1976).

[17] See, e.g., Lowenfels, Expanding Public Responsiblities of Securities Lawyers: An Analysis of the New Trend in Standard of Care and Priorities of Duties, 74 Colum. L. Rev. 412 (1974).

This is not to say that the Supreme Court assessed the SEC policy on its merits, weighing the desirability of using accountants' and lawyers' superior access to information about fraudulent schemes against the alleged harm to professional-client relationships that might come from making the professional a policeman. Unlike Justices Rehnquist's and Powell's opinions in *Blue Chip,* which develop a substantive policy argument to justify their legal holding, Justice Powell's opinion in *Ernst & Ernst* is restricted to considerations of statutory language, legislative history, the fit of Section 10(b) with other securities law provisions, and the history of Rule 10b-5. The main explicit argument was simply that the language in Section 10(b) referring to "any manipulative or deceptive device or contrivance" strongly suggests an intention to proscribe knowing or intentional conduct, not negligence. In a sense, the opinion's narrowness is odd, because a reasonable argument could have been made that a scienter requirement was a good filter for straining out vexatious litigation. On the other hand, putting such an argument in the opinion would have highlighted the relative unpersuasiveness of a similar argument made previously in *Blue Chip.* It might have shown the court's strict interpretation of the purchaser-seller doctrine to have been a symbolic act of hostility to plaintiff's attorneys rather than a result compelled by neutral policy considerations.

Basis of result?

Ernst & Ernst explicitly did not settle some important questions about the mental state that must be shown in actions under Section 10(b). Subsequent opinions of the courts have had to deal with such questions as whether scienter needs to be proven in an action brought under Section 10(b) by the SEC to obtain an injunction,[18] whether scienter is present if the defendant showed a reckless disregard for the truth,[19] and the conditions under which defendants can be held liable for aiding and abetting a primary fraud.[20]

Questions for later cases

[18] Aaron v. SEC, 446 U.S. 680 (1980) (scienter required).

[19] Courts of Appeals that have considered the issue have held that recklessness, in at least some circumstances, satisfies the scienter requirement. See, e.g., G. A. Thompson & Co. v. Partridge, 636 F.2d 945 (5th Cir. 1981); Mansbach v. Prescott, Ball & Turben, 598 F.2d 1017 (6th Cir. 1979); Rolf v. Blyth, Eastman Dillon & Co., 570 F.2d 38 (2d Cir.), cert. denied, 439 U.S. 1039 (1978); Sanders v. John Nuveen & Co., 554 F.2d 790 (7th Cir. 1977), cert. denied, 450 U.S. 1005 (1981). Review of these cases shows, however, that the courts disagree as to what recklessness means.

[20] Courts have been willing to hold an aider and abettor liable based on recklessness. See, e.g., Rolf v. Blyth, Eastman Dillon & Co., note 19 supra. See generally Note, Liability for Aiding and Abetting Violations of Rule 10b-5: The Recklessness Standard in Civil Damage Actions, 62 Tex. L. Rev. 1087 (1984). A standard formulation is that for a defendant to be liable as an aider and abettor of a primary wrongdoer, the following must be present: (1) an

No one seems to doubt seriously that Section 10(b) still applies to conventional insider trading. The point of *Ernst & Ernst* in this context would seem to be only that the defendant must have known that the information to which he had access while trading was material and nonpublic.

§8.10.4 Materiality

The cases differ somewhat in the verbal formulae they use to describe which misrepresented or omitted facts are material for purposes of Rule 10b-5 and other antifraud provisions. In the landmark case of *Securities and Exchange Commission v. Texas Gulf Sulphur Co.*,[21] the court construed material facts as those to which a reasonable man would attach importance in determining his choice of action in the transaction in question. The class of reasonable investors includes speculators and chartists, not just conservative investors. The reasonable investor would consider it important to know facts that in reasonable and objective contemplation might affect the value of the corporation's securities.

***TSC Industries* case**

As of this writing, the Supreme Court has not yet squarely declared a specific formula to be the official one in Rule 10b-5 cases. But in the related context of Rule 14a-9, the general antifraud provision of the SEC's proxy rules,[22] the Court held, in *TSC Industries, Inc. v. Northway Inc.*,[23] that an omitted fact is material "if there is a substantial likelihood that a reasonable shareholder *would* consider it important in deciding how to vote," and rejected an appellate court formulation that described as material "all facts which a reasonable shareholder *might* consider important." You may be surprised that such a semantic choice should have occupied the resources of the nation's highest court. Perhaps the significance of this post-1974 decision is that it fits into the court's program of getting tough, symbolically as well as actually, with litigation brought under the federal securities laws.

Applicability in 10b-5 cases

It seems likely that the Court would apply the *TSC* formulation of materiality to actions brought under Rule 10b-5, after replacing the words "important in deciding how to vote" with "important in deciding whether and on what terms to buy or sell a security." Indeed, the court took pains in footnote 9 of the *TSC* opinion to reconcile its holding with its prior lan-

---

independent wrongful act; (2) knowledge by the aider and abettor of the wrongful act; and (3) substantial assistance in effecting that wrongful act.

[21] 401 F.2d 833, 848-849 (2d Cir. 1968), cert. denied, 394 U.S. 976 (1969).

[22] See section 9.2 infra.

[23] 426 U.S. 438 (1976).

guage in a 10b-5 case, *Affiliated Ute Citizens v. United States*.[24] There it had held that when a Rule 10b-5 violation involves a failure to disclose, "positive proof of reliance is not a prerequisite to recovery. All that is necessary is that the facts withheld be material in the sense that a reasonable investor might have considered them important in the making of [his] decision." The *TSC* opinion categorizes this explanation of materiality as given simply to convey a sense of the term rather than as a precise definition designed to be part of the holding in *Ute*.[25]

§8.10.5 Causation, Reliance, and Privity

We turn now to issues whose case law development reflects not the ideology of the Supreme Court but the difficulties of devising specific rules when the underlying theory of a cause of action is not clearly perceived or agreed upon. In general tort law, a plaintiff has to show not only that a duty was owed by the defendant to him and that it was violated but also that the violation caused him injury. The causation requirement is traditionally divided into two parts: (1) the violation must have been a cause in fact, or "but-for" cause of the injury and (2) it must have been a legal or proximate cause of the injury.[26] The phrase *but for* comes from the stipulation that "violation A caused injury B" means that "but for A, the injury B would not have occurred." That is, A was a necessary condition of B.

Two causation requirements

In some tort actions, such as that for deceit, the defendant's behavior is conceived to have caused injury to the plaintiff by means of an impact, in the first instance, on the plaintiff's mental processes. The defendant lies; the plaintiff believes the lie and acts upon his belief to his detriment; the plaintiff's reliance upon the lie was thus a part of the causal chain from violation to injury. Perhaps because common law courts could not readily conceive how a lie about a factual matter could hurt a plaintiff who did not believe and act upon it, they made proof of reliance a necessary part of the plaintiff's action for deceit. But it is important to remember that reliance is only one way of specifying for *some* contexts the general and primary requirement of but-for causation in tort law. Once this point is grasped, it is easier to think about alternative chains of causation of injury in fraud cases, and to recognize the possibility that even "non-relying" plaintiffs can be hurt by fraud.

Reliance as the causal link

[24] 406 U.S. 128, 153-154, reh. denied, 407 U.S. 916 (1972).

[25] Later decisions have in fact agreed that the *TSC Industries* definition of materiality applies to Rule 10b-5 cases. See, e.g., Kidwell ex rel. Penfold v. Meikle, 597 F.2d 1273 (9th Cir. 1979); Joyce v. Joyce Beverages, Inc., 571 F.2d 703 (2d Cir.), reh. denied, 437 U.S. 905 (1978).

[26] W. Prosser, Handbook of the Law of Torts 263-279 (5th ed. 1984).

Reliance not always required

There are three substantial reasons why courts have chosen not to make positive proof of reliance on the part of each plaintiff an essential element of all Rule 10b-5 causes of action: (1) the fraud on the market theory, (2) the practical problems of litigation, and (3) the conceptual problems that arise in some cases. The first two reasons apply less to insider trading cases than to cases involving misrepresentations or failures to disclose information that the defendant had an unconditional duty to disclose, but they are treated here to facilitate study of the potentially confusing judicial pronouncements on reliance.

Fraud on the market theory

Fraud on the market. The first reason concerns real chains of causation. A materially false statement made available to the general investing public, such as a press release issued by a corporate official, may have been read, believed, and used for purposes of valuing the company's stock by only a relative handful of stock market professionals—the securities analysts at some large brokerage firms and the institutional investors. Other investors, who do not read the press release but who perhaps rely on their investment counselors or on efficient markets theory, simply buy or sell the stock at the current market price. The fact that they don't engage personally in valuing the stock on the basis of the raw informational material doesn't mean that they aren't hurt by the false statements. If the professional investment analysts affect the market price by their valuations and trades, and if their valuations are based on materially false statements, the market price of the stock will deviate from what it ought to be, and all investors who trade at that price will be affected.

Thus, suppose we can assume that most material statements released to the public are considered by the professionals and do affect their valuations and that the professionals are a large enough group to affect stock market prices. From these rather modest assumptions, we can reasonably expect that any *materially* false statement released to the public affects the price of the securities concerned. It therefore hurts those who innocently buy the stock (if bad news is being suppressed, or good news exaggerated) or sell it (vice versa) during the lifetime of the false information. We can therefore dispense with the requirement that each plaintiff must prove actual reliance on the false statement.

Judicial support

A version of this argument moved the court in *Blackie v. Barrack*,[27] which held in a Rule 10b-5 class action context that "proof of subjective reliance on particular misrepresentations is unnecessary to establish a 10b-5 claim

[27] 524 F.2d 891 (9th Cir. 1975), cert. denied, 429 U.S. 816 (1976).

for deception inflating the price of stock traded in the open market."[28] Subsequent case law has generally favored this approach, which has often been referred to as the fraud on the market theory.[29]

Relation to economic theories

The general point is reminiscent of one made in the law and economics literature, that a small ratio of comparison shoppers to noncomparison shoppers may be enough to keep a market competitive, since the former's activities in gathering and assessing information and making valuations may determine the market price.[30] The fraud on the market theory is also associated sometimes with a belief in the efficient capital markets hypothesis.[31] But a little thought suggests that it does not depend on any strong belief in that hypothesis—for example, a belief that the stock markets are "perfectly" efficient or that they efficiently allocate real resources. The fraud on the market theory really only depends on the modest beliefs that most publicly announced material statements about companies are considered by market professionals and therefore affect the market prices of the companies' securities.

Rebuttable presumption

In any event, note that the *Blackie* case created only a presumption of reliance. The presumption can be rebutted by the defendant's showing that (1) the misrepresentation was not really material, (2) not even the minimum number of investors needed to affect the securities' market price received and relied on the misrepresentation, or (3) the particular plaintiff knew of the falsity or for some odd reason clearly would have traded on the same terms even if the false statement had not been made.

[28] 524 F.2d at 906. But see Huddleston v. Herman & MacLean, 640 F.2d 534, 547 (5th Cir. 1981) (plaintiff must prove reliance); Wilson v. Comtech Telecommunications Corp., 648 F.2d 88 (2d Cir. 1981) (affirmative misrepresentation; plaintiff must prove actual reliance); Sharp v. Coopers & Lybrand, 649 F.2d 175 (3d Cir. 1981) (district judge has discretion in allocating burden of proof of reliance), cert. denied, 455 U.S. 938 (1982).

[29] E.g., Panzirer v. Wolf, 663 F.2d 365, 368 (2d Cir. 1981), vacated on mootness grounds, 459 U.S. 1027; Shores v. Sklar, 647 F.2d 462 (5th Cir. 1981), cert. denied, 459 U.S. 1102 (1983). See Grzebielski, Should the Supreme Court Recognize General Market Reliance in Private Actions Under Rule 10b-5? 36 Baylor L. Rev. 335 (1984); Note, The Fraud-on-the-Market Theory, 95 Harv. L. Rev. 1143 (1982).

At least one court has held that while the fraud-on-the-market theory is valid when considering fraud perpetrated on an actively traded market, it loses its persuasive value when applied to undeveloped markets. In such cases, the plaintiff must establish greater proof of reliance. Lipton v. Documation Inc., 734 F.2d 740 (11th Cir. 1984), cert. denied, 105 S. Ct. 814 (1985).

[30] Schwartz and Wilde, Intervening in Markets on the Basis of Imperfect Information. A Legal and Economic Analysis, 127 U. Pa. L. Rev. 630 (1979).

[31] E.g., T.J. Raney & Sons, Inc. v. Fort Cobb, Oklahoma Irrigation Fuel Authority, 717 F.2d 1330 (10th Cir. 1983), cert. denied, 104 S. Ct. 1285 (1984). See also Fischel, Use of Modern Finance Theory in Securities Fraud Cases Involving Actively Traded Securities, 38 Bus. Law 1 (1982).

Proof problems in class actions

Practical problems. The second reason for dispensing with reliance concerns the practicalities of adjudication. Effective enforcement of an antifraud provision in the context of the national securities markets, where a given fraud may cause a large investor loss that is nevertheless spread among many investors, requires a relatively streamlined judicial procedure such as the class action. If each of the thousands of members in a class of plaintiffs in a Rule 10b-5 suit has to prove affirmatively that he relied on a false statement, then either the class will not be certified because individual questions outweigh common ones or the class action will lose the economy for which it was designed. It is frequently practical and reasonable to assume that if the false statement was directed to all the class members, then its very materiality — the fact that the statement is found to be such that reasonable investors would be substantially likely to consider it in making decisions — indicates that it probably affected the class members' decisions. This train of thought also influenced the court in *Blackie.* It was also at work in a pre-1974 Supreme Court decision under the antifraud provision of the proxy rules, according to which reliance was presumed from materiality in a class action context.[32]

Reliance on a nondisclosure??

Conceptual problems. The third reason for dispensing with reliance in some cases is a conceptual one. Let's consider this point in two contexts: straight nondisclosure cases and insider trading cases. First, the pure nondisclosure context: When defendant had a duty to disclose certain material information and did not do so, what does it *mean* to say that the plaintiff relied on the defendant's nondisclosure? Must the plaintiff show that he consciously experienced something like the following thought: "Defendant owes me a duty but has not disclosed any information that would lead me to reconsider the action I am about to take, so I can safely proceed"? Of course not; such a requirement would be absurd. The court should simply infer the truth of the counterfactual proposition that if defendant had disclosed the material information to plaintiff the latter would have given it weight in making his decision and that, since this did not occur, plaintiff suffered a legally cognizable harm. Thus, as noted earlier, the Supreme Court held in the *Affiliated Ute Citizens* case,[33] that in a case involving primarily a failure to disclose, positive proof of reliance was not necessary to recovery. It was enough for causation purposes to show that the facts withheld were material.

[32] Mills v. Electric Auto-Lite Co., 396 U.S. 375, 384 (1970).

[33] Affiliated Ute Citizens v. United States, 406 U.S. 128 (1972).

The problem of alternative "but fors"

Now consider the paradigmatic insider trading cases, where the question of reliance has also been debated. Satisfaction of the causation requirement in these actions involves a very important, special difficulty. The problem is that the trading insider, under the conventional case law formulations, has violated the disclose or abstain rule, a duty that could have been satisfied in alternative ways. The but-for test of causation in fact always leads one to ask whether, if the defendant had fulfilled his duty instead of violating it, the plaintiff would have been harmed anyway. If the answer is yes, the defendant did not cause the harm; if no, he did cause it. As applied to the disclose or abstain rule, this procedure produces a conundrum. If, contrary to fact, the insider had satisfied his duty by *disclosing* the inside information in order then to be free to trade, then presumably the market would have efficiently digested the information and the price at which investors were willing to buy or sell the stock would have quickly adjusted. Then the plaintiff either would not have traded or would not have traded on the bad terms on which he did trade. Under this analysis, the defendant's violation *did* cause harm to the plaintiff. But if, contrary to fact, the insider had satisfied his duty by *abstaining* from trading in order not to have to make disclosure, then presumably the market price would have remained essentially as it was, and the plaintiff would have traded to his detriment on the same bad terms on which he did trade. Under this analysis, the defendant's violation did *not* cause harm to the plaintiff.

A red herring

(There is actually a slight complication, the perception of which has thrown some courts off the track of the main problem. If defendants' trading was substantial enough, one might infer that their abstention, simply by altering the volume of supply or demand for the stock, would have altered the market price of the stock somewhat and that some plaintiffs faced by the adjusted price might not have traded and been hurt. But convincing proof that the defendants' failure to abstain from trading caused injury in this sense is extremely difficult, and accurate measurement of damages under this approach is almost impossible.)

Proper response not obvious

General tort law does not provide a clear rule as to how the causation requirement should be understood in the case of duties which have a logical structure like that of the disclose or abstain rule. What, then, should a court do about the causation requirement in insider trading cases? Should it require proof that it was more likely than not that the particular defendants, if they had fulfilled their duty, would have fulfilled it by making disclosure rather than abstaining from trading? Could convincing proof of such a counterfactual situation often be given? Or should the court simply assume, as an empirical guess, that most illegally trading insiders would have satisfied their duty by disclosure and thus find the causation requirement satisfied in all cases of trading on material inside information? Or should the courts make the opposite empirical guess and deny private recovery of damages in all insider trading cases? Or may a court simply admit that it cannot responsibly make these empirical assumptions and somehow declare them irrelevant? Or might a court say that the plaintiffs' "losses" (as computed by comparison to what their position would have been had there been disclosure) should be arbitrarily viewed as "half caused" by insider trading?

Courts' recharacterizations of issue

In fact, the courts that have principally dealt with the causation problem have tried to get out of the dilemma by failing to state it clearly and refusing to face up to it squarely. They have developed semantic recharacterizations of the disclose or abstain rule that only appear to resolve the dilemma. In the process, they sometimes confuse the issue of causation in fact with the issues of proximate causation and the proper purpose and measure of damages.

Case emphasizing nondisclosure aspect

Thus, in the important case of *Shapiro v. Merrill Lynch, Pierce, Fenner & Smith, Inc.*,[34] which held the disclose or abstain rule applicable in a private action for damages against both nontrading tippers of inside information and trading tippees,[35] the Second Circuit rejected the defendants' argument that they had not caused harm to the plaintiffs. The court invoked *Affiliated Ute Citizens* and asserted that causation in fact was established "by the uncontroverted fact that defendants traded in or recommended trading in the Douglas stock in question without disclosing material insider information. . . ."[36] But, of course, the court's holding does not follow from *Ute*'s by logical deduction. The Supreme Court in *Ute* prefaced its statement on the nonnecessity of proving reliance with the words, "(U)nder the circumstances of this case, involving primarily a failure to disclosure. . . ." In essence, the Second Circuit tried to characterize insider trading as involving "primarily" a failure to disclose by the semantic trick of reformulating the defendants' violation of the disclose or abstain rule as consisting of

[34] 495 F.2d 228 (2d Cir. 1974).

[35] *Shapiro* involved trading in the common stock of Douglas Aircraft Co. On June 7, 1966, Douglas released a favorable earnings report for the first five months of the year. Merrill Lynch, then involved in underwriting a new issue of Douglas debentures, was privately informed by Douglas management between June 17 and June 22 that earnings for the rest of 1966 and 1967 were expected to be substantially lower. It was alleged that between June 20 and June 24, Merrill Lynch, through certain directors and employees who were named as defendants, divulged this information to some of its institutional clients (also named as defendants). These investors, between June 20 and June 23, sold their Douglas shares on the New York Stock Exchange without disclosing the inside information. The revised earnings projection was released publicly on June 24. Between June 22 and July 1, the price of Douglas stock declined from 87½ to 61¾.

[36] 495 F.2d at 238.

trading without disclosing inside information. This formulation makes it seem that what the defendants should have done was to disclose the information, period. In fact, however, they had a choice whether to disclose or abstain. It is obvious that one could just as well reformulate the violation as consisting of "*trading* on undisclosed inside information *instead of abstaining*." This formula would make the real violation appear to be the defendants' failure to keep out of the market. It would facilitates a finding that defendant caused no harm to plaintiffs.

Case emphasizing trading aspect

It is essentially this alternative reformulation that was used by the Sixth Circuit in *Fridrich v. Bradford*.[37] A district court judgment in favor of plaintiffs who sold during a period of nondisclosure of good news was reversed on the ground that the defendants — trading insiders, none of whom bought their stock from the actual plaintiffs — had caused no injury to the plaintiffs. The court stated flatly, "We conceive it to be the act of trading [rather than not disclosing] which essentially constitutes the violation of Rule 10b-5, for it is this which brings the illicit benefits to the insider. . . ."[38] It thus played the same semantic game as the *Shapiro* court, but in reverse.

Two questions arise at this point. Can the differing orientations of the *Shapiro* and *Fridrich* cases be understood or even justified in light of the facts of the cases? And, more generally, how should the causation in fact requirement be specified in insider trading cases?

Contrast in fact patterns

On the first question, one should note a striking contrast in factual patterns. In *Shapiro*, the defendants were the country's largest brokerage firm, which had tipped off its institutional investor clients about nonpublic bad news concerning a large public corporation, and the institutional investors themselves, who had engaged in massive selling on the basis of the tip. The institutional investors thus avoided their share of the losses allocable to investors who held the public corporation's stock at the time of the bad corporate developments by shifting the losses to uninformed buyers. The Second Circuit was not clear about whether the defendants would be liable to pay full compensation to all investors who bought Douglas stock during the period of nondisclosure (or the period starting with defendants' trading and ending with disclosure of the bad news) or only to give up their "profit" (the amount of losses illicitly avoided by the trading defendants). It left this question to the district court on remand.[39] But even if it had decided that the logic of its reasoning called for full compensation, it

[37] 542 F.2d 307 (6th Cir. 1976), cert. denied, 429 U.S. 1053 (1977).

[38] Id. at 318.

[39] The district court never reached the issue; the case was settled. See Dooley, Enforcement of Insider Trading Restrictions, 66 Va. L. Rev. 1, 22 n.106 (1980).

might well have perceived no injustice. Since the trading defendants' activities accounted for nearly half the activity in the public corporation's stock on some crucial days, their damages would have been only a small multiple of their actual illicit profits.

By contrast, the defendant focused upon in the *Fridrich* opinion was an individual who received a tip from his father about an insurance company traded on the over the counter market, bought stock in the company, and made an illicit profit of $13,000, which he had already disgorged pursuant to a consent decree in an SEC proceeding. Yet if this individual were found to have caused injury to the whole class of persons who sold stock during the period of nondisclosure, and if (as the Sixth Circuit assumed) the tort-like nature of the Rule 10b-5 action mandates that he pay them full compensation, then he would be liable to pay more than $361,000. Understandably, the court saw itself as rejecting a "view where its application leads us inexorably to an unjust and unworkable result."[40]

Semblance of privity compromise

The *Fridrich* court's decision to impose a just limitation on the defendant's liability for damages by means of a holding on what appears to be another subject — whether defendant in fact caused injury — must leave jurists uncomfortable. A concurring opinion by Judge Celebrezze, who sensed the problem, tried to preserve some role for Rule 10b-5 class actions against insider trading on the open markets by suggesting that the majority's holding did not preclude liability in appropriate cases. According to Celebrezze, defendants trading on inside information ought to be liable, on a full compensation basis, to all those who traded in the opposite direction on the public market *during the period while the insiders were trading* (not during the entire period of nondisclosure of the inside information). The idea is that this class of plaintiffs includes those who actually sold to or bought from the defendants. In a rough sense, the whole class can be viewed as consisting of persons who were "connected" to the defendants' wrongful trading; they had a "semblance of privity" with the defendants and can be viewed as having been injured by them. The reason for not insisting that those who *actually* sold to or bought from the insiders be precisely identified, so that they and only they can sue, is that such precise identification is impractical in public market transactions.

Has problems too

Celebrezze's compromise is by no means an ideal one, of course. A case may well arise in which, even given his semblance of privity limitation, an individual defendant will be held liable for damages vastly exceeding his illicit profits. Furthermore, from the point of view of the public investors, all of them who traded the wrong way in the dark and were injured,

[40] 542 F.2d at 320.

relative to what would have happened had there been timely disclosure, the compromise position seems arbitrary. And, of course, if the harm of insider trading is viewed as including its tendency to create a bias against timely disclosure of important information, the Celebrezze compromise appears to make an irrational distinction between public traders who can and cannot be plaintiffs.

Contemporaneous trading rule

Nevertheless, this compromise position, under the label of the contemporaneous trading rule, has been followed. Indeed, subsequent case law suggests that it may soon become the prevailing rule.[41]

§8.10.6 Proximate Causation and Privity

Proximate causation

In tort actions, a plaintiff usually must show not only that defendant's violation caused an injury in fact but that it proximately caused his injury. Judicial opinions have varied greatly in describing proximate causation. Some say that a violation proximately causes an injury when it directly did so. Perhaps the now prevailing view is that a violation proximately causes those injuries that were reasonably foreseeable by the violator.[42]

Liability-limiting aim

Astute courts and commentators recognize that whatever the formula, a main consideration is to limit a defendant's liability for damages to an amount that is just or socially efficient. Under such an approach, the court in *Fridrich* could have said — although it did not — that, whether or not not Mr. Bradford may have caused injury to the plaintiffs, he did not proximately cause it.

Privity concept similar

The idea of limiting the defendant's damages to sensible proportions also seems to account for the notion that privity should be required in certain court actions, that is, that the plaintiff must show that the defendant dealt with him. Just as reliance can be viewed as one specification of the causation-in-fact requirement, so privity can be considered as one specification of the proximate causation requirement. (It can also be considered a precondition of standing to bring suit.) Nevertheless, the federal courts have rejected the notion that plaintiffs in Rule 10b-5 cases involving insider trading on the open markets must show privity, that is, that they actually bought from or sold to the plaintiffs.[43] Without such a rejection, the Rule 10b-5 class action could hardly have developed.

[41] See Wilson v. Comtech Telecommunications Corp., 648 F.2d 88, 94-95 (2d Cir. 1981); Backman v. Polaroid Corp., 540 F. Supp. 667, 670 (D. Mass. 1982).

[42] See W. Prosser, Handbook of the Law of Torts, Chap. 7 (5th ed. 1984).

[43] Shapiro v. Merrill Lynch, Pierce, Fenner & Smith, Inc., 495 F.2d 228, 239 (2d Cir. 1974). See 3 A. Bromberg & L. Lowenfels, Securities Fraud & Commodities Fraud, §8.5 (511) (1984).

Example of exchange-listed options

An interesting question about the possible extent of an insider's liability involves exchange-listed options. It represents a special case that is increasingly important in view of the recent rapid growth and development of markets in options and futures. It also shows neatly how extent-of-liability questions tie in with decisions about the scope of duty and the criteria of causation. The question may be put by a hypothetical. Suppose Matthew, president of Video Corp. and therefore a clear insider, sells Video stock on the basis of important undisclosed bad news. On the same day, Alex and a dozen others buy call options on Video stock on an options exchange. When the bad news comes out, their options drop greatly in value. Can they bring a successful 10b-5 suit against Matthew?

Of course, they have to contend with a causation-in-fact problem. Some courts may think that assessing the existence and amount of damages to the option buyers is too speculative an inquiry.[44] By what formula do stock price changes affect the prices of options on the stock? How important are stock price changes versus other determinants of an option's price? In principle, and in practice through the use of expert witnesses, answers to these questions can be given.

But then another serious problem rears its head. Assuming, as is usually the case, that the call options were created and issued not by Video Corp. but by someone or something else, such as an institutional investor owning Video stock, is it right to regard Video Corp. and its officers and directors as having fiduciary duties to those trading in the options? If not, then Matthew's violation of the disclose or abstain duty he owed to investors in Video stock may not support a private action for damages on the part of the option buyers.[45]

§8.10.7 Damages

Principles flow from other decisions

As indicated in the previous discussion, the basic principles governing damages in an insider trading case flow from the court's understanding of the harm caused by insider trading; its choices with respect to the issues of

[44] See, e.g., Laventhall v. General Dynamics Corp., 704 F.2d 407 (8th Cir.), cert. denied, 464 U.S. 846 (1983). But see Backman v. Polaroid Corp., 540 F. Supp. 667 (D. Mass. 1982); O'Connor & Assocs. v. Dean Witter Reynolds, 559 F. Supp. 800 (S.D.N.Y. 1983).

[45] See, e.g., Laventhall v. General Dynamics Corp., 704 F.2d 407 (8th Cir. 1983). But see O'Connor & Assocs. v. Dean Witter Reynolds, 529 F. Supp. 1179 (S.D.N.Y. 1981) (insider's breach of duty to common shareholders supports option holder's suit against insider for trading in inside information on the options market). The latter case might seem suspect in light of Moss v. Morgan Stanley, 553 F. Supp. 1347 (S.D.N.Y. 1983), aff'd, 719 F.2d 5 (2d Cir. 1983), cert. denied, 104 S. Ct. 1280 ("A plaintiff claiming damages under Section 10(b) must establish the existence of a special relationship by the defendant with an insider or the plaintiff.").

causation, reliance, and privity; and its view of the major purpose of damages (compensation of appropriate plaintiffs or deterrence of the insiders).

Disgorgement approach

Thus far, we have seen that, in considering how to limit the defendant's damages to reasonable amounts, courts have favored one device — the contemporaneous trading rule — and rejected another — strict privity. A third device is to limit damages to the disgorgement of the defendant's profits from (or losses avoided by) insider trading, instead of making him liable for all losses suffered by those trading in the opposite direction during the relevant time period. The disgorgement approach seems now to have become the prevailing one.[46]

Subsidiary issues

Even within this approach, there is a question whether to hold the defendant liable for the full profits (or avoided losses) or only the portion attributable to the nondisclosed information. For example, in *SEC v. MacDonald,*[47] the insider bought on undisclosed good news. Upon disclosure, the stock went up 20 percent, but the insider held on for another year to get long-term capital gain treatment, and during that time the stock went up some more. The court held that he had to disgorge only that part of his profits (the 20 percent) attributable to the impact of the good news. The dissent argued that holding the insider liable for his full profits would have created a desirable deterrent effect.[48] In another case,[49] the court did hold the insider liable for his full profits.

Multiple damages approach

As we discussed earlier in this chapter, there is much to be said for a rule that would make insiders liable for some fixed multiple of — say, three times — their illicit profits, in order to create a real deterrent against insider trading. As I noted, Section 21(d)(2) of the Securities Exchange Act, which was added by the Insider Trading Sanctions Act of 1984, empowers the SEC to seek a civil penalty of three times the profit gained or loss avoided by insider trading. But no formula was legislated for private civil actions.

There are numerous additional issues involved in choosing a specific formula for actually measuring or computing damages in an insider trading case. These issues will not be explored here,[50] but the difference between

[46] See, e.g., Elkind v. Liggett & Myers, Inc., 635 F.2d 156 (2d Cir. 1980) (an evaluation of three damage measures, with the court adopting the disgorgement alternative).

[47] 699 F.2d 47 (1st Cir. 1983).

[48] On the other hand, this policy could prompt victims of insider trading to wait until the market is as high as possible in order to get greater recovery if the "full profits" measure is used. See Thompson, The Measure of Recovery Under Rule 10b-5: A Restitution Alternative to Tort Damages, 37 Vand. L. Rev. 349, 381-397 (1984).

[49] Cf. Nelson v. Serwold, 687 F.2d 278 (9th Cir. 1982) (officer who fraudulently purchased majority of corporation stock liable for *all* profits received).

[50] See Grenier, Damages for Insider Trading in the Open Market: A New Limitation on Recovery Under Rule 10b-5, 34 Vand. L. Rev. 797 (1981); Jacobs, The Measure of Damages in

general damages principles and specific measurement formulas will be illustrated in the next section in connection with Rule 10b-5 cases based on misrepresentations.

§8.11 *Beyond Insider Trading: Misrepresentations and Omissions*

As already suggested by our discussion of *Ernst & Ernst,* the coverage of Section 10(b) and Rule 10b-5 extends beyond conventional insider trading to cases where (1) the defendant makes a material misrepresentation in connection with the purchase or sale of securities, (2) omits to state a material fact needed to make other statements not misleading — that is, tells a half-truth — or, more generally, (3) fails to make a disclosure when he has an unconditional duty to disclose.

These misrepresentation and omission cases involve several important issues that should be treated separately.

§8.11.1 Fraud versus Breach of Fiduciary Duty

A federal corporate law?

Can Rule 10b-5 be used to remedy conduct that essentially amounts to a breach of fiduciary duty under state corporate law? If so, the Rule would provide an entree into the federal courts and a basis for developing a "federal corporate law" with a wide reach. This in turn would delight potential plaintiffs and their attorneys, if they believe that a federal action will often be heard more quickly, carefully, and sympathetically than an action in the relevant state court. Put another way, may the federal courts interpret the concept of fraud so broadly as to catch conduct by a fiduciary that is objectionable because it was substantively unfair, even if it did not involve lies or half truths?

***Santa Fe's* negative answer**

In *Santa Fe Industries, Inc. v. Green,*[1] the Supreme Court seemed to answer these questions with a decisive no. The case involved a freeze-out merger — one in which minority shareholders are forced to take cash in exchange for their shares[2] — which allegedly lacked a corporate business purpose and was accomplished without notice to the minority shareholders. Plaintiff shareholder claimed that such a merger was fraudulent and a

Rule 10b-5 cases, 65 Geo. L. Rev. 1093 (1977); Note, Damage to Uninformed Traders for Insider Trading on Impersonal Exchanges, 74 Colum. L. Rev. 299 (1974).

§8.11 [1] 430 U.S. 462 (1977).

[2] See chapter 12.

violation of Rule 10b-5, even though there was no misrepresentation or failure to disclose information that was required to be disclosed. The Supreme Court rejected this claim. Rule 10b-5 cannot be used to remedy above-board unfairness, even if it constitutes a breach of fiduciary duty under state law. Section 10(b) of the statute is aimed only at deception and manipulation, not substantive unfairness, and the rule must not be interpreted to go beyond these concerns. Thus, the facts that exceptionally unfair conduct might be described as fraudulent in some state court decisions, and that Rule 10b-5 contains the word *fraudulent*, are beside the point.

How to circumvent it

Soon afterwards, the important case of *Goldberg v. Meridor*[3] showed how the apparent force of *Santa Fe* could be legitimately weakened. Two points of general interest were made. First, misleading disclosures by management about a substantively unfair transaction may be remedied under Rule 10b-5 where the misrepresentations preclude shareholders from obtaining an injunction or other remedy in state court. Thus, full and accurate disclosure can be called for as a matter of federal law when it is needed for adequate enforcement of state created fiduciary duties.

Second, when a corporation was an actual purchaser or seller of securities and the Rule 10b-5 suit is brought derivatively on its behalf, the knowledge of the corporation's directors will not be imputed to it if they are interested in or controlled by the other party to the transaction. Thus, an unfair self-dealing transaction may result in deception *of the corporation* and so be subject to attack under Rule 10b-5.

***Goldberg v. Meridor* case**

Goldberg itself involved a purchase by a partially owned subsidiary of parent company assets at an allegedly inflated price, using subsidiary stock as the means of payments. The subsidiary was thus an actual seller of shares and met the usual standing requirement. "It" could be found, under the reasoning of Judge Friendly's opinion for the Second Circuit, to have been "deceived" about the unfairness of the transaction despite the fact that the actual directors and officers involved knew all the essential facts, because the knowledge of interested or controlled managers should not be imputed to the corporation. When the managers are so interested, the relevant question becomes whether the public or minority shareholders were informed. If they were not, there may have been a legally cognizable harm, even if they had no power under state law to block the transaction in

[3] 567 F.2d 209 (2d Cir. 1977), cert. denied, 434 U.S. 1069 (1978). See generally Ferrara & Steinberg, A Reappraisal of *Santa Fe:* Rule 10b-5 and the New Federalism, 129 U. Pa. L. Rev. 263 (1980); Hazen, Corporate Mismanagement and the Federal Securities Act's Antifraud Provisions: A Familiar Path with Some New Detours, 20 B.C.L. Rev. 819 (1979).

question by voting against it, since full disclosure would have enabled shareholders to seek other kinds of redress under state law, such as seeking to enjoin the transaction.[4]

Application to mergers

The *Goldberg* technique is especially useful in the context of corporate acquisitions. For example, in *Healey v. Catalyst Recovery of Pennsylvania, Inc.*,[5] the court held that where a misrepresentation or omission deprives a plaintiff minority shareholder of an opportunity under state law to enjoin a merger, there is a cause of action under Rule 10b-5. It also held that the plaintiff must demonstrate, at the time of the misrepresentation or omission, that there was a "reasonable probability of ultimate success" in securing an injunction had there been no misrepresentation or omission.

When corporation is deceived

In *Maldonado v. Flynn*,[6] the Second Circuit returned to the concept of deception of the corporation and explored it further. The court enunciated and applied several principles.

(1) Where corporate action requires shareholder approval, full disclosure of material information must be made to the shareholders.
(2) Where their approval is not necessary, full disclosure to a disinterested board of directors will do. Even if some of the directors are interested, then, absent domination or control of the board by interested officers, approval of the transaction by a disinterested majority of the board possessing authority to act and "fully informed of all relevant facts" will suffice to bar a Rule 10b-5 claim that the corporation or its stockholders were deceived. (This can be a critical point where none of the "disinterested" but informed outside directors wants to take action against possible unfairness, but one of the minority shareholders, had he been informed, would have done so.)
(3) The test of disinterest is lack of any financial stake by a director in the transaction under consideration. Thus, the corporation's outside lawyer who sits on the board would normally be treated for these purposes as a disinterested director, even though he has an obvious incentive to approve what management wants so that his

[4] Query what the result would be if the shareholders' only remedy was appraisal. One might argue that the remedy forestalled by nondisclosure has to be a corporate one since the theory is that the "corporation" was deceived. But this seems to take the corporate fiction too literally.

[5] 616 F.2d 641 (3d Cir. 1980).

[6] 597 F.2d 789 (2d Cir. 1979).

law firm will continue to get lots of business from the corporation. This weak test of disinterest has been criticized in the law journals.[7]

§8.11.2 Problems with Recovery Against the Corporation

The misrepresentation and omission cases also involve the issue of finding a proper fit between harms and remedy — who should have a right of recovery against whom for what — but the discussion of the issue in this context must be somewhat different from the one that occupied us in connection with conventional insider trading.

The *TGS* litigation

The *Texas Gulf Sulphur* litigation[8] provides a good starting point. Corporate personnel had made discoveries that seemed to indicate a major body of commercially minable ore. Rumors of the discovery began to circulate. The corporation issued a misleading press release that downplayed the significance of the company's exploratory efforts. While the press release was having its depressing effect on the market price of the company's stock, various officers and employees frantically bought up company shares. That is, they engaged in conventional insider trading, and would have profited handsomely had it not been for the ensuing torrent of litigation. Both the corporaton and a *nontrading insider,* an executive vice president of the company who participated in drafting and issuing the fraudulent press release, were also sued in a private action for damages under Rule 10b-5. In *Mitchell v. Texas Gulf Sulphur Co.,*[9] they were held liable to plaintiffs who had sold stock in reliance upon the misleading press release.

Hypo for analysis

Suppose the following simplified case. Officer *O,* who never buys or sells any stock, causes X Corporation to issue a fraudulent press release on April 1. The effect is to produce a market price of $1 per X share, whereas (our expert investment analyst later tells us, at trial) a true press release would have resulted in a market price of $2 per share. These conditions, a $1 actual market price and $2 intrinsic value, persist until April 15, when

[7]See, e.g., Note, The Propriety of Judicial Deference to Corporate Boards of Directors, 96 Harv. L. Rev. 1894 (1983).

[8]See SEC v. Texas Gulf Sulphur Co., 401 F.2d 833 (2d Cir. 1968), cert. denied, 394 U.S. 976 (1969); Mitchell v. Texas Gulf Sulphur Co., note 9 infra; In re Texas Gulf Sulphur Securities Litigation, 344 F. Supp. 1398 (1972) (listing 70 suits); Cannon v. Texas Gulf Sulphur Co., 55 F.R.D. 308 (S.D.N.Y. 1972) (settlement).

[9]446 F.2d 90 (10th Cir. 1971), cert. denied, 404 U.S. 1004 (1971), reh. denied, 404 U.S. 1064 (1972).

the falsity is uncovered and the market price jumps to $2. During the 15 day interim, half of the investors who owned X stock just before April 1 sold at $1; the other half are continuing shareholders. Understandably, the selling shareholders now want to sue to recover damages, which for the moment we assume will be so-called actual damages of $1 per share sold. They would like to reach certain X directors who bought on the basis of the undisclosed correct information during the interim period, but these individuals have absconded.

Recovery from buyers is unfeasible

In principle, the courts might analyze and evaluate five alternative approaches to the question of remedies for the selling shareholders. First, the sellers might obtain recovery from all those who bought stock during the 15 day period on the theory that each buyer has a windfall gain which should have gone to the sellers. But this approach is practically unfeasible. It also seems unjust to the noninsider buyers since they played no role in issuing the fraudulent release which caused the sellers' problem.

From officer, inadequate

Second, the selling shareholders might recover their actual damages solely from *O*, the corporate official responsible for the press release. While the prospect of liability of this sort might very well deter some future officers form falsifying press releases, this approach would frequently impose a staggeringly disproportionate personal liability on them. Moreover, because of the limits to the officers' personal wealth, it would frequently leave selling shareholders greatly undercompensated.

From corporation, unfair to others

Third, the selling shareholders might recover their actual damages solely from the corporation on whose behalf the press release was issued. A close variant of this approach would be to make *O* and and X jointly and severally liable but with the practical understanding that plaintiffs would first seek, and usually get, full payment from the corporation. This variant is the approach taken in the *Mitchell* case, with the modification (soon to be discussed) that a "cover" measure of damages rather than an actual damages measure was used in the computations. The variant approach will in practice often be substantially equivalent to recovery against the corporation alone. The corporation might in principle seek contribution from the officer, but it often will not, and it might not be able to collect any judgment if it did. The main problem with recovery against the corporation is, of course, that it is very unfair to the continuing shareholders. In effect, it taxes them a part (in our hypothetical, half) of their share of the value of the favorable corporate developments in order to give the selling shareholders the full amount of their share. In addition, it only partly takes away the putative windfall gain from the buying shareholders.

No remedy is also bad

In disgust over the apparent absence of the perfect remedy, the court might consider a fourth alternative, giving the selling shareholders no right of recovery. But this would leave the sellers with no compensation for the injury they suffered by virtue of the fraud. It would leave all efforts to deter people like *O* in the hands of public enforcement agencies like the SEC, which may simply lack the resources to do a complete job. In light of these considerations, perhaps the *Mitchell* court's approach is the least unpalatable alternative.

Equal sharing approach

Yet there is a fifth alternative, which I call "the equal sharing approach," and it deserves to be considered by the courts. This approach views the impact of the fraud as similar to that of an unfortunate accident which alters the natural or ideal distribution of rewards among selling, buying, and continuing shareholders. It seeks to spread the impact of the accident evenly among all three of these groups. Thus, solely for purposes of determining claims to the increment in total corporate value represented by the corporate event or condition that the press release falsified, the plaintiff selling shareholders would be treated as if they were still shareholders.

In our hypothetical, suppose the sellers had sold 50 shares during the April 1-15 period, the buyers had bought and now still possess 50 shares, and the continuing shareholders have held 50 shares. At all times, the outstanding X stock amounted to only 100 shares. During the April 1-15 period, the total market value of the company's stock was $100 whereas its intrinsic value was twice that amount. Under the approach suggested, the $100 difference ought to be allocated proportionately among the selling, buying, and continuing shareholders. This is done by letting the sellers recover, from the corporation, 66 cents for each share they sold, which is computed as follows:

(1) The corporation's "equal sharing claims" are calculated. Here the number is 150 claims, the sum of the actual shares plus those sold by the defrauded sellers.
(2) The defrauded sellers' portion of these claims is computed. The answer is 50 sold shares divided by 150 equal sharing claims, that is, one third.
(3) The defrauded sellers' share of the misrepresented increment in corporate value is figured: ⅓ times $100 = $33. Finally, this is translated into a per share figure — $33/50 shares = 66 cents — so that each plaintiff's damages can be easily computed.)

This compares with a *Mitchell*-type recovery of $1 per share, which is much harsher on the innocent continuing shareholders.

§8.11.3 Measures of Damages

Restitution

Under the courts' actual approach to the general problem of a damage remedy for defrauded sellers in *Mitchell*-type situations — that is, give them full recovery from the corporation — there still remain problems concerning the precise measure of damages. Unlike the alternatives just discussed, some of these alternative measures were analyzed in *Mitchell.* The plaintiffs wanted restitution, or damages equivalent to restitution, for the stock they sold in reliance on the false press release. Thus, they wanted damages equal to the number of shares they sold times the market price of the corporation's shares at the time of suit, minus their sales proceeds. In effect, they claimed a right to the value of increases in the price of the corporation's stock occurring long after the fraud had been uncovered.

Actual damages

The defendants, of course, wanted another measure, so-called actual damages: the difference between the price at which the plaintiffs actually sold and the true or intrinsic value on that date. True value means the fair market value the stock would have had on the plaintiffs' selling date had there been no fraud. The true value of the stock on the sale date is not directly observable, of course, so the courts have to decide which bit or bits of objective data to use as evidence of what the true value was and how conclusively to treat the evidence. Unfortunately, they sometimes seem unaware of the basic theory of actual damages and fail to recognize what they are really doing is seeking evidence of an essentially unobservable figure. A favorite candidate for the key evidentiary figure is the actual market value reached by the stock soon after dissemination of the information correcting the fraud. It is also possible to use an average of actual market prices observed over some short time period (say, 10 days) after the truth has been disseminated.

Choice depends on counterfactual scenarios

As a matter of legal analysis, the choice between restitutionary and actual damages is difficult because of a causation problem somewhat reminiscent of the one underlying the dispute between the *Shapiro* and *Fridrich* opinions. Consider the question put by the but-for test of causation. What would have happened had the corporation not violated its duty but had issued an accurate press release? In the first instance, the market price of the company's stock would have been higher. Faced with the higher price, what would the plaintiff have done? Something other than what he did, obviously. But there is more than one possibility. He might have held on to the stock, on the basis of a judgment that the accurate press release and the higher stock price signified even greater things to come. If this is our view of what he would have done, then restitution may seem the proper measure of damages. On the other hand, if the plaintiff had been faced by an accurate press release and a higher market price, he might simply have sold his stock at the higher price. If this is our image of what he would have done, then actual damages are clearly the proper measure of damages.

But actual damages are better

Since both views have some plausibility, the choice is not easy. My own view is that the actual damages measure is preferable. The restitutionary measure requires one to make a large number of speculative, counterfactual assumptions about the plaintiff's behavior, namely, that on each day since the inaccuracy was corrected until the time of suit the plaintiff would have decided not to sell his stock. The actual damages measure requires the court to make one counterfactual determination — what the stock's price would have been had accurate information been publicly available when the plaintiff sold — and this task seems more manageable.

"Cover" measure, occasionally

What do the courts do in fact? The answer varies. In *Mitchell,* the Tenth Circuit, obviously perceiving the logical dilemma at some intuitive level, rejected both restitutionary and actual damages, and instead adopted a compromise "cover" measure of damages, the rationale of which is hard to fathom. The plaintiff can recover the difference between the price at which he sold and the price that he would have had to pay to cover himself, that is, to reinvest in TGS stock during a reasonable time period after he actually learned about the press release correcting the impression created by the earlier false release.[10] On the particular facts, this gave a somewhat different result than the actual damages measure, because the plaintiffs were somewhat slow to learn about the corrective press release. In many situations, the actual and cover measures may be fairly close in outcome. In any event, many cases have applied the actual or out of pocket measure of damages in cases involving defrauded *buyers.*[11]

§8.12 Beyond Insider Trading: Trading on Nonpublic but Noninside Information

Market information

In this section we turn to issues similar to those explored in subsection 8.10.2 (who can be sued) but focus more on types of information than types

[10] Reynolds v. Texas Gulf Sulphur Co., 309 F. Supp. 548, 564 (D. Utah 1970), aff'd sub nom. Mitchell v. Texas Gulf Sulphur Co., cited supra note 9 to subsection 8.11.2.

[11] E.g., Madigan Inc. v. Goodman, 498 F.2d 233, 239 (7th Cir. 1974); Occidental Life Ins. Co. v. Pat Ryan & Assoc., 496 F.2d 1255, 1264-1265 (4th Cir.), cert. denied, 419 U.S. 1023 (1974). See also Green v. Occidental Petroleum Corp., 541 F.2d 1335, 1341-1346 (9th Cir. 1976) (Sneed, J., concurring). But see Thompson, The Measure of Recovery Under Rule 10b-5: A Restitution Alternative to Tort Damages, 37 Vand. L. Rev. 349 (1984).

of defendants. No one seriously doubts that Section 10(b) and Rule 10b-5 cover conventional insider trading, as well as material misrepresentations and omissions made by anyone in connection with sales or purchases of securities. But what about trading by *non*insiders on the basis of nonpublic information that *is* relevant to valuation of the traded security but does not *originate* within the corporation and perhaps does not *directly* concern its assets and operations? In the past, some commentators called this the issue of whether to disclose market information,[1] and the SEC tried to extend the antifraud provisions beyond corporate-generated information by use of the phrase *material nonpublic information*. We may usefully analyze several distinct examples.

§8.12.1 Information about One's Own Trading Activity

The self-fulfilling prophet

Suppose an investment analyst, who writes a financial column for a newspaper, buys stock in X Corporation and then immediately publishes a column that strongly urges all readers to buy as much X stock as they can. The column contains no factual misstatements, but it does not disclose that the writer has just purchased a large block of the stock or that he intends to sell it in the near future if the price rises. Many readers follow the columnist's advice, and the increase in the volume of buy orders for X stock raises its price significantly. The columnist then sells his X stock at a hefty profit. Has he violated Section 10(b) and Rule 10b-5?

The answer would appear to be yes.[2] One analysis is that his recommendation was deceptive because there was a misleading omission: He knowingly failed to reveal material information about his own position in the stock and his intent to benefit from his readers' reactions to his advice. In addition, the columnist's behavior is arguably a form of stock manipulation, and manipulative as well as deceptive practices are outlawed by Section 10(b). Manipulation is behavior aimed at creating trading, or the appearance of active trading, in a security for the purpose of inducing others to buy or sell the security.[3]

Compare to standard manipulation

A more standard example of manipulation would not involve a verbal communication such as a financial column. For instance, Mo and Flo might

§8.12 [1]Fleischer, Mundheim, and Murphy, An Initial Inquiry into the Responsibility to Disclose Market Information, 121 U. Pa. L. Rev. 798 (1973).

[2]The practice described in the text is known as "scalping." See SEC v. Capital Gains Research Bureau, Inc., 375 U.S. 180 (1963); Zweig v. Hearst Corp., 594 F.2d 1261 (9th Cir. 1979); Note, A Financial Columnist's Duty to the Market under Rule 10b-5: Civil Damages for Trading on a Misleading Investment Recommendation, 26 Wayne L. Rev. 1021 (1980).

[3]See Hundahl v. United Benefit Life Ins. Co., 465 F. Supp. 1349, 1359-1363 (N.D. Tex. 1979); 3 L. Loss, Securities Regulation 1529-1570 (1961).

agree to sell 10,000 shares of X stock back and forth to each other on the over-the-counter market in the following way: On Day 1 Mo sells to Flo at 51; on Day 2, Flo sells back to Mo at 52; on Day 3, Mo sells to Flo at 53; and so on until Mo gets the stock back at 60. At that time, if other investors have been led by the apparently large volume of trading and rising price of X stock to be willing to buy X stock at 60, perhaps because they think that other people have independently valued X Corporation and arrived at an optimistic appraisal of its prospects, then Mo may unload the X stock at 60 to a group of such investors.

Problem is similar

While the original hypothetical about the columnist involved a verbal promotion of trading activity, the problem in the two hypotheticals is similar. If public investors had known the columnist was self-interested because of his stock holdings and his intention to sell on a price rise, they might well have assessed his advice differently. If public investors had known of the Mo-and-Flo arrangement, which was not based on an assessment of X's prospects, then they might also have discounted the significance of the active trading in X stock. Hence both behavior patterns seem to fall within the concept of manipulation.

§8.12.2 Market Information Obtained by Chance or Industry

Accidental recipient

Suppose that Jones is sitting in a bar in Switzerland and inadvertently overhears two Arab oil ministers discussing a major OPEC policy decision that has yet to be announced to the world. Calculating how the new policy will tend to affect the business environment and profits of various U.S. companies, Jones rushes to phone his stockbroker in New York and to make purchases and sales accordingly. As a result, he makes risk-adjusted returns on his investments that are very much above those reaped by other public investors. Has he violated Section 10(b)?

Diligent searcher

Or consider Y Corporation, which devotes a great deal of management time to an intensive analysis of the world market for expandrium products, concludes that the market's potential has been widely unappreciated, and then proceeds to purchase stock in X Corporation, a leading expandrium producer, without disclosing the results of its study. Has it violated Section 10(b)? In either case, the traders may be characterized as trading on the basis of material nonpublic information.

Positive response to searcher

But most observers would balk at making these traders liable for their outsider trading. At the least, one wants to excuse Y Corporation because a rule requiring it to disclose its research or refrain from trading would substantially deprive it of the incentive to search out and develop undervalued opportunities. For once its favorable view of the expandrium market is known, existing shareholders will be reluctant to sell X stock to Y except at a higher price. Y will therefore lose most of the value uncovered solely by its research efforts. Since research efforts are economically desirable, it is desirable to have legal rules that allow searchers to capture the value of their work.

Mixed one to chance recipient

By contrast, Jones did little that smacks of superior skill, industry, knowledge, intelligence, or entrepreneurial effort or that otherwise might seem to call for a reward. Sound economic policy does not seem to dictate that people should be able to capture the value of information obtained by mere chance. A strained argument could be made that people should have incentives to be in places where random but occasionally useful bits of information are more likely to be received, but one doubts that this argument is sensible as applied to barrooms. One might also argue that Jones had to have acquired certain basic knowledge about the stock market in order to use the information he acquired by chance, and that this acquisition of knowledge should be rewarded. This argument also seems strained. And because the economic virtues of letting Jones make a superior investment return are tenuous or nonexistent, some analysts may want to place on him a duty to disclose or abstain, on the ground that it is unfair that he get the value of an *unearned informational advantage* that is not available to other investors. Courts have not gone this far, however. Perhaps this is because cases precisely like that of Jones are rare and actual situations raise the difficulty of determining whether an informational advantage has been earned.

§8.12.3 Market Information Received in Confidence

A more realistic class of cases includes people like law clerks who have advance knowledge of judicial decisions that will affect the price of certain corporations' stock or governmental employees with advance knowledge of other governmental decisions that will have such an effect. An apt instance of this class of cases was the subject of the Supreme Court's decision in *Chiarella v. United States.*[4] Chiarella was employed by a financial printer that had been engaged by certain corporations to print corporate takeover bids. Although the copies of documents that he received at work had blank spaces instead of names of the principal companies (to maintain confidence until the final printing was ready), he decoded the names of the target companies from information in the documents. Without disclosing

***Chiarella* case**

[4] 445 U.S. 222 (1980).

his knowledge, he purchased stock in the target companies and sold the shares immediately after the takeover attempts were made public. The SEC investigated, and he entered into a consent decree in which he agreed to return his profits to the sellers of the shares. Afterwards, he was criminally prosecuted and convicted for violating Section 10(b) and Rule 10b-5. In a 6-3 decision, the Supreme Court reversed.[5]

Duty based on fiduciary relationship

The Court held that a duty to disclose (or abstain) under Section 10(b) does not arise from the mere possession of nonpublic market information. In reasoning toward this result, Justice Powell stressed the need for defendant to be in a fiduciary-like position. He admitted that silence in connection with the purchase or sale of securities may operate as a fraud under Section 10(b). But he argued that liability under the statute presupposes a duty to disclose (or abstain) that arises from a relationship of trust and confidence between the parties to a transaction. He pointed out that the classic insider trading cases involved corporate insiders who violated their duties to shareholders (including, in some cases, those investors who became shareholders as a result of the transaction at issue). According to Powell, Chiarella had no such duty to sellers of stock of the target companies. He was not an insider of the targets by virtue of his job or position, and he received no confidential information from them. He had no prior dealings with the sellers of the stock; he was not their agent; and he was not a person in whom they had placed their trust. According to Powell, this meant that no duty could arise from his relationship to them. Finally, however, Powell noted that the Court did not have to decide whether Chiarella's conviction could be supported on the theory that he reached a duty to the *acquiring* corporations, since such a theory was not submitted to the jury.

Court's rationale

The pattern of reasoning in Powell's opinion is odd. Its essence is that the disclose or abstain rule depends on some position or relationship creating a quasi-fiduciary duty, but that the federal courts cannot say that being in the position of a stock market professional or otherwise having access to nonpublic information gives rise to the requisite duty. But why not? The language and legislative history of Section 10(b) contain no such prohibition. Nor does Powell adduce any substantive policy reasons as to why one should be implied. His argument depends on identifying a factual pattern in leading Section 10(b) cases of the past and simply declaring that it would be wrong to go beyond the boundaries of those fact patterns. Thus, he

[5]The Justices covered a large part of the spectrum of possible attitudes with their five opinions: by Powell, for the Court; by Stevens, concurring; by Brennan, concurring in the judgment; by Burger, dissenting; and by Blackmun, with whom Marshall joined, dissenting.

reviews the SEC's opinion in *Cady, Roberts,*[6] the Second Circuit's in the *Texas Gulf Sulphur* case,[7] and the Supreme Court's in *Affiliated Ute Citizens,*[8] notes faithfully that they involved defendants who were insiders, tippees, or persons with a specific fiduciary duty to the plaintiffs, and then assumes that only persons with these statuses can have a duty under Section 10(b) to public investors. The closest thing to a reason for this assumption is the question-begging set of assertions,

> No duty could arise from petitioner's relationship with the sellers of the target company's securities, for petitioner had no prior dealings with them. He was not their agent, he was not a fiduciary, he was not a person in whom the sellers had placed their trust and confidence. He was, in fact, a complete stranger who dealt with the sellers only through impersonal market transactions.[9]

Critique

But, of course, corporate insiders like the chief executives of publicly held companies are usually complete strangers to the investors who have traditionally sued them in insider trading suits. And it is quite clear that courts have placed a disclose or abstain duty on them, not because any particular plaintiffs place specific trust and confidence in them as individuals, but because of the nature of the role or status they occupy in the developed system of relationships that characterize the modern corporation and the national capital markets. The directors, officers, and controlling shareholders of public corporations occupy standardized roles: Much of what they do is determined not by specific contracts but by law or custom — by "implicit form contracts." Their rights and duties have been determined as much by the cumulative effects of the not-predetermined decisions of courts applying general principles to new situations as by any concrete statutory directives. The courts, if they so choose, can exercise the power, which they possess legitimately, to help define the legal contours of other crucial roles in the great web of patterned relationships that make up the securities markets, including the role of the financial printer. Nothing written in Section 10(b) or in the stars prevents this. Justice Powell's opinion can only be understood as part of a program "to hold the line" against further developments in federal securities fraud litigation, and to freeze established patterns, whatever they might happen to be.

[6] 40 S.E.C. 907 (1961).
[7] 401 F.2d 833 (2d Cir. 1968), cert. denied, 394 U.S. 976 (1969).
[8] 406 U.S. 128 (1972).
[9] 445 U.S. at 232-233.

By contrast, Chief Justice Burger's dissent makes a refreshing foray into policy considerations. He focuses upon the *reason* for the general rule in torts that neither party to an arm's length transaction has a duty to disclose information to the other unless the parties stand in some confidential or fiduciary relation: It gives businessmen an "incentive for hard work, careful analysis, and astute forecasting."[10] Thus, the way in which material nonpublic information is obtained is crucial. Those who get it by virtue of their skill, industry, and the like, in contexts where their efforts are generally economically productive and have not been pledged to another's benefit, may capture its value. But, according to Burger, Section 10(b) builds on the principle that a person who has *misappropriated* nonpublic information has an absolute duty to disclose that information or refrain from trading. The securities laws' antifraud provisions aim "to assure that dealing in securities is fair and without undue preferences or advantages among investors."[11] A person who, like Chiarella, "purchases securities on the basis of misappropriated nonpublic information possesses just such an 'undue' trading advantage; his conduct quite clearly serves no useful function except his own enrichment at the expense of others."[12]

Misappropriation theory

Burger's stress on the unproductiveness and unfairness of Chiarella's behavior comes close to the view that investors should not trade on unearned informational advantages, but he adds the element of misappropriation. His view in the case was essentially that Chiarella had misappropriated information belonging to the acquiring companies. Justices Powell and Brennan, and perhaps the other Justices, disagreed with the Chief Justice on whether the jury was adequately charged with this theory, but no one on the Court expressly disagreed with this theory. The opinions thus left it open for the government to try to convict future Chiarellas by simply altering the stated theory of the case and the jury instructions.

Left open in *Chiarella*

Subsequent case law demonstrated that this possibility was a real one. In *United States v. Newman,*[13] the Second Circuit upheld the legal sufficiency of an indictment against Newman, a securities trader for a brokerage firm. Newman had been tipped off by two investment banking firm employees about impending acquisitions by clients of the firm and had arranged purchases of stock in the various target companies. The case is thus quite

Subsequently adopted and applied

[10] Id. at 240.

[11] H.R. Conf. Rep. No. 94-229, 94th Cong., 1st Sess., reprinted in 1975 U.S. Code Cong. & Ad. News 323.

[12] 445 U.S. at 241.

[13] 664 F.2d 12 (2d Cir. 1981), cert. denied, 104 S. Ct. 193 (1983). See also SEC v. Materia, 745 F.2d 197 (2d Cir. 1984) (misappropriation theory applied to a financial printer), cert. denied, 105 S. Ct. 2112 (1985).

analogous to *Chiarella* and shows that the use of the misappropriation theory could well have changed the result in that case.

Rule 14e-3

Another reason why a present-day Chiarella would have legal trouble is that the SEC subsequently adopted Rule 14e-3, pursuant to the tender offer provisions of the 1934 Act, to outlaw precisely the kind of conduct in which Chiarella had engaged.[14]

Enforcement problem

Nevertheless, a serious problem of enforcement remains. In a case like *Chiarella* or *Newman,* involving someone who is not an insider with respect to a target company but who trades on nonpublic information about an impending acquisition of it, can public investors who traded opposite such a person bring a successful private civil action for damages under Rule 10b-5? For example, does the susceptibility to criminal liability of Newman and the investment banking firm employees who tipped him mean that sellers of the target company stock during the period when Newman and the employees were buying on the basis of undisclosed information could recover damages from them under Rule 10b-5? In *Moss v. Morgan Stanley,*[15] the answer given to this question was no. The basic reason was that the investment banking firm and its employees had no fiduciary relationship *to the plaintiffs,* that is, the target company stockholders.

§8.12.4 Market Information Obtained by Structural Insiders

Particularistic reasoning

As developed by the courts, the reach of Rule 10b-5, even as it has been boosted by the misappropriation theory, still depends on a rather specific vision of a quasi-fiduciary relationship: For example, financial printers and their employees have duties to their clients but not necessarily to public investors who are deeply affected by the information they handle. This view of the matter seems to oust the possibility of private actions for damages under Section 10(b): The selling shareholders in a Chiarella-type situation are not owed a duty by the printer, and the printer's client might run afoul of the purchaser-seller doctrine.

More universal concepts

The only position taken by any Supreme Court Justices that broke away from specific-relationship reasoning and proposed a fairly general rule governing relationships among participants in the securities markets was that of Justices Blackmun and Marshall in the *Chiarella* case. They seem to

[14] Rule 14e-3 imposes a duty to disclose or abstain from trading on any person obtaining inside information about a tender offer from either the offeror or the target company.

[15] 553 F. Supp. 1347 (S.D.N.Y. 1983), aff'd, 719 F.2d 5 (2d Cir. 1983), cert. denied, 104 S. Ct. 1280 (1984).

have adopted much of the reasoning of Professor Brudney.[16] Blackmun would have found Chiarella's conduct fraudulent under Section 10(b) even if Chiarella had obtained the blessing of the acquiring companies whose documents he was working on. For Blackmun believed that a structural disparity in access to material information is a critical factor under Rule 10b-5. Accordingly, although unsure that he would fully accept the market insider category created by the Second Circuit, he would have held that "persons having access to confidential material information that is not legally available to others generally are prohibited by Rule 10b-5 from engaging in schemes to exploit their structural informational advantage through trading in affected securities."[17]

A vision of the *system*

In my own view, something like the approach of Blackmun or the Second Circuit is warranted. One can speak meaningfully about the characteristics and appropriate duties of people like financial printers, SEC employees who receive documents for filing, accountants and lawyers for acquiring companies in takeovers, and even union officials who have advance knowledge that their members will strike certain companies and affect the value of their stock. These and similar persons occupy standardized roles in the securities market system or, as in the case of the union official, in organizations whose activities have regular impacts on the securities markets. By virtue of their roles, they may have access to material nonpublic information not legally available to public investors. But their roles were not created for the purpose of giving them special information for their own benefit. The activities called for by their jobs do not consist of personally gathering, analyzing, and evaluating publicly available raw data in order to form specific judgments about securities values. Individuals who fit this description — let us call them structural insiders as opposed to corporate or market insiders — can reasonably be asked to refrain from trading on the basis of material nonpublic information that they get through their roles. Such a duty would promote fairness among investors. By reducing investor discouragement and distrust of the market because of the structural insiders' perceived advantages, it might even further the goal of economic efficiency. The duty would be construed as running from structural insiders to public investors generally. Those investors who so traded in a security as to be at a disadvantage while the structural insider was reaping the benefit of his informational advantage would have standing to bring suit under Section 10(b).

[16] Brudney, Insiders, Outsiders and Informational Advantages under the Federal Securities Laws, 93 Harv. L. Rev. 322 (1979).

[17] 445 U.S. at 251.

Climax of this chapter

The proposed duty on the part of structural insiders would reflect the true nature of the modern securities markets: not a disjointed assemblage of particular relationships between individuals but a connected system of universal relationships among role players — where corporations that differ in their businesses are all just so many competitors for funds; where investors reduce stocks to fungibility by focusing on the abstract characteristics of risk and return; where institutions shift holdings at the drop of an index; where established institutions like unions often have impacts on stock prices; and where, in order to make the vast numbers of shifting relationships manageable, everyone is expected to fit himself into the nearest available role, and to orient himself to its functions, its tasks, its expectations — and its duties.

CHAPTER 9

THE VOTING SYSTEM

Before looking into the matters discussed in the next several chapters, it is desirable to get a more detailed sense of how shareholder voting works.

Anyone who has ever owned a small block of shares in a publicly held corporation and received annual proxy materials probably has wondered whether shareholder voting rights amount to anything or serve any useful purpose. Before examining this question (section 9.5), we shall explore the basic legal rules governing the voting system, both at the state (section 9.1) and the federal (sections 9.2-9.4) level.

§9.1 State Law of Voting Rights

Approach

In this section I will simply give brief explanations of some key concepts that are met in the state law governing voting rights. As in many other areas of corporate law, there are numerous variations in the detailed provisions of different state statutes. Thus, for the person who wants to become a practicing corporate lawyer, there is no substitute for painstakingly careful study of the actual text of all provisions of the relevant state statute. Nevertheless, it will help greatly to know beforehand what the basic ideas and patterns are.

§9.1.1 When Votes Are Cast

Annual meetings

Shareholder votes are cast at both annual meetings and special meetings. There are several elementary points that you should know about annual meetings. First, corporations are usually supposed to hold them. Statutes usually assume, if they do not state, that corporations are required to hold annual meetings. If an annual meeting is not held in timely fashion, a shareholder can often get a judicial order forcing one to be held.

Second, the usual business of an annual meeting is to vote for the election of directors, but other matters on which shareholders can act may be brought up, even if not described in the notice of the meeting.

Third, for a valid meeting at which binding action can take place, it is necessary that notice and quorum requirements be satisfied. For example, the statute may require that an officer of the corporation give shareholders notice of the date, time, and place of each meeting no fewer than 10 nor more than 50 days before the meeting date, and that holders of 50 percent or more of the shares must be present (in person or by proxy) in order to make a quorum. The statute will often allow these requirements to be modified in the articles or bylaws, although it may also impose limits on such modifications. For example, it might say that the articles cannot prescribe a quorum of fewer than one-third of the outstanding shares.

Special meetings

Special meetings are held episodically. Usually they may be called by the company's board of directors or by certain individuals authorized to do so in the articles or bylaws. Only business described in the notice of meeting can be conducted at a special meeting. Notice and quorum requirements have to be met, of course.

Written consents

A number of state statutes now allow action by shareholders apart from shareholder meetings, by means of written consents obtained from some specified proportion of shareholders — say, those holding more than 50 percent of the shares. These provisions were originally adopted to make life easier for close corporations. But in recent years they have been used by persons attempting hostile takeovers of corporations, as a way of achieving certain tactical objectives, such as removing current directors or modifying bylaw provisions, in a somewhat speedier and less formal way.

Those soliciting such consents will often have to comply with the filing and disclosure requirements of the federal proxy rules, however, so the net advantages of the technique may be modest. Moreover, as a defensive maneuver, many corporations have adopted bylaw or charter provisions that preclude shareholder action by means of written consents.

§9.1.2 Who Votes and How

Consequences of wide ownership

The fact that the modern public corporation is designed to have widespread ownership and freely transferable ownership interests has led to the evolution of a number of distinctive practices concerning voting rights. These practices are reflected in at least three basic concepts: the record date, street name ownership, and the proxy.

Record dates

A record date determines who is entitled to notice of a particular upcoming shareholder meeting and who may vote at it — namely, those persons who were registered as shareholders "of record" on that date. The record date is often set in the bylaws, subject to limits laid out in the governing corporate statute.[1] A corporation might set the record date before its annual meeting at 30 days before the meeting date, for example. If it could not do so, but sent out notices and proxy materials to shareholders of record 30 days before the meeting *and* to all others who became such right up to the time of meeting, it would incur greater administrative costs and might generate confusion. Obviously, these problems become more serious the more widespread and actively traded the shares are. A similar set of problems would arise if the corporation decided to determine who was entitled to vote at the meeting on the basis of actual ownership at the time of vote.

Street name ownership

Similarly, widespread and constantly shifting ownership of stock is one factor behind the holding of stock in street name. For example, suppose a brokerage firm is the nominal, registered owner of a large number of XYZ shares. Hundreds of its customers have claims to specified numbers of these shares,[2] which they are constantly buying and selling. But for the most part, the buying and selling doesn't require changing the name of the registered owner and having new share certificates issued.[3]

Depositories

A further reduction in the costs of issuing and transferring physical

§9.1 [1] See MBCA §7.07.

[2] Customers have the option of buying stock in their own names and holding the actual certificates, of course.

[3] At most, the brokerage firm has only to buy or sell shares to the extent of *net* changes in street name ownership by its customers, and there will be a single nominal owner.

certificates occurs when the brokerage firm itself becomes equitable owner of an interest in a super XYZ certificate that is owned by a depository trust company, represents many shares, and is equitably owned by numerous brokerage firms. Then only one new giant certificate need be issued for all the brokerage firms' street name customers each day, reflecting only changes in the net level of ownership by those customers. Records of customers' ultimate equitable claims are maintained and updated as computer entries.

Obviously, when there are one or two intermediaries of this sort between the ultimate owner and the corporation, care has to be taken that brokerage firms receive and forward proxy materials, annual reports, and the like to their customers and cast votes in accordance with customer instructions. The SEC has long applied pressure, by rules and otherwise, to foster this practice.

Proxy voting

Finally, the fact that the stock of public corporations is held by numerous, widely scattered shareholders, many of whom have only a small stake in a particular company, means that most shareholders cannot be expected to attend shareholder meetings in person in order to cast their votes. Instead, they sign proxies or proxy cards authorizing specified other persons, often management, to vote their shares in a specified way.

Split ownership puzzles

The facts that shares are continually being transferred and that, in an advanced economy, rights in shares are often split in complex ways (between trustee and beneficiaries, for example) generate many run-of-the-mill legal puzzles. For example, when a borrower pledges XYZ stock to secure a loan from a lending bank, who has the right to vote the shares? As far as the issuing corporation is concerned, the registered owner, which may be either pledgor or pledgee. The rights of the pledgor and pledgee depend on their agreement. Some pledge agreements contemplate that the pledgee will register the stock in its own name at the outset, with a promise to retransfer it when the loan is paid; whether the pledgee promises also to vote the stock as the pledgor wishes depends on the agreement. Under other pledge agreements, the lender takes possession of the stock certificate and an already signed stock transfer power but doesn't have the stock registered in its own name unless and until the pledgor defaults on the loan. Under such an arrangement, the pledgor usually keeps the voting rights.

Subsidiary with parent shares

A rather different kind of problem results from the fact that corporations themselves are allowed, under modern statutes, to own shares in other corporations. Suppose P is a publicly held corporation with 10 million outstanding common shares and S is its wholly owned subsidiary. The board of P selects and controls the directors of S. They cause S to buy 11 million newly issued common shares of P. May they (really, the board and top management of P; technically, the board of directors of S) vote these P shares at shareholder meetings? If so, then management will have usurped voting control of P from its shareholders. But such shares would probably lack voting power, just as treasury shares do.[4]

§9.1.3 How Voting Power Is Distributed

One share – one vote rule

One vote per share? Generally, unless the articles of incorporation provide otherwise, each outstanding share of stock is entitled to one vote on each matter voted on at a shareholders' meeting.[5] Usually, common shares are governed by this one share – one vote rule. But preferred shares are often created so as to have lesser voting rights — for example, no rights to vote for directors unless and until specified dividend payments to the preferred shareholders have been skipped for two years.

Attack on rule

The one share–one vote rule has been maintained for public corporations with the help of the major stock exchanges, whose listing rules have prohibited or discouraged nonvoting shares or shares with restricted voting power. As of this writing, however, a movement has recently been launched, mainly by managers who fear their firms will become the object of hostile takeover attempts,[6] to pressure the exchanges into allowing restricted and nonvoting shares. But the movement is being resisted — for example, by pension funds and other institutional investors that generally benefit from takeover attempts — and the outcome is uncertain. The theory of the distribution and separate transferability of shareholder voting rights has received a modest amount of academic commentary.[7]

Cumulative voting. A related concept that is of greater importance to close corporations than to public corporations is cumulative voting. I will dis-

[4]Treasury shares are shares that are authorized and issued but not outstanding; that is, they are held by the issuing corporation. Obviously, if treasury shares had voting power, management could always and easily arrogate voting control to itself. For example, the board of P could cause it to sell 1 million newly issued P shares to P's top managers at the going market price, then cause P to buy the stock back at the same price and keep it as treasury shares, then do the same with another 1 million shares, and so on, until the treasury shares amounted to more than half of the authorized and issued shares. By mere paper transactions, without any permanent parting with money on the part of P or its managers or directors, the public would have been disenfranchised.

[5]MBCA §7.21(a).

[6]These are discussed in chapter 13.

[7]See, e.g., Clark, Vote Buying and Corporate Law, 29 Case Wes. Res. L. Rev. 776 (1979); Easterbrook & Fischel, Voting in Corporate Law, 26 J.L. & Econ. 395 (1983).

cuss, in turn, how it works, arguments for and against it, and some typical legal provisions and issues.

Straight voting example

To understand cumulative voting, consider first the ordinary system of straight voting. Under this system, each share entitles its owner to cast only one vote for each candidate, although the shareholder may vote for as many candidates as there are seats to filled.[8] For example, assume that Family Corporation has 300 shares outstanding. Alex owns 199 shares, and Brother owns the remaining 101. The annual meeting is imminent, and three directors are to be elected. (Family has a three person board, and each directorship is refilled every year.) There are six candidates: three supported by Alex and three by Brother. Under a straight voting system, Alex could cast 199 votes for each of his candidates, while Brother would cast 101 votes for each of his candidates. Even though Brother controls over one-third of the votes, each of his candidates will lose. Under a straight voting system, any person who controls a majority of the votes in a particular election can elect *all* the directors.

Cumulative voting example

Under the system of *cumulative voting,* however, Brother could elect one of his candidates to the board. Under cumulative voting, each shareholder has a number of votes equal to the number of shares he owns times the number of directorships to be filled (as under straight voting) but can distribute them among candidates as he wishes. Thus, Brother could cast all of his 303 votes for a single candidate rather than spread them among three candidates. No matter how Alex splits his 597 votes, he can elect only two board members. If he splits his votes evenly among his three candidates, for example, they each will have 199 votes. But Brother's candidate will have 303 votes and will therefore be elected ahead of them; there will be only two seats left, to be allocated (somehow) to two of Alex's candidates. Brother is therefore assured of a seat on the board.

On the other hand, there is no way (short of a foolish miscalculation by the majority shareholder) that cumulative voting will result in a change in control of the corporation. If, for example, Brother tried to get pushy and elect two of the three directors of Family, by allocating 152 votes to one candidate and 151 to the other, he could not succeed and would run a risk of not electing either. Alex would either split his votes 299/298, thus winning the first two directorships anyway, or split them 199/199/199, thus winning all three directorships.

General rule

As suggested, the general rule by which cumulative voting is imple-

[8] Alternatively, you could think of each directorship as a box (or seat) that can and must be filled by only one person; each share entitles its owner to cast one vote toward determining the occupant of that box.

mented is that each shareholder receives as many votes as he has shares, multiplied by the number of directors to be elected at the meeting. Furthermore, the statutes authorize the shareholder to distribute those votes "among as many candidates as the shareholder sees fit."

Formula

Cumulative voting allows minority shareholders to make precise calculations as to whether they can elect representatives to the board and, if so, how many. The usual general formula[9] used to determine the minimum number of shares that a shareholder needs to elect a given number of directors is

$$X = \frac{Y + N' + 1}{N + 1}$$

where

Y — the total number of shares outstanding (400 in our example).

N — the total number of directors to be elected (3 in the example).

N′ — the number of directors the shareholder desires to elect (1 in the example)

X — the number of shares needed to elect N′ directors (101 in the example).

Argument pro

Is cumulative voting a good idea? The strongest argument for cumulative voting is that it provides a large minority shareholder with a "look-in" at the board and at management decisions that affect his investment. Furthermore, the presence of a minority director may force other directors in the corporation to weigh their policy decisions more carefully, because they realize that an independent and self-interested director is alert to signs of a breach of fiduciary duty. In particular, the minority director may lead nominally unaffiliated directors, who otherwise would go along with any and all management proposals, to exercise some independent judgment.

Argument con

The customary argument against cumulative voting is that it disrupts the optimal relationship between the board of directors and the management of the corporation. Ideally, it is said, the directors and managers must fully trust one another and should exude an atmosphere of willingness to cooperate. Directors must work with managers and each others to assure

[9] A more sophisticated approach is developed and explained in Glazer, Glazer, & Grofman, Cumulative Voting in Corporate Elections: Introducing Strategy into the Equation, 35 S. Car. L. Rev. 295 (1984).

the smooth day-to-day operation of the firm and a continuity between short-range decisions and long-term planning. But (it is argued) cumulative voting is likely to polarize the board and transform it into a turmoil-ridden group in which constant bickering deflects energies away from rational efforts to identify and respond to the corporation's problems and opportunities.

Resolution difficult

Weighing these competing arguments is difficult. How much extra protection of a minority shareholder's interests is given by his having a seat on the board? The answer depends in part on our beliefs about how likely it is that majority shareholders will try to take advantage of minority shareholders and about how effective other protective mechanisms (such as the ability to bring a derivative lawsuit) are. How important is blissful or even unquestioning cooperation to the running of a profitable corporation? And how much, if at all, does cumulative voting really affect constructive cooperation? Obviously, cumulative voting might launch paralyzing board-level warfare in some companies, might positively promote better business decisions in others, and might have little effect on business operations in others. Forming a general judgment involves many guesses about how things usually work.

States' approaches

Most states permit cumulative voting, leaving the matter optional with the corporation.[10] Some states have statutes mandating cumulative voting,[11] and a few state constitutions require it as well.

Devices undercutting cumulative voting

Significant legal problems may arise when corporations in states requiring cumulative voting attempt to use mechanisms that have the effect of reducing or eliminating minority representation on the board, despite the formal existence of cumulative voting. Recall that cumulative voting assures a board seat not to all minority shareholders but only to those (if any) who have more than a certain percentage of shares. What the critical percentage is depends on, and varies with, the number of directors to be elected at a meeting. If, for any reason, that number is reduced, a minority shareholder who previously could get a person on the board may suddenly find it impossible, even though he can still cumulate his votes. For example, as the formula shown earlier indicates, if there are 11 directors to be elected, an 8.5 percent shareholder is assured of a board seat. But if there are three directors to be elected, that shareholder cannot win a seat; only a minority shareholder with 25.5 percent or more of the shares could do so. The number of directors up for election can be reduced in various ways.

[10] See, e.g., MBCA §7.28(b)-7.28(d); Del. §214; N.Y. §618.
[11] Cal. §708.

The articles (or perhaps the bylaws) could be amended to change the number of directorships. Or the total number could be retained, but the articles amended to classify the board so that it has "staggered" directors; for example, directors serve three year terms but only one-third of the directorships are up for election each year. Or different classes of directors could be created, with each class to be voted on only by holders of a corresponding class of stock.

An example

Consider, for example, the case of *Bohannon v. Corporation Commission.*[12] The Arizona Constitution mandated cumulative voting. The appellants had attempted to incorporate a company with a nine member board of directors. The directors were to be staggered, so that they each would serve three year terms, but only three would be elected in any given year. As compared to a straight nine member board, the staggered board (1) would lessen the likelihood that a change in control of shareholder votes would lead to an immediate change in the control of the board of directors (thus, it was a mild anti-takeover measure) and (2) would increase the minimum minority shareholding needed to elect one director from just over one-tenth of the voting stock to just over one-fourth. In this way the incorporators proposed to gain the benefits of a large board of directors without the worry that a relatively small owner could gain board representation. The Corporation Commission rejected the proposed articles of incorporation, stating that a staggered board of directors was conceptually incompatible with the cumulative voting clause of the constitution and the policy favoring minority representation that the clause expresses.

The Supreme Court of Arizona rejected the Commission's argument and held that, because the cumulative voting system can only function as a crude minority representation device, staggered boards are permitted as long as they merely restrict the effect of the cumulative voting system without destroying the right entirely. The court also spoke about the contribution that the staggered board system makes to "corporate stability and continuity of experienced management,"[13] and the long history (presumably successful?) of the use of the staggered board in Arizona. Perhaps the court believed that cumulative voting was potentially disruptive and should not be given unrestricted scope. But the opinion never addresses the conflict between the goal of management stability and continuity and the cumulative voting system's goal of facilitating minority shareholder oversight of management.

[12] 313 P.2d 379 (Ariz. 1957).
[13] 313 P.2d at 380.

Similar problems appear in other cases. For example, constitutionally mandated cumulative voting may conflict with the constitutionally permitted practice of creating classes of shares with different voting rights.[14]

§9.1.4 What Issues Are Voted On

Director election and organic changes

As described earlier (section 3.1.1), shareholders generally have the right to vote for the election of directors and the right to vote for or against director-initiated organic changes such as mergers, sales of all assets, and dissolution of the corporation. Occasionally they may vote on whether a director should be removed from office. They may also vote on shareholder-sponsored resolutions requesting the directors to take certain actions (see subsection 9.3 below).

Greater rights, sometimes

In the close corporation context, shareholders as such sometimes have a greater set of voting rights. As will be discussed below (in subsection 18.3.5), some modern corporation statutes allow the articles of incorporation to provide that a corporation will be managed by its shareholders rather than its directors.

§9.2 The Federal Proxy Rules

Stress on disclosure

Section 14 of the Securities Exchange Act of 1934 is the source of federal regulation of the process and procedures by which proxies are obtained from shareholders of public corporations. Like other aspects of securities regulation, the focus is on assuring that public investors have true and adequate *information* before they exercise their right to vote. The statute does not purport to preempt or add to state corporate law on questions of the existence, distribution, and content of voting power — which classes of securities may vote on which matters and to what effect.

§14(a) authorizes proxy rules

Section 14(a) makes it unlawful for "any person" to solicit "any proxy or consent or authorization" from holders of registered[1] securities in violation

[14]Diamond v. Parkersburg-Aetna Corp., 122 S.E.2d 436 (W. Va. 1961). The court held in favor of allowing the separate classes of stock. The dissent argued strenuously that such special classes of stock effectively eviscerated the cumulative voting requirement.

§9.2 [1]Unless expressly exempted, all securities traded on any national securities exchange (including the New York Stock Exchange, the American Stock Exchange, and the various regional exchanges) are required to be registered with the SEC. Securities Exchange Act §12(a). In addition, when an issuer has total assets of more than $3 million and a class of equity security held of record by 500 or more persons, it has to register the securities. Securities Exchange Act §12(g); Rule 12g-1 (raising the dollar amount from $1 million to $3 million). This provision picks up many over-the-counter stocks.

of SEC rules. Thus, the subsection cannot be violated if there are no SEC rules to implement it. There are such rules, and they will be explained shortly. A major effect of them is that when corporate management solicits proxies from the shareholders, for example, proxies giving someone the power to vote for the management's candidates for directorships, the company must supply the shareholders with documents called proxy statements, which contain a medley of information that the rules require to be furnished.

§§14(b) and 14(e)

Similarly, Section 14(b) authorizes the SEC to make rules defining when it is unlawful for a registered broker-dealer to give or withhold a proxy, consent, or authorization in respect of a registered security carried for a customer's account. Section 14(c), which was added in 1964, covers the case where the management of the corporation (or other issuer of registered securities) is not making a Section 14(a) – regulated solicitation of proxies, consents, or authorizations in connection with the meeting of the security holders. (It is, however, relatively uncommon for management of a public corporation not to be soliciting some proxies for an annual meeting of the shareholders. Usually, management at least requests proxies to vote for the management slate of nominees for directorships.) In such situations, the issuer must file with the SEC and give to the security holders information similar to that which would be provided if a management solicitation were being made. Thus, even if management is not going to request a shareholder vote at a planned meeting, the corporation must nevertheless furnish the shareholders with information statements that are similar to proxy statements. One conceivable instance of this situation would be a special meeting called to consider a shareholder-sponsored resolution about which management was not prepared to make a solicitation.

Sections 14(d), (e), and (f) deal with tender offers and are covered separately in chapter 13.

Proxies and solicitations covered

Regulation 14A under the Securities Exchange Act implements Section 14(a) and comprises the SEC rules governing solicitation of proxies. Rule 14a-1 (definitions) gives definitions of key terms used in the other rules. Most notably, it defines proxy to include *every* proxy, consent, or authorization within the meaning of Section 14(a). It expresses the SEC's intention

---

As a result of these two provisions, most stock issued by the 9,000 or so U.S. corporations that could be described as publicly held corporations is registered. As a consequence, the issuing corporations are governed by important provisions of the Securities Exchange Act: the requirement that they file periodic reports with the SEC (§§13(a)-13(c)), the proxy provisions (§§14(a)-14(c)), the tender offer provisions (§§13(d)-13(f) and 14(d)-14(f)), and the provision giving them a right to recover short-swing trading profits from their insiders (§16(b)).

that the term have the broadest meaning consistent with the statute. It is clear from the definition that a proxy need not be a piece of paper; a shareholder's oral consent to a request may count. Rule 14a-2 (solicitations to which rules apply) provides that the other proxy rules will apply to all proxy solicitations, with a few exceptions: a solicitation for securities not registered under Section 12 of the Securities Exchange Act; a nonmanagement solicitation of 10 or fewer persons; and a request by a nominee, broker, or the like for instructions as to how to vote stock he holds for others, providing he meets certain conditions, such as that he receive no commission for the request other than reimbursement of reasonable expenses.

Example of *Studebaker* case

The combined sweep of these two rules covers a surprisingly wide field of activities. For example, in *Studebaker Corporation v. Gittlin,*[2] a shareholder, who hoped to achieve certain changes in the board of directors, wanted to solicit proxies for the forthcoming annual meeting. In order to solicit those proxies, he first tried to get a list of shareholders from the company. The relevant state's statutory right to inspect the list of shareholders was available to shareholders who had owned their stock for more than six months or whose shares constituted more than 5 percent of the company's stock. Not meeting either test by himself, the shareholder sought to get other shareholders to join with him. He obtained authorization from 42 other shareholders to make the request to inspect the shareholder list. (Together, their holdings topped the 5 percent mark.) The Second Circuit affirmed a district court holding that those authorizations were "proxies or consents or authorizations" within the meaning of Section 14(a) and Rule 14a-1 and that Gittlin had solicited them in violation of Rules 14a-3 to 14a-6 (see below), since he did not make the required filings with the SEC or give the 42 shareholders (and any others solicited) the required proxy statements.

Rationale

The *Studebaker* case may seem harsh at first blush, since Gittlin was caught by the rules before he made his substantive solicitation of all shareholders for proxies to vote on changes in the board of directors. But several mitigating factors should be noted. If Gittlin had obtained a shareholder list and made the substantive proxy solicitation he was planning to make, he would have had to prepare, file, and distribute a proxy statement containing much of the same information required to be given to the shareholders he asked to authorize him to seek a list. Thus, if he had done as the courts required in the first stage, at least some of his expenses for the second-stage solicitation would have been saved.

[2] 360 F.2d 692 (2d Cir. 1966).

Moreover, Gittlin had alternative courses of action. Invoking common law rather than statute, he might have tried to compel inspection of a shareholders' list without getting the authorization of other shareholders (although under this approach he probably would have had the burden of proof on the proper purpose issue). Or, again without preliminary communications to other shareholders, he might have sought to take advantage of Rule 14a-7, which if properly invoked would have obligated Studebaker either to mail his proxy materials to the other shareholders (at his expense) or to furnish a list of shareholders.

Furthermore, the purpose of the proxy rules, protection of the shareholders, seems to have been furthered by the court's holding. As Judge Friendly pointed out, Gittlin presumably told other shareholders something when he obtained their authorizations, and any misinformation spread at that time may have been very hard to undo at the later stage. And since a shareholder list is a valuable thing to one seeking control over the affairs of a corporation, shareholders ought to have full information before they help someone obtain a list.

Proxy statements and annual reports

Rule 14a-3 requires that certain information be furnished to security holders in connection with proxy solicitations. With or before the solicitation, the target person must be given a *proxy statement* conforming to Schedule 14A, which appears at the end of the rules. Among other things, Schedule 14A requires disclosure of conflicts of interest, management remuneration, and the details of major corporate changes that are to be voted upon. In addition, if the solicitation is by management, relates to an annual meeting, and involves the election of directors, then the corporation must also send the security holders an *annual report*. This document may be in a form deemed suitable by management. Typically, it will be printed on glossy paper, liberally sprinkled with photographs and logos, and written in optimistic, nontechnical style.

Yet you should not suppose that the rule doesn't regulate the annual report's content. There is, for example, a requirement that it contain *audited* financial statements for the last two years and information, for each quarter of the last two years, about the company's dividends and the high and low sales prices of its securities. Subsection (c) of the rule requires the company to send the SEC copies of the annual report "for information" although not for filing. (If a document is considered filed, certain persons may bring civil actions for damages under Section 18 of the statute against persons who caused false or misleading statements to be made in it.)[3] Subsection (d)

[3]But actions under §18 are hard to win. The statute has a strict period of limitations, requires a showing of actual reliance, and is subject to a defense of good faith ignorance of the falsehood.

imposes a duty on the issuing corporation to make inquiries of holders of record — for example, bank trust departments and broker-dealer firms — concerning the beneficial owners and to supply the record holders with proxy statements, annual reports, and the like and money for forwarding them to the beneficial owners.

Proxy cards

Rule 14a-4 lays out "requirements as to proxy," that is, some requirements as to the form and content of the proxy cards that security holders are asked to check, sign, and return. For example, the proxy form must indicate in bold face type whether the proxy is solicited on behalf of management, and if directors are to be elected, there must be a checkable box or similar device by which the security holder can withhold his authority to vote for each nominee.

Presentation of information

Rule 14a-5 deals with the presentation of information in the proxy statement. Besides exhorting preparers to write in clear and readable terms and outlawing small type, it creates some important relaxations of the disclosure requirements of Schedule 14A and Rule 14a-3. For example, with an exception for information that may be stated in terms of present knowledge or intention, "information which is not known to the persons on whose behalf the solicitation is to be made and which is not reasonably within the power of such persons to ascertain or procure may be omitted, if a brief statement of the circumstances rendering such information unavailable is made." This rule may be crucial to outsiders seeking to mount a proxy contest against management, since the outsiders may lack access to the information otherwise required to be disclosed.

Filing

Rule 14a-6 specifies filing requirements. Not only formal proxy statements conforming to Schedule A but also other proxy solicitation materials such as press releases and television scripts have to be filed with the SEC.

Mailing for shareholders

The next three rules are the most important ones, for they often apply to situations of conflict between management and outsiders. Rule 14a-7, on mailing communications for security holders, establishes what I would call the "mail their stuff or give them a list" rule. A straightforward example of its application might be a situation in which management wants the shareholders to vote their approval of a merger with another corporation, but a group of shareholders wants to solicit votes against the merger.

The rule first says that if corporate management has made or intends to make a proxy solicitation covered by the rules, the corporation must also mail out proxy materials supplied by a security holder that deal with the same subject matter or meeting. This duty arises only if the security holder is entitled to vote on the subject matter or at the meeting, makes a proper request in writing, and, most importantly, defrays the reasonable expenses incurred by the corporation in forwarding the materials. The rule, however, does not impose any limits on the length of the material supplied by the security holder, and it gives management no basis for censorship and little basis for objection.

The rule then states an alternative method of compliance. Instead of forwarding the security holder's materials, the corporation may, at its option, give the security holder a current list of the names and addresses of the security holders that are to be solicited. Since such a list might be used for other purposes than the dispute at hand — for example, to facilitate a later takeover attempt by the shareholder getting it or by their allies — management is often reluctant to choose this alternative method of compliance.

Promptness requirement

Basically, the corporation must mail a security holder's materials "with reasonable promptness" after tender of the materials and payment for postage. But in order to put the outside security holder and management on an equal footing, the rule sometimes allows the corporation to delay mailing the security holder's materials. In the case of an annual meeting, mailing may be delayed until the earlier of (1) a day corresponding to the first date on which the corporation's proxy soliciting material was released to security holders in connection with the last annual meeting of shareholders or (2) the first day on which solicitation is made on behalf of management.

The second part of this formula reflects a decision to enable management to start its own solicitation at the same time as the outsiders. The first part aims to prevent their abuse of this power. Without the alternative date, management might prepare an elaborate and apparently devastating rebuttal of the outsiders' materials, push the release of their and the outsiders' materials as close as possible to the annual meeting date, and effectively foreclose the outsiders from making a counterargument in a second solicitation. With the alternative date, management may have to release the outsider's materials fairly early and will usually feel compelled to respond quickly.[4]

Shareholder proposal rule

Rule 14a-8 is the very important shareholder proposal rule. It is the vehicle by which shareholders have tried to use the shareholder voting

[4] There are some nice questions as to the meaning of the second part of the timing formula for annual meetings. If a couple of top officers of the corporation make oral or written statements disparaging the outside shareholders' proposals and these statements are picked up and spread by the newspapers, has a solicitation on behalf of management begun for purposes of Rule 14a-7? The court answered no in Rosen v. Alleghany Corp., 133 F. Supp. 858 (S.D.N.Y. 1955), and chose to view the rule as simply mandating that the plaintiffs' material had to be mailed when the defendants' material was mailed. Query whether this view is consistent with the holding in *Studebaker*.

system as a forum for debate about issues of "corporate social responsibility," such as the propriety of a corporation's doing business in South Africa. When applicable, the rule allows security holders to have their own proposals for action at a forthcoming meeting of the corporation's security holders included in *management's* proxy statement. In contrast to a shareholder solicitation in Rule 14a-7, the printing and the mailing expenses are borne by the company rather than by the shareholder. And unlike the security holder's rights under Rule 14a-7, the right under Rule 14a-8 does not depend on management's intention to make a solicitation on the same subject matter or at the same meeting. Rule 14a-8 thus goes beyond allowing fair opposition to management proposals to positive facilitation of *shareholder-initiated* proposals. Indeed, a shareholder proposal that is counter to a proposal to be submitted by management at the forthcoming meeting (for example, a merger plan), as well as a shareholder proposal relating to election to office (for example, directorships), are specifically excluded from the kinds of proposals that may qualify under Rule 14a-8.[5]

Stringent requirements and exclusions

On the other hand, the rule imposes stringent requirements as to security holder eligibility, notice to management, timeliness of submissions, and the number and length of proposals; and it contains a long list of types of proposals that do not have to be included in management's proxy statements. Currently, a proponent must own at least 1 percent or $1,000 in market value of securities entitled to be voted at the meeting and must have held them for at least one year. He may submit only one proposal for inclusion in the proxy materials. The proposal and its supporting statement in the aggregate must not exceed 500 words. The word limit obviously curbs verbosity and saves corporations from being forced to mail out a blizzard of paper, but it also leaves little room for a thoroughly reasoned argument or a good philosophical discourse on difficult or elusive issues like corporate social responsibility.

"Not a proper subject" exclusion

As for the thirteen exceptions from the duty to include shareholder proposals, the most important is the first, which applies "[i]f the proposal is, under the laws of the issuer's domicile, not a proper subject for action by security holders." This exception reflects the SEC's interpretation of the securities laws as giving it power to mandate disclosure and to assure fair use of voting power but not to usurp the states' role in defining the existence, distribution, and subject matter of voting power. Since, as we have seen, state law generally leaves very few corporate business matters to be voted on by shareholders (election of directors and approval of organic changes, essentially), the exception seems to leave only modest scope for

[5] Rule 14a-8(c)(8), 14a-8(c)(9).

shareholder proposals under the SEC rules. But an SEC note to the first exception cautions that a proposal that is improper when framed as a mandate or directive may be proper when framed as a recommendation or request. It is for this reason that the more interesting shareholder proposals are generally framed as requests: For example, "Resolved, that the shareholders of Widget Corporation request its board of directors to consider the advisability of ceasing to do business in South Africa."

Spelled out by other exclusions

Many of the other exceptions can be interpreted as simply spelling out the implications of the first one. For example, the seventh exception, for proposals dealing with a matter relating to the conduct of the corporation's "ordinary business operations," reflects the SEC's understanding that virtually all state corporation laws leave decisions about ordinary business operations to corporate management, and, with special exceptions inspired by the needs for flexibility of close corporations, they generally do not allow shareholders to intervene in such matters. Among the other exceptions to the inclusion rule are proposals dealing with matters not significantly related to the issuer's business (as determined in part by a mechanical 5 percent test),[6] and proposals dealing with matters that are beyond the corporation's power to effectuate.[7] In their best uses, these exceptions help management get rid of "crackpot" proposals, such as "Resolved, that the antitrust laws are bad for business and should be abolished" or "Resolved, that taxation is a form of theft." They also force proponents of shareholder proposals to relate their reform ideas to the existing operations of the particular corporation and to scale them down accordingly. A resolution that the management consider not manufacturing a dangerous product now in its line is likely to qualify, while a resolution that the product is excessively dangerous and should be abandoned by all manufacturers, or even a resolution that management should try to get a law passed to regulate the product, are not likely to qualify.

Because of the special importance of Rule 14a-8, it will be discussed further in a separate section (9.3).

Antifraud rule

Rule 14a-9 outlaws false and misleading statements or omissions in connection with proxy solicitations. Its language is very similar to that of Rule 10b-5 (which we discussed at length in chapter 8) except that the latter concerns statements or omissions in connection with the purchase or sale of a security. The significant jurisprudence developed under this rule is treated in a separate subsection (9.4).

[6]Rule 14a-8(c)(5), which allows exclusion of a proposal that relates to operations accounting for less than 5 percent of the issuer's total assets, net earnings, and gross sales, "and is not otherwise significantly related to the issuer's business."

[7]Rule 14a-8(c)(6).

Other rules Rule 14a-10 prohibits solicitation of undated or post-dated proxies. The final two rules give some leeway to persons who want to react promptly against the proxy solicitations of others but who might be disabled from doing so by the requirement of first preparing a full-fledged proxy statement. Rule 14a-11 contains special provisions applicable to contests over the election of directors. A person opposing another person's solicitation may file a special, relatively short statement conforming to Schedule 14B provided that certain conditions are met. Similarly, Rule 14a-12 allows a person to make a solicitation prior to furnishing a 14A proxy statement, provided certain conditions are met, when the solicitation is in opposition to a prior solicitation, invitation for tenders, or other publicized activity other than an election contest.

§9.3 *Shareholder Proposals*

A study in federalism Experience with the shareholder proposal rule shows the uneasy tensions that exist between the federal and state roles in regulating public corporations. The federal rule, as interpreted by the federal courts, has had a modest impact on the relative power of managers and stockholders and on the conception of legitimate purposes for action by participants in the corporation.

Two eras These points can be seen by examining two major cases, each of which appeared early in a distinctive era of shareholder proposals.

In the first era, around 1950, most shareholder proposals were aimed at protection of the public stockholders' interests by installing controls on the managers. Stockholders sought to establish security holder selection of auditors, move the place of the annual meeting, require post-meeting reports to shareholders, institute cumulative voting, and control executive compensation.[1]

In the second era, around the late 1960s and early 1970s, the attention of activist stockholders was focused on general political controversies, many of which had a basis in economic shortages or conflicts between nations, races, and sexes. For example, in the 1974 proxy season the major shareholder proposals concerned corporate political activities — for example, resolutions prohibiting corporate political contributions or requiring a pub-

§9.3 [1]See Bayne, Caplin, Emerson, and Latcham, Proxy Regulation and the Rule Making Process: The 1954 Amendments, 40 Va. L. Rev. 387 (1954).

lished account of them — strip mining, equal employment, doing business in South Africa, energy conservation, and women as directors.[2]

The *Transamerica* case

SEC v. Transamerica[3] is from the first era. It is a difficult but significant case. Gilbert, a shareholder, wanted, among other things, to propose a bylaw change so that Transamerica's independent public auditors would be elected by the security holders rather than appointed by management — this on the theory that watchdogs ought not to be chosen by those they are supposed to watch. Management was inclined to omit the proposal on the ground that it would not be a proper subject for shareholder action under the law of Delaware, where Transamerica was incorporated. Their reasoning had several steps: another bylaw (47) declared that shareholders could not vote validly on a bylaw amendment unless notice of the proposed amendment was given in the notice of the annual meeting; management prepares that notice, and no law or rule clearly required them to include items suggested by other people; and management would refuse to put Gilbert's proposed amendment in the notice.

Gilbert's response to this problem was to propose a second amendment to amend bylaw 47 itself, to eliminate the notice requirement. Management's stance was that even *this* proposed amendment could not be voted upon by the stockholders unless they, management, decided to put it in the notice of meeting — which they would not. In effect, the managers were interpreting bylaw 47 as giving themselves virtually unlimited discretionary power to filter or screen out shareholder-proposed bylaw amendments that were not to their liking. They were also claiming that they had a unilateral right to decide when or whether to give up or modify this power. Gilbert pushed for inclusion of his resolutions in management's proxy material under the predecessor of Rule 14a-8. The SEC insisted that the corporation include them; the corporation refused; the SEC brought suit to enjoin the corporation's use or solicitation of proxies until it conformed to the SEC's demand. The Third Circuit sided with the SEC.

Need to assemble the rules

In order to understand what the court's opinion did and, just as important, what it could have done, it is helpful to arrange the relevant rules in a hierarchical fashion. From top to bottom, these comprise provisions in a federal statute, a federal rule, a state statute, a corporate charter, and the corporation's bylaws.

[2]See Weiss, Proxy Voting on Social Issues: A Growth Industry, Business & Society Rev. 16 (Autumn 1974).

[3]163 F.2d 511 (3d Cir. 1947), cert. denied, 332 U.S. 847 (1948).

Federal law and rule

First of all, there was Section 14(a) of the 1934 Act, which simply makes it unlawful to solicit proxies in violation of such rules as the SEC may prescribe "as necessary or appropriate in the public interest or for the protection of investors." Obviously, legislative history would have to be consulted to see how this literally open-ended language should be limited and when an SEC rule might be construed as exceeding congressional intent. Implementing the statute was a predecessor to Rule 14a-8, which obligated management to include, in its proxy material, a properly presented "proposal which is a proper subject for action by security holders." An SEC release indicated what is nowadays explicitly in the rule, that the reference was to such matters as were proper subjects for security holders' action "under the laws of the state under which [the corporation was] organized."[4]

State law and articles provisions

Section 9 of the Delaware Corporate Law contained the usual provision that the business of a corporation shall be managed by its board of directors, except as otherwise provided in the Delaware statute or in the certificate of incorporation. Article XIII of Transamerica's certificate stated that "[a]ll of the powers of this corporation, in so far as the same may be lawfully vested by this Certificate of Incorporation in the Board of Directors, are hereby conferred upon the board of directors. . . ." But these rather sweeping and indefinite provisions had to be read in conjunction with some more specific ones. Section 12 of the Delaware General Corporation law provided that, after incorporation, the power to make, alter, or repeal bylaws would be in the shareholders, although any corporation might, in its certificate, confer that power upon the directors. If a certificate provision adopted pursuant to this authorization simply stated that the directors have the power to amend the bylaws, period, it would raise serious questions. Would it mean that *only* the directors could amend the bylaws or both directors and shareholders? If the latter, which group has final say? These questions seemed mooted by Transamerica's implementing provision, in Article X of its certificate, which gave its board the power to make or alter bylaws without shareholder action and then added "but the bylaws made by the directors and the power so conferred may be altered or repealed by the stockholders." Thus, it appeared that Transamerica's founders clearly contemplated that the shareholders would have the right to undo bylaw changes made by the directors, that is, to have the final say.

[4]This crucial expression of deference to state law was mentioned by the district court, 67 F. Supp. 326, 329 (D. Del. 1946), but slighted by the Third Circuit.

Finally, at the low end of the hierarchy of rules, the controverted bylaw 47 said, **Bylaw**

> These by laws may be altered or amended by the affirmative vote of a majority of the stock issued and outstanding and entitled to both thereat, at any regular or special meeting of the stockholders *if notice of the proposed alteration or amendment* be contained in the notice of the meeting, or [by a directors' resolution, if certain procedures were followed]. (Emphasis added.)

Case involved interpretation of bylaw?

Given the whole hierarchy of rules, the court could have rejected management's view as simply being an *erroneous interpretation of bylaw 47*. Especially in view of the certificate provision giving the shareholders ability to undo management's bylaw changes, a court could reasonably conclude that the purpose of the notice provision in bylaw 47 was simply to make sure that shareholders knew about proposed bylaw amendments before the meeting at which they could vote on them, not to give management an unfettered discretion to decide what proposed amendments shareholders could and could not vote upon.

Or of state statute?

A second approach would have been to interpret the Delaware statute against the company. Even if the court conceded that the certificate and bylaws could be interpreted to mean that management had discretion to decide which proposed amendments would be voted on, the court could have interpreted Delaware law as imposing a duty on management to act in good faith in exercising their discretion or even as forbidding a certificate-and-bylaw-arrangement that completely and irrevocably ousted shareholders of the power to initiate and amend by laws.

Or of federal law?

A third approach would be to construct an expansive reading of federal law. Even assuming that bylaw 47 and Article XIII gave management the absolute power they claimed, and that Delaware permitted or did not outlaw such an arrangement, the court could declare these rules in conflict with, and preempted by, the federal proxy rule and the accompanying statute.

The court's blend

In its opinion, the Third Circuit actually seems to blend the first and third approaches. It is the court's passage on the third approach, federal priority, that is the most intriguing:

> If this minor provision [bylaw 47] may be employed as Transamerica seeks to employ it, it will serve to circumvent the intent of Congress in enacting the Securities Exchange Act of 1934. It was the intent of Congress to require fair opportunity for the operation of corporate suffrage. The control of great corporations by a very few persons was the abuse at which Congress struck in enacting Section 14(a). We entertain no doubt that [the predecessor of 14a-8] represents a proper exercise of the authority conferred by Congress on the

> Commission under Section 14(a). This seems to us to end the matter. The power conferred upon the Commission by the Congress cannot be frustrated by a corporate by-law. . . .[5]

Broad approach unnecessary and wrong

The strong language of this passage, especially the last sentence, suggests that Section 14(a) empowers the Commission, where necessary, to change the distribution and subject matter of the shareholder voting rights that would exist under state law as implemented by a valid charter and bylaws. But if the court meant this, its position seems wrong, and its decision a mere usurpation of power by a federal court on behalf of a federal agency.

Supporting argument

To see this, suppose that, like the MBCA, a state statute provides what is basically a two-step procedure for effectuating a valid merger of one company into another one: (1) the directors adopt a resolution recommending the merger and submit the resolution to a vote of the shareholders and (2) the shareholders may then authorize the merger by a vote. It is fairly clear that most state statutes of this type *intend* to deny shareholders a right to initiate the merger procedure by submitting a resolution for shareholder vote (thus bypassing the directors) or by forcing the directors to adopt a resolution and then submit it to the shareholders. The most the shareholders can do is to request that the directors consider adopting such a resolution and then submitting it to shareholder vote. In effect, shareholders are given only a veto power over mergers, not a power to bring them about despite the directors' opposition.[6] By passing the Securities Exchange Act, did Congress intend to allow the SEC to give shareholders greater voting power over mergers if the SEC deems doing so appropriate for the public interest and investor protection? Could the SEC do so if the state statute positively prohibits charters that purport to give shareholders the right to initiate merger proposals? Could the SEC negate a state's decision to charter corporations in which shareholders would have no voting rights whatsoever?

The limited federal concern

I think the responsible answer to all these questions is no. This fact is itself a reason for rethinking the restrictions that Congress has placed on federal laws governing corporations. But Congress's historical intent was to make sure that shareholders have adequate information and fair opportunity to exercise their voting rights, but not to create such rights. As *Transamerica* illustrates, though, it is hard to keep this distinction sharp. This is understandable, for information and power tend to go together.

[5] 163 F.2d at 518.

[6] Of course, a large block of shareholders might be able to elect directors more disposed to their views about the desirability of a merger.

In any event, the applicability of Rule 14a-8 to precatory proposals has opened up a large forum for shareholder debate and expression of opinion by vote. Precatory proposals are a subject on which state law is generally neither hostile nor receptive but simply silent. This silence makes it difficult to contend that the SEC is impermissibly "creating" voting rights by facilitating shareholder voting on precatory proposals.

Precatory proposals avoid the problem

We turn now to the second case, *Medical Committee for Human Rights v. SEC,*[7] which grew out of the Viet Nam War. The Committee first submitted to Dow Chemical Company a proposal that the shareholders would vote to request the directors to consider initiating a certificate amendment stating that napalm would not be sold to any buyer unless the buyer gave reasonable assurance that the substance would not be used against human beings. The company's general counsel informed them that their proposal had arrived too late for inclusion in the 1968 proxy statement. The committee tried again the next year, this time requesting an amendment that the company would not make napalm at all. Dow's management resolved instead to omit the proposal from the company's proxy materials, and the SEC's Chief Counsel of the Division of Corporate Finance sent them a no action letter saying that if Dow omitted it as planned, the division would not recommend any action against them; this was later approved by the Commission itself. The Committee brought suit against the SEC in the circuit court for the District of Columbia, and much of the SEC's argument centered on whether the court had jurisdiction. The court held that it did,[8] found the SEC's decision to be puzzling, remanded the case for a "more illuminating consideration and discussion," and gave a long advisory opinion to "aid" the SEC's reconsideration.

***Medical Committee* case**

The Supreme Court granted certiorari and vacated the judgment for mootness, because Dow management finally saw the light and simply included the committee's proposal in its 1971 materials. Less than 3 percent of all voting shareholders supported the proposal.[9] It thus appeared that management's fear — that too many of their shareholders would be affected by their social consciences rather than their desire for profit — was grossly overblown and that the resistance to inclusion of the proposal was a waste of corporate resources. Despite this history, the substance of the circuit court opinion has enduring value.

Aftermath

[7]432 F.2d 659 (D.C. Cir. 1970), vacated as moot, 404 U.S. 403 (1972).

[8]The correctness of this holding was not free from doubt. See Kixmiller v. SEC, 492 F.2d 641 (D.C. Cir. 1974).

[9]404 U.S. 403, 406 (1972).

Two exceptions invoked

How could Dow's management oppose the committee's proposal, which was cast as a mere *request* that the directors *consider* something? It invoked two of the then existing exceptions to Rule 14a-8: one allowing management to omit a proposal submitted "*primarily* for the purpose of promoting *general* economic, political, racial, religious, social or similar causes," and the other allowing omission of recommendations with respect to the conduct of "the ordinary business operations" of the issuer.

Political causes exception

The committee admitted that its objections to sale or manufacture of napalm were primarily based on concern for human life rather than for Dow's profits (although it did note that its investment advisors thought the product was bad for Dow's business). But the court deemed this primary purpose nondispositive, apparently because the proposal was not framed to promote their cause *generally* — as were some of the crackpot proposals that gave rise to the exception — but was limited to actions that were or could be taken by the particular corporation being petitioned. Furthermore, the court's advisory opinion seems to suggest that the SEC's adoption of a clearly contrary rule would violate congressional intent behind Section 14(a). The SEC seems to have agreed with the court, for after the *Medical Committee* decision it revised the exception to omit reference to primary purpose and to apply only to proposals for actions with respect to "any matter, including a general economic, political, racial, religious or social or similar cause that is not significantly related to the business of the issuer or is not within the control of the issuer." In 1976 it went further and simply dropped the reference to "general economic . . . cause[s]," so that now there are simply two exceptions for proposals not related to the company's business or not within its power to effectuate. (It later added, effective in 1984, the 5 percent tests of relationship to the business.) In essence, the compromise worked out for social responsibility proposals was: Make them precatory rather than mandatory and relate and limit them to the company's major existing operations, and they will be includable, even if your purpose is to improve the general good at the expense of the company's profits.

Ordinary business exception

As for the ordinary business operations exception, it was clear that both sides in the *Medical Committee* case could make an argument: the corporation, that the decision to make and sell certain products was normally considered just the sort of thing that is clearly left to management's discretion; the committee, that the manufacture and sale of *this* product, napalm, was clearly no "ordinary" business matter — certainly in social, if not in economic, terms — for it was intimately linked with widespread unrest and contention about the ongoing Viet Nam war. Remarkably, the court sidestepped this obvious issue — whether social importance "counts" in determining what is an extra-ordinary business matter or whether only an impact on the company's finances does — and returned to the theme of federalism. Its reasoning: The phrase *ordinary business operations* is to be interpreted with reference to state law; Delaware law provided that a company's certificate could be amended to change, substitute, enlarge or diminish the nature of the company's business; the committee could be viewed as requesting a charter amendment to change the nature of the company's business; therefore, exclusion of the proposal as relating to ordinary operations would be unwarranted. In effect, the federal court was using the notorious flexibility of Delaware law and the idea of deference to state law as a device for advancing its conception of shareholder democracy against managerial prerogatives.

Inflation of federal role, again

But the deference to state law seems to have been lost sight of just a few paragraphs later. Judge Tamm insisted that the "overriding purpose [of Section 14(a)] is to assure corporate shareholders the ability to exercise their right — some would say their duty — to control the important decisions which affect them in their capacity as stockholders and owners of the corporation."[10] And in response to management proclamations that Dow was making napalm not because of business considerations but in spite of them — evidently *management's* conception of social responsibility was to help America win the Viet Nam war by liberal use of napalm — the court referred contemptuously to "management's patently illegitimate claim of power to treat modern corporations with their vast resources as personal satrapies implementing personal political or moral predilections"[11] and spoke approvingly of "the philosophy of corporate democracy which Congress embodied in section 14(a). . . ."

Critique

These are noble sentiments and probably not misleading in the context of the particular case. But consider this: Couldn't a state statute, without running afoul of Section 14(a), explicitly authorize the incorporation of a type of corporation in which the directors (and only the directors) have the discretion to devote a certain portion of the firm's profits to social goals as *they* conceive them? Presumably yes, if the intent of the federal statute was neither to fix the substantive goals of corporations (e.g., to pursue only profit, or charitable and social objectives, or some combination of the two), nor to determine the existence and distribution of substantive voting rights. (Note that state corporation laws already provide for the creation of so-called charitable as well as business corporations. In the former the

[10] 432 F.2d at 680-681.
[11] Id. at 681.

management may well have full power, not restrained by "member democracy," to implement their personal political or moral predilections, as long as they fit within the activity constraints specified in the corporate charter.) It seems just as doubtful that Section 14(a) could be fairly used to undo a state supreme court opinion to the effect that directors of ordinary business corporations do have discretion to devote a reasonable portion of the corporation's resources to social causes or to make product line decisions with a view to their conception of what would further the general good. If this is so, then, even in the absence of such a clearcut opinion, the federal courts ought to realize that they are searching for the meaning of state law, not federal law, when they try to decide whether claims to such discretionary powers are "patently illegitimate."

Analogy to *Transamerica*

And yet, in *Medical Committee* as in *Transamerica,* the *rhetoric* of the federal court opinion seems to extend federal control of shareholder voting rights beyond what Congress intended. (Admittedly, the holding could be read as merely creating law in the sense of filling in ambiguities left by state law.)

Underlying "social responsibility question

The experience with shareholder proposals raises an important theoretical question. Is it good policy to allow either directors or a majority of shareholders, over the objection of a minority of the shareholders, to devote resources of a corporation primarily engaged in business to non–profit-maximizing goals? This general question will be discussed in the later chapter on corporate personality (chapter 16). It should be noted here that most shareholder-initiated social responsibility proposals that are voted upon are rejected by overwhelming margins. The proponents are not discouraged by this fact, since they are primarily seeking a forum for public dissemination of their views. They may also hope that managements will voluntarily respond to the concerns they raise, as managements sometimes do.

Wide access to corporate mailings?

The theoretical question could therefore be rephrased. Ought all individuals in a society to have the power, contingent only upon their buying and holding a relatively modest amount of stock and submitting a timely resolution in proper form, to commandeer the resources of any public corporation to the extent necessarily involved in these shareholder proposal matters? That is, should concerned citizens be able to force corporations to print and mail their proposals to thousands of investors? Should they all be given this nearly free access to all of these direct mailing operations?

Perhaps, if properly structured

Several factors would support a positive answer. First, the *marginal* costs to corporations of their compliance with such requests are fairly small, since in virtually all cases management would have printed and mailed proxy materials anyway.

Second, the shareholder proposal rule as now interpreted limits the privilege to proposals that relate to the petitioned company's business and are within its power to change. Consequently, qualifying proposals will often relate to alleged negative externalities, or impositions of costs on society, for which the company is responsible and as to which it may be in a good position to act. It may be more efficient to "raise hell" at the doorstep of the company that might correct the problem (or explain why it doesn't really exist or can't be corrected) rather than to lobby a governmental unit into launching a cumbersome regulatory scheme. This possibility seems more vivid when we consider the problems, such as crowded agendas and biased access to information, that afflict legislative operations.

Third, a broad shareholder proposal rule can be viewed as a legitimate delegation of governmental power. If governments can delegate part of the lawmaking function to administrative agencies, it seems that they should be able to delegate another part, that of providing a forum for citizen discussion, to governmentally chartered corporations.[12]

§9.4 *Antifraud Actions*

A weapon for shareholders

The proxy rules may have affected shareholders less by the fact that required disclosures to them sometimes change the way they vote than by the fact that the antifraud provision of the rules gives disaffected shareholders a weapon with which to challenge corporate practices and transactions that they think are infected with a conflict of interest or otherwise bad. (Of course, a third possible effect of the rules is that the *prospect* of having to disclose executive compensation, conflicts of interest, and the like deters some corporate managers from taking improvident actions that they would otherwise be tempted to take or forces them to be more careful and self-conscious when forming corporate policies.) In any event, a case law jurisprudence somewhat similar to that under Rule 10b-5 has arisen under Section 14(a) and Rule 14(a)-9. Some main points worked out by the courts will be briefly mentioned.

[12] See generally Schwartz & Weiss, An Assessment of the SEC Shareholder Proposal Rule, 65 Geo. L.J. 635 (1977); Schwartz, The Public Interest Proxy Contest: Reflections on Campaign GM, 69 Mich. L. Rev. 419 (1971).

§9.4.1 Private Right of Action

Private actions

Early on, the Supreme Court acknowledged an implied private right of action under Section 14(a).[1] The action may be for damages or other relief as the merits of the controversy may require.

§9.4.2 Materiality

What's material

In the post-1975 period of limiting and defining private plaintiffs' rights under the securities laws, the Supreme Court decided upon the following verbal formula for determining what omissions are material enough to support a cause of action: "An omitted fact is material if there is a *substantial likelihood* that a reasonable shareholder *would* consider it important in deciding how to vote."[2] (Emphasis supplied.) The Court thereby rejected a standard that would consider any omitted fact material because shareholders *might* consider it important.

On the other hand, it also rejected the notion that a material omitted fact is one that probably would have caused the reasonable shareholder to *change* his vote; the true test is only whether the fact would have "assumed actual significance" in his deliberations. "Put another way, there must be a substantial likelihood that the disclosure of the omitted fact would have been viewed by the reasonable investor as having significantly altered the 'total mix' of information made available."[3]

You may wonder, of course, how important these linguistic distinctions are to the outcome of particular cases. In the case just mentioned, which involved the validity of a shareholder vote approving a merger, the Supreme Court decided that the omitted facts, when viewed against disclosures actually made, did not warrant entry of summary judgment against the defendants. To reach this decision, it only had to reject the contention that the omissions were so obviously important to an investor that rea-

§9.4 [1] J. I. Case Co. v. Borak, 377 U.S. 426 (1964). *Borak* is from an era in which the Supreme Court seemed readier than it later was to imply private rights of action. In Touche Ross Co. v. Redington, 442 U.S. 560 (1979), the Court specified that its holding in *Borak* acknowledged a private cause of action only for 14a-9 violations and should not serve as a bellwether for further implied private actions under other provisions of the 1934 Act. 442 U.S. at 577.

How effective this admonition has been in guiding lower courts is another question. Consider, for example, the Seventh Circuit's holding that *Borak* leads logically to the conclusion that a private action should lie under Rule 14a-7 when a corporation refuses to mail a shareholder's proxy materials. Haas v. Wiebolt Stores, Inc., 725 F.2d 71, 73 (1984).

[2] TSC Indus., Inc. v. Northway, Inc., 426 U.S. 438, 449 (1976).

[3] Ibid.

sonable minds could not differ on the question of their materiality. Nevertheless, the Court's formulation of the materiality standard did help to justify its rejection of this claim.

§9.4.3 Culpability

Negligence may be enough

On whether a private plaintiff suing under Rule 14a-9 must prove scienter on the part of the defendants, there is some uncertainty, since the Supreme Court has not ruled squarely on the issue. In *Gould v. American-Hawaiian Steamship Company,*[4] the Third Circuit based an outside director's liability on negligence: He would have known that the proxy statement in its final form was false if he had read it, which it was his duty to do. The court thought that the analogy between a Rule 14a-9 action and a private action under Rule 10b-5, which according to the Supreme Court ruling in *Ernst & Ernst*[5] does require a showing of scienter, was not as good as an analogy to a private action under Section 11 of the Securities Act, where negligence is the test. Section 11 concerns false registration statements used in connection with the issue and sale of new securities. Unlike Section 10(b), both Section 14(a) as implemented by Rule 14a-9 and Section 11 of the Securities Act require affirmative disclosures through single specific documents — proxy statements and registration statements, respectively — and they enumerate specific classes of individuals who are responsible for meeting the disclosure standards. Other courts have made similar holdings.[6]

§9.4.4 Causation, Reliance, and Standing

Relations among the three ideas

Consider first the connections among these three ideas. The fact that plaintiff actually relied on a misleading proxy statement is one way he might have been caused injury by it. But reliance is not the only mechanism by which falsehoods can cause injury. Fraud may have affected other stockholders' behavior (their decision as to how to vote, for example) or the

[4] 535 F.2d 761 (3d Cir. 1976).

[5] Ernst & Ernst v. Hochfelder, 425 U.S. 185, reh. denied, 425 U.S. 986 (1976).

[6] Gerstle v. Gamble-Skogmo, Inc., 478 F.2d 1281 (2d Cir. 1973); SEC v. Wills, 472 F. Supp. 1250 (D.D.C. 1978); Management Assistance Inc. v. Edelman, 584 F. Supp. 1021 (S.D.N.Y. 1984) ("knowing, reckless or negligent" omission of material fact is actionable under 14a-9); Fradkin v. Ernst, 571 F. Supp. 829 (N.D. Ohio 1983). But the Sixth Circuit held that a §14(a) action brought against an outsider requires proof of scienter. Adams v. Standard Knitting Mills, 623 F.2d 422 (6th Cir. 1980) (accounting firm not liable for failure to detect error in proxy statement where there was no intent to deceive), cert. denied, 449 U.S. 1067 (1980).

market and thus led indirectly to plaintiff's injury. The standing issue is often the issue of whether a particular plaintiff was or could have been injured (through reliance or otherwise) by defendant's alleged misconduct. But sometimes standing cases deal with the purpose and coverage of a statute: Was the plaintiff, although perhaps injured by defendant's conduct, within the class of persons intended to be protected by the statute?

Proof of reliance excused in *Auto-Lite*

The Supreme Court, in its 1970 decision in *Mills v. Electric Auto-Lite Co.*,[7] rejected the position that plaintiffs had to prove actual reliance on the falsehoods or omissions in the proxy statements. Instead, it allowed causation of injury to be presumed from the materiality of the falsehood or omission plus the connection between the proxy solicitation and the transaction complained of.

> Where there has been a finding of materiality, a shareholder has made a sufficient showing of causal relationship between the violation and the injury for which he seeks redress if, as here, he proves that the proxy solicitation itself, rather than the particular defect in the solicitation materials, was an essential link in the accomplishment of the transaction.[8]

The idea behind the holding is, of course, that when a court finds a misstatement or omission to be material, that finding itself embodies a conclusion that the defect probably would have been considered important by a reasonable shareholder trying to decide how to vote; it would have affected her decision making process if not the ultimate decision. The Court's holding also avoids the need to try to determine how many votes were affected by the defect — an inquiry that would be speculative and impractical.

Inadequacy of proxy statement

In the *Auto-Lite* case, plaintiffs complained that the proxy statement soliciting shareholder approval of a proposed merger of Auto-Lite into another company, Mergenthaler, failed to bring out in an adequate way the relationship between Auto-Lite's board members, who were conspicuously represented in the proxy statement as having given careful consideration to the merger and as believing it to be fair and equitable to the shareholders, and Mergenthaler, which owned 54 percent of Auto-Lite's outstanding shares and could influence the identity and actions of its directors. In other words, there was a potential conflict of interest. Mergenthaler could control the decisions of both companies' boards of directors, and its managers had an incentive to make the terms of the merger deal unfavorable to the public shareholders of Auto-Lite. In essence, the plain-

[7] 396 U.S. 375 (1970).
[8] Id. at 385.

tiffs' argument, basically adopted by the Supreme Court, was that the facts relevant to this conflict were not adequately disclosed and emphasized and that if they had been they would have been material to the public shareholders' decision whether to vote against the merger or to take other protective actions. Other protective actions included: (1) examining the proposal with special care to determine whether the terms were really optimal, (2) bringing a derivative suit challenging the fairness of the terms of the merger and seeking an injunction or damages; and (3) taking the first steps in the procedure of exercising appraisal rights under state law.[9] Subsequent cases have explored other variations on the causation theme.[10]

§9.4.5 Remedies

Discussion in *Auto-Lite*

What remedies are available to a private plaintiff on account of a violation of Rule 14a-9? In the *Auto-Lite* case, the Supreme Court said that its conclusion about the causation issue implied nothing about the form of relief to which the plaintiffs might be entitled, but it did give the lower courts some advice to guide them on the remand. The Court acknowledged that courts could and should provide such remedies as are necessary to make effective the congressional purpose behind the violated provision and that the remedies might be prospective or retrospective. At least three forms of remedy were contemplated.

[9] In contrast to the Supreme Court's ruling on causation, the Seventh Circuit would have allowed the defendants to show by a preponderance of the evidence that the merger would have received a significant vote even if the proxy statement had not been misleading. Mills v. Electric Auto-Lite Co., 403 F.2d 429, 436 (7th Cir. 1968), rev'd, 396 U.S. 375 (1970).

[10] For example, the Ninth Circuit held that a shareholder who did not grant a proxy to management in reliance upon the allegedly misleading proxy material lacked standing to assert a nonderivative equitable action under the proxy provisions. Gaines v. Haughton, 645 F.2d 761 (9th Cir. 1981). But a district court, following an earlier Sixth Circuit opinion, held that shareholders who themselves did not rely on misleading proxy statements still had an action under §14(a) on their claim that other shareholders were misled. Leff v. CIP Corp., 540 F. Supp. 857 (S.D. Ohio 1982). And in an SEC injunctive action for proxy violations, the Second Circuit rejected a defendant's argument that the nondisclosure in question could have made no difference to shareholders whose choice was to accept the offering price or exercise their appraisal rights. The court ruled that, unlike the situation in the *Santa Fe* case, the minority shareholders could have had the merger enjoined under New York law as one undertaken for no valid business purpose. SEC v. Parklane Hosiery Co., Inc., 558 F.2d 1083 (2d Cir. 1977).

In Bolton v. Gramlich, 540 F. Supp. 822 (S.D.N.Y. 1982), the court opined that proxy contestant shareholders should not be denied standing under §14(a) simply because they are also making a tender offer. But it resisted a claim for reimbursement of plaintiff's expenses in the failed effort to gain control on the ground that such reimbursement would indirectly benefit the company shareholders who were the persons for whose "special benefit" Congress chose to regulate proxies.

Injunction

First, the court might enjoin a corporate merger or other transaction that has not yet occurred, if the shareholders' proxies were solicited by means of false or misleading proxy statements. In such a case it might order a new proxy solicitation. This approach was unavailable in the *Auto-Lite* case since the merger had occurred seven years before the Supreme Court rendered its decision.

Rescission

Second, it might set aside such a transaction. But the Court stressed that the lower courts were not required to unscramble a merger merely because a proxy violation occurred. Rather, they should exercise their discretion to achieve the most equitable reconciliation between the public interest and private needs as well as between competing private claims. Again, the seven year delay assured that the courts would find the *Auto-Lite* merger immune from this remedy, since unscrambling it would have been a messy, expensive, and harsh remedy.

Damages

Third, the court could award damages. When a misrepresentation relates to the consideration to be received by the solicited shareholders, this remedy may be easy and natural. For example, if the shareholders were misled into thinking they would get a package of securities worth $80 for every share they gave up, and the package was only worth $60, the court could simply require defendants to pay them an extra $20 per share. But when the misrepresentation concerns some other matter, such as the conflict of interest inherent in a controlled merger, determining monetary damages is often very difficult. The Court suggested that if showing direct injury from the merger were impossible, relief might be predicated on a determination of the *fairness* of the terms of the merger at the time when it was approved. Admittedly this is somewhat odd. As at least one commentator has observed, a remedy consisting of damages based on the substantive unfairness of the terms of the merger exchange is not closely related to the wrong of nondisclosure for which it is supposedly a remedy.[11] The effect of the Court's recommendation is to allow a federal remedy for substantive unfairness, as long as there is a material defect in the proxy materials.

Irony of fair merger standard

The net result of the Supreme Court's views on causation and damages in the *Auto-Lite* case is odd for another reason. In the beginning of its opinion it rejected the Seventh Circuit's ruling that the fairness of the merger deal was a defense to the plaintiffs' suit. The Seventh Circuit reasoned that if the merger was in fact fair to the minority shareholders, the trial court would be justified in concluding that a sufficient number of

[11] Lorne, A Reappraisal of Fair Shares in Controlled Mergers, 126 U. Pa. L. Rev. 955, 966-967 n.35 (1978).

minority shareholders would have approved the merger even if there had been no deficiency in the proxy statement. But when the Supreme Court moved from the causation issue to the question of remedies, it re-inserted the issue of fairness in a way that was crucial to the case before it. The upshot was that the case went back down to the district court and then again to the Seventh Circuit,[12] where it was finally determined, according to the court's understanding of a fairness test for controlled mergers developed by two law professors,[13] that the merger *was* fair and that the plaintiffs should therefore receive no damages. In summary, it took seven years and three reported decisions to find that plaintiffs had a cause of action and another seven years and two reported decisions to determine that they were nevertheless not entitled to relief.[14]

Interim award of attorney's fees

About the only immediate beneficiaries of the struggle were the lawyers. In the Supreme Court's 1970 decision in the case, for example, one of the holdings was that the petitioner-plaintiffs, having established a violation of the securities laws by their corporation, were entitled to reimbursement by the corporation or its survivor in the merger for the cost of establishing the violation, namely, an interim award of litigation expenses and reasonable attorneys' fees. Perhaps this is the best way to understand the significance of the *Auto-Lite* litigation: It gives attorneys something like a bounty hunter's incentive to police the accuracy of proxy statements.

§9.5 *The Theory of Voting Rights*

Control in residual owners, why

From an economic point of view, there is a strong argument that the power to control a business firm's activities should reside in those who have the right to the firm's residual earnings, that is, those earnings that are left over when all fixed and definite obligations of the firm have been provided for. The intuition behind this argument is that giving control to the residual claimants will place the power to monitor the performance of participants in the firm and the power to control shirking, waste, and so forth in the hands of those who have the best incentive to use the power.[1]

[12] Mills v. Electric Auto-Lite Co., 552 F.2d 1239 (7th Cir.), cert. denied, 434 U.S. 922 (1977).

[13] See Brudney & Chirelstein, Fair Shares in Corporate Mergers and Takeovers, 88 Harv. L. Rev. 297 (1974). The test is discussed in section 11.3 infra.

[14] Lorne, note 10 supra, at 955.

§9.5 [1] See generally Alchian & Demsetz, Production, Information Costs, and Economic Organization, 62 Am. Econ. Rev. 777 (1972); Jensen & Meckling, Theory of the Firm: Managerial Behavior, Agency Costs, and Ownership Structure, 3 J. Fin. Econ. 305 (1976).

To be sure, the nature of the modern firm complicates this argument, since the benefits of managerial expertise and the need to prevent wasteful duplication of decision making have led to a professional class of managers distinct from public shareholders. Managers have control over ordinary business operations, even though they do not have full ownership rights to their firm's residual earnings. (Of course, they usually own substantial residual claims because of stock option programs and similar arrangements.) Yet it can still be argued that ultimate control ought to reside in the ultimate claimants on the residual earnings.

Application to common shareholders

This viewpoint supports the conclusion that common shareholders should possess voting rights that, at a minimum, give them the power to select or remove the directors and, therefore, the indirect power to control the identity of top management. We could argue further that voting rights should be proportional to one's share of the residual interest in the firm.[2] Otherwise, there would be some misalignment between the power and the incentive to monitor and enforce company performance.

Voting rights valuable?

Common shareholders generally do possess voting rights. But observation of how they are exercised in the public corporation raises a new problem: Do these voting rights actually amount to anything? Are they worthwhile rights or mere symbolic nods to the vague general ideal of democracy? In the rest of this section, I will explore the problems afflicting shareholder voting and some of the devices for protecting shareholder interests.

Collective action problems

Whenever shareholders of a publicly held company vote upon matters affecting the corporation, they engage in collective action that suffers from many systemic difficulties.[3] Such difficulties include "rational apathy" of shareholders, the temptation of individual shareholders to take a "free ride," and unfairness to certain shareholders even where collective action is successful. Each of these three problems merits discussion.

§9.5.1 The Rational Apathy Problem

When costs exceed benefits

Often the aggregate cost to shareholders of informing themselves of potential corporate actions, independently assessing the wisdom of such actions, and casting their votes will greatly exceed the expected or actual

[2] Easterbrook and Fischel, Voting in Corporate Law, 26 J.L. & Econ. 395, 408-410 (1983).

[3] See generally K. Arrow, Social Choice and Individual Values (2d ed. 1963); D. Black, The Theory of Committees and Elections (1958); J. Buchanan & G. Tullock, The Calculus of Consent (1962); A. Downs, An Economic Theory of Democracy (2d ed. 1971); A. Hirschman, Exit, Voice, and Loyalty (1970); M. Olson, Jr., The Logic of Collective Action (2d ed. 1971). Of these works, those by Hirschman and Olson are the most pertinent to the issues discussed in this section.

benefits garnered from informed voting. Recognition of this phenomenon accounts for the usual rules that entrust corporate management with all ordinary business decisions. But the same problem still exists with respect to the major subjects of shareholder voting: the election of directors and the approval or rejection of major organic changes such as mergers.

Example

Consider a simplified case. Outta Control Corp., with 1 million voting common shares outstanding, has 10,000 shareholders, each of whom owns 1 block of 100 shares. The directors propose a plan to merge Outta Control into Purchaser Corp., which would result in the acquisition by the former Outta Control shareholders, in exchange for their old shares, of voting common shares in Purchaser with a total market value of $50 million. In fact, Purchaser would have been willing to exchange $60 million worth of its shares if it had not agreed, under prodding by Outta Control's managers and in return for their cooperation in recommending the merger, to give extraordinary salary increases to those officers of Outta Control who would continue their employment after the merger. Payments would also be made to departing officers under so-called consulting and noncompetition agreements. Moreover, a majority of Outta Control's directors are not officers and would seek a new merger agreement at a much higher price if the current proposal were not approved by the shareholders.

Assume that all of this information is contained in a 240 page proxy statement that is sent to Outta Control's shareholders and that any rational shareholder who reads it would decide to vote against the merger. Assume further that if the merger proposal were disapproved, a new one would be adopted that would yield these shareholders the additional $10 million gain which Purchaser Corp. was prepared to pay. Thus, the actual benefit to be derived from collective shareholder action against the merger plan would be $1000 per shareholder.

Expected benefits are relevant

Shareholders do not expect, however, to discover a reason for concluding that disapproval will avert a corporate harm or open the door to a larger corporate gain every time they read a proxy statement. To make our problem complete, assume that the shareholders in it make a rational assessment of the probabilities of such an occurrence. Because of their assessment, they assign an expected benefit of $50 per shareholder to collective action of the sort described, that is, action based on each shareholder's reading the proxy statement, making up his mind, and voting.

Costs of becoming informed

Now suppose the average cost of informed shareholder action is simply the opportunity cost[4] of reading the proxy statement before sending in the

[4] The cost attributable to doing one thing to the exclusion of another stems from opportunities sacrificed to pursue the chosen course. This sacrifice is called "opportunity cost."

proxy card and that this amount is $120 per shareholder (three hours of reading at $40 per hour — a rather low estimate). Thus the total cost of collective action would be $1.2 million. This cost would still be less than the *actual* benefit to be gained, in this case, from collective action by informed voters. But the cost of such collective action greatly exceeds the *expected* benefit — $120 versus $50 per shareholder — so sensible shareholders will not read the proxy statement. They will be rationally apathetic. At the same time, management will be shielded from shareholder policing of their fiduciary duties, thereby allowing them to receive compensation that is unnecessary to induce their services.

§9.5.2 The Free Rider Problem

Benefits exceed costs

One legal approach toward improving the efficiency of collective action is to make it cheaper for each shareholder to act in an informed way. Suppose that in our example the opportunity cost of reading the proxy statement concerning the proposed merger were only $10 per shareholder, because the SEC had devised a system of proxy rules that produced extremely concise, quickly understandable proxy statements that emphasize crucial data. Suppose that the SEC also monitors the statement and requires that the crucial information appear in bold face type. The expected benefit of collective action by informed voting is still $50 per shareholder, but the cost of such action is now only $10 per shareholder. The net expected benefit is therefore $40 per shareholder.

But leave it to others

Yet the desired collective action still may not occur. Any one shareholder may realize that only 50 percent of the shareholders are needed to block the merger. If the shareholder believes that enough other shareholders will respond to the incentive of the $40 net expected benefit and will act accordingly to produce the desirable collective result, he might decide to save himself the cost of reading the streamlined proxy statement. He can still participate in any benefits of collective action that arise through the work of the other shareholders. He will be a free rider on their efforts. The net expected benefit of his action as a free rider would be $50 rather than $40.

Of course, it may also occur to him that if all the other shareholders thought similarly, no collective action would be taken, and everyone would lose the chance of reaping the benefits. He might realize that giving in to the temptation to achieve an individual gain superior to everyone else's would jeopardize the attainment of collective benefits. Conceivably this realization might prompt him to read the proxy statement. But it is doubtful whether this would happen in practice and, as a matter of theory (game theory, that is), a rational, self-interested shareholder would not do so.[5] The situation is like the prisoner's dilemma of game theory[6] and may call for solutions similar in strategy to those that would solve that dilemma.

Prisoner's dilemma

We might try to solve the free rider problem by having the corporation reimburse each shareholder who incurs reasonable investigative costs with respect to a proposed corporate action. This procedure would spread the costs of collective action among all the shareholders in accordance with their pro rata interest in the company. It would be quite impractical, however, since the transaction costs of processing reimbursements would be prohibitive, and adequate verification of the shareholders' investigative efforts would be virtually impossible.

Reimbursement of all costs impractical

§9.5.3 The Fairness Problem

Let the giant do it

Let us again alter the hypothetical so that the free rider problem, like the rational apathy problem, effectively disappears. Suppose that one shareholder, Ajax, owns 200,000 shares, while every other shareholder owns only one block of 100 shares. The other facts remain the same. The expected benefit to Ajax is now $100,000, which is, let us assume, more than the expected cost of reading the proxy statement and convincing the holders of 300,100 other shares also to vote against the merger. (He would do this by waging a proxy contest — a technique discussed in the next subsection.) Unless it deeply galls Ajax to think that he will be treated unfairly, he will take action to achieve the collective benefit even if he cannot be reimbursed for the costs and risks of such action.[7] Acting strictly for his own benefit, he will nevertheless have created a collective good for all the other shareholders in the company. The smaller shareholders will get the benefit of his concern without bearing a pro rata share of the cost. This phenomenon is an example of what one economist calls the systematic exploitation of the large by the small.[8]

Nature of problem

The obvious problem here is one of fairness to the guardian shareholder. Less obviously, problems of allocative efficiency may also arise. The pros-

[5] Why not? Because, whether he assumes the other shareholders will read or will not read, he will expect to be better off if he doesn't. Assume the others will read: His own expected benefit is $50 if he doesn't read, and $40 if he does. Assume the others will not read (so the original merger plan goes through): His own expected benefit is $0 if he doesn't read, but *minus* $10 if he does.

[6] See M. Bacharach, Economics and the Theory of Games 61-64 (1977).

[7] We can assume that Ajax will not try to be a free rider because his particular expected benefit is so high that he would not risk depending on action by other shareholders.

[8] See M. Olson, Jr., note 3 supra, at 35.

pect of being taken advantage of by the smaller shareholders may deter investors from becoming dominant shareholders in the first place. The problem once again resembles the prisoners' dilemma, but in this situation the players are all investors as they contemplate buying into any publicly held corporation. But in the real world there are many factors that tempt investors to obtain large percentage interests in companies, not the least of which is the chance of acquiring the various special benefits of controlling the corporation on an ongoing basis. Any force toward misallocation created by the phenomenon of exploitation of the large by the small is likely to be more than offset by these factors. Thus, the only remaining problem will be unfair treatment of the large, but not controlling, shareholder who undertakes a proxy contest or similar action for the corporation's benefit.

§9.5.4 Solutions to the Collective Action Problems

Three alleviating devices

Legal rules have been crucial in the creation of three devices that offer some hope of overcoming the collective action problems: the proxy contest, the shareholders' derivative suit, and the corporate takeover. The first of these turns out not to live up to its promise, but the other two are powerful and important mechanisms for protecting shareholder interests. The second, the derivative lawsuit, does not depend at all on the transferability of shares, or on the fact that common shares typically have voting power. But the takeover mechanism does. Let's examine each mechanism in turn.

Example of proxy contest

The proxy contest. Consider some factors that at first blush might seem to result in effective shareholder control despite rational apathy. A shareholder who is not aligned with management may solicit proxies in opposition to management from his fellow shareholders. Suppose Bustle, an ordinary shareholder of Outta Control Corp., incurs an opportunity cost of $120 in reading its proxy statement and discovering a reason to disapprove the merger plan and then expends $50,000 in conducting a (very economical) proxy solicitation. The solicitation reduces the opportunity cost of investigation by other shareholders to an amount that induces collective action. Just reading the first few sentences of the countersolicitation, for example, leads the average solicited shareholder to revise upward the expected benefit of reading further, and the body of the counterstatement greatly reduces the total time and cost that the shareholder spends on reading, because the points to consider are highlighted. Consequently, the undesirable merger proposal is disapproved. The shareholders gain $1,000 per block less whatever opportunity costs they actually incur.

Difficult to recover costs

But will this scenario occur? It will not, if Bustle, the guardian shareholder, can't recover his $50,120 in costs, for that figure greatly exceeds his own actual and expected benefits. (As an ordinary Outta Control shareholder, he holds the usual 100-share block.) In some jurisdictions, it appears that successful insurgents in a proxy contest may recover their expenses from the corporation if certain requirements are met.[9] But this rule apparently has been applied only in cases in which the insurgents succeeded in electing a controlling majority of the directors.[10] Thus it won't help Bustle. This restriction on reimbursement occurs because the corporation is not generally obligated to make reimbursement.[11]

Or compensate for risk taking

Moreover, even if an insurgent who successfully caused a proposed merger or other corporate action to be defeated were regularly reimbursed for all his expenses, Bustle still would not be induced to take action. This is because he does not know ex ante whether investigating any particular proposed corporate action will pay off. Therefore, in order to elicit guardian behavior from Bustle, he must be compensated for the *risk* of engaging in such behavior. Conceivably, this could be done by paying him some *multiple* of his actual expenses in those cases where his efforts succeed. The multiplier would be based on the frequency of successful investigation.

But for several reasons, it is difficult to implement this procedure in a satisfactory way. Awareness of this fact may discourage policy makers from allowing the insurgent shareholder to receive risk-adjusted reimbursement. Ascertaining a frequency figure would depend on whether or not particular activities were classified as "investigations" — a determination that would engender tremendous definitional problems. If the frequency were based on past investigations of a particular corporation, an adequate sample of data might not be available. If it involved investigations of all public corporations, or some class of corporations, the figure might be considered unfair by managers and shareholders who believe their company to be more responsive to ordinary voting procedures than

[9] Successful insurgents may be reimbursed from corporate funds for expenses incurred in a proxy fight, provided (1) reimbursement is ratified by a majority of the shareholders, (2) the contest is for corporate policy control rather than personal control, and (3) the expenses were reasonable both in nature and amount. See Steinberg v. Adams, 90 F. Supp. 604, 607-608 (S.D.N.Y. 1950); Rosenfeld v. Fairchild Engine & Airplane Corp., 128 N.E.2d 291, 293 (N.Y. 1955), both discussed in E. Aranow & H. Einhorn, Proxy Contests for Corporate Control 569-574 (2d ed. 1968).

[10] See Phillips v. United Corp., 5 SEC Jud. Dec. 758 (S.D.N.Y.), appeal dismissed, 171 F.2d 180 (2d Cir. 1948), discussed in E. Aranow & H. Einhorn, note 9 supra, at 575-577. But see Friedman, Expenses of Corporate Proxy Contests, 51 Colum. L. Rev. 951, 958 (1951).

[11] See Rosenfeld v. Fairchild Engine & Airplane Corp., 128 N.E.2d 291, 293 (N.Y. 1955).

the average corporation. Moreover, payment of a multiple of actual expenses might result in inefficient and aimless investigation.

Summary

Of course, any cost-based system of reimbursement encourages extravagant spending. But the problem is greatly magnified by a system that in effect reimburses the investigators for the cost of *all* their investigations. To try to control extravagant spending, each guardian shareholder might be paid on the basis of a fixed fee schedule and a legally mandated multiplier. But then other difficulties would ensue. The fees fixed by the courts or regulators would tend to be arbitrary, since they would have no practical way of finding the ideal figure.

In summary, the shareholder-sponsored proxy context is not an adequate solution to the rational apathy problem or the free rider problem. Partly, this results from the practical difficulties that would arise from trying to identify deserving insurgent shareholders and compensate them for their costs and risks they incur. Even more importantly, the proxy contest is limited because current law doesn't even try to provide for such compensation as a matter of right.

An ingenious solution

The shareholder's derivative suit. The derivative suit, or action brought on behalf of the corporation by a shareholder, solves collective action problems in an ingenious way. It allows the burden of taking action on behalf of the collectivity of shareholders to be transferred to the plaintiff's attorney. The plaintiff-shareholder is really a figurehead who has little concern for the costs of the suit, since the attorney's compensation is customarily contingent upon success. The system further ensures that the successful attorney is compensated both for the immediate costs of litigation and for the risks of taking action, because court awards of attorney's fees in derivative actions do allow the risk element to be taken into account.[12] And it automatically spreads the costs among all shareholders who benefit from the

[12] See section 15.8 infra. To be sure, this procedure is subject to difficulties similar to those that would plague risk-adjusted reimbursement of insurgent shareholders who lead proxy contests. The special dispensation to shareholder suits may simply reflect the courts' belief that judicial scrutiny of managerial actions yields better outcomes than the reactions of public shareholders subjected to propaganda campaigns, or that courts are more competent to measure and award litigation expenses than proxy contest expenses. Or it may be an historical "accident," i.e., a fact that is hard to rationalize.

For factors sometimes considered in awarding fees to a successful plaintiff's attorney in a derivative suit, see Angoff v. Goldfine, 270 F.2d 185, 188-189 (1st Cir. 1959); Newmark v. RKO General, Inc., 332 F. Supp. 161, 163-164 (S.D.N.Y. 1971). See also Cole, Counsel Fees in Stockholders' Derivative and Class Actions — Hornstein Revisited, 6 U. Rich. L. Rev. 259 (1972).

successful derivative suit, since the plaintiff's attorney is generally paid out of the benefit conferred by the suit upon the corporation.[13]

Example of derivative suit

Consider any of the three variations of our hypothetical. Champpe, an enterprising plaintiff's attorney, might assess the expected benefit to Outta Control Corp. of his reading the proxy statement and making related investigations at $500,000 or more.[14] If Champpe were successful in a suit after the merger against the officers of X, alleging that they were taking part of the merger price as a bribe, he might recover a large amount for the corporation and risk-adjusted compensation for all his own costs provided that they did not exceed the limit for contingency fees.[15] Prospectively, he might contemplate an expenditure of time and effort that, billed at a rate reflecting a normal risk of failure, would yield himself $150,000. As his investigation proceeded and new facts emerged, this estimate would of course be revised — in our example, upward. The amount of upward revision would depend on the details of the particular case. While the cost of a derivative suit is not always less than the cost of a proxy context, it is often the cheaper or more feasible alternative.

Remedy for wrongs, not under-performance

There is, however, a great problem with the derivative suit. Even apart from procedural restrictions on its use (which are examined in chapter 15), the derivative suit is well designed only for remedying violations of legal norms, not for policing underperformance, slack, or incompetence. And even when the impetus for collective action springs from managerial wrongdoing, the wrongdoing may not be effectively addressable in a lawsuit. This is often true of actions based on an alleged violation of the duty of care. It would also be true of a claim such as the one in our hypothetical that the managers were taking an implicit bribe. Champpe's suit would be hard to win. Some other protective device should be available.

How takeover is a solution

The takeover. The derivative suit solves collective action problems by making it possible for any shareholder, acting unilaterally, to *authorize an agent* to seek a collective benefit and to be compensated by all shareholders if he succeeds. The corporate takeover, on the other hand, solves collective action problems by making it possible for any person, whether or not an existing shareholder, to *become the principal part of the collectivity of interests* whose welfare the corporation is designed to serve. A person establishes this status by acquiring a majority of the corporation's voting shares. Sup-

[13] See Cole, note 12 supra, at 261-262.

[14] He might assess the expected benefit as being substantially below this amount. While shareholders may take remedial action, such as voting for new, more competent directors, the recovery in a derivative suit would be the loss of anticipated profits resulting from the directors' misbehavior. This amount is often difficult to prove.

[15] A typical limit would be 30 percent of the recovery. See Cole, note 12 supra, at 283-285.

pose, in our hypothetical, that Darth foresees an expected benefit to Outta Control Corp. of $500,000, to be gained from investigating the proposed merger and pursuing a desirable course of collective action. After conducting a minimal investigation and discovering that the company is really worth $60 million, Darth might attempt to capture part of the potential benefit to Outta Control by buying as many of its shares as he can at the lowest available price.

Value of voting rights

And now for the observation that ties this whole discussion to the theory of voting rights. For the takeover to succeed and be a socially useful mechanism, several conditions must be satisfied: (1) *There must be voting rights;* (2) they must be susceptible to being bought and sold (along with the shares that have them, usually); and (3) their purchaser must be able to obtain a reward for having expended funds to obtain control. The value of the takeover does *not* depend, however, on whether the voting rights are ever exercised by the shareholders in ordinary times. If the corporate takeover is of great value in solving collective action problems, and if no better solution exists which renders it unnecessary, then it need not bother us that shareholders are generally apathetic about voting or that most shareholder votes are mere expressions of confidence in management. Nor is it a fatal problem that the voting system creates costs because companies must comply with the associated disclosure requirements and proxy rules.[16]

Why not lawsuits as only control?

Yet the expense of maintaining a voting system — a system justified primarily by the relatively rare transfers of corporate power it makes possible — and the realization that not all corporate takeovers are for the better may lead you to wonder whether the derivative suit alone is an adequate device for overcoming barriers to collective action. Why not complete the process of separating ownership and control by making all shares nonvoting or by removing obstacles to the use of nonvoting shares? Why not trust litigation, including class actions and SEC proceedings as well as derivative suits, to ensure managerial accountability?

Complementary virtues theory

I've already mentioned the drawbacks of using the derivative suit to redress a problem of the sort raised by our hypothetical. The more general point to grasp is this: The derivative suit and the takeover mechanism are

[16]For similar views, see M. Eisenberg, The Structure of the Corporation 66-68 (1976); Manne, Mergers and the Market for Corporate Control, 73 J. Pol. Econ. 110, 112-113 (1965); Manne, Some Theoretical Aspects of Share Voting, 64 Colum. L. Rev. 1427, 1430-1434 (1964); Manne, The "Higher Criticism" of the Modern Corporation, 62 Colum. L. Rev. 399, 410-413 (1962).

both desirable as remedies for the failure of corporate fiduciaries to maximize the welfare of their beneficiaries because the strengths inherent in each tend to compensate for the weaknesses of the other.

Strengths of derivative suit

Derivative suits deal well only with cases of managerial fraud, self-dealing, and other misconduct, but in such situations they may have a strong relative advantage. A derivative suit may be aimed at specific past instances of misconduct and can produce a recovery for the corporation that exceeds the costs of the suit. A small shareholder and her lawyer can feasibly bring such a suit. By contrast, the enormous amount of investment capital required for a successful tender offer may cause substantial financing problems for the aggrieved shareholder. Furthermore, the transaction costs of a takeover may be great enough to render the entire process counterproductive for any shareholder. Moreover, taking control of the company may enable the purchaser to halt managerial theft and self-dealing, but it will not automatically effect recovery of past misappropriations. Consequently, the prospect of being taken over does not deter managers from engaging in large, "one-shot" raids on the corporate treasury. In other words, market-based controls like the takeover discipline managers only in the case of repeated or continuing wrongs, whereas legal controls like the derivative lawsuit can respond to singular wrongs.[17]

Strengths of takeover mechanism

A takeover, on the other hand, may be prompted by *any* sag in the ratio of a firm's market value to its potential value, whether caused by continuing misconduct, by managerial incompetence or negligence, or simply by the fact that some outsiders are so positioned that they can take the firm in new directions to a higher value. Even an honest, capable, and hard-working management may sometimes find its firm the subject of a takeover attempt that would produce net social benefits if it succeeded.

[17]In this context, "controls" means practices that guide one's behavior toward a social norm, such as honesty or efficiency. Market controls influence those who voluntarily enter into commercial transactions. For example, it is a generally held norm that individuals should repay money lent to them. Persons who default on their promises to repay may find it difficult to obtain credit on favorable terms in the future. Because many people will observe this consequence of default and consider its relevance to themselves, the rate of default may be lower than it would be if it were always possible to get new loans on the same terms as anyone else, regardless of one's credit record. In this terminology, the difference between the rate of default in the real and hypothetical state of affairs would be described as due to market controls.

"Legal controls" are controls that operate through the promulgation and enforcement of statutes, regulations, and decisional law. For example, if the rate of default on loans is lower than it would be if creditors could not seize and sell the property of debtors pursuant to judicial authority, then the difference would be described as the result of legal controls. Derivative suits are, of course, part of a system of legal controls.

Summary

To summarize: I've argued in this section that the traditional proxy contest is often an ineffective method of collective action and that the corporate takeover is a necessary device for staving off prospective wrongs and therefore must exist in addition to the derivative suit as a means for ensuring managerial accountability. The takeover, in turn, depends on shares having voting rights and being freely salable.

CHAPTER 10

THE GROUND RULES OF CORPORATE COMBINATIONS

§10.1 The Simple Polar Cases: Sale and Merger

Approach

Throughout the next three chapters, I shall discuss important problems of alleged unfairness and conflict of interest among managers and shareholders in the context of sales and combinations of corporations. Before taking up these topics, one must have a good idea of the different forms of sales and combinations, the numerous legal consequences that attach to each form, and the rationale for the legal rules.

Two polar cases

The best way to start is with two relatively clear cases that have rather different characteristics and consequences. It should then be possible to explore some major variations on these polar cases in a more intelligent way (see sections 10.3 and 10.4 infra). The two cases involve, respectively, a simple *sale* for cash of all of a corporation's assets and a simple *merger* of one corporation into another. (Incidentally, the term *merger* is used here in accordance with its original meaning rather than in accordance with the technical usage of modern business corporation statutes. The original concept has substantive connotations and denotations; whereas, as we shall see, things that count as mergers under the statutes are unified more by procedures and technicalities.)

It may be useful to focus on examples.

A simple sale

Sale. Suppose that Sound Corporation, which has hitherto operated a wholesaling business in phonograph records and tape cassettes, wants to acquire Records Corporation, which owns and operates a retail outlet for such products. The directors and officers of Records are all planning to retire after the acquisition. Records is valued at $1 million as a going concern; Sound, at $9 million. Records has 100,000 outstanding shares of common stock, owned in varying amounts by 100 shareholders; it has issued no other kinds of stock and has no bonds or debentures outstanding. Sound has 900,000 outstanding shares of common stock, owned by 9,000 shareholders; it has issued no other kinds of stock and has no bonds or debentures outstanding. The management of Records agrees to a proposal whereby Sound will pay Records $1 million cash for all its assets. After the sale, Records Corporation will be dissolved and the cash distributed pro rata to the Records shareholders, who will receive $10 per share.

A simple merger

Merger. Message Corporation owns a number of retail stores in the South, and from them it sells health food, jogging equipment, and achievement-oriented religious literature. Nirvana Corporation owns retail stores in the West, from which it sells health food, jogging equipment, and relationship-oriented religious literature. Each corporation is valued at $5 million, has about 500 shareholders owning about 500,000 common shares, and has no other kinds of stock, bonds, or debentures outstanding. The managers of the two companies would like to merge Message into Nirvana. They will be careful to follow the merger procedure set forth in the business corporation statutes of the two states under whose laws Message and Nirvana are incorporated. Pursuant to these statutes and the terms of their particular merger agreement, Message will cease to exist as a corporate entity and all of its assets and liabilities will become assets and liabilities of Nirvana. Each shareholder of Message will receive newly issued common shares of Nirvana in exchange for his old Message shares, on a one-share-for-one-share basis. Collaterally, it is agreed that the directors and officers of Message will be given positions of various sorts with Nirvana, the surviving corporate entity.

Some differences and similarities. Close analysis of the differences and similarities between these simple cases is a prerequisite to a good understanding of how corporate combinations are treated for tax and accounting purposes, as well as under the securities laws, business corporation statutes, and antitrust laws. Six distinct aspects of the transactions should be examined.

Disinvestment vs. changed investment

(1) From the point of view of the *acquired company's shareholders*, perhaps the key difference between the sale and merger has to do with the consideration received. After the sale and liquidation, the Records shareholders have cash instead of shares. They have been entirely *disinvested* from their prior indirect claim on the assets and earnings of the business conducted by Records, and no longer possess the rights of shareholders, such as inspection rights, voting rights, and rights to dividends. (Of course, some or all of the former Records shareholders may turn around and reinvest their cash, perhaps even in shares of Sound Corporation. But this would be a separate course of action from the sale initiated by the former managers of Records.)

After the merger, however, the former Message shareholders still own *shares* of stock, and these Nirvana shares represent an indirect interest in a pool of business assets that includes, as a substantial part of itself, the assets of their former corporation. They have not been disinvested, although of course the nature of their *investment* has *changed*. Instead of representing a five hundred thousandth interest in the retail stores in the South, each share becomes converted by law and the merger agreement into a one millionth interest in the retail stores in the South and in the West.

Independently valuable consideration

(2) Correlatively, from the point of view of the *acquiring company*, a major difference between the sale and the merger has to do with the consideration given. In the sale transaction, Sound Corporation paid cash. It thus had to give up pre-existing, independently valuable corporate assets to purchase Records' business. (Indeed, it may have had to sell or pledge less liquid assets to raise the money for the acquisition.) In effect, it has replaced some assets (the cash) with others (Records' business assets). Consequently, the total size — say, in terms of the total value of its assets — of Sound Corporation after its purchase is not ipso facto increased. Rather, Sound Corporation will become larger and more valuable if it turns out that the acquisition makes good sense as a business proposition; if, for example, the combination of the record store and the record wholesaling

business under one management enables the company not merely to add the businesses' pre-existing profits together but to increase sales and reduce costs.

vs. securities

On the other hand, in the Message-Nirvana merger, Nirvana Corporation does not relinquish any of the pre-merger assets, such as cash, buildings, inventory, or patents, that were owned by it. It does not pay out independently valuable assets that it held in its own name as owner but simply issues certain paper claims against itself, that is, shares of common stock, which represent a complex, indirect interest in whatever its real assets happen to be.[1] Nirvana's assets are not replaced, even in part; they are *combined* with those of another entity. It is as if the Nirvana business operations were surrounded by a kind of legal cell membrane, and this membrane were then snipped open, stretched to engulf the former business operations of Message as well as the old ones of Nirvana, and the membrane's ends reconnected. The size or real value of the real business assets owned by Nirvana as a legal entity is automatically increased by the merger. In fact, Nirvana doubles in size. Of course, whether the post-merger value of Nirvana will be more than the pre-merger value of Message and Nirvana will depend on various factors, such as whether the merger enables the managers to reap the benefit of real efficiencies.

Size disparities

(3) From the point of view of the *acquiring company's shareholders,* both the sale and the merger involve a change in the nature of the business assets in which their shares give them an indirect claim. In our polarized examples, however, the change is much smaller in the sale transaction, because Sound Corporation was nine times larger than Records while Nirvana was the same size as Message. The impact on Sound's shareholders is similar to that of buying an unusually large new machine or building a new outlet or two. The impact on Nirvana's shareholders is more drastic. Although the relative sizes of combining companies vary from case to case, even apart from the kind of acquisition, it is proper, I think, to associate radical size disparities with the idealized notion of a sale-purchase transaction and rough equality of size with the paradigmatic case of a merger.

Dilution of voting power

On another front, the difference between sale and merger is clearer: The pre-sale shareholders of Sound do not have to share their claims on its post-acquisition assets with anyone else, but the pre-merger shareholders of Nirvana find that they have been joined by an additional 500 sharehold-

§10.1 [1] To convince yourself that shares issued by a corporation are not independently valuable assets of that corporation, ponder this question: How much would a corporation be worth that owned only a single asset, namely, 5 million shares of itself?

ers. Consequently, the relative voting power of the old Nirvana shareholders is diluted, while that of the old Sound shareholders is not.

In sum, the idealized merger involves a greater impact than does a sale on the acquiring company's shareholders, both in terms of the nature of their investment and in terms of their rights as shareholders.

End of acquired company

(4) The *acquired company* in a sale transaction does not cease to exist as a legal entity merely because it sells all its assets to some other legal person. The merging company in a merger does cease to exist by virtue of the terms of the relevant merger statute. Nevertheless, when, as in our example, a corporation does sell all of its assets, the controlling persons often cause it to be dissolved by resort to the formal dissolution procedures specified in the relevant corporate law statute, and the assets are then distributed to the shareholders. In such cases, the end result for the acquired corporation is similar to that obtained in a merger.

Management unified

(5) The next point relates to the decision making power of *managers*. An important theme to both the polarized sale and merger cases is that what were once two separate sets of business operations under the control of two different groups of managers will now be operated under the ultimate control of a single group of managers. Real decision making power over business decisions — with respect to pricing and the amount of output to be produced, for example — will have been consolidated. From certain public policy perspectives, such as that of antitrust law, this is a crucial fact.

Need to document transfers

(6) Some *technical differences* between the sale and merger cases may be mentioned. In the sale transaction, the parties must make sure that title to each individual asset of Records is transferred by some legally efficacious document. Records' real property will be conveyed, for example, by a properly executed and recorded deed, and its personal property should be clearly identified in a bill of sale. In addition, if the parties desire that Sound assume any or all of Records' liabilities as part of the consideration paid for the assets, then they must do so by an explicit agreement that identifies the liabilities. In the merger transaction, however, the parties need not prepare separate deeds and bills of sale nor need they identify all the liabilities that will be assumed. Unless transferred or gotten rid of before the merger, *all* assets and liabilities of Message will become assets and liabilities of Nirvana, by operation of law (namely, the merger statute), when the merger becomes effective.[2] This automatic transfer includes assets and liabilities of which the acquiring corporation had no knowledge, as well as unliquidated and contingent assets and liabilities. Thus, for

[2]See, e.g., MBCA §11.06(a)(2), 11.06(a)(3); Cal. §1107(a); Del. §259(a); N.Y. §906(b).

example, Nirvana Corporation might later find itself the defendant in a tort action brought by customers who claim they were poisoned by health food bought from Message stores several months before the merger. By the merger transaction, Nirvana "steps into the shoes" of Message in a more complete way than it would in a sale transaction.

§10.2 Legal and Other Treatment of the Polar Cases

The characteristics of our simple sale and merger examples are relevant to the legal and accounting treatment of the transactions. Let us examine, in turn, their tax, accounting, securities regulation, corporate law, and antitrust aspects.

§10.2.1 Federal Income Tax

Continuity of interest the key

The sale-merger distinction is a critical one for federal income tax purposes, because it makes the difference between a taxable and a tax free transaction. (The term *tax deferred* is technically more accurate than tax free.[1]) Essentially, the tax law focuses on the first of the differences that were identified in section 10.1 supra: the fact that in the sale transaction the selling company's shareholders *terminate* their investment, whereas in the merger the merging company's shareholders *continue* their investment, albeit in greatly modified form. As the reader may know, in our income tax system, an increase in the value of an asset is not treated as taxable gain until the owner realizes and recognizes it: He must sell his stock, for example, before his investment profit is measured and taxed. In our simple sale transaction, the selling shareholders' investments were "cashed out," and that is the clearest and most definite kind of realization of gain. (It is not the only kind that produces taxability, of course. Presumptively, any exchange of an asset for another valuable asset of a different kind will count as a taxable termination of the original investment.[2]) In a merger transaction, the tax law could take the position that the merging company shareholders receive a new investment that is different enough from their old stock to trigger measurement and recognition of taxable gains and

§10.2 [1]This is so because any appreciation in the value of the affected assets may still be taxed if and when a taxable transaction later occurs. For example, if a Message shareholder has a cost or basis of $10,000 in his Message shares and gets Nirvana shares worth $25,000, treating the merger as a nontaxable transaction means he is not taxed now. But if he turns around and sells the Nirvana shares for $25,000 in cash, he will have $15,000 of taxable gain.

[2]I.R.C. §1001(c).

losses with respect to their old stock. But it has long eschewed such a stringent interpretation of the realization requirement. Instead, the basic philosophy is that, as long as the shareholders retain a substantial *continuity of ownership interest* in the surviving company, the merger should be treated as not being an appropriate occasion for taxation. The continuity-of-interest concept not only provided the impetus to the creation of a large number of particular rules in the statutes and the regulations, but it retains independent force as a notion by which judges flesh out those rules and decide the more complicated cases.[3]

Capital gain on seller's side

Let us be more specific. When Records sells its assets to Sound, the regular rules applicable to sales and purchases of assets presumptively apply. Records as seller will have recognizable gains or losses on the sale of its assets, unless it has the benefit of a special provision in the Internal Revenue Code — as it probably would in our example. Section 337 provides that if, during the 12 months beginning on the date on which a corporation adopts a plan of complete liquidation, all of its assets are distributed (less assets retained to meet claims), then no gain or loss shall be recognized to the corporation from the sale or exchange by it of property within those 12 months (with various exceptions, of course.) In other words, if Records' directors take the simple precaution of adopting a formal plan of complete liquidation before they sell all the company's assets to Sound, Records will have no taxable gain or loss on the sale transaction. (Section 337 was enacted to help equalize the tax treatment among different methods of effectuating a sale of all of a corporation's assets; this is a point that will be explained further in section 10.3 below.) Accordingly, the provision has the result that, in a situation where there has been gain on the selling side, instead of *both* a corporate-level and a shareholder-level income tax on the seller's side, there will be only a shareholder-level tax. Furthermore, each shareholder's gain will be measured by the difference between the proceeds received in liquidation and the basis (or adjusted cost) of his or her shares, and will be treated as capital gain for tax purposes.[4]

Stepped-up basis on buyer's side

Sound, being a mere cash purchaser, recognizes no gain or loss in the sale transaction, but it does get a tax basis[5] in each acquired asset that is equal to the cash paid for it. Thus, if certain depreciable assets, such as Records' store building, have increased in value over their original cost and

[3] See generally B. Bittker & J. Eustice, Federal Income Taxation of Corporations and Shareholders, ¶14.11 (4th ed. 1979).

[4] See I.R.C. §331(a), 331(b).

[5] Basis is a concept that operates in tax law like book value in accounting practice. It is usually determined by the *cost* of the asset, with various adjustments. See I.R.C. §1012.

Sound has paid for them accordingly, it will be able to take larger depreciation deductions against taxable income than the selling company did. A similar point is true of appreciated inventory that is later sold by Sound; its basis in the inventory will be what it paid for the inventory, so its taxable income on sale will be less than that which Records would have had to report. Finally, the sale transaction has no direct tax impact on the purchasing corporation's shareholders.

Nonrecognition of gain or loss in merger

The merger, by contrast, would qualify as a tax free reorganization under the Internal Revenue Code. Statutory mergers are among the six categories of reorganizations[6] that are eligible for special treatment. Accordingly, Message, the transferring corporation, recognizes no gain or loss,[7] nor do the Message shareholders recognize any gain or loss by virtue of their giving up Message shares in exchange for Nirvana shares of stock.[8] Ordinarily, of course, an individual shareholder who, by arrangement with another investor, swaps stock in X Company for stock in Y Company would recognize taxable gain or loss equal to the difference between the value of the Y stock received and his cost or basis in the X stock. On the other hand, Message shareholders' basis in their new Nirvana stock will be the same as the basis in their old Message stock; the basis is said to be carried over.[9] As a result, if the Nirvana stock has a market value much higher than what the old Message shareholders originally paid for their Message stock, these shareholders may still recognize substantial taxable gain if and when they later sell their Nirvana stock. (That is why the transaction is more correctly called tax deferred rather than tax free.) Likewise, the survivor corporation, Nirvana, gets only the same tax basis in the old Message assets that Message itself had.[10] It is not taxed, however, by virtue of the fact that it has issued new shares in itself in exchange for the old Message assets.[11] Finally, as in the case of the buying corporation shareholders and the sale transaction, the Nirvana shareholders are unaffected by the merger.

§10.2.2 Accounting Treatment

Two kinds of treatment

Our polar cases of a sale and a merger transaction will also result in different accounting treatment: purchase treatment for the sale transaction

[6] See I.R.C. §368(a)(1)(A).
[7] I.R.C. §361(a).
[8] I.R.C. §354(a).
[9] See I.R.C. §358(a) and the example in note 1 supra.
[10] I.R.C. §362(b).
[11] I.R.C. §1032(a).

and pooling for the merger. The reasoning for this different treatment is similar to that which explains the difference in tax treatment for the polar cases. The emphasis, however, is now upon the position of the acquiring company rather than upon the continuing interest of the acquired company's shareholders.

Purchase treatment for the sale

When the acquiring company pays out cash — or any other independently valuable assets it owns — for the acquired company, it can be viewed as buying a large number of assets at once, and the accounting treatment should basically follow this notion. There must be appropriate adjustment, of course, for the fact that the acquired company usually has a going concern value over and above the sum of the separate fair market values of its individual assets. Accordingly, the purchase price paid by Sound for Records will be allocated to particular assets of Records, and these allocated amounts will become the new book values of those assets in Sound's hands. Book value, of course, is similar to the concept of basis for tax purposes and is used in measuring depreciation deductions for depreciable assets and profits or losses on the resale of those and other assets. Sound will treat the amount of the total purchase price that is not thus allocated to particular assets as paid for goodwill (that is, going concern value) and will henceforth show that amount as an asset on its balance sheet.

Pooling treatment for the merger

When the acquiring company does not replace independently valuable assets with others, however, but extends or increases them by issuing stockholder-type claims against itself to the acquired company's shareholders, it can be argued that a different accounting treatment is appropriate. Nirvana simply loops its cell membrane around Message's assets and liabilities, one might say, so why not regard the two companies as simply fusing or putting together their assets, rather than as one buying the other? If this view is taken, all of Message's assets as well as those of Nirvana should simply *retain* the book value they had before the merger. The amounts in the various categories on the asset side of the two companies' premerger balance sheets will simply be added together to get the amounts for those categories of assets on the post-merger balance sheet of the survivor. There will be no need for a purchased goodwill account. Liabilities and net worth will also be added, although there will have to be some nonadditive adjustments among the accounts that make up net worth (namely, stated or legal capital, capital surplus, and earned surplus or retained earnings), since there will only be one corporation with outstanding stock.[12]

[12] Suppose the Message common shares were originally issued at $5/share with a par value

Contra pooling treatment of merger

Just as the characteristics of a simple merger do not *necessarily* imply tax free treatment (because the investment of the merging company's shareholders is changed as well as continued), so the characteristics of the simple merger do not inevitably imply pooling type accounting treatment. This is because the parties have not only put their assets together but have also bargained at arms' length about their relative values. The managers of Message and Nirvana clearly did this when they decided how many shares of Nirvana stock would be given in exchange for each share of Message. Furthermore, where the acquiring company's shares are publicly traded, their market value, and hence the bargained-for value of the acquired company, can be readily expressed in dollars. It can then be argued that, because ownership of the old Message assets changed hands on terms set by independently bargaining parties, the merger, just like the conventional sale, does provide an eminently appropriate occasion to rewrite (up or down) the book value of the Message assets. Doing so seems quite consistent with the accounting profession's notorious preference for objectivity. To be sure, there will be problems of allocation: which book value should be written up or down in which amounts, and so forth. But presumably the managers of the two companies will have done some of this work during the negotiating process leading to the merger.

---

of $2/share, and Nirvana's were issued at $3/share with a par value of $1/share. Assume the two balance sheets indicate the following:

	Message	*Nirvana* (pre-merger)
Assets	$6 million	$7 million
Liabilities	$1.5 million	$2.5 milion
Stated capital	$1.0 million	$0.5 million
Capital surplus	$1.5 million	$1.0 million
Retained earnings	$2.0 million	$3.0 million

After the merger, Nirvana will have one million shares outstanding, each with $1 par value; stated capital will thus be $1 million. Assets, liabilities, and retained earnings are simply added. Capital surplus is obtained by adding the two pre-merger capital surpluses and then adding the amount by which Message's stated capital exceeded the par value of the *newly issued* Nirvana shares. In this example, that excess is $.5 million. Thus, the new balance sheet would show:

	Nirvana (post-merger)
Assets	$13 million
Liabilities	$4 million
Stated capital	$1 million
Capital surplus	$3 million
Retained earnings	$5 million

Discretion creates problems

Because there is validity in both of these concepts — a merger is a fusion or pooling of two businesses; a merger is an occasion when assets are revalued by parties bargaining at arms' length in a market transaction — it might seem that the accounting profession should be free to choose, on a case by case basis, which accounting method to employ for any given merger. But discretion creates possibilities of abuse. The most obvious is that corporate managers of acquiring companies will pressure their accountants to account for a merger by the pooling method when the acquired company's assets have increased over their adjusted historical cost or book value but to use the purchase method when the acquired company's assets have declined below book value.

Example

Suppose that Message corporation owned a building whose book value, to it, was $100,000, while Nirvana figured the building's current fair market value to be $500,000 and, as payment for the building, it was going to issue new Nirvana stock that was expected to have a market value, right after the acquisition, of $500,000. Suppose further that Nirvana will take depreciation deductions by the straight line method and calculates that the building will last 10 years and then be worth nothing. If it records the building at $500,000 on its books — as it would under the purchase method of accounting for the acquisition — it will have to take depreciation deductions against its gross revenues of $50,000 a year. If it records the building on its books at $100,000 — which it would do under the pooling method of accounting — it will take depreciation deductions of only $10,000 a year, and its reported — that is, its nominal or apparent — net income will be substantially higher in the years following the acquisition. It might therefore appear, to casual investors and stock analysts looking at the sharp increase in reported corporate earnings in the years before and after the merger, that the managers of Nirvana were running the business ever more efficiently and successfully. (By the same token, managers of an acquiring company could make themselves look good in the opposite case, where the fair market values of the acquired company's assets are *less* than their book values, by using the *purchase* method of accounting.)

But a little thought should show that these apparent spurts of growth and net income may be illusory, at least as far as the investors are concerned. If, in payment for a particular building of Message, Nirvana actually issues enough new shares to be worth $500,000 on the stock market, Nirvana is obviously "costing" its old shareholders five times as much as if it were issuing a smaller number of shares that would be worth only $100,000. Whatever the corporate accounting records may say, the old Nirvana shareholders are giving away a greater portion of their claims to the net income of the surviving company. From their perspective, it is more accurate to view themselves as if they were paying something worth $500,000, not $100,000. To be sure, the Nirvana managers may drive a hard bargain and succeed in paying the Message shareholders stock worth less than the full value to Nirvana of the Message assets. If they do, it will benefit the old Nirvana shareholders. But this benefit will not be the result of using one accounting method rather than another. The only way that selective use of accounting methods can itself create real gains to a person or group is by misleading another person or group. And indeed, there is empirical evidence for the view that the stock market often sees through and adjusts for different methods of accounting for essentially similar economic performance.[13] It is hard for a company to change the market price of its stock merely by changing how it accounts for what it does.

Having it both ways? Another sort of anomaly would occur if the managers in an acquisition by merger wanted to account for it by the pooling method for purposes of financial reporting to investors (to make earnings growth look better) but wanted to treat it as a sale-purchase transaction for tax purposes (in order to get larger depreciation deductions against taxable income). They might be able to do this by deliberately failing to meet some technical requirement for having an acquisition treated as tax free (see section 10.4), while not going so far as to make the use of the pooling method of accounting completely indefensible. In other words, they might try to have their cake and eat it too.

APB No. 16 Thus, giving discretion in the use of accounting methods has its problems. Because of them, Accounting Principles Board Opinion No. 16, adopted in 1970 and still in force,[14] tries to eliminate discretion. Under it, a business combination that meets specified conditions — our polar merger would be an easy paradigm case — *requires* accounting by the pooling method. All other business combinations — including our polar sale transaction, again an easy case — must be accounted for as purchases.

The precise conditions for pooling treatment will be summarized in the section on hybrid transactions (section 10.5).

[13] Hong, Kaplan, & Mandelker, Pooling vs. Purchase: The Effects of Accounting for Mergers on Stock Prices, 53 Accounting Rev. 31 (1978).

[14] Prior to 1973, the Accounting Principles Board of the American Institute of Certified Public Accountants (AICPA) issued statements on standard practices for the profession. The power to issue authoritative statements on these matters then shifted to the Financial Accounting Standards Board (FASB), which was designed to be more independent, better financed, better staffed, and more continuously devoted to the task of formulating accounting principles. Section III(k) of the FASB's Rules of Procedure (adopted effective March 29, 1973 and amended January 1, 1978), however, states that the opinions of the Accounting Principles Board, as well as the Accounting Research Bulletins (from an earlier AICPA-sponsored group), should be treated as continuing in force except to the extent altered, amended, supplemented, revoked, or superseded by statements of the FASB.

§10.2.3 Securities Regulation

Differing needs for information

The federal securities laws are concerned with making sure that investors receive information adequate to make prudent decisions in certain recurring transactions involving corporate securities. When the shareholders of Records decide to vote in favor of the simple corporate sale, they are making an important decision and need information. But, since Sound is planning to pay cash, there appears to be little need to give them extensive information about the business operations and financial performance of that acquiring company. When the shareholders of Message are asked to vote for the merger into Nirvana Corporation and to receive the latter's shares, however, they are being asked, in effect, to make an investment in the acquiring company. They therefore ought to have extensive information about its business operations and financial performance.

Reflected in Exchange Act rules

The actual provisions of the securities laws and the rules under them are rather complicated, but they do reflect this basic dichotomy. Under state corporate law rules (see section 10.2.4), the shareholders of the company to be acquired would have to vote for the proposed transaction in both the sale and the merger transactions. Because their votes or proxies would thus be solicited by their management, their corporation would have to supply them with proxy statements in accordance with Section 14(a) of the Securities Exchange Act of 1934 and its implementing rules.[15] In both situations, extensive information about the business operations and financial performance of the acquired company would have to be disclosed; this would assist the shareholders in judging the value of what they are being asked to give up. In the merger transaction, similar information would have to be disclosed about the business operations and finances of the acquiring company; this would assist the acquired company shareholders in judging the value of the paper claims they are being asked to take. But in our simple sale transaction, where Sound is issuing no securities of any kind to Records or its shareholders, this information would not be required with respect to the acquiring company.[16]

And in Securities Act rule

The basic thrust of the Securities Act of 1933 is to require companies to disclose elaborate information about themselves when they sell stock or other securities to the public. Rule 145 under that Act takes the position that, *when* the merging or transferring corporation's shareholders are to

[15] See Securities Exchange Act §14(a); 17 C.F.R. 240.14a-2(a)(3), which makes it clear that the other, substantive proxy rules would apply in the sale and merger transactions; and 17 C.F.R. 240.14a-101, Item 14, which requires disclosure of various information in connection with mergers and acquisitions.

[16] See 17 C.F.R. 240.14a-101, Items 14(b), 15(b).

receive *securities* of another party to the transaction, mergers and transfers of substantial parts of the corporation's assets to another company are to be treated as involving "offers to sell" securities to the target company shareholders. Such transactions will therefore trigger the registration and prospectus-delivery requirements of the 1933 Act and, in our simple merger transaction (but not in our sale transaction), this would mean that the acquiring company, Nirvana, would have to make elaborate disclosures about itself. Fortunately, Rule 145 would also allow Nirvana to use a simplified form of registration statement, according to which the proxy statement prepared under the 1934 Act (see previous paragraph) would simply be incorporated in toto, supplemented by a modest amount of additional information.[17]

§10.2.4 Treatment Under State Business Corporation Statutes

A different key needed

The discussion to this point shows that our analytical distinction between a simple sale and a simple merger transaction supplies the key to understanding some very basic distinctions in the tax, accounting, and securities regulation rules applicable to business combinations. In each of these normative fields, there is a dichotomy that is closely analogous to the sale-merger dichotomy. But when we turn to traditional corporate law, the distinctions cease to be neatly parallel. This is partly because of the odd way in which corporate statutes have evolved and partly because of the different policy objectives behind the corporate law provisions.

Concept of organic change

The basic idea underlying the corporate law provisions on sales and mergers seems to be that sudden, deliberate (that is, manager-initiated), major or "organic" corporate changes that affect shareholder interests ought to be approved or consented to by some majority of the shareholders. (It should not be thought, however, that the statutes pursue this idea with complete consistency or efficacy.)

Impact on shareholders is key

From this policy standpoint, the first two differences between our simple sale and merger cases are irrelevant. Whether the acquired company's shareholders terminate their investment or continue it in substantially altered form, or whether the acquiring company exchanges or extends its assets, the effect on the acquired company's shareholders is fairly drastic, as well as being both sudden and manager-initiated, in *both* the sale and merger cases. Accordingly, in both cases these shareholders should have a right to vote.

[17]Rule 145 is discussed at length in section 17.3.5 infra.

On acquiring side too

Nevertheless, the third difference between our simple sale and merger cases has some relevance to the policy of the corporate law. We saw that in the simple sale transaction the acquiring company was much larger than the acquired company and that in the simple merger the size disparity was less. We also saw that, in any event, the merger but not the sale would have a substantial impact on the voting power of the acquiring company's shareholders. Both differences suggest that it is more important in the merger case to give the acquiring company's shareholders a vote. Yet, since many real life mergers (as defined by corporate statutes or by our first two differences) may involve great size disparities, statutory draftsmen might consider dropping this voting right in those cases. For example, does it really make sense to require that the public shareholders of a giant corporation running a nationwide chain of supermarkets must vote to approve an acquisition by merger of a Mom and Pop corner grocery store? And since some real life sales of one corporation to another may occasionally involve companies of similar size — when they are basically exchanging or swapping their assets, for example — perhaps the law should give a voting right to both companies' shareholders in those cases.

Sales under typical statutes

To test these ideas let us see what some typical statutory provisions actually provide. Delaware Corporation Law (Section 271) provides that a corporation may sell, lease, or exchange all or substantially all of its assets on such terms as its board of directors deems expedient and for the best interest of the corporation, when authorized by a majority vote of the outstanding stock of the corporation. The MBCA is similar except that it explicitly restricts this approach to sales that trigger the basic policy decision to focus on sudden or unexpected major changes. Thus, Section 12.01 declares that a sale, lease, exchange, or other disposition of all or substantially all of a corporation's assets "in the usual and regular course of its business" does not require shareholder approval. Section 12.02 provides that, when such a transaction would not be in the usual and regular course of the corporation's business, the standard pattern for authorizing organic corporate changes must be followed: The board of directors must adopt a resolution recommending the transaction and directing that it be submitted to a vote at a shareholder meeting; notice must be given to the stockholders; and the transaction must be approved by affirmative vote of the majority of the shares entitled to vote on it, with provision for class voting in certain circumstances. Although the decision is debatable, neither the Delaware law nor the MBCA requires a shareholder vote when the corporation mortgages or pledges all its assets. Furthermore, both statutes are silent about the rights of shareholders of purchasing corporations; nothing in them explicitly gives such shareholders a right to vote. This feature of the statute is consistent with my earlier description of the basic idea behind the sale and merger provisions. For in the polar case sale, the acquiring company shareholders will be much less affected than the acquired company shareholders.

Exchanges covered too

But, you may ask, since some sale transactions may involve companies of roughly equal size, doesn't the law go too far by not giving voting rights to purchasing company shareholders in those situations? The answer is that the law does so provide — indirectly. Suppose that X Corporation is to be bought by Y Corporation, which just before the transaction has assets roughly equal in value to those of X. The reference is to gross assets; the point I will make doesn't depend on whether or not Y has large liabilities or had to borrow heavily to acquire assets needed to make the acquisition. It also doesn't matter theoretically whether Y's assets consist entirely of cash, or or marketable securities, or of widgets, or of buildings, or of some mixture of these and other items. But, to have a more specific image in mind, imagine that X is a family-owned discount department store business whose owners want to retire from involvement in active business operations and Y is a closed-end investment company, holding only treasury bills and other unexciting marketable securities, whose managers want to put their talents to use in a hopefully more profitable nonfinancial business. It should be obvious that, if anything remotely like a fair deal is struck, both X *and* Y will be *exchanging* substantially all their assets. As noted above, both Delaware law and the MBCA require a shareholder vote when a corporation exchanges substantially all of its assets in a transaction not in the regular course of business. This rule would apply to Y as well as to X. There is thus an automatic provision of voting rights to purchasing company shareholders in the equal-sizes case.

Mergers under MBCA

Now let us turn to merger provisions. Under the MBCA, statutory mergers are governed by a set of formal and substantive requirements. Section 11.01 requires the board of directors of each of the corporations involved to adopt a resolution approving a plan of merger, which must contain certain specified kinds of information, such as the terms and conditions of the proposed merger and the manner of converting the shares of the merging company into other kinds of assets.[18] Section 11.03 requires the board of directors of each of the corporations involved in the merger to resolve to submit the plan of merger to the shareholders at a properly noticed meeting (annual or special), requires approval by an affirmative vote of the

[18] Many state statutes also have a similar provision for consolidations — transactions in which two or more corporations fuse to become a new corporation. A consolidation is very like a merger except that none of the merging corporations survive.

majority of shares entitled to vote on it, and provides for class voting in certain situations.[19] Section 11.05 provides that after shareholder approval, the surviving corporation must deliver to the appropriate secretary of state, for filing, articles of merger, a document that must set forth the plan of merger plus certain other information, such as the numerical results of the shareholder voting. Unless a delayed effective date is specified, the merger takes effect when the articles of merger are filed. (Of course, the terminology and procedures of individual states may be different. For example, the state statute may refer to a merger agreement instead of a plan of merger and to a certificate of merger instead of articles of merger.)[20]

Consequences of merger

However determined, the exact moment when a merger takes effect is of legal and practical significance. MBCA §11.06 tells us what happens when a merger takes effect: It elaborates the intuitive notion that the surviving corporation "steps into the shoes" of the corporation merging into it and automatically acquires all of its assets and liabilities. Upon effectiveness, the Message Corporation of our original example would cease to exist. The title to all of its real estate and other property would vest in Nirvana. All liabilities of Message would become liabilities of Nirvana. Lawsuits against Message would become lawsuits against Nirvana, as if the merger hadn't even occurred. The shares of Message would become converted into the right to receive what was promised their holders in the plan of merger.

Rules related to impact on shareholders

Now to test our earlier formulation of the basic policy objective. Are the merger procedures restricted in applicability to cases where the merging companies are of roughly equal size? On the acquired or merging company side the answer is no. But this is as it should be, since the shareholders of that company are always affected rather drastically by the merger and therefore should have a vote. On the acquiring or surviving company side, many corporate statutes now have a refinement consistent with the postulated policy. Section 11.03(g) of the MBCA provides that if the number of post-merger voting shares of the survivor corporation will not exceed the

[19] Compare Cal. §§1103, 1200-1201; Del. §251(b), 251(c); N.Y. §903. Under MBCA §§11.03(f)(1) and 10.04, a class of shares must separately approve a merger if:

(1) the number of authorized shares in the class will be changed;
(2) the class will be exchanged or reclassified into shares of another class;
(3) the relative rights or preferences of the class will be modified;
(4) a new class of shares with prior and superior rights will be created or the rights of existing prior stock strengthened;
(5) the preemptive rights of the class will be limited or denied; or
(6) accumulated but undeclared dividends for the class will be affected.

[20] See, e.g., Del. §251(c).

number of its premerger voting shares by more than 20 percent, and certain other conditions are met, the votes of its shareholders need not be obtained. (The 20 percent test is also applied, separately, to the number of participating shares, those that entitle their holders to participate without limitation in distributions of earnings or surplus.) Delaware law has a similar provision.[21] In other words, the giant corporation that makes a relatively small acquisition by merger need not go through the trouble and expense of getting the approval of *its* shareholders. The merger's impact on those shareholders is assumed to be not so great as to necessitate triggering the voting procedure and its costs.

§10.2.5 Antitrust Treatment

Indifferent to sale-merger distinction

Antitrust law is concerned with business combinations that pose a threat to competition. From its standpoint, what matters is the major common element between our polar sale and merger: the fact that two businesses once run by separate top managements are now controlled by one top management. Formerly independent decisions about pricing, output, and the like may now be coordinated. In some circumstances, for example, when the two merging corporations were direct competitors of one another in an oligopolistic market, this may mean a significant reduction in the number of competitors in a relevant market and perhaps even in the strength of competition in the market. Consequently, antitrust courts and commentators pay relatively scant regard to the sale-merger difference and to the host of variations and hybrids that will occupy us in the next two sections.

Concern for motives and effects

What antitrust analysis — as practiced by commentators, anyway — does pay attention to are the substantive, business aspects of combinations. What were the corporate managers' *motives* or *reasons* for attempting the combination? What, in any event, will be its economic *effects*, especially on variables relevant to the strength of competition? Antitrust law is a vast subject treated in many other sources.[22] It will not be explored here.

§10.3 Variations: Forms of Sale

In these next two sections I continue to refrain from introducing complications that would make it hard to tell whether a combination is more like a

[21] Del. §251(f).

[22] See, e.g., 4, 5 P. Areeda & D. Turner, Antitrust Law Chs. 9-12 (1980); R. Bork, The Antitrust Paradox 198-262 (1978).

polar case sale or a merger. But I will introduce complications in the technical methods used to carry out transactions that are clearly like either sales or mergers in their basic effects.

Figure 10.3-A presents diagrams of three major variations of the sale of one corporation to another. The polar case we dealt with in sections 10.1 and 10.2 is variation II in the figure.

Variation I — Liquidation-and-sale

Variation I may be called the liquidation-and-shareholder-sale transaction or *liquidation-and-sale* for short. (In the hyphenated names for the different variations, the word *and* is used as a shorthand for *followed by*. It should be clear that in variation I, for example, the sale by shareholders occurs after the dissolution and liquidation of the selling corporation.) The management and shareholders of X Corporation, the company to be acquired, cause it to be dissolved and its assets distributed to them in proportion to their respective stockholdings. Thereafter, the shareholders as individuals all sell the assets so obtained to Y Corporation for agreed-upon amounts of cash (or for assets that are close substitutes for cash).

Variation II — Sale-and-liquidation

Variation II may be called the corporate-sale-and-liquidation transaction or the *sale-and-liquidation* for short. The steps are exactly those described in

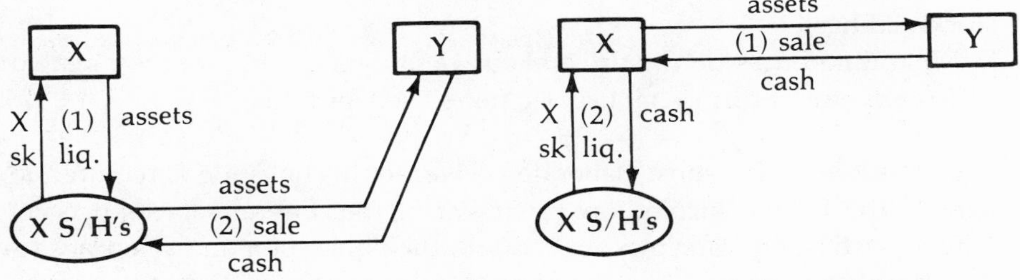

I. Liquidation and Sale

II. Sale and Liquidation

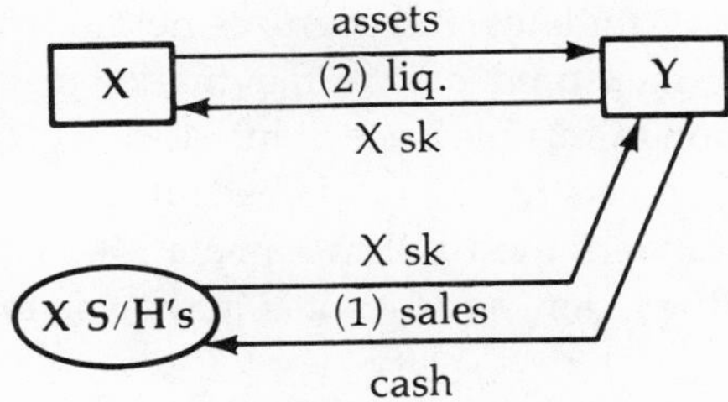

III. Stock Sale (and Liquidation)

Figure 10.3-A
Forms of Sale

our polar case of a corporate sale. The management and shareholder of X Corporation vote to approve a sale for cash of all of X's assets to Y Corporation, and this transaction is effected. They also vote to dissolve the corporation. When this transaction is carried out, they receive the cash as a liquidating distribution, in proportion to their respective shareholdings. The pattern is thus the same as variation I, except that the temporal order of the steps is reversed.

Variation III — Stock sale

Variation III may be called the *stock sale* or, when the sale is followed by dissolution of the acquired company, the *stock-sale-and-liquidation* transaction. Here Y Corporation simply buys stock directly from the individual shareholders of X. Subvariations are obviously possible (and will assume importance in later chapters). Y Corporation may make a single, publicly announced offer to buy X stock from any X shareholders willing to sell it (a classic tender offer), or it may privately negotiate purchases from individual shareholders at different times and places. Y may or may not pay all X shareholders the same price per share. Y may buy literally all the X stock or only a hefty majority of it. After acquiring all or a controlling block of X stock, Y may or may not take a second step: formally dissolving X and transferring X's assets as a liquidating distribution to itself (and if there are some other X shareholders, to those shareholders in proportion to their stockholdings).

What differences do the three major variations make? Are they treated differently under our previously examined sets of rules?

Taxation of variation I

Tax treatment. The most elaborate answer to this question is required to explain the federal income tax treatment of the different forms of sale. Under established principles, variation I, the liquidation-and-sale transaction, results in one tax, on the selling company shareholders at the favorable capital gain tax rates, and the acquiring company gets a new basis in the acquired assets equal to their cost to the acquirer. More specifically, when X Corporation liquidates, it recognizes neither gain nor loss.[1] Each X shareholder's gain, measured by the fair market value of the assets he receives in liquidation minus his basis in his stock, is taxed as capital gain,[2] and the basis of the assets in his hands becomes their fair market value.[3] When the X shareholders then sell the assets for cash to Y Corporation, they will have neither gain nor loss if Y pays fair market value for the

§10.3 [1]I.R.C. §336(a). There are exceptions pertaining to LIFO inventory, §336(b), and installment obligations, §453B.

[2]I.R.C. §331.

[3]I.R.C. §334(a).

assets. Y, as purchaser, recognizes no income but gets assets that will have a tax basis equal to what is paid for them. The Y shareholders are not directly affected.

Taxation of variation II

Variation I, under which the X shareholders as individuals sell various bits of X's assets, is basically abnormal and cumbersome. It would hardly have been used had it not been for the tax burdens that once afflicted variation II, the sale-and-liquidation transaction. In the latter, there were once two occasions for recognition of gain or loss: when X Corporation sold the assets and when X liquidated and gave the proceeds to X shareholders. As mentioned earlier, Section 337 of the Internal Revenue Code attempts to achieve a rough equivalence between the tax treatment of the two variations by providing for nonrecognition of gain or loss on corporate sales made within 12 months of the adoption of a formal plan of liquidation. Thus, for many purposes,[4] the corporate-level tax can be escaped.

Taxation of variation III

When X shareholders sell their stock to Y for cash, as in variation III, they are taxed as in any other sale of their stock to third parties. The gain, meaning the money they receive minus their bases in their stock, is taxed as capital gain, and the acquiring company has a basis in the acquired stock equal to the price paid. Without more, however, the basis of Y's assets — and therefore the allowable amount of depreciation deductions that could offset taxable income after the sale — would not be changed. From the acquiring company's point of view, this would be a good tax result if the acquired company had a total asset basis higher than what was just paid for all the stock. It would be a bad thing if, as is more common, the purchase price of the stock exceeded the acquired company's old basis in its assets; for then the post-sale depreciation deductions would be smaller than if the acquirer had bought the assets instead of the stock.

Election re basis

This problem, however, can be solved if Y makes an election under Section 338 of the Internal Revenue Code. If it does, X's assets may be written up or down (as appropriate in the particular case), even though X is not dissolved and liquidated. (Technically, the statute achieves this result by "deeming" X to have sold its assets to itself in an §337-type sale, at a price determined by reference to the price Y paid for its X stock.)

There are restrictions on the use of this election. One of them is that Y must treat stock acquisitions of different target companies consistently — it must make the election for all or none of the acquired companies — if the acquisitions are made within a specified time period. The "consistency" time period varies according to a rule set out in the statute.

[4] But note that §337 has a number of special rules. For example, gains on the sale of inventory items during the 12 month period only benefit from nonrecognition if the inventory is sold to one person in one transaction.

Purchase treatment for all

Accounting treatment. For accounting purposes, the differences among the three major methods of sale often fail to be crucial ones. All three are subject to "purchase" treatment on the acquiring company's side.

Amortization of good will avoidable?

One special issue worthy of note is whether Y, by taking the first but not the second step of variation III — that is, by simply buying and holding the X stock — can somehow avoid having to amortize the goodwill element of its purchase price. Remember that in the direct purchase of X's assets the purchase price will have to be allocated among X's various assets but that, when a healthy business with a sizable going concern value is bought, there will often be an amount left over, which is recorded on Y's books as an asset called purchased goodwill. Accounting authority requires companies to amortize[5] purchased good will over a certain number of years,[6] and this will cause an unpleasant reduction in Y's reported net income. Without the rule of amortization, of course, management would be greatly tempted to allocate as much of the purchase price as possible to the goodwill element, which, as an asset without a determinate lifespan, might not be written off at all. Can management avoid the rule of amortization by simply having the company buy stock instead of assets?

Not if consolidated statements used

In the kind of situation we have been considering, the answer is no. When a corporation acquires control in an investee company — as in our variation III — it should generally employ *consolidated financial statements.* The presentation of information will then be quite similar to that which would occur if the company had bought the acquired company's assets directly. In particular, the purchased good will element would have to be amortized.[7]

Compare cost and equity methods

Notice how this contrasts with the treatment of other situations where one corporation buys stock in another. When a company buys a small proportion of another company's stock — say, 5 percent — it will usually account for this investment by the *cost method:* It will record the cost of its investment on its books, writing that down only if and when adverse developments in the investee company's business clearly call for a devaluation; it will treat dividends paid on the stock as income to itself; and it will

[5]To amortize an asset is to deduct portions of its book value from gross revenues, year by year, until the book value has been exhausted. Amortization is thus very similar to depreciation. Usually the difference is one of terminology: one depreciates plant and equipment but one amortizes an intangible asset. Sometimes the term *amortization* is used as the generic term that encompasses depreciation, depletion, and amortization of intangibles.

[6]AICPA, Accounting Principles Board Opinion No. 17, ¶9. The maximum amortization period is 40 years.

[7]AICPA, Accounting Principles Board Opinion No. 18, ¶4; AICPA, Accounting Research Bulletin No. 51, ¶1-5, 7-8 (1959).

generally ignore fluctuations in the investee company's earnings or losses.[8] But when a corporation has a more substantial investment in another company — for example, when it owns more than 20 percent but less than 50 percent of the other company's stock — it should usually employ the *equity method of accounting*.[9] The investor company will initially record the investment at cost but will periodically adjust the carrying amount of the investment to recognize the investor's share of the earnings or losses (not just the dividends) of the investee after acquisition. Among other things, the adjustment should be accomplished so as to "amortise, if appropriate, any difference between investor cost and underlying equity in net assets of the investee at the date of investment," that is, to amortize the goodwill element of the purchase price.[10]

Securities regulation. As for securities regulation aspects: Variations I and II would call for X to furnish proxy statements to its shareholders, whereas variation III would often require Y to make disclosures to the X shareholders under the tender offer rules.[11]

Variation I: corporate action plus contracts

Corporate law. The treatment of the three variations under the business corporation statutes is more interesting. To accomplish variation I under the typical statute, there would have to be director initiation and approval of the liquidation step, followed by a shareholder vote.[12] There is no corporate procedure for binding the individual shareholders of X to take step 2, the sale by them to Y of the assets they have received in liquidation, so Y would have to arrange this step by negotiating a contract or contracts with the X shareholders. Since a majority of the X shareholders could not compel the minority to enter such contracts, Y might run into problems. This is especially likely if there were numerous X shareholders and it was considered essential to get virtually all of X's assets.

Variation II: two corporate acts

The difficulty of dealing with individual shareholders recedes in variation II. Here both director initiation/approval and a majority shareholder vote will be required for both the corporate sale of assets step[13] and for the subsequent liquidation[14] and distribution to the cash proceeds to the X shareholders. But, since the steps are linked, both could be described in

[8] AICPA, Accounting Principles Board Opinion No. 18, ¶6(a).

[9] Id., ¶14-17.

[10] Id., ¶6(b), 19(b).

[11] See section 9.2 supra and section 13.3 infra.

[12] See MBCA §14.02; §§14.03-14.07 describe other procedural aspects and legal consequences of the dissolution procedure.

[13] MBCA §12.02.

[14] MBCA §14.02.

the same proxy statement and the votes on both taken at the same meeting of shareholders. In this variation, a majority of approving shareholders can force the sale and liquidation of the entire business over the objection of the minority. (More accurately, this is true when the minority objects simply because they think the sale and liquidation are a bad business proposition. When a minority shareholder objects because the proposed corporate sale is fraudulent or grossly unfair, afflicted with a serious conflict of interest, or illegal, he may be able to enjoin it. These kinds of problems are discussed in later chapters.) The shareholders who object to a sale of substantially all their corporation's assets often have a right to be bought out at an appraised value,[15] but this right doesn't apply where, as in variation II, the sale is for cash and the proceeds are to be distributed to the shareholders within a year after the sale.[16]

Variation III: circumvents target's directors

In both of the asset-sale variations (I and II), corporate law requires director initiation and approval of key transactions. What then can Y Corporation do if X's board of directors is hostile to the proposed acquisition? How can it circumvent X's management? One answer is that it can try to buy shares directly from the X shareholders. The permission of X's board is not needed for that, although, as we shall see,[17] X's board can take many defensive actions in an effort to defeat such a takeover attempt. If Y succeeds in gaining a controlling block of shares in X, it can vote in its own directors and can then have them initiate a liquidation procedure, if that step is thought desirable.

Share exchange statutes

Incidentally, some statutes[18] now have a provision by which an acquisition of *all* of a corporation's *shares* can be accomplished through the procedure of director initiation and approval followed by majority shareholder vote. If such a share exchange procedure is available and is followed, a majority of X's shareholders could force the minority to go along with a variation III–type stock sale to Y. The minority, however, would have appraisal rights.[19] The reasons for adoption of the new share exchange provisions will become apparent in the next subsection when we consider the reasons for so-called triangular acquisitions.

[15] See, e.g., Ill. Rev. Stat. ch. 32 §11.65(a)(2); N.J. Stat. Ann. §14A:11-(1)(b); N.Y. §910(a)(1)(B). Delaware does not provide for appraisal in this situation unless the corporation so specifies in its certificate of incorporation. Del. §262(c).

[16] MBCA §13.02(a)(3); see also the New Jersey and New York statutes cited in note 15 supra.

[17] Section 13.6 infra.

[18] MBCA §11.02; Md. Corp. & Assns. Code Ann. §3-105; Va. Code §13.1-69.1. The New Jersey statute, passed in 1967, was the first such provision enacted. The Model Act section was added in 1976.

[19] See, e.g., MBCA §13.02(a)(2).

§10.4 *Forms of Merger*

"Practical" mergers

The key idea of this section is that an acquiring company can achieve the same net result as a simple merger done in accordance with a business corporation statute's formal merger provisions by using other techniques. For example, it can buy all of the target company's stock, using its own stock as the means of payment, and can then liquidate the target. Or it could buy all of the target company's assets, using its own stock as means of payment, after which the target company would liquidate and give the acquiring company shares to the old target company shareholders. Many of these techniques are called practical mergers, or even mergers simply, by corporate lawyers who are aware of their functional equivalence. The reasons why businessmen and their lawyers resort to the variations instead of always sticking to the simple merger will be explored later in this subsection, after the variations and their legal and other treatment have been described.

Tax law's "reorganizations"

Figure 10.4-A diagrams two of the more important variations on the simple merger transaction. The breakdown and labels used here follow corporate tax law very closely. Section 368(a) of the Internal Revenue Code defines certain transactions to be corporate reorganizations, and related provisions of the Code spell out the details of the tax deferred treatment for which they are eligible.[1] Like the term *merger* the term *reorganization* can be used in various senses. In many contexts it means a reshuffling of the creditor and the shareholder claims on a corporation in a bankruptcy or other insolvency proceeding. But in Section 368 of the Code there is no such connotation. The term there comprises our simple statutory merger and a number of ways of effecting a practical merger or fusion of businesses, as well as certain kinds of divisive transactions (by which operating units are spun off, or split off, from the original corporation), recapitalizations, and mere changes in the identity, form, or place of organization of a corporation, however effected.

"A" reorg

Section 368(a)(1)(A) of the Code defines the term *reorganization* to include "a *statutory merger* or consolidation." Tax lawyers often call such a transaction an "A reorganization" or "A reorg." It means a corporate combination carried out in accordance with the merger provisions of a business corporation statute, for example, a merger following the procedures of, and having the legal effect specified by, some state's version of MBCA Sections 11.01, 11.03, 11.05, and 11.06. Our polar case merger of section 10.1 is a good example.

§10.4 [1]I.R.C. §§354-358, 361-363, 381-383.

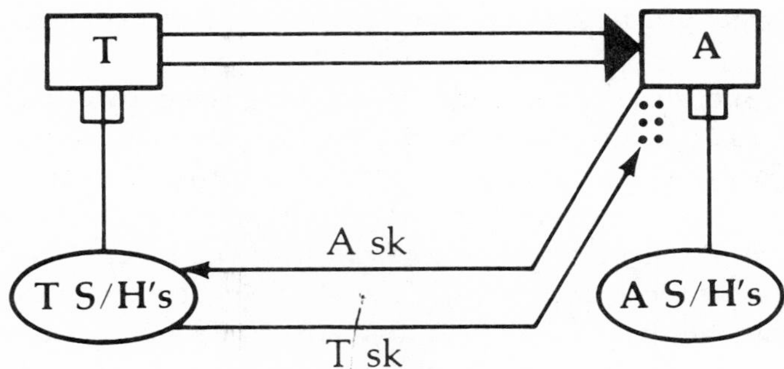

"A"—Statutory Merger

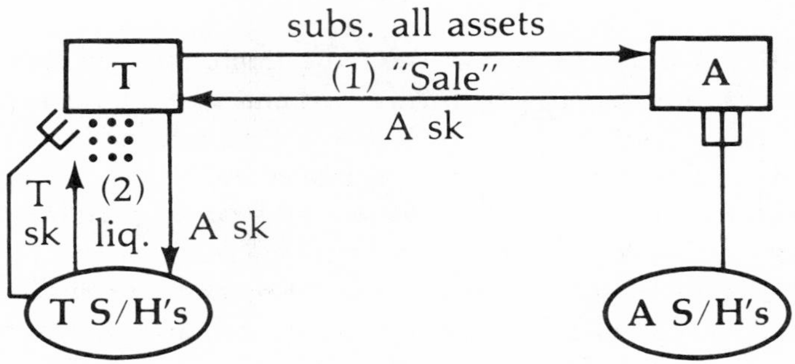

"C"—Sale of All Assets for Stock
(and maybe Liquidation)

Figure 10.4-A
Forms of Merger

"B" reorg The "B reorganization," or *stock-for-stock-exchange,* is an acquisition by one corporation, in exchange solely for all or a part of its voting stock, of stock of another corporation if, immediately after the acquisition, the acquiring corporation has control of the other corporation. Control means that the acquirer owns stock possessing 80 percent of the total combined voting power of all classes of stock entitled to vote and at least 80 percent of the total number of shares of all other classes of acquired company stock.[2]

[2] I.R.C. §368(c).

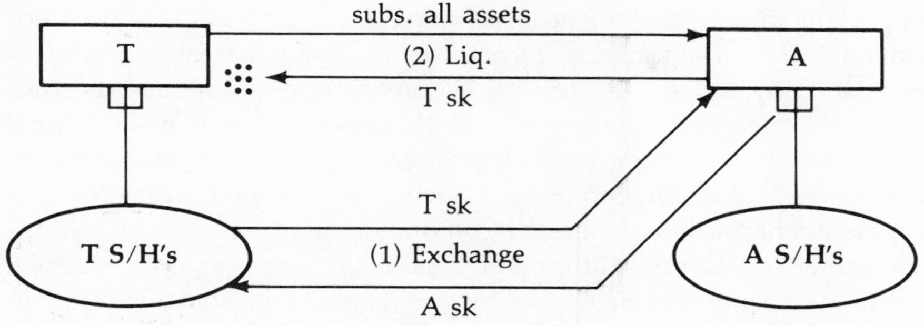

"B"—Stock-for-Stock Exchange
(and maybe Liquidation)

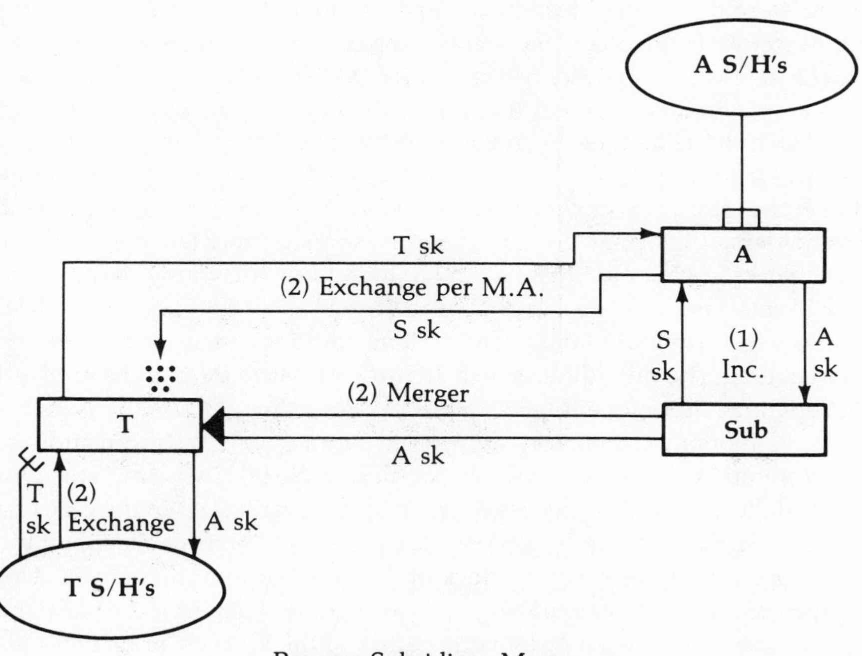

Reverse Subsidiary Merger
(a "triangular acquisition")

Figure 10.4-B
Forms of Merger, continued

In deciding whether a share acquisition is a B reorganization, it does not matter whether the acquiring corporation also had control immediately before the acquisition. The term *B reorganization* also includes the case where the acquiring company gets stock of the target in exchange solely for all or a part of the voting stock of a parent corporation of the acquirer.

Application to original hypo

To go back to our hypothetical of section 10.1, suppose that Nirvana Corporation had acquired Message Corporation, not by invoking the statutory merger procedures, but by individual purchases from each Message shareholder, using a formula whereby the shareholders would be paid one share of Nirvana stock for each share of Message stock that they gave up. If Nirvana obtained at least 80 percent of the Message stock this way, and paid nothing but Nirvana voting stock to the old Message shareholders, it would have effected a B reorganization. It might or might not then take a second step: dissolving Message assets in a liquidating distribution. (This second step is analogous to the second step sometimes taken in the type III or stock sale variation described in section 10.3.1.)

If the second step is taken, the net result is quite obviously very similar to that of a simple merger. Even without the second step, there are striking similarities: Like our simple statutory merger but unlike our sale transaction, the stock-for-stock exchange pools the Message and Nirvana shareholders, that is, it continues rather than terminates the Message shareholders' ownership interest, and it does dilute the voting rights of the old Nirvana shareholders; it pools the two pre-existing operating businesses in one corporate family; and it de facto brings them under one top management. The only difference is that the Message operations are kept in a separate corporate entity.

"C" reorg

The "C reorganization," or *assets-for-stock-exchange,* is the acquisition by one corporation, in exchange solely for all or a part of its voting stock, of substantially all of the properties of another corporation. As in the case of a B reorganization, the acquisition may still count as a C reorganization if the acquiring company uses voting stock of a parent corporation of itself. Unlike the case of a B reorganization, however, the requirement that the acquisition be paid for solely by voting stock of the acquirer or its parent is tempered by the statute.

Liabilities assumable

For one thing, the definition of a C reorganization directs that, in determining whether an exchange is solely for voting stock, the fact that acquired property is subject to a liability shall be disregarded. By contrast, if the acquiring company in a stock-for-stock exchange assumed liabilities of the target company shareholders, the deal would not qualify as a B reorganization.

Rough parallel to A and B

Economically, of course, when a corporation not only gives stock but agrees to assume a liability in order to get some assets, its assumption of liability constitutes part of the consideration paid for those assets. On the other hand, when a corporation acquires a target company by a simple merger, it automatically acquires whatever liabilities the target company has. And when a corporation acquires a wholly owned subsidiary by use of its own voting shares, the target company's liabilities do not thereby evaporate but continue to constitute a claim on the subsidiary's assets that is prior to the equity claim of the subsidiary's corporate shareholder. Thus, the rule about disregarding assumed liabilities for purposes of classifying a transaction as a C reorganization can be viewed as a way of achieving parallel treatment with A and B reorganizations.

Some "boot" allowed

A second liberality is that the solely for voting stock requirement is not deemed violated in a C reorganization as long as the acquiring company does get, solely for voting stock, property of the target company that has a fair market value of at least 80 percent of the fair market value of all of the target's property. The rest may be acquired for money or other property. In a sense, this achieves something like a parallel with the B reorganization, where the acquirer need only get 80 percent of the target stock.[3]

Distribution needed

Under a 1984 amendment to the Code, an acquisition will only qualify as a C reorganization if the target company distributes both the consideration it receives from the acquiring company and any other property it may still have pursuant to the plan of reorganization.[4] Thus, the acquired company could not be kept alive indefinitely as a vehicle for holding the stock and other property received from the acquirer. Normally, therefore, the acquired company will be dissolved as part of the C reorganization.

Recall continuity of interest idea

Apart from the details, the reader should remember the basic reason for making it a precondition of favorable tax treatment that the acquired company shareholders receive voting stock of the acquiring company in reorganizations. That reason is the continuity of interest doctrine: A merger is an inappropriate occasion to recognize shareholder gains or losses only when the shareholders' investments are being continued rather than terminated.

Application to hypo

Once again, reconsider our hypothetical from section 10.1. Suppose Nirvana simply acquired all of Message's assets from Message, in exchange for assumption of Message's liabilities and the payment to Message of a certain amount of voting common stock of Nirvana. Message, through director approval and shareholder vote, then took the obvious second step: It dissolved itself and distributed its assets (the Nirvana shares) in liq-

[3]But if an acquirer obtained 100 percent of a target company's stock all at once, yet gave a few of the shareholders cash instead of voting stock, it might have difficulty satisfying the requirements for a B reorganization. See note 10 infra.

[4]I.R.C. §368(a)(1)(G).

uidation to its shareholders. The net effect would clearly be quite similar to that of the simple merger transaction. Such a transaction would qualify as a C reorganization.

Triangular acquisitions

Now consider a class of variations in which there are at least three corporations involved: a target company and, on the acquiring side, both a parent corporation and a wholly owned subsidiary. These variations are sometimes referred to as triangular acquisitions because diagrams of them suggest that name. (See Figure 10.4-B). The parent corporation is often a public corporation with publicly traded securities, and one aim is to give the target company shareholders securities issued by this parent company. The subsidiary is often, but not always, a shell corporation (that is, a corporation without a real operating business) formed specifically for the purpose of effecting the acquisition in question, and one aim of the parties is to run the target company's business operations in a separate subsidiary of the parent company. For simplicity, let us refer to the corporation to be acquired as T, the acquiring subsidiary as S, and the acquiring parent corporation as P.

Direct subsidiary acquisitions

One set of triangular acquisitions is generated if S makes the acquisition in the first place but uses P stock as the means of payment. (P would previously have contributed stock in itself to S, perhaps in return for S shares.) For example, T may merge into S under a merger agreement whereby T stock would be converted into stock of P. Most modern merger statutes would allow this form of consideration to be paid in a merger.[5] And the transaction could count as a reorganization for tax purposes.[6] Alternatively, S could acquire all of T's stock or all of T's assets in exchange for voting stock of P. As we saw previously, these transactions could count as B and C reorganizations. All of these triangular acquisitions might be called direct subsidiary acquisitions. (But remember that subsidiaries may sometimes make acquisitions using their own stock. Such acquisitions are not at issue here.)

Drop down acquisitions

Another set of triangular acquisitions is generated by the possibility that P could first acquire, in exchange for its own voting stock, the assets or stock of T by means of an A, B, or C reorganization, and could then convey the newly acquired assets or stock to S. These variations might be called drop down triangular acquisitions. (Why? Because subsidiaries are often

[5] See, e.g., MBCA §11.01(b)(3) referring to conversion of shares of either corporation in the merger into "shares, obligations, or other securities of the surviving or any other corporation or into cash or other property in whole or part").

[6] I.R.C. §368(a)(2)(D).

placed under their parents in diagrams. Not a profound reason, I admit.) They can qualify as tax deferred reorganizations.[7]

Reverse subsidiary merger

Finally, a more elaborate, yet quite common and useful, kind of triangular acquisition occurs when, as a formal or technical matter, S merges into T, and the T shareholders' old T stock is changed into or exchanged for P stock. This transaction is often called a reverse subsidiary merger and by some lawyers a reverse B merger. The reverse subsidiary merger, which can qualify as a tax deferred reorganization,[8] is diagrammed in figure 10.3-C, and it merits some explanation. Typically, the would-be acquirer, P, will create a separate subsidiary corporation, S, and pump into it, in exchange for the newly issued S shares, the shares of P voting stock (and other consideration, perhaps) that it wants to use in the acquisition.

That is the first step. A merger agreement is then negotiated, approved, and voted by all the relevant parties whereby S is to merge into T. Under the merger agreement, P, the sole shareholder of the merging corporation, S, is to have its shares in S converted into shares of T. Also under the merger agreement, the old T shareholders' stock is to be converted into P stock; the actual shares they receive will be those that were owned by S but become assets of T by virtue of the merger itself.

This second aspect of the merger agreement seems unorthodox, of course. In our simple merger transaction, and perhaps in most two-company mergers, the surviving company's preexisting shareholders do not have their shares converted into something else. But it is clear that, at least under modern merger statutes, such conversions can be provided for in the merger agreement. After the transaction is over, then, the old T shareholders are shareholders of P, and T is wholly owned by P; S has simply dropped out of the picture. *The net result is just what would have happened if P had made a stock-for-stock exchange directly with the T shareholders (a B reorganization) and had succeeded in getting 100 per cent of the T shareholders to agree to the exchange.* Apparently that is why this rather complicated form of triangular acquisition is sometimes called a reverse B merger: The formal merger proceeds in a counterintuitive direction (*into* the target), and the net effect is like a B reorganization between the target and the real acquiring company (the parent).

Why merger instead of "B" reorg

You may be wondering why businesspersons and their lawyers resort to shell corporations and other such rigamarole. In our last example, why didn't they use the simple old "forward" B reorganization and skip both

[7] I.R.C. §368(a)(2)(C).
[8] I.R.C. §368(a)(2)(E).

the shell subsidiary and the hocus pocus? The answer, in part, is that the simple B reorganization may be obstructed by some minority shareholders of T. P can easily offer its shares in exchange for any and all T shares that the old T shareholders wish to tender for exchange. But even when its exchange ratio is highly favorable — enough to induce a large majority of T shareholders to tender eagerly, for example — some T shareholders may refuse to tender. They may be holding out for a higher price or simply opposed to the acquisition in principle. P could then pay whatever it had to buy them out — an expensive proposition — or it could content itself with simply acquiring control, but not entire ownership, of the target.

Neither alternative is satisfactory. The first may risk charges of unfairness from other T shareholders if they are not given the same high price, it may make the transaction prohibitively expensive if they are given that price, and it may jeopardize the transaction's tax status if consideration other than voting stock is demanded by the holdouts. The second alternative creates an ongoing messy situation. No rational top management wants to worry about whether someone could plausibly allege that minority shareholders of its partially owned subsidiaries are being treated unfairly in some one or more of the multitude of intercompany transactions that later occur. The beauty of the reverse subsidiary merger is simply that of majority rule: A majority of the T shareholders can force the minority to go along, and P can be sure of winding up with 100 percent of T. (Even if some of the old T shareholders invoke their appraisal rights and demand to be bought out with cash in a judicial proceeding, that will usually not cause the deal to fail.)

Note that in states that allow stock-for-stock exchanges to occur as corporate action, after director approval and shareholder vote, there can be a ordinary, "forward" B reorganization without a stubborn minority problem.

Two other aspects of the reverse subsidiary merger remain unexplained. Granted that a simple B reorganization may be undesirable because of the stubborn minority problem — so that some form of corporate action (a statutory merger or C reorganization) is desired — why have a subsidiary acquisition at all, instead of a merger of T into P? And if there's some answer to that question, why not have T merge into S, rather than vice versa?

Subsidiary reduces liability exposure

One answer to the first question is that P may not want to expose its preexisting assets to responsibility for the liabilities of T. In general, of course, managers often try to magnify the benefits of limited liability by keeping separate business operations within separate legal entities that are part of the same corporate family. How important it is to do this will vary with the facts of each situation. Separation will be particularly important when P is worried that the putative acquired company T may have large unknown liabilities or contingent liabilities whose risk of actualization is larger than P was led to believe. (In a merger of T into P, P would be stuck with such liabilities, regardless of whether it foresaw them.)

And avoids shareholder vote

A second and often more important reason for P's using a subsidiary to carry out the acquisition is that it avoids the need to get the vote of P's shareholders. When P is a public company, the costs of preparing a proxy statement, soliciting proxies, and holding a special shareholders' meeting can be considerable.

Reverse motion for tax reasons

Finally, a major reason why the managers of P and T do not arrange for T to merge into S, rather than the reverse, is to make certain that any post-acquisition losses that might be generated by the acquired company's business can still be carried back and offset against preacquisition earnings of T. Prudent tax planners would fear that if T were tc cease to exist (as would happen in a merger of T into S), so would the ability to invoke the tax law's loss carryback provisions.[9]

Summary

Thus, the various aspects of the reverse subsidiary merger do have rationales:

(1) use of an A rather than a B reorganization gains the benefits of majority rule;
(2) acquisition by a subsidiary multiplies the benefits of limited liability and avoids the need to seek the votes of the acquirer's public shareholders; and
(3) making the target the survivor of the merger assures retention of desirable tax characteristics.

So far I have explained only why reverse B mergers are a common mode of acquisition. This does not mean that they are ideal for all situations. Other reasons for the choice among forms of merger may point to different conclusions. Some of these reasons will emerge in our brief discussion of the legal and other treatment of these forms.

Nonrecognition for all

Tax treatment. Virtually all of the forms of merger identified above can qualify for tax deferred treatment under the Internal Revenue Code. As

[9]Certainly, this result seems mandated by I.R.C. §381(b)(3). Aetna Casualty and Surety Co. v. United States, 568 F.2d 811 (2d Cir. 1976), and Bercy Indus., Inc. v. Commissioner, 640 F.2d 1058 (9th Cir. 1981), appear to say that this rule need not apply in the case of mergers with shell corporations, but a tax lawyer might be wary of testing that proposition in other circuits and other fact situations.

indicated, however, the extent to which the acquiring company may use consideration other than voting stock is greater for A and C reorganizations than for B reorganizations.[10]

Pooling too

Accounting treatment. Virtually all of the examples in this section of forms of merger will qualify for the pooling-of-interest method of accounting. The relevant financial accounting principles do impose stringent conditions on the use of the pooling method, but, as in the tax law context, the main ways in which a combination can run afoul of these conditions has to do with the use of consideration other than voting stock — or more generally, features of the transaction that violate the continuity of interest notion.[11]

Various disclosure rules

Securities regulation. As in the simple merger, most of the variations are governed by the Securities Act, which mandates disclosures by the acquir-

[10]For A reorganizations, any consideration permitted by the state merger statute may be used, but the transaction must preserve a continuity of interest on the part of the acquired company's shareholders. This requirement was created by the courts, but is now codified in Treas. Reg. §1.368-1(b). The acquired company's shareholders must receive some stock in the acquiring company, but exactly how much is not settled. The IRS has indicated that the requirement is satisfied for ruling purposes if 50 percent of the consideration is in the form of stock. Rev. Proc. 77-37, 1977-2 C.B. 568; Rev. Rul. 66-224, 1966-2 C.B. 114. One early case held that 25 percent was sufficient. Miller v. Commissioner, 84 F.2d 415 (6th Cir. 1936).

In a triangular merger, the acquired company's shareholders may receive stock in the parent of the acquirer but not of both parent and subsidiary. I.R.C. §368(a)(2)(D); Treas. Reg. §1.368-2(b)(2). Reverse subsidiary mergers can qualify as A reorganizations, but the requirements are more stringent. I.R.C. §368(a)(2)(E).

Section 368(a)(1)(B) specifies that solely voting stock may be used in a B reorganization, and few exceptions have been developed. Cash may be paid in lieu of fractional shares. Rev. Rul. 66-365, 1966-2 C.B. 116. Expenses incurred by the acquired company that are directly related to the acquisition may be paid by the acquirer. Rev. Rul. 73-54, 1973-1 C.B. 187. A share exchange may be disqualified due to cash purchases of small amounts of stock in a separate, earlier transaction. Chapman v. Commissioner, 618 F.2d 856 (1st Cir. 1980), cert. denied, 451 U.S. 1012 (1981). An exchange will not be disqualified by cash payments by the *acquired* corporation to its dissenting shareholders, but the acquirer may not furnish the funds. Rev. Rul. 68-285, 1968-1. C.B. 147.

In a C reorganization, voting stock must be exchanged for at least 80 percent of the value of the acquired assets; the balance may be in cash or other property. If *only* voting stock is used, liabilities of the acquired corporation that the acquirer assumes and liabilities to which the acquired assets are subject will be ignored; otherwise, these liabilities will be treated as cash paid by the acquirer. For example, if a corporation's only asset is land with a market value of $1 million, subject to a $500,000 mortgage, the land can be acquired in a C reorganization only if no consideration other than voting stock is paid. (This requirement, however, is subject to the exceptions noted above for the B reorganization.) If the acquirer issues bonds in exchange for the bonds of the acquired corporation, this may be regarded as an assumption of liabilities. Helvering v. Taylor, 128 F.2d 885 (2d Cir. 1942).

[11]See AICPA, Accounting Principles Board Opinion No. 16, par. 46-48. See also the discussion of criteria of pooling in section 10.5.2 infra.

ing company. Some, like the B reorganization, are fairly obviously covered by the statute; others, like the A and C reorganizations, are covered by virtue of Rule 145. Transactions involving shareholder voting, such as the A and C reorganizations and the reverse B merger, also trigger the proxy rules. Those involving a public offer to acquire shares, such as a B reorganization when the acquired company has many shareholders, will trigger the tender offer rules.

Corporate statutes. All A reorganizations are, by definition, statutory mergers or consolidations, and they therefore often require director and shareholder approval on the part of both companies. The reverse is not true, however: Not everything that would be a merger under a modern business corporation statute would qualify as a tax deferred reorganization. The reason is that, in relatively recent times, corporate merger statutes have been liberalized to allow for payment to shareholders of the merging company (or even to shareholders of the surviving company) to be made, not only in shares of stock, but also in debentures, notes or other obligations, or even in cash.[12] Thus, as a matter of terminology and procedure in such business corporation statutes, Message Corporation could merge into Nirvana Corporation even though, as a part and result of the transaction, all of the old Message Corporation shares were to be converted entirely into cash. This usage of merger conflicts with the sense I assigned the term in section 10.1 supra, of course. In its essential characteristics, if not in its corporate law procedures, the cash merger is clearly a sale. Moreover, it is quite clear that, despite the Internal Revenue Code's simple statement that reorganization includes a statutory merger or consolidation, a cash merger of the sort just described would *not* qualify for tax deferred treatment, because it would run afoul of the judicially created continuity of ownership interest requirement. Furthermore, the cash merger would not qualify for the pooling method of accounting treatment, and it would not trigger the Securities Act registration and prospectus-delivery requirements under Rule 145. The cash merger is like the simple merger, however, in the technical sense that the merging company would cease to exist and all of its assets and liabilities would pass over to the surviving corporation by operation of the law rather than by deed or bill of sale.

Cash mergers not reorganizations

Another variation in the corporate merger statutes is the so-called short-form merger. Numerous statutes now provide that, if a parent corporation owns more than a certain percentage of a subsidiary's stock, such as 90

Short-form mergers

[12]Del. §251 (liberalized in 1967). The MBCA adopted a similar provision in 1969. 2 Model Bus. Corp. Act Ann. 2d §71(c) (1971). For the current version, see note 5 supra.

percent, the board of directors of the parent, by resolution, may merge the subsidiary into the parent.[13] The procedure does not require a vote on the part of either company's shareholders, nor even a resolution of the subsidiary's board. These statutes, since they save the cost and uncertainty of soliciting shareholder votes, give managers some encouragement to rearrange the corporate family so as to eliminate partially owned subsidiaries and the conflict of interest problems they continually create. The minority shareholders are supposed to be protected against abuse of this power to effect a short form merger by their appraisal rights[14] and their ability, in appropriate situations, to attack the short-form merger in a lawsuit.[15]

"B" reorg B reorganizations often require no action by the acquired company's board and no vote of either corporation's shareholders. From the acquiring company's point of view, the stock-for-stock exchange is simply a purchase transaction, which, like any major corporate purchase, requires a board resolution. If the number of shares it proposes to give the shareholders of the target company is already authorized, it can usually issue them by board resolution. If that number of shares is not authorized, however, the acquiring company may have to amend its articles of organization to increase the number of authorized shares — a procedure that does require a shareholder vote as well as director initiation and approval.[16]

On the target company side, the B reorganization is usually just a matter of contracts for sale of stock on the part of many individual shareholders. As noted several times, however, in some jurisdictions the target company directors and shareholders can act collectively to bind the minority, in a procedure similar to that of a merger.[17] If, after the stock exchange, it is proposed to liquidate the target into the acquiring company, the latter may be able to avail itself of a short-form merger statute; otherwise, it might invoke the standard dissolution and liquidation provisions[18] or the regular merger provisions.[19]

"C" reorg In modern business corporation statutes, a C reorganization is not distinguished from our simple sale transaction. Both come under the provision dealing with sale of substantially all assets of a corporation other than in the ordinary course of business, and they therefore require, on the target company's side, director initiation/approval and a shareholder vote. (There

[13] MBCA §11.04; Cal. §1110; Del. §253; N.Y. §905.
[14] MBCA §13.02(a)(1)(ii); Cal. §1300; Del. §253(d); N.Y. §910(a)(2).
[15] See, e.g., Roland Int'l. Corp. v. Najjar, 407 A.2d 1032 (Del. 1979).
[16] See, e.g., MBCA §§6.01(a), 10.03, 10.04(a)(1).
[17] See section 10.3 note 18 supra, and accompanying text.
[18] See, e.g., MBCA §§14.02-14.07.
[19] See, e.g., MBCA §§11.01, 11.03, 11.05, 11.06.

is a parallel here to the modern merger statutes: In each case, the provision may apply regardless of the form of consideration received.) On the acquiring company's side, the situation is similar to that in a B reorganization: The transaction can be approved by board resolution unless new shares have to be authorized. When, after the sale of all its assets, the target company is to be liquidated, then the normal dissolution and liquidation provisions apply.

Four practical parameters

Summary of some practical considerations. It may be useful to recapitulate some of the more obvious pros and cons of the major forms of merger. First, in terms of ability to insulate the acquiring company from liabilities — including hidden and contingent ones — of the acquired company, the C reorganization is best, the B reorganization is next best, and the A reorganization is worst. (Remember that, with occasional exceptions aimed at helping tort victims,[20] in the C reorganization the acquiring company gets only those assets and liabilities that are identified in the purchase contract.)

Second, in terms of ability to circumvent the opposition of a target company's management, the B reorganization is clearly better than the A and the C.

Third, in terms of ability to circumvent the opposition of stubborn minority shareholders of the company to be acquired, the A and C reorganizations are clearly better than the B.

Fourth, in terms of ability to reduce the number of proxy solicitations and sets of shareholder votes required, the B reorganization is best (it may require no shareholder vote, or only one), the C reorganization is next best (one or, sometimes, two), and the A reorganization is worst (usually two). The acquiring company can usually avoid a vote of its shareholders by using a subsidiary to effect the acquisition.

§10.5 *Variations: Hybrids Between Sale and Merger*

Sometimes an acquisition transaction has some aspects characteristic of our simple sale, and some aspects characteristic of our simple merger. Which of the polar cases the hybrid most resembles can be a vitally important question for tax and accounting purposes. The question of transactional

[20] Some courts have imposed successor liability on acquiring companies in C reorganizations for the benefit of tort victims. See the discussion of the *Knapp* case in section 10.7 infra. Some states courts have rejected the doctrine, however, and many have no squarely relevant decisions.

characterization is of little importance for securities law and corporate law purposes, however, so those sets of rules will not be explored further in this section. I shall mention briefly some salient points of tax law and accounting treatment — enough only to suggest the vast range of particular questions that can arise in practice, and that are dealt with in more specialized courses of study.

§10.5.1 Tax Treatment

Two questions

For federal income tax purposes, it is important to distinguish two questions: (1) when an acquisition transaction is or is not deemed to be a "reorganization" and (2) how consideration other than voting common stock is treated in a transaction that is nevertheless deemed to be a reorganization.

Relevant factors

Classification as reorganization. The first question leads to an inquiry as to whether the continuity of interest requirement for reorganization treatment is met. This is turn depends on the kinds and relative amounts of consideration paid and on the extent to which specific transactions (which may not all occur at the same time) are lumped together and treated as parts of "the" acquisition transaction.

Example with nonstock consideration

Consider an example that illustrates the first question. Hardware Corp., with several dozen shareholders, is to be acquired by IBN Corp., a large publicly traded company with thousands of shareholders. In accordance with the desires of Hardware's shareholders, Hardware shareholders holding 70 percent of Hardware's common shares will receive, in exchange for their shares, voting common stock of IBN. Holders of the other 30 percent will receive, in exchange for their shares, some cash and some 20 year IBN bonds paying interest at the rate of 12 percent.

Not a "B"

If this acquisition were structured as a simple securities-for-securities exchange, not involving formal corporate action under statutory merger or statutory sale-of-all-assets provisions, it would not qualify as a tax free B reorganization. To have a B reorganization, IBN would have to use *only* voting stock of itself (or a parent) to acquire Hardware's stock.

Not a "C"

If the transaction were structured as an exchange of all of Hardware's assets for securities under a statutory sale-of-all-assets provision, it would not qualify as a C reorganization. To have a C reorganization, at least 80 percent in fair market value of Hardware's property must be acquired by IBN solely for voting stock of itself (or a parent).

Maybe an "A"

If the transaction were structured as a statutory merger, however, it might qualify as an A reorganization. Section 368(a)(1)(A) of the Code expresses no explicit continuity-of-interest test, but it is clear that courts would apply one. The Internal Revenue Service, before ruling in favor of reorganization treatment, would have to be assured that its guidelines are met.[1] Currently, this includes the requirement that holders of at least 50 percent in value of the Hardware stock would have to obtain a continuing interest through stock ownership in IBN.[2] In our example, a sufficient number of Hardware shareholders will become shareholders of IBN.

Decoupling strategy fails

Suppose that the holders of only 40 percent in value of Hardware stock want to become shareholders of IBN; the rest want senior securities or cash. What would happen if the designers of the acquisition transaction tried to get around the 50 percent requirement for a ruling on an A reorganization by simply accelerating or delaying the exchanges that will give the majority of the Hardware shareholders their cash or bonds?

Suppose, for example, that Hardware borrows a lot of money and repurchases 60 percent of its common shares (from those who want to sell); then, a month later, it merges via statute into IBN pursuant to a merger plan under which all of the then remaining Hardware shareholders get IBN voting common stock, and nothing else. Alas, this will not do. The IRS guidelines state that

> [s]ales, redemptions, and other dispositions of stock occurring prior to or subsequent to the exchange [effected by the technical merger] *which are part of the plan of reorganization* will be considered in determining whether there is a 50 percent continuing interest through stock ownership as of the effective date of the reorganization.[3]

Assuming that the redemption is "part" of the larger acquisition plan, it would torpedo the chances for a favorable ruling.

Step-transaction doctrine

Would the courts adopt the same or a similar substance-over-form approach in deciding whether the redemption transaction destroyed reorganization treatment for the ensuing merger? Of course they would. Courts dealing with purported reorganizations frequently use the step-transaction doctrine, under which specific steps in a series of transactions may be integrated, or treated as parts of one transaction, if doing so seems appropriate.[4]

§10.5 [1] Participants in an important acquisition usually want to get an IRS ruling before proceeding, and in any event they rarely have a positive desire to test their interpretation of case law doctrine against that of the IRS in court.

[2] Rev. Proc. 77-37, 1977-2 C.B. 568.

[3] Ibid. (Emphasis supplied.)

[4] See B. Bittker and J. Eustice, Federal Income Taxation of Corporations and Shareholders ¶14.51 (4th ed. 1979).

Implementing tests

Whether particular steps would be integrated in a given case might depend in part on which of several tests the court would use or emphasize. For example, under the end result test, purportedly separate transactions will be amalgamated with another transaction when it appears that they were really component parts of a single transaction intended from the outset to be taken for the purpose of reaching the ultimate result.

A second test is the interdependence test, which focusses on whether the steps are so interdependent that the legal relations created by one transaction would have been fruitless without a completion of the series.

Finally, a binding commitment test forbids use of the step-transaction doctrine unless, when one transaction to be integrated into a single whole is accomplished, there is a binding commitment to take the later steps. In our example, the redemption and later merger would be integrated under the first two tests. Depending on additional facts and on how the court interpreted the third test, it might not be integrated under that test.

Other points about the doctrine

Note that when two transactions are integrated, the resulting single transaction may or may not qualify as a nontaxable reorganization. Note also that the step-transaction doctrine might well be used by a court to find a single transaction when the Service happens to want the opposite result; that is, in principle the doctrine is to be applied evenhandedly.[5] Finally, note that the step-transaction doctrine is not at all restricted to determining whether a certain transaction is really part of a statutory merger. It can be applied to determine whether redemptions, large dividends, sales, and the like should be integrated with earlier or later acquisition transactions taking many forms. It might, for example, foil an attempt to make an end run around the 80 percent requirement for a C reorganization.[6] Indeed, the doctrine might be used in contexts where classification of transactions as a reorganization was not an issue.

Treatment in nonreorganization

Treatment of boot in a reorganization. Let's reconsider the case where some but not all of Hardware's shareholders will wind up as continuing, bona

[5]See McDonald's Restaurants of Ill. Inc. v. Commissioner, 688 F.2d 520 (7th Cir. 1982). This case involved the question whether a merger and a subsequent sale of stock should be "stepped together" for purposes of applying the continuity of interest doctrine. The court thought that they should be, regardless of which of the three tests discussed in the text were used. This favored the taxpayers (wholly owned subsidiaries of the acquiring company), who wanted to treat the acquisition as a sale-purchase transaction so they could get a stepped-up basis in the assets.

[6]Suppose that Hardware transferred all its assets to IBN solely for IBN voting stock, which was distributed to Hardware shareholders, and that three months later IBN, by prearrangement, buys 30 percent of these distributed shares for cash. A nontaxable reorganization? Not likely.

fide shareholders of IBN after a statutory merger. If there are not enough continuing shareholders to make a reorganization, then *all* of the Hardware shareholders will be treated as being involved in a taxable transaction, including those who gave up Hardware voting common stock and received nothing but IBN voting common stock. Gain (or loss) will be recognized by them. But what happens if there is a reorganization, yet (as in our original hypothetical) holders of 30 percent of the Hardware stock now receive cash and IBN bonds?

Treatment in reorganization

The holders of the 70 percent of Hardware stock who receive IBN stock would be treated as engaged in a nontaxable exchange. They would recognize neither gain nor loss. The basis in their old stock would be carried over and would become the basis of their new IBN stock.[7] The holders of the other 30 percent, who receive cash and bonds, will be taxed on their gain, if any,[8] but will not be able to recognize any loss that they might have.[9] If a particular Hardware shareholder received IBN stock as well as cash and bonds, she would also recognize her gain, but not to the extent (if any) by which it exceeded the amount of the cash and bonds.[10] Colloquially, the cash and bonds would be referred to as boot. They are taxable for the usual reason, namely, that a shareholder who receives them is not continuing her ownership interest but is disinvesting.

Exchange of debt

Until now, we have ignored any debt holders that Hardware might have. Consider again our statutory merger where most of the Hardware shares are to be exchanged for IBN stock, with an additional complication. Hardware has a class of debt securities outstanding: debentures that pay 13 percent interest and have 10 years to maturity. Holders of the debentures will receive, in exchange for the debentures, 20 year IBN bonds paying 11

[7] Suppose Algo originally bought 150 shares of Hardware at $20 per share. His basis in his Hardware stock is therefore $3,000. In the merger, he gets 80 shares of IBN which, at $93.75 per share, have a total market value of $7,500. Algo's gain is therefore $4,500, but it will not be recognized and taxed. His total basis in the IBN shares, however, will only be $3,000, which when allocated among the shares would give a basis of $37.50 per share.

[8] I.R.C. §356(a)(1). So, if Bass bought 150 Hardware shares for a total of $3,000 and now receives $2,000 in cash and IBN bonds with a market value of $7,000, he will have taxable gain of $6,000. Furthermore, if the exchange has "the effect of the distribution of a dividend," the gain might be treated as dividend income, taxable at ordinary rates. I.R.C. §356(a)(2).

[9] I.R.C. §356(c). Thus, if Compil bought her 150 Hardware shares for $10,000 and now receives $2,000 in cash and bonds with a market value of $7,000, she could not recognize her $1,000 loss.

[10] Suppose Doss has a basis of $3,000 in her 150 Hardware shares. In the merger, she receives IBN stock with a market value of $7,000 and IBN bonds with a market value of $2,000. Her gain is $6,000 but she will only have to recognize $2,000 of it, the amount of her boot. If the relative weight of the kinds of consideration were switched, so that she received $2,000 of IBN stock and $7,000 of IBN bonds, then she would recognize her full $6,000 gain.

percent interest. Each Hardware debenture has a principal or face amount of $1,000 and will be exchanged for an IBN bond with a principal amount of $1,200. This exchange will not affect the classification of the merger as a reorganization. (Nor would it matter if the debenture holders were simply given cash for their debentures; it is the continuity of the *equity* owners' interest that is crucial to the classification issue.) The holder of each debenture would recognize his gain (if any) on the exchange to the extent of the market value (if any) of the "excess principal amount," that is, the $200 by which principal amount of the bond received exceeds the principal amount of the debenture that was given up for it.[11]

§10.5.2 Accounting Treatment

Criteria for pooling

Accountants face similar issues of characterization. To a large extent, these are handled by resort to the criteria for pooling treatment that are described in APB Opinion No. 16. They resemble the guidelines for reorganization classification developed by tax authorities (the Code, regulations, rulings, and judicial opinions) but differ in detail and seem to be somewhat more mechanical.

90 percent voting common stock requirement

Pooling treatment requires that a 90 percent voting common stock interest in the acquired company be acquired with voting common stock of the acquiring company that is substantially like its existing common stock. (This need not be done by a straightforward stock-for-stock exchange, however, but might be accomplished in a statutory merger or in some other form of acquisition.)

Supporting rules

This combining-of-equity-interests requirement is bolstered by a number of other rules:

(1) There can be no changes in equity interests in contemplation of the combination within two years before the plan of combination is initiated or between the initiation and consummation of the plan. (Thus, the target company couldn't simply buy out a large minority shareholder who didn't want to participate in the upcoming merger.)

(2) Between initiation and consummation of the plan, each company may reacquire shares of its voting common stock only for purposes other than business combinations. The combination must be effected in a single transaction or within one year.

(3) It must be resolved at the date the plan is consummated, so there

[11] I.R.C. §§354(a)(1), 354(a)(2), 356(a)(1), 356(d)(2)(B).

can be no contingent consideration. (This rule has the important effect of precluding earn-out clauses in acquisitions where pooling treatment is insisted upon. Under such a clause, the acquired company shareholders are promised additional consideration if the post-acquisition performance of the acquired company exceeds specified benchmarks.)

(4) There can be no plan to retire or reacquire stock after the acquisition. (Thus, the acquiring company couldn't simply promise the large minority shareholder of the target who didn't want to participate in the merger that it would buy him out a few months after the merger.)

(5) The surviving company must have no plan to dispose of acquired company assets within two years, other than in the ordinary course of business or in transactions aimed at eliminating duplicate facilities or excess capacity.

Pooling treatment also requires that each of the combining companies be independent of the other and that neither corporation was a division or subsidiary of another company within two years before the plan of combination was initiated.

Hold on to the talisman

As should now be obvious, the rules and principles governing hybrid acquisitions form a complex labyrinth of pitfalls and resting places. Should you ever enter this maze of rules in connection with a case, remember the continuity of interest concept that lies at the heart of the idea of a merger, for it is the talisman that will keep you from losing your way.

§10.6 Appraisal Rights

§10.6.1 Introduction

Basic concept

Corporate statutes often give a shareholder who dissents from certain major corporate transactions the right to be bought out by the company at a price reflecting the value of his shares as determined in a judicial proceeding. Typically, this right of appraisal is given in connection with mergers, sales or exchanges of substantially all assets of the corporation, and charter amendments that materially and adversely affect the rights of the dissenting shareholder.

Origin

Historically, appraisal rights seem to have been given to shareholders as the quid pro quo for abandonment of the old nineteenth century rule that major corporate changes like mergers require the unanimous consent of all the shareholders.[1] Today, the apologists for appraisal rights can proffer two serious arguments for them — one based on a claim of defeated expectations and one based on the risk of unfair treatment in major corporate transactions.

Defeated expectations argument

The first argument, which resembles the historical rationale, is that a person who buys shares in a company with a certain identity and set of characteristics may rightfully expect to continue as investor in *that* enterprise and that no one should be able to force him to become an investor in a quite different business. If I buy a block of stock in a company publishing books and outlines about the law, I may not want to wake up one day and find out that it has merged into a multimedia conglomerate, most of whose revenues derive from television programming, and that my stock now represents an interest in an entirely different business. In the interest of facilitating major corporate changes desired by corporate managers and a majority of the shareholders involved, however, the law will not let me block such changes whenever they affront my expectations. It will only give me a remedy — the remedy of being cashed out at a fair price, so that, instead of being dragged along unwillingly into a venture in which I do not want to invest, I can turn around and invest in something more to my liking.

Difficulties

This defeated expectations argument is fraught with difficulties. One objection is that investors nowadays care only about the risks and expected return presented by their investments. They are not usually attached, out of sentiment or ideology, to a particular company or kind of company. This observation is probably right. But it doesn't necessarily lead to the conclusion that mergers and the like do not seriously defeat investor expectations. In connection with a major merger or other organic change, the shareholder is often given consideration that presents a very different risk-and-return mix than that presented by his original investment.

A second objection to the defeated expectations argument is that shareholders in today's large publicly held companies do expect mergers and other major changes in the nature of their investments to occur with some frequency, and on the basis of majority vote. An argument based on people's actual expectations can easily lead us to an impasse, though. The supporter of appraisal rights can simply observe that investors today do expect to have appraisal rights and that, therefore, such rights ought not to be disturbed absent a compelling reason. What this debate shows us is that people's expectations may adjust to whatever assignments of rights and

§10.6 [1]Manning, The Shareholder's Appraisal Remedy: An Essay for Frank Coker, 72 Yale L.J. 223, 228-229 (1962).

duties the law in fact imposes. In such a context, it requires a different set of considerations than people's actual expectations to decide which expectations the law ought to encourage.

Remedy-for-unfairness argument

The second major argument for appraisal rights tries to supply such a consideration. The notion is that mergers, sales, and charter amendments are occasions on which there is a significant risk that public shareholders will be unfairly treated and that appraisal rights are a desirable intermediate remedy against such unfairness. Major organic changes pose a risk to public shareholders because managers initiate, shape, and carry out the changes and can do so in ways that further their own interests at the expense of noncontrolling shareholders. For example, the managers of an acquired company may cause the total consideration that the acquiring company is willing to pay to be allocated in such a way that an excessively large proportion will go to themselves in the form of new employment contracts or consulting and noncompetition agreements. This diversion may not be detected and corrected by shareholders during the voting process. This may happen not only because of flaws in the information disclosure system, but also because of the now familiar rational apathy and free rider problems that afflict collective shareholder action in the public corporation. (See section 9.5)

Other remedies often drastic

One could object, against the risk-of-unfairness argument, that an individual shareholder who thinks he has spotted unfairness could simply bring a suit to enjoin the merger or, if it has already occurred, to have it undone. The supporter of appraisal rights would point out that injunctions and rescission are very drastic remedies that courts are reluctant to grant except in the clearest cases. Blocking a merger could also block the increase in real value to which the merger might lead. Similarly, even a suit for damages based on alleged self-dealing in a merger may have relatively high costs — the costs of a fault-based lawsuit. It is therefore prudent to have a less drastic remedy that can be invoked by as many dissident shareholders as think they are being treated unfairly in any given case.

***Locus poenitentiae* argument**

Another argument for appraisal rights is that they are a fairly nonintrusive check on management's occasional bad business judgments. The idea is that managers will occasionally arrange a merger or other transaction on terms that are not the best that could be obtained for the company. The greater the number of shareholders who have this perception of a proposed deal, the greater the number of dissenters who will demand to be bought out, and the more likely it is that management will reconsider its position. Of course, if more than a majority of the shareholders think the deal is bad and vote against it, it will fail, whether or not there are appraised rights. The appraisal remedy only adds something when a significant minority dissents and thereby succeeds in getting management to rethink its position.

Arguments con

Granted that a prima facie case for appraisal rights can be constructed, we must note three common arguments against appraisal rights that do not depend on which rationale is thought to support them. We might label these as the consistency argument, the cash drain argument, and the stock market argument.

Consistency argument

The first argument is that various corporate changes besides mergers, charter amendments, and the like may create a risk of unfairness (or defeat shareholder expectations or constitute bad business judgments), yet do not give rise to appraisal rights. For example, the board of directors may completely change the corporation's line of business without taking a shareholder vote or triggering appraisal rights, and such change could easily be as drastic as the average merger. This argument from consistency, however, only tells us that the present law doesn't seem to be consistent and that if lawmakers want to be perfectly consistent they should either abolish appraisal rights or extend them to some other transactions.[2] (To how many others is not at all clear.) This is not a good argument against appraisal rights per se.

Cash drain argument

The second argument is the view that, when many minority shareholders exercise their appraisal rights, the resulting cash drain on the corporation may lead it to abandon an otherwise desirable transaction. This turns out to be merely a debater's point. On the factual side of the debate, we may well doubt whether a significant number of major corporate transactions have been deterred or called off because of heavy exercise by minority shareholders of their appraisal rights. No one seems to have carried out a sophisticated study of this empirical question. But anyone who has regularly read business newspapers and journals for a number of years would have his doubts about the seriousness of the alleged problem. As for the logic of the argument, we may wonder why, if a corporate transaction is a genuinely good one that will increase the value of the corporation's shares, the managers will be unable (1) to convince the minority shareholders of this fact and of the desirability of participating in the transaction (especially since shareholders seeking appraisal are legally barred from sharing in gains arising from the transaction to which they dissent) and/or (2) to obtain financing with which to buy out the dissenting shareholders.[3]

[2] Also, achieving perfect consistency in a set of legal rules is costly, yet there is often no significant practical gain to be had from the achievement. There may even be losses, if the drive for consistency makes people neurotic.

[3] The argument that management proposing a truly value-enhancing transaction ought to be able to get financing to take care of dissenters is not completely satisfactory, however. In

Alternative solution

Even if cash drain caused by dissenters' appraisal rights were to become a significant problem in the real world, and managers were somehow unable to convey information effectively and raise money in reasonably efficient capital markets, it would seem as if there were less drastic solutions than abolishing appraisal rights. For instance, the laws could be changed to require dissenters to sell their stock on the market and sue their former corporation for the difference (if any) between what they received and what they can convince a court was the true fair value of their shares under traditional standards of appraisal. This would substantially reduce the cash drain problem, without compromising the degree of protection given to dissenters by existing law.

Stock market argument

A third general argument against appraisal rights is that they are unnecessary in the large class of cases where the corporation's shares are publicly traded. The underlying notion is that the organized stock markets — the New York Stock Exchange, the American Stock Exchange, the recognized regional stock exchanges, and the national over-the-counter market operated through the computerized quotation system of the National Association of Securities Dealers — are economically quite efficient. Thus, the price a dissenting-selling shareholder can get on these markets usually reflects all the information that is publicly available and relevant to valuation of the stock. Accordingly, the market price of stock on these markets ought to be deemed to be equivalent to the stock's fair value or intrinsic value for most legal purposes. And market price seems especially helpful in the appraisal context, for the dissenter is supposed to be given the value of his shares shorn of any contribution made by the transaction to which he objects.

If we trust the market, why not simply give him the market price of his shares before announcement of the proposed transaction? Why indulge the hope or fantasy that a single judge will somehow be able to get a better fix on the true value of the shares than did the market, which reflects the cumulated decisions of hundreds or even thousands of investors, all trying to be rational and to maximize their own self-interest? And if market price is thus to become the touchstone, why have any appraisal proceedings at

---

some cases, the financing capacity used to satisfy dissenters might otherwise have been used to maintain or expand real business operations, thus leading to further enhancement of value. And in any event, taking the argument as far as it will go seems to lead us to the conclusion that every shareholder ought to be able at any time to demand that his company buy him out at appraised value. That is, the argument seems to do away with limits on the ability of individual shareholders to cause termination or contraction of the corporate enterprise. These limits, as we saw in chapter 1, seem to be efficient ones in the context of the publicly held corporation.

all? The dissenter who doesn't like a forthcoming merger can simply sell on the market and cash himself out of the unwanted new enterprise.

Reflected in some statutes

As a result of arguments of this sort, the MBCA (in 1969)[4] and the laws of a number of states such as Delaware (in 1967)[5] were amended to create a so-called stock market exception to the appraisal remedy. Shareholders in companies the shares of which were traded on certain specified markets — the list varied — were generally denied their traditional appraisal remedy. In 1978, however, the framers of the MBCA reversed themselves and eliminated the stock market exception.[6] Why the change of heart?

One apparent reason lies in the going private phenomenon of 1974-1975, when the controlling insiders of a number of publicly held corporations took advantage of a depressed stock market to forceably squeeze out public shareholders — through cash mergers and other techniques — at prices widely felt to be unfair. In these transactions, the public shareholders were inevitably paid amounts that were above current market prices of their stock but which seemed unfairly small in relation to the prices which they had paid when the company went public (during the booming market of the late 1960s, typically) or in relation to the market prices to which the stock of similar companies rose during the subsequent market upturn.

Whether these going private transactions were really unfair is an issue that will occupy us later.[7] Certainly many corporate lawyers, including some who otherwise saw eye to eye with management, thought that something quite unfair was happening. This perception weakened reliance on market price as the ultimate touchstone of the value that dissenters ought to be able to realize. Some commentators added fuel to these suspicions by expanding on reasons why market prices, although generally reliable, might occasionally be flawed,[8] and suggesting that the flaws were more likely to be present in just those cases where minority shareholders were

[4] See Scott, Changes in the Model Business Corporation Act, 24 Bus. Law. 291, 303 (1968).

[5] 56 Del. L. c. 50. This exception to the appraisal remedy applies to shares listed on a national exchange or held of record by not less than 2000 shareholders, unless the corporate charter provides otherwise. But, as amended in 1969, 57 Del. L. c. 148, §29, if the holder's stock is converted by merger or consolidation into anything other than stock in the survivor, stock listed on a national exchange or held by at least 2000 holders, or cash in lieu of fractional shares, he is still entitled to an appraisal. See Del. §§262(b)(1), 262(b)(2), 262(c).

[6] See Conard, Amendments of Model Business Corporation Act Affecting Dissenters' Rights, 33 Bus. Law. 2587, 2595-2596 (1978).

[7] See chapter 12.

[8] Brudney, Efficient Markets and Fair Values in Parent Subsidiary Mergers, 4 J. Corp. L. 63 (1978). See also Note, A Reconsideration of the Stock Market Exception to the Dissenting Shareholder's Right of Appraisal, 74 Mich. L. Rev. 1023 (1976).

protesting a transaction.[9] These reasons included the proposition that the managers initiating the dissented-to transactions and setting their terms may have been acting on the basis of inside information or on the basis of something similar but more subtle — *positionally superior insight,* as I prefer to call it. This question will be discussed in the chapter on freezeouts (chapter 12).

§10.6.2 Statutory Coverage and Procedures

MBCA's approach

The coverage and mechanics of the appraisal statutes vary from state to state. For the sake of illustration, let us consider MBCA Sections 13.01 through 13.31. It should be noted that these sections reflect a strenuous attempt to make the appraisal remedy fairer and more workable than it was perceived to be in many traditional statutes.

Some commentators had observed that, because of procedural pitfalls and the delay and expense necessitated by the traditional appraisal statutes, the appraisal remedy was virtually worthless to aggrieved shareholders in most situations where it was technically available.[10] Others worried that the remedy was a vehicle for strike suits. The new MBCA provisions attempt to ameliorate these problems. Its strategy is to try to motivate the parties to settle their difference in private negotiations, before resorting to judicial appraisal proceedings. Consistent with this hope, it refers not to "appraisal rights" but "dissenters' rights" to obtain payment for their shares.

Transactions covered

Coverage. Besides granting appraisal rights in the case of mergers, sales of substantially all assets, and amendments of the articles of organization that adversely affect shareholder rights of certain sorts (preferential rights, redemption rights, preemptive rights, or voting rights), MBCA Section 13.02 gives them in connection with Section 11.02 share exchange plans where the corporation's shares are to be acquired and in connection with any other corporate action taken pursuant to shareholder vote and as to which the articles, the bylaws, or a board resolution grants appraisal rights.[11]

[9] See, e.g., Francis I. DuPont Co. v. Universal City Studios, Inc., 312 A. 2d 344 (Del. Ch. 1973), aff'd, 334 A.2d 216 (Del. 1975); Bell v. Kirby Lumber Corp., 413 A.2d 137 (Del. 1980).

[10] E.g., Manning, note 1 supra, at 230-233.

[11] The California appraisal statute applies to mergers, consolidations, and B and C reorganizations. Cal. §1300. Delaware limits appraisal rights to mergers and consolidations, unless the certificate of incorporation extends them to transactions involving the sale of substantially all the corporation's assets or to amendments of the certificate of incorporation. Del. §262(c).

Exception for our simple sale

The exceptions are of some interest. The appraisal remedy is not available in a sale of all assets when the sale is for cash and the net proceeds are to be distributed pro rata to the shareholders within one year of the date of sale — that is, in pure sale-and-liquidation transactions of the kind discussed in Section 10.3. These transactions, we saw, are similar from the selling shareholders' point of view to a stock sale, which also does not result in appraisal rights.

And some nonvoting shareholders

Two other exceptions arise out of the fact that, in a merger, the statute generally gives dissenter's rights only to shareholders who are entitled to vote on it. (There's an exception for the subsidiary's shareholders in a short-form merger, as we shall soon see.) Thus, the appraisal remedy does not apply to shareholders of a surviving corporation in a merger when the vote of the survivor's shareholders is not necessary to authorize the merger. The main examples of this are whale-minnow mergers and short-form parent-subsidiary mergers.

The former are described (without my fishy metaphor) in Section 11.03(g). To simplify, when X corporation merges into Y corporation and the number of Y voting shares outstanding right after the merger is not more than 20 percent greater than the number outstanding before the merger, and other conditions are met, the vote of the Y shareholders is not required to approve the merger. They also do not have appraisal rights. The theory is that from their point of view (though not from the point of view of the X shareholders) the mergers is more like a purchase of investment assets than a major corporate change.

Short-form mergers

Under MBCA Section 11.04, when a parent corporation owns at least 90 percent of the outstanding shares of each class in its subsidiary, the parent's board of directors may, by resolution, merge the subsidiary into itself without the vote of *either* company's shareholders. Nor is a resolution of the subsidiary's board of directors necessary. MBCA Section 1302(a)(1) doesn't give dissenter's rights to shareholders of the parent but does give them to the minority shareholders of the merged subsidiary. This makes sense, for it is the minority shareholders who are most likely to be treated unfairly.

Procedures. Consider Apple Corporation, whose directors have resolved to merge it into a fruit juice conglomerate. Each share of Apple common is to be converted into a share of preferred stock newly created by the conglomerate, in such a way that two Apple dissidents, Worm and Bug, are sure to object. The MBCA establishes a number of practically important rules to govern the process by which they exercise their dissenters' rights. Apple must notify its shareholders of their rights in the notice of the meet-

Notices required

ing to vote on the merger.[12] Moreover, if Worm and Bug intend to preserve and exercise their appraisal rights, they must file notice with Apple of their intent before the vote is taken, and they must not vote in favor of the merger.[13] The advance notice will help management to know what kind of cash drain to expect and to plan accordingly. Next, if the merger is approved by a majority of the shareholders, Apple has to send Worm and Bug a second notice, which will tell them where and when they must make demand for payment and where and when to deposit their share certificates (if their shares are certificated).[14] Worm and Bug will lose their appraisal rights if they don't make the demand and deposit their shares.[15]

Share deposit requirement

The requirement of depositing share certificates (like the provision for restricting the transferability of noncertificated shares[16]) is designed to prevent the Apple shareholders from trying to have it both ways. Without the requirement, even a shareholder who thinks the merger is good might decide to hedge his bets by pursuing his appraisal remedy until the situation became clear. If the merger turned out to be unexciting for the old Apple shareholders, he could continue with appraisal, in the hope of doing better. If the merger turned out favorably to the old Apple shareholders he could abandon the appraisal process and sell his Apple stock on the market, at a high price reflecting the fact that the buyer could turn the stock in for preferred shares in the fruit juice conglomerate. Of course, if every Apple shareholder tried to hedge in this manner, it would wreck the merger. That is why the law tries to prevent the practice.

Payment of estimated fair value

After Worm and Bug have deposited their shares, the ball is in Apple's court. Unlike many traditional appraisal statutes, the MBCA would not allow Apple to wait until the end of judicial appraisal proceedings to pay something to Worm and Bug. (This delay is a major reason why more shareholders have not attempted to exercise their appraisal rights.) Immediately upon effectuation of the merger — or upon receipt of the demands for payment, if that happens afterwards — Apple must pay Worm and Bug the amount it estimates to be the fair value of their shares.[17]

Deficiency claim and hearing

If Worm and Bug don't think this amount is adequate, they may send Apple their own estimate of the fair value of the shares and demand payment of the deficiency.[18] If the deficiency claim is not settled within 60

[12] MBCA §13.20(a).
[13] MBCA §13.21.
[14] MBCA §13.22.
[15] MBCA §13.23(c).
[16] MBCA §13.24.
[17] MBCA §13.25.
[18] MBCA §13.28.

days, the *corporation* must file a petition in an appropriate court requesting that the fair value of the shares be determined.[19] It must make *all* the dissenters who have properly made demand, deposited their shares, and claimed a deficiency parties to the same proceeding,[20] and it must pay the costs and expenses of the proceeding, including the compensation of the court-appointed appraiser.[21] Obviously, the drafters hoped to create a system in which most disputes would be resolved out of court.

Incentives to play fair

What happens if Apple is supposed to initiate the judicial valuation proceeding but doesn't? Then Worm and Bug must be paid the amount they demanded for their shares, no questions asked.[22] Moreover, if Apple fails to comply substantially with the requirements of the statute, the court in the appraisal proceeding may assess the fees of Worm and Bug's lawyers and experts against Apple.[23] More generally, the court may assess fees and expenses against either corporation or dissenters if it finds the assessed party to have acted arbitrarily, vexatiously, or not in good faith.[24]

Query impact

The MBCA, by requiring prompt partial payment to dissenters, by requiring corporate initiative and expense bearing in valuation proceedings, and by combining such proceedings, has attempted to make the appraisal remedy a more effective one than it has been in the past. Whether these provisions will be widely adopted and whether they will have any serious impact on shareholders' resort to appraisal remains to be seen.

§10.6.3 Valuation Methods

Pre-transaction value, often

Appraisal statutes generally do not specify how the court or appraiser is to value the stock in question. They do often make the point that the objective is to give the dissenter the fair value of his shares, construed to mean "their value immediately before the effectuation of the corporate action to which the dissenter objects, excluding any appreciation or depreciation in anticipation of such corporate action unless such exclusion would be inequitable."[25] The thought behind such provisions seems to be that if a shareholder elects to opt out of the enterprise because he objects to a proposed transaction and also refuses to help bring about the transaction

[19] MBCA §13.30(a), 13.30(b).
[20] MBCA §13.30(c).
[21] MBCA §13.31(a).
[22] MBCA §13.30(a), second sentence.
[23] MBCA §13.31(b)(1).
[24] MBCA §13.31(b)(2).
[25] MBCA §13.01(3). Compare Del. §262(h), which is similar but doesn't expressly grant the judicial discretion embodied in the MBCA's "unless" clause.

(by voting for it), he ought not to share in any value or disvalue created by the transaction but should be bought out at a price reflecting the pre-transaction value of the corporation. As a result, it is perfectly conceivable and proper that a dissenter who pursues his appraisal remedy will receive substantially less than the amount received by nondissenting shareholders. Occasionally this does in fact happen.[26]

Traditional valuation methods

In valuing stock in appraisal proceedings, courts have generally employed a weighted average of the results of several different valuation methods: the market value, asset value, and earnings value methods.

Market value of stock

The first method of valuation is to look at the market value of the corporation's stock before announcement of the transaction in question. This method is less helpful and is typically given less weight under certain circumstances: when (as in the case of most closely held corporations) the stock is not traded actively in a liquid, reasonably efficient market; when the market price is believed to have been flawed for some identifiable reason, such as nondisclosure of relevant information, past uncorrected self-dealing by management, and the like; or when news of the merger or other transaction was leaked to the market so long before its effectuation that the last untainted market price is simply stale.

Asset value

The second method of valuation is to sum the separate market values of the corporation's assets. What could the company get if it were to sell all of its assets at a reasonable speed in appropriate markets for them? This method is given considerable weight when it is in fact likely that the company or its successor will sell most of its assets within the near future. It is also weighted heavily when the company owns a substantial proportion of assets that are valuable, yet not currently generating income, so that the third method of valuation cannot readily be used. An example is a corporation that has purchased land for future development or sale. But in the ordinary case, asset value would seem to have little relevance. Since the ordinary corporation is planning to use its capital assets rather than sell them, the touchstone value to the shareholder is what the corporation will produce for him by way of dividend payments and earnings for retention and expansion.

Earnings value

Accordingly, the third valuation method, the construction of the firm's investment (or earnings) value, is often crucial. Conceptually, the basic goal is for the court, after hearing the experts on both sides, to project the *future* earnings of the corporation, and to discount them to a present value figure at a discount rate that reflects the time value of money (that is, the

[26] In re Valuation of Common Stock of Libby, McNeil and Libby, 406 A.2d 54 (Me. 1979); Lucas v. Pembroke Water Co., 135 S.E.2d 147 (Va. 1964).

risk-free interest rate, such as that paid on government securities), the riskiness of the earnings projection for the particular corporation, and the expected growth pattern of those earnings.[27]

Valuation is prospective

Consider that valuation is always prospective. When I buy a car, a house, a widget-making machine, a bond, or a block of stock, the value I place on these things, and hence the maximum amount I will be willing to pay for them, depends on my estimate of the benefits they will yield to me after I own them. The benefits they may have yielded anyone in the past are not directly relevant to my evaluation. They are relevant only as evidence as to what the future may be.

Courts' past-oriented formulae

The courts often seem to have forgotten the fundamentally prospective nature of a correct valuation of capital assets. Instead they have often traded relevance for certainty. Delaware law, as it was developed before the important case of *Weinberger v. UOP, Inc.*,[28] illustrates this point.

Over the years, the Delaware courts had developed a practice of computing investment value in formulaic terms. Typically, they would consider the company's past five years of earnings, factor out the profits or losses due to nonrecurring events, and calculate the adjusted average earnings. To this earnings figure they would then apply a multiplier in order to obtain the company's investment value. Since an earnings multiplier of this sort is logically just the mathematical reciprocal of the discount rate being used,[29] the multiplier should depend on such factors as the riskiness of the company's projected earnings, the relevant trend factors or growth rates, and so forth. In fact, the courts seemed to rely quite heavily on the average price-earnings multiple that one could compute by looking at the market prices of the stock and the published per share earnings of a group of comparable companies. Not surprisingly, of course, plaintiffs and defendants would often have very different ideas about which other companies in the industry were truly comparable.

Problems with approach

While this "objective" procedure is not indefensible, it does have the problem that it makes the courts unreceptive to evidence that the corporation in question has growth prospects and a risk level that are different from those in its past or from those characteristic of other firms in the industry. Indeed, it may be that unfair squeezeout transactions — the kind

[27] See generally V. Brudney and M. Chirelstein, Cases and Materials on Corporate Finance 1-78 (2d ed. 1979); R. Brealey and S. Myers, Principles of Corporate Finance 10-39, 89-109 (2d ed. 1984). *For an example, see Appendix B.*

[28] 457 A.2d 701 (Del. 1983).

[29] The reciprocal of the discount rate (R) is l/R. Thus, dividing by the discount rate is equivalent to multiplying by l/R; l/R is the multiplier.

to which public shareholders seem most likely to dissent — occur more frequently in just those situations where managers have temporarily impacted information about an unexpectedly bright future for their company.[30] Oddly enough, shareholders might be better served if the courts were more receptive to the admittedly vague and open-ended but theoretically more relevant process of considering the parties' explicit earnings projections and company-specific data about the riskiness and growth prospects of the company's future stream of earnings.

Weinberger case modernizes Delaware law

Perhaps partly for this reason, and certainly because it wanted to modernize its practices and allow use of valuation methods actually used by today's investment analysts, the Delaware Supreme Court announced in *Weinberger v. UOP, Inc.* that, henceforth, the Delaware courts could take account of earnings projections in doing valuations for appraisal purposes and, more generally, could use other rational and recognized valuation techniques.[31]

[30] A curious fact about the reported appraisal cases is consistent with this hypothesis. If you do some calculations on the typical law review article's table of reported results under the three usual valuation methods, you will discover a very striking and consistent relationship:

$$AV > MV > EV$$

where AV means the asset value that was accepted by the court; MV, the market value; EV, the earnings value. See, e.g., Note, 30 Okla. L. Rev. 629, 640-641 (1977), where AV exceeded MV in 9 of 10 cases where both were found, and by an average of 144 percent; AV exceeded EV in 11 of 13 cases, by an average of 261 percent; and MV exceeded EV in 8 of 11 cases, by an average of 38%. The AV:MV:EV ratio is therefore something like 2.6:1.4:1. See also Note, 79 Harv. L. Rev. 1453 (1966); Note, 78 Dickinson L. Rev. 582 (1974).

These figures are anomalous if one accepts the standard theory expressed in the cases that the three methods are just different ways of getting at the same thing, and the use of three different procedures using different data is simply a diversification strategy to reduce the risk of serious error. If this theory were true and complete, there would be no reason to expect a *systematic* difference in the results of the three methods, as there clearly is.

One of several possible explanations is that EV's in the cases are artificially low because courts insist on using past earnings to project future earnings, yet insiders expect a better future in precisely those cases where they cause a merger, freezeout, etc., as to which some shareholders object to the merger price so strongly that litigation and reported opinions result. Asset values come out higher because the appraisers can put values on assets in light of current market conditions, which do reflect (at least to some extent) expected improvements in the company's future. The traded price of the company's stock (MV) could also reflect these prospects; in fact that MV is usually less than AV suggests that not everything about the company's (bright) future prospects was disclosed to investors.

[31] 457 A.2d 701, 704, 712-714 (Del. 1983). The facts of the case suggest that two particular kinds of evidence of value will often be relevant in future appraisal proceedings: internally prepared valuation studies and expert testimony about typical acquisition premiums in comparable situations.

§10.6.4 Exclusivity

Pro and con exclusivity

When the appraisal remedy is available to shareholders who object to a corporate transaction, is the remedy exclusive? Or may the shareholder elect to try the harder route of enjoining or setting aside the transaction? On the side of nonexclusivity , one can argue that the appraisal remedy, as it has been implemented in most jurisdictions, is a very imperfect remedy. It is slow, expensive, and risky (that is, rights may be lost if one makes a misstep in the complicated statutory procedures), and it does not facilitate collective action in which dissidents can share costs and pool resources. Moreover, even in a jurisdiction that has adopted the MBCA procedures, one could argue that if a major corporate transaction is seriously alleged to be unfair or otherwise objectionable, and there is a conflict of interest or other reason to doubt the efficacy of normal safeguards against unfairness, the law should allow an enterprising shareholder or group of them to try to assert and protect the rights of shareholders as a group, and to recover expenses if they prevail. Allowing such actions may be efficient in the same way that derivative suits generally can be efficient vehicles for policing nonrecurring or noncontinuing managerial misconduct. (See section 9.5.4) On the side of exclusivity, one might argue that giving the option of a suit to attack the transaction itself simply gives greater leverage to strike suitors.

MBCA approach

The law on exclusivity varies. MBCA Section 13.02(b) tries to make the appraisal remedy exclusive for most purposes. It says that the shareholder entitled to dissenter's rights may not challenge the corporate action creating the entitlement unless the action is "unlawful or fraudulent with respect to the shareholder or the corporation." This may seem to preclude a shareholder from attacking a merger as unfair in its terms of exchange, unless he can show that crucial information was misstated in or omitted from the proxy statements and other documents connected with the merger. Nevertheless, the word *fraudulent* is not as narrow or confining as the word *deceptive*, and the courts are legitimately free to give it a generous reading. Remember the law of fraudulent conveyances (see chapter 2): It clearly was never restricted to transfers that are deceptive but has also included transfers that are unfair to creditors in specified ways. Similarly, it should be noted that a New York court has held that a freezeout merger effected without a valid corporate business purpose was fraudulent and could therefore be enjoined under New York's Martin Act.[32] Moreover,

[32] People v. Concord Fabrics, Inc., 371 N.Y.S.2d 550 (Sup. Ct.) aff'd per curiam, 377 N.Y.S.2d 84 (App. Div. 1975).

these generous readings of *fraudulent* may make good policy sense. There seems to be little reason to make a radical distinction between the rules governing injury to creditors by deceiving them from those governing injury to creditors by making unfair transfers on the eve of insolvency. Nor is there great reason to distinguish between a management's taking value away from shareholders by lying to them and their taking value away from shareholders by means of an unfair self-dealing transaction that is fully disclosed.

Cal. §1312

The California statute is sensitive to these concerns. Section 1312 of the General Corporation Law basically makes the appraisal remedy exclusive, with an important exception for situations where the objecting shareholder holds shares in a corporation that is controlled by, or under common control with, another corporation that is a party to a reorganization or short-form merger — that is, when there is an organizational conflict of interest. (By reorganization the California law includes statutory mergers and transactions like the B and C reorganizations of tax law.[33]) In these situations, if the shareholder attacks the validity of the transaction or seeks to have it set aside, the controlling corporation has the burden of proving that the transaction is just and reasonable as to the shareholders of the controlled corporation.

Some might want the law to go a step further along the spectrum and to make appraisal nonexclusive not only in controlling mergers but also in other major transactions that have a potential for abuse. The theory would be that, even in an apparently arm's-length merger, the acquired company's management may succumb to the temptation to demand and receive side payments — overly generous compensation arrangements and consulting agreements with the acquirer — at the expense of the acquired company shareholders.

Delaware approach

Perhaps partly in recognition of such possibilities, the Delaware courts, beginning with *Singer v. Magnavox Co.*,[34] expressed views that suggested that appraisal would be a nonexclusive remedy in an even wider range of corporate transactions than in California. In the *Weinberger* case, the Delaware Supreme Court seemed to cut back on this trend, at least nominally. It said that the plaintiff's monetary remedy should "ordinarily" be confined to the liberalized appraisal remedy it established. But it also said it did not intend to limit the Chancellor's discretion to give other appropriate relief and noted that the appraisal remedy may not be adequate where

[33] See Cal. §181.

[34] Singer v. Magnavox Co., 380 A.2d 969 (Del. 1977).

"fraud, misrepresentation, self-dealing, deliberate waste of corporate assets, or gross and palpable overreaching are involved."[35]

§10.7 *The De Facto Merger Cases*

Basic concept

The de facto merger doctrine refers to a set of case law principles to the effect that certain corporate transactions that are not mergers in the technical statutory sense will nevertheless be treated as functionally equivalent to them. In most cases applying the doctrine the result is that shareholders who otherwise would not have gotten appraisal rights do get them. If you have followed the discussion in this chapter up to this point, you will find it very easy to grasp these superficially complicated cases.

Delaware's rejection

Let us start with a 1963 Delaware case, *Hariton v. Arco Electronics*,[1] which rejected a de facto merger argument. Loral, a New York corporation, acquired Arco, a Delaware corporation, in a C reorganization. Instead of merging Arco into Loral under Delaware's statutory merger provisions, Arco sold substantially all of its assets to Loral for Loral stock, and Arco was then dissolved and the Loral stock distributed to the old Arco shareholders. Under Delaware law, a statutory merger would have given rise to voting and appraisal rights on the part of the Arco shareholders. But although the Delaware sale of all assets and dissolution provisions each required a shareholder vote, neither gave rise to appraisal rights. The complaining shareholder argued that when a sale of all assets is followed by dissolution and liquidation of the selling corporation, the transaction has the same result as a merger and ought to be treated accordingly. The Delaware court refused to grant appraisal rights, arguing that to do so would offend the "independent legal significance" or "equal dignity" of the asset sale and dissolution provisions of the corporate statute. The court saw no reason, at least in this context, why the statute couldn't provide different routes, with different rules of the road, to the same result.

Farris v. Glen Alden

The classic case adopting the de facto merger doctrine is the 1958 Pennsylvania decision in *Farris v. Glen Alden Corporation*.[2] Here List, a large conglomerate incorporated under Delaware law, wanted to acquire Glen Alden, a Pennsylvania corporation engaged in mining. To that end, List bought 38.5 percent of Glen Alden stock for cash. Nevertheless, the final set of transactions was staged as an acquisition of List by Glen Alden. The

[35] 457 A.2d at 714.

§10.7 [1] 182 A.2d 22 (Del. Ch. 1962), aff'd, 188 A.2d 123 (Del. 1963).

[2] 143 A.2d 25 (Pa. 1958).

specific technique was a C reorganization. List transferred substantially all of its assets to Glen Alden, which paid for them by assuming List's liabilities and giving List a large amount of newly issued Glen Alden stock. List then dissolved and distributed this Glen Alden stock to its shareholders. Finally, Glen Alden's name was changed to List Alden.

Explanation of acquisition technique

Why was the transaction formally cast as if Glen Alden were acquiring List, when any businesspersons would have surmised that in a substantive sense the opposite was happening? The answer lies in the vagaries of corporate law. Under Pennsylvania law, if Glen Alden either merged into List *or* sold all its assets in exchange for stock, the Glen Alden shareholders would have had appraisal rights. On the other hand, the Pennsylvania statute did not give shareholders of Glen Alden an appraisal remedy when the company merely made purchases of assets — and there was no explicit exception for purchases of whole companies that were paid for by stock. This explains why management wanted the acquisition to proceed in reverse. As for why they wanted List to transfer its assets by way of a C reorganization rather than a statutory merger, the answer is the same as that uncovered in *Hariton:* Under Delaware law, List shareholders would have appraisal rights in the statutory merger but not in the two separate steps of the C reorganization.

Pennsylvania court's response

The Pennsylvania Supreme Court decided that the transactions were a de facto merger and the Glen Alden shareholders had appraisal rights. The court emphasized the fact that the dissident Glen Alden shareholders were being projected into a different new business enterprise against their will, on terms not of their own choosing, and in this respect their position was similar to what it would have been in a formal merger of Glen Alden into List, or a sale of all its assets to List. In both of these latter situations they clearly would have been entitled to appraisal.

"B" reorg as de facto merger

Subsequent decisions have tried to grapple with other variations in fact patterns and to be somewhat more specific about the conditions under which a corporate combination will be assimilated to a statutory merger. In *Applestein v. United Board and Carton Co.,*[3] for example, a New Jersey court construed a B reorganization as a de facto merger and therefore gave the acquiring company's shareholders appraisal rights that they would not otherwise have had. In doing so, the court listed a number of factors that were usually present in formal mergers and observed that they were present in the transaction before it. The factors included the facts that:

(1) the acquired company transferred all its assets, had all its liabilities assumed, and was legally dissolved;

[3] 159 A.2d 146 (N.J. Super. Ct. Ch. Div.), aff'd, 161 A.2d 474 (N.J. 1960).

(2) the pooling method of accounting was used;
(3) there was a joinder of officers and directors and a retention of key personnel; and
(4) the acquired company shareholders received shares in the acquiring company, that is, there was continuity of ownership interest.

This aspect of the opinion has a plodding and unsatisfactory character. One immediately wants to ask: *Why* are these factors relevant? Are there others? How many have to be present to find a de facto merger? Are some factors to be weighted more heavily than others? And so forth.

***Applestein* court's philosophy**

Far more interesting is the court's general reasoning behind its result. Paraphrased somewhat, the court said that to determine properly the nature of a corporate transaction, courts must look not only to the provisions of the agreement — the form, if you like — but also to its substance, that is, to the *consequences of the transaction* and the *purposes of the provisions of the corporate law* said to be applicable.[4] In this statement there lies an entire judicial philosophy and a strong basis for judicial power to try to achieve equity in corporate transactions.

Assessment linked to views about appraisal

Since most de facto merger cases involve not only the general question whether different corporate transactions yielding the same practical result should receive the same legal treatment but also a particular question as to which situations ought to trigger appraisal rights, one's assessment of the cases is likely to be colored by one's assessment of the appraisal remedy per se. Commentators like Folk[5] and Manning,[6] who were impressed by the cash drain and inconsistency arguments against appraisal rights, and who viewed public shareholders as being pure passive investors, naturally thought that courts ought not to extend what they saw as a bad remedy to start with to situations where the statutes do not clearly call for it. Commentators like Professor Eisenberg, who think that some shareholders' expectations do center on the enterprise rather than the stock market, that one can make a viable distinction between "business changes" and "structural" changes (the latter but not the former calling for shareholder voting and appraisal rights), and that in any event the appraisal remedy is a good emergency switch to check management improvidence, would naturally be more inclined to applaud *Farris* and its progeny.[7]

[4] 159 A.2d at 154.

[5] Folk, De Facto Mergers in Delaware: Hariton v. Arco Electronics, Inc., 49 Va. L. Rev. 1261 (1963).

[6] Manning, The Shareholder's Appraisal Remedy: An Essay for Frank Coker, 72 Yale L.J. 223 (1962).

[7] Eisenberg, The Legal Roles of Shareholders and Management in Modern Corporate Decision Making, 57 Calif. L. Rev. 1 (1969).

Doctrine used in successor liability case

It should be noted, however, that it is possible for courts to apply the de facto merger doctrine for purposes other than granting appraisal rights. This possibility is illustrated by successor liability cases. In *Knapp v. North American Rockwell,*[8] for example, the de facto merger doctrine was applied to help a tort victim. The issue on a summary judgment motion was whether a person injured by a defective machine could be barred from recovery from the corporation that purchased substantially all the assets of the manufacturer of the machine on the ground that corporate liabilities generally don't carry over to the acquiring corporation in an asset acquisition (as opposed to a statutory merger). The court's answer was no, at least in the kind of case before it. In effect, the court used the de facto merger doctrine as a substitute for our old friend, Fraudulent Conveyance Law.

Possible reasons

It is interesting to speculate about why the court felt compelled to do so. It appears that the tort victim could no longer sue the manufacturing corporation, which had dissolved and liquidated after the sale of its assets. Nor could he sue the selling company's shareholders, as putative fraudulent transferees, since doing so would be unfeasible. Nor could he sue the selling company's directors and officers, since they had complied with the creditor-protection procedures imposed by the business corporation statute on the managers of the dissolving corporation. In effect, the court wanted to expand the scope of creditor protection afforded by fraudulent conveyance principles (including bulk sales law) and statutory dissolution and liquidation provisions. Possibly it wanted to do so because of the normal reasons for expanding product liability — for example, to put the costs of product-related accidents on the cheapest cost avoider. From this viewpoint, it seems that both the manufacturer and its business successor were better suited than customers to make the proper trade-off between building safer machines and pooling residual risks through insurance. That these considerations played a part is suggested by the fact that the court noted, and seems to have been influenced by, the circumstance that the selling corporation's product liability insurance policy could have been assigned to the acquiring company, although it was not.[9]

[8] 506 F.2d 361 (3d Cir. 1974), cert. denied, 421 U.S. 965 (1975).

[9] For a good discussion of successor liability problems, see Roe, Mergers, Acquisitions and Tort: A Comment on the Problem of Successor Corporation Liability, 70 Va. L. Rev. 1559 (1984).

CHAPTER 11

CONTROL SHIFTS AND INSIDER OVERREACHING: MERGERS AND SALES OF CONTROL

Plan of chapters 11-13

In this and the next two chapters we will examine some conflict of interest problems that arise in corporate combinations and other transactions affecting corporate control. This chapter deals with control shifts in which the insiders of the affected corporation are cooperating in the shift but are alleged either to have overreached in their attempt to grab benefits for themselves or at least to have deflected values that otherwise would have gone to the corporation's shareholders.

Chapter 12, on freezeouts, also deals with corporate transactions that the insiders of the affected corporation initiate or favor. But in those transactions the insiders consolidate their own influence or control to the exclusion of, and perhaps at the expense of, the corporation's outside or minority shareholders.

By contrast, chapter 13, on tender offer and takeovers, deals mainly with attempted control shifts that management of the target corporation actively resists. The legal question raised is whether their resistance serves their own interests at the expense of public investors. In a sense, chapter 17, on the regulation of public offerings of stock, should be added to this group of chapters on control shifts, because it deals with fairness problems that arise when insiders give up some of their control (their de jure voting power, at least) by inviting public investors into the enterprise.

Two broad classes of cases are covered in this chapter: those involving complete acquisitions of a corporation (sections 11.1 to 11.3) and those involving sales of controlling blocks of stock (section 11.4).

§11.1 *Arm's-Length Mergers*

Hypo for analysis

Consider a friendly merger between two previously unrelated companies, Burger Corp. and Pizza, Inc. The merger may be statutory or practical, that is an A, B, C, or triangular reorganization. The shareholders of the merging company, Burger Corp., are to receive stock or other securities of Pizza, Inc. No one is being forceably disinvested or cashed out. The terms of the exchange have been negotiated by management teams from the two companies. Each two shares of Burger Corp. will be converted into one share of Pizza, Inc.

Business judgment rule

At first blush, it seems that no situation could be a better candidate for application of the business judgment rule. There appears to be no conflict of interest that would justify declaring the rule inapplicable. If a minority shareholder of Burger Corp. feels that the company's managers have not bargained hard enough or have incompetently agreed to transfer the company for less than its worth, so the argument would go, he should nevertheless not be able to attack their business judgment in court, in a suit to enjoin or set aside the merger. If he feels the two for one exchange ratio does not give him something worth the value of his old investment, he should at most be given an appraisal remedy. And as we have seen (section 10.5), even that much is debatable.

Attack possible but difficult

In fact, the case law of some states has permitted shareholder attacks on the validity of arm's-length mergers. In the past, at least, Delaware cases have held that even an arm's-length combination is subject to judicial review for fairness, although the plaintiff has the burden of proof and must show that the consideration paid is so inadequate as to constitute "constructive fraud."[1] To be sure, the courts rarely strike down a transaction under this standard of review; but the legal remedy is there for the egregious case. And, of course, managerial misstatements or nondisclosures in even an arm's-length merger can give rise to a shareholder suit based on

§11.1 [1]Baron v. Pressed Metals of America, Inc., 123 A.2d 848, 855 (Del. 1956); Allied Chemical & Dye Corp. v. Steel & Tube Co., 120 A. 486, 494 (Del. Ch. 1923).

the antifraud provisions of the federal securities laws — for example, Rules 14a-9 or 10b-5.

Side payments problem

Do the courts have a good reason for allowing some possibility of shareholder-initiated judicial review of arm's-length mergers? Yes. The most important problem is that the managers of the acquired company may have a conflict of interest that will lead them to accept unfair "side payments" at the expense of their shareholders. Consider these further facts about our example. Pizza, Inc.'s managers had first proposed to Burger Corp.'s managers that $10 million worth of Pizza securities be paid to acquire Burger Corp. Nothing much else was said. Burger Corp.'s managers hemmed, hawed, and delayed, saying they were not sure they were happy about the proposal and would have to sleep on it. Pizza's managers then made some inquiries and found out that the key Burger Corp. officers would very much like to continue as corporate executives in the combined venture, although they were dissatisfied with their present level of compensation. Pizza's managers then came up with a second proposal. Burger Corp. would be acquired for Pizza securities worth only $8 million. But, in collateral agreements, Pizza would sign five year employment contracts with the key Burger Corp. officers. Under the contracts the officers would receive compensation substantially in excess of what they were receiving from Burger Corp. Indeed, Marvin Pesky, a dissident shareholder of Burger Corp., has calculated that the discounted present value of these excess compensation amounts is about $1 million.

Plaintiff's argument: a bribe

Even in this highly simplified example — real world transactions are usually more complicated and harder to decipher — there are substantial problems of interpretation. Pesky could claim that Burger Corp.'s managers converted an amount that should have gone to the shareholders into personal benefits. His argument would be that the $1 million of extra compensation to the officers was really being paid by Pizza, not to obtain the post-merger personal services of those officers, but to obtain their present cooperation — their implicit promise not to use their official positions with Burger Corp. to block the acquisition or make it more costly. Pizza was willing to go along with this, he would say, because it was indifferent as to who got the consideration, as long as it got Burger Corp., and because the Burger Corp. officers were willing, because of the bribe, to convey their corporation's assets for $1 million less than Pizza was willing to pay. (Instead of the $10 million bid made at first, the buyer would pay the $8 million second bid plus the $1 million of extra compensation to the officers.) Now, it is as clear as anything can be in corporate law that corporate directors and officers may not take personal payments from third parties for the exercise of their official powers ostensibly on behalf of the corporation. It is also clear that a noncooperative management, solely by use of delaying tactics and defensive maneuvers (and apart from mere hard bargaining), can greatly raise the acquisition costs of the acquiring company. To sum up: Target company managers do have the power to demand bribes, and acquiring companies do have incentives to pay them.

Defendant's argument: a raise

Where Pesky's argument runs into trouble, however, is in the area of specific proof in the particular case at hand. Burger Corp.'s and Pizza's managers will say that the $1 million "raise" in the compensation of the former is exactly what it appears to be: a recognition of those officers' achievements and a set of payments to induce them to contribute their valuable talents to the merged companies. They will correctly point out that it is perfectly proper for an acquiring company to hire the officers and employees of an acquired company. Indeed, doing so may be positively desirable, for investors and for overall economic efficiency, because it may facilitate smooth transitions and take advantage of company-specific expertise. They will explain the $2 million drop in the nominal purchase price of Burger Corp. as merely reflecting the normal vicissitudes of the bargaining process.

Choice often difficult

The choice between the plaintiff's and the defendants' interpretations of the merger process will be made even more difficult if the facts are more complicated, as they usually are. For example, suppose the positions of the Burger Corp. officers with the surviving company will be different in their scope and titles from those of their old jobs. Suppose also that the second acquisition proposal varies from the first in ways that make it difficult to place a value on the consideration. In the second proposal, for example, Pizza might offer to give the Burger Corp. shareholders newly created convertible preferred stock that is said by some expert — an investment banker hired by Pizza — to have a probable ultimate market value of $10 million. Now the true motivations of the managers and the effects of the bargaining are thoroughly obfuscated.

Impact on plaintiffs

In short, in all but the clearest cases, it will be difficult for watchdogs like Pesky to prove that arrangements beneficial to merging company managers were actually illegitimate side payments or bribes. And no judge sympathetic to economic efficiency would adopt a flat rule prohibiting all such arrangements. As a result, plaintiffs have often failed to win such cases.[2] What plaintiffs might hope for is a ruling that generous employment contracts (or consulting and noncompetition agreements, and so forth) for acquired company managers will lead the courts to consider the

[2]See, e.g., Smith v. Good Music Station, Inc., 129 A.2d 242 (Del. Ch. 1957); Mitchell v. Highland-Western Glass Co., 167 A. 831 (Del. Ch. 1933).

acquisition a conflict of interest transaction (of the mixed motive type — my fourth paradigm),[3] so that the fairness of the acquisition is subject to a high degree of judicial scrutiny and the burden is placed on the defendant companies and officers to show such fairness. So far, this approach seems not to have been taken by courts.

In conclusion, it can be said that no one has yet devised an elegant solution to the side payments problem.

§11.2 *Two-Step Acquisitions*

Sometimes combinations between previously unrelated corporations occur not at once but in several stages. The stages may be part of a single general plan of acquisition and may occur within a relatively short period of time, such as one year. Suppose, for example, that Pizza, Inc. had first made a tender offer for the shares of Burger Corp. (perhaps because it was not willing to pay the latter's managers a bribe to agree to a friendly merger) and had thereby acquired 60 percent of its 1 million shares for $6 million, or $10 per share. Three months later, after Pizza had installed it nominees on Burger Corp.'s board, Pizza causes a merger of Burger Corp. into itself, and gives the remaining 40 percent shareholders of Burger Corp. newly issued Pizza common shares. Note that in this example no one is being forced to disinvest entirely or to be cashed out.

Hypo for analysis

These two transactions are much like an arms' length merger in their net effect, except that the merger has been split up and dragged out. If we conceptually integrate the two transactions, as business sense suggests we ought, we can argue that Pizza is acting essentially as an arms' length bargaining party with respect to Burger Corp. and its shareholders. We might conclude that Pizza is not to be viewed as a fiduciary with respect to them; thus, courts need not feel called upon to scrutinize carefully the fairness of the terms of the acquisition, nor the existence of valid business purposes for it. Assuming that the side payments problem does not raise its head here, the acquisition seems to call for complete protection by the business judgment rule.

Basic legal approach

But are there nevertheless fairness questions in this case? Consider the fact that, after the first step of the acquisition, Pizza is in fact a controlling shareholder and thereby acquires a fiduciary status with respect to the remaining Burger Corp. shareholders. In the second step merger, it has both controlling power and an interest adverse to the Burger Corp. minor-

Some fairness questions

[3] See section 4.1 supra.

ity shareholders. There is, therefore, self-dealing, and this justifies special rules.

But perhaps the problem is greatly mitigated here, because the terms of the recent tender offer (which *were* set in an arm's-length rather than a self-dealing transaction) are readily available to serve as an easy check on the fairness of the terms in the second step. This line of thought leads to a major question. At the second step, should it be impermissible for Pizza to design and carry out a merger in which the 40 percent shareholders will be paid consideration worth less than that received by the 60 percent shareholders in the first step?

Let us call this the equal treatment problem. It is the salient problem posed by two-step acquisitions, just as the side payments problem is the salient problem posed by arm's-length acquisitions. Some commentators would raise a second question about the two-step acquisition. At the time of the tender offer, should Pizza be obligated to disclose its intention to take the second or "mop up" step?

Notice, stampedes, and equal treatment

Professors Brudney and Chirelstein would answer yes to both of these questions.[1] Their view is that nondisclosure of a planned coercive merger is unfair to the tender offerees; the offerees ought to know what the offeror has in store for them if they refuse the offer. But they think that disclosure by itself will generate an undesirable "whipsaw" effect. The offerees will know that if they do not accept the $10 per share offer now they may be forced to accept $7 per share later, if the offeror succeeds in gaining control. Even if an offeree thinks $10 per share is not adequate, he will fear that a majority of his fellow shareholders are being tempted to accept the offer. Other offerees will be in a similar position. Being risk-averse, they will rush to join the stampede, and collectively their fears will turn into a self-fulfilling prophecy. On the other hand, so the argument goes, if this coercive aspect had not been present, the offeree shareholders may have assessed the terms of the offer more soberly and arrived at a more careful judgment as to whether it reflected the intrinsic value or potential of their investment. Accordingly, say Professors Brudney and Chirelstein, the merger price ought to be at least equal to the tender offer price, and this equality should be known to the offerees.

§11.2 [1]Brudney & Chirelstein, Fair Shares in Corporate Mergers and Takeovers, 88 Harv. L. Rev. 297, 336-340 (1974); Brudney & Chirelstein, A Restatement of Corporate Freezouts, 87 Yale L.J. 1354, 1359-1365 (1978); Brudney, Equal Treatment of Shareholders in Corporate Distributions and Reorganizations, 71 Calif. L. Rev. 1072, 1118-1122 (1983). For a different view as to the equal treatment question, see Toms, Compensating Shareholders Frozen Out in Two-Step Mergers, 78 Colum. L. Rev. 548 (1978).

A contrary view

Other commentators, such as Professors Easterbrook and Fischel, would strongly oppose the equal treatment rule.[2] The gist of their view is that the rule would tempt shareholders too strongly to be holdouts (or free riders), that this would in turn reduce the number of successful takeovers, and that takeovers are simply too important as mechanisms for increasing business values and keeping managers on their toes to be thus impeded.

Holdout argument

The holdout argument can be briefly elaborated. Consider the shareholder of Burger Corp. who receives an offer to sell his shares for $10. The equal treatment rule assures him that, if the tender offeror is successful at getting control and later employs a merger to forcibly acquire his shares, he will nevertheless be paid at least $10. What will he do? He may very well decide to sit out the tender offer, in the hope that in a later offer or transaction of some sort he will receive more than $10. He may as well delay if he feels sure of getting at least $10 anyway.

Of course, it may occur to him that if most of his fellow shareholders do likewise, the tender offer will fail, the market price of Burger Corp.'s stock may fall back to its pre-tender offer level — say, $5 — and they will all have lost a fine opportunity. Perception of this possibility — a kind of prisoner's dilemma problem — may lead the offerees not to be greedy holdouts. But opponents of the equal treatment rule would discount the significance of this possibility. (How important it actually could be is an empirical question, of course.) They would predict that offeree shareholders would engage in holdout behavior frequently enough to reduce the number of successful takeovers significantly. As for the final prong of the argument, the notion that corporate takeovers are (in general) economically desirable, there are in fact strong arguments and evidence for this belief, and it will be examined more closely in chapter 13.

Benchmark for two-tier pricing

Would opponents of the equal treatment rule impose *any* constraint on the second step of the acquisition? Some would. Easterbrook and Fischel, for example, would hold that the second step merger price is fair so long as the shareholders received consideration equal to or better than the pre-tender offer fair value of their shares.[3] In this example, if the pre-tender offer market prices were found to reflect the true value of the company, the fair value would be $5, so that the $7 merger price would easily qualify as adequate.

Competing analogies

A seasoned corporate lawyer might be tempted to reconceptualize the debate as a battle between competing analogies. Brudney and Chirelstein stress the fact that the paradigmatic two step acquisition is functionally

[2] Easterbrook & Fischel, Corporate Control Transactions, 91 Yale L.J. 698, 727-728 (1982).
[3] Id. at 728.

equivalent to an arm's-length merger that occurs in one fell swoop and that in such a merger all shareholders of the merging company would have to be treated equally — that is, would get consideration that has the same value (if not the same form) per share given up. Their opponents could stress the fact that the shareholders who refused the tender offer and are being forced to sell in the second-step merger are more like dissenters to an arm's-length merger — dissenters who are in effect remitted to something like appraisal rights. That is why the floor they would put on the price paid in the second step is the fair value of the minority's shares apart from any value added or subtracted by the tender offer and the merger transactions. Such a floor corresponds precisely to the valuation standard in appraisal statutes.

A compromise

Of course, the appraisal analogy falls apart when the first step in a two-step acquisition is an offer that is *not* equally available to all the target's shareholders. Suppose, for example, that the first step was not a public tender offer made to all shareholders but a negotiated private purchase of a controlling block of stock. The minority shareholders could hardly be viewed as dissenting from an opportunity they didn't have. Thus, a possible compromise position is to accept the appraisal analogy when the merging company shareholders actually did have the chance to sell their shares on the same terms as other shareholders in the first step of the acquisition sequence but to follow the equal treatment rule when they did not have such a chance.

Empirical questions

In the end, however, the important questions have to do with empirical realities rather than the fitness of legal analogies. Would an equal treatment rule contribute to or detract from aggregate shareholder welfare? The argument that it contributes might rest on a judgment that the stampede effect of two-tier pricing will result in corporate resources not being moved into their most valuable uses.[4] The argument that equal treatment would reduce shareholder welfare depends on judgments about the real net effects of takeovers and the extent to which an equal treatment rule would actually impede them. It is hard to be certain about the correct answers to these empirical questions.

[4]Note that it is not necessarily better for shareholders, in the aggregate, if an equal treatment rule thwarts a particular takeover attempt, with the result that other bidders come in and pay the shareholders more. One has also to consider the possible negative impact of the rule in reducing the rate of takeover attempts. The more plausible argument, at least on its surface, is that two-tier pricing will allow first bidders to get their way more often, even though delay would cause companies willing to pay more to come into the picture, and that once a first bidder has acquired a company there are institutional factors that would make it costly for a subsequent bidder to convince the first bidder to resell the target to it.

State courts' decisions

What is the law on the equal treatment question? State courts do not appear to impose an equal treatment rule, although they do occasionally note with obvious approval that the shareholders in a coercive later-stage merger were paid the same amount as shareholders whose interests were acquired earlier.[5]

Federal law issue

In the federal courts, the issue has arisen whether the use of a two-tier price structure in a multistep acquisition attempt constitutes a "manipulative" device or practice in violation of one of the antifraud provisions of the federal securities laws. In *Radol v. Thomas*,[6] the court found that plaintiffs seeking a preliminary injunction had "not shown to a substantial likelihood" that the two-tier price structure of U.S. Steel's tender offer and merger plan for Marathon Oil Company was manipulative in violation of Sections 10(b) or 14(e) of the Securities Exchange Act. (Section 14(e) is the general antifraud provision applicable in connection with tender offers.) Plaintiffs had argued that the price structure created artificial market influences by coercing Marathon shareholders into tendering to U.S. Steel in order to avoid the risk of later being forced out at a lower price. The court first noted the Supreme Court's statements to the effect that manipulative conduct under the securities laws means intentional conduct designed to deceive or defraud investors by controlling or artificially affecting the price of securities. It could then have contented itself with simply noting that, even if the two-tier pricing structure could somehow be construed as artificially affecting market prices, it clearly did not *deceive* the target shareholders in any way.

Oddly enough, however, the court went into a substantial discussion of the extent to which the two-tier pricing structure was "coercive." It noted that all tender offers were coercive to some degree because they put pressure on offerees; that the offer didn't foreclose Mobil, U.S. Steel's rival, from making its own, essentially noncoercive offer, to which the target shareholders did not respond as warmly; and so on. This discussion is odd because coercion, however objectionable it might be in some contexts, is not itself a basis for finding deception or manipulation. In any event, the court's result seems consonant with prior understandings of the concept of manipulation.

[5]See Alcott v. Hyman, 184 A.2d 90, 94-95 (Del. Ch. 1962), aff'd, 208 A.2d 501 (Del. 1965); Brundage v. New Jersey Zinc Co., 226 A.2d 585, 601-602 (N.J. 1967). But see Northway, Inc. v. TSC Indus., Inc., 512 F.2d 324, 339 (7th Cir. 1975), rev'd on other grounds, 426 U.S. 438 (1976).

[6]534 F. Supp. 1302, 1311-1314 (S.D. Ohio 1982).

§11.3 Parent-Subsidiary Mergers

Hypo for analysis

Consider now the merger of a long-standing subsidiary corporation into its parent. Suppose, for example, that Pizza, Inc. has owned 60 percent of the shares of Burger Corp. for many years. It has become difficult or impossible to use the terms of the original acquisition as a useful point of reference for assessing a proposed merger of Burger Corp. into Pizza, Inc. The businesses have grown; markets and personnel have changed; lines of business are different; intercompany transactions have occurred; intervening business opportunities have been assigned to one company or the other. The question arises as to whether the fairness of the merger may be scrutinized by a court and, if so, how fairness should be determined.

A form of basic self-dealing

Ordinarily, a parent-subsidiary merger can be properly characterized as a self-dealing transaction. (Specifically, it matches the first paradigm, basic self-dealing, set out in section 4.1.) This is true in the obvious institutional sense that the parent corporation controls both sides of the transaction and unilaterally sets the terms of the deal. It is also true in the more realistic human sense that the top managers of the parent, who have the real power on both sides, will often have a greater personal financial interest in the welfare of the parent. This happens because incentive compensation arrangements for top managers are generally tied to the overall performance of the parent. Their personal stockholdings tend to be in the parent, and the subsidiary is, by hypothesis, party owned.

For example, if Mr. Pepperoni, the chairman, president, and dominant personality in Pizza, Inc., owns 5 percent of the stock of that corporation, he will have a $50,000 share in each additional $1 million of net assets held by Pizza but only a $30,000 share (that is, 5 percent times 60 percent times $1 million) of each additional $1 million of net assets held by Burger Corp. So when the question is whether Pizza should pay an additional $1 million of consideration for the assets of Burger Corp. in a merger, his strong incentive will be to answer no. Since he controls or strongly influences the decisions of both companies, he may be able to implement this answer. Furthermore, even when a majority of the public shareholders of the subsidiary (and not just a majority of all its shareholders, including the parent) vote for such a merger, rational apathy and free-rider problems may well mean that such approval should count for little in deciding whether the transactions should be subject to judicial scrutiny at the instigation of a dissident shareholder. (See section 9.4.)

Subject to fairness scrutiny

Since parent-subsidiary mergers may often constitute self-dealing transactions, the courts tend to subject them to fairness scrutiny and to declare that the parent corporation and its management are fiduciaries with respect to the minority shareholders of the subsidiary. In the leading Delaware case of *Sterling v. Mayflower Hotel,*[1] for example, involving a merger between Mayflower and its parent, Hilton Hotels, the court relied upon

***Sterling* case**

> the settled rule of law that Hilton as majority stockholder of Mayflower and the Hilton directors as its nominees, occupy, in relation to the minority, a fiduciary position in dealing with Mayflower's property. Since they stand on both sides of the transaction, they *bear the burden* of establishing its *entire fairness,* and it must pass the test of *careful scrutiny* by the courts.[2] [Emphases added.]

Although the opinions are informative about where the burden of proof lies and what the reviewing court's attitude toward such mergers ought to be, they are less clear about what fairness is supposed to mean.

Fairness and market price

Two important sets of questions about the fairness issue should be noted. The first set concerns the *market price* of the minority shares in the subsidiary. In assessing fairness, what is the proper weight to be given to the price(s) at which the subsidiary's minority shares were being traded in the period before the parent-subsidiary merger? Is market price adequate evidence of what the minority shareholders should have been paid? The best evidence? The only evidence? What other kinds of information are relevant? When and why should market price be given little weight? This set of questions will be explored in the next chapter, on freezeouts, which raise the issues in even more pointed form.

Fairness and merger gains

The second set of questions concerns *merger gains* — the increases in business values that often result from parent-subsidiary mergers. Does the fairness standard require that the minority shareholders be given a share in such gains, or only the pre-merger value of their shares? If the former, what portion of the gain is due them, and how is it to be computed? These questions are dealt with in this section.

Some courts appear to focus on whether the value of what is surrendered by the subsidiary's public shareholders is equivalent to what they receive in exchange.[3] Is what they get equivalent to what they give? Occasionally cases suggest that fairness requires a sharing of gains from the merger,[4] but more often they suggest something akin to the appraisal

§11.3 [1]93 A.2d 107 (Del. 1952).

[2]Id. at 109-110.

[3]Alcott v. Hyman, 184 A.2d 90 (Del. Ch. 1962), aff'd, 208 A.2d 501 (Del. 1965); Allied Chemical & Dye Corp. v. Steel and Tube Co., 120 A. 486 (Del. Ch. 1923); Willcox v. Stern, 219 N.E.2d 401 (N.Y. 1966).

[4]Jones v. Missouri-Edison Electric Co., 199 F. 64, 69 (8th Cir. 1912), cert. denied, 229 U.S. 615 (1913).

standard, that is, that the minority must be given at least the pre-merger value of their shares.[5] What is the proper approach? Should subsidiary public shareholders be entitled to share in any gains from the merger, and if so, to what extent?

Arm's-length bargain test fails

Professors Brudney and Chirelstein, in an important law review article on this problem,[6] observed that the cases have commonly seen the fiduciary norm as directing them to test such mergers against a hypothetical arm's length bargain.[7] In effect, the court is supposed to imagine what the minority shareholders of Burger Corp. would have received in a merger with Pizza, Inc. if the two companies had been completely independent and their managers had engaged in serious bargaining with each other. The problem, as the professors point out, is that this exercise is indeterminate. When two parties are bargaining over a deal that they expect to create a net gain, the portion of the gain that will in fact go to each party will depend very much on variables like the parties' relative bargaining strength and negotiating skills, their differing information and expectations, and so forth. In the face of this indeterminacy, of course, the courts might arbitrarily decree that expected merger gains should be split equally between parent and subsidiary in a merger. Or they might throw up their hands and say that the division of gains is fair as long as the subsidiary gets some not insignificant portion of the gains — since that result could have occurred in an arm's-length bargain.

Analogy to multiple trust accounts

What Brudney and Chirelstein suggest, however, is that courts should not postulate a fictional and indeterminate bargaining session but should emphasize the joint character of management's responsibility to the stockholders of both parent and subidiary. The analogy should be made to a trustee managing multiple accounts. In their view, such a trustee should treat all of his beneficiaries evenhandedly. More particularly, this means that the trustee or parent company management should try to allocate gains and savings so that all beneficiaries receive the same return per dollar of resources managed. Merger gains should therefore be subject to a rule of proportionate sharing. The minority shareholders' proportionate interest in the combined value of the parent and subsidiary should be as great after the merger as before it.

A proposed sharing rule

To carry out this idea in the simple case where the minority shareholders of the subsidiary are receiving common shares of the parent, they suggest

[5] Sterling v. Mayflower Hotel Corp., 93 A.2d 107 (Del. 1952).

[6] Brudney and Chirelstein, Fair Shares in Corporate Mergers and Takeovers, 88 Harv. L. Rev. 297 (1974).

[7] Id. at 309.

the following guideline: The subsidiary's old minority shareholders must possess, immediately after the merger, a percentage of the total parent company common shares that at least equals the percentage which the pre-merger value of the minority's stock was of the total pre-merger value of the two companies. Using this approach, the court would *not* have to determine whether there actually would be or were gains from the merger; nor would it have to put a dollar value on such gains. The court, however, would have to determine the relative pre-merger values of the two companies. In doing so it would not necessarily treat the market prices of the two companies' publicly outstanding stock as conclusive evidence of intrinsic values.

In cases where the subsidiaries' minority shareholders receive consideration other than common stock of the parent, implementation of the proportionate sharing rule could be much more difficult. The court would have to value this other consideration, in order to determine what percentage it constituted of the total post-merger value of the combined companies. Since it would probably value the other consideration (say, preferred stock) at least partly by looking at its market price after the merger, there would be an element of hindsight in the valuation, to which managers would surely object.

Critics, besides noting that it might be hard to implement the proportional sharing rule in some cases, have raised various objections against the rule. Four will be mentioned here.

Arbitrary?

First, it is claimed that the rule is arbitrary.[8] It is not really supported by analogy to the law of trusts, which isn't clear about the precise duties owed by a trustee of multiple accounts. Moreover, why couldn't fairness mean equal return to asset values, rather than to equity values, an even split, or some other rule of division? This sort of objection, however, amounts to cavilling. Granted that the choice of a specific fairness rule has to be somewhat arbitrary; that does not mean that the proportional sharing rule is an unreasonable choice (it's as reasonable as any of the common alternatives) or that there is no point in making the fairness ideal more specific.

Ignores causes of gain?

Second, it is argued that the rule wrongly ignores the causes of gains. One view of the "proper" apportionment of gains is that they should be split according to the relative contributions made by the parent and the subsidiary.[9] Unfortunately, in many cases it is virtually impossible to make

[8]See Lorne, A Reappraisal of Fair Shares in Controlled Mergers, 126 U. Pa. L. Rev. 955, 971-973 (1978); Easterbrook & Fischel, Corporate Control Transactions, 91 Yale L.J. 698, 728 (1982).

[9]Lorne, note 8 supra, at 974-976.

a justified determination of the relative contributions to the later increases in value.

Hinders creation of gain?

Third, it is argued that a sharing rule may deter value-creating transactions and thus reduce aggregate shareholder welfare. This argument is based on the contention that the creation of merger gains may *depend* on unequal division of them. How so? One scenario suggested by Professors Easterbrook and Fischel is that, if the parent company has to share merger gains in the event the merger turns out well but must bear all the loss if it turns out poorly, the deal may become unprofitable, when viewed before the fact, and will not be attempted.[10] But this possibility seems unimpressive: At least in the case where the subsidiary's minority shareholders receive parent company common stock (as Brudney and Chirelstein recommend), the proportional sharing rule will lead to proportional sharing of losses as well as gains. Conceivably there are other ways in which the sharing rule might deter a desirable parent-subsidiary merger (although concrete examples are hard to think of). But then the question becomes the empirical one: How often would this actually happen?

Not needed?

A fourth objection is that the proportional sharing rule is not needed to protect shareholders against self-dealing because they can easily diversify away the risks of unequal treatment in parent-subsidiary mergers.[11] To appreciate this point, recall my analysis of basic self-dealing in chapter 5. I urged that, in order to protect investors against unnecessary and unproductive risks of unfair treatment, basic self-dealing should be prohibited unless a self-dealing surplus could be shown and there would be sharing of it. It could be argued that, in the context of parent-subsidiary mergers, a surplus can usually be presumed and there is no need to enforce sharing of gains in each transaction. Investors, if they are well advised, will have broadly diversified portfolios. Thus, they are likely to have equity positions in parent companies as well as in partially owned subsidiary companies. Although they will be on the losing side in some parent-subsidiary mergers, they will be on the winning side in others. In the long run, these differences should even out.

Pro and con diversification argument

One reply to this argument is that many public investors are not in fact optimally diversified, so that their gains and losses from parent-subsidiary mergers will not in fact balance each other. A possible counterargument is

[10] Easterbrook & Fischel, note 8 supra, at 728.

[11] Easterbrook & Fischel, note 8 supra, at 711-714. Professor Brudney's reply to this and other arguments against his sharing-of-gains approach is given in Brudney, Equal Treatment of Shareholders in Corporate Distributions and Reorganizations, 71 Calif. L. Rev. 1072, 1098-1106 (1983). See also Hoffman, The Efficiency and Equity of Corporate Sharing Rules, 7 Corp. L. Rev. 99 (1984).

that if some investors are not broadly diversified, it is their own fault and they should bear the consequences. Against this it could be pointed out that professional investment advisers still vigorously promote the notion, which academic economists generally think is wrong, that investors can make superior returns by eschewing complete diversification and picking investments selectively. It seems harsh to penalize public investors who give more credence to their brokers than to finance professors.

A second possible counterargument would challenge this last point and insist that the legal rules should be such as to reward rational rather than irrational investor behavior, that is to reward broad diversification. In fact, of course, the question is not whether to give a bonus to diversifiers but whether to penalize nondiversifiers who happen to find themselves in a minority position. By the hypothesis of the diversification argument, a broadly diversified investor should do as well in the long run whether or not there is proportionate sharing of gains in parent-subsidiary mergers.

Another reply to the diversification argument is that it is sometimes *impossible* for *public* investors to diversify into the investment positions held by the controlling parties in a controlled merger. Suppose, for example, that the parent company is closely held. Or suppose the parent company is a recently created shell corporation founded by the managers and controlling stockholders of the operating company for the precise purpose of then freezing out the public, noncontrolling shareholders of the operating company. Even the optimally diversified public investor investing for the long run may find herself injured by the absence of a sharing rule if controlled mergers of this sort are fairly frequent.

It might be countered that the market prices of stocks will be discounted to reflect the risk of getting a raw deal in this way so that investors won't really be hurt. But any such discounts will have to be large enough to reflect the *uncertainty* investors face about the number and magnitude of future raw deals they'll endure. As stated on other occasions in this book, the thrust of corporate law rules should be, and often is, to prevent the creation of uncertainties which are not an essential aspect of some productive activity. Thus, the real inquiry turns out to be the one raised earlier in connection with the third argument against proportionate sharing: In the real world, does the occurrence of value-creating parent-subsidiary mergers often depend critically upon unequal division of gains?

Impact on case law?

But enough of theory, you say: Tell me about the law. Has the generally ambiguous and amorphous body of case law mentioned earlier in this section been changed as a result of the commentators' discussions of sharing proposals? Slightly. The proportionate sharing proposal was explicitly adopted by the Seventh Circuit in the *Electric Auto-Lite* litigation.[12] In a merger involving Christiana Securities and the du Pont company, however, a federal district court not only observed that the Brudney and Chirelstein rule would not apply (because Christiana, although a significant shareholder of duPont, was not a parent of it) but went on to opine that Delaware law did not require a sharing of merger gains and to express an unwillingness to adopt such an approach.[13]

§11.4 *Sales of Control*

The issue May a shareholder who owns a controlling block of stock in a corporation sell it at a price significantly higher than that available to noncontrolling shareholders who also wish to sell? The conventional answer given by the courts is that the sale of a control block of stock at such a premium price is not wrong per se.[1] It becomes wrong only under special circumstances. These special circumstances comprise an important class, however, and a great deal of legal commentary has been devoted to figuring out what its boundaries are or ought to be. Let us look at several of the major categories.

§11.4.1 Sale to Looters

Hypo for analysis Suppose Mr. Dominant owns 55 percent of the common stock in the Liquid Investment Co., which owns a portfolio of stocks, bonds, and money market instruments.[2] The current market price of Liquid stock is $9 per share, though the net asset value per share is $12. (Net asset value is the sum of the current market prices of the securities owned by Liquid, minus its liabilities.)[3] Mr. Dominant is approached by Robert Mesco, a

[12] Mills v. Electric Auto-Lite Co., 552 F.2d 1239 (7th Cir.), cert. denied, 434 U.S. 922 (1977).

[13] Harriman v. E. I. du Pont de Nemours and Co., 411 F. Supp. 133 (D. Del. 1975). A later case suggested that sharing of merger gains might be required by Delaware law in certain situations. Lynch v. Vickers Energy Corp., 429 A.2d 497 (Del. 1981) (3-2 decision). This suggestion was in turn placed in doubt by the fact that Weinberger v. UOP, Inc., 457 A.2d 701 (Del. 1983), overruled *Lynch* to the extent that it purports to limit a shareholder's monetary relief to a specific damage formula.

§11.4 [1] Clagett v. Hutchinson, 583 F.2d 1259 (4th Cir. 1978) (applying Maryland law); McDaniel v. Painter, 418 F.2d 545 (10th Cir. 1969) (applying Kansas law); Roby v. Dunnett, 88 F.2d 68 (10th Cir.), cert. denied, 301 U.S. 706 (1937).

[2] Technically, Liquid Investment is a closed-end investment company.

[3] It may sound impossible for market price to fall much below net asset value, but it frequently happens. For an analysis of some of the explanations that have been proposed for

charming man with a deep tan and a Latin-style mustache, who offers to buy Dominant's controlling block of stock at $15 per share. Mesco says emphatically that he is not interested in buying any other Liquid stock. Dominant recalls that someone with the name of Mesco once looted a large mutual fund, by carrying out scores of unfair self-dealing transactions with it, and was pursued by authorities but escaped to Costa Rica. He wonders if he is free, without making inquiries, to sell his stock to Mesco for $15 a share.

No sale to looters

The answer is probably no. Case law appears to have established that a holder of controlling shares may not knowingly, recklessly, or perhaps negligently, sell his shares to one who intends to loot the corporation by unlawful activity.[4] Presented with both a suspicious character and a suspicious price, Dominant may be reckless if he doesn't investigate further. (Why is the price suspicious? Consider this: The price of $15 per share for an investment company that would only give its shareholders $12 a share if the company were efficiently liquidated on the securities markets is hard to understand if Mesco is honest but easy to understand if one supposes that he plans to take more than his pro rata share of the assets and earnings after he gains control.) If Dominant does breach his duty and the corporation is harmed, he will be liable for the forseeable injuries.[5] He might even have to account for the premium received for his shares.[6] In legal terms, the controlling shareholder's duty has been described as part of his fiduciary duty of care to the corporation with respect to the transfer of control.[7] Some judges have seen it as a mere application of standard tort principles.[8]

Modest case law

Interestingly, after several key decisions of the late 1930s involving investment companies, most of the small number of reported later cases involving an alleged sale of control to looters involved public corporations with relatively illiquid assets and were lost by plaintiffs. The one case that did clearly involve a close corporation imposed liability on the selling stockholder.[9] A reason for the paucity of cases may be that situations

---

these discounts, see Malkiel, The Valuation of Closed-End Investment Company Shares, 32 J. Fin. 847 (1977).

[4] Insuranshares Corp. v. Northern Fiscal Corp., 35 F. Supp. 22 (E.D. Pa. 1940); De Baun v. First Western Bank & Trust Co., 120 Cal. Rptr. 354 (Cal. App. 1975); Gerdes v. Reynolds, 28 N.Y.S.2d 622 (Sup. Ct. 1941).

[5] See Insuranshares Corp. v. Northern Fiscal Corp., 35 F. Supp. 22 (E.D. Pa. 1940).

[6] Gerdes v. Reynolds, 28 N.Y.S.2d 622 (Sup. Ct. 1941).

[7] Insuranshares Corp. v. Northern Fiscal Corp., 35 F. Supp. 22 (E.D. Pa. 1940).

[8] Perlman v. Feldmann, 219 F.2d 173, 179 (2d Cir.), cert. denied, 349 U.S. 952 (1955) (Swan, J., dissenting).

[9] De Baun v. First Western Bank & Trust Co., 120 Cal. Rptr. 354 (Cal. App. 1975).

where sellers of control can be shown to have acted recklessly are very rare because looters don't advertise their intentions.

§11.4.2 Sale of Office

Basic concept and simple example

A corporate director or officer will often have actual power, if not formal power, to influence the identity of his successor. Outgoing directors as a group, for example, may arrange to have certain nominees for directorships put forward to the shareholders as management's slate of candidates, a label that in the ordinary course will insure the election of those nominees. But directors and officers are forbidden to demand or accept payment from someone other than their corporation to exercise the powers they have, by virtue of their positions, to influence the corporation's fortunes. This principle would clearly extend to a simple or bald sale of office. Thus, retiring director John could not properly take a secret $1,000 payment from Henry in exchange for a promise to put Henry's name before the nominating committee and push it vigorously. If John recommends anyone, he should recommend whoever he thinks is best for the job, and his compensation for doing so is to be found in his official director's fee. The temptation for any manager to confuse the best candidate for the company with the candidate who does that manager the biggest favor is simply too great to permit side payments.

Example connected with control shift

But suppose the case is more complicated: The transfer of office occurs in connection with the sale of a controlling block of stock. Henry, for example, is about to buy 51 percent of the stock of The New Tech Company from shareholders John, Jackie, and Jorg, who are also the company's present directors. The price would be $15, which is $4 more than the minority shareholders could now get on the thin market for The New Tech Company's stock. As part of the deal, Henry insists that the three J's engage in seriatim resignation and appointment of his men to directorships. Jorg would resign and John and Jackie would elect Henry to be his successor; Jackie would then resign and John and Henry would appoint Hart to be his successor; and then John would resign and Henry and Hart would elect Hulk — all in one meeting. (Remember that in most corporations shareholders elect the directors annually, but if a director resigns during the year the other directors can appoint a successor to serve until the next shareholder election.) Could a minority shareholder successfully bring a suit based on a claim that part of the control premium of $4 per share was "really" a forbidden payment to the three J's for the sale of their offices (their directorships) to the three H's?

Essex Universal case

Most likely the answer is no. In a leading case discussing the issue, *Essex Universal Corp. v. Yates,*[10] both Chief Judge Lumbard and Judge Friendly inclined to the view that a contract provision providing for a mass resignation and election procedure of the sort described did not violate public policy when it was entirely plain that a shareholder election would be a useless formality — that is, when the sellers transferred more than 50 percent of the stock. In a way, this amounts to saying that a sale of office is proper when it is part of a sale of control, since the buyer will control the offices anyway. Another reason for not objecting is that the buying party, because of his heavy investment interest, will be more motivated than a mere office holder to increase the company's value and refrain from looting it.

"Working" control enough?

But the judges disagreed on the approach to take to a case where the buyer was getting a less than 50 percent block that was nevertheless alleged to give him working control. Judge Lumbard thought a resignation-and-election clause is proper when it is practically certain that the buyers' wishes will prevail in shareholder voting in due course. He stressed the points that easy and immediate transfer of corporate control to new interests is often beneficial to the economy, yet it would hinder transfers if the seller could not assure the buyer of immediate control over operations.

Judge Friendly was inclined to insist on formal certainty, that is, to allow the resignation-and-election clause only if the buyer were getting more than fifty percent of the relevant voting stock. He stressed the difficulty of knowing — other than by hindsight, looking at several years' operations — whether a smaller block of stock actually does constitute working control and thought that it was an affront to principles of corporate democracy and to public stockholders' expectations to presume that it did. He pointed out that if the purchaser of so-called working control did not want to wait until the next annual meeting to have his henchpersons elected, he could have the existing managers call a special meeting of the stockholders. (Conveniently, Judge Friendly neglected to weigh the considerable extra expense this alternative would entail for a public company against its benefits.) He also noted that sudden shifts in control have sometimes led to serious injury to corporations — an observation from which one is apparently supposed to make the inference that control shifts should be slowed down, and also put more fully in the open, by procedures such as the special meeting of stockholders and the disclosures it would entail.

[10] 305 F.2d 572 (2d Cir. 1962).

§11.4.3 Diversion of Collective Opportunity

Basic concept and terminology

Sometimes a sale of control at a premium can be characterized as a taking by the seller of something akin to a corporate opportunity, or to the taking of an opportunity that it seems right to say should have been developed for all shareholders on a pro rata basis. I refer to these sales of control as diversions of "collective opportunities." My reason for this terminology is to avoid confusion with the more traditional phrase, *corporate opportunities,* which has connotations that are not usually appropriate here.

The traditional doctrine of corporate opportunities (see chapter 7) is usually applied in cases where it is alleged that the corporation had a chance to *buy* and exploit some business opportunity that an insider took for himself. But in the collective opportunity cases, the opportunity or potentiality that the actual sale of controlling stock is compared to is an opportunity for the company to *sell* all its assets (or transfer them in a merger) or for all the shareholders to sell their stock at a single price, as in a tender offer for all of the shares.

Moreover, conventional corporate opportunities are usually only business opportunities that can be said to belong, as against the fiduciary, to the corporation itself, considered as an entity. In some of the collective opportunity cases, the opportunities taken by the insiders arguably belonged, as against the insider-fiduciary, to all shareholders as a group, rather than to the corporate entity. This difference makes it hard for courts to conceptualize the problem, or to relate it to corporate law precedents. For as we saw in our discussion of insider trading, some state courts, especially those that have dealt mostly with close corporations, have had trouble conceiving of fiduciary duties being owed by corporate managers directly to groups of their corporation's investors, much less to the investing public generally.

Three kinds of cases

The collective opportunity cases can be assigned to three points along a line of intellectual development pointing ultimately toward fully equal treatment of the shareholders. The three kinds of cases involve what I would call (1) displaced company-level opportunities, (2) opportunities first designed for all shareholders, and (3) opportunities naturally and fairly developed for all shareholders.

Displaced opportunities

Displaced company-level opportunities. As suggested, the first stage of development involves an insider's taking, by means of a control premium, a displaced company-level opportunity, that is, an opportunity (in the broad sense, including opportunities to sell products) that has become unavailable to the corporation itself for extraneous reasons, but the benefit of which could easily be reaped by the shareholders as a group. The question presented in such cases is whether the displaced corporate opportunity ought to be considered to belong to the shareholders as a group as against a controlling shareholder or corporate fiduciary.

Perlman v. Feldmann

For example, suppose, as in the famous case of *Perlman v. Feldmann,*[11] a corporation manufacturing steel faces a lucrative market — supply is tight and demand is high — but it is barred, by ethical guidelines adopted by the industry during wartime, from selling steel at a price reflecting purchasers' willingness and ability to pay. Absent the ethical guidelines, which constitute a kind of virtual price ceiling, the corporation would be selling steel at a higher price to the most eager buyers, and the extra profit thus made would benefit all the shareholders pro rata in accordance with their holdings.

Suppose further that the ethical guidelines refer only to steel prices; they can be avoided if the most eager steel buyers form a group and buy or obtain control of the steel manufacturer itself and then cause it to direct all its output — at the prices fixed in the ethical guidelines, of course — to themselves. These eager buyers are willing to put, into the price they will pay for the common stock of the steel manufacturer, the extra money they would normally have paid to the steel manufacturer itself for the steel, in order to make sure that they and not others will get the steel. Call this amount $X million.

Suppose that, instead of arranging for a sale of *all* of the manufacturer's stock at a price per share that reflects this $X million premium, Mr. F., the president, chairman of the board, and controlling stockholder of the steel manufacturer, negotiates a sale only of a controlling block of shares, at a price that includes the $X million premium. Note that the buying corporation can cause the manufacturer to sell the steel to itself whether it owns 51 percent or 100 percent of the manufacturer's stock. From its viewpoint, the distribution of the $X million premium across the pocketbooks of the shareholders is not terribly important. In other words, the controlling shareholder arranges things so that he and his friends get all of the premium the eager buyers will pay, instead of the pro rata share of the premium they would get if either the steel were being sold directly, or the manufacturer's entire common stock were being purchased in a tender offer or similar transaction. May Mr. F. do so with impunity?

Breach of fiduciary duty found

One way reading the *Perlman* case is to see it as answering this question in the negative. The facts of *Perlman* were similar to those in my hypothetical, but they involved some complications to which we shall have to return in a few paragraphs, since they affect one's assessment of the result in

[11] 219 F.2d 173 (2d Cir.), cert. denied, 349 U.S. 952 (1955).

the case. In any event, the court found that the selling stockholder had breached his fiduciary duty in selling the controlling stock at a premium price not available to the other shareholders. The court required him to share the control premium. The district court was ordered to determine the value of the defendants' stock without the appurtenant control over the corporation's output of steel. It could then compute from this the amount of the control premium that had been received and could make it available to all the old shareholders on a pro rata basis.

Interesting remedy

Interestingly, although the suit was a derivative one, the circuit court ordered payment to be made directly to the old minority shareholders, rather than to the corporation. The remedy, if not all the language in the opinions in *Perlman,* thus suggests that the court conceived the interests needing protection to be those of a particular set of shareholders, namely, all those owning stock at the time of the sale of control, rather than the interests of the corporation as an entity with a changing and disregardable set of shareholders.[12]

Relevance of market price rise?

Now let's return to the complications of the *Perlman* case. Two facts may suggest that the court's ruling was unnecessarily harsh. One is that the market price of the publicly held stock of Newport (the steel company) rose a bit when the control block was sold and remained strong thereafter. This seems to negate any idea that the buyers of control were going to take for themselves alone something of value to Newport. If they were usurping a corporate opportunity, and their actions were public, wouldn't there be a fall in the price of the noncontrolling stock?

Not necessarily. Remember that the displaced opportunity analysis is very different from the normal analysis of corporate opportunity cases. The opportunity in question, that of selling Newport's product at a high price, is assumed to have been not fully realizable in the normal way (selling the product to the highest bidders). Thus, there is no good reason to have

[12]Suppose the entire control premium paid was $10 million, and that the buyer group acquired 60 percent of the stock from the old controlling shareholder. If the court orders the latter to pay $10 million to the corporation, it will presumably cause an indirect benefit of $4 million to the old minority shareholders — which seems to be the proper amount of their claim. But this remedy will also take $6 million from the selling stockholder and return it in effect to the buyer's group, and this result seems to be punishment to the seller and a windfall to the buyer's group. Such a result does not seem warranted.

In addition, many of those who were shareholders at the time of the sale of control may have sold their stock, so that a corporate recovery would not benefit them. That is, despite the form of the lawsuit, the interests that are sought to be protected in this kind of case really do seem to be the interests of a particular group of shareholders, whose identity is fixed at a particular point in time.

expected that buyers and sellers of the noncontrolling stock would have been trading at prices reflecting the scarcity value of the product. Of course, they might have done so if they could have foreseen the ruling in *Perlman*. But the very fact of extended litigation suggests that there was uncertainty about whether efforts to realize the full scarcity value of the product in nonnormal ways would succeed and would result in benefits for all shareholders. Indeed, the slight rise in the price of noncontrolling stock after announcement of the sale of control might have been due to shareholders' perceptions that the scarcity value would now be realized and the control buyers would appropriate most but not quite all of it. The rise might also have been due to the shareholders' guess — correct, as it turned out — that litigation would ensue and would result in their getting some part of the control premium.

Relevance of Feldmann Plan?

A second complicating fact is that some of the scarcity value of Newport's steel *was* being realized by Newport before the sale of the controlling block of stock. Under the so-called Feldmann Plan, prospective purchasers gave Newport interest-free advances on the purchase price of steel products they would later buy, in return for Newport's commitments to sell those products to them. By not charging Newport interest on these advances, the prospective purchasers were effectively paying a premium over the nominal price of the steel products, and were circumventing the ethical guidelines.

The critical question is whether Newport was realizing the full scarcity value of its products in this way. If it was, then the case did not actually involve a displaced or thwarted company-level opportunity. This conclusion would in turn reopen the question as to why the buying group paid a large premium for the controlling block of Newport stock. The obvious alternatives are that it wanted to loot Newport, which seems unlikely on the facts, or that it thought it could make Newport more profitable, which is the normal, good reason for control premiums and which traditionally does not lead to the conclusion that the premium should have been shared.

On the other hand, if the interest-free advances were not yielding Newport the full scarcity value of its products, then the displaced opportunity analysis would retain its applicability, at least to some extent.

Did the Feldmann Plan realize for Newport the full scarcity value of its products? The answer to this question is hard to determine from the reported opinions.

Conversion of offer

Opportunities first intended for all shareholders. A second stage in the development of the collective opportunity cases involves an insider's taking an opportunity originally intended to be presented to the shareholders as a group, by converting it into an opportunity available only to himself. A clear example is that of the insider who dissuades an outsider who intended to buy all of the corporation's stock at $X per share and convinces him to buy the insider's controlling block of shares at a per share price of $X + Y. The insider might perhaps also convince the outsider to acquire the minority shares at $X − Z.

Brown v. Halbert

An important California case, *Brown v. Halbert,*[13] presents a good illustration, although not the sharpest possible one. McDonald, a potential buyer of financial institutions, came to see Mr. Halbert in his office at the Tulare Savings and Loan Association. Mr. Halbert was president, manager, chairman of the board, and (with his wife) the owner of 53 percent of the stock of the association. McDonald asked if the association was for sale. Halbert replied flatly that it was not for sale but that he and his wife would sell their controlling stock in it for $1,548 per share. Halbert did not tell the association's board of directors or its shareholders about McDonald's interest in acquiring the association.

After further negotiations, McDonald eventually accepted the $1,548 per share price for the Halbert stock. Besides agreeing to sell his stock, Halbert also agreed to cause the association to withold paying dividends pending settlement. After settlement, Halbert, who had not yet relinquished his corporate offices, actively helped the buyer solicit the minority shareholders' shares and even advised them that, since McDonald was going to withold dividends for 10 or 20 years, they ought to take his offer of $300 per share. McDonald bought some of the minority shares at $300 and others at prices between $611 and $650.

Fiduciary duty to minority shareholders

Although the minority shareholders who later learned of Halbert's private deal and his other conduct probably wanted to hang him, they had to settle for a lawsuit based on breach of fiduciary duty. The California court first had to free itself of the tendency to find a fiduciary relationship only to the corporate entity. It decided that the "special facts" doctrine, which required that special facts be found before a major stockholder-director would be held to have a fiduciary relationship to shareholders, should not be applied in cases where such a person sells his stock to outside purchasers and thereby causes the minority stock to be devaluated. Instead, the court thought that simply by virtue of his acting in the capacity of president, chairman of the board of directors, and dominant stockholder,

[13] 76 Cal. Rptr. 781 (Cal. App. 1969).

Halbert stood in a fiduciary relationship to the corporation *and* to the minority stockholders as beneficiaries thereof.[14]

Duty elaborated

The court then found that the record clearly showed that Halbert failed to perform his obligations as fiduciary. It adopted

> the rule . . . that . . . the duty of the majority stockholder-director, when contemplating the sale of the majority stock at a price not available to the other stockholders and which sale may prejudice the minority stockholders, is to act *affirmatively and openly with full disclosure* so that *every opportunity is given to obtain substantially the same advantages* that such fiduciary secured and for the full protection of the minority.[15] [Emphases added.]

Prior judicial opinions had suggested that someone in Halbert's position should at least have to disclose the third party's interest in buying the corporation to the board, and perhaps to the other stockholders, before trying to nail down a sale for himself.[16] But the California's court's use of the term *affirmatively* and its reference to obtaining the "same advantages" for the minority indicates that it was imposing a more active duty upon the fiduciary. This interpretation is bolstered by the fact that earlier in its opinion the court had faulted Halbert not only for actively helping McDonald buy the minority's stock cheaply but also because he "failed to make any effort to obtain for the minority substantially the same price that he received. . . ."[17]

Prejudice to minority

Note that in the above-quoted formulation of its "rule," the California court did not explicitly say that the fiduciary's affirmative duties were triggered by the fact that the original offer to buy the company was an undifferentiated one for the whole company. Instead, the court suggests that the duties are triggered whenever the majority stockholder contemplates a premium-price sale that "may prejudice the minority stockholders." Conceivably, minority stockholders can be prejudiced in other ways than by having a uniform offer twisted into a two-tier one. But the operational meaning of the term *prejudice* is not clear.

Opportunities deemed to belong to all shareholders. The third stage of development of the collective opportunity concept involves opportunities that were not actually presented by some outside third party in a way that

[14] Id. at 789.
[15] Id. at 793-794.
[16] Low v. Wheeler, 24 Cal. Rptr. 538 (Cal. App. 1962); McManus v. Durant, 154 N.Y.S. 580 (App. Div. 1915).
[17] 76 Cal. Rptr. at 791.

offered pro rata benefits for all stockholders but are nevertheless judged by a court to be opportunities that ought to be developed for all shareholders rather than only the controlling group.

***Ahmanson* case**

The leading case is a decision by the California Supreme Court, *Jones v. H. F. Ahmanson & Co.*,[18] which involved not a sale or transfer of control but an exchange of a controlling block of shares for shares of a holding company. Defendants owned 85 percent of the stock of United Savings and Loan Association of California. There was a boom in the price of publicly traded savings and loan stocks at the time, but United's closely held nature, plus the fact that each one of its shares had a very high value, made it unsuitable for participation in the stock markets. Defendants determined to fix this situation. Chief Justice Traynor decided that there were two paths open to them.

First, they could cause United to effect a stock split (this would enable a normal 100 share block to trade in a customary price range) and could take steps to make a market for the stock as by having United's shares listed on some stock exchange or by encouraging a securities firm to be a dealer in the stock. Or they could accomplish the same result by the technically different route of creating a holding company for United's shares, permitting all United shareholders to exchange their shares for holding company shares, which would be divided into appropriately sized units, and for which an active trading market would then be developed. In either case the market could be developed further by the old stockholders selling part of their new holdings (after the stock split or the holding company exchange) to the general investing public.

Second, they could solve the numbering problem, create a trading market, and sell interests to public investors in a way that would exclude the minority shareholders of United.

The second path is the one they chose. The 85 percent block of controlling shares was transferred to a holding company, United Financial, at an exchange ratio of 250 United Financial shares for one United share. United Financial then created a market for its own stock. It sold new shares in itself to the investing public, and the benefits of this offering went to the controlling group. Meanwhile, it became apparent that an active trading market would never be developed for the 15 percent of United shares not held by the holding company. When the market value of 250 United Financial shares (the equivalent of one share of United) had increased to $8,800, United Financial offered to exchange $2,400 of its stock for each one share

[18] 460 P.2d 464 (Cal. 1969).

of United still outstanding in the hands of minority shareholders. A minority shareholder then brought a class action against the controlling group.

The decision

The California Supreme Court decided that plaintiff's complaint stated a cause of action, and that if the facts supporting it were established, she would be given damages based on the notion that she should have been allowed to participate in the exchange plan on the same basis as the controlling group. At her election, she could receive either the appraised value of her shares on the date of the exchange of United Financial shares (plus interest), *or,* for each United share, a sum equal to the fair market value of 250 shares of United Financial on the date of the action plus the amount ($927.50) paid by United Financial to its original shareholders when it sold new shares to the public (again, plus interest).

Holding and philosophy

The holding of the case is difficult to state in a precise and generally applicable way. In a narrow sense, the court simply decided that, when no active market in a corporation's shares exists, the controlling parties can't use their power over the corporation to promote a marketing scheme that benefits themselves alone to the detriment of the minority. But in reaching this result, Chief Justice Traynor deploys a variety of high-minded thoughts about the identity and role of the corporate fiduciary. He declares that California has long repudiated the view, taken by the defendants, that shareholders owe no fiduciary duties to other shareholders, except when they rely on inside information, use corporate assets, or commit fraud. Instead, he says, majority stockholders do have a duty to use their power in a fair, just, and equitable manner.

> Majority shareholders may not use their power to control corporate activities to benefit themselves alone or in a manner detrimental to the minority. *Any use to which they put the corporation or their power to control the corporation must benefit all shareholders proportionately* and must not conflict with the proper conduct of the corporation's business. . . .[19] [Emphasis added.]

Like many other good judges, Traynor quotes with approval the "seven commandments" for the fiduciary that were laid out in Justice Douglas' immortal opinion in *Pepper v. Litton.*[20] And he states that, although a controlling shareholder who sells or exchanges his shares is not under an obligation to obtain for the minority the consideration he receives in all cases, when he does sell or exchange his shares the transaction is subject to close scrutiny. The defendants' exchange was flawed in his eyes because

[19] Id. at 471.
[20] 308 U.S. 295 (1939).

"they used their control . . . to obtain an advantage not made available to all stockholders," and "[t]hey did so without regard to the resulting detriment to the minority shareholders [namely, their loss of a *potential* market for active trading in their shares] and in the absence of any compelling business purpose."[21]

Reach unclear

It is not easy to tell how far the opinion in *Ahmanson* reaches. But it seems clear that this uncertainty was a deliberate and necessary aspect of Justice Traynor's philosophy. His aim was to define the duties of the corporate fiduciary in open-ended terms, so that fiduciaries could never think that their duties consist merely in literal compliance with technical rules.

Critique of result

Apart from the opinion's noble philosophy and aspirations, was the result reached a good one in the particular case? There are reasons for doubt. The controlling persons who formed the holding company were not trying merely to make an indirect market for interests in the savings and loan association. They were also trying to create the business advantages that can flow from operating a financial institution in the same corporate family with other, related businesses (which would be operated in other subsidiaries of the holding company).[22] From their point of view, they bore all the costs and risks of launching the holding company, only to be forced later to share some of the gains with others.

With this thought as background, the fact that the minority shareholders waited until *after* the holding company structure had proved its value before demanding admission into the project becomes important. One can infer rather easily that they would have made no such demand if the holding company had flopped. Giving the minority shareholders an option to share in the gains but not the losses[23] seems terribly unfair to the majority. Moreover, future entrepreneurs contemplating similar corporate restructurings might be discouraged from going ahead by such a lopsided sharing requirement. The requirement could therefore be inefficient.

Response to critique

Whether the *Ahmanson* sharing rule actually deters value-creating transactions is unclear. If the initial fact pattern were repeated, the controlling parties could presumably satisfy the exhortations of the *Ahmansom* opinion

[21] 460 P.2d at 476.

[22] See Clark, The Regulation of Financial Holding Companies, 92 Harv. L. Rev. 787, 816-833 (1979).

[23] Note that the probabilities of both gain *and loss* were lower for shareholders in the savings association. Even if the occasion of the holding company's failure were such as to result in a decline in the price of the savings association's stock, this decline would most likely be much less than the decline in the stock price of the highly leveraged holding company. By holding savings association stock as protection against loss but possessing an option to convert it into holding company stock at a previously fixed ratio, an investor would have the best of both worlds. This is essentially what the court gave the minority shareholders.

by offering to let the minority participate in the initial formation of the holding company on the same basis as themselves. (*Same basis* would mean giving shares relative to *total* contributions of resources. Thus, if some controlling parties devoted substantial personal time and effort into launching the venture, other shareholders might have to pay more for their holding company shares.) If the minority refused to get in at the beginning, and thus bear the risk of loss as well as the risk of gain, then surely they could not complain about their nonparticipation later. If all this is so, then the *Ahmanson* rule might have little or no discouraging effect on the promoters of such new ventures.

§11.4.4 Control a Corporate Asset?

The Berle theory

Several decades ago, Adolph Berle, a distinguished writer on the modern corporation, maintained that if the control function in the corporation has a value, that value "belongs" to the corporation. His view is often characterized as being that control is a corporate asset. At first glance, this position seems to represent a semantic mistake: Surely the control *of* a corporation is not the sort of thing that can meaningfully be said to be owned *by* that corporation. But the phrase *corporate asset* is merely a shorthand reference to the theory's operational meaning, which is that the power to control corporate activities, even as it is represented in ownership of voting stock, should be treated for many legal purposes like the power that is given to one who occupies an official corporate position such as that of director or officer. That is, such power is supposed to be exercised for the benefit of the corporate entity and for all its shareholders, rather than for the exclusive or disproportionate benefit of the holder of the power. (Recall that Justice Traynor spoke in similar terms in the *Ahmanson* case.) The Berle theory thus seeks to generalize the imposition of fiduciary responsibilities that clearly lie on named corporate officers and directors to all holders of control over corporate activities.

Possible implications

One possible implication of this theory is that when control is transferred, as in the sale of a controlling block of stock, the transferor should not receive any payment *for* the giving up of control. Rather, he should only be paid for giving up his claim as equity holder in the net worth of the company. Alternatively, the theory might mean that if a transferor for control is paid for giving up control, the amount received must be shared pro rata with all stockholders. The first possible implication seems to some people to lead to an unenforceable rule. The second implication seems to other observers to create a conceptual puzzle. If an outsider pays a premium for control, doesn't he then own it so that when *he* later sells it he may do so without sharing the proceeds? In fact, though, the Berle theory can lead to an implementable rule. For example, courts could rule that sellers of a control block may never sell at a price significantly higher than that available to minority stockholders.

Case law reception

Has any case law accepted the theory that control is a corporate asset in the sense described above? Professor Berle thought that *Perlman v. Feldmann* went far toward doing so,[24] and this view was apparently shared by Judge Swan, who dissented in that case. A close reading of Judge Clark's opinion for the court, however, discloses that he nowhere clearly adopted the theory. He does report the *plaintiffs'* contentions in terms showing that they were asking the court to adopt a corporate asset theory, but he does not express agreement with their theory of the case. In fact, his opinion is so rich and open-textured that it can support a wide variety of theories. It has been read by various commentators as

(1) constituting an extension of the looting cases,[25]
(2) involving the sale of a corporate policy or opportunity,[26]
(3) being grounded on the notion that the control premium was a disguised increase in the price of the company's product (a view much like the one I expressed in the section on diversion of collective opportunities),[27] and even
(4) being explainable only on the supposition that judges condemn profiteering activities that threaten a country's voluntary efforts to make itself better able to fight a war perceived as just.[28]

***Green Giant* case**

One of the cases that has explicitly declared that the Berle theory is *not* the law is worthy of note. In *Honigman v. Green Giant Co.*,[29] a successful company had two classes of common that were identical except that the 44 shares of class A possessed voting power and the 428,998 shares of class B did not. The class A stock was owned by Cosgrove, the dominant person in the business, and by his relatives; most of the class B was owned by the public.

[24] Berle, "Control" in Corporate Law, 58 Colum. L. Rev. 1212, 1221 (1958).

[25] Leech, Transactions in Corporate Control, 104 U. Pa. L. Rev. 725, 812-813 (1956).

[26] Bayne, A Philosophy of Corporate Control, 112 U. Pa. L. Rev. 22, 50 (1963).

[27] Andrews, The Stockholder's Right to Equal Opportunity in the Sale of Shares, 78 Harv. L. Rev. 505, 514 (1965).

[28] Deutsch, Perlman v. Feldmann: A Case Study in Corporate Legal History, 8 U. Mich. J.L. Ref. 1 (1974).

[29] 309 F.2d 667 (8th Cir. 1962), cert. denied, 372 U.S. 941 (1963).

A recapitalization plan was proposed, and approved by all of class A and 92.3 percent of class B, whereby the owners of class A would give up most of their voting power to the class B owners, but would get a larger share of the company's equity (and therefore, for example, a larger share of the company's dividends). At the end of 10 years, there would be one class of common stock, with one vote per share; the old class A owners' share of voting power would have gone from 100 percent down to 9.3 percent while their share of the equity would have gone from .01 percent up to 9.3 percent.

Plaintiff, a class B shareholder, attacked the plan and objected to the fact that the class A shareholders were being paid to extend corporate democracy, that is, to transfer voting power. If the control function is a corporate asset, then it would seem, according to plaintiff, that the class A should not be allowed to receive a benefit at the expense of other shareholders for relinquishing or sharing it.

Plaintiff (and Berle) rebuffed

The court found this argument "unrealistic," since it would be "wholly unreasonable" to expect that a recapitalization to extend voting power to all shareholders could be effected without some dilution of the class B's equity. Apparently the court meant that since the class A shareholders elected the directors, and under statutory procedures governing charter amendments no plan of recapitalization changing class B into voting stock could occur without the directors' initiation and approval, it was idle to expect that any such recapitalization would occur unless the class A shareholders were paid for not blocking it. Thus, the court viewed class A's power to block a charter amendment effecting a change in the nature of class B's rights not as a mere de facto power, but as a property right that could rightfully be sold — at least in the factual situation before it.

Factors supporting result

Lest one conclude that it is always and everywhere proper for shareholders to sell voting power or control, however, one must look at the situational factors that led the court to think of the actual recapitalization plan as both fair and desirable. No one was arguing that the class B shareholders didn't know when they became such that they were getting nonvoting stock and that the control was lodged in class A; they had no reasonable expectations of getting voting power without paying for it.

Moreover, the recapitalization plan promised benefits to both the class B public shareholders and the corporation. Stock Exchange rules often forbid listing of nonvoting stock; after the recapitalization Green Giant common could be listed and the shareholders would have a more liquid and efficient market in which to sell their shares. Further, the spreading of voting power among numerous publicly traded shares would mean that the company's managerial displacement mechanisms would be improved; the company would be more easily subject to a takeover if its management underperformed and the stock's market value sank far beneath its potential value.

While not using "displacement mechanism" language, the court was clearly concerned about the effects on shareholder welfare it the successful dominant person in the firm died or retired, while effective control over operations could not easily pass to outsiders over the relatives' opposition. An economist would suggest that the mere existence of a potent displacement mechanism helps to keep share market values up. As for the corporation itself, the existence of publicly traded voting shares would enable it more readily to raise money for expansion — for example, by means of public offerings of its stock on major stock exchanges — and to engage in desirable mergers and acquisitions with other companies. The court was impressed with the fact that the recapitalization did indeed enable the company to effect a merger with another company, immediately after the recapitalization.

Summary

In sum, the court thought the recapitalization opened the door to real benefits for the corporation and the class B shareholders, did not thwart any reasonable expectations of the class B shareholders, and yet might not have occurred if there were a flat rule prohibiting the class A shareholders from charging for their release of voting power. Note, however, that the court *did* perceive the recapitalization as a conflict-of-interest transaction, because only the class A shareholders had elected the directors who proposed the plan. It therefore put the burden of proof on the defendants to show the plan's fairness. Because of the arguments mentioned above, and because of the overwhelming approval given by most class B shareholders, it nevertheless found the plan fair.

§11.4.5 An Equal Opportunity Rule?

Andrews' proposal

Professor Andrews, in a well-known law review article, proposed a rule that

> [W]henever a controlling stockholder sells his shares, every other holder of shares (of the same class)[30] is entitled to have an equal opportunity to sell his shares, or a prorata part of them, on substantially the same terms. Or . . . before a controlling stockholder may sell his shares to an outsider he must

[30] The rule would therefore not disturb the holding of the *Green Giant* case.

> assure his fellow stockholders an equal opportunity to sell their shares, or as high a proportion of theirs as he ultimately sells of his own.[31]

In a sense, the rule would assimilate sales of control blocks to a tender offer for all shares of a target, where equal treatment is the norm.

Arguments pro

Among the main arguments for the equal opportunity rule are that it would have a beneficial impact on cases involving diversions of collective opportunities and on those involving sales to looters. In cases like *Brown v. Halbert*, the rule would make it easier for plaintiffs to prove and win their case, and this reduction of enforcement costs would help deter the kind of conduct condemned in that case. As for sales to looters, the equal opportunity rule would tend to have an automatic screening effect.

Distinguish two reasons for premiums

To understand the last point, consider two major reasons why a third party would be willing to pay a premium over the current market price of a company's shares to get a controlling number of those shares. One reason is to *enhance the company's value:* If the buyer thinks well of his own abilities, he may think that having control over the company's management will enable him to run the company more profitably or at least to assure that he will be able to correct any future underperformance by key employees. He will therefore be willing to pay a premium for control. The other reason is to *obtain some nonshareholder relationship* with the company: If the buyer has control, he can force the company to deal with himself or his affiliated businesses, rather than with others, when the company needs to get itself a supplier, lender, chief executive, consultant, major customer, or the like. If he expects these nonshareholder relationships to be lucrative, he will be willing to pay a premium for control.

Problems with second kind

Now, a little thought will show that paying something to assure a nonshareholder relationship with the corporation can be a perfectly good thing but that making the payment by means of a control premium for a block of stock is an indirect and suspect way of doing it. If Manufacturing Co. wants to beat out its competitors in the struggle to secure scarce materials from The Raw Materials Corp., it can simply bid a higher price for the materials and thereby become the favored customer. If Able wants to secure the position of chief executive officer at The Raw Materials Corp., he can win over his rivals by making more subtle forms of higher bids and payments — working harder and better, demanding somewhat less compensation, and so forth. If First Bank wants to secure the relationship of

[31] Andrews, note 27 supra, at 515.

lender to The Raw Materials Corp., it can outbid its rivals by asking a lower interest rate for loans.

Why should Manufacturing Co., Able, or First Bank ever try to achieve their ends, not by competitive bidding, but by buying a controlling block of stock and thus becoming able to *force* The Raw Materials Corp. to enter the desired relationship? One obvious answer is that, with control, the potential customer, executive, or lender can have the company enter the relationship on terms that are more favorable to the controlling person than those it could get by arm's-length bargaining in a competitive market. That is, the controlling party will be able to engage in unfair self-dealing (alias looting, construed broadly). This is profitable to the controlling person, as we have often noted in this book, whenever he owns less equity in the entity treated unfairly than in the other party to the relationship.

Entrepreneur vs. looter

Note, then, the following disparity in the positions of a control buyer who seeks only to enhance the company's value (the bold entrepreneur) and a control buyer who wants to engage in unfair self-dealing (the looter). The bold entrepreneur has no reason, if he can get financing to do so, not to want to buy *all* of the company's stock at the same premium price he is willing to pay for the controlling block. If he thinks that after getting control he can run the company so much more profitably that it will have a net increase in investment value of $20 per share, and yet he can acquire stock by payment of only a $14 per share premium over market price, he will expect a profit of $6 per share for each and every additional share he buys at the $14 premium, not just for the controlling shares.

By hypothesis, the bold entrepreneur thinks he has found a true bargain, a risk-adjusted rate of return superior to that which he could get as a purely passive investor in the capital markets. One would therefore expect him to be eager to buy as much of this bargain as he could. On the other hand, the looter has exactly the opposite preference. He wants to buy the smallest amount of stock that will nevertheless enable him to gain control — say, 51 percent, or whatever amount the present controlling person owns and insists on selling to him. To the extent he buys more than this minimum amount, his later looting gains will come unnecessarily out of his own pocket.

Relevant to proposed rule

What is the relevance of these observations to the equal opportunity rule? The rule naturally tends to discourage the looter without discouraging the bold entrepreneur, because in practice it will pressure, although not require, the control buyer to buy all of the corporation's shares. Under the equal opportunity rule, if the seller of controlling shares is selling 70 percent of his stock, the other shareholders need to be given only an opportunity to sell 70 percent of their stock at the same price. In fact, of course, sellers of control, such as the company founder who now wants to retire, often insist that the buyer take all of their stock interests. Under the equal opportunity rule, the minority shareholders would then have to be given an opportunity to sell all of their stock at the same price.

"Financing problems" objection

Three main objections have been raised against the equal opportunity rule. First, even the control buyer who wants only to enhance the company's value may find it impossible to *finance* the acquisition of all of the company's stock, so the equal opportunity rule may thwart some perfectly good sales of control.[32] How important this financing problem actually would be is an empirical question to which no one has a definitive answer. It should be noted, though, that the objection assumes imperfections in the capital markets — the bold entrepreneur will somehow be unable to find other lenders or co-investors and convince them of the potential value he has discovered — and econometric work on the efficiency of the capital markets makes it implausible to assume that such imperfections are systematically very large, at least for companies operating in regional and national markets.

Diversification objection

Second, the pressure to buy all of a particular company may impede control buyers' efforts to achieve optimal *diversification* of their own investment interests.[33] This objection really builds and depends on the first, for if the potential buyer can find co-investors to join with him when he doesn't want to use all of his fixed capital for one investment, the problem disappears.

Direct regulation alternative

Third, it could also be objected that the equal opportunity rule doesn't do anything *directly* to prevent looting, and therefore may be an inferior way of dealing with the problem. If possible unfair self-dealing in the future is the problem, if it doesn't necessarily follow all shifts in control, and if it may very well occur in the future even when there is no shift in control, why fiddle with rules governing control shifts? Why not design better rules about self-dealing (see my recommendations in chapter 5, for example), and design better monitoring and enforcement mechanisms for these rules?

An answer to these questions might be that, if the equal opportunity rule imposes few significant costs (such as the alleged cost to financing and diversification efforts), then it may wisely be added to the complex of rules designed to control unfair self-dealing directly. Conceivably, even though the rule is an indirect control mechanism, it may achieve more bang for the

[32] Javares, Equal Opportunity in the Sale of Controlling Shares: A Reply to Professor Andrews, 32 U. Chi. L. Rev. 420, 425-426 (1965).

[33] Id. at 426.

buck than direct ones. And in an uncertain world, where control mechanisms of any particular sort may not in fact be maintained or implemented properly, it seems prudent to have a diversified mix of them.[34]

[34] One objection students sometimes raise to allowing sellers to get any control premiums, after hearing about the distinction between enhancement of company value and linking up to nonshareholder relationships, is that if a "good" control buyer (a bold entrepreneur) is willing to pay a premium over the current market price, the implication must be that the incumbent controlling persons have failed to maximize the value of the company, and so they don't seem to *deserve* to get a control premium. Allowing them to get one seems to amount to rewarding persons who were either negligent, incompetent or dishonest.

But this view is too harsh. A buyer in a sale-of-control situation may foresee a later increase in the company's investment value under his own management, not because the incumbents were bad or incompetent in the use of resources available to them, but simply because he has resources that, when injected into or combined with those of the company, may produce previously unavailable synergistic gains. This is especially likely when the buyer is another corporation which has complementary resources. Furthermore, one should not forget that the buyer's willingness to pay a premium represents a gamble on his part, a subjective estimate that he can do better, and in many cases he may well be wrong.

CHAPTER 12

CONTROL SHIFTS AND INSIDER IMPERIALISM: FREEZEOUTS AND BUYOUTS

§12.1 Introduction

In this section I define freezeouts and similar transactions and describe some techniques for accomplishing them. Subsequent sections discuss the alleged merits and demerits of these transactions (section 12.2) and legal developments affecting them (sections 12.3 and 12.4).

Freezeouts

Freezeouts are transactions in which those in control of a corporation use their control to force noncontrolling shareholders to lose their status as shareholders with any equity interest in the business operations of that corporation. Freezeouts occur when the insiders force the noncontrolling shareholders to sell their shares or otherwise disinvest. The net effect of most freezeouts, if they survive litigation arising out of them, is to treat common shareholders as if they had been holding redeemable preferred stock without knowing it. (Common stockholders generally expect that they themselves have the power to decide when to sell their stock; the holder of redeemable preferred knows that his investment can be bought out by the issuing corporation at its option.)

Squeezeouts

The term *squeezeouts* is sometimes used interchangeably with *freezeouts,* but may have a different connotation: a transaction or set of transactions that does not coerce the noncontrolling shareholder in any formal legal sense, but that has the purpose and practical effect of making his situation so unrewarding that he is virtually disinvested or so unpleasant that he will inevitably sell out on the insider's terms.

Going private

The term *going private* refers to the process of changing a publicly held corporation into a closely held corporation. This occurs when the corporation's stock ceases to be registered under the Securities Exchange Act, listed on a stock exchange, or actively traded on the over-the-counter market. Going private may be accomplished by a freezeout of public shareholders. But freezeouts of noncontrolling shareholders do not necessarily result in a public company's becoming a close corporation, and freezeouts may occur in companies that are already closely held. Furthermore, while some going private transactions are formally coercive — the noncontrolling shareholders who object to the transaction lack voting power or legal ability to refuse it — other going private transactions are, at least in their early stages, only coercive in a practical sense.

Management and leveraged buyouts

The term *management buyout* refers to transactions whereby a group of executives acquire all or a dominant equity interest in a corporation. It might refer to a case where the company is going from public to private status, but it need not. Some management buyouts arise when a subgroup of executives in a large conglomerate buy one subsidiary that the conglomerate's top managers want to sell. Many management buyouts are also *leveraged buyouts,* that is, a large part of the funds used to buy the company in question is borrowed, usually from a consortium of institutional investors put together by one of the investment banking firms specializing in such buyouts. The borrowed funds are often paid out of subsequent earnings of the company.

Early techniques: dissolution

In the past, controlling persons have tried a variety of freezeout techniques. Suppose Ebenezer owns 60 percent of Scrooge Trading Company and wants to kick out the minority shareholders at a price Ebenezer has set. A few decades ago he might have tried working with the statutory provisions on corporate dissolutions, sales of assets, or mergers. In a dissolution freezeout, Ebenezer would cause the trading company to adopt and carry out a plan of dissolution under which he would receive, in the corporation's final distribution, the productive assets of the company — that is, the real heart of the business enterprise, which he would continue to operate — while the minority shareholders would receive cash or notes. Courts tended to find that such plans ran afoul of norms of equal treatment.[1]

Sale of assets

In a sale-of-assets freezeout, Ebenezer would first organize a corporation — call it Quickie Corp — and become its sole shareholder. He would then cause Scrooge Trading Company to sell its assets to Quickie Corp for cash or notes. If cash were used, it might be contributed to Quickie Corp by Ebenezer from his own resources or from funds borrowed for the purpose. In either case, Ebenezer could get 60 percent of the money back very promptly by dissolving the trading company after it sells all its assets. Scrooge Trading might thus be liquidated. Whether or not it is, Ebenezer now owns a 100 percent equity interest in the old and continuing *business* that was previously operated by Scrooge Trading. Courts were inclined to disapprove such transactions, however.[2]

Redeemable preferred

In a freezeout using an exchange in a merger of stock for debt or redeemable preferred stock, Ebenezer would again start by forming a shell corporation, Quickie Corp, of which he would be sole shareholder. He would then cause Scrooge Trading to merge into Quickie Corp, in a plan under which Scrooge Trading's shareholders would exchange their shares for short-term debentures or redeemable preferred stock issued by Quickie Corp. After a certain period of time, the debentures would be paid off or the preferred stock redeemed. In other words, the minority shareholders would be cashed out over a somewhat longer period of time than in the other two variations. In one well-known case, *Matteson v. Ziebarth,*[3] a deal of this kind was held to be attackable only by resort to the appraisal remedy (which plaintiff had failed to pursue), but the opinion of the court showed that it was heavily influenced by the fact that the freezeout seemed to be in aid of a substantial business purpose.

Modern techniques: (1) cash merger

The use of redeemable preferred stock or debt securities was necessary for a freezeout by merger around the time of the *Matteson* case because merger statutes then did not always provide, as they now usually do, for

§12.1 [1]Mason v. Pewabic Mining Co., 133 U.S. 50 (1890); Kellogg v. Georgia-Pacific Paper Co., 227 F. Supp. 719 (W.D. Ark. 1964); Zimmerman v. Tide Water Associated Oil Co., 143 P.2d 409 (Cal. App. 1943). But see Rossing v. State Bank of Bode, 165 N.W. 254 (Iowa 1917).

[2]Cathedral Estates, Inc. v. Taft Realty Corp., 157 F. Supp. 895 (D. Conn. 1954), aff'd, 251 F.2d 340 (2d Cir. 1957); Cardiff v. Johnson, 218 P. 269 (Wash. 1923). But see Alcott v. Hyman, 208 A.2d 501 (Del. 1965).

[3]242 P.2d 1025 (Wash. 1952).

cash mergers.[4] Nowadays Ebenezer would skip the rigamarole of the debt securities or preferred stock and simply effect a cash merger of Scrooge Trading into Quickie Corp. Use of this technique is now common.

(2) Short-form merger

A second modern freezeout technique is to use a short-form merger statute where one is applicable. If 90 percent or more of Scrooge Trading's stock were owned by Wealth Maximizing Corp., for example, the latter's board of directors might be able to adopt and effectuate a parent-subsidiary merger in which the minority shareholders of the subsidiary were paid off in cash. Here, it could sensibly be argued that the short-form merger statutes were designed precisely to facilitate and encourage elimination of a generally undesirable relationship — that between parent and partly owned subsidiary.[5] It is less plausible to argue, however, that this elimination must be accomplished under a plan whereby the minority shareholders are cashed out rather than given stock in the parent. (Note that even when there is no pre-existing parent company, controlling shareholders like Ebenezer might pool their stock, put it into a newly formed corporation that would thereby become a holding company, and then, if the holding company has held a large enough percentage of shares, effect a short-form cash merger of the original corporation into the holding company.)

(3) Reverse stock split

A third modern freezeout technique is the reverse stock split. Since a corporation may occasionally find it sensible for legitimate reasons to change the numbering system for investor units in itself, business corporation statutes allow corporate charters to be amended so that all outstanding stock of a certain class is divided into some larger number of new shares (a stock split), or so that each x number of shares already held by a shareholder is consolidated into one new share (reverse stock split). The latter procedure will often result in some shareholders being entitled to a fraction of a new share. For example, if the recapitalization plan provides for each two existing common shares to be converted into one new common share, a stockholder owning an odd lot of 25 shares will find himself entitled to 12-1/2 new shares. Because of the inconvenience of keeping track of fractional shares, however, statutes frequently provide that the plan can provide for payment by the corporation of cash in lieu of fractional shares. Thus, our odd-lot shareholder might actually be entitled to get 12 new shares and $6 in cash, the latter figure being, let us say, half of the current market price of one existing share.

[4] See subsection 10.2.4 and section 10.4 supra.

[5] See section 7.8 supra.

Misuse of fractional shares proviso

But what, you may ask, does all this have to do with freezeouts? The answer is that some corporate insiders who are not at all interested in effecting a change in the numbering system of the corporation's investor units for the usual business reasons have tried to take advantage of the "cash in lieu of fractional shares" provisions to effect freezeouts. Suppose, for example, that Ebenezer's 60 percent interest in Scrooge Trading consisted of 60,000 common shares, and that the 40,000 other common shares were held in variously sized blocks by 400 shareholders. Ebenezer might cause the corporation to adopt by charter amendment a reverse stock split plan under which "every shareholder will receive one new share for each 60,000 shares he already owns, but $9 in cash for every fraction of a new share to which he would otherwise be entitled." Under this plan, Ebenezer gets one share — which is the only one issued — and the other shareholders are cashed out at $9 a share. In effect, Ebenezer has used his ability to control transactions under the organic change provisions of the statute to force the other shareholders to sell their stock to the company, at a price Ebenezer names, with the result that he becomes 100 percent owner.

Variations

In addition to the three pure versions of modern techniques for accomplishing freezeouts, there are various combinations and extensions. For example, the insiders may cause the corporation to make a tender offer to repurchase its own shares, accompanied by a thinly veiled threat that the corporation will later use a cash merger to "mop up" the shareholders who don't tender. The shareholders have therefore been presented with a choice: "Voluntarily" sell your shares to us now, at our price, or find yourself forced to sell them later at our later-named price. This pattern was found in some of the going private transactions of the mid-1970s. Voluntary going private transactions like share-repurchase offers also tended to be accompanied by other kinds of threats, which were usually presented quite clearly in the corporation's disclosures of possible effects of the transaction that shareholders ought to know about. These disclosures might point out, for example, that if enough shareholders accepted the repurchase offer, the company might cease to be subject to SEC disclosure and reporting requirements, so that important sources of information to remaining shareholders would dry up. They might also point out that if enough shareholders were to accept the offer, the company's shares would cease to be listed on a stock exchange or traded over the counter, so that the remaining shareholders' investment would become quite illiquid.

The fate of attempted freezeouts using the modern techniques will be examined in sections 12.3 and 12.4.

What are the motives behind freezeouts? These vary greatly, but the not unreasonable fear that courts have is that the insiders may simply be trying to buy out other shareholders at a cheap price. Before drawing any sweeping conclusions about freezeouts, however, it is important to examine what their possible harms and benefits might be.

§12.2 The Rationale of Judicial Regulation

§12.2.1 Harms

Market price sole touchstone?

Most freezeouts involving public corporations occur at a price that is at or above the current market price of the publicly held shares. Suppose, for example, that Jacob is a minority stockholder of Scrooge Trading and the latter's stock is selling at $12. Ebenezer tries to freeze out Jacob and the others at $14. The $2 premium may suggest that the deal poses no serious problems. Isn't the sole real objection to freezeouts that the freezees will not be paid enough money? If the freezees receive more than the current market price and the market is reasonably thick rather than thin, won't they be paid enough to make the deal fair? What else is there to worry about? Don't the freezees lack a basis for claiming they have been harmed?

Possible harms

The "no problem" argument overlooks at least five ways in which freezees may be harmed by a freezeout. The first, second, and third are harms usually restricted to freezeout transactions. The fourth and fifth not only represent more serious problems, but are also harms that may attend insider-controlled organic changes in which the outsiders are not cashed out — such as a parent-subsidiary merger in which the minority shareholders are given stock in the parent.

(1) Tax burden

The first possible harm is one that occurs frequently in freezeouts: the freezeout may force the freezees to bear a significant tax burden. If Jacob bought his stock long ago at $4, he will have $10 per share of taxable capital gain income when he is cashed out. By contrast, if Jacob were to receive new stock for his old stock in an insider-controlled merger it is quite possible that no tax liability would have been triggered. If Jacob had been able to pick the time of selling or otherwise disposing of his shares — and as owner, he probably expected that he would be able to do so — he might very well have improved his position. He could have waited until he was in a lower tax bracket. He could have kept the stock until his death, at which time it would obtain a stepped-up basis and could have been sold by his heirs free of any income tax burden, or he could have simply deferred the income tax burden until such time as he needed the income from the sale of the stock or could offset a capital loss against a capital gain. Even deferral by itself has substantial value: Other things being equal, it is always better to pay $1 of tax several years in the future than to pay it now. The government's allowing one to have that option is equivalent to its making an interest-free loan. The freezeout forecloses Jacob from making any of these potentially desirable decisions. It should be noted, however, that in most freezeouts and management buyouts reported in the financial press the premiums paid are large enough that the vast majority of freezees are probably well compensated for the value of their lost tax-planning flexibility.

(2) Reinvestment costs

A second harm is that the freezeout forces Jacob, if he still wants to be invested at the same level he previously was, to incur reinvestment costs. He must spend some of his valuable time and pay his broker a fee to find and acquire another investment or investments that suit his particular portfolio and preferences. The costs to all the freezees of reinvesting may be significant in the aggregate. Once again, though, the typical freezeout premium seems large enough to cover these costs as well as the tax-related ones.

(3) Defeated expectations

A third arguable harm is that a freezeout may frustrate the expectations of those investors who, regardless of the freezeout price (within limits, of course), want to remain investors of *the* particular enterprise from which they are being excluded. Such investors are likely to say, "I don't care if the freezeout price is fair. I want to continue to be a stockholder of Scrooge Trading. Being a stockholder in some other company will not be an adequate substitute for me. And you should not have any right to force me out."

One's first response to this line of argument might be to say that the objector is just being irrational, or perhaps overly sentimental in an arena of life where sentiment is strangely out of place. But a little thought will show that this response is too facile. Some investors may be strongly attached to the particular corporation for a variety of perfectly legitimate reasons. They may have exceptional faith in the business acumen (if not the business morals) of the management. They may believe that the company owns a product or operates in an industry that the market systematically undervalues but that will eventually come into its own. Or they may simply like to think of themselves as investors in that company. Put another way, there may be some investors in a company who place a very high value on their investment — a value that is not likely to be matched by any normal freezeout price, even a price including a hefty premium over current market price.

Based on option to sell

There need be nothing abnormal about this. Every economist recognizes, for example, that if Scrooge Trading's stock is selling for $12 on the market, then those shareholders who are holding the stock rather than selling it must have assigned it a value to themselves of $12 *or more*. There is little reason to think that the range of valuations made by these holders is very narrow. If the market price were increased to $13, then, in the usual case, some but by no means all of the holders would sell. The distribution of holders' valuations of the stock is likely to be spread upward over a significant range — like half of a bell-shaped curve in a statistics book, perhaps — and there will be some statistical "outliers" who are not prepared to sell voluntarily unless the premium over current market price becomes very large — larger than the premium likely to be offered in a freezeout situation. Whatever other observers might think of the validity of the reasons for these "outlier" persons to place a high value on the shares, they might agree that each shareholder has the right to *choose his own reasons* for selling or holding and should usually have the right to decide on which terms he will sell. In any event, the courts have occasionally acknowledged that the stockholder's desire to remain invested in a particular company is a legitimate interest entitled to some legal protection.[1]

Circularity problem

The real problem with the defeated-expectations argument is not investor irrationality but long-run circularity. Remember that the common stockholder's right to decide whether and on what terms to dispose of his shares has been less than absolute for a very long time. In an ordinary merger, for example, a dissenting shareholder has to go along with the transaction or seek appraisal; he can't enjoin the merger so that he can continue being a shareholder in the same, unchanged company until he chooses to sell. This restraint on freedom is desirable because it allows transactions to go forward that the majority thinks are value-creating; the dissenter can only insist on fair compensation. Since everyone knows that these are the basic rules of the road, the dissenter can't raise a defeated-expectations argument.

Transition problem

Similarly, once the power of a controlling group to freeze out other shareholders becomes clearly established by case law or statute and the governing rules become widely known, shareholders can't raise the defeated-expectations argument anymore. To be sure, while the legal rules are changing or developing, there may be all sorts of unfair surprises that should somehow be taken into account. (Perhaps, for example, courts might not countenance new waves of insider-initiated transactions that defeat the likely expectations and assumptions of most public shareholders. This would remit insiders to state legislatures, where they could lobby

§12.2 [1]E.g., Singer v. Magnavox, 380 A.2d 969, 977-978 (Del. 1977).

for prospective rule changes that would permit the new transactions they have in mind.) But what expectations the legal rules *should* generate is the ultimate question for lawmakers.

(4) Loss from impacted information

The fourth harm is that, because of information and insight not communicated to the market and reflected in stock prices, the freezeout may deprive the freezees of part of the true investment value of their shares. Two factors conspire to make this possible: The insiders rather than the freezees control the *timing* of the transaction, and they may temporarily have more *insight* than the market has into the company's future prospects. Suppose the law were such that over a ten-year period Ebenezer continually has the de facto option of freezing out the other shareholders, so long as he pays $2 a share more than the current market price of Scrooge Trading stock just before announcement of the freezeout. Suppose further that, because of his fiduciary position in the company, Ebenezer is occasionally able to forecast with considerable confidence that the company's future earnings will be significantly smaller or larger than the stock's current market price implicitly indicates. If Ebenezer is as thoroughly mastered by the love of gain as was his Dickensian namesake (before his Yuletide conversion) and is also unmindful of his fiduciary obligations to his fellow shareholders, at what time is he likely to stage a freezeout? The answer is clear: when he knows that the company is really worth more than its current market price. The other shareholders may argue that they have a right to be free from such one-sided decision making so long as they have not sold Ebenezer an explicit option to purchase their shares. More to the point, from the lawmaker's perspective, they can plausibly claim that the insider's option is not the sort of arrangement that investors and managers would agree to in a hypothetical ideal bargaining session that aims to set out all the standard or presumptive rules to govern their relationship. Investors in the original position would likely insist that such options be bargained for explicitly in each individual case or, at the least, that the rules regulating minimum freezeout prices be strict.

Inadequacy of insider-trading remedy

Two objections may be raised against the importance of the fourth possible harm. One is that, if the pre-freezeout market price of the company's stock is distorted because of suppressed inside information, the freezees can simply bring a lawsuit under Rule 10b-5. But this objection misses the point. A successful 10b-5 suit presupposes the insider had access to definite bits of information of fairly obvious importance. He knows of an ore discovery, a forthcoming merger, the disastrous results of the current quarter, a new product, or some other discrete chunk of nonpublic news. The premise of my argument here is that insiders occasionally have insight into their companies' futures that is better than the market's because of continual exposure to numerous bits and pieces of information and opinion that come their way by virtue of their being in their official positions and that have value as a totality. This total picture is based in part on numerous small items that, individually considered, are not important enough to be labelled material and that never get communicated to market analysts because of the cost of formulating and transmitting them. Consequently, it is important to consider the possible misuse of managers' temporarily superior insight, and not to restrict one's thinking to the conventional category of "suppressed inside information." If superior insight is, as I suspect, an important factor in many buyouts and freezeout transactions, then lawmakers might tailor rules accordingly — for example, by insisting on a detailed, independent investigation into the value of a firm that is being taken private, and not relying heavily on market prices.[2]

Inadequacy of appraisal

A second objection is that any mismatch between true investment value and market price can be handled in an appraisal proceeding. But this objection neglects the fact that appraisal is often a cumbersome remedy. It looks only to pre-transaction values, and in practice courts may exclude special evidence that future earnings will be different from those of the past. It may not allow or require the amount of detailed investigation into the facts that is warranted by the acute conflict of interest and the potential for investor harm that is inherent in freezeout transactions. Historically, an appraisal proceeding was based on the assumption of a dissenter who doesn't want to be forced to continue his investment in a substantially changed enterprise — exactly the opposite of the position of a minority shareholder who objects to a freezeout.

(5) Loss from self-dealing

A fifth possible harm is that a freezeout may deprive the freezees of the true investment value of their shares because the market price reflects a substantial discount for the negative value of past and (expected) future self-dealing by the controlling parties. Some commentators refer to this as "control overhang" and urge it as a reason why (1) courts should not rely heavily on pre-freezeout market price as an indicator of what a fair freezeout price would be, and (2) courts should even adjust detailed independent

[2] Of course, some may argue that insider trading is a good thing because of its incentive effects on managers and that the same conclusion holds a fortiori for managers' buyouts based on positionally superior insight. But this point implicates the whole set of arguments for and against regulating insider trading. These arguments were discussed in sections 8.2 through 8.4 supra.

valuations of the company that have not added in something to compensate for control overhang.[3]

Separate problem objection

Here again it can be objected that the problem, if it exists, can be analyzed and treated separately from the freezeout context. If the controlling parties have in fact taken specific improper actions in the past that have depressed the company's market price, then the public shareholders can institute a suit for breach of fiduciary duty, invoking whichever of the numerous traditional duties and doctrines are applicable. If the controlling persons usurped a corporate opportunity, improperly altered dividend policy, or engaged in unfair basic self-dealing transactions prior to the freezeout attempt,[4] these actions can all be remedied directly.

Response

While this objection has force, it does not offer a reason why the claims of past self-dealing and breach of duty should not be handled in the same lawsuit that determines the acceptability of the freezeout price. Indeed, combining the investigations will economize on the use of judicial and lawyerly resources. Moreover, it seems reasonable to argue that the very *possibility* of past overreaching, together with the possibility of insider trading on positionally superior insight, justifies courts in making an independent valuation of the company involved in the freezeout. What remains of the objection, then, is simply an insistence that courts should not simply presume that past overreaching has actually occurred and make an arbitrary, compensating addition to the value of the company as it is otherwise assessed. Rather, they should make actual findings of past misconduct before boosting the firm's appraised value as a remedy.

Assessing market-anticipated self-dealing

The possibility that the company's stock price was depressed because the market anticipated that the controlling parties would engage in future self-dealing (perhaps in a freezeout!) is one that is hard to assess and put to use. It seems only to bolster the conclusion, which as we've seen is supported by other considerations, that the court should not accept market price as the litmus test of value, but should consider detailed independent valuations.

[3]See V. Brudney & M. Chirelstein, Corporate Finance 689-691 (2d ed. 1979).

[4]Some litigated freezeout cases do raise these issues. See, e.g., Berkowitz v. Power/Mate Corp., 342 A.2d 566 (N.J. Ch. 1975), where a temporary injunction was issued against a freezeout merger, despite an above-market freezeout price, partly because there were indications of premerger self-dealing transactions (such as large bonuses to the principal officers). In close corporation cases involving freezeout tactics other than merger, a more direct remedy against self-dealing behavior may be more likely. See, e.g., Corbin v. Corbin, 429 F. Supp. 276 (M.D. Ga. 1977).

§12.2.2 Benefits

So far we have been stressing the seamy side of freezeouts. Is there a positive side? Can proponents argue convincingly that these transactions do something more than redistribute wealth and power? That they can actually lead to increases in total social welfare?

Possible synergies, sometimes

When a freezeout involves a merger or combination of two real businesses, of course, then any of the usual benefits from corporate combinations may be the expected result. These benefits include possible economies of scale in financing, management, marketing, or production; complementary uses of resources; and so forth. Even here it may be doubted that the benefits *depend* on the freezeout of shareholders, as opposed to an ordinary merger. But where the existence of benefits meets with greatest skepticism is in the case of going private transactions and management buyouts where no combination of real business operations is about to occur.

Costs of being public

One early reason urged as a justification for going private was that it saved the costs of operating as a public company. These costs include the attorney's and accountants' fees and related costs involved in preparing and filing periodic reports with the SEC, as well as the expenditures made to prepare and distribute annual reports. Some commentators and observers treated this justification with severe skepticism, since it seemed that, in cases involving any but the smaller public companies, the discounted present value of these savings was apt to be equalled or exceeded by the sizable costs of the going private transaction itself.

Helpful secrecy

Another alleged benefit is that a private company is better able to keep its plans and finances secret from its rivals, and this secrecy enables it to compete more effectively. How important this possibility is — how much the extra secrecy really increases profitability — is hard to assess.

Reduction of "agency" costs

A third possibility is the most significant: the reduction of "agency" costs. This benefit includes two related subparts, an improvement in incentives and a reduction in monitoring costs. In a privately held company, the usual diversity of interests is reduced. Top management and the shareholders consist largely of the same persons. Managers are now working much more for themselves. They therefore work harder, and the business may be run more efficiently and become more valuable. (True, they had a duty of care before going private, but adherence to this duty simply does not produce the driven entrepreneurial activity of the person who runs his or her own business.) Furthermore, the fact that there is no separate group of public investors who have to monitor what the managers do, and no group of minority shareholders that has to monitor what the controlling shareholders are doing, means that over time many costs are saved. These include not only the costs incurred by outside investors and their advisers in evaluating financial and other reports about the company ("monitoring" costs in the narrow sense), but also the occasional, dramatic costs of derivative lawsuits and proxy fights.

Qualification

Of course, the controlling persons in a private company do have to monitor each other. And the history of the law concerning close corporations[5] doesn't at all suggest that they will be immune from disputes and bitter litigation. The hope is that there will be a net reduction in total agency costs.

Application to LBOs

Note that in the typical modern leveraged buyout (LBO) of public investors, several classes of investors have claims on the resulting company. A consortium of banks may own a large amount of senior debt; a group of pension plans or wealthy individuals may own subordinated but high-yielding debt (called "junk bonds" by detractors of LBOs); the LBO promoter and some of its more adventuresome clients may own preferred stock and some of the common; and the managers may own a large but not controlling percentage of the common. (Also, some of the investors may possess interests in more than one of these "strips" of financing.) But despite the existence of all these nonmanagement investors there may be net gains in monitoring efficiency, as compared to a public company, because the outside investors are relatively small in number and are sophisticated, and they possess powerful means of controlling wayward managers.

Though businesspersons don't usually couch their reasons in terms of "agency costs" jargon, they do frequently point to particular examples of alleged benefits from going private that fall into this category. There is no a priori reason to doubt that these kinds of benefits might be real and significant. How frequent and quantitatively important these benefits are is an empirical question that at present has no well-grounded answer.

Incidental benefits

Businesspersons also adduce benefits of going private transactions that can be described as "incidental," that is, the benefits are of the sort that might indeed flow from the transaction but could also be achieved in other ways that do not involve cashing out all the public shareholders. For example, it is often pointed out that a buyout gets the fruits of the company's enterprise into investor hands in a way that triggers a capital gains tax rather than a (higher) ordinary income tax, as a large dividend would. But an occasional, genuinely voluntary repurchase offer will often achieve the same result, and in many cases reinvestment of company earnings is even better for company and stockholders. In LBOs a major claim is that, be-

[5]See chapter 18 infra.

cause the company is borrowing so much, it will get the tax benefits of increased leverage. But leverage can be increased without going private or letting managers become dominant shareholders. The company could simply borrow more money and use it to finance either expansion or a truly voluntary stock repurchase offer.

§12.2.3 Nonlegal Controls

Rival bids as safeguard

An argument sometimes made against serious legal regulation of going-private transactions is that if the proposed freezeout price is too low, other companies and investors will spot the opportunity to offer the shareholders more money and still come out with a bargain investment. Bidding will therefore drive the price up toward where it should be. Indeed, management buyout proposals do sometimes provoke rival bids. There is no doubt that the process occurs and can be important.

Not always available or adequate

The bidding mechanism suffers from two serious limitations, however. First, it is not available in the many cases where the group wishing to effect a freezeout already controls a majority of the stock. As a control mechanism, rival bids seem restricted to management buyouts; they don't touch most freezeout mergers involving parents and subsidiaries. Second, to the extent that the initiators of the freezeout or going-private transaction do have positionally superior insight about the future prospects of their company, they have an advantage in the bidding process. A rival does not know how much it can safely bid above the last bid of the insiders. If it overbids, it may win but turn out to have made a bad investment. This means that rival bidding will be an imperfect control mechanism. (Whether we can reasonably expect legal controls to do better is another question, of course, and its answer is not obvious.) It should also be noted that promoters of some LBOs have tried to block effective rival bidding by such practices as giving "lockup options" (discussed below in section 13.6.1) to the management-affiliated group.

Other safeguards

In many well-advised LBOs the management group is careful to have the proposed deal assessed for fairness by both the independent directors and by an independent investment banking firm. How good these safeguards are is a debatable question.

§12.2.4 Summary of Harms and Benefits

So far we have seen that even freezeouts at a premium price may impose costs and harms on noncontrolling investors. These costs include loss of tax planning flexibility, reinvestment (or capital reaggregation) costs, defeat of reasonable expectations about one's rights (at least in those transitional periods when the legal right to effect freezeouts is not clearly established, defined, and publicized), and deprivation of investment values because market prices are depressed by self-dealing or don't reflect insiders' positionally superior insight into the company's future. This recitation may suggest either that freezeouts are too dangerous and should be prohibited, or that the law should insure that the freezeout premium is large enough to compensate for all the costs. The latter alternative seems the better one in light of the possible benefits: the usual benefits of corporate combinations in some freezeout cases, the reduction of agency costs in going private cases, the transaction cost savings of not operating as a public company subject to special regulation, the possible benefits of more secret operations, and various incidental benefits. How important each of the possible harms and benefits are in the real world is a difficult empirical question. Uncertainty over the aggregate net effects of these transactions suggests we should avoid extreme rules — like a rule forbidding all freezeouts or a rule permitting all of them so long as they are effectuated at the stock's market price or better.

Avoid extreme rules?

§12.2.5 Self-Dealing Analysis

Review of self-dealing analysis

It may now be useful to analyze the problem within a broader framework. Freezeouts often fall within our first category of conflict-of-interest transactions, basic self-dealing. (See section 4.1.) The three defining elements are present. (1) There is a transaction between referent persons — the noncontrolling stockholders — and other persons. (2) Certain controlling persons (corporate managers and majority shareholders) have decision making power or influence and thus set the timing and terms of the deal unilaterally, or virtually so. (3) The controlling persons have an interest adverse to that of the referent persons. My argument in chapter 5, you will recall, was that, because of the uneliminable risk that unfairness might occur and go undetected and/or uncorrected, basic self-dealing transactions of the sort there analyzed should be flatly prohibited, *unless* the controlling persons can show (a) that the transaction would produce a self-dealing surplus — a unique advantage not obtainable by an other-dealing or market transaction — and (b) that the vulnerable entity or persons would share in it, that is, would receive some compensation for being made by their fiduciaries to bear the risk of undetected and uncorrected unfairness.

This argument can now be applied to freezeout transactions. Indeed, because freezeouts pose several significant risks that are not usually presented by ordinary self-dealing between an officer and his company, the case for going beyond the business judgment rule and even the fairness test is stronger in this context.

Comparison to courts' approach

Have the courts done so? Not exactly. They have generally put aside the business judgment rule in favor of a stricter fairness test. They have not, however, enunciated a "more-than-fair-plus-sharing" test. Interestingly, in 1977 the Delaware Supreme Court adopted an approach, which it followed until 1983, that is similar in spirit to the one suggested in chapter 5. Under this approach, a freezeout merger was valid only if it could be shown to have a corporate business purpose *and* to be fair.

Business purpose test

Let's consider each part of this test in turn. The requirement of a business purpose is analogous to the argument that self-dealing should not be allowed unless it produces a surplus. True, the business purpose test does not by its terms stress the *comparative* aspect of the self-dealing surplus test: Could the controlling persons have achieved the proper business purpose in some way that would not involve self-dealing or the risk of treating the noncontrolling shareholders unfairly? In practice it is often open to the parties and the judge to inquire into the existence of less drastic ways of achieving the proper business purpose as part of the inquiry into the legitimacy and substantiality of the business purpose justification.

Why dropped

So why was the business purpose test eventually dropped in Delaware? In large part, I think, because it was so easy for proponents of freezeouts to allege plausible-sounding business reasons for what they were doing, and so hard for courts to second-guess the reality and weight of these reasons. Also, the growing realization that benefits might be frequent, so that a flat prohibition of freezeouts was not warranted, prompted courts to focus instead on insuring that freezees are adequately compensated.

Fairness test

Let us turn, then, to the fairness test. It is analogous to the surplus sharing requirement I recommended for basic self-dealing. But because the term *fairness* is so malleable, it might be interpreted to be a weaker test. For example, a court might define a freezeout to be fair so long as the minority or public shareholders receive at least as much money as they would be due under an appraisal standard of valuation. What courts actually mean by "fairness" will be explored in section 12.3.

§12.2.6 The Implications of Different Contexts

Commentators vs. courts

Several commentators have concluded that there are several distinct categories of freezeout transactions, and that different legal rules ought to govern them.[6] Courts have thus far declined to enunciate different, fairly precise rules for these different categories and have instead preferred to resort to highly general, open-ended language such as statements of the fairness test. Perhaps they think a categorical approach would hamper them in reaching equitable results in the myriad factual situations that might arise, and some situations might not fit neatly into any of the categories or might present factual variations not taken into account during the original construction of rules for the categories.[7]

Contextual analysis useful

Distinguishing among kinds of freezeouts is nevertheless a useful exercise. For one thing, the courts' reluctance to adopt the commentators' categories and their rather fixed rules for them doesn't mean that courts are insensitive to the contextual differences pointed out by the commentators.[8] Courts simply want to leave legal doctrine fluid and to consider contextual differences as part of a large, undefined array of factors relevant to decision. Moreover, the SEC, in its going-private rules, has relied on a categorical approach and, to a lesser extent, so has the California legislature.[9]

[6]Brudney & Chirelstein, A Restatement of Corporate Freezeouts, 87 Yale L.J. 1354 (1978); Greene, Corporate Freeze-Out Mergers: A Proposed Analysis, 28 Stan. L. Rev. 487 (1976).

[7] [A]s I perceive it, the Court is tending to flesh out broad equitable principles into rules and formats that automatically hold mergers "made for the sole purpose of freezing out minority stockholders [are] an abuse of the corporate process" . . . . The very uniqueness of equity is its ability to react on a case-by-case basis without the rigidity of pigeonholes. Roland Intl. Corp. v. Najjar, 407 A.2d 1032, 1038 (Del. 1979) (Quillen, J., dissenting).

See also Young v. Valhi, Inc., 382 A.2d 1372 (Del. Ch. 1978). *Young* involved a freezeout merger of a partially owned subsidiary. Brudney and Chirelstein had suggested that, in this category of cases, eliminating the potential for conflicts of interest would almost always supply the justifying business purpose that Delaware courts then required. But the court rejected this viewpoint because the parent was merely a holding company.

[8]Some commentators have suggested that the standard of review should vary according to the type of merger involved. . . . While such a pragmatic approach has much to commend it in maintaining corporate flexibility, in our judgment, the duty involved should not be dependent upon the type of merger. When and how the majority stockholder gained that position may be relevant in determining the *bona fides* of a business purpose when a freeze-out merger is challenged, or it may be helpful at the remedy stage, but such facts are not the measure of the majority's duty to the minority. Our law applies to all majority shareholders, no matter how, nor how recently such majority was obtained. Roland Intl. Corp. v. Najjar, 407 A.2d 1032, 1034 n.4 (Del. 1979).

[9]Rule 13e-3 under the Securities Exchange Act regulates going private and related transactions by corporations that are registered with the SEC. How it operates will be discussed in section 12.3 infra. For now, note that subsection g(1) provides that the rule will not apply to a transaction that takes place within one year of a tender offer through which the party engineering the transaction gained control. To qualify for this exemption, the controlling party must have disclosed in the course of the tender offer the plans for the later transaction and

Two-step acquisition

One noted analysis distinguishes three kinds of freezeout transactions. The first is a cashout merger that occurs as the later step of a multistage acquisition of one company by another, independent one. This is just a variant of the two-step acquisition analyzed in section 11.2, in which the minority shareholders in the second or final step get cash instead of stock. As before, one could take the position that, so long as shareholders received as much per share in the second step as in the first, courts need not inquire further. There need be no focus on the fiduciary status of the acquiring company, no shifting of the burden of proof to it, and no business-purpose test. Others would argue further that the second-step price need not be as high as the first. In any event, there is no objection to the cashout aspect of such an acquisition, any more than there would be to the cashout of dissenters to a one-step sale of business to another, independent one for cash, followed by dissolution and liquidation of the seller.

Merger of long-term affiliates

The second category of freezeout mergers is the merger of long-term affiliates. This is a variant of the parent-subsidiary merger analyzed in section 11.3. The variation is that now the minority shareholders of the subsidiary get cash instead of parent company stock. As before, the merger is clearly a basic self-dealing transaction and seems to call for a requirement that the parent company show that a surplus will result from the merger and that it will be shared with the minority shareholders — or that, in the language once used in Delaware, the parent company's managers must show a business purpose for the merger and that it is entirely fair. We can readily omit a requirement of an explicit showing of business purpose or self-dealing surplus in this category of freezeout cases, because an important advantage can almost always be presumed to result in a merger of this sort, namely, the elimination of an undesirable relationship, that between parent and partly owned subsidiary. (The relationship is thought to be undesirable because of the continual tensions, monitoring costs, and risks

---

must compensate shareholders being frozen out at a level at least as high as the highest consideration offered during the tender offer. As we shall see, this exemption corresponds with one of the commentators' categories of transactions: the multistage acquisition.

California statutes on merger and sale of assets provide for special rules in certain classes of transactions. For example, although a sale of assets usually requires majority shareholder approval, when the buyer controls or is in common control with the seller, 90 percent approval is needed. Cal. §1001. Similarly, in controlled mergers, where one constituent corporation owns a majority of the voting shares of another, the nonredeemable common shares of a constituent corporation may be exchanged only for similar shares in the surviving corporation. An exception is made for short-form mergers. Cal. §1101. The use of reverse stock splits is limited by the restriction that a corporation may not pay cash in lieu of fractional shares if this would result in elimination of more than 10 percent of any class. Cal. §407.

of unfair transactions that afflict it.) As for the fairness test, commentators Brudney and Chirelstein suggest it be interpreted to require not only a sharing of gains from the transaction between the shareholders of the two companies (as discussed in section 11.3), but also that payment to the subsidiary's minority shareholders *must* be made in the form of shares of the parent, rather than cash. Courts have not adopted this rule, however.

Pure freezeouts

The third category of freezeout mergers might be called pure freezeouts, a class that in the context of publicly held corporations consists mostly of going-private transactions. In this category, unlike the first two, the controlling insiders are typically *not* trying to combine two separate business operations, nor to eliminate continual conflicts of interest between shareholders of two separate but related corporations. Here the freezeout is not viewed as ancillary to such corporate business purposes. Rather, the exclusion of some shareholders, usually the public investors, from the continuing enterprise is the primary objective. This is the kind of case that was implicitly assumed in most of the analysis of harms and benefits of freezeouts in subsections 12.2.1 and 12.2.2. There is little question that it is appropriate to analyze the pure freezeout as involving basic self-dealing by a fiduciary and to set legal rules accordingly. Even in the case of "voluntary" deals, such as the typical LBO (where a majority of the public shareholders have to respond to a tender offer or vote for a cash-out merger), the insiders have sufficient self-interest and decision making influence to justify considering the transactions to be self-dealing that can provoke careful judicial scrutiny.

Independent valuation vs. prohibition

Because of the possible benefits of going private transactions, I suggested that judicial focus be on a detailed independent valuation of the company taken private, in order to determine whether the freezeout price was "more than fair" — a question that includes within itself the inquiry whether the freezeout premium compensates for the possible costs and risks imposed on the freezees. But other commentators, not seeing (or believing in) the possible benefits, would take a harsher approach. For example, because going-private transactions have great potential for abuse, and because the proffered business reasons for them often appear to be flimsy excuses, some commentators would flatly prohibit them.[10]

Other approaches

Others have suggested a medley of less drastic remedies.[11] One of the

[10] Brudney & Chirelstein, note 6 supra, at 1368-1369.

[11] In Borden, Going Private — Old Tort, New Tort or No Tort?, 49 N.Y.U. L. Rev. 987 (1974), it is suggested that flat prohibition should apply only to "fully bootstrapped takeouts," in which insiders with no significant equity interest use corporate assets to gain control and "shake-down tender offers" affording no reasonable protection against panic selling.

most appealing ideas is that before a freezeout can be effected a majority of the minority's shares must be voted in favor of the transaction.[12] The most important consequence of such a rule may not be immediately obvious: It would create the possibility of an auction even when the initiators of the freezeout plan held a majority of the stock. Note that the rule gives holders of the minority shares a veto power. An outside company or group that feels the plan initiators are offering too low a price (say, $14 a share) may decide to make a tender offer for all the minority shares at a higher price (say, $17 a share). If successful in getting the minority shares, the outside group may then demand a higher freezeout price (say, $20 a share) as a precondition of their assent to the plan. Even if their tender offer isn't successful, because the plan initiators raise their proposed freezeout price (to, say, $18 a share — $1 higher than the tender offer price), the minority shareholders will still have benefited from the rival bidding.

True auctions for LBOs

With respect to the typical voluntary LBO, commentators like Louis Lowenstein and Bevis Longstreth have suggested that genuine auctions be mandated: Managers may try to buy out their public shareholders, but others must be allowed to make rival bids on as nearly equal terms as possible.[13] This approach would outlaw lockup options and similar devices and suggests that rival bidders be given a reasonable opportunity to investigate the company.

§12.3 *Legal Developments: Public Corporations*

A story with many plots

Starting in the mid-1970s, the case law concerning freezeouts and going private began to develop in a remarkable way. The story is one that addresses several larger themes: It is a story about federalism, about relations between legislatures and the judiciary, and about the amazing vitality of the concept of the fiduciary.

Rules proposed for general going-private transactions include a sharing of profits with frozen out shareholders if the company is sold within some fixed time after the freezeout, an offer of rescission if the company goes public again within some fixed time, and the distribution of financial statements covering the year after the freezeout. This last requirement is an effort to use disclosure to insure a fair price.

Note, Going Private, 84 Yale L.J. 903 (1975), reiterates the need for a valid corporate purpose and suggests that shareholders who are frozen out be given warrants that will enable them to share in any gains from going public again.

[12] See Note, Approval of Take-Out Mergers by Minority Shareholders: From Substantive to Procedural Fairness, 93 Yale L.J. 1113 (1984).

[13] Lowenstein, Management Buyouts, 85 Colum. L. Rev. 730, 779-784; Longstreth, Fairness of Management Buyouts Needs Evaluation, in Legal Times, Oct. 10, 1983, at 15.

§12.3.1 The Supreme Court's Renunciation

Perhaps the first high point in the story is the Supreme Court's decision in *Santa Fe Industries, Inc. v. Green.*[1] The case falls into the commentators' category of a merger of long-term affiliates. Santa Fe used the Delaware short-form merger statute to cash out the remaining minority shareholders of Kirby Lumber Corporation, a 95 percent subsidiary. Instead of pursuing their appraisal remedy in a Delaware court, plaintiffs brought suit in federal court under Rule 10b-5 to set aside the merger or to recover what they claimed to be the fair price of Kirby's shares ($772, rather than the $150 offered in the merger). Plaintiff's legal theory was that a freezeout merger without a corporate business purpose is fraudulent under Rule 10b-5. They thought that such a merger is not saved by a finding that defendants made no material misstatements and fully disclosed certain appraisals of the merging company's assets and stock, as well as other relevant information. But the Supreme Court, through Justice White, held that if the transaction were carried out as alleged in the complaint, it was neither "deceptive" nor "manipulative" and therefore did not violate either Section 10(b) or Rule 10b-5. In other words, Rule 10b-5 cannot be used as the basis for the development of a federal corporate law of fiduciary duties. The rule is not available to redress mere breaches of fiduciary duty or substantive unfairness in transactions initiated by fiduciaries, but only violations of federal duties to avoid deception or manipulation in stock transactions. Put crudely, when corporate managers harm their stockholders by guile, both federal and state law may help; but when they harm them "out in the open," through self-dealing, the stockholder must seek state remedies.

***Santa Fe* case**

Justice White's argument was based mainly on the language of the relevant federal statute, Section 10(b), and on the principle that Rule 10b-5 should be interpreted to implement that statute but not extend its reach. He also made the arguments that creating a private federal cause of action in these situations was unnecessary to fulfill congressional intent, that plaintiffs had a state remedy as an alternative, and that acknowledging plaintiffs' theory would open the flood gates of litigation.

Rationale

A neutral observer who read Section 10(b) and its legislative history carefully, but who had not been influenced by a knowledge of the expansive growth in the late 1960s and early 1970s of case law under Rule 10b-5, would probably have found nothing surprising about the Supreme Court's holding. It seems the most likely, if not the inevitable, result. Why then did the plaintiffs attempt so vigorously to establish a federal cause of action, instead of invoking state corporate law that obviously was applicable?

A puzzle

§12.3 [1] 430 U.S. 462 (1977).

Plaintiff's preference for federal court

One educated guess is that plaintiffs wanted to get something akin to an appraisal remedy in federal court, because their lawyers believed, as many then did, that plaintiff shareholders have a better chance of succeeding in a federal rather than a state court. In particular, they probably thought that Delaware courts were too pro-management: Those courts would interpret the appraisal remedy as being the exclusive remedy for shareholders dissatisfied with the merger and would apply the appraisal remedy in a niggardly way. This attitude would have fit in with the published views of one eminent corporate law commentator and former SEC chairman,[2] who had stirred considerable debate in the profession over the desirability of a federal law imposing minimal standards of fiduciary conduct on corporate managers. A similar attitude may also have been adopted by the Supreme Court itself, which accepted without question the parties' assumption that the plaintiffs would only have had an appraisal remedy under Delaware law.

§12.3.2 Delaware Responds to the Challenge

Singer v. Magnavox

Not long after the *Santa Fe* decision, the Delaware Supreme Court handed down a landmark opinion in the case of *Singer v. Magnavox Co.*[3] The case involved a multistage acquisition. T.M.C. Development Corporation, by use of a newly formed subsidiary, bought 84 percent of Magnavox's shares for $9 per share in a tender offer and then, within a year, caused a long-form cash merger between Magnavox and the subsidiary under which the remaining Magnavox shareholders received $9 per share. Plaintiff shareholders sued to nullify the merger and receive compensatory damages. Reversing a dismissal of the action by the Court of Chancery, the Delaware Supreme Court held that

> a §251 [long form] merger, made for the sole purpose of freezing out minority stockholders, is an abuse of the corporate process; and the complaint which so alleges in this suit, states a cause of action for breach of fiduciary duty for which the Court may grant such relief as it deems appropriate under the circumstances.[4]

[2] Cary, Federalism and Corporate Law: Reflections Upon Delaware, 83 Yale L.J. 663 (1974) (characterizing the alleged competition among states to provide the most pro-management corporation statute, with Delaware the traditional leader, as a "race for the bottom").

[3] 380 A.2d 969 (Del. 1977).

[4] Id. at 980.

Consequently, defendants must show a corporate business purpose for the merger. Moreover, the court reaffirmed the requirement laid down for parent-subsidiary mergers in *Sterling v. Mayflower Hotel Corp.*,[5] that the defendants must show the merger's "entire fairness." Finally, the court also held that plaintiffs' statutory appraisal remedy was not the exclusive remedy for their dissatisfaction.

Speculations about motives

Among the many interesting aspects of Justice Duffy's rich opinion for the majority is the placement of its reaction to *Santa Fe.* At the end of a sentence asserting that defendants' duties are to be measured by fiduciary standards, Justice Duffy drops a footnote reference to *Santa Fe* in which he remarks that it is "a current confirmation by the Supreme Court of the responsibility of a State to govern the internal affairs of corporate life. . . ." In the text he then goes on to say, "Delaware courts have long announced and enforced high standards which govern the internal affairs of corporations chartered here, particularly when fiduciary relations are under scrutiny."[6] He then cites Delaware opinions that use strenuous language in describing the duties of corporate fiduciaries. The cases stretch back to the 1939 opinion in *Guth v. Loft, Inc.*,[7] from which the court quotes at length. The court also takes pains to distinguish a line of Delaware precedents that seem to suggest an opposite attitude. Is it too much to surmise that at least some members of the Delaware Supreme Court were offended by the apparent assumptions by lawyers, professors, and even other courts that Delaware corporate law offered inadequate protection to shareholders?

Subsequent case law

Subsequent Delaware case law elaborated the principles of *Singer*. *Tanzer v. International General Industries, Inc.*[8] held that a cashout merger made primarily to advance the business purpose of a majority stockholder — a parent corporation — was proper so long as it was a bona fide purpose (not a subterfuge for the real purpose of ridding itself of unwanted minority shareholders in the subsidiary) and the transaction was entirely fair to the minority.[9] Another case seemed to establish that it was not enough for defendants to allege a plausible business purpose: the court would look

[5] 93 A.2d 107 (Del. 1952).

[6] 380 A.2d at 976 and n.6.

[7] 5 A.2d 503 (Del. 1939).

[8] 379 A.2d 1121 (Del. 1977).

[9] Though some observers regarded *Tanzer* as a retreat from *Singer,* the two cases were not logically inconsistent. What presented greater cause for concern among would-be plaintiffs was the vice-chancellor's decision on the remand from *Tanzer*. 402 A.2d 382 (Del. Ch. 1979). He granted defendants' motion for summary judgment, finding it no affront to the entire fairness test that the price offered the minority failed to recognize a merger gain and that the minority was forced to take cash instead of parent company stock.

into the real existence and substantiality of the alleged purpose.[10] In *Roland International Corp. v. Najjar* the Delaware Supreme Court established that the rule announced in *Singer* would also apply to short-form mergers.[11] And in *Lynch v. Vickers Energy Corp.*[12] the court dealt with some aspects of a going-private transaction of the "voluntary" type — a share purchase offer with threats of illiquidity and delisting. In reversing the vice-chancellor's decision for defendants, the court reached only the plaintiffs' nondisclosure claim — the claim that the defendants violated their fiduciary duty of candor by failing to disclose all the information in their possession that was germane to the issue. It therefore did not deal with the more interesting argument that defendants, through use of their superior bargaining position and control over corporate assets and process, had actually coerced the minority shareholders into selling for an inadequate price.[13]

Some other state courts followed the lead of *Singer*,[14] and other courts may yet decide to use the business purpose test, despite Delaware's eventual rejection of it.

§12.3.3 The Lower Federal Courts Stand Ready to Assist

Disclosure in aid of state law rights

A third stage in the story began with the realization by parties and courts that minority shareholders might have valuable disclosure-oriented rights under federal law to information they need to determine *whether management has breached its fiduciary duties under state law*. In *Santa Fe* the United States Supreme Court, in footnote 14, had rejected the plaintiffs' contention that the majority stockholder's failure to give the minority ad-

[10]Young v. Valhi, Inc., 382 A.2d 1372 (Del. Ch. 1978). The claim was that the cashout parent-subsidiary merger would produce tax savings and eliminate conflicts of interest. The court found that there were alternative ways to achieve the tax savings and that the desire to eliminate conflicts was contrived, given the respective sizes of the two companies and their meager record of past intercorporate dealings. (The parent was little more than a holding company.)

[11]407 A.2d 1032 (Del. 1979).

[12]383 A.2d 278 (Del. 1977).

[13]On remand, the vice-chancellor found that plaintiffs had suffered no damages. 402 A.2d 5 (Del. Ch. 1979). The Delaware Supreme Court again reversed, 429 A.2d 497 (Del. 1981), and held, among other things, that the plaintiffs did not have to show injury or economic loss to be entitled to a remedy, and that the majority stockholder would be required to pay "rescissory damages" to plaintiffs, measured by the equivalent value, at the time of judgment, of the corporate stock received by defendant.

[14]Gabhart v. Gabhart, 370 N.E.2d 345 (Ind. 1977); Perl v. IU Intl. Corp., 607 P.2d 1036 (Hawaii 1980). But see In re Jones & Laughlin Steel Corp., 412 A.2d 1099 (Pa. 1980) (appraisal is sole *post*merger remedy for aggrieved minority shareholders).

vance notice of the freezeout merger was a material nondisclosure under Rule 10b-5, saying

> . . . respondents do not indicate how they might have acted differently had they had prior notice of the merger. Indeed, they accept the conclusion of both courts below that under Delaware law they could not have enjoined the merger because an appraisal proceeding is their sole remedy in the Delaware courts for any alleged unfairness in the terms of the merger. Thus, the failure to give advance notice was not a material nondisclosure. . . . [15]

Since *Singer* showed the minor premise of this syllogism to be wrong — appraisal is not the exclusive remedy, at least in some states in some kinds of mergers — it has become feasible for frozen out shareholders to claim that various nondisclosures were material in that they thwarted the plaintiffs' ability to pursue their rights under state law.

Indeed, circuit courts writing in the post-*Santa Fe* era have recognized, in a variety of situations, a right to information with respect to corporate transactions in securities that shareholders could have attacked under state law had they known the facts.[16] There is no obvious reason why the basic principle of these decisions would not apply to freezeout mergers.

§12.3.4 The SEC's Reaction

Rule 13e-3

In the same vein as those federal court decisions, but more specifically addressed to the topic of this section, is the SEC's Rule 13e-3,[17] which was adopted in 1979. This rule applies to going-private transactions. These are defined in very broad terms to include share repurchases, tender offers, mergers with affiliates, recapitalizations, reverse stock splits, and so on, wherever the effect will be either deregistration under the Securities Exchange Act, delisting of exchange-traded securities, or the removal of securities from the NASD's stock quotation system (that is, from the chief "over the counter market"). Therefore, the rule might cover many transactions

[15] 430 U.S. at 474 n.14.

[16] Healey v. Catalyst Recovery of Pennsylvania, Inc., 616 F.2d 641 (3rd Cir. 1980); Alabama Farm Bureau Mut. Cas. Co. v. American Fidelity Life Ins. Co., 606 F.2d 602 (5th Cir. 1979), cert. denied, 449 U.S. 820 (1980); Kidwell ex rel. Penfold v. Meikle, 597 F.2d 1273 (9th Cir. 1979); Goldberg v. Meridor, 567 F.2d 209 (2d Cir. 1977), cert. denied, 434 U.S. 1069 (1978); Wright v. Heizer Corp., 560 F.2d 236 (7th Cir. 1977), cert. denied, 434 U.S. 1066 (1978). See also Ferrara & Steinberg, A Reappraisal of Santa Fe: Rule 10b-5 and the New Federalism, 129 U. Pa. L. Rev. 263, 282 (1980).

[17] See also SEC Release No. 34-17719, 46 Fed. Reg. 22,571 (1981) (interpretation of 13e-3); SEC Release No. 34-17720, 46 Fed. Reg. 22,602 (1981) (proposed amendments to 13e-3).

falling in the commentators' second category of freezeouts (mergers with long-term affiliates), as well as purer going-private transactions. There is, however, an exception for the first category (freezeouts pursuant to a multistage acquisition) even when the result is delisting or the like.

Special disclosure requirements

When a going-private transaction is proposed, the rule subjects the issuer of the affected securities to an antifraud rule and requires it to file and distribute a disclosure document conforming to Schedule 13E-3. This form requires information reminiscent of that required under Schedule 13D, the form for individuals and groups who have just acquired more than five percent of the equity securities of a public corporation. But it also requires more. First, the document must disclose the true purpose of the going-private transaction and must also discuss alternative ways of achieving that purpose, and the reasons for the timing and structuring of the transaction. Second, it must analyze the probable benefits and detriments of the transaction to the issuer, to any affiliates of it, and to the minority shareholders. Third, the document must also state whether the issuer or its affiliate believes the transaction is fair or unfair to unaffiliated security holders. It must also discuss in reasonable detail the material factors on which this belief is based. Evasive answers — for example, "The issuer doesn't have sufficient information to form a belief as to the fairness of the transaction" — are not acceptable.

Strategy of rule

From the regulatory point of view, these disclosure requirements reflect a clever drafting strategy. Consider the dilemma into which it puts the insiders who want to take a company private primarily in order to make profits for themselves, although they can point to some corporate advantages such as elimination of SEC filing costs. If they fail to disclose their true beliefs about the basic purpose and the fairness of the transaction, together with all the material information and analysis relevant to the support or disconfirmation of the validity of these beliefs, they will be in violation of the rule and may eventually be found out and made liable thereunder. But if they make the full and complete disclosures required by the rule, they may have given aid and evidence to minority shareholders who wish to challenge the transaction under substantive standards of fiduciary conduct in a state court action. And yet the rule does not run afoul of the basic notion affirmed in *Santa Fe,* that the antifraud provisions of the federal securities laws are aimed at inadequate disclosures and misrepresentations, not at breaches of fiduciary duty generally.

Rule 13e-3 appears to have had little impact on the development of the case law on going-private transactions. It may nevertheless have had good effects. The typical disclosure document in LBO deals is elaborately informative.

§12.3.5 Delaware Takes a Second Look

Weinberger v. UOP

In 1983 the Delaware Supreme Court decided *Weinberger v. UOP, Inc.*,[18] which overhauled the Delaware law concerning freezeout mergers. Five aspects of the opinion are worthy of note.

Duty and procedures clarified

First, the court clarified the existence of a fiduciary duty and the location of burdens of production and proof. It reaffirmed the position that, in a merger between a partially owned subsidiary (UOP) and its controlling parent company (Signal), the parent company and the directors of the parent and the subsidiary are fiduciaries with respect to the minority shareholders of the subsidiary, that the merger involves an inherent conflict of interest, and that the burden of proof is therefore on the fiduciaries to prove the entire fairness of the transaction, in sufficient detail to survive the careful scrutiny of the courts. It then went on, however, to discuss the preliminary burdens that the plaintiff in such a case must meet. The plaintiff must allege specific acts of fraud, misrepresentation, or misconduct that show unfairness to the minority, and he must demonstrate some basis for invoking the fairness obligation. In terms of the standard formulations of evidence law, the court seems to have meant that the plaintiff has to meet a burden of production of initial evidence, even though defendants have the ultimate burden of proof.

Vote of minority

Significantly, the *Weinberger* court also complicated the procedural issues by declaring that an *informed vote of a majority of the minority* stockholders would result in a shifting of the burden of proof to the plaintiff. Nevertheless, the burden of proof as to whether the vote was informed — that is, whether all relevant material disclosures were made to the minority shareholders — remains always on the defendants. In the case itself, the court found that adequate disclosures had not been made.

Business purpose test rejected

Second, the court expressly rejected the business purpose test laid down in the *Singer* case. (It did not deny, however, that the nature of the reasons and purposes behind a merger might be one factor among others that a court would consider in the course of its inquiry into a merger's overall fairness.)

Fairness test explicated

Third, the court explicated and applied the concept of fairness. In assessing a parent-subsidiary merger, the court must determine whether the fiduciaries satisfied their duty of complete candor, and whether the transaction was entirely fair in that there was *both* fair dealing *and* a fair price.

Application

In the *Weinberger* case itself, the court found the merger deal sadly lacking in all three of these dimensions of fiduciary duty. There was a lack of

[18] 457 A.2d 701 (Del. 1983).

complete candor in several important respects. An internal feasibility study of Signal's possible acquisition of UOP, which was done by two Signal officers who were also directors of UOP and which concluded that any price up to $24 a share would yield a good investment for Signal, was not disclosed to UOP's outside directors or to the minority shareholders. (The actual price set for the merger was $21, and $24 would have meant an additional $17 million for the minority.) Nor was there disclosure of the hurried nature of the preparation of a fairness opinion letter by an investment banking firm hired to examine the deal. And the disclosures that were made to the public gave the misleading impression that there were real negotiations between the parent and the subsidiary managements over the merger price. An absence of fair dealing was indicated not only by these nondisclosures, but also by the very facts that the investment banker's work was done hurriedly and that there were no negotiations as to the merger price. On the subject of fair price, doubts were raised by the contents of the feasibility study.

Remedies indicated

Fourth, the court made important pronouncements about the plaintiff's remedy. In a freezeout merger, the plaintiff's monetary remedy should ordinarily be confined to appraisal.[19] The court thus cut back substantially on the impression created by *Singer* of the nonexclusivity of the appraisal remedy. Its remarks suggest that the plaintiffs will rarely be able to get an injunction against a merger or damages for the entire class of frozen out shareholders. Nevertheless, the court was careful not to make its new principle an absolute one. It stated that it did not intend to limit the chancellor's historic power to give other equitable and monetary relief where doing so would be appropriate. It noted that such other remedies might be called for when the transaction involved fraud, misrepresentation, self-dealing, deliberate waste of corporate assets, or gross and palpable overreaching.

The court's remarks about the availability of remedies raise numerous problems. For example, does the inclusion of the term *self-dealing* in its list of conditions justifying special remedies mean that plaintiffs can always escape confinement to the appraisal remedy when challenging a parent-subsidiary merger where top management owned any significant amount of stock in the parent? Probably not. The Delaware Supreme Court seems to use the term *self-dealing* for conflict-of-interest transactions where the conflict is fairly substantial and serious.

Question of fit

Another question is how the parts of the court's opinion fit together.

[19]The plaintiff in the case, as well as certain others, were grandfathered against the possibly devastating effect of applying this new principle to them.

Apparently, appraisal is ordinarily the only remedy that will be available in the future to plaintiffs like the one in the *Weinberger* case. Yet appraisal is ordinarily a matter of right in mergers. Those who invoke this statutory remedy aren't required by the statute to meet some burden of production or proof concerning unfairness, and the company in question isn't required to meet any burden of proving that the merger was fair. The court is simply asked to determine the fair value of the shares. Of course, what the fair value is may be illuminated by an inquiry into whether there was complete candor and fair dealing in connection with the merger, but surely these are collateral issues in an appraisal proceeding. And if appraisal is a statutory right anyway, why all the talk about burdens of proof, fiduciary duties, and fair dealing?

One possibility is that a finding that a parent-subsidiary merger was unfair would allow a court to give an appraisal remedy to shareholders who would not have it under the Delaware statute — because, for example, of its stock market exception to the appraisal remedy. (See section 10.6.1.)

Valuation methods liberalized

A fifth aspect of the opinion is that it declared a liberalization of the valuation methods to be used in appraisal proceedings. Instead of being bound to use the mechanical "Delaware block" or weighted-average method of figuring an appraised value, courts are now empowered to use any techniques or methods that are generally considered acceptable in the financial community and otherwise admissible in court. This permission is subject to the statutory rule that fair value as computed in appraisal proceedings may not include elements of gain or loss arising from the merger itself. But the court interpreted this rule narrowly to refer only to "speculative elements of value" that may arise from the accomplishment or expectation of the merger.

Discounted cash flow

What are some of the new methods appraising courts may use? Certainly, plaintiff's experts may now use the usual discounted cash flow techniques of valuing a firm's projected earnings. We know this because the court in *Weinberger* was partly moved to liberalize its law of valuation by the observation that such a technique was used by Signal's officers to value UOP for their internal feasibility study, which played a key role in Signal's decision to acquire the rest of UOP.

Average premiums

Another newly permissible technique may be the use of expert testimony to show how the parent's proposed premium over market price for the subsidiary's minority shareholders compares to average premiums over market in comparable acquisitions. This was one of the two techniques plaintiff's expert sought to use in the court below (the other was a discounted cash flow analysis), and the *Weinberger* opinion does not suggest it would be impermissible or irrelevant. Incidentally, if it becomes accepted that fairness requires that there be a freezeout premium of normal size, the result would be an indirect requirement that merger gains be shared.

§12.4 Close Corporation Cases

Drastic consequences

Freezeouts and squeezeouts of close corporation shareholders present some problems beyond those already encountered. These stem from the peculiar characteristics of close corporations. Consider, first, the fact that in many close corporations the shareholders will earn their livelihood, or a significant amount of their income, by working for the company. Consequently, since a freezeout of a stockholder's share interest in a close corporation will usually lead also to his no longer being employed by the company, the damage typically done by a freezeout may be greater in the close corporation context. Alternatively, one may look at the coerced termination of a participant's employment status as one part of the process of squeezing him out.

Subtler tactics

Second, consider the fact that the close corporation's stock is usually illiquid: There is no ready market for it. This fact widens the range of squeezeout techniques. It permits tactics that are somewhat more subtle — more ambiguous and less obviously coercive — than a simple cashout merger. For example, the controlling persons can cause the company to cease paying dividends and can continue to receive the same overall return for themselves from the company by paying themselves higher salaries. This action may have the effect of making the stock of the noncontrolling shareholder virtually worthless. (Such a shareholder may be unemployed by the corporation, e.g., a widow of a deceased former participant, and in any event may be unable to obtain a raise in his or her own salary from the corporation.) Indeed, squeezeouts in close corporations come in such a rich variety of forms that O'Neal has devoted an entire book to the study of them.[1]

More fighting

Third, consider the small number of participants in the typical close corporation and the fact that their life situations will change over time (creating conflicts of interest where previously there was harmony), they have many face-to-face and therefore emotionally tinged interactions with

§12.4 [1] F. O'Neal, "Squeeze-Outs" of Minority Shareholders: Expulsion or Oppression of Business Associates (1975 & supp.). O'Neal deals mainly with close corporations, though cases involving public corporations are also cited and discussed.

one another, and they tend to confuse the separate and distinct roles of investor, manager, employee, and corporate entity that are established by corporate law. In such a context, personal feuds are apt to arise. Some feuding participants may try to freeze or squeeze the others out of spite, as well as out of a desire for profit. Some feuding participants may try unfairly to obstruct the operations of the company or the legitimate business plans of the others to such an extent that the latter are provoked into buying or freezing the former out in order to enable the corporation's business to avert failure or to seize significant new opportunities. These feuds will take a wide variety of forms, and it will not always be easy to say on which side the equities lie.

Courts' hard task

Taken together, these differences suggest that in close corporation cases involving freezeouts or squeezeouts the courts should be especially solicitous of freezees or squeezees, while at the same time not tying their hands by adoption of an inflexible categorical rule.

Matteson v. Ziebarth

There is some evidence that courts are sensitive to the special situation of close corporation participants in this context. In the venerable case of *Matteson v. Ziebarth*,[2] for example, a court faced with a challenge to a freezeout of a close corporation shareholder held, in an apparently wooden and strict manner, that the relevant corporate statutes didn't forbid a merger with a shell corporation for the purpose of effecting a freezeout, and that the statutory appraisal proceeding was the exclusive remedy in such a case for any unfairness or breach of fiduciary duty short of actual fraud. Nevertheless, a close reading of the case shows that the court was heavily influenced by the perception that the freezeout was necessary to clear the way for a sale of the company to a larger, independent firm, and that this sale was the only feasible way of saving something of value from the otherwise unprofitable company. The court thus perceived the freezee as trying to block realization of the company's only good hope. To the extent it acted on this perception, it was implicitly applying a kind of business purpose test.[3]

Sensitivity to business purpose

In a superficially contrasting case, *Bryan v. Brock & Blevins Co.*,[4] the active shareholders of a close corporation tried to freeze out a retired 15 percent shareholder by merging the company into a newly formed shell corporation to which they had contributed their controlling stock. Applying Georgia law, the Fifth Circuit upheld a district court's issuance of an

[2] 242 P.2d 1025 (Wash. 1952).

[3] See Vorenberg, Exclusiveness of the Dissenting Stockholder's Appraisal Right, 77 Harv. L. Rev. 1189, 1195-1197 (1964).

[4] 490 F.2d 563 (5th Cir.), cert. denied, 419 U.S. 844 (1974).

injunction against the merger on the ground that the merger lacked a "business purpose" and that the shell was therefore purely a sham party created to circumvent the majority's inability, absent a contrary charter provision, to force the minority shareholder to surrender his stock. More generally, the court stressed that the corporate statute should be interpreted in a way that comports with equity in good conscience.

"Doing equity"

Even courts that take a permissive stance to freezeouts may be observed to reach rather far in their efforts to "do [at least some] equity" in the particular case. In *Yanow v. Teal Industries, Inc.,*[5] which involved a freezeout of a close corporation shareholder, the court found it was forced by the clear and express language of the Connecticut statute to hold that appraisal was the plaintiff's only remedy against the freezeout merger. It also held that the plaintiff was precluded by the "continuing ownership rule"[6] from bringing a derivative suit against the surviving corporation for pre-merger breaches of fiduciary duty that harmed the merging corporation, since he no longer owned shares. (They were extinguished in the merger!) Nevertheless, the court did allow the plaintiff to maintain a direct suit in his individual capacity against the controlling party for 19 allegedly unfair pre-merger transactions involving that party and the controlled corporation. In the case of some of those transactions — for example, an alleged usurpation of corporate opportunity — the characterization of them as giving rise to a direct rather than a derivative claim seems rather generous to the plaintiff, and perhaps was a product of the court's misgivings about its other rulings.

[5] 422 A.2d 311 (Conn. 1979).
[6] See section 15.4 infra.

CHAPTER 13

CONTROL SHIFTS AND INSIDER RESISTANCE: TENDER OFFERS

§13.1 Introduction

This chapter deals with controls shifts that are opposed by those currently in control of the corporation. The focus is on unfriendly takeovers attempted by means of tender offers.

Characteristics of tender offers

A tender offer occurs when one company (or an individual, or a group of persons) invites or solicits shareholders of a target company to tender their shares for sale at some specified consideration. The consideration may be formulated as a cash price or as a package of securities, or both. In recent years, cash tender offers have been more common. The value of the consideration offered usually exceeds the current market price of the target company's stock by a substantial premium. Shareholders are therefore usually delighted to hear that their company has become the target of a tender offer. The offer is usually made for some fixed, limited period of time, though the time period may be extended. In a conventional or standard tender offer, the offeror usually publishes a notice of its offer in newspapers that are widely read by investors, so the offer is effectively made available to all shareholders of the target. (Not everything that courts have called tender offers have this characteristic, however.) Stockholders of the target who wish to respond to the tender offer will often "tender" their shares by having their broker forward them to a depository bank that acts as agent for the tender offeror. Usually, the tender offeror words its offer so that it is obligated to buy the tendered shares only if certain conditions have been satisfied. A frequent, and very important, condition is that some specified minimum number of shares must have been tendered by a certain date. The minimum number might equal 51 percent of the target's stock, or such lesser percentage as the offeror thinks would give it working control of the target. Another important condition might be a "litigation out" clause — a statement, for example, that the offeror will not be bound to buy tendered shares if the Justice Department or the Federal Trade Commission brings or threatens an antitrust action against the proposed acquisition. The offeror may or may not limit the maximum number of shares it will buy. It may promise to buy all shares that are tendered (subject, perhaps, to there being a minimum number tendered). Or it may promise to buy up to a specified percentage of the target company's outstanding stock, so that if too many shares are tendered it will buy from each tendering shareholder on a pro rata basis and return the excess. For example, if it commits itself to buying 60 percent of the target's stock and 70 percent is tendered, it will buy six-sevenths of the stock tendered by each shareholder. Or it may commit itself only to buying some specified percentage of shares, while indicating that it may decide to buy all or a greater portion of the tendered shares anyway.

When employed

Would-be acquiring companies usually resort to a tender offer when a "friendly" acquisition cannot be arranged. As indicated in chapter 10, acquisition by a merger or sale of substantially all assets of a target company requires, as a matter of corporate law, the approval of the target's board of directors before the transaction can be submitted to the target's shareholders for a vote. When the target's directors don't want the company to be acquired, the would-be acquirer must make its offer to the individual shareholders themselves; it must try to get individual shareholders to sell their stock to itself. As we shall see, target company management has techniques for trying to make a tender offer fail. Tender offers therefore tend to involve a great deal of litigation and other forms of struggle.

Regulation

In the United States, tender offers are primarily regulated by the Williams Act, which added certain sections to the Securities Exchange Act, by state takeover statutes, and by general corporate law doctrines. Before examining these bodies of law, however, it is important to consider the pros and cons of takeovers by tender offer, so that we may better understand legislators' and courts' beliefs about why and how takeovers should be regulated. Anyone who reads the relevant case law carefully is likely to be impressed with the view that many judges seem to have a personal image or paradigm of a standard takeover, to use this image as the basis for their attitudes towards takeovers in general, and to let this attitude shape their choice of formulation of particular rules and case law holdings.

§13.2 *Theories of Tender Offers*

Why are tender offers made? What side effects do they have? The answers to these questions have a bearing on the kind of regulation of tender offers and of managerial responses to tender offers that one would like to see.

§13.2.1 Explanations of Tender Offers

Five explanations

There are at least five common explanations as to why corporations make tender offers. After discussing these explanations, I will introduce some systematic empirical evidence that bears on which of these explanations is most nearly correct and complete.

(1) Gains from better management

The first explanation is that the acquisitor wants to capture the target company's potential value, which has been made possible by the suboptimal performance of the target and its management. As some commentators have put it,[1] tender offerors are crucial forces in the "market for corporate control": they monitor the performance of other companies and act as vehicles for disciplining suboptimal performance. When lawmakers accept this explanation, they ought to regard tender offers as very good things indeed, both for shareholders and for society in general.

Hypothetical case

This point may be developed by a hypothetical. Ernest Shaker, the chief executive officer of Calvinist Chemical Corporation, has discovered that one moderate-sized publicly held oil company, The Quiet Oil Company, is

§13.2 [1] The seminal work in this genre is Manne, Mergers and the Market for Corporate Control, 73 J. Pol. Econ. 110 (1965).

selling for $40 a share, a figure that is less than the book value per share. (Or perhaps he discovers only that Quiet Oil's ratio of market value to book value is much lower than that of other oil companies.) Since this fact suggests that Quiet Oil has not been getting as high a return on stockholders' investment as other companies, he orders a cadre of vice presidents to investigate further. After diligent searching, they find many suggestive bits of evidence. Admittedly, Quiet Oil has always had positive earnings (but how often do oil companies have losses?) and is now sitting on an unusually large amount of accumulated cash. But its earnings growth has been unspectacular and management seems tardy about putting the accumulated cash to work. Fatty Laidback, the president of Quiet Oil, is fairly honest and benign, but he has not acted in a particularly dynamic or daring way. The company doesn't sell its products at the best available prices. It mounts no market research efforts. It doesn't attempt to speed collection of aging accounts receivable. It employs an unusually large number of clerks to do paper work that in most firms is handled by computer. It has failed to pursue specific exploration and development opportunities that were within its reach. It owns new and expensive machines that it hardly uses, and it uses old machines that are technologically primitive. Its employees are not disgruntled, but neither are they euphoric; mostly, they are just somnolent.

After digesting these reports, Shaker decides to have Calvinist Chemical make a tender offer for all Quiet Oil shares at $60 per share. He and his advisors think that, once Quiet Oil comes under their control, they can, by ousting Laidback and his cronies and instituting various operating reforms, easily make the company worth $70 per share. After a short and furious struggle the tender offer succeeds.

Shaker replaces Quiet Oil's top managers by his own nominees, who then upgrade marketing and bill collecting efforts, dismiss redundant clerks, pursue new opportunities aggressively, and modernize the physical plant and equipment. As a result, Calvinist Chemical's stock rises in market value in a total amount equivalent to a rise from $40 to $62 per share in the market value of the old Quiet Oil shares.

Happy ending

The story has a happy ending. Just about everybody is better off, or not significantly worse off, because of the takeover. The Quiet Oil shareholders received a gain of $20 per share over what they might have gotten in the market had there been no tender offer. The Calvinist Chemical shareholders received a far smaller benefit than Shaker originally contemplated, but they did come out ahead. The general public is not harmed by any new monopolistic practices, since Calvinist Chemical has not increased its market power or share in any reasonably defined product or geographical market. If anything, the general public is benefited by Quiet Oil's newly obtained innovativeness and its streamlining of operations. The redundant clerks of Quiet Oil resented the takeover at first, of course, but most of them went back to school, became computer programmers, and were pleasantly surprised to find that their incomes and job satisfaction increased. Even Fatty found out that there could be life after a takeover. He took a job as head of a career counselling firm. The pay wasn't as good, but he was happy and he greatly supplemented his income by the speaker's fees he got from going before innumerable groups and talking about the evils of "corporate cannibalism" — a subject on which he could speak with an almost supernatural eloquence.

Aspects of the scenario

Notice several points about this model scenario. The tender offeror engaged in a significant amount of *monitoring* the *performance* of another company and its management; it served as a kind of policeman for Quiet Oil's shareholders. Because of its own expenditures and efforts, it discovered a potential for increasing the value of another company through improved operating efficiency, and actually brought about *increased efficiency*. The total gains of this sort seem clearly to have been far larger than the net losses to some of the affected parties (the target's top managers and some of its employees); there were *net gains*. And the gains were *shared* with the stockholders of the target. In this scenario, Calvinist Chemical and its managers appear as value creators who deserve to be rewarded for what they have done.

How frequent?

It is certainly *plausible* to suppose that tender offerors might act as did Calvinist Chemical in our hypothetical, but is it *probable* that this model of monitoring and correcting suboptimal performance represents many takeover attempts? Perhaps surprisingly, the answer is yes. The evidence for this answer appears in the lesser plausibility of some of the other explanations for tender offers and in certain systematically collected data that will be discussed in the next subsection (13.2.2).

(2) Synergy gains

The second explanation for tender offers is that acquiring firms attempt them for many of the same, basically good, business reasons that prompt firms to embark on friendly acquisitions like mergers. The reasons for takeovers may be the same as the business reasons for corporate combinations generally. Among such reasons are expectations of economies of scale in operations, management, or finance; "synergistic" gains from combining two complementary lines of business; elimination of the sometimes high costs of coordinating activities by contracting with the other firm instead of subjecting both activities to a common boss; and so forth. Perhaps, for example, Calvinist Chemical has some secret, valuable, but unpatentable information about how best to convert petroleum products into oils for use in the paints it manufactures, but is afraid to give this information to an independent supplier of the oils. Theoretically, it could contract against adverse use or dissemination of such confidential information, but in reality it might find it very difficult to detect or remedy a breach of such a contract.

Plausibility problem

The main problem with the second explanation for tender offers is that it seems implausible that acquiring companies motivated solely by such reasons would resort to a hostile tender offer rather than a friendly merger. Hostile offers are generally much more costly to the acquiring company than friendly ones. If Calvinist Chemical saw that combining with Quiet Oil could produce some operating synergy or reduction in contracting costs, why wouldn't it take its case to Quiet Oil's managers, show them the desirability of a merger to both companies and their managements and shareholders, and then negotiate the terms of a deal that would distribute these advantages? Notice that this kind of question does not embarrass the first explanation of tender offers: When the reason why the target could become more valuable if owned by the acquirer is that the target's management is suboptimal and must therefore be replaced (or, more realistically, shunted into nominal executive positions with little real power) then obviously there is less likelihood that potential acquirers will attempt or succeed in carrying out a friendly merger. But when the anticipated gain is expected to come from more impersonal forms of efficiency-increasing changes, it becomes implausible to think that potential acquirers would frequently have to resort to tender offers.

Theory better as partial explanation

There are some caveats to this criticism of the second explanation. For one thing, conventional business reasons for combination may be a *part* of the total set of motivations behind an attempted takeover. Calvinist Chemical might want both to shake up Quiet Oil's management and to achieve a reduction in contracting costs, and the fact that the former reason determines the form of acquisition does not mean that the latter is not important. Moreover, some tender offers may result when a desired friendly merger for conventional business reasons is thwarted because target managers insist on getting such a large share of the expected synergistic gains that the acquirer thinks it is cheaper to incur the usually higher transaction costs of a tender offer. (Even here, though, one could construe the target management's insistence on huge side payments for themselves as suboptimal performance toward their shareholders and thus classify the situation as falling under the first explanation.)

(3) Monopoly benefits

The third explanation of tender offers is that the offeror is attempting to monopolize trade or commerce, or to embark on some other anticompetitive course of conduct. Imagine, for example, that Calvinist Chemical and

Quiet Oil are both major manufacurers and sellers of lubricants for motors and tools, that the market for such products is extremely concentrated, and that Calvinist Chemical hopes that by acquiring Quiet Oil it will eventually be able to raise prices and make supranormal profits. If this scenario is representative of most tender offers, policy makers ought to be concerned about them.

Plausibility problem

The monopoly benefits explanation is not plausible, however. Most tender offers do not appear to present serious anticompetitive risks. They do not usually involve a horizontal combination of two firms operating principally in a single, dangerously concentrated market. Frequently, tender offerors propose vertical and conglomerate acquisitions. Although courts and commentators, especially in the past, have envisioned numerous conceivable anticompetitive risks that could be created by such acquisitions, much informed current commentary regards these risks as greatly exaggerated.[2] Moreover, because tender offers are highly visible, controversial, and subject to the waiting period requirements of the Hart-Scott-Rodino Antitrust Improvements Act,[3] as well as to suits by the Justice Department, the Federal Trade Commission, and various private parties, rational tender offerors are unlikely to think they can get away with a significantly anticompetitive acquisition. Yet many tender offers are made. This at least suggests that many of them are not motivated by anticompetitive desires. Finally, one can ask, as in the case of the second example, why monopolistic acquisitors would not usually resort to a friendly merger rather than a tender offer.

(4) Managerial benefits

The fourth explanation for tender offers is that they yield benefits to bidding company managers. This viewpoint comes in many varieties. Perhaps the bidding company managers expect that, as bosses of bigger companies, they will acquire greater power and prestige. Perhaps they expect to obtain greater executive compensation, another often alleged correlate of company size. Or, since so much of their personal wealth is tied up with the fortunes of their company — they own substantial stock, stock options, and similar rights in it — they may simply be trying to diversify their portfolios of investment assets. (Ordinary passive investors, by contrast, can diversify more cheaply and simply, and in a more fine-tuned way, by investing in a mix of securities. They don't need managers to diversify for them at the company level by making conglomerate acquisitions.) Or they

[2]See, e.g., 3 P. Areeda & D. Turner, Antitrust Law ¶¶ 701(c), 711(a) n.3, 730 (1978); R. Bork, The Antitrust Paradox 144-145, 250-260, 380-381 (1978); R. Posner, Antitrust Law 122-124, 182 (1976); F. Scherer, Industrial Market Structure and Economic Performance 335-347 (2d ed. 1980).

[3]15 U.S.C. §18a.

may launch takeovers because they like a good fight. A takeover battle is more exciting than the painstaking and sometimes boring job of actually running a company.

Bad for shareholders

If managerial benefits are the sole motive and effect of hostile takeovers, then takeovers are bound to be bad for shareholders. By hypothesis, the bidding company managers will be indifferent to the hard task of identifying and making just those acquisitions that present the best opportunities for increasing shareholder wealth. They will make acquisitions when no synergistic gains or gains from better management can be expected or even when declines in efficiency, or synergistic losses, are likely to occur.

Impact on bidding company: bad

What would be the average, long-run impact on the wealth of the bidding company shareholders, if this theory is correct? The answer depends in part on whether we think that bidding company managers motivated solely by personal benefits would make, on average, "neutral" acquisitions — business combinations that result neither in gains nor in losses to real efficiency — or would be driven by their unquenchable thirst for targets to make "bad" acquisitions — those having a detrimental effect on efficiency. This choice might depend in turn on which of the varieties of the managerial benefits theory we have in mind. Even if the managers made only neutral acquisitions, their own shareholders' wealth would decrease because of two factors: (1) the very considerable costs of the acquisition transactions themselves — for example, investment bankers' fees and lawyers' fees, and the loss of top management's services during the busy acquisition period; and (2) the premium paid to the target company shareholders. If their managers made economically bad acquisitions, then there would also be shareholder loss because of (3) the efficiency losses following the successful acquisitions.

As for shareholders as a whole, they would be worse off by the amount of the transaction costs and the efficiency losses. Society as a whole would also be worse off by this amount minus the gains to the managers, whose welfare, like that of everyone else, counts as part of the total.

Point of analysis

Probably no well-informed observer thinks that managerial benefits are the *sole* motive and effect of hostile takeovers, of course, and few indeed would contend that benefits to managers are completely irrelevant. The point of considering the explanation in its pure form is to see better what its implications are. As we have seen, its implications for shareholder wealth are negative. If we were to discover strong evidence that, on average, shareholders are not hurt by hostile takeovers or that they are greatly benefited by them, we would have to conclude that managerial benefits cannot be a predominant factor in explaining takeovers, however intuitively appealing that factor may be.

(5) Looting gains

The fifth explanation for tender offers is that the acquirers want to get control so that they can loot the target company. Sometimes the term *raider*, when applied to a tender offeror, has this connotation, but often it merely connotes the speaker's dislike of the probability that the tender offeror will oust the current management of the target. Suppose, for example, that Calvinist Chemical wants to acquire control of Quiet Oil so that it can "rip off" its accumulated cash, strip it of inventory and other items easily converted into cash, and liquidate the remaining assets for the exclusive benefit of itself. In the real world, one occasionally sees businessmen pointing an accusatory finger at offerors who they think will liquidate X Company if they get control of it, rather than maintain it as a going concern.

Distinguish rational liquidations

Almost by definition — a *proper* definition, that is — "looting"-oriented takeovers are bad. But the real issue is whether the critics of tender offerors as looters and raiders are objecting to activities that can sensibly be characterized as looting. Suppose it is true that Calvinist Chemical plans, if it gets control of Quiet Oil, to sell all of the latter's assets piecemeal, dissolve the corporate entity, and pay out the proceeds in a final liquidating distribution. So what? This will be a good thing for any remaining (now minority) shareholders of Quiet Oil if two conditions are satisfied: (1) The distribution is paid to shareholders on a pro rata basis, in accord with the clear, normal rules of corporate law; and (2) The business of the corporation has a liquidating value that is higher than its going concern value — it is actually worth more dead than alive. Satisfaction of the first condition is a legal requirement that may be policed by a lawsuit, if necessary. It is in the self-interest of Calvinist Chemical to determine whether the second condition is met before it causes a liquidation. It wants to liquidate if and only if doing so is the economically sensible course of action. As major owner of the target, it has *no incentive* to waste assets or to destroy a truly flourishing business — that is, a business that has an excess of going-concern value over liquidation value.

The plant-closing bugaboo

Other aspects of tender offers, if not explanations of them, are sometimes alleged as bases for regulation. Often the arguments are casual and emotional. For example, managers of potential targets sometimes contend that hostile takeovers destroy jobs or injure local communities. They may invoke the specter that the bidder, once in control, will close plants or relocate them. Several points are worth noting about this argument. First, there seems to be no good systematic evidence showing that bidding firms as a class are very likely to do such things. The evidence usually invoked is quite anecdotal. Second, plants are closed and employees are laid off, obviously, mostly by companies in trouble, quite apart from any recent shift in the ownership of their shares. (Since only a small percentage of companies are subject to takeovers, it's likely that the great majority of plant closings are done by firms that have not been subjected to a takeover bid.) If there ought to be further legal regulation or governmental assistance programs concerning these problems, then surely the rational approach is to deal with them directly, rather than by making takeovers difficult. Third, plants are usually closed because they are losing money — they are less efficient than competing plants elsewhere. For the longer-run good of the economy, they should be closed. Abrupt plant closings may indeed cause losses for employees and local communities, and these may well be a legitimate cause for governmental reaction. But the better response would appear to be some form of governmental or private transition assistance, not a flat prohibition on closings. And preventing takeovers as an indirect way of pursuing that flawed second strategy is doubly irrational.

§13.2.2 Evidence About the Theories

Use of stock price data

One approach to choosing among the five explanations is to look at stock prices. Is the total value of the acquiring and target companies, as measured by the stock market, greater (on average) after a successful hostile takeover than it was before it? If the answer is yes, and if we trust the collective judgment of players in the market, we are reduced to choosing among the first three explanations. And if we could then rule out the third choice, the monopoly benefits explanation, on other grounds, then we might conclude that hostile takeovers are, on average, value-creating transactions. If the answer is no, and again we trust the collective judgment of the players in the market, then the choice is between the fourth and fifth explanations. We might then conclude that hostile takeovers are, on average, value-destroying transactions.

Not a simple matter

Using data about market prices is not a simple matter, however. To do the job right, the researcher has to identify many difficult issues and respond to them. For example, should she consider price changes before and after completion of the acquisition, or before and after *announcement* of the acquisition attempt? On reflection, the announcement date seems the better choice; market participants quickly reflect their expectations about the (bad or good) consequences to shareholders of a transaction in stock trading prices, and their expectations are largely formed when a transaction is proposed and seems likely to occur. (This is just an offshoot of the basic principle that the value a rational person places on a capital asset is the discounted present value of the benefits or detriments she expects it to yield to herself in the future.) Another problem is how to decide on time periods before and after the announcement date. Too short a period after the announcement may not tell us about the long-term consequences of the takeover bid. But looking at data over too long a period after the bid is apt to yield no detectable or meaningful pattern, because the influence of the acquisition per se will begin to be swamped by the effects of many other factors affecting market prices and company fortunes.

Factoring out market changes

An even more important problem is the need to factor out price changes that simply reflect changes in market prices as a whole or changes in the market's perceptions of the future of the whole industry of which the bidder or target is part. Unless this adjustment is made, any positive or negative results we discover may be spurious; they may really tell us nothing about hostile tender offers per se. Moreover, the researcher ideally should measure shareholder returns in relation to risk, and should attempt to measure and adjust for changes in risk levels that are caused by takeovers. Otherwise, the before-and-after comparisons will have an apples-and-oranges flavor.

Econometric studies

The statistics reported in the popular financial press or assembled by practicing lawyers sometimes fail miserably to take adequate account of the problems mentioned in the last paragraph. Economists and statisticians have, in general, done much better. Some have used the technique of measuring "cumulative average residuals" (CARS) before and after the announcement of takeover bids. Roughly speaking, CARS measure "abnormal" returns or losses: those not due simply to fluctuations in the market as a whole or to changes in risk level, or to other factors in the economist's capital-asset pricing model, but to the market's reaction to the specific takeover bid. Using this technique, they have compared successful and unsuccessful takeovers, takeovers in different time periods, hostile takeovers versus friendly acquisitions, and many other things. There has been a rather substantial body of research.

Results

What are the results? They are hard to convey adequately in a short space, but the gist of them can be indicated here. Professors Jensen and Ruback offered a thorough summary of CARS studies of mergers and tender offers using announcement date as reference point.[4] For target firms, abnormal *positive* returns are found to be 29 percent for successful

[4]Jensen & Ruback, The Market for Corporate Control: The Scientific Evidence, 11 J. Fin. Econ. 5 (1983). This article is the introductory piece for an entire issue of the Journal of Financial Economics that covered the market for corporate control and summarizes most of the other new research therein.

takeovers, over the month or two surrounding the announcement.[5] Targets of *un*successful takeovers maintain high returns, provided they receive a new offer within two years.[6] Do the bidding firms' shareholders lose what the target companies' shareholders gain? No. For the bidding company shareholders, abnormal *positive* returns are found to be 4 percent for successful takeovers,[7] but in the case of unsuccessful takeover attempts, bidders have a negative abnormal return of 1 percent.[8]

Takeovers seen as value-creating

To summarize, in percentage terms, shareholders of target firms gain *substantially* from takeover attempts, and shareholders of bidding firms gain, though by more modest amounts, when attempts are successful. The results are impressive, and they strongly suggest that takeovers are perceived by the stock market as *value-creating* transactions.

Why uneven split of gains

One puzzle with such findings is why the bidding company shareholders get so little of the gain created by takeovers. Several explanations have been ventured. First, the disparity is to a large extent illusory because acquiring firms are, on average, much larger than acquired firms. Even if the two companies' shareholders split the absolute amount of the expected gain half and half, it would result in a much lower percentage increase in the market price of an acquiring company share, as compared to a target company share. Second, the disparity may be partly illusory because the market capitalizes the expected gain to a bidding company from a program of acquisitions as soon as the market perceives that there is such a program. Thus, bidding company shareholders realize some of their abnormal positive returns long in advance of particular acquisition attempts by their companies. Empirical research suggests that this explanation does have validity.[9] Third, low abnormal returns to bidders may simply reflect competition in the market for control.[10] The resistance tactics employed by target managements may also be an important factor.

[5] By contrast, the abnormal positive returns found for mergers were only 16 percent. Why the difference? Perhaps because mergers involve only the prospect of ordinary synergies — the second type of explanation proposed earlier in this section — whereas hostile takeovers may produce *both* ordinary synergies and better management, alias "reduction of agency costs."

[6] Again by contrast, abnormal returns to shareholders are lost in the case of mergers as soon as the failure of the proposed merger becomes known.

[7] For mergers, the comparable figure is only 1.4 percent, and the results from study to study are less consistent than in the takeover case.

[8] For mergers, the negative return figure is about 2.5 percent.

[9] Schipper & Thompson, Evidence on the Capitalized Value of Merger Activity for Acquiring Firms, 11 J. Fin. Econ. 85 (1983); but see Asquith, Bruner, & Mullins, The Gains to Bidding Firms from Merger, 11 J. Fin. Econ. 121 (1983).

[10] Incidentally, this explanation casts doubt on the claims of those who say the law should encourage, more than it already does, "auctions" in which rival bidders compete vigorously for targets.

Attacks on such studies

Proponents of curbs on takeovers have attacked the CARS studies, sometimes with vehemence. Of the many points that have been or could be raised, several are worth noting. One is that tests of the financial performance of acquired targets, as measured by accounting data before and after the acquisition, would be a more relevant test of the real impact of takeovers. If bidders can improve management or realize synergies, these effects ought to show up after the acquisition in the financial statements.

Accounting data studies have drawbacks too

In fact, early studies of the effects of mergers tended to rely on accounting data. Unfortunately, this method of research has severe drawbacks. Real operating gains or losses after an acquisition may take years to materialize, and by then it will be hard to sort out the effects of the acquisition from numerous other factors. (This is, once again, the "swamping" problem that plagues attempts to measure long-term effects in a complicated world.) Moreover, it takes a trained investment analyst to properly decipher financial statements and to hunt intelligently for extraneous facts that will reveal their sometimes-hidden meanings. It is doubtful that the typical academic economist or statistician, however smart and well trained, could do the job well. Yet stock market prices already reflect the cumulative judgment of professional securities analysts, many of whom will have probed both the company's financial statements and a myriad of associated nonfinancial data.

Costliness of in-depth research

Why not place highly trained analysts, accountants, economists, and even sociologists in acquiring companies to see how they actually change the operations of target companies? This sort of research would surely yield rich and illuminating material. Unfortunately, it is very expensive to do, and it requires managerial cooperation that will not always be forthcoming. And if it is done in a few cases, there will be serious questions about whether the results can be generalized. This is an especially acute problem with open-ended, in-depth studies, because they present many opportunities for the interpretive biases of the researchers to shape the findings.

Challenges to wisdom of market

The most serious attack on the CARS studies has to do with their underlying assumptions and relevance to policy making. Why should we take the stock market's reactions to business combinations as saying anything about whether they are really good or bad? Does the fact that the market thinks a transaction creates value mean that, in some more basic economic sense, the transaction does increase value?

Stock market speculatively efficient

In technical terms, the question resolves to whether the stock market is allocatively efficient as well as speculatively efficient. A great amount of research supports the notion that the organized stock markets *are* efficient in the sense that investors without access to inside information can expect only a competitive return on their investments. For example, studies suggest that the number of mutual funds that outperform the market by getting a higher-than-normal risk-adjusted return over a substantial time period is no greater than would be expected on the basis of chance. Few investors could demonstrate (though many imagine that they get) reliable, consistent "monopoly rents" resulting from their investment activities. The market seems to have many buyers and sellers and fairly low transaction costs, and information deemed relevant by investors is very quickly reflected in prices after it is made public.

Maybe not allocatively efficient

Conceivably, however, the market might not be efficient in an allocative sense. This could happen if all investors valued stocks not by considering information about the actual and expected economic performance of issuing companies but by considering other, irrational factors. The market could then be an efficient game for the investors in that few players could systematically get the jump on everyone else, but stock prices would tell us little about which companies were really creating value and generating high earnings and dividends. A stock market with these characteristics would have a bad effect on the real economy. For example, the market might value Firm A's stock much higher than Firm B's, even though the latter had better future earnings prospects, with the unfortunate result that relatively inefficient A might have an easier time raising money to expand its lackluster operations.

Debate among economists

The extent to which the market is allocatively efficient is a lively topic of debate among contemporary economists.[11] Resolution of the debate is not expected soon.

Policy implications

Probably most economists think that the stock market is allocatively efficient to a significant extent. If it is not, the implications for policy about takeovers are not at all clear. True, the CARS studies would not then be able to be interpreted as showing that takeovers create "real" efficiency in business operations. But neither could they — or any other systematic

[11] Contrast Shiller, Do Stock Market Prices Move Too Much to Be Justified by Subsequent Changes in Dividends? 71 Am. Econ. Rev. 421 (June 1981), with Leroy, Efficiency and the Variability of Asset Prices, 74 Am. Econ. Rev. 183 (May 1984). Roughly speaking, the Shiller paper explores the idea that, because over time the stock prices of public companies are very much more volatile than the companies' dividend payouts, the market must be responding to factors foreign to a rational capital asset pricing model; it may therefore be allocatively inefficient to a significant degree. Leroy criticizes this type of study and some of the conclusions sought to be based on it. There are many debatable issues, of course. For example, a large part of the relative volatility of stock prices might be explained by fluctuations in the general level of interest rates. This phenomenon would not impugn the market's efficiency because the usual capital-asset pricing model depends on the risk-free rate of interest, which clearly fluctuates greatly from time to time.

evidence now in print — be interpreted to show that takeovers produce a bad effect on real efficiency. On the real effects on business operations of takeovers, the rational policy maker who didn't trust the market would simply have to be agnostic, which might lead to a neutral set of legal rules — such as the Williams Act supposedly embodies. Or it might lead to restraints on costly defensive tactics, since the empirical evidence does at least suggest that *shareholders* benefit from takeovers.

§13.2.3 Possible Implications

As just noted, there is substantial evidence that shareholders benefit from takeovers and that defensive tactics may harm them. The policy implications of this evidence are not entirely certain, however. The debate over defensive tactics is discussed in subsection 13.6.4 infra. Some views on regulation of offerors are mentioned here.

A mixed review

In a comprehensive review of explanations of takeovers,[12] Professor Coffee admits the force of the arguments and evidence for the disciplinary hypothesis (the first explanation discussed in 13.2.1), but also notes apparently contrary kinds of evidence (such as surveys of what acquiring company managers say they are trying to do) and alternative interpretations of the evidence. He also stresses the costs of takeovers, including the more subtle and unmeasurable ones. He argues that having *more* takeovers than we already have would not necessarily be better for shareholder welfare, since, as with any sanctioning mechanism, there can be such a thing as overdeterrence of undesired conduct. These reflections lead him to only modest suggestions for tinkering with existing regulation.

Partial bids, two-tier offers, and "distorted choice"

Many commentators, including Coffee and persons sympathetic to the disciplinary hypothesis, have been bothered by partial bids and two-tier offers. In a partial bid, the offeror seeks only bare control of the target. In a two-tier offer, the offeror makes a bid for bare control at one price and, if successful, then effects a freezeout merger of remaining shareholders, usually at a lower price. One argument — developed, for example, by Professor Bebchuk[13] — is that these practices lead to a distorted choice. Target shareholders may tender because they fear they will be left out of a sale at a premium price and will become minority shareholders who are (relatively) poorly treated, not because they think the offeror's bid price reflects the

[12] Coffee, Regulating the Market for Corporate Control: A Critical Assessment of the Tender Offer's Role in Corporate Governance, 84 Colum. L. Rev. 1145 (1984).

[13] Bebchuk, Towards Undistorted Choice and Equal Treatment in Corporate Takeovers, 98 Harv. L. Rev. 1693 (May 1985).

company's full value. Put another way, a single owner of control of the target, not being affected by such strategic considerations, might demand and get a higher price for the target's shares.

A proposed solution

Bebchuk's solution is to allow target shareholders to tender "approvingly or disapprovingly," that is, with a yes or no vote on the proposed shift in control. Shareholders might vote no, for example, if they think that the bid is inadequate and its defeat will be followed by another, better bid, perhaps by another offeror. If a sufficient number of tendering shareholders vote yes, the tender offer and shift in control is allowed to proceed; however, all tendering shareholders, even those voting no, have their shares taken up. But if most shareholders vote no, the tender offer is precluded and no shares are taken up. Thus, if the offer really was an optimal one that won't be bettered, the shareholders will have lost an opportunity. This approach is designed to encourage shareholders to express their true beliefs about the desirability of a takeover instead of letting them be browbeaten or enticed into gaming behavior.

We now turn to the existing regulation of tender offers.

§13.3 The Williams Act: Basics

§13.3.1 Background and Purposes

Rise of cash offers

Before the 1960s, persons trying to take over a company did so mainly by starting a proxy contest.[1] During the 1960s, however, takeovers were increasingly effected through outright stock purchases, typically solicited by a tender offer.[2] Tender offers and other methods of stock acquisition were less complicated and less time-consuming than proxy contests. Persons who bought a controlling amount of stock for cash were exempt from federal disclosure requirements, but federal law required significant disclosures by those seeking control of a corporation through a proxy contest or an exchange offer. Thus, the cash tender offer provided an opportunity for secrecy and surprise, both of which helped the acquirer to carry out the takeover, even in the face of bitter resistance by management.

Pressure on investors

As a result of the rise of tender offers, investors increasingly faced situations in which they were forced to make quick and arguably ill-informed decisions about whether to sell their stock or retain it. The investor faced

§13.3 [1]See Note, The Developing Meaning of "Tender Offer" Under the Securities Exchange Act of 1934, 86 Harv. L. Rev. 1250, 1253 (1973).

[2]See H.R. Rep. No. 1711, 90th Cong., 2d Sess. 4, reprinted in 1968 U.S. Code Cong. & Ad. News 2811, 2812.

by a tender offer might not know the identity or goals of those who would end up in control of the corporation. One could at least argue — how convincingly is another matter — that this knowledge would be important to the investor. She might decide not to tender her shares if she thought the offeror would get control anyway and improve the company's performance, thus making her shares worth more than even the tender offer price. Even if she tendered shares, she might not know whether all of them would be purchased. If she waited to see whether a better offer developed, eager fellow shareholders might fill up the offer, and she would lose the chance to tender at a premium price.

The Williams Act

The argument was advanced that investors faced with a bid for their shares were no less entitled to an opportunity to make a rational investment decision based on all the relevant information than were investors facing a proxy contest or exchange offer. Congress apparently bought this argument,[3] for in 1968 it passed the Williams Act,[4] which amended the Securities Exchange Act of 1934. The Williams Act added Sections 13(d)-(e) and 14(d)-(e) of the Exchange Act. It deals with both acquisitions of control through market purchases and with acquisitions through tender offers, and places similar disclosure requirements on the two types of acquisitions. In addition, some provisions subject tender offers to further regulations designed to relieve investors of some of the pressure attendant on offers limited with respect to time or number of shares requested. Ultimately, the Act sought to place tender offers under regulations designed to give investors the same protections that are accorded investors facing proxy contests or exchange offers,[5] but was not intended, however, either to encourage or discourage tender offers.[6]

A need for information?

Should investors who are asked to sell to offerors be entitled to such protection? In support of the Williams Act, one could argue that, from a shareholder's point of view, a shift in control virtually produces a new company and is equivalent to a forced exchange for a wholly new security. The investor's decision whether to sell to the acquirer is like the investor's initial decision whether to invest, so the investor seems entitled to similar treatment. The counterargument is that the two situations are not the same: An investor who sells to an acquirer no longer has any interest in the company, whereas the investor asked to make a decision in a proxy contest

[3]See id. at 2812-2813; 113 Cong. Rec. 854 (1967) (remarks of Senator Williams).

[4]Act of July 29, 1968, Pub. L. No. 90-439, 82 Stat. 454 (codified as amended at 15 U.S.C. §§78m(d)-(e), 78n(d)-(f) (1982).

[5]See report cited in note 2 supra.

[6]Id. at 2813.

or exchange offer will still be invested in the company regardless of what he decides.[7]

§13.3.2 The Rules of the Road

13(d) disclosures by 5 percent owners

Let's first consider the disclosure requirements that are triggered whenever a person acquires more than 5 percent of a class of stock of a public company. Note that this rule is not restricted to acquisitions by tender offer. In its usual application, for example, it would apply to purchases on the open market, through ordinary broker's transactions, that put the buyer over the 5 percent mark. Specifically, Section 13(d) requires any person who has "directly or indirectly" acquired the beneficial ownership[8] of more than 5 percent of any equity security of a class registered pursuant to Section 12 of the Exchange Act to send, within 10 days of the acquisition, certain information to the issuer of the security and the exchanges on which the security is traded, and to file that information with the SEC. The information includes facts about the identity and background of the purchaser, the source of the funds used in the acquisition, and the number and percentage of shares held. If the purchaser intends to acquire control of the issuing company, the purchaser must divulge "any plans or proposals which such person may have to liquidate such issuer, to sell its assets to or merge it with any other persons, or to make any other major change in its business or corporate structure. . . ." Although 13(d) does not say in express and unconditional terms that the acquirer must disclose an intent to gain control, it has been supplemented by SEC regulations requiring disclosure of such intent as well as further information regarding the purchaser's future plans for the issuer.[9]

[7]See Brudney, A Note on Chilling Tender Solicitations, 21 Rutgers L. Rev. 609, 616-620 (1967).

[8]Rule 13d-3 codifies the rule in Bath Indus., Inc. v. Blot, 427 F.2d 97 (7th Cir. 1970), that beneficial ownership exists whenever a person (with certain exceptions, e.g., a broker) has voting power or investment power over a security or has the right to acquire either of these powers.

[9]Schedule 13D, Item 4, requires a statement of the purpose(s) of acquiring the securities and a description of any plans that relate to or would result in 1) the acquisition of additional securities of the issuer; 2) any change in the present board of directors or management of the issuer; 3) any merger, reorganization, liquidation, or major sale of assets of the issuer; 4) changes in the issuer's business or corporate structure, and changes in its capitalization or dividend policy; 5) amending the issuer's charter or bylaws to make a takeover of the issuer more difficult; 6) causing a class of the issuer's securities to be delisted from a national stock exchange, or no longer quoted in a system under a registered national securities association; or 7) making a class of the issuer's securities eligible for deregistration by reducing the number of shareholders to less than 300. Any action similar to one of those listed above should also be

Exceptions

Section 13(d)(6) specifies certain exceptions to the disclosure requirements, including an exception for acquisitions that, together with all purchases over the last 12 months, would not exceed 2 percent of the security. Thus, a person already holding 15 percent of a company's stock might buy up to 2 percent more per year without having to file a 13D. There is also an exception for any acquisition of an equity security by the issuer of the security. But Section 13(e) subjects issuer purchases to "such rules and regulations as the Commission, in the public interest or for the protection of investors, may adopt." The SEC has adopted a number of rules pursuant to this authorization.

13(e)

Definition of *person*

Section 13(d)(3) defines *person* for the purposes of the Williams Act to include "two or more persons act[ing] as a partnership, limited partnership, syndicate, or other group for the purpose of acquiring, holding, or disposing of securities of an issuer. . . ." Thus, if two individuals each buy 3 percent of the common stock of a public company but they are acting in concert, their actions will trigger the 13(d) disclosure requirement.

14(d) disclosures by tender offerors

Now let us consider the rules about tender offers. Section 14(d) and SEC Schedule 14D-1 require any tender offeror who, if the offer were consummated, would be the beneficial owner of more than 5 percent of a security of the same class covered in 13(d), to disclose, to the SEC and the target company, the same information as that which the market purchaser is required to disclose under Section 13(d), plus certain other specified items relating to the purchaser's financial condition and any agreements with the target company. Significantly, the offeror must disclose the purpose of the tender offer and its plans or proposals for the target.[10]

---

reported. A later addition, Section 13G, imposes somewhat lesser disclosure requirements on all owners of more than 5 percent of a qualifying security, and permits certain acquirers to file under 13(g) in lieu of filing under 13(d). (Note that no acquisition is required to trigger 13(g).) Any material change in the facts disclosed must also be reported promptly, under Section 13(d)(2) and Rule 13d-2(a).

[10] See Schedule 14D-1. Specifically, the bidder must describe any plans that relate to or would result in:

1) a merger, reorganization, or liquidation of the target company or any of its subsidiaries;
2) a sale of a material part of the assets of the target or any of its subsidiaries;
3) any change in the present board of directors or management;
4) any material change in the capitalization, dividend policy, corporate structure or business of the target company;
5) causing a class of the target company's securities to be delisted from a national securities exchange or lose its trading authorization on an inter-dealer quotation system; or
6) a class of equity securities of the target company becoming eligible for deregistration under Section 12(g)(4) of the Exchange Act.

Antitrust disclosure

It should be noted that tender offers are also subject to the disclosure provisions of the Hart-Scott-Rodino Antitrust Improvements Act of 1976,[11] which requires companies with $100 million or more in sales or assets to notify the FTC and the Antitrust Division of the Justice Department of any plans to acquire 15 percent or more of the assets or voting securities of a company with $10 million or more in sales or assets. After notifying the government, the acquirer must wait 15 days before any acquisition for cash can begin, and 30 days before any other kind of acquisition can begin.

Exceptions to 14(d)

Section 14(d)(8) lists exceptions to the 14(d) disclosure requirement. These include acquisitions by the issuer of its own securities and offers that, together with all purchases over the last 12 months, would result in acquisition of less than 2 percent of the target's stock. The Section also gives the SEC power to exempt other tender offers, provided they do not have the purpose or effect of changing or influencing control of the issuer.

Regulation of recommendations

In addition, Section 14(d) allows the SEC to regulate any solicitation or recommendation to accept or reject the tender offer. Accordingly, through Rule 14d-4 the SEC has applied the disclosure requirements of 14(d) to such communications. It has created two exemptions, however. First, Rule 14d-2(e) exempts advice concerning a tender offer that is given by a bank, investment adviser, attorney, or fiduciary who is not otherwise participating in the tender offer to a client who either made an unsolicited request for the advice or has a general contract to receive such advice. Second, Rule 14d-2(f) exempts communications by the target if they say no more than that management is considering the tender offer and shareholders should not decide whether to accept or reject the offer until they have received management's recommendation on the matter, which will be given by a specified date not later than ten days before the close of the offer. Whether a particular communication falls within this latter exemption or is a recommendation against a tender offer appears to depend on its precise wording. For instance, in *Anaconda Co. v. Crane Co.*,[12] Anaconda responded to a tender offer from Crane by issuing the following press release: "When Crane does file a registration statement and preliminary prospectus with the S.E.C., Anaconda will be in a position to consider an evaluation of the situation. Until that time it should not be assumed that the Anaconda management is sympathetic to the proposed offer."[13] The court held that this statement was exempted.

[11] 15 U.S.C. §18a.
[12] 411 F. Supp. 1210 (S.D.N.Y. 1975).
[13] Id. at 1213.

"Person"

Section 14(d)(2) mirrors Subsection 13(d)(2) by deeming a group acting in concert to be a "person" for purposes of the 14(d) requirements.

Traffic rules too

In addition to affirmative disclosure requirements, the statute has three important provisions that create what might be thought of as "traffic rules" for tender offers. These pertain to withdrawal rights, a proration requirement, and price increases. Arguably, they all contribute to fair play and a reduction of pressure on shareholders.

Withdrawal rights

Specifically, Subsection 14(d)(5) gives target shareholders a chance to change their minds: Securities deposited pursuant to a tender offer may be withdrawn by the depositor at any time within seven days after the tender offer is published. But SEC Rule 14d-7 further extends this withdrawal period to 15 business days, so that, not seven days, is the relevant period. The rule also adds a withdrawal period of ten days after a competing tender offer is made.

Proration

Section 14(d)(6) provides that when an offeror offers to purchase only a portion of the outstanding stock of an issuer and a greater number of shares than it wants are tendered, the offeror must purchase the shares on a pro rata basis from each tendering shareholder. This is known as the "pro rata rule." The statute speaks of proration rights for those tendering in the first ten days of an offer, but Rule 14d-8, adopted in 1982, extends them to all tenders made while the offer is open. By rule, as we shall soon see, an initial offer must be kept open for at least *20* days.

Best price rule

Section 14(d)(7) provides that an offeror who, before expiration of the offer, increases the consideration offered to shareholders, must pay the increased consideration to each shareholder whose shares are purchased, including those who tendered before announcement of the price increase. This is known as the "best price rule."

14(e) antifraud provision

Finally, Section 14(e) contains a general antifraud provision, similar to that of Rule 10b-5, that applies to all statements made and acts done in connection with tender offers. Perhaps oddly, it is a rule adopted under this general antifraud provision, Rule 14e-1, that requires tender offers to be kept open at least 20 business days. And if the offeror increases the price during an offer, it must keep the offer open for at least ten days after the announcement of the increase, even if the 20-day period was almost up.

Minimum offer period

Summary

In summary, the Williams Act's regulation of tender offers consists of three major components: mandatory disclosure requirements, a general antifraud provision, and some modest "traffic rules" designed to protect target shareholders.

§13.3.3 An Illustrative Hypothetical

Enter Joe Bob Briggs

In order to see how these dry rules work in practice and to understand the human impulses they are designed to curb, let us imagine a hypothetical case. Joe Bob Briggs is an aggressive Texan and an expert on horror movies. His main activities have been watching movies and writing a weekly newspaper column, but recently he has formed bigger ideas. He wants to buy a controlling interest in the Texas Chain Saw Company, a public corporation, and to use its inventory to make a horror film of epochal proportions. You are Joe Bob's lawyer, and he has come to you for advice.

Secret purchases of 20 percent?

Joe Bob wants to buy 20 percent of Chain Saw's stock on the market before making a tender offer. His idea is that it would be desirable to get a foothold, and not just a measly toehold, before springing the offer on the shareholders. He hopes to keep his actions secret until the offer is announced. He wonders if this is possible.

It is your sad duty to inform him that it is not. Under 13(d) he has ten days to file a Schedule 13D after getting 5 percent of the Chain Saw stock. You then discuss the kinds of information that he must disclose.

Split purchases among friends?

Upset at your advice, Joe Bob comes up with a counter proposal. He and his friends — Buckaroo, Sally, and Dolly — will each buy 4.9 percent of Chain Saw stock on the market. Joe Bob may later buy their shares, and in any event he can always count on their cooperation if he needs it to control the company. Joe Bob's thought is that when all four blocks are purchased, then and only then will he announce and make a tender offer.

No; group equals person

You must now tell him that his new plan would also run afoul of 13(d), because he and his three friends would undoubtedly constitute a "group" acting together to acquire shares and therefore would be considered a "person" that is required to make disclosure. You might even point out how sweeping the 13(d) provision about a "group" really is. For example, if Joe Bob and his friends each had separately acquired 4.9 percent of Chain Saw stock long ago and now simply agree — informally, not necessarily expressly or in writing — to cooperate if Joe Bob's tender offer is made and is successful, then they would be considered a group and would have ten days in which to file a 13D, even though they haven't yet started doing anything such as making offers or buying more stock.

Buy during ten-day filing period?

Still determined to make a surprise attack from the strongest possible position, Joe Bob proposes another idea. He will buy 5 percent of Chain Saw's stock on the market, through ordinary broker's transactions, and wait until the last day of the ten-day period before filing his Schedule 13D and announcing his takeover attempt. During that ten-day period he will buy as much stock as he can on the market. Is this permissible?

Finally (at least as of this writing), you are able to give him an answer he likes. Market purchases during the ten-day period are permissible. But the SEC would like to require Joe Bob to file the day after getting 5 percent or not to buy any more shares after passing the 5 percent mark until he has made his filing. There is some question whether the SEC needs new statutory power to impose such a rule.

Joe Bob then pursues a different set of worries. After he has bought what he can on the market and filed his 13D, he will make a tender offer. He realizes, of course, that he will have to make filings and disclosures at the start of the tender offer (not, say, within ten days after the offer is announced). He is concerned about whether he is required to disclose his intention to gain control and his business plan — namely, to redeploy Chain Saw's assets into a shockingly new kind of business.

Disclosure of business plan?

Of course, Joe Bob does have to disclose major plans for changing the target company's business. Would you think it ethical to point out to him that if he looked again into his thoughts, he might discover that his business plans were not really so definite after all, so that he could make do with an extremely vague disclosure? It might not bother him to make a statement of this kind: "If the offeror succeeds in gaining control of the target company, he will study its business operations and prospects carefully, and such examination of the business may lead him to design an alternative plan of operations." In practice, many offerors make disclosures that are not much more informative than this.

The vagueness alternative

Joe Bob then raises another concern. He is worried that if he keeps his offer open too long, his arch rival, J. R. of Dallas, will come in with a rival bid. He therefore wants to put pressure on the target company shareholders to "fish or cut bait" before this happens. He wants the offer to be open for only three days.

Three-day offer?

Now you must convey the unwelcome information that under Rule 14e-1 the offer must be kept open at least 20 business days and that under Rule 14d-7 any shareholders tendering within the first 15 business days will have withdrawal rights during that time period. The effect of these rules is to encourage auctions of the sort Joe Bob wishes to avoid.

No: 20 business days

Joe Bob, who is nothing if not persistent, wants to pressure the shareholders anyway. His next idea is to make a bid for only 51 percent of Chain Saw. If more than that is tendered, he will only buy shares up to 51 percent on a first-come, first-served basis. This, he hopes, will get the shareholders to tender quickly for fear of losing out on his high-priced offer.

"First come, first served"?

But again you must throw the lawyer's wet blanket on his plans. Under Rule 14d-8 all shares tendered during the period of the offer must be taken up pro rata, not on a first-come, first-served basis.

No: pro rata

Price discrimination?

Irritated at the thought that you will send him a hefty bill for this discouraging advice, Joe Bob shifts to a new concern. He is well aware that some shareholders might be willing and eager to sell at $12 per share, but others will not sell until the price is raised a few dollars more, and so on. In order to minimize his expenditures, he would like first to offer $12 and see who tenders; he will then offer a higher price that will be available only to those who tender after he announces it. Will this work?

No: higher price to all

You must point out that it will not work if the price increase is announced during the period when the offer is open. Section 14(d)(7) requires that the highest price be given to all shareholders who tender pursuant to the offer. Moreover, even apart form this provision, there is a practical problem: Shareholders possessing withdrawal rights would simply withdraw their shares when the price increase is announced and then re-tender them after a day or so.

Unless new offer made

Nevertheless, as you point out in an eager attempt to be of service to your client, Joe Bob might well consider making a tender offer at $12 and buying as many shares as are tendered when the offer ends, and then making an entirely new tender offer at a higher price a few days later. Under the law current as of this writing he could do this, but it has been proposed that a rule be adopted making the higher price available to persons whose shares were tendered and bought in an earlier offer that ended within the 30-day period before the subsequent one began.

What's a tender offer, anyway?

After engaging in as much reflection as his rednecked temperament is capable of, Joe Bob wonders aloud whether he should attempt his acquisition in some way that does not involve making a tender offer. In that way he could avoid the 14(d) disclosure requirements, the frustrating substantive regulations such as withdrawal and proration rights, and potential liabilities under Section 14(e). In order to know the boundaries within which he could act if he made such a decision, he asks you to explain to him the Williams Act's definition of a tender offer.

No statutory definition

Embarrassed that you have to reveal the careless drafting of fellow lawers, you tell him that the Act has no definition of *tender offer*. The meaning of the term has had to be explored in a rather messy set of judicial opinions (which we shall examine in the next section of this chapter).

As the last part of our hypothetical suggests, the Williams Act left considerable room for statutory construction. Therefore, having looked at the basic statutory provisions, we will now examine certain interpretations of the Act that have been developed by the courts and the SEC.[14]

[14] For extensive treatments of the issues covered in this and the next section of the text, see E. Aranow, H. Einhorn, & G. Berlstein, Developments in Tender Offers for Corporate Control chs. 1-3 (1977); 1 M. Lipton & E. Steinberger, Takeovers and Freezeouts chs. 2 and 3 (1984).

§13.4 *The Williams Act: Litigation*

§13.4.1 Acquisitions Covered by Section 13(d)

What counts as an acquisition that triggers the application of Section 13(d)? Legal developments show how surprisingly difficult this question can be.

Unintentional acquisitions

For example, how should the law regard actions by the issuer itself that cause a shareholder to cross the 5-percent line? The SEC has ruled that a shareholder was not required to file a disclosure statement when his interest in the issuer rose above 5 percent simply as a result of a repurchase by the issuer.[1] This ruling seems to indicate that only purposeful action by a shareholder will invoke the disclosure rules. Yet this policy might be read to conflict with the fact that the Williams Act includes indirect acquisitions, depending on whether one thinks the term "indirect acquisitions" includes "unintentional acquisitions." The possibility of differing interpretations is reflected in the case law. For example, courts have differed over whether inheriting more than 5 percent of a corporation's securities should trigger the disclosure requirements.[2]

Acquisition of what?

What must be acquired to trigger the Act is also problematic at times. Acquisition of nonvoting securities does not require filing under Section 13(d) (although they are included under the definition of equity security for the purposes of Regulations 14D and 14E). Thus, acquisition of preferred stock will require filing under Section 13(d) only if it includes voting rights, whether or not the shares are voted as a special class.[3]

What's a group or person?

What constitutes a "group" and when a group makes an acquisition also present legal line-drawing dilemmas. As noted above, Subsection 13(d)(3) defines a *person* to include "two or more persons act[ing] as a partnership, limited partnership, syndicate, or other group for the purpose of acquiring, holding, or disposing of securities of an issuer." In favor of an expansive reading of this language, courts cite the basic purposes of Section 13(d): to alert investors to potential changes in corporate control and to give them a chance to evaluate the effect of such changes.

§13.4 [1]Drico Indus. Corp. [1977-1978] Fed. Sec. L. Rep. (CCH) ¶81,270 (SEC 1976). Nor does the disclosure duty of an acquiring corporation vanish when a public offering by the issuer causes the acquirer's interest to drop below 5 percent. American Pepsi Cola Bottlers, Inc., [1971-1972] Fed. Sec. L. Rep. (CCH) ¶78,765 (SEC 1972).

[2]Compare Sisak v. Wings & Wheels Express, Inc., [1970-1971] Fed. Sec. L. Rep. (CCH) ¶92,991 (S.D.N.Y. 1970) (inheritors must file), with Ozark Air Lines v. Cox, 326 F. Supp. 1113, 1117 (E.D. Mo. 1971) (inheritors not required to file because no "purposeful acquisition").

[3]1 M. Lipton & E. Steinberger, Takeovers & Freezeouts, §2.01[2] (1984).

Agreement to act in concert

To find that such a group exists, a court need only find an agreement among two or more persons to act together for one of these stated purposes. No written agreement is necessary, since the court will infer a joint venture from circumstantial evidence.[4] In *General Aircraft Corp. v. Lampert,*[5] for instance, the court found three persons to constitute a group when the shares of one person were held in another's name, the three persons filed and signed a disclosure statement, and copies of the correspondence with the target from any one of the three were sent to the others. In another case, a court held that such an agreement existed when, at a meeting of the corporation's board of directors, several insiders engaged in a discussion of a proposed sale and liquidation of the corporation.[6]

On the other hand, it was held in *Texasgulf, Inc. v. Canada Development Corp.,*[7] that a "[m]ere relationship, among persons or entities, whether family, personal or business, is insufficient to create a group which is deemed to be a statutory person. There must be agreement to act in concert." Thus, the court refused to aggregate the shares in the plaintiff corporation that the defendant and a third company held, even though an officer and director of the defendant corporation was also president of a concern that controlled the third company. Similarly, in *Corenco Corp. v. Schiavone & Sons, Inc.,*[8] the court found no agreement under Section 13(d) between the defendant, a 4.8-percent shareholder of the plaintiff corporation, and a broker who controlled 4.996 percent of the plaintiff's stock and who was to receive from the plaintiff a finder's fee if the plaintiff acquired the defendant. The court reasoned that, although the broker was in communication with the defendant, his fee depended on the plaintiff's acquiring the defendant, not vice versa.

When does group acquisition occur?

Another issue concerns *when* an acquisition by a group occurs that triggers the filing requirement. This issue can be framed by the following hypothetical. Assume shareholder *A* owns 4.5 percent of X Corporation

[4] See Water & Wall Assocs., Inc. v. American Consumer Indus., Ind., [1973] Fed. Sec. L. Rep. (CCH) ¶93,943 at ¶93,756 (D.N.J. 1973) (requiring a written agreement "could render nugatory the purpose of the statute"); see also M. Lipton & E. Steinberger, note 3 supra, at §2.01[5].

[5] 556 F.2d 90, 95 (1st Cir. 1977).

[6] Scott v. Multi-Amp Corp., 386 F. Supp. 44, 59-61 (D.N.J. 1974). See also Financial General Bankshares v. Lance, [1978] Fed. Sec. L. Rep. (CCH) ¶96,403 (D.D.C. 1978) (series of meetings at which substantial acquisitions were planned and agreed on); Ozark Air Lines v. Cox, 326 F. Supp. 1113 (E.D. Miss. 1971) (explicit written agreement to take control).

[7] 366 F. Supp. 374, 403 (S.D. Tex. 1973).

[8] 488 F.2d 207, 217-218 (2d Cir. 1973). See also Lane Bryant, Inc. v. Hatleigh Corp., [1980] Fed. Sec. L. Rep. (CCH) ¶97,529 (S.D.N.Y. 1980) (mere discussions of possible arrangements among purchasers of a target's stock does not constitute a 13(d) group).

and shareholder *B* owns 4.5 percent of X. Assume further that a 9-percent interest in X would be sufficient for control of X. Neither *A* nor *B* is subject to the provisions of Section 13(d). Now *A* and *B* agree to get together and take control of X. At this point *A* and *B* have neither purchased any more shares of X nor agreed to purchase any more X stock. Under Section 13(d)(3), are *A* and *B* considered to be two persons who have acted or are acting as a group for the purpose of acquiring, holding, or disposing of securities?

In *Bath Industries, Inc. v. Blot,*[9] the court denied that Section 13(d)(3) would apply to such a situation and held that a group must agree to acquire more shares before the filing requirements of Section 13(d) are triggered. The Second Circuit disagreed with the *Bath* court, in *GAF Corp. v. Milstein,*[10] and held that the moment individuals agree to attempt together to gain control of a corporation, a group has come into being and has "acquired" shares. If the total number of shares exceeds 5 percent, as in the above example, the filing requirements of Section 13(d) apply. The *GAF* view, adopted in 1977 by the SEC in Rule 13d-5, is tied to the statutory language by the argument that *A* and *B* have at least acted as a group for the purpose of "holding" securities. Indeed, the *Corenco* court interpreted *GAF* as holding precisely this, although the *GAF* court expressly grounded its decision, not on the "holding" concept, but on a (broad) interpretation of "acquisition."[11]

§13.4.2 Remedies for Violation of Section 13(d)

Troublesome issues

The scope of relief under Section 13(d) has been a troublesome issue for several reasons. First, Congress did not make explicit what remedies were to be available and to whom. The questions whether private parties can sue under Section 13, whether equitable relief is available and, if so, in what form, have been much litigated. Moreover, because Section 13, in contrast to Section 14, does not itself contain any antifraud provision, the issue has arisen whether suit can even be brought under Section 13 when a party's disclosures are false and misleading. This latter question seems to have been resolved in favor of permitting fraud actions.[12]

[9] 427 F.2d 97, 109-110 (7th Cir. 1970).

[10] 453 F.2d 709, 715-719 (2d Cir. 1971), cert. denied, 406 U.S. 910 (1972).

[11] It should also be noted that a number of *sellers* of stock who cooperate to effect a shift in control of the corporation could be a group obliged to make disclosure under 13(d). See Wellman v. Dickinson, 682 F.2d 355 (2d Cir. 1982), cert. denied, 460 U.S. 1069 (1983).

[12] See GAF Corp. v. Milstein, note 10 supra, at 720 n.22.

With respect to remedies available, the law is in flux. It is clear that the SEC may obtain relief against any person for a material violation of the Section 13(d) disclosure requirement. Possible remedies include orders to comply and injunctions against future violations. Private actions, however, are more limited in availability.

No action implied

Private actions for damages? Courts have declined to read an implied private right of action for damages into Section 13(d).[13] They have noted that such actions are possible under either of two other provisions: Section 18(a) of the Exchange Act, which provides that anyone who, in reliance on a materially false or misleading statement in a report filed under the Exchange Act, purchases or sells a security at a price "affected" by that statement may collect damages from the person filing the report, unless that person had no knowledge that the statement was false or misleading and acted in good faith;[14] and the more well-known Section 10(b) of the Exchange Act. But both of these other provisions require that a person have been a purchaser or seller to sue. Thus, a continuing shareholder or an issuer will lack standing to assert damages under either of them.

Who sues for what?

Private actions for equitable relief. The issue of private equitable actions under Section 13 is complex. It encompasses two distinct questions. First, who may sue — the shareholder, the issuer, or both? Second, what kinds of relief are available? The possibilities are numerous. A court might prohibit the violator from further purchases of the company's stock, order him to divest himself of his stock, or enjoin him from voting it. Or, focusing more directly on the disclosure violations, the court might simply require corrective disclosure or enjoin future violations. The multiplicity of possible forms of relief makes it difficult to judge the importance of any one case addressing only certain requested remedies. Nevertheless, a summary follows.

Shareholders and issuers

Early cases seemed to establish that both shareholders and the issuer of a security have standing to sue to enjoin a violator of Section 13(d) from further purchases of stock and from voting the stock.[15] Although it might

[13]Weisman v. Darneille, [1977-1978] Fed. Sec. L. Rep. (CCH) ¶96,278 (S.D.N.Y. 1978). See also Moyers v. American Leisure Time Enter., Inc., 402 F. Supp. 213 (S.D.N.Y. 1975), aff'd, 538 F.2d 312 (2d Cir. 1976).

[14]It should be noted that suit under Section 18 is not a particularly attractive option for plaintiffs.

[15]See, e.g., Grow Chemical Corp. v. Uran, 316 F. Supp. 891 (S.D.N.Y. 1970) (shareholders may obtain injunctive relief); GAF Corp. v. Milstein, note 10 supra (issuer may sue to enjoin further purchases by section 13(d) violator).

appear that only the shareholders are harmed, there is an argument that the issuer, too, should be able to seek injunctive relief. In *GAF Corp v. Milstein*,[16] the Second Circuit permitted an issuer to sue for injunctive relief for false and misleading disclosures under Section 13(d) on the grounds that the issuer is in the best position to enforce the statute: It is most likely to know about a failure to file and to be able to appraise the accuracy of statements that are filed. Further, it has the resources and the self-interest to bring and maintain an action.[17] We might object that, on the other hand, the issuer's management is likely to be overzealous, if not fanatical, in its invocation of the statute. The lawsuit could be a mere defensive tactic of no real value to investors.

Irreparable harm requirement: *Rondeau* case

As suits under Section 13(d) multiplied, the ability to get injunctive relief other than in rare cases was cast in doubt by the Supreme Court in *Rondeau v. Mosinee Paper Corp.*[18] The Court rejected a claim for injunctive relief on the ground that the standard of irreparable harm, along with the other traditional principles of equity, applies to private actions for injunctive relief under Section 13(d) and was not satisfied. In *Rondeau* the defendant, ignorant of his obligations under the Williams Act, failed to file disclosure statements after acquiring more than 5 percent of the plaintiff corporation's stock. After the plaintiff notified the defendant of his failure, the defendant belatedly filed the correct document, in which he stated his intent to obtain control of the plaintiff through further purchases and to make changes in the plaintiff's management. The plaintiff then sought a court order enjoining the defendant from voting or pledging his stock and directing him to divest himself of his stock in the plaintiff. The Supreme Court rejected the claim for injunctive relief. The Court reasoned that the plaintiff was facing no irreparable harm, because the proper information had now been disclosed. Although the *Rondeau* court reserved the question when, if ever, an injunctive remedy exists under Section 13(d), the effect of the case has been to set the standards for equitable relief high enough that few claims for injunctions have succeeded.

§13.4.3 Meaning of "Tender Offer"

Importance of the issue

If a particular action by an acquirer is not a tender offer, the acquirer may be subject only to Section 13(d)'s post-acquisition disclosure requirements. If the action is a tender offer, the acquirer will have to make disclosure

[16] 453 F.2d 709 (2d Cir. 1971), cert. denied, 406 U.S. 910 (1972).
[17] Id. at 719, 721.
[18] 422 U.S. 49 (1975).

before acquisition, abide by the pro-rata, withdrawal, and best-price rules, and submit to the risk of an action under Section 14(e), the general antifraud provision covering tender offers. Given the importance of deciding whether conduct constitutes a tender offer, you would probably guess that the Williams Act defines the term in a complex way. As noted earlier, however, the Act does not define the term. Nonetheless, the scant legislative history suggests that by *tender offer* Congress was referring to the conventional tender offer, consisting of an announced bid, a premium price, tender by those solicited, and conditional acceptance by the offeror.[19]

Conventional tender offer

Eight factors approach: *Wellman* case

Both courts and the SEC have elaborated on this definition, though not always with the same results. One case that does present a helpful list of tender offer characteristics is *Wellman v. Dickinson.*[20] The court took the view that an unadorned series of open market purchases and a number of privately negotiated purchases were "traditional exceptions" to Section 14. At the same time, the statute covers more than the conventional tender offer. The court looked with favor on and applied a list of eight[21] elements that the SEC had suggested were characteristic of a tender offer:

(1) active and widespread solicitation of public shareholders for the shares of an issuer;
(2) solicitation made for a substantial percentage of the issuer's stock;
(3) offer to purchase made at a premium over the prevailing market price;
(4) terms of the offer are firm rather than negotiable;
(5) offer contingent on the tender of a fixed number of shares, often subject to a fixed maximum number to be purchased;
(6) offer open for a limited period of time;
(7) offeree subjected to pressure to sell his stock; and
(8) public announcement of a purchasing program concerning the

[19] House Report, supra note 2 in §13.3, at 2811:

> The offer normally consists of a bid by an individual or group to buy shares of a company — usually at a price above the market price. Those accepting the offer are said to tender their stock for purchase. The person making the offer obligates himself to purchase all or a specified portion of the tendered shares if certain specified conditions are met.

The use of the word *normally,* however, is arguably evidence that Congress did not intend to limit the applicability of §14 to such transactions.

[20] 475 F. Supp. 783 (S.D.N.Y. 1979), aff'd, 632 F.2d 355 (2d Cir. 1982), cert. denied, 460 U.S. 1069 (1983).

[21] In the *Wellman* case itself, the SEC suggested only seven factors, apparently because the eighth, which it had included in other cases, wasn't satisfied. The court ignored this strategic omission and considered the eighth factor relevant anyway.

> target company, before or during the rapid accumulation of large amounts of target company securities.[22]

In the *Wellman* case, which involved a series of telephone solicitations of 30 institutions owning stock in the target, the factors that most obviously set the facts apart from the ordinary "plain vanilla" series of privately negotiated purchases were factors (4) and (6) on this list. The court found the first seven factors, and therefore a tender offer, were present. How many of the factors are needed is unclear. The court said that "[t]he absence of one particular factor . . . is not necessarily fatal to the Commission's argument because depending on the circumstances involved in the particular case, one or more of the above features may be more compelling and determinative than the other."[23] Such language obviously leaves courts with much discretion.

Broader interpretations

Even broader interpretations of what constitutes a tender offer have been suggested. In 1979 the SEC proposed a rule that would have prohibited virtually any acquisition of more than 5 percent of the issuer's shares other than by a formal tender offer.[24] The SEC's proposal was attacked as going far beyond the congressional intent embodied in the Williams Act.[25] It would seem to erase the line between large stock accumulations calling only for disclosure (Section 13) and those calling for the more substantive provisions of Section 14 as well. Had Congress wanted to treat as tender offers all accumulations for control purposes, it

[22] Id. at 823-824.

[23] Id. at 824.

[24] Proposed rule 14(d)-1(b), SEC Release No. 34-16385, Fed. Sec. L. Rep. (CCH) ¶82,374 (Nov. 29, 1979), offers a bifurcated definition of tender offer. A solicitation is a tender offer if it meets either of these two conditions:

> 1. it constitutes one or more offers to purchase or solicitations of offers to sell securities of a single class during any 45 day period, directed to more than 10 persons, and seeking the acquisition of more than five percent of the class of securities; or
> 2. it exhibits these three characteristics:
>
>   2.1. the offers to purchase must be widely disseminated;
>   2.2. the price offered must exceed the current market price by 5 per cent or $2, whichever is greater; and
>   2.3. the offers do not provide a meaningful opportunity to negotiate the price.

See E.H.I. of Florida, Inc. v. Insurance Co. of North America, 652 F.2d 310 (3d Cir. 1981), in which the court relied on the proposed rule.

[25] M. Lipton & E. Steinberger, note 3 supra, at §2.15[1]. They also note that similar overreaching is present in the SEC's proposed amendments to the Williams Act, which would require certain stock acquisitions to be made only by tender offer. Id.

would not have created two separate categories of regulated activity — or, at least, so courts have consistently held.[26]

Line-drawing problems

You could argue that, in order to effectuate Congress's intent to protect investors from facing hurried, ill-informed choices, courts should not exalt form over substance but should classify as a "tender offer" any request to sell that places investors in such a situation.[27] This view, however, has found only limited acceptance in the case law.[28] The concern effectuating Congress's purposes has led to much judicial line-drawing in cases that fall somewhere between the series of ordinary market transactions and a narrowly defined tender offer. Let us look at some of the more commonly litigated types of transactions and their treatment by the courts.

(1) Market purchases plus publicity

Consider first the series of ordinary, on-exchange purchases with one additional feature: the acquirer has made it publicly known that it wishes to obtain a controlling percentage of the issuer's stock. The public's knowledge may come from newspaper accounts of the acquirer's activities and plans, from a press release by the acquirer itself, or even from an announcement by the acquirer that it will make a formal tender offer at some near-future date. Rumor might even suffice.[29] Under the view that the tender offer provisions of the Williams Act are directed at all situations placing pressure on uninformed investors, some courts have held that such public knowledge would arguably turn a series of ordinary market transactions into a tender offer.[30]

Examples

In *S-G Securities, Inc. v. Fuqua Investment Co.,*[31] for example, the court declared that a tender offer occurs when "there is (1) a publicly announced intention by the purchaser to acquire a substantial block of the stock of the

[26] See, e.g., Copperweld Corp. v. Imetal, 403 F. Supp. 579, 598 (W.D. Pa. 1975); Gulf & Western Indus. v. Great Atlantic & Pacific Tea Co., 356 F. Supp. 1066, 1074 (S.D.N.Y.), aff'd, 476 F.2d 687 (2d Cir. 1973).

[27] See Note, note 1 supra in §13.3, at 1251.

[28] In Panter v. Marshall Field & Co., 486 F. Supp. 1168 (N.D. Ill. 1980), aff'd, 646 F.2d 271 (7th Cir. 1981), cert. denied, 454 U.S. 1092 (1981), for example, the court excluded from the category of tender offers an actual offer to purchase shares of the target company, mainly on the grounds that the offeror never took the steps necessary to meet certain conditions precedent, to purchase shares, or to solicit shareholders. Another court held that an announcement by a tender offeror of an increase in the number of shares the offeror would purchase was not a new tender offer. McDermott, Inc. v. Wheelabrator-Frye, Inc., [1980] Fed. Sec. L. Rep. (CCH) ¶97,687 (7th Cir. 1980).

[29] See Financial Gen. Bankshares, Inc. v. Lance, note 6 supra (suggesting that rumor might be sufficient to trigger §14 provisions, but finding no rumor).

[30] See, e.g., S-G Sec., Inc. v. Fuqua Inv. Co., 466 F. Supp. 1114 (D. Mass. 1978) (press release); Applied Digital Data Sys., Inc. v. Milgo Elec. Corp., 425 F. Supp. 1145, 1153-1155 (S.D.N.Y. 1977) (announcement of forthcoming tender offer).

[31] 466 F. Supp. 1114 (D. Mass. 1978).

target company for purposes of acquiring control thereof, and (2) a subsequent rapid acquisition by the purchaser of large blocks of stock through open market and privately negotiated purchases."[32] The court found that a public announcement creates "a risk of the pressure on sellers that the disclosure and remedial tender offer provisions of the Williams Act were designed to prevent."[33] Not all courts give such great importance to the fact of public knowledge of an acquisition attempt. In *Corenco Corp. v. Schiavone & Sons, Inc.*,[34] for example, the court held that a newspaper announcement of a forthcoming tender offer did not trigger Section 14 because it stated it was not a tender offer.

(2) Market purchases with secret intent

What if an acquirer makes market purchases with the intention eventually of making a tender offer but does not make that intent known? Even under the "pressure" view, there is no good argument for considering these purchases to be part of the tender offer, and courts have so held.[35] It would seem that until the 5-percent threshold is reached or until substantial steps are taken toward the tender offer, no such disclosure of intent is presently required.[36]

(3) Privately negotiated purchases

Now let us consider a very different kind of acquisition plan. Suppose the acquirer personally communicates to the shareholders of the issuer an offer to purchase their shares. The situation might sometimes exhibit the same qualities that led Congress to pass the Williams Act: Uninformed investors facing a decision to sell, perhaps under great time constraints. The pressure of a tender offer might be magnified by direct persuasion. Such activity thus might warrant invoking Section 14.

Example

Precisely this reasoning was applied to a series to privately negotiated purchases in the early case of *Cattlemen's Investment Co. v. Fears*,[37] in which the defendant, an owner of 4.86 percent of the stock of the target company, brought his ownership well above the 5-percent mark over a six-week period by means of "an active and widespread solicitation of public shareholders in person, over the telephone and through the mails." The court held that this method of purchase should be considered a tender offer because "the contacts utilized by the defendant seem even more designed than a general newspaper advertisement, the more conventional type of 'tender offer,' to force a shareholder into making a hurried investment

[32] Id. at 1126-1127.
[33] Id. at 1126.
[34] 488 F.2d 207, 216 (2d Cir. 1973).
[35] See, e.g., Copperweld Corp. v. Imetal, note 26 supra.
[36] M. Lipton & E. Steinberger, note 3 supra, at §2.08[3].
[37] 343 F. Supp. 1248 (W.D. Okla. 1972).

decision without access to information, in circumvention of the statutory purpose."[38]

Courts disagreeing with the result in *Cattleman's* have pointed to relevant statements of the sponsor of the Williams Act.[39] Moreover, in cases in which the investor was able to engage in actual bargaining, courts have been reluctant to find tender offers.[40] The most common example is the negotiated private purchase from institutional or otherwise sophisticated investors.[41]

§13.4.4 Actions Under Section 14(e)

This subsection discusses the basic elements of a cause of action under Section 14(e) of the Exchange Act. Some important litigation invoking this provision to challenge takeover defenses is discussed below in subsection 13.6.2. Section 14(e) states:

14(e) It shall be unlawful for any person to make any untrue statement of a material fact or omit to state any material fact necessary in order to make the statements made, in the light of the circumstances under which they are made, not misleading, or to engage in any fraudulent, deceptive, or manipulative acts or practices, in connection with any tender offer or request or invitation for tenders, or any solicitation of security holders in opposition to or in favor of any such offer, request, or invitation.

Comments The language of Section 14(e) thus explicitly applies to any tender offer for any security. The provision neither imposes a 5-percent requirement nor limits itself to equity securities. On its face, Section 14(e) seems to bar

[38] Id. at 1252. See also Nachman Corp. v. Halfred, [1973-1974] Fed. Sec. L. Rep. (CCH) ¶94,455 (N.D. Ill. 1973) (adopting view but finding no tender offer).

[39] Senator Williams stated:

> Substantial open market or privately negotiated purchases of shares may . . . relate to shifts in control of which investors should be aware. While some people might say that this information should be filed before the securities are acquired, disclosure after the transaction avoids upsetting the free and open auction market where buyer and seller normally do not disclose the extent of their interest and avoid prematurely disclosing the terms of privately negotiated transactions.

See 113 Cong. Rec. 856 (1967), quoted in, e.g., Brascan Ltd. v. Edper Equities Ltd., 477 F. Supp. 773, 790 (S.D.N.Y. 1979).

[40] See, e.g., Nachman Corp. v. Halfred, note 38 supra.

[41] See, e.g., Kennecott Copper Corp. v. Curtiss-Wright Corp., 584 F.2d 1195, 1206-1207 (2d Cir. 1978); Stromfeld v. Great Atlantic & Pacific Tea Co., 496 F. Supp. 1084 (S.D.N.Y.), aff'd, 646 F.2d 563 (2d Cir. 1980); *Brascan*, note 39 supra; Financial Gen. Bankshares, Inc. v. Lance, note 6 supra; D-Z Inv. Co. v. Holloway, [1974-1975] Fed. Sec. L. Rep. (CCH) ¶94,771 (S.D.N.Y. 1974); Water & Wall Assocs., Inc. v. American Consumer Indus., Inc., note 4 supra.

two distinct categories of activity: nondisclosure (misstatement or omission) on the one hand, and manipulation, deception, or fraud on the other. This linguistic division might be read to support the idea that some sorts of things forbidden by the provision — manipulation, for example — may occur even in the absence of material misstatements or omissions. The lower federal courts generally required an act of nondisclosure or misrepresentation as an element of a claim under Section 14(e), however, and the issue now appears to have been settled by the Supreme Court's decision in *Schreiber v. Burlington Northern, Inc.*,[42] which required misrepresentation or nondisclosure. Thus, one of the central issues in a case brought under Section 14(e) is whether a material fact has been misstated or omitted.

Scienter needed?

Culpability. The issue of what degree of culpability, if any, is necessary for a violation of Section 14(e) has provoked some controversy in the courts. At least one court facing the issue has held that in SEC actions no culpability is required and a negligent misstatement or omission is actionable.[43] Most courts, however, following the law under Rule 10b-5, have required, for both SEC and private actions, at least some culpability — either knowledge of falsity or reckless disregard of the truth.[44]

***TSC* formulation used**

Materiality. Courts addressing the issue of materiality have used the standard of materiality for proxy solicitation cases enunciated by the Supreme Court in *TSC Industries, Inc. v. Northway, Inc.*[45] An omitted fact is material if there is "a substantial likelihood that, under all the circumstances, the omitted fact would have assumed actual significance in the deliberations of the reasonable shareholder," that is, "a substantial likelihood that the disclosure of the omitted fact would have been viewed by the reasonable investor as having significantly altered the 'total mix' of information made available."[46]

Applications

The materiality of specific types of information has occupied considerable judicial attention. Courts have sometimes excused the omission of

[42] 105 S. Ct. 2458 (1985). The case is discussed below in subsection 13.6.2.

[43] See SEC v. Wills, [1979] Fed. Sec. L. Rep. 1 (CCH) ¶96,712 (D.D.C. 1978) (negligence is sufficient; omission of material facts in defendants' knowledge is negligence per se).

[44] A&K Railroad Materials v. Green Bay & W.R. Co., 437 F. Supp. 636, 642 (E.D. Wis. 1977); SEC v. Texas Intl. Co., 498 F. Supp. 1231, 1252-1253 (N.D. Ill. 1980) (scienter required); Chris-Craft Indus. v. Piper Aircraft Corp., 480 F.2d 341, 362-363 (2d Cir.), cert. denied, 414 U.S. 910 (1973); Smallwood v. Pearl Brewing Co., 489 F.2d 579, 606 (5th Cir.), cert. denied, 419 U.S. 873 (1974); Lowenschuss v. Kane, 520 F.2d 255, 268 n.10 (2d Cir. 1975).

[45] 426 U.S. 438 (1976). See also, e.g., Flynn v. Bass Brothers Enterprises, Inc., [1978] Fed. Sec. L. Rep. (CCH) ¶96,611 (E.D. Pa. 1978), aff'd, 744 F.2d 978 (3d Cir. 1984).

[46] 426 U.S. at 449.

material information if it was readily available to shareholders in annual reports or newspapers.[47] Similarly, certain financial and accounting knowledge may be imputed to shareholders, and its omission or misstatement will not be considered material.[48] On the other hand, omission or misstatement of facts from which a reasonable shareholder could infer the possibility that a tender offer will violate antitrust laws is a material violation of Section 14(e).[49]

Information regarding the value of the target's stock is important to a shareholder's decision whether to sell to a tender offeror. Nonetheless, several courts have hesitated to require an offeror to state the basis on which the offering price was calculated.[50] But if this offeror has based its bidding price on information gained from the target, other cases suggest this is a material fact that should be disclosed.[51] Moreover, the target company has a duty, both in the case law and through SEC Schedule 14D-9, to explain why it believes an offer to be either acceptable or inadequate.[52]

Clearly material are a tender offeror's future plans with respect to the target and its management.[53] Failure to disclose an intent to gain control is a material omission, and any structural changes contemplated must also be

[47] Valente v. Pepsico, Inc., 454 F. Supp. 1228, 1243 (D. Del. 1978) (no duty to disclose earnings per share since information was provided in financial reports of company and in newspapers).

[48] Compare Emhart Corp. v. USM Corp., 403 F. Supp. 660, 663 (D. Mass. 1975), vacated on other grounds, 527 F.2d 177 (1st Cir. 1977) (offeree held to knowledge that book value and market value may differ), with Weeks Dredging & Contracting, Inc. v. American Dredging Co., 451 F. Supp. 468 (E.D. Pa. 1978) (offeree not held to knowledge that asset value is relevant only in liquidation proceedings).

[49] See Gulf & Western Indus. v. Great Atlantic & Pacific Tea Co., 476 F.2d 687 (2d Cir. 1973); Copperweld Corp. v. Imetal, note 26 supra. But see Missouri Portland Cement Co. v. Cargill, Inc., 375 F. Supp. 249, 268 (S.D.N.Y. 1974), rev'd on other grounds, 498 F.2d 851 (2d Cir. 1974), cert. denied, 419 U.S. 883 (1974) (no duty to disclose if possibility of antitrust violation is unclear). Obviously, this area offers no bright lines as to when the possibility of antitrust violations must be disclosed.

[50] See, e.g., Weeks Dredging & Contracting, Inc. v. American Dredging Co., note 48 supra, at 484-485 (E.D. Pa. 1978) (no violation of §14(e) to offer, without having done detailed analysis, a price of $30.25 per share in expectation that shareholders would infer from precision of price that offeror did such analysis); Alaska Interstate Co. v. McMillian, 402 F. Supp. 532 (D. Del. 1975).

[51] See, e.g., Seaboard World Airlines, Inc. v. Tiger Intl., Inc., 600 F.2d 355 (2d Cir. 1979); Alaska Interstate Co. v. McMillian, note 50 supra.

[52] See Humana Inc. v. American Medicorp, Inc., Fed. Sec. L. Rep. (CCH) ¶96,286 (S.D.N.Y. 1978). See also Royal Indus., Inc. v. Monogram Indus., Inc., [1976-1977] Fed. Sec. L. Rep. (CCH) ¶95,863 (C.D. Cal. 1976), in which the court held that due to management's fiduciary duty to treat its shareholders fairly, it must, under §14(e), provide a reasonable basis for its characterization of an offer as "inadequate."

[53] Weeks Dredging & Contracting, Inc. v. American Dredging Co., supra note 48 at 480.

disclosed, although the disclosure need not be any more definite or specific than are the plans themselves.[54]

Reliance requirement

Reliance. For a claim under Section 14(e), it is not enough that a misrepresentation or omission be material; it must also have been one on which shareholders relied.[55] The interpretation of "reliance" in Section 14(e) suits tracks that in the Rule 10b-5 and proxy solicitation contexts. Thus, when reliance is likely but burdensome to prove, as in the case of a nondisclosure (as opposed to misrepresentation), reliance is often presumed from materiality.[56] When an offer has been voluntarily withdrawn, however, courts have held that a material omission preceding the withdrawal will not suffice to support an action, because reliance is impossible (no tenders were accepted).[57]

Actions allowed

Private actions. Since *Electronic Specialty Co. v. International Controls Corp.*[58] authorized them, private actions have constituted the bulk of the litigation under the antifraud provision.[59] Unlike Rule 10b-5, Section 14(e) has not been read to embody a standing requirement that the plaintiff have purchased or sold securities.[60]

Standing rules

Damages. The target corporation and the tendering and nontendering shareholders have standing to sue a violator of Section 14(e) for damages.[61] In *Piper v. Chris-Craft Industries,*[62] however, the Supreme Court held that a tender offeror (though also a shareholder) lacks standing to assert damages, on the grounds that an offeror is not within the class of intended beneficiaries of the Williams Act. Plaintiffs must prove injury,[63] caused

[54] Electronic Specialty Co. v. International Controls Corp., 409 F.2d 937, 948 (2d Cir. 1969).

[55] Lewis v. McGraw, 619 F.2d 192, 195 (2d Cir.), cert. denied, 449 U.S. 951 (1980) (citing Chris-Craft Indus. v. Piper Aircraft Corp., 480 F.2d 341 (2d Cir. 1973)).

[56] Id. (citing Mills v. Electric Auto-Lite Co., 396 U.S. 375 (1970); Affiliated Ute Citizens v. United States, 406 U.S. 128 (1972)).

[57] See Lewis v. McGraw, note 55 supra; Panter v. Marshall Field & Co., note 28 supra.

[58] 409 F.2d 937 (2d Cir. 1969).

[59] While the SEC may, of course, seek injunctions for violations of the tender offer rules through §14(e), it rarely does so. See E. Gadsby & A. Sommer, 1A The Federal Securities Exchange Act of 1934, §7A.03[3], at 7A-80 (1985).

[60] Neuman v. Electronic Specialty Co., [1969-1970] Fed. Sec. L. Rep. (CCH) ¶92,591 (N.D. Ill. 1969).

[61] Electronic Specialty Co. v. International Controls Corp., note 58 supra (target corporation and tendering shareholders have standing); Dyer v. Eastern Trust and Banking Co., 336 F. Supp. 890, 914 (D. Me. 1971) (nontendering shareholders of target have standing).

[62] 430 U.S. 1, reh'g denied, 430 U.S. 976 (1977).

[63] Emmi v. First-Manufacturers Natl. Bank, 336 F. Supp. 629 (D. Me. 1971).

either directly by defendant or through reliance (see discussion above) on defendant's misrepresentation or omission.

Injunctions. All private parties involved in a tender offer may also assert a claim for injunctive relief under Section 14(e).[64] As under Section 13(d), the plaintiff must show a substantial probability that a violation has occurred and must demonstrate that it will be irreparably harmed if an injunction is not issued.[65] Preliminary injunctions are often lifted after the offeror corrects the misstatement or omission.[66]

§13.5 State Takeover Regulation

Origin of trend

Unfriendly takeover attempts emerged as a salient phenomenon in the middle and late 1960s. Many interest groups that reflected the fears of managers who thought their companies might become targets lobbied for federal legislation that would chill tender offers. When the Williams Act was finally passed in 1968, however, it embodied a stance of neutrality as between offerors and targets. The groups wishing to curb tender offers therefore turned to state legislatures.

A wave of statutes

Many states responded.[1] When the Williams Act was passed, only one state had a statute regulating attempted takeovers of ordinary business corporations.[2] By the time of the Supreme Court's 1982 decision in *MITE* (which will be discussed shortly), about 37 states had adopted statutes regulating takeovers.[3]

Designed to hinder takeovers

For the most part, the state statutes were the result of lobbying by management interests who feared that their companies might become takeover targets, and so were designed to make hostile takeovers quite difficult. The chief strategy for doing this was to slow down the offeror; all

[64] The cases cited above, which establish private rights of action, apply to injunctive relief as well as to damages, with the exception of *Piper,* which does not bar a tender offeror from seeking injunctive relief. See especially Humana, Inc. v. American Medicorp, Inc., note 52 supra, which explicitly affirms that an offeror may seek an injunction against further violations of §14(e).

[65] See Rondeau v. Mosinee Paper Co., 422 U.S. 49 (1975).

[66] See, e.g., Corenco Corp. v. Schiavone & Sons, Inc., note 8 supra; Chromalloy Am. Corp. v. Sun Chem. Corp., 474 F. Supp. 1341 (E.D. Mo.), aff'd, 611 F.2d 240 (8th Cir. 1979).

§13.5 [1] See Wilner & Landy, The Tender Trap: State Takeover Statutes and Their Constitutionality, 45 Ford. L. Rev. 1 (1976).

[2] That state was Virginia. See SEC Release No. 34-16384, 44 Fed. Reg. 70326, 70329 n.14 (1979).

[3] Edgar v. MITE Corp., 457 U.S. 624, 631 n.6 (1982).

takeover experts recognized the great value of delay to the defending target company management. Of course, a number of alleged public policies, such as the need to give shareholders greater protection than they received under federal law, were invoked as justifications.

Typical elements

A typical state anti-takeover statute in the wave of laws passed in the early 1970s created several barriers. First, it would require filing of disclosure documents well in advance of the making of a tender offer, plus notice to the target company's management. This would give the target more time to prepare its defensive strategy. Second, it would require more burdensome disclosure than under the Williams Act. Third, it would require an administrative hearing before a state official or commission. The hearing might be at the option of a state official or, sometimes, at the option of the target company's management. The hearing would be about the adequacy of the offeror's disclosure documents or, under the more severe statutes, about compliance with newly created substantive standards. Among such standards were the following: the terms of the tender offer must be found by the hearing body to be "fair" to the target company shareholders; the offeror must be willing to buy all of the target's shares; the offer must be found to "benefit the people of this state." Whatever the ostensible purpose of the hearing, a major effect of requiring it was to impose great and perhaps fatal delay upon the offeror, since the statutes usually gave the state official or hearing body plenty of time to have the hearing and then to decide what to do. Finally, the statute would create special, easier rules for tender offers that were not opposed by the target company's managers. In effect, the offeror was strongly urged to come to terms with the managers instead of dealing directly with the shareholders.

Typically, any of a number of jurisdictional links might trigger the application of such an anti-takeover statute: the target's being incorporated in the state, its having a principal office or major operations in the state, or the existence of a significant number of target shareholders in the state.

The *MITE* case

In 1982, the validity of many of the anti-takeover statutes was thrown into doubt by the Supreme Court's decision in *Edgar v. MITE Corp.*[4] The Court struck down the Illinois Business Takeover Act on the ground that it impermissibly burdened interstate commerce. The Illinois statute was fairly typical. It required tender offerors to register their offers with the Illinois Secretary of State 20 days before they were to become effective. During this period, the Secretary could call a hearing on the fairness of the offer. If the Secretary found the offeror's disclosures inadequate or found the offer otherwise fraudulent or unfair, the Secretary would bar the offer.

[4] 457 U.S. 624 (1982).

It was this power to block the offer that the Supreme Court held to constitute a substantial burden on commerce that was not counterbalanced by any benefit to local interests. The alleged benefits were in any case thought to be merely speculative.

Statutes invalidated

After the decision in *MITE* — and indeed, even before it — a number of cases invalidated state takeover statutes, or certain provisions or applications of them.[5] Furthermore, the SEC adopted Rule 14d-2(b), under which a bidder's public announcement of certain material terms of a cash tender offer causes the offer to commence under Section 14(d) of the Securities Exchange Act. Since many of the state statutes required bidders to announce their intent to make an offer and then wait for several weeks before commencing it, this rule created a direct conflict between the federal and state regulatory schemes: It was impossible to satisfy both.[6] It thus became fairly clear that the conflicting state law provisions would be found invalid if challenged, on the ground that the federal statute and rules properly adopted under it preempt conflicting state law.[7]

A new wave of statutes

Thus, in the early 1980s it began to look as if the time had come to mourn the passing of the state anti-takeover statutes. However, as usually happens when powerful competing interests have access to at least some lawmaking bodies, there was soon a counterattack. Within a few years some states began adopting a new type of takeover statute. The new statutes aimed to put into law several kinds of defensive tactics that had been developed by lawyers specializing in takeover battles.

Pennsylvania example: broadened discretion

A good example is given by the 1983 Amendments to Pennsylvania's business corporation law.[8] One provision gave a target company's board of directors broader discretion in exercising its fiduciary duties in connection with a takeover attempt.[9] Management is declared to have such duties not only to shareholders, but also to employees, customers, suppliers, and the surrounding community. The obvious thrust of this provision is to give management more room to create (nonfalsifiable) business reasons for opposing a takeover, and thus a greater shield against shareholder lawsuits

[5] 1 M. Lipton & E. Steinberger, Takeovers and Freezeouts §§5.02 nn. 25, 28, 37, 5.02[4][c] (1984).

[6] See SEC Release No. 34-16384, 44 Fed. Reg. 70326 (1979).

[7] In the *MITE* case, the preemption analysis was also urged as a basis for invalidating the Illinois statute, but a majority of the Court neither accepted nor rejected this approach. At the time, however, Rule 14-d(2) was not yet in force.

[8] See Comment, The 1983 Amendments to Pennsylvania's Business Corporation Law: Unconstitutional? MITE Be, 89 Dick. L. Rev. 401 (1985).

[9] Pa. Stat. Ann. tit. 15, §1408 (Purdon Supp. 1984-1985).

claiming that certain defensive tactics represented a waste of corporate assets or improper self-dealing.

A second provision imposed a supermajority voting requirement for certain controlled mergers.[10] When a tender offeror succeeds in getting a controlling block of a target's shares, it often completes the acquisition by effecting a cashout merger between the target and some affiliate of itself. The statute requires the vote of a majority of the minority shareholders in such a merger. This requirement can be avoided, however, if the cashout price is as high as was the price paid in the first step of the acquisition, or if certain independent directors approve the transaction.

Supermajority vote

A third provision might be classified as a statutory poison pill plan: When a person becomes a holder of 30 percent or more of the company's shares, the remaining shareholders then have the right to be bought out by that person at a fair price plus a premium.[11]

Statutory poison pill

A major question about this and similar recent statutes is whether they will survive constitutional challenge.

§13.6 Defenses to Takeover Attempts

§13.6.1 Tactics

We can put devices used by target company managers to resist hostile tender offers into two broad classifications, depending on whether the devices are typically invoked after a particular takeover attempt is on the horizon, or as a prophylactic measure well before such an attempt.

Two broad classes

Before considering these two broad classes and the various species that fall within them, however, it is important to realize that any taxonomy of takeover defenses is apt to be partial and to become outdated soon. The technology and the law of resistance tactics have been continually evolving since the adoption of the Williams Act. There is no reason to expect a cessation of this evolution soon.

Constant changes

Post-Offer tactics. There are at least six important general categories of post-offer resistance tactics.

The first category might be labelled propaganda. The target managers, using company funds, can issue press releases, take out newspaper advertisements, and otherwise communicate arguments to the shareholders as

"Propaganda"

[10] Id. at §1409.1(C).

[11] Id. §1910. See generally Special Report, 16 Sec. Reg. L. Rep. 1392 (1984) (panel discussion by ABA Committee on the Ohio, Maryland, and Pennsylvania approaches to post-*MITE* state takeover legislation).

to why they shouldn't tender. Absent misrepresentation or material omissions, this kind of defense is legally unproblematic. One could even argue that the managers have a positive duty to communicate their viewpoint to the shareholders. The main problem is practical. Alongside a premium bid, propaganda has a hollow sound.

Defensive suits

A second category consists of defensive lawsuits. Management can cause the target company to sue the offeror, alleging a variety of legal violations. Claims under the federal securities laws and the antitrust laws are the staples of this litigation. Though standing is usually not a problem, the federal courts seem to have developed a certain amount of cynicism about claims of this kind.[1] Consequently, target management can rarely hope for a final victory on the merits in such litigation. They can hope that it will buy valuable time.

Defensive acquisitions

A third type of tactic is the defensive merger or acquisition. The target can try to arrange hasty acquisitions of companies that, if acquired, will create an antitrust problem for the offeror (because, for example, the acquired company is a direct competitor of the offeror in a concentrated market). Such acquisitions are not always feasible, however, and the offeror may try to neutralize the antitrust problem by promising to divest itself of the acquired company when it gets control of the target. This tactic poses an obvious and substantial risk that the target managers will waste corporate assets — by making a poor acquisition at an excessive price — in their desperate scramble to preserve their control and their jobs. It therefore invites shareholder litigation against the target managers.

White knights

A more benign variation, from the shareholders' viewpoint, is target management's search for a "white knight," that is, a rival bidder that will save them from the first offeror by offering both the shareholders and themselves a more attractive deal.

Lockups

A fourth kind of post-offer tactic is the lockup.[2] Suppose Targg, the target company, has a valuable asset, such as a remarkably productive oil field, which is an important or critical attribute of Targg in the eyes of

§13.6 [1]See, e.g., Electronic Specialty Co. v. International Controls Corp., 409 F.2d 937 (2d Cir. 1969) (Friendly, J.) (arguing that, in view of the stressful, warlike nature of the takeover context, Congress intended to assure "basic honesty and fair dealing, not to impose an unrealistic requirement of laboratory conditions that might make the new statute a potent tool for incumbent management to protect its own interests against the desires and welfare of the stockholders."); Missouri Portland Cement Co. v. Cargill, Inc., 498 F.2d 851 (2d Cir.) (Friendly, J.) (warning against imposition of "a duty of self-flagellation" on offerors), cert. denied, 419 U.S. 883 (1974). For a contrasting attitude, expressed in the context of a review of a ruling granting a motion for preliminary injunction, see Gulf & Western Indus., Inc. v. Great Atlantic & Pacific Tea Co., 476 F.2d 687 (2d Cir. 1973) (Timbers, J.).

[2]See Note, Lock-Up Options: Toward a State Law Standard, 96 Harv. L. Rev. 1068 (1983).

potential acquirers, but which does not constitute "substantially all the assets" of the target within the meaning of the relevant corporation statute. Under the typical corporation statute, the board of directors is therefore able, without seeking shareholder approval, to sell the asset or grant an option to buy it. Omen, a hostile bidder, makes a tender offer to buy all of Targg's stock at $50 per share. Targg's managers solicit Gunn, a white knight that implicitly promises to treat them better after a takeover. Gunn makes an offer at $55, which Omen quickly matches. In order to make sure that Gunn wins the bidding war, Targg's directors vote to grant Gunn, for a fixed consideration, an option to buy the oil field for $100 million. Thereafter, Gunn has a crushing advantage. If Omen were to raise its price high enough — say, to $100 — to win the bidding contest, Gunn would still be able to buy the oil field at the same fixed price. Omen could find that it had paid far too much for what was left of Targg. This would not happen to Gunn.

Variations

There are variants. Targg could sell Gunn newly-issued Targg shares or an option on such shares at a fixed price. If Targg were already authorized, without a current shareholder vote, to issue enough shares in this way, the result of the bidding war might indeed be "locked up."

Avoiding shareholder vote

In either case, the strategy depends on the ability of the target management to sell a major interest in the company to the favored bidder *without getting the approval of the majority of the shareholders.* During a bidding war, of course, the shareholders would not approve any such deal, but would prefer a free and unhampered auction for their shares. Moreover, the strategy poses an obvious danger to shareholders: In their haste to retain control, target managers will not sell or option the "crown jewels" or the new shares at the best price.

Share manipulations

A fifth class of post-offer resistance tactics consists of various kinds of share manipulations. Four kinds will be mentioned here.

Sale to friends

(1) The target might sell stock to friendly entities that can be trusted not to tender to the hostile bidder, thus making it harder for the bidder to buy enough shares to make a controlling percentage. For example, Targg's managers might consider selling some stock to the pension plan sponsored by the company, if they dominated the plan's trustees or could trust them to see things their way.

Repurchase from other shareholders

(2) If the incumbent controlling group held a substantial block of stock (say, 35 percent), the target might offer to repurchase some of its own stock from other shareholders. If such a repurchase were large enough (say, 32 percent), it would result in the incumbent group's getting de jure voting control (say, 35/68 or 51 percent, instead of 35 percent). In any event, it would make it easier for the group to then use its own resources to buy enough additional shares to clinch control.

Greenmail

(3) A more direct repurchase approach is to pay "greenmail," that is, to cause the target company to buy the shares already obtained by the hostile would-be acquirer at a substantial premium over the latter's cost, with the understanding that he, she, or it will stop the takeover attempt.[3] Understandably, other shareholders are likely to be outraged by this tactic. Suppose Targg stock has been selling for around $50. Ike files a Schedule 13D that reveals that he has amassed, through open market and privately negotiated purchases, 8 percent of Targg's stock at an average price of $60. Reliable rumor has it that Ike is considering a takeover bid at $75. In addition to preparing various other defenses, Targg's board negotiates with Ike to sell his shares to Targg at $90; Ike will agree not to pursue a takeover. Not only have the other Targg shareholders lost a possible chance to sell at a premium, but they may also find that their shares' value has been diluted by Targg's exorbitant payment to Ike.

Poison pill plan

(4) Yet another species of share manipulation is the "poison pill" plan. (It might be adopted before or after a hostile tender offer is imminent, so it is not necessarily a post-offer tactic.) As originally conceived, it was to be effective against two-tier takeover attempts, in which the acquirer first makes a tender offer not for all shares but for a controlling interest, with the intent or possibility of later freezing out the remaining shareholders, perhaps at a lower price. There are several varieties, three of which will be mentioned.

Conversion rights version

First, the target's board might cause it to create a new class of preferred stock and distribute shares of it to the common stockholders as a stock dividend. The charter provisions defining the rights of the preferred would say that the company could not consummate certain transactions, such as a merger with another entity or a transfer of substantially all assets, unless the acquirer undertook to comply with certain provisions of the preferred stock contract. Under these provisions the preferred stock would become convertible into voting stock of the acquirer. The conversion ratio would reflect the highest acquisition price paid by the acquirer or, if higher, the current market value of the target's stock. If the plan worked as intended, it would reduce the incentives of target shareholders to tender, since they might think they had nothing to lose by waiting.

Problems

The poison in the conversion feature might be nullified, however, if the acquirer were an individual or a nonpublic firm such as a limited partner-

[3] See Macey & McChesney, A Theoretical Analysis of Corporate Greenmail, 95 Yale L.J. 13 (1985); Note, Greenmail: Targeted Stock Repurchases and the Management-Entrenchment Hypothesis, 98 Harv. L. Rev. 1045 (1985); Note, The Standstill Agreement: A Case of Illegal Vote Selling and a Breach of Fiduciary Duty, 93 Yale L.J. 1093 (1984).

ship rather than a public company that had outstanding publicly traded stock. Moreover, the conversion might not be at all unmanageable in the case of an acquirer that was a large public corporation with diffuse ownership.

Redemption rights version

Second, the target might issue preferred stock in which the poisonous aspect resided in the stock's redemption rights instead of its conversion rights. Suppose, for example, the preferred stockholder is empowered to compel the target to redeem her preferred shares at any time within 30 days after a "stock acquisition date." The latter is defined to occur when anyone acquires a certain amount, e.g., 40 percent, of the target's equity. The redemption price is based on the highest price the acquirer paid for the common stock of the target, plus all unpaid dividends on the preferred. This feature might deter the hostile bidder because if it gained control, it might find itself with a company that had just seriously depleted its assets in order to redeem the preferred. Obviously, this problem could be made even more serious if the redemption price were set arbitrarily high — say, three times the acquirer's acquisition price — but then the plan might be much harder to justify if subjected to legal attack. Mixing our metaphors in the wild manner that is customary when discussing takeovers, we might say that this second type of poison pill embodies a "scorched earth" policy.

Problems

The sting in the redemption feature might be blunted if the contemplated redemption were to run afoul of norms designed to protect the target's creditors: for example, the corporation statute's legal-accounting rules governing redemptions, covenants in loan agreements with financial institutions, and the rules of fraudulent conveyance law. Because of these problems, the redemption usually couldn't be so large that it would completely (and perhaps substantially) deplete the target's net worth.

Rights plan version

A third poison pill involves giving the target's common shareholders, as a dividend on their shares, "rights" or warrants instead of preferred stock. The governing document might provide that the rights could be detached and sold separately from the common on which they were issued when a person or group acquired 20 percent of the target's common, or when a tender offer for 30 percent of the common was announced. The holder of a right would be entitled to buy new preferred stock on certain terms or, in the event of a merger of which the target was not the survivor, $200 worth of the *acquiring* company's equity for $100! Thus, an offeror corporation making a classic two-tiered offer might find the interests of its own preexisting shareholders being *substantially* diluted.

Turnabout

A sixth general category of takeover defenses might be described as "turnabout." For example, the target might respond by making a tender offer for the offeror's shares. Conceivably, they might devour each other —

that is, each might wind up liquidating itself to pay the other's shareholders. (This was once described as the Pac Man defense, after a now almost-forgotten computer game.)

Shark repellents

Pre-Offer tactics. In addition to the tactics already discussed, there is a large set of precautions that can be taken before a particular tender offer is about to be made.[4] Many of these precautions require amendment of the corporation's charter and therefore a shareholder vote. They are often called "shark repellents."

Supermajority voting rules

One anti-takeover charter amendment is a provision requiring a supermajority vote — say, 80 percent of the common shares instead of the usual bare majority rule — in order to effect a merger or sale of all assets. Since tender offerors often complete their acquisitions by following their acquisition of a control block with a freezeout merger, this would make their effort somewhat harder and riskier. To prevent the change from being easily undone, the charter would also have to be changed so that further amendments of it (or of the anti-takeover provision) would also require a supermajority vote. Notice that the supermajority provision would not absolutely block a takeover attempt, especially by a bidder willing to buy all the target stock.

Veto stock

Similarly, the charter might be amended to create a class of stock that has the power to veto a merger or other organic change, and the stock could be placed with persons friendly to management.

Staggered board

Yet another amendment would create a staggered board of directors. For example, a board with 12 directorships, each up for shareholder vote every year (as is normal practice) might be reclassified so that only three positions would be voted on each year. Thus, a hostile offeror that buys a control block might (in theory) have to wait two or three years before it could vote in a majority of the directors, and thus have legal authority to change the management and operations of the target. (In practice, of course, the incumbent directors would often find it in their interest to come to terms with the new controlling shareholder.)

Accelerated loans

Another idea, not involving a charter amendment, is to arrange for provisions in the target's major loan agreements that the loans will become due and payable in the event of a hostile takeover. If the banks, insurance companies, or other creditors actually pursued their rights under these loan acceleration clauses, the effect would be that of a scorched earth strategy: the successful tender offeror would find itself with a target im-

[4] An excellent analysis of these is found in Gilson, The Case Against Shark Repellent Amendments: Structural Limitations on the Enabling Concept, 34 Stan. L. Rev. 775 (1982).

mediately obligated to pay out huge amounts of money. In practice, of course, the major creditors might find they were scorching their own feet. If the target actually had to liquidate many assets to repay the loans, the loans might not be repaid in full. If, more realistically, the offeror simply paid off the loans and refinanced them with other lenders, the original lenders would have lost a potential customer and the offeror would be subjected only to some transaction costs and perhaps to a higher interest rate — that is, to an irritant rather than a repellent.

Golden parachutes

Finally, the potential target might manufacture "golden parachutes" for its top managers. These are contractual arrangements with the managers whereby very large increases in their compensation will be triggered by a successful takeover bid. The kind of compensation — for example, vested pension benefits — could take many forms. The main idea is that, if the managers are about to be blown out of their cockpits, they might as well float down in style. The parachutes are like severance pay for ordinary workers, but a lot more generous, of course. Consequently, this technique is more a form of insurance for managers than a true shark repellent.[5] Indeed, some have argued that golden parachutes, unlike many other defensive measures, actually benefit shareholders because they reduce the personal incentive of target managers to stop takeover bids at all costs.[6] Consider, for example, that a series of defensive acquisitions could cost a target and its shareholders much, much more, in terms both of wasteful use of assets and lost opportunities for better management, than a successful takeover that is accompanied by generous payments to departing managers.

§13.6.2 Federal Case Law

Case law involving challenges to defensive and offensive tactics in takeover struggles is in a state of rapid development. It is important to distinguish actions brought under provisions of the federal securities laws

[5] Of course, a golden parachute might be a true repellent if it were glaringly outrageous — if, for example, it called for the departing top managers to get half the assets of the target company. But it is hard to imagine such an arrangement surviving a derivative lawsuit for waste. Actual plans usually refrain from provisions that would administer violent shocks to the conscience of a reviewing court.

[6] This view is now supported by an empirical study that purports to show a positive security market reaction to the adoption of golden parachute plans. Lambert & Larcker, Golden Parachutes, Executive Decision Making, and Shareholder Wealth, 7 J. Accounting & Econ. 179 (1985). See also Note, Golden Parachutes and the Business Judgment Rule: Toward a Proper Standard of Review, 94 Yale L.J. 909 (1985).

from those invoking principles of state law, such as the fiduciary duties of care and loyalty.

Lockups as 14(e) "manipulation"?

The case law on defensive tactics under the securities laws indicates that challengers will often have a tough time. Consider this paradigmatic issue: If a target's directors cause it to grant lockup options on its "crown jewel," or on a substantial block of authorized common shares, to one of two rival bidders (a white knight) and this helps defeat the original bidder's offer, does such conduct constitute illegal "manipulation" within the meaning of Section 14(e) of the Exchange Act? Though the Sixth Circuit answered yes,[7] the Second Circuit later took the opposite view in *Data Probe Acquisition Corp. v. Datatab, Inc.*[8]

Arguments pro and con

In the former case, the fact that the lockups made it virtually impossible for the hostile bidder to win was thought to have "artificially affected" market prices — to wit, the prices the bidders were willing to offer — in a way characteristic of manipulative schemes. In the latter case, Judge Winter reasoned that "manipulation" under 14(e) involves not only artificially affecting the price of a security, but doing so in a way that misleads other investors into misinterpreting market activity and acting on their misinterpretation to their detriment. Certainly the classic manipulation schemes of the '30s had these characteristics. (Example: Mo and Flo sell the same shares back and forth to each other on the stock exchange at successively higher reported prices so that other investors will think insiders must know something good and will be willing to buy at a higher price when Mo eventually sells to them instead of Flo.) More generally, Section 14(e) is basically just an antifraud statute, but the real gist in *Data Probe* of the plaintiff's objections to the lockup scheme was that the target's managers breached their fiduciary duties — a state law claim. By trying to transform this claim into a securities law violation, plaintiff was attempting the same "end run" around the intended coverage of the securities laws as was unsuccessfully attempted with respect to Rule 10b-5 in *Santa Fe Industries, Inc. v. Green.*[9] Such an end run attempt neglects the fact that the basic philosophy of the securities laws is to insure full and honest disclosure, not (for the most part) to impose substantive rules of conduct.

Supreme Court rejects broader theory

Subsequently, the *Data Probe* view was adopted by the Supreme Court in *Schreiber v. Burlington Northern, Inc.*,[10] which held that misrepresenta-

[7] Mobil Corp. v. Marathon Oil Co., 669 F.2d 366 (6th Cir. 1981), cert. denied, 455 U.S. 982 (1982).

[8] 722 F.2d 1 (2d Cir. 1983) (Winter, J.), cert. denied, 465 U.S. 1052 (1984).

[9] 430 U.S. 462 (1977).

[10] 105 S. Ct. 2458 (1985).

tion or nondisclosure is a necessary element of a 14(e) violation. The case involved the rescission of a hostile tender offer and its replacement by a friendly acquisition agreement. Though the substitution resulted in a diminution in payment to those shareholders who had tendered pursuant to the tender offer, it was found not to have constituted manipulative conduct. (The case therefore rejects the broader conception of manipulation argued for by some commentators.)[11]

Manipulation as nonverbal fraud

Note how the *Schreiber* viewpoint can be understood to make sense out of the pattern of drafting in 14(e). *Deception* refers to fraud that is accomplished by verbal misrepresentations or omissions. *Manipulation* refers to nonverbal fraud, that is, frauds accomplished by engaging in behavior or causing activity, such as a heavy volume of trading, that others are likely to misinterpret to their detriment. The second concept simply recognizes that in most cultural contexts many human acts, and not just words, have standardized meanings that can be exploited by the deviant.

Related holdings

In a similar vein are holdings that a two-tiered offer does not by itself constitute a violation of Section 14(e),[12] nor does a poison pill plan.[13]

Similar issues under 10b-5

A related set of questions arises under Rule 10b-5, of course. Suppose a person buys a significant percentage of the stock of a company and then says loudly and clearly, "Buy me out or face a takeover bid!" Would such a greenmail attempt constitute a manipulative or deceptive scheme prohibited by Rule 10b-5? No, said the Fourth Circuit;[14] the very frankness of the greenmailer, who after all has an interest in conveying his message clearly, negates such a conclusion.

§13.6.3 State Case Law

Five possible rules

Before examining the emerging case law, it is useful to get a sense of what the possibilities are. There are at least five types of rules that could be adopted to govern the behavior of target company directors and officers

[11] E.g., Weiss, Defensive Responses to Tender Offers and the Williams Act's Prohibition Against Manipulation, 35 Vand. L. Rev. 1087 (1982).

[12] Radol v. Thomas, 534 F. Supp. 1302 (S.D. Ohio 1982), partial summary judgment granted to defendants in 556 F. Supp. 586 (S.D. Ohio 1983), aff'd, 772 F.2d 244 (6th Cir. 1985). Perhaps because this decision was rendered in the Sixth Circuit after the *Mobil* decision but before the Supreme Court's decision in *Schreiber,* the court emphasized that the two-tier pricing structure did not amount to a significant "coercion" of shareholders or "interference with the market of other potential offerors," rather than the theory that manipulation is a form of fraud.

[13] Gearhart Indus., Inc. v. Smith Intl., Inc., 741 F.2d 707 (5th Cir. 1984).

[14] Dan River, Inc. v. Icahn, 701 F.2d 278, 284-285 (4th Cir. 1983).

who cause their company to take defensive measures against a takeover attempt. They are set out below in order of decreasing severity.

(1) Pure passivity

The first rule is a rule of pure passivity: apart from arguing their case to the shareholders (the "propaganda" tactic), target managers should refrain from defensive tactics.[15] They should simply let the shareholders decide whether they want to sell their shares to the tender offeror. This rule is based on the belief that defensive tactics raise the cost of takeovers and reduce their frequency, and therefore decrease shareholder welfare in the long run. It can also be based on a perception of the severe conflict of interest faced by managers who use corporate resources for defensive purposes and a disbelief in the ability of the legal system regularly to sort out good defensive maneuvers from bad ones in real cases.

(2) Modified passivity

A second rule is one of modified passivity: target managers would be allowed only to engage in propaganda and in the solicitation of rival bids.[16] Proponents of this view, unlike those who support the first rule, usually tend to support legislation that requires tender offers to be kept open for some minimum time period. The idea behind the second rule is to allow auctions to flourish. Supposedly, target shareholders will be better off if their managers and the legal system combine to encourage competitive bidding for their shares. At the same time, this rule would strictly prohibit target managers from engaging in defensive tactics that are likely to waste corporate resources and hurt shareholders.

(3) Differential regulation

A third approach is differential regulation: different categories of defenses would be governed by different rules.[17] For example, greenmail

[15] See Easterbrook & Fischel, The Proper Role of a Target's Management in Responding to a Tender Offer, 94 Harv. L. Rev. 1161 (1981).

[16] See Bebchuk, The Case for Facilitating Competing Tender Offers, 95 Harv. L. Rev. 1028 (1982); Gilson, A Structural Approach to Corporations: The Case Against Defensive Tactics in Tender Offers, 33 Stan. L. Rev. 819 (1981). As between this viewpoint and the stricter notion developed by Easterbrook & Fischel, note 15 supra, see the following exchange: Easterbrook & Fischel, Auctions and Sunk Costs in Tender Offers, 35 Stan. L. Rev. 1 (1982); Bebchuk, The Case for Facilitating Competing Tender Offers: A Reply and Extension, 35 Stan. L. Rev. 23 (1982); Gilson, Seeking Competitive Bids Versus Pure Passivity in Tender Offer Defense, 35 Stan. L. Rev. 51 (1982).

[17] In this category I would put the recommendations of Greene & Junewicz, A Reappraisal of Current Regulation of Mergers and Acquisitions, 132 U. Pa. L. Rev. 647 (1984). In responding to the recommendations of the SEC's Advisory Committee on Tender Offers, they urge Congress to consider giving the SEC plenary rule-making authority in the tender offer area. Id. at 737. They are doubtful of the efficacy of judge-made restraints on defensive tactics and urge a requirement of shareholder approval of directors' conduct in responding to tender offers. Like other moderates, they look also at possible abuse on the offeror side and recommend regulation of partial offers — at the least, that substantially equal consideration be paid in each tier.

might be flatly prohibited,[18] defensive lawsuits would be allowed and shielded by the business judgment rule, poison pill plans would be regulated so that "backloaded" plans were illegal but plans merely assuring equal treatment of shareholders in different stages of an acquisition were proper, and so on. The idea behind this approach is that some types of defenses pose a much greater risk to shareholder welfare than others, and that regulators can distinguish between types where a strict preventive rule is desirable and types where other considerations justify a more permissive rule. Note that this approach calls for rather definite rules, even though types of takeover defenses are continually being created and are always evolving. Consequently, it would probably have to be administered by a rule-making regulatory agency such as the SEC, rather than embodied in a detailed statute or developed by the courts.

(4) Primary purpose test

A fourth rule is a primary purpose test: if a defensive tactic were challenged by target company shareholders in a derivative lawsuit, the target's managers would have the burden of proving that the tactic was engaged in for the primary purpose of implementing a bona fide corporate business purpose, rather than the self-regarding purpose of preserving their own control. This rule recognizes that managers are fiduciaries and that defensive tactics usually involve them in a conflict of interest. It reflects a typical judicial response to such a situation. Note, for example, that it is analogous to the usual rule about challenges to basic self-dealing transactions:[19] the fiduciary has the burden of proving that the transaction was entirely fair to the corporation.

(5) Business judgment rule

A fifth rule is the business judgment rule: the decision to commit corporate resources to a takeover defense is a matter within the normal business discretion of the target's directors and officers, and could not be successfully challenged unless the plaintiff could prove some serious failure on the

---

A similarly selective approach is recommended by Professor Coffee in his Regulating the Market for Corporate Control: A Critical Assessment of the Tender Offer's Role in Corporate Governance, 84 Colum. L. Rev. 1145 (1984). He would prohibit greenmail and require most defensive tactics to be subject to specific shareholder approval but would allow target management to make an effective counter bid. He would also severely restrict partial bids.

Professor Lowenstein would limit certain defensive tactics that he calls "structural changes" — for example, defensive acquisitions and lockups — and would require that, when a takeover bid is in progress, *no* person or group may buy more than 5 percent of the target except pursuant to a tender offer. But he would also require offerors to keep bids open for 6 months — a rather draconian recommendation. Lowenstein, Pruning Deadwood in Hostile Takeovers: A Proposal for Legislation, 83 Colum. L. Rev. 249, 317-318 (1983).

[18] See Note, Greenmail: Targeted Stock Repurchases and the Management-Entrenchment Hypothesis, 98 Harv. L. Rev. 1045 (1985).

[19] See section 5.2 supra.

defendants' part — such as gross negligence or palpable overreaching. Since target managers usually go through the forms of carefulness — they hire expensive counsel and investment bankers, hold many meetings, and leave a justificatory paper trail — and since they can and do allege the corporate good as a basis for their defensive maneuvers, this rule makes it impossible to attack any but the most outrageous defensive maneuvers.

Supporters of these rules

Who supports which of the five approaches? A number of respected scholars in the law and economics tradition argue about whether the first or second rule is the better one,[20] but courts, as we shall soon see, seem to hover between the fourth and fifth approaches. Something like the third approach has been urged by the SEC's Advisory Committee,[21] by trade associations and other interest groups, and by the more middle-of-the-road commentators.[22] This alignment of views and adherents seems to reflect the idealism, the ineffectuality, and the love of compromise, respectively, of the three supporting groups.

Federal courts on state law

Federal courts, acting on their pendent jurisdiction over state law claims in cases also alleging violations of the federal securities laws, have rendered a fair number of decisions on substantive challenges to defensive maneuvers.[23] Because it represents a low-water mark in the protection of investor interests, a noteworthy case is *Panter v. Marshall Field & Co.*[24] For several years the target had responded to unwanted acquisition attempts by making defensive acquisitions that created antitrust problems for the prospective acquirers. After a lucrative tender offer was withdrawn because of this tactic, angry shareholders of Field's sued the company and its directors. The Seventh Circuit first disposed of several securities law claims. Section 14(e) was not applicable because the proposed tender offer had been withdrawn, and thus there could be no fraud "in connection with" a tender offer. Claims of misrepresentation and omission under Rule 10b-5 were also rejected. For example, plaintiff's objection to the board's failure to disclose its alleged policy of keeping the company independent regardless of the merits of any acquisition policy was characterized as being no more than a claim that the directors breached the fiduciary duty

***Marshall Field* case**

[20] See sources cited in notes 15 and 16 supra.

[21] SEC Advisory Committee on Tender Offers, Report of Recommendations (July 8, 1983). Note, however, that though the Committee would have regulated shark repellents in certain ways, it leaned rather heavily toward the business judgment rule approach, and basically manifested a pro-target-management stance.

[22] See sources cited in note 17 supra.

[23] See 1 A. Fleischer, Tender Offers: Defenses, Responses, and Planning 160-193 (1983); 1 M. Lipton & E. Steinberger, Takeovers and Freezeouts §6.01 (1984).

[24] 646 F.2d 271 (7th Cir. 1981).

they owed shareholders under state law. The court then opined that the relevant state law, that of Delaware, would analyze claims such as those made by the plaintiffs under the business judgment rule. Specifically, the plaintiffs proposed that in the takeover context the burden be placed on the directors to establish the compelling business purpose of any transaction that would have the effect of consolidating or retaining their control. The court rejected this proposal. Nevertheless, though stating that evaluation of possible acquisition offers and responses to them were properly within the scope of the directors' duties, the court seemed to leave room for the plaintiffs to present "evidence of self-dealing, fraud, overreaching or other bad conduct sufficient to give rise to . . . [a] reasonable inference that impermissible motives predominated in the board's consideration. . . ."[25] Its consistent finding was that they had not done so. Thus, the main legal point seems to have been about the burden of proof: Instead of requiring the directors to prove a compelling business purpose for their defensive tactics, the court required the plaintiffs to prove that impermissible motives predominated.

Dissenting view

In a stinging and well reasoned dissent, Judge Cudahy charged the majority with moving "one giant step closer to shredding whatever constraints still remain upon the ability of corporate directors to place self-interest before shareholder interest in resisting a hostile tender offer for control of the corporation."[26] He emphasized that the rationale for the business judgment rule was the directors' relative expertise, as compared to the court's, and that it was standard practice to set aside the rule when directors were afflicted with a conflict of interest, as they are in the hostile takeover context. He thought that the presence of a majority of nonmanagement directors on the board was not enough to negate the existence of a conflict of interest, in view of the usual relationship of symbiosis that exists between such directors and the inside directors. He protested the conclusion that plaintiff's evidence wasn't even sufficient to withstand a motion for a directed verdict, and he pointed out that Field's shareholders were injured: the price of their stock plunged dramatically upon the announcement of the withdrawal of the tender offer.

A query about state law

An interesting question raised by such decisions of federal courts is whether they correctly state and apply state law. (Most of the decisions relied on by the majority in *Panter* were decisions by *federal* courts purporting to apply Delaware or other state law.

[25] Id. at 296.
[26] Id. at 299.

For example, would the Delaware Supreme Court apply the business judgment rule to a target board's adoption of takeover defenses, as long as the board had a majority of nonmanagement directors? After some years of suspense, the answer appears to be yes, although the court has added some important guidelines as to how the rule should be applied in the takeover context.

***Cheff's* proper purpose test**

Let us look at some of the Delaware decisions. *Cheff v. Mathes*[27] was decided by the Delaware Supreme Court in 1964, before the rise of modern-style takeover bids. The directors of a company were attacked for causing it to buy out an insurgent shareholder (who was attempting a hostile takeover) at a premium price. (In modern jargon, they caused the company to pay greenmail.) The court said that the directors faced a conflict of interest and had the burden of proving that a legitimate corporate business purpose lay behind their action, rather than a mere desire to retain control. It found, however, that they had met that burden. Their stated purpose, which the court credited, was to prevent control from passing into the hands of someone who would change business policies and practices in a way that would damage the corporation.

***Pogostin's* business judgment rule**

In 1984, the Delaware Supreme Court decided *Pogostin v. Rice,*[28] in which it held that the business judgment rule, including the standards by which director conduct is judged, is applicable in the context of a takeover.[29]

***Unocal's* synthesis**

In 1985, the same court decided *Unocal Corp. v. Mesa Petroleum Co.,*[30] wherein it purported to reaffirm and apply the principles of both of the cases just mentioned, despite the apparent tension inherent in them. The main facts are worth noting. Mesa, already owner of about 13 percent of Unocal's stock, began a two-tier cash tender offer for an additional 37 percent of the stock at $54 a share. If successful in gaining control, it planned to eliminate the remaining shareholder by an exchange of securities purportedly worth $54 a share, but arguably worth less. Unocal's board, consisting of eight independent outside directors and six insiders, held several lengthy board meetings, listened to presentations by investment bankers and appropriate company officers, and deliberated about the proper reaction. Unocal then offered to repurchase up to 49 percent of its shares in exchange for a package of debt securities with an aggregate par

[27] 199 A.2d 548 (Del. 1964). See also Bennett v. Propp, 187 A.2d 405 (Del. 1962); Kors v. Carey, 158 A.2d 136 (Del. Ch. 1960).

[28] 480 A.2d 619 (Del. 1984).

[29] Id. at 627.

[30] 493 A.2d 946 (Del. 1985).

value of $72 per repurchased share (though the debt securities were arguably worth less than their par value). At first the repurchase offer was conditioned on Mesa's obtaining a controlling interest by its tender offer. This condition (the Mesa Purchase Condition) created an obvious problem for Unocal shareholders. If too many of them held back from tendering to Mesa, hoping to get the higher price from Unocal, then the tender offer would fail and the repurchase offer would expire; they would not get a premium price from either source. And Mesa might be so discouraged by the possible "scorched earth" character of the repurchase that it would find a way to back out of its offer. After shareholders protested and Mesa had brought suit, however, the Mesa Purchase Condition was essentially waived. The board did stick to another feature of its repurchase offer, however: Mesa was excluded from tendering its shares to Unocal pursuant to that offer. It is this exclusionary feature that was the focus of the court's opinion.

Target's repurchase offer

Exclusion of bidder

The court found the exclusion to be proper. It announced several principles. The board of a Delaware corporation has power to cause it to make selective stock repurchases; that is, the corporation is not absolutely forbidden from buying some shareholder's stock without giving the others an equal opportunity to sell.[31] This power is restricted by the directors' fiduciary obligations, however. In the tender offer context, this means that the board must not act "solely or primarily out of a desire to perpetuate themselves in office"; defensive measures should be motivated by a good faith concern for the welfare of the corporation and its stockholders. Furthermore, the defensive measure must be reasonable in relation to the threat posed.

Exclusion found proper

What, then, were the valid business purposes that, in the court's view, justified the selective repurchase? The court accepted the Unocal board's claim that its objective was either to defeat the Mesa offer, which it honestly believed to be inadequate or, if the offer should succeed, at least to give a fair deal to the remaining shareholders, who otherwise would be forced to accept what they considered to be "junk bonds." This objective called for exclusion of Mesa, thought the court, because otherwise Unocal would be subsidizing Mesa's efforts to buy cheaply, and because "Mesa could not, by definition, fit within the class of shareholders being protected from its own coercive and inadequate tender offer." The board also claimed it wanted to forestall a greenmail attempt by Mesa.

Valid business purposes found

[31] Indeed, *Cheff* had already established this much. But there, ironically, the court *sanctioned* the payment of greenmail, and here it found Unocal's exclusion of Mesa partly justified as a device to thwart a bidder who might soon demand greenmail!

Importance of outside directors

The court was heavily influenced by the fact that a majority of the directors were outsiders (and so not motivated by a selfish desire to hold on to their principal jobs, as inside directors presumably would be) and had gone through the forms of diligence in deliberating about their response to the tender offer. Indeed, this fact may explain why the court apparently saw no inconsistency between the "business judgment rule" approach of *Pogostin* and the "primary purpose" test of *Cheff.* The court reiterated the point made in earlier case law that a defensive share repurchase involves the directors in a conflict of interest, and thus the directors must show reasonable grounds for believing that there exists a danger to corporate policy and effectiveness from a certain person's stock ownership. But, said the court, they can satisfy this burden by showing "good faith and reasonable investigation," and their proof is "materially enhanced" when the board is composed of "a majority of outside independent directors."

Reactions to decision

Not surprisingly, some observers think the Delaware court was being naive, perhaps willfully so, in giving so much weight to the technical independence of outside directors and in minimizing the conflict of interest affecting all takeover defenses. Others simply dislike the blessing given to unequal treatment of shareholders in connection with repurchase offers. A more considered response of some commentators is to recommend that defensive stock repurchases should not be flatly prohibited, but should be subjected to two conditions: (1) They should be treated under federal law as tender offers ("self" tender offers) and therefore subject to the disclosure and other rules governing tender offers (such as the minimum time period, withdrawal, pro rata, and best price rules); and (2) They must be made for no less than the number of target shares for which the external offeror is bidding.[32] The proponents of this view argue that, given these two conditions, the target managers could not use a defensive repurchase offer to defeat a value-increasing bid.[33]

A poison pill case: *Household International*

In the same year, the Delaware Supreme Court decided another case involving a modern-style defensive tactic. *Moran v. Household International,*

[32] Bradley & Rosenzweig, The Law and Economics of Defensive Stock Repurchases and Defensive Self-Tender Offers, forthcoming in 99 Harv. L. Rev. (1986).

[33] On the positive side, Bradley and Rosenzweig argue that the ability to make a self-tender offer means that target managers can defeat bids by raiders, i.e., those who offer less than the company is really worth, since the target can always top such bids. Obviously, they think that looting and low bids aren't adequately deterred by existing legal rules and by competition among acquirers. They also argue that a self-tender offer may effectively signal the market about the target's true value. Whatever one may think about these reasons for permitting repurchases, their arguments for the two conditions are well developed.

Inc.[34] involved a poison pill "Rights Plan" similar to the one described above in section 13.6.1. The plan was challenged by John Moran, the largest shareholder and a director, who voted against adoption of the plan. The Delaware Supreme Court upheld the plan. The court first held that the board's adoption of the rights plan was within the scope of its authority. It bolstered this conclusion by stating that the plan did not, at least in theory, usurp the shareholders' right to receive tender offers. The court noted that would-be offerors could avoid the lethal aspects of the poison pill by several methods, such as by making a tender offer with a condition that the board redeem the rights or by acquiring 50 percent of the shares and causing Household to self-tender for the rights.

More important, the court reaffirmed the *Unocal* decision and the applicability of the business judgment rule to takeover defenses. Its restatement of this view indicates, however, that the rule is subject to three important guidelines or subrules in the takeover context.

First, the target directors have the initial burden of showing a reasonable belief that a takeover would threaten corporate policy and welfare. Among the beliefs that, if reasonably held, will apparently qualify for this purpose are a belief (as in *Cheff*) that the offeror will change business practices in a way that will be disastrous for the company, a belief (as in *Household* itself) that the most likely offerors will resort to "coercive takeover tactics" such as two-tier pricing that can be countered by the particular defensive measure in question, and a belief that the offeror will resort to "junk bond" financing and then cause a "bust up" of the target to pay for the enormous debt burden thereby acquired.

Second, the defensive action taken by the board must be reasonable in relation to the threat posed to corporate welfare. The court thought the rights plan in *Household* was not unreasonable because it did not absolutely preclude a takeover bid. Presumably, then, a defensive tactic that *did* foreclose all genuine bidding for the target's shares would be subject to attack. Also vulnerable would be a defensive tactic that demonstrably wasted corporate assets.

Third, the presence and the informed activity of independent directors will help the board to meet the burden of making the two initial showings just described. Once these showings are made, the burden of proof shifts to the plaintiffs and is difficult to meet.

At least one other court has refused to follow the Delaware Supreme Court's approach. A federal court applying New Jersey law decided that a

[34] 500 A.2d 1346 (Del. Nov. 19, 1985), aff'g 490 A.2d 1059 (Del. Ch. 1985).

somewhat different poison pill plan amounted to a discriminatory and illegal reclassification of common stock.[35] It also held that a series of scorched earth measures, including some very generous golden parachute arrangements, raised an inference that management intended to entrench itself and therefore shifted the burden to them to show the fairness and propriety of their actions.

Although greenmail, discriminatory repurchase offers, and poison pills seem to have fared reasonably well under state law, lockups have been overturned by a number of courts including the Delaware Supreme Court.[36] The case law in this area is actively evolving.

§13.6.4 Assessment

Conflict-of-interest argument

The case against allowing managers to engage in takeover defensive tactics can be put in several ways. One is a traditional legal argument. Directors and officers of a corporation whose shares are subject to a hostile takeover bid face a serious conflict of interest. Indeed, we could well conclude that *in no other context is the conflict of interest as serious as in the takeover situation.* Often the managers' jobs are at stake. The temptation to find that what is best for oneself is also best for the corporation and shareholders (for example, to assert that the company's stock is "undervalued" and that shareholders will eventually do better if the pending offer fails), the temptation to spend corporate resources extravagantly in the attempt to fend off the raider (it's always easier to spend other people's money), and the temptation to sacrifice the shareholders' interests (as by paying exorbitant amounts of greenmail), must be overwhelming. No human being can be expected to resist such temptations. Nor does it matter much if a majority of directors are outside directors. They still have a social bond with the inside directors and officers, not with the diffuse public shareholders, and they may care about the status and perquisites that go along with being a director.

[35] Minstar Acquiring Corp. v. AMF Inc., [1985] Fed. Sec. L. Rep. (CCH) ¶92,066 (S.D.N.Y. 1985) (opinion of Lowe, J.). The court flatly stated its belief that the courts of New Jersey would not follow the *Unocal* opinion.

[36] In MacAndrews & Forbes Holdings, Inc. v. Revlon, Inc., [1985] Fed. Sec. L. Rep. (CCH) ¶92,333, aff'd, — A.2d — (Del. 1986), the Delaware courts decided that the business judgment rule doesn't protect a lockup extended to foreclose further bidding in an active bidding situation. In another case applying New York law, Hanson Trust PLC v. ML Acquisition Inc., 781 F.2d 264 (2d Cir. 1986), the court held that plaintiffs had shown a likelihood of success on the merits of their claim that the directors did not exercise honest business judgment in granting a lockup option, and so reversed the district court's denial of a preliminary injunction.

For several reasons, the adoption of takeover defensive tactics usually involves extremely severe self-dealing. The managers' temptation to act out of self-interest and to ignore shareholder welfare is extraordinarily strong. The possible harm to shareholder welfare is much greater than in the ordinary run-of-the-mill basic self-dealing transaction. And the probability of otherwise unobtainable benefits to the corporation seems low. In such a situation, the law should either impose a strict standard of assessment of the defensive action's impact on the corporation and shareholders, *if it can devise one that is meaningful and administrable,* or it should flatly prohibit this type of behavior.

Severity of problem

A second line of argument against defensive tactics is cast in economic terms. When successful, these tactics deprive shareholders of significant gains.[37] Moreover, defensive tactics raise the cost of effecting a takeover, sometimes significantly so. If the law permits them and allows the average level of takeover costs to rise, there will be fewer takeover attempts. With a lower probability of facing a takeover attempt and possible ouster, managers will feel less pressure to perform as well as they can. There will be more managerial discretion and slack, since the market price of a company's shares will have to fall further below its potential value before the gap triggers a takeover attempt. For example if defensive tactics are outlawed and takeover costs are thereby kept down to, say, 10 percent of an acquired company's market value, the gap between the company's actual performance and its potential performance (as judged by potential acquirers) only has to exceed 10 percent to trigger a takeover bid. If defensive tactics are freely allowed and average takeover costs rise to, say, 35 percent of a company's market value, then the gap between actual and potential performance must be at least that large before a takeover attempt is triggered. Managers will have much more discretion that is unpoliced by market forces, and companies will be run much less efficiently. In the aggregate, shareholder welfare and general economic efficiency will be sharply reduced.

Lost gains and higher costs argument

An important point about this argument is that *it holds true even though, after a particular tender offer has been made, the shareholders of that particular company might get a higher price for their shares than the original tender offer price*

Occasional gains vs. overall loss

[37] See Easterbrook & Jarrell, Do Targets Gain from Defeating Tender Offers? 59 N.Y.U.L. Rev. 277 (1984). The authors claimed that the then-available empirical studies of post-offer movements in the prices of target stocks show clearly that successful defensive tactics have deprived target shareholders of appreciation gains worth between 15 and 52 percent of the value of targets shares. They attacked the methodology of one study that seemed to show a contrary result.

if their managers are allowed to engage in some sorts of defensive tactics, such as those that force the offeror to up its bid. The fact that this can and does happen does NOT mean that shareholders are better off *in the aggregate* because such defensive tactics are allowed. Quite the reverse is likely to be true. Shareholders as a group may be better off in the long run if the cost of takeovers is kept low and the number of takeovers high. Rational shareholders who realize this should desire legal rules that uniformly ban defensive tactics that have the overall effect of raising costs and reducing the frequency of takeovers. Over the course of their investing careers, they will be better off with such rules.

What are the arguments for permitting defensive tactics? One is that they may allow the directors to protect the corporation against raiders or new managers who would not run the company as well as the incumbent ones. As discussed in section 13.2 above, the empirical evidence does not support a belief that most tender offerors fit into this category. Yet defensive tactics are resorted to in response to almost all hostile tender offers.

Another argument is that defensive tactics may have the result that the shareholders eventually get a better price. This argument, as we have just seen, neglects the systemic effect of such tactics: Overall, they may reduce shareholder welfare.

Soliciting rival bids

Commentators sometimes suggest that some tactics are not subject to the "bad systemic effects" argument. When target management solicits rival bidders, for example, their activity does not consume much in the way of corporate resources, and it may lead to competitive bidding. Competitive bidding is usually thought to be good, since it is likely to lead to resources being channeled into their most valuable uses. (Those who can make the most out of a business are those who will be willing to pay the most.)

Objections

This suggestion is not without problems, however. Some feel that first bidders incur special costs in identifying good targets and that rival bidders should not get a "free ride" on the first bidders' search efforts. This counsels against making rival bids too easy; the result could be a discouragement of takeover attempts, since few would want to take the risks of being first bidders. Moreover, it seems practically difficult to allow target management to solicit rival bids that don't involve more questionable aspects like lockups, side payments to the target managers, and so on. Finally, one could argue that all that is required to generate an auction among rival bidders is a legal rule that, as the Williams Act now does, requires a tender offer to be kept open for a modest amount of time. Letting target managers actively solicit or pick the rival bidders seems unnecessary.

There is some systematic empirical evidence on the effects of defensive maneuvers.[38] A study of greenmail payments and standstill agreements found they were bad for nonparticipating shareholders.[39] There were negative average returns associated with these transactions.

Empirical evidence: greenmail bad

On the other hand, a study of the effect of certain types of anti-takeover charter amendments on shares prices provided only weak preliminary support for the view that these had a negative impact.[40] The weak result might be explained by the fact that the amendments in question — staggered boards, supermajority merger approval provisions, and associated fair price provisions — do not preclude a successful takeover and may not significantly deter takeover attempts.

Charter amendments, maybe

Similarly, a study of reincorporations to Delaware found that reincorporations motivated by fear of possible takeover had neither a positive nor a negative effect on investor returns, so far as statistical tests could reliably tell.[41] This might be explained in several ways. Perhaps protection against takeovers is not significantly better in Delaware than elsewhere, though managers hope so and are willing to spend corporate money to give it a try. Or perhaps the reincorporating companies do acquire a bit more insulation against takeovers and this does exert a negative force on stock prices, but the force is offset by a "signalling" effect: the market appreciates, more emphatically than it did before the reincorporation, that the company's managers fear a takeover and that therefore the company may very well be a prime candidate for a takeover attempt at a premium price.

Reincorporations neutral

Finally, I should mention a study of defensive litigation by target companies.[42] It found that litigious targets were more likely to generate auctions than were nonlitigious companies acquired by merger, with the result that the targets' shareholders usually got higher premiums and higher adjusted returns on their stock. From this data one might conclude that this particular type of defensive tactic conduces to shareholder welfare rather than to managerial entrenchment. Perhaps, then, we should encourage or at least continue to allow defensive litigation.

Defensive litigation may help shareholders

[38] See generally Easterbrook & Jarrell, note 37 supra.

[39] Dann & DeAngelo, Standstill Agreements, Privately Negotiated Stock Repurchases, and the Market for Corporate Control, 11 J. Fin. Econ. 275 (1983).

[40] DeAngelo & Rice, Antitakeover Charter Amendments and Stockholder Wealth, 11 J. Fin. Econ. 329 (1983).

[41] Romano, Law as Product: Some Pieces of the Incorporation Puzzle, 1 J. Law, Econ. & Org. 225 (1985).

[42] Jarrell, The Wealth Effects of Litigation by Targets: Do Interests Diverge in a Merge? 28 J. Law & Econ. 151 (1985).

Counterarguments

Several arguments can be made against this conclusion, however. First, defensive litigation rarely succeeds on the merits, if and when the litigation is resolved on the merits. This suggests that it is simply dilatory in nature. If there are good effects from having offers kept open longer, they could be achieved more cheaply by simply extending the minimum tender offer period under the Williams Act.

Second, in those cases where defensive litigation *does* succeed in discouraging the offer (as happened in 21 of 98 studied cases) instead of leading to a takeover at a higher price, the target's shareholders are hurt quite badly. Their stock's value plummets.

Systemic effects are what matter

Third, and most important, we should recall the point made earlier about systemic effects. The fact that a particular defensive tactic leads to a higher price for shareholders already faced with a tender offer does not show that it has an overall good effect on shareholder wealth. The systemic impact of the tactic on the *frequency* of takeovers must also be considered. If it is negative, the net result for shareholders may also be negative.

But difficult to measure

Unfortunately, it is very difficult to devise a test to measure systemic effects. Arguments about some defensive tactics must therefore be based more on theory than on hard evidence. By contrast, empirical evidence showing that certain other defensive tactics (such as greenmail) have negative near-term effects is fairly damning, since there is little theoretical reason to expect positive systemic effects that might offset the observed bad effects.[43]

[43] But even this point can be questioned, at least as to greenmail. See Macey & McChesney, cited in note 3 supra, who argue inter alia that greenmail may be a desirable way of compensating persons who perform the valuable service of discovering undervalued companies and signaling their discovery to other market participants by means of their purchases of stock in target companies.

CHAPTER 14

DISTRIBUTIONS TO SHAREHOLDERS

Kinds of distribution

This chapter deals with distributions of property by corporations to their shareholders in their capacity as shareholders.[1] The major kinds of distributions are dividend payments, payments made to the shareholder by the corporation when it redeems or repurchases the shareholder's stock, and payments to the shareholders when the corporation is dissolved or when its business is totally or partially liquidated.[2] The property distributed is often money, as in the case of ordinary dividends, but it could be any other

[1] A corporate payment might be made to a shareholder receiving it in some other capacity. An example is a rental payment to a shareholder who is leasing property to the corporation.

[2] A distribution by X Corporation to its shareholders of additional X stock would be called a *stock dividend.* A distribution by X Corporation to its shareholders of its excess inventory of widgets would be called a *dividend in kind.*

form of property, including stock, bonds, and other securities issued by the distributing corporation itself.[3]

Plan of chapter

The plan of this chapter is straightforward: The first three sections deal with dividends; the second three deal with redemptions and repurchases. In each group I first discuss questions of business practice and financial theory, move on to legal restrictions developed by case law for the protection of shareholders, and, finally, review the statutory legal accounting rules that are designed mainly for the protection of creditors.

§14.1 *Dividend Policy*

What business judgment?

It is often said that the directors' decision to declare dividends is a matter of business judgment. But what is the business judgment that the directors are trying to make? Though their decisions about dividends are usually shielded from legal attack, directors still have a fiduciary duty of care that requires them to attempt to maximize shareholder wealth. If a director is trying to do this in connection with dividend policy, at what specific objective should he be aiming? Should he want to pay out all current earnings as dividends, or none, or some specific proportion? Does the answer depend on other factors? If so, which factors, and how? These turn out to be surprisingly difficult questions.

Practice

There is some good evidence on what managers in fact aim to do in setting dividend policy.[1] Many of them try to achieve a target payout ratio. For example, the company may tend to pay out half of each year's current net earnings as dividends. The company does not hit the target exactly every year, however, but smooths out dividend payments in relation to earnings fluctuations. As a result, fluctuations in dividend payments are not as great as fluctuations in earnings. Thus, if a company's net earnings go up $1 per share this year as compared to last, the directors might increase this year's per share dividend by one-third that amount; if the high earnings persist next year, they will then take the dividend payments up further toward the long-term target ratio of half of earnings. Moreover, when managers do raise regular dividends, they generally do so only

[3]Some major occasions for invoking the dissolution and liquidation provisions of corporate statutes were discussed in chapter 10, particularly in section 10.3.

§14.1 [1]Lintner, Distributions of Incomes of Corporations among Dividends, Retained Earnings, and Taxes, 46 Am. Econ. Rev. 97 (1956). See also Fama & Babiak, Dividend Policy: An Empirical Analysis, 63 J. Am. Statistical Assn. 1132 (1968); Watts, The Information Content of Dividends, 46 J. Bus. 411 (1973).

when they expect that future earnings will grow or that recent high levels of earnings will be maintained. They seem to fear having to cut dividends.

Theory: M & M irrelevance proposition

But what sense does a target payout ratio make? Is there, in theory or practice, some ideal payout ratio for a company that will increase shareholder wealth more than any other? On this question there is much debate among financial theorists. In considering this debate, the best starting point is the "irrelevance" proposition of Modigliani and Miller.[2] Their view applies to a world with no transaction costs, perfect information, and efficient capital markets. They assume that a firm has independently made its investment decisions — it knows which machines, factories, and other investments in business opportunities it wants to make — and that it does not want to borrow any more. In other words, it faces a choice between two financing options: It can finance its investment decisions by retaining earnings, which in turn involves forgoing dividends, or it can raise money for its investment projects by selling new shares of stock, in which case it will pay out net earnings as dividends. [3] (Obviously, combinations of the financing options are also possible.) M and M believe that the choice of financing method (or of any combination of retained earnings financing and new equity financing) cannot influence the value of the firm or the value of its stock. In this sense, dividend policy is irrelevant to shareholder wealth. Consequently, managers should not worry about finding an optimal dividend policy; any policy will do. To be sure, shareholders might appreciate knowing what the policy is in advance, and being forewarned of any changes; but the payout ratio itself is of little concern.

The tax factor

In the real world, of course, there are transaction costs and other imperfections. The most obvious of these, and in the minds of many theorists the one most likely to have a powerful influence on real decisions, is federal income taxation. Whether a company pays out its net income as dividends or not generally does not affect the size of its tax liabilities, but a shareholder who receives a dividend is treated as receiving ordinary income that is taxable at the individual's marginal tax rate for ordinary income. If the shareholder does not receive a dividend but the value of his shares increases because the corporation has retained net income instead of distributing it, the shareholder is not taxed. True, he may be taxed on this

[2] Miller & Modigliani, Dividend Policy, Growth and the Valuation of Shares, 34 J. Bus. 411 (1961).

[3] A lawyer would immediately notice one difference between these two strategies that would sometimes affect the control of the corporation. If the corporation always sells new shares to finance new projects (and preemptive rights are not available, as is usually the case with public corporations), the voting power of existing shareholders will be diluted. An old group may lose or jeopardize its working control.

gain in value if he should sell his shares, but then the tax rate will be that for capital gains, which for most individuals is much lower than their rate for ordinary income. (At present, only 40 percent of net capital gains are included in the taxable income of an individual investor. Therefore, an individual investor is normally taxed much more lightly on capital gain income than on dividend income.)

Implies no dividends? This major real world factor seems to argue quite strongly that companies usually should pay no dividends at all. Even a shareholder who needs a steady stream of cash from his stock investment would do better by simply selling off a few shares now and then, rather than demanding that the company pay dividends. The only obvious exception would be for companies that simply have no good investments to finance. This might happen, for example, because the company is restricted by regulation to a particular geographical area and line of business, such as banking. Such a company might even run a serious risk of incurring a penalty tax if it retained income without having a good business purpose for doing so. In any event, the company without expansion prospects is presumably a rare case in a well-functioning economy, so this possibility can hardly explain why so many companies pay substantial dividends.

A paradox As suggested, the tax factor raises a great conceptual puzzle for financial theorists. In the real world it is definitely not the case that most corporations are trying to move toward a no-dividend policy. It is also clear that many shareholders would find it abhorrent if their corporations did so. Why? Are shareholders and managers simply irrational? If not, how can we explain their behavior?

Seven factors Many factors have been adduced to try to resolve the paradox. Indeed, the possibility, or probability, that actual behavior is the result of a number of individually minor influences all acting together may be what leads people to feel unsatisfied that the paradox has been properly resolved. (Most people, I think, would feel better if there were a "single factor" explanation.) In any event, let us consider seven possibly relevant factors. Three have to do with the special tax situations of some investors; the others deal with regulatory requirements, transaction costs, information costs, and agency costs.

(1) Reversed tax preferences First, some holders of stock, namely, ordinary business corporations, are taxed more heavily on capital gains than on dividend income.[4] Such

[4] I.R.C. §1201(a)(2) (tax rate of 28 percent on a corporation's net capital gain); §§11 (corporate tax rates — top rate being 46 percent), 243(a)(1) (85 percent dividends received deduction, which results in a top marginal tax rate of 6.9 percent for dividend income received by corporations).

investors have a preference for dividends, and managers will be influenced by it. This factor is probably a minor one.

(2) Untaxed investors

Second, many shareholders aren't taxed at all. Among the shareholders that are untaxed are the private and the state and local pension funds, which today hold a very substantial fraction of all publicly traded stock. These holders of stock are not driven by tax factors to prefer a low dividend payout policy. Of course, their tax situation by itself doesn't mean that they will have a positive preference for dividend-paying companies, but it does clear the way for other factors to shape their preferences. Some of these other factors are discussed below. (Consider especially the fifth, sixth, and seventh factors.) These factors might play little role in shaping the preferences of ordinary individual investors, for whom the desire to avoid paying ordinary income taxes on dividends may dwarf all other factors, but they may be very important factors for pension funds and other untaxed investors.

(3) Lightly taxed investors

Third, there are numerous investors in rather low tax brackets. For them, if factors like five, six, and seven below are significant, they may have a net preference for corporations with positive dividend payout ratios. Among such investors are life insurance companies, retired persons, and personal trusts established for minor children.[5]

(4) Regulated preferences

Fourth, some investors are legally or morally bound to prefer high dividend payout companies. Life insurance companies governed by New York law, for example, must invest only in a legal list of presumably safe, statutorily specified kinds of investments, including some high dividend-yielding stocks.[6] The investments of property and liability insurers are also restricted, though not as severely.[7] In many personal trusts, the beneficial interest is divided between life beneficiaries and remaindermen, and the governing document specifies that the life beneficiaries will receive all current net income, which is defined to be that attributable to interest, dividends, and the like. A trustee in such a case may very well be bound to invest substantial amounts in "income-producing," that is, dividend-

[5]Financial economists have analyzed the possible effects of taxes on dividend policy in rather more abstruse terms. The effect of differential rates of tax on dividends and capital gains is analyzed in Brennan, Taxes, Market Valuation and Corporate Financial Policy, 23 Natl. Tax J. 417 (1970). The view that dividend policy is irrelevant even in the presence of taxes is developed in Black & Scholes, The Effects of Dividend Yield and Dividend Policy on Common Stock Prices and Returns, 1 J. Fin. Econ. 1 (1974); Miller & Scholes, Dividends and Taxes, 6 J. Fin. Econ. 333 (1978).

[6]N.Y. Ins. Law §§1403(a)(1) and 1402, 1403(d), 1405, 1406, 1440 (McKinney's rev. 1984 Ins. Law Special Pamph.).

[7]N.Y. Ins. Law §§1403(c) and 1402, 1403(d), 1404, 1407 (McKinney's 1984 Ins. Law Special Pamph.).

paying, stocks. Incidentally, this factor is probably not a minor one. We know that trusts managed by bank trust departments hold several hundred billion dollars' worth of stock, and that some very large but not precisely known amount of "individually" owned stock is held by other kinds of trustees.

(5) Transaction costs considerations

Fifth, investors who want a steady stream of cash from their investments — for example, in order to meet living expenses — may experience minor but real transaction cost savings if their cash flow comes in the form of dividends as opposed to proceeds from stock sales. This is true even if we assume that the bookkeeping and mailing fees incurred by companies when paying dividends are ultimately borne by shareholders, for these amounts are undoubtedly smaller than the brokerage fees and other costs (including opportunity costs like inconvenience) that would be involved in having the same number of shareholders all individually sell a small portion of their stock in the company every quarter. Put another way, a corporation can realize some economies of scale in the periodic liquidation of investment interests by paying dividends. On the other hand, however, the company that pays significant amounts of dividends will presumably have to make public offerings of its stock somewhat more frequently than a low-payout company (in order to finance its new projects), and the costs of making public offerings are themselves substantial. Whether these costs would outweigh the transaction cost savings we just discussed is an empirical question. The answer might vary from company to company.

(6) Credible signals

Sixth, some investors may distrust the information that companies give out about their earnings. They may therefore prefer corporations that have made it a long practice to "put their money where their mouths are" by paying regular and gradually increasing dividends. Presumably, a company that exaggerates its reported income could not follow a high payout dividend policy indefinitely. In the United States, skepticism about reported net earnings is most likely to be rational if based not on the supposed malleability of financial accounting principles but on imperfections in the auditing process. That is, outside auditors don't always discover and report insider frauds, embezzlements, and the like. It may be that some investors exaggerate the possibility of such misbehavior, because they are overly influenced by news of dramatic scandals. Since successful frauds are by definition undiscovered, however, and may express themselves in unexpected earning declines in later years, who can say what the proper degree of investor suspicion is?

(7) Agency costs reduction

The seventh theory also has to do with the reduction of agency costs — roughly, the costs of monitoring and policing managerial behavior. The theory is that investor preferences for high dividend-paying companies constitute a device for shifting companies toward less costly methods of capital-market discipline of the companies' investment decisions.[8] Shareholders may want net income to be paid out in dividends partly because that will mean that when their managers want to finance new ventures they will have to "go to market," that is, to institutional lenders for a loan or to investment bankers for a stock offering. The managers will therefore have to submit their past performance and their current plans to outside review and evaluation. This evaluation will affect the feasibility and terms of financing and will lead to definite constraints on the managers' freedom of action. For example, before a large bank approves a loan to a corporation whose performance has been less than glistening in the recent past, it may demand that the corporation give it a security interest in its inventory (which involves bothersome procedures), promise not to create other debt, promise not to participate in any mergers or acquisitions without the bank's permission, and make many other restrictive agreements. The bank may even demand that if certain financial ratios fall below specified figures, all proposed increases in executive compensation will have to be submitted to the bank for prior approval. It might also obtain the right to replace the managers under certain conditions. A manager looking forward to these possible consequences of the process of going to market for money will be more likely to try to keep the company house in good condition. Sophisticated investors (such as the institutional investors who account for so much of the trading in today's markets) appreciate this phenomenon and will therefore want to see managers frequently faced with the need to seek outside financing. This will add to their reasons for preferring dividend-paying companies.

Objection and response

Against this seventh theory, you might object that when managers retain earnings instead of paying dividends and use the retained earnings to finance a project, the merits of the project will eventually be tested in the capital market anyway. Specifically, if the project is a bad one and leads to a decline in share prices, a takeover attempt may follow. This is true, but the important point concerns the relative costs of the different types of capital-market discipline. Takeovers are very expensive transactions. The size of takeover costs may even be taken as a measure of the amount of leeway that managers have, that is, the amount of slack they can create or tolerate, or the amount of deviation from profit maximization, before pro-

[8] This theory is my own conjecture, which I have long presented to my students for classroom discussion. It is put forward only as an hypothesis, not as a firm belief. For a similar, independently developed explanatory effort, see Easterbrook, Two Agency-Cost Explanations of Dividends, 74 Am. Econ. Rev. 650, 654 (1984).

voking a corrective response from market forces. The costs of two other types of transaction that impose capital-market discipline — namely, making a private placement of debt and making a public offering of stock — are quite small by comparison. Yet these transactions may also influence the identity and behavior of managers in directions favorable to shareholder interests.[9] If sophisticated shareholders appreciate these facts, however dimly, their expressed preference for dividends may be a way of encouraging more frequent and competent testing and monitoring of managerial performance.[10]

Different clienteles

Our discussion to this point suggests that there are both high payout and low payout clienteles among investors. Some shareholders prefer companies with high dividend payout policies, and other prefer low payout companies. Companies have acted to satisfy these preferences and have sorted themselves out into different kinds. With any luck, the forces of supply and demand work towards an equilibrium, in the normal way that markets do. This, at least, seems to be the view of the more moderate financial theorists.

Impact on irrelevance proposition?

Note, however, that this state of affairs may well be consistent with a belief in the irrelevance proposition, as applied to individual corporations. If the different investor clienteles are all basically satisfied, any particular company might find it impossible to lower its cost of capital (and increase shareholder wealth) by altering its dividend policy.[11] (Note also that there are commentators on the financial scene who still think that corporations and shareholders are irrationally doing the wrong thing — paying and demanding dividends instead of financing new projects as much as possible out of retained earnings.)

Caveat regarding close corporations

For the lawyer, I must add one very big caveat and one middle-sized caveat to the preceding discussion. The big caveat is this: the irrelevance

[9] And indeed, unlike the takeover mechanism, they result in serious outside review of investment projects *before* the projects are undertaken. This may be a crucial factor in lowering overall agency costs.

[10] Incidentally, this seventh theory would help to explain an otherwise puzzling phenomenon asserted to exist by some researchers: the rate of return on projects financed by retained earnings tends to be lower than the rate of return on new equity. If this difference really exists — it's been disputed — it might simply reflect the different relative costs of capital-market discipline in the two contexts. See Baumol, Haim, Malkiel & Quandt, Earnings Retention, New Capital and the Growth of the Firm, 52 Rev. Econ. & Stat. 345 (1970). As noted, the claim generated dispute. See, e.g., Whittington, Profitability of Retained Earnings, 54 Rev. Econ. & Stat. 152 (1972); Friend & Husic, Efficiency of Corporate Investment, 55 Rev. Econ. & Stat. 122 (1973); Racette, Earnings Retention, New Capital and the Growth of the Firm: A Comment, 55 Rev. Econ. & Stat. 127 (1973); and Baumol, Haim, Malkiel & Quandt, Efficiency of Corporate Investment: A Reply, 55 Rev. Econ. & Stat. 128 (1973).

[11] See Black & Scholes, cited in note 5 supra.

proposition of M and M does not apply, even in theory, to close corporations. It assumes efficient capital markets as a critical feature of its argument. It doesn't apply where the shareholders do not have the option of selling their shares in a reasonably efficient market. This is an absolutely critical point for lawyers because virtually all litigated cases involving alleged managerial dereliction by failing to pay dividends (or, more rarely, by paying allegedly excessive dividends) involve closely held corporations, or cases where the complainants are shareholders in a partially owned subsidiary or in a company whose management is dominated by a controlling stockholder. That is, the cases involve contexts in which the shareholder has no active market, or no market untainted by distorting factors, to which he can turn. In these contexts a particular dividend policy very definitely can be (though of course it need not be) a weapon of oppression or a means of violating a fiduciary duty of loyalty. The next section will explore some of these problems; issues involving close corporations will be examined more comprehensively in chapter 18.

Caveat regarding changes in policy

The lesser caveat is that, even though directors of any particular company may rest assured that they are not likely to be violating their duty of care or failing to maximize shareholder wealth by blindly following a traditional target payout ratio policy (or by adopting a target ratio as "optimal" on the basis of some half-baked, unproven theory), they should nevertheless have some concerns about abrupt *changes* in their company's dividend policy. Ideally, the company's dividend policy should be made reasonably clear to the investing public. Shifts should be preceded by a fair warning, so that investors in particular personal situations (for example, a high or a low tax bracket) will not be caught holding the wrong kind of stock for them. In other words, the directors should aspire toward consistency and openness in setting dividend policy.

Managers' vs. shareholders' preferences

Finally, it should be noted that at least one legal commentator believes it to be likely that management preferences with respect to dividend policy may be systematically different, rather than occasionally different (as in the conflict-of-interest cases dealt with in the next section), from those of shareholders.[12] If this view is valid, it may serve as a reason, or as an additional reason, for mandating disclosures about the bases of dividend decisions. Consider, for example, an unusual increase in a company's quarterly dividend. The increase may reflect a judgment by management that it has no better use for the funds, or it may reflect their expectation that earnings will increase enough to cover both expansion needs and future dividends at the increased rate. An unusual dividend decrease

[12] Brudney, Dividends, Discretion, and Disclosure, 66 Va. L. Rev. 85 (1980).

might also be ambiguous: a very special good opportunity has come along and will be financed by the extra retained earnings, or the managers expect future revenues to decline, so that the extra retention of earnings will be needed just to maintain normal operations. Presumably, the managers' duty of care implies that they should make reasonably sure that investors will not put the wrong interpretation on a particular change in dividend policy. (This would not mean, of course, that they have to explain every change in dividend policy. The way that investors can be expected to read a change — most dividend increases are judged to be good, for example — may well be the appropriate way in a particular case.) If one believes that managers will frequently be tempted not to fulfill this duty to prevent misinterpretation, one may see greater need for explicit disclosure requirements about the bases of dividends. The conclusion and its supporting arguments have been vigorously disputed, however.[13]

On balance, it appears that routine business decisions to pay dividends will and should be little affected by corporate law. But then, the law often gets its life not in the ordinary or common situation but in the peripheral and the deviant.

§14.2 Protection of Shareholders

The fourth paradigm reappears

Judicial opinions use various linguistic expressions to describe what will overcome the business judgment rule and lead a court to find that a given dividend policy was improper. But they suggest that the plaintiff must show that the policy complained of is not justified by any reasonable business objective, and/or that the policy resulted from improper motives and harmed the corporation or certain shareholders. In other words, the cases fall into my fourth, or "mixed motive," category of conflict of interest transactions:[1] The corporation is caused to take an action or enter a transaction in which the controlling parties have no direct financial interest, but which has collateral consequences that are of personal interest to those controlling parties. As noted earlier, this is the most difficult kind of conflict for courts to deal with effectively, and the law often tries to govern these cases by a "proper purpose" test or similar formula that inevitably seems unsatisfactory.

Dodge v. Ford Motor Co.

Let us consider the classic American case in which a court did order the payment of dividends. *Dodge v. Ford Motor Co.*[2] involved a closely held

[13] Fischel, The Law and Economics of Dividend Policy, 67 Va. L. Rev. 669 (1981).

§14.2 [1] See chapter 4.

[2] 170 N.W. 668 (Mich. 1919).

corporation. Henry Ford owned 58.5 percent of the stock and was the dominant person; the Dodge brothers owned 10 percent. The company was extremely successful. It had profits of about $60 million a year and a surplus[3] of $112 million against liabilities and stated capital of only $20 million. It had been paying regular dividends of $1.2 million per year and so-called special dividends of about $10 million a year.[4] But Ford caused the company to cease paying the special dividends, and the disaffected Dodge brothers sued.

Why no dividends

The court appeared to accept at face value Ford's explanation of the cessation of dividends: the company needed money for expansion (it wanted to build a second plant) AND Ford didn't want the company to get the money for the expansion from future sales (which easily could have funded the expansion) because he wanted to lower the price of cars for social and altruistic reasons. Ford didn't argue that lowering the price of cars would increase sales volume sufficiently that it would lead to an increase in company profits; that is, he didn't claim that demand was price-elastic. Rather, it was conceded that the company could sell all cars it could possibly make in the old and new plants at the existing price and that, therefore, the price-lowering policy would hurt corporate profits. But Ford's position was that the stockholders had made enough money — full maximization of profits would be indecent, so to speak — and that American consumers and workers deserved a break.

Response to "social benefit" explanation

The Michigan Supreme Court was not impressed. In a famous, oft-quoted passage, it told Mr. Ford, in effect: it is morally good to be generous, but please be generous with your own money, not that of other persons.

> There should be no confusion (of which there is evidence) of the duties which Mr. Ford conceives that he and the stockholders owe to the general public and the duties which in law he and his codirectors owe to protesting, minority stockholders. A business corporation is organized and carried on primarily for the profit of the stockholders. The powers of directors are to be exercised for that end. The discretion of directors is to be exercised in the choice of means to attain that end and does not extend to a change in the end

[3] "Surplus" is the excess of total net worth (or "stockholders' equity") over the company's legal (or stated) capital. These concepts are explored and illustrated in the next section. The point here is that Ford Motor Co. was very profitable and had more than ample room to pay very large dividends without running afoul of any statutory restriction on dividends.

[4] The terms *regular* and *special* in this context are not legal terms used in corporate statutes or case law holdings. They are terms used by management to suggest to shareholders what sort of dividends can and cannot be expected to be repeated regularly in the future.

itself, to the reduction of profits or to the nondistribution of profits among stockholders in order to devote them to other purposes.[5]

Other explanations

Many people who have read the case, and perhaps the court itself, have wondered whether Ford's "eleemosynary" explanation of the cessation of special dividends was genuine. The Dodge brothers were planning to start their own automobile company. Perhaps Ford was really just trying to make it hard for them to finance what could become a rival company. If this were so, Ford's motive was a corporate business purpose connected with profit maximization, but one that might raise antitrust problems or questions of unfair competition. Or Ford may simply have wanted, by turning off the faucet of financial return, to weaken the position of the Dodge brothers so that he could later get them to sell their stock to him more cheaply. (Indeed, he later did succeed in buying them out, at a price that in hindsight looked quite favorable to him!) In other words, the decision to suspend dividends could have been one step in a rather garden variety squeezeout plan. If so, Ford's purpose was even less proper than the one the court expressly rejected. (Squeezeouts in close corporations will be dealt with at greater length in chapter 18. As will appear there, courts don't always see that the steps in a squeezeout are part of a larger pattern, and therefore they may fuss with the too-narrow question whether a particular step violated "the rules" that are said to govern that kind of transaction. Ideally, courts should always be sensitive to the whole factual context in which challenged transactions, like dividend policies, occur.)

Bad faith test

On the legal question in the case, the court enunciated a "bad faith" test for dividend decisions. Dividends are basically matters of business judgment; courts will interfere only if the directors' action in paying or not paying dividends is such an abuse of discretion as would constitute a fraud, or a breach of that good faith that they are bound to exercise towards the shareholders. Ford acted in bad faith by deciding to suspend special dividends in order to accomplish a non-profit-maximizing objective dear to himself. The court ordered the payment of substantial dividends.

Fiduciary duty approach: close corporations

A much more recent decision applied the Massachusetts theory that holders of power in a close corporation owe a fiduciary duty of utmost good faith and loyalty to one another. In *Smith v. Atlantic Properties, Inc.*,[6] each of four shareholders in a close corporation owning real estate properties had a veto power over policy decisions. Against the wishes and warn-

[5] 170 N.W. at 684.

[6] 422 N.E.2d 798 (Mass. App. 1981).

ings of the others, one, a Dr. Wolfson, refused to accede to the payment of substantial dividends despite the presence of very large retained earnings, ostensibly because he wanted to devote them to repairs and improvements of the real estate. As a result, the Internal Revenue Service twice imposed sizable penalty taxes on the corporation for unreasonable accumulation of earnings.[7] Dr. Wolfson's refusal to consent to dividends was found to be unreasonable, and he was held liable to the corporation for the penalty taxes. The trial court was ordered to tell the parties to try to agree to a specific dividend policy for the future, with the threat that the court would impose one if they couldn't agree.[8]

A Delaware example

Consider now a case exemplifying the Delaware approach. In *Sinclair Oil Corp. v. Levien,*[9] the plaintiffs were minority shareholders in a corporation (Venezuelan) that was 97 percent owned by another (Sinclair). The charge was that Sinclair caused Venezuelan to pay excessive dividends and took various corporate opportunities for itself and for other, wholly-owned subsidiaries. Venezuelan had been engaged in the oil business in Venezuela; legal restraints made business growth there unfeasible. Sinclair, rather than direct Venezuelan into opportunities elsewhere, was essentially letting it phase down, and one result of this was that Venezuelan was now paying massive dividends, 97 percent of which were going to Sinclair, of course. The Delaware Supreme Court disposed of the corporate opportunity point, against the plaintiffs, by applying the familiar "line of business" test. (See chapter 7.)

Self-dealing not found

On the dividend issue, the court held that the business judgment rule applied. The plaintiffs claimed, and the court conceded, that if the dividend decisions amounted to self-dealing, the burden would shift to the defendant corporation to prove the entire or intrinsic fairness of those decisions. The plaintiffs' view was that there was self-dealing, inasmuch as the decisions of the subsidiary were controlled by Sinclair, which received

[7] Note that this imposition of penalty taxes indicates that at least the IRS was *not* convinced that earnings were being retained for bona fide business purposes, such as repair and improvement of the buildings. Apparently, the retained earnings were not in fact used to a large extent for repairs and improvements. Perhaps this was because Dr. Wolfson's business reasons for retention were not his real reasons, or perhaps it was because the others obstinately refused to go along with the idea of using the retained earnings as he proposed. The court discussed both possibilities and seemed to conclude that Dr. Wolfson was the major cause of the penalties. Note that Dr. Wolfson conceivably might have been motivated by a self-interested reason, if he personally didn't pay taxes on dividends, and this would put the case in our mixed motive category.

[8] See also Keough v. St. Paul Milk Co., 285 N.W. 809 (Minn. 1946); Miller v. Magline, Inc., 256 N.W.2d 761 (Mich. App. 1977).

[9] 280 A.2d 717 (Del. 1971).

97 percent of all the dividends and allegedly wanted them solely to satisfy its own desires for cash. The court disagreed, asserting that the transactions did not involve self-dealing, because the controlling party and the minority shareholders were all treated equally in each disputed transaction: the minority got its pro rata share, so the majority did not receive anything to the exclusion of the minority. The court drew a contrast to interested-director transactions, which, it said, do involve self-dealing.

Proper purpose approach

By characterizing the subsidiary's dividend payments as not involving self-dealing, the court did not mean to imply that there was no way that a plaintiff could challenge them successfully. The point about there being no self-dealing concerned the burden of proof and the applicability of the business judgment rule. Even though the latter rule applied, a plaintiff could get a court to find the dividends improper if he could sustain the burden of proving that the "dividends were not grounded on any reasonable business objective."[10] Somewhat later, the court also pointed out that a plaintiff could prevail by showing that the challenged dividends "resulted from improper motives" and amounted to waste.[11] The court did not make it clear whether a plaintiff would have to show both lack of business purpose and presence of improper purpose, or whether either alone would do. Nor did it make clear whether the improper purpose would have to be the sole or primary purpose behind a dividend policy, or simply a significant one.

Why no self-dealing

Perhaps the most interesting aspect of the case is why the court refused to see self-dealing in a dividend policy caused by a controlling parent corporation. Remember that in many situations involving parents and partially-owned subsidiaries, the top management of the parent not only exerts ultimate control over the subsidiary's actions but also has a stronger personal interest in the welfare of the parent than in the welfare of the subsidiary. This differential interest arises because the managers get incentive compensation based on the financial or stock market performance of the parent. Thus we seem to have a transaction between the two entities (dividends), insiders with decision making influence over the vulnerable entity, and a greater interest on the part of the insiders in the welfare of the other entity. Do not these together make up a conflict-of-interest situation, that is, self-dealing in a comprehensive sense?

Self-interest neither shown nor plausible

One reason why the court may have neglected to pursue this approach is that the plaintiffs did not argue their case in terms of a personal self-interest of the parent company managers, nor did they adduce convincing

[10] Id. at 721.
[11] Id. at 722.

specific evidence of such an interest. Furthermore, any such self-interest may well have been small in this context. Suppose the chief executive of the parent corporation owned 1 percent of its common stock (a large amount, in the case of a sizable public corporation). Whether any given $100 is kept in a 97 percent subsidiary, or $97 of it is moved to the parent while $3 is paid to other shareholders, cannot, *by itself* and directly, change the value of the executive's stock in the parent one little bit. (A 1 percent interest in a 97 percent interest in $100 is the same as a 1 percent interest in $97. Both are indirect claims on 97 cents.) A conflict would only arise, it seems, if both the parent and the subsidiary have good investment opportunities to pursue but neither can get outside financing at a reasonable price. This hardly seems like a plausible occurrence. Or to put the point another way, even if the parent's chief executive generally has a greater personal interest in the welfare of the parent than of the subsidiary, he has little or no personal reason to prefer the particular transaction in question, payment as opposed to nonpayment of dividends.

Contrast other parent-subsidiary dealings

Note well: the same point could not be made about a sale of goods or services, or a loan, between the parent and the subsidiary. In that sort of transaction, treating the subsidiary unfairly will benefit the parent's managers. For example, charging the subsidiary $100 over fair market value for goods sold to it by the parent will lead, in our example, to the chief executive's being richer than if the deal had been fair. (A 1 percent interest in a 97 percent interest in $100 is *not* the same as a 1 percent interest in $100. The first is an indirect claim on 97 cents; the second, an indirect claim on $1. The difference in this example is trivial. But raise the amount of the overcharge of the subsidiary to realistic levels and lower the parent's percentage interest in the subsidiary, and the difference can become very great.) Accordingly, the Delaware Supreme Court could find, consistently with the *Sinclair Oil* case, that the latter situation did involve self-dealing sufficient to shift the burden of proof and trigger the fairness rule.

Shareholders in conflict

Consider now how differences in shareholder preferences can complicate the application of the "bad faith" or "improper purpose" test. Shareholders J. P. and Smith are both shareholders in Dicey Corporation, but they are in different tax brackets and have different liquidity needs. Accordingly, J. P. strongly prefers that Dicey not pay any dividends, whereas Smith strongly prefers that it pay substantial dividends. Must the directors of Dicey seek out, or at least take note of and act on, information about the dividend preferences of their existing shareholders? If the shareholders have different preferences, as in our example, should the directors try to accommodate the preferences of holders of a majority of the shares or should it try to effect a compromise dividend policy? In the context of public corporations, it does not appear that any courts have held that managers must take note of and accommodate the actual dividend policy preferences of the existing shareholders. This seems acceptable, given the continually changing character of the shareholder roster and the freedom of shareholders to switch investments to companies with dividend policies to their liking. The emerging, special interpretation of fiduciary duties in the close corporation context (see chapter 18) may mean, however, that courts would consider shareholder preferences in cases involving close corporations. Doing so could be quite important, given the inability of the dissatisfied close corporation shareholder to sell his shares in an active market.

And one in control

Suppose now that the J. P. of our example was also in *control* of Dicey Corporation, and had caused it to implement the dividend policy of his choice. There is now a potential conflict of interest; J. P. may be causing the corporation to adopt the no-dividend policy to further his own personal interests, even though it decreases the corporation's value overall. Conceivably, his personal tax savings outweigh his personal share of the decline in the company's value, even though this is not true of most other shareholders. Accordingly, it would seem that Smith could challenge the no-dividend policy and attempt to prove that it was the result of bad faith and improper purpose.

But adduces business purpose

But suppose, as is likely, that J. P. can easily show that the earnings retained because of the no-dividend policy are being used for business expansion that seems to make sense. Dicey is building a new factory, for example, that everyone expects to be profitable. Should the court stop the inquiry at this point, and hold for defendant? Or should it go on to examine (if plaintiff Smith is willing and able to produce the requisite evidence) questions designed to address the relative causal weight of the good motive and the bad motive?

Possible judicial scrutiny

If the court did go further, it would face at least three sets of such questions. (1) The first set goes to *how* good the program of expansion is. Granted that the new projects are reasonably expected to be profitable, will they be profitable enough to enhance or at least maintain the corporation's net present value? In financial jargon, is the corporation's cost of capital less than the expected return from the projects financed by the retained earnings?[12] (2) Other questions concern how important financing by means

[12] Strictly speaking, this is the proper comparison only when the new projects have the same risk as the firm's existing operations. On how to handle the risk factor, see R. Brealey & S. Myers, Principles of Corporate Finance 164-187 (2d ed. 1984).

of withheld earnings is. Are there equally good alternative sources of financing? That is, is there a way of achieving the corporate objective of financing desirable expansion that is less injurious to the interests of non-controlling shareholders but equally good or better for the corporation? (3) The court might then examine verbal and personal behavior of controlling parties for evidence of their intent. Was J. P. a dominant influence in getting the board to adopt the no-dividend and expansion policies? Was his primary motive the selfish, tax-related one, rather than a desire to further the corporate good? (In a sense, this question is just a psychologistic version of the first two.)

Judicial practice?

Conceivably, a court could hold that if the answer to any of these questions is yes, the no-dividend policy should be reversed, or the court should exercise its own business judgment and impose a dividend policy on the corporation. Existing judicial authority does not suggest, however, that courts would shift the burden to defendants of producing evidence relevant to these questions, just because plaintiff had alleged and given some evidence of a conflict of interest on the defendant's part. Whether they would even go into these three sets of questions at the insistence of a well-prepared plaintiff is a more difficult question — the answer to which is not, I think, certain.

Example of *Mission Development*

In a complex case that roughly resembles our simplified hypothetical, *Berwald v. Mission Development Co.*,[13] the Delaware court found for defendants after deciding that a no-dividend policy was in fact a means of financing the expansion and modernization of the company's oil refining facilities. The subtler questions of expected return versus cost of capital and of alternative sources of financing were unasked and unanswered. Perhaps surprisingly, the court even finessed the primary-purpose issue, by speaking as if the choice before it were a simple either-or choice: to decide whether the dividend policy in question was "designed to further the selfish interest of Mr. Getty [the controlling person] *and not* to further its own [the controlled corporation's] corporate interests," or whether "the opposite is true."[14] This phrasing obviously avoids the hard question of what to do when, as one would often expect, the controlling party acted both to serve his own interest and to implement a corporate policy that has some business justification but is arguably not the optimal policy.[15]

[13] 185 A.2d 480 (Del. 1962).

[14] Id. at 482 (emphasis added).

[15] The plaintiffs got even shorter shrift in Kamin v. American Express Co., 383 N.Y.S.2d 806 (Sup. Ct. 1976), aff'd on opinion below, 387 N.Y.S.2d 993 (App. Div. 1976). American Express (AE) distributed as a dividend in kind some stock in another corporation (DLJ) that

Recommendation

My view is that, when a plaintiff shows that controlling parties have caused the corporation to adopt a particular dividend policy that is in their own self-interest and also introduces evidence that the resulting policy was suboptimal for the company or unnecessarily injurious to noncontrolling shareholders, the burden of proof should then shift to the defendant controlling parties to show the entire business wisdom of the dividend policy. The reviewing court, if not satisfied with their showing, should then exercise its own judgment as to a proper policy and order such relief, including payment of dividends in specified amounts, as seems appropriate.

§14.3 *Protection of Creditors: The Dividend Statutes*

Warm-up

After the high financial theory of section 14.1 and the tales of struggle between insiders and investors in section 14.2, it may be something of a letdown to consider the so-called dividend rules in the business corporation statutes. But here, too, an active imagination can find an interesting theme: the steady historical corruption of creditor-protecting principles by the mad desire for objectivity and bright lines. One sees in the statutes the increasing power of professional managers, which leads to the closing off of scrutiny of their decision making through the adoption of objective and mechanical, but trivial, rules. On the other hand, the exercise reveals little to get up in arms about. Through their loan agreements, institutional lenders have installed better protective devices than these statutes ever provided, and in appropriate cases creditors may still invoke the judicially developed bodies of creditor-protecting law: the doctrines of fraudulent conveyances, equitable subordination, and piercing the corporate veil. So maybe this section is bound to be less than rousing. But it has its value,

---

had declined greatly in value since AE bought it. Plaintiffs argued that the decision to declare the dividend was imprudent: If AE had sold the DLJ stock it would recognize a capital loss that could be used to offset income from other sources and lower AE's taxes, but the dividend would not result in tax savings by either AE or its shareholders. While not challenging plaintiffs' tax analysis (which appears to have been correct), the court nevertheless dismissed the complaint. Its reason was that the plaintiffs' objection was purely to the merits of a business decision and alleged no fraud, self-dealing, bad faith, or the like.

Interestingly, however, there were two ways in which the case arguably *did* present conflict-of-interest issues. First, if AE had sold the DLJ stock at a loss, it would have had to report smaller net earnings on its income statements. This would have made the officers and directors look bad. (Arguably, when the DLJ stock was distributed as a dividend, the loss on it could be charged against capital surplus instead of earned income.) Second, the same drop in reported net earnings might have adversely affected the incentive compensation owed to the four-out-of-20 inside directors. The court noted this argument but found it "highly speculative" and insufficient to infer self-dealing.

for every corporate lawyer should be generally familiar with these technicalities.

(And if you, reader, are a law student, count your blessings. Reliable senior colleagues tell me that many corporate law professors used to spend a substantial fraction of class time on this subject. Innate optimism leads me to believe that this misfortune will not happen to you.)

Creditor protection and legal capital

Most of the state corporation *statutes* having to do with when dividends are permissible are designed primarily to provide a minimal level of protection to a corporation's creditors, not to insure fairness among shareholders or to regulate the fulfillment of management's duties to shareholders. State statutes vary, but most of them still restrict dividends by reference to the concept of legal capital. This notion will be explored more fully in section 17.1. For now, it should be said that the concept was originally intended to signify the amount of money and other assets contributed to the corporation by its shareholders and committed to use in the corporation's business for the indefinitely long term — that is, the shareholders' "permanent investment." To creditors, the amount also signified the absolute minimum amount that shareholders were pledged not to withdraw from the company while any of its debts were unpaid. Legal capital was even regarded as the quid pro quo for granting limited liability to shareholders. Technically, "legal capital" or "stated capital" refers to the sum of the "par values" of all of the outstanding stock of a corporation, or, if the corporation's stock is "no par," the "stated capital" refers to an amount that the directors decide to attribute to all the outstanding stock.

Example

Thus, the directors of a newly formed corporation might decide to have it issue 100,000 shares of common stock, each share having a par value of $3, to the founding shareholders. Suppose the latter pay $5 per share for their shares. The corporation's opening balance sheet will look like this:

Assets	*Liabilities and Shareholders' Equity*	
Cash $500,000	Debt	$ 0
	Shareholders' equity:	
	Stated capital	300,000
	Capital surplus	200,000
$500,000		$500,000

With the original understanding about the concept of legal capital, a potential lender to the corporation who is looking at this balance sheet will conclude that the founding shareholders were willing to risk $300,000 of their money as a long term investment. He might find the $200,000 capital surplus (that is, the capital contributed in excess of legal capital by the founding shareholders) to be more "iffy" since, as we shall see, the shareholders can take it back more easily than they can take back the legal capital. In an age when (a) accounting principles were not regulated by an independent standard-setting body like the FASB of today, or at least by a committee of a nationwide professional association of accountants, (b) corporate financial statements were not routinely audited by independent accounting firms, as they are today, and (c) there was no SEC and no system of securities regulation that mandated detailed financial disclosures, a potential creditor of a young corporation might have found a use for such conclusions. The amount of a corporation's legal capital is a publicly available figure (one can usually find it on a document required to be filed with a secretary of state), and those who assert what this amount is run a legal risk if they do so falsely. The potential creditor might therefore use the purported amount of legal capital, plus the amount of the corporation's already outstanding debt and a lot of other information, in deciding whether and on what terms to make a loan. This he might do because the amount of a corporation's legal capital bears on its degree of leverage (its ratio of debt to equity capital), which will affect the riskiness of his own loan: A $100,000 loan to a corporation with $300,000 of legal capital is, all other things being equal, less risky than a $100,000 loan to a corporation with legal capital of only $1,000.

Then and now

Whether the concept of legal capital was ever relied on in this way by a substantial number of creditors and, if so, for how long a period of American business history, are elusive historical questions. But it is fairly clear that the original concept was understood in the way described and that it stopped being of much possible utility to creditors many decades ago.[1]

With this introduction as background, let us turn to ten separate topics about the regulation of dividends. They are arranged in a way that shows the ultimate insignificance of this kind of legislation.

§14.3.1 The Earned-Surplus Test

Widely prevailing approach

Before its financial provisions were subject to a sweeping revision and modernization in 1979, the MBCA provided an earned-surplus test of the legality of dividends. A majority of state statutes still do, and still others use another version of the concept of surplus, so it is still useful to under-

§14.3 [1] See generally B. Manning, A Concise Textbook on Legal Capital (1977).

stand the test. Section 45 of the old MBCA prohibited a corporation's board from declaring and paying dividends when their payment would render the corporation insolvent. This insolvency test is an ultimate one found in the statutes of almost all jurisdictions. The section also said, however, that dividends may be declared and paid "only out of the unreserved and unrestricted earned surplus of the corporation," unless otherwise provided in the section.

Example

Suppose that High-Tech Corporation has operated for several years and now has the following simplified balance sheet (000's will be omitted, from now on, in this section):

Assets		*Liabilities and Shareholders' Equity*	
Cash	$ 300	Current liabilities	$ 100
Marketable securities	200	Long-term debt	500
Inventory	100	Shareholders' equity:	
Other assets	600	Stated capital	100
		Capital surplus	200
		Earned surplus	300
	$1,200		$1,200

The earned surplus amount of $300 represents net income that the corporation has earned from its operations but has so far kept rather than distributed. (On a real balance sheet today, the term *retained earnings* would probably be used instead of *earned surplus*.) Unless the directors had placed some restrictions on the earned surplus account, the directors would be free under the old Section 45 to pay $300 in cash to the shareholders as a dividend. After that, the balance sheet would be rewritten as follows:

Assets		*Liabilities and Shareholders' Equity*	
Cash	$ 0	Current liabilities	$100
Marketable securities	200	Long-term debt	500
Inventory	100	Shareholders' equity:	
Other assets	600	Stated capital	100
		Capital surplus	200
		Earned surplus	0
	$900		$900

The directors could not, however, now cause the corporation to pay out a single additional dollar's worth of property to the shareholders as a dividend without violating old Section 45.

§14.3.2 Distributions out of Capital Surplus

Beyond earned surplus

Suppose the directors really want to distribute even more of the corporation's assets to the shareholders, and the latter are insisting on it. Suppose, for example, they want to distribute the $200 worth of marketable securities, which are virtually equivalent to cash, to the shareholders. Is there a way around the earned-surplus test? Yes. The directors may be able to cause the corporation to distribute the securities, although they will have to call it "a distribution out of capital surplus" rather than "a dividend."

Prerequisites

Under old MBCA Section 46, a distribution out of capital surplus is permissible either if the articles of incorporation provide that the corporation may make such a distribution or if the directors obtain a majority vote of shareholders approving the distribution. If there was advance permission in the articles, then arguably the creditors of High-Tech ought to have known about it. If not, the delay and publicity involved in getting a shareholders' vote may lead to most creditors being tipped off about the impending distribution. Oddly enough for a statutory provision that basically makes sense in creditor-protection terms, however, old Section 46 does not expressly require that creditors be given notice of an impending distribution

Example

out of capital surplus. After the distribution, High-Tech's balance sheet will look like this:

Assets		*Liabilities and Shareholders' Equity*	
Cash	$ 0	Current liabilities	$100
Marketable securities	0	Long-term debt	500
		Shareholders' equity:	
Inventory	100	Stated capital	100
Other assets	600	Capital surplus	0
	$700		$700

At this point, creditors of High-Tech who know what is going on will be getting quite nervous.

§14.3.3 Changing Legal Capital to Capital Surplus

Suppose that the directors of High-Tech want to distribute even more of the company's assets to their loyal shareholders without waiting for the company to earn more income. (Perhaps it is Christmas, and they have a Santa Claus complex.) Can they distribute, say, most of the corporation's inventory without violating the old MBCA? Yes, if they follow proper procedures. They would proceed in two steps.

First, they would adopt a resolution changing the corporation's stated capital from $100 to, say, $1 and would submit it to the shareholders for a vote. Under old MBCA Section 69, a majority vote is required. The resolution would be filed with the secretary of state. Once again, the statute does not require notice to creditors. After this procedure, the net worth, or shareholders' equity, portion of High-Tech's balance sheet would look like this:

Changing stated capital

Shareholders' equity:	
Stated capital	$ 1
Capital surplus	99
Earned surplus	0

The rest of the balance sheet would not have been changed. Incidentally, if High-Tech had had par value stock outstanding instead of no-par stock, it could have achieved a similar result by an amendment to the articles of incorporation.[2] The amendment might, for example, change the par value of each share from one dollar to one cent.[3]

Subsequent distribution

Second, the directors would then proceed to give the shareholders $99 worth of inventory as a "distribution out of capital surplus." Here they would follow the procedure described in the previous subsection. If they needed a shareholder vote, they might get it at the same meeting at which the shareholders were to vote on the alteration of the stated capital account. After the distribution, High-Tech's balance sheet would be as follows:

Assets		*Liabilities and Shareholders' Equity*	
Cash	$ 0	Current liabilities	$100
Marketable securities	0	Long-term debt	500
		Shareholders' equity:	
Inventory	1	Stated capital	1
Other assets	600	Capital surplus	0
		Earned surplus	0
	$601		$601

At this point any creditors aware of these events would be in a state of panic. For the company now has $600 of liabilities and only $1 of net assets.

[2] See old MBCA §§58-64.

[3] See, especially, old MBCA §58(e), which explicitly allows charter amendments to decrease or increase the par value of authorized shares, whether issued or unissued.

Yet all distributions were perfectly legal as far as the business corporation statute is concerned.

§14.3.4 Insolvency Test

Example Suppose the directors of High-Tech are still unsatisfied, and they want to distribute $100 worth of "other assets" to the shareholders. May they do so? Finally, the answer seems to be no. The distribution would make the corporation insolvent, and distributions that do that are explicitly forbidden under both old Sections 45 and 46. More specifically, if the distribution were made, High-Tech's balance sheet would be as shown below. (Note that, for simplicity, we now drop items with 0 amounts.)

Assets		*Liabilities and Shareholders' Equity*	
Inventory	$ 1	Current liabilities	$100
Other assets	500	Long-term debt	500
		Shareholders' equity:	
		Stated capital	1
		Surplus (deficit)	(100)
	$501		$501

A company with this balance sheet is insolvent in a balance sheet sense: its assets ($501) on the balance sheet are less than its liabilities ($600). Furthermore, its legal or stated capital is impaired, that is, the total amount of its shareholders' equity (*minus* $99) is less than its legal capital (plus $1). The latter point is worth noting because a few corporation statutes speak in terms of dividends that would "impair capital."

A genuine limit When various procedural maneuvers are taken into account, therefore, the insolvency test appears to be the only real, ultimate limit on management's ability to make distributions to shareholders legally — even when the governing statute seems to impose a tougher, "earned surplus" test. Note that the insolvency test is a common feature of virtually all statutes, and it applies not only to dividends in a technical sense, but also to distributions out of capital surplus and to most redemptions and repurchases of stock.[4]

But our Santa Clausian managers may not have been completely thwarted yet. There are other ways to get into a house than by going down a straight and narrow chimney. Let us look at some of them.

[4] See, e.g., old MBCA §§6, 66.

§14.3.5 The Nimble Dividends Test

Delaware version

Some states, such as Delaware,[5] have a nimble dividends test of legally permissible dividends. Indeed, an alternative version of old MBCA Section 45 was suggested for state legislatures that might want to adopt this approach. Under this alternative test a corporation can pay dividends out of its earned surplus or out of its *net earnings* of the current and previous fiscal years taken as a single period.[6] The alternative test is useful when a company has had a history of earnings deficits, but earnings have become positive for two years, the future looks brighter, and the directors would like the shareholders to participate in the new prosperity before the net deficit in the retained earnings account can be wiped out.

Example

Suppose, for example, that High-Tech had not made the illegal dividend discussed in the previous subsection, but sold some stock for $399 (and increased stated capital to $400) and then proceeded to operate at a loss for ten years so that its balance sheet became

Assets		*Liabilities and Shareholders' Equity*	
Cash	$100	Debt	$700
Other assets	700	Stated capital	400
		Earned surplus (deficit)	(300)
	$800		$800

In the previous fiscal year, the corporation broke even: it had neither positive nor negative earnings. In the current year it has earned $100 of net income from operations. Giving effect to those earnings, its balance sheet should be rewritten:

Assets		*Liabilities and Shareholders' Equity*	
Cash	$200	Debt	$700
Other assets	700	Stated capital	400
		Earned surplus (deficit)	(200)
	$900		$900

[5] Del. §170(a).

[6] Delaware's statute speaks of dividends paid out of the corporation's "surplus" or out of its "net profits for the fiscal year in which the dividend is declared and/or the preceding fiscal year."

The corporation still has a net deficit in earned surplus; it could not pay dividends under the earned surplus test. But if the directors want to pay a dividend of $100, equal to the corporation's net earnings of the last two years, the nimble dividends test would let them do so.

§14.3.6 Dividends out of Revaluation Surplus

Write up assets? Go back to the last High-Tech balance sheet presented in 14.3.3. Note that the corporation's balance sheet shows only $1 of net assets, so that any significant dividend would violate the ultimate, nonwaivable, insolvency test. Is there nevertheless some way that the directors, short of improving operations and causing the corporation to have net income, could justify a dividend? Perhaps. One possibility is to claim that the corporate assets in the "other assets" category are greatly undervalued on the balance sheet and to write them up to their true market value.

Background Remember that for financial reporting purposes accountants typically insist on valuing assets like land and buildings at their historical cost (less depreciation computed according to a mechanical formula, in the case of buildings) rather than at their estimated market value. Moreover, except when a new owner has purchased a business, the balance sheet of a business normally does not record its estimated "goodwill" value, that is, the excess of the business's going-concern value or estimated total market value over the sum of the values of particular assets.

Example Suppose, however, that the directors of a corporation do want to reflect these values on a balance sheet in order to justify a payment of dividends. Suppose, for example, that the High-Tech directors hired appraisers to put an up-to-date value on the corporation's land, buildings, other fixed assets, and to determine the firm's total market value as a going concern, and then adopted the following balance sheet:

Assets		*Liabilities and Shareholders' Equity*	
Cash	$ 1	Current liabilities	$ 100
Other assets	1,000	Long-term debt	500
Goodwill	300	Stated capital	1
		Revaluation surplus	700
	$1,301		$1,301

Could the directors then pay a legal dividend in the form of $700 worth of other assets to the shareholders?

Randall v. Bailey

There is famous authority for doing so in New York. In *Randall v. Bailey*[7] a reorganization trustee of a corporation sued its former directors to recover from them about $3.6 million, the amount of allegedly unlawful dividends that they approved. The applicable New York statute said only that dividends had to come out of surplus; it did not specify earned surplus. At the time when the dividends were declared, the corporate books showed positive surplus amounts, because the corporation had revalued its assets to their estimated fair market value. The Court of Appeals found the dividend consistent with the statute. It held, for the purpose of interpreting the dividend statute, that good will was a recognizable element of value; that the value of assets, not their cost, must be used in determining whether a surplus exists, and value includes unrealized appreciation; that unrealized *depreciation* in the value of assets must also be considered; and that the surplus computed by the directors was adequate to support dividends.

Assessment

It may well be that most courts faced with the same legal issue, and presented with facts indicating that the redetermined values were valid, would reach the same decision.[8] In principle a fair estimate of the market value of the corporation's assets should lead to a surplus computation such that, even if all surplus is paid out as dividends, creditors would still be protected. A "fair value" surplus test of dividends is similar to an insolvency test using live valuations rather than dead historical figures. The danger, of course, is that the "fair values" picked by an ever-optimistic board of directors with Santa Clausian tendencies may be used to justify dividends that deplete the corporation's wealth so much that creditors are left unsatisfied — as were the creditors in *Randall v. Bailey*. This fear of manipulation of subjective estimates must be weighed against distaste for the theoretical irrelevance of objective accounting techniques.

§14.3.7 Increasing Surplus by Accounting Changes

Boosting reported income

To a certain extent a corporation may be able to influence its reported earnings or earned surplus, and therefore its ability to pay legal dividends under many state statutes, by its choice of accounting methods. In an

[7] 23 N.Y.S.2d 173 (Sup. Ct. 1940), aff'd without opinion, 29 N.Y.S.2d 512 (App. Div. 1941), aff'd, 43 N.E.2d 43 (N.Y. 1942).

[8] See generally D. Herwitz, Materials on Accounting for Lawyers 198-228 (1980). The new MBCA, in §6.40(d), would codify a version of Randall v. Bailey by allowing the directors' determination as to whether the statute's dividend tests are met to be based "on a fair valuation or other method that is reasonable in the circumstances."

inflationary time, a company that switches from the last in-first out (LIFO) to the first in-first out (FIFO) method of valuing inventory may boost its reported net income.[9] So might a company that switches to a slower depreciation schedule for its fixed assets. It should be noted, however, that increases of this sort in reported net income are likely to be modest and of a one-shot rather than continuing nature, and that companies that must have, or want to have, certified financial statements will be restricted to using generally accepted accounting principles and will therefore have only limited room for such maneuvering.

Example of debt extinguishment

Some increases in reported earned surplus, although they do not stem from a change in sales or in other aspects of underlying business operations, do involve financial as well as accounting changes. Let us consider the extinguishment of debt as an example. Suppose that a few years ago High-Tech Corporation issued $500,000 in face amount of 20-year bonds paying interest at the rate of 10 percent. The corporation's balance sheet (000's *not* omitted here) is now as follows:

Assets		*Liabilities and Shareholders' Equity*	
Cash	$100,000	Current liabilities	$100,000
Inventory	100,000	Long-term debt	500,000
Other assets	500,000	Stated capital	100,000
		Earned surplus	0
	$700,000		$700,000

[9]For income tax purposes, where the game is to reduce nominal net (taxable) income, a corporation may want to make exactly the opposite switch.

FIFO and LIFO have to do with estimating the costs of goods sold. Suppose Ace Department Store bought 50 class A widgets over the past year, in the following pattern: 10 for $78, 20 for $84, 8 for $86, and 12 for $95. Previously, it had never bought a class A widget. It now, finally, sells 6 class A widgets to customers for $200 apiece. How does it calculate its profits from these sales? By subtracting the actual price paid for each individual widget it sold (plus other expenses) from the sales price? Exact tracing of this sort would entail cumbersome and expensive record keeping when there are many items in Ace's inventory, so shortcuts are used.

Under the FIFO method, Ace assumes it sold the first six widgets that it purchased. Its profit per sale (forgetting other costs) is $200 − 78, or $122. The total cost of its remaining class A widget inventory for balance sheet purposes is:

$$[(4 \times \$78) + (20 \times \$84) + (8 \times \$86) + (12 \times \$95)], \text{ or } \$3820.$$

Under the LIFO method, Ace assumes it sold the last six widgets it bought. Its profit per sale (forgetting other costs) is $200 − 95, or $105. Notice that this is a smaller amount than profit reported under the FIFO method. The total cost of its remaining class A widget inventory for balance sheet purposes is:

$$[(10 \times \$78) + (20 \times \$84) + (8 \times \$86) + (6 \times \$95)], \text{ or } \$3718.$$

In a jurisdiction with the earned surplus test, High-Tech cannot now pay dividends.

Depressed debt retired

Because of changes in general interest rate levels, however, bonds of the same rating or risk class as those of High-Tech can be issued and sold to investors only if the bonds pay 15 percent interest. Accordingly, the market value of already outstanding, low interest-bearing bonds has dropped. Each $1,000 amount of High-Tech bond has a market value of only $666.67.[10] The total market value of all the High-Tech bonds is therefore $333,335. Suppose that the directors, because they wish to continue paying dividends, cause the corporation to sell $333,335 of other assets at cost and use the proceeds to buy back all of the bonds, which are then cancelled. The corporation's long-term debt account has gone from $500,000 to 0, even though its assets have decreased by only $333,335. Suppose its accountants let the corporation recognize all of this gain currently in income,[11] and though the gain is treated as extraordinary[12] rather than recurring, it increases earned surplus. High-Tech's new balance sheet will therefore be

Assets		*Liabilities and Shareholders' Equity*	
Cash	$100,000	Current liabilities	$100,000
Inventory	100,000	Long-term debt	0
Other assets	166,665	Stated capital	100,000
		Earned surplus	166,665
	$366,665		$366,665

Followed by dividend

Could the directors now, consistent with a dividend statute that imposes an earned-surplus test, pay out the corporation's $100,000 of cash as a dividend to the shareholders? Apparently it could, since there is an adequate earned surplus computed according to accepted accounting principles. Even after the dividend, the balance sheet would show an earned surplus of $66,665.

Possible waste if refinancing ensues

Though not violating the dividend statute, the directors may have violated their duty of care. This may happen because they caused the corpora-

[10] One $1,000 face amount High-Tech bond pays $100 of interest per year. A bond with a face amount of $666.67 and a 15 percent interest rate will also pay $100 of interest per year. Since the market rate is currently 15 percent, no one should pay more than $666.67 for a High-Tech bond.

[11] Could the accountants properly do this? See AICPA, Accounting Principles Board Opinion No. 26 (1972) (yes).

[12] See AICPA, Accounting Principles Board Opinion No. 30 (1973); FASB No. 4 (1975).

tion to give up a financing arrangement that was, in terms of current interest rate levels, a bargain for the corporation. This may affect shareholders and the short-term creditors adversely if the corporation wasn't ready to retire its long-term debt. Suppose, for example, that in order to maintain the company's business operations, the directors must now replace the company's just distributed $100,000 of cash and its recently sold $333,335 of other assets, and they do so by having the corporation issue new 20-year bonds paying interest at 15 percent. The new balance sheet is as follows:

Assets		*Liabilities and Shareholders' Equity*	
Cash	$100,000	Current liabilities	$100,000
Inventory	100,000	Long-term debt	433,335
Other		Stated capital	100,000
assets	500,000	Earned surplus	66,665
	$700,000		$700,000

In terms of balance sheet comparisons, this may suggest that, despite the corporation's recent large dividend payment, the refinancing operations have caused the corporation to be in a stronger financial position: it has gone from $100,000 to $166,667 of reported net worth.

Impaired earnings/interest coverage

From a rational creditor's perspective, however, this change is an illusion. Such a creditor will be more interested in the capacity of the corporation's earnings stream to cover its debt payments. Previously, the corporation had to make payments on long-term debt of $50,000 a year; now, its interest burden on such debt is about $65,000 a year. (That is, $433,335 times 15 percent). If the underlying business operations are unchanged — the expected sales revenues, the expenditures for labor and materials, and so forth, are not affected by all the financial restructuring — the risk that the corporation will become unable to pay its debts is clearly *greater* than before.[13] When all is said and done, a mere replacement of old for new debt at current market rates does not, in and of itself, increase corporate wealth.[14]

[13]Indeed, rational lenders would have foreseen this and probably would have demanded that the company pay an interest rate on the new long-term bonds of greater than 15 percent, to compensate for the extra risk. Unfortunately, the short-term creditors will not be so compensated.

[14]Of course, if the old debt was a bad deal — the interest rate was higher than it should have been, for example — or the new debt is an especially good deal, refinancing may have positive benefits. There may be other positive reasons for refinancing in particular cases.

In fact, the replacement decreases corporate wealth by the amount of the transaction costs. These costs include the hefty fees paid to investment bankers, lawyers, and printers; to the extent of these costs the shareholders will be injured. Furthermore, a large dividend made legally possible by such refinancing raises the risk level faced by preexisting creditors, such as the short-term creditors. So perhaps the policy, if not the literal terms, of the dividend statute has been offended. Indeed, a court that saw the debt extinguishment, the dividend, and the reissuance of new debt as part of a single plan might conclude that these events, taken together, did constitute a violation of the dividend statute.

Transaction costs

§14.3.8 Financial Ratios as Tests

Some states, influenced by the perception that traditional dividend tests are so porous as to be practically meaningless, have revised their statutes to provide rules that mimic those that well-informed lenders would impose on corporate borrowers by contract. In bank loan agreements, for example, the borrowing corporation often promises not to pay dividends unless its financial statements meet certain ratio tests. The California dividend statute adopts a similar approach, but since its aim is only to provide a minimal level of creditor protection, the ratios are not as severe as those found in some loan agreements. With various refinements and provisos, Section 500 of the California statute allows dividends out of retained earnings or when, after the dividend, (1) the corporation's total assets will be at least 1¼ times as great as its total liabilities and (2) its current assets will at least equal its current liabilities.[15] Note that this test does not depend on the concept of legal capital. It is harder to evade than the nimble dividends test or the system of concepts embodied in the old MCBA.

California statute

§14.3.9 The New MBCA

As indicated earlier, the MBCA provisions on dividends and related matters were revised in 1979.[16] The new MBCA has rejected the concept of

Two insolvency tests

[15] Some corporations have to meet a "1¼" ratio even for current assets and liabilities. These are corporations whose average earnings before interest expense and taxes for the two preceding fiscal years were less than their average interest expense for those years.

[16] See Changes in the Model Business Corporation Act — Amendments to the Financial Provisions, 34 Bus. Law. 1867 (1979); Goldstein & Hamilton, The Revised Model Business Corporation Act, 38 Bus. Law. 1019 (1983); Kummert, State Statutory Restrictions on Financial Distributions by Corporations to Shareholders, Pt. II, 59 Wash. L. Rev. 185 (1984). See also Current Issues on the Legality of Dividends from a Law and Accounting Perspective: A Task Force Report, 39 Bus. Law. 289 (1983).

legal capital. In what is now Section 6.40, its approach is to impose insolvency tests on *all* kinds of distributions. In order to make a distribution, the corporation must be solvent after the distribution in both a balance sheet sense and an "equity" sense. The corporation is insolvent in the equity sense when it is unable to meet its debts as they become due in the usual course of business. This test focuses more on ability to meet current liabilities, and it is more flexible than a balance sheet test. In theory, the equity-sense insolvency test could be applied by courts in a way that would give creditors more real protection against excessive dividends than the earned surplus test does. But, while usually applauding the new MBCA's abandonment of the concept of legal capital, critics have objected to its failure to demand any "cushion" or margin of safety for creditors (as the California statute, which also abandoned legal capital, does).

In the first five years after the new MBCA approach was put forward, only a handful of states adopted provisions based on it.[17]

§14.3.10 Fraudulent Conveyance Law

An alternative approach?

As indicated in section 2.5, there are substantial arguments that the rules of the Uniform Fraudulent Conveyance Act or of other expressions of fraudulent conveyance law apply to a corporation's dividends and other distributions. If so, they provide an additional level of minimum protection to creditors, which in some cases will be much more meaningful. Thus, for example, a corporation that can pay a dividend, so far as the business corporation statute is concerned, because it has earned surplus equal to the amount of the proposed dividend, but that has a woefully small amount of legal capital (or more generally, net worth) in relation to its size and liabilities, may be precluded from doing so because of Section 5 of the UFCA. That section prohibits transfers of property without fair consideration that leave a transferor that is a business with "unreasonably small capital."

It has been argued that the possibility of an argument under Section 5 is of little or no practical significance.[18] The drafters of the revised MBCA apparently thought otherwise, for they proposed an optional section the intent of which was to allow a state to "override" its fraudulent convey-

[17] Haw. Rev. Stat. §416-491 (effective July 1, 1986); Ill. Ann. Stat. ch. 32, §9.10 (Smith-Hurd 1984 Pamphlet); Minn. Stat. Ann. §320A.551 (West 1985 Special Pamphlet); Mont. Code Ann. §35-1-711 (1983); N.M. Stat. Ann. §53-11-44 (1983 Replacement Pamphlet).

[18] Kummert, note 16 supra, at 281.

ance doctrine in favor of its dividend statute when both legal rules could be applied.[19]

§14.4 *Repurchases: Theory and Practice*

Terminology

In this section we shall examine the business rationale of redemptions and repurchases of shares. But before looking at the why's of these transactions, let us clarify some terminology. Corporate lawyers and business corporation statutes often distinguish between "redemptions" and "repurchases" of shares. Both terms refer to a corporation's buying back shares in itself. In a redemption the corporation buys pursuant to a previously arranged contract. For example, the provisions in the corporation's articles of organization that define the attributes of a particular class of preferred stock may specify that any time after five years from the date of issuance of the preferred stock the corporation will have the right to buy it at a price equal to 110 percent of the stock's par value. A purchase pursuant to this right would be called a redemption, and the shares themselves would be called redeemable preferred shares. (Some lawyers would use the term *callable* rather than *redeemable* to describe such stock.) Similarly, the contract might give the shareholder the right to sell the preferred stock back to the corporation under certain specified conditions. By contrast, *repurchase* connotes a purchase not done pursuant to a charter provision defining the rights and obligations of the kind of stock in question. For example, a public corporation may buy some of its own shares of common stock through a brokerage firm, paying a price near the going market price to any stockholder who wants to sell to it. Or the directors of a close corporation may agree with a shareholder who is retiring from active participation in the business that the corporation will purchase her shares at a certain price.

The difference between a redemption and a repurchase has certain technical consequences for the corporation's legal-accounting treatment of the transaction. (See section 14.6 below.) Corporate tax lawyers and subchapter C of the Internal Revenue Code do not make the distinction, however. They often use the term *redemption* to refer to either type of buyback of a company's shares.

Why redeemable preferred

Why do corporations engage in redemptions and repurchases? Redeemable preferred shares are fairly easy to understand. Preferred shares usu-

[19] Changes, note 16 supra, at 1889. Of the five states cited in note 17, only two (Minnesota and New Mexico) adopted the optional provision.

ally pay a fixed dividend that represents a claim on corporate earnings that is prior to the rights of common shareholders. From the common shareholder's perspective, the preferred stock is like a form of long-term debt; the major difference is that the preferred dividend rights are not absolute, as the rights to contractually-specified interest payments on bonds are. Management almost inevitably identifies with the common shareholders more than with the preferred shareholders, both because their basic obligation is seen to be to maximize the wealth of the corporation's "residual" claimants and because they themselves are often holders of common stock in the corporation (or of options on such stock, or of incentive compensation rights whose value depends on the value of the common, and so forth). Accordingly, for reasons similar to those that lead managers to want to retire long-term debt when the corporation is able to do so, the managers will want the corporation to be able to redeem preferred shares. There is also a major additional reason: dividend payments on preferred stock, unlike interest payments on debt, cannot be deducted in computing the corporation's taxable income.[1]

Why repurchases of common?

Why a corporation should want to repurchase its common shares is a more difficult problem. Perhaps surprisingly, it may be that *public* corporations rarely have a good reason for repurchasing their shares. In any event, it is instructive to look at the usual explanations with a critical eye.

§14.4 [1]This point raises the question: Why do firms issue preferred stock in the first place? Often, it comes about at the conjunction of special preferences of investors and issuing corporations.

Unlike individual investors, investors that are corporations often prefer interest income or dividend income to capital gain income, since the latter is taxed more heavily to them. As between the same amount and quality of interest income and dividend income, they may be indifferent. But if a kind of stock offers a greater yield (albeit with a higher risk), the corporate investor may prefer to invest in it. (Whether this is so will depend on what else is in the investor's portfolio and how much risk it wants the whole portfolio to have.) It might often satisfy such a preference simply by investing in high payout common stocks. In the case of some corporate investors, such as insurance companies, however, regulation of their permissible investments restricts this possibility and steers them toward preferred stock.

On the issuing side, companies often want to issue additional securities paying holders of them at a fixed rate. Usually they prefer to do this by issuing debt securities, so that they can deduct the interest payments from otherwise taxable income. But some issuers of fixed-rate securities, such as regulated public utilities, may be fairly indifferent to the extra tax costs of issuing high payout stock because they know the regulated rates they charge customers will be set to cover their costs.

So we find public utility companies issuing preferred stock to investors who are often insurance companies. This explanation, as well as other convincing explanations of preferred stock issues, may strike you as very particular and special. Note, however, that the total amount of outstanding preferred stock in the economy is very small in relation to the amount of outstanding common stock and debt securities, so special explanations may be all that are needed.

Dividend-type functions. One category of alleged reasons is that a repurchase may fulfill the functions that are usually performed by dividends. For example, a corporation having no investment projects with an expected return greater than its cost of capital might wish to distribute its excess funds to shareholders, as might a company that wished to satisfy shareholder preferences for actual cash distributions.

Distribute excess funds

The problem is that this explanation, by itself, is inadequate. Since a corporation can pay dividends under the same circumstances, why isn't the power to pay dividends enough for fulfillment of these dividend-type functions? One possible response is that a corporation's offer to repurchase its shares allows those shareholders who prefer a cash flow from the corporation to sell some of their shares, while allowing shareholders who prefer a low payout investment to stand pat: therefore, shareholder preferences will be better satisfied. But this argument neglects the fact that it is quite unnecessary for any particular corporation to try to be all things to all types of shareholders. Investors who want high yielding stocks can and do invest in companies with high dividend payout ratios, and investors who want low yielding stocks do the opposite.

Dividends would do same?

Nevertheless, you may ask, why worry about it? If, for whatever reasons, a corporation wants to make distributions to shareholders and can do so via dividends or repurchases, why worry if it arbitrarily chooses the latter? Is there some reason for lawmakers to worry about repurchases more than dividends?

Yes, there is. Repurchases have a greater potential for creating unequal treatment of shareholders of the same class. If a repurchase is made for more than the shares' fair market value, for example, the deal will hurt the remaining shareholders. If it is made at less than the stock's true value, it will hurt the selling shareholders and confer a windfall on the remaining shareholders. When dividends are paid on a class of common stock, however, every shareholder receives the same amount per share. The occasions on which the dividend policy of public corporations may pose serious questions of unfair treatment of shareholders are therefore limited. (See section 14.2.)

Repurchases more dangerous

Legal-capital adjustments. A second category of alleged reasons for repurchases are technical reasons relating to the corporation's capital structure. Although these seem to justify even pro rata repurchases as against dividends, they generally turn out to be of dubious validity. For example, it could be claimed that by repurchasing a large number of the company's shares and cancelling them the corporation could decrease its stated capital. Under most state statutes, however, the directors can reduce stated

Sleight of hand

capital by following a voting procedure. Again, it is not clear why a repurchase is needed.

Non-pro rata repurchases by public corporation. A third class of reasons relates to non-pro rata repurchases by public corporations. Let us consider a number of these.

Shareholder tax savings

(1) By repurchasing stock rather than paying dividends, the corporation's distributions of cash to shareholders may generate capital gain rather than ordinary income to the shareholders and thus reduce their taxes. This is a common, plausible, and often valid explanation of a share repurchase plan. There are pitfalls to the technique, however. If the corporation simply bought a pro rata portion of each shareholder's shares, the Internal Revenue Service would treat the redemptions as equivalent to dividends and tax them accordingly.[2] Even with non-pro rata repurchases — such as those resulting from the company's publicized tender offer for a certain number of its own shares — the shareholders run a risk of being treated as having received dividends if their corporation makes it a regular practice to repurchase shares.[3] The prime candidate for recharacterization would be the corporation that baldly decided to stop paying dividends altogether and switched to quarterly repurchase offers involving similar amounts of money. The Service, however, might well recharacterize "repurchases" as dividends in situations that were much less clear-cut. Therefore, in the public corporation context the occasions for tax-motivated repurchases are real but limited.

"Correcting" market value theory

(2) A common explanation by managers of their causing their corporation to repurchase shares on the market is, "The market has persisted in undervaluing our shares and the repurchase program will, we expect, help bring the stock's market price up to its true value." On one level this explanation seems readily understandable and credible. All of us can sympathize with the manager who thinks the brilliance and wisdom of his strategy for his company is simply not perceived by those thickheaded, uninspired stock market analysts. ("No imagination. No long term view. All they care about is short-run profits." Etc.)

A suspect argument

On closer examination, though, the manager's reasoning appears highly suspect. If we credit the efficient-markets theory — and there is now substantial evidence in support of that theory[4] — we will find it difficult to

[2]See I.R.C. §302(a), 302(b)(1); §301(a), 301(c).

[3]See I.R.C. §305(c), Treas. Reg. §1,305-3(e), example (9) (concerning effect on shareholders who don't sell); but see I.R.C. §302(b)(2), 302(b)(3).

[4]See, e.g., Fama, Efficient Capital Markets: A Review of Theory and Empirical Work, 25 J. Fin. 383 (1970); J. Lorie & M. Hamilton, The Stock Market: Theories and Evidence (1973); R.

believe that the market systematically and persistently undervalues public corporations. At any rate, even if the efficient market occasionally goofs, the number of goofs is unlikely to be as high as the number of actual repurchase programs.

Better correctives

A second difficulty with the manager's "correction of undervaluation" theory is that the socially preferred way to correct misvaluation is to supply better information. If the managers of a company think the market misunderstands them, shouldn't they simply work harder at communicating those facts, plans, opinions, judgments, and the like that lead them to place a high value on their corporation? Under what causal theory will having the company buy back shares, as opposed to having the company give out better information and explanations, lead more certainly to a valid "correction" of market values? Basically, the corporation's repurchase of shares will affect market price in one of two ways. Market participants may read the repurchase program as a signal that management knows information that leads it to predict a brighter future for the company. But why shouldn't management simply convey such information and predictions directly? Or if the market trusts nonverbal signals more, why shouldn't they simply raise their regular dividends? Alternatively, the repurchase may lead to a rise in market price because it creates an appearance of active trading based on favorable nonpublic information that in reality does not exist. But if this is what the repurchase program amounts to, it constitutes manipulation, which is a crime under the federal securities laws[5] and performs no economically useful function.

"Good investment" theory

A variation on the undervaluation argument is, not that the repurchase will help correct the market's valuation, but that the repurchase will take advantage of it for the benefit of the shareholders. As a manager might express it, "We feel the stock is undervalued in the market and that, therefore, it represents an exceptional investment opportunity. So we are really 'investing' corporate funds by buying back the stock."

Nonsensical and suspect

But "the repurchase is an investment" is a form of doubletalk. After the repurchase, the funds used for it will no longer be in the corporation or invested in its real business operations. Even if the repurchased shares are not cancelled but are kept as "treasury stock," they still will not constitute a true investment, for there are only minor technical differences between treasury stock and authorized but unissued shares. What the repurchase

---

Brealey, An Introduction to Risk and Return from Common Stocks ch. 2 (1983). Admittedly, more recent work has focused on facts that are hard to square with the theory. See, e.g., Symposium, Valuation Anomalies — Empirical, 39 J. Fin. 807 (1984).

[5] E.g., Securities Exchange Act §§9(a)(2), 10(b); Rule 10b-5.

really does, if the managers are right about the market's undervaluation, is shift wealth from the shareholders who sell to those who don't. Perhaps managers see this as a division between investors who lack faith in them and those who have it and consequently think the repurchase is a fine method of punishing the doubters and rewarding the faithful. But it hardly seems appropriate for management to be doing this. Shareholders who have more faith in the company's future are perfectly able to buy additional shares from those valuing it less highly, without management's help. Indeed, by raising the demand for the corporation's shares, the repurchase offer will induce some shareholders to sell who otherwise would have stood pat and, under the managers' own theory of undervaluation, would have participated in the company's bright but unappreciated future. Such shareholders are affirmatively injured by the repurchase offer.

Buying off the insurgent

(3) A corporation's board of directors might cause the company to buy the shares of a shareholder who is trying to take control, as by leading a proxy fight or buying up as many shares as he can, with the understanding that the shareholder will then give up trying to get control. Clearly this can be a real reason for a share repurchase, but it is extremely doubtful whether such repurchases are often, or ever, in the best interests of the shareholders.[6] One obvious problem is that the incumbent managers may simply be trying to save their jobs and status with the corporation's money. For his part, the insurgent is unlikely to agree to go away unless paid a price for his shares that is substantially higher than that which the other shareholders can get in the market.

Going private

(4) Sometimes a share repurchase offer is the first step in a "going private" set of transactions engineered by the corporate insiders. As we saw in chapter 12, there are arguments for severely restricting attempts to go private, as well as arguments for thinking that such transactions may often be good.

Other reasons

Various other reasons occasionally motivate non-pro rata repurchases of stock in public corporations. The discussion above was not intended to list all possible reasons, but to illustrate the kind of critical scrutiny that ought to be applied to many of the major reasons put forward for repurchases.

Substitute for trading market

Repurchases in close corporations. There is, finally, a fourth category of reasons for share repurchases. These relate to non-pro rata repurchases of stock in closely held corporations. In contrast to the situation with public corporations, these reasons are often positively good ones, at least in prin-

[6]Recall our discussion of takeover defenses in section 13.6 supra.

ciple. A repurchase can provide a substitute for an active stock market, which the close corporation shareholder lacks. For example, when one shareholder in a three-person corporation wishes to liquidate her investment because she is retiring, a sale to the corporation may be the only, or at least the best, alternative. Repurchases may also be means of resolving deadlocks, which are not uncommon in close corporations. Of course, both the retiring shareholder and the deadlocked one might have sold their shares to the other shareholders, but in many situations the latter may lack the means to do so, or to do so in an expeditious way.

§14.5 *Repurchases and Shareholder Protection*

Directors and other controlling parties who cause their corporations to repurchase shares are of course bound by the general fiduciary duties of care and loyalty. In some types of situations, the courts have made these duties somewhat more specific.

Buying off raider: *Cheff v. Mathes*

Consider first the example of a corporate repurchase that is made in order to buy off an insurgent who was trying to take control. Essentially, this situation was presented in the notable Delaware case of *Cheff v. Mathes,*[1] which was mentioned in section 13.6.2 but merits separate examination here. In that case, defendants caused the corporation to buy the insurgent's shares at a premium above the then-current market price of the corporation's shares. Understandably, plaintiffs thought that this diluted the value of the other shares, such as their own, and that it constituted a wasteful use of corporate assets. In addition, it was clear that defendants had a substantial conflict of interest — one falling squarely under my fourth paradigm — because their own jobs and positions of power would undoubtedly have been lost if the insurgent had succeeded in taking control. In this context the Delaware Supreme Court held that the defendants had the burden of proof to show that the primary purpose of the repurchase was to further their honest conception of good business policy for the corporation rather than to retain control. In the case before it, it found that defendants had met their burden. (This aspect of the case provoked bitter criticism and seemed by hindsight to have been a mistake, inasmuch as the vaunted "business policies" that the chief defendant was allegedly trying to preserve by the repurchase later turned out to constitute viola-

§14.5 [1] 199 A.2d 548 (Del. 1964).

tions of the Federal Trade Commission Act and landed that defendant in jail.[2])

Primary purpose test is troublesome

As for the primary purpose test itself, it inevitably appears unsatisfactory on reflection (though devising a better test is no easy task). How on earth can a judge tell what the true motive or purpose of incumbent management is in a situation like *Cheff?* Isn't it obvious that defendants can almost always produce some seemingly plausible rationalizations of their actions? In *Cheff,* for example, a basic defense was that the insurgent (Maremount) intended to change the corporation's system of selling furnaces — from door-to-door selling to selling through retail outlets — and the incumbents asserted it to be their best business judgment that such a change would be disastrous for the company, and that this perception of impending doom to the company — not, of course, a base fear of losing their own jobs — was what was leading them to resist the shift in control. Is a court well-equipped to decide whether such a claim is genuine and serious? Defendants also argued that Maremount was known to have a reputation for buying companies and then liquidating them, and that this gave them further reason to fear for the company's welfare. The court was impressed by this argument, perhaps because it lacked sophistication about business decision making. Consider this: why would anyone buy all of a company and then liquidate it? Answer (in most cases): because he honestly believed that the company's liquidation value was greater than its going concern value. And clearly, from the point of view of maximizing shareholder wealth, a company of which this is true ought to be liquidated: liquidating it is positively good, and keeping it alive is positively bad. Moreover, situations can readily occur when incumbent managements ought to liquidate their companies but out of their own self-interest fail to do so. For example, this may happen because the managers' jobs with the company are more important to them than their shareholdings in it.

Another objection

Another objection to the primary purpose test is that it fails to take into account the existence of less dangerous or less restrictive alternative methods of accomplishing the alleged business policy that the incumbents say they want to pursue. In *Cheff,* for example, the defendants could simply have conducted a proxy fight against Maremount: they could have revealed to the shareholders all the data and reasoning that led them to the judgment that the company's shares would eventually have a higher value

[2]See Cheff v. Schnackenberg, U.S. Circuit Judge, 384 U.S. 373 (1966). For a graphic description of the company's sales practices, see In the Matter of Holland Furnace Co., 55 FTC 55 (1958), order aff'd, 269 F.2d 203 (7th Cir. 1959) and 295 F.2d 302 (7th Cir. 1961), cert. denied, 361 U.S. 932 (1960).

under their continued control than the price Maremount was paying for shares, and the shareholders could then decide for themselves whether to give a proxy to Maremount or sell to him. Or the defendants could simply have let the control shift take place, and if the imagined mismanagement and self-dealing of Maremount actually did occur, it might have been subject to the usual sorts of remedial actions: an SEC suit, an FTC suit, a criminal prosecution, a stockholder's derivative suit, and so forth. It is not as if Maremount could do anything he wanted with impunity after taking control. It seems reasonably clear that either alternative would have posed much less risk of a substantial waste of corporate assets and of unfair treatment of shareholders.[3]

An alternative

Accordingly, one alternative approach would be for courts to lay down a "no repurchase" rule whenever the repurchase was designed to thwart a shift in control. In other words, repurchase would be a forbidden defensive maneuver.

Remember in this connection that there are substantial arguments in favor of rules restricting all active kinds of defensive maneuvers in attempted takeover situations (see section 13.6.3).

Example invoking first paradigm

Note that it is unfeasible to have one specific formulation of the fiduciary duty of loyalty that could apply to all share repurchase transactions. This is because different repurchases may invoke different conflict-of-interest patterns. We have been analyzing a type-IV or mixed-motive conflict. Now consider one that falls into the type-I or basic self-dealing category. Bigg, a dominant corporate insider, prevails on his fellow directors to cause the corporation to repurchase his shares at an excessive price. Or suppose that the corporate insiders, who are also major shareholders, cause the corporation to repurchase a minority shareholder's shares at an unfairly low price; the minority shareholder sells because favorable inside information has been withheld from him. In the first case the repurchase could be governed by the rules applicable to basic self-dealing and in the second by Rule 10b-5.

Conflict among classes

Repurchases and redemptions may raise issues of fairness, not only as between insiders or controlling shareholders and public or minority shareholders, but as between different classes of shareholders. If the exercise of redemption rights by the corporation would help one class of shareholders at the expense of another and nonexercise would do the opposite, how should the directors proceed? If they themselves have a substantial interest in one of the two classes of stock, should that fact make a difference? For

[3] Compare Comment, Buying Out Insurgent Shareholders with Corporate Funds, 70 Yale L.J. 308 (1960).

example, should the rule be that in such a situation they should, in the strictest fiduciary fashion, make the choice that favors the other class of stock?

Zahn v. Transamerica facts

A case that seems to raise these issues is *Zahn v. Transamerica Corp.*[4] The facts are complex, but they need to be grasped in order to understand the issues in the case. A corporation held a vast inventory of tobacco that had appreciated greatly in value, although that fact was not known by investors. It had issued two classes of so-called common stock, class A and class B. The controlling shareholder, a corporation, held mostly class B stock. The two classes of stock differed along five main dimensions. (1) Dividends: The class A was entitled to cumulative annual dividends of $3.20 per share. The class B was entitled to annual dividends of $1.60 per share, payable only after the specified dividend on the A stock was paid. If dividends exceeding these specified amounts were paid in a given year, every share of class A and class B would share equally in them. (2) Redemptions: Class A stock was callable; that is, the company could, after giving 60 days' notice, buy it back at a price per share of $60 plus accrued dividends. The class B stock was not redeemable, however. (3) Liquidation: Should the company dissolve and liquidate, each share of class A was to receive $2 for every $1 received by a share of class B. (4) Conversion: A holder of class A shares could convert them into class B shares on a one-for-one basis. (5) Voting: In ordinary times, class A stock did not have voting power to elect directors, but if the company failed to pay the specified dividends for four quarters, the class A would have voting power, on a one-share, one-vote basis. The class B always had voting power on a one-share, one-vote basis.

Challenged action and alternatives

With this background, the controlling corporate shareholder caused the company to redeem the class A and to distribute only then the valuable tobacco inventory to the remaining shareholders as a liquidating distribution.[5] The effect of this course of action, as compared to others that might have been taken, was bad for the class A stockholders. Management of the company had essentially three options. First, they could — as they did — simply redeem the class A stock, without revealing the extent of the appreciation in the value of the inventory or their plans to liquidate the company. Under this course of action, each share of A stock received $60 plus accrued dividends (say, $80 per share). Second, they could have disclosed the corporation's true value and the liquidation plan and could then have given notice of intent to redeem the class A stock. In this scenario, all

[4] 162 F.2d 36 (3d Cir. 1947).

[5] No, the company did not deliver truckloads of tobacco to the shareholders' doorsteps. It distributed warehouse receipts for the tobacco (plus some cash).

rational class A stockholders would presumably have converted their A shares into B shares before the 60-days' waiting period was up, so that no shares would in fact be redeemed. In the ensuing liquidation, each new share of class B (derived from the conversions) would share equally with each old B share and would receive, say, $120 per share. Third, whether or not they made disclosures as just indicated, the managers could have declined to issue a notice of redemption and simply gone ahead with the liquidation. In this scenario, no rational class A shareholder would convert his shares, but would hold them and therefore receive in the liquidation twice as much as the holder of an equal number of B shares — say, $240 per share.

Courts' responses

The federal court in *Zahn* seemed to hold that the managers had a fiduciary duty to choose the third course of action and violated their duty by causing a redemption, which would needlessly harm the class of stock in which they were not interested.[6] But in a later decision involving the same case, *Speed v. Transamerica Corporation*,[7] the court characterized the defendants' violation as being a failure to disclose the hidden value and the liquidation plan — that is, a failure to pursue the second option above. Clearly, the nondisclosure was a violation of the "disclose or abstain" interpretation of Rule 10b-5.[8] The real question of interest was whether the defendants had a fiduciary duty not to exercise the corporation's redemption rights. In essence, the *Speed* court answered no.

***Speed* court's was better**

Was it right? Under the circumstances, yes. An examination of how the class A stock differed along the five main dimensions from the class B stock, together with some basic familiarity with corporate financing practices, shows that the class A stock, despite its name, was really a kind of preferred stock.[9] Part of the contract creating this stock granted the corporation an option to buy the stock back at a fixed price, should it see fit. The purpose of such a contract is to allocate risk between more and less conservative investors: the class A had various preferences over the class B, and thus was a safer stock to be holding if the company's affairs turned out badly. By contrast, the class B was designed to take second place in many ways but to be able to garner the lion's share of the profits if the company

[6] See 162 F.2d at 46.

[7] 235 F.2d 369 (3d Cir. 1956).

[8] See section 8.10 supra. The "connection with a purchase or sale" requirement is met because the shareholders subject to redemption were selling to the corporation. Nor were they completely "forced" sellers (a status that might negate a finding of causation of injury by nondisclosure) in the relevant sense, for they had the power to convert instead of submitting to redemption, and full disclosure would have affected their choice.

[9] See Taylor v. Axton-Fisher Tobacco Co., 113 S.W.2d 377 (Ky. 1943).

did exceptionally well — and it seems clear that one purpose of the company's redemption rights against class A was precisely to enable class B to do so. Compare: when you give an option on your IBM stock to someone in return for a price you agreed to and he later tries to exercise the option, it is unfair to complain that he is doing so when the stock has risen greatly in price. That's just what he bargained for and what you gambled would not happen.

Primary duty to residual owners

To put the matter a different way, management's primary duty is to the residual owners, alias common shareholders in most contexts, and in the *Transamerica* case that turned out, on analysis, to mean the class B shareholders. Toward bondholders and preferred stockholders the managers must act, as they must toward suppliers and other parties with whom the corporation contracts, with justice; they must live up to defined contractual and other legal obligations. But toward the residual owners they must act as fiduciaries; they must strive to fulfill an open-ended duty to maximize the beneficiaries' welfare.

§14.6 *Repurchases: Legal Accounting Treatment*

Similarity to dividend regulation

The statutory provisions regulating redemptions and repurchases are similar in aim and method to those regulating dividends. The basic aim is to provide a minimal level of protection against depletion of corporate assets available for creditors, though protection of shareholders of higher rank is also a goal. Methods are also similar to those involving dividends. For example, the rules are often based on the concept of legal capital. Thus, the old MBCA provided (as do many existing state statutes) that repurchases could be made only out of earned surplus or, if done pursuant to permission in the articles of organization or pursuant to a director resolution and majority shareholder vote, out of capital surplus.[1] That is, the amounts paid by the corporation to buy back the stock had to be equalled or exceeded by the amounts in these net worth accounts. Repurchases were also subject to the basic, nonwaivable insolvency limit.

Redemptions

Redemptions were subject to a somewhat easier set of rules.[2] This is as one would expect, since the timing and price of redemptions are usually specified in advance in the articles of organization and are therefore mat-

§14.5 [1]Old MBCA §6. See also Del. §160(a) (impairment of capital test); N.Y. §513(a) ("out of surplus"). California lumps repurchases with dividends as "distributions" and governs both by its financial ratio tests. Cal §§166, 500.

[2]Old MBCA §66. See also N.Y. §513(c).

ters of which contract creditors may easily take notice. The insolvency limit applied, of course: redemptions may not be made when the corporation will be insolvent immediately afterwards. Other than that, the basic restraint was that immediately after the redemption the corporation's net assets must equal or exceed the liquidation preference amounts of prior stock (if there is any). For example, suppose a corporation has two classes of preferred stock, "prior preferred" and "subordinated preferred," and one class of common stock. The charter provisions governing the prior preferred state that if the corporation should ever be dissolved and liquidated, each share of prior preferred will receive $110 worth of property distributed in liquidation before other classes of stock may receive anything. In order to redeem subordinated preferred stock, even according to a contractually fixed schedule, the corporation's financial condition would have to be such that, just after the redemption, its net assets would have to at least equal $110 times the number of outstanding shares of prior preferred stock.

Balance sheet adjustments

The balance sheet adjustments that must be made after a redemption or repurchase generally depend on whether the stock bought back is cancelled or not. (Usually, redeemed stock is automatically cancelled, while repurchased stock is cancelled only if the board of directors adopts a resolution cancelling it.[3] The basic difference is that when stock is cancelled the corporation's legal capital account must be written down to reflect that fact — for example, by subtracting the total par value of the cancelled stock or, if no par stock was cancelled, the amount of stated capital attributable to the cancelled stock.

Installment purchases

One of the interesting issues that has arisen under statutory restraints on repurchases is the proper treatment of installment purchases. Suppose Williams, the sole stockholder of H.D. Corporation, wants to help a buyer make a "bootstrap acquisition" of the corporation. (That is, the buyer is unable or unwilling to pay cash for all of the assets or stock and must, in effect, finance part of the acquisition price by borrowing against the future earnings of the corporation.) Specifically, Williams sells two-thirds of his stock to the buyer in exchange for a seven-year promissory note paying interest at X percent and having a principal amount of $200,000, and he simultaneously sells the remaining one-third of his stock back to the corporation in exchange for a seven-year promissory note paying X percent interest and having a principal amount of $100,000. At the time the corporation gives the note to Williams, the corporation's balance sheet shows more than $100,000 of earned surplus. But seven years later, when the

[3]See, e.g., old MBCA §§67, 68.

corporation is supposed to pay that amount to Williams, according to the note, it has an earned surplus deficit. Will the payment be legal under a statute that says simply that "repurchases" must be made out of "earned surplus"?

Two-time vs. one-time tests

In one case with essentially these facts, a Texas civil court of appeals adopted what amounted to a "two-time" test: the corporation had to have enough earned surplus to cover the repurchase, both at the time the note was given and at the time cash payment was to be made on the note.[4] One may guess that it strained toward this result because it (accurately) perceived that bootstrap acquisitions frequently impose a serious risk on creditors and that a mechanical, legal-accounting rule like the earned-surplus test is easily avoided unless courts step in to strengthen it. The Texas Supreme Court reversed, however.[5] It went off on a linguistic context approach to statutory interpretation. Since the statute distinguished in another provision between the "purchase" of shares and "payment" for them, and the provision in question simply applied the earned-surplus test to repurchases, it thought that the test needed to be satisfied only at the time when the corporation gave the note. Other jurisdictions responded differently to the problem. California imposed a two-time test by statute,[6] for example, though New Jersey's statute made it quite clear that only the time of purchase was relevant.[7] The revised MBCA follows the latter approach.[8]

Fraudulent conveyance analysis

As in the case of excessive dividends, objecting creditors and bankruptcy trustees seem to have failed to appreciate the possibility of attacking an installment repurchase as a fraudulent conveyance. If, for example, when Williams caused the corporation to give him the $100,000 note, the transaction left the corporation with "unreasonably small capital" — as determined not by merely looking at its balance sheet but by considering the real likelihood that its total net worth was adequate for a corporation of its size, line of business, amount and timing of liabilities, and so forth — then there would have been a fraudulent transfer under Section 5 of the Uniform Fraudulent Conveyance Act.[9]

[4] Williams v. Nevelow, 501 S.W.2d 942 (Tex. Civ. App. 1973).

[5] Williams v. Nevelow, 513 S.W.2d 535 (Tex. 1974).

[6] Cal. §§166, second sentence, and 500, final sentence.

[7] N.J. §14A:7-16(6).

[8] MBCA §6.40(e)(1), 6.40(f).

[9] Remember that there is never "fair consideration," in the sense meant by the statute, when a corporation makes a distribution to shareholders, because the corporation receives nothing the creditors could levy on or, if they did levy on it (as in the case of repurchased stock) nothing that would have value in their hands equivalent to the assets transferred to the shareholders. That is, from the creditor's perspective, distributions clearly reduce or deplete "the estate of the debtor."

CHAPTER 15

SHAREHOLDERS' SUITS

§15.1 Introduction

The derivative suit

The common law countries have devised one of the most interesting and ingenious of accountability mechanisms for large formal organizations: the shareholder's derivative suit. In such a suit, the shareholder sues on behalf of the corporation for harm done to it. Ordinarily, therefore, any damages recovered in the suit are paid to the corporation. Historically, the derivative suit was conceived of as a double suit, or two suits in one: The plaintiff (1) brought a suit in equity against the corporation seeking an order compelling it (2) to bring a suit for damages or other relief against some third person who had caused legal injury to the corporation. Although not inevitably, the third person was usually an officer, director, or other fiduciary of the corporation. Although each derivative suit is now very definitely treated in the courts as a single case, the historical conception survives in the customs of making the corporation a nominal defendant in the action and allowing it to raise various objections to the suit. Many of these possible objections are treated in succeeding sections of this chapter.

Direct actions

Shareholders may also bring direct actions, both as individuals and as a class, for injuries done to them in their individual capacities by corporate fiduciaries. Recovery in these individual or class actions goes to the suing shareholders, not their corporation. Because these kinds of actions, unlike derivative suits, do not raise procedural issues that are dramatically special to the corporate context, they are left for books and courses on civil procedure. (Section 15.9 wrestles with the problem of assigning actions to the direct or the derivative category, however.) Furthermore, my treatment will focus on major issues. A number of miscellaneous procedural questions, such as those pertaining to jurisdiction, venue, statutes of limitations, intervention, and consolidation of derivative suits, will be ignored.

The last section of the chapter deals with the important topic of the extent to which corporate fiduciaries can escape the full force of derivative actions by means of indemnification agreements and liability insurance.

§15.2 Demand on Directors

A microcosmic issue

Perhaps the most important issue raised in derivative litigation is the struggle between shareholder control and director control over the corporation's power to bring and pursue a lawsuit. Under what conditions may an individual shareholder maintain a suit on behalf of his corporation in disregard of the directors' wishes? This question is, of course, only one instance of a broader question: What are the limits of centralized management, and under what conditions should this basic principle be held not to govern?

Demand requirement everywhere

The general rule in virtually all United States jurisdictions is that before bringing a derivative suit a shareholder must first make a demand on the corporation's board of directors to act so as to remedy the situation about which the shareholder complains. If the directors respond affirmatively, as by suing the parties that allegedly caused harm to the corporation or taking other corrective action, their action usually precludes a shareholder-initiated suit. If the directors decline to take action, then, depending on factors to be discussed, the shareholder may or may not be able to proceed with his derivative action.

Assumed in statutes

The procedural codes of virtually all jurisdictions assume the demand requirement without directly stating it. For example, Rule 23.1 of the Federal Rules of Civil Procedure says that a complaint in a derivative action shall "allege with particularly the efforts, if any, made by the plaintiff to obtain the action he desires from the directors or comparable authority and, if necessary, from the shareholders or members, and the reasons for his failure to obtain the action or for not making the effort.[1]

Reasons

Judicial opinions offer several reasons for the demand requirement. First, and most obviously, it helps to implement the basic principle that management of the corporation is entrusted to the board of directors, not to the shareholders. Whether to sue or not to sue is ordinarily a matter for the business judgment of directors, just as is a decision that the corporation will make bricks instead of bottles. Second, the requirement may serve judicial economy. Since some demands will be handled by corrective action short of suit, the courts will be saved from ruling on those matters. And where the directors' judgment not to take action is binding, the courts will be saved from examining business decisions. Third, the requirement protects directors from the harassment of litigious shareholders who might otherwise contest ordinary business decisions. Fourth, the requirement may help discourage "strike-suits" — those based on reckless charges and brought for personal gain.

In fact, these objectives all depend as much on the business judgment rule as on the demand requirement. Furthermore, the various reasons really reduce to only two, furthering centralized management and deterring strike suits, and it is not clear how well the demand requirement furthers the latter objective.

Issues

Three important questions about the demand on directors requirement need to be asked. When will demand be excused? When demand is made and the directors refuse to cause the corporation to sue, what is the effect of their refusal? When a derivative suit is brought against directors and the board sets up a committee of independent directors that investigates the claim and then moves to dismiss the suit as not in the corporation's best interest, how should a court rule on such a motion?

§15.2.1 Excuse

Basics

Opinions often say that demand on the directors will be excused when it would be futile. Typically, demand is considered futile where the alleged wrongdoers *comprise* or *control* a majority of the directors. Thus, many courts would excuse demand when the plaintiff shareholder was alleging (nonfrivolously) that a majority of the directors had directly engaged in basic self-dealing with their corporation or had usurped a corporate oppor-

§15.2 [1]Note that many derivative actions, although based on state law claims, are brought in federal courts because they are attached to claims under the federal securities laws and the court exercises pendent jurisdiction over them.

tunity. No one would expect the defendant directors to give adequate consideration to a shareholder demand for corrective action. Courts may differ, however, over whether relatively passive directors should be considered wrongdoers for the purpose of excusing demand.

Example

Consider two cases. In *Barr v. Wackman,*[2] the shareholder claimed that the directors of Talcott National Corporation had converted a merger offer at a price of $24 per Talcott share into an acquisition at $20 per Talcott share plus favorable employment and consulting agreements for Talcott insiders. In effect, the insiders were accused of taking bribes for the exercise of their power to facilitate or block the acquisition and therefore violating their fiduciary duty of loyalty. Only five of Talcott's 16 directors were also officers or employees, however; the rest were unaffiliated. As to these 11 directors, the shareholder's complaint was that they violated their duty of due care by authorizing and approving the wrongful transactions. The New York Court of Appeals held that demand was excused. At least in some contexts, then, a nonfrivolous allegation that unaffiliated directors violated their duty of due care is a good excuse.

Example with a different slant

By contrast, in *In re Kaufmann Mutual Fund Actions,*[3] a federal appellate court asserted that "[w]here mere approval of the corporate action, absent self-interest or other indication of bias, is the sole basis for establishing the directors' 'wrongdoing' and hence for excusing demand on them, plaintiff's suit should ordinarily be dismissed. . . ." In the case before it, the primary claim was that the mutual funds' investment advisers and affiliated directors had violated antitrust law by charging excessive advisory fees. Unaffiliated directors are required to approve, and commonly do approve, such advisory contracts, so the case seems contrary to *Barr v. Wackman.* Nevertheless, the court went on to distinguish between a case where a director goes along with a colleague in an act on its face advantageous only to the colleague and not the corporation (in which case the court might well decide that the colleague controlled that director and that demand on him would be futile) and a case where a director merely made an erroneous business judgment in approving what was plainly a corporate act (in which, however, some colleague had a personal financial interest). Furthermore, the quoted language seems to be dicta. As the concurring judge pointed out, the plaintiff hadn't alleged that the unaffiliated directors who would have voted on a demand, had plaintiff made one, were the same directors who were on the board when it approved the allegedly wrongful contracts. Thus, dismissal could be justified on the

[2] 329 N.E.2d 180 (N.Y. 1975).

[3] 479 F.2d 257, 265 (1st Cir. 1973), cert. denied, 414 U.S. 857 (1973).

ground that it hadn't been alleged that a majority of the directors participated in the wrongs, even to the extent of approving them.

Need to show domination

Kauffman and other cases[4] do show that courts will not simply accept conclusory allegations that independent directors were controlled or dominated by wrongdoing affiliated directors. Plaintiffs must allege particular facts showing domination or control.

Aronson v. Lewis

Emphasis upon this principle seems to have been taken to extreme lengths by the Delaware Supreme Court in *Aronson v. Lewis.*[5] Plaintiffs challenged an exceptionally generous consulting package awarded by the board to a Mr. Fink, who was retiring as a director at age 75 and who was a 47-percent shareholder in the corporation. Plaintiffs argued that a demand on directors would be futile because Fink had chosen all the directors personally, the directors had already approved the deal, and making a demand would be, in effect, asking directors to sue themselves, "thereby placing the conduct of this action in hostile hands and preventing its effective prosecution." The court dismissed the third argument as a "bootstrap." The other two arguments were judged insufficient to excuse demand. In the absence of more particularized facts that would support an allegation of control and domination, the mere evidence of Fink's 47-percent ownership and personal selection of directors was insufficient, according to this court, to overcome the judicial presumption that director's decisions are the product of a valid exercise of business judgment.

Though the court might be argued to have blinded itself to reality, the result is not as harsh on plaintiffs as first appears. The issue in the case was whether demand should be excused, not whether a demand made and rejected (by an independent directors' committee, for example) should preclude the action from proceeding. The latter question is governed in Delaware by somewhat different principles, as we shall see in subsection 15.2.3.

§15.2.2 Refusal

Effect of refusal?

What happens if a shareholder does make a demand on the directors to sue someone and the directors refuse to do so? Is their refusal a decision

[4]See, e.g., Jones v. Equitable Life Assurance Society, 409 F. Supp. 370 (S.D.N.Y. 1975).

[5]473 A.2d 805 (Del. 1984). See also Pogostin v. Rice, 480 A.2d 619 (Del. 1984), which applied the standards of *Aronson* to stockholders who alleged that a stock option plan was a waste of assets and that the board's refusal to accept a premium takeover bid or to negotiate with the bidder was a breach of fiduciary duty. The stockholders failed to demonstrate the first point by particularized allegations and failed to overcome the presumption of sound business judgment with respect to the second, so demand was not excused.

protected by the business judgment rule, so that a court would not allow the shareholder to maintain a derivative action and would not examine the merits of the directors' decision? In a simple case involving a potential suit against a third party, the answer is usually yes. Whether to sue or not really is a matter of business judgment. It depends not only on whether the corporation's decision makers think the corporation has a valid claim, but also on their assessment of their costs of trying to enforce it and the likelihood of success.

Typical approach

The simple case, however, arises very rarely indeed. The vast majority of derivative actions involve claims that some or all of the corporation's managers violated their duties toward the corporation. A standard formulation of the rule for this common context is that when the directors have refused to sue, the shareholder can maintain a derivative action if he can allege and prove that the directors are "personally involved or interested in the alleged wrongdoing in a way calculated to impair their exercise of business judgment on behalf of the corporation, or that their refusal to sue reflects bad faith or breach of trust in some other way."[6]

Participation and domination key ideas

As in the case of excuse, then, the courts can look into whether the directors refusing to sue somehow participated in the alleged wrong or were dominated or controlled by the primary wrongdoers. In principle, an affirmative finding on either score permits the derivative suit to go forward, despite the directors' refusal. Once again, however, the inevitable variations in operative facts and in judicial attitudes make it difficult to apply these abstract principles with certainty.[7]

Why two issues?

An interesting question to consider is this: if case law in a state shows that the rules governing excuses for not making demand are basically the same as those governing what overturns the directors' refusal to sue, why should the issue be able to come up at two points in the litigation process? Since a shareholder can make demand very cheaply — it's a mere matter of typing up a letter and mailing it to the board — why not say that share-

[6]Issner v. Aldrich, 254 F. Supp. 696, 699 (D. Del. 1966), quoting Ash v. International Business Mach., Inc., 353 F.2d 491, 493 (3d Cir. 1965).

[7]For example, Issner v. Aldrich, cited in note 6 supra, superficially seemed similar to Barr v. Wackman. Plaintiff was a shareholder in D Corporation. D and P corporations each had a 50 percent interest in N.H., a joint venture. P had 12 percent of the stock of D and 3 of D's 17 directors were affiliated with P. Plaintiff charged that P engaged in unfair self-dealing transactions with N.H. to the detriment of D, and brought a derivative action against all three corporations and the directors of D and N.H. The court treated the D directors' refusal to sue as dispositive. Note, however, that a majority of D's directors were unaffiliated with P, that there was no convincing evidence that P dominated those directors (the 12-percent stock ownership was thought to be insufficient evidence), and that the D directors hadn't authorized or approved the self-dealing transactions and thus they were not participants in the wrong.

holders must always make demand, and *then,* if and when the directors refuse or decline to sue, apply the rules to assess the shareholders' argument that they should nevertheless be able to maintain a derivative action? A possible reason for not following this suggestion is that demand creates delay and expense. When directors receive a demand they inevitably embark on a flurry of defensive maneuvers at corporate expense, and the plaintiff's lawsuit is at least delayed until a reasonable time for their response has passed. Accordingly, if the demand is truly futile — if a negative decision by the directors is quite likely to be made but not to preclude the suit — there is reason not to incur these costs.

§15.2.3 Independent Committees

A new defensive strategy

In the mid-1970s, starting with cases in which managers were alleged to have been guilty of waste of corporate assets by approving or failing to stop illegal foreign payments, corporate managements began to employ a new device to ward off derivative suits. After the derivative suit was filed, the board of directors would set up a committee of supposedly disinterested directors to investigate the plaintiff's claims and recommend action with respect to them. (Recall that modern corporation statutes allow the board to delegate some or most of its functions to working committees, and that large corporations have increasingly made use of this power.) The committee might be composed of two or three directors who were not named as defendants in the suit, perhaps because they were not directors at the time of the alleged wrongdoing or because they were outside directors who were obviously ignorant of the alleged wrongdoing. Indeed, the existing directors might appoint new directors in order to have persons to put on such a committee. Sometimes, if all of the directors were named as defendants, the board might appoint to the committee those ouside directors who had no personal financial interest in the challenged transactions and hope that they would be considered disinterested. In some cases one committee member would be a person who was not a director, or the committee would at least retain an outside party as consultant. The consultant might be, for example, a retired chief judge of a state supreme court or an eminent professor of corporate law. The committee would then examine records, conduct interviews, hold meetings, write discussion drafts, and eventually, after a suitable display of investigative activity and collective deliberation, would produce a report that concluded, unsurprisingly, that the committee thought it was in the corporation's "best interest" not to proceed with the lawsuit. The corporation would then bring a motion to dismiss the lawsuit.

Committee's power

Courts faced with these motions had to decide several questions. One was whether a committee of the type described had power to dismiss or request a dismissal, or, put another way, whether the court would ever pay any deference to such a committee's recommendations. Most courts answered yes. One federal court applying Virginia law seemed to take the position that the derivative suit could routinely go on despite the recommendations of such a committee,[8] but other courts decided that even a board tainted by the self-interest of a majority of its members may delegate its authority to a committee of disinterested directors.

Scope of judicial review

A second question was what the scope of judicial review of the special committee's recommendation would be. After considerable litigation, two main positions seemed to emerge. One, which was articulated by the New York Court of Appeals in *Auerbach v. Bennett,*[9] allows only minimal review.

Minimalist position

After the special committee recommends dismissal, the plaintiff may try to show that the committee members were not truly independent or disinterested, that they did not act in good faith, or that their investigations and deliberations were not sufficiently diligent. If the plaintiff can establish any of these things, the motion to dismiss is denied. If he cannot, the substantive merits of the committee's recommendations will not be scrutinized by the court. Rather, the decision will be treated as shielded by the business judgment rule. Thus, if the defendant board of directors can assemble a few new directors and if the latter go through an adequate sequence of investigatory steps, the court will hardly ever reexamine the decision not to sue by asking about the true likelihood of success on the merits, the true costs of suit, and so forth.

Delaware's two-step test

The other position, expressed by the Delaware Supreme Court in *Zapata Corporation v. Maldonado,*[10] provides for moderate scrutiny. The court is supposed to apply a two-step test to the motion to dismiss. First, it should inquire into the "independence" and "good faith" of the committee and the "bases supporting its conclusions." The *corporation* has the burden of proving independence, good faith, and a reasonable investigation. If the court determines that the committee wasn't independent, didn't act in good faith, or hasn't shown reasonable bases for its conclusions, or if the court is "not satisfied for other reasons relating to the process," it should

[8] Abella v. Universal Leaf Tobacco Co., 495 F. Supp. 713 (E.D. Va. 1980). See also Miller v. Register & Tribune Syndicate, Inc., 336 N.W.2d 709 (Iowa 1983), holding that directors who are parties to a derivative suit cannot delegate to a special committee the power to bind the corporation as to the conduct of the litigation.

[9] 393 N.E.2d 994 (N.Y. 1979). See also Lewis v. Anderson, 615 F.2d 778 (9th Cir. 1979), cert. denied, 449 U.S. 869 (1980).

[10] 430 A.2d 779 (Del. 1981).

deny the corporation's motion. Even if the court is satisfied on all these procedural grounds, it may proceed, "in its discretion," to the next step. In this second step, the court should determine, *"applying its own business judgment,"* whether the motion should be granted. The court may consider matters of law and public policy in addition to the corporation's best interest, and it should try to balance legitimate corporate claims as expressed in a stockholder suit against the corporation's interest as expressed by an independent investigatory committee. "The second step is intended to thwart instances where corporate actions meet the criteria of step one, but the result does not appear to satisfy its spirit, or where corporate actions would simply prematurely terminate a stockholder grievance deserving of further consideration in the corporation's interest."[11]

Followed in *Joy v. North*

The *Zapata* approach was followed and amplified in a noteworthy federal court opinion, *Joy v. North,*[12] that applied Connecticut law. The court frankly noted the reality that special litigation committees are appointed by the defendants to the litigation and opined that it was not cynical to expect that such committees will tend to view derivative actions against the other directors with skepticism. The court also rejected the argument that courts are not competent to make the relevant business decision (whether to continue the litigation), since courts do have a special aptitude for analyzing the termination of lawsuits.

Criticisms

The *Zapata* decision has been denounced by lawyers who usually represent defendants in derivative suits, principally on the ground that it gives courts open-ended flexibility rather than laying down sharp, bright lines and therefore will generate more litigation — more derivative suits and more briefing and arguing of the issues left open by the decision.[13] It is also claimed that courts are not competent institutions for exercising business judgment on behalf of corporations. One commentator argues that the decision whether to sue is not significantly different from ordinary business decisions,[14] but other commentators disagree.[15]

Analysis of the alternatives

In any event, the problems that the Delaware Supreme Court dealt with were serious ones, and its refusal to follow *Auerbach* has much to be said for it. The basic problem is this: When the board of directors as a whole is

[11] Id. at 788-789.

[12] 692 F.2d 880 (2d Cir. 1982), cert. denied, 460 U.S. 1051 (1983).

[13] See Block & Prussin, The Business Judgment Rule and Shareholder Derivative Actions: Viva Zapata? 37 Bus. Law. 27 (1981).

[14] Fischel, The "Race to the Bottom" Revisited: Reflections on Recent Developments in Delaware's Corporation Law, 76 Nw. U.L. Rev. 913, 938 n.150 (1982).

[15] Coffee & Schwartz, The Survival of the Derivative Suit: An Evaluation and a Proposal for Legislative Reform, 81 Colum. L. Rev. 261, 281-283 (1981).

disabled from making a decision on behalf of the corporation about whether to maintain a suit because a majority of its members are alleged wrongdoers, to whom should decision making power shift? The alternatives that have been considered, explicitly or implicitly, are (1) the complaining stockholder, (2) stockholders as a group, (3) a special committee appointed by the directors for the purpose, and (4) the court. The first alternative is rejected because it would arguably give too much power to individual stockholders to run up corporate expenses, even when their claims were basically frivolous, and would therefore tempt them to bring strike suits. This argument assumes, of course, that courts do not have adequate means or incentives for penalizing plaintiffs who bring frivolous suits. Note, however, that the first alternative satisfies the desire for a bright-line rule that avoids litigation about the conditions under which a committee recommendation to dismiss a suit is dispositive. For under this alternative, *all* such recommendations are simply disregarded.

The second alternative, letting shareholders as a group decide whether or not the corporation should pursue a suit against the managers, is obviously suboptimal in the public corporation context. The shareholders are simply an inappropriate decision making body. They will either succumb to rational apathy or engage in wastefully duplicated decision making.

The third alternative, as sanctioned by *Auerbach*, falls prey to the objection that when the members of the "independent" committee are selected by or under the influence of the defendant directors, the almost inevitable result in practice is that the committee will make a recommendation that favors the defendants' interest. This is true even when the independent committee members act in a way that seems, to their own consciences, to be perfectly earnest and honest. Subjective good faith simply does not insure lack of bias in an objective sense. Bias in results can occur because the defendants will always urge the appointment of independent persons who think and have opinions in certain predictable ways — ways that accord with the defendants' own thinking.

Support for Delaware approach

These thoughts about the first three alternatives may seem, then, to force us to consider the fourth alternative, that of the Delaware Supreme Court, which may be the best of the four. After all, the open-endedness of the two-step test is probably exaggerated, and it simply isn't the case that courts have not exercised business judgments over corporate disputes in the past. They do so every time they examine the substantive fairness of a self-dealing transaction, for example, or otherwise look at the fairness of a corporate transaction.

Court-appointed committee?

There is a fifth possible alternative, however. When requested by the board of directors in a derivative suit, the *court* might, in its discretion, appoint a special committee of independent and knowledgeable persons to determine whether continuance of the lawsuit would be in the corporation's best interest.[16] This committee's decision would be reviewed as in *Auerbach,* thus saving the court from the perils of decision making about business matters. The difference would be that the committee might be less likely to have a pro-defendant bias.

§15.3 Demand on Shareholders

Demand requirement not universal

Although all jurisdictions have a demand on directors requirement, in some important jurisdictions there is no requirement for demand on shareholders,[1] and in others the contours of the requirement are murky. The uncertainty is reflected in procedural statutes like F.R. Civ. P. 23.1, which requires the plaintiff to allege in his complaint, "if necessary," the efforts made to obtain the action he desires from the shareholders.

Reasons against it

There are several reasons for not imposing a demand on shareholders requirement. (1) With a publicly held corporation, making such a demand would be quite expensive and burdensome[2] and would unduly deter the bringing of derivative lawsuits. (2) In a publicly held corporation, the shareholders are simply an inappropriate body for making a complicated judgment about the merits, costs, and likelihood of success of suit and therefore about whether suing or not suing is in the corporation's best interest. (3) A majority of a company's shareholders should not be allowed to ratify a fraud over the objection of the minority, any more than they can vote to give away corporate assets over the protests of the minority.

Judicial reactions

The first two reasons suggest that the demand on shareholders requirement might be adopted for close corporations but not for public corporations. Courts have not adopted this obvious distinction in any clear-cut way, however. The third reason was adopted as the chief basis of decision in the Delaware decision of *Mayer v. Adams.*[3] The court held that the demand on shareholders was not necessary where the derivative claim was based on "frauds" by the directors. In speaking about "frauds and wrongs," the court seemed to include self-dealing as well as deception. In a similar vein, a Pennsylvania decision held that shareholder ratification of alleged lack of due care was proper and could bar a derivative suit, al-

[16] See, e.g., Miller v. Register and Tribune Syndicate, Inc., 336 N.W.2d 709 (Iowa 1983).

§15.3 [1] See, e.g., Cal. §800(b)(2); N.Y. §626(c).

[2] See Levitt v. Johnson, 334 F.2d 815 (1st Cir. 1964), cert. denied, 379 U.S. 961 (1965).

[3] 141 A.2d 458 (Del. 1958).

though the court would not have said that about "fraud, self-dealing, personal profit or intentional dissipation or waste of corporate funds."[4] But there is opposite authority. For example, an Ohio court concluded that a majority of the shareholders could ratify fraud.[5]

Reasons for the requirement

The reasons for having a demand on shareholders requirement seem to be the following: (1) The power to make business judgments should switch to shareholders as a group when the directors are disabled from acting; and (2) Without the requirement, there may be a plague of vexatious litigation. The second reason seems clearly overbroad for the purpose. Given the great expense of the demand on shareholders requirement in the public corporation context, the requirement is bound to deter meritorious as well as vexatious lawsuits. Surely there must be better filters against frivolous suits. The first reason seems sound in principle — the decision whether it is in the corporation's best interest to pursue a claim against directors, even one based on fraud, really is a question of business judgment — but it simply cannot withstand the rebuttal that in the public corporation context the shareholders en masse are rarely a good decision making body.

The same problem infects a proposal made by some commentators: don't require plaintiffs to make demand on shareholders, and thus don't impose on them the enormous expense of doing so, but do allow a majority vote of the shareholders to stop the derivative suit.[6] But this majority vote would always be solicited by the alleged wrongdoers, who would do so at corporate expense, using their control of the proxy machinery.

Conclusion

On balance, it seems unwise that there should be any demand on shareholders requirement in a derivative suit brought on behalf of a public corporation.

§15.4 *The Contemporaneous Ownership Rule*

Concept

A majority of jurisdictions, whether by statute, court rule, or judicial decision, still have the contemporaneous ownership rule. As expressed in F.R. Civ. P. 23.1, the derivative suit plaintiff must allege that he was a shareholder at the time of the transaction of which he complains or that his shares thereafter devolved on him by operation of law, for example, because the prior owner died and he inherited the shares.

[4] Smith v. Brown-Borhek Co., 200 A.2d 398, 400-401 (Pa. 1964).

[5] Claman v. Robertson, 128 N.E.2d 429 (Ohio 1955).

[6] Note, Demand on Directors and Stockholders as a Prerequisite to a Derivative Suit, 73 Harv. L. Rev. 746, 751-752 (1960).

Origin and rationale

Originally the rule was designed simply to deter the buying of shares in order to create diversity of citizenship and thereby gain access to the federal courts. Nowadays one may attempt to rationalize the rule as applied by state courts, by arguing that it prevents the buying of shares by litigious persons who might bring frivolous suits. But it is easy, of course, to argue the opposing view that a cause of action for wrongdoing by directors and officers is part of the assets in which a shareholder has a transferable interest. If a person thinks he has a valid derivative claim against his corporation's directors and officers but is reluctant to start a lawsuit himself — perhaps because he lacks time or is risk-averse — it would appear to be a good thing, for himself and other shareholders, if he could sell his shares to a more daring investor who is willing to act as prosecutor on behalf of all the shareholders. Thus, it is difficult to justify the continued existence of the contemporaneous ownership rule.

Statutory exception

Some appreciation of the unsteady basis for the rule is apparent in the California statute enacted in 1976.[1] The statute expresses the rule but provides for an elaborately defined exception to its application: a strong prima facie case, absence of similar action elsewhere, acquisition of shares before there was disclosure to the public or to the plaintiff of the alleged wrongdoing, and so forth.

Continuing-wrong doctrine

Courts have carved out a more widespread exception, the continuing-wrong doctrine. If the alleged misconduct can be construed as having "continued" until plaintiff acquired his shares, the plaintiff does not run afoul of the contemporaneous ownership rule. For example, suppose defendant insiders transfer overvalued property to their company for shares of stock to be issued later, the plaintiff later acquires his shares, and the corporation finally issues the shares to the defendants. In such a case the court might find that the wrong continued until the issuance of shares to the defendants, so that the contemporaneous ownership rule is satisfied.[2] A policy reason for this result would be that the original wrong is more likely to be discovered if the share issuance appeared of record. On the other hand, if the defendants sold land to the corporation for an inflated price in shares plus an assumption of the debts secured by the land, the plaintiff then acquired his shares, and the corporation later paid off the assumed debts, the court might very well find that the wrong was completed before the plaintiff's acquisition of shares, so that the contem-

§15.4 [1] Cal. §800(b)(1). See generally Harbrecht, The Contemporaneous Ownership Rule in Shareholders' Derivative Suits, 25 U.C.L.A.L. Rev. 1041 (1978).

[2] Maclary v. Pleasant Hills, Inc., 109 A.2d 830 (Del. Ch. 1954).

poraneous rule was not satisfied.[3] In this situation the alleged wrong would be in the entering of the contract, not in the mere mechanical carrying out of its terms. There would be no policy reason analogous to that behind the discovery rule in fraud cases, for construing the debt payment to be an important part of the wrongful sequence of behaviors.

Corporate incapacity rule

In addition to carving out exceptions to the contemporaneous rule, courts have also extended it. Some courts have applied a corporate incapacity rule under which a corporation may be barred from bringing suit if all its shareholders would be barred — usually, by the contemporaneous ownership rule — from bringing a derivative action against the same defendant for the same wrong. An example is where a shareholder buys all of a corporation's shares and then causes the corporation to sue the former controlling shareholder for having misappropriated corporate assets before the purchase.[4] Part of the justification for the doctrine would appear to be that the price plaintiff pays for the shares already reflects the impact of past misbehaviors of the defendants, so that any recovery would be a windfall. This suggests that when the price does not reflect the results of allegedly wrongful past behavior, the corporate incapacity doctrine ought not to apply.

For completeness, I should mention the rather basic point that the plaintiff must hold shares at the time he brings suit (and throughout the suit). Indeed, he should hold them continuously from the time of the wrong to the time of the suit.

§15.5 *Security for Expenses*

New York's older approach

About a third of the states have enacted statutes under which derivative suit plaintiffs may be required to post security for the expenses of the defendants. New York Section 627 is typical of the older sort of statute,[1]

[3] Goldie v. Yaker, 432 P.2d 841 (N.M. 1967). See also Lewis v. Anderson, 477 A.2d 1040 (Del. 1984) (a plaintiff who ceases to be a shareholder as a result of a merger loses standing to continue a derivative suit).

[4] Capitol Wine & Spirit Corp. v. Pokrass, 98 N.Y.S.2d 291 (App. Div. 1950), aff'd, 98 N.E.2d 704 (N.Y. 1951), rehearing denied, 100 N.E.2d 37 (N.Y. 1951). See also Courtland Manor, Inc. v. Leeds, 347 A.2d 144 (Del. Ch. 1975), where the court found corporate incapacity to sue when two shareholders would be barred from doing so derivatively and the other shareholder had "acquiesced" in the wrongs.

§15.5 [1] Old MBCA §49 was similar, but the current MBCA §7.40(d) simply declares that on termination of the proceeding the court may require the plaintiff to pay any defendant's reasonable expenses (including counsel fees) incurred in defending the proceeding if it finds the proceeding was commenced without reasonable cause.

which gives the corporate defendant in a derivative suit an entitlement to demand that *small* derivative suit plaintiffs (those holding less than 5 percent of the company's stock, unless their stock has a market value greater than $50,000) post security for the payment of defendants' reasonable expenses. The statute does not limit the amount of security that may have to be posted to any dollar figure. As for when the security may be used, the statute is open-ended. "[T]he corporation shall have recourse [to the security] in such amount as the court having jurisdiction of such action shall determine upon the termination of such action."

California's modern one

Section 800(c)-(f) of the California statute, by contrast, reflects the misgivings that lawmakers and commentators have long had about security-for-expenses statutes. Defendants must request the posting of security within 30 days after service of summons on them; the New York statute allows defendants to request it at any time before final judgment. Under the California statute, defendants may only move the court for an order requiring security; under the New York statute, defendants are "entitled" to require security. The moving defendants in California must show that there is no "reasonable possibility" that the suit will benefit the corporation or its shareholders or that the moving party did not participate in the transaction complained of; under the New York statute, the defendants need show no reasons, but only that the plaintiff shareholder has small stockholdings. The court under the California statute may not fix security requirements greater than $50,000; under the New York statute, as stated, there is no such limit. On the other hand, the California statute may be invoked by defendants other than the corporation; under the New York statute, only the corporate defendant can require security. Nevertheless, it should be noted that, because the corporate defendant's expenses may also include its indemnification payments to the individual defendant directors and officers for their expenses, the New York statute may expose plaintiffs to liability for, and the need to post security for, most of the defendants' expenses.

History of statutes

To understand security-for-expenses statutes, it is necessary to know something of their history. During the Great Depression, there was an increase in stockholders' derivative suits, which may have been due to a number of factors. With many business failures occurring, disappointed shareholders were eager to find someone at fault to sue. Several spectacular recoveries in derivative actions may have encouraged lawyers to be willing to bring such suits. In any event, a committee of the New York Chamber of Commerce prepared a report (the Wood Report) in 1944 that analyzed a decade's worth of derivative suits in the New York courts. The report found that only 8 percent of the nearly 1,300 suits produced corporate recoveries and concluded that the derivative suit mechanism was being abused by "strike suiters" — plaintiffs with minor interests in the corporation who brought unmeritorious claims for the purpose of harassing the corporation and being bought off by it, and who suffered little if the corporation suffered because of their activity. New York enacted a security-for-expense statute forthwith, and other states followed.

Commentators' criticisms

Some commentators of that era, especially Professor Hornstein, sharply criticized the statutes. Hornstein pointed out that if the legislators had really been concerned with stopping the identified abuse, the extortionate secret settlement with a frivolous plaintiff, the obvious remedy was to bar secret settlements, by simply requiring that once a plaintiff has filed a derivative suit, it may not be dismissed, discontinued, or settled without the approval of the court. The court will look to the best interests of the corporation and will therefore refuse to award any payments to mere strike suiters. (In fact, since Hornstein wrote, states have enacted statutes requiring such judicial approvals.) He also pointed out that the Wood Commission was dominated by management-oriented defense attorneys who hoped to bar derivative suits entirely, and that in the two and a half years after the New York law was enacted, there was only a handful of derivative suits.[2]

Death knell or false alarm?

At this point one might have been persuaded to sound the death knell for the derivative suit. But the judicial process in a common law system is an amazing phenomenon. It has its own ways of reaching equilibrium, ways that often seem to have little to do with legislative enactments. Accordingly, when law students did an empirical study for the Columbia Journal of Law and Social Problems some 23 years later, they found that derivative suits were again numbering in the hundreds per decade, and that the security-for-expenses statute was a minor factor in the bringing of such suits.[3]

What had happened?

Reasons for small impact

One development was that when defendants moved for the posting of security by a small shareholder-plaintiff, courts would allow the action to be stayed while the plaintiff got a shareholders' list and solicited other shareholders to join with him so as to pass the 5-percent test and avoid the need for posting security. Of course, the prospect of the plaintiff publiciz-

[2] Hornstein, New Aspects of Stockholders' Derivative Suits, 47 Colum. L. Rev. 1, 3, 5 (1947); see also Hornstein, The Death Knell of Shareholders' Derivative Suits in New York, 32 Calif. L. Rev. 123 (1944).

[3] Note, Security for Expenses in Shareholders' Derivative Suits: 23 Years' Experience, 4 Colum. J. Law & Social Prob. 50 (1968).

ing his complaints to other shareholders was one of the last things that defendant managers wanted to see, so they eventually began to think it better not to request security at all. Another development was that plaintiffs could often avoid the security requirement by casting their claims in terms of a federal securities law violation and going to federal court, or sometimes they could avoid it by filing suit in a jurisdiction without such a statute. Delaware, to take the most prominent example, never adopted a security-for-expenses statute.

§15.6 *Conflicts of Interest in the Defense of Derivative Suits*

Whose defense?

Two types of conflict of interest are of concern here. One pertains to the kinds of defenses that may or must be raised by the corporation as nominal defendant in a derivative suit, as opposed to defenses that should be raised by the real defendants. When the real defendants are directors and officers of the corporation who are being sued for breach of duty, they may have a personal interest in causing the corporation to raise and attempt to prove, at *its* expense, as many defenses as possible. This may happen because they are not entirely sure that their own legal expenses will ultimately be indemnified by the corporation or covered by directors' and officers' liability insurance.

Guidelines

Judicial opinions are relatively sparse and do not give unambiguous answers to all the questions one might ask, but it seems feasible to venture a few guidelines.[1] Consider a derivative suit in which plaintiff alleges that several directors usurped a corporate opportunity for themselves. Conventional defenses on the merits ought generally to be raised only by the real defendants, rather than by the corporation. This would include the defense that the opportunity in question was not a corporate one or that the corporation was incapable of financing it. Conventional procedural defenses also should generally be raised by the real defendants. Examples are claims that venue is improper or that defendants were not properly served. On the other hand, most defenses peculiar to the derivative suit should belong to the corporation. This is especially true of defenses aimed at preserving the integrity of the principle of centralized management, that is, at keeping the corporation's decision making apparatus in proper hands. Such defenses include the claim that the plaintiff failed to make a demand

§15.6 [1]See Note, Defenses in Shareholder Derivative Suits — Who May Raise Them? 66 Harv. L. Rev. 342 (1952).

on the board and/or on the shareholders, that a special committee has recommended that the suit not proceed or that plaintiff was not a shareholder at the time of the alleged wrong. The corporation, of course, should be able to raise any procedural defenses related to its role in the suit — for example, that it was not properly served.

Separate counsel issue

A second type of conflict springs from the fact that the corporation and the real defendants will often have opposing interests in how the suit is resolved or settled. A recovery for the corporation will hurt the defendants, and vice-versa. Should the corporation and the real defendants therefore have separate counsel? Modern opinions say yes.[2] They stress the potential for conflicts of interest and betrayal of confidences, whereas judges in earlier times might have been more impressed by the extra cost of having two sets of defense attorneys and by the observation that the corporation's role in the suit was actually rather minimal in most cases.

Who gets which lawyers?

Suppose it is the practice in an area of the country that when a corporation's top managers are sued in a derivative suit, the *corporation's* regular outside law firm will take the lead in representing those individuals. It is the corporation for whom new outside counsel is sought. This might lead us to question whose interest — that of management or that of the corporation and its shareholders — the regular outside law firm previously saw itself as trying to advance. Furthermore, it seems odd that it is not the court, but defendant management, in consultation with the corporation's regular law firm, that chooses the law firm to represent the corporation in the derivative suit. This practice also raises questions about the vigor and vitality of legal representation for the corporation and its public shareholders. At present, however, there is no solid evidence that law firms representing corporations in derivative suits often fail to represent them well.

Attorney-client privilege

Incidentally, the United States Supreme Court has taken a broad view of the reach of the attorney-client privilege when the client is a corporation. The privilege runs not just to attorney communications with the "control group" of managers, but to those with lower-level executives as well.[3]

§15.7 *Settlement*

Settlement regulated

Since the great majority of derivative actions are settled rather than litigated to an outcome on the merits, it is imperative for any corporate

[2] Cannon v. U.S. Acoustics Corp., 398 F. Supp. 209 (N.D. Ill. 1975), aff'd in part and rev'd in part, 532 F.2d 1118 (7th Cir. 1976). See generally Note, Developments in the Law — Conflicts of Interest in the Legal Profession, 94 Harv. L. Rev. 1244, 1339-1342 (1981).

[3] Upjohn Co. v. United States, 449 U.S. 383 (1981).

lawyer to know the rudiments of settlement regulation. Federal Rule of Civil Procedure 23.1 declares that derivative actions shall not be dismissed or compromised without the approval of the court and that notice of a proposed settlement or dismissal shall be given to the shareholders in the manner the court directs. Many jurisdictions now have similar rules. There are subtle variations. New York Section 626(d), for example, adds the word "discontinued" to "compromised or settled," and it gives the court discretion to decide whether notice, by publication or otherwise, must be given to the shareholders in a particular case, and which one or more of the parties should bear the expense of giving notice.

Hearings

Courts usually hold hearings on proposed settlements. Generally, the proponents of the settlement have the burden of convincing the court that the settlement is in the best interests of the corporation and its shareholders. The court will consider factors such as the attorney's opinions of the likelihood of the suit's success on the merits, the costs and delays of continued litigation, the defendants' solvency, and so forth.[1] At the hearings on the settlement, interested shareholders may appear and present their objections to or opinions about the settlement. Amounts paid under settlement agreements must go to the corporation, not to the plaintiff shareholder, although the plaintiff's attorney's fees are usually paid out of the recovered amount.

Former approach

In earlier times, it was not the case that settlements had to be approved by the court. Consequently, many suspect settlements occurred. Frequently, observers were tempted to label them hush payments or extortion money for strike suiters. To understand more precisely why these secret settlements were not always in the corporation's best interest, you should consider how the personal interest of the settling individuals frequently differs from the interest of the corporation's shareholders.

Hypo for analysis

Suppose that plaintiff has sued the directors and officers of X Corporation for unfair self-dealing with the corporation. The case is about to go to trial. The defendants have just offered to settle the case for $1 million. If this settlement occurs, the plaintiff's attorney will receive (by virtue of a prior agreement with his client) $0.2 million as his fee. At this point in time the plaintiff's attorney, who is of course the real party in interest on the plaintiff's side, estimates that there is a 25-percent chance that if the case goes to trial the plaintiff will win, and therefore, damages of $5 million will be awarded, out of which he will take a fee of $0.8 million.[2] In this situa-

§15.7 [1] See generally Haudek, The Settlement and Dismissal of Stockholders' Actions — Part II: The Settlement, 23 Sw. L.J. 765 (1969).

[2] For purposes of this example, assume that the plaintiff's attorney's additional costs from

tion, the corporation — alias the public shareholders — has a different expected value from the two courses of action. Settlement has an expected value of $0.8 million to the corporation (that is, $1 million, the settlement amount, minus $0.2 million, the fee to the plaintiff's attorney, times 1, the probability of getting that amount if settlement is pursued). Trial on the merits has an expected value of $1.05 million to the corporation (that is, $5 million, the amount of a judgment if plaintiff wins, minus $0.8 million, the fee to the plaintiff's attorney, times .25, the probability that plaintiff will win at trial). The best interests of the corporation seem to favor trial. As for the plaintiff's attorney, it seems at first blush that he should be indifferent. Settlement has an expected value to him of $0.2 million, but so does a trial. (His fee if he wins, $0.8 million, times .25, the probability of winning, equals $0.2 million.)

Attorney's urge to settle

Nevertheless, the plaintiff's attorney may be strongly inclined to settle rather than go to trial. Why? Because trial exposes him to a greater *risk* than does settlement, and most ordinary persons are averse to taking risks. The attorney will only undertake the trial if the risk is compensated for by a sufficiently high additional amount of expected value. How large an additional amount of expected value is needed will depend on his personal attitudes toward risk, which will in turn depend in part on his wealth level. Presumably, the plaintiff's attorney who is simply making an ordinary lawyer's living will be more risk-averse than one who is already rolling in wealth.

Conflict with shareholder interests

But, you may ask, might not the public shareholders of the corporation also be risk-averse (they undoubtedly are), and doesn't this imply that they too may prefer settlement to trial? Perhaps, but not likely. Ordinarily, shareholder investments represent discretionary funds, not the money that the investors are counting on for next year's food and shelter, and the shareholders have often diversified their investment risk by assembling a balanced portfolio of assets. Shareholders in general are not likely to be nearly as risk-averse about the trial-or-settlement decision as is the plaintiff's attorney, whose very livelihood depends on the outcome.

Defendant's urge to settle

As for the real defendants, *their* personal degree of risk aversion will often lead them to want to settle long before the corporation (alias the public shareholders), if rational and well informed, would want to do so. Together with the typical incentives of plaintiff's attorney, this means that there will be a rather constant tendency for settlement agreements to be

---

going to trial can be disregarded; the difference would only complicate the analysis without affecting the basic point.

reached that are not really in the corporation's best interest. That is why there are requirements for judicial approval of settlements, notice to other shareholders, and a chance for shareholders to raise objections. One may have doubts about how well these control mechanisms work, of course, but in principle they seem preferable to not having controls.

Arguments for old view, and its demise

This view was not always taken. In 1942 a noteworthy New York decision[3] confirmed the notion that the parties to a derivative suit could stipulate a discontinuance without court approval. In that case the settlement provided that plaintiff shareholders would have their shares bought at seven times their market value. The court rationalized the result by noting that other shareholders could have intervened and taken over the suit, that other shareholders could have filed separate complaints, that the discontinuance would have no res judicata effect on other shareholders, and that it was fair to the plaintiff to let him decide when to quit, since he was bearing the risk and expense of maintaining the suit. Even before this result was reversed by statute, however, it was partly chipped away by a subsequent New York decision that insisted that even in private settlements the amounts paid over must go to the corporation rather than to the plaintiff shareholder.[4] Admittedly, the latter rule is hard to police when courts don't formally approve the settlements, but that only argues for the superiority of the approach taken in the modern statutes.[5]

§15.8 Fees

Pay-your-own-lawyer principle

The ordinary principle about litigation expenses in American courts is that each party bears his own. In the derivative suit context, a mechanical interpretation of this principle would have unfortunate results. It would always require the plaintiff shareholder to pay his attorney the substantial fees involved in bringing the suit even though any recovery from the real defendants, whether by judgment or settlement, generally must go to the corporation rather than to the shareholder. There would be no lawsuits brought on a contingent fee basis under such a regime. Very few shareholders would ever have an incentive to bring a derivative suit on any realistic fee arrangement — even when a suit would be meritorious and clearly justified, on a cost-benefit analysis, for the shareholders as a group.

[3]Manufacturers Mut. Fire Ins. Co. v. Hopson, 43 N.E.2d 71 (N.Y. 1942).

[4]Clarke v. Greenberg, 71 N.E.2d 443 (N.Y. 1947).

[5]But there are problems under the current system, especially when it is the *corporation* (itself controlled by the real defendants) that settles the claims. See, generally, Note, Director Independence and Derivative Suit Settlements, 1983 Duke L.J. 645.

True, recovery by the corporation will increase the value of the plaintiff's shares somewhat. But except in an extreme case only the plaintiff shareholder who owns a very substantial percentage of the stock will find that this increase in share value exceeds the attorney's fees he would have to pay under the strict pay-your-own-lawyer rule. For example, if the attorney's fees that plaintiff must pay are expected to equal 20 percent of any amount recovered by the corporation — a percentage that is a realistic one — then only the shareholder who owns more than 20 percent of the corporation's stock will ever find it worthwhile to sue derivatively under the pay-your-own-lawyer rule. Rational smaller shareholders will not want to sue, even when the chance of winning is almost 100 percent and the corporate recovery far exceeds all lawyers' fees. And since the very large shareholder is likely to be in control of corporate management, he is more likely to find himself defending a derivative suit than wanting to bring one.

Common fund doctrine

Not surprisingly, then, the courts have developed a more flexible interpretation of the principle that each side ordinarily pays its own lawyers. It is called the "common fund doctrine." Under it, if the litigation brought by plaintiff produces a fund or recovery that benefits an entire class of persons, or an entity in which he along with others has an interest, the plaintiff's reasonable litigation expenses may be taken out of the recovery. Not only does this doctrine promote efficiency by eliminating a free-rider problem that would deter the bringing of meritorious suits, it also satisfies intuitive notions of fairness. If all stockholders share in the benefits of the suit, they should all share in the costs.

Several interesting extensions of the common fund doctrine have been developed. (Some courts have called these extensions "exceptions" to the doctrine, because they have focused too literally on the exact words in which the guiding idea of the common fund doctrine was expressed in prior opinions.) One extension is the "substantial benefit" doctrine, under which a court might order a corporation to pay a derivative suit plaintiff his attorney's fees, even though the suit did not produce a monetary recovery or "fund" for the corporation, because the plaintiff did succeed in producing some other kind of "substantial benefit" to the corporation. Benefits that have been considered substantial for this purpose include a major change in the corporation's power structure, designed to reduce the risk of questionable transactions by the previously dominant personality,[1] a determination that a purported election of directors and a proposed bylaw amendment were illegal,[2] and a determination that a proxy statement is-

Substantial benefit doctrine

§15.8 [1]Fletcher v. A.J. Indus., Inc., 72 Cal. Rptr. 146 (Ct. App. 1968).

[2]Bosch v. Meeker Cooperative Light & Power Assn., 101 N.W.2d 423 (Minn. 1960).

sued by the corporation was materially misleading to minority shareholders in violation of Section 14(a) of the Securities Exchange Act.[3] Not all courts are receptive to the substantial benefit analysis, however, and it is unclear how far courts would go with the idea.

Threatened litigation

A second extension concerns benefits produced by the threat of litigation rather than by actual litigation. At least in the context of Section 16(b) of the Securities Exchange Act, the shareholder may recover attorney fees in such a situation. In *Blau v. Rayette-Faberge, Inc.*,[4] for example, the shareholder employed an attorney to discover (by reading Section 16(a) reports on file with the SEC) whether the corporation was entitled to recover short-swing profits under the mechanical rule of Section 16(b). After discovering a violation, as to which about three-fourths of the statute of limitations had run, the attorney asked the corporation to institute suit against the offending officer, and stated that his client would sue derivatively if the corporation did not commence action or receive payment within 60 days. When the 60 days were almost up, the corporation told the attorney that the officer had agreed to pay. The Second Circuit, inferring that under the circumstances the activities of the plaintiff and the plaintiff's attorney were important in causing the corporate recovery, ordered an award of attorney's fees. Important to the result was the fact that it was fairly clear that the corporation would not have acted on its own. Thus, if a shareholder's attorney wrote a letter to the corporation's board of directors immediately after a Section 16(a) report indicating a violation had been filed, it is unlikely that a court would award fees.

Note too that causation problems can arise even when a plaintiff has actually instituted a derivative suit. For instance, suppose a plaintiff shareholder brings a derivative suit against a corporation's management for various breaches of duty, and while it is pending a regulatory agency that doesn't know about the suit (or isn't acting because of such knowledge) discovers the same violations and has them corrected. The corporation could argue that plaintiff was not the proximate cause of the benefit to itself, and so should not recover his litigation expenses.

Court approval of fee amounts

When fees are awarded, their amount must be determined or approved by the court. Courts often profess that in awarding fees to plaintiffs' attorneys they do not simply apply some standardized percentage to the amount recovered by the corporation, but look instead at a wide range of relevant factors. Nevertheless, surveys of fees actually awarded in stockholders' derivative and class actions show that they cluster around 20

[3] Mills v. Electric Auto-Lite Co., 396 U.S. 375 (1970).
[4] 389 F.2d 469 (2d Cir. 1968).

percent.[5] In addition to the amount of recovery and other benefits to the corporation, courts consider the hours reasonably spent on the case by plaintiffs' attorneys, the contingent nature of the lawsuit (that is, courts do allow plaintiffs' attorneys some "risk premium" to reflect the fact that they cannot win all the derivative suits they bring on a contingent fee basis), the skill and reputation of counsel, and the novelty and complexity of the issues in the case.[6]

§15.9 Characterization of Suits

The question What determines when a shareholder's suit should be brought derivatively, and when it should be brought directly by the individual shareholder or on behalf of a class of shareholders? The question is important because of the special procedural requirements that apply to derivative suits. In a borderline case plaintiffs may prefer to have their suit characterized as direct rather than derivative.

A formal answer A formal answer to this question is that a derivative suit is called for when the wrong complained of primarily constituted an injury to the corporation, whereas a direct suit is appropriate when the injury was primarily to the shareholder(s) as such. But to get a sense of the operational meaning of this abstract proposition, one must look at a fair number of specific cases.

Kinds of direct suits The following kinds of suits are usually classified as direct: a suit by a shareholder to enforce her rights to inspect the corporation's books and records, to enforce voting rights, to enforce preemptive rights,[1] to compel the declaration of dividends,[2] to enforce rights of redemption, to have the

[5]See Cole, Counsel Fees in Stockholders' Derivative and Class Actions — Hornstein Revisited, 6 U. Rich. L. Rev. 259, 283-285 (1972). A subsequent, detailed study of over 100 cases, mostly between 1960 and 1977, is described in Mowrey, Attorney Fees in Securities Class Action and Derivative Suits, 3 J. Corp. Law 267 (1978).

[6]See, e.g., Newmark v. RKO General, Inc., 332 F. Supp. 161 (S.D.N.Y. 1971).

§15.9 [1]See subsection 17.1.4.

[2]This one is more subtle than courts seem to realize. Generally, the board of directors has discretion whether or not to declare and pay dividends. In exercising their discretion they are supposed to determine which payout policy is in the best interests of the corporation and its shareholders, that is, maximizes shareholder wealth. This is a difficult financial decision, both in theory and in practice. Their decision is ordinarily protected by the business judgment rule, but the latter can be overcome when the directors' decision was tainted by "bad faith," self-dealing, or other improper conduct. Accordingly, a shareholder's suit to compel dividends can reasonably be looked at as a challenge to the board's decision about the corporation's optimal financial policy and, therefore, as derivative in nature. See, e.g., Gordon v. Elliman, 119 N.E.2d 331 (N.Y. 1954). Most courts, however, have focused on the fact that a successful

corporation dissolved and liquidated, and against the managers for having defrauded the shareholder into buying or selling shares. Sometimes these direct suits can be brought as class actions. One defrauded selling shareholder, for example, may sue on behalf of all similarly situated shareholders.

Kinds of derivative suits

The kinds of suits that are derivative in nature include most cases based on breach of the fiduciary duties of care and loyalty. These include, for example, suits based on gross negligence, waste of corporate assets, basic self-dealing, excessive compensation, or usurpation of a corporate opportunity. Perhaps the most interesting twist in the case law occurs when the plaintiff seems really to be concerned about some such violation of duty, but wants to bring a suit that will be classified as direct so he can avoid the security-for-expenses statute.

Example of derivative-direct transformation

Consider an example of how such a transformation of the cause of action may come about. A corporation bought property owned by its majority shareholder. The shareholders, including the majority shareholder, voted to approve the deal; a majority of the outstanding shares were cast in favor of it. But plaintiff thinks the price paid was excessive and sues to rescind. He alleges not that there was unfair self-dealing (a derivative injury), but that his *voting rights* were impaired (a direct injury)! How so? Because, he alleges, the majority shareholder should not have voted on the transaction, and if he had abstained the resolution would have been defeated. Had there been abstention, therefore, plaintiff's voting rights would have carried more weight. A court basically unsympathetic to security-for-expenses statutes might well accept this theory.[3]

Now from defendant's side

Now consider a move by a defendant to partially transform a derivative suit into something more individual. Defendant directors were paid excessive salaries, although a large number of shareholders had voted to ratify the directors' actions in setting the salaries. Minority shareholders brought a derivative suit and succeeded in having the directors' actions declared a fraud on the corporation. The defendants, attempting to limit their damages, argue that damages should be paid only to the shareholders who didn't vote to ratify, and in proportion to their interest in the corporation.

---

recovery in such a suit (that is, the mandated dividends) will go into the pockets of the shareholders, not into the corporate fisc. Accordingly, they view the suit as clearly direct in nature. Incidentally, the New York legislature reversed the *Gordon* case by describing a derivative suit as one brought in the right of a corporation to procure a judgment "in its favor." N.Y. §626.

[3]Reifsnyder v. Pittsburgh Outdoor Advertising Co., 173 A.2d 319 (Pa. 1961). See also Eisenberg v. Flying Tiger Line, Inc., 451 F.2d 267 (2d Cir. 1971), which involved a similar plaintiff's gambit.

(Thus, for example, if the excessive amount of compensation were $10 million, and 20 percent of the shareholders had not voted to ratify, the defendants would only have to pay $2 million.) In a case similar to this, the Delaware Supreme Court held against individual recovery, even though it realized that there can be special circumstances in which individual recovery might be appropriate even in a derivative action.[4] The court may well have thought that the ratifying shareholders should not be penalized for their consent to the wrong, because in such cases (shareholder approval of executive compensation arrangements) the public shareholders are simply not an appropriate, well-informed decision making body.

§15.10 *Indemnification and Liability Insurance*

Conflicting extreme views

Occasionally, critics of the modern corporation complain that liberal indemnification statutes and plentiful directors' and officers' liability insurance (hereafter, D&O insurance) are major reasons why directors do not police management more vigorously and effectively. Some even think that reform in these areas would greatly improve the working of the corporate system. At the same time, some businessmen complain about being exposed to crushing liability for "honest" mistakes of judgment. Which view is right?

The moderate reality

Neither view is really on the mark. It is true that a large majority of public corporations have come to acquire sizable D&O policies. But neither the policies nor the indemnification statutes provide certain assistance to directors or officers guilty of serious managerial misconduct. They do provide a fair measure of protection, however, for directors who negligently fail (or "honestly negligently" fail) to monitor and respond to managerial miscreants, but such protection makes sense as a policy matter. This is not to say that the indemnification statutes and D&O policies are optimal; there are various features in them that can be criticized. Yet major improvement in the monitoring of managerial conduct is unlikely to come from reforms in this area.

Plan of this section

To show these points, I will assess the coverage that is and is not af-

[4] Keenan v. Eshleman, 2 A.2d 904 (Del. 1938). Special circumstances justifying individual recovery may exist when the corporation is in liquidation (there's no point, then, in giving money to the corporation), when defendants sold stock for an unlawful premium that if recovered by the corporation would largely benefit the buyers of control, or when the wrongdoers are themselves substantial shareholders. Usually, though, bypassing the corporation is disfavored because it (1) impairs the directors' normal discretion as to whether to pay dividends and (2) may increase risks to creditors.

forded the corporation, its directors, and its officers by D&O insurance. I will also compare the insurance coverage with the coverage of some representative indemnification statutes. The particular insurance policy form that I will refer to is a variant of the Lloyd's D&O policy form that is widely copied and used in the D&O market.[1] The particular indemnification laws selected for purposes of comparison are Section 145 of the Delaware Corporation Law,[2] and, because of their importance and distinctiveness, the New York and California statutes.[3]

Directors and officers of corporations are in fact sued for many kinds of alleged wrongs. However, to understand the basic principles of indemnification and insurance it is better to focus in the first instance on the rather formalistic categories of third party suits and suits brought by or in the right of the corporation. (For the most part, this second category means derivative suits.)

§15.10.1 Third Party Suits

Hypo for analysis

Suppose that a major customer of Cruncher Corporation, which makes and sells accounting software for businesses, sues Bluster, a marketing vice president and a director of Cruncher, for negligently representing that the customer's needs would be met by certain software that turned out to be woefully inadequate. Suppose also that a shareholder of Cruncher sues Slye, the president and also a director, for intentionally misstating the degree of readiness for commercial distribution of certain key software packages being developed by Cruncher, with the result that the shareholder rescinded an order to his broker to sell his Cruncher stock and later suffered losses when the stock price declined. Note that both of these actions are third party suits, not suits on behalf of the corporation. One is based on negligence; the other on fraud. The three obvious possibilities in either suit are that the defendant officer will win, lose, or settle. Consider each possibility in turn.

Indemnification if defendants win

Suppose Bluster and Slye win their suits. Each obtains a final judgment in his favor. Each has incurred $80,000 in legal fees. Clearly, the corporation may indemnify them for their reasonable costs and expenses, including reasonable attorney's fees. Indeed, under the statutes they have a right

§15.10 [1] Lloyd's Directors' and Officers' Liability Insurance Form "Lydando No. 1," reprinted in J. Bishop Jr., The Law of Corporate Officers and Directors (1980), at App.-71 to App.-85 (hereafter cited as Lloyd's Policy).

[2] This is similar to MBCA §§8.50-8.58.

[3] N.Y. §§721-727; Cal. §317.

to indemnification.[4] In Delaware and New York, they have the right if they were successful "on the merits or otherwise," but in California they must have been successful "on the merits."[5] Thus, under the California statute, if Bluster won because of a procedural misstep by his plaintiff, he might not be indemnified as of right for his legal fees. (The corporation might choose to indemnify him, however.)

What insurance adds

What would a D&O policy do in this situation? Under it, the insurer would pay the corporation, up to the policy limit, for the amount ($160,000) it is obligated to pay to the two successful officers as indemnification.[6] In this context the policy simply adds the financial capacity of the insurer to that of Cruncher Corporation, which may be insolvent or financially pressed when called on to give indemnity.

Indemnification when defendants lose or settle?

Now suppose the officers lose or settle their third party civil suits. Bluster loses the negligence action and is ordered to pay plaintiff $1 million in damages. Slye settles the fraud action for $100,000. Each, as before, also incurs legal fees of $80,000. The consequences are less simple. Generally, as far as corporate law itself (as opposed to other bodies of law) is concerned, Cruncher Corporation has the power, though not a duty,[7] to indemnify the two officers for both their legal (and other) expenses and the amounts payable under the judgment or settlement agreement *under certain conditions.* The principal condition is that the officer to be indemnified must be determined by some statutorily specified person or entity to have met a specified standard of conduct.

Standard of indemnifiable conduct

Under the New York and California statutes, the standard of conduct is that the officer must have acted, with respect to the matter giving rise to the lawsuit, (a) in good faith and (b) for a purpose or in a manner that he reasonably believed to be in the best interests of the corporation.[8] Delaware's standard is similar, except that in part (b) it is enough if the officer acted in a manner "in or not opposed to the best interests of the corporation,"[9] a phrase that has received various interpretations by commentators.[10]

[4] Del. §145(c); N.Y. §724(a); Cal. §317(d).

[5] See provisions cited in preceding note.

[6] See Lloyd's Policy, clause 1(B); see also definitions in clauses 2(A) (DIRECTOR or OFFICER), 2(E) (Loss), 2(F) (Wrongful Act).

[7] But note that the corporation may have a duty to indemnify in these situations if it has entered into a contract with the officer to indemnify him and if the governing statute is interpreted to allow such contracts.

[8] N.Y. §723(a); Cal. §317(b).

[9] Del. §145(a).

[10] According to one source, Richard Corroon, a member of the Delaware Law Revision

Application to hypo

It should be easy for Bluster to satisfy these requirements. Though he was judged to be negligent, he probably acted in good faith and for Cruncher's interests when he misstated the fitness of the software for the customer's purpose. But Slye will have a harder task. An officer who engaged in intentional misstatement may have acted within the scope of his authority and for what he thought was the corporation's best interest, but did he act in good faith? One would assume that intentional misconduct of this sort implies bad faith as a matter of definition. Slye's argument has to be that he did not engage in deliberate fraud at all. He will be helped by the fact that because he settled, there has been no adjudication that he behaved fraudulently. (If Slye had lost the fraud suit on the merits, getting indemnification of his expenses and the damages he must pay would be very hard indeed.)

***Who* applies the standard**

Obviously, the question of *who makes the determination* as to whether Bluster and Slye satisfied the statutory standard of indemnifiable conduct will be very important. The statutes differ on this crucial point.

Delaware, the most liberal, allows the determination to be made by the board of directors (if there is a quorum of directors who are not themselves parties to the action), by the stockholders, or, most comfortingly and most commonly, by independent legal counsel.[11] New York's provision is somewhat similar, except that the officer apparently cannot resort to independent legal counsel if the directors who are not themselves parties to the action make up a quorum. The statute's wording suggests that if such directors do make a quorum, they, if anyone, should make the determination.[12] This provision obviously puts the uninvolved directors in a difficult position. They would often like, if possible, to pass the buck to an outside law firm. California, in a burst of realism — or, if you will, cynicism — would allow the saving benediction to be uttered by the unsued directors,

---

Commission who had been given responsibility for drafting the indemnification provision but whose draft had not included the "not opposed to" phrase, the provision was added to reach good-faith takings of corporate opportunities. Others, such as S. Samuel Arsht and Orvel Sebring, thought the phrase was included to cover the case where a director is engaged in a purely personal transaction, such as trading in the company's stock. See Comment, Law for Sale: A Study of the Delaware Corporation Law of 1967, 117 U. Pa. L. Rev. 861, 878-879 (1969). But see Bishop, New Problems in Indemnifying and Insuring Directors: Protection against Liability Under the Federal Securities Laws, 1972 Duke L.J. 1153, 1161-1166 (expressing reservations about the Delaware act's applicability to litigation based on federal securities laws).

[11] Del. §145(d).

[12] N.Y. §724(b). It is not clear, however, whether New York courts would insist on this interpretation. As for when legal counsel is independent, see Schmidt v. Magnetic Head Corp., 468 N.Y.S.2d 649 (App. Div. 1983).

by the stockholders, or by the court that heard the lawsuit, but not by independent legal counsel.[13]

Role of insurance

Once again, let's consider the role of insurance. Would D&O insurance make it substantially easier for Bluster to get reimbursed for his $80,000 expenses and his $1 million obligation under the judgment? For Slye to get reimbursed for his $80,000 of expenses and the $100,000 he owes under the settlement agreement? Generally it would, for several reasons.

Financial back-ups

First, there is the obvious point that in some cases the insurer's financial ability or its willingness to pay the officers' losses will be greater than that of the corporation. Remember that Cruncher may have the power but not a duty to indemnify, whereas the insurer may be contractually bound.

Coverage of some nonindemnifiable expenses allowed

Second, it is permissible under many statutes to insure expenses and payments that could not be indemnified. When that is so, the director or officer who is insured may not have to pass (or even submit to the application of) the statutory test of conduct that must be met before indemnification is allowed. Thus, to be reimbursed by the insurer, Bluster and Slye would not have to seek and get the formal blessing of disinterested directors, shareholders, independent counsel, or a court, as to their good faith and the corporate orientation of their conduct. As indicated, not having to pass this test of conduct could be a real boon in California. (Of course, Bluster and Slye do have to hope that the *insurer* judges the claims against them to be covered by the policy.)

Specifically, Delaware and California authorize their corporations to purchase insurance to cover liabilities incurred by their directors, officers, and agents and arising out of their status, whether or not the corporation could indemnify for the liabilities.[14] On the other hand, New York's statute forbids the corporation's purchase of D&O insurance for nonindemnifiable liabilities unless the insurance policy provides for a deductible and for coinsurance in a manner acceptable to the New York Superintendent of Insurance.[15] The idea is obviously to make the individual director or officer feel some of the sting in the case where indemnification was not possible.

And promised by policies

A third consideration in favor of D&O insurance relates not to what insurance is legally permissible but to what policies actually are available. The typical D&O policy is not restricted to indemnifiable liabilities of the directors and officers. It combines two contracts: (1) a promise by the insurer to the directors and officers to pay for their losses (as defined) arising out of claims made on account of their wrongful acts (as defined),

[13] Cal. §317(e).
[14] Del. §145(g); Cal. §317(i).
[15] N.Y. §727(a)(3).

and (2) a promise by the insurer to the corporation to cover its indemnification payments to the directors and officers.[16] In clause 1 there is no qualification that the insurer will pay only losses for which the corporation could indemnify the promisees.

But see policy definitions

Of course, the insurance policy's definition of insured wrongful acts may or may not cover particular conduct of the director or officer, and the policy's exclusions may not be applicable. These provisions must be studied carefully. Our sample policy form defines *wrongful act* to mean

> . . . any actual or alleged breach of duty, neglect or error by or accountability of the directors and officers as directors and officers or any actual or alleged misstatement, misleading statement or other act or omission by the directors or officers in their respective capacities as directors or officers.[17]

And exclusions

This language would appear to cover the misstatements of Bluster and Slye. But the inquiry is not over. We must look at the exceptions and exclusions in the policy too.

Five common exclusions. The thrust of most of the policy exclusions is to preclude insurance in self-dealing situations. The exclusions therefore are more relevant to derivative suits than to third party suits. However, some of the exclusions will bear on third party suits, such as those alleging a fraud. Under the usual exclusions[18] the insurer is not liable for losses arising from certain claims made against the directors or officers: (1) a claim based on their gaining a personal profit or advantage to which they were not legally entitled, (2) a claim based on their having acted dishonestly or acted in bad faith with knowledge or reasonable cause to believe that their action violated the law (including the rights of others), (3) a claim for return of illegal remuneration, (4) a claim for libel or slander, and (5) various other special claims based, for example, on certain kinds of pollution or on the federal pension law (ERISA). These exclusions may eliminate insurance for a very large proportion of the lawsuits successfully brought against directors and officers, but it is hard to see how a reasonably honest director or officer could complain about them.

Application to hypo

In our hypothetical the second exclusion listed above means that Slye (but not Bluster) may have trouble getting reimbursed by the insurer; if Cruncher has already indemnified Slye, it may also have trouble. True,

[16] Lloyd's Policy, clauses 1(A) & 1(B).
[17] Id., clause 1(F). Words in all capital letters in the policy have been lower-cased here.
[18] Id., clause 4. The listing in the text reorders them.

Slye was not adjudicated to have been fraudulent, but the claim against him was *based* on his alleged dishonesty, and therefore the insurer may claim that it is not obligated to reimburse. In practice, insurers often make their own decisions as to whether someone like Slye (or his indemnifying company) deserves to be reimbursed. If the insurer and insured disagree, as often happens, they may settle on a compromise payment. (Note too that a large part of the practical game under both indemnification and insurance is to get advance payments, that is, payment of the officers' legal fees as they accrue, not just at the resolution of the suit. If the insurer has been persuaded to make advances, it will rarely try to get them back when the suit is finally settled, on the ground that the policy didn't cover the expenses, but it may resist additional payments at that point.)

Fines, penalties, and punitive damages. So far this discussion has centered on third party civil suits. Administrative and criminal proceedings that seek to impose fines and penalties add one major twist: D&O policies generally do not cover fines and penalties.[19] This is partly a matter of the insurer's own self-interest. Fines and penalties are usually a consequence of intentional misconduct, and the insurer does not want to give the insureds a blank check to finance their intentional wrongdoing. The lack of coverage also reflects a public policy determination that it should not be possible to insure against legal liabilities whose major purpose is to deter wrongdoers rather than to compensate injured parties. In this latter connection, it should be noted that D&O policies explicitly remind the insureds that they are not insuring matters deemed uninsurable under applicable law.[20] Many courts would probably decide that punitive damages in civil suits are uninsurable. Some might even hold — wrongly, I think — that all damages, compensatory or punitive, in a suit based on intentional wrongdoing, are uninsurable.[21]

[19] Id., clause 2(E)(i) & (ii). The exclusion is absolute for fines and penalties in criminal actions. Other fines and penalties, as well as punitive damages, are excluded if they are deemed uninsurable under the law governing the policy.

[20] Id., clause 2(E)(iii).

[21] Northwestern Natl. Cas. Co. v. McNulty, 307 F.2d 432 (5th Cir. 1962), is sometimes cited for the proposition that it is against public policy to provide insurance coverage for willful, wanton, and reckless conduct. In that case, however, the insurer had paid compensatory damages to an injured party under an automobile liability policy; the only issue was whether the policy also covered punitive damages. Generally, in insurance law it is recognized that certain policies may cover liability for injuries sustained by a third person (as contrasted to one's own property) as a result of willful, wanton or reckless conduct. See 12 Couch on Insurance §45.35 (2d ed. 1964).

In my view, the question of insurability is not one that can be answered by a simple black

At first glance, indemnification looks better than insurance for proceedings that result in fines, penalities, or punitive damages. The corporate statutes generally permit indemnification for fines and penalties if certain standards of conduct are determined to have been met — such as good faith, action in what was thought to be the corporation's best interests, and not having reasonable cause to believe that one's conduct was unlawful.[22]

Indemnification statutes look better here

However, two very important caveats should be noted. First, a court might decide that federal policy as expressed, for example, in the federal securities laws, antitrust laws, or the pension reform law, will be deemed frustrated if certain damages can be indemnified. If so, the federal policy would preempt state law and impose a limit on the state indemnification statutes. Second, a court might even decide that certain state policies, as expressed in the state's particular criminal and regulatory statutes, would be frustated if indemnification of the particular fines and penalties in question were permitted. The corporate statutes, after all, deal with the general question of corporate power to indemnify, not with the question whether the deterrence objective of particular statutes would be defeated if the impact of penalties can be shifted from wrongdoing individuals to the corporation that employs them.

But may be preempted

§15.10.2 Derivative Suits

Now consider actions against officers that are by or in the right of the corporation. Suppose, for example, that a shareholder of Cruncher brings a derivative action against Bumbler, a senior vice-president, for negligently wasting corporate assets. Another shareholder brings a derivative action against Siphon, Cruncher's chairman of the board, for selling it computer equipment at a grossly inflated price. Roughly speaking, D&O insurance

New hypo

---

and white rule of universal validity. Certainly, the dividing line is not between intentional wrongdoing and other kinds of wrongdoing. A dividing line based on the distinction between compensatory damages and punitive damages does much better. Since the former are given primarily to compensate plaintiffs, insurance would seem to be positively desirable. Since the latter are aimed at deterrence, insurance would seem to be against public policy. However, if one looks behind labels, the distinction is not so neat in practice. Damages given in some kinds of lawsuits may be nominally compensatory, yet much of the award may go to plaintiffs' attorneys, and statutes or courts may in fact be aiming primarily to encourage them to act as private attorneys-general so that other, potential defendants will be deterred. Fines imposed on individuals under certain laws arguably might serve their purpose just as well if the cost were shifted to an insurer or an employing corporation (via indemnification or purchase of insurance for the individual), since either type of entity might, in some circumstances, be able to control the individual's conduct.

[22] Del. §145(a); N.Y. §723(a); Cal. §317(b).

would cover expenses and payments in Bumbler's case (errors and omissions) but not in Siphon's case (self-dealing). This is usually an advantage over indemnification.

Indemnification of expenses restricted

The New York statute, for example, forbids indemnification of any expenses in a derivative suit, even one based on negligence, if the officer is adjudged to have breached his duty to the corporation.[23] Thus, if either Bumbler or Siphon lost his case on the merits, he could not be indemnified under this statute for his legal expenses, let alone for amounts payable under the adverse judgment itself.

Judgment and settlement amounts not indemnified

In no event does the New York statute (or the California statute) permit amounts payable *to the corporation* under an adverse judgment or under a settlement agreement to be indemnified.[24] The interpretation of the Delaware statute is more complicated, but its basic rule is similar.[25] Obviously, to determine that Siphon is liable to his corporation for, say, $2 million because of harm he did to it and then to allow Cruncher to reimburse him for paying over the $2 million, would be something only appropriate in Wonderland. The same would be true of a judgment against Bumbler.

Sometimes covered by insurance

By contrast, if Bumbler is adjudged liable to the corporation for, say, $1 million in damages or agrees to settle the derivative suit for $500,000, the amount he thus becomes liable for (plus his expenses) could be covered by insurance, even though it was purchased by the corporation.

Virtues of insurance

This fact may prompt critics to argue that the laws are defective in allowing wrongdoing insiders to be made whole for the losses they cause their corporations. The argument is not a strong one, however. Insurance has two special virtues. First, insurance, unlike indemnification, spreads the risk of losses due to negligent directors and officers like Bumbler among all insured corporations rather than leaving it on the particular corporations actually harmed by them. Second, insurance, as compared to a bare claim against an individual officer (who may be judgment-

[23] N.Y. §722(a). Expenses also cannot be reimbursed in an action settled without court approval. N.Y. §722(b)(2). Compare Del. §145(b): it is similar to N.Y. §722(a), but the court may grant indemnity for expenses to which the officer is "fairly and reasonably entitled" despite adjudication of liability. See also Cal. §317(c)(1) (same as Delaware).

[24] N.Y. §722(b)(1); see also Cal. §317(c)(2).

[25] Unlike Del. §145(a), which deals with third party suits, Del. §145(b), which deals with derivative suits, does not authorize indemnity for "amounts paid in settlement." Rather, it authorizes indemnification of "expenses" — counsel fees, mostly — in derivative actions, subject to certain conditions. However, the tantalizing language of Del. §145(f), which declares the indemnification statute nonexclusive, conceivably might be construed to permit indemnity of amounts paid in settlement if previously agreed to by the corporation and the individual.

proof), also makes it more likely that an injured corporation will in fact be compensated.

Irrelevant who buys it

Notice, too, that no one could properly object to letting the individual director or officer buy his own insurance for the kinds of liabilities covered by the typical D&O policy, and, moreover, it would be practically impossible to forbid the corporation's reimbursing him, in one way or another, for the premiums. If both points are true, it would be pointless to prohibit the corporaton from purchasing the insurance.

Policies don't cover self-dealing

But the key fact in assessing the social desirability of D&O insurance may be that actual policies do not cover self-dealing. Siphon could not get the insurer to reimburse him for amounts he owed Cruncher pursuant to an adverse judgment in the derivative suit against him, nor could he get reimbursed for his attorney's fees. If Siphon settles the suit, the interpretation of the D&O policy becomes more arguable, as in Slye's case. The policy, as noted above, excludes losses arising out of claims "based upon or attributable to" self-dealing. Nevertheless, he *might* prevail upon the insurer to pay him something. In cases of negligent misbehavior, D&O policies cover judgments as well as settlement amounts but that seems positively desirable, for the reasons mentioned in the last two paragraphs.

Settlement problem

This last point may tempt you to skepticism about the value of D&O insurance for protection against derivative suits. As we have noted before (in section 3.4), successfully litigated suits against directors and officers that impose liability for mere negligence are rare.[26]

§15.10.3 The Value of D&O Insurance?

It may be helpful to summarize the preceeding discussion by asking, "Given the existence of indemnification statutes, on the one hand, and policy limits and exclusions, on the other, what if anything is added by D&O insurance? Why should anyone buy it?"

Advantage to corporation

From the point of view of the corporation, the advantages of D&O insurance are twofold. First, the corporation will obtain protection against having to pay out as indemnification more than it considers prudent in any given year. Second, the insurance may enable the corporation to obtain

[26] It should be pointed out, however, that malpractice lawsuits against *lawyers* because of their errors or negligence are fairly frequent. Often, the lawyer successfully sued for malpractice has let a statute of limitations run against a client, or neglected to make a promised title search — from overwork, no doubt — or has engaged in some other form of simple, but insurable, sloppiness. Accordingly, the lawyer employed by a corporation would do well to make sure that he is covered by its D&O policy or, if that is not feasible, to get his own malpractice insurance — known in polite circles as lawyer's professional liability insurance.

better directors and officers. Many persons will flatly refuse to consider serving as directors of a large corporation unless it carries substantial liability insurance.

Advantages to manager

From the point of view of the director or officer of the corporation, the advantages of D&O insurance are fairly numerous. First, the insurance enables payment to be made to him when the corporation would be legally able but financially unable or unwilling to indemnify him. Second, it will enable him to be covered when his conduct might not be determined by the appropriate person or entity to have met the statutory tests for indemnification but was nevertheless of such a kind as not to be uninsurable. Third, in some instances insurance, unlike indemnification, will enable him to provide for payments under adverse judgments or settlement agreements. Fourth, D&O insurance, by its very presence, may expedite the resolution of threatened or actual litigation against the individual director or officer.

Other considerations

Obviously, none of these considerations dictates the purchase of insurance. Before making a purchase the representatives of the corporation must also consider the costs of the insurance, the likelihood of lawsuits, the degree of cooperation that can be expected of a particular insurer once a claim has been made, and the fact that many of the most suable activities of directors and officers — namely, those involving variations on the theme of self-dealing — are not covered by insurance. But when these factors are taken into account, the decision to purchase insurance will often appear inevitable.[27]

[27] A good extended treatment of indemnification and insurance is J. Bishop, Jr., note 1 supra.

CHAPTER 16

THE MEANING OF CORPORATE PERSONALITY

§16.1 Introduction

Ultra vires problem

The fact that the law conceives corporations to be legal persons with certain powers and purposes raises many interesting problems. For example, what happens when a corporation acts in a way that goes beyond the powers given to it by the governing corporate statute and articles of incorporation? This is the so-called *ultra vires* problem. In the United States, it is now a problem that is largely of historical interest. Early corporate statutes expressly granted only limited powers to corporations and allowed them to engage only in certain specified lines of business. A corporation that gave a guarantee of another person's debts, tried to own stock in another corporation, tried to repurchase its own stock, or entered a contract involving business activities not in the line of business specified in its charter, might find these actions declared beyond its powers. The difficulty of then sorting out the rights, if any, of third parties with whom the corporation had contracted beyond its powers gave rise to a significant body of case law. Guidelines for these situations were eventually put into statutes.[1] Modern statutes have also caused the underlying problem to fade away by granting corporations legal powers almost coextensive with those of natural persons[2] and by allowing them to engage in any lawful line or lines of business.[3]

Application of criminal law

Another major set of problems arising from corporate personality has concerned the law's attempts to define criminal conduct by corporations and to impose criminal sanctions in the most effective way. Obviously, there is a problem in deciding when a corporation might be deemed to have had a criminal intent. Equally obviously, corporations as such cannot be put in jail. Criminal sanctions for misconduct by corporate agents must be imposed in other ways. Determining the best way is very difficult.[4]

Constitutional issues

A related kind of problem is the extent to which constitutional provisions protecting or binding persons should be interpreted to include corporations.[5]

Social responsibility issues

This book does not deal with the three kinds of problems just mentioned. However, this chapter does deal with a very large and sprawling group of topics that have to do with the proper role or purpose of corporations in society. These topics are sometimes placed under the headings of "corporate social responsibility" or "corporate governance." More precisely, this chapter discusses the business corporation's role with respect to objectives traditionally thought to be the responsibility of governmental units. My focus is on actual and possible legal norms that define what the purposes of a business corporation are. I first examine some major conceptions of the corporation's role and what can be said for and against each of them. In the second part of the chapter I suggest a different analytical approach to the concerns that underlie these traditional debates.

§16.1 [1]See, e.g., MBCA §3.04.

[2]See, e.g., MBCA §3.02.

[3]See, e.g., MBCA §3.01.

[4]See generally Coffee, "No Soul to Damn: No Body to Kick": An Unscandalized Inquiry into the Problem of Corporate Punishment, 79 Mich. L. Rev. 386 (1981); Fisse, Reconstructing Corporate Criminal Law: Deterrence, Retribution, Fault, and Sanctions, 56 S. Cal. L. Rev. 1141 (1983); Stone, The Place of Enterprise Liability in the Control of Corporate Conduct, 90 Yale L.J. 1 (1980).

[5]See, e.g., Note, Constitutional Rights of the Corporate Person, 91 Yale L.J. 1641 (1982).

§16.2 *Views About the Corporation's Proper Role*

Five ideal types

I discern five major clusters of views concerning the corporation's proper role in relation to governmental tasks. For ease of analysis and reference, I present these views as ideal types and give them labels usually applied to major strands of thought in philosophy: dualism, monism, modest idealism, high idealism, and pragmatism. In each case, I will first present a statement of the view, describe its legal status, and then consider reasons for the viewpoint and objections to it.

Legislator's concern with corporation's role

Before examining these views, I should point out the limited, special sense in which they are about "the corporation's role." In a larger sense, the corporation's role in society depends on one's social philosophy. For example, if you are a utilitarian, as many people seem to be, you will see the corporation's role as being to aid in maximizing total welfare or happiness. You would not accept assertions that the corporation's sole purpose is to maximize profits for shareholders, gains to consumers, or the welfare of any special group. As a utilitarian legislator, you would insist on considering the net effects of the corporation on all affected groups of people. If corporations are generally maximizing the welfare of their consumers but harming other groups, for example, you would want to know whether there is a way to rearrange things so as to increase the surplus of benefits over harms.

Vs. manager's concern

But there is also a more limited sense in which the phrase "the corporation's role" is meant: as a shorthand way of referring to the affirmative, open-ended goals that a particular corporation's ultimate decision making group should try to pursue. (In our current system, this decision making group consists of the corporation's "managers" — its directors and officers). Granted that these decision makers should cause the corporation to abide by specific legal duties imposed by lawmakers (who have, let us hope, taken a fully comprehensive look at all affected interests), how should they conceive their *residual* duty? Should they adopt the legislator's stance, or some other? These are the questions to which the following views relate.

§16.2.1 Dualism: the Norm of Strict Profit Maximization

Profit maximization norm

Statement. The dualist, who is also the traditionalist, regards the private and public spheres as having distinct functions that ought to be kept distinct. Accordingly, from the traditional legal viewpoint, a corporation's directors and officers have a fiduciary duty to maximize shareholder wealth, subject to numerous duties to meet specific obligations to other groups affected by the corporation.

Not just short-run profits

Several comments about this norm are needed to forestall some common misunderstandings. First, under appropriate conditions and definitions, different formulations of the thing to be maximized — "profits," the company's net present value," "the market value of the company's common shares," and "shareholder wealth" — turn out to be equivalent to one another. Similarly, the profit-maximizing norm does *not* imply a commitment to short-run profits at the expense of long-run profits. All intelligent formulations of the norm, such as the "net present value" or "stock market value" ones, implicitly assume that a wealth-maximizing balance should be struck between long- and short-run profits. In any event, for my purposes most of the alleged differences in formulations can be ignored.

Many obligations to nonshareholders

Second, the profit-maximizing norm does *not* imply that corporations and their managers have only minimal legal obligations to persons other than shareholders. Quite the contrary is true. Every major relationship between the corporation and persons or groups it affects is subject to vast and intricate bodies of legal doctrine and to legal enforcement mechanisms. These legal controls are ineffective in some instances and suboptimal in others, but they exist. (A brief outline of this maze of legal controls was given in section 1.4. It would be useful to review it at this point.) Corporations owe many contractual, common law, and statutory duties to their customers, suppliers, creditors, employees, and to the environment, the general public, and numerous governmental entities.

Theory concerns residual goal

If the legal system as a whole imposes so many duties to so many constituencies and thus mandates a wide-ranging (though perhaps inadequate and not ultimately coherent) accommodation of diverse interests, what, if anything, is the real meaning of the profit-maximizing norm? The answer is that it tells corporate managers what their *residual* goal is — or, in economic jargon, what the company's "objective function" is. The duties to all other groups need simply be satisfied — they function as constraints — but the duty to shareholders is open-ended: Profits should be made as large as possible, within the constraints.

Background assumption

Legal status. Perhaps surprisingly, the state business corporation statutes under which corporations are chartered generally do not say explicitly that the purpose of a business corporation is to make or maximize profits. When the statutes do refer to the corporation's purposes, they usually mean its lines of business. The general profit-maximizing purpose has nearly always been assumed by courts and lawyers, however, and legal authorities sometimes state and use the general purpose as a basis of decision. In the famous case of *Dodge v. Ford Motor Co.*,[1] for example, the Michigan Supreme Court viewed as "bad faith" and a breach of fiduciary duty Henry Ford's use of his power to withhold corporate dividends, over the objection of minority shareholders, in order to be able to sell cars more cheaply and benefit the American public at the expense of corporate profits. The court told Mr. Ford that the corporation was not an eleemosynary institution and that, though his objective was laudable, he should not be generous with other people's money. In addition, the statutory[2] and case law[3] formulations of the directors' and officers' duty of care can easily be read to imply profit maximization as the ultimate goal.

Double-sided argument

Rationale. Perhaps the most notable justification of the strict profit-maximizing goal was Milton Friedman's essay entitled The Social Responsibility of Business Is to Increase Its Profits.[4] In subsection 1.2.3, I presented a similar but differently structured argument. The argument had a positive and a negative side: we gain a lot from strict profit maximization in terms of private-sector performance, but we don't really jeopardize the attainment of public policies.

(1) Better private-sector performance

It is worth repeating that argument here. A single, objective goal like profit maximization is more easily monitored than a multiple, vaguely defined goal like the fair and reasonable accommodation of all affected interests. It is easier, for example, to tell if a corporate manager is doing what she is supposed to do than to tell if a university president is doing what she is supposed to do. Since shareholders do have some effective control mechanisms (the proxy contest, the takeover bid, and the derivative lawsuit) better monitoring means that corporate managers will be kept more accountable. They are more likely to do what they are supposed to do, and do it efficiently. Better accountability thus encourages people to participate in large organizations, in which claims on the organization and the power to manage it are necessarily separated; it helps such organizations exist and function well. Large organizations are in turn often desirable for everyone. They increase social welfare, because without them

§16.2 [1] 170 N.W. 668 (Mich. 1919).

[2] See, e.g., MBCA §8.30(a): ". . . A director shall discharge his duties as a director . . . in a manner he reasonably believes to be in the best interests of the corporation."

[3] See, e.g., Selheimer v. Manganese Corp. of America, 224 A.2d 634 (Pa. 1966); Barnes v. Andrews, 298 F. 614 (S.D.N.Y. 1924); Bates v. Dresser, 251 U.S. 524 (1920).

[4] N.Y. Times, Sunday, Sept. 13, 1970, magazine section, 33.

certain large-scale business ventures would be impossible or would be carried out in a wasteful way.

(2) No preclusion of regulation

On the other side, no one need be made worse off by the corporation's having a single goal of profit maximization. The interests of nonshareholder groups like employees can be protected by contract, common law developments, and special legislation. Negative externalities like pollution can be corrected by tort law or pollution laws telling companies not to pollute or taxing them when they do. The production of public goods and the redistribution of wealth from rich to poor can be better accomplished by actual governments, which have a more legitimate claim to do these things. And corporate resources can still be diverted to these governmental activities, in small or great measure, as elected representatives see fit, because governments can tax both corporations and their shareholders. Profit maximization is therefore a legitimate and desirable goal for business corporations.[5]

First argument hard to attack

Objections. Objections to the preceding line of argument should be considered in two parts. The first concerns the dualist view that strict profit maximization promotes better monitoring and enforcement of the corporation's economic performance. No truly persuasive critique of this view has been offered. Although it is difficult to make any definitive comparison between the relative tightness of controls on managerial performance as between business corporations and governmental units, and though the total set of market and legal controls on corporate managers clearly leaves them with a significant amount of slack, or uncontrolled discretionary power to deviate from strict profit maximization, the evidence for the power of capital market controls on managerial behavior is very strong.

Doubts about external regulation

That leaves us with the negative side of the dualist argument. The most serious criticisms of the dualist viewpoint are those that attack the notions that external governmental regulation of corporations can be an effective way of correcting market failures, and that strictly profit-maximizing corporations won't seriously distort political mechanisms for deciding collectively about the size and nature of redistributive programs. So much evidence of governmental and regulatory failure has accumulated in the last decade or so that many critics have urged that corporations must be involved more directly in setting and pursuing public goals, if we are to achieve them at all well.

[5] For other presentations that basically uphold the traditional dualist viewpoint, especially against claims of the sort I attribute to "high idealism," see Eisenberg, Corporate Legitimacy, Conduct, and Governance — Two Models of the Corporation, 17 Creighton L. Rev. 1 (1983-1984); Williamson, Corporate Governance, 93 Yale L.J. 1197 (1984).

Implications?

As the committed dualist would quickly point out, however, even massive regulatory failure doesn't necessarily imply a change in the corporation's residual goal of strict profit maximization. It does so only if (1) an alternative to external regulation were available that would result in better achievement of the legitimate public goals behind regulation, (2) the alternative would necessitate a change in the profit-maximizing goal, (3) the cost of the alternative (in terms of reduced monitoring and control of corporate managers' performance, for example) would not outweigh the gains, and (4) no other alternative reform strategy exists that would yield a better cost-benefit ratio but not involve a change in the corporation's goal.

Many analysts have pressed vigorously for regulatory reforms that do not impinge on the dualist norm. An example is the call to greater deployment of market-mimicking incentives like user fees on polluters rather than simple prohibitions against effluents exceeding a single standard.[6] But others, like Professor Elliot Weiss, have bitten the bullet and argued, in effect, that the four conditions listed above do obtain.[7]

§16.2.2 Monism: Long-Run Identity Between Public and Private Interests

Conventional images of responsible acts

Statement. The monist viewpoint is that many types of corporate activities that appear to be profit-reducing voluntary expenditures for the public good are really conducive to profit maximization in the long run. Virtually no one is a strict or absolute monist, that is, one who believes that all public-spirited tasks a corporation may engage in will conduce to long-run profits. The typical monist believes rather that there is some set of "socially responsible" corporate activities that it is good for corporations to foster, because doing so will eventually create a better climate or culture in which business can operate. The set of socially responsible activities is usually understood (not defined) in an extremely conventional sense to include contributions to recognized charities and nonprofit organizations, modest investments in blighted urban areas, employment of minority or handicapped workers, and the like.

Legal acceptance

Legal status. Limited monism has been sanctioned by both courts and legislatures. In an earlier time, a board of directors that caused a corporation to make a gift to a university might find itself sued in a stockholder's

[6] See C. Schultze, The Public Use of Private Interest (1977).

[7] Weiss, Social Regulation of Business Activity: Reforming the Corporate Governance System to Resolve an Institutional Impasse, 28 U.C.L.A.L. Rev. 343 (1981).

derivative action based on the theory that there had been a waste of corporate assets. After some initial uncertainty, courts were inclined to accept at face value managerial arguments that, in their honest business judgment, their corporation's charitable contributions would promote its long-run profitability and thus did not constitute waste.[8] State corporation statutes now routinely allow boards of directors to make charitable contributions,[9] and the Internal Revenue Code facilitates them to the extent of allowing a limited deduction for such contributions.[10] Notice, however, that these statutory authorities deal only with conventional charitable contributions. If directors are attacked for causing their corporation to embark on other kinds of socially responsible activities that take away from tangible short-run opportunities to increase profits, they have to invoke the business judgment rule.

Need to invoke corporate interest

With a possible exception or two,[11] courts have not retreated from the assumption that the primary or residual purpose of a business corporation is to make profits for its shareholders. Accordingly, it is important for managers to make the right noises — namely, some version of the monist argument — when they cause their corporations to embark on some socially responsible activity. On the other hand, if they are at all careful to

[8] See, e.g., A. P. Smith Mfg. Co. v. Barlow, 98 A.2d 581 (N.J. 1953), appeal dismissed, 346 U.S. 861 (1953).

[9] See, e.g., MBCA §3.02(13).

[10] I.R.C. §170(b)(2).

[11] In the *A. P. Smith* case, cited in note 8 supra, the court remarked that ". . . modern conditions require that corporations acknowledge and discharge social as well as private responsibilities as members of the community within which they operate." 98 A.2d at 586. But this language seems unnecessary to the holding, given the court's espousal of the theory that the gift in question was for the corporation's indirect benefit, and it is unclear that the court intended anything more than to express a rationale for traditional corporate giving, which was sanctioned by statute in New Jersey, where the corporation was domiciled and the donee organization located. In Medical Committee for Human Rights v. SEC, 432 F.2d 659 (D.C. Cir. 1970), vacated for mootness, 404 U.S. 403 (1972), the circuit court expressed the view that Congress's concern for shareholder democracy meant that a proposed shareholder resolution to ask the directors to consider causing the company to cease making napalm was a fit subject for shareholder action within the meaning of the federal proxy rules, even though the proponents were motivated primarily by humanitarian rather than profit-making concerns. But the court nowhere declared explicitly that profit making was not the corporation's residual purpose; and in any event, such a pronouncement by a federal court about a state law question would not have been definitive.

Other lines of decision, such as those determining when a shareholder does or does not have a right to inspect corporate books and records, tend to confirm the realist viewpoint emphatically. See, e.g., State ex rel. Pillsbury v. Honeywell, Inc., 191 N.W.2d 406 (Minn. 1971) (purpose to persuade company to adopt certain social and political concerns, irrespective of economic benefit to company, was not proper purpose justifying inspection).

do so, it is almost impossible for shareholders to attack their actions successfully.

As the preceding paragraph suggests, the abstractly stated monist view is logically consistent with the dualist viewpoint, as I defined it earlier. In practice, of course, some observers will disagree with the judgment that the sorts of activities that monists like to foster really do promote long-run maximization of a corporation's profits.

ALI proposal

It should be noted that in its proposed principles of corporate governance the American Law Institute reaffirms the profit-making goal of business corporations but states certain exceptions. In the conduct of its business, the corporation is "(a) obliged, to the same extent as a natural person, to act within the boundaries set by law, (b) may take into account ethical considerations that are reasonably regarded as appropriate to the responsible conduct of business, and (c) may devote a reasonable amount of resources to public welfare, humanitarian, educational, and philanthropic purposes."[12] The latter two exceptions seem to reflect the conventional monist philosophy.

Political activities

A more debatable form of corporate activity outside of normal business operations consists of corporate political activities, including expenditures for political speech.[13] Though some might view these activities as an aspect of socially responsible corporate behavior, many academic and other critics would strongly disagree.[14] Clearly, the liberal elite is more interested in urging corporations to donate money to its preferred charities than in seeing them influence the political process against regulation of business.

[12] American Law Institute, Principles of Corporate Governance: Analysis and Recommendations, tent. draft no. 2 (April 13, 1984), §2.01, at 25. See Comment, Corporate Ethics and Corporate Governance: A Critique of the ALI Statement on Corporate Governance Section 2.01(b), 71 Calif. L. Rev. 994 (1983).

[13] See First Natl. Bank of Boston v. Bellotti, 435 U.S. 765 (1978), reh. denied, 438 U.S. 907, declaring unconstitutional as an abridgement of speech protected under the First Amendment a Massachusetts statute prohibiting corporations from making expenditures to influence the vote on "any questions submitted to the voters, other than one materially affecting any of the property, business or assets of the corporation." The statute also created an *irrebuttable* presumption that no referendum issue concerning the taxation of the income, property, or transactions of individuals would be deemed to be one "materially affecting" the business of a corporation. (Obviously, incumbent political forces were trying to keep corporations from arguing to the public against tax increases. Corporations like the First National Bank of Boston thought that tax increases on individuals *were* materially relevant to their businesses. High taxes, for example, might make it harder to recruit out-of-state personnel.)

[14] See Baker, Realizing Self-Realization: Corporate Political Expenditures and Redish's *The Value of Free Speech*, 130 U. Pa. L. Rev. 646 (1982); Brudney, Business Corporations and Stockholders' Rights Under the First Amendment, 91 Yale L.J. 235 (1981).

Big picture needed

Rationale. The basic argument for the monist view is that received notions of profit maximization were too narrow-minded, because they were overly biased toward tangible short-run payoffs, and ultimately self-defeating, because they led corporations to behave in a way that caused society at large to be permanently suspicious of corporations.

A cover for plutocrats?

Objections. The main argument against monist views is that they are a façade for the illegitimate accumulation and exercise of managerial prerogatives. This argument can be broken down into four steps.

First, managers almost always enjoy some slack, or freedom to deviate from strict profit maximization, because market and legal controls are never perfect.

Second, because of the differential effectiveness of controls on different kinds of deviation from profit maximization, managers do not capture the value of slack only in the form of excessive pay; they also secure perquisites of many kinds.[15]

Third, one kind of perquisite is managerial power to direct corporate resources toward nonbusiness goals that suit the managers' political preferences.

Fourth, these managerially chosen public goals often (1) don't have much to do with long-run profit maximization by the particular corporation, (2) don't reflect their shareholders' preferences, and (3) don't reflect the public policy preferences of citizens at large.

The more readily managers' monist arguments can be shielded from challenge by the business judgment rule, the more likely it is that these disparities will occur. In short, monism is plutocracy in disguise.

Other objections

Less sophisticated arguments against monist activities are that they won't in fact create a significantly better climate for business; they can't do much to solve social problems, given current and foreseeable levels of monist activities; and they may deflect governments from adopting much needed taxing and regulatory measures.

§16.2.3 Modest Idealism: Voluntary Compliance with the Law

Statement. The essence of modest idealism is that corporate managers should cause their corporations to comply with applicable laws and regula-

[15] See generally O. Williamson, The Economics of Discretionary Behavior: Managerial Objectives in a Theory of the Firm (1967).

tions even when noncompliance would increase the corporation's net present value.

Example

Consider, for example, a complex water pollution statute and the elaborate administrative regulations that implement it. For a given corporation that has long been accustomed to discharge pollutants into rivers next to its factories, the estimated cost of compliance is $10 million. There is no honest doubt, let us assume, about which regulations apply to the corporation, whether they are legally valid, and how they are supposed to be met. There is only a small probability, however, that if the corporation fails to comply with the regulations its noncompliance will be both discovered and corrected (through successful legal proceedings) by the regulators. The corporation expects that if there is discovery and successful enforcement, it will incur additional legal fees, a modest fine, and delayed expenditure of $10 million for compliance. Using their best business judgment, the managers discount these costs by their probability of occurrence and by their futurity, and they conclude that the estimated present value of these costs of noncompliance is only $2 million. Thus, compared to compliance, noncompliance has a net present value of $8 million. From a purely profit-maximizing point of view, the managers may decide not to comply with the pollution regulations, unless and until the regulators bring legal proceedings specifically against their corporation. The modest idealist would say that the managers should not be guided by a cost-benefit analysis that takes the probability of successful enforcement into account, but should cause their corporation to comply with the regulations promptly.

Modest but perhaps important

Two cautionary points are worth noting. First, modest idealism is only modest in its conception of idealistic behavior: the corporate manager is not asked to create public policy, but only to help carry it out. But to its proponents, modest idealism is not at all modest or trivial in its economic significance. Professor Christopher Stone, for example, has argued vigorously and persuasively that the main problem in making corporations socially responsible is the problem of enforcement of defined public policies.[16] Many of the most shocking examples of corporate misbehaviors involve conduct that violates existing law.

Relation to dualism

Second, as with monism, modest idealism is not logically inconsistent with the traditional dualist viewpoint, as it was defined earlier. Dualism holds that managers should maximize shareholder wealth, *subject to* the constraint that the corporation meet its specific legal obligations to other persons. In a sense, modest idealism merely postulates that the constraint should not be interpreted as containing an implicit qualification that man-

[16] C. Stone, Where the Law Ends: The Social Control of Corporate Behavior (1975).

agers may or must take the likelihood and cost of enforcement activities into account when deciding whether to meet specific legal obligations.

Legally acceptable

Legal status. Though clear and explicit legal authority is hard to come by, it seems obvious that modest idealism would be acceptable to the courts. For example, suppose a shareholder brought a derivative action for waste against his corporation's directors, claiming that they caused the corporation to spend $10 million to comply with (valid and clearly applicable) water pollution regulations even though any rational cost-benefit analysis would have led them to opt for noncompliance. It is difficult to believe that any court would give more than short shrift to such an argument. Nor is this prediction a function of the business judgment rule. It would make little difference, I would think, if the plaintiff offered clear and convincing evidence to show that the directors completely neglected to make any sort of cost-benefit analysis of compliance versus noncompliance. Indeed, one suspects that if corporate managers did commission and act on an explicit cost-benefit analysis of this sort and left a written record of it that later came to light in a legal proceeding to enforce the pollution laws, their activity would be a target of judicial condemnation rather than a recognizable excuse.

Rhetoric of noncompliers

These intuitions are consistent with the rhetoric that corporations actually use when resisting regulation. When challenged, noncompliers never say they made a rational decision to "run for it," in the hope that they wouldn't be caught. Typically, they try to argue that the regulations do not apply to them, at least not in the manner alleged; that the agency followed improper procedures in adopting or enforcing the regulations; that the regulations exceeded the agency's statutory authority (here, for example, is where cost-benefit analyses come into play); and so forth. All of this seems to assume the legal validity of modest idealism.

Outside of litigation settings, one sometimes hears corporate managers and attorneys try to rationalize corporate noncompliance with regulatory statutes by complaining that the devil of fiduciary duties to shareholders made them do it. What they are complaining about, it seems to me, is not corporate law, which certainly does not tell them to break other laws in order to make their shareholders richer, but the unfortunate fact that if they do not take advantage of lax legal enforcement they may be ousted by aggressive managers who will.

Reducing business's bad side effects

Rationale. One major argument for modest idealism is that, if corporate managers lived up to its mandate, the bad side effects of profit-seeking activity in the private sector would be greatly mitigated. If corporations voluntarily complied with the antitrust laws as interpreted by the courts, more of the surplus from economic transactions would go to consumers in general rather than to strategically situated clumps of investors, managers, and employees. If corporations voluntarily complied with the environmental laws, they would greatly curtail important negative externalities of modern business enterprise. If corporations fully complied with workplace safety regulations or drug testing regulations, they would curtail other kinds of bad side effects of business activity. And so forth. This argument assumes that the antitrust laws, the environmental laws, and other major laws whose implementation would benefit from voluntary compliance are socially desirable on balance. The modest idealist may postulate this assumption as reflecting his own best judgment, or may appeal to the idea that the laws reflect the outcome of a more or less legitimate political process, and should not be second-guessed in the enforcement context.

A major part of the modest idealist's first line of argument is to convince everyone that (1) noncompliance with regulation is a major problem, and (2) compliance would have important and desirable effects. I submit that they have had more success with (1) than with (2).

Transaction costs saved

A second line of argument for modest idealism is that voluntary compliance reduces the transaction costs generated by the legal system. When law is internalized, when citizens follow the rules even when the policeman isn't looking, when, in short, law becomes morality — then the costs of enforcing law will drop.

Better business climate

A third line of argument is that, if most business leaders act as modest idealists most of the time, society at large will upgrade its estimate of the legitimacy of the modern business corporation, and there will be a truly better climate for business. This is because the corporate manager who acts as a modest idealist is bound to be seen by the public as a nobler and more trustworthy figure than the calculating opportunist.

Limits on workability

Objections. One drawback of modest idealism is that it is subject to the familiar difficulties of voluntary collective action, such as the free rider problem and the prisoner's dilemma, and so is only likely to be possible within a range of action that corresponds to managerial slack. In short, it is not likely to work very well; its economic effects are likely to be modest after all. For example, if any one corporation's board of directors decides to comply voluntarily with an expensive regulatory statute but their competitors do not, their company may take a beating in the market for its products. In addition, when the company's actual stock market value drops (because of its reduced earnings) relative to its potential value (as revealed by comparison to the stock market values of noncomplying competitor companies), the company may well become the subject of a takeover bid, after which the idealistic managers will be replaced. To be sure, these adverse reactions from the product and capital markets would not occur if managers of all firms in the industry acted as modest idealists. But how, short of coercive collective action of some sort, is this state of affairs going to come about? Any individual corporation will observe that the best of all possible worlds would be for the other corporations to act as modest idealists while it acted as a calculating opportunist, because then it would gain an enormous competitive advantage.

Doubt about the laws

A second major objection to modest idealism is the same as one raised against dualism: The laws and regulations that are actually adopted do not reflect optimal public policy, for there are systematic imperfections in the traditional law making process. Accordingly, corporations should be enlisted in the work of defining public policies, not just in pursuing them.

§16.2.4 High Idealism: Interest Group Accommodation and the Public Interest as Residual Goals

Change the goal itself

Statement. High idealism holds that the business corporation's residual goal, and not just its specific, externally imposed legal obligations, should be defined to include a much wider set of interests than those of the shareholders. One variation is that the purpose of the corporation, and the general residual duty of those who hold decision making power over its activities, is to achieve a reasonable accommodation of the interests of all groups affected by the corporation. Another version is that the basic purposes of a corporation include not only the objective of making profits but also that of furthering the public interest, as conceived by its decision makers.

Usually vague

Other variants could also be stated. Most of them avoid the concept of maximization (of an interest, of a variable, of a sum of interests or variables, or anything else), and in effect they reject or ignore the concept of an identifiable group of owners of the corporation's residual value. Consequently, they are inevitably vague and do not imply an operational meaning or measure of good corporate performance. Unlike the other views considered in this part, high idealism *is* logically inconsistent with the traditional dualist viewpoint.

Example of plant closing

A prototypical example of how the interest-group variation of high idealism might apply is a proposed plant closing. Suppose a corporation in a northeastern city operates a factory that is losing money and its directors are considering whether to close it and open a substitute plant in a Sunbelt town where taxes are lower, labor is cheaper, energy use would be less, shipping facilities are more modern and convenient, and the surrounding environment is more pleasant. The workers at the old factory, as well as some activists who reside in the city, protest the proposed plant closing, claiming that it will cause a hardship to the workers and will lead to all the bad consequences of increased unemployment in a declining local economy. The high idealist would say that the directors should consider the interests of the employees and of the neighborhood, and might justifiably decide to continue operating the old plant, even though it would continue to lose money or make a subnormal rate of return. Perhaps the high idealist would draw a line at operating losses and say that they would almost always justify a plant closing, although inability to maximize profits would not. The important conceptual point, however, is that the corporate decision makers might properly consider the interests of the affected workers even though they were not bound to do so by contract or by the labor laws.

Example of unhealthy product

An example of the application of the public interest variant of high idealism would be the cigarette manufacturing company that voluntarily ceases to make cigarettes, even though business is highly profitable, because its decision makers have finally become convinced that cigarette smoking does indeed cause some 350,000 premature deaths per year in the United States. Once again, the important conceptual point is that the corporate decision makers would not be acting to fulfill an explicit governmental command. Instead, they would be making their own determination as to what was a negative externality or "public bad" and would be voluntarily adopting a policy to reduce it.

Traditional justifications too

These examples suggest an important caveat. The corporate actions involved might also be justified in traditional, nonidealistic terms — specifically, within the monist framework. The directors might decide that not closing a currently unprofitable plant would promote the company's long-run profitability by improving labor relations. This need not be a disingenuous or mistaken judgment. Observers of Japanese companies have long suggested that a policy of lifetime employment can have sizable benefits, such as fewer strikes and a more loyal work force, for the sponsoring corporation. Similarly, though perhaps less persuasively, deciding to cease production of a major health hazard might improve public relations and solidify long-term profitability. Thus, though in theory the monist and high idealist positions will result in radically different actions in some situations, it is difficult to assess beforehand how their implications will differ in practice. And it is misleading to assign particular classes of "socially responsible" activities exclusively to one or another of the theoretical viewpoints.

Change decision makers too?

More acutely than the other viewpoints, high idealism raises the question, "*Who decides* how the corporation's general purpose is to be accomplished?" The traditional view, as embodied in the business corporation laws of all states, is that the business of the corporation is to be managed by (or under the supervision of) its board of directors, who are elected by shareholders. Logically, the high idealist might want decision making power over particular corporate activities to reside in shareholder-elected directors, or directly in shareholders, or in a board composed of directors elected by members of a number of different constituencies, or in a board containing representatives appointed by an explicit governmental unit. Let us call these options managerial decision making, investor decision making, interest-group decision making, and government-influenced decision making, respectively.

Employees and interest groups

In practice, idealists of the interest-group variety tend to support reforms that would promote interest-group decision making. The most common yet the most limited proposal of this sort is to have employee representation on the board of directors, as is done in some other countries.[17] More ambitious interest-group representation has been urged by the Nader group.[18] For the high idealist of the public interest variety, such as Professor Weiss, government-appointed directors seem to be a more natural reform proposal.[19]

Not embodied in law

Legal status. High idealism, as defined in the first paragraph of this subsection, is not embodied in current statutes and case law: Its various formulations are to be found in the writings of reform-oriented commentators. Occasionally, corporate managers will say that what they are trying to do, what they ought to do, and what they think the law allows or requires them to do is to effect an accommodation of the whole family of

[17] See Hopt, New Ways in Corporate Governance: European Experiments with Labor Representation on Corporate Boards, 82 Mich. L. Rev. 1338 (1984); Vagts, Reforming the "Modern" Corporation: Perspectives from the German, 80 Harv. L. Rev. 23 (1966).

For analyses of the pros and cons of union representation on boards in the United States, see Comment, An Economic and Legal Analysis of Union Representation on Corporate Boards of Directors, 130 U. Pa. L. Rev. 919 (1982); Note, Serving Two Masters: Union Representation on Corporate Boards of Directors, 81 Colum. L. Rev. 639 (1981).

For an economic analysis that goes beyond "codetermination" to examine (and criticize) labor-managed and labor-owned firms, see Jensen & Meckling, Rights and Production Functions: An Application to Labor-Managed Firms and Codetermination, 52 J. Bus. 469 (1979).

[18] R. Nader, M. Green, & J. Seligman, Taming the Giant Corporation (1976). A carefully worked out criticism of their viewpoint is given by Engel, An Approach to Corporate Social Responsibility, 32 Stan. L. Rev. 1 (1979).

[19] See Weiss, note 7 supra, at 418-434.

interests in their corporation, not to maximize profits. But such statements seem to reflect either ignorance of legal authorities or a bid for greater discretionary power. (It should be pointed out, though, that some things desired by some idealists, such as worker-owned firms and cooperatives, can readily be achieved under existing law. A worker-owned firm could be organized as an ordinary business corporation governed by special provisions in its articles and bylaws, as a partnership, or, in some states, as a cooperative. As with any business, there are costs and benefits associated with the use of each form. But there is no serious obstacle to the creation of such firms. What seems lacking is a strong demand for them.)

"Government failure" argument

Rationale. Perhaps the main reason for high idealism is "government failure." Explicit lawmaking and regulatory activities are said to be flawed in many ways. The legislatures and agencies suffer from informational problems, perverse agenda-setting processes, capture by vested interests, nonrepresentation of diffuse interests, poor incentive structures and role definitions for the lawmakers and regulators, and more.[20] In view of these failures, it seems prudent to encourage private enterprise, perhaps only on an experimental basis, to participate actively in the definition and execution of public policies. Since the setting and implementation of public policy is in such bad shape, so the argument goes, we must try something new.

Dispersal of government power

A second argument for high idealism is that it would help to disperse governmental power and responsibility, thus reducing the likelihood of a wholesale abuse of that power and promoting participatory democracy. For this argument to work, one should, it seems, furnish reasons why the thousands of local governmental units in our federal system do not provide an adequate dispersal of power and responsibility.

Increase in participation

Another argument sometimes offered for interest-group variations of high idealism is that a large corporation always has a powerful impact on the lives of certain groups of people, such as employees, consumers, and neighbors. These groups, therefore, ought to have a direct voice in determining how the corporation runs, in order both to protect their interests and to develop participatory decision making as an end in itself. To the extent that this argument is not based on simple romanticism or deep confusion about the nature of decision making in a complex economy, it seems to reflect a belief that the kinds of controls on corporations that affected groups do have are either impotent or inadequate, and cannot be

[20] See Weiss, note 7 supra, at 378-393; see generally S. Breyer, Regulation and Its Reform (1982).

made adequate at reasonable cost. These currently available controls include market forces, for example, corporate behavior is powerfully affected by consumer choices; legal mechanisms, for example, consumers can sue under existing tort law and consumer protection laws; and the right to lobby governments to tax and regulate corporations in certain ways. To this combination of opportunities for "exit" and "voice,"[21] the interest-group idealists would add an opportunity for a more direct voice in ordinary business decision making.

Decreased economic performance

Objections. One main argument against high idealism is that, to the extent it would make a difference, it would have a very high cost in terms of decreased economic performance by corporations. It might impair overall allocational efficiency. For example, the corporation that quickly accedes to demands not to close an unsuccessful plant may be adding to immobility in the flow of resources to more productive uses; it may be merely putting a costly drag on changes that eventually ought to be made. Indeed, high idealism may lead to a low level of managerial performance even in terms of its own, partly noneconomic, objectives. This point is the reverse side of the main positive argument for dualism. Since corporate decision makers would not be assigned the task of maximizing a single, objective, easily monitored goal, it would be very difficult to keep them truly accountable to a vague statement of purposes.

Ineffective with managerial decision making

A second argument is that high idealism might be largely ineffective. Consider this point under three assumptions. (1) If the idealist viewpoint were implemented by some form of managerial decision making, the managers might well lack the incentive or the slack to pursue the more broadly defined goals to a significant extent, unless they were somehow shielded more effectively than they now are from takeover bids, derivative lawsuits, and competition in their product markets. A deliberate governmental weakening of these present controls, in order to give managers more discretionary power to serve the general good as they saw fit, would probably do more harm than good. Among other things, the newly increased discretionary power might in fact be used by managers for their own benefit, just as existing amounts of slack seem inevitably to be turned into perquisites or excessive compensation.

Or shareholder decision making

(2) Could high idealism be implemented by shareholder decision making? It seems unlikely that shareholders would often sacrifice their self-interest to the interest of other affected groups. The poor voting record on

[21] The terminology is from A. Hirschman, Exit, Voice and Loyalty (1970).

corporate social action proposals under the federal proxy rules supports this prediction.

Perhaps with interest-group decision making

(3) If high idealism were implemented by interest-group decision making of some sort, it might indeed have real effects. But caution is needed even here. Labor representation on boards of directors, in countries where it has been tried, seems not to have made nearly as much difference as early proponents thought it might. Partly, this is because corporate behavior must often bend to other controlling forces, such as consumer choices in the product markets. If a company keeps a relatively inefficient plant in operation, for example, it may have to charge more than competitors, lose business, and eventually be forced to change its practices or seek a governmental bailout. This need not happen if competitors are following similar policies of accommodating nonshareholder interests. But, once again, one must realize the limits of voluntary collective action.

Illegitimate form of government

A third argument against high idealism (the main one, in the eyes of some observers) is that it would constitute an illegitimate form of government — a case of oligarchy in disguise, and on a very grand scale indeed. When implemented by managerial or shareholder decision making, the high idealist's brand of social responsibility will reflect mostly upper class preferences. Consider, for example, that over half of the corporate stocks and bonds owned by individuals (or estates, trusts, and the like) in the United States are held by the wealthiest one percent of the population,[22] and that managers of large publicly held corporations are paid incomes that send them into orbits far above the ordinary ground-level income.[23] Policies defined by such persons will have a very different scheme of priorities and effects than policies made by democratically elected representatives of the entire population. This is true even though democratically elected bodies are in fact heavily influenced by elite interest groups.

Wide and good participation difficult

If high idealism is implemented by some form of interest-group decision making, it may or may not be legitimate from the point of view of one who insists on broad representation and participation. Unless great care is taken in institutional design, some groups who ought to have power (or direct voice) may not get it. Consider, for example, the possible implications of a board composed of directors elected by shareholders and employees. The interests of these groups may conflict seriously with those of consumers and governmental units. For example, featherbedding may be desired by employees but may raise prices to consumers and result in lower profits,

[22] U.S. Bureau of the Census, Dept. of Commerce, Statistical Abstract of the United States: 1979, at 544 (table 897); id. at 470 (table 775).

[23] See section 6.1 nn. 2 and 3 supra.

thus reducing corporate income tax revenues to certain governments. Unless there is some good reason to think that these latter groups already possess adequate controls on corporations, whereas labor does not, the premises of interest-group idealism seem to suggest that they also be given direct voice. More generally, participatory systems (like markets) can be afflicted by a wide variety of problems that may be quite costly to solve.[24]

Incoherence in public policy

A fourth argument against high idealism is that, with so many thousands of mini-governments (namely, the newly transformed business corporations) acting independently to define and implement public policy, overall public policy is likely to be even more incoherent and uncoordinated than it is now. The strength of this argument varies with one's estimate of the importance of overall coherence in public policy making, and may be different in different substantive areas, for example, more important for health care policy than for land use policy.

Caveat

Despite these many objections,[25] it should be stressed that no one knows with certainty that corporations transformed in accord with some leading version of high idealism would fail to make a net improvement in the overall welfare of our society. The hard questions are ultimately empirical ones, and high idealism has not yet been tried on a significant scale in the American setting.

§16.2.5 Pragmatism: Contracting to Provide Public Services

More contracting out

Statement. Pragmatism holds that governmental units should make greater use of business corporations to implement public policies, and that business corporations should design, develop, and seize opportunities to perform public services on a profit-making basis. For example, the typical pragmatist wants the realm of government contracting to expand well beyond traditional activities like making weapons for the Defense Department and office buildings for other governmental units. He envisages more contracting by business corporations to provide job training for members of minority groups, to redevelop urban areas, to educate children, and to run municipal hospitals. Like its counterpart in academic philosophy, pragmatism in this sense is as American as apple pie.[26]

[24] For an interesting account of the need for, and the costs of, "participation-perfecting strategies," see Reich, Corporate Accountability and Regulatory Reform, 8 Hofstra L. Rev. 5, 19-28 (1979).

[25] See also Eisenberg, note 5 supra; Wiliamson, note 5 supra.

[26] *Pragmatism* seems to describe the philosophy of corporate social responsibility worked

Legal status. Nothing in corporate law encourages or restrains the pragmatist viewpoint, which is logically quite consistent with the traditional dualist viewpoint. Such legal norms as there are that bear on the possibility of realizing pragmatist hopes are to be found in the numerous laws that influence when governments may or may not contract with private, for-profit corporations.

Consistent with dualism

Rationale. A major argument for pragmatism is the claim that business corporations can bring more expertise and more efficient management and production techniques to bear on the solution of social problems and the provision of social services. This effect is seen as flowing from the fact that private corporations are more tightly disciplined by product market forces and capital market forces than are government bureaucracies.

Expertise and efficiency

Another argument for pragmatism is that it may ultimately reduce the "we-they" feeling that now exists between persons who work for business corporations and those who work for governmental and nonprofit organizations. That there is such an opposition seems confirmed by the literature that emphasizes the cultural differences between the "productive class" and the "new class."[27] On the other hand, increased corporate participation in the provision of public services may simply exacerbate the existing tensions, since it would threaten the established turfs of some members of the new class.

Reduction of "we-they" feeling

Objections. The main argument against pragmatism is that profit-maximizing private corporations that contract to provide public services will be tempted to cut corners and to neglect noneconomic values and policies. For example, a for-profit elementary school that is paid by a local government on the basis, say, of the number of students it graduates from each grade each year who can pass certain standardized tests, will be tempted to skimp on the acquisition of library books and the development of social skills, and it may try to keep out or discourage applicants who are likely to be poor learners, a group that may contain disproportionately more members of minority groups. These tendencies could be controlled by explicit rules, but, so the objection would go, the rule making that would ultimately be needed would be extremely cumbersome and costly to enforce.

Corner-cutting fear

---

out by William C. Norris, chairman and chief executive officer of Control Data Corp. See his essay, A New Role for Corporations, in Public-Private Partnership: New Opportunities for Meeting Social Needs 243 (H. Brooks, L. Liebman, & C. Schelling, eds. 1984).

[27] See D. Bell, The Cultural Contradictions of Capitalism (1976). Another prominent writer sounding this theme is Irving Kristol.

How potent this objection is will obviously depend on the context. I will say more about this problem below.

§16.3 *A Reconceptualization*

Most discussions of the business corporation's role in meeting social needs approach the problem with a focus on the *corporation and its decision makers.* One typically considers what corporations do, what their managers are legally required to do, and what the managers might be encouraged to do. That is the approach reviewed in the previous section of this chapter. A more productive approach might be to focus on *activities* oriented to the general public interest, and to ask whether we can develop a good theory of the proper *location* of such public-regarding activities. This approach suggests that we start by considering which activities are considered and which should be considered to "belong" in some sense to the public sector; then consider why a governmental unit sometimes internalizes its characteristic activities and sometimes externalizes them; and finally consider why, when a governmental unit does externalize activities, it sometimes delegates only to private nonprofit corporations, and sometimes delegates also to private for-profit corporations.

Location of public-regarding activities

§16.3.1 Distinguishing Among Public Sector Activities

Social welfare theory of government's role

Social welfare theory as developed by economists[1] makes a coherent and reasonably clear distinction between activities that belong to the private sector and those that belong to the public sector. The public sector is supposed to produce "public goods,"[2] prevent and correct market failures, and redistribute wealth; the private sector is supposed to do everything else. In my view, however, this statement of the division does not isolate in adequately precise terms the essence of governmental institutions. A distinction should be made between essential governmental functions and appropriate types of governmentally mandated activities. At the core of government is coercive resolution of collective action problems, not public-regarding activities themselves.

§16.3 [1] For a classic early statement, see W. Baumol, Welfare Economics and the Theory of the State (rev. 2d ed. 1952; 1965).

[2] *Public goods* are those characterized by nonrivalry in consumption and high exclusion costs. See Samuelson, The Pure Theory of Public Expenditures, 36 Rev. Econ. & Stat. 387 (Nov. 1954), and his Diagrammatic Exposition of a Theory of Public Expenditure, 37 Rev. Econ. & Stat. 350 (Nov. 1955).

Some key definitions

Perhaps this point can be made clearer by a series of definitions. By *the government* I shall mean the set of organizations in society that carry out core governmental functions. By *core governmental functions* I shall mean (1) the setting up of rules mandating the principal kinds of public-regarding activities and (2) the control and deployment of ultimate means of coercion for the purposes of enforcing such rules. By *the principal kinds of public-regarding activities* I shall mean the redistribution of wealth (for example, through taxing and spending programs), the establishment and maintenance of basic institutions that form the matrix in which the nongovernmental activities take place (for example, such institutions as contract law, property law, and the antitrust laws in our political system); the production of public goods, and the correction of market failures. Under these definitions, it is logically possible that many or even all of the principal kinds of public-regarding activities will not be carried out by the government. Sometimes the very organizations that comprise the government will internalize the conduct of those activities, but sometimes they will externalize them. Internalization is a process that usually corresponds to using employees of the governmental organizations, while externalization usually corresponds to some form of contracting out. Ideally, however, one should not equate "externalization" to "contracting out," a technical legal concept that may lack clear meaning in some political systems and contexts, but should understand it in a more institutional sense as referring to activities not done within some actual, sociologically recognizable government organization.

Examples of internalization and externalization

History and contemporary practice give us many examples of both externalization and internalization of public-regarding activities. The collection of taxes is certainly a public-regarding activity in my sense, but it has sometimes been accomplished by independent tax collectors rather than by government organizations and employees. Similarly, redistributive spending and the provision of social services is often accomplished externally. Consider, for example, that the federal Medicare program not only relies on private hospitals and private physicians to provide the services paid for by the program, but also contracts out the payment function itself to numerous fiscal intermediaries, principally the Blue Cross and Blue Shield plans, that are private corporations. National defense is a prototypical public good, but many governments have hired mercenaries, even mercenary armies, and in our own system most of the design and production of weapons has been contracted out to private enterprises. Reducing the negative externalities of a market economy is also a classic public-regarding activity, but the degree to which its actual accomplishment is assigned to governmental versus nongovernmental organizations varies substantially over time and across jurisdictions. In particular, there are shifts in the balance between private versus public enforcement of rules about externalities. In an earlier phase of our industrial history, pollution generated by business tended to be attacked, if at all, by private plaintiffs in tort actions. In more modern times, government bureaucracies have been created to grant and deny licenses, to make inspections, and to bring enforcement actions.

§16.3.2 Determining the Degree of "Vertical Integration" of Governmental Organizations

What factors determine the mix between internalization and externalization of public-regarding activities? I do not have a satisfying general theory to answer this question, but I will mention several apparently major influences. Perhaps they can be divided into normatively appropriate factors and normatively irrelevant or objectionable factors.

Coordination and control

First, a major form of justification for internalization is that it permits better coordination of governmental activities and better assurance of reliability and stability in their performance. Or, more abstractly and with somewhat different connotations, it permits a reduction in transaction costs, namely, the costs (defined very broadly) of contracting out. This kind of rationale is parallel to the reasons given by managers of business corporations, and by historians of business,[3] to explain why so many business corporations have resorted to vertical integration.

Efficiency and external expertise

Second, a major form of argument for externalization is that nongovernmental organizations exist that can perform the public-regarding activities more efficiently and expertly. Whether this is true, and the nature of the public-regarding activities with respect to which it is true, obviously depends heavily on the actual nature and level of development of the particular governmental and nongovernmental organizations that exist in a society when the question is raised. Consequently, even as a purely normative matter, the optimal equilibrium between internalization and externalization will be extremely contingent on the historical and cultural context. It may make sense for governmental organizations, as the society in which they operate becomes larger, more complex, and more technologically advanced, to become significantly more vertically integrated in some respects and much less so in others.

Turf-building factor

In addition to the two factors mentioned, there are undoubtedly others that are important but regrettable. One obvious possibility is that top level

[3] A. Chandler, Jr., Strategy and Structure (1962).

bureaucrats in government have a natural tendency to expand their bureaus, since doing so will often give them greater prestige and power, and thus a tendency to internalize public-regarding (and other!) activities well beyond the optimal point. This tendency may be bolstered by an ideological framework that leads them to a systematic discounting of the value and potential value of nongovernmental organizations.

§16.3.3 Allocating Activities to NonProfits and For-Profits

Readier delegation to nonprofits: why?

An extremely important fact about government's externalization of public-regarding activities is that government is not equally ready to delegate to or to contract with private nonprofit and private for-profit corporations. The government is willing to contract for weapons manufacture and highway construction with for-profit corporations, for example, but seems willing to give tax subsidies for education only to nonprofit corporations. Many similar withholdings of governmental support to for-profits can be found in our medical care delivery system.[4] (To facilitate the present discussion, I am here assuming, as many people do, that education, or at least elementary education, and the provision of medical care contain significant public-regarding elements and are therefore appropriate arenas for substantial government intervention.) What determines when public-regarding activities may be contracted out or delegated to for-profit corporations?

Theory of nonprofit corporations

The answer to this question should be sought in the emerging theory of the nonprofit corporation. The main legal distinction between the for-profit and the nonprofit corporation is the application to the latter of a rule that might be labeled "the nondistribution constraint." Ordinary business corporations have shareholders who are allowed to receive the residual earnings of the enterprise by means of distributions, that is, dividends, stock redemptions, and payouts on liquidation of the enterprise. By contrast, the members of a nonprofit corporation are expressly prohibited from receiving any part of the assets or property of the corporation for themselves. This means that all residual earnings must be rededicated to the corporation's activities, which are usually specified in the charter to be of a charitable, religious, scientific, educational, or similar nature. The leading current theory of nonprofit enterprises[5] claims that the rationale for use of the

[4]See Clark, Does the Nonprofit Form Fit the Hospital Industry? 93 Harv. L. Rev. 1416, 1473-1476 (1980).

[5]Hansmann, The Role of Nonprofit Enterprise, 89 Yale L.J. 835 (1980); see also Clark, note 4 supra (discussing applicability of this theory versus a counter theory). An attempt to critique

nonprofit form lies in the chief function of the nondistribution constraint, namely, that it helps to overcome contractual failure in situations where such failure is quite likely to occur.

Contractual failure and the nondistribution constraint

Contractual failure is characterized by the inability of a buyer of services to assure himself that he is getting what he intends to be contracing for; in more general terms, it denotes high monitoring and enforcement costs. The nondistribution constraint is supposed to be helpful in such situations because it gives the buyer some reason to believe that those who appoint and control the actual providers of services and goods will not have an incentive to take advantage of his vulnerability as consumer. In a for-profit enterprise, by contrast, both the shareholders and the managers (who are accountable to shareholders, and whose interests are usually made to coincide in part with those of the shareholders by such means as stock option plans) have an incentive not only to be as efficient as possible and thus to outperform competitors, but also to take advantage of all market imperfections.

Examples: redistribution

Some examples may illuminate this theory. First, consider privately initiated redistributive activities, that is, gifts. Nationwide flower-delivery services are operated by decidedly for-profit corporations, yet the donors who pay the corporations for helping to carry out their redistributive programs are not deterred by this fact. By contrast, an international food-delivery service is operated by CARE, a nonprofit corporation, and its nonprofit status seems very important in encouraging donors to contribute to it. Why the difference? One important distinction is that if the flower-delivery firm fails to perform, or performs badly, the donor is likely to find out about it, at least eventually, and to take remedial measures. She may demand a refund, complain to the Better Business Bureau, spread the bad word about the corporation among potential customers, and so forth. If an organization like CARE fails to perform adequately, however, the donor is unlikely to find out about it. This is because the donor and the intended donees are unlikely to have a personal relationship to each other, such that reliable feedback on performance would naturally be sent along established lines of communication. In short, this donor faces a serious monitoring problem — a form of contractual failure afflicts him — and he may be comforted to know that CARE's sponsors are legally prohibited from getting a personal benefit out of its activities.

Hansmann's views is made in Ellman, Another Theory of Nonprofit Corporations, 80 Mich. L. Rev. 999 (1982). Implications of Hansmann's approach are explored in his Reforming Nonprofit Corporation Law, 129 U. Pa. L. Rev. 497 (1981), and The Rationale for Exempting Nonprofit Organizations from Corporate Income Taxation, 91 Yale L.J. 54 (1981).

Consider, as a second example, basic scientific research, an activity that, if successful, leads to production of a public good. Many organizations for basic research are in nonprofit form, whereas firms that do applied research are often in for-profit form. Why? The problem facing government agencies and private donors who "purchase" basic research is that even the most diligent, competent, and well-conceived basic research may yield no clearly valuable output. If the research organization receives and spends a large sum of money and then comes up with nothing but an apologetic report, the situation may reflect the luck of the draw just as readily as a waste of resources. Unless the purchaser is willing to become an ever-present policeman watching the researchers' processes and activities, and has the technical and professional confidence to second-guess the quality of their activities, she will be hard-pressed to tell the difference. In short, she faces a serious monitoring problem and therefore may seek protection against her consumer vulnerability by going to a nonprofit organization. The purchaser of applied research, for example, a marketing survey done for a particular business, is much less afflicted by such problems. He can go to a firm that is driven by competitive forces and a profit-making purpose to be as efficient as possible, yet still have reasonable protection against overreaching and poor performance.

"Public good" example

Finally, consider complex personal services like education and medical care. Much more than with other essentially private goods and services, these services are often provided by nonprofit organizations. Why? One possible justification again relates to severe monitoring problems and the consumer vulnerability that they generate. For one thing, the recipients of such services lack the professional's esoteric knowledge and canons of judgment needed to evaluate the quality of services they are getting. Perhaps even more important, there is often profound disagreement among professionals and expert observers of their behavior as to what constitutes good education or good medical care, and these disagreements reflect, among other things, vast areas of ignorance about relevant empirical questions. For example, with respect to a very large percentage of practiced medical procedures, physicians have no solid evidence, such as the results of randomized clinical trials, of the procedures' effectiveness, let alone their rationality in cost-benefit terms.

Complex personal services

When general goals cannot be reduced to an agreed upon, operationally defined set of particular objectives and results, it is obviously difficult or impossible to monitor and assess performance of those who undertake to provide services aimed at achieving the general goals. Accordingly, consumers may have a preference for nonprofit service-delivery organizations. To be sure, the question whether, in a given context, nonprofit organizations actually do serve to mitigate the problem of consumer vulnerability is a difficult and separate inquiry, and there is a basis for answering the question in the negative in the case of nonprofit hospitals in the United States.[6] The notions of contractual failure and consumer vulnerability may at least help us to understand why many people have an intuitive bias in favor of nonprofit organizations in certain contexts.

Implication of theory

The principal implication of this theory of nonprofit enterprise for our present purposes is that *contracts by for-profit business corporations to provide services to governments are likely to flourish only where governmental goals have been clearly defined and the services are specified in terms of outputs and activities that are easily monitored yet meaningfully related to the goals.* Since many unmet social needs seem to call for activities that involve complex personal services or other hard-to-monitor activities — they resemble elementary education more than weapons manufacture — this implication is an extremely important one. What it suggests is that priority ought to be given to attempts to define public policies in operational, but sensible, terms. Business corporations may be able to help in these attempts, by offering and justifying such operational definitions of public policies, but the final determinations will undoubtedly have to be made by governmental organizations.

§16.4 Conclusion

Drawbacks to existing views

In trying to make the corporation's role with respect to social needs a more fruitful one, the most important task facing the legal system is not that of choosing among different conceptions of corporate purpose. Such an exercise is likely to be inconsequential or misguided. In addition, each of the main conceptions of purpose has serious drawbacks. The dualist viewpoint has great strengths but presupposes and depends on a just distribution of wealth and acceptable institutional arrangements in government. Monism tends to be uncritically conventional and merely palliative. Modest idealism is not likely to be widely practiced. High idealism, if it were ever adopted, would simply spread the basic failure of government, confusion of ends and absorption of energies in the endless squabbling of interest groups, while destroying the chief virtue of business corporations, their capacity to achieve definite goals efficiently. Pragmatism is a benevolent idea, but it will not be implemented on a truly significant scale unless government puts its house into better order.

[6] Clark, note 4 supra.

Reform of governmental processes

A much more important task is to reform collective decision making processes in ways that will faciliate sharper definitions of public policies. How to do this in a world where political consensus is often impossible to achieve is a difficult question, but the need to attempt answers cannot be avoided. At least it is not *inevitable,* I think, that lack of consensus will lead to statutes that express multiple, vaguely expressed, and unranked goals. Without clearer definitions of public goals, private sector involvement in meeting social needs is unlikely to increase significantly — or, if it does, it is likely to have questionable consequences. When public policies are conceived of in more nearly operational terms, however, good governmental monitoring of corporate commitments to meet them will be feasible, and expanded corporate involvement in public-regarding activities will tend to follow naturally.[1]

§16.4 [1]On the general themes of this chapter, see Public-Private Partnership: New Opportunities for Meeting Social Needs (H. Brooks, L. Liebman, & C. Schelling eds. 1984).

CHAPTER 17

THE ISSUANCE OF SECURITIES

§17.1 State Corporate Law Issues

When stock is sold to investors, a number of technical issues may arise under the relevant state's corporation law. In contrast to questions arising under federal and state securities laws, many of these issues have receded in importance in recent decades, but they still have to be understood by the corporate lawyer.

§17.1.1 Subscription Agreements

Motivation

Less often today than in the past, potential investors in a newly formed business may be asked to sign subscription agreements in which they promise to buy a certain number of shares at certain times and prices. The promise might be a contingent one. For example, the subscriber might agree, "I will buy 1,000 shares if and when other potential investors have signed subscription agreements covering 50,000 shares all together." In this example the motivation for having a subscription agreement, rather than simply buying shares outright, might be the investor's not wanting to commit herself until enough other people have also agreed to invest in the business. Being sure of this was especially important in days when statutes required new corporations to meet significant minimum capitalization requirements. Or it might simply be that the investor wants to pay for stock in installments. Nowadays, neither reason applies in the typical case when a company is going public. The new issue of stock is almost always sold out quickly, and in any event the underwriters may agree to take any unsold portion. In the close corporation context where only a few investors are involved, a subscription agreement may appear unnecessary.

Revocability

A question that used to arise with some frequency was whether subscription agreements entered into before the issuing corporation was incorporated were revocable by the signing investor, at least before the corporation was formed and adopted or had accepted the subscription agreement. The case law was split and confused.[1] Statutes in a majority of the states now provide that subscriptions of a corporation to be organized are irrevocable for a specified period of time (such as six months) unless all of the subscribers consent to a revocation or the agreement provides otherwise.[2]

Subscriber's status

Subscribers in the post-incorporation period are usually treated as having the status of shareholders for many purposes. They may have voting and inspection rights, although their right to receive dividends may be limited to those shares for which they have paid.[3] The corporation might restrict the transfer of shares until the buyer's note is paid or promise of future services fulfilled.[4]

Not surprisingly, subscribers are liable for the unpaid portions of their subscriptions unless they have a valid contractual defense. Jurisdictions

§17.1 [1] See W. Cary & M. Eisenberg, Cases and Materials on Corporations 1017-1019 (5th ed. 1980).

[2] Id. at 1019. See, e.g., MBCA §6.20(a).

[3] See id. at 1019-1021.

[4] See, e.g., MBCA §6.21(e).

are split as to whether the liability runs to the creditors or to the corporation.[5]

§17.1.2 Par value

Vestigial remains

Par value and associated terms, like *watered stock* and *no par stock*, refer to practices that now have little economic significance but that still must be understood by every corporate lawyer. In this subsection we review how the concept of par value originally functioned, some of the legal problems it led to, and the changes that led to the demise of par value's significance.

Fairness function

The original concept. One main early function of the concept of par value was to help assure equality and fairness among shareholders in a new corporation. (The word *par*, by the way, means "equal.") This function depended on the practice of selling stock at a price equal to its par value, neither more nor less. Suppose that in 1870 Mr. Black, promoter of the then newly formed Box Corporation, approaches Mr. Input with an offer to invest in the corporation's common stock at a price of $100 per share. Black has been soliciting many potential investors in person, on an individual basis. He says that two dozen other investors have already bought shares in Box, and that several dozen others are expected to do so. Input is worried that the other investors have or will put in less money per share then he is being asked to contribute, thus diluting his claim to Box's earnings. What, he asks, is to keep Black from selling the next batch of shares at $60 apiece if he has trouble getting rid of them? Black replies that the par value of each share is $100 (he shows Input a certified copy of the corporate charter and a sample stock certificate, which demonstrate that this is so) and says that there would be legal trouble for him and the other investor if shares were sold for less. Input is reassured by this answer.

Creditor-helping function

The second main function of the concept of par value was to help creditors, both in assessing the riskiness of a proposed extension of credit and in guarding against unfair transfers by their debtor. Suppose that Box Corporation succeeded in issuing 100,000 shares with a par value of $100 per share. Its legal capital now equals $1 million, that is, the par value per share times the number of shares sold. This amount is supposed to signify the stockholders' long-run commitment of investment capital to the new enterprise. If there were ever a bankruptcy of Box, the creditors' claims could be satisfied out of the corporate assets acquired by this investment capital; stockholders would only get what was left — usually nothing.

[5] See W. Cary & M. Eisenberg, note 1 supra, at 1021.

Thus, if all other things are equal, the greater the amount of Box's legal capital, the smaller the risk presented to a creditor contemplating an extension of credit to Box. The potential creditor could therefore use the amount of legal capital as one relevant factor in deciding whether and on what terms to extend credit. If the loan were risky because Box's capital is quite small, for example, the lender might demand a higher interest rate or a mortgage.

"Permanent" investment

Furthermore, it will be much harder, at least in theory, for the shareholders of Box to take back the amounts they invested as legal capital than to receive distributions out of the corporation's earnings or out of any capital contributed in excess of legal capital.[6] Basically, under many statutory schemes directors of Box will not be able to make legal distributions of corporate property to the shareholders unless the value of the property remaining just afterwards matches or exceeds the amount of its debt plus its legal capital. The legal capital amount therefore creates a kind of "minimum collateral" requirement to help protect creditors against excessively large uncompensated transfers of property by their corporate debtor.[7]

Quid pro quo for limited liability

Another way of trying to understand the second, or creditor-protecting, function historically attributed to par value is to see the conceptual linkage between legal capital and limited liability. Consider this often-quoted passage:

> Some Seven men form an Association
> (If possible, all Peers and Baronets)
> They start off with a public declaration
> To what extent they mean to pay their debts.
> That's called their Capital.
> — The (English) Companies Act of 1862, satirized by W. S. Gilbert.

The playwright was not only clever; he sensed an historically important connection between two then-emerging ideas. Imagine the creditors of businesses, as a group, all addressing the newly created large business firms:

[6] See section 14.4 supra.

[7] The creditors could also bargain for explicit additional collateral, of course. The bondholders might take a mortgage on the corporation's real property, for example, and a lending bank might take a security interest in the corporation's inventory and accounts receivable. Nondistribution of legal capital, however, is a minimum protection that all the creditors are entitled to assume will be there, without explicit bargaining in each case.

> We grant you it is not feasible that your numerous stockholder-type investors will put all their personal assets at risk in the business, and expose them to our claims. So we'll let them have limited liability. But at least be good enough to tell us how much of their assets they *do* intend to commit indefinitely to the business and to put at risk, subject to our claims. Declare that amount, and call it legal capital. It will help us know our risks and bargain accordingly.[8]

Does par value perform these two functions — insuring fairness among investing shareholders and rationalizing creditors' risk-taking — today? The answer is clearly no: these functions are performed by other practices and institutions. What, then, is different about the corporate financing environments of 1870 and of today that accounts for the change, and what are these other protective practices? Before answering these questions, however, let us look at some of the legal problems generated by the use of par value stock. Doing so will help us understand the historical changes.

Legal problems associated with par value. Three kinds of problems may be distinguished. They relate to the kind of consideration that legally may be paid for shares, the amount of consideration, and the valuation of noncash forms of consideration.

Example of goods and services

(1) Kind of consideration. Suppose, in our hypothetical, that Mr. Black sold 1,000 of the Box Corporation's $100 par value common shares to Mr. Raw, not for cash but for timber and other materials that were said to be worth $100,000. And suppose he sold another 100,000 shares to Mr. Star, a promising young business executive, not for cash but for Star's promise to work three years for Box Corporation at a low salary. If our cautious potential investor, Mr. Input, learns about these transactions, he may be very alarmed. So may First Bank, a potential creditor of Box. They will worry that Raw's timber and materials were overvalued and that Star's future services won't really be worth $100,000 to the corporation or, worse yet, won't in fact be provided for the full three years. In either case, the result will be to dilute the value of Input's stock and to increase the riskiness of First Bank's loan.

Disclosure vs. restrictions

The worried potential investors could proceed in one of two ways to protect against these contingencies. One way is to insist on full and complete disclosure of all issues of Box stock for noncash consideration, to

[8] See also Hospes v. Northwestern Mfg. & Car Co., 50 N.W. 1117, 1121 (Minn. 1892): "The capital of a corporation is the basis of its credit. It is a substitute for the individual liability of those who own its stock."

evaluate each such transaction, and to invest or not invest in light of these evaluations. Another method is simply to insist that Box issue stock only for cash equal at least to the par value of the issued stock. And, of course, potential investors as a class could act to have their preferences embodied in state corporation statutes, since doing so would simplify common practice and save contracting costs.

Present/future distinction

The way the law settled out in many jurisdictions is exemplified by Section 504(a) of the New York statute.[9] The line is drawn between present and future consideration rather than between cash and noncash consideration. Shares may be issued for money, for other property, (tangible or intangible, for example, patents or copyrights), or for labor or services actually performed for the corporation. However, neither promissory notes nor future services may constitute payment or part payment for the issuance of a corporation's shares. Thus, in our example, the sale of stock to Raw could be valid, while the sale of stock to Star could not.

Bonus, discount, and watered shares

(2) *Amount of consideration.* Stock can be issued for less than par value in a number of different ways. Shares issued without consideration are called *bonus* shares. Shares issued for a positive amount of money less than par value are called *discount* shares. Shares issued for overvalued property or services, so that the true value of the consideration given is less than the shares' par value, are called *watered* shares. Over time, different courts have adopted several supposed rules or theories to deal with the liabilities of shareholders in these situations: the trust fund theory, the fraud or "holding out" theory, and the statutory obligation theory. Let us consider these in turn.

Trust fund doctrine

The trust fund doctrine was probably invented by Justice Story in 1824.[10] An instructive application was made in *Sawyer v. Hoag,*[11] decided in 1873. There the Supreme Court said that "the capital stock of a corporation, especially its unpaid subscriptions, is a trust fund for the benefit of the general creditors of the corporation." Accordingly, a stockholder not making valid payment for his shares could be liable for the shortfall to the company's creditors in a bankruptcy proceeding.

Facts of *Sawyer v. Hoag*

The actual facts in *Sawyer v. Hoag* are infinitely more interesting than this abstract description. They show (1) how the spirit of naive deviousness was alive in the hearts of businessmen and lawyers even a century ago, (2) how an astute court can see through form to substance, and (3) that the

[9] The old MBCA §19 was similar. But MBCA §6.21(b) allows issuance of shares for promissory notes or for contracts for future services.

[10] Wood v. Dummer, 30 F. Cas. 435, No. 17,944 (C.C.D. Me. 1824).

[11] 84 U.S. 610 (1873).

ultimate rationale of the trust fund theory was not really very different from the rationale of the later-developed fraud theory. The company involved was Lumberman's Insurance Company of Chicago. Then, as now, a corporation had to have a substantial, statutorily specified amount of legal capital before it could begin to operate an insurance business. It was clear that if the corporation sold stock with the requisite total par value to investors who actually paid only a fraction of the par value in cash (say, 15 percent), with a promise to pay the rest in installments in the future, the objective behind the minimum capital requirement would not be met and the subscribing shareholders could be held liable for the 85 percent balance in an insolvency proceeding. In essence, Lumberman's tried to get around this problem by magically converting the subscriber's liability for the unpaid subscription amount into debt for money lent by the corporation. The technique was as follows: An investor would actually pay cash equal to 100 percent of the par value of the Lumberman's stock he was getting. But then the company would immediately "loan" him 85 percent of that amount, so that he actually parted with cash equal to only 15 percent of the stock's par value. After Lumberman's was set up this way, the great Chicago fire occurred and the resulting claims under the company's policies made it insolvent. The company determined how much it owed under its policies to the various policyholders whose buildings had burned down and issued them not cash but "certificates of adjusted loss" — that is, creditor claims against the company's assets. Understandably, the value of these certificates was uncertain. Sawyer, one of the "15 percent down" stockholders, bought one of these certificates for 33 percent of its face value. When Lumberman's trustee in bankruptcy[12] demanded that he pay up on his note to the company, Sawyer insisted on "setting off" the full amount of the certificate of loss against this note.

Court looks at substance

Obviously, if Sawyer succeeded with this argument, his total loss on his bad investment in the insurance company would have been much less than the par value of his common stock in the company. The Supreme Court, however, held that his liability to the insurance company on the note was really a liability for the unpaid stock subscription. Under the trust fund theory he therefore had to pay up on this liability for the benefit of creditors. Furthermore, and more important, he could not set off the certificate of loss against this liability, because "mutuality" was lacking. In other words, his liability as a subscriber for stock was not on the same level as his claim as a transferee of a policyholder (who is a creditor), because the whole purpose of his liability as stock subscriber was to make sure that

[12] The trustee in bankruptcy was then referred to as the "assignee."

funds equal to the legal capital of the company were available to meet its creditors' claims. (Also, if the set-off had been allowed, the holder of that certificate of loss would have received preferential treatment as compared to the treatment received in the bankruptcy proceeding by other policyholders.)

Fraud on the public

Interestingly, the Supreme Court was quite aware that Lumberman's initial financing scheme was an evasion of regulatory requirements for insurance companies and/or an attempt to defraud the general public (and policyholders in particular) by treating as "fully paid" stock that, by any common sense analysis of the business realities, was not fully paid. The Court said, "We do not believe we characterize it too strongly when we say it [the two-step financing scheme] was a fraud upon the public who were expected to deal with them."[13] Moreover, the Court's basis for holding that Sawyer did not make valid payment for its stock was not that no money actually passed to the corporation (it did); it objected to the "intent and purpose" of the transactions, that is, to the transparent attempt to change the character of the debt, from one on a stock subscription to one for loan of money, by a mere shuffling of words on paper.

Misrepresentation theory — the *Hospes* case

In 1892 in *Hospes v. Northwestern Manufacturing & Car Co.*,[14] the Minnesota Supreme Court rejected the trust fund doctrine as "not sufficiently precise or accurate" and substituted a misrepresentation theory that was later adopted in other jurisdictions.[15] It would let a creditor recover only if defrauded by the issuance of bonus stock. Yet the creditor need not prove that he relied on an actual belief that the stock was paid for and represented so much capital; he need only allege that he became a creditor after the issuance of the bonus shares. It would then be the defendant's job to prove, if he could, that the creditor actually knew of the bonus shares arrangement and thus was not defrauded. But the Minnesota legislature, although it generally adopted the *Hospes* approach, required the creditors to bear the burden of proof.

Constructive fraud approach criticized

The "constructive fraud" approach has been criticized as no better than the trust fund doctrine, on the grounds that the holder of bonus or watered shares doesn't actually represent to any creditor that he paid for them in full and that modern creditors usually don't know and rely on a corporation's amount of legal capital.[16]

[13] 84 U.S. at 622.

[14] 50 N.W. 1117 (Minn. 1892)

[15] See, e.g., Ballantine, Stockholders' Liability in Minnesota, 7 Minn. L. Rev. 79, 89 (1922); Note, Watered Stock — Shareholder's Liability to Creditors in Arizona, 8 Ariz. L. Rev. 327 (1967).

[16] See Ballantine, note 15, supra.

Some jurisdictions would find a holder of bonus, discount, or watered stock to be liable to the corporation's creditors on the grounds that he incurred a "statutory obligation" to give consideration at least equal to the stock's par value.[17] This is an issue of statutory interpretation, however, and it is very easy for courts to construe a state statute as not imposing such an unbending obligation to creditors, and to adopt the misrepresentation theory instead.[18]

Statutory obligation theory

(3) *Valuation of consideration.* Suppose, in our original hypothetical, that Box Corporation issues shares with a par value of $100,000 to Mr. Raw in exchange for timber that is said to have a fair market value of that amount. If new management takes over Box, or if it goes into bankruptcy and a trustee is appointed to pursue the creditors' interests, can this valuation be challenged as inflated, with the result that Raw's shares will now be characterized as watered stock? And if there is liability for the water under a misrepresentation or statutory obligation theory, who will be liable, Box's former directors, or Raw, or both?

Challenge to original valuation

At common law there were two rules: a "true value" rule, under which the property's value simply could not be less than the stock's par value at the time of the transfer, regardless of what the parties thought; and a "good faith" rule, under which the parties were safe if they honestly appraised the property as being at least equal in value to the stock's par value.

True value and good faith rules

Today, however, the question is usually governed by statute. For example, MBCA Section 6.21(c) requires the directors to make a judgment on the adequacy of consideration but makes that judgment conclusive for purposes of determining whether the shares are "validly issued, fully paid, and nonassessable." Delaware Section 152 is similar.[19] Thus, in our example Mr. Raw could feel sure of avoiding watered stock liability if the Box directors made the requisite valuation of the timber given for the stock, as long as he did not defraud them. (This assumes, however, that Mr. Raw is independent of the board of directors. If he were a promoter or otherwise

Modern statutes

[17] See, e.g., Easton Natl. Bank v. American Brick & Tile Co., 64 A. 917 (N.J. Ct. Err. & App. 1906); DuPont v. Ball, 106 A. 39 (Del. 1918).

[18] See Bing Crosby Minute Maid Corp. v. Eaton, 297 P.2d 5 (Cal. 1956). In 1976, however, California abandoned the concept of corporate capital in its new General Corporation Law. Newly issued shares therefore do not have a "par value" or a "stated value." But §410 does say that "every subscriber to shares and every person to whom shares are originally issued is liable *to the corporation* for the full consideration agreed to be paid for the shares." (Emphasis added.)

[19] It makes the directors' valuation conclusive "[i]n the absence of actual fraud in the transaction." On the problems treated in this subsection, see generally Israels, Problems of Par and No-Par Shares: A Reappraisal, 47 Colum. L. Rev. 1279 (1947).

controlled or strongly influenced the corporation's valuation and its issuance of stock to himself, the governing rules could be quite different, even in a jurisdiction with a statute like MBCA Section 6.21(c). We shall soon examine what his duties might be in the subsection on promoter's fraud.) As for the Box directors, they could presumably escape liability for watered stock as long as they did not act fraudulently or in bad faith.

Sales above par

The demise of par value. Par value ceased long ago to have a role in promoting equality among shareholders. Ironically, this happened at least in part because the concept of par value was too potent for its own good, and generated cautious practices. Precisely in order to reduce the chance of liability for watered stock, corporations began selling stock for substantially more than its par value. For example, Box Corporation might issue 100 shares with a par value of $1 each to Mr. Raw, in exchange for timber valued at $100,000. Box's balance sheet, in so far as it was due to this transaction, would appear as follows:

Assets		*Liabilities*	
Raw Materials	$100,000	Legal Capital	$100
		Capital Surplus	99,900
	$100,000		$100,000

To be sure, the directors might incur liability to certain creditors for misrepresentation or fraud if these figures were deliberately misleading and the creditors relied on them. But that would be of no concern to Mr. Raw, and in any event no one would be liable on a watered stock theory.

Subverted equal treatment function

But this "super safe" technique contained within itself the seeds of destruction of the concept of par value. Corporations were free under liberal statutes to set the par value of stock at any figure and to sell shares at any price in excess of par: $1 par stock might sell for $10 or $10,000. Consequently, after the practice of issuing stock above par got under way, a potential investor solicited by a promoter could not be sure he was getting equal treatment with the other shareholder simply by noting the stock's par value.

Little help to creditors

Another reason for the demise of par value is that it ceased to be of any significant help to creditors (if, indeed, it ever was), either by protecting them against distributions or by aiding them in assessing credit risks. As state corporation statutes whittled down or abandoned their requirements that new corporations have some specified minimum amount of legal capital, and as creditors developed a vast array of techniques for investigating and measuring creditworthiness and for monitoring and securing loans, the debtor's legal capital became a trivial consideration in most lending situations.

No-par stock

All states today allow corporations to issue "no-par value" stock if they wish. No-par shares may be sold at whatever price is deemed reasonable by the board of directors. The statutes permitting them were designed to help eliminate the problem of watered stock liability. They make it safer to issue stock for property of uncertain or speculative value. But many of the statutes, such as Delaware Section 153(b), require the directors to determine or state the value of the consideration to be received by the corporation for no-par shares. The total amount thus determined for the outstanding no-par shares is shown on the balance sheet as "stated capital." If the assets received for no-par shares are worth less than their stated value, problems of watered stock liability may re-emerge.

§17.1.3 Promoters' Frauds

Hypo for analysis

Imagine the following classic sequence of transactions. (1) Peter and Paula Promoter buy certain mining properties for $1 million in cash. (2) They later form the Copper Corporation. (3) They transfer the mining properties to Copper for stock with a total par value of $3.25 million. They also value the properties at that amount on Copper's financial statement. At the time of transfer, Peter and Paula are the only shareholders, directors, and officers of Copper. The mining properties' true fair market value at the time of transfer is $2 million. (4) Copper sells shares to public investors, who pay an amount per share that equals or exceeds par value. Igor is one such investor. (5) Several months later, Peter and Paula sell their shares and thereby lose control of Copper. (6) The new management discovers that the actual fair market value of the mining properties is less than $3.25 million and decides to sue Peter and Paula.

Harm to uninformed investor

Before considering the law's reactions to this hypothetical, let us ask who has been harmed by the Promoters' conduct, and how. The most plausible answer, it seems, is that investors like Igor may have been harmed if they knew and relied on Copper Corporation's financial statements or on the information that the corporation had already issued stock with a certain par value.[20] Igor may have concluded from either source that

[20] Alternatively, Igor's financial advisor, or those market professionals who actually shop around for companies and set the market price at which investors like Igor buy, may have done the knowing and relying. Igor would still have been hurt.

In addition, the buyers of the stock sold in step (5) of the hypothetical may have been injured, depending on whether or not the price they paid reflected the actual value of the mining properties, i.e., on whether the inflated par value had been "found out" by the time they bought.

the corporation already owned property with a fair market value of at least $3.25 million. This conclusion may have affected the price at which he was willing to buy Copper shares. Granted, Igor may have been quite willing to pay more per Copper share than the Promoters did, if he had a favorable view of the company's prospects. Granted, also, that the apparent fair market value of the company's already purchased properties was surely only one of many factors that went into his evaluation of the company's prospects. But the important assumption for our purposes is only that, other things being equal, his view of the fair market value of the company's properties would affect the price at which he would be willing to buy. Had the truth been known, the price paid by Igor and other investors for Copper's shares would have been lower.[21] Moreover, Igor's willingness to buy Copper stock, and the terms on which he would buy, may have been different if he had known what the Promoters had originally paid for the mining properties. This information might affect him because it could influence his own opinion as to the property's fair market value or because it could influence his opinion as to how grasping the Promoters were.

Four lines of attack

In the United States, four main lines of legal attack on promoters like Peter and Paula have developed:

(1) common law rules concerning the promoter's duty to disclose;
(2) the disclosure requirements of the federal Securities Act;
(3) case law interpretations of Rule 10b-5; and
(4) common law rules about the fiduciary's duty to deal fairly with beneficiaries.

Promoter's fiduciary duty to disclose

1. At common law, promoters owe a fiduciary duty to the corporation they are promoting. This duty calls for full disclosure of their personal interests and information relevant to fairness when they are dealing with the corporation. But in two early, well-known cases quite similar to our hypothetical, the state and federal courts took different approaches to the meaning of this duty when the promoters constituted the shareholders and directors at the time of the transaction in question. In *Old Dominion Copper Mining & Smelting Co. v. Bigelow*,[22] the Massachusetts Supreme Judicial Court faulted the promoters for not procuring independent representation

[21] How much lower? The answer is difficult to find, given that factors other than the market value of a company's existing properties do, and rationally should, affect the price at which its stock would sell. This difficulty makes it hard to calculate damages based on what would have happened had there been no fraud.

[22] 89 N.E. 193 (Mass. 1909), aff'd, 225 U.S. 111 (1912).

for the corporation. All the persons interested in the corporation or representing it at the time of the transaction knew the relevant facts, but the sale was part of a plan that contemplated that outside investors would be invited into the business soon afterwards. In *Old Dominion Copper Mining & Smelting Co. v. Lewisohn,*[23] however, the United States Supreme Court took the narrower view that the corporation could not have been deceived at the time of the transaction, because at that time all the individuals whose knowledge could be attributed to the corporation knew the relevant facts. Justice Holmes was also impressed by the consideration that a corporate recovery against the promoters would benefit guilty and innocent shareholders alike — that is, the shareholders who were part of the original syndicate of investors with the two principal promoters and the shareholders who were later invited to buy. (In this respect, remember that corporate recovery is problematic in other situations involving insiders' frauds on some but not all of a corporation's shareholders. See, for example, the discussion of corporate recovery for insider trading in subsection 8.5.2.) Most states followed the *Bigelow* approach, however, and the force of the *Lewisohn* opinion was blunted by later decisions in the federal courts.[24]

***Old Dominion* cases**

The *Bigelow* approach, it should be realized, was a way of getting around limits on direct actions by injured investors. They could not bring a common law fraud action, which required an intentional misrepresentation by the Promoters to the investors; nor, of course, could they then bring a class action. Consequently, a "corporate" action was used, because it invoked the fiduciary's affirmative duty to disclose and offered a remedy. But the *Bigelow* approach doesn't necessarily result in a remedy for the right persons, nor does it focus clearly on the truly harmful conduct.

Circumventing old limits

2. The federal Securities Act removed much of the uncertainty of the common law approach by affirmatively mandating elaborate disclosures in registration statements and prospectuses when corporations offer stock to the general public.[25] Among the many things that have to be disclosed are the facts concerning promoters' and insiders' acquisitions of the corporation's stock. Compliance with these rules would have prevented frauds of the kind occurring in the *Old Dominion* cases. Noncompliance would have given a clear, statutorily defined right of action to the buyers of the corporation's stock.[26] Because the right is defined by statute and resides in the

Securities Act disclosure requirements

[23] 210 U.S. 206 (1907).

[24] See McGowan, Legal Control of Promoters' Profits, 25 Geo. L.J. 269, 282 (1937); San Juan Uranium Corp. v. Wolfe, 241 F.2d 121, 123 (10th Cir. 1957).

[25] See section 17.2 infra.

[26] See subsection 17.4.1 infra (on Section 11 of the Securities Act).

investors rather than in the corporation, there is no need to engage in the metaphysical exercise of deciding whether the corporation was deceived. Where the Securities Act (or a similar state blue sky law) is applicable, there is less impetus to bring a case along the lines of the *Old Dominion*-type promoters' duty to disclose.

Rule 10b-5

3. Occasions do arise when a corporate action seems more feasible or convenient, however, and this, surprisingly, has led to suits based on Rule 10b-5. In our hypothetical, the theory would be that the corporation was a defrauded seller of shares to the promoters. The corporation was deceived in the sense developed by the *Bigelow* line of cases: the promoters had a duty to disclose to the corporation; but their knowledge could not be attributed to the corporation because of their self-interest and the plan to make offers to other investors without disclosure; yet the promoters obtained no independent representation for the company. In *Miller v. San Sebastian Gold Mines, Inc.*,[27] essentially this theory was adopted by a federal appellate court.

Doubts

One may wonder whether such holdings in favor of *corporate* recovery fit the spirit of the Supreme Court's insistence in the *Santa Fe* case[28] on the need for actual fraud or deception to support a 10b-5 action. If the basic objection to the promoters' behavior is that they gave inadequate value to their corporation in return for their shares, the wrong is one that seems redressable only by invoking the state law fiduciary duty of loyalty. If the basic objection is actually fraud, however, the persons hurt by the promoters' nondisclosure must be later-purchasing public investors, a class that might well be different from the class consisting of all of the shareholders of the corporation at the time of the corporate suit. Hence, it is hard to see how the corporation could properly invoke Rule 10b-5. On the other hand, a corporate action has certain economies of scale as compared to a class action by individual shareholders.

Fiduciary duty to deal fairly

4. Finally, apart from rules concerning fraud, a promoter's stock acquisition like that in our hypothetical may be attacked as unfair basic self-dealing. Remember that promoters are fiduciaries to the corporation they are promoting and that they therefore have an affirmative duty to deal fairly with it. In dealing with the corporation they are not allowed to get the best deal for themselves that they can manage, as are ordinary contracting parties. This means that the adequacy of the consideration they give for shares may be examined and found wanting by a court. In *Pipelife Corpora-*

[27] 540 F.2d 807 (5th Cir. 1976). See also Bailes v. Colonial Press, Inc., 444 F.2d 1241 (5th Cir. 1971).

[28] Santa Fe Indus., Inc. v. Green, 430 U.S. 462 (1977).

tion v. Bedford,[29] for example, a Delaware court held that the *promoters* had the burden of proving that their acquisition of stock from the corporation was "entirely fair" to the latter. The case is especially interesting because Delaware had a statutory provision that, like MBCA Section 6.21(c), asserted that when stock is issued for property (as it was in the case before the court), the directors' good faith valuation of the property shall be conclusive. The court held that this statute was inapplicable because of the self-dealing: the promoters, who were fiduciaries, controlled the corporation and were dealing with it. That is, such a statute is designed to create repose on difficult valuation issues for the benefit of arms' length purchasers of stock, not to nullify basic fiduciary duties.

§17.1.4 Preemptive Rights

Basic concept

Sometimes shareholders have so-called preemptive rights: when the corporation issues new shares, the shareholder has the right to purchase a percentage of the new issue that equals his or her percentage of ownership of the already outstanding stock (of the same class) of the corporation. Whether preemptive rights are created by the corporation statute and have to be stipulated away in the articles of incorporation if the incorporators so wish, or whether preemptive rights have to be expressly granted in the articles, depends on the particular state's statute.

Prevalence

In the case of public corporations, preemptive rights are very rare. They exist in some close corporations, where they can serve both to protect some shareholders against unwanted changes in the balance of power and to frustrate those who think a change is needed.

§17.2 The Securities Act: Basics

§17.2.1 The Disclosure Philosophy

Goals of Securities Act

The federal Securities Act of 1933 (the Securities Act) is based on a philosophy of full disclosure rather than on an ideal of substantive regulation. One of its major goals is to deter promotional frauds. It also aims at making sure investors have adequate information for rational investment decision making. The Securities Act is designed to ensure that when offering securities for sale to potential investors, corporations and other issuers of securities provide adequate and accurate information about themselves

[29] 145 A.2d 206 (Del. Ch. 1958).

and the securities they are offering. More specifically, this means that a corporation wishing to sell stocks, bonds, or other securities to the investing public must first file a *registration statement* with the SEC, the registration statement must become *effective,* and every buyer of the securities must receive a copy of a document called a *prospectus,* which is actually part of the registration statement. There are, of course, many important refinements and exceptions to the statement; some are explored in the rest of this chapter.

To perfect, not constrain, choice

The Securities Act does not attempt to prevent people from making and acting on their own judgments about which investments are desirable. The SEC will not refuse to let a registration statement become effective on the ground that the securities are overpriced, or that the investment is too risky for the average investor, or that the issuers' business plans are harebrained. Nor does the SEC produce ratings of securities or otherwise pass on their merits for the guidance of potential investors. It simply requires disclosure of certain kinds of information as a precondition to the public offering and sale of securities. Its goal is to mitigate imperfections in the securities markets by making it easier for participants to engage in informed decision making.

§17.2.2 The Key Provision: Section 5

Registration and prospectus delivery

The key provision of the Securities Act is Section 5, which imposes registration and prospectus delivery requirements on public offerings of securities. The issuing company must prepare and file a registration statement containing extensive, detailed information about itself and the offering, as specified by the statute[1] and the implementing rules and forms. After the SEC staff reviews the statement and the issuer responds to its suggestions about changing it, the registration statement may become effective. The issuer must also see to the dissemination and delivery of copies of the statutory prospectus, which is a smaller, more manageable document containing the most essential parts of the registration statement.[2]

Three time periods

In examining the impact of Section 5, it is customary to distinguish three time periods that are marked off by points in the registration process: the period when a public offering is planned but a registration statement has not yet been filed with the SEC (the pre-filing period), the period between filing and the date when the registration statement becomes effective (the

§17.2 [1]Section 7 and Schedule A.
[2]See §10.

waiting period), and the period after the registration statement has become effective, during which sales are made (the post-effective period).

Offers forbidden

The pre-filing period. The basic rule in the pre-filing period is that offers to sell and offers to buy the securities in the planned offering are fobidden. More precisely, Section 5(c) makes it unlawful for "any person" to make use of any means or instruments of transportation or communication in interstate commerce or of the mails to "offer to sell or offer to buy . . . any security" unless a registration statement has been filed as to such security.[3] Since the terms *person* and *security* are defined quite broadly[4] and the subsection repeatedly uses the term *any*, the sweep of this rule is extremely broad. If any offer to sell securities when no registration statement has been filed is to be legal, either it must not involve any of the stipulated links to interstate commerce or it must fit within an express exemption found elsewhere in the statute. Sections 3 and 4 list numerous exemptions.

Includes stirring up interest

The statute declares that the term "offer to sell" includes "*every* attempt or offer to dispose of, *or solicitation of an offer to buy*, a security or interest in a security, for value."[5] Thus, most efforts to stir up interest in the forthcoming public offering would be forbidden. For example, if X Corporation is planning to file a registration statement, the president of X should not telephone her friends, family members, and customers to ask them if they wish to buy X securities when the offering is finally made. On the other hand, X might properly gather up information about market conditions.

Offers but not sales

The waiting period. In the waiting period there can be offers to sell or buy,[6] but no sales. Section 5(a) prohibits sales until the registration statement becomes effective. Since the terms *sale* and *sell* are defined quite broadly to include "every contract of sale or disposition of a security or interest in a security, for value,"[7] this rule precludes binding agreements to

[3] The full text of §5(c):

> It shall be unlawful for any person, directly or indirectly, to make use of any means or instruments of transportation or communication in interstate commerce or of the mails to offer to sell or offer to buy through the use or medium of any prospectus or otherwise any security, unless a registration statement has been filed as to such security, or while the registration statement is the subject of a refusal order or (prior to the effective date of the registration statement) any public proceeding or examination under section 8.

[4] Sections 2(1) (*security*), 2(2) (*person*).
[5] Section 2(3) (emphases added).
[6] Section 5(c) only prohibits offers before a registration statement has been filed.
[7] Section 2(3).

purchase during the waiting period. For example, during the waiting period a broker whose firm is part of the selling group for the public offering may call up one of his customers, describe the offering, make an offer to sell some of the securities to the customer, and receive the customer's tentative expression of interest (or lack of interest), but may not solicit or receive a firm acceptance of the offer. This is so even if the customer agrees to take delivery of the securities and pay for them only after the effective date; a firm acceptance would still create a *contract* of sale, which is forbidden. Put another way, the customer could tentatively express interest in buying a certain number of the securities during the waiting period, but would be free to renege when the registration statement becomes effective.[8] During the interim, the customer might have read the preliminary prospectus and decided that the offering wasn't so great as the broker's glowing phone call suggested.

Oral vs. written communications

Oral offers like the broker's phone call can be presented in fairly free and unregulated fashion, so long as there are no material misrepresentations. But the use of written or printed materials during the waiting period is tightly regulated. Thus, the selling group brokers are essentially restricted to sending their customers preliminary prospectuses, or "red herrings." They may not also send them "free writings," such as a research report written by the brokerage firm's research staff, that concludes that the offering is a good one for investors.

Statutory basis

Let's examine a bit more closely how the statute produces this result. Section 5(b)(1) makes it unlawful for any person to carry or transmit any "prospectus" relating to any security with respect to which a registration statement has been filed unless the prospectus meets the requirements of Section 10. The term *prospectus* is defined very broadly to mean "any prospectus, notice, circular, advertisement, letter, or communication, written or by radio or television, which offers any security for sale or confirms the sale of any security,"[9] with certain exceptions. Because the brokerage firm's research report appears designed to stir up interest in the offering, it constitutes an offer to sell; because it is also a written communication, it is a prospectus. It would not meet the requirements of Section 10, however, and thus cannot be sent during the waiting period.

The brokerage firm might send out a "bare bones" letter noting the upcoming offer and saying little more than where the customer might get a

[8] The phrase "free to renege" is an overstatement. You can imagine for yourself how many times a customer could do this before his broker stopped making calls to tell him about upcoming public offerings.

[9] Section 2(10).

preliminary prospectus,[10] but this exception gives it no scope for serious selling efforts.

The post-effective period. In the post-effective period, both offers and sales may be made. In addition, free writing is permissible if it is preceded or accompanied by a statutory prospectus in final form.[11] Furthermore, Section 5(b)(1) makes it unlawful to deliver any of the securities (through the mails or otherwise in interstate commerce) unless they are accompanied or preceded by a statutory prospectus.

Offers, sales, and prospectus deliveries

The requirement just mentioned is an odd way for a disclosure-oriented statute to specify a mandated document delivery. If a buyer need be sent a prospectus only when the securities are delivered to her and delivery takes place *after* she has made up her mind and agreed to buy the securities, then the required disclosure document may be quite irrelevant to her investment decision making. In recognition of this anomaly and to counter its possible effects, the SEC emphasizes the obligation of the issuer, underwriter, and selling group brokers to disseminate the preliminary prospectus during the waiting period.[12]

A timing anomaly

§17.2.3 The Registration Process

Contents of registration statements

What is required to be in a registration statement? You can get an abstract sense of the answer to this question by reading the list of 32 items set out in Schedule A to the Securities Act. You can get a more vivid sense of what registration statements are like simply by reading a sample registration statement, or at least a prospectus. Both exercises are highly recommended, and there is no quick substitute for them. As you will discover, the issuer must disclose a great deal of information about its business operations and its capital structure, its financial condition and performance, its directors and officers and their personal relationships to the issuer, the terms of the offering, the uses to which the proceeds of the offering will be put, commissions to the underwriters, and so forth. (Note, however, that under the modern system of "integrated disclosure," which is discussed below in subsection 17.5.1, much of the information that is required to be disclosed may actually appear in other publicly available documents that the registration statement incorporates by reference.)

[10] See §2(10)(b).

[11] See §2(10)(a).

[12] If the SEC staff believes the preliminary prospectus has been inadequately distributed, it may refuse to grant "acceleration," a concept explained in the next subsection.

Effective date

A few points about registration procedures deserve to be mentioned here. Consider first this basic question: How soon after a registration statement is filed may securities covered by it be sold? According to Section 5(a), sales may only take place when the registration statement is "in effect." Section 8(a) declares that, except as otherwise provided, the "effective date" of a registration statement is the twentieth day after it is filed *or* such earlier date as the Commission may determine, having due regard to the adequacy of the information publicly available about the issuer and other related factors. The Commissioner's power to set such an earlier date is called its power to "accelerate" the effectiveness of the statement.

Need for acceleration

It might seem, then, as if the issuer could simply file a registration statement, wait 20 days, and then begin selling, with or without the SEC's permission. But this does not happen. In order to have a complete and legally adequate registration statement, the price at which the securities will be offered to the public must be stated. But since market conditions constantly change and the investment banking firm that is doing the underwriting will decide the optimal offering price just before making the offer — for example, on the day before the effective date — the actual offering price cannot be inserted into the registration statement when it is originally filed. To get it in, there has to be an amendment to the registration statement. But an amendment starts the 20-day period running again![13] By the end of that 20-day period the inserted price will be stale, and a new amendment will be needed. So the issuer and the underwriter are caught in an immobilizing infinite regress, unless the Commission agrees to accelerate the effective date on receipt of the price amendment. And how do they induce the Commission to agree to acceleration? By playing ball with the SEC staff. That is, they should follow the agency's guidelines as to what should be in the statement and should respond cooperatively and diligently to the staff's suggestions (for example, in a "letter of comment") about the original version of the registration statement. The Commission's power to accelerate is thus a very important one, and it has served as the vehicle by which many of the agency's policies about desirable disclosures have been implemented.

Enforcement powers

Note also that the SEC has numerous other enforcement powers. For example, Section 8(b) authorizes the Commission to issue "refusal orders": If a registration statement appears on its face to be inaccurate or incomplete in any material respect, the Commission may, after notice and opportunity for a hearing, issue an order refusing to permit the statement to become effective. Under Section 8(d), it can issue a "stop order" suspend-

[13] Section 8(a), second sentence.

ing the effectiveness of a registration statement, if it appears to contain material misstatements or omissions; again, however, this is done after notice and opportunity for a hearing. The SEC is empowered to conduct examinations — by demanding the production of books and papers, administering oaths and questioning relevant persons, and so on — in order to determine whether a stop order should issue.[14] Section 20(a) empowers it to demand statements from suspected violators of the Act; 20(b), to bring injunctive actions in the federal district courts and to refer matters to the Attorney General for possible criminal proceedings; and 20(c), to apply in the district courts for writs of mandamus to compel compliance with the Act.

Staff review

Despite the fact that the SEC staff reviews registration statements (primarily to see if they appear, on their face, to be complete and adequate), it makes no official findings as to their truthfulness and completeness, and the fact of such review should have no weight in a civil action brought by an investor on the basis of misrepresentations and omissions in a registration statement. Indeed, Section 23 makes it a crime to represent to a potential purchaser that by letting a registration statement become effective the SEC has found it to be true and accurate on its face, or has found it not to contain untruths and omissions.

§17.3 The Securities Act: Exemptions

Importance of topic

Though the actual shepherding of corporations through the Securities Act registration process is specialized work done mostly by relatively few law firms, many lawyers counseling business clients have occasion to investigate whether a proposed transaction invokes the Act's registration requirements or is exempted from them. The question is an extremely important one to clients because the registration process is quite expensive.[1] As might be expected, given the stakes involved and the endless variety of business financing arrangements, there is a complex body of lore on exemptions.

Need for a map

Perhaps the most useful first step in studying this subject is to obtain a

[14] Section 8(e).

§17.3 [1] Public offerings create two major categories of costs: the administrative costs of the offering (those run up by the lawyers, accountants, financial printers, etc.) and the underwriters' fees. For sample figures, see R. Brealey & S. Myers, Principles of Corporate Finance 303 (2d ed. 1984). Issue costs, as a percentage of proceeds for registered issues of common stock over a five-year period, averaged 6.2 percent (5 percent underwriters' compensation and 1.2 percent other expenses). By contrast, unregistered private offerings of securities have much lower costs. However, there are economies of scale in public offerings.

map of the major types of transactions involving an ordinary small business that raise the exemption question. Once we grasp the basic types and their relationships to one another, we can begin to study the details in a more sensible way.

Three types of transactions

Three types of transactions may be distinguished. (1) The first type consists of offers and sales of securities by a corporation to a small and/or sophisticated set of investors. These may qualify for exemption as "private offerings" pursuant to Section 4(2) of the Act and Regulation D. (They are also known as "private placements.") Related to this are exemptions for offerings involving only a small dollar amount of new capital, which are also covered by Regulation D. (2) The second type consists of resales by private placees or others of stock originally issued in a private offering or other exempted offering. These may qualify for exemption under Section 4(1) and Rule 144 if certain requirements are met. (3) The third type involves sales or resales of securities by a controlling person of an issuing corporation. Such sales may cause problems for both the controlling person and his or her broker, unless exemptions are available pursuant to Sections 4(1) or 4(4) and Rule 144.

Happy Hospital hypo: initial offering

Let us consider a hypothetical case. Ed forms the Happy Hospital Consulting Corporation to run a business that will consult with hospitals and show them how to maximize the reimbursements they can get from governmental and private insurance programs. On January 1, 1985, he raises $2 million of initial capital by causing Happy Hospital to sell newly issued shares of common stock to himself and to four close friends, as follows: Arlene, 10 percent; Baker, 5 percent; Charlene, 15 percent; Doug, 10 percent; Ed, 60 percent. Ed uses the telephone to negotiate some aspects of the sales, and he causes Happy Hospital to mail stock certificates to each of the investors. Happy Hospital does not file a registration statement with the SEC, nor does it deliver prospectuses to the investors.

Application of §5

If we read only Section 5 of the Securities Act and the associated definitions in Section 2, we would conclude that Ed and Happy Hospital have violated the Act. Section 5(a), for example, prohibits "any person, directly or indirectly," from using instruments of communication in interstate commerce (such as telephones) to "sell" "a security," unless a registration statement is in effect. It also prohibits using the mails to deliver the securities unless a registration statement is in effect. Section 5(b), requiring the delivery of a statutorily satisfactory prospectus, and Section 5(c), requiring the filing of a registration statement before making offers to sell any security, also appear to have been violated.

Exemption under §4(2)?

To avoid a violation, the offering and sale to the five friends would have to fit under an exemption. The most likely candidate is the Section 4(2) exemption. That subsection says the provisions of Section 5 shall not apply to "transactions by an issuer not involving any public offering." Thus, Happy Hospital and Ed would argue that the sale is pursuant to a *private* offering, not a public one.

What's "public" vs. "private" offering?

But what is a "public" and what is a "private" offering? Obviously, when a large corporation hires a major investment banking firm to sell millions of shares to the general public and the shares are then to be traded on a stock exchange, the offering is a public one. Equally obviously, a single individual who incorporates her business and takes all of its stock is not engaged in a public offering. Intermediate cases are often governed by case law and Regulation D, which are discussed in subsection 17.3.1. Let's assume that the offer and sale of Happy Hospital stock to the five friends does qualify as a private offering, so Section 5 was not violated.

Resale by initial investor

Suppose that a year later, on January 1, 1986, Arlene wants to sell her Happy Hospital stock and use the proceeds to buy a vacation home. She is willing to solicit possible buyers from among her numerous acquaintances, or to ask a broker to try to find a buyer.

Application of §5

Do these would-be sales by a private placee of stock not issued pursuant to a registration statement create any legal problems? Yes. Once again, the sweeping terms of Section 5 cause a problem. Arlene would be "selling" "a security" while no registration statement is in effect. Therefore, she must undertake to have her offer and sale registered or must find an explicit exemption.

Exemption under §4(1)?

Assume that the private offering exemption would not be available, because she or her broker would have to solicit many buyers. Could she nevertheless fit under Section 4(1)? That provision says that Section 5 shall not apply to "transactions by any person other than an issuer, underwriter, or dealer." Surely Arlene is not an issuer; Happy Hospital Consulting Corporation is the issuer of the stock. Nor does she appear to be an "underwriter" in the ordinary business usage of that term: she is not running an investment banking firm that is engaged in the business of helping companies raise money by selling stocks and bonds to the general public. Nor does she appear to be a "dealer" within the meaning of Section 2(12), because she is not, let us assume, engaged "*in the business* of offering, buying, selling, or otherwise dealing or trading in securities issued by another person." (Emphasis added.)

What's an "underwriter"?

But there is a catch. It involves the Act's broad definition of *underwriter* in Section 2(11). That provision defines *underwriter* to mean "any person who has purchased from an issuer with a view to, or offers or sells for an issuer in connection with, the distribution of any security, or participates or has a direct or indirect participation in any such undertaking, or participates or has a participation in the direct or indirect underwriting of any such undertaking. . . ." Arguably, Arlene's sales would simply be part of a general process by which Happy Hospital made a "distribution" of its securities to the investing public. The fact that Happy Hospital initially sold only to five investors is arguably a mere detail; what has to be looked at, to see if it is making a distribution to the investing public, is the net result of the whole set of transactions in its stock over a several-year time period. If Arlene's sales are deemed to be part of such a distribution, then perhaps it can also be argued that she originally "purchased with a view to" the distribution. Perhaps it is enough for this purpose that she considered it possible on January 1, 1985, that she might want to resell her stock within a few years. If so, then she would be acting as an underwriter in January, 1986, and so the Section 4(1) exemption would not be available.[2]

The crucial question for Arlene is whether the SEC and the courts would place such a broad construction on the concept of "underwriter" and on its defining elements. What then is a "distribution"? What does it mean to "purchase with a view to" a distribution? What does it mean to "offer or sell *for*" an issuer? These questions are taken up in subsections 17.3.3 and 17.3.4.

Sale by controlling person

Suppose now that seven years later, on January 1, 1993, Ed wants to retire and to sell all of his stock in Happy Hospital (which has never sold securities pursuant to a registration statement). He does not want to file a registration statement covering his sales. He plans to ask Worthy Broker to sell the shares to any potential buyers he can find.

Not same problem

Because of the long time period between the initial offering and Ed's resale, his problem, if any, is different from Arlene's. Surely no one will seriously argue that his resales are part of a distribution to the public which began with the initial sales in 1985. Thus, Ed is not an "underwriter" in connection with such a distribution. Nor does he appear to be an issuer or dealer, so perhaps the Section 4(1) exemption applies.

Broker "underwriting" a "distribution"?

But again there is a catch. Ed, with his 60 percent common stock interest in Happy Hospital, is clearly a controlling person of Happy Hospital. This puts him in the somewhat more general category of an *affiliate*: one who controls, is controlled by, or is under common control with, the issuer. If we go back to Section 2(11) and look at the rest of its definition of *underwriter*, we find a curious final sentence. It says that for purposes of applying the definition of *underwriter* the term *issuer* shall include any affiliate of the

[2] Another problem with the §4(1) exemption is that, if Arlene uses a regular stockbroker to help sell her shares, the broker will appear to be a "dealer" under the §2(12) definition, and the transactions would thus "involve" a dealer.

actual issuer.[3] (By "actual issuer" — my term, not the statute's — I mean the entity against which the securities represent an investment interest. Here it is Happy Hospital.) Thus, if Ed's sales are large and substantial enough to be considered a distribution of securities to the investing public, then anyone who "offers or sells *for*" Ed will be offering or selling for an issuer in connection with a distribution, and will therefore be deemed an "underwriter" within the meaning of Section 2(11). In our hypothetical, this means that Worthy Broker will be deemed an underwriter of the distribution of securities. Sales by Ed through Worthy will therefore *not* qualify under Section 4(1) as "transactions by any person other than an issuer, underwriter, or dealer." Unless some other exemption is available, the sales will be in violation of Section 5.

Counterarguments

Worthy could try two counterarguments. One is that Ed's sales don't amount to a "distribution," whatever that undefined term in the statute might mean. The other is that the sales are covered by the Section 4(4) exemption for "brokers' transactions executed upon customers' orders on any exchange or in the over-the-counter market but not the solicitation of such orders."

Under what conditions will these counterarguments work? This question is considered below in subsection 17.3.4.

Summary of overview

To recapitulate the main points of our discussion: (1) Happy Hospital's initial sales of its stock raise the question whether the offers and sales are exempted as a private offering; (2) Arlene's resales of stock bought in a private offering raise the question whether she is an underwriter acting in connection with an unregistered distribution of securities; and (3) the sales by controlling person Ed raise the question whether Worthy Broker is acting as an underwriter in connection with an unregistered distribution. We turn now to authorities that help answer these and related questions.

§17.3.1 Private Offerings

Traditional applications

What does Section 4(2) mean by "transactions not involving any public offering"? Several traditional applications of the provision may be noted.[4] One consists of sales of bonds, debentures, or notes by corporations to one or more institutional investors, such as life insurance companies or pension funds. A related kind of private placement is the issuance by a corpo-

[3]The last sentence of §2(11) states, "As used in this paragraph the term 'issuer' shall include, in addition to an issuer, any person directly or indirectly controlling or controlled by the issuer, or any person under direct or common control with the issuer."

[4]See D. Ratner, Securities Regulation 54-55 (2d ed. 1982).

ration of a promissory note to a commercial bank when it takes out a term loan. In these cases the exemption makes obvious sense. Institutional investors are usually sophisticated and powerful enough to demand and get the information they need before committing their money. The legal system does not have to protect them with a superimposed mandatory disclosure system.[5] Another use of the exemption is for sales of securities to a few key, well-informed, and well-positioned employees of the issuing corporation. It could also apply to the issuance of securities by a corporation (say, a large, publicly held one) to acquire all the shares of a closely held corporation, and it often may apply to promotional offerings of securities to a limited number of people. This last case is the one on which we shall focus.

***Ralston Purina* case**

In 1953 the Supreme Court decided the important case of *SEC v. Ralston Purina Co.*[6] In that case the offering was made to employees of the issuer. The Court decided that the availability of the 4(2) exemption depends on the offerees' "need for the protection" provided by the Act. Whether this need is present turns on (1) whether the offerees have access to the kind of information that registration would provide and (2) whether they are able to fend for themselves. Thus, the exemption is not available merely because the offering was made to a small number of people, or to a sharply delimited class of people.

Access and sophistication factors

Implementation problems

The concepts employed in the *Ralston Purina* decision were clearly related to the policies behind the Securities Act, but were not so easy to apply to real cases. In 1962, in Securities Act Release No. 4552, the SEC elaborated the meaning of those concepts and offered a balanced and fairly complete listing of factors relevant to the availability of the exemption. Practicing lawyers did not find this sufficiently definite or objective enough to give them confidence about their advice in many cases, however. The SEC was induced in 1974 to adopt Rule 146, a complex and technical but supposedly objective rule. This rule was in turn superseded in 1982 by Regulation D, which comprises Rules 501 through 506 under the Securities Act.[7]

Reg D a safe harbor

The first thing to note about Regulation D is that it is only a safe-harbor rule. If a transaction meets its requirements, it is safe from attack by the

[5] If the legal system were to do anything about the typical negotiations between corporations and consortia of commercial banks involving a term loan, its most useful act might be to provide post-bargaining psychiatric care to the officers of the borrowing corporations.

[6] 346 U.S. 119 (1953).

[7] Regulation D also superseded old Rules 240 and 242, which had to do with exemptions for small offerings. This aspect of the Regulation is treated in the next subsection.

SEC as an illegally unregistered offering of securities.[8] If a transaction does not meet the Regulation's requirements, however, it *might* still qualify as an exempted private offering or other exempt transaction. In deciding whether such a noncomplying transaction does so qualify, the lawyer has to look at other sources, such as Release No. 4552, for guidance.

Rule 506's main features

Rule 506 is the part of the Regulation that exempts certain private offerings. Generally speaking, its strategy is to focus on the number of unsophisticated investors who can buy securities without making the transaction a public offering. More precisely, the Rule has four salient features. First, under it an issuer may sell to any number of accredited investors but only up to 35 nonaccredited investors. Roughly speaking, "accredited investors" are those who are deemed on the basis of certain rather mechanical tests[9] to be able to fend for themselves — for example, insurance companies, millionaires, and individuals who make more than $200,000 a year.[10]

Second, there is no dollar limit to the amount of sales under Rule 506.

Third, certain procedural requirements must be met: The issuer must not engage in general advertising of the offer;[11] it must file a notice of the sales with the SEC;[12] and it must take reasonable care to assure itself that the buyers are not underwriters and and that they understand the limits on resales.[13]

Fourth, if (but only if) the issuer sells any securities to any nonaccredited investor, it has to meet additional requirements. (1) It must make certain specified disclosures.[14] These are generally much less expensive to make than those required in a full-scale registration. The exact type of information to be furnished to purchasers depends on the size of the offering and the company's status (whether it reports under the Securities

[8] Nor could it be attacked on this basis by private parties.

[9] See the lengthy definition of *accredited investor* in Rule 501(a). Note too that Rule 506 focuses on the number of purchasers. Previously, lawyers and courts worried about the number of *offerees*. (They may still do so when a party claiming there is a private offering does not rely on Regulation D.)

[10] More exactly, you are an accredited investor if you had more than $200,000 of individual income in each of the last two years and reasonably expect to top that mark again in the current year.

[11] Rule 502(c).

[12] Rule 503.

[13] Rule 502(d). The basic limit is that the securities cannot be resold without registration under the Act or an exemption from registration. This point has to be conveyed to purchasers in written form before sale and must be noted on the stock certificates or other evidences of the securities.

[14] Rule 502(b). Notice that, if required, the disclosures must be made to *all* purchasers during the course of the offering and prior to the sale.

Exchange Act, for example). (2) Prior to making any sale to a nonaccredited investor, the issuer must also "reasonably believe" that the latter, either alone or with his "purchaser representative" (a kind of financial guardian angel defined in the Regulation), has "such knowledge and experience in financial and business matters that he is capable of evaluating the merits and risks of the prospective investment." This last requirement retains a dose of subjectivity in the Rule and makes lawyers feel that the harbor is a little less than absolutely safe. (3) With respect to the provision of information by the issuer, nonaccredited investors must be treated equally with accredited investors. (4) The nonaccredited investors must be given an opportunity to ask questions and receive answers.

§17.3.2 Small Offerings

§3(b) Section 3(b) of the Securities Act authorizes the SEC to adopt rules exempting issues of securities "by reason of the small amount involved or the limited character of the public offering," as long as the aggregate amount at which the issue is offered to the public doesn't exceed a certain amount ($5 million, as of this writing). For such cases, Regulation D has two exemptions, Rules 504 and 505, that depend on the dollar amount of offerings.

Rule 504 Rule 504 is the purer example. Remember that Rule 506 (on private offerings) focused on a small number of (nonaccredited) purchasers as the key to the exemption, but imposed no dollar limit. By contrast, Rule 504 focuses on a small amount of money ($500,000 or less, currently) as the key to an exemption, but imposes no limit on the number of nonaccredited purchasers. Specifically, to qualify under Rule 504 the aggregate offering price for the securities cannot exceed $500,000 *less* the aggregate offering price for all securities sold by the issuer in the previous 12 months in reliance on a 3(b) exemption or in violation of the Act. That is, multiple offerings within any 12-month period have to be lumped together in determining whether the dollar limit is exceeded.

If the dollar limit is met, there are few other restrictions. Unlike the case under Rule 506 when some sales are made to nonaccredited investors, Rule 504 does not impose specific disclosure requirements.[15] The rules limiting general advertising and requiring communication of restraints on resale do apply, unless the offers and sales are made exclusively in a state or states that require registration and delivery of disclosure documents before sale and the state requirements are actually met.

[15] See Rule 502(b)(l)(i).

Return to our hypothetical case. Suppose that Ed wants Happy Hospital to make its initial offering of stock to 50 doctors (all general practitioners), none of whom is an accredited investor, but is willing to raise only $500,000. The offering would not qualify under Rule 506, since there are too many nonaccredited investors, but it could qualify under Rule 504. **Example**

Rule 505 can be understood as a rule that straddles 504 and 506. Like 504, it imposes a dollar limit on the offering (here, $5 million). Like 506, it imposes a limit on the number of nonaccredited purchasers (35). Moreover, the other restrictions affecting transactions exempted under Rule 506 generally apply. Thus, if there are any sales to nonaccredited investors, the specific information disclosure requirements of Rule 502 are triggered. **Rule 505**

This last point suggests a question: If both 505 and 506 impose a limit on nonaccredited purchasers, specific disclosure requirements, and similar procedural restraints, but only 505 has a dollar limit, why does anyone ever try to get under Rule 505? The answer is that under it the issuer is not required (as it is under 506) to form a "reasonable belief" about the knowledge, experience, and evaluative capability of the nonaccredited investors. Thus, the lawyer counseling her client about the availability of this exemption may be able to achieve greater certainty than if the private offering exemption were invoked. **Why use 505 rather than 506**

Return again to our hypothetical. Suppose Ed wants Happy Hospital's initial offering to be a sale of stock for a total price of $2 million to 30 doctors who are not accredited investors. Rule 504 would not be applicable because the dollar amount is too large. Rule 506 might be, but it would trigger the "reasonable belief" problem, which Ed might well prefer to avoid. He would thus turn to Rule 505. **Example**

Note that if Happy Hospital were to sell $2 million of stock to more than 35 nonaccredited investors, then none of the three exemptions in Regulation D would apply. Happy would have to register or find some other exemption. (It might argue, for example, that the transaction was a non-Regulation D private offering fitting under case law precedents.)

§17.3.3 Resales of Restricted Securities

Recall our discussion of Arlene's problem in the introductory part of this section. Having bought stock from a corporation that did not register the offering, she wants to sell it a year later to other investors. I suggested that there could be a problem, namely, that she might be considered an "underwriter" with respect to an (unregistered) distribution of the corporation's securities to the investing public. The question now is whether the law **Meaning of *underwriter?***

would really adopt such an expansive interpretation of the concept of "underwriter."

Chinese Consol. Benev. Assn. **case**

Case law indicates that it is proper to interpret the term quite broadly. Consider the Second Circuit's decision in *SEC v. Chinese Consolidated Benevolent Association.*[16] The case did not involve a resale of privately placed securities, but it did interpret the term *underwriter* in an eye-opening way. The Chinese government was then engaged in a losing war with Japan and was trying to finance its efforts by the sale of bonds. The Association, on its own motion and without having any contractual relationship with the Chinese government, set up a committee that began to drum up interest in the bonds among Chinese-Americans. The committee also offered to act, and did act, as a conduit by accepting funds from prospective purchasers for delivery to the Bank of China in New York. Neither the committee nor its members received compensation from any source for these activities. The bonds were not registered under the Securities Act.

"Selling for" an issuer

The court held that there was a violation of Section 5(a) and that the exemption for transactions not involving an issuer, underwriter, or dealer was not available. The Association was an underwriter because it was "sell[ing] *for* an issuer in connection with a distribution," and therefore fitted the statutory definition. It was irrelevant that its activities were not authorized by the issuer and were not compensated by anyone. Nor could it be argued that the Association's activities were for the purchasers but not for the Chinese government. "Selling for" an issuer occurs when one sells "for the benefit of" the issuer; it is not necessary that one also sell "on behalf of" the issuer, in the sense of being its agent.[17]

Purpose of exemption

Looked at another way, the court stressed the narrowness of the fundamental purpose of the Section 4(1) exemption: to exempt trading between investors in securities already issued, not to exempt distributions by issuers. Notice that, were it not for Section 4(1), most of the millions of dollars' worth of trades that are done every day on the major stock exchanges would be in violation of the Securities Act. Even if we say that all the subsection does is to exempt such ordinary secondary trading, that interpretation leaves it with quite an impressive role.

Why this case?

On reflection, the result in the case seems harsh. Surely most Chinese-Americans knew how the war was going, and it is plausible to suppose that most of the investors in the bonds didn't really expect to get their money back. The whole bond issue could be viewed as a face-saving way of

[16] 120 F.2d 738 (2d Cir. 1941).

[17] The court would have found the exemption unavailable even if the Association were not an "underwriter," because it participated in transactions that *did* involve "an issuer."

soliciting patriotic contributions. If this interpretation is correct, it seems silly to suppose that the "investors" needed or wanted the detailed, cautionary disclosures that would be provided under the Securities Act. Why, then, did the SEC choose to use its scarce legal resources to bring an enforcement action in this situation?

Possible answer

Perhaps because it wanted to establish emphatically that the Act's definition of *underwriter* has an extremely broad reach. (It may also have taken a dim view of foreign bonds at that time.) With the perimeters of the statutory prohibitions set so far out, it would then have plenty of room in which to carve out exemptive rules to its own liking.

Rule 144

The relevant rule governing resales of privately placed securities is Rule 144, which was adopted in 1972. Let's examine its major features.

Two types of transactions

Coverage. Rule 144 covers two types of transactions: (1) sales of "restricted securities" by any person for his own account; and (2) sales of "restricted *or any other securities*" by any person "for the account of an affiliate" of the issuer of such securities.[18] If the conditions of the Rule are met, then either type of selling person is deemed not to be engaged in a "distribution" of the sold securities and therefore not to be an "underwriter" under the Act.

Restricted securities

Restricted securities are those acquired directly or indirectly from the issuer or an affiliate of the issuer in a transaction or chain of transactions not involving any public offering.[19] The Rule therefore covers the very common case of resales of securities that were originally issued pursuant to an exempt private offering. Remember Arlene in our hypothetical case: She bought shares from Happy Hospital; the company (properly) didn't register the offering; she later wants to sell her shares. She will be assured of not violating the Act if she complies with Rule 144. The same is true of persons who buy the stock from her when it comes time for them to resell.

Sales for affiliates

The second type of transaction covered by the Rule, sales for the account of an affiliate of the issuer of the sold securities, will be discussed in the next subsection (17.3.4.).

[18] Rule 144(b).

[19] Rule 144(a)(3). Notice a problem that this definition creates. Suppose a private placee (like Arlene in our hypothetical) resells her stock to various people, including Buyer. Assume that, under the facts, Arlene *should* have registered but didn't. May Buyer, when he wants to resell some of the shares, invoke the Rule? Arguably not. He does not seem to hold "restricted securities" *as defined* in the Rule, for it is not the case that he bought them in a chain of transactions "not involving any public offering." His chain of transactions did involve a public offering (Arlene's sale); it simply wasn't registered. Nor is Buyer an "affiliate." Therefore, neither of the operative provisions of Rule 144(b) seems to apply. Admittedly, though, this reading of the Rule is quite literal.

Safe harbor

Approach. The basic approach of Rule 144 is to provide a safe harbor for persons who might otherwise be classified as underwriters of an illegally unregistered distribution of securities, as long as certain objective criteria are met. Thus, failure to satisfy all the conditions of the Rule doesn't *necessarily* mean that Arlene will be violating the Act when she resells her stock.[20] The existence of a violation would be finally determined, if at all, in litigation. But if her transactions satisfy the Rule, she should be safe from the risk of such a finding.

Conditions. For the safe harbor to be available, five conditions must be met.

Information requirement

First, adequate and current public information must be available about the issuer of the securities.[21] The Rule specifies what this means. An issuing company that reports under the Securities Exchange Act must be current in filing required reports. Other companies must have made publicly available the information specified in certain clauses of another rule.[22]

Holding period

Second, if the securities sold are restricted securities, a holding period requirement applies.[23] The person for whom they are sold must have been the beneficial owner for at least two years. There are elaborate subrules about how to count the two-year period in particular situations. For example, if Arlene makes a *gift* of her stock to her son and he later wants to sell it, he can count the period she held the stock toward satisfaction of the two-year requirement. Note that in our original hypothetical, she wanted to sell only one year after the original private offering, so she could not claim the protection of the Rule.

Volume limits

Third, there are volume limits on the sales. The safe harbor is unavailable if the seller wants to sell too much too fast. Basically, the limit in each three-month period is the greater of (1) 1 percent of the units of the outstanding securities in question or (2) the average weekly trading volume in the securities during the prior four weeks.[24] Thus, even assuming that Arlene waited two years after Happy Hospital's private offering before trying to sell her stock, and assuming that Happy Hospital stock is not actively traded, Arlene would be restricted under the Rule to selling only 1 percent of Happy's outstanding stock every three months. Since she owns

[20] See Rule 144(j) (the "non-exclusive rule").

[21] Rule 144(c).

[22] Rule 15c2-11 under the Securities Exchange Act.

[23] Rule 144(d).

[24] Rule 144(e). As with the holding period requirement, there are elaborate subrules about how to "count": whether, for example, the separate sales of a husband and wife have to be aggregated for purposes of applying the volume limit.

10 percent, the volume limit would seem to force her to take about two and a half years to dispose of her stock — if she wishes to rely on Rule 144.

Lifted after three years

In fact, though, under an amendment to the Rule the volume limit is lifted for a nonaffiliate who has held restricted securities for three years.[25] (Indeed, the public information requirement and the requirements discussed in the next two paragraphs are also lifted after three years.) Thus, Arlene could sell one percent of Happy Hospital stock each quarter during her third year of holding such stock and her remaining 6 percent interest immediately after the third year.

Manner of sale

Fourth, there are limits on the manner of sale.[26] Arlene would have to sell her stock in ordinary "brokers' transactions"[27] or directly to a "market maker."[28] The thrust of this requirement is to limit sharply her broker's ability to solicit customers' orders to buy the stock — that is, to act as an aggressive salesman rather than simply responding to buy orders or the inquiries of potential buyers. For this condition to be met, there would almost have to be a pre-existing market in the shares of Happy Hospital stock.

Notice

Fifth, a notice of the proposed sale must be filed with the SEC and the exchange (if any) on which the securities are traded.[29]

Though Rule 144 aims to provide objectivity and certainty, a very large number of interpretive questions have arisen under it.

§17.3.4 Sales by Controlling Persons

The problem

Recall the third problem raised in our introductory hypothetical: years after the initial private offering, Ed, controlling stockholder of Happy Hospital, wants to sell his stock through Worthy Broker, but the latter is worried that he might be considered an underwriter of an illegally unregistered distribution of securities.

***Ira Haupt* case**

The nature of the problem is well illustrated and analyzed by *In the Matter of Ira Haupt & Co.*,[30] an SEC decision. Schulte and two controlled entities owned over 90 percent of the common stock of Park & Tilford, Inc., which was planning a distribution of whiskey at cost to its shareholders.

[25] Rule 144(k).
[26] Rule 144(f).
[27] Rule 144(g) defines the term.
[28] As defined in Section 3(a)(38) of the Securities Exchange Act.
[29] Rule 144(h).
[30] 23 S.E.C. 589 (1946).

Because of the wartime shortage of liquor, this plan was expected to create very active trading in Park & Tilford stock, as thirsty investors scrambled to get under the corporate spigot. To take advantage of this interest, Schulte asked Ira Haupt & Co., a brokerage firm, to sell a substantial part of his stock on an orderly basis (in other words, in small lots, and not in a hurry). In about six months Haupt sold stock for Schulte amounting to some 38 percent of the outstanding Park & Tilford stock. A proceeding was brought before the SEC to determine whether *Haupt* had violated Section 5(a) of the Securities Act and should be sanctioned.[31] A willful violation was found.

Why Haupt is an underwriter

One major issue was whether Haupt was an underwriter. The SEC decided it was, because it sold for an issuer in connection with a distribution. There was little question that Haupt "sold for" Schulte, who as controlling stockholder was an "affiliate" of Park & Tilford and therefore, under the final sentence of Section 2(11), was himself deemed to be an "issuer" of the stock. The only serious question was whether the sales were in connection with a "distribution." This term, which is not defined in the statute, was described as comprising "the entire process by which in the course of a public offering the block of securities is dispersed and ultimately comes to rest in the hands of the investing public." The SEC thought the facts clearly showed a distribution in this sense.

Brokers' transactions exemption not applicable

A second major issue was whether Haupt could invoke the exemption for "brokers' transactions executed on customers' orders or on any exchange or in the over-the-counter market but not the solicitation of such orders," which now appears as Section 4(4). After all, Haupt did act as broker (that is, agent) on the orders of Schulte, its customer. But the SEC staff argued that this exemption could never apply to exempt an underwriter engaged in a distribution for a controlling stockholder or, alternatively, that Haupt's activities exceeded normal brokers' functions and thus destroyed the exemption's availability. The Commission basically agreed with the first argument, stressing that the congressional intent was focused on exempting secondary *trading* by investors in already issued securities, as distinct from the *distribution* of securities to investors. In the words of the Commission's own summary,

> Section [4(4)] permits individuals to sell their securities through a broker or in an ordinary brokerage transaction, during the period of distribution or while a stop order is in effect, without regard to the registration and prospectus

[31] The sanctions might have included revoking Haupt's registration as broker-dealer or expelling it from the National Association of Securities Dealers. It was merely suspended from membership in the NASD for 20 days.

requirements of Section 5. But the process of distribution itself, however carried out, is subject to Section 5.

(Incidentally, this reading of Section 4(4) shows how it is simply a counterpart to Section 4(1), when considered in relation to the millions of ordinary stock trades that are carried out every day on the stock exchanges. Section 4(1) is what gives the investors their exemption from Section 5; Section 4(4) is what gives it to their brokers.)

§§4(4) and 4(1)

It should also be noted that the controlling person, or affiliate — one who is in a position such as Schulte's — may also be found to have violated the Securities Act by making an unregistered distribution through brokers.[32]

Controlling person has problem too

The *Ira Haupt* decision left open many disturbing questions. It suggested that brokerage firms were at risk of being found to be underwriters whenever they undertook to sell a significant amount of stock for a customer who had a large interest in the issuing company. Rule 154 was adopted to help define what the brokers could and couldn't do in such a situation. It was followed by a flood of requests to the SEC for "no action" letters, however, so its ability to provide guidance and quell doubt left much to be desired. Furthermore, the SEC perceived the opposite problem among the less scrupulous brokerage firms: They did not try hard enough to become aware of the possibility that they might be assisting controlling persons to make distributions, or they would rely on vacuous letters of counsel.[33] In 1972, Rule 154 was superseded by Rule 144, which, it was hoped, would create clearer guidelines.

Questions and rules

We discussed Rule 144 in the preceding subsection, so only a few points need be made here. First, notice that the Rule covers sales for the account of affiliates of "restricted *or any other* securities" of the issuer. Thus, suppose that Happy Hospital *had* originally sold its stock pursuant to a properly registered public offering, in which Ed acquired 60 percent. Worthy Broker *still* has to worry about being an underwriter of an illegally unregistered distribution when, years later, Ed wants him to sell his stock. Broker may therefore want the guidance and protection of the Rule.

Rule 144 points:

Nonrestricted securities

Second, in the case of sales for *affiliates,* the volume limit on sales under the Rule is *not* lifted when the affiliate has held the securities for three years.[34] Thus, as long as Broker wants to proceed under the Rule and Ed remains an affiliate of Happy Hospital, Ed's stock must be trickled out to

Volume limit not lifted

[32] Indeed, he may be sent to jail for doing so. See United States v. Wolfson, 405 F.2d 779 (2d Cir. 1968), cert. denied, 394 U.S. 946 (1969).

[33] See Securities Act Rel. No. 5168 (1971).

[34] See Rule 144(e)(1)&(2), 144(k).

buyers, rather than sold with dispatch. Consequently, in the common case where the controlling person wants to dispose of his entire interest in a corporation, he will often be forced to register. (It may sometimes happen, of course, that an exemption other than the Section 4(1) exemption will be available to such a controlling person.)

§17.3.5 Mergers

Merger a sale

In a merger or sale of all of a corporation's assets for securities, the acquired company's shareholders often receive newly issued securities of the acquiring company. Can the transaction be considered a sale by the acquiring company of the securities, so that their issuance must be registered under the Securities Act (or covered by some exemption)? For many years, the SEC took the position that no sale was involved in such acquisition transactions.[35] The theory was that a merger or sale of all assets involves only corporate action, with management doing the real bargaining and setting the terms, not a series of individual purchase decisions by the acquired company shareholders. But in 1972 the SEC reversed itself and adopted Rule 145, which rejects the no-sale theory. Now the action of shareholders in voting for the merger or sale of all assets was to be seen as sufficiently akin to a voluntary investment decision to be considered a purchase of acquiring company securities.

Rule 145

Among other things, Rule 145 provides sadistic law professors with great opportunities for classroom fun, because law students almost always misunderstand it when they first read it. The purpose and operation of the Rule are not what they might seem on the surface to be.

Acquirer must register

Let's explore this point. By rejecting the no-sale theory, Rule 145 makes the acquisition transactions it covers subject to Section 5. The acquiring company therefore has to file a registration statement and supply prospectuses, unless some explicit exemption applies. (Sometimes, for example, the acquired company shareholders are small enough in number that the deal might be considered a private offering to them.) This suggests that the main point of the Rule is to mandate a new level of disclosure from the combining companies.

Not so drastic

Upon investigation, this suggestion proves weak. Even apart from Rule 145, the acquired company, assuming it was subject to Securities Exchange

[35] More specifically, it opined in old Rule 133 that there was no sale for purposes of the Securities Act registration provisions. But the Supreme Court held that such an acquisition transaction did involve a "sale" for purposes of Rule 10b-5. SEC v. National Sec., Inc., 393 U.S. 453 (1969).

Act reporting requirements, would be responsible for giving its shareholders a proxy statement containing substantial amounts of information about itself, the acquiring company, and the acquisition transaction. The registration statement that is required because of Rule 145 is in fact usually just a "wraparound proxy statement": you take the proxy statement and add a very modest amount of additional writing to it. In terms of the quantity and value of information disclosed, the Rule makes little difference.

Other goals?

But if a need for fuller disclosure to the acquired company shareholders was not the main problem addressed by Rule 145, what was?

Effect on resales

The answer is: resales by acquired company shareholders not accompanied by an adequate and accurate supply of information to the new buyers. Before the Rule many investors in acquired corporations assumed they were free to resell the acquiring company's securities at will. Some abusive schemes were based on this belief.

Example

To see how the Rule operates with respect to resales, let us examine a hypothetical case. Suppose Happy Hospital grows and prospers after the departure of Arlene and Ed. The shares are now held as follows: Alvin, 40 percent; Beth, 40 percent; and 400 other shareholders, including Charlie, each holding 1/20th of a percent. A merger plan has been negotiated whereby Happy will merge into Honest International Hospital Organizations, Inc. (HIHO), a publicly traded corporation that owns a number of for-profit hospitals. Under the terms of the plan, Alvin will receive HIHO common stock; he will receive so much that he will be considered an "affiliate" of HIHO after the merger. Beth will receive only 7-year bonds in HIHO and will therefore not become an affiliate of HIHO. Both Alvin and Beth, of course, are large enough shareholders to be affiliates of Happy Hospital right now, before the merger. Charlie and the other shareholders will receive HIHO common stock in amounts proportionate to their small interests.

Affiliates are "underwriters" if they resell

Rule 145(c) declares that affiliates of the merging party, such as Alvin and Beth, will be deemed to be "underwriters" engaged in a distribution if they publicly offer or sell the HIHO securities they acquired in the acquisition. Charlie, not being such an affiliate, would not be an underwriter if he immediately resold the HIHO stock he received in the merger.

Exceptions

Rule 145(d) then provides a partial out for Alvin and Beth. Alvin can avoid being classified as an underwriter if he resells in compliance with some of the conditions of Rule 144: the current public information requirement, the volume limit, and the manner of sale limits.[36] In other words, his resales won't cause him to be an underwriter if they amount to a mere

[36] See Rule 145(d)(1) and provisions cross-referenced therein.

trickle, modest in amount and spaced out over time. Beth can also avoid being classified as an underwriter by meeting these conditions. If she is patient, however, she can invoke two other outs that are not available to Alvin because he, unlike her, will be an affiliate of HIHO. First, after holding the HIHO bonds for two years, she can resell all of them without being deemed an underwriter as long as HIHO then meets the current public information requirement of Rule 144.[37] Second, if she holds the bonds for three years she can resell without worrying even about that requirement.[38]

Note this, however: Neither Alvin nor Beth can avoid being classified as underwriters if they insist on selling all of their HIHO securities soon after the merger.

What difference does it make?

Now let's consider what difference it makes whether, under Rule 145(c) and (d), Alvin and Beth are classified as underwriters. Is the effect of this classification that Alvin and Beth are flatly prohibited from immediately reselling all their HIHO securities? No. Remember that under Rule 145 HIHO's issuance of securities in the merger *will* be registered under the Securities Act. Thus, although Alvin and Beth are underwriters if they immediately resell, there would be little basis for claiming that they were underwriters in connection with an illegally unregistered distribution.[39]

§11 liability

The effects of calling them underwriters are rather more subtle. First, as underwriters they will be subject to civil liability under Section 11 of the Securities Act for misstatements in HIHO's registration statement. If the statement misrepresents HIHO's true financial condition, for example, buyers from Alvin and Beth may be able to sue *them* under Section 11. In various ways, suit under this Section (which is discussed below in subsection 17.4.1) may be easier for plaintiffs to maintain than a suit under some general antifraud rule such as Rule 14a-9 or Rule 10b-5. Similarly, even if Alvin and Beth don't resell, the fact that Rule 145 subjects HIHO to the registration requirement means that a whole set of other people will become subject under Section 11 to possible civil liability for misrepresentations and omissions. The threat of Section 11 liability may in turn encourage more complete disclosure in the statement sent to the shareholders.

[37] Rule 145(d)(2).

[38] Rule 145(d)(3).

[39] Contrast the situation that would be presented if HIHO's issuance of securities were considered an exempt private offering rather than one covered by Rule 145. The securities received by *all* of the Happy shareholders would be "restricted" securities, and therefore all of them would have to meet Rule 144's holding period requirements before they sell anything (assuming they wanted the protection of Rule 144).

Second, if Alvin and Beth are going to become underwriters by reselling soon after the merger, they should be named as underwriters in HIHO's registration statement. If they are not, that omission may itself be deemed a material omission in violation of Section 11 and could furnish ammunition for a lawsuit.

Naming in registration statement

Third, if Alvin and Beth are underwriters engaged in a distribution when they resell, the prospectus-delivery requirement of Section 5(b)(2) will apply. They will have to see to it that buyers from them get prospectuses; it will not be sufficient that all the Happy Hospital shareholders received disclosure documents before they voted on the merger.[40]

Prospectus-delivery requirement

Thus, the major effects of Rule 145 are to broaden the scope and deepen the extent of possible liability on the part of those responsible for disclosure documents, and to subject some resales by major shareholders of acquired companies to Rule 144's trickle-out approach.

Summary of Rule's effects

Our discussion so far has slighted questions concerning the coverage of Rule 145.[41] The Rule does not cover cash mergers, of course, since the merging company shareholders in such a situation are not being asked to invest in new securities. The Rule does cover not only business combinations but also reclassifications that involve the substitution of one kind of security for another. It does not cover acquisitions accomplished by a direct stock-for-stock exchange (or securities-for-stock exchange) with the target company shareholders, that is, the so-called B reorganization (discussed above in subsection 10.3.2) and similar transactions. Such transactions were already understood, before adoption of Rule 145, to involve a sale by the acquiring company of its securities that, absent exemption, would have to be registered. On the other hand, a merger or sale of all assets in which the acquired company shareholders get securities, but that doesn't qualify as a tax-free reorganization, would still be covered by Rule 145. Mergers for the mere purpose of reincorporating in another state are not covered by Rule 145, even if there are some changes in shareholder rights (for example, preemptive rights and cumulative voting rights are eliminated). And so on; interpretative questions never cease to arise.

Coverage

[40] Note this further problem: what happens to Alvin and Beth if they want to sell all their securities when the HIHO registration statement has become stale or ineffective — say, a year and a half after the merger? They would still be deemed underwriters under 145(c), it seems, but even if willing to bear the risk of Section 11 liability and to deliver prospectuses they would not be selling while a registration statement was in effect. Their alternative, of course, is to have a new registration statement prepared and filed.

[41] Many such questions, and others concerning Rule 145, are discussed in Securities Act Rel. No. 5463 (1974).

§17.3.6 Other Exemptions

Caution

This subsection merely flags the fact that there are numerous other exemptions possible under the Securities Act.[42] Some, such as that for interests in a railroad equipment trust,[43] are quite specialized. Others, such as that for purely intrastate offerings,[44] are of more general interest.

§17.4 The Securities Act: Liabilities

§17.4.1 Liability under Section 11

Explicit cause of action

Section 11 of the Securities Act creates civil liability on account of false registration statements. The statute is rather explicit about the parameters of the cause of action it authorizes.

Falsehoods in registration statement

The Section is triggered when the registration statement becomes effective and any part of it contains an untrue statement of a material fact or omits a material fact required to be stated or necessary to make statements in the document not be misleading. Remember, in this connection, that the prospectus is part of the registration statement.

Who sues

Who can sue? Any person who acquires a security issued pursuant to the registration statement.[1]

Who can be sued

Who can be sued? Signers of the registration statement; directors of the issuer at the time of filing of the statement or persons named with their consent as about to become directors; accountants, engineers, appraisers, and other professional experts who prepare or certify a part of the registration statement; every underwriter of the security; and, of course, the issuer itself.[2] According to Section 6(a), those who must sign the registration statement include the issuer, its principal executive officer(s), its principal financial officer, its comptroller or principal accounting officer, and a majority of its board. If the alleged wrongdoer, such as legal counsel to the underwriter, is not within the statutorily listed class of possible defendants, then he probably cannot be held liable under Section 11.[3]

[42] See §§3 and 4.

[43] Section 3(a)(6).

[44] Section 3(a)(11), which is elaborated in Rule 147.

§17.4 [1] Note that if a corporation already has outstanding, publicly traded securities of a certain class — say, common stock — and makes a public offering of new securities of that class, a plaintiff under §11 has to show that the securities of that type that he bought were among those listed in the offering. See, e.g., Klein v. Computer Devices, Inc., 591 F. Supp. 270 (S.D.N.Y. 1984).

[2] Section 11(a)(1)-(5). The issuer comes into the list because it is a signer.

[3] See In re Flight Transportation Corp. Securities v. Reavis & McGrath, 593 F. Supp. 612 (D. Minn. 1984).

Mental element and "due diligence"

What is the standard of conduct, or mental element, that applies to defendants? The issuer can be held liable under Section 11 even in the absence of scienter or negligence on the part of anyone. As for the other possible defendants, they can try to show that they acted with due diligence in relation to the registration statement. Notice, however, that the burden of proof to show due diligence is on the defendants; it is not the plaintiff's burden to show their negligence. Generally, to successfully invoke the defense a defendant must prove, as to each material misstatement or omission in the registration statement, that "he had, after reasonable investigation, reasonable grounds to believe and did believe" that the statement was true or that there was no such omission.[4] However, with respect to a false statement or omission in a part of the registration statement "expertised"[5] by some expert other than himself (such as financial statements certified by independent public accountants or a valuation report supplied by an appraiser) a defendant need only prove that "he had no reasonable grounds to believe and did not believe" that the statement was false or that there was such a material omission.

Reliance?

Must the plaintiff prove reliance on the false statement or material omission? Normally, no. But the defendant may establish a defense by proving that the plaintiff, when she bought the security, knew of the falsehood or omission. Also, if the plaintiff bought her securities after the corporation had made generally available to its security holders an earnings statement covering 12 months after the effective date of the registration statement, she must prove reliance.[6]

Damages

What is the measure of damages? It is (1) the price the plaintiff paid for her securities (but not to the extent this exceeds the price at which the securities were offered to the public) minus (2) their value at the time of suit or the price at which she disposed of them.[7] She does not have to prove that the falsehood or omission in the registration statement caused the price decline. Defendant, however, can try to prove that some or all of the decline was due to other factors, and thus mitigate damages to that extent.

Limitations

What is the statute of limitations? One year after the falsehood or omission was discovered or should have been discovered by the exercise of reasonable diligence.[8]

[4] Section 11(b)(A) & -(C).
[5] This is securities lawyers' handy jargon, not a term in the statute.
[6] Section 11(a), final sentence.
[7] Section 11(e).
[8] Section 13.

Though Section 11 was originally thought by some observers to be a draconian provision that would impose crushing liabilities on participants in public offerings, very few cases arose under it for many years. In 1968, a major case was finally decided against numerous defendants involved in a

BarChris **case**

public offering. This case, *Escott v. BarChris Construction Corp.*,[9] created new concern, and even some temporary hysteria, among members of the practicing securities bar, and it still serves as an instructive cautionary tale.[10]

§17.4.2 Liability under Section 12

§12(1)

Under Section 12(1), a person who offers or sells a security in violation of Section 5, such as stock that should have been registered but wasn't, is liable to the person buying from him. The plaintiff may sue to recover the amount paid for the security[11] on tendering it back to the defendant, or for damages if he no longer owns it.

§12(2)

Under Section 12(2), a more broadly applicable provision, any person who offers or sells a security by means of a written or oral communication that contains a material falsehood or omission is liable to the person buying from him. The provision applies even to offers or sales of securities exempted from registration by Section 3.[12] The defendant may establish a defense by proving that "he did not know, and in the exercise of reasonable care could not have known" of the untruth or omission. As under 12(1), the remedy is rescission or damages. Section 13's one year statute of limitations applies to actions under Section 12(2).

To understand the features of a private civil action under Section 12(2), you may find it helpful to contrast it with an action under Section 11. Five points may be noted.

Falsehoods covered

First, Section 11 is triggered only by falsehoods or omissions in registration statements; it therefore wouldn't help a plaintiff when there was no registration statement with respect to the security he purchased. But Section 12(2) is triggered by falsehoods or omissions in any prospectus (i.e.,

[9] 283 F. Supp. 643 (S.D.N.Y. 1968). See also Feit v. Leasco Data Processing Equip. Corp., 332 F. Supp. 544 (E.D.N.Y. 1971).

[10] See Folk, Civil Liabilities under the Federal Securities Acts: The *BarChris* Case, 55 Va. L. Rev. 1 (1969).

[11] Plus interest, minus income received from the security.

[12] This is not true of securities exempted by Section 3(a)(2), however. That provision exempts government securities, interests in bank-sponsored common trust funds, interests in certain pension and annuity plans, and various special items.

written communication) or oral communication that is used to sell the security.

Defendants suable

Second, Section 11 makes liable a broad but sharply defined class of participants in the registration process. Suit under Section 12(2) may be against "any person" who offered or sold the security. In fact, a fair number of courts have interpreted this restriction broadly to allow suit under Section 12(2) against persons other than the actual, immediate seller of securities to the plaintiff. Though courts differ in their degree of liberality, perhaps the dominant approach is to allow suit against a person who was a proximate cause of, or a substantial factor in, the sale. Under this approach, for example, a plaintiff was allowed to sue a company that lent money to plaintiff and other investors to buy shares in a fraudulent scheme, even though it didn't itself sell the shares.[13]

Standards of conduct

Third, the standard of conduct defendants must show they have met in order to establish a good defense is somewhat different under Section 11 than under Section 12(2). Section 11 requires the defendant to show that she did believe in the truth of something after actually engaging in reasonable investigation. Section 12 requires the defendant to show that she couldn't have known of its untruth even if she had exercised reasonable care. I leave it for you to decide which is more difficult.

Privity

Fourth, a plaintiff under Section 11 need not have been in privity with the defendant(s). He needs to show that he acquired the securities, not that he acquired them from the defendants. But a Section 12(2) plaintiff probably must have bought the securities from the defendant, or from someone who was a substantial factor in the sale.[14]

Remedy

Fifth, the remedies are slightly different. A Section 12(2) plaintiff who still owns the securities is entitled to rescission, while a Section 11 plaintiff who still owns them is entitled to damages for the price decline.

Case law: reliance, materiality

Case law has wrestled with some of the obvious interpretive questions that may be raised about actions under Section 12(2). For example, courts have held that Section 12(2) imposes liability without regard to whether the buyer shows reliance on the misrepresentation or omission,[15] and that the standard of materiality in such actions is the same as under Rule 10b-5.[16]

[13] Davis v. Avco Fin. Serv., Inc., 739 F.2d 1057 (6th Cir. 1984).

[14] For example, in Wright v. Schock, 571 F. Supp. 642 (N.D. Cal. 1983), the courts held that liability under §12 is imposed only if the defendant was in privity by being the immediate seller of the securities or a substantial factor in the sale. In dicta it noted that there is considerable doubt that aiding and abetting liability exists at all as to §12 violations. Id. at 658.

[15] E.g., Klein v. Computer Devices, Inc. 591 F. Supp. 270 (S.D.N.Y. 1984).

[16] Simpson v. Southeastern Inv. Trust, Inc., 697 F.2d 1257 (5th Cir. 1983); see also SEC v. Seaboard Corp., 677 F.2d 1301 (9th Cir. 1982).

§17.4.3 Liability under Section 17

General antifraud provision

Section 17(a) makes it unlawful in the offer or sale of any security for any person

(1) to employ any device, scheme, or artifice to defraud;
(2) to obtain money or property by means of material falsehoods or omissions; or
(3) to engage in any transaction, practice, or course of business which does or would operate as a fraud or deceit upon the purchaser.

In other words, it is a general antifraud provision so worded that it might catch objectionable behavior not clearly covered by the more specific strictures of the Act. Its language is similar to that of Rule 10b-5 under the Securities Exchange Act. A major difference is that Section 17 covers only frauds by fraudulent sellers, whereas Rule 10b-5 covers fraudulent buyers as well.

Implied private right of action?

Section 17(a) is a criminal statute and clearly can be enforced by criminal prosecution or by a civil action for injunctive relief brought by the SEC. In sharp contrast to Sections 11 and 12, however, it does not by its terms create any right of action in private parties. The question then arises: Will the courts find an implied private right of action under Section 17(a)? The circuits have split on this issue.[17] The weight of recent opinions seems to be against a private right of action.[18] The negative opinions typically express the thought that it would be inappropriate to add an implied remedy when the Securities Act already creates detailed and explicit private rights of action, with corresponding limitations on liability. They also suggest that the implied action might even throw a monkey wrench into Congress's carefully wrought machinery.

[17] Recognizing a private right of action: Stephenson v. Calpine Conifers, Ltd., 652 F.2d 808 (9th Cir. 1981); Kirshner v. United States, 603 F.2d 234 (2d Cir. 1978); Newnan v. Prior, 518 F.2d 97 (4th Cir. 1975). Not recognizing a private right of action: Landry v. All American Assurance, 688 F.2d 381 (5th Cir. 1982); Shull v. Dain, Kalman and Quail, Inc., 561 F.2d 152 (8th Cir. 1977). Undecided: Peoria Union Stockyards v. Penn Mut. Life Ins. Co., 698 F.2d 320 (7th Cir. 1983); Gutter v. Merrill Lynch, 644 F.2d 1194 (6th Cir. 1981).

[18] Bruns v. Ledbetter, 583 F. Supp. 1050 (S.D. Cal. 1984); Kilmartin v. H. C. Wainwright & Co., 580 F. Supp. 604 (D. Mass. 1984); Kimmel v. Peterson, 565 F. Supp. 476 (E.D. Pa. 1983); North Am. Fin. Group Ltd. v. S.M.R. Enterprises, 583 F. Supp. 691 (N.D. Ill. 1984); Warner Communications v. Murdoch, 581 F. Supp. 1982 (D. Del. 1984). But see Geller v. Prudential-Bache Securities, 591 F. Supp. 27 (W.D. Okla. 1983); Roskos v. Shearson/American Express, Inc., 589 F. Supp. 627 (E.D. Wis. 1984).

Proving a violation of Section 17(a)(1) requires a showing of scienter on the defendant's part, but Sections 17(a)(2) and 17(a)(3) do not.[19]

Scienter?

§17.5 Critiques of the Mandatory Disclosure System

Cold climate for critics

Criticisms of the federal securities laws are something like criticisms of mother's milk: Onlookers may think that the critic is unusually mean-spirited. Even opponents of substantive regulatory schemes often see disclosure regulation as a good, less intrusive, alternative approach to dealing with market imperfections. As for the SEC, it has long been at the top of people's lists of good regulatory agencies. At times, observers have claimed that it attracts the best and brightest of young lawyers wishing to go into government service. It supposedly is not "captured" by the firms it regulates, the way other agencies are thought to be. It appears to be fairly competent and efficient. The regulatory scheme it administers seems to oil the securities markets rather than to put a brake on them. Indeed, the securities laws seem important as a symbol of our society's commitment to maintaining a vigorous and honest system of private enterprise. A typical pattern for developing countries that begin to experience booming growth and all the delights of an entrepreneurially active capitalist economy is to study and imitate the securities laws of the United States, regardless of where they may have borrowed the bulk of their legal system. Perhaps businessmen in such economies have a nagging suspicion that securities regulation may be a guard rail that helps keep the system from falling over into the horrid miasma of socialism.

Most criticisms concern implementation

As we shall see in the next two subsections, the most common criticisms of the securities laws go to questions of implementation rather than to the basic idea. Yet it is instructive and illuminating to ponder the fundamental theory behind mandatory disclosure. (See subsection 17.5.3.) After discussing criticisms, I shall discuss briefly the issue of evidence for the effects of the securities laws.

§17.5.1 Imbalance Between Continuous and Episodic Disclosure

Wrong-emphasis argument

A criticism that came to be levelled against the federal securities laws with increasing frequency was that the relative emphasis on disclosures

[19] Aaron v. SEC, 446 U.S. 680 (1980).

under the Securities Act and under the Securities Exchange Act was misconceived.[1] For the typical public corporation, required disclosures under the Securities Act were highly episodic: they had to be made only on the relatively infrequent occasions when the corporation wanted to sell new stocks, bonds, or other securities to the general public. On those occasions the required disclosure was very extensive indeed, and strict compliance was usually induced by the SEC staff, which was very serious about its review of registration statements and the decision to accelerate their effectiveness. Many businessmen complained that the requirements were unduly burdensome and expensive. By contrast, disclosures required of companies that have to register under Section 12 of the Securities Exchange Act[2] were periodic in nature: the annual reports on Form 10-K, the quarterly reports on Form 10-Q, and miscellaneous other documents. Yet these reports filed with the SEC were not generally required to be distributed to investors, were not reviewed as carefully by SEC staff, and did not have to be filed until some generous time period after the end of the year or quarter had passed — that is, when the information in them was quite stale. To make things worse, numerous companies missed even these generous filing deadlines.

To some observers, this relative emphasis on the episodic disclosures was backwards: It is as or more important to the protection of investors to make sure that timely and relevant information about public corporations is *continuously* being supplied to the market. Other observers were simply impressed by what seemed to be the needlessly high costs imposed on new issuances of securities by companies that were already disclosing lots of information under the Securities Exchange Act and, more important, in response to the continuous demands for information by professional investment analysts, institutional investors, and the financial press.

Needlessly high costs

Integrated disclosure program

In response to these criticisms, the SEC proposed[3] and in 1982 adopted[4] registration forms to implement a program of "integrated disclosure." The basic idea was that, depending on the degree of dissemination of information about the company in the market place (as indicated by some fairly objective criteria), the company might be eligible to use a new, streamlined, and simplified (and therefore less expensive) registration form. Under the new system, registrants are classified into three categories: (1) companies that are widely followed by professional analysts; (2) companies

§17.5 [1]See Cohen, "Truth in Securities" Revisited, 79 Harv. L. Rev. 1340 (1966).
[2]Note 1 to section 9.2 above discusses when this is necessary.
[3]Securities Act Rel. No. 6235 (1980); Securities Act Rel. No. 6331 (1981).
[4]Securities Act Rel. No. 6383 (1982).

that have been subject to the periodic reporting requirements of the Securities Exchange Act for three or more years, but that are not widely followed; and (3) companies that have been in the Exchange Act reporting system for less than three years. Similarly, the main registration forms were reduced to three: S-1, S-2, and S-3, with the latter allowing the most abbreviated disclosure and being available only to widely followed registrants. The precise eligibility rules and the requirements of each form may be found in the regulations.

Comments

Whether this integrated disclosure system responds to all of the concerns raised about the basic design and relationship of the Securities Act and the Securities Exchange Act is doubtful. Arguably, it even created new problems, such as exposing various persons to Section 11 liability for misstatements in the cross-referenced Securities Exchange Act reports. On the other hand, the reform seems to have made registration cheaper for many companies in many contexts, and this has tended to quiet the critics who count.

Shelf registration rule

A reform having a similar pacifying effect was Rule 415, which was adopted in 1982 to make "shelf registration" more widely available.[5] The basic idea of shelf registration is simple enough. In certain contexts an issuing corporation would like to be able to prepare and file a registration statement covering the possible sale of new securities, get the statement reviewed and basically approved by the SEC staff, and then "put it on the shelf," that is, wait a few months or years until market conditions seem ideal for actually making the offer to the investing public. At that time the issuer would simply stick a few more bits of information, such as the offering price and the precise number of securities to be sold, into the registration statement, and without having to wait for a laborious further review by the SEC staff, go quickly to market. Even more flexibility would be provided if multiple offerings could be made under the shelf registration statement.

Origin and basis

Shelf registration had long been permitted for a few special types of offerings, such as offerings of shares by mutual funds, which continuously offer investors a chance to buy shares at a constantly changing price and therefore need some such permission. It had been prohibited for most public offerings, however. The concern, presumably, was that information publicly available to investors when the offering was actually made to them would be stale. (The legal basis for restricting shelf registration was thought to lie in Section 6(a).) The liberalization of the availability of shelf registration by Rule 415 was based on the perception that the traditional

[5] See Securities Act Rel. No. 6383, 6423 (1982).

types of shelf registration had not spawned major abuses to the detriment of investors and that the new integration program provided an increasingly efficient system for keeping disclosures about public companies up-to-date. The SEC appreciated that shelf registration might facilitate the development of new, cheaper, and more flexible capital-raising techniques. It first adopted Rule 415 on a trial basis, however, in part because the Rule, though liked by many potential issuing corporations, was feared by some investing banking firms that thought it might hurt their traditional ways of doing business and their revenues. Later the Rule was made permanent.

Restrictions

Rule 415 is not without its own restrictions. Generally, for example, the securities covered by a shelf registration must be offered and sold within two years of the effective date of the statement. There are guidelines concerning when and how new information must be added to the registration statement. Fundamental changes require a post-effective amendment, while other material changes may be noted by the simpler "stickering" procedure, for example, and "S-3" companies (the big, widely followed ones) may incorporate by reference changes noted in their Exchange Act reports. "At the market" offerings of equity securities must meet special conditions. In practice, the Rule has been employed most often in connection with the offering of high-grade debt securities.[6]

§17.5.2 Irrelevance of Data Disclosed

Attack on accounting data

A major theme of critics in the later 1960s and throughout the 1970s was that the information required to be disclosed under the federal securities laws was largely irrelevant to rational decision making by investors. The principal object of these charges was disclosure of accounting data, such as financial statements prepared in accordance with generally accepted accounting principles and in conformity with the SEC's own special rules about accounting.

Accounting statements backward-looking, conservative

The principle theme of this criticism is that valuation is forward-looking but accounting statements are backward-looking. Traditional accounting principles have a strong conservative bias, especially in periods of inflation.[7] Assets are usually recorded at their historical cost (less depreciation, if applicable), instead of at their current fair value. Depreciation deductions

[6] Issuance costs for Rule 415 offerings have in fact been lower than for traditional offerings. It seems to have resulted in increased competition among underwriters.

[7] See Benston, The Effectiveness and Effects of the SEC's Accounting Disclosure Requirements, in Economic Policy and the Regulation of Corporate Securities 26-30 (H. Manne ed. 1969).

against gross income are also based on asset cost, without adjustment for the changing replacement cost of the assets. But when potential investors in securities value a business, they are interested in the discounted present value of what it will yield them in the future. Not only does traditional accounting data fail to tell them directly about future prospects, but it misrepresents the company's current condition and performance, which might help inform guesses about the future.

Variations on the theme

The criticism comes in many variations. It has been alleged that in making investment decisions, sophisticated institutional investors don't look much at figures prepared by accountants.[8] Others have shown analytically how a series of accounting data, such as a company's annual reported net income for the past five years, can be a very poor basis for extrapolations to the future.[9] In particular, the accountants' rules as to when value increases can be recognized (when goods are finally sold, for example) often assign value increases to the wrong years, making apparent trends misleading. And inflation may increase a company's reported net income by more than the general inflation rate, because it affects revenues but not the historical asset costs used for computing depreciation deductions.

Bias against projections

Apart from criticizing conventional accounting data that were required to be disclosed, many critics faulted the SEC for its traditional, longstanding bias against allowing management's projections of their company's future performance in documents filed with it. The SEC's pessimism was a natural corollary, of course, of its mission to prevent frauds of the *Old Dominion* type.

***Gamble-Skogmo* case**

The double-edged nature of the SEC's traditional strictures on projections and similar kinds of "information" was nicely illustrated by *Gerstle v. Gamble-Skogmo, Inc.*[10] The plaintiffs brought a challenge under Rule 14a-9 against a proxy statement sent to the minority shareholders of a subsidiary in connection with its merger into the parent company. One claim was that the proxy statement failed to disclose *asset appraisals* of the subsidiary's plants, an omission that was quite important in view of management's intent to continue to sell the plants. In essence, Judge Friendly replied that disclosure of asset appraisals was a good idea and could be required by the SEC, but that it would be unfair to base liability on such an omission, given the SEC's longstanding and consistent policy of refusing to allow such

[8] Ross, The Wonderful World of Accounting, in Empirical Research in Accounting: Selected Studies 108 (1970).

[9] See Note in V. Brudney & M. Chirelstein, Cases and Materials on Corporate Finance 1110 (2d ed. 1979).

[10] 478 F.2d 1281 (2d Cir. 1973).

information in official disclosure documents. (Asset appraisals involve projections, of course: The appraised value represents a prediction as to what the asset could be sold for.) The holding is thus ironic. To protect *buyers* of securities from the charms of hype-creating promoters, the SEC had adopted a pessimistic, conservative bias about required disclosures. The case shows how this bias jeopardizes the flow of relevant information to *sellers,* such as merging company shareholders.

Fortunately for the plaintiffs, the court also opined that the proxy statement's failure to disclosure the parent company's *intent* to pursue aggressively the merging company's policy of trying to sell its plants was an actionable omission, and so found the statement to have violated Rule 14a-9. It also reasoned that failure to disclose *firm offers* for the plants might support the action, though it questioned the materiality of the offers actually received. The resulting set of pronouncements seems odd: Management's business plans and outsiders' firm offers both involve predictions about what people will do in the future that will affect the shareholders' wealth, just as much as asset appraisals do, yet only the latter escapes the obligation to be disclosed.

Arguments for projections

In any event, the proponents of allowing predictive information in SEC filings and required documents stressed two main arguments: One was that such information is valuable to the investment decision making process; the other was that fairness required disclosure of management's projections to the ordinary investor, because the projections were already being given to professional securities analysts.

Arguments con

Opponents of the disclosure of projections argued that ordinary investors would give too much weight to projections (and needed to be protected against their own gullibility), that disclosure would create civil liability problems for managers and accountants, and that the not-infrequent failure of events to live up to projections would create a credibility problem for managers. A cynic or two might even have suggested that disclosure of projections would reduce management's ability to trade on a form of soft but valuable inside information.

Liability problem

One legal problem often raised about disclosure of projections was how such a disclosure would be assessed under antifraud provisions. What does it mean to make a "fraudulent prediction"? Surely you are not guilty of fraud every time you make a prediction about the future that does not come true! As a matter of strict logic, a predictive statement is not the sort of linguistic entity that is either true or false when uttered; the prediction can either be borne out or not, but that is a different matter. Yet surely you could not go to the other extreme and claim that there is no sense whatever in talking about a fraudulent prediction. Usually, when you make a serious predictive statement to other people, you are *implicitly* making a collateral statement about a matter of fact, namely, that you yourself believe your prediction. If you solemnly utter a prediction you don't believe, without cluing the audience in to your disbelief, you may well be accused of defrauding them, perhaps to their detriment.

Case law response

The case law response to this conundrum seems to be that management's projections of a company's future performance involve an implicit representation that they have an informed and reasonable belief in the validity of their predictions.[11]

Rule 175's safe harbor

Eventually the SEC responded to the debate about disclosure of predictions. In 1979, it adopted Rule 175, a safe harbor rule for some projections. Statements covered by the rule are deemed not to be fraudulent if they are made by or on behalf of the issuer or by an outside reviewer retained by the issuer, unless it is shown by the plaintiff that the statements were made without reasonable basis or were disclosed other than in good faith.

Limited coverage

Note, however, that Rule 175 covers only some kind of statements in some kinds of documents produced by some kinds of companies. It covers forward-looking statements with respect to income, revenues, earnings per share, and the like, management's plans for future operations, and certain statements about future economic performance. It also covers statements about the likely effects of changing prices on the issuer's business. It does not obviously cover predictions about many nonfinancial events, for example, a prediction that the company will complete construction of five new factories in the coming year. The forward looking statements must be in certain documents filed with the SEC: the annual report to shareholders, the annual 10-K, or Part I of its 10-Q's. Predictions in a press release would not be covered.[12] The companies covered are those making filings under the Securities Exchange Act, or that are going public or registering under

[11] See, e.g., Marx v. Computer Sciences Corp., 507 F.2d 485 (9th Cir. 1974). The case actually involved failure to update projections fast enough, i.e., failure to disclose that the company wasn't going to expense certain development costs on schedule but would write them off at once due to serious development problems. But it contains an interesting general discussion of the application of Rule 10b-5 to forecasts.

[12] On the other hand, statements in press releases have never been constrained by the SEC's past, conservative bias against permitting forward-looking statements. If predictions in a press release are attacked as fraudulent, for example, in a Rule 10b-5 action, the standards for assessing the defendant's conduct in making the predictive statements are probably the same as those in Rule 175: the "reasonable basis" and "good faith" standards. See the *Marx* case, note 11 supra. But some courts have taken a stricter approach. E.g., Beecher v. Able, 374 F. Supp. 341 (S.D.N.Y. 1974) (earnings forecast must be based on facts from which a reasonably prudent investor would conclude that it was highly probable that the forecast would be realized). So perhaps the Rule 175 safe harbor does give significant protection.

the Exchange Act for the first time. Thus, statements by privately held corporations are not covered.

§17.5.3 Mandatory Disclosure Unnecessary or Bad?

A basic critique

A more fundamental criticism is that for the federal government to mandate disclosures by corporations to investors is a bad idea in principle. It should be noted at the outset that this most basic attack is not widely made, but is restricted to a rather small subset of critics. Even ardent proponents of deregulation in general are wont to have a soft spot in their hearts for the basic concept of the securities laws.

What's wrong with markets?

A basic move behind this criticism is to wonder what is wrong with unregulated securities markets. Granted that information relevant to the valuation of securities is a valuable thing, what reason is there to expect that this good won't be produced by ordinary market forces in more or less optimal quantities, just as toothpaste and haircuts are? What reason is there for government to give an artificial boost to production in this area, in contrast to others? What answer can be given to the charge that the artificial boost will most likely lead to excessive production of information, that is, will create more costs than benefits?[13]

Information as a public good

One answer to these aggressively skeptical questions is to state that investment-related information is a "public good" (as economists use that term) so that market forces left to themselves won't produce enough of it. A public good, at least in its pure form, is characterized by "nonrivalry in consumption" and "high exclusion costs." National defense is often thought to be a prototypical public good. Your consumption of its benefits doesn't prevent other citizens of your country from obtaining its benefits also; in this respect it is quite unlike a piece of pizza, which cannot be eaten by others if it is eaten by you. Because of nonrivalry in consumption, the total benefits to all persons who enjoy a public good may be very great. National defense also has high exclusion costs: if a group of private citizens undertook to defend the entire United States from foreign attack, it would be hard for them to get everybody who benefits from their expenditures of time and resources to pay them for it (if they had to rely on voluntary payments). It would be very hard for them to provide defense *only* to those who agree to pay for it, and to exclude others. Consequently, since the benefits are so great but the private producers would not be paid by many

[13]The remainder of this subsection is indebted to an article that develops quite similar arguments in a more elaborate way: Easterbrook & Fischel, Mandatory Protection and the Disclosure of Investors, 70 Va. L. Rev. 669 (1984).

or most benefited parties, the private producers would not produce enough defense. So government steps in and forces people, through taxes, to pay for it.

Application to investment-related information

How does the argument apply to investment-related information? You might imagine that it applies neatly, if you focus on individual investors as the would-be producers of such information. Suppose investor Smart devotes a whole year to researching the future prospects of several dozen public corporations, and as a result acquires an excellent sense of the likely risks and returns that would flow from investment in each company's stock. This research will therefore help Smart make much more rational decisions than he would have made a year earlier. Moreover, if his research and opinions are better than any that are already publicly known, their release to other investors would benefit many other people without hurting him (at least if we assume he has already invested all of his own money on the basis of his research before conveying it to others). He would like to charge people for his hard-earned predictions and advice, of course. If other investors paid anything approaching what the value of his advice would be to them, he might be inspired to spend many years doing further research. But in fact he may well be paid poorly. The first buyers of information from him may leak it to others, who won't pay and will leak it to still others. Even if the law says his advice is proprietary information whose dissemination he can control, his right would be largely unenforceable. He'll be discouraged and won't do enough research — enough, that is, in relation to all the good it could create for so many investors. What is worse, other potential researchers will be similarly discouraged from investigating deeply and trying to sell results widely. They will tend to search in the shallows and only for themselves. Even their feeble efforts will be wastefully duplicated. The rational faculties of investors will be bloated from malnourishment.

Counterargument based on firms' incentives

Before we recoil in dismay from this information-starved world, though, let us consider the counterargument. It is a mistake to imagine the investors as the primary producers of information. Firms have an incentive to get information about themselves communicated to investors. Doing so will reduce the uncertainty investors face, and, other things being equal, will reduce the rate of return that they demand on their invested money. Since gains from uncertainty reduction are possible and each firm can produce and distribute information about itself, thus automatically spreading the information costs among all of its investors, plenty of information should be forthcoming, without too much duplication of effort.

Problems of verification

Are there problems and costs with such an approach (production of investment-related information by individual firms)? Yes, of course. Firms may be able to make one-shot killings against new investors by defrauding them as to the condition of the company. Therefore, investors will have to incur the costs of attempting to verify or check up on the information supplied by firms. Firms that have genuinely good things to tell investors about themselves will try to distinguish themselves from defrauding firms by finding some way to guarantee or certify the accuracy of their disclosures to investors, and in doing so will incur costs. The issue is not whether there are verification and "bonding" costs of this sort — there are — but whether they are very high and can only be reduced effectively by government intervention.

Responsive mechanisms

In thinking about this issue, consider some of the mechanisms, apart from the federal securities laws, that have arisen to help firms and investors deal with the verification problem. Firms use professional "information intermediaries": investment banking firms, when they sell new securities to the public, and independent accounting firms, when they periodically issue audited financial statements. These intermediary firms are repeat players in the market. Their very business is to continually supply information to investors that will be trusted, and therefore they have their reputations to worry about. A corporation going public might be eager to make a killing by defrauding investors if it doesn't expect to have to go back to the market for new money; its investment banker is apt to be distinctly less enthusiastic, and is apt to play the role of private policeman with respect to what potential investors are told about the corporation. Independent accountants are arguably in a similar position. In addition, they may invent new and better ways of formulating and presenting information and spread the cost of doing so among many clients.

Other mechanisms for coping with the verification problem are the stock exchanges. Those who control a stock exchange and benefit from its well-being have an incentive to promote trading on it, which in turn entails promoting investor confidence, partly by assuring accurate disclosures about listed companies and cracking down on frauds. Yet another mechanism (a governmental, but nonfederal, one) consists of the disclosure rules of individual states. One could even point out that those investors who do engage in research and verification will inform other investors of the results of their endeavors, whether they want to or not, by their trading behavior.

Gaps?

Given that firms have natural incentives to produce investment-related information and there are various mechanisms for certifying and verifying it, are there likely to be gaps or excessive costs that might be dealt with by federal intervention? Perhaps so. Professors Easterbrook and Fischel identify three candidates. The first problem they label as "third party effects."

Third party effects

For example, Ajax Corporation may be able to produce and distribute information, such as predictions of the future growth of market demand for the types of goods it makes, that will be of use to many investors other than those who invest in Ajax, namely, investors or potential investors in all its competitors. Yet Ajax will not give weight to gains to those other investors when it decides how much to spend on market research, and thus it may not research as deeply as is optimal. Competitor firms will do the same, so there will be duplicated and shallow research. Similarly, no one may have an adequate incentive to produce the optimal amount of *comparative* information about firms.

States' parochialism and costs

A second problem, which afflicts state disclosure systems, is that state legislatures may have a tendency to enact rules that benefit their residents even though they reduce investor welfare as a whole.[14] A third problem is that a state-based, common law approach to developing and enforcing rules about fraud may be more costly than a system driven mainly by a rule making federal agency.

Conclusion

Enough has been said to suggest that, as a matter of theory, one can argue with some plausibility both for and against the proposition that the federal securities laws have increased the welfare of investors and of the general public (or that they could increase welfare if suitably reformed). Like many other issues in the rational design and evaluation of government policy, the crucial questions are empirical ones. What really are all the important effects of law, and how significant are those effects?

§17.5.4 Evidence about Effects?

Stigler study

Unfortunately, there has been only a small amount of systematic research into the actual effects on investors of the federal securities laws. A pioneering study by George Stigler on returns to investors before and after the passage of the laws failed to detect any effects.[15] The study was soon subjected to intense criticism, however.[16] Later commentators have ob-

[14]For a good example, see Easterbrook & Fischel, note 13 supra, at 697-698.

[15]Stigler, Public Regulation of the Securities Market, 37 J. Bus. 117 (1964).

[16]Friend & Herman, The S.E.C. Through a Glass Darkly, 37 J. Bus. 382 (1964). Among other things, they claim the study data showed a decrease in the variance of investor returns. This suggests that investors may have benefited from a reduction in the uncertainty surrounding their investments. Subsequent papers in the Stigler vs. Friend & Herman exchange appear in 37 J. Bus. 414 (1964) and 38 J. Bus. 106 (1965).

A similar effort was George Benston's study to determine whether '34 Act reporting requirements benefited investors. Benston, Required Disclosure and Act of 1934, 63 Am. Econ. Rev. 132 (1973). His negative findings were challenged by Friend & Westerfield, Reserved that, depending on one's model of the operation of the securities markets and the securities laws, the latter may have produced gains that would not accrue to investors but to other parties. Thus, some have suggested that any gains from mandated disclosure would probably be reaped by investment intermediaries;[17] others, by issuing corporations. Neither possibility has yet been carefully studied.

More research welcome

In general, there is room for a great deal of additional research on the effects of the securities laws. Until it is forthcoming (if it ever is), policy makers will continue to proceed on the basis of habit and faith.

---

quired Disclosure and the Stock Market, 65 Am. Econ. Rev. 467 (1975). See also Benston's rejoinder, 65 Am. Econ. Rev. 473 (1975).

[17] Gilson & Kraakman, The Mechanisms of Market Efficiency, 70 Va. L. Rev. 549, 638-639 (1984).

CHAPTER 18

CLOSE CORPORATIONS

§18.1 Introduction

Problems with the four principles

In the first chapter of this book, we explored what might be called the "bright side" of the four basic principles of the corporate form of organization. In the succeeding chapters, we explored the "dark side" of those principles — their susceptibility to abuse — and the efforts of corporate law doctrines and legal enforcement mechanisms to deal with that dark side. Now we shall explore yet another aspect of the four principles: their frequent unsuitability to the needs and wants of participants in close corporations. We might refer to this as the "clumsy side" of the four principles.

Limited liability

The problem with limited liability for close corporations, for example, is simply that some major creditors will find it unacceptable. These creditors can and do insist in such cases on getting personal notes or guarantees from the individual participants. This part of the clumsy side will not be discussed further.

Free transferability

Among the problems posed by free transferability of corporate shares are impediments to the wishes of many close corporation participants to control the identity of new shareholders, to preserve an existing balance of power, or to assure that there will be a way to disinvest themselves (for example, on retirement, when cash needs can no longer be satisfied by salary), even though there is no active market for the shares of their company. At least in the past, and to some extent even today, legal rules have put up obstacles to agreements restricting the transferability of shares in ways designed to meet these objectives. The evolution of the law to a more flexible and accommodating system and the character of the remaining restraints are the subject of one section (18.2) of this chapter.

Centralized management

A third principle of the corporate form, centralization of management, has proven most troublesome in the close corporation context. In the standard model, which makes good economic sense for public corporations, shareholders are passive investors and a majority of them elect the directors, a majority of directors appoint the officers and provide ultimate management and supervision of the business, and the officers actively run the business and receive substantial compensation for doing so. With many close corporations, only a majority stockholder would find this arrangement acceptable. This is so because many of the shareholders will also expect to be actively engaged in helping to form and implement the corporation's business decisions, and they will want to be compensated as officers or employees. These shareholders, if they have forethought, will want to make these expectations secure, and will not trust solely to the continued good will of the other persons in the enterprise. For example, a prudent 20 percent shareholder may want to make sure that she will always have a right to be both a director of the company and a full time officer sharing in a reliable way in the corporation's growth and profits. She might also insist on getting a veto power with respect to certain classes of business decisions, such as the appointment of a chief executive, the sale of all the company's assets, or a reclassification of its shareholdings. In order to achieve such objectives, shareholders have often tried to adjust by contract the standard authority structure of the corporate form. The law's regulation of these efforts and the change toward legal rules more accepting of them are examined in another section of the chapter (18.3).

Legal personality

Finally, a major problem with legal personality as it has been developed for public corporations has been presented by the "hard to kill" character of the corporation. Remember that, in order to safeguard going concern values, the standard model requires a directors' resolution followed by a majority vote of the shareholders in order to accomplish the voluntary dissolution of a corporation. Many close corporation shareholders, however, would like to have a rule resembling the right of a partner to terminate a partnership at will and to liquidate her investment. As time goes on, close corporation participants will retire, die, change their likes and dislikes, and have fights with each other. When faced with such changes, a less than controlling shareholder may want to withdraw and liquidate her investment, but unlike a public corporation shareholder, she has no market on which to sell her stock, and there may be no acceptable outside buyers. For liquidity she may look to the other shareholders or to the corporation itself. She may want to be able to force the corporation to buy her out, or to force a dissolution and liquidation of the corporation (because that would also achieve a liquidation of her investment). Ideally, she would like an absolute right to force a buyout or liquidation. Corporate law has not gone this far, however. In response to the needs of close corporation participants, the standard pattern of dissolution by majority vote has been supplemented in most states by statutes allowing shareholders to seek involuntary dissolution, but only upon a showing that certain statutory grounds, such as deadlock among directors that threatens injury to the corporation's business, have been met. The meaning and rationale of these kinds of statutes, as well as some alternatives to them, are discussed in the final section (18.4).

§18.2 *Restricting the Transferability of Shares*

§18.2.1 Policies

Inevitability of changed relationships

As time passes, the personal relationships among the major participants in a close corporation always change in important ways. One of several participants will retire or die, leaving a gap in a shareholding or managerial role that might or might not be filled. Participants who were once friendly to each other will accumulate grudges. Some participants will want to go on to other ventures. Others will want to bring in new associates, who may or may not be acceptable to the others.

Planning with transfer restrictions

Shareholders who look ahead to these possibilities will usually want to restrict the transferability of their shares. When one shareholder wants to sell his or her stock, for example, the continuing shareholders would often like to be able to keep out any newcomers, or at least to be able to control their identity. Sometimes the continuing shareholders will want the exiting shareholder to sell to the corporation, rather than to any of themselves, in order to preserve the existing balance of power. Some types of contractural restrictions are used to give shareholders a more liquid investment. These include, for example, those by which the corporation or other shareholders are obligated to buy when the exiting shareholder retires or wants to get out. Liquidity is a big problem for close corporation shareholders, of course, since there is usually no developed market for their shares.

Past reluctance to enforce

Traditionally, courts hesitated to enforce restrictions on the transferability of shares, but in recent decades they have become much more accepting of them, and legislatures have acted to give express permission for certain kinds of restrictions. The courts' hesitation had several apparent bases. In seemingly mechanical fashion, some courts would invoke a general common law policy against restraints on alienation of personal property. Others would invoke a more particular policy that shares of stock in business corporations ought to be freely transferable, a policy that tends to promote economic efficiency but doesn't necessarily make sense when applied to close corporations. Whatever their rhetoric, many judges who hesitated to enforce restrictions appear to have been troubled by issues of fairness among shareholders.

Reasons for concern

This can be seen, I believe, by a careful reading of the facts of the cases. The factual patterns often suggest the following questions as being the real issues: (1) Did all the parties know about and freely consent to the restrictions? (2) When the restrictions were agreed to, what was the contemplated range of application? That is, did the parties foresee or consider, in any meaningful sense, the kind of situation that later did arise and cause the controversy in question? (3) If not, can one judge with any degree of confidence or plausibility what they would have provided for had they expressly considered such a situation? (4) What would reasonable persons similarly situated have agreed to, or understood, or expected?

Even today, when the idea of transfer restrictions is looked upon more favorably, courts are sensitive to these issues. The difference is that the courts are quite unlikely to invoke a supposed policy of flatly prohibiting transfer restrictions to justify a decision.

§18.2.2 Techniques

Some of the more important kinds of agreements restricting share transfers are those that create

(1) rights of first refusal,
(2) first options,

(3) consent powers,
(4) buyback rights, and
(5) buy-sell arrangements.

First refusal

A right of first refusal may be given to the corporation, or to the other shareholders, or to both (with the corporation having the first chance to exercise the right, usually). Under such an arrangement, if a shareholder wishes to sell to a third party, he or she must first offer the stock for sale to the holder of the right, who might or might not decide to buy. If the right holder declines to buy within the time specified in the agreement, the shareholder may sell to the third party. If the right holder does decide to buy, he, she, or it will buy on the same terms as were offered by the third party.

First option

A first option is similar to a right of first refusal, except that if the right holder decides to buy, the price paid is one that is determined by the agreement creating the option, rather than by the third party's offering price. (Some pricing methods are discussed below under the heading of "valuation.")

Consent power

Consent powers are given to the corporation's board or to the continuing shareholders; their permission must be obtained before a shareholder can transfer his stock to a third party.

Buyback right

Buyback rights are often given to the corporation. Under a typical arrangement, the corporation will have the right to repurchase the shareholder's shares, even if the shareholder doesn't want to sell, on the happening of certain events, such as the shareholder's ceasing to be employed by the company. Various methods may be used for fixing the price at which the shares will be repurchased.

Buy-sell agreement

Buy-sell agreements obligate the owner of shares to sell them, and the corporation or other shareholders to buy them, on the happening of certain events, such as the death or retirement of a shareholder. These agreements are immensely important for estate planning. When a shareholder in a close corporation dies, the estate will often be called on to pay taxes or meet other needs requiring cash. To meet these liquidity needs, it may be necessary or desirable to sell the shares in the close corporation rather than other assets. Because the corporation is closely held, however, there will be no ready market for them, and, in the absence of a buy-sell agreement, the executor of the estate might be in a poor bargaining position vis-à-vis the only potential buyers — the corporation and the other shareholders. Once again, various pricing methods may be specified in the relevant agreement.

§18.2.3 Valuation

Book value

Many approaches to the pricing problem are possible. Some typical ones are as follows. (1) The right holder may pay the shares' *book value*. The book value of a share is usually understood to mean the company's net worth as taken or computed from its latest balance sheet, divided by the number of outstanding shares. An agreement might or might not specify that the balance sheets and net worth figure must be prepared in accordance with "generally accepted accounting principles, applied on a consistent basis from year to year." If it does, such a provision may reduce the range of possible disputes. Book value has the advantage of being an objective figure. But, because accountants normally record the value of major corporate assets at their historical cost (less depreciation computed by some mechanical formula) and for other reasons, the book value of assets will often reflect neither what they could be sold for, either alone or as part of the whole business, nor the present value of the earnings the assets are expected to generate. Consequently, the total book value or net worth of a business may be much, much less (or greater) than its market value. With a book value pricing formula, the selling shareholder may be paid a price that he will feel to be shockingly low, or one that the others will feel to be shockingly high.

Earnings value

(2) The right holder may pay the *capitalized earnings value* of the shares. In principle, this is the soundest method of valuation. At the time of the proposed sale of stock, the future earnings that the company is expected to generate and that are attributable to the shares in question are discounted to a present value using a discount rate that corresponds to an appropriate rate of return for a business with similar characteristics. (See Appendix B, "Valuation," at the end of this book.) Though proper as a matter of economic theory and business practice, this approach is fairly subjective and manipulable. The parties to a transfer restriction agreement may therefore bargain for a more confined version of the technique. For example, the average of the past five years' earnings, increased by x percent, may be used instead of an actual estimate of future earnings, and the discount rate might be specified as the current rate for treasury bills plus y percent. Alternatively, or in addition, the parties to the agreement may bargain carefully over the identity of the persons who are to perform the capitalized earnings evaluation, to make sure that it will be done by competent, honest individuals acceptable to all participants.

Dollar value or formula

(3) The agreement might specify a *dollar value* for the stock sale price, but provide that it will be changed in accordance with a certain formula, or periodically revised by agreement of the parties. Obviously, this technique

has drawbacks very similar to those of book value. A mechanical formula for adjusting the dollar value may easily turn out to be inappropriate. A provision to adjust it by mutual agreement from time to time may fall apart when, much later on, the shareholders who expect that they will retire or leave the business first want a high valuation, and the other shareholders want it to be kept low.

Specification of evaluator

(4) Another alternative is to have the price fixed by an arbitrator. The agreement creating the restriction would specify how the arbitrator is to be selected, and might lay down some guidelines for valuation techniques.

§18.2.4 Rules

State law about the validity of restrictions on transfer of stock can be divided into three main groups: common law, permissive statutes, and statutes creating special rules for close corporations.

Reasonableness and notice

In states with corporation statutes that, like the MBCA, are not very detailed on the question of the validity of restrictions, the restraints will be tested under the basic judge-made rule: Restraints must be "reasonable" and shareholders subject to them must have had "notice." (The notice requirement is today embodied almost everywhere in a governing statute — usually, in both the Uniform Commercial Code and the Business Corporation Statute of a state.[1]) This group also includes states like California, where the corporation statute simply codifies the common law concept of reasonableness.[2]

Delaware statute

Other states have corporation statutes that list and bless various types of transfer restrictions. Section 202(c) of the Delaware statute, for example, explicitly permits transfer restrictions that create first refusal rights, buyout obligations, and consent powers. It also allows restrictions that prohibit transfers "to designated persons or classes of persons, [when] such designation is not manifestly unreasonable." This latter provision might cover a prohibition on stock sales to persons affiliated with businesses that compete with the corporation, for example, but not a prohibition on sales to members of a certain racial group.

Maryland statute

Finally, there is the approach of the Maryland statute, which creates a fairly rigid set of special rules for close corporations.[3] These rules apply

§18.2 [1]UCC §8-204 (absent actual notice, issuer's restrictions on transfer must be noted on certificate); MBCA §6.27(b) (similar requirement for restrictions imposed by agreements among shareholders, or between shareholders and corporation, as well as those imposed in articles or bylaws); Del. §202(a) (like MBCA).

[2]Cal. §204(b).

[3]Md. Corp. & Assns. Code §§4-503, 4-602.

even when the participants haven't explicitly adopted them in a stock transfer agreement. Under the Maryland approach, a shareholder in a close corporation cannot transfer stock without the consent of all of the other shareholders. But if the other shareholders don't consent, the would-be transferring shareholder has the right to require dissolution of the corporation — and thus, in effect, to be bought out by the corporation. This right to require dissolution can be waived or modified in a unanimous shareholders' agreement, however.

Application of reasonableness test:

To consent powers

Characteristic problems have arisen under these different legal approaches. Consider first, for example, the test of reasonableness. It has had to be applied to a wide array of types of restrictions. Most courts would uphold typical first refusal rights as being reasonable. But consent restrictions have been more problematic, because they restrict the transfer of stock more severely. Across jurisdictions, judicial authority seems to be split,[4] and even within a jurisdiction, judicial opinions may seem reconcilable only by making quite elusive distinctions. For example, in *Rafe v. Hindin,*[5] two persons each owned 50 percent of a corporation. There was a restriction making the stock of each nontransferable except to the other, and requiring the written consent of the other shareholder before either one could transfer his stock to a third party. The New York court (Appellate Division) held the restriction to be an unreasonable restraint on alienation. It was influenced by the fact that the agreement didn't say that consent would not be unreasonably withheld and didn't restrict the other shareholder's buying price at all. But earlier, in *Penthouse Properties, Inc. v. 1158 Fifth Ave., Inc.,*[6] a provision barring stock transfer without the written consent of the board or of two thirds of the shareholders had been upheld. In that case, the corporation operated a cooperative apartment house, and all the shareholders were also tenants in it. The court there was influenced by the special nature of the ownership situation. The court in *Rafe* tried to distinguish the *Penthouse* decision in a more definite way by saying that the case before it involved the sale of stock of a corporation organized for profit and therefore didn't come within the principle of *Rafe.*

To first options

Whether first option rights will pass scrutiny under the test of reasonableness may depend on the pricing method that is used. A fair procedure for determining the capitalized earnings value of stock at the time of exercise of the option is undoubtedly valid. In view of the problem of subjectivity in valuation, most book value approaches are probably also acceptable.

[4] See 2 F. O'Neal, Close Corporations: Law and Practice §7.08 (2d ed. 1971 & 1985 Supp.).
[5] 288 N.Y.S.2d 662 (App. Div.), aff'd, 244 N.E.2d 469 (N.Y. 1968).
[6] 11 N.Y.S.2d 417 (App. Div. 1939).

An agreement that gives the holder the right to buy the departing shareholder's stock at the *original purchase price* for that stock is more troublesome, since over time the shares' market value is likely to drift very far away from that price. Nevertheless, in *Allen v. Biltmore Tissue Corp.*,[7] the New York Court of Appeals upheld such a restriction. The court relied heavily on the notion that, since fair market value was such a manipulable and therefore litigable and expensive concept in the close corporation context, it was reasonable for drafters of transfer restrictions to resort to objective pricing formulas. By itself, of course, this reasoning only justifies use of some kind of mechanical formula, such as current net book value; it hardly justifies any and all formulas. What really seems to have set the court at ease was the perception that the parties freely and knowingly agreed on a price formula that suited them.

Analogy to call option

To use an analogy, knowing consent must be the reason why it is acceptable for a pension plan to issue a call option against shares of IBM stock that it owns. To be sure, the pension plan takes the risk that if IBM stock rises sharply in market price, it will have to sell the stock at a much lower price. But dividing up different portions of the risk-and-return characteristics of an investment is precisely the point of the option agreement, and it is acceptable — indeed, it is economically efficient — to let private parties bargain with each other as to how such divisions of an investment risk will be made. The problem with this analogy is, of course, that in some close corporation situations the parties accepting stock subject to transfer restrictions will not be nearly as aware of and self-conscious about the risks of gain and loss that they are taking as is the typical buyer of options on the organized stock markets.

Equitable restraints on statutory authorizations?

Now let us consider a problem arising under the Delaware approach to transfer restrictions: whether to read a "business purpose" test or similar requirement into the bland statutory permissions. In one noteworthy situation,[8] a large brokerage firm had adopted stock transfer restrictions in order to comply with the rules of the New York Stock Exchange, of which the firm was a member. The restrictions provided that on the happening of certain events, such as the death of a shareholder, the firm would have an option to buy back the stock at its net book value. The gist of the stock exchange rules was to insure that no persons would be stockholders of member firms who were not also full-time officers or employees of the

[7] 141 N.E.2d 812 (N.Y. 1957).

[8] St. Louis Union Trust Co. v. Merrill Lynch Pierce Fenner & Smith, Inc., 562 F.2d 1040 (8th Cir. 1977), rev'g 412 F. Supp. 45 (E.D. Mo. 1976), cert. denied, 435 U.S. 925 (1978); see also Kerrigan v. Merrill Lynch Pierce Fenner & Smith, Inc., 450 F. Supp. 639 (S.D.N.Y. 1978).

member firms. The intent was to prevent member firms from being owned by public investors. After conducting a lengthy study, however, the New York Stock Exchange changed its mind and decided to allow member firms to go public. After this, one of the brokerage firm's shareholder-employees died. Plaintiffs, the executors of his estate, claimed that after the management of the brokerage firm had learned of the new stock exchange policy and had decided to cause the brokerage firm to go public, but before it did so, they exercised the option to buy back the deceased shareholder's shares at net book value. Compared to what would have happened if the firm had not exercised the option, this resulted in serious financial loss to the deceased shareholder's estate. This is true because, when a company with a bright future makes a successful distribution of securities to the public at large, the old shareholders tend to have great gains in the realizable value of their investment.[9]

Arguments and holdings

The plaintiffs claimed that the defendants violated Rule 10b-5 by failing to disclose the intent to go public at the time the decedent's shares were purchased pursuant to the option. The main difficulty with this theory had to do with causation of injury. If plaintiffs *had* to sell at the net book value price, because the defendant brokerage firm had an absolute right to exercise its option, then nondisclosure of material inside information was beside the point. Plaintiffs argued in response that under Delaware law the transfer restriction was invalid as applied, so that they were not in fact under an enforceable obligation to sell the stock, and the nondisclosure of the decision to go public was therefore harmful to them. But Section 202 of the Delaware statute appeared on its face to authorize first option provisions and did not mention a requirement of reasonableness. Plaintiffs' response to that was the important argument that, for exercise of the option to be valid, it must be done for a proper business purpose of the corporation. In this context, such a purpose was arguably not present. Since the original, explicitly acknowledged reason for the transfer restric-

[9]Suppose *A*, *B*, and *C* founded X Corporation and bought 1,000 shares each for $10 per share. The business is successful, and a few years later the company has retained earnings to such an extent that its book value per share is $20. In addition, the future growth of the corporation's earnings looks so promising that the corporation is able to sell 30,000 shares to public investors at $100 per share. If a market for the shares is maintained after this public offering and the market price remains at about $100, a founder could sell some or all of his shares for ten times more than what he paid for them. Or, to take another perspective, the public offering has caused the book value per share of his investment to go from $20 to about $93. (The company's book value immediately after the public offering is $3,060,000, that is, $60,000 (3,000, the number of old shares, times $20, the old book value per share) plus $3,000,000, the proceeds from the public offering. Dividing this sum by 33,000, the number of shares outstanding after the public offering, gives the new book value per share.)

tions — the stock exchange rules — no longer existed, there was no proper purpose for invoking those restrictions. Though a federal district court bought the argument, the Eighth Circuit rejected it, as did another federal district court in a strikingly similar case involving the same brokerage firm.[10] Relying on a prominent commentator on Delaware law,[11] the latter court reasoned that one purpose of Section 202(c) was to eliminate the uncertainty of prior case law by validating the first option provisions and removing the need for a specific showing of business purpose.

Two caveats

Two comments about these holdings should be made. First, whether the federal courts' interpretation of the Delaware statute corresponds to what the Delaware Supreme Court would say in a similar case is not entirely clear. In a variety of contexts (such as squeezeout mergers, dividends, and share repurchases), that court has made proper purpose a test in situations involving alleged breach of fiduciary duty. Admittedly, its general attitude toward such a test has been thrown in doubt by its decision[12] to stop using the "business purpose" approach in freezeout mergers. In fairly recent years, however, it has also delivered decisions that highlight the notion that literal compliance with the terms of an authorizing statute is no shield against liability for breach of fiduciary duty.[13] Second, the federal courts in the cases just discussed may not have appreciated fully that they were being asked to look at transactions affected by a conflict of interest. That is, not only did the decedent's estate lose because it was forced to sell its stock to the brokerage firm rather than participate in the gains from the later public offering, but this loss most likely benefited the remaining shareholder-employees, including the management personnel who decided to exercise the option. By excluding the decedent's estate from the gains of going public, the remaining shareholders would get a larger share of those gains. It is precisely in this sort of situation that the Delaware courts have been inclined to look into charges of unfairness or lack of purpose.

§18.2.5 Other issues

Many other issues may arise in connection with stock transfer restrictions. For example, there are innumerable issues of interpretation. If a first

[10] See cases cited in note 8 supra.

[11] E. Folk, The Delaware General Corporation Law 198-199 (1972).

[12] Weinberger v. UOP, Inc., 457 A.2d 701 (Del. 1983).

[13] For example, in its opinion in Fliegler v. Lawrence, 361 A.2d 218 (Del. 1976), the court decided that compliance with the procedures of the interested-director provision of the Delaware statute does not prevent the court from scrutinizing a self-dealing transaction to see if it was entirely fair.

refusal agreement refers simply to "transfers" of stock, should that be read to include transfers by means of a will or the intestacy laws? Questions also arise as to whether restrictions can be imposed on shareholders who have not consented to them, or removed when some shareholders who originally agreed to them do not want them removed. These and related issues are left for texts on business planning.

§18.3 *Adjusting the Authority Structure*

Why participants want adjustments

Participants in close corporations generally expect to receive returns from the enterprise in ways other than and in addition to those received by purely passive investors. They generally expect to be actively involved in managing or operating the business. Consequently, a participant who will hold only a minority block of stock should normally be concerned to obtain a veto power over managerial decisions with which he strongly disagrees. In most cases, the minority shareholder would also like to secure a commitment that he will be able to participate in corporation decision making, at least to the extent of making sure that certain very important affirmative goals are achieved, such as the shareholder's employment as an officer or a right to a certain percentage of corporate net income before salaries and dividends. Unfortunately, however, the basic rule is that the board of directors shall manage the business of the corporation, and directors are normally elected by a majority vote of the stockholders. How, then, can the minority shareholder achieve and secure the decision making power that is so important to him?

Cumulative voting rights

Some possibilities have already been discussed. For example, the shareholder might think of relying on cumulative voting rights.[1] The practical significance of these rights can be eroded in many ways, however. The majority might cause the corporation to issue new common stock to itself or to adopt a classified board of directors. With a greater number of outstanding shares, the minority's proportion of voting power is lessened, and with a classified board and a consequent smaller number of directors up for election each year, it takes a larger percentage of shares to elect a director, even when there is cumulative voting. Accordingly, at the beginning of the enterprise, the minority shareholder might want to bargain not only for cumulative voting rights but also for preemptive rights, for a prohibition against staggered boards, and for an enforceable provision in the articles under which there would be no way to change the articles (and

§18.3 [1]See section 9.1.3 supra.

thus, the preemptive rights provisions, and so forth) without his consent. Even then, the shareholder might fear that not all conceivable loopholes were closed, and that the whole network of agreements made for a cumbersome structure. The shareholder might therefore look for alternative ways of adjusting the authority structure.

Other techniques

There are a fair number of standard alternatives, and they are discussed below under five headings. The first four topics deal with ways of modifying shareholders' voting to elect directors and approve or disapprove organic changes. The fifth topic deals with the more difficult issue of agreements that restrict the actions of directors as such, that is, agreements that attempt to determine certain aspects of managerial decision making in advance.

§18.3.1 Voting Agreements

Vote pooling

One common approach is for a majority, or some, or all of the stockholders of a close corporation to sign an agreement with each other to vote their shares in a certain way, for example, to elect each other as directors. Though generally held valid today, these agreements created difficulties for courts in the past.

Reasons for past reluctance to enforce

It is instructive to consider why. What possible reason might courts have for objecting to so-called pooling agreements? They do not, after all, seem to fly in the face of any of the four basic principles of the corporate form of organization. The main answer may be that courts were concerned with nonsigning shareholders. A potential investor obviously has an interest in knowing about preexisting control arrangements among other shareholders before she invests money in an enterprise. This perception might lead lawmakers to insist that agreements affecting control should be matters of public record rather than secret. One thing that legislatures did do in some states fairly early on was to enact voting trust statutes that embodied this policy of publicity. Yet earlier corporate law statutes were often silent about voting agreements. This duality created an obvious problem. Should voting agreements be invalidated as de facto but noncomplying voting trusts? Or should they all be allowed ad libitum, under freedom of contract principles? Or should only some voting agreements be upheld, and if so, which? Those that in a formal sense were not too much like voting trusts? Or those that were not secret? (We return to case law dealing with these issues below.)

Validation by statutes and cases

In any event, modern authorities often explicitly validate voting agreements. MBCA Section 7.31 provides flatly that shareholder voting agreements are "specifically enforceable" and not subject to the voting trust provisions. Case law has reached a similar conclusion. In *E. K. Buck Retail Stores v. Harkert,*[2] the court announced its perception that the "correct rule" is that a stockholders' control agreement is valid "where it is for the benefit of the corporation, where it works no fraud upon creditors or other stockholders, and where it violates no statute or recognized public policy." In that case, the shareholders' agreement obliged each shareholder to vote for the others' nominees. The agreement was prompted by one shareholder's contributing needed capital to the business. After a falling out, however, another shareholder wanted to renege on the agreement and say that it was against public policy. The court found that it was not.

Compliance with statute

Voting agreements may still be invalid, of course, if they fail to comply with a governing statute. In one case, a voting agreement giving a minority shareholder a proxy to vote shares of the other was found invalid where it failed to meet the terms of a North Carolina statute authorizing such agreements. In particular, the agreement was not limited, as the statute suggested that it should be, to the election of directors, but applied to all corporate business to be transacted at stockholder meetings. In addition, the agreement did not provide that all the shares of the signing shareholders would be voted as a unit. Furthermore, the court found that a proxy given by one shareholder to the other had expired, again, under the terms of the governing statute.[3] The moral is that attorneys for close corporation participants should read the statutes of the relevant states very carefully before drafting shareholder voting agreements.

Enforcement problem

A practical problem with voting agreements is the possible need to go to court to enforce them. If one minority shareholder decides not to comply with an agreement to vote in the same way as another minority shareholder, the inspector of elections may well regard this as a matter to be remedied between the stockholders themselves, and to count as valid whatever votes are submitted by the record holders of shares, unless a court order to the contrary is received. One possible way around this problem is for all the signers of the agreement to give a proxy to someone who will actually vote the shares in accordance with the agreement. Unfortunately, the traditional rule is that proxies given by shareholders can be revoked right up to the time of the shareholders' meeting. There is a traditional exception, however, for "proxies coupled with an interest," and some state corporation statutes, like that of Connecticut,[4] make it quite clear that a proxy given in connection with a valid shareholders' voting

[2] 62 N.W.2d 288 (Neb. 1954).
[3] Stein v. Capital Outdoor Advertising, Inc., 159 S.E.2d 351 (N.C. 1968).
[4] Conn. Stock Corp. Act §33-337.

agreement is an irrevocable proxy. The same result can be fairly implied under the laws of other states, such as that of Delaware.[5]

§18.3.2 Supermajority Provisions

Veto power

A more negative form of power for the minority shareholder is the veto right that comes with a supermajority provision. For example, if the articles of incorporation provide that it shall take the affirmative vote of the holders of 80 percent or more of the common stock to elect a director, a 33 percent shareholder can block any given person from being elected a director. Similarly, a provision that directors shall be elected by an affirmative vote of 100 percent of the shares being voted will give a veto power to even the smallest shareholder. Presumably, in a typical case the possession of a veto power will help assure that other shareholders will not put in directors who are completely unacceptable to the minority shareholders or who bid fair to adopt policies that will oppress them, and it will induce other shareholders to cooperate in electing a representative of the minority shareholder to the board. In practice, when relations among shareholders become strained, the veto power may simply result in a deadlock: no one is able to elect anyone to the board.

Valid under modern statutes

Modern statutes frequently make it clear that supermajority provisions are valid. For example, the MBCA adopts a presumption of majority rule but allows other patterns if they are properly embodied in the articles. Specifically, Section 7.25(a) says that a majority of the votes entitled to be cast by a voting group of shares constitutes a quorum unless the articles or the Act provide otherwise, and Section 7.25(c) states, with the same exception, that if a quorum exists, an action carries if the votes for it exceed those against it. Section 7.26 governs how greater quorum or voting requirements may be imposed. The articles amendment creating them must be approved under the voting rule then in effect or to be adopted, whichever is greater. Thus, if a corporation with an ordinary bare-majority voting rule is to have a new 80 percent voting requirement, 80 percent of the shares must be voted in favor of the amendment to change the rule.

***Benintendi* case and legislative response**

In the past, some close corporations have run into difficulty over their attempted supermajority provisions. In *Benintendi v. Kenton Hotel*,[6] for example, the bylaws of a close corporation required the unanimous vote of all shares present when sufficient notice was given, the unanimous vote of all shareholders voting for the election of directors, and the unanimous vote

[5] See Del. §§212(c), 218(c).
[6] 60 N.E.2d 829 (N.Y. 1945).

of all three directors for any board action. A minority shareholder sued to have these bylaws declared valid and to enjoin any action inconsistent with them. The court held for the defendant. The New York statute set up a structure of corporate governance based on plurality votes for the election of directors. The unanimity requirement for electing directors violated state policy as expressed in that statute. The bylaw giving a single shareholder absolute veto power was deemed contrary to the state's scheme of allocating power to certain fractions (sometimes one-half, sometimes two-thirds) of the shareholders. Finally, the bylaw concerning directors' voting made a deadlock too likely and contradicted the statute fixing the quorum for director action at between one-third and a majority of the directors. (The court thought that the common law notion of a quorum incorporated the concept of majority voting, and was not changed by the legislature.) Perhaps fortunately for close corporations, the New York legislature responded to this decision by enacting a statute authorizing supermajority provisions in the certificate of incorporation.[7]

Restraint on exercise of power

Even when a statute is flexible and the participants in a close corporation take advantage of it, a court may not allow a minority shareholder or director to exercise a full, unfettered veto power. In *Gearing v. Kelly*,[8] a corporation had three directors and one vacant directorship. The bylaws required a majority of the board, that is, three out of the four, to be present for a quorum. Two directors met to fill the vacancy, but the third refused to attend precisely in order to prevent a quorum. This third director sued to invalidate the attempted filling of the vacancy. The court held for the defendants. It decided that the equitable relief requested, the ordering of a new election, was barred because the defect in the election was caused by the plaintiff's own conduct. The dissent argued that the effect of allowing the election to stand was to strip the plaintiff of all control, and that if there were to be a deadlock in a new election, the shareholders would have other remedies. Professor O'Neal, the leading commentator on close corporation law, called the decision highly questionable.[9] Nevertheless, after *Gearing* the New York Legislature adopted a provision that board vacancies may be filled by vote of a majority of the directors then in office, even though less than a quorum exists, unless the certificate or bylaws provide for filling the vacancy by vote of the shareholders.[10] Presumably, the prevention of paralysis and facilitation of the vital function of director succession were

[7] N.Y. §§616, 709.
[8] 182 N.E.2d 391 (N.Y. 1962).
[9] 1 F. O'Neal, Close Corporations: Law and Practice §4.22 (2d ed. 1971).
[10] N.Y. §705(a).

seen as more important than allowing minority shareholders to secure an absolute veto power.[11]

§18.3.3 Voting Trusts

Basic points

In lieu of using a voting agreement, shareholders in a close corporation may coordinate their efforts by establishing a voting trust. Each shareholder formally transfers legal title to his shares to trustees who will have the right to vote all the transferred shares in the manner stipulated in the document setting up the voting trust. The shareholders become beneficial or equitable owners of the shares. They retain the right to receive dividends and other asset distributions, and normally receive transferable voting trust certificates evidencing their interests. Depending on the context, close corporation participants may be somewhat discouraged from using a voting trust because a state stock transfer tax might be triggered by transferring shares to the trust, and shares of interest in a voting trust may be even more illiquid than the shares themselves. Until recently, they might also have worried that the trust would make the corporation and shareholders ineligible for "flow through" type tax treatment under Subchapter S of the Internal Revenue Code.[12]

Incidentally, voting trusts are sometimes used to hold the shares of public corporations. This might happen, for example, when the creditors of a financially troubled corporation refuse to approve a reorganization plan unless they are given control, or participation in control, through the device of having their representatives become some or all the trustees of a voting trust.

Validating statutes

Today, most state business corporation statutes have provisions authorizing and regulating voting trusts. Typically, the statutes require that the trust be created by an agreement in writing, that a copy of the agreement and of a record of the holders of voting trust certificates be available at the corporation's registered office for inspection by any shareholders or certificate holders, that the trust will be valid only for a limited term (usually, up to ten years), and that the trust will be irrevocable during its designated life.[13] Since statutes and courts differ on whether an ambiguous voting trust agreement will give the trustees power to vote on matters other than the election of directors (for example, on a proposed sale of all of

[11] See also Jacobson v. Moskowitz, 261 N.E.2d 613 (N.Y. 1970).
[12] I.R.C. §1361(c)(2) now eliminates this problem, however.
[13] See MBCA §7.30; Cal. §706(b); Del. §218; N.Y. §621(d).

the company's assets) it is important for voting trust agreements to be carefully drafted to provide for such contingencies.

How to square with voting agreements?

Ringling **case**

A famous trio of Delaware cases illustrate the difficulty courts have had in making sense of the simultaneous existence of voting trust statutes and other voluntary devices for regulating shareholder voting power. In a 1947 case, *Ringling v. Ringling Bros.-Barnum & Bailey Combined Shows, Inc.*,[14] two shareholders in a three-shareholder corporation had a voting agreement that provided for them to vote as a block, with disagreements to be settled by arbitration. At a meeting to elect directors, a disagreement arose and the arbitrator was called in. One shareholder voted her shares according to the arbitrator's decision, but the other refused. The chairman of the meeting ruled that the refusing shareholder's vote would be counted as though she had followed the agreement. That shareholder and the third one objected. The complying shareholder filed suit. The Vice Chancellor held that the agreement was binding and ordered a new election. On appeal, defendant argued that the agreement was invalid because voting power cannot be separated from ownership unless a voting trust is created under the state statute or unless there is a proxy coupled with an interest. The court held, however, that the agreement was not an assignment of voting rights, but simply an agreement by each shareholder to vote her shares in a particular way. As such, it did not violate any public policy, did not take advantage of any other shareholder, and was not an attempt to circumvent the voting trust statute. The relief granted was that the noncomplying shareholder's votes were not counted at all. (From the plaintiff's point of view, this was not a very effective remedy. It meant that one principal purpose of the original agreement, the deployment of a controlling block of votes, could not be obtained.)

Abercrombie **case: disguised voting trust**

In 1957, however, in *Abercrombie v. Davies*,[15] the Delaware Supreme Court held a voting agreement among shareholders invalid because it operated essentially as a voting trust agreement yet failed to comply with the voting trust statute. In this case the agreement provided that a group of shareholders holding 54½ percent of the stock would deposit their shares in escrow after endorsing the share certificates and delivering them to certain designated agents. The agents were to get proxies for all shareholder votes and were to vote as a block. The vote was to be determined by the agreement of at least seven out of the eight agents or, failing such agreement, by arbitration. Proxies were given for ten years, but could be terminated by seven agents. On request by seven agents, the parties would

[14] 49 A.2d 603 (Del. Ch. 1946), on appeal, 53 A.2d 441 (Del. 1947).
[15] 130 A.2d 338 (Del. 1957).

execute a voting trust to replace the escrow, with the agents becoming trustees. In holding that the agreements operated essentially as a voting trust, the court declared that the parties' subjective intention to avoid creation of a trust was irrelevant. The court seemed to identify three elements that, if present, would make a pooling agreement a de facto voting trust: (1) separation of voting rights from beneficial ownership, (2) transfer of voting power irrevocably for a definite period, and (3) a principal object of the agreement being voting control of the corporation. *Ringling* was distinguished on the ground that the agreement there did not involve a transfer of voting rights.

Together, these two cases suggest that courts should draw a sharp distinction between an agreement under which *X* gets the right to vote *Y*'s shares and one under which *Y* promises to vote her shares according to *X*'s direction. If the latter kind of agreement is specifically enforced, it seems to have the same effect as the former. The only difference would be that a lawsuit is needed before *X*'s wishes are carried out. Accordingly, it is not clear what sense the distinction makes as a policy matter, nor is the distinction one that will be easy to apply in hybrid situations.

It might be suggested that the *Abercrombie* result was nevertheless a sound one, because the agreement made by the parties in that case was apparently not made public and therefore violated the publicity policy that underlies the voting trust statutes. Granting the validity of this point would indicate, however, that ordinary voting agreements of the type examined in Ringling should be held invalid whenever a copy of such an agreement is not filed with the corporation and made available to inspection by all shareholders. It does not appear, however, that the Delaware courts would insist on this. Indeed, a court in a jurisdiction following the MBCA probably could not impose a publicity requirement on voting agreements. Section 7.31 of that act provides both that shareholder voting agreements are specifically enforceable and that such agreements shall not be subject to the section of the statute (7.30) on voting trusts. This provision may provide a clear rule but it simply emphasizes the basic policy puzzle: Why should the law impose a publicity requirement on voting trusts but not on voting agreements?

***Lehrman v. Cohen:* classified stock OK**

The final case in the trio is *Lehrman v. Cohen*,[16] which involved classified stock. The corporation had two classes of shares, one owned by the defendant and one owned by the plaintiff, each of which was entitled to elect two of the company's four directors. To avoid a deadlock, it was unanimously agreed to create one share, with $10 par value, of a new class of

[16] 222 A.2d 800 (Del. 1966).

stock possessed of the right to elect a fifth director but having no right to dividends or the distribution of assets on liquidation. The share of the new class of stock was issued to the company's counsel. Eventually, however, the attorney and the defendant combined to elect the attorney as president and to give him a long-term executive employment contract. The plaintiff brought suit and contended that the new class of stock was in substance and effect a voting trust, and was illegal because it was not limited to a ten-year period as required by the voting trust statute. The court held for the defendants. It said that the arrangement creating a deadlock-breaking third class of stock with only voting rights did not separate the voting rights of the older classes of stock from the other attributes of ownership of those classes of stock. In the court's view this meant that the arrangement was valid under the first *Abercrombie* test. Having held that the stockholders of the older two classes did not divest themselves of their voting rights, although they did dilute their voting powers, the court did not feel a need to reach the remaining *Abercrombie* tests, both of which assume the divestiture of voting rights.

As in the case of the court's distinction between the *Abercrombie* arrangement and that in *Ringling,* the distinction between the *Lehrman* device and that in *Abercrombie* seems technical and elusive rather than pragmatic.

§18.3.4 Classified Shares

Statutory authorization

As the discussion of the *Lehrman* case might suggest, shareholders may often be able to create a flexible yet valid adjustment of their relative voting rights by use of different classes of stock. Statutes seem to offer no impediments. For example, MBCA Section 6.01(a) provides for the creation of classes of stock possessing such "preferences, limitations, and relative rights" as shall be described in the articles of incorporation. Section 8.04 specifically authorizes the articles of incorporation to provide that specified numbers of directors will be elected by certain classes of shares. Since such a provision will appear in the articles of incorporation, which are available for public inspection, one could not object to classified shares by raising the argument against secret control arrangements.

Useful device

Perhaps many attorneys advising close corporation participants would prefer the use of classified shares to other devices adjusting the authority structure among shareholders. To be sure, the worried minority shareholder might well insist on safeguarding the rights she acquires under a system of classified stock by insisting that there be a supermajority voting requirement for charter amendments. Otherwise, the articles might be amended against the minority's will to allow for the creation of new classes of stock with their own rights to elect directors.

§18.3.5 Agreements Restricting Actions of Directors

A tougher problem

Agreements that restrict the actions and decisions of directors as such are more directly important to many close corporation participants than are shareholder voting agreements, because directors make a wide range of particular business decisions, such as who will be employed as such and such an officer at a particular level of pay, that do not fall within the purview of shareholder voting rights. Yet director-restricting agreements are more troublesome as a legal matter, because they seem to offend one of the four basic principles of the corporate form, namely, centralized management.

Inapplicable policies

To understand the positions that have evolved in the statutes of important states, let us consider three questions in turn. First, why does corporate law normally provide that directors rather than shareholders shall make business decisions? The answer is that the basic rule of centralized management eliminates redundancy and waste in decision making and facilitates the coordination of the multitude of activities that are carried out by a large, complex business. Both aspects of this answer lose their force in the context of the close corporation, however. It is therefore not surprising that some corporation laws were eventually amended to allow the founders of such corporations to provide in the articles of organization, if they so wished, that management would be carried out directly by shareholders.[17]

Danger to public shareholders

Second, why would courts view it as improper, in the public corporation context, for the directors to agree with each other (outside of directors' meetings) to pursue and support certain business decisions, for example, to vote for the appointment of one another as officers with certain fixed salaries? The answer is that such agreements might be inconsistent with the best interests of the public shareholders, whom the directors are supposed to be representing. Indeed, such back-scratching arrangements might be devices for exploiting shareholders.

Danger to nonparties

Third, why, in the close corporation context, might courts be reluctant to allow directors to agree with each other to pursue certain business decisions? The answer is that the interest of the minority shareholders who are not parties to the agreement may be hurt. Nevertheless, if *all* shareholders in a close corporation were also directors and were parties to the director-

[17] E.g., Del. §351.

restricting agreement, there would appear to be little objection to such agreements, even though they might involve business decisions such as who has what job with the corporation.

Statutory approaches

Legislatures have taken several different approaches toward liberalization of the rule against director-restricting agreements in the case of closely held corporations. One approach, followed by New York,[18] is to allow restrictions on the directors' exercise of power if they are imposed by unanimous consent of the shareholders, appear in the certificate of incorporation, and if notice of them is given to all subsequent shareholders. A second approach, followed by Delaware,[19] is to allow even the holders of a majority of the stock to agree in writing among themselves to restrict their actions as directors. Under either approach, the quid pro quo is that the effect of any such agreement shall be to impose on the parties to it the liability for managerial acts or omissions that is normally imposed on directors, to the extent that the discretion of the board is controlled by such agreement. Accordingly, under the Delaware approach, if several shareholders agree with each other to act in certain ways as directors (for example, to have each other appointed as officers at certain salaries) and this results in injury to the interest of a non-signing minority shareholder (for example, because the officers are paid excessive salaries) the shareholders who are party to the agreement will be liable for breach of a fiduciary duty of loyalty, even if they elected other people to be the actual directors who then carried out their policies.

Minnesota approach

A most comprehensive, modern approach is taken by the Minnesota statute that authorizes "shareholder control agreements."[20] It allows shareholders to make specifically enforceable agreements relating to the control of *any phase* of the business and affairs of the corporation. Without limitation, the agreement may cover general business decisions, dividend payments, employment of shareholders, election of directors and officers, and arbitration of disputes. Certain requirements must be met, however. The agreement must be written. *All* shareholders must sign it. A copy must be filed with the corporation. Notice must appear on each share certificate of the existence and location of the agreement. Every shareholder, beneficial owner, or holder of a security interest in a share has a right to get a copy of the agreement. If all these requirements are met, the agreement will apply to subsequent (nonsigning) holders of stock. Creditors are bound if they

[18] N.Y. §620(b).
[19] Del. §350.
[20] Minn. Bus. Corp. Act §302A.457.

have actual knowledge of it. As usual, to the extent powers are shifted from directors to shareholders, so are the duties and liabilities.

A New York trio

To appreciate the practical significance of these modern statutes, it is necessary to review the older case law. A well-known trio of New York cases illustrates the perils that close corporations faced. In 1934, the New York Court of Appeals decided *McQuade v. Stoneham and McGraw.*[21] McQuade and McGraw bought shares from Stoneham, who was, even after the purchase, majority shareholder of the New York Giants baseball team. The purchase agreement required all three to "use their best endeavors" to keep themselves as directors and officers of the company. Later, McQuade was replaced as treasurer when Stoneham and McGraw refused to support him at a board meeting. McQuade contended that under the agreement, he could not be replaced unless he had been disloyal to the corporation, which he was not. Defendants claimed the agreement was void as an infringement of the powers of the directors. Though the lower court had allowed damages, the New York Court of Appeals held for defendants. It emphasized that directors may not abdicate responsibility to exercise their independent judgment on behalf of the corporation, and that there was no evidence that the corporation would be harmed by McQuade's replacement. Indeed, its view was that contracts restricting directors would be void, even without inquiry by the court into the motives of the directors. An alternative basis of decision was that, since McQuade was a city magistrate at the time the contract was made, his employment as officer of the corporation was illegal under local statute.

***McQuade* case**

***Clark v. Dodge*: different result**

Just two years later the court decided *Clark v. Dodge.*[22] Here the plaintiff, a 25-percent shareholder, and the defendant, a 75-percent shareholder, made an agreement that required the defendant to vote his stock to preserve the plaintiff's position as director and officer, and his income from the corporation, so long as plaintiff remained competent and loyal. Plaintiff claimed breach, and the defendant argued that the agreement was void under the *McQuade* rule. The court held that the complaint did state a cause of action. Why the different outcome from *McQuade?* Now the court stressed that the plaintiff and the defendant were the only shareholders and there was no indication that the agreement threatened harm to any-

[21] 189 N.E. 234 (N.Y. 1934).

[22] 199 N.E. 641 (N.Y. 1936). A later New York case, Zion v. Kurtz, 405 N.E.2d 681 (N.Y. 1980), points out that New York §620(b), discussed supra at note 18, was thought by the legislature to overrule, at least in part, both *Long Park* and *McQuade.* The court did not reach this conclusion itself, since it decided the case on other grounds.

one, including the public, that any invasion of the directors' powers was negligible, and that under these conditions the participants should be able to structure their deal as they see fit.

***Long Park* and long agreements**

If lawyers in New York thought that *Clark v. Dodge* opened up a field for fully free contracting to modify the governance structure of the corporate form, they were mistaken. In 1948, in *Long Park, Inc. v. Trenton-New Brunswick Theatres Co.,*[23] the Court of Appeals struck down an agreement among three shareholders, who owned all the shares of their company, that one of them would manage the company for nineteen years. This agreement was deemed invalid as a significant violation of the statutory requirement that the directors shall manage the corporation. *Clark v. Dodge* was distinguished as involving only an insignificant variation from that requirement.

In the last couple of decades, courts seem to have become much more sympathetic to the attempts of close corporation participants to adjust by contract the standard authority structure of the corporate form, even when not explicitly authorized to do so by the governing corporation statute.

Galler v. Galler

Perhaps the leading case in this regard is *Galler v. Galler,*[24] a 1964 Illinois decision. Two 47½-percent shareholders entered into an agreement concerning the conduct of their family business. Among other things, the agreement provided that the parties would vote to elect themselves directors, that dividends would be declared according to a certain formula (which preserved a $500,000 earned surplus), and that at the death of either owner a pension would be paid to his widow. When the plaintiff's husband died, however, the defendant refused to honor the agreement. The lower court found that the agreement violated the state corporation statute, but on appeal the court held for plaintiff. In its view, the minimum dividend required by the agreement was unobjectionable because the required surplus would protect creditors, and the promised pension, which was to be paid only if deductible by the corporation, was not detrimental to the corporation. Furthermore, the 5-percent minority shareholder had not complained about the arrangement.

Recognition of special problems

More important, however, the court in *Galler* explicitly recognized that special treatment should be afforded to close corporations. It observed that agreements such as the one before it are necessary to protect close corporation participants, who have no market for their shares. Its position was that such agreements should be given effect if they violate no explicit statutory language and they harm neither creditors nor minority shareholders.

[23] 77 N.E.2d 633 (N.Y. 1948).
[24] 203 N.E.2d 577 (Ill. 1964).

§18.4 *Dissolving the Legal Person*

§18.4.1 Problems and Policies

The difference a market makes

In a public corporation, the shareholder who disagrees with the identity of the management or with the wisdom of their business decisions has the option of selling his shares on an active market. Furthermore, since he looks to dividends or share price increases for a return on his investment, rather than to employment by the corporation, most acts of unfairness or breach of duty by the corporation's management will not bear on him in particular, but will afflict all shareholders pro rata. An enterprising fellow shareholder and his lawyer may come forward to redress such unfair acts by means of a derivative action in which the benefits and costs of suit can be easily spread among the many investors. In a close corporation, however, the participant who disagrees with the personalities or policies of the others and cannot get a decisive upper hand in management has no active market for his shares to which he can turn. Unless he has contracted for a buyout, his investment is illiquid. Moreover, many possible acts of unfairness by controlling parties could indeed be aimed at him in particular. For example, antagonistic controlling parties might force him out of his employment with the company.

Courts as managers?

If the disgruntled shareholder tries to seek legal redress for such unfair acts by invoking fiduciary principles and seeking equitable remedies, he will often put the court in an uncomfortable position. He may be asking it to measure unquantifiable harms and to give remedies that seem to interfere with the company's decision making as to business matters. Should the court order a squeezed-out participant to be re-employed? For how long? At what salary? How can the court be sure that the plaintiff will be reasonably competent and diligent? The risk that the court will not give a satisfactory remedy is significant.

Need for planning

Here, of course, as elsewhere in the close corporation context, the problem might well have been avoided or mitigated by careful planning. If the participant had had the advice and counsel of a good lawyer, he might have obtained a satisfactory long-term employment agreement, a set of arrangements insuring some power in decision making, and a right to have his investment bought out by the corporation or other shareholders on the happening of certain events, or whenever he wanted. But even the best laid plans of lawyers and men go oft astray. Moreover, in many close corporations there simply has been no adequate advance planning. The participants failed to take seriously the likelihood that they would one day be at odds with one another. Furthermore, the basic rules of the "form contract" that is corporation law were designed with the public corporation in mind, so corporate law does not offer streamlined, efficient, and satisfactory rules for resolution of disputes among the close corporation participants.

Liquidity via dissolution

Consequently, the dissatisfied participants in the close corporation frequently want to be bought out by the corporation or other shareholders at an acceptable price. Or they want to achieve a similar result, withdrawal of their investment, by forcing dissolution of their corporation. The law has tried to respond to the needs of such dissatisfied shareholders by allowing petitions for involuntary dissolution. It has also tried to respond to two other concerns that traditionally have been thought to be important.

Destruction of going concern

One is the desire not to facilitate wanton destruction of going concern values. If dissolution results in a corporation's business being terminated and its assets being sold piecemeal, going concern values will have been sacrificed. In the case of a public corporation, of course, this sacrifice could amount to an enormous deadweight loss.

Hold-up problem

The other concern is a desire to deter minority shareholders from using the threat of dissolution as a way of "holding up" the majority. Because of these policies, courts in the past were notably reluctant to order dissolution of solvent going concerns on the request of a dissatisfied shareholder. Even today, when judicial attitudes are more favorable and courts are more disposed to treat close corporation problems as distinct, state statutes allow involuntary dissolution only under certain conditions, such as a showing of deadlock among shareholders. These conditions will be discussed in the next subsection.

Hetherington & Dooley's critique

In an important law review article,[1] Professors Hetherington and Dooley strongly criticized the traditional viewpoint. Their empirical research indicated that when shareholders bring petitions for involuntary dissolution the ultimate result is rarely that the corporation's business is actually terminated or liquidated. Typically, the dissenting shareholder is bought out by the others, either before judicial resolution of the lawsuit or after a dissolution order has been entered.[2] There is therefore almost no destruc-

§18.4 [1]Illiquidity and Exploitation: A Proposed Statutory Solution to the Remaining Close Corporation Problem, 63 Va. L. Rev. 1 (1977).

[2]Remember, dissolution means an ending of the corporation as a separate *legal person,* with the ability to sue and be sued in its own name, with limited liability for its owners, and so forth. Dissolution per se does not imply that the business that had been operated by the corporation ceases to function as a going concern. For example, when a corporation starts a formal dissolution process, it could transfer the entire business (physical assets, employees, customer relations, and all) to outsiders for cash, or to the shareholders as individuals. Granted, however, that as part of many voluntary dissolutions of corporations, the corporate

tion of going concern values as a result of the involuntary dissolution procedure. Rather, the aggrieved shareholders use their power to petition for involuntary dissolution as a bargaining chip. The model that seems to underlie some dissolution statutes — a picture of a corporation in which two rival factions are deadlocked as to decision making power, as a consequence of which the business cannot function properly and is steadily losing money or has even become insolvent — is rarely the model that is presented to the courts.

Their analysis and proposal

Under the Hetherington and Dooley view, the disgruntled shareholder is usually seeking not a judicial order that will help cut his losses on a money losing venture but a judicial order (or the threat of one) that will either (1) prod the others into buying him out at an acceptable price or causing the corporation to do so, (2) prod the others into letting him buy them out, or (3) prod the others into agreeing to some change in the business arrangements or formal balance of power, such as agreeing to give him a seat on the board and a particular position of employment. Hetherington and Dooley respond to this situation by arguing that dissolution proceedings are a cumbersome and costly way for a shareholder to pursue any of these objectives. The main reason for the costliness is that the dissolution remedy is discretionary and based on fault, features that inevitably create large litigation costs. One consequence of these costs is that minority shareholders with smaller interests are less likely to try to invoke the remedy, no matter how oppressed they think they are. Hetherington and Dooley therefore propose a statutory reform that would respond more directly to the concerns of a dissatisfied shareholder in a close corporation: an automatic buyout right that is roughly similar to a partner's right to force dissolution.

Specifics

More specifically, under their proposal a minority or 50-percent shareholder would be entitled to demand that the corporation buy all of his shares. The corporation would have a right of first refusal but would not be obligated to buy. If it did not, it would have to offer the shares to the remaining shareholders, who could then make pro rata offers to purchase. If the parties could not agree on a purchase, however, the demanding shareholder could bring an action for a judicial determination of the value of the shares. The corporation and the other shareholders would then have 90 days to buy at the price fixed by the court. If they did not agree to buy all the demander's shares by the end of that period, the court would be required to order dissolution. No proof of the majority's "fault," or the

business is also "liquidated piecemeal" in the sense that various assets are sold to different buyers.

like, would be necessary. Presumably, this ultimate possibility of dissolution would encourage the parties to negotiate a buyout on mutually acceptable terms, or at least to accept those fixed by an impartial judge.

Refinements

In order to make the scheme more flexible and to prevent abuses, there would be important refinements on this basic procedure. For example, to protect the corporation and the other shareholders against sudden cash drains, the court could provide for installment payments of the purchase price for a period of up to five years. In addition, a shareholder could not exercise her buyout right until more than two years after acquiring her shares. Furthermore, shareholders could explicitly contract to waive their buyout rights, though only for two years at a time. Waiver might be necessary, for example, to induce a creditor to lend money to the corporation.

Criticism

Perhaps the basic criticism that could be leveled against Hetherington and Dooley's automatic buyout right is that minority shareholders would use it as a way of holding up majority shareholders. Arguably, the holdup potential would be greater than under current law, where, in order to make a credible threat of dissolution, the minority shareholder must have prima facie evidence that one of the statutory grounds of dissolution, for example, "oppression" by the majority, has been satisfied. Hetherington and Dooley would counter with the point that the holdup power is mitigated by their provision that the corporation might pay for a buyout over several years and their intuition that minority shareholders in fact are not usually trying to extort unfair concessions from the majority.

§18.4.2 Rules

Grounds of dissolution

MBCA Section 14.30(2) gives the courts power to liquidate a corporate business when a shareholder establishes one of four conditions: director deadlock; shareholder deadlock; illegality, fraud, or oppression by those in control; and misapplication or waste of corporate assets. Many states have similar statutes. Others have statutes that contain a narrower list of grounds. New York law provides, for example, that holders of 50 percent of the voting shares can petition for dissolution on grounds of director or shareholder deadlock or internal dissension, and that any holder of voting shares can petition for dissolution on the ground that shareholders are so divided that they have failed, for a period including two successive annual meeting dates, to elect a successor to directors whose terms were due to expire; but it restricts dissolution petitions based on illegality, fraud, oppression, and misapplication or waste to holders of more than 20 percent of the company's stock.[3] Still other states have statutes with a more inclusive list of grounds of dissolution. California, for example, has made several additions to the MBCA pattern.[4] The two most notable ones are a showing that those in control have been guilty of "persistent unfairness towards minority shareholders" and a showing that "liquidation is reasonably necessary for the protection of the rights or interests of any substantial number of the shareholders, or of the complaining shareholders."

Each of these grounds for dissolution has spawned issues for resolution by case law. The decisions reflect both the importance of variations in statutory language and the weight given to perceived equities in the particular case.

Dissolution for deadlock

(1) Consider two cases involving a claim of deadlock. In *Wollman v. Littman*,[5] a New York case, plaintiffs and defendants each controlled 50 percent of the shares and 50 percent of the board. Plaintiffs also had an indirect interest in the corporation's main supplier. When defendants in a separate suit charged plaintiffs with luring customers away to the supplier, plaintiffs sued for dissolution, charging that differences among the owners made management impossible. The court held for the defendants, vacating a lower court's dissolution order and remanding for trial. It thought that dissolution would accomplish the wrongful purpose with which the plaintiffs were charged in the other suit, since only the supplier was in a position to buy the corporation's assets. Dissolution would therefore be inequitable. Furthermore, dissolution is a discretionary remedy, and the New York statute provided that in deciding whether to grant a petition for dissolution, the court should consider the *benefit to the shareholders* to be of paramount importance.

Benefit-to-shareholders factor

A contrary case

In apparent contrast is *Strong v. Fromm Laboratories, Inc.*,[6] a Wisconsin case. After the death of a leading participant in the business, serious friction developed between two 50-percent factions. The court held that whether or not a liquidation of the corporation would be beneficial or detrimental to the shareholders was *not* a material factor to be considered in exercising the power to order involuntary liquidation under the Wiscon-

[3]N.Y. §§1104, 1104-a. The latter provision, adopted in 1979, was part of a liberalization of New York law. The legislature intended that proof of the most egregious misconduct be no longer required for dissolution and that the profitability of the business not be a reason to deny dissolution. The statute instructs the court to "take into account" whether liquidation is the only feasible means to give petitioners a fair return on their investment and whether it is reasonably necessary for the protection of shareholder interests.

[4]Cal. §1800(b).

[5]316 N.Y.S.2d 526 (App. Div. 1970).

[6]77 N.W.2d 389 (Wis. 1956).

sin statute. Furthermore, said the court, since there was no alternative corrective remedy — none other than that granted by the statute — and the conditions of the statute were met, it was an abuse of discretion for the trial court not to have decreed a liquidation. This ruling seemed clearly to limit judicial discretion with respect to the dissolution remedy.

Based on a different statute

The apparent contrast in judicial attitudes in these cases can be explained in part by reference to the different statutes involved. The Wisconsin statute applied in *Strong* was similar to the MBCA provision. It mentioned as one ground of dissolution that directors are deadlocked in the management of corporate affairs, the shareholders are unable to break the deadlock, *and* irreparable injury is being suffered or is threatened by reason thereof. (That corresponds to the more traditional judicial attitude that dissolution of a solvent going concern should not be ordered unless continued life would injure the corporation and its shareholders and/or dissolution would benefit them.) But another ground of dissolution, the one invoked by the court, is that shareholders are deadlocked in voting power and have failed, for a period that includes at least two consecutive annual meeting dates, to elect successors to directors whose terms were due to expire. In this latter ground, there is no mention of irreparable injury resulting from the deadlock. The Wisconsin court seized on this difference and on the fact that the Wisconsin statute did not, like those of New York and Minnesota, impose an explicit general requirement that courts consider benefits to stockholders when deciding whether to order involuntary dissolution or liquidation. It therefore concluded that an MBCA-type shareholder deadlock provision is designed to provide a fairly objective test (the two meetings rule) and thus to preclude protracted arguments about benefits and detriments.

Similar issue in waste cases

(2) The same basic issue — whether a court should undertake to decide if nondissolution would result in irreparable injury — arises when the alleged ground for dissolution is misapplication, waste, or maladministration of corporate assets. It is hard enough to bring a derivative action for waste or lack of due care, given the business judgment rule. When a claim in the nature of waste has been alleged as a ground for involuntary dissolution, some courts have added the difficult requirement of a showing of injury. In *Johnston v. Livingston Nursing Home, Inc.*,[7] two sisters who owned a nursing home corporation engaged in a fair amount of bickering and quarreling, and one charged the other with mismanagement of the business. The court held that she might have judicial redress to correct such alleged abuses, but that dissolution would not be ordered in the absence of

[7] 211 So. 2d 151 (Ala. 1968).

fraud or "maladministration that is destructive or injurious to the corporation." The court was influenced by the fact that the corporation operated at a substantial profit. Presumably, such a court would order dissolution only if the maladministration or waste were of a repeated or continuing character and it was unrealistic to expect that it could be ended by less drastic means.

"Oppression"

(3) "Oppression" is surely the most intriguing, yet least clear-cut, of the grounds for involuntary dissolution. Courts are at least clear that controlling parties' conduct can be "oppressive" within the meaning of the relevant statute even when their acts were not illegal or fraudulent and did not constitute misapplication or waste of assets, if for no other reason than the fact that these terms are also mentioned separately in the dissolution statutes and therefore seem to be separate bases of decision. Influential British decisions describe oppression as a departure from fair dealing.[8] A noteworthy Illinois decision can be read for the proposition that a continued course of conduct to exclude the minority party from meaningful participation in corporate decision making may constitute oppression.[9] There, the court found deadlocks at shareholder and director meetings for a period of years, evasion by the president of a bylaw requirement that he report to the directors and shareholders, self-dealing by the president, "numerous acts of hostility toward and deprivation of the rights" of the complaining stockholders, and nonpayment of dividends. It is still very hard to get any coherent general idea from the court's decision as to what constitutes oppression.

Example of *White v. Perkins*

A Virginia decision may be taken to illustrate the elusive character of the concept. In *White v. Perkins*,[10] White (owning 55 percent) and Perkins (45 percent) had a falling-out over the conduct of their business. White refused to allow a dividend, which put pressure on Perkins because they had elected subchapter S treatment. White gave Perkins a salary increase but (1) continued to refuse dividends; (2) refused Perkins' request for additional equity to make their holdings 50/50; (3) allowed the corporation to extend excessive credit to another business owned by White; (4) claimed the corporation owed him rentals for facilities for which there was no lease agreement. Perkins sued for dissolution. The lower court ordered assorted relief, including payment of the dividend, but no dissolution. The appellate court affirmed as to the finding of oppressive conduct, but reversed as

[8] See Elder v. Elder & Watson, Ltd., (1952) Sess. Cas. 49, 55; Scottish Co-op. Wholesale Society, Ltd. v. Meyer, 3 All E.R. 66, 86 (H.L. 1958).
[9] Gidwitz v. Lanzit Corrugated Box Co., 170 N.E.2d 131 (Ill. 1960).
[10] 189 S.E.2d 315 (Va. 1972).

to the remedy. The court opined that "oppressive" does not require fraud or illegality and quoted with approval the description of oppression as a departure from fair dealing. As for remedies, it held that the two possibilities under the statute, dissolution or custodianship, were exclusive.

An interpretation of the concept

My view is that "oppression" should be interpreted in a way that corresponds to the emerging case law concept of a breach of the majority shareholder's *fiduciary duty of loyalty* to the minority. There are two main categories of behavior patterns that the courts considering a claim of oppression should look for. The first is *self-dealing* by the controlling party that may be unfair to the corporation, and hence to the minority. For example, has the controlling party caused the corporation to buy supplies from some other business in which he has a significant interest? The more numerous and continuing the self-dealing transactions, the more ready the court should be to call them an oppressive course of conduct. The second category consists of *squeezeout moves,* that is, a configuration of decisions that together indicate that the majority is trying to exclude the minority from meaningful participation in either (1) the economic returns generated by the corporation or (2) corporate decision making processes, when there is a good basis for thinking that the minority had a right to participate in decision making or a justifiable understanding of being able to so participate.

Squeezeout moves

It is crucial to note that in the close corporation context, a controlling party wishing to take advantage of minority shareholders need not effectuate an easily visible, clear-cut freezeout transaction of the type discussed in connection with public corporations. (See chapter 12 supra.) He may achieve his ends by a more subtle combination of moves, which will make the minority's stock certificates worthless without actually taking them away. The term *squeezeout* connotes these subtler moves better than the term *freezeout.* One common squeezeout pattern, which may well constitute the prototype of "oppression," has three elements. (1) The controlling party has caused the corporation to cease paying dividends, or the corporation has never paid dividends and the controlling party is unwilling to change this policy. (2) The controlling party has excluded the minority shareholder from employment with the corporation, or has made life so miserable for the minority shareholder that the latter has resigned, or has refused to cause the company to hire a new shareholder, for example, the daughter of a former shareholder who has just died and bequeathed his shares to the daughter. (3) After the first two elements have been in place — that is, after the spigot of financial return from the business has been shut off to the minority — the controlling party offers to buy out the minority shareholder at a price that would seem rather low to a disinterested outsider performing a capitalized-earnings evaluation of the business. (To some extent, this third element is optional, like frosting on a cake.) This description is not meant to be a statement of necessary and sufficient conditions for finding the squeezeout type of oppression, but only to convey the crucial idea that a configuration of corporate and individual behavior patterns, when seen as a coherent whole, may indicate a probable squeezeout.

Different from breach of loyalty suit

There is perhaps one important respect in which the courts should approach a claim of oppression differently from one of breach of the duty of loyalty. Since the former is raised in a proceeding that seeks involuntary dissolution, a decision for plaintiff means that every shareholder, including the oppressive controlling shareholder, will be given her pro rata share in the proceeds of the liquidated business. The defendant is not required to pay damages for specific wrongful acts, nor is there need to measure the extent of the harm she has caused. But since an allegation of breach of fiduciary duty is usually brought in a derivative or direct action for damages, a decision for plaintiff means that money will be taken from defendant and given to the corporation or the plaintiff. In view of this difference, courts faced with suggestive but imperfect evidence of improper behavior by controlling parties may well find oppression more readily than they would find a breach of the fiduciary duty of loyalty.

Protection-of-interests approach

(4) In California, where dissolution may be ordered when reasonably necessary for the protection of the rights or interests of the complaining shareholder, there is less pressure to give content to the concept of oppression. The court may focus on the plaintiff's plight, without having to decide whether the controlling parties acted badly. This could make quite a difference when evidence suggesting oppression is soft or difficult to interpret. For example, consider a family corporation in which one of two sons ceases to be employed by the business as a result of a managerial dispute. The company pays no dividends; for tax reasons it has never done so. No one has tried to buy the son out at an unfair price. Without more, this pattern is hard to construe as a squeezeout. Yet the estranged son nevertheless has an investment interest that is practically worthless. In precisely this situation, a California court could order relief (namely, a dissolution decree) that in fact would probably lead to the other brother buying him out.[11]

Nonstatutory dissolution?

(5) Incidentally, it should be mentioned that some state courts allow, at least in principle, for *nonstatutory* dissolution. This approach appears not to be frequently invoked today, however, and the success rate of plaintiffs

[11] See, e.g., Stumpf v. Stumpf & Sons, Inc., 120 Cal. Rptr. 671 (Cal. App. 1975).

appears not to be high.[12] The grounds recognized by courts in such actions are similar to those stated in statutes like the MBCA.

§18.4.3 Alternatives to Dissolution

There are various alternatives to dissolution proceedings as a way of resolving disputes in close corporations. One major group consists of ways of injecting new personnel into the corporation's affairs, for the purpose of breaking ties or managing the business. Another group of alternatives consists of expanding the menu of orders that courts can give. Let us briefly examine some of these alternatives.

(1) Arbitration

(1) One alternative to resolving suits by litigation is *arbitration.* Arbitration is thought by its proponents to be prompter and more private, to result in more workable decisions (including specific performance and the making of managerial decisions, from which courts tend to shy away), to be carried out by a decision maker with a better understanding of the business, and to leave the disputing parties more satisfied. Arbitration is available, of course, only when all the disputants have agreed to resort to and be bound by it.

Past legal obstacles

In the past, use of arbitration was afflicted by legal obstacles. Agreements to arbitrate future disputes were held unenforcable as attempts to oust courts of jurisdiction. Thus, when a dispute finally arose, a party to the agreement might revoke his agreement and sue in court anyway, or at least refuse to participate in the arbitration. Many current statutes have changed this rule, however.[13] Another problem was that some arbitration statutes would authorize arbitration only for controversies that could be the subject of lawsuits; this left arbitrators without explicit statutory authorization to handle disputes about questions of business decision making. But some of these arbitration statutes have been amended to make arbitration agreements "enforceable without regard to the justiciable character of the controversy."[14]

Consistency with corporate law

From the standpoint of the themes of this book, perhaps the most interesting legal question that arose about arbitration is whether, and when, the general statutes authorizing arbitration should be construed as fatally inconsistent with the particular corporate law provision that the business of a corporation shall be managed by its board of directors. If an arbitrator is

[12] See, e.g., Nelkin v. H.J.R. Realty Corp., 255 N.E.2d 713 (N.Y. 1969); 2 F. O'Neal, supra note 9 to §18.3, §9.27.

[13] See 2 F. O'Neal, supra note 9 to §18.3, §9.14.

[14] See, e.g., N.Y. Civ. Prac. Law & Rules §7501; Mich. Comp. Laws Ann. §600.5025.

asked to resolve a major question of business decision making for a firm, does his doing so run afoul of the basic principle of centralized management? In *Application of Vogel,*[15] an appellate court in New York gave a qualified no as answer. Two 50-percent shareholders disagreed over whether the corporation should exercise an option to buy warehouse property it was leasing. There was an arbitration agreement. The court held the controversy to be arbitrable and not in conflict with the directors-shall-manage statute in New York, because, it seems, the question at issue was essential to the "continued life" of the organization and the arbitrator would not assume "any burden of continuing management." This seemed to mean that a little bitty violation of a statutory norm is okay when it is very important. Not only does this principle make courts uncomfortable, but it also casts doubt on the validity of arbitration in many less extreme situations. In any event, the New York Court of Appeals affirmed the lower court's order in a deliberately noncommittal way: "We decide only that, when viewed against the factual background of the case, the arbitration clause . . . encompasses the controversy which has arisen and that such controversy is a proper subject for arbitration. . . ."[16] In other words, the court wasn't sure of the lower court's reasoning, but it agreed with the result. Furthermore, Section 620(b) of the New York Business Corporation Law now provides that a provision in the certificate of incorporation that restricts the board's management of the business or transfers it to other persons is valid if all the incorporators or shareholders authorized the provision and if all subsequent shareholders took their shares with knowledge or notice or consented to it in writing. This provision would not have directly saved the agreement in *Vogel,* because that agreement was not embodied in the certificate of incorporation. It does, however, give participants in New York close corporations an effective way to agree to arbitrate disputes over managerial policies.

***Vogel* case**

N.Y. §620(b)

This result is as it should be, for arbitration agreements in close corporations do not really impinge in an unacceptable way on the policies behind the principle of centralized management. As we saw in chapter 1, the function of that principle in the paradigmatic public corporation context was not to make sure that all of a corporation's business decisions will in fact be made by the board of directors, but that they will have ultimate authority over such decisions, including the ability both to delegate and to take back power over particular kinds of decisions. And the functions of centralizing ultimate control over the allocation of authority within the

Justification of arbitration

[15] 268 N.Y.S.2d 237 (App. Div. 1966).
[16] 224 N.E.2d 738 (N.Y. 1967).

enterprise were in turn seen to be those of facilitating the coordination of a large, complex business operation and pinpointing the persons who would be ultimately responsible for corporate operations and primarily accountable to the investors. In the close corporation racked by disputes among persons who are both investors and employees, however, allowing an arbitrator to resolve disputes is hardly likely to impair the coordination activities of management (quite the reverse is true), nor is it apt to further confuse shareholders as to who is responsible for particular decisions. Yet its positive effects may be quite substantial.

(2) Receivers

(2) Courts of equity have long had the power to appoint *receivers* for troubled corporations. The function of a receiver is basically to sell off all of the corporation's assets. She differs from the sheriff or liquidator in that the sale need not be done as soon as possible, or in a short time period, but over an extended stretch of time, so that the receiver can get the best price for the assets and perhaps can sell the business as a going concern. Typically, receivers are appointed at the behest of creditors of an insolvent corporation. But courts may also appoint them at the behest of shareholders when dissension is so great in the corporation that the business cannot be conducted without incurring serious losses. Appointment of a receiver is discretionary with the court, however, and this drastic remedy is not ordered lightly.[17] It is basically only appropriate for dying corporations and therefore does not touch a large majority of close corporation disputes.

(3) Custodians

(3) Some state statutes allow for the appointment of *custodians* for close corporations. Custodians are like receivers (courts appoint them and they usually have full power to run the business), but their job is to continue the business, not to liquidate it. Delaware allows a shareholder to apply to the Court of Chancery for the appointment of a custodian when shareholder deadlock has resulted in nonelection of successors to directors, director deadlock has caused or threatened irreparable injury to the corporation's business, or the corporation has abandoned its business but has taken no steps to dissolve.[18] In addition, a shareholder in a close corporation may also apply for an appointment of a custodian when the shareholders had opted (under Delaware provisions) to manage the business but are so divided that the business is suffering or threatened with irreparable injury, or when the petitioning shareholder has the right to dissolution of the corporation under a valid provision in the certificate.[19]

[17] See, e.g., Recarey v. Rader, 320 So. 2d 28 (Fla. App. 1975); Duval v. Severson, 304 N.E.2d 747 (Ill. App. 1973); see also Del. §§226, 291.

[18] Del. §226.

[19] Del. §352.

Criticism

The custodianship remedy has been sharply criticized and in fact it seems to be used only rarely.[20] Custodianships substitute judicially controlled management for management by the owners. This in itself seems objectionable to many persons. They are also likely to generate significant costs, including both legal expenses and lost opportunities. The custodian is likely to see himself as a caretaker, preserving the status quo and keeping the peace, and is likely to have little incentive to cause the business to take risks and develop new opportunities. Even worse, the custodian may try to prolong his management role. Moreover, the custodian is unlikely to achieve a long-term resolution of the underlying disharmony among the owners. His term is therefore likely to be indefinitely long, unless the court appointed him solely as a means of temporizing while deciding whether to order dissolution.

(4) Provisional directors

(4) Some states also allow courts to appoint *provisional directors.* Unlike receivers or custodians, such persons do not have extensive powers over the business. They have the powers and duties of ordinary directors, and the reason for appointing them is to break ties. When the deadlock is broken, the provisional director is supposed to go away. The statutes may vary on crucial details. For example, Delaware allows appointment of a provisional director "in lieu of appointing a custodian for a close corporation,"[21] but the New Jersey statute contains no such limitation.[22]

Problems

A problem with provisional directors is that they are likely to be useful only in resolving trivial disagreements. Where stakes are high and dissension is great, the provisional director is unlikely to be able to create harmony. Moreover, some would argue that as a matter of principle no state or public interest justifies taking away the right to veto corporate decisions from either of the deadlocked factions.

(5) Flexible remedies

(5) Another alternative is to give courts *wide discretion* to grant relief other than dissolution. Critics would describe this as the power of "direct judicial management" of the dispute-ridden close corporation. South Carolina, for example, provides that in an involuntary dissolution action the court may grant such relief other than dissolution as it deems appropriate, including orders altering the articles or bylaws, cancelling or altering corporate resolutions and acts, directing or prohibiting "any act" of the corporation or shareholders, directors, officers, or other persons party to the action, and providing for the purchase at their fair value of the shares of any shareholder, either by the corporation or other shareholders.[23]

[20] Hetherington & Dooley, note 1 supra, at 23-26.
[21] Del. §352(b).
[22] N.J. Bus. Corp. Act §12-7.
[23] S.C. Bus. Corp. Act §33-21-155.

Illustration

The Oregon Supreme Court asserted a similarly broad set of powers by deciding that a showing of "oppressive" conduct did not require the court to exercise its statutory dissolution power, but permitted "various alternative remedies," many examples of which the court proceeded to list. Two of the more interesting possibilities it imagined were ordering the declaration and payment of dividends and ordering that minority shareholders be permitted to buy additional stock under conditions specified by the court.[24] Note, however, that other courts faced with the question might well decide that the statutory remedies of dissolution, and appointment of a custodian, and so forth, are exclusive — as did the Virginia court in *White v. Perkins*.[25]

Once again, such remedies represent displacement of management by the parties with judicial management, yet are unlikely to achieve a long-term resolution of the underlying problem. On the other hand, giving the courts only a narrow range of drastic remedies is likely to hamper them in doing justice in the particular case.

(6) Statutory buyout right

(6) Yet another alternative is the *statutory buyout right* proposed by Professors Hetherington and Dooley and already discussed. Some states have superficially similar provisions. An example is California's provision that in an action to dissolve the corporation or appoint a receiver, holders of 50 percent or more of the corporation's stock may avoid these remedies by purchasing the plaintiff's stock at its "fair cash value," which, if the parties can't agree, will be fixed by the court.[26] But with this type of provision, the aggrieved minority shareholder has no control over the use of the alternative remedy (the defendants may or may not decide to buy him out), and in any case he has to have prima facie evidence that the statutory grounds for dissolution are met before he can bring a credible action.[27] In both these respects, the Hetherington and Dooley proposal offers a sharp contrast and provides more direct and certain help for the disgruntled shareholder holding illiquid stock.

(7) Fiduciary duty approach

(7) Finally, some courts have developed the theory of *fiduciary duties* in a way that may be of great utility to participants in close corporations. A pathbreaking decision in this regard is the Massachusetts case of *Donahue*

[24] Baker v. Commercial Body Builders, Inc., 507 P.2d 387 (Or. 1973).

[25] 89 S.E.2d 315 (Va. 1972).

[26] Cal. §2000. Note also that N.Y. §1118, as a counterbalance to the liberalized right to petition for dissolution created by N.Y. §1104-a, discussed in note 3 supra, grants the majority the right to make an irrevocable election to buy out the minority's shares and thus end the dissolution proceeding. If the parties can't agree on a price, the court must determine the fair value of the shares and the other terms and conditions of the purchase.

[27] Minn. Bus. Corp. Act §302A.751 allows the court to order a buyout (specifically, a sale by either party to the other or the corporation) on the motion of either party. But one of the grounds of dissolution has to have been established.

Donahue v. Rodd Electrotype

v. Rodd Electrotype Co.[28] Defendant, a close corporation, repurchased shares of a controlling shareholder (who was retiring from the business and leaving effective control in the hands of his children), while refusing to repurchase the plaintiff's minority shares on similar terms. Plaintiff was the widow of a formerly active participant. Plaintiff sued to set aside the repurchase, alleging breach of fiduciary duty owed to the plaintiff. The Supreme Judicial Court held that in the operation of a close corporation, shareholders owe each other fiduciary duties as though they were partners.[29] The reasons for imposing a duty of "utmost good faith and loyalty" are the practical resemblance between a close corporation and a partnership, the inherent danger to minority interests of being subjected to squeezeout attempts and other such behavior, and the lack of adequate other protections for the minority (such as the absence of a market out). More specifically, the court decided that a share repurchase by a close corporation should be subject to an "equal opportunity" rule: Provision of a market and access to corporate assets or benefits must be provided without discrimination among shareholders.

Subsequent extension

A subsequent Massachusetts decision extended and refined the concept of a special fiduciary duty in another classic close corporation dispute. In *Wilkes v. Springside Nursing Home, Inc.*,[30] plaintiff was one of four shareholders in defendant corporation. He had been a director and treasurer, and had been involved in the daily operation of the business. He received a regular salary; the corporation paid no dividends. After a transaction between the corporation and another shareholder, relations between plaintiff and that shareholder deteriorated. Plaintiff gave notice of intent to sell his shares, and at the next annual meeting he was stripped of his salary and of his positions with the corporation. He sued, alleging breach of fiduciary duty. The court held for plaintiff. The court reiterated that, as in a partnership, a fiduciary duty is owed among close corporation shareholders. It found that the plaintiff was ready and able to carry out his duties and that the other shareholders acted in bad faith to freeze him out at a low price.

Procedural aspects

The court in *Wilkes* proceeded to elaborate the procedural aspects of the utmost good faith and loyalty rule. When a plaintiff alleges bad faith on the part of the majority, the majority may justify their actions by demonstrat-

[28] 328 N.E.2d 505 (Mass. 1975).

[29] As to what the court meant by the phrase "close corporation," it said that such a corporation is typified by (1) few shareholders, (2) no ready market for the stock, and (3) substantial majority-shareholder participation in management.

[30] 353 N.E.2d 657 (Mass. 1976).

ing a "legitimate business purpose" for them. The plaintiff may then respond by showing that the same objective could have been obtained in a way less harmful to the minority. The court would then have to balance these factors in the circumstances of the individual case.

Other developments

The *Donahue-Wilkes* decisions have been followed in some other jurisdictions[31] and are likely to be influential. Some courts have refused to apply the duty of utmost loyalty, without rejecting it as an appropriate legal concept, in particular kinds of close corporation disputes. For example, in *Zidell v. Zidell, Inc.,*[32] two brothers owned 37.5 percent each in certain corporations and one J. R. owned 25 percent. The plaintiff brother asked J. R. about selling his stock and told the defendant brother about J. R.'s interest in doing so. But the defendant brother acted more quickly and bought the shares of J. R. Plaintiff then sought an order that the corporations should be able to buy J. R.'s shares, thus preserving the balance of power between the brothers. The court held that the defendant was under no duty to maintain proportionate control, and said that the protective approach taken in *Donahue* (which this Oregon court seemed to approve) would not require such a result. The court seems to have been strongly influenced by the fact that there was no evidence that the Zidell corporations had made it a practice of purchasing their own stock or that it was contemplated that they would do so in order to maintain proportionate control. Other decisions involving similar factual situations and seeming to go different ways can to some extent be reconciled in terms of whether or not the court thought that there was an original agreement or understanding that proportionate control would be maintained.[33] Note that, in general, it will be easier and more realistic to presume that the original participants shared an understanding that their claims to financial returns would be maintained than to presume an agreement that all would maintain the same share ownership.

[31] See, e.g., Alaska Plastics, Inc. v. Coppock, 621 P.2d 270 (Alaska 1980); Comolli v. Comolli, 246 S.E.2d 278 (Ga. 1978).

[32] 560 P.2d 1091 (Or. 1977).

[33] See, e.g., Cressy v. Shannon Continental Corp., 378 N.E.2d 941 (Ind. App. 1978); Johns v. Caldwell, 601 S.W.2d 37 (Tenn. App. 1980).

APPENDIX A

A SPECIAL NOTE ON HIERARCHIES

At least three different kinds of explanation of hierarchies can be given. One, the most cynical, emphasizes *the interests of elites.* Hierarchies exist because the more dominant persons or groups in society find it in their interest to have them. Hierarchical organizations help those at the top of the social class structure to consolidate and extend their power and to increase the benefits they reap from their power. Among these benefits may be princely financial renumeration and satisfaction of a psychological lust for domination over other human beings.

A second kind of theory emphasizes *the resolution of conflict.* Hierarchical structures of authority mitigate the wasteful aspects of struggle and rivalry that occur when large numbers of people live or work together. In fact, archaeologists and anthropologists have developed substantial, intricate arguments and evidence for the view that, when ancient hunter-gatherer bands switched to an agricultural life-style, their populations and their levels of intra-society conflict both increased dramatically. Accumulations of property, jealousy, theft, hostility, fighting, and murder all took an upswing. Hierarchical authority structures eventually followed and became established because they succeeded in reducing and controlling conflict. The same process has actually been observed in modern-day hunter-gatherer bands that have switched to agricultural life-styles.[1]

The third kind of theory emphasizes *the facilitation of cooperation* in the carrying out of large-scale tasks. This is the kind of theory that will be developed in this appendix. By setting it forth, I do not mean to imply that the processes postulated by the other two kinds of theories do not exist or that they are not important. With respect to some social institutions and historical epochs, they may offer the most important and valid way of

[1]For a highly readable account of the archaeological and anthropological evidence, see J. Pfeiffer, The Emergence of Society ch. 4 (1977).

understanding events. With respect to corporations, they have some explanatory value. I do think, however, that the modern corporation cannot be understood unless primary emphasis is given to the third kind of theory.

To understand why corporate hierarchies exist, one must first understand why managers exist — although an understanding of managerial activity is by no means sufficient. The need for managers may be seen as a consequence of the division of labor and the resulting need for coordination. The argument proceeds as follows: Complex technologies and the limited abilities of individual persons, as well as mundane practical factors like time lost when an employee shifts from one task to another, make it efficient for people's jobs to be *specialized.* Specialization may be carried to a self-defeating extreme, of course, and a too-narrow job may rob a life of all its lustre; the literature on management is full of books trying to prove the value of "job enlargement" and the like.[2] But there is little doubt that an advanced industrial society requires an enormous amount of specialization if it is to survive in competition with other societies.

But specialization promotes blindness about how one's work fits into a larger pattern, both generally and in specific situations; it creates a need for *coordination* of specialized activities. Somehow the plumber must put the pipes in after the carpenter builds the basic structure but before he puts up the walls. Somehow the production department must produce enough widgets to satisfy the orders that the salesmen get, but not too many extra ones. Much coordination can take place by market transactions. The plumber and the carpenter may both contract with a general contractor to do the work as called for by the latter. But when technology or market conditions are such that people want to embark on large-scale projects, many of whose component tasks are highly interrelated, as in automobile production or the building of a railroad, then much of the coordination tends to take place within a single firm.[3]

Coordination makes up a large part of what is referred to as managerial activity.[4] Quite clearly, a very large portion of any manager's job consists of

[2]E.g., D. McGregor, The Human Side of Enterprise (1960); R. Likert, The Human Organization (1967). For a critique, see C. Perrow, Complex Organizations: A Critical Essay 112-128 (2d ed. 1979).

[3]Some of the leading literature on why activities take place within firms, rather than in markets, should be mentioned here. Coase, The Nature of the Firm, 4 Economica (n.s.) 386 (1937); Alchian & Demsetz, Production, Information Costs, and Economic Organization, 62 Am. Econ. Rev. 777 (1972); Williamson, The Modern Corporation: Origin, Evolution, Attributes, 19 J. Econ. Lit. 1537 (1981).

[4]Henry Mintzberg has studied managers' actual activities in detail. In his The Nature of

gathering, evaluating, relating, and dispensing pieces of *information*. He or she is an information processor par excellence. The term *information* is used here in a broad sense: it includes not only bits of factual data, judgments, opinions, and predictions, but also requests, advice, and commands within a firm, and bids and offers among those who potentially might make a deal of some sort. Included within the manager's information processing tasks is the activity of making business *decisions*, for some of his informational outputs (advice, commands) are designed to implement a specific idea about how specific tasks should be coordinated. Furthermore, it should be clear that the amount and range of any manager's decision making power in a well-functioning organization will depend heavily on his place in the communications network. How often an individual should make decisions, at what level of generality or specificity, and about which tasks and activities — those with narrow or with wide-ranging consequences, for example — should depend, in an efficient organization, on the amount, quality, and range of information that the individual normally receives.

That managerial activity largely consists of information processing, and that the power to make decisions should correlate with possession of the information needed to make them, does not tell us what kind of communication network is called for by a large organization, however. This is a variation of my earlier point that the division of labor and the need for coordination cannot by themselves explain the existence of hierarchies. Fortunately, reflection on the properties of communication networks helps to complete the explanation. I will examine five possible communication networks, after first specifying four criteria for evaluating them.

One important feature of an organization's communication network is the ratio of communication channels to persons (C/P). A *channel* is simply a line of communication from one individual person to another that has been established and that receives a significant amount of use. It might be thought of concretely or metaphorically as a private telephone line, but of course it need not be. The significance of the ratio of channels-to-persons figure is that it is a rough indicator of the relative expensiveness, or *cost*, of the organization's communication network — what proportion of its resources are devoted to coordinative communications as opposed to the basic work of its operating corps. A second important feature of the net-

---

Managerial Work 54-99 (1973), he classifies them into ten job functions: figurehead, leader, liaison, monitor, disseminator, spokesman, entrepreneur, disturbance handler, resource allocator, and negotiator. Many of these relate to the coordination of activities within the organization.

work is the maximum number of channels handled by any one person (MAX C/P). This figure should serve as a rough indicator of the probability that at least one person will succumb to information *overload* and consequently do a poor job. How important the overload threat is to the organization will depend on the role of the overloaded individual.

Other things being equal, one would want to minimize both C/P and MAX C/P in a communications network. Other things are not equal, of course, in real systems. On the cost side, the actual expensiveness of a given network will depend on the intensity with which the channels are used and the specific characteristics of the persons communicating, the information-handling technology they use (telephone versus letters, for example), and the kind of information they exchange. On the benefits side, it may happen that an increase in the channels-to-person ratio, by increasing the amount of useful communication among persons in the organization, may increase the quality of the decision making. How one then determines an optimal C/P is easy to specify in theory but difficult in practice. In theory, the network designer simply increases C/P until the marginal cost of doing so is no longer less than the marginal benefit — that is, until the net gains are exhausted. In practice, this determination will vary among organizations and will be based on numerous guesses. There are some general points, however, that may be extremely useful for the network designer. Most important, relative rates of increase of cost, overload danger, or benefits may be routinely linked to a particular kind of network. If one kind results in an extremely rapid increase in C/P (and therefore costs) as the network becomes larger, as compared to another kind of network, and there is no specific reason to believe that the benefits of the network will continually increase at the same rapid rate, this network may be regarded as presumptively unfit for very large organizations.

A third important feature of a communications network is the *average path* of messages, here defined (somewhat arbitrarily) as the average number of channels in a linked series of channels in the network. (If *A* has a channel with *B*, and *B* with *C* and *C* with *D*, the path is three units long.) "Average path" is a rough indicator of the amount of *systematic distortion* of information that can be expected in the system. Everyone who has ever participated in the familiar psychology experiment, where each person in the class hears a story in private from one person and repeats it in private to another until the story has gone back to the instructor, will appreciate the statement that, at least with oral communications, distortion can be severe after information is relayed through a fairly small number of persons. And distortion can be expected to be worse when the persons in the line are expected not just to relay information but to filter, aggregate, or interpret it before passing it on. A fourth feature is the *maximum path* of messages, that is, the longest linked series of communication channels in the network. It is a rough indicator of the *maximum distortion* in a particular area of the system, and it may be important if the particular area is crucial to the organization.

Again, other things being equal, one wants to minimize the average path and the maximum path of messages in a communications network. As before, there are qualifications. Information distortion will depend on factors like the character of the persons in the network, the nature and form of the information (oral or written, for example), the amount of selection and reformulation that is supposed to occur at each relay point, and the kind of information technology used. But in this context, it is hard to imagine benefits (such as the receipt by persons of usefully refiltered and reformulated information) being continually associated with larger message paths, at least beyond rather small lengths.

We turn to the five communication networks.

The equal partners' communication network. Conceivably, the workers in an organization might all participate equally in management in the way that (absent contrary agreement) partners are supposed to do. Each person would have power to decide matters within her jurisdiction and would have an equal vote on all collective decisions. To get the information flows necessary to make this kind of decision making yield coordinated and efficient results, each partner would establish a direct communication channel with every other partner. (See Figure A-1. Note that this pattern is not just restricted to equal partners. It may very well characterize the patterns of communications among persons and firms in some *markets*.) Each partner would give information and advice that might bear on the tasks performed by any other. Certainly there should be little information distortion in such an organization (the average path and the maximum path are both only one), and perhaps there should be a happy feeling of siblinghood. And if the enterprise is engaged in an activity, such as scientific research, that depends critically on an intense exchange of ideas, the open system of communication may yield rich rewards.

But the equal partner network is very expensive and, more important, its cost increases at a much faster rate than the number of persons in the system. When there are nine people already in it, for example, adding a tenth person entails the installation of not one, but nine new communication channels. With five partners, the ratio of channels to persons is only two; with 17 partners, the C/P is eight; with 500 partners, the C/P is 249.5. With 50,000 persons — the number of workers, let us say, that were in-

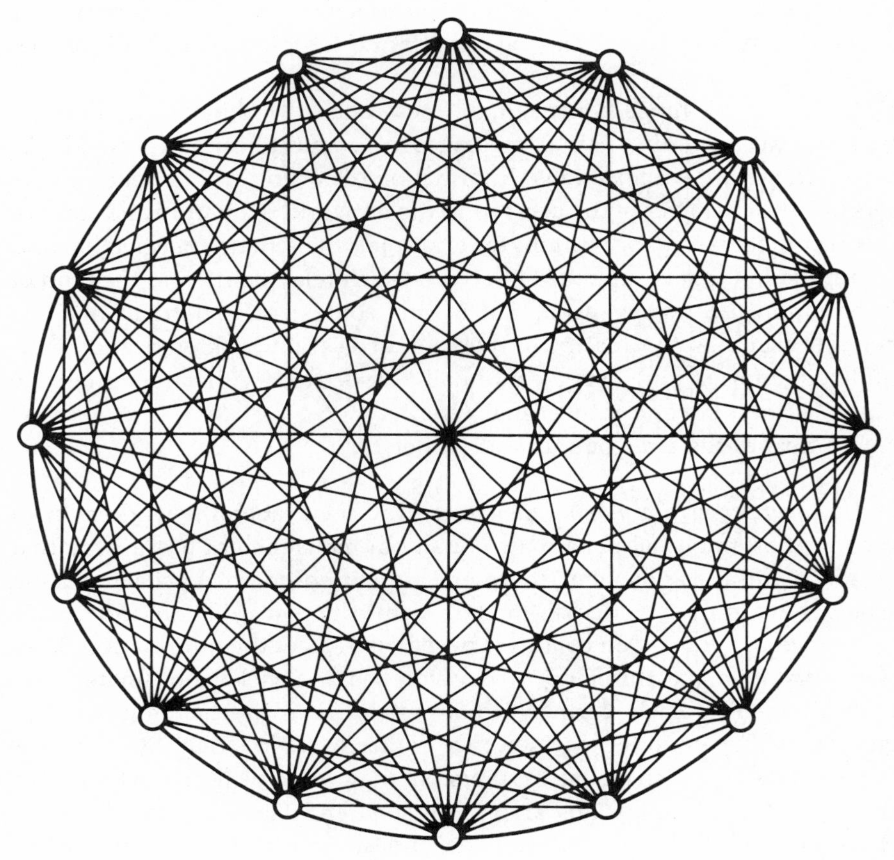

17 persons (P).
Each P has 16 channels (C).

—C/P = 136/17 = 8 —C goes up much faster than P —C/P goes up too	**Too Expensive for Large Organization**

Figure A-1
The Equal Partners' Communication Network

volved in the jet rail project of Chapter 1 — the C/P is a staggering 24,999.5. One therefore doubts whether, if the channels were actually used, any real work would get done. It is rather hard to imagine that many large industrial organizations would find that the increased benefits resulting from an open system of communication would outweigh the costs. Rather, the equal partners' network seems suitable for an organization only when it has a relatively small number of members.

How small is small enough will be contingent on other factors. When the organization benefits greatly from many members participating heavily in a variety of informational exchanges, as in a research firm, or when the members carry out tasks that are largely self-contained, as in many law firms, then the feasible number of members may be larger than it otherwise would be. But it seems unlikely that the equal partners' network could ever encompass, in a meaningful or efficient way, more than a few hundred members. It is therefore unsuitable for many modern enterprises.

The strict chain of command. In an effort to avoid the cost of a partnership network of communication, a modestly large firm (say, 500 members) might (momentarily) consider going to the opposite extreme of arbitrarily restricting each person to no more than two channels. For example, the members could be linked in a circular pattern. Each person would continue to have power within his own sphere of operations and a vote on collective decisions. Each would send messages around the communications circle that might be of value to some other person further on. Requests would be sent in the same way. In effect, everyone would be a manager to the extent of trying to coordinate or fit his own activities in with those of all the other participants, but would not be able to communicate directly with more than two other persons.

It is implausible that even with a small number of persons such a network could lead to adequate coordination of activities. The basic problem is that no one has responsibility for gathering information and making decisions relevant to fitting all activities together into an optimal, coherent whole. Because of this, the firm might consider adopting a strict chain-of-command approach. (This is represented in Figure A-2 as a spiral; it could also be drawn as a straight line with person nodules — a "chain.") At one end of the chain is The Boss. All information relevant to the organization's activities is sent up to her, and she sends coordinating commands — in a firm trying to be humanistic rather than authoritarian, they are called "advice" — down the chain. The reported data may be filtered and aggregated as it moves upward; the commands or advice may be made more opera-

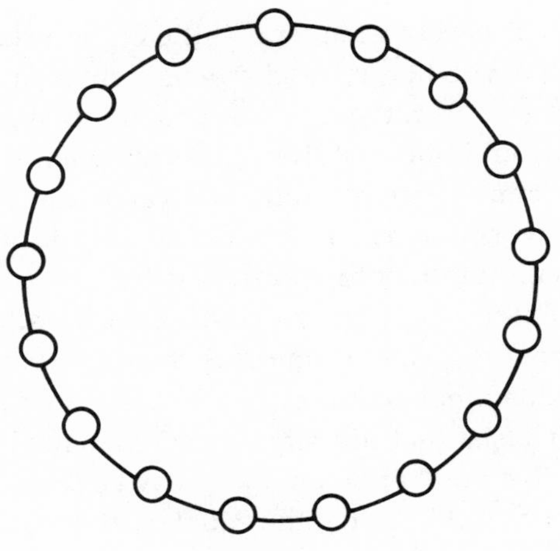

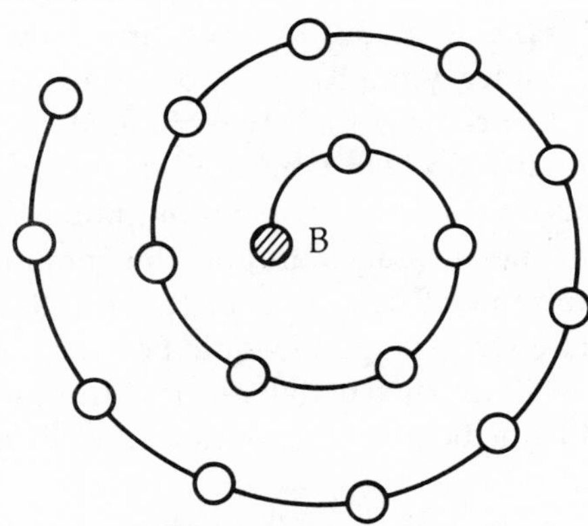

—C/P = 16/17 = < 1 —C/P doesn't increase with size	**Inexpensive** **(Re Fixed Costs)**

But

—Average & Maximum Path long —They increase linearly with size	**Too Much** **Distortion**

Figure A-2
The Strict Chain-of-Command Approach

tional as they move down, until they reach the person charged with actual implementation. All this happens at a C/P of less than 1.

One major problem with both the circular and the spiral patterns of communication is that they entail a large average message path, and therefore a great amount of systematic distortion in information flows. (Other problems include increased use intensity of the channels — adding to costs, despite the original plan — and extreme stratification.) Moreover, the risk of distortion increases linearly with the addition of new persons to the network. Imagine a message being relayed through 500 persons in the modestly sized firm! This systematic distortion is likely to become serious when there are still only a small number of people in the organization, and at such numbers the equal partner network might very well have not become too costly. Because of these problems, one very rarely finds a strict chain network of communication in organizations, even in very small ones.

The accessible leader network. In adopting a communication network, a firm might try to minimize simultaneously both distortion and cost — including the psychological cost of ranking and stratifying persons, as is done in extreme form by the strict chain — by appointing only one person as leader, who then communicates directly with every operative. (This is represented in Figure A-3 as a kind of spoked wheel without the rim, or perhaps more fittingly, as a pin cushion stuck full of pins.) At first blush this system seems absolutely wonderful. The ratios of channels to persons is low throughout the entire range of sizes: with five persons, C/P is 4/5; with 17 it is 16/17; with 500, 499/500, and so on — always less than one. The network is therefore a cheap one. The average path is one, so the network should generate minimal distortion, and the amount of stratification and hierarchy is about as low as it can feasibly be.

The problem in many contexts is that with large numbers the system simply won't work. The leader will be overloaded and will soon be burnt out. The MAX C/P (the number of channels that the leader has to attend to) increases in direct proportion with the number of other persons in the organization. Needless to say, no leader who has to receive individualized information and give individualized advice to all the operators can possibly communicate meaningfully with 50,000 or even 500 of them. In many situations, a mere handful of persons is the threshold limit before overload occurs.

An important qualification concerns the general spoked network pattern rather than the accessible leader network as just envisioned. A central leader or office can communicate meaningfully, cheaply, and directly with all operating units if the message to all of them is the same. All that is

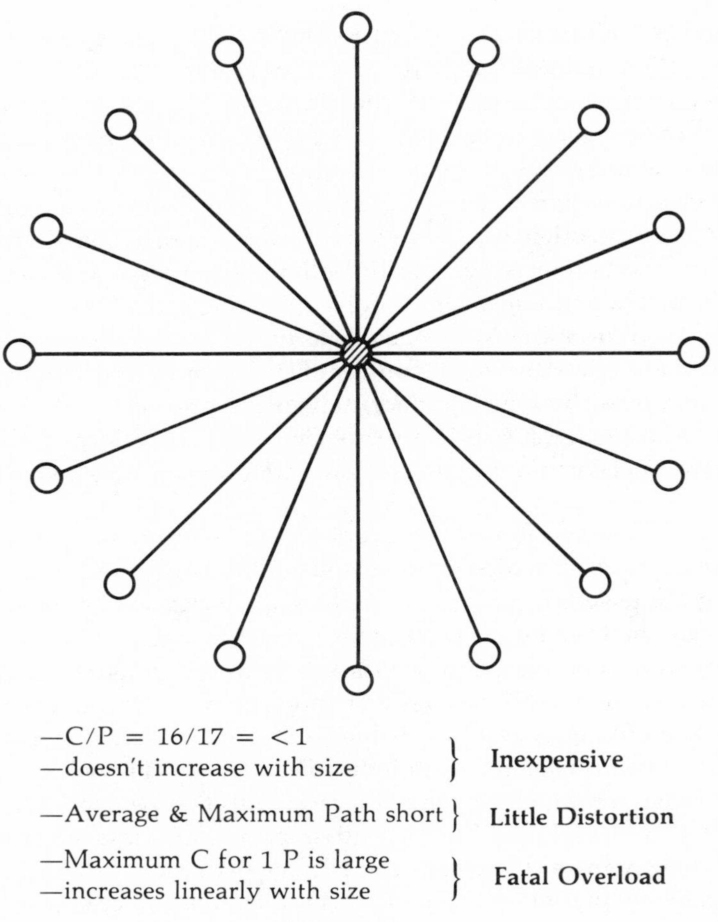
—C/P = 16/17 = <1
—doesn't increase with size
Inexpensive
—Average & Maximum Path short
Little Distortion
—Maximum C for 1 P is large
—increases linearly with size
Fatal Overload

Figure A-3
The Accessible Leader Approach

needed for this is a copying machine and a message delivery system, or a podium from which the leader can address the assembled multitude. Many fast food chains employ this technique, for example. They supply every manager of every one of their thousands of hamburger stores with an operating manual that explains, in excruciating detail, every aspect of operations, from the exact weight of each kind of hamburger to the exact timing and method of cleaning the floors. Conversely, every one of the operators can communicate directly with central headquarters, if the messages are in standardized form (as are routine financial reports from the stores, for example) and can be digested by the center's computers. Thus, standardization and good information processing technology can greatly extend the range of organization sizes for which the spoked network makes sense. By the same token, however, the nature of the task that the organization does, and the nature of its environment, will influence the extent to which standardization is feasible.

According to writers in the so-called contingency school of organization theory[5] (thus named because they hold that the proper form for a given organization is contingent on its tasks and environment) organizations facing uncertain environments and tasks cannot resort so much to formalization and standardization. For these organizations, the overload problem I identified will resurface with great vigor. And in fact, even organizations using the spoked network do it for only some of their communications. In the fast food chains, for example, more individualized information and advice are officially supposed to be handled in a hierarchy that includes store managers, district managers, regional managers, the national store manager, and the company's chief executive officer.

Interestingly, Max Weber, the great German sociologist who developed the theory of bureaucratic organizations at the turn of the century, seems to have regarded hierarchy, or the existence of numerous levels of formal authority, and a set of impersonal, official operating rules as going hand in hand.[6] But our analysis, which is supported by the more recent research on organizations,[7] suggests that they are basically substitutes or alternative methods of coordination.

The explosive organization. Let us assume that most large enterprises have many individualized situations that have to be coordinated, so that the spoked network is inadequate for them. The overload threat caused by that network can be ameliorated, without reintroducing the cost and distortion problems in their extreme forms, by the simple trick of adding more persons to each spoke. The leader becomes the head of a number of shorter chains of command. (This pattern is represented in Figure A-4 as similar to a number of rays streaking out from an impact crater, hence the term *explosive*.) With 17 persons in the organization and four chains, the values of *all* of our four criterion variables become appealingly low — certainly by comparison with the values given off by the three previously described

[5]See P. Lawrence & J. Lorsch, Organization and Environment: Managing Differentiation and Integration (1967); J. Thompson, Organizations in Action (1967).

[6]M. Weber, The Theory of Social and Economic Organization 329-341 (trans. by A. Henderson & T. Parsons 1947).

[7]See H. Mintzberg, The Structuring of Organizations 3-9 (1979).

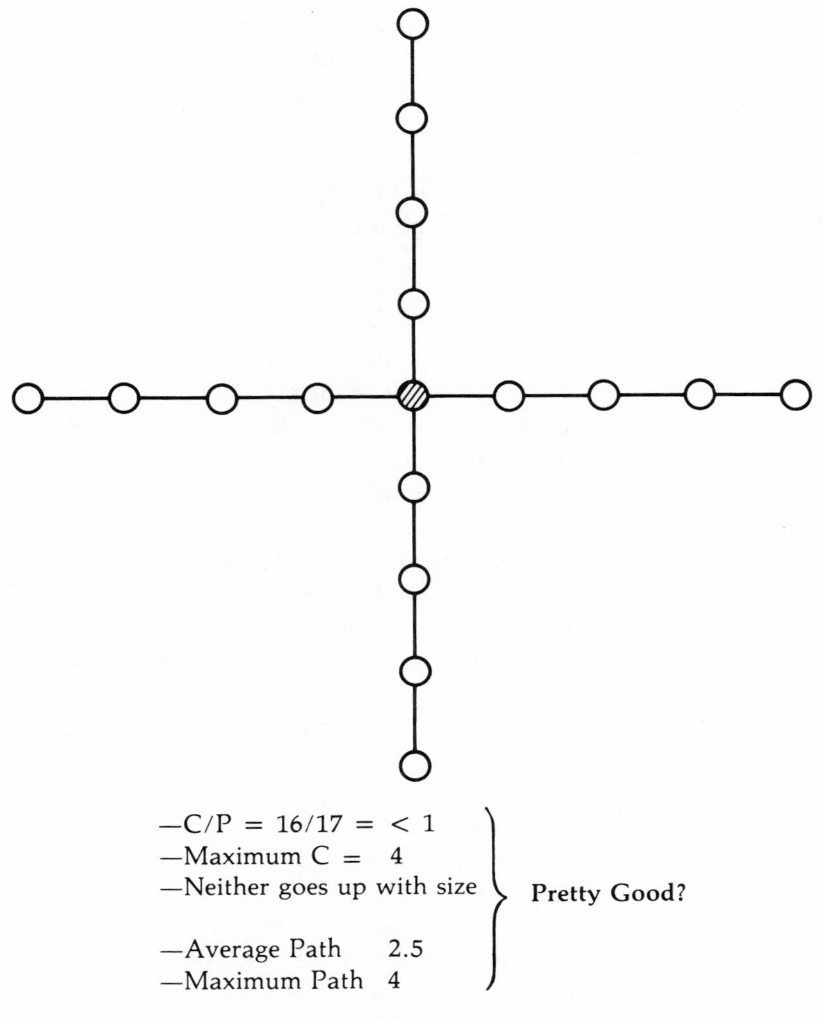
—C/P = 16/17 = < 1
—Maximum C = 4
—Neither goes up with size
—Average Path 2.5
—Maximum Path 4
Pretty Good?

Figure A-4
The Explosive Organization

network patterns. The C/P is less than 1 (communication system is cheap); MAX C/P is 4 (little danger of leader overload); average path is 2.5 and maximum path is 4 (little danger of systematic or particular distortion).

The branching hierarchy. The explosive network can itself be easily bettered by putting persons into small groups, each of whose members has a direct channel to the same person, who is himself a member of another

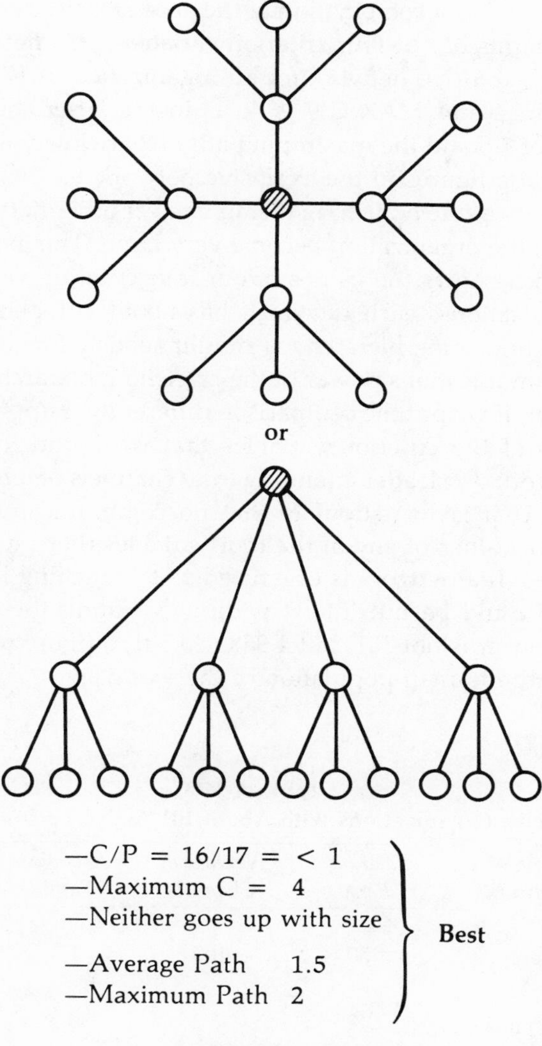
or
—C/P = 16/17 = < 1
—Maximum C = 4
—Neither goes up with size
—Average Path 1.5
—Maximum Path 2
Best

Figure A-5
The Branching Hierarchy

such group, and so on until the leader is reached. With 17 persons, for example, there could be four groups of three operators; the members of each group would communicate with their particular "middle manager"; and the four middle managers would communicate with the chief executive. (This pattern is represented in Figure A-5 as a branching system. It is first drawn with a leader at the center rather than the top, so that the pattern can be seen as a combination of the accessible leader and explosive networks.) In terms of our four criterion variables, this network is clearly superior to the explosive network for an organization of 17 members: AV C/P is less than 1 and MAX C/P is 4, as in the latter, but the average message path of 1.5 and the maximum path of 2 are lower and better than the corresponding figures in the explosive network.

The superiority of the branching hierarchy over other networks becomes dramatic when the organization become very large. This point is made in Table A-1, which shows the values of our four criterion variables for five different organizations, each of which has about 101 persons. The one organized as a branching hierarchy is simultaneously low on all four variables. The communications power of the branching hierarchy is illustrated better, however, if we put the comparison differently. Suppose we take the specific values of the criterion variables that we found in a 101-person explosive network (the leader attending to 10 channels of ten persons each) as *constraints.* That is, we stipulate that no communications network is allowed to have values of any of the four variables that exceed those constraining values. If a network is organized as a branching hierarchy, how many persons could be put into it without violating these constraining values? The answer is not 101, but 4,358,480,501, a figure roughly comparable to the entire human population of the world.

Table A-1
Five Organizations with About 101 Active Persons

	Form of Network	*Channels/ Person*	*Maximum Channels*	*Average Path*	*Maximum Path*
I.	Equal Partners	50	100	1	1
II.	Chain of Command	1	2	50.5	100
III.	Accessible Leader	1	100	1	1
IV.	Explosive Organization	1	10	5.5	10
V.	Branching Hierarchy	1	5	2.5	4

Question: Taking the values given on line IV as constraints (maximum permissible values of the four communication-system variables), how many people could be put into a branching hierarchy?

Answer: 4,358,480,501 people.

The point should now be clear. As a network of communication designed to achieve the coordinated execution of a very large organization's tasks, the branching hierarchy far surpasses alternative networks in a number of abstract, but practically important, general characteristics. Other things being equal, it tends to be cheaper, less distorting, and less likely to create critical overloads. Because organizational power tends, however imperfectly, to correlate with the range of information to which the organizational member has access, it is not really surprising that the formal authority structures of very large organizations are perceived to be hierarchical and that the top managers are those who have formal and informal access to the most wide-ranging and comprehensive kinds of information.

What is surprising, perhaps, is that large organizations are like trees. (That's right: not like families, chains, impact craters, machines, animals, or blobs, but like trees.) The communication and control networks of the former are like the literal branching systems of the latter, and for parallel reasons. A tree's problem is to reduce both the ratio of branches to leaves (compare: channels to persons), since a high ratio makes for a heavy structure that cannot both withstand gravity and grow large, and the average path between leaves and roots, since long length multiplies the energy needed to transport liquids between them.[8]

Some additional qualifications. The preceding discussion of conditions favorable to the rise of hierarchies is greatly simplified. It merely suggests a strong set of reasons to expect that the basic authority and communication structure of a large organization will tend to have the pattern of branching hierarchy. The typical organizational chart confirms this tendency. The intent, however, was not to minimize or deny the many phenomena that are ignored by organizational charts. De facto power is often distributed somewhat differently from formal authority, and all organizations have not only formal communication systems but informal ones that both help and hinder the achievement of organizational goals.[9] Nor does the existence of a branching hierarchy entail any specific form or quantity of delegation of decision making authority to lower units. (In terms of the branching net-

[8]See P. Stevens, Patterns in Nature 37-48, 135-143 (1974), for an extended treatment of the reasons why natural phenomena may have tree-like shapes. Many things besides organizations have tree-like structures, for course: the circulatory systems of vertebrates and the structures of many complicated computer programs are two wildly different examples. The causes of these patterns are often analogous.

[9]The pattern of the informal communication network may not be a neat or symmetrical branching system, and it may resemble such a system only faintly, as a spider web does, but it will never be like the equal partners' network or the spoked network.

work, greater delegation simply means that fewer messages have to go up and down the whole length of the hierarchy.) Depending on the nature of its tasks and environment and the design decisions of its top managers, a corporation may be relatively centralized or decentralized.[10] It may be organized into functional divisions or profit center divisions,[11] and it may or may not rely on many lateral relationships among members or on other attributes of a "matrix" design.[12] In different subunits, it may emphasize one or the other of three basic coordinating mechanisms: mutual adjustment, standardization and formalization (as by official rules), and direct supervision. It may be more or less authoritarian, and it may be more or less open to employee initiatives and job enlargement proposals. What it will not do, however, is depart from a fundamentally hierarchical authority structure. There will be a central or "top" core of managers who have access to a comprehensive diversity of relevant information and who make many of the most structural or far-reaching decisions about the organization.

[10] See H. Mintzberg, note 7 supra, at 181-213.

[11] A leading analysis of the reasons for the two forms is O. Williamson, Markets and Hierarchies, esp. ch. 8 (1975).

[12] See, e.g., S. Davis & P. Lawrence, Matrix (1977).

APPENDIX B

VALUATION

Here is a greatly simplified example of valuation of a company's stock determined by discounting expected earnings to present value. Suppose X Corp. is earning $3 per share this year and that earnings are expected, for the indefinite future, to grow at a constant rate of 6 percent per year, compounded. The prediction of X's earnings is not certain, however; there is a risk of error associated with it. Suppose also that the current rate of return on the best available alternative investment of comparable riskiness is 17 percent. This is a good benchmark for our evaluator to use: why should he invest in X unless he can expect it to yield him a return of at least 17 percent? (In economist's jargon, this represents his "opportunity cost.") This 17 percent rate itself represents the sum of two others: the current risk-free rate of interest (say, 8.7 percent, as indicated by the current yield on long-term United States government bonds) and a premium to compensate investors for taking risk (say, 8.3 percent, which is the estimated risk premium — not the total return — paid on a portfolio of stocks that mimics the entire stock market). Our evaluator could use the following simple formula:

$$PV = \frac{E}{k - g}$$

where PV means the present value of a share of X stock; E, the earnings per share projected for the coming year; k, the capitalization rate; g, the constant rate of growth expected for E. Plugging in the numbers, he gets the following:

$$PV = \frac{\$3}{.17 - .06}$$

$$PV = \$27.27$$

He should buy X stock if there will be a *positive net* present value from the purchase, that is, if he can buy it for any amount less than \$27.27. (*Net present value* means present value less cost.)

Several of many possible complications should be noted at once. First, the above example stipulates that investing in X is as risky as investing in a portfolio mimicking the whole stock market. If X is judged to be more or less risky than the market, the risk-premium part of the capitalization rate (the 8.3 percent part of the 17 percent) will have to be adjusted up or down accordingly. This may be done by multiplying the market's risk premium by a "beta factor" appropriate for the particular industry in which X operates. See R. Brealey & S. Myers, Principles of Corporate Finance 164-188 (2d ed. 1984).

Second, the above formula won't work if E is not expected to grow at a constant rate, or if earnings are not expected "in perpetuity." Suppose, for example, the investment is expected to yield \$3 at the end of the first year, \$5 at the end of the second, \$2 at the end of the third, and nothing thereafter. A different formula would have to be used, one that separately discounts to present value each future year's expected yield and then adds up the results. Thus,

$$\begin{aligned} PV &= \frac{E_1}{1 + k} + \frac{E_2}{(1 + k)^2} + \frac{E_3}{(1 + k)^3} \cdots \\ &= \frac{3}{1.17} + \frac{5}{(1.17)^2} + \frac{2}{(1.17)^3} \\ &= \$7.46 \end{aligned}$$

Third, the above formula shouldn't be used when k and g are close together (for example, 17 percent and 15 percent). Among other reasons, the assumption of *constant perpetual* growth is always fictitious; usually this idealization causes little trouble, but it can lead to silly results when near-term g is expected to be very high in relation to k.

Fourth, the evaluating investor's direct interest is not in X's earnings but in the *cash flow* that owning X stock will yield to him — that is, in the dividends and capital gain (on resale) that he anticipates. Company earnings are relevant only insofar as they predict these cash flows. The investor might try to predict dividends and capital gain more directly and precisely and use *them* in a valuation formula.

Fifth, taxes have to be handled consistently. If the capitalization rate (k) reflects, as it does in our example, a return on an alternative investment (viz., a portfolio of market-mimicking stocks) that would be taxable to the evaluating investor, then he must identify an expected yield figure for an investment in X that is pre-tax *as to him*. In our example, this means that E should be net of X's corporation-level taxes but not net of the investor's expected tax payments on dividends and capital gain. In other words, E should be X's after-tax income per share.

TABLE OF CASES

Table of Cases

Table of Cases

Table of Cases

Table of Cases

Table of Cases

INDEX

Index